Handbook of Research
on the Education
of Young Children

The *Handbook of Research on the Education of Young Children* is the essential reference on research on early childhood education throughout the world. This outstanding resource provides a comprehensive research overview of important contemporary issues as well as the information necessary to make knowledgeable judgments about these issues.

Now in its fourth edition, this handbook features all new sections on social emotional learning, non-cognitive assessment, child development, early childhood education, content areas, teacher preparation, technology, multimedia, and English language learners. With thorough updates to chapters and references, this new edition remains the cutting-edge resource for making the field's extensive knowledge base readily available and accessible to researchers and educators.

It is a valuable resource for all of those who work and study in the field of early childhood education including researchers, educators, policy makers, librarians, and school administrators. This volume addresses critical, up-to-date research on several disciplines such as child development, early childhood education, psychology, curriculum, teacher preparation, policy, evaluation strategies, technology, and multimedia exposure.

Olivia N. Saracho is Professor at the Department of Teaching and Learning, Policy and Leadership of the University of Maryland, College Park, USA. She has published extensively in the field of early childhood education.

Handbook of Research on the Education of Young Children

FOURTH EDITION

Edited by

Olivia N. Saracho

Routledge
Taylor & Francis Group

NEW YORK AND LONDON

Fourth edition published 2020
by Routledge
52 Vanderbilt Avenue, New York, NY 10017

and by Routledge
2 Park Square, Milton Park, Abingdon, Oxon, OX14 4RN

Routledge is an imprint of the Taylor & Francis Group, an informa business

First edition published by Macmillan. 1993.
Second edition published by Lawrence Erlbaum Associates, Inc. 2006
Third edition published by Routledge 2013

Library of Congress Cataloging-in-Publication Data
A catalog record has been requested for this book

ISBN: 978-1-138-33683-4 (hbk)
ISBN: 978-1-138-33684-1 (pbk)
ISBN: 978-0-429-44282-7 (ebk)

Typeset in Times
by codeMantra

Contents

Part I. Early Childhood Education and Child Development

Part II. Early Childhood Educational Curriculum and Instruction

Contributors

Joana Acha is an associate professor at the Department of Basic Psychological Processes and Development, Faculty of Psychology, University of the Basque Country. She is a member of the Research Group Haezi UPV/EHU. Her research interest is focused on cognitive development and language acquisition.

Monirah A. Al-Mansour is an assistant professor of education in Early Childhood Education at King Saud University and the founder of the "My Game" program at King Saud University. She is a certified trainer by the King Abdulaziz Center for National Dialogue, specializing in Dialogue in early childhood. Her research interests are open-ended play, creative expression, and early childhood communication/dialogue, multiculturalism, and third kid culture.

Karin Archer is responsible for research and evaluation of STEM-based programs for school-aged children at Let's Talk Science. She also lectures in the area of Developmental Psychology at Wilfrid Laurier University in Waterloo, Ontario, Canada. Her research interests include early introduction of technology and the educational implications of introducing and using technology as educational tools.

Tuğçe Burcu Arda Tunçdemir is a PhD student in Early Childhood Education at the Pennsylvania State University where she is researching play and creative drama. She has shared research results at national and international conferences and published chapters and journal articles. She teaches play courses and supervises teacher candidates in Early Childhood Education field settings. She is the 2018 recipient of NAEYC's Play Policies and Practices Emerging Play Scholar Award.

Enrique B. Arranz-Freijo is a professor at the Department of Basic Psychological Processes and Its Development at the University of the Basque Country, Spain. He is a co-director of HAEZI-ETXADI group. His priority research lines are family context and child development, positive parenting policies, family-school coeducation, perinatal family context and child development, and family context and executive functions development. He is a member of the Expert Group on Positive Parenting of the Spanish Ministry of Health, Social Services and Equity and the Spanish Federation of Municipalities and Provinces.

W. Steven Barnett is a Board of Governors Professor and Senior Co-Director of the National Institute for Early Education Research (NIEER) at Rutgers University. His research includes benefit-cost analyses of the Perry Preschool and Abecedarian programs beginning and research on effectiveness of early childhood programs including long-term impacts.

Florencia B. Barreto-Zarza, PhD, is at the Department of Basic Psychological Processes and Development, Faculty of Psychology, University of the Basque Country UPV/EHU. She is a member of the Research Group Haezi-Etxadi UPV/EHU as well as the Research Group "Environmental Epidemiology and Child Development" at the Biodonostia Health Research Institute. Her research interest is focused on family context and executive functions development.

Ali Brian is Associate Professor at the College of Education in the University of South Carolina. She is a Certified Adapted Physical Educator and her research focuses on creating ecologically valid intervention strategies to support the social-emotional and motor development of young children with and without disabilities. She has published over 60 peer-reviewed articles and 7 book chapters as well as made over 140 international/national presentations.

Margaret Bridges is a developmental psychologist and research scientist at the Institute of Human Development at Berkeley. She leads the Early Development and Learning Science Program, a teaching and research effort focusing on children through eight years of age. Margaret Bridges studies how family and preschool experiences influence social-emotional growth and early academic skills, along with how diverse families prepare children for school.

Jeanne Brooks-Gunn is the Virginia and Leonard Marx Professor of Child Development at Columbia University's Teachers College and Professor of Pediatrics at the College of Physicians and Surgeons. She directs the National Center for Children and Families (which focuses on policy research on children and families) at the University (www.policyforchildren.org). As a life-span developmental psychologist, she is interested in how lives unfold over time and factors that contribute to well-being across childhood, adolescence, and adulthood. She conducts long-run studies beginning when mothers are pregnant or have just given birth of a child (sometimes following these families for thirty years). Other studies follow families in different types of neighborhoods and housing. In addition, she designs and evaluates intervention programs for children and parents (home visiting programs for pregnant women or new parents, early childhood education programs for toddlers and preschoolers, two-generation programs for young children and their parents, and after-school programs for older children). She is the author of several books including *Adolescent Mothers in Later Life*, *Consequences of Growing Up Poor*, and *Neighborhood Poverty: Context and Consequences for Children*. She has been elected into both the National Academy of Medicine and the National Academy of Education, and she has received lifetime achievement awards from the Society for Research in Child Development, American Academy of Political and Social Science, the American Psychological Society, American Psychological Association, and Society for Research on Adolescence. She holds an honorary doctorate from Northwestern University and the distinguished alumni award from the Harvard University Graduate School of Education.

Cristina Carrazza is a PhD student in Developmental Psychology at the University of Chicago, where she is also part of the Interdisciplinary Training Program in the Education Sciences. Her research explores how the early learning environment affects children's understanding and future academic achievement, particularly in the domain of math, and the role parents and teachers play in supporting this learning. Cristina is a National Science Foundation Graduate Student Research Fellow and an Institute of Education Sciences Pre-Doctoral Fellow. She is also an affiliate of the DREME (Development and Research in Early Math Education) network (https://dreme.stanford.edu/) funded by the Heising-Simons Foundation.

Douglas H. Clements – Distinguished University Professor, Kennedy Endowed Chair in Early Childhood Learning, and Executive Director of the Marsico Institute for Early Learning and Literacy at the University of Denver – is widely regarded as a major scholar in the field of early childhood mathematics education, one with equal relevance to the academy, to the classroom, and to the educational policy arena. At the national level, his contributions have led to the development of new mathematics curricula, teaching approaches, teacher training initiatives, and models of "scaling up" interventions, as well as having a tremendous impact on educational planning and policy, particularly in the area of mathematical literacy and access. He has served on the U.S. President's National Mathematics Advisory Panel, the *Common Core State Standards* committee of the National Governor's Association and the Council of Chief State School Officers, the National Research Council's Committee on Early Mathematics, the National Council of Teachers of Mathematics national curriculum and Principles and Standards committees, and is co-author each of their reports. A prolific and widely cited scholar, he has earned external grant support totaling over $20 million, including major grants from the National Science Foundation, the National Institutes of Health, and the Institute of Education Sciences of the U.S. Department of Education. Additional information can be found at http://du.academia.edu/DouglasClements, http:// www.researchgate.net/profile/Douglas_Clements/, and http://portfolio.du.edu/dclemen9.

Delis Cuéllar is a research faculty member at the University of Wisconsin in Madison (UW-Madison). She specializes in the education of young bilingual Latino children. She has experience working with children, parents, and teachers of dual language learners across the United States. Previous to her work at UW-Madison, she held a research associate position at the Center on Teaching and Learning of the College of Education in the University of Oregon. She received a doctorate degree in educational policy from Arizona State University where she worked for the National Task Force on Early Childhood Education for Hispanics. She also held a one-year post-doctoral position at the National Institute for Early Education Research at Rutgers, the State University of New Jersey.

Domenica De Pasquale is currently employed at the University of Waterloo in the role of Educational Research Associate. She is responsible for assessing the impacts of online learning. She also lectures in the area of Psychology at Conestoga College. Domenica De Pasquale's research interests focus on early social and cognitive development, and educational interventions. Specifically, she examines scaffolding in formal and informal educational environments and how technology can be used as an instructional tool.

Susanne A. Denham is an applied developmental psychologist with particular expertise in the social and emotional development of children. After graduating Summa Cum Laude from Western Maryland College, Dr. Denham went on to receive her MA from the Johns Hopkins University and her doctorate from the University of Maryland Baltimore County. Prior to coming to George Mason University in 1985, Dr. Denham was an instructor at the University of Maryland, College Park, and a Guest Scientist at the National Institute of Mental Health Developmental Psychology Laboratory. Dr. Denham has also used her 11 years of hands-on experience as a school psychologist to aid in her research, which focuses on the role of emotional competence in children's social and academic functioning, its assessment, and the role that parents and teachers play in fostering it. She has been funded by the Institute for Education Sciences, National Institute of Mental Health, National Institute for Child Health and Human Development (in partnership with Head Start and the Administration for Children and Families), the W.T. Grant Foundation, the John Templeton Foundation, and the National Science Foundation. She has served on numerous editorial boards, and is past co-editor of the journal *Social Development*, as well as current editor of *Early Education and Development*. As she is now retired, she is finding time to do more writing and editing.

Stacy DeZutter is Associate Professor and Chair of the Education Department at Millsaps College, where she teaches foundations of education courses to aspiring teachers. She

Contributors

also works with the Early Oral Intervention for the Deaf and Hard of Hearing program at the University of Southern Mississippi. DeZutter holds a PhD in Learning Sciences with specialization in social contexts for teaching and learning from Washington University in St. Louis. Her published work includes research on distributed creativity in small groups and studies of play as an improvisational context for literacy development. Both lines of research draw on DeZutter's background as a performer, director, and teacher of theater. DeZutter has held several offices in the American Educational Research Association, including Chair of the Teaching Educational Psychology Special Interest Group, Chair of the Graduate Student Council, and Newsletter Editor for the Studying and Self-regulation Special Interact Group. At Millsaps College, DeZutter has served as the Director of Student Teaching, the Director of Ventures (First-Year Seminar), Chair of Theatre, and Interim Director of Peace and Justice Studies. She is currently developing a line of research on preparing teachers to foster self-regulation in the early childhood classroom.

Karen E. Diamond is Professor Emerita of Developmental Studies at the Department of Human Development and Family Studies in Purdue University. She is past Editor of the *Early Childhood Research Quarterly*. Her research focuses on classroom interventions to improve outcomes for preschool children from lower-income families and for children with disabilities.

Pool Ip Dong is a part-time instructor at Early Childhood Education in Changwon National University, South Korea. She is conducting some studies including young children's digital play and their understandings of social class via popular culture. Her research interests are young children's popular culture, visual culture, digital technology, media, and digital play.

Shyrelle Eubanks is the Senior Policy Analyst for School Readiness at the National Education Association (NEA), responsible for the development of policy, programmatic, and advocacy initiatives both within and outside of NEA. Prior to her work at NEA, Dr. Eubanks was an Associate Professor in the Early Childhood Department of Prince George's Community College, Largo, Maryland. She is also a former Training Development Coordinator for the Massachusetts Office of Child Care Services (OCCS) where she worked with OCCS staff to provide diversity training as well as child care resource and referral agencies to ensure quality training and educational opportunities for family child-care providers in African American and Hispanic communities. Dr. Eubanks is also a former pre-kindergarten and kindergarten teacher. She received a Doctor of Education in Education Policy from the University of Maryland, a Master of Arts in Child Development from Tufts University, Medford, Massachusetts, and a Bachelor of Arts Degree in Early Childhood and Lower Elementary Education from Xavier University of New Orleans.

Ruri Famelia is a postdoctoral researcher at the Crane Center for Early Childhood Research and Policy in The Ohio State University. Her research agenda is interested in understanding how motor skill programs promote children's motor skill competence and investigating the association between motor skills and cognitive development in young children. She has published six peer-reviewed articles and presented at the national and international level.

Dale C. Farran is Professor Emerita of Peabody College at Vanderbilt University and is also a Research Professor of the Peabody Research Office. Dr. Farran has been involved in research and intervention for high-risk children and youth for all of her professional career. She was a researcher on the Abecedarian Project for ten years at the Frank Porter Graham Child Development Center in Chapel Hill, NC and also at the Kamehameha Schools Early Education Project in Hawaii. Dr. Farran is the editor of two books both dealing with risk and poverty, and the author of more than 90 journal articles and book chapters. Her recent research involves several longitudinal studies of children from low-income families including directing an evaluation of the State of Tennessee's Prekindergarten program and evaluating the effectiveness of alternative preschool curricula.

Rebecca C. Fauth is a developmental psychologist specializing in research and evaluation of social policies and programs on children and families. Her research aims to unpack whether, how, and for whom programs are or are not effective. Dr. Fauth's expertise on the influence of family- and community-level poverty and how it relates to children's development is complemented by her extensive knowledge of mixed methods research, evaluation design, and research-practice integration. She is a research assistant professor at the Eliot-Pearson Department of Child Study and Human Development in Tufts University working with the Tufts Interdisciplinary Evaluation Research (TIER) group and a senior research fellow at Child Trends. Rebecca serves as a principal investigator on a number of evaluations, focused on home visiting and other dual-generation family support programs and community-wide place-based initiatives. Previously, Dr. Fauth was the assistant research director at the National Children's Bureau in London, England, and a research scientist at the National Center for Children and Families in Columbia University. At the start of her career, Rebecca worked as a preschool teacher and a family support case worker.

Barbara H. Fiese is a clinical and developmental psychologist whose research focuses on family factors that promote health and well-being in children. She holds the Pampered Chef, Ltd., Endowed Chair in Family Resiliency and is Professor and Director of the Family Resiliency Center at the University of Illinois at Urbana-Champaign, with affiliated appointments in the Departments of Pediatrics and Psychology. She is considered one of the national experts in the role that shared family mealtimes may play in promoting health.

She is a Principal Investigator or Co-Investigator on multiple federally funded projects aimed at examining environmental and biological factors contributing to early nutritional health including the STRONG Kids2 Project which takes a cell-to-community approach to dietary habits from birth. She is Past-President of the Society of Family Psychology, Editor of the *Journal of Family Psychology*, and Inaugural Editor of *Advances in Child and Family Policy and Practice*.

Meghan Fisher is currently a doctoral candidate at the Department of Human Development and Family Studies (HDFS) in the University of Illinois at Urbana-Champaign (UIUC). She has spent the past five years involved with co-ordinating and executing research projects at the university's Child Development Laboratory (CDL). Her research focuses on early childhood educators' professional development, specifically on nutrition and feeding practices.

Allison H. Friedman-Krauss is an Assistant Research Professor at the National Institute for Early Education Research (NIEER), where she leads work on the annual State of Preschool report. Her research interests focus on the effects of early childhood education programs for children growing up in poverty, preschool quality, and teacher stress and well-being.

Bruce Fuller is a professor of education and public policy at Berkeley as well as the author of *Standardized Childhood*. His work centers on the sociology of families and the institutions that host young children. Fuller served as a research sociologist at the World Bank, then taught at Harvard University before returning to California.

Claudia Galindo is an associate professor of education policy at the University of Maryland, College Park. Her research and teaching focus on improving opportunities for racial and ethnic minority students, emphasizing the Latino community. Current projects highlight the cultural assets and strengths of underserved families and children, grounded in ecocultural perspectives. Galindo studies full-service community schools in Baltimore, centering on the holistic needs of families.

David L. Gallahue is Professor and Dean Emeritus of the School of Public Health at Indiana University. His scholarship involved the applied aspects of the motor development and movement skill learning of young children and youth in physical activity and sport settings. He is the author of numerous textbooks, book chapters, and journal articles. His work has been translated into Chinese, Greek, Japanese, Portuguese, Turkish, Farsi, and Spanish. Dr. Gallahue has been a visiting professor, guest lecture, and keynote speaker on over 300 occasions at universities and professional conferences in 23 countries.

Eugene E. García is Professor Emeritus at Arizona State University (ASU). He served as Professor and Vice President for Education Partnerships at ASU from 2006 to 2011 and as Dean of the Mary Lou Fulton College of Education from 2002 to 2006. He joined ASU from the University of California, Berkeley, where he was Professor and Dean of the Graduate School of Education (1995–2001). He has served as an elected member of a local school board and a senior officer in the U.S. Department of Education. He received an honorary doctorate from the Erikson Institute and is an AERA Fellow. García has published extensively in the areas of early learning, bilingual development, and equal educational opportunity. He has published 16 books and over 200 articles and book chapters. His most recent books include *Understanding the Language Development and Early Education of Hispanic Children* (2012) with Erminda García, Teachers College Press, and *An Asset-Based Approach to Latino Education in the United States* (2018) with Dali Ozturk, Routledge Press.

Madelyn Gardner is a Researcher and Policy Advisor at the Learning Policy Institute (LPI) and doctoral student at the Harvard Graduate School of Education. At LPI, she is a member of LPI's Early Childhood Learning Team and is a co-author of *On the Road to High-Quality Early Learning: Changing Children's Lives*. Her work at LPI focuses on issues of access and quality in state early learning systems, and on strategies for effective educator preparation and development. Previously, Gardner worked at the Next Generation think tank, where she supported the development of evidence-based policies affecting children and families in California. She also taught English as a foreign language at Payap University in Thailand. She holds an MA in International Education Policy from Stanford University, and a BA with honors in Anthropology and Global Development Studies from Grinnell College.

Herbert P. Ginsburg is the Jacob H. Schiff Professor of Psychology and Education Emeritus at Teachers College, Columbia University. He holds a BA from Harvard University and his MS and PhD from the University of North Carolina, Chapel Hill. He has conducted basic research on the development of mathematical thinking, with particular attention to young children, disadvantaged populations, and cultural similarities and differences. He has drawn on cognitive developmental psychology to develop a mathematics curriculum (*Big Math for Little Kids*), print and interactive storybooks for young children, tests of mathematical thinking, computer-based assessment systems, and math software for little children. He is a member of the DREME (Development and Research in Early Math Education) network (https://dreme.stanford.edu/) funded by the Heising-Simons Foundation. With DREME colleagues, he is currently creating materials to help teachers, parents, and university students to gain insight into children's mathematical thinking and how it can serve as the foundation for early mathematics education.

Jacqueline D. Goodway is Professor of Kinesiology at The Ohio State University. Dr. Goodway's research agenda focuses on promoting an "Active Start" in young children who are economically disadvantaged and elucidating the role motor competence plays in leading a physically active lifestyle and maintaining a healthy weight. She has a leading textbook in motor development, over 70 peer-reviewed articles, 8 book chapters, 50 keynotes, and over 200 presentations, receiving numerous awards for her work. Dr. Goodway actively works to promote motor development and physical activity for young children in underserved communities across the world.

Mileidis Gort is Professor of Educational Equity and Cultural Diversity at the University of Colorado Boulder School of Education. Previously, she held faculty appointments at the University of Connecticut (Assistant Professor of Bilingual/Bicultural Education), University of Miami (Associate Professor of Language and Literacy Education), and The Ohio State University (Associate Professor of Bilingualism and Biliteracy). Dr. Gort's research interests include bilingual and biliteracy development in young children, bilingual education policy and practice, culturally and linguistically sustaining pedagogies, genre-based literacies, and the ethnography of biliteracy education. Her scholarship has been published in premier academic journals such as the *Elementary School Journal, Journal of Literacy Research, Journal of Early Childhood Literacy, Research in the Teaching of English, Bilingual Research Journal, Educational Policy, International Multilingual Research Journal, Language and Education,* as well as various edited volumes. She is a co-editor, with Eurydice Bauer, of *Early Biliteracy Development: Exploring Young Learners' Use of their Linguistic Resources* (Routledge, 2012), and an editor of the recently released volume: *The Complex and Dynamic Languaging Practices of Emergent Bilinguals* (Routledge, 2018). Dr. Gort serves as co-editor of the *International Multilingual Research Journal* and series editor of the Research in Bilingual Education book series (Information Age Publishing).

Vasilis Grammatikopoulos is Professor of early childhood education assessment and Head of the Department of Early Childhood Education and Care in International Hellenic University (IHU), Thessaloniki, Greece. He was previously Senior Lecturer in Teesside University, UK and Assistant Professor in University of Crete, Greece. He was also Postdoctoral Teaching Fellow in Liverpool Hope University, UK, in University of Macedonia, Greece. He has participated as a coordinator and key staff member in numerous funded national and international research projects, and his main research interests are educational assessment, early childhood education assessment, and evaluation of physical activity in early childhood education. He has published over 30 research papers in peer-reviewed international journals.

Athanasios Gregoriadis is an Associate Professor of Early Years at Aristotle University of Thessaloniki, Greece. In the past he has been a visiting professor in the University of Bielefeld, Germany and a visiting research fellow in the University of Oxford, UK. His main research interests include teacher-child relationships, early educators' professional development, home learning environments and the evaluation of the quality of early childhood education environments. He is the author and co-author of numerous articles, book chapters and books. Dr. Gregoriadis is the scientific director of the Experimental Early Childhood Center of Thessaloniki and was the chair of the 29th EECERA conference in 2019. He has also participated as a coordinator and a key staff member in many internationally and nationally funded research projects.

Mary Harrill is Senior Director of Higher Education at the National Association for the Education of Young Children (NAEYC). In this role, she contributes to NAEYC's higher education policy work, and oversees NAEYC's higher education accreditation system for early childhood degree programs and NAEYC's national recognition system of higher education programs through its partnership with the Council for the Accreditation of Educator Preparation (CAEP). Prior to working at NAEYC, Mary worked at Achieving the Dream (ATD) overseeing grants to improve student success in community colleges and managing the recruitment and retention of colleges in the ATD network. From 2001 until 2014, Mary worked for the American Association of Colleges for Teacher Education (AACTE) in many roles – including overseeing federal and state policy, managing state chapters, overseeing governance operations, and leading initiatives to improve principal preparation and advance clinical preparation of educators.

Susan E. Hill is an Associate Professor of Early Childhood, School of Education at the University of South Australia. She is a researcher in the field of early language and literacy. She is the author and co-author of numerous articles and book chapters on early literacy, family literacy, and literacy and new technologies. She has written a number of books for researchers, teachers, and children. She has worked for many years in Australia, as an early childhood teacher, reading adviser, and literacy consultant, and presents at national and international conferences in the areas of early literacy, family literacy, and early childhood education.

Mairéad Hourigan works as a mathematics teacher educator within the STEM Education Department of Mary Immaculate College, University of Limerick, Ireland. Her research interests include mathematics education, STEM education, children's mathematical thinking, effects of pre-tertiary education, educational transitions, the characteristics of pre-service teachers, and the impact of initial teacher education and research methodologies to support understanding.

Wu-Ying Hsieh is an Associate Professor at the Department of Special Education in the University of Northern Iowa. Dr. Hsieh is involved in a pre-service teacher program to prepare Early Childhood Special Education teachers. Her research interests center on early childhood inclusive education, coaching teachers in using literacy strategies, and early math teaching and learning.

David Imig teaches courses in teacher education policy and practice at the University of Maryland in College Park in the Department of Teaching and Learning, Policy and Leadership. He co-coordinates the College's cohort-based Education Doctorate Program. Prior to coming to the University of Maryland, Dr. Imig was the president and chief executive officer for the Washington, DC-based American Association of Colleges for Teacher Education for 25 years. Dr. Imig has served as chair of the NCATE executive committee, chaired the National Policy Board for Educational Administration, the Forum for Education Organization Leaders and the Board for the Carnegie Project on the Education Doctorate. He currently serves as a Senior Fellow for the Carnegie Foundation for the Advancement of Teaching and is co-lead on the Foundation's iLEAD initiative. He has consulted in the US and abroad on matters of educator preparation policy and practice. He holds three academic degrees from the University of Illinois, Urbana-Champaign and an honorary doctorate from Bridgewater State University.

Douglas Imig is the lead for evidence and outcomes for Early Childhood Action Strategy, a statewide collective impact effort designed to improve outcomes for young children in Hawaii. Before joining ECAS, Dr. Imig directed research and evaluation for the Indianola (Mississippi) Promise Community and was a professor of political science at the University of Memphis. Dr. Imig has also worked as a resident fellow at the Urban Child Institute, as a research fellow at the University of Oklahoma's Center for Infants, Toddlers, Twos and Threes (IT3), and as a director of the Benjamin L. Hooks Institute for Social Change at the University of Memphis. He is the author of books and articles on children's advocacy, social movement mobilization, and political representation.

James E. Johnson is Professor of Early Childhood Education at Penn State and Past President of The Association for the Study of Play and current Series Editor of *Play & Culture Studies*. His current research interests concern digital play during the early years and parental and teacher influences.

Becky Kochenderfer-Ladd is a Professor at the T. Denny Sanford School of Social and Family Dynamics in Arizona State University. She is an editor in chief of the *Journal of Applied Developmental Psychology* and Director of the Class Act Project, a long-term study of the risk factors and consequences of school bullying and peer victimization. She is also Co-Director (with Dr. Gary W. Ladd) of the 4R-SUCCESS Project, a program that promotes children's social, academic, and character development in elementary-school classrooms. She has published empirical studies, theoretical articles, and reviews of research on peer victimization and children's social development, and is interested in how children respond to peer victimization and how such responses affect risk for future victimization and adjustment problems.

Gary W. Ladd is the Cowden Distinguished Professor in the T. Denny Sanford School of Social and Family Dynamics at Arizona State University. Previously, he was a Professor at Purdue University and the University of Illinois at Urbana-Champaign, and a Fellow at the Center for Advanced Studies in the Behavioral Sciences at Stanford. Gary W. Ladd was Associate Editor for the scientific journals such as *Child Development* and *Journal of Social and Personal Relationships*, and currently is Editor of *Merrill-Palmer Quarterly*. He is Director of the Pathways Project, a long-term study of children from kindergarten through high school and Co-Director (with Dr. Becky Ladd) of the 4R-SUCCESS Project, a program that promotes children's social, academic, and character development in elementary-school classrooms. Dr. Ladd has published books, empirical studies, theoretical articles, and reviews of research on children's social development, and is interested in how socialization experiences with peers, parents, and teachers influence children's early psychological and school adjustment.

Bernadette M. Laumann is the Co-Principal Investigator for the Illinois Early Learning Project at the University of Illinois Urbana-Champaign. Dr. Laumann holds a PhD in Special Education from the University of Illinois at Urbana-Champaign. She has taught undergraduate and graduate courses in early childhood special education. She has been an early childhood special education teacher, principal of an inclusive preschool program, researcher, and a project coordinator for federal and state-funded grants. Her research interests include mentoring and induction support for beginning teachers, professional development, and the use of technology in teacher education

Aisling M. Leavy is Head of the Department of STEM Education at Mary Immaculate College. She lectures in mathematics education and STEM education. Her research interests include children's mathematical thinking, the development of statistical reasoning, problem solving, the mathematics preparation of pre-service teachers, STEM education, and the development of conceptual understanding of mathematics in primary classrooms.

Susan C. Levine is the Rebecca Anne Boylan Professor of Education and Society at the Department of Psychology in the University of Chicago, joining the faculty after receiving her PhD in Psychology at MIT. Her research focuses on early spatial and numerical thinking, and particularly on the kinds of adult-child interactions that foster learning in these domains. She studies how particular kinds of mathematical language contribute to children's mathematical learning, and how the use of this language can be encouraged through interventions involving shared book reading and math apps. She also studies intergenerational effects of negative math attitudes, specifically the role of parents' and teachers' math attitudes on the mathematical achievement and attitudes of children. Dr. Levine is a member of the DREME (Development and Research in Early Math Education) network (https://dreme.stanford.edu/) funded by the Heising-Simons Foundation. She served as co-PI of the NSF Spatial Intelligence and Learning Center (SILC) and is the inaugural faculty director of the University of Chicago Science of Learning Center.

Kristi H. Liverette received her PhD in Applied Developmental Psychology from George Mason University. Currently she is a District Support for KinderCare Education. Her research interests are social emotional development in child-care settings and the implementation of curriculum to help support social emotional development.

Esther Elena López-Mulnix is an experienced Senior Administrator in Higher Education with demonstrated results with regional and programmatic accreditation, innovation, and sustainability in the United States as well as internationally. She has strong professional and research skills in Leadership, Instructional Design, Multicultural Education, Public Speaking, Editing, Publishing, Translation (Spanish), Wellness, Mentorship, and Faculty Development. She is editor-in-chief of the Journal of Hispanic Higher Education, a blind, peer reviewed, interdisciplinary, international academic journal published by SAGE. She was one of the founding editors nearly twenty years ago.

Camille C. Martínez is a doctoral student and a Graduate Teaching Assistant at the Department of Teaching, Learning and Sociocultural Studies in the University of Arizona and a Graduate Teaching Assistant at the Department of Mexican American Studies. She is a former kindergarten, elementary, and middle-school teacher and holds a BA in Business Administration and B.S. in Sociology from the University of California, Riverside; an MEd in Curriculum and Teaching with a major in early childhood education from the University of Southern California; an MEd in Learning and Teaching from the Harvard Graduate School of Education; and an MEd in Educational Leadership from the University of Arizona. She holds multiple teaching and administrative credentials in Arizona and California. Ms. Martínez was the former Director of Project Native III, funded by the U.S. Department of Education, to prepare Native American Teachers and Principals. She is also an alumnus of the Harvard Graduate School of Education's Management in Educational Leadership Institute. She has worked as a Coordinator for the American Cancer Society, a nationally Certified Public Health Specialist, the Director of the Emergent Literacy Project, and a Senior Education Director. Over the past six years, she has worked at the University of Arizona in several positions: University Supervisor for Student Teaching, Coordinator of the Early Childhood Teacher Preparation Program, and Adjunct Instructor for Teacher Preparation Program (Educational Foundations courses and Instructional Practices courses). Ms. Martinez's ancestral heritage originates in the Southwest geographical region as she represents the Pascua Yaqui and the Tohono O'odham Indigenous people. Her professional interests are in the sociology of education, early childhood, and family literacy.

Tiana Moore is a Graduate Fellow at the National Center for Children and Families (NCCF) in Columbia University and a Robert Wood Johnson Foundation Health Policy Research Scholar. Before arriving at the NCCF, she attended Stanford University, where she earned her BA in Human Biology with a concentration in children's health in underserved communities, and her MA in Sociology with a concentration in poverty and inequality. Her current research interests include examining features of neighborhoods that contribute to health and education disparities and two-generation interventions that improve outcomes for both children and parents.

Kimberly T. Nesbitt is an Assistant Professor of Human Development and Family Studies at the University of New Hampshire. Dr. Nesbitt's research focuses on the processes that enhance or disrupt cognitive development in early childhood, including differential outcomes associated with socio-economic status. She also pursues a line of applied research examining instructional practices that contribute to the emergence of more sophisticated cognitive abilities and enable young children from diverse backgrounds to learn in early educational environments. Dr. Nesbitt has collaborated on various longitudinal studies examining the co-development of young children's executive function and academic skills as well as randomized control trials evaluating the effectiveness of early educational curricula and pedagogy. Her work appears in education and psychology journals, including *Child Development*, *Developmental Psychology*, *Journal of Educational Psychology*, and *Early Childhood Research Quarterly*.

Michaelene M. Ostrosky is Grayce Wicall Gauthier Professor of Education and Head of Special Education at the University of Illinois at Urbana Champaign (UIUC). Throughout her career, Dr. Ostrosky has been involved in research and dissemination on the inclusion of young children with disabilities, social emotional competence, and challenging behavior. She strives to promote caring, inclusive communities where all children are accepted, and where differences are celebrated. As a former teacher of young children who were deaf and blind, and adults with severe disabilities, Professor Ostrosky is committed to making research accessible to practitioners and family members through her writing and presentations. She has published more than 100 peer-reviewed articles, book chapters, and books, and she is a frequent speaker at state, national, and international conferences. Professor Ostrosky has mentored approximately 30 doctoral students, and she has been recognized for her professional accomplishments with honors such as UIUC University Scholar, Goldstick Family Scholar, College of Education Senior Scholar, and the Division of Early Childhood of the Council for Exceptional Children's Award for Mentoring.

John C. Ozmun is a professor at the Division of Health and Human Performance in Indiana Wesleyan University. He received his doctorate from Indiana University with major areas in motor development and adapted physical education. Dr. Ozmun is active in the study of early childhood motor development and physical fitness. He is a co-author of the textbook *Understanding Motor Development: Infants, Children, Adolescents, Adults,* and has authored or co-authored several book chapters and journal articles.

Douglas R. Powell is a Distinguished Professor Emeritus at the Department of Human Development and Family Studies in Purdue University. His research focuses on professional development and parenting interventions to improve young children's school readiness outcomes. He led the development of the evidence-informed Early Learning Matters (ELM) Curriculum for the U.S. Department of Defense Child Development Program.

Robert Rueda is Professor Emeritus of Educational Psychology at the Rossier School of Education in the University of Southern California. His research has centered on the sociocultural basis of motivation, learning, and instruction, with a focus on reading and literacy in English learners, and students in at-risk conditions. He is a member of the National Academy of Education, and is a fellow of the American Psychological Association and the American Educational Research Association. He recently served as the associate editor of the *American Educational Research Journal (Teaching, Learning, and Human Development),* and has served on the editorial boards of several other educational journals.

Rebecca M. Ryan is a Provost's Distinguished Associate Professor at the Department of Psychology in Georgetown University. She came to Georgetown after completing a post-doctoral fellowship at the University of Chicago's Harris School of Public Policy Studies in Fall 2009. She earned a PhD in Developmental Psychology from Columbia University in 2006. Most broadly, her research explores the implications of socioeconomic disadvantage for children's home environments and well-being as well as the relationship between parenting and children's development in at-risk contexts. Both strains of research explore two fundamental influences on child well-being: the quality of parent-child interactions and parents' ability to invest time and money in children's environments. Her research has been continuously funded by both federal and private institutions, including the National Institute for Child Health and Human Development, the National Science Foundation, the Russell Sage Foundation, and the Spencer Foundation. Her overarching aim is to link developmental psychology to child and family policy in an effort to enrich both fields.

Julie Sarama is the Kennedy Endowed Chair in Innovative Learning Technologies and Distinguished University Professor at the University of Denver. She conducts research on young children's development of mathematical concepts and competencies, implementation and scale-up of curricula, professional development models and their influence on student learning, and implementation and effects of learning technologies (including those she has created) in mathematics classrooms. These studies have been published in more than 77 refereed articles, 6 books, 55 chapters, and over 80 additional publications. Dr. Sarama has directed over 25 projects funded by the National Science Foundation (NSF), the U.S. Department of Education's Institute of Education Sciences (IES) and the National Institute of Health (NIH), the Bill and Melinda Gates Foundation, and the Heising-Simons Foundation.

She is currently conducting research on learning trajectories and developing tools and activities for teachers and caregivers who want to implement learning trajectories in early mathematics. Dr. Sarama has taught secondary mathematics and computer science, gifted math at the middle school level, preschool and kindergarten mathematics enrichment classes, and mathematics methods and content courses for elementary and secondary teachers. She designed and programmed over several computer programs and apps for children birth-grade 6 and is interested in the unique role technology can play in learning. See https://www.researchgate.net/profile/Julie_Sarama.

Christopher M. Schulte is an Endowed Associate Professor of Art Education in the School of Art at the University of Arkansas. He earned his BA and MA in Art Education from the University of Northern Iowa and his PhD in Art Education from Penn State University. His research on the study of childhood art, specifically drawing in early childhood, has appeared in handbooks and other edited volumes as well as in national and international journals in art education, early childhood education, and qualitative studies. He is the editor of *Ethics and Research with Young Children: New Perspectives* and co-editor with Christine Marmé Thompson of *Communities of Practice: Art, Play, and Aesthetics in Early Childhood.* He also serves as senior editor of the *International Journal of Education & the Arts* and as Associate Editor for the *Journal of Curriculum and Pedagogy.*

Serap Sevimli-Celik is an Assistant Professor of Elementary and Early Childhood Education at the College of Education in the Middle East Technical University (METU), where she teaches courses on movement education, play, and creativity at the undergraduate level and embodied learning at the graduate level. Her research interests center on teacher education, embodied learning, active designs for indoors and outdoors, play pedagogy and cross-cultural play, and creative thinking. She has recently written a book chapter on active designs for movement in early childhood education.

John A. Sutterby is an associate professor at the University of Texas San Antonio. His research interests include children's play and play environments, children's literature, and action research. He has twice served as the president of The Association for the Study of Play.

Christine Marmé Thompson is Professor Emerita at the School of Visual Arts in Penn State University, where she taught from 2001 to 2017. Her research focuses on children's culture and art learning, especially the social contexts of early childhood art. She is a co-editor, with Christopher M. Schulte, of *Communities of Practice: Art, Play and Aesthetics in Early Childhood* (2018) and, with Liora Bresler, of *The Arts in Children's Lives: Context, Culture, and Curriculum* (2002); an editor of *The Visual Arts and Early Childhood Learning* (1997); a section editor and contributor to

The International Handbook of Research in Arts Education (2007), and an author of numerous publications.

Nikolaos Tsigilis is an Assistant Professor at the Aristotle University of Thessaloniki, Greece. He has published more than 100 articles in international and national scientific journals regarding quantitative research methods in early childhood education and in education in general. He is highly recognized and cited in prestigious international peer-reviewed journals. He is a member of several scientific associations and he has taught in several workshops organized by the Northern Greek Psychological Society and the South East European Research Center. His research interests are quantitative research methods, applied statistical techniques, psychometrics instrument development and validation, occupational burnout, job satisfaction, and self-efficacy.

Colleen Uscianowski is a postdoctoral researcher at the Department of Human Development in Teachers College, Columbia University. Her research interests include developing and evaluating resources to help parents and teachers promote young children's math learning and improving the mathematical thinking of children with learning disabilities. Dr. Uscianowski is an affiliate of the DREME (Development and Research in Early Math Education) network (https://dreme.stanford.edu/) funded by the Heising-Simons Foundation. She was formerly an elementary and middle school special education teacher, where she developed a deep interest in math teaching and learning. She also served as an adjunct lecturer at Hunter College, City College, and Teachers College and provided professional development for middle school administrators and early childhood teachers.

Ann-Marie Wiese focuses on issues related to the education of young dual language learners at WestEd's Center for Child and Family Studies and currently directs the Parent Involvement Project. She has contributed to the development of various resources in collaboration with the California Department of Education to support the education of young dual language learners. She co-directed the project that developed the *California's Best Practices for Young Dual Language Learners Research Overview Papers* which informed the *California Preschool Program Guidelines* and accompanying videos. Dr. Wiese most recently co-authored a chapter titled "Pathways to Relational Family Engagement with Culturally and Linguistically Diverse Families: Can Reflective Practice Guide Us?" for the edited volume *Family Involvement in Early Education and Child Care, Advances in Early Education and Day Care*. Wiese received a PhD in education from the University of California, Berkeley. She began her career as a Spanish–English bilingual teacher in a two-way immersion program.

Eileen Wood is a professor and full-time faculty member at the Department of Psychology in Wilfrid Laurier University. Her primary research interests involve examining how children, youth, and adults (young through old) acquire and retain information especially in educational contexts. One focus involves investigating instructional strategies that facilitate learning and memory. A second focus targets the impact of new technologies as instructional tools across the lifespan and in formal and informal learning contexts. Topics covered in her research span cognition, memory, metacognition, reading, writing, social development, multitasking, and learning strategies. An adjacent line of inquiry examines gender issues and gender stereotypes and how new technologies impact on these domains.

David B. Yaden, Jr. (PhD, University of Oklahoma) is Professor of Language, Reading and Culture at the Department of Teaching, Learning and Sociocultural Studies in the University of Arizona (UA) and was co-editor of the *Journal of Literacy Research* from 2013 to 2016. Prior to his present position at UA, he held appointments at Emory University, the University of Houston, and the University of Southern California. He was a Principal Investigator (1997–2002) in the federally funded Center for the Improvement of Early Reading Achievement (CIERA) where he oversaw the implementation of an early literacy curriculum for Spanish-speaking preschoolers in inner-city Los Angeles. In 2009–2012, he directed a statewide consortium of researchers from Arizona's three major universities in the evaluation of the state's early childhood initiative, *First Things First*, a study of over 9,000 children, ages birth to seven years of age, to evaluate health, developmental, and educational factors contributing to school readiness. His research interests and specializations include developmental issues in early childhood education, the acquisition of literacy and biliteracy in young children, family literacy, theories of reading disability, microgenetic and developmental research design, and the application of complex adaptive systems theory to growth in reading and writing.

Susan Young recently retired as a senior lecturer in Childhood Studies and music education at the University of Exeter, UK. She is Senior Research Fellow at the Applied Music Research Group (AMRG), University of Roehampton, London and Research Associate of the Centre for Research in Early Childhood, Birmingham. Her career has combined university lecturing with a range of freelance research, evaluation, and consultancy specializing in early years arts, music and education. Originally trained as a pianist at the Royal College of Music London, she spent her early career teaching music in secondary and primary schools before gaining a PhD in music education from the University of Surrey. She has published widely in professional and academic journals and has authored, and co-authored, several books. Last year she completed a Master of Letters (MLitt) in anthropology from the University of Bristol.

Evridiki Zachopoulou is Professor and Dean of the School of Social Sciences in International Hellenic

University (IHU), Thessaloniki, Greece. She was a lecturer at the Department of Physical Education and Sport Science in Democritus University of Thrace, Greece (1999–2003). Her main research interests are focused on the enhancement of the professional development of early childhood professionals, the evaluation of the quality of early childhood education, the implementation of intervention programs for preschool aged children and their effects on children's development, and the creativity in teaching and the creative child. She has published over 40 papers in international scientific journals. Prof. Zachopoulou has been extensively involved as a coordinator and key staff member in national and international research projects.

About the Editor

Olivia N. Saracho is a professor of education at the Department of Teaching and Learning, Policy and Leadership of the University of Maryland. Her areas of scholarship include family literacy, cognitive style, play, and teaching and teacher education in early childhood education. She is widely published in the field of early childhood education. Olivia N. Saracho authored the book titled *An Integrated Play-Based Curriculum for Young Children* (Routledge/Taylor and Francis Group) and co-authored with Mary Jalongo the book titled *Writing for Publication: Transitions and Tools that Support Scholars' Success* (Springer Publishing Company). Olivia N. Saracho is a co-editor, with Bernard Spodek, of the *Handbook of Research on the Education of Young Children*, 3/ed. (20013, Routledge). She is also a editor of the Contemporary Perspectives in Early Childhood Education series (Information Age Publishing). She also edited the *Handbook of Research Methods in Early Childhood Education: Research methodologies*, Volume I and *Handbook of Research Methods in Early Childhood Education: Review of Research Methodologies*, Volume II (Information Age Publishing).

Editorial Advisory Board

Additional Reviewers

Susan Adler
University of Hawai'i-West O'ahu

Enrique B. Arranz-Freijo
University of the Basque Country. Spain

Steven Asher
Duke University

Lisa Michele Barnett
Deakin University

William M. Bart
University of Minnesota

Angela C. Baum
University of South Carolina

Doris Bergen
Miami University

Natalie H. Brito
New York University Steinhardt's

Liane Brouillette
University of California, Irvine

Stuart Brown
Founder and President, The National Institute for Play

Dina C. Castro
University of North Texas

Ang Chen
University of North Carolina at Greensboro

Lori Custedero
Teachers College Columbia University

Karen Diamond
Purdue University

Paul Angus Duncum
University of Illinois at Urbana Champaign

Bronwyn S. Fees
Kansas State University

Karen A. Ferneding
Southern Arkansas University

Daisy E. Fredericks
Grand Valley State University

Manuel Freire Morán
Universidad Complutense de Madrid

Douglas Frye
University of Pennsylvania

Claudia Galindo
University of Maryland

Kyra D. Gaunt
University at Albany

Cyndi Giorgis
Arizona State University

Paul Gorski
Equity Literacy Institute and EdChange

Peter Gray
Boston College

Dominic Gullo
Drexel University

Frances Hancock
Orlando, Florida

Emily Hoffman
Ball State University

Berchie Holliday
Cincinnati, Ohio

Jason Hustedt
University of Delaware

Mary Jensen
The State University of New York, Geneseo

Jennifer Kampmann
South Dakota State University

Laurie Katz
The Ohio State University

Barbara Z. Keifer
The Ohio State University

Jason Kosnoski
University of Michigan – Flint

Vicki Lake
The University of Oklahoma – Tulsa

Riikka Mononen
University of Oslo, Norway

Jennifer Neitzel
University of North Carolina

Larry Nucci
University of California, Berkeley

Rebecca Oxford
Maxwell Air Force Base - Air University

Jane Page
University of Melbourne

Shana Rochester
University of Michigan

Stephanie Sanders-Smith
University of Illinois at Urbana-Champaign

Wayne Slater
University of Maryland

Susan Sonnenschein
University of Maryland, Baltimore County

Patricia St. John
Teachers College Columbia University

Stephen Thornton
University of South Florida

Margaret Walker
University of Maryland

Thomas Weible
University of Maryland

Nancy Wiltz
Towson University

Preface

Early childhood education is a field that includes practitioners in nursery schools, elementary schools, Head Start centers, child care centers, family homes, and other institutions. Its practitioners are referred to as teachers, child development specialists, early childhood educators, child care givers, and by other names. As a field it serves children whose ages range from birth to approximately eight years; occasionally parents of these children are also considered as its clients. The purposes of early childhood education include education, child care, and the nurturing of development. Seldom does a single program of early childhood education serve children across this entire age range. Nor do programs for all children in this educational range look alike. Programs for infants and toddlers include activities and physical settings that are different from one another. Some early childhood programs emphasize the caring function, whereas other programs emphasize the educational function and some engage in what Magda Gerber calls "educaring," which refers to caring and treating infants with respect and trust in their abilities to develop naturally at their own pace. In addition, there are programs for children within the same age range that differ from one another. They may serve children with different characteristics, for example, children with disabling conditions, children who are gifted, children who are at risk of academic failure, or children for whom English is not their initial language. Thus, although there is a coherence to the field of early childhood education, programs in the field vary by age, by characteristics of their clients, by purpose, and by institutional sponsorship.

In the 1960s early childhood education was a minor field, although it was still evolving. Public kindergartens for children in the southeast or the central parts of the United States were not available. There were limited teacher preparation programs in colleges or universities at that time. In addition, community colleges had not been established. In 1964, the National Association for Nursery Education (NANE) became the National Association for the Education of Young Children (NAEYC) with less than 1,500 members throughout the United States, although there were many more members of local and regional groups that later became affiliates of NAEYC. The Association for Childhood Education International (ACEI) was the other national association that focused its attention in early childhood education. At that time, it had tens of thousands of members, but it only concentrated on the education of children in nursery schools, kindergartens, and elementary schools, with its special attention on kindergarten and primary education. Since 1948 the World Organization for Early Childhood Education (OMEP) has been the international organization that had national committees functioning in many of the 70 countries represented in the organization. The OMEP Committee in the United Sates was a small organization at that time and continues to be relatively small.

Although the field of early childhood education has a history of more than 150 years, research specific to early childhood is more recent. The scientific study of education is only about 100 years old, as is the scientific study of the development of children. Much of the early child development research, from the work of G. Stanley Hall through the studies conducted by the illustrious early childhood research centers funded by the Laura Spellman Rockefeller Foundation, focused primarily on understanding young children. The research attempted to establish patterns of development, the range of individual differences in those patterns as well as the influence of various environmental factors.

As the field continued to evolve in the 1960s, we began to see the creation of a broad range of educational interventions to enhance young children's learning and development through the creation of program "models." The reaction toward these models of early childhood education, and their implementation, especially with children who might risk academic failure in their later school careers, led to research on the short- and long-term outcomes of programs for young children. Much of the early research in early childhood education programs now seems naive. Often the objective of these experimental programs was to increase IQ scores through short periods of attendance in early childhood education programs. However, this research led to a realization that early childhood programs can have serious short- and long-term educational consequences for many populations of young children.

Since the era of the 1960s, the field of early childhood education has expanded greatly. Today, the majority of children entering kindergarten have previously been in some type of early childhood education program, and kindergarten education has become almost universal. With this growth has come increased research in the field of early childhood education. One indication of that increase is the creation of early childhood journals in recent years, such as the *Early Childhood Research Quarterly*, the *Journal of Research in Childhood Education*, *Early Child Development and Care*, *Early Education and Development*, and *Early Childhood Education*. These journals were devoted to almost exclusively to reporting research in early childhood education. Not only has the number of studies in the field expanded over the years, but the range of research topics and research methodologies used has expanded as well.

Research and practice in early childhood education are still closely allied with the field of child development. What children in this age range are capable of learning is determined to a great extent by their level of development. In addition, how children develop at this stage is determined by what they learn and many environmental factors including education and cultural contexts. As a result, practice and research in early childhood education are informed by and related to child development research.

Whereas research in the various domains of early child development has generated significant knowledge related to early childhood education, so has research on young children's learning in the various educational content areas. Early childhood research, however, goes well beyond classroom practices. Increasingly, research is being used as a basis for suggesting new social policies as well as for looking at the consequences of those already established social policies. Setting standards for programs and for personnel requires the establishment of legal requirements that programs must meet. Such standards are found in state school codes, state licensing regulations for child care centers, and state teacher certification requirements. Standards are also set voluntarily, through the accreditation of early childhood programs and of programs that prepare early childhood personnel. Such standards should not be arbitrary; they should enable the profession to improve the quality of the education offered to young children. Therefore, regulatory agencies must continually seek knowledge upon which to base these standards. Increasingly in the last several years, research in early childhood education has been policy oriented.

Just as early childhood educational practice changes, so does early childhood educational research change. Understanding the nature of the research process and the new approaches to educational research that are evolving is important to educators who utilize research as well as to those who produce research. Thus, the chapters in this volume review and critically analyze studies that use different types of research methodologies grounded in its academic field. For example, studies in children's literature are conducted based on a literary perspective, most of them use literary criticism or critical theories for their methodology.

The development of any book requires that choices be made – choices in what to include and exclude. There is no way that everything that everyone might consider relevant can be addressed in a single volume. Authors who have written specific chapters have been forced to select carefully what to include. As editor, I had to make similar choices. Important areas of research and theory have not been included. Although some of this might be the result of oversight, generally, it is the result of forced choices in the context of what seemed to be of critical importance at this point in the development of the field. If this *Handbook* had been developed at another time, another set of choices might have been made.

This book is designed to be used by students of early childhood education at all levels of professional development and levels of sophistication such as mature scholars seeking research outcomes in areas to be further studied in depth as well as others searching for summary statements of various aspects of the field. It should be of use to administrators and policy makers as a source of information to be consulted in policy development. It should also be a resource to classroom teachers as a way to help them reflect on practice, acquaint them with theories and empirical research to explain classroom circumstances, and provide suggestions for what might become classroom activities.

It is hoped that this *Handbook of Research on the Education of Young Children* will serve the needs of many in the educational community. Scholars seeking the current state of research knowledge in various areas should find this volume useful. Practitioners who are trying to seek knowledge of research and its practical implications should find that this volume serves their needs. Policy makers who shape the early childhood educational enterprise through law and regulation will also find this volume useful. I have tried to make this *Handbook* both informative and accessible, with individual chapters presenting a review and critical analysis of relevant and current research and identifying the implications of this research for practice and policy development.

Olivia N. Saracho

Acknowledgments

The preparation of this volume involved the work of many people. The contributions of the individual chapter authors are evident, and these authors deserve thanks for their careful attention to the domains they surveyed. A special thanks needs to be given to members of the *Handbook's* Editorial Advisory Board. They have provided excellent advice from the very beginning; they reviewed and commented on the basic conception of the book; and they made suggestions about topics to be covered and scholars who might be interested in contributing a chapter. Individual members of the Editorial Advisory Board also served as chapter reviewers; they carefully read drafts of chapter manuscripts and provided suggestions for their improvement. In addition, I sought the assistance of several scholars to also help me review the chapters. I want to wish to thank those colleagues who helped me review the chapters. They read, critically reacted, and provided recommendations for each of the chapters in the *Handbook*. Both the names of the members of the *Handbook's* Editorial Advisory Board and other reviewers are acknowledged in a separate section of the *Handbook*. The help and support of the editorial staff at Routledge/Taylor & Francis must also be acknowledged, especially Alex Masulis who helped to initiate the fourth edition of the *Handbook* and Misha Kydd who provided continued support and encouragement toward its completion.

Introduction

A Contemporary Researcher's vade mecum (Redux) Sequentia

OLIVIA N. SARACHO

For numerous decades early childhood education programs have been developed all over the world. Programs for young children in different countries have encountered numerous challenges and concerns. Presently society has acknowledged the importance of young children's learning, which is evident in the increase in early childhood teacher education programs at both community colleges and four-year institutions. Nationally, approximately two million early childhood educators care and educate nearly ten million children whose ages range from birth to eight years. Roughly half of those educators are in center-based programs and are home-based providers (Whitebook, McLean, Austin, & Edwards, 2018). Similarly, nearly 1.9 million educators teach children in public schools (McFarland et al., 2018).

This acknowledgment is evident in the increased enrollments in early childhood education programs. In 2016, enrollment in preprimary programs included 42% of three-year-olds, 66% of four-year-olds, and 86% of five-year-olds. The enrollment was higher for five-year-olds, although the percentage for four-year-olds was higher than for three-year-olds. Approximately, 54% of three- to five-year-old children were in full-day programs, whereas 81% of three- to five-year-olds were in kindergarten and attended full-day programs. More three- to five-year-old kindergarten children attended full-day programs than three- to five-year-old preschool children who were attending full-day programs (McFarland et al., 2018). Approximately 1.58 million children were enrolled in state-funded preschool programs. Such enrollment had more than 1.3 million four-year-olds, which consists of one-third of all four-year-olds in the country. In relation to three-year-olds, the enrollment was more than 227,000, which is almost 5.7% of three-year-olds (Friedman-Krauss et al., 2019). In the year 2020–2021, it is projected that this population will increase to 37.4 million students (Aud et al., 2011). Typically, the preschool children's enrollment in classrooms appears to be stable, but the development of preschool programs in the public schools prompted an increase of preschool children in the public school programs (U.S. Department of Education,

2018a, 2018b). In 2017, the majority of four-year-olds and a considerable (but lesser) percentage of three-year-olds were enrolled in state and locally supported preschool programs (Friedman-Krauss et al., 2018). Within all public programs (e.g., preschool, federal and state-funded Head Start), 44% of four-year-olds and 16% of three-year-olds were served. Since 2002, there has been an increase in enrollment across these programs where four-year-olds increased 13.5 percentage points and three-year-olds increased merely 2.8 percentage points (Friedman-Krauss et al., 2019).

The importance of young children's learning is also evident in the increases in early childhood teacher education programs at the community college and university level. Parallel to this growth has been the increase in knowledge-generating activities in the field, part of which might be attributed to the general knowledge explosion in our society and throughout the world. Evidence of this can be seen in the increase of research activities in the field and the growth of research journals and research associations (Spodek & Saracho, 2003) and government funding.

During the past decade the importance on the quality of early childhood education has considerably improved, which may be the result of a nationwide demand to improve the accountability for schools and funded government education programs by agencies such as the National Research Council (2009) and the Administration for Children and Families (U.S. Department of Health and Human Services, Administration for Children and Families, 2010). In addition, the Head Start Act (2007) focuses on getting young children ready for school before they enter kindergarten (Waterman, McDermott, Fantuzzo, & Gadsden, 2011). Throughout the United States, the implementation of standards-based accountability education reforms such as the federal government's *No Child Left Behind Act* (NCLB) is generating a new set of challenges in early childhood education (Brown, 2011).

Funding has increased to emphasize the need for effective education and care for children at the earliest ages, well before they enroll in the public schools. For example, the Pew

Center on the States has been conducting groundbreaking research in early childhood education to provide feedback to policy makers. Pew released a research report that indicates that the public education systems in America need to admit children below kindergarten. It describes strategies to revamp public education to include preschool children, which refers to children ages three to five. This transformation is supported in their rigorous research where leading scholars and institutions have (1) determined the knowledge and skills that children will need to succeed in school and (2) identified the teaching practices that are most appropriate for them. Pew's report concludes that for more than 40 years, pre-kindergarten education has been one of their most well-researched public education areas. Their results support that young children who attend quality pre-kindergarten programs are more academically and socially prepared when they make their transition to public school and more likely to finish high school and become productive adults in society (Pew Center on the States, 2011).

This explosion of knowledge and the related increase in research results related to early childhood education that are available require that this knowledge be more available and readily accessible to the field. This requirement led earlier to the publication of the first, second, and third editions of the *Handbook of Research on the Education of Young Children* and now to the creation of this fourth edition. The *Handbook* can be a valuable tool to all who work and study in the field. Thus, the *Handbook* can be referred to as a *vade mecum* (a ceaseless companion) that revives (*redux*) and focuses (*sequentia*) on important contemporary research issues in early childhood education that provide researchers and scholars the information necessary to make judgments about these research issues and in important areas that are currently changing theoretical frameworks in early childhood education.

Knowledge of Early Childhood Education

Knowledge of the field of early childhood education consists of three domains: theory, research, and practice. Although these spheres often seem independent of one another, they are interrelated. The process of knowledge generation is *cyclical*, rather than being deductive (top down) or linear (one step always follows another). The forms all overlap. The process usually begins with a problem or issue that needs to be studied through research; this research is driven by theory and practice. The results also contribute to theory and practice, which then provide directions for future research studies. This cyclical process is presented in Figure 0.1 (Saracho & Spodek, 2013; Spodek & Saracho, 2006).

This *Handbook* focuses on research conducted over the past decade or so. The decision to focus on the most recent research was made so that there would be minimum overlap with the work presented in the first, second, and third editions of the *Handbook*. The editor recognizes that this is a limitation. She also acknowledges, as she has noted elsewhere, that the current research is only possible because of

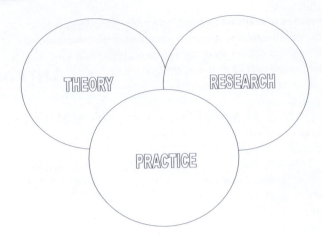

Figure 0.1 Interaction process.

the theoretical work and the research studies that have been conducted in the past. We very much "stand on the shoulders of giants" (Spodek & Saracho, 2003). However, the field has seen a significant amount of new theory building as well as the development and use of new research paradigms to study early childhood education. These are acknowledged here.

Current social and historical conditions have also aroused a more dynamic focus on the potential for practical contributions to the systematic study of early childhood education. These circumstances have led many early childhood education scholars to respond by focusing their research attention to applied problems, such as improving teaching techniques and raising the children's educational and intellectual status. Empirical investigations in these problem areas have contributed to both theoretical and practical underpinnings. By using knowledge generated in the past along with knowledge that is being generated in the contemporary scene, we can best understand early childhood education and serve the teachers and children who engage in it.

History of Early Childhood Education

The field of early childhood education has a history of more than 150 years. The first educational programs in the United States that were specifically designed for young children were *infant schools*. This program was based on the ideas that Robert Owen had developed in Scotland (Owen, 1824). Even before Owen himself came to America, his ideas had crossed the ocean. Infant schools were established in a number of communities in the eastern United States during the first quarter of the nineteenth century. These programs did not flourish for long. The infant school educated young children separately from their families. The idea of educating young children outside the home was counter to the family ethic of the time (Strickland, 1983).

Later, German immigrants brought the *kindergarten*, created by Freidrich Froebel in Germany, to the United States. The kindergarten slowly expanded in the United States, sponsored by various organizations to serve a number of purposes in addition to educating young children. By the late nineteenth century, kindergartens began to be incorporated into public school systems (Shapiro, 1983). Today, kindergartens are part of public elementary schools throughout the United States and almost all five-year-olds go to kindergarten. Recently, some public elementary schools have also begun to admit children ages three and four.

Other approaches to early childhood education were imported to the United States in the first quarter of the twentieth century. The *nursery school*, which originated in England with Margaret Macmillan at the beginning of the twentieth century to serve low-income children and their families, was soon established in America. The *Montessori method*, which originated in Italy, was brought to the United States after World War I, though these schools closed during the Great Depression of the 1930s. However, the movement was resurrected in the late 1950s and early 1960s.

The nature of the early childhood programs evolved over the years. Nursery schools and Montessori schools, which were originally designed to serve children of poor families, became programs from more affluent families in America. Kindergarten, that was originally Froebelian, was influenced by American progressive education and reconstructed to become the American kindergarten that can be observed today. Even now changes are taking place. With kindergartens essentially part of the elementary school in America, it has been influenced by the program of the primary grades; at the same time it has influenced the program of the primary grades. Today, American kindergartens are more academically oriented, especially since the Federal *No Child Left Behind Act* (2001) was passed. In addition to the original Montessori method, a modified method was developed in the United States that was supported by the American Montessori Society. Similar changes have taken place in other approaches to early childhood education. The changes that have taken place over the years were the result of many influences, but they had little influence by research over the years.

The changes in early childhood education programs took place as programs originally developed in other countries were modified to better fit into American society. In addition, as American society has changed, programs for young children have changed. Seldom were early childhood education programs modified by recourse to research, however, until the 1960s.

Early Childhood Education Research

Research in early childhood education has had a much shorter history than practice. It seems that research in early childhood education follows practice and that it needs a strong foundation of practice before research can become established in the field. Until about 70 years ago the only research on young children was research in child development, even though the field of early childhood education is older than the field of child development. While universities often established "laboratory nursery schools" on their campuses, these often served to provide "laboratory experiences" for students in child development, home economics, and education or to provide research subjects for studies of child development. Seldom were these laboratory nursery schools used to inquire into the nature and consequences of the educational process for young children or as a way of testing new curriculum ideas in early childhood education.

Only in the late 1950s and early 1960s did we see a movement toward establishing a research base that was specifically in early childhood education. The impetus came from several major changes: changes in developmental psychology, a concern for America's national defense, and a concern for social justice.

For years in America, the maturationist theory of Arnold Gesell and his followers was the accepted theory in child development. This theory posited that most human attributes were determined genetically and were therefore fixed at birth. It was believed that one could thwart developmental attributes by not providing a proper environment, but one could not increase a person's intelligence or modify any other such attribute than make her or him taller. Thus, any attempt to increase the intelligence of individuals or change any other attribute was futile. Academic learning was the domain of the elementary and secondary school. The nursery school and kindergarten were designed to keep children healthy and safe so that their genetic makeup would unfold. Readiness was a naturally occurring maturational process. Real education, it was believed, began in the primary grades when children were taught to read.

This changed when new English translations of the work of Jean Piaget and Lev Vygotsky reached our shore. The arguments regarding the impact of environment were further supported when J. McVicker Hunt (1964), an American psychologist, pulled together a range of studies supporting this notion in a book that had a major impact on psychology and education—*Intelligence and Experience*. Others further argued that preschool experiences could have a greater impact on human development than experiences provided to children later in life (Bloom, 1964). In addition, behavioral psychologists were arguing that environmental conditions could shape human development (Bijou, 1977). It was further found that children growing up in poverty suffered from significant environmental deficiencies that impacted on their learning and development. By offering these children early educational experiences, it was argued, society might be able to ameliorate the consequences of poverty—and ultimately even eliminate poverty.

A second influence was the consequence of the Soviet Union's space efforts, which took place when the Soviets launched orbiting rockets in the 1950s, well before our own space program got underway. There was a concern that we were losing the Cold War and that Soviet technology was overshadowing our own. As a result, there was a press to improve the education of children and youth in our schools. This led to the enactment of the National Defense Education Act of 1958 that was designed to improve public education in America. Teachers were provided with additional education to increase their competence. In addition, a series of curriculum development projects were launched to improve elementary and secondary education. These projects were designed to bring the subject matter of the school more closely in line with the knowledge that scholars in the various fields were currently developing.

These projects in science, mathematics, social studies, and language were focused on the education of children from kindergarten to the upper grades. Among the products of the curriculum research projects were materials from the *Elementary Science Study* (Allen, 1970), which consisted of three activity-based programs—Elementary Science Study (ESS), Science-A Process Approach (SAPA), and the Science Curriculum Improvement Study (SCIS). Bredderman (1983) provides the following descriptions for these science programs.

- The ESS was developed at the Educational Development Center, Newton, Massachusetts, from 1961 until 1971. In comparison to the other activity-based programs, the ESS was the least structured. It lacked sequenced objectives and detailed instructional procedures. The program included 56 independent units with no fixed sequence across the elementary grades. The ESS included life and physical science units and some units that entailed activities in spatial relations, logic, and perception. Its activities were considered to be motivating and provided children with opportunities for problem solving and understanding natural phenomena. In the activities children were introduced with a challenge, problem, or perplexing situation; then they were engaged in open-ended exploration, and concluded with a class discussion. Teachers informally observed the children to evaluate them.
- The development of the SAPA was directed by the Commission on Science Education of the American Association for the Advancement of Science (AAAS, 1993/2009), Washington, DC, from 1963 until 1974. SAPA was a very structured program that focused on teaching specific science processes. It had approximately eight basic and six advanced science processes. Each process was broken down to additional small procedures for instructional purposes. All procedures were described using behavioral terms and were hierarchically organized. SAPA's content was drawn from both the life and physical sciences and was considered to be understandable and applicable. The sequenced objectives were used to evaluate individual children or the whole class.
- The SCIS was developed at the Lawrence Hall of Science at the University of California at Berkeley from 1962 until 1974. The main goal of the program was to develop scientific literacy. It had a combination of basic knowledge about the natural environment and focused on the children's investigating ability and curiosity. SCIS had

12 units that included one life and one physical science unit at each elementary grade level. Approximately ten key concepts were developed each year. These concepts were interconnected and were supposed to provide a conceptual framework for the children's thinking. SCIS provided children with opportunities to develop their science processes. The regular instructional pattern encouraged children to explore new materials, learn a new concept, and apply the new concept in a variety of new situations. Children were evaluated through observation during activities, through examination of their work, and through assessment with special evaluation instruments.

These three innovative science programs, which were developed and tested as part of the curriculum reform movement, began at the kindergarten level. The first two of these programs used Piagetian theory to justify the design of their activities. The third used a behavioral approach. Each of them ran counter to the uses of kindergarten suggested by the maturationist theorists of child development who saw kindergarten primarily as either a place for children to adjust to the rigors of the elementary school or a place that supported the development of children's readiness for school learning.

The third influence was the concern for social justice in America. In many ways, early childhood education had been historically linked to a concern for social justice, as the history of the kindergarten movement showed. Kindergartens early on were used as a way to ameliorate the damages to children caused by poverty or to deal with other social ills impacting on children (Shapiro, 1983). This influence was further felt as President Lyndon Johnson established the Head Start program as part of his War on Poverty. Even before the creation of Head Start, a number of research projects, funded by educational foundations, had been developed to test the influence of different curriculums on the development of children from low-income families. These various programs were based on different assumptions about what might be considered an effective early education. See Spodek (1973) for a description of these program assumptions.

These early research projects were the basis later for a major national study of Head Start programs called the Planned Variations project—an attempt to compare the outcomes of different approaches to early education in terms of children's intelligence and school success. These outcomes were to show which curriculum was most effective for young children. Unfortunately, the evaluation of the outcomes of these various projects was controversial and no "one best system" prevailed. However, the idea that various early educational curriculums can be tested in practice and that various aspects of early childhood education are worthy of study led to a growth in research relating to early education in the United States. In addition, various research studies were undertaken to test the impact of Head Start on children's learning and development. It can be argued that this was the beginning of early childhood educational research in the United States.

Conditions that Support Early Childhood Education Research

There are a number of conditions that are necessary for research in a field to flourish. There needs to be a place where research will be nurtured or at least allowed to develop. There needs to be a cadre of well-trained researchers who are knowledgeable of their field. There needs to be financial support for research to be conducted. And there needs to be a way for researchers to share their work—to communicate with one another and with others: practitioners, administrators, and policy makers. These conditions would slowly develop in America.

The majority of research in the United States is conducted in universities. After World War II many of the state teachers' colleges expanded to become multipurpose colleges and finally full-fledged universities. Thus, a number of venues were created in which research could flourish and there was an increase in the output of research in this era, but not in early childhood education.

However, early childhood education was a small field well into the 1960s. There were no public kindergartens for children in the southeast or the central parts of the United States. There were few teacher-training programs in colleges or universities at that time nor were community colleges yet established. Starting in the 1970 there was an expansion of kindergarten education as well as an expansion of the entire field of early childhood education. With that came the establishment and expansion of early childhood education programs in colleges and universities. As that happened, doctoral programs in early childhood education also grew and as did the number of PhDs in early childhood education, trained in research, since one of the requirements of such a program was a dissertation. In addition, most universities require that their faculty engage in research and that the research be published.

While the production of research in early childhood education increased in the United States, the vehicles for disseminating that research were limited. Over the past years, both American organizations began to sponsor research journals: the *Early Childhood Research Quarterly*, sponsored by the National Association for the Education of Young Children (NAEYC) and published originally by Ablex and currently by Elsevier which began publication in 1986. The *Journal of Research in Childhood Education* published by the Association of Childhood Education International (ACEI) began publication at the same time. Although it was originally published by ACEI, it is currently published by Taylor and Francis/Routledge. Additional journals related to research in early childhood education have developed over the years, such as *Early Child Development and Care*, *Early Education and Development*, and *Early Childhood Education*; these have become more scholarly and research-oriented.

There were two other organizations that have served to disseminate research in early childhood education. One of these is the Society for Research in Child Development (SRCD).

This organization focuses primarily on child development research and has paid less attention to early childhood education in recent years, both in its journal and in its conference programs. The SRCD publishes *Child Development*, their research journal, and has a biennial research conference. The other organization is the American Educational Research Association (AERA). In addition to sponsoring a number of journals, the AERA holds an annual conference. Its divisions and its special interest groups (SIGs) determine the content of that conference. Many early childhood studies are presented in sessions sponsored by Divisions B (Curriculum Studies) and C (Learning and Instruction) of the organization. Most importantly, there are two SIGs that are specifically devoted to early childhood education: the Early Education and Child Development SIG and the Critical Perspectives in Early Childhood Education SIG. In addition, the conference of the NAEYC includes a research track. Thus, there have been avenues for the reporting of research and these have increased in the recent past.

While the production and dissemination of research in early childhood education has increased substantially in recent years in the United States, it has also increased substantially in other parts of the world. The European Early Childhood Education Research Association with its annual research conference and journal, the *European Journal of Research in Early Childhood Education*, and the Pacific Early Childhood Education Research Association with its annual research conference and journal, the *Asia-Pacific Journal of Research in Early Childhood Education*, give evidence of this.

The *Handbook of Research in Early Childhood Education* (Spodek, 1982) and the three editions of the *Handbook of Research on the Education of Young Children* (Saracho & Spodek, 2013; Spodek, 1993; Spodek & Saracho, 2006) were developed to bring together in one source the research available at that time in early childhood education. Since the field has changed significantly since 2013, there is a need for an update of these handbooks and one that focuses primarily on studies conducted during the last decade of scholarly activity in the field. Hence, there is a need for this volume.

Organization of the Current Volume

This *Handbook* is organized into three sections: (1) Early Childhood Education and Child Development, (2) Early Childhood Educational Curriculum and Instruction, and (3) Foundations of Early Childhood Educational Policy. This is very similar to the sections of the first, second, and third editions except that we eliminated the fourth section on research and evaluation strategies for early childhood education. This section was included in the first and second editions but not in the third and the fourth editions. Although some of the chapters cover the same areas of research as the previous editions and in a few cases the authors are the same, all the material in this edition is new. In addition, some areas that were covered in the first, second, and third editions of the *Handbook* are not covered here while new areas are covered.

The section on child development and early childhood education has the same chapters from the third edition but eliminated the one on creativity. The areas that were maintained are taking on increasing importance in the study of early childhood education.

In the section on early childhood educational curriculum, we deleted the chapters on language, science, and movement. The content for the chapter on social studies was changed to consider children as active citizens in their classrooms and local communities. In addition, we have added two three chapters on outdoor play environments, technology, and media exposure in early childhood and infancy. To enhance the chapter on technology, a chapter was added that focused on traditional media (TV) and mobile digital technologies. These chapters were added because we found that important research had been conducted in these areas in the last few years.

The final section on Foundations of Early Childhood Educational Policy includes chapters on childhood poverty (which the authors refer to as "low-income"), bilingual children, multicultural education, children with disabilities, families, and the professional development (PD) of teachers. Although we no longer include the chapter on children who are at risk, child care, and assessing children's learning, we have added two chapters that focus on teachers. One is on the preparation of early childhood educators and the second one is on assessing teacher-child relationships from a cultural context perspective, because we believed that studies in these areas are making an impact in the study of early childhood education.

This edition of the *Handbook* includes a number of new authors. Among those are scholars in early childhood education and related fields from countries other than the United States including Spain, Greece, Ireland, Australia, Turkey, Saudi Arabia, Indonesia, South Korea, Thailand, Canada, and Great Britain. This provides some recognition that the study of early childhood education is not limited to to this country, the United States of America. Rather, it is an international endeavor.

Overview of the *Handbook*

The chapters that are included in the three parts of this *Handbook* present current reviews of research and theory within the various areas of early childhood education. The chapters provide a review and critical analyses of the research in important areas that are currently changing theoretical frameworks in early childhood education.

Early Childhood Education and Child Development

Much of the theory and research in early childhood education are derived from the field of child development. Indeed, there are some educators who view the field as one of applied child development. The first part of this *Handbook* presents reviews of research in the areas of child development that are of particular significance to early childhood education. Also

included is a discussion of the uses of child development knowledge for early childhood education.

Although early childhood education is allied with cognitive psychology, the social nature of early childhood education means that only certain *parts* of psychology have direct usefulness for teachers. For example, cognitive research related to neuropsychology cannot really give specific advice about how young children learn in classrooms. Areas that focus on cognitive processes (e.g., information processing) can be specific and thus helpful, but only if envisioned within the social ecology of early childhood classroom life. Yet many areas (e.g., joint attention, pretend play, or bilingualism) have direct classroom implications because of the forthrightly social way they are framed. The social basis of early childhood education needs to be understood more fully so that developmental psychology can focus its support for early childhood education more effectively.

In Chapter 1, Enrique B. Arranz-Freijo, Joana Acha, and Florencia Belén Barreto provide several sections where they provide an updated overview of the basic landmarks of cognitive development during early childhood. The first section focuses on the so-called classical theories, which marked the beginning of the scientific study of cognitive development is presented. The contributions made by Piaget's genetic epistemology and Vygotsky's cultural-historical theory are explored and the historical origins of developmental scales are expounded. Then the section outlines the most important contributions made by information processing theories. The second section analyzes the early progress of basic cognitive processes as prerequisites for developing higher-level cognitive functions. The third section focuses on the executive functions and their cross-cutting nature in the cognitive, emotional, and behavioral self-regulation domains. The fourth section analyzes the development of language and theory of mind, which have some similarities but develop differently. The fifth section presents and discusses the implications of all the previous findings for preventive-educational interventions focusing on cognitive development and its optimization within different development contexts.

Cultural roots, philosophical perspectives, history, and scientific theories have motivated current members of societies to embrace the premise that early experience plays a critical role in human development. Researchers have become interested in early relationships and their role in children's growth and development. For many years, theory and research on early socialization have focused on parent-child relationships, but it has become increasingly clear that the age mates or peers also contribute to the young children's development.

Decades of research has demonstrated the importance of positive peer relationships and social competence to children's psychological, social, and emotional well-being as well as their academic success. In Chapter 2, Becky Kochenderfer-Ladd and Gary W. Ladd consider several issues that have motivated research on young children's peer relations and the evidence that has been gathered to address these issues. They review this extensive literature on children's social competence and peer relationships, and consider the significance of these aspects of children's development. Becky Kochenderfer-Ladd and Gary W. Ladd organized their chapter around several primary social challenges, or tasks, such as gaining entry into peer activities, earning acceptance among classmates, and forming and sustaining positive relationships, that confront young children, and then consider the social competencies or skills that are needed to master such tasks. They conclude the chapter with recommendations for promoting healthy peer relationships and facilitating the development of social competence. Successful, independent interactions with their peers is a critical predictor for the children's later mental health and well-being, beginning during preschool, continuing during the grade school years when peer reputations solidify.

The current educational environment focuses on the children's cognitive development, which promotes their pre-academic skills. Recent early childhood educational research trends reveal an increasing focus on children's school readiness and predicting their academic success. However, their emotional competence is essential for their social development. The elements of emotional competence help to ensure effective social interactions built upon specific skills such as listening, cooperating, seeking appropriate help, joining interactions, and negotiating.

Emotional competence, such as expressing, understanding, and regulating emotions in an adaptive manner, is crucial in its own right, and for young children's social and pre-academic development. In Chapter 3, Susanne A. Denham and Kristi H. Liverette review the nature of and skills involved in emotional competence, and their interrelation and acquisition during early childhood. Each aspect of emotional competence undergoes important transformations during early childhood. The ways in which emotional competence contributes to the preschoolers' social and pre-academic progress are emphasized: a positively expressive emotional style, more developmentally appropriately sophisticated emotional knowledge, and increasing ability to regulate emotional expression and experience are the hallmarks of successful social interaction and learning. Then Susanne A. Denham and Kristi H. Liverette examine how intrapersonal and especially interpersonal contributors (i.e., parents and teachers), as well as gender and culture, can impact early childhood emotional competence. Each of these contributors can affect the acquisition and demonstration of early childhood emotional competence. Finally, they discuss issues regarding educational programming and assessment to foster early childhood emotional competence, given its foundational importance to concurrent and later development in several domains.

Motor development examines the individuals' changes in motor behavior across their lifespan. These changes are the results of experiences rather than age. In 2009 the National Association of Sport and Physical Education (NASPE, 2009) revised "Active Start", a set of national physical activity guidelines for children whose ages range from birth to five years. In Chapter 4, Jacqueline D. Goodway, Ruri Famelia, Ali Brian, John Ozmun, and David L. Gallahue first provide a brief overview of an emerging concept of physical literacy, define motor development, and discuss principles of motor development. Then they describe and compare models of motor development and the emergence of key fundamental motor skills (FMS). Then they summarize gender differences in motor skills, along with developmental delays in FMS of young children. Then the authors provide a list of resources to assist early childhood teachers select developmentally appropriate instructional activities including lesson ideas provided by several professional organizations. They conclude with a summary of the literature seeking to improve motor skills and physical activity behaviors via intervention, along with implications for promoting an active start in young children.

Early Childhood Educational Curriculum and Instruction

During the last century, children's literature has come to be valued and appreciated as an art form for children. Research evidence supports that it provides young children with the foundation for later literary understanding and aesthetic development. The young children's aesthetic experiences assist them in all facets of their lives, including their language and linguistic development. In addition, studies suggest that children's literature has a significant effect on the young children's intellectual and emotional experiences in their wider world (Kiefer, 2004). In Chapter 5, Hebert P. Ginsberg, Colleen Uscianowski, Cristina Carrazza, and Susan C. Levine examine young children's picture books, both print and electronic, that focus either explicitly or implicitly on mathematical concepts and methods. A focus on mathematics picture books is valuable because they can serve as a friendly and meaningful introduction to mathematics for both children and adults. Their perspective derives in good measure from developmental psychology and cognitive science, because they believe that science-based ideas about children's thinking and development can contribute to the understanding and betterment of children's literature and its uses. At the same time, Hebert P. Ginsberg, Colleen Uscianowski, Cristina Carrazza, and Susan C. Levine are sensitive to a humanistic perspective that values picture books as literature. They examine the effectiveness of picture books in promoting children's learning of mathematics concepts and methods, as well as their acquisition of relevant vocabulary in mathematics. To help adults select high-quality picture books, they present an analysis of generally (there are always exceptions!) desirable and undesirable picture book features. Their analysis focuses on literary merit as well as on special features that are essential for conveying mathematical ideas. Hebert P. Ginsberg, Colleen Uscianowski, Cristina Carrazza, and Susan C. Levine conclude with a discussion of practices that can promote sensitive mathematics picture book reading, a suggestion about writing mathematics picture books, and a description of future directions for research.

Research exploring the efficacy of mathematics curriculums designed for young children has shown that high-quality mathematics programs produce learning gains for young children in their number and geometrical understandings (Presser, Clements, Ginsburg, & Ertle, 2015). The outcomes that show that specific numerical knowledge developed prior to entry to elementary school is a strong predictor of later achievement (National Mathematics Advisory Panel, 2008; National Research Council, 2009) have resulted in growing support for an emphasis on early number. In Chapter 6, Aisling Leavy and Mairéad Hourigan explore the emerging research relating to young children's mathematical understanding in the area of statistics and probability. They focus on research that examines young children's statistical understandings as they engage in rich data modeling, mathematical inquiry, and cycles of statistical investigation alongside examining their emerging understandings of the big ideas in probability. Specifically, they reviewed research examining young children's ability to (1) represent and structure data, (2) generate and select attributes, and (3) make predictions and generate informal inferences about data. Aisling Leavy and Mairéad Hourigan provide insights into the crucial role of contexts, the language of chance, understandings of randomness, quantification of chance, and combinatorial reasoning. They argue that these studies reveal the nascent potential of young learners to grapple with complex concepts and processes fundamental to statistics and probability. They maintain that young children are not only capable of deeper statistical and probabilistic thinking than was previously thought but that the origins of these ideas appear at ages earlier than generally anticipated. Instruction based on comparisons between quantities has the potential not only to increase children's numerical knowledge but also to build links between numeracy and other important components of early childhood mathematics.

Research into early literacy has often been of a predictive nature to find discrete elements of literacy that may be precursors of future development. Recently, changes in policy and practice have led to an increase in research focus on young children's language and literacy development (Pelatti, Piasta, Justice, & O'Connell, 2014). In a wide-ranging review of quantitative and qualitative early literacy research, Teale, Whittingham, and Hoffman (2018) identified four patterns in early literacy: accretion or a gradual growth in knowledge, the influence of "scientifically valid" research, limited response to the increasingly diversified student populations, and a greater focus on very young children. There is a more academic emphasis within preschools and the early years of school that D'Agostino and Rodgers (2017) maintain that kindergarten is now the new first grade, which is supported by Bassok, Latham, and Rorem (2016). In Chapter 7, Susan E. Hill reviews how early literacy begins by considering different theoretical perspectives and their implications for research and practice. She examines a move toward multimodal, semiotic approaches to early literacy research as literacy is increasingly viewed as multimodal within young

children's digital worlds. The semiotic approach focuses on context, incorporating oral and written language as well as other modes of representing and communicating meaning. Susan E. Hill concludes with a call for early literacy researchers to consider research from a semiotic theoretical position with close observation of how children are making meaning with new multimodal forms of literacy.

In early childhood education young children are prepared to become participants in a democratic society. Foundational thinkers like John Dewey, Frederick Froebel, and Maria Montessori emphasized the importance of citizenship preparation in the education of young children (Saracho & Spodek, 2007). The United Nations Educational, Scientific, and Cultural Organization (UNESCO, 2010) defines "Citizenship education as educating children, from early childhood, to become clear-thinking and enlightened citizens who participate in decisions concerning society" (UNESCO, 2010). Education for young children (ages birth to eight years) on citizenship education has traditionally been a concept in social studies and has focused on the first of UNESCO's (2010) goals, "educating people in citizenship and human rights through an understanding of the principles and institutions [which govern a state or nation]." However, in Chapter 8, Stacy DeZutter goes beyond the discussion about social studies. Rather, she assumes a broader approach, asking how recent research might inform the education of young children for participatory citizenship in a democratic society. She has structured the chapter according to the three most recent and prominent areas of inquiry in social studies. Stacy DeZutter examines research on the education of young children in a democratic society. She focuses on three areas of research: (1) research that aims to position children as active citizens in their classrooms and local communities; (2) research that examines specific methods for advancing civic learning in early childhood; and (3) research on content area literacy in social studies. She presents the promises and challenges of each of these strands of research and requests the extension and deepening research on democratic education in early childhood.

Research on the visual arts in early childhood traditionally focused on issues of development approached within a psychological paradigm compatible with a modernist understanding of the origins and functions of art making in human life. Since the latter part of the twentieth century, attention has shifted from an emphasis on preservation of the innate creativity of individual children toward recognition of art making, even in its earliest manifestations, as a social and historical activity, undertaken in dialogue with peers, adults, and the surrounding culture. In recent years, this shift has continued, reflecting the influence of postmodern thought on our conceptions of children and childhood art. In Chapter 9, Christine Marmé Thompson and Christopher M. Schulte present contemporary research as it extends, critiques, and exists alongside earlier understandings of what child art is, what it means for human functioning, and how it is influenced by formal and informal teaching and learning. These issues of development, context, and curriculum are addressed from the perspective of early childhood art education as a palimpsest in which modernist and postmodernist concepts of childhood, art, and education continue to coexist, often in contradictory relationships, reflecting the complexity of attitudes that shape research, theory, and practice.

Until recently early childhood music education research was mostly focused on the preschool years and on the types of activity typical of educational settings. Over the last decade this focus has expanded in two directions. The age phases of focus have expanded to include babies and children who are under three years of age. In addition, the contexts of focus have expanded beyond educational settings to include diverse contexts, including a keen interest in the home and family. Both expansions reflect contemporary social, cultural, and technological changes and how they have impacted on the lives of infants and very young children. In Chapter 10, Susan Young provides an overview of scholarly activity in early childhood music across the age phase of birth to five-years-old. She focuses on the last decade but also introduces earlier research and theory that has paved the way for the more recent activity. Susan Young strives to be broad in scope, including research at all levels from the micro level of brain activity to macro cultural and political issues in international contexts. She plots the paradigm and practice shifts that have characterized early childhood music education in the last 10–15 years. In her individual sections, she discusses musical development, musical play, musical engagement, and pedagogy and learning. Although many topics are introduced, the substantial references lead the reader to explore further sources in order to expand their knowledge and understanding.

Play in early childhood education is a very broad topic that continues to create much discussion and debate. It is also complex and difficult to define, which threatens the place of play in the field. As a result, kindergarten is becoming the new first grade (Bassok et al., 2016; D'Agostino & Rodgers, 2017). Fortunately, professional and public interest in children's play is growing and seems to be relentless. Cambridge University's first "Professor of Play" David Whitebread calls play "in fashion" academically and clinically; "the new renaissance" is reflected in current academic journals such as *The International Journal of Play* and many recent books (Whitebread, 2018). At the level of use, this contemporary interest is revealed by amplified media awareness, community "Play Days," conferences, and other signs. In early childhood education, which covers birth to eight years of age according to the NAEYC, play is definitely the furthermost investigated subject with outcomes frequently worthwhile for practice and policy. Research on play is very perplexing because of the absolute quantity of studies on many areas. In Chapter 11, James E. Johnson, Serap Sevimli-Celik, Monirah A. Al-Mansour, Tugce Burcu Arda-Tuncdemir, and Pool Ip Dong discuss (1) several specific research studies and (2) selected general play concepts, issues, and applications to practice and policy. They examine research on play and

early education that they organized into three sections: (1) definitions and concepts, including content pertaining to play and learning and play and assessment; (2) importance of play, including subsections for self-regulation, social competence, literacy, numeracy, physical well-being, and creative expression; and (3) play pedagogy, including sections on narrative approach, creative drama, use of open-ended objects and activities, and the use of electronic technology. With nuanced understanding of play concepts and with knowing the importance of play in child development, professionals in the field are better positioned to articulate and implement pedagogies of play involving child-initiated play.

Many assume that the landscape of outdoor play consists of the display of available playground equipment. It is important to also consider the green scaping around the equipment to be a function of the environment and other elements beyond playground equipment. In Chapter 12, John A. Sutterby examines outdoor play environments and some of the historical and cultural forces which have shaped the appearance of the present environments. He emphasizes the concept of the playground as a force for democratic ideals. He describes how play environments are situated in a larger social context which includes the historical park and playground movements that have underscored the importance of play and recreation for creating opportunities for everyone to develop a better understanding of each other. Then John A. Sutterby examines the present landscape for play which is currently being removed from the society's democratic ideals by obstacles such as adult fear, an emphasis on safety, and increased attention to academic outcomes. The standardization of the outdoor play experience prompted for environments to become sterile and monotonous for children. Lastly, he identifies movements which are at this time resisting these forces in order to allow children to continue to play as they have in the past.

Foundations of Early Childhood Educational Policy

Growing up in poverty can significantly affect young children's readiness to learn upon school entry. In 2017, approximately one in five of all children under the age of six years in the United States is living below the official poverty threshold (Fontenot, Semega, & Kollar, 2018). These children are at a higher risk of living in poor or near-poor households than older children; therefore; they are regularly characterized as "low-income." Living in low-income households is associated with lower levels of well-being for children across a range of domains. In Chapter 15, Tiana Moore, Rebecca M. Ryan, Rebecca C. Fauth, and Jeanne Brooks-Gunn first explore the complexities in measuring poverty and identify relationships to child development. Then they reflect on potential pathways through which poverty may influence child development. Next, they review federal programs and policies that provide money as well as food, housing, and health care to poor and near-poor families with the aim of reducing poverty. Finally, the authors conclude with a discussion of how programs available to low-income families have changed over time and the role that these programs play in reducing child poverty.

Recently, society in the United States has been directing their attention to the education of young emergent bilingual (EB) learners whose ages range from birth to eight years. Such attention is evidenced by the publication of numerous summary research reports from government sources, non-profit organizations, and researchers concerning the education of young children who many (e.g., Carnock, 2018; Guzman-Orth, Lopez, & Tolentino, 2017; National Institute for Early Education Research [NIEER], 2018; Takanishi & Le Menestrel, 2017) frequently termed as *Dual Language Learners* (DLLs). Publications explain in great detail numerous issues and challenges related to the academic achievement of young EBs (e.g., Mulligan, McCarroll, Flanagan, & Potter, 2018; Rathbun & Zhang, 2016). Repetitive research outcomes revealing the history of academic achievement in bilingual programs (e.g., Collier & Thomas, 2017) and their fully supported economic benefits (Garcia, Heckmann, Leaf, & Prados, 2018) for underserved children speaking languages other than English and for the communities in which they live, purposeful resistance to and failure to fully support young EB children, are still very much a reality. In Chapter 16, David Yaden, Mileidis Gort, Camille Martinez, and Robert Rueda adopt the term EB to more accurately index and designate those whose bilingualism is still emerging. In spite of a significant increase in recent asset-based national policy statements aimed at recognizing the language diversity of young children, much of the language research on EBs still emanates from a deficit perspective. Nonetheless, the authors advance the hypothesis that the reasons for lower performance are less likely to be due to learner-based deficits and more likely to be due to policy, programmatic, and instructional factors. They also suggest that a reconceptualizing of traditional research categories is needed since these categories are socially constructed and descriptive, not theoretical or explanatory of language learning. Similarly, as scholars have identified a "special education symbolism" that is evoked about individuals with various "dis/ability" labels that marginalize them, David Yaden, Mileidis Gort, Camille Martinez, and Robert Rueda believe that there is also an *EB symbolism* or mindset that is evoked about young multi-language learners in schools or research settings, creating an overall negative ideology about their performance outcomes. Finally, they advocate for a "contrapuntal" theoretical approach for studying young EBs in hopes of generating improved research designs that result in deeper insights into children's language learning abilities.

Recent studies indicate that young DLLs make up a growing percentage of the school age population. The education of children who speak a language other than English at home is a major concern given that they represent almost one-third of the population of children ages birth to eight years in the United States. Approximately more than 5.5 million—or 10% of

students in the United States lack sufficient proficiency in English to engage academically without support. Young children in the United States who have at least one parent who speaks a language other than English at home has increased by 24% since the year 2000. In fact, young DLLs now make up close to one-third of all young children (ages birth to eight years) in the United States (Park, O'Toole, & Katsiaficas, 2017). Simultaneously, the educational system has traditionally underserved these children which has detained them from keeping pace with their monolingual English-speaking peers (Takanishi & Le Menestrel, 2017). Maximizing opportunities for DLLs requires an understanding that language development is interdependent with multiple factors and an array of other institutional conditions and cultural practices (García & Ozturk, 2017). The education of children who speak a language other than English at home is a major concern given that they represent almost one-third of the population of children ages birth to eight years in the United States. In Chapter 17, Ann-Marie Wiese, Delis Cuéllar, and Eugene E. García summarize past and present federal legislation and provide an overview of state-level policies that guide the education of English learners and DLLs, with an emphasis on preschool age children. They describe California's approach to DLLs as an exemplar, focusing on recent changes in the state's educational language policy and California's Early Learning and Development System. They conclude by proposing research-based recommendations for the early childhood education field and addressing assessment and early learning approaches at both program and classroom levels.

The contemporary multicultural movement includes children who are not part of the mainstream, middle-class White culture, including children of color, girls, children with disabilities, sexual orientation, immigrants, the poor, and non-English-speaking children. The 1954 Supreme Court decision, Brown versus the Board of Education of Topeka, provides a good place to begin the history of multicultural education in the United States (Wardle, 2013).

In the United States, early childhood classrooms have children who are identified as White, Hispanic, Black, Asian, American Indian or Alaska Native, and Pacific Islander. Hence, nowadays, it is vital that educators learn effective multicultural teaching skills. There is a "… pervasiveness of institutions to privilege one set of racial experiences over another" (González & Morrison, 2016, p. 89). Thus, cultural differences among teachers and students make it necessary for prospective teachers to develop multicultural skills. In Chapter 18, Esther López-Mulnix describes a cultural journey for early childhood education teachers. The journey's goal is to develop multicultural skills and recommend policy applications for multicultural education. She presents literature and research to frame multicultural teaching effectiveness. She begins with the teachers' awareness of their values—grounded on their intersecting groups of reference (e.g., race, ethnicity, gender, socioeconomic status, sexual orientation, religion, mental and physical abilities). Esther López-Mulnix continues with exploring the values of diverse students as well as the impact of power and privilege in society in the United States. Then she advocates the development of multicultural skills that are demonstrated by the reflective practice of dialogic pedagogy. She concludes with recommendations for policy applications.

Young children with disabilities are increasingly attending inclusive early childhood programs with their typically developing peers. For over 30 years of research, policy in early childhood special education (ECSE) has supported inclusive environments for children with disabilities. High-quality inclusive educational experiences include a combination of exemplary practices in general early childhood (EC) education along with recommended practices in ECSE. Two documents highlight recommendations for the inclusion of children with disabilities in educational and community settings. The first document, *Early Childhood Inclusion: A Joint Position Statement of the Division for Early Childhood of the Council for Exceptional Children* (DEC) *and the National Association for the Education of Young Children* (NAEYC) IDivision for Early Childhood of the Council for Exceptional Children and the National Association for the Education of Young Children (DEC/NAEYC, 2009), was co-authored by the two largest organizations representing EC and ECSE professionals. It provides a definition for the inclusion of children with disabilities and offers recommendations to expand inclusive opportunities (DEC/NAEYC, 2009). The second document, co-authored by the U.S. Department of Health and Human Services and the U.S. Department of Education (2015), provides recommendations that state to further the inclusion of children with disabilities in early education and care settings. In Chapter 19, Bernadette M. Laumann, Michaelene M. Ostrosky, and Wu-Ying Hsieh draw upon these statements to highlight research on high-quality inclusive settings for preschoolers with disabilities. They include suggestions for research and increased support for inclusive preschool education.

All children are raised in some form of family. But families take different forms in terms of number of adults in the household, contact with extended families, and sheer size of the group. Families differ in the beliefs that they hold about trustworthiness of relationships and in their daily practices and routines. Families live in neighborhoods that reflect available resources for healthy foods, physical activity, social support, and quality of education. In Chapter 20, Barbara H. Fiese and Meghan Fisher describe how families are dynamic systems with shared practices and beliefs that contribute to child well-being and preparedness to learn. These practices and beliefs are embedded in a socio-economic context that includes cultural influences as well as neighborhood context. Thus, they propose Bronfenbrenner's ecological model (Bronfenbrenner & Morris, 1998) to situate the family in a larger developmental context.

In some cases, and at some times, families function in such a way that children's growth is fostered and there is optimal development. In other cases, however, individual and socio-economic forces compromise the family's ability to provide a supportive environment for their children. Fiese and Fisher provide examples of the effects of cumulative risk under high-risk child-raising conditions such as poverty or parental psychopathology that may derail the positive family process and make children vulnerable to behavioral and learning problems. There is reason for optimism, however, as protective factors may promote positive development through responsive parent-child interactions and structured home environments.

Family life is often marked by transitions. Marriage, the birth of a child, going to school, leaving home, marriage of children, and becoming grandparents are just a few of the transitions that members experience as part of normative changes (Walsh, 2003). Several transitions are apparent during early childhood—gaining autonomy through learning to walk, asserting opinions in learning to talk, and being poised to learn when transitioning from home to school. An important transition where characteristics of the child, family, social institutions, and culture transact is the transition to formal school. The family plays an important role in easing these transitions by establishing partnerships with child care providers and school personnel. However, this transition is moderated by available resources in the community and the cultural context in which education is provided. In the third section of the chapter, Fiese and Fisher discuss family partnerships with early childhood care providers and educators and transition to kindergarten as important settings for early learning. Further, in this section they highlight the importance of establishing partnerships between early child care settings in light of increasing diversity in family life.

Early childhood teacher preparation programs assume an important function in preparing teachers to work with young children. Unfortunately, the field lacks the knowledge about how these programs perform this essential role (Sumrall et al., 2017). The preparation of early childhood educators is composed of multifaceted process because teachers of young children (birth through age eight) must respond to the cognitive, physical, social, and emotional needs of young children, which are intertwined and rapidly changing in their first years (Institute of Medicine & National Research Council, 2015). In addition, it (1) focuses on a large age span (birth through age eight), (2) has an assortment of settings (e.g., family child care, Head Start, Early Head Start, private centers, elementary schools, and public pre-K), (3) requires a curriculum among preparation programs, (4) demands that they learn to serve both regular early childhood education and the inclusion of a far more diverse student population, (5) gives teachers challenging working conditions, and (6) extends across all degree levels including often preparing individuals for the same role in the profession degrees at the associate and baccalaureate level (Whitebook et al., 2018). In addition, the policy landscape has different education requirements based on the children's age. For example, individuals teaching in birth through age five private settings only need a high school diploma. In contrast, states require that those teaching young children (ages three to five years) in the public settings are required to have both a bachelor's degree and teaching certificate but provide PD opportunities and requirements. The preparation of early childhood educators has many of the commonalities in terms of features and challenges that face the preparation of K-12 teachers (Chen, 2018; Leachman, Masterson, & Figueroa, 2017; Litvinov, Alvarez, Long, & Walker, 2018), but there are distinct constraints and challenges specific to early childhood preparation. In Chapter 21, Mary Harrill, Madelyn Gardner, Shyrelle Eubanks, Douglas Imig, and David Imig survey the early childhood teacher preparation landscape with a primary focus on higher education programs. They provide an overview of why preparation matters, the education credentials and demographics of the current workforce, characteristics of current higher education pathways, and challenges facing those pathways. Mary Harrill, Madelyn Gardner, Shyrelle Eubanks, Douglas Imig, and David Imig offer a high-level exploration of the early childhood preparation landscape and its complexities as well as developments that can point the early childhood preparation profession forward. While there remains a need for a more robust research agenda to examine what kinds of preparation best prepares individuals to become early childhood educators, the research is consistent about higher education having a positive impact on the quality of early childhood educators.

PD for in-service teachers is increasingly used as a tool to strengthen the impact of early childhood classrooms on children's outcomes. Currently there is considerable interest in PD for in-service teachers as a tool for strengthening the impact of early childhood classrooms on children's learning and development. PD is a major focus of recent policy and programmatic initiatives aimed at improving the effects of programs for young children across a range of early childhood sectors, including child care, state-supported prekindergarten, and Head Start (Martínez-Beck & Zaslow, 2006). The concept of PD as the pathway to improve student outcomes goes beyond the early childhood period. Increasingly education reform is synonymous with teachers' PD. In Chapter 22, Douglas R. Powell and Karen E. Diamond briefly describe an emerging conceptualization of PD that emphasizes intensity, duration, and linking content to the realities of teachers' classrooms and contexts. They examine characteristics and outcomes from research related to three promising approaches to PD. Then they discuss the approaches that are needed for professional learning communities, coaching and similar forms of individualized work with teachers, and uses of innovative technologies in the delivery of PD. Powell and Diamond conclude with a discussion of factors associated with variations in the implementation and engagement of PD and identify needed directions in PD research.

Assessing the quality of teacher-child relationships is a challenging attempt, because of the difficulty in conceptualizing and describing such relationships. All-inclusive methodological customs (e.g., person centered, variable centered) and techniques have been used in this time-consuming task, but in spite of the cumulative size of accessible literature,

the well-validated techniques, especially in early childhood education, continue to be restricted. Until the late 1990s, most of the studies assessing teacher-child relationships consisted of teacher-reported measures, parents' perceptions, or classroom observations. Particularly for investigations in early childhood education, researchers typically evaded including young children either because they thought (1) it was developmentally inappropriate to ask them about their feelings for a specific relationship or (2) children under six years of age were unreliable sources of information (Harcourt & Einarsdottir, 2011) or basically because there was a lack of accessible instruments. Nevertheless, from a methodological perspective, the assessment of teacher-child relationships is more reliable when using several points of view and mostly both the insider's and the outsider's interpretation. The increasing recognition of the importance of teacher-child relationships on children's development, school adjustment, and academic trajectory increases the mandate and emphasizes the need for even more accurate and precise assessment and measurement of the quality of these relationships (Tsigilis, Gregoriadis, Grammatikopoulos, & Zachopoulou, 2018). During the beginning of the new century numerous researchers established developmentally appropriate measures for young children (Papadopoulou & Gregoriadis, 2017). In Chapter 23, Athanasios Gregoriadis, Vasilis Grammatikopoulos, Nikolaos Tsigilis, and Evridiki Zachopoulou reflect on (1) teacher-child relationship assessment and attachment theory and (2) the influence of cultural contexts in the development and interpretation of this relationship. Specifically, it undertakes the problem about the central role of sociocultural processes and cultural contexts assume the assessment of teacher-child relationships and interpreted in different cultural settings. The authors describe important outcomes about the significance of teacher-child relationships, especially in early childhood settings. Then they present the most common techniques for assessing early teacher-child relationships and introduce key aspects of attachment theory to demonstrate the central role it holds in conceptualizing teacher-child relationships. Next they describe the main points of criticism regarding the universality of attachment theory and also summarize brief literature findings about the influence, the role, and the characteristics of cultural contexts. In addition, they provide an example of the construct of dependency in order to build the case for the influence of the cultural context, while measuring teacher-child relationships. Finally, Athanasios Gregoriadis, Vasilis Grammatikopoulos, Nikolaos Tsigilis, and Evridiki Zachopoulou discuss some conclusions and proposals for future research efforts.

While preschoolers may soon begin their formal schooling years, approximately 15 years later, most of these children will enter the country's work force. The recent extension of public education into the prekindergarten years makes early childhood education settings the first introduction for many children to the world of more formal learning in a group setting. These early experiences are critical for establishing learning and dispositional patterns that may affect children's interactions with classrooms for years to come. Over the years, however, no clear or coherent consensus has emerged for the purpose of early childhood education nor whether there should be different purposes in caring for or educating young children. In Chapter 24, Dale C. Farran and Kimberly Nesbitt provide an update of an earlier review (Farran & Hofer, 2013) of measures evaluating the quality of early childhood education, due to efforts complicated by the different histories and missions of programs in this field. In the six years between our original chapter and this one, Quality Rating Improvement Systems (QRISs) have been adopted by many states. They review the research on the utility of QRIS overall and then examine their individual components, all of which have been used separately in research for many years. They confirm that the child outcomes found to be most important for later school success are mathematics, reading (language/literacy), and attention (self-regulation). They report that none of the quality measures currently in the field have demonstrated much capacity for identifying classrooms that are more effective in helping children learn those skills. Dale C. Farran and Kimberly Nesbitt review some newer, alternative efforts to measure quality and delineate issues that make the earlier ones deliver so much less than promised. They believe that the next steps in developing effective measures of classroom quality have to be empirical investigations of the behaviors of teachers and children demonstrated to be linked to gains in those three skill areas.

Researchers disagree on how to define key elements of quality in early education settings, stimulated by the sequence of fluctuating phases of individual caregivers and early childhood programs that have persisted over the past half-century. Unbalanced long-term benefits of several preschool attempts—particularly after quality delays—continue having educators and scholars challenging *which ingredients of quality* can improvement maintainable benefits for children. Concepts of child-care and preschool quality reflect structural features of organizations or social processes that unfold between youngsters and caregivers or teachers. Less attention is paid to how elements of quality respond to the cognitive demands, language, and behavioral norms that young children learn in culturally bounded homes and communities. In Chapter 25, Bruce Fuller, Margaret Bridges, and Claudia Galindo first review conventional definitions of early education quality. Next, they describe how these signs of quality have neglected culturally situated practices, especially how young children learn to become competent members of their social collectives. They focus on how early educators often miss the cultural strengths that Latino children, as one case, demonstrate in care or early childhood settings. These include cooperative skills, engaged approaches to learning, respect for adult authority, and discourse patterns. Finally, Bruce Fuller, Margaret Bridges, and Claudia Galindo identify promising practices through which early educators do scaffold from children's cultural strengths, advancing early growth, and enriching how the field conceives of quality.

State and local education agencies account for most of the four-year-olds enrolled in public preschool and a substantial percentage of three-year-olds, though they often contract with private providers to deliver the service. All of these programs are considered public education, but many are neither located in nor directly operated by public schools. In Chapter 26, W. Steven Barnett and Allison H. Friedman-Krauss describe these programs in detail with particular: governance and administration, evidence of effectiveness, eligibility criteria and enrollment levels, program quality standards, and funding. Each of these features or dimensions of "public school" early childhood education programs varies tremendously among the states. This variation is much more extreme than for K-12 education. Most worrisome is the variation in program effectiveness in recent studies indicating that some programs can even be harmful. W. Steven Barnett and Allison H. Friedman-Krauss explore the role of continuous improvement processes as a key quality component required to assure success. They also assess the extent to which each state has made progress and attained high levels of enrollment and spending per child over the past 15 years. They identify those with the most and least growth and that attain the highest and lowest levels of access and funding.

A Final Note

In the first, second, and third editions, we ended the introduction with the following paragraph. We believe it is as valid today as it was several years ago:

> A book such as this is often seen as more theoretical than practical. Research studies in educational practice seldom lead to the creation of educational practice. Yet research informs practice. By helping practitioners reflect on practice and assess their ideas about their work, the Handbook can suggest new visions of early childhood education. In this way it may be among the most practical of educational endeavors.

References

Allen, L. R. (1970). An evaluation of certain cognitive aspects of the material objects unit of the Science Curriculum Improvement Study elementary science program. *Journal of Research in Science Teaching, 7*(4), 277–281.

American Association for the Advancement of Science. (1993/2009). *Benchmarks for science literacy*. Washington, DC: American Association for the Advancement of Science.

Aud, S., Hussar, W., Kena, G., Bianco, K., Frohlich, L., Kemp, J., & Tahan, K. (2011). *The condition of education 2011* (NCES 2011–033). U.S. Department of Education, National Center for Education Statistics. Washington, DC: U.S. Government Printing Office.

Bassok, D., Latham, S., & Rorem, A. (2016). Is kindergarten the new first grade? *AERA Open, 2*(1). doi:10.1177/2332858415616358

Bijou, S. W. (1977). Behavior analysis applied to early childhood education. In B. Spodek & H. J. Walberg (Eds.), *Early childhood education: Issues and insights* (pp. 138–156). Berkeley, CA: McCutchan.

Bloom, B. (1964). *Stability and change in human characteristics*. New York, NY: John Wiley & Sons.

Bredderman, T. (1983). Effects of activity-based elementary science on student outcomes: A quantitative synthesis. *Review of Educational Research, 53*(4), 499–518.

Bronfenbrenner, U., & Morris, P. A. (1998). The ecology of developmental processes. In W. Damon & R. M. Lerner (Eds.), *Handbook of child psychology* (pp. 993–1028). Hoboken, NJ: John Wiley & Sons.

Brown, C. (2011). Searching for the norm in a system of absolutes: A case study of standards-based accountability reform in pre-kindergarten. *Early Education & Development, 22*(1), 151–177.

Brown v. Board of Education of Topeka, 347 U.S. 483 (1954).

Carnock, J. T. (2018). *Dual language learner data gaps: The need for better policies in the early years*. Washington, DC: New America.

Chen, G. (2018, November 12). 10 major challenges facing public schools. *Public School Review* [Web log post]. Retrieved from https://www.publicschoolreview.com/blog/10-major-challenges-facing-public-schools

Children and youth learning English: Promising futures [A consensus study report of the National Academies of Sciences, Engineering, & Medicine]. Washington, DC: The National Academies Press. doi:10.17226/24677

Collier, V. P., & Thomas, W. P. (2017). Validating the power of bilingual schooling: Thirty-two years of large-scale, longitudinal research. *Annual Review of Applied Linguistics, 37*, 203–217. doi: 10.1017/S0267190517000034

D'Agostino, J., & Rodgers, E. (2017). Literacy achievement trends at entry to first grade. *Educational Researcher, 46*(2), 78–89. doi:10.3102/0013189X17697274

Division for Early Childhood of the Council for Exceptional Children and the National Association for the Education of Young Children (DEC/NAEYC). (2009). *Early childhood inclusion: A joint position statement of the Division for Early Childhood (DEC) and the National Association for the Education of Young Children (NAEYC)*. Chapel Hill: The University of North Carolina, FPG Child Development Institute. Retrieved from https://www.naeyc.org/sites/default/files/globally-shared/downloads/PDFs/resources/position-statements/DEC_NAEYC_EC_updatedKS.pdf

Farran, D. C., & Hofer, K. (2013). Evaluating the quality of early childhood education programs. In O. N. Saracho & B. Spodek (Eds.), *Handbook of research on the education of young children* (pp. 426–437). New York, NY: Routledge/Taylor & Francis.

Fontenot, K., Semega, J., & Kollar, M. (2018). *U.S. Census Bureau current population reports, income and poverty in the United States: 2017*. Washington, DC: U.S. Government Printing Office.

Friedman-Krauss, A. H., Barnett, W. S., Garver, K. A., Hodges, K. S. Weisenfeld, G. G., & DiCrecchio, N. (2019). *The state of preschool 2018: State preschool yearbook*. New Brunswick, NJ: National Institute for Early Education Research.

Friedman-Krauss, A. H., Barnett, W. S., Weisenfeld, G. G., Kasmin, R., DiCrecchio, N., & Horowitz, M. (2018). *The state of preschool 2017: State preschool yearbook*. New Brunswick, NJ: National Institute for Early Education Research.

García, E. E., & Ozturk, M. (2017). *An asset-based approach to Latino education in the United States*. New York, NY: Routledge.

Garcia, J. L., Heckmann, J. J., Leaf, D. E., & Prados, M. J. (2018). *Quantifying the life-cycle benefits of a prototypical early childhood program* [NBER Working Paper No. 23479]. Retrieved from http://www.nber.org/papers/w23479.pdf

González, R. G., & Morrison, J. (2016). Culture or no culture? A Latino critical research analysis of Latino persistence research. *Journal of Hispanic Higher Education, 15*(1), 87–108.

Guzman-Orth, D., Lopez, A. A., & Tolentino, T. (2017). *A framework for the dual language assessment of young dual language learners in the United States* [ETS Research Report No. RR-17-37]. Princeton, NJ: Educational Testing Service.

Harcourt, D., & Einarsdottir, J. (2011). Introducing children's perspectives and participation in research. *European Early Childhood Education Research Journal, 3*(19), 301–307.

Head Start Act, 42 U.S.C. §9801 (2007). Public Law 110–134–Dec. 12, 2007, 121 Stat. 1363. Retrieved October 4, 2011 from http://www.gpo.gov/fdsys/pkg/PLAW-110publ134/pdf/PLAW-110publ134.pdf

Hunt, J. McV., (1964). *Experience and intelligence*. New York, NY: Roland Press.

Institute of Medicine and National Research Council. (2015). *Transforming the workforce for children birth through age 8: A unifying foundation*. Washington, DC: The National Academies Press.

Kiefer, B. Z. (2004). Children's literature and children's literacy: Preparing early literacy teachers to understand the aesthetic values of children's literature. In O. N. Saracho & B. Spodek (Eds.), *Contemporary perspectives on language policy and literacy instruction in early childhood education* (pp. 161–180). Greenwich, CT: Information Age.

Leachman, M., Masterson, K., & Figueroa, E. (2017). *A punishing decade for school funding*. Washington, DC: Center on Budget and Policy Priorities.

Litvinov, B., Alvarez, B., Long, C., & Walker, T. (2018, August 3). Ten challenges facing public education today [Web log post]. Retrieved from http://neatoday.org/2018/08/03/10-challenges-facing-public-education-today/

Martínez-Beck, I., & Zaslow, M. (2006). The context for critical issues in early childhood professional development. In M. Zaslow & I. Martinez-Beck (Eds.), *Critical issues in early childhood professional development* (pp. 1–16). Baltimore, MD: Brookes.

McFarland, J., Hussar, B., Wang, X., Zhang, J., Wang, K., Rathbun, A., ... Mann, F. B. (2018). *The condition of education 2018* (NCES 2018–144U). U.S. Department of Education, National Center for Education Statistics. Washington, DC: U.S. Government Printing Office. Retrieved from https://nces.ed.gov/pubsearch/pubsinfo.asp?pubid=2018144

Mulligan, G. M., McCarroll, J. C., Flanagan, K. D., & Potter, D. (2018). *Findings from the fourth-grade round of the early childhood longitudinal study, kindergarten class of 2010–2011* [ECLS-K:2011; NCES 2018–094]. U.S. Department of Education, Washington, DC: National Center for Education Statistics. Retrieved from http://nces.ed.gov/pubsearch

National Association for Sport and Physical Education. (2009). *Active start: A statement of physical activity guidelines for children birth to five years* (2nd ed.). Oxon Hill, MD: Aahperd Publications.

National Defense Education Act of 1958 (P.L. 85–864; 72 Stat. 1580). Copy of the original National Defense Education Act of 1958 can be found in https://federaleducationpolicy.wordpress.com/2011/06/03/national-defense-education-act-of-1958-2/

National Institute for Early Education Research. (2018). *Special report: Supporting dual language learners in state-funded preschool: State of the preschool yearbook, 2018*. New Brunswick, NJ: National Institute for Early Education Research (NIEER), Graduate School of Education at Rutgers, The State University of New Jersey.

National Mathematics Advisory Panel. (2008). *Foundations for success: The final report of the national mathematics advisory panel*. Washington, DC: U.S. Department of Education, Office of Planning, Evaluation and Policy Development.

National Research Council. (2009). *Mathematics learning in early childhood: Paths toward excellence and equity*. Washington, DC: National Academy Press.

No Child Left Behind Act (2001). Conference report to accompany H.R. 1 [Rep. No. 107–334, 107th] Congress, 1st session.

Owen, R. D. (1824). *Outline of the system of education at New Lanark*. Glasgow, UK: Wardlaw and Cunningham.

Papadopoulou, E., & Gregoriadis, A. (2017). Young children's perceptions of the quality of teacher-child interactions and school engagement in Greek kindergartens. *Journal of Early Childhood Research, 15*(3), 323–335. doi:10.1177/1476718X16656212

Park, M., O'Toole, A., & Katsiaficas, C. (2017). *Dual language learners: A national demographic and policy profile*. Washington, DC: Migration Policy Institute.

Pelatti, C. Y., Piasta, S. B., Justice, L. M., & O'Connell, A. (2014). Language- and literacy-learning opportunities in early childhood classrooms: Children's typical experiences and within-classroom variability. *Early Childhood Research Quarterly, 29*(4), 445–456. doi:10.1016/j.ecresq.2014.05.004

Pew Center on the States. (2011). *Transforming public education: Pathway to a Pre-K-12 future.* Washington, DC: Pew Charitable Trusts. Retrieved from http://www.pewcenteronthestates.org/uploadedFiles/wwwpewcenteronthestatesorg/Initiatives/Pre-K_Education/Pew_PreK_Transforming_Public_Education.pdf

Presser, A. L., Clements, M., Ginsburg, H., & Ertle, B. (2015). Big math for little kids: The effectiveness of a preschool and kindergarten mathematics curriculum. *Early Education and Development, 26*(3), 399–426. doi:10.1080/10409289.2015.994451

Rathbun, A., & Zhang, A. (2016). *Primary early care and education arrangements and achievement at kindergarten entry* [NCES 2016-070]. Washington, DC: National Center for Education Statistics, U.S. Department of Education.

Saracho, O. N., & Spodek, B. (2007). Social learning as the basis for early childhood education. In O. N. Saracho & B. Spodek (Eds.), *Contemporary perspectives on social learning in early childhood education* (pp. 303–310). Charlotte, NC: Information Age Publishing Inc.

Saracho, O. N., & Spodek, B. (2013). *Handbook of research on the education of young children* (3rd ed.). New York, NY: Routledge/Taylor and Francis Group.

Shapiro, M. S. (1983). *Child's garden: The kindergarten movement from Froebel to Dewey.* University Park: Pennsylvania State University Press.

Spodek. B. (1973). *Early childhood education.* Englewood Cliffs, NJ: Prentice-Hall.

Spodek. B. (Ed.). (1982). *Handbook of research in early childhood education.* New York, NY: Free Press.

Spodek. B. (Ed.). (1993). *Handbook of research on the education of young children.* New York, NY: Macmillan.

Spodek, B., & Saracho, O. N. (2003). On the shoulders of giants: Exploring the traditions of early childhood education. *Early Childhood Education Journal, 31*(1), 3–10.

Spodek, B., & Saracho, O. N. (2006). *Handbook of research on the education of young children* (2nd ed.). Mahwah, NJ: Lawrence Erlbaum Associates.

Strickland. (1983). Paths not taken. In B. Spodek (Ed.), *Handbook of research in early childhood education.* New York, NY: Free Press.

Sumrall, T. C., Scott-Little, C., La Paro, K. M., Pianta, R. C., Burchinal, M., Hamre, B., … Howes, C. (2017). Student teaching within early childhood preparation programs: An examination of key features across 2 and 4 year institutions. *Early Childhood Education Journal, 45*(6), 821–830. doi:10.1007/s10643-016-0830-x

Takanishi, R., & Le Menestrel, S. (2017). *Promoting the educational success of children and youth learning English: Promising futures* (Report of the National Academies of Sciences, Engineering, and Medicine). Washington, DC: The National Academies Press. doi:10.17226/24677

Teale, W. H., Whittingham, C. E., & Hoffman, E. B. (2018). Early literacy research, 2006–2015: A decade of measured progress. *Journal of Early Childhood Literacy.* doi:10.1177/1468798418754939

Tsigilis, N., Gregoriadis, A., Grammatikopoulos, V., & Zachopoulou, E. (2018). Applying exploratory structural equation modeling to examine the Student-Teacher Relationship Scale in a representative Greek sample. *Frontiers in Psychology, 9*, Article 733. doi:10.3389/fpsyg.2018.00733

U.S. Department of Education. (2018a). *The condition of education at a glance.* Retrieved from https://nces.ed.gov/programs/coe/indicator_cfa.asp

U.S. Department of Education. (2018b). *Digest of education statistics.* Retrieved from https://nces.ed.gov/programs/digest/d17/tables/dt17_202.10.asp

U.S. Department of Health and Human Services, Administration for Children and Families. (2010, January). *Head start impact study, final report.* Washington, DC: Administration for Children and Families, Administration on Children, Youth, and Families, & Head Start Bureau.

U.S. Department of Health and Human Services & U.S. Department of Education. (2015). *Policy statement on inclusion of children with disabilities in early childhood programs.* Retrieved from https://ed.gov/policy/speced/guid/earlylearning/joint-statement-full-text.pdf

United Nations Educational, Scientific and Cultural Organization (UNESCO). (2010). Citizenship education for the 21st century. Retrieved from http://www.unesco.org/education/tlsf/mods/theme_b/interact/mod07task03/appendix.htm

Walsh, F. (2003). *Normal family processes* (3rd ed.). New York, NY: Guilford.

Wardle, F. (2013). U. S. early childhood education multicultural education. In O. N. Saracho & B. Spodek (Eds.), *Handbook of research on the education of young children* (3rd ed., pp. 275–300). New York, NY: Routledge/Taylor and Francis Group.

Waterman, C., McDermott, P. A., Fantuzzo, J. E., & Gadsden, V. L. (2011). The matter of assessor variance in early childhood education—Or whose score is it anyway? *Early Childhood Research Quarterly.* doi:10.1016/j.ecresq.2011.06.003

Whitebread, D. (2018). Play: The new renaissance. *International Journal of Play, 7*(3), 237–243. doi:10.1080/21594937.2018.1532952

Whitebook, M., McLean, C., Austin, L. J. E., & Edwards, B. (2018). *Early childhood workforce index – 2018.* Berkeley, CA: Center for the Study of Child Care Employment, University of California, Berkeley. Retrieved from http://cscce.berkeley.edu/topic/early-childhood-workforce-index/2018/

Part I

Early Childhood Education and Child Development

1

Cognitive Development and the Education of Young Children

ENRIQUE B. ARRANZ-FREIJO, JOANA ACHA, AND FLORENCIA B. BARRETO-ZARZA

This chapter offers an updated overview of the basic landmarks of cognitive development during early childhood. First, the so-called classical theories are presented; these theories marked the beginning of the scientific study of cognitive development and provide key frameworks of reference for understanding the developmental and educational importance of this complex process. The historical origins of developmental scales will be expounded, and the contributions made by Piaget's genetic epistemology and Vygotsky's cultural-historical theory will be explored. Finally, the section will outline the most important contributions made by information processing theories, which offer a new framework to understand the early progress of basic cognitive processes as prerequisites for developing higher-level cognitive functions, with special attention being paid to executive functions and their cross-cutting nature in the cognitive, emotional and behavioural self-regulation domains. The third section will analyse the major cognitive development challenges of early childhood, namely the development of language and theory of mind (ToM), which, while sharing common areas, nevertheless develop differently. Phonological, lexical and grammatical development culminates in basic learning processes such as reading and writing, which enable children to attend school, while ToM has deep-rooted implications for children's cognitive and social development. Finally, the last section presents and discusses the implications of all the previous findings for preventive-educational interventions focusing on cognitive development and its optimisation within different development contexts.

Internal Cognitive Mechanisms and External Mediators for Child Development: The Classical View and the Transition towards Information Processing Theories

The contributions of Swiss psychologist Jean Piaget (1896–1980) underpin our current understanding of human cognitive development, and indeed, many aspects of Piaget's

work are still relevant even today. His theory will be presented in accordance with the summary drafted by Arranz (1998). To understand Piaget's theoretical proposal of the evolution of the cognitive structure, known as *genetic epistemology*, one must first comprehend and accept the concept of *functional invariants*, which are basically functions which are present in a stable manner throughout the entire development process, but which manifest themselves differently in the different developmental stages identified by Piagetian theory. The first of these invariants is *Organisation*, which reflects the fact that the internal *cognitive structure* is always organised in accordance with a certain set of operating rules. This structure and its operating rules change over time as the result of the actions of another invariant function known as *Adaptation*, an interactive and dialectic process that operates in a bidirectional way between the structure and the physical and social environment. These *functional invariants* constitute what Piaget called an individual's *modus operandi*, a way of functioning that is innate to each member of the human species.

Adaptation is twofold in nature. Its first component is *Assimilation*, or in other words the distortion of the external in accordance with the internal. Here, the *cognitive structure* itself is not modified, but rather new experiences and information are distorted to fit pre-existing categories in a process known as *distorting assimilation*. One example of this would be a child saying that a horse is a big dog because it has four legs. The opposite process consists of modifying the internal cognitive structure in accordance with the characteristics of the external object. This process is called *Accommodation*. To continue with the previous example, an instance of *Accommodation* would be to create a new category for horses, thus giving rise to an evident enrichment of the *cognitive structure*.

It is important to highlight the fact that no adaptive act is either pure *Assimilation* or pure *Accommodation*. Rather, the two processes coexist and complement each other. If an external object or piece of information resists the cognitive structure's attempts at assimilation, such as, for example, when a little girl applies the same motor patterns to a golf ball as to the tennis ball she had earlier, the old structure enters into conflict with the object and becomes unbalanced in its relationship with it. The search for a new balance will force the cognitive structure to accommodate the object by generating new resources that enable the individual to explore its characteristics. The dynamic process of searching for *Balance* is the cornerstone of the model of change proposed in Piaget's theory. *Assimilation* is behaviourally represented through play, understood as a repetitive, reassuring activity that serves to consolidate the cognitive structure while at the same time being enjoyable. *Accommodation* is behaviourally represented through imitation, an activity which seeks to integrate the new and which is flexible by nature and vital to ensuring developmental crises within the *cognitive structure*. The constant action of functional invariants enhances the active role that the individual plays in his or her own development process, through the construction of increasingly more complex representations of reality. *Constructivism* is therefore a key element in Piagetian theory.

Perhaps the most significant legacy bequeathed by Piaget's theory to our understanding of cognitive development is its identification of the importance of both play and imitation in this process. In relation to play, the recent clinical report published by the American Academy of Pediatrics (Yogman et al., 2018) is worth mentioning, since it highlights the role of play in cognitive development, the construction of brain architecture and the development of executive functions and self-regulation abilities, among others. As regards imitation, research into its impact on cognitive development continues to be a vibrant field of study today, as regards both its innate and acquired components (Heyes, 2016), its cross-cultural components (Wang, Williamson, & Meltzoff, 2015) and the development of its neurological infrastructure within the mirror neuron system (Campbell & Cunnington, 2017). The educational implications of play and imitation will be discussed in the final section of this chapter.

Another key element in Piaget's theory is the clinical and experimental work he carried out on children's egocentrism. Early childhood is the stage in which this characteristic of children's thinking is manifested most clearly, with egocentrism being a *representation of* the world as *animist*, to think that everything in nature has a soul and is alive, *artificialist*, to think that everything has been created by anyone, *realist*, to think that non-material things have a real matter, for example dreams, *finalist*, to think that everything has a purpose and *phenomenic*, to think that everything is observable. The Piagetian assumption that egocentrism is a cross-cutting characteristic of children's thinking, which they do not start to overcome before age seven, marked the start of a fruitful avenue of research which has given rise to more recent work on the development of ToM. This construct has key implications for understanding normative and atypical cognitive development, as well as for designing effective interventions on developmental delays. Section in this chapter devoted to cognitive challenges in the early years explores the study of ToM development in more detail.

It may be interesting to highlight the fact that Piaget's theory found a source of inspiration in the previous developmental approach of the French psychologist Alfred Binet (1857–1911). Binet's proposal is basically an experimental assessment of intelligence which views this construct from a developmental perspective. The American version of the scale was developed by Lewis Terman (1857–1956), who also developed the concept of IQ (intelligence quotient), which is the result of dividing a person's mental age (as assessed by the scale) by their chronological age. The historical forerunner of modern-day development scales is still used today by psychologists as a basic diagnostic instrument for measuring cognitive development in the educational, social and health fields, in which a precise assessment of cognitive competences is a prerequisite for planning any kind of intervention. The *Merrill Palmer* scales and the different versions of the *Bayley* scales are also worth mentioning.

A very enriching complement to the classic understanding of cognitive development can be found in the work of L. S. Vygotsky (1896–1934), also known as the Mozart of Psychology due to his early demise and brilliant contributions. A concise and integrating summing up of his theory would be that it combines the idea of Piaget's active subject or builder of cognitive structures with a solid yet flexible proposal regarding the influence of the social context on this process of construction. His emphasis on the influence of the social context illustrates the deep influence of Marxist theory on Vygotsky's work, particularly as regards the anthropological and psychological contents stemming from it and highlighting the typical dialectical background understanding human development as a bidirectional interactive process by nature.

One key concept in Vygotsky's theory is the *Law of the dual origin of higher psychological processes*. This law explains the process known as the individuation of the social, which gives rise to *higher psychological processes*, conceived as the result of the gradual internalisation of social interactions. In modern-day terms, we would speak of the internalisation of an interaction that is meaningful for the subject. It is in this process that we find the origin of the symbol as a higher psychological process. According to Vygotsky's theory, *interpsychic* interactions (between people) attain an *intrapsychic* symbolic nature (within a person) following internalisation. An *interpsychic* interactive event, such as, for example, the agreement to ring a bell to indicate the end of class, is constituted in the form of an *intrapsychic* symbol for each of the subjects participating in the event, who internalise it. This symbol maintains its potential even in other interactive contexts, thereby expressing its decontextualised nature, just like the words in a language, which are defined as *decontextualised mediation instruments*. This is the case of the decontextualised power of the word "summer" brought to a conversation that is being maintained in winter.

The *Law of the dual origin of higher psychological processes* is further specified and complemented by the concept of the *Zone of Proximal Development* (ZPD). It is in the ZPD that the social dialogue that is later to be internalised takes place. It is defined by the distance between *effective development* – i.e. that which the child is able to do by themselves – and their proximal development – consisting of those activities, skills, abilities, etc. that they are able to do with the help of an adult. The ZPD characterises cognitive development not retrospectively, but rather prospectively, revealing the proximal achievements inherent to the maturing process. This prospective view of development is one of Vygotsky's most important contributions, since it has the virtue of apprehending the development process itself, while at the same time successfully combining the dialectic approach and processes of social interaction.

The key activity carried out in the ZPD is imitation. The importance attached to imitation constitutes a vital nexus between Piaget's and Vygotsky's work, even though they both interpret this activity in terms of their respective theoretical constructs, with Piaget considering it to be generated inside the cognitive structure, and at the service of said structure, and Vygotsky viewing it as stemming from social interaction. J. Bruner (1915–2016) was perhaps the author who explored the idea of the ZPD in most detail and depth, making seminal contributions in this field, mostly linked to *language acquisition formats* and the help and structuring that the more competent adult offers the child during the development process. Together, all these activities make up what is known as the *scaffolding* (Wood, Bruner, & Ross, 1976) on which interactions in the ZPD take place. Both imitation and scaffolding are particularly important from the perspective of fostering cognitive development through education.

Finally, it should be mentioned that research into the internalisation of social interactions converges in studies on language. This is key issue in Vygotsky's work, in which language is seen as a decontextualised mediation *tool*. Vygotsky applies Engels' concept of tool in a masterful manner, claiming that words are human beings' special tools and that it is through their subsequently internalised mediation that higher psychological processes are constructed. Language constitutes an agent for self-regulation and helps structure psychological activity. Even basic processes such as hearing and distinguishing pitch are developed under the influence of existing social conditions and, above all, language.

To conclude this overview of the contributions made by classical theories to our current understanding of children's cognitive development, mention must be made of those theories that fall within the *information processing paradigm*, which uses the computational metaphor as its framework of reference. The first of these is Pascual-Leone's theory of *constructive operators* (1987), which amends Piaget's theory by focusing on the quantitative increase in memory capacity which occurs throughout the development process trying to find an explanation to the so-called *decalage* phenomenon, in which a subject carries out a good performance in a task with a low demand of memory and a bad performance in a task with a higher demand of memory, having both tasks

the same logical structure. Another theory worth bearing in mind is Case's automata theory (Case, Hayward, Lewis, & Hurst, 1985), which points to the reduction in conscious processing space required when an activity becomes automatic. For their part, by creating an actuation programme, Klahr and Wallace (1976) aimed to simulate the process followed by humans to resolve a specific problem. The tasks the subject was asked to carry out in order to solve the problem were formulated as processing routines, in a direct reference to computers. Finally, mention should also be made of Karmiloff-Smith's *representational redescription* theory (2018), which views the structure of the mind as being made up of modules which contain the subject's representations of a certain domain. The common active process responsible for cognitive development is representational redescription, defined by the author as a process by which information, which is implicit in the mind, becomes explicit knowledge. One example of the proposed mechanism would be the concept of a *zebra crossing*, which evokes the appearance of an animal. All these theories have opened up different avenues of research which have used different approaches to the study of the development of both basic and other cognitive and meta-cognitive processes.

Cognitive science has drawn on these historic contributions and has focused on striving to understand the way in which different mental mechanisms explain the appearance and development of intellectual functions and sophisticated behaviours. With this aim, and based on neuroscientific evidence about the link between neuronal connectivity and the development of brain functions, recent research has offered a new explanatory framework about how the progressive sophistication of basic processes such as perception, attention or memory supports the emergence of complex knowledge and high-order intellectual abilities. Hence, cognitive psychology has enabled researchers to refine the theories outlined above, explaining, for instance, the construction of early visual or auditory representations for objects and words in terms of basic mechanisms such as perceiving environmental regularities and internalising them bias recurring experiences (Gervain, Berent, & Werker, 2012). Also object permanence has been explained in terms of memory – remembering that an object is still there even when it is out of vision – and executive function – being able to control the habit boosted by the experimenter to look for the object in a certain place (Diamond, Kirkham, & Amso, 2002). In the same vein, symbolic capacity has been explained as a cognitive consequence of being able to retain and operate with various representations – real object and its picture, real house and house toy – simultaneously (Deloache, 2000) and ToM as the result of a successful understanding of communication cues – eye gaze following, pointing – within the joint attention framework (Tomasello & Rakoczy, 2003). Given the importance of these mechanisms in the constitution of the cognitive architecture in childhood, this framework will be the starting point to describe the development of psychological processes that support the acquisition of superior skills in the light of recent contributions made by cognitive psychology. Finally, we will emphasise the role of education and its potential to modulate the developmental trajectory of these mechanisms and, therefore, of cognitive development during early childhood.

The Development of Basic Processes and Their Role in Higher Cognitive Abilities

One of the most interesting questions in the field of children's cognitive development is how the cognitive infrastructure that enables learning during early childhood is organised and evolves. Current perspectives have enabled the establishment of a theoretical framework which facilitates our understanding of this process. This framework assumes, first, that as the central nervous system (CNS) matures, it lays the groundwork for the development of different intellectual abilities (biological perspective). Second, it also assumes that basic abilities are vital to the acquisition and appearance of more complex ones (cognitive perspective). Finally, it holds that the way in which certain basic cognitive mechanisms evolve affects the pace and timing of intellectual development (information processing perspective). The integration of these perspectives enables cognitive development to be conceptualised as follows: brain development supports the emergence of certain cognitive processes which evolve as the CNS matures (Johnson, 2001), and the learning of complex abilities depends on their progressive sophistication throughout childhood (Gooch, Snowling, & Hulme, 2011). The basic processes which condition development and learning in the early years are perception, attention and working memory – a key component of executive function – although processing speed is also sometimes included in this network (Magimairaj & Montgomery, 2012).

It is important to highlight the fact that the basic condition required for the development of these mechanisms is that the sensory system perceives stimuli that can be processed mentally. Perception skills are therefore necessary to access external stimuli, and this is particularly important during the first few months of an infant's life. Indeed, without a perceptual system capable of capturing external stimuli and mentally processing experiences, babies would be incapable of constructing internal mental realities based on such stimuli, and would therefore lack the basic starting point for the entire learning process. For example, visual perception enables infants to internalise shapes and colours and to bestow identity and stability on objects, people or letters (McCandliss, Cohen, & Dehaene, 2003), and auditory perception enables them to build internal representations of sounds, words and grammatical structures to which they are exposed (Gervain et al., 2012). In this sense, there is a large body of evidence supporting the important role played by stimulus perception in the development of initial adaptive behaviours and learning (Rose, Feldman, & Jankowski, 2001). Nevertheless, in itself, a perceptual system is not enough to guarantee the construction of internal representations. It must be complemented by the existence of an attentional mechanism dedicated to focusing attention on the stimulus and codifying the information perceived in the environment.

Attention is one of the key mechanisms for learning, first because it is the earliest mechanism to emerge, and second because it is therefore the foundation for other mechanisms such as memory and executive function, which depend on its development and increasing sophistication. The development of attention depends on the connection between the subcortical regions involved in involuntary attention, with the thalamus and temporal and parietal areas involved in orientation, and changes in attentional focus and prefrontal areas involved in voluntary attentional control (Casey, Giedd, & Thomas, 2000). From a developmental perspective, this progress can be detected as early as during the first year of life. Acquisition of attentional control implies not only that infants are capable of orienting the focus of their attention towards relevant stimuli in their environment, but also that they are able to change the focus of their attention quickly in response to a new stimulus.

Recent evidence on this field has revealed that, in addition to its adaptive function, the level of and moment at which the capacity for voluntary attention is developed is directly linked to subsequent learning. For example, the ability to pay controlled attention to auditory stimuli enables infants to find auditory anchor points and gather adjacent sounds also, thereby broadening their sound representations of language and facilitating its internalisation (de Diego-Balaguer, Martinez-Alvarez, & Pons, 2016). This same mechanism enables pre-readers to construct orthographic representations from letters (Bental & Tirosh, 2007). The explanation for this relationship between attention and learning lies in the progressive control of our mental processes, which determines the amount and type of information learned. Consequently, the development of attentional processes has been studied in relation to our capacity for control and our ability to ignore those stimuli which may distract our attention (inhibition). Recent studies have evaluated the whole of this potential attentional network using paradigms which aim to measure alerting (speed at which the attentional mechanism engages with the stimulus), orienting (efficacy for directing attention towards one position or another in accordance with the location of the stimulus) and inhibition (ability to inhibit irrelevant information and respond only on the basis of the stimulus of interest) during a single task (see Rueda et al., 2004).

These studies have revealed that the efficacy of this circuit evolves gradually throughout childhood, with the first developmental peak being the one corresponding to alerting (age five), followed by orienting (around age six) and finally inhibition and control over attention (between ages seven and ten). The findings support previous evidence suggesting that by age seven, children reach peak development in attention tasks, but continue to progress in relation to their capacity for control. For example, the development of inhibition determines selective attention, but the capacity for controlling and planning responses continues to evolve even after peak attentional maturity levels have been attained (Klenberg, Korkman, & Lahti-Nuuttila, 2001). Thus, the evidence reveals that it is necessary to focus on the development of children's capacity for control as an additional mechanism to attention, not only because the two abilities follow different developmental timelines, but also because each can independently explain distinct developmental trajectories (Manly et al., 2001).

Recent findings have shown that a key and common element in the development of attention and control processes is the ability to operate and monitor information, a capacity also known as working memory. This mechanism is concerned with holding coded information in mind temporarily while it is processed, avoiding any processing loads derived from distractors or from the execution of another task. It is a sophisticated cognitive mechanism that enables certain information to be activated while inhibiting other, or which permits various mental representations to remain active while a task related to one of them is carried out. The fact that working memory enables a cognitive load to be withstood while voluntarily keeping some kind of mental information active explains the interdependent nature of attention and voluntary control over mental processes, and this in turn makes it one of the most important mechanisms in children's intellectual development (Gray et al., 2017).

In terms of Baddeley's model of memory (2000), working memory would be the equivalent of the central executive, a component of the model which operates with verbal and visual information in order to store it in short-term memory. Recent studies have shown that although short-term memory is modular in nature – the ability to store verbal information in infancy is quite independent from the ability to store visual material, for instance – working memory is a general processing mechanism, devoted to monitor and operate with any kind of information, either visual or verbal. For example, while a discrepancy between the level of visual and verbal short-term memory may be the cause of a phonological disorder linked to language or reading (Gathercole & Pickering, 2000), a deficit in working memory underlies almost all development disorders, regardless of their form (Henry & Botting, 2017). For this reason, recent works conceptualise the basic cognitive system as one in which attention, working memory and executive control jointly modulate cognitive development. These mechanisms are interdependent and form the basic cognitive infrastructure which determines learning and linguistic and intellectual development during early childhood (Gooch, Thompson, Nash, Snowling, & Hulme, 2016).

It is precisely the relationship between attention, working memory and executive control that has been the object of much research in recent years, as part of an attempt to conceptualise the basic infrastructure on which all subsequent learning depends (McCabe, Roediger, McDaniel, Balota, & Hambrick, 2010). The complexity of the executive control construct makes it difficult to systematise specific functions, although there is a certain degree of consensus regarding the fact that it includes aspects related to control, inhibition and flexibility for resolving mental conflicts or making decisions

(Zelazo et al., 2003). The development of executive functions depends on the level of connectivity in the prefrontal region, which suggests that executive function itself depends on the maturity of this particular area of the brain (García, Eseñat, Tirapu, & Roig, 2009). Since this area matures very slowly, the development of voluntary control of mental processes is also slow and gradual (Lamm, Zelazo, & Lewis, 2006), and therefore extremely vulnerable to environmental effects during childhood (Hughes, 2011).

In fact, an adequate development of executive mechanisms is related to the development of behavioural control and reflexive capacity during this period, as well as to the development of coordination skills and the ability to unite all the other mental mechanisms in order to generate integrated knowledge. Therefore, a failure to develop these control mechanisms is linked to an incapacity to plan and the inattentive and impulsive behaviours typical of attention-deficit hyperactivity disorder (ADHD) (see Barkley, 1997), as well as to difficulties integrating and generalising knowledge to new situations, which is also characteristic of autism (Hill, 2004).

In sum, evidence suggests that attentional and inhibition/control mechanisms together support the cognitive structure whose evolution influences general intelligence and the development of specific higher-level abilities such as language (Gray et al., 2017), ToM (Hughes & Devine, 2015) and metacognition (Fernandez-Duque, Baird, & Posner, 2000); this in turn suggests that in order to understand the relative role of each process in intellectual development, we must focus on both the progression of each process individually, and the way they interact throughout development.

The Development of Self-Regulation

Over the last few decades, there has been widespread consensus among scientists regarding self-regulation (which begins to develop during early childhood) as one of the skills associated with success in the academic, occupational and social fields. Indeed, poor self-regulation has been linked to school dropout (Kitsantas, Steen, & Huie, 2009), addictions (Zucker, Heitzeg, & Nigg, 2011), eating disorders (Dohle, Diel, & Hofmann, 2015), poor social skills (Moilanen & Manuel, 2017), ADHD (Brocki, Forslund, Frick, & Bohlin, 2017) and internalising and externalising problems (Eisenberg, Hernández, & Spinrad, 2017), among others, during both childhood and adolescence, with the resulting problems persisting into adulthood. These findings indicate that self-regulation is a vital skill, necessary to ensuring both adequate adaptation to the environment and healthy development. As Montroy, Bowles, Skibbe, McClelland and Morrison (2016) point out, early childhood, between ages three and seven, is a critical developmental period in which a qualitative change occurs regarding the normative evolution from a reactive or co-regulated behaviour to a proper self-regulation.

First, it is important to clarify the fact that the term "self-regulation" refers to an individual's capacity to modulate and inhibit their thoughts, feelings and actions either automatically or voluntarily, with the aim of defining goals and establishing the means necessary to achieve them. Moreover, this ability is underpinned by attention and executive functions (working memory, cognitive inhibition and flexibility). These cognitive processes enable an individual to undertake any type of learning, from riding a bicycle or learning to read, to thinking before acting, resisting temptation, setting oneself goals and focusing on the tasks required to achieve them (Diamond, 2013). McCoy (2013) also identifies two other important elements in the concept of self-regulation: emotional regulation, which enables an individual to adapt their response to different levels of emotional arousal, such as anger or joy, and effortful control, which enables them to control their behaviour, inhibiting impulsiveness or postponing gratification. An example of this would be, for instance, when you decide to change the enjoyable plans you had made for this weekend in order to stay at home studying so as to pass the exam you have next week. Effortful control is also involved in emotional self-regulation. Thus, the aforementioned processes correspond (respectively) to the cognitive, emotional and behavioural components of self-regulation.

In the specific case of the cognitive component, Piaget's observations (1954) regarding object permanence in children under age one, detected underlying indications of the development of working memory and inhibition (Johnson, 2001). Children only begin to successfully resolve the classic "A not B" task, in which they are asked to say in which of the two boxes the researcher has hidden an object, between the ages of seven and a half months and one year. Nevertheless, adult-equivalent levels of working memory are not reached until approximately age 12 (Johnson, 2001).

In the case of inhibitory control, using magnetoencephalography (MEG), Vara, Pang, Vidal, Anagnostou and Taylor (2014) found that neural inhibition patterns continue to mature even during adolescence, particularly between the ages of 13 and 17. The initiation of both these mechanisms marks the passage to a higher level of development, in which cognitive flexibility begins to emerge, which in turn enables individuals to understand an issue from two different angles and to switch between tasks almost seamlessly (Diamond, 2013; Nigg, 2017). The combination of these three types of process enables high-level executive development which includes reasoning, problem-solving and planning (Nigg, 2017).

As regards the emotional component, it should be highlighted that emotional regulation starts to develop during early childhood as the result of the interaction between brain maturation, settlement of cognitive functions to attend and understand social cues, and social experiences, particularly the extent to which parents are capable of identifying and responding to their child's emotional states. For example, when a child starts crying because they do not want to go to school, their parents should intervene in order to calm them down and give meaning to the situation through words, since these actions help the child organise their experiences around predictable routines. Shonkoff and Phillips (2000) underscore the fact that this environmental predictability reduces the emotional demands made by the child by daily experiences, thereby encouraging them to make an effort to regulate their emotions. Moreover, another variable to bear in mind is the establishment of secure attachment, which provides children with the confidence and security they need to begin internalising these regulatory processes (Pallini et al., 2018).

Similarly, emotional self-regulation also requires an effortful control process in which executive functions also play a key role. According to Casey (2015), an emotion is an specific type of information that must be controlled by higher cognitive domains (Nigg, 2017). Indeed, Zelazo and Carlson (2012) distinguish between cool and hot executive function. Specifically, cool executive function is associated with the lateral prefrontal cortex and traditionally assessed using tests such as the Stroop Task or the Eriksen Flanker Task. Hot executive function is controlled by the orbitofrontal cortex and medial regions and is assessed using high-risk decision-making tests such as the Iowa Gambling Task, which contain a motivational component in emotionally meaningful situations. In a study carried out with a sample of children and adolescents aged between 8 and 15, Prencipe et al. (2011) found age-related improvements in both types of executive function (cool and hot), although only older subjects performed well in the Iowa Gambling Task. Thus, it seems that the two processes follow different developmental timelines, with the area of the brain associated with resolving tasks containing a motivational and emotional component maturing slightly later in life. This seems to explain why some adolescents take risks without taking into account the negative consequences of their behaviour (Zelazo & Carlson, 2012).

Finally, the variable associated with the behavioural component is effortful control, which also requires executive function. This concept was defined by Rothbart, Sheese and Posner (2007) as "the ability to inhibit a dominant response in order to active a subdominant response, to plan, and to detect errors" (p. 3). This ability progresses quickly during the preschool years, gradually moving up a continuum from more or less automatic responses to stimuli (a basic dimension of infant temperament during the first year of life) to self-regulation, understood as a process which regulates this activity and which becomes stable at around age three. According to Rothbart et al. (2007), the feeling of fear, which is developed during the first year of life, serves as a control mechanism which has been linked to inhibition throughout childhood and adolescence, and which can also be considered a precursor of awareness. In this sense, it is important to point out that the feeling of fear may be affected by children's individual temperament, as well as by the characteristics of their principal carers and environmental factors such as stress, parental conflict and family engagement and cohesion (Crawford, Schrock, & Woodruff-Borden, 2011). Moreover, effortful control is determined by inhibitory control, by the ability to focus attention, and by the ability to change the focus of one's attention (Nigg, 2017; Rothbart et al., 2007), which demonstrates that it is influenced by processes within the executive domain.

Following this overview of the processes underlying the capacity for self-regulation, let us now analyse some general aspects. The first consideration to bear in mind is that the development of these underlying processes begin in early childhood and reach peak maturity during early adulthood because the brain areas on which their development depends, such as the fronto-parietal network, mature gradually over the course of many years. Nevertheless, there are several critical periods in which the nervous system is more sensitive to environmental factors, thus giving rise to changes in the brain structures that govern the ability for self-regulation. The work of Lyall et al. (2015) shows how brain thickness, which is related to cognitive functioning, increases during the first two years of life to, on average, 97% of adult values.

For their part, Raznahan et al. (2011) found that towards the end of childhood and during adolescence, annual cortical growth was around ±0.5% (Geng et al., 2017). Moreover, it is during early childhood that the first neuron networks are established, which in turn enable the development of higher-order cognitive domains during subsequent stages. In this sense, as we have tried to explain throughout the course of this section, the capacity for self-regulation follows a developmental cascade model, in which basic capacities gradually become part of more complex ones, which in turn become stable as a result of both the passage of time and life experience (Nigg, 2017).

As stated earlier, another particular characteristic of self-regulation is that its development is influenced by multiple different variables. This is basically the essence of Bronfenbrenner's Bioecological Theory (2005), which postulates that development occurs as the result of continuous interaction between four different levels: Process-Person-Context-Time. This theory is further complemented by Gottlieb's concept of *probabilistic epigenesis* (2007; Johnston, 2015), which advocates a bidirectional interaction between genetic, biological and contextual variables, which together result in the individual's final phenotypical expression. In this sense, negative affect, which includes fear, frustration and sadness, has been associated with poor self-regulation during childhood (see Putnam, Rothbart, & Gartstein, 2008). Specifically, Crawford et al. (2011) found that both negative affect and the quality of family functioning were directly related to internalising problems in children aged between three and five. Moreover, traumatic experiences such as poverty, chronic stress, chaos at home and violence (among others), disrupt self-regulatory processes, thus making it harder for children in such situations to cope with external demands (Evans & Kim, 2013; McCoy, 2013).

A third characteristic of the capacity for self-regulation is that it is governed by cognitive processes such as executive functions which, as explained earlier, constitute a cross-cutting process present at all the different levels outlined above. Individuals are not born with these levels or domains; rather, they develop on the basis of interactions with the environment and are particularly sensitive to experiences. This sensibility is the reason why it is vital for children to

have meaningful interactions on their most immediate microsystem, namely the family, which due to its continuity and significance has a major influence on their development. Consequently, one variable to bear in mind during early childhood is carers' sensitivity in terms of being alert to, correctly identifying and responding to the signals sent out by infants. A study by Frick et al. (2018) found an association between high levels of maternal sensitivity and the promotion of emotional regulation during early childhood. Therefore, mothers' sensitivity in responding to their children's distress is a predictor for child well-being in both the short and long term (Leerkes, Weaver, & O'Brien, 2012).

In sum, the capacity for self-regulation is initially based on external regulation which, during subsequent developmental stages, enables the internalisation of models and processes that empower individuals to function independently within cognitive, emotional and behavioral ways. Moreover, this capacity is acquired through a slow process involving a series of different cognitive domains, including executive functions, which are highly dependent on environmental interactions, with the family being the most influential microsystem. Future research may wish to explore which specific mechanisms and family variables foster the capacity for self-regulation, which is such an urgent and necessary human skill for adapting to one's environment.

Cognitive Challenges during the Early Years: Language Development and ToM

Language and ToM are the two major intellectual milestones in early childhood development. Interestingly, these milestones share a common origin exclusive of human evolution, and based on the emergence of symbolic capacity and the understanding of communicative intention (Tomasello, 2003). The search for this common origin leads to the emergence of joint attention as a means of establishing a communicative framework, and the understanding of the referential intention and the possibility of influencing another human being during a shared experience (Tomasello, Carpenter, & Liszkowski, 2007). The understanding of what communication means, together with the baby's attempt to communicate through gestures or words, takes place during the first year. This boosts the symbolic capacity that enables the child to use language as a means of communication, and to learn how it can influence the minds of adults. Despite these shared features, language development and ToM are governed by different processes and follow specific developmental trajectories.

Regarding language, recent evidence has challenged the traditional view of generative language that studies the evolution of infant grammar by comparing it with adult structures (see Tomasello, 2000). This view assumes that grammatical categories are operative early in development, and that the differences between the child and the adult are based on external factors such as processing limitations, maturation or lexical experience with a specific language. Without denying the importance of these factors, neither this vision nor the learning views explain how children integrate new words and new grammatical structures based on their daily experience. Studies in recent years have tried to overcome this caveat by showing that the acquisition of language is governed by the same mechanisms that intervene in other aspects of cognition: extraction of perceptual regularities, application of analogies and inclusion of new linguistic items in frequently heard structures.

These mechanisms can be applied to different linguistic dimensions: phonological, lexical or syntactic (van der Lely, 2005). This systematisation allows us to examine the evolution of different linguistic levels in isolation, as well as to evaluate specific language dimensions in clinical practice; yet taking into account these dimensions are interdependent during the course of development. The first year of life is characterised by the development of the phonological dimension, implying knowledge of sounds and their permissible combinations in the language. Babies use perceptual categorisation mechanisms to identify and classify the sounds of their language, so that when they are born they have the ability to distinguish the full range of sounds, but after a few months of exposure, they only recognise those sounds of their language.

The above-explained process occurs around the sixth month in monolingual children (Werker & Tees, 2002) and around the tenth month in bilingual children (Albareda-Castellot, Pons, & Sebastian-Gallés, 2011). At the same time, babies extract regularities of frequent sound combinations (Marcus, 2000), so that by seven months they react to combinations of illegal sounds in their language (Curtin, Mintz, & Christiansen, 2005) and begin to recognise word's boundaries based on clues such as accent, prosodic patterns or most frequent grammatical structures (Yurovsky, Yu, & Smith, 2012). This tuning is the result of neuronal pruning and it is the reflection of an efficient cognitive system. In fact, an earlier tuning predicts a higher lexical and linguistic level later on (Kuhl et al., 2008).

Evidence in favour of the hypothesis that babies extract perceptual regularities is the temporal continuity between the internalisation and production of linguistic sequences. That is why at about eight months babie's babbling includes frequent syllabic sequences in their native language (Shaffran, Aslin, & Newport, 1996). In the same vein, sensitivity to the relative position of specific structures in a sentence influences the ability to locate frequent specific stimuli within those structures (Gervain et al., 2012). This explains the transition from phonological to lexical and grammatical development using the same mechanisms. Thus, at eight months, babies discriminate sounds within words, and between 14 and 17 months they discriminate words within grammatical contexts (Byers-Heinlein, Fennell, & Werker, 2012) producing combinations of two words, that is, simple grammatical structures (Iverson & Goldin-Meadow, 2005). It has been observed that phonological memory plays a fundamental role in the child's ability to record and internalise these combinations, and to create lexical representations (Gathercole, 2006). This ability, together with the understanding of the communicative function, explains this transition towards the use of words and grammatical structures with a clear communicative intention.

In this line, research has tried to solve two key questions: on the one hand, how lexical development is linked to statistical learning (how children locate the word within the grammatical structure), and on the other hand, how the lexical-semantic association occurs (how they discover which object corresponds to the word). Regarding the first question, it has been observed that children recognise and locate words using statistical learning, specifically extracting regularities from frequent lexical combinations and integrating new words in known structures by means of construction of grammatical categories, comparison of structures and bootstrapping (Kidd & Arciuli, 2016). Regarding the second question, it has been observed that the linguistic and iconic cues provided by adults (visual guidance, declarative pointing, gesture-word contingency) serve as a guide to associate lexical label and reference (Xu, Cote, & Baker, 2005) activating some principles by which children assign referents to words: complete object, mutual exclusivity or taxonomic relationship (Markman, 1990). These findings support the hypothesis that language learning requires: (i) children to discover similarities between internalised sequences and extract "semi-abstract" constructions or patterns, and (ii) a social experience (inference of the speaker's intention, visual guides) that facilitates lexical exposure and semantic assignment (Tomasello, 2000).

In sum, language development during early childhood implies the construction of exhaustive phonological representations that facilitate the development of subsequent abilities involved in reading such as phonological awareness (Duncan et al., 2013), as well as the attainment of syntactic rules and verbal morphology (Theodore, Demuth, & Shattuck-Hufnagel, 2011) in this way at the end of this period, the organisation of the linguistic system culminates, through its phonological, lexical and syntactic components.

Another major landmark of cognitive development during early childhood is the development of ToM or, in other words, the capacity to attribute mental states such as desires, beliefs, intentions and emotions to both oneself and others. ToM involves both cognitive and affective aspects. From a developmental perspective, children gain this ability between the ages of two and seven. According to Wellman (2012), three phases can be identified in children's development of ToM. During the first phase, children come to understand the existence of a non-observable mental reality which motivates both their own actions and those of others. In other words, they come to realise that they act in accordance with their own wishes and desires, and so do other people, and those wishes and desires may not always coincide. The second phase is characterised by the realisation that people have different beliefs and that one's belief can be verified (or refuted) in the real world. Finally, during the third phase, children come to understand that people may have different states of knowledge, i.e. you may know something someone else does not. Once they have gained this understanding, they comprehend that people act in accordance with their beliefs, even though these may be erroneous, something which is known as *false belief*. It is this concept that lends its name to the *false belief task* (Wimmer & Perner, 1983), which is the procedure used to assess this understanding. In order to respond correctly to false belief tasks, a process of *mentalist inference* must be carried out to enable the individual to fully understand the situation and correctly predict that the other person will not act in accordance with reality, but rather with their own false belief.

The majority of children aged between three and four do not possess this capacity for mentalist inference, although they do generally develop this skill from age four onwards. The development of ToM gradually becomes more complex, until children are able to understand that people may feel one thing and express another. In other words, they gradually come to understand the concept of pretending. Between the ages of 7 and 11, they begin to use second-level recursive thinking: "I think that you think that he/she thinks…"; and third-level recursive thinking: "I think that you think that he/she thinks that he/she (other) thinks…" develops during adolescence and early adulthood (Valle, Massaro, Castelli, & Marchetti, 2015).

There is much debate regarding the origins of ToM. It has been suggested that mirror neurons and joint attention are two biological and cognitive mechanisms (respectively) that are innately designed to enable individuals to recognise and imitate gestures and behaviours associated with different mental states. One piece of evidence which supports this hypothesis is the absence of these mechanisms in babies and autistic children (Peterson, Welman, & Slaughther, 2012). Another finding which supports an innate basis for the development of ToM is the detection of deceptive behaviour and perspective-taking skills in primates (Call & Tomasello, 2008).

Nevertheless, previous studies have demonstrated the fact that ToM is also sensitive to contextual variables such as secure attachment, sibling relations, the use of decontextualisation strategies by parents and references by adults to desires, beliefs and motivations (McAlister & Peterson, 2013). Moreover, ToM is also closely related to other development processes, such as vocabulary level, the complexity of the grammatical structures used (Farrant, Maybery, & Fletcher, 2012) and the development of executive function. Children with better control over their attentional processes are more flexible and able to process more information, which in turn enables them to develop an earlier understanding of false beliefs.

Educational Implications

The evidence presented in this chapter attests to the basic, underlying mechanisms involved in early childhood development, and serves to strengthen the idea of the vital importance of cognitive abilities in this process. This prompts us directly to consider the possible educational implications of that outlined above for psychologists, parents and education professionals. In this section, we will outline those implications considered by authors to be most important.

First, it is worth highlighting the legacy left by classical theories in relation to the importance of play and imitation as natural activities which foster cognitive development, and which should clearly be encouraged in all children's interactive environments. In relation to play, Yogman et al. (2018) advocate a mixed approach which combines formal learning and learning through play (or guided play). Within this context, one key activity is *scaffolding*, understood as a process deliberately instigated by an adult to foster the development of executive function. Scaffolding constitutes a key element of *school readiness*, a construct that reflects a child's maturity level in terms of school adjustment and which can be assessed with a view to designing individualised intervention programmes to facilitate this adjustment. The educational promotion of imitation also emerges as an important element, in connection with the fostering of play activities. The two concepts merge, for example, in the practice of symbolic play or imitation games. It is worth mentioning that Harvard University's Center on the Developing Child offers an online resource for parents and children containing specific activities for fostering play and executive function (Center on the Developing Child, 2014).

Second, existing evidence points to the importance in early development of very subtle and basic processes such as attention and working memory, not only because they influence learning during this period, but also because they lay the groundwork for academic development and behaviour during adulthood. In this sense, one cannot overstate the importance of assessing these processes at an early age through screening tests, not only due to the expedient nature of early prevention interventions but also due to two key pieces of evidence. The first is the finding that interventions focused on attention and working memory can bring about direct improvements in the completion of the tasks which measure these processes, and indirect improvements in reasoning and academic performance (Klingberg et al., 2005), and that the demands and richness of the school environment may also make an additional contribution to this improvement (Rueda, Checa, & Combita, 2012).

The second is that predictive relations between these processes and higher abilities have only been verified within a very narrow timeframe, thus indicating the existence of only a short period in which certain specific abilities are sensitive to development. In other words, once children reach a certain age, interventions focused on attention or working memory may have a weaker impact on their learning, since after that age learning depends more on prior knowledge or experience.

Third, there are many reasons why education professionals should be involved in promoting attentional control and self-regulation. Simple aspects such as gaze and verbalisation synchrony between adult and child and the contingency of the gestural and linguistic response may help regulate attentional control and foster the development of sustained attention during the early years. In the opposite sense, the association detected between the use of technological devices and decreased attentional control during childhood warns of a possible danger in the development of executive function among the children of the high-tech generation. This in turn prompts the need to provide educators with the knowledge and strategies they require to improve children's attention and concentration and regulate their use of technological devices. This implies not only regulating screen time, but also assessing the impact of specific programmes on the processes studied. Indeed, factors such as spending more than two hours a day in front of a screen or using electronic devices, failing to ensure between 9 and 11 hours' sleep and not engaging in sport for at least one hour every day are all related to poorer cognitive development (Walsh et al., 2018).

An argument which stems from this idea and which also supports the evidence outlined so far in this chapter is that the direct fostering of self-regulation behaviours during childhood may have a positive impact on development through two different pathways. First, external regulation based on rules aimed at fostering autonomy and responsibility challenge these functions, generating cognitive demands that result in greater internal control. And second, the internal regulation of emotions and behaviour may have an impact on the processes which support executive functions, which in turn form part of the self-regulation construct and are involved in the learning of higher abilities (Hughes & Ensor, 2009, 2011).

Fourth, the evidence reported by previous studies shows that frequent exposure to a rich and varied language during childhood may influence a child's language development trajectory. A rich linguistic input during the first two years of life contributes to the internal construction of the key phonological structures of a language, thereby enabling the establishment of a mental system prepared for lexical integration and grammatical construction. For example, maternal speech, which entails prosodic and sound-related characteristics, can facilitate the extraction of linguistic cues by the child (Hoff, 2003). Similarly, exposure to a rich and elaborate language input during later years, accompanied by shared experiences and good reading habits, may help foster the semantic richness, background knowledge and grammatical flexibility necessary for constructing a more complex mental world, thereby enabling the individual in question to cope more successfully with future social and academic challenges.

In this sense, it is worth remembering that educational fostering of ToM is also an important issue. All activities aimed at promoting contact between children and the desires, intentions, emotions and emotional states of others are beneficial to their development. ToM can be viewed as a vital cognitive infrastructure for understanding other people's rights, and therefore for facilitating peaceful and democratic coexistence in our society. There are a number of initiatives and programmes aimed at promoting ToM during the development process (Galende, de Miguel, & Arranz, 2011).

Fifth, recent research points to the need for adult training as a means of impacting child development. For example, interventions focusing on enhancing parents' executive function and self-regulation capacity improve any programme (Shonkoff, 2011), a fact which justifies the establishment of positive parenting programmes and the involvement of educators in order to try and ensure the full and effective deployment and development of the processes and faculties described in this chapter. It is important for the progress made in cognitive psychology and neuroscience to be translated into preventive training policies aimed at all adults responsible for establishing a safe relational space for children. These policies should foster the adequate development of brain structures in order to enable children to reach optimum levels of cognitive, emotional and behavioural maturity right from the earliest years of their development.

Finally, it's important stating that all the recommendation and implications mentioned above should be integrated under a general framework of *co-education*. Given the early contact that children nowadays have with institutional learning and care, an accurate and synchronised action of family, school and community is highly required to properly support children' psychological development.

References

Albareda-Castellot, B., Pons, F., & Sebastián-Gallés, N. (2011). The acquisition of phonetic categories in bilingual infants: New data from an anticipatory eye movement paradigm. *Developmental Science, 14*(2), 395–401.

Arranz, E. (1998). *Modelos del desarrollo psicológico humano*. Bilbao, Spain: Servicio Editorial de la Universidad del País Vasco.

Baddeley, A. (2000). The episodic buffer: A new component of working memory? *Trends in Cognitive Sciences, 4*(11), 417–423.

Barkley, R. A. (1997). Behavioral inhibition, sustained attention, and executive functions: Constructing a unifying theory of ADHD. *Psychological Bulletin, 121*(1), 65.

Bental, B., & Tirosh, E. (2007). The relationship between attention, executive functions and reading domain abilities in attention deficit hyperactivity disorder and reading disorder: A comparative study. *Journal of Child Psychology and Psychiatry, 48*(5), 455–463.

Brocki, K. C., Forslund, T., Frick, M., & Bohlin, G. (2017). Do individual differences in early affective and cognitive self-regulation predict developmental change in ADHD symptoms from preschool to adolescence? *Journal of Attention Disorders*, 1–11. doi:10.1177/1087054717693372.

Bronfenbrenner, U. (2005). *Making human beings human: Bioecological perspectives on human development. The SAGE Program on Applied Developmental Science*. London, UK: Sage Publications.

Byers-Heinlein, K., Fennell, C. T., & Werker, J. F. (2013). The development of associative word learning in monolingual and bilingual infants. *Bilingualism: Language and Cognition, 16*(1), 198–205.

Call, J., & Tomasello, M. (2008). Does the chimpanzee have a theory of mind? 30 years later. *Trends in Cognitive Sciences, 12*(5), 187–192.

Campbell, M. E., & Cunnington, R. (2017). More than an imitation game: Top-down modulation of the human mirror system. *Neuroscience & Biobehavioral Reviews, 75*, 195–202. doi:10.1016/j.neubiorev.2017.01.035

Case, R., Hayward, S., Lewis, M., & Hurst, P. (1988). Toward a neo-Piagetian theory of cognitive and emotional development. *Developmental Review, 8*(1), 1–51. doi:10.1016/0273-2297(88)90010-X

Casey, B. (2015). Beyond simple models of self-control to circuit-based accounts of adolescent behavior. *Annual Review of Psychology, 66*, 295–319. doi:10.1146/annurev-psych-010814-015156

Casey, B. J., Giedd, J. N., & Thomas, K. M. (2000). Structural and functional brain development and its relation to cognitive development. *Biological psychology, 54*(1–3), 241–257.

Center on the Developing Child at Harvard University. (2014). *Enhancing and practicing executive function skills with children from infancy to adolescence.* Retrieved from www.developingchild.harvard.edu

Crawford, N. A., Schrock, M., & Woodruff-Borden, J. (2011). Child internalizing symptoms: Contributions of child temperament, maternal negative affect, and family functioning. *Child Psychiatry and Human Development, 42*(1), 53–64. doi:10.1007/s10578-010-0202-5

Curtin, S., Mintz, T. H., & Christiansen, M. H. (2005). Stress changes the representational landscape: Evidence from word segmentation. *Cognition, 96*(3), 233–262.

De Diego-Balaguer, R., Martinez-Alvarez, A., & Pons, F. (2016). Temporal attention as a scaffold for language development. *Frontiers in Psychology, 7*, 44.

DeLoache, J. S. (2000). Dual representation and young children's use of scale models. *Child Development, 71*(2), 329–338.

Diamond, A. (2013). Executive functions. *Annual Review of Psychology, 64*, 135–168. doi:10.1146/annurev-psych-113011-143750

Diamond, A., Kirkham, N., & Amso, D. (2002). Conditions under which young children can hold two rules in mind and inhibit a prepotent response. *Developmental Psychology, 38*(3), 352.

Dohle, S., Diel, K., & Hofmann, W. (2018). Executive functions and the self-regulation of eating behavior: A review. *Appetite, 124*, 4–9. doi:10.1016/j.appet.2017.05.041

Duncan, L. G., Castro, S. L., Defior, S., Seymour, P. H., Baillie, S., Leybaert, J., … Lund, R. (2013). Phonological development in relation to native language and literacy: Variations on a theme in six alphabetic orthographies. *Cognition, 127*(3), 398–419.

Eisenberg, N., Hernández, M. M., & Spinrad, T. L. (2017). The relation of self-regulation to children's externalizing and internalizing problems. In C. A. Essau, S. S. LeBlanc, & T. H. Ollendick (Eds.), *Emotion regulation and psychopathology in children and adolescents* (pp. 18–42). Oxford, UK: Oxford University Press.

Evans, G. W., & Kim, P. (2013). Childhood poverty, chronic stress, self-regulation, and coping. *Child Development Perspectives, 7*(1), 43–48. doi:10.1111/cdep.12013

Farrant, B. M., Maybery, M. T., & Fletcher, J. (2012). Language, cognitive flexibility, and explicit false belief understanding: Longitudinal analysis in typical development and specific language impairment. *Child Development, 83*(1), 223–235. doi:10.1111/j.1467-8624.2011.01681.x

Fernandez-Duque, D., Baird, J. A., & Posner, M. I. (2000). Executive attention and metacognitive regulation. *Consciousness and Cognition, 9*(2), 288–307.

Frick, M. A., Forslund, T., Fransson, M., Johansson, M., Bohlin, G., & Brocki, K. C. (2018). The role of sustained attention, maternal sensitivity, and infant temperament in the development of early self-regulation. *British Journal of Psychology, 109*(2), 277–298. doi:10.1111/bjop.12266

Galende, N., de Miguel, M. S., & Arranz, E. (2011). The role of physical context, verbal skills, non-parental care, social support, and type of parental discipline in the development of ToM capacity in five-year-old children. *Social Development, 20*(4), 845–861.

García-Molina, A., Enseñat-Cantallops, A., Tirapu-Ustárroz, J., & Roig-Rovira, T. (2009). Maduración de la corteza prefrontal y desarrollo de las funciones ejecutivas durante los primeros cinco años de vida. *Revista de Neurología, 48*(8), 435–440.

Gathercole, S. E. (2006). Nonword repetition and word learning: The nature of the relationship. *Applied Psycholinguistics, 27*(4), 513–543.

Gathercole, S. E., & Pickering, S. J. (2000). Assessment of working memory in six-and seven-year-old children. *Journal of Educational Psychology, 92*(2), 377–390. doi:10.1037/0022-0663.92.2.377

Geng, X., Li, G., Lu, Z., Gao, W., Wang, L., Shen, D., … Gilmore, J. H. (2017). Structural and maturational covariance in early childhood brain development. *Cerebral Cortex, 27*(3), 1795–1807. doi:10.1093/cercor/bhw022

Gervain, J., Berent, I., & Werker, J. F. (2012). Binding at birth: The newborn brain detects identity relations and sequential position in speech. *Journal of Cognitive Neuroscience, 24*(3), 564–574.

Gooch, D., Snowling, M., & Hulme, C. (2011). Time perception, phonological skills and executive function in children with dyslexia and/or ADHD symptoms. *Journal of Child Psychology and Psychiatry, 52*(2), 195–203.

Gooch, D., Thompson, P., Nash, H. M., Snowling, M. J., & Hulme, C. (2016). The development of executive function and language skills in the early school years. *Journal of Child Psychology and Psychiatry, 57*(2), 180–187.

Gottlieb, G. (2007). Probabilistic epigenesis. *Developmental Science, 10*(1), 1–11. doi:10.1111/j.1467-7687.2007.00556.x

Gray, S., Green, S., Alt, M., Hogan, T., Kuo, T., Brinkley, S., & Cowan, N. (2017). The structure of working memory in young children and its relation to intelligence. *Journal of Memory and Language, 92*, 183–201.

Henry, L. A., & Botting, N. (2017). Working memory and developmental language impairments. *Child Language Teaching and Therapy, 33*(1), 19–32.

Heyes, C. (2016). Imitation: Not in our genes. *Current Biology, 26*(10), R412–R414. doi:10.1016/j.cub.2016.03.060

Hill, E. L. (2004). Executive dysfunction in autism. *Trends in Cognitive Sciences, 8*(1), 26–32.

Hoff, E.(2003). The specificity of environmental influence: Socioeconomic status affects early vocabulary development via maternal speech. *Child Development, 74*, 1368–1378.

Hughes, C. (2011). Changes and challenges in 20 years of research into the development of executive functions. *Infant and Child Development, 20*(3), 251–271.

Hughes, C., & Devine, R. T. (2015). Individual differences in theory of mind from preschool to adolescence: Achievements and directions. *Child Development Perspectives, 9*(3), 149–153.

Hughes, C. H., & Ensor, R. A. (2009). How do families help or hinder the emergence of early executive function?. *New Directions for Child and Adolescent Development, 2009*(123), 35–50.

Hughes, C., & Ensor, R. (2011). Individual differences in growth in executive function across the transition to school predict externalizing and internalizing behaviors and self-perceived academic success at 6 years of age. *Journal of Experimental Child Psychology, 108*(3), 663–676.

Iverson, J. M., & Goldin-Meadow, S. (2005). Gesture paves the way for language development. *Psychological Science, 16*(5), 367–371.

Johnson, M. H. (2001). Functional brain development in humans. *Nature Reviews Neuroscience, 2*(7), 475–483.

Johnston, T. D. (2015). Gilbert Gottlieb and the biopsychosocial perspective on developmental issues. In S. D. Calkins (Ed.), *Handbook of infant biopsychosocial development* (pp. 11–21). New York, NY: The Guilford Press.

Karmiloff-Smith, A. (2018). Précis of beyond modularity: A developmental perspective on cognitive science. In A. Karmiloff-Smith, M. S. C. Thomas, & M. H. Johnson (Eds.), *Thinking developmentally from constructivism to neuroconstructivism* (pp. 64–94). London, UK: Routledge.

Kidd, E., & Arciuli, J. (2016). Individual differences in statistical learning predict children's comprehension of syntax. *Child Development, 87*(1), 184–193.

Kitsantas, A., Steen, S., & Huie, F. (2009). The role of self-regulated strategies and goal orientation in predicting achievement of elementary school children. *International Electronic Journal of Elementary Education, 2*(1), 65–81.

Klahr, D., & Wallace, J. G. (1976). *Cognitive development. An information processing view.* Hillsdale, NJ: Lawrence Erlbaum Associates.

Klenberg, L., Korkman, M., & Lahti-Nuuttila, P. (2001). Differential development of attention and executive functions in 3-to 12-year-old Finnish children. *Developmental Neuropsychology, 20*(1), 407–428.

Klingberg, T., Fernell, E., Olesen, P. J., Johnson, M., Gustafsson, P., Dahlström, K., … Westerberg, H. (2005). Computerized training of working memory in children with ADHD–A randomized, controlled trial. *Journal of the American Academy of Child & Adolescent Psychiatry, 44*(2), 177–186.

Kuhl, P. K., Conboy, B. T., Coffey-Corina, S., Padden, D., Rivera-Gaxiola, M., & Nelson, T. (2008). Phonetic learning as a pathway to language: New data and native language magnet theory expanded (NLM-e). *Philosophical Transactions of the Royal Society of London B: Biological Sciences, 363*(1493), 979–1000.

Lamm, C., Zelazo, P. D., & Lewis, M. D. (2006). Neural correlates of cognitive control in childhood and adolescence: Disentangling the contributions of age and executive function. *Neuropsychologia, 44*(11), 2139–2148.

Leerkes, E. M., Weaver, J. M., & O'Brien, M. (2012). Differentiating maternal sensitivity to infant distress and non-distress. *Parenting, 12*(2–3), 175–184. doi:10.1080/15295192.2012.683353

Lyall, A. E., Shi, F., Geng, X., Woolson, S., Li, G., Wang, L., … Gilmore, J. H. (2015). Dynamic development of regional cortical thickness and surface area in early childhood. *Cerebral Cortex, 25*, 2204–2212. doi:10.1093/cercor/bhu027

Magimairaj, B. M., & Montgomery, J. W. (2012). Children's verbal working memory: Relative importance of storage, general processing speed, and domain-general controlled attention. *Acta Psychologica, 140*(3), 196–207.

Manly, T., Anderson, V., Nimmo-Smith, I., Turner, A., Watson, P., & Robertson, I. H. (2001). The differential assessment of children's attention: The Test of Everyday Attention for Children (TEA-Ch), normative sample and ADHD performance. *The Journal of Child Psychology and Psychiatry and Allied Disciplines, 42*(8), 1065–1081.

Marcus, G. F. (2000). Pabiku and Ga Ti Ga: Two mechanisms infants use to learn about the world. *Current Directions in Psychological Science, 9*(5), 145–147.

Markman, E. M. (1990). Constraints children place on word meanings. *Cognitive Science, 14*(1), 57–77.

McAlister, A. R., & Peterson, C. C. (2013). Siblings, theory of mind, and executive functioning in children aged 3–6 years: New longitudinal evidence. *Child Development, 84*(4), 1442–1458. doi:10.1111/cdev.12043

McCabe, D. P., Roediger III, H. L., McDaniel, M. A., Balota, D. A., & Hambrick, D. Z. (2010). The relationship between working memory capacity and executive functioning: Evidence for a common executive attention construct. *Neuropsychology, 24*(2), 222.

McCandliss, B. D., Cohen, L., & Dehaene, S. (2003). The visual word form area: Expertise for reading in the fusiform gyrus. *Trends in Cognitive Sciences, 7*(7), 293–299.

McCoy, D. (2013). Early violence exposure and self-regulatory development: A bioecological systems perspective. *Human Development, 56*(4), 254–273. doi:10.1159/000353217

Moilanen, K. L., & Manuel, M. L. (2017). Parenting, self-regulation and social competence with peers and romantic partners. *Journal of Applied Developmental Psychology, 49*, 46–54. doi:10.1016/J.APPDEV.2017.02.003

Montroy, J. J., Bowles, R. P., Skibbe, L. E., McClelland, M. M., & Morrison, F. J. (2016). The development of self-regulation across early childhood. *Developmental Psychology, 52*(11), 1744–1762.

Nigg, J. T. (2017). HHS public access. *Journal of Child Psychology and Psychiatry, 58*(4), 361–383. doi:10.1111/jcpp.12675

Pallini, S., Chirumbolo, A., Morelli, M., Baiocco, R., Laghi, F., & Eisenberg, N. (2018). The relation of attachment security status to effortful self-regulation: A meta-analysis. *Psychological Bulletin, 144*(5), 501–531.

Pascual-Leone, J. (1987). Organismic processes for neo-Piagetian theories: A dialectical causal account of cognitive development. *International Journal of Psychology, 22*(5–6), 531–570. doi:10.1080/00207598708246795

Peterson, C. C., Wellman, H. M., & Slaughter, V. (2012). The mind behind the message: Advancing theory-of-mind scales for typically developing children, and those with deafness, autism, or Asperger syndrome. *Child Development, 83*(2), 469–485.

Piaget, J. (1954). *The construction of reality in the child.* Abingdon, UK: Routledge.

Prencipe, A., Kesek, A., Cohen, J., Lamm, C., Lewis, M. D., & Zelazo, P. D. (2011). Development of hot and cool executive function during the transition to adolescence. *Journal of Experimental Child Psychology, 108*(3), 621–637. doi:10.1016/j.jecp.2010.09.008

Putnam, S. P., Rothbart, M. K., & Gartstein, M. A. (2008). Homotypic and heterotypic continuity of fine-grained temperament during infancy, toddlerhood, and early childhood. *Infant and Child Development, 17*, 387–405. doi:10.1002/ICD.582

Raznahan, A., Shaw, P., Lalonde, F., Stockman, M., Wallace, G. L., Greenstein, D., … Giedd, J. N. (2011). How does your cortex grow? *Journal of Neuroscience, 31*(19), 7174–7177. doi:10.1523/JNEUROSCI.0054-11.2011

Rose, S. A., Feldman, J. F., & Jankowski, J. J. (2001). Visual short-term memory in the first year of life: Capacity and recency effects. *Developmental Psychology, 37*(4), 539.

Rothbart, M. K., Sheese, B. E., & Posner, M. I. (2007). Executive attention and effortful control: Linking temperament, brain networks, and genes. *Child Development Perspectives, 1*(1), 2–7. doi:10.1111/j.1750-8606.2007.00002.x

Rueda, M. R., Checa, P., & Combita, L. M. (2012). Enhanced efficiency of the executive attention network after training in preschool children: Immediate changes and effects after two months. *Developmental Cognitive Neuroscience, 2*, 192–204.

Rueda, M. R., Fan, J., McCandliss, B. D., Halparin, J. D., Gruber, D. B., Lercari, L. P., & Posner, M. I. (2004). Development of attentional networks in childhood. *Neuropsychologia, 42*(8), 1029–1040.

Saffran, J. R., Aslin, R. N., & Newport, E. L. (1996). Statistical learning by 8-month-old infants. *Science, 274*(5294), 1926–1928.

Shonkoff, J. P. (2011). Protecting brains, not simply stimulating minds. *Science, 333*, 982–983.

Shonkoff, J. P., & Phillips, D. A. (2000). *From neurons to neighborhoods: The science of early childhood development.* Washington, DC: National Academy Press. Retrieved from http://www.nap.edu/catalog/9824.html

Theodore, R. M., Demuth, K., & Shattuck-Hufnagel, S. (2011). Acoustic evidence for positional and complexity effects on children's production of plural-s. *Journal of Speech, Language, and Hearing Research, 54*(2), 539–548.

Tomasello, M. (2000). Do young children have adult syntactic competence? *Cognition, 74*(3), 209–253.

Tomasello, M. (2003). On the different origins of symbols and grammar. *Studies in the Evolution of Language, 3*, 94–110.

Tomasello, M., Carpenter, M., & Liszkowski, U. (2007). A new look at infant pointing. *Child development, 78*(3), 705–722.

Tomasello, M., & Rakoczy, H. (2003). What makes human cognition unique? From individual to shared to collective intentionality. *Mind & Language, 18*(2), 121–147.

Valle, A., Massaro, D., Castelli, I., & Marchetti, A. (2015). Theory of mind development in adolescence and early adulthood: The growing complexity of recursive thinking ability. *Europe's Journal of Psychology, 11*(1), 112.

Van der Lely, H. K. (2005). Domain-specific cognitive systems: Insight from Grammatical-SLI. *Trends in Cognitive Sciences, 9*(2), 53–59.

Vara, A. S., Pang, E. W., Vidal, J., Anagnostou, E., & Taylor, M. J. (2014). Neural mechanisms of inhibitory control continue to mature in adolescence. *Developmental Cognitive Neuroscience, 10*, 129–139. doi:10.1016/j.dcn.2014.08.009

Wang, Z., Williamson, R. A., & Meltzoff, A. N. (2015). Imitation as a mechanism in cognitive development: A cross-cultural investigation of 4-year-old children's rule learning. *Frontiers in Psychology, 6*, 562. doi:10.3389/fpsyg.2015.00562

Wellman, H. M. (2012). Theory of mind: Better methods, clearer findings, more development. *European Journal of Developmental Psychology, 9*(3), 313–330.

Werker, J. F., & Tees, R. C. (2002). Cross-language speech perception: Evidence for perceptual reorganization during the first year of life. *Infant Behavior and Development, 25*(1), 121–133.

Wimmer, H., & Perner, J. (1983). Beliefs about beliefs: Representation and constraining function of wrong beliefs in young children's understanding of deception. *Cognition, 13*(1), 103–128. doi:10.1016/0010-0277(83)90004-5

Wood, D., Bruner, J. S., & Ross, G. (1976). The role of tutoring in problem solving. *Journal of Child Psychology and Psychiatry, 17*(2), 89–100.

Xu, F., Cote, M., & Baker, A. (2005). Labeling guides object individuation in 12-month-old infants. *Psychological Science, 16*(5), 372–377.

Yogman, M., Garner, A., Hutchinson, J., Hirsh-Pasek, K., Golinkoff, R. M., & Committee on PsychosociaL Aspects of Child and Family Health. (2018). The power of play: A pediatric role in enhancing development in young children. *Pediatrics, 142*(3), e20182058.

Yurovsky, D., Yu, C., & Smith, L. B. (2012). Statistical speech segmentation and word learning in parallel: Scaffolding from child-directed speech. *Frontiers in Psychology, 3*, 374.

Zelazo, P. D., & Carlson, S. M. (2012). Hot and cool executive function in childhood and adolescence: Development and plasticity. *Child Development Perspectives, 6*(4), 354–360. doi:10.1111/j.1750-8606.2012.00246.x

Zelazo, P. D., Müller, U. B., Frye, D., Marcovitch, S. D., Argitis, G., Boseovski, J. J., ... Sutherland, A. E. (2003). The development of executive function in early childhood. *Monographs of the Society for Research in Child Development, 68*(3), 8–137.

Zucker, R. A., Heitzeg, M. M., & Nigg, J. T. (2011). NIH public access. *Child Development Perspectives, 5*(4), 248–255. doi:10.1111/j.1750-8606.2011.00172

2

Peer Relationships and Social Competence in Early Childhood

Becky Kochenderfer-Ladd and Gary W. Ladd

Evidence gathered over several decades suggests that children who form positive peer relationships and possess higher levels of social competence experience better outcomes in multiple areas of development, including social, emotional, and academic domains (Denham, Zinsser, & Brown, 2013; Elliott, Frey, & Davies, 2015; Ladd, 2005; Parker & Asher, 1993; Torres, Domitrovich, & Bierman, 2015). Such children appear to be better equipped to cope with social challenges and contexts, form new and rewarding relationships, and succeed academically (DeRosier & Thomas, 2018; Elliott, Davies, Frey, Gresham, & Cooper, 2018; Zins, Bloodworth, Weissberg, & Walberg, 2007).

Conversely, children who lack healthy peer relationships and critical social skills are more likely to engage in disruptive classroom behaviors, continue to participate in problematic peer relationships (e.g., peer rejection bullying, victimization; Ettekal, Kochenderfer-Ladd, & Ladd, 2015), and fail or fall behind academically (Medford & McGeown, 2016; Zins et al., 2007). Indeed, the established links between children's early peer relations and social competence and their later development and school performance have motivated calls for universal, early screening to identify those children who are most at risk for problematic peer relationships and poor social-emotional skills (Diamond, 2016; Elliott et al., 2018; Humphrey & Wigelsworth, 2016).

Several aims are addressed in this chapter and, to the extent feasible in the space provided, explicated with relevant theory and evidence. The first aim is to profile young children's peer relationships and consider how their participation in these relationships may, for better or worse, affect the course of their development. The second aim is to consider the meaning of social competence during early childhood, and identify abilities or skill sets that children need to form and manage peer relationships, and to successfully negotiate frequently encountered interpersonal contexts and challenges. The third aim is to identify practices and policies that early educators can use to help young children acquire essential social competencies and successfully launch and maintain their peer relationships.

Identifying Pivotal Social Challenges in Early Childhood Environments

In addition to intellectual, language, and physical development, preschool teachers and childcare providers have been entrusted with the responsibility of promoting children's social development. However, because social development has many facets, it may be challenging for teachers and caregivers to decide which aspects of children's social development they should facilitate. One way to address this dilemma is to identify fundamental interpersonal challenges that are inherent in early childhood environments, and then enumerate the types of skills or competencies that young children need to address or successfully adapt to those challenges. This logic dictates that we begin by identifying some of the social challenges that young children routinely confront in early childhood settings.

Transitions across interpersonal settings or environments, such as from home to preschool or childcare, and from preschool or childcare to grade school, present young children with many challenges. Early in development, most young children migrate from smaller familiar settings, such as the home and neighborhood, to larger social contexts, such as childcare, preschool, and kindergarten, where they are encouraged to interact with peers in unstructured (e.g., play) and structured activities (e.g., peer-oriented learning groups, activity centers). As children enter these new settings, they must interact, play and work cooperatively, and form ties with other children. Thus, initiating and responding to peers, entering and participating in peer activities, and forming positive or constructive relationships with agemates or near-agemates constitute fundamental social challenges for young children (Ladd, 2008).

Subsequent transitions, such as entrance into grade school, create both similar and new challenges. As children enter kindergarten, they often lose many of their preschool friends and playmates and are thrust into new and larger peer groups with unfamiliar classmates (Ladd & Price, 1987). Moreover, because the adult to peer ratio is often smaller in kindergarten classrooms than it is in preschool or childcare environments, interactions with peers become more common than those with adults.

Collectively, then, the following are among the pivotal social challenges that young children routinely confront during early childhood: (a) navigating an ever-expanding and complex set of social settings and peer contexts, (b) entering or gaining access to peer activities, (c) initiating peer interactions and responding positively to peers' social overtures, (d) cooperatively participating or collaborating with peers in structured or unstructured activities, and (e) forming and sustaining positive peer relationships.

In the next section, the challenge of forming peer relationships is considered in greater detail. Not only do we consider the types of peer relationships that young children form with peers, but we also consider the role that these relationships play in their development. Three types of peer relationships have garnered the most research attention and, therefore, received the most consideration: friendships, peer group acceptance/rejection, and aggressor-victim relations.

Types of Peer Relationships

Research suggests that at least three types of peer relations emerge and become significant to children during the early childhood years: friendship, peer group acceptance/rejection, and aggressor-victim relations (Ladd, Kochenderfer, & Coleman, 1997; Parker & Asher, 1993). *Friendship* refers to a voluntary, dyadic relationship that is built on an affiliative tie (Howes, 1983, 1988; Ladd & Kochenderfer, 1996). In contrast, *peer group acceptance/rejection* is defined as the degree to which an individual child is liked and/or disliked by the members of his or her social group (Asher, Rose, & Gabriel, 2001; Parker & Asher, 1993). *Aggressor-victim relations* refer to a form of association in which one child is frequently aggressed upon by one or more members of his or her peer group (Kochenderfer-Ladd & Ladd, 2001; Ladd, Ettekal, & Kochenderfer-Ladd, 2017; Perry, Kusel, & Perry, 1988).

Although each of these concepts refers to a distinct form of relationship, it should be recognized that children often participate in multiple types of peer relationships simultaneously (Ladd et al., 1997). For example, it is possible for preschoolers or grade-schoolers to be rejected by the majority of their classmates and still have a friend in their peer group (Parker & Asher, 1993). Likewise, children who are victimized by their peers are not necessarily disliked or rejected by a majority of their classmates (Perry et al., 1988). Further, friendship, peer group acceptance/rejection, and victim-aggressor relations may look different across various age groups; therefore, it is essential to consider how researchers have defined and measured friendship, peer acceptance/rejection, and victimization specifically in early childhood.

Friendships in Infants, Toddlers, and Preschoolers

With infants and toddlers, friends have often been identified on the basis of a peers' familiarity, the frequency with which pairs of children interact, and the likelihood that partners reciprocate each other's emotions (Howes, 1988). Toddlers' friendships are unique in the sense that they adjust to suit their partners, and relate with them differently than they do with other children (Howes, 1983, 1988). Moreover, such friendships have been shown to be relatively long lasting. For example, Howes (1983) found that 60% of toddler friends sustained their relationship over a period of months, and Howes and Phillipsen (1992) reported that toddlers' friendships often lasted well into the preschool years.

For preschoolers, criteria such as companionship, intimacy, affection, and proximity have been used to identify friendships (Howes, 1988). For example, to identify friends, researchers have noted the peers with whom preschoolers often play and measured the duration of their interactions and proximity with those peers (Hinde, Titmus, Easton, & Tamplin, 1985). Others have used evidence of complementary or reciprocal play, mutual positive affect, and agreement in children's friendship nominations as means of identifying preschooler's friendships (Howes, 1988; Price & Ladd, 1986). As with toddlers, stability is a defining feature of preschoolers' friendships. Studies show that many preschoolers remain friends for as long as one to two years (Howes, 1988), and that it is not uncommon for preschoolers to maintain their friendships from preschool into kindergarten (i.e., across school transitions; Ladd, 1990).

Peer Group Acceptance/Rejection

This form of relation has been examined primarily with preschoolers, and in school settings (e.g., classrooms, playgrounds). The goal is to assess group members' sentiments toward individuals, and typically this is accomplished by asking each member of the peer group to either (a) rate how much they like ("not at all", "somewhat", or "a lot") to play with each of the other members of the peer group or (b) nominate those group members that they most "like" or "don't like" to play with. When ratings are used, peer acceptance or rejection is determined by averaging and standardizing the scores children receive from all group members. High standardized scores indicate peer acceptance and low standardized scores denote rejection. With nominations, it is possible to classify children into peer status subtypes (i.e., popular, average, controversial, neglected, and rejected; Coie & Dodge, 1983). Preschoolers are considered popular if they receive a large number of positive nominations and few negative nominations, and deemed rejected if they receive few positive nominations and many negative nominations.

Aggressor-Victim Relations

Young children who are frequently teased, harassed, or otherwise aggressed upon by peers have been termed *victims* of peer aggression or bullying (Kochenderfer-Ladd & Wardrop, 2001). To identify young victims, investigators tend to use either multi-informant (Ladd & Kochenderfer-Ladd, 2002) or multimethod (see Vlachou, Botsoglou, & Andreou, 2013) approaches. For example, Ladd and Kochenderfer-Ladd (2002) used teacher-, self-, and peer-reports to obtain estimates of the frequency with which children had been harassed or abused by a peer or peers. Additional strategies include peer nominations or naturalistic observations (Vlachou et al., 2013).

Although prevalence estimates for peer victimization vary, and some periods of schooling have been investigated more than others, evidence suggests that the occurrence of peer victimization varies by age or grade level. Moreover, findings indicate that victimization tends to be more widespread in earlier as opposed to later years of schooling (Nylund, Bellmore, Nishina, & Graham, 2007; Reavis, Keane, & Calkins, 2010; Rudolph, Troop-Gordon, Hessel, & Schmidt, 2011) with studies demonstrating that many children experience peer abuse as they begin school. For example, in their K through grade 12 longitudinal study, Ladd et al. (2017) found that over 20% of kindergarteners could be classified as "severe victims". Further, for some children, victimization is a pervasive experience that continues through the school years and affects their engagement in the classroom as well as their academic progress (Ladd et al., 2017).

Children who fail to develop allies within their peer groups appear to be at greater risk for victimization than those who do. Children who are friendless or highly disliked by members of their peer groups are particularly vulnerable to this kind of maltreatment (Perry, Hodges & Egan, 2001) and tend to become increasingly victimized over time (Hodges & Perry, 1999). In contrast, children who have friends are less likely to be victimized, even when they exhibited other risk factors that predict peer maltreatment (e.g., physical weakness, poor family relationships; Hodges, Malone, & Perry, 1997; Hodges & Perry, 1999).

In sum, making friends, establishing oneself as a member of a peer group, and coping with peer harassment are three principal relationship tasks that confront young children during the early childhood years. Next, we consider the significance of these relationships for children's socialization, development, and adjustment.

Role of Peer Relationships in Young Children's Development

A common premise within socialization theories is that peers play an important role in shaping young children's development. As the following findings indicate, this hypothesis has received considerable support.

Friendship

Friendships provide children with psychosocial benefits dependent upon the quality, or features, of those relationships. For example, friendships characterized by sharing, helping, and companionship offer young children a sense of closeness, or belonging, security, and a social context for motivating and honing interpersonal social skills (Bukowski & Hoza, 1989; Ladd & Kochenderfer, 1996; Parker & Asher, 1993). Children with close friendships not only view themselves more positively, but also experience greater perceived social support and less loneliness (Ladd, Kochenderfer, & Coleman, 1996; Parker & Asher, 1993).

Friendships also have been linked with young children's school readiness and adjustment. Studies show that children adapt better to kindergarten if they begin school with a pre-established friend (e.g., a friend they knew in preschool), and children who make new friends in kindergarten, compared to those who do not, develop more favorable school attitudes and do better scholastically (Ladd, 1990). What occurs within children's friendships may also have an important bearing on their school adjustment. Ladd et al. (1996) found that kindergartners' views of their classrooms were more positive when they saw their classroom friends as sources of affirmation (support) and aid (assistance). In contrast, kindergarteners (especially boys) who reported conflict within their classroom friendships exhibited lower levels of classroom engagement and participation (Ladd et al., 1996).

Collectively, research on friendship suggests that young children benefit from having a friend, and that friends contribute to multiple aspects of children's health and development. In contrast, children who lack friends, or who participate in poor quality friendships, appear to be at greater risk for maladjustment (Ladd, 2005).

Peer Group Acceptance and Rejection

Of particular concern are children who fail to become accepted members of their peer groups. Although estimates vary across studies, about 12%–16% of children in community samples tend to be identified as rejected (Ladd, Herald, & Kochel, 2006; Ladd, Herald-Brown, & Reiser, 2008). Moreover, once children are rejected, they often remain so, and rejection becomes more stable as children get older (Coie & Dodge, 1983; Ladd, 2006). Evidence also shows that children who suffer longer periods of rejection are more apt to develop social, psychological, and scholastic problems (Ladd, 2006).

Longitudinal studies have corroborated the hypothesis that peer group rejection antecedes many forms of psychological maladjustment (McDougall, Hymel, Vaillancourt, & Mercer, 2001). For example, during both early and middle childhood, links have been found between peer rejection and particular types of internalizing (e.g., loneliness) and externalizing problems (e.g., misconduct, delinquency, violence). Further, several investigators have discovered that the severity of children's maladjustment increases as a function of how long they have been rejected (i.e., rejection chronicity; Ladd et al., 2008).

Children's school adjustment, in particular, appears to suffer when they fail to become accepted by their classmates. Classroom peer rejection at school entry predicts problems such as negative school attitudes, school avoidance, and underachievement during the first year of schooling (Buhs & Ladd, 2001; Ladd, 1990). Later, in the elementary years, low peer acceptance has been linked with loneliness (Parker & Asher, 1993), emotional problems, and academic deficits (Ladd et al., 1997, 2008). If children are rejected across multiple school years, they appear to be at significant risk for school disengagement (Ladd et al., 2008).

Thus, it appears that negative developmental consequences often await children who fail to become accepted by their peers, particularly in classroom settings. Most likely, this is because rejection by one's agemates prevents children from participating in important learning experiences and exposes them to adverse social processes (e.g., exclusion; Asher et al., 2001).

Aggressor-Victim Relations

Children who are victimized by peers are more likely to develop certain types of psychological maladies, including loneliness, depression, and anxiety (Ettekal et al., 2015), hopelessness (Bonanno & Hymel, 2010), and suicidal ideation and self-injury (Heilbron & Prinstein, 2010). Further, they are at risk for poor academic outcomes (Ladd et al., 2017; Nakomoto & Schwartz, 2010). Studies indicate that, among those who are frequently victimized, many tend to act either passively or aggressively around agemates. Shy or withdrawn children who are victimized (e.g., passive victims) tend to report moderate to severe levels of anxiety and somatic complaints (e.g., headaches, stomachaches, and other minor physical ills) following bouts of bullying at school (Perry et al., 2001). In contrast, children who are aggressive and victimized (i.e., aggressive victims) tend to develop higher levels of externalizing problems such as misconduct and delinquency (Perry et al., 2001).

Victimized children, regardless of their behavioral propensities, are also more likely to develop mild to severe school adjustment problems. Research on school transitions has shown that, following children's entrance into kindergarten, the frequency of children's exposure to peer abuse forecasted significant gains in loneliness and school avoidance over their first year in school (Kochenderfer & Ladd, 1996). Pronounced or prolonged (e.g., chronic) peer abuse has been linked with more serious or debilitating forms of school maladjustment (Kochenderfer & Wardrop, 2001; Ladd et al., 2017; Troop-Gordon & Ladd, 2005).

As was the case for peer group rejection, it appears that many young children are exposed to peer victimization, and that experiences of this type place them at risk for multiple forms of maladjustment. Here again, it is likely that abusive physical and verbal processes—ones that may be more severe than those associated with peer rejection (e.g., hitting, teasing, ridicule, exploitation; Ladd et al., 2017)—are responsible for the negative developmental outcomes that are associated with peer victimization.

Participation in Multiple Forms of Peer Relationships

Researchers have also examined children's participation in multiple forms of peer relationships and the relative (differential) "contributions" they make to specific adjustment outcomes. Evidence suggests that children's classroom peer relationships appear to be specialized in the types of resources or constraints they create for socio-emotional and academic adjustment (Ladd et al., 1997; Parker & Asher, 1993). For young children, it has been shown that these types of peer relationships contribute uniquely to the prediction of changes in kindergartners' school perceptions, avoidance, and performance (Ladd, 1990; Ladd et al., 1997). For example, although both peer group rejection and peer victimization appear to hinder children's adaptation to school, peer victimization is more closely linked with the development of loneliness and school avoidance (Ladd et al., 1997) whereas peer rejection appears to play more of a role in limiting children's participation in classroom activities and, therefore, tends to be a stronger predictor of subsequent achievement (Buhs, Ladd, & Herald, 2006; Ladd, Birch, & Buhs, 1999; Ladd et al., 1997).

Friendships may be particularly beneficial for children in school contexts and may, under some circumstances, compensate for the adverse effects of negative peer relationships. Children who form higher quality friendships with classmates tend to fare better in school than those who are rejected or remain friendless (Ladd, 1990; Ladd et al., 2008, 1997). In contrast, children who are rejected or victimized by peers are more likely to develop a range of adjustment problems, including school avoidance, loneliness, and negative attitudes toward classmates, and disengagement from the school environment (Ettekal et al., 2015; Kochenderfer-Ladd & Wardrop, 2001; Troop-Gordon & Ladd, 2005).

Other findings imply that the contributions of classroom peer relationships to children's adjustment depend not only on the resources or constraints they confer upon children, but also upon the duration of children's participation in these relationships. Findings show that prolonged instead of brief exposures to relational adversities (e.g., longer periods of peer group rejection or victimization) or relational supports (e.g., history of peer group acceptance) are more predictive of children's school adjustment trajectories (Ladd et al., 2017; Troop-Gordon & Ladd, 2005).

In sum, findings from research on friendships, peer group acceptance, and peer victimization are largely consistent with the hypothesis that peer relationships affect children's development. That is, existing findings lend support to three major premises: (1) peer relationships *provide* or *prevent* children from obtaining interpersonal resources (support, aid) that are essential for human development. (2) Participation in certain kinds of peer relationships alters the child's social environment (how they are seen, treated by peers), or the child's response to the peer system (they may approach, withdraw, move against it), both of which may have consequences for their development and adjustment. (3) Peer relationships may alter the child by socializing specific assets or vulnerabilities (e.g., self-worth, fears) that make him or her more (or less) resilient or vulnerable to adjustment problems. Further, available evidence suggests that the relationships young children form with peers play an important role in establishing the social, intellectual, and psychological conditions that underlie school adjustment and scholastic progress. Ultimately, it is the combination of children's social competence and success at establishing supportive ties with classmates that appears prognostic of their school adjustment.

Defining Social Competence in Early Childhood

One way to define social competence during early childhood is to identify the types of skills that young children need to successfully address social challenges that are specific to this age period. In keeping with this logic, we return to the pivotal social challenges that were delineated earlier in this chapter and, using theory and evidence, attempt to define forms of social competence (e.g., types of social skills) that may be relevant to these challenges.

The task of defining relevant competencies is aided by the plethora of perspectives and frameworks that researchers have developed to conceptualize social competence as a construct and enumerate its forms (Darling-Churchill & Lippman, 2016; Diamond, 2016; Elias & Moceri, 2012; Gresham, Elliott, & Kettler, 2010; Ladd, 2005; Weissberg, Durlak, Domitovich, & Gullotta, 2015). Frameworks such as these have, for example, been utilized for tasks such as developing social emotional learning (SEL) programs for children, devising methods to assess children's social competence, and evaluating children's skill learning and progress (Darling-Churchill & Lippman, 2016; Elliott et al., 2018; McKown & Taylor, 2018). From these perspectives, we adopt the view that social competence is a multi-faceted construct, and that its forms or manifestations can be parsed into three principal domains: behavioral, cognitive, and emotional.

Behavioral Indicators of Social Competence

In general, studies of the antecedents of friendship, peer group entry, and peer group status show that whereas some of children's behavior patterns (e.g., prosocial) predict positive relational outcomes, others (e.g., anti-social) forecast negative relational consequences (for review, see Ladd, 2005; Putallaz, 1983). Thus, the typical behavioral indictors of social (in)competence among preschool children include engaging in (a) prosocial (e.g., friendly overtures, sharing, cooperation, helping), (b) antisocial (e.g., fighting, conflict,

betrayal), and (c) asocial (e.g., anxious shyness, extreme wariness or reticence) behaviors. In general, findings show that prosocial behaviors tend to predict the formation of positive relationships, such as friendship and peer group acceptance, whereas antisocial behaviors have been linked with negative relationship outcomes, such as friendlessness and peer group rejection. In addition, certain types of asocial behaviors, such as anxious shyness and social withdrawal, have been linked with peer victimization (Ettekal et al., 2015; Ladd, Ettekal, & Kochenderfer-Ladd, 2019).

Further, children's prosocial versus aggressive behaviors in classrooms is a robust predictor not only of the quality of their peer relationships (e.g., peer group acceptance, friendships) but also of their school adjustment, even at very early stages of their school careers. In particular, prosocial behaviors are linked with positive social and scholastic outcomes (e.g., school readiness, including emergent literacy; Medford & McGeown, 2016; Romano, Babshiskin, Pagani, & Kohen, 2010) during early schooling and thereafter.

Antisocial behaviors, in contrast, are associated with incipient and persistent forms of school maladjustment (e.g., loneliness, peer rejection, classroom misconduct; Ladd, 2005). Children who frequently engage in aggressive behaviors elicit reactions from peers (e.g., ignoring, exclusion) that reduce their participation in classroom activities. These environmental restrictions, in turn, appear to interfere with children's learning and achievement, and promote the development of negative attitudes toward school, classroom activities, peers, and teachers (Buhs & Ladd, 2001; Buhs et al., 2006).

Cognitive Indicators of Social Competence

Another premise that has guided research on social competence is that children's success at social challenges stems from their thinking or "theories" about social relations (see Dweck & London, 2007). Evidence links two types of cognitions with children's success at social challenges: *inter*personal cognitions, including how children think about peers, social interaction, and purposes and actions in social situations, and *intra*personal cognitions, such as how children conceive of themselves and their social skills and abilities.

It has been discovered that how children construe the purposes of peer interactions and relationships, make sense of interpersonal encounters, and regard themselves, peers, and social situations are important predictors of their success at many types of social challenges (see Crick & Dodge, 1994; Dweck & London, 2007). For example, findings show that children who are friendless, rejected, or victimized by their peer groups are more likely to have self-centered or antisocial goals and strategies for social interaction, biased interpretations of peers' motives, and debilitating self-perceptions (for review, see Ettekal et al., 2015). Further, as has been shown in "theory of mind" research, preschoolers increasingly make reference to their friends' cognitions and mental states, and this growing metacognitive capacity is predictive of their skillfulness in peer interactions (Dunn, Cutting, & Fisher, 2002;

Watson, Nixon, Wilson, & Capage, 1999), and their success at forming friendships (Fink, Begeer, Peterson, Slaughter, & de Rosnay, 2015).

These findings support arguments that the construct of social competence should incorporate a cognitive component and, thus, refer to more than just skilled social behavior. Children's ability to think about peers, and how they think about social interactions and relations may also determine their competence or incompetence in social situations.

Emotional Indicators of Social Competence

Researchers have also examined the tenet that emotions affect children's thoughts and actions and, therefore, play a role in their success with social and learning tasks. Those investigating the emotional basis of social competence have searched for differences in how children express or display emotions, interpret or understand their own and peer's emotions, and regulate their own emotions (Denham et al., 2013; Denham & Brown, 2010; Eisenberg, Champion, & Ma, 2007).

Accruing evidence implies that each of these aspects of emotion is associated with children's success or difficulties in peer relations. For example, young children who frequently express positive emotions have greater success at making friends and becoming accepted by peers (Denham et al., 2013). Conversely, children who frequently display facial and verbal anger tend to become disliked or rejected by peers (Hubbard, 2001). Other findings show that children who have difficulty interpreting peers' emotions tend to be disliked or rejected by peers (Cassidy, Parke, Butkovsky, & Braungart, 1992; Fabes et al., 1999). Further, it has been discovered that children who are better able to manage their negative emotions during peer interactions have greater success in their peer relations (Eisenberg et al., 2007).

In sum, it has been established that children who frequently express positive emotions, are accurate at interpreting peers' emotions, and are able to control negative emotions during peer interactions, and have greater success at making friends, becoming accepted by peers, and succeeding at other types of social challenges. These findings have encouraged investigators to broaden the definition of social competence to include an emotional component.

Relation between Social Competence and Specific Early Childhood Social Challenges

Here we consider findings that illustrate how various forms of social competence—behavioral, cognitive, and emotional—are linked with pivotal social challenges that occur during early childhood. Due to space limitations, and the expansiveness of available evidence, four pivotal social challenges are considered: (a) entering peer group activities and forming positive peer relationships, (b) setting and achieving positive social goals, (c) acquiring increasingly sophisticated social skills to meet new challenges, and (d) handling conflict and negative peer interactions.

Entering Peer Group Activities and Forming Positive Peer Relationships

As children venture forth into neighborhoods, childcares, or school systems, they are confronted with the challenge of joining ongoing peer activities. Studies show that some children are more skilled at this task than others and that certain social skills are more "competent" than others (i.e., have a higher probability of producing positive results). Failure to acquire these requisite skills can have serious effects on children's adjustment. Less skilled and disliked children often fail to develop consistent play companions and, even after considerable periods of time, wander from playmate to playmate on the periphery of the peer group (Ladd et al., 1990). Other findings show that disliked or rejected children not only have difficulty gaining inclusion into peer activities, but in the face of such barriers tend to seek out younger children as play companions (Ladd, 1983; Ladd et al., 1990). These consequences appear to come about because less skilled and disliked children are increasingly avoided by peers, forcing them to repeatedly search out different playmates in their peer group or, if necessary, find companionship outside their peer group (Ladd et al., 1990).

Successfully entering new peer groups and forming positive bonds is no small challenge, but evidence implies that certain skills increase young children's chances of success at this task. Studies show, for example, that children tend to fare better during early childhood transitions if they exhibit higher levels of social initiative and lower levels of social reticence. Thus, skilled children attempt to initiate interactions with classmates and teachers, approach and join classmates' ongoing activities, reciprocate peers' social overtures, and accept classmates' play invitations. Moreover, researchers have found that young children are more likely to gain admission to peers' ongoing play activities (instead of being told "You can't play!") if they observe peers' activities before attempting entry (e.g., hovering), consider peers' perspectives or frame of reference, and then enact entry behaviors that complement or accommodate peers' ongoing activities (Corsaro, 1981; Putallaz, 1983). Conversely, less-skilled children habitually avoid classmates, shrink from social interaction, act disinterested in or refuse to join peer activities, ignore classmates' overtures, and consistently pursue solitary rather than social activities (Ladd et al., 2006).

In addition to the ability to gain entry into group activities, children need social skills for developing positive reputations as well as establishing friendships within new peer groups or classrooms (see Ladd, 1990; Ladd et al., 1999). Evidence indicates that, soon after children enter new classrooms, peers begin to develop sentiments about the "likeability" of their associates, or the extent to which they prefer some group members over others as play partners, workmates, or frequent companions (see Howes, 1988; Ladd, Price, & Hart, 1990; Ladd et al., 1999). Findings from these and other studies indicate that children who become accepted members of their peer groups tend to interact with others in a friendly and prosocial manner. Those who more often interact in aggressive, unfriendly ways tended to be become disliked, or rejected members of their peer groups. These findings underscore the importance of specific behavioral skills in that children who lack prosocial skills, or frequently interact aggressively, appear less likely to earn acceptance among agemates.

Forming friendships is a related but different social task that nearly all young children confront as they enter any novel peer context. Consequently, the abilities that make young children skillful at forming friendships may not be the same the skills needed to join and become accepted members of peer groups (for similar arguments, see Ladd, 2005). As indicated earlier, friendships differ from children's peer group relations (e.g., peer group acceptance, rejection) because they occur between *pairs* of children (dyads), are created by mutual consent, and exist only as long as both participants choose to be in the relationship. In new peer groups, most young children show strong preferences for specific companions, and associate with these children more frequently than they do with others (see Howes, 1988; Ladd et al., 1990). Studies of preschoolers' conversations reveal that, as pairs of young children become acquainted, the most important determinants of friendship are skills such as communication clarity and connectedness, reciprocity of information exchange, establishment of common activities, and conflict resolution (Parker & Gottman, 1989). Perhaps not surprisingly, some young children who lack these skills tend to be less successful at forming and maintaining friendships.

In addition to forming specific types of relationships, greater social skill proficiency appears to help children attain leadership roles, attract play partners and workmates, and work collaboratively with peers in many types of interpersonal contexts (Ladd, Kochenderfer-Ladd, Ettekal et al., 2014; Ladd, Kochenderfer-Ladd, Visconti et al., 2014). Studies of preschooler's classroom and playground behavior show that, as children become acquainted, they increasingly direct their interactions toward socially skilled and well-liked classmates. Eventually, these preferred playmates become the leaders of the peer group's interactions and activities (Ladd & Price, 1993; Ladd et al., 1990). These findings suggest that young children gravitate toward skilled interaction partners, and that socially competent children tend to establish consistent social ties (e.g., stable networks), become leaders or central members of their peer groups, and develop supportive and sustained peer companionship. The reverse appears to be true for children who lack social skills or manifest lower levels of social competence.

Setting and Achieving Positive Goals

Studies of children's success at social challenges suggest that socially competent children, when entering social situations or interacting with peers, tend to pursue prosocial purposes (e.g., shared, cooperative, or other-centered aims) instead of uniformly pursuing self-centered or antisocial goals

(Putallaz, 1983). Thus, the actions that socially competent children take when attempting to achieve their goals tend to be friendly and considerate in the sense that they are performed in ways that protect rather than usurp other's interests or rights. For example, rather than hit to obtain a peer's toy, the socially competent child might ask to play with the toy, try various persuasive tactics, or simply wait until the peer has abandoned the toy. By using these strategies, children eventually succeed at their social tasks (e.g., getting the toy) without harming the peer or potentially damaging their relationships with peers. Further, when their aims or behavioral strategies are thwarted, socially competent children tend to be flexible rather than rigid in their rejoinders, often devising options, or experimenting with alternative approaches to social problems (see Rubin & Krasnor, 1986).

In sum, socially competent children exhibit a range of cognitive competencies. They set goals to achieve their ends in social situations and, as much as possible, seek to fulfill their objectives using behaviors or strategies that are respectful of others, consistent with social norms and rules, and conducive of interpersonal harmony. They also monitor the effects of their actions on others, and adjust their goals and strategies in light of the observed interpersonal consequences. By pursing their goals in this manner, children maximize the likelihood that they will preserve rather than damage their relationships with peers.

Acquire Increasingly Sophisticated Social Competencies

Studies conducted with very young children have shown that social competence and social development are mutually intertwined and facilitative processes (Ladd, Kochenderfer-Ladd & Sechler, 2014; Weissberg et al., 2015). Although children's first peer interactions are driven by simple gestures such as smiling or imitating peers, this kind of "relational" experience rapidly leads to the development of progressively more sophisticated, reciprocal, and synchronized skills for relating with agemates. Moreover, as children mature, their spiraling growth in social competence creates ever-richer social experiences that "teach" them about themselves, peers, and the connections that transpire between these entities (e.g., basic principles of social interaction; Ladd, 2005; Weissberg et al., 2015).

These findings illustrate that young children learn and change as a result of their interactions with peers, and that early peer interactions are an important staging area for the growth of social competence. Social competence fuels early social learning, and the child's interpersonal growth promotes the development of increasingly sophisticated social skills.

Handling Conflict and Negative Peer Interactions

Sadly, young children also need skills for coping with conflict and peer harassment. The nature and dynamics of peer groups are such that young children must be able to deflect teasing, repel bullies, and evade other forms of peer maltreatment (e.g., peers' aggressive behaviors; see Asher, Rose, & Gabriel, 2001; Kochenderfer & Ladd, 1996; Perry, Kusel, & Perry, 1988). Additionally, an important challenge for children who become mired in abusive, demeaning, or exploitive peer relations is to extricate themselves from these persistent or chronic "victim" roles and relationships.

Many of the same skills that are essential for making friends and earning acceptance in peer groups appear relevant for these purposes. Evidence suggests that social skills and supportive ties with peers are essential resources for young children's psychosocial well-being as well as their academic progress (Kochenderfer-Ladd & Ladd, 2016). There is substantial evidence to suggest that the propensity to interact with others in a friendly and prosocial manner not only promotes success in social relations, but also prevents children from maladaptive relationships and consequences. Conversely, poor or underdeveloped social skills appear to place children at risk for a variety of interpersonal and academic difficulties (for a meta-analytic review, see Nakamoto & Schwartz, 2010).

Children prone toward withdrawn or aggressive behavior are among those who appear to be at greatest risk. Withdrawn behavior frequently has been linked with problems such as immaturity and low self-esteem (Coplan, Prakash, O'Neil, & Armer, 2004). Aggressive behavior, in contrast, has been found to be a significant predictor of later misconduct, violence, and school adjustment problems (Coie, Terry, Lenox, Lochman, & Hyman, 1995). Moreover, evidence indicates that both direct (e.g., physical, verbal) and indirect (e.g., relational) forms of aggression are predictive of children's adjustment problems (Coie & Dodge, 1998).

Overall, these findings are consistent with the view that multiple forms of social competence are needed for children to meet the social challenges of early childhood, including gaining entry into peer activities, forming and sustaining positive relationships, expressing emotions in socially appropriate ways, and refraining from negative behaviors, such as aggression (Darling-Churchill & Lippman, 2016; Elias & Moceri, 2012; Gresham et al., 2010). How caregivers, service providers, and teachers can facilitate children's social competence is considered next.

Facilitating Young Children's Positive Peer Relationships and Social Competence

During the early childhood years, adults who work with children are in a pivotal position to help young children acquire critical social competencies and launch their peer relations successfully. Often this goal is best achieved by collaborating with children's parents or other child-rearing partners. SEL programs specifically targeting two- to five-year-old children, such as the *Incredible Years* (Webster-Stratton, Reid, & Stoolmiller, 2008) and *Head Start Redi* (Bierman, Welsh, Heinrichs, Nix, & Mathis, 2015; Bierman et al., 2014; Nix et al., 2016), could be used to support such collaborative efforts (for other high-quality SEL programs, see www.

blueprintsprograms.org). For example, Webster-Stratton's (2016) *Incredible Years* is a series of training programs targeting distinct developmental stages, including baby/toddler (1 month to 2 years), preschool (3–5 years), and school age (6–12 years). Training at each stage provides childcare workers, teachers, and parents with a variety of age-appropriate behavior management and disciplinary strategies to promote children's social competence and decrease problem behaviors. Thus, such programs offer excellent resources for childcare providers who can then serve an educational and preventive function by increasing parents' and other socializers' (e.g., grandparents, babysitters, pediatricians) awareness of the importance of children's social competence.

Ideally, prevention would take the form of educating parents about the importance of healthy peer relationships before their children enter childcare or preschool, as well as during the time that children are receiving these services. This type of prevention may shape caregivers' socialization efforts (e.g., attempts to create and supervise play opportunities, screen playmates; see Finnie & Russell, 1988; Ladd & Golter, 1988; Ladd & Hart, 1992), and help them make more informed choices about childcare arrangements.

Childcare providers can also promote positive peer relations and prevent later problems by raising questions about this aspect of children's lives in their meetings and conferences with parents, and in their screening procedures with children. Evidence or concerns about lack of friends, peer rejection, bullying or victimization, and related problems (e.g., loneliness, low self-confidence around peers, extreme aggressiveness or shyness) can be important warning signs and signal a need for further assessment. Numerous measures are available to aid in the assessment of social skills and identify peer problems (see Darling-Churchill & Lippman, 2016; Elliott et al., 2015, 2018; Gresham et al., 2010; McKown & Taylor, 2018).

Conclusions

Research conducted over the last several decades has helped to create a better understanding of the types of interpersonal challenges that confront young children, and the types of skills that young children need to effectively master these social challenges. A substantial body of evidence indicates that healthy peer relations are an essential resource for children's development. Much of what has been learned reinforces the conclusion that high-quality, satisfying peer relationships promote children's health and welfare, and that problematic or adverse peer relations are prognostic of dysfunction and maladjustment. In general, evidence suggests that young children who form supportive friendships, become accepted members of their peer groups, and avoid victimization by peers have healthier developmental trajectories.

Early childhood educators play an essential role in preparing children for social challenges of early and later childhood, and in identifying children who need assistance with social skills and peer relations. Essentially, they are "first responders" when it comes to assessing children's social competence and devising strategies that will guide the course of children's peer relations and social development. It is encouraging that a number of programs and intervention strategies (preventive and remediative) have been created to help young children develop social competence and succeed in their peer relationships, and that early childhood service professionals are in a unique position to utilize these strategies and collaborate with other socializers to achieve positive outcomes for young children.

References

Asher, S. R., Rose, A. J., & Gabriel, S. W. (2001). Peer rejection in everyday life. In M. R. Leary (Ed.), *Interpersonal rejection* (pp. 105–142). Oxford, UK: Oxford University Press.

Bierman, K. L., Nix, R. L., Heinrichs, B. S., Domitrovich, C. E., Gest, S. D., Welsh, J. A., & Gill, S. (2014). Effects of Head Start REDI on children's outcomes 1 year later in different kindergarten contexts. *Child Development, 85*(1), 140–159.

Bierman, K. L., Welsh, J. A., Heinrichs, B. S., Nix, R. L., & Mathis, E. T. (2015). Helping Head Start parents promote their children's kindergarten adjustment: The research-based developmentally informed parent program. *Child Development, 86*, 1877–1891.

Bonanno, R. A., & Hymel, S. (2010). Beyond hurt feelings: Investigating why some victims of bullying are at greater risk for suicidal ideation. *Merrill-Palmer Quarterly, 56*, 420–440.

Buhs, E. S., & Ladd, G. W. (2001). Peer rejection as antecedent of young children's school adjustment: An examination of mediating processes. *Developmental Psychology, 37*, 550–560.

Buhs, E. S., Ladd, G. W., & Herald, S. (2006). Peer exclusion and victimization: Processes that mediate the relation between peer group rejection and children's classroom engagement and achievement? *Journal of Educational Psychology, 98*, 1–13.

Bukowski, W. M., & Hoza, B. (1989). Popularity and friendship: Issues in theory, measurement, and outcome. In T. J. Berndt & G. W. Ladd (Eds.), *Peer relationships in child development* (pp. 15–45). New York, NY: John Wiley & Sons.

Cassidy, J., Parke, R. D., Butkovsky, L., & Braungart, J. M. (1992). Family-peer connections: The roles of emotional expressiveness within the family and children's understanding of emotions. *Child Development, 63*, 603–618.

Coie, J. D., & Dodge, K. A. (1983). Continuities and changes in children's social status: A five-year longitudinal study. *Merrill-Palmer Quarterly, 29*, 261–282.

Coie, J. D., & Dodge, K. A. (1998). Aggression and antisocial behavior. In W. Damon (Series Ed.) and N. Eisenberg (Vol. Ed.), *Handbook of child psychology, Vol. 3: Social, emotional, and personality development* (5th ed., pp. 779–862). New York, NY: John Wiley and Sons.

Coie, J. D., Terry, R., Lenox, K., Lochman, J., & Hyman, C. (1995). Childhood peer rejection and aggression as predictors of stable patterns of adolescent disorder. *Development and Psychopathology, 7*, 697–713.

Coplan, R. J., Prakash, K, O'Neil, K., & Armer, M. (2004). Do you "want" to play? Distinguishing between conflicted-shyness and social disinterest in early childhood. *Developmental Psychology, 40*, 244–258.

Corsaro, W. A. (1981). Friendship in the nursery school: Social organization in a peer environment. In S. R. Asher & J. M. Gottman (Eds.), *The development of children's friendships* (pp. 207–241). New York, NY: Cambridge University Press.

Crick, N. R., & Dodge, K. A. (1994). A review and reformulation of social information processing mechanisms in children's social adjustment. *Psychological Bulletin, 115*, 74–101.

Darling-Churchill, K. E., & Lippman, L. (2016). Early childhood social and emotional development: Advancing the field of measurement. *Journal of Applied Developmental Psychology, 45*, 1–7.

Denham, S. A., & Brown, C. (2010). "Plays nice with others": Social-emotional learning and academic success. *Early Education & Development, 21*, 652–680.

Denham, S. A., Zinsser, K. M., & Brown, C. A. (2013). The emotional basis of learning and development in early childhood. In B. Spodek & O. Saracho (Eds.), *Handbook of research on the education of young children* (3rd ed.). New York, NY: Erlbaum.

DeRosier, M. E., & Thomas, J. M. (2018). Establishing the criterion validity of Zoo U's game-based social emotional skills assessment for school-based outcomes. *Journal of Applied Developmental Psychology, 55*, 52–61.

Diamond, A. (2016). Why improving and assessing executive functions early in life is critical. In J. A. Griffin, P. McCardle, & L. S. Freund (Eds.), *Executive function in preschool-age children: Neurodevelopment and translational research* (pp. 11–43). Washington, DC: American Psychological Association.

Dunn, J., Cutting, A. L., & Fisher, N. (2002). Old friends, new friends: Predictors of children's perspective on their friends at school. *Child Development, 73*, 621–635.

Dweck, C. S., & London, B. (2007). The role of mental representation in social development. In G. W. Ladd (Ed.), *Appraising the human developmental sciences* (pp. 121–137). Detroit, MI: Wayne State University Press.

Eisenberg, N., Champion, C., & Ma, Y. (2007). Emotion-related regulation: An emerging construct. In G. W. Ladd (Ed.), *Appraising the human developmental sciences* (pp. 97–120). Detroit, MI: Wayne State University Press.

Elias, M. J., & Moceri, D. (2012). Developing social and emotional aspects of learning: The American experience. *Research Papers in Education, 27*(4), 423–434.

Elliott, S. N., Davies, M. D., Frey, J. R., Gresham, F., & Cooper, G. (2018). Development and initial validation of a social emotional learning assessment for universal screening. *Journal of Applied Developmental Psychology, 55*, 39–51.

Elliott, S. N., Frey, J. R., & Davies, M. (2015). Systems for assessing and improving students' social skills to achieve academic competence. In J. Durlak, C. Domitrovish, R., Weissber, & T. Gullott (Eds.), *Handbook of social & emotional learning: Research and practice* (pp. 301–319). New York, NY: Guildord Press.

Ettekal, I., Kochenderfer-Ladd, B., & Ladd, G. W. (2015). A synthesis of person-and relational-level factors that influence bullying and bystanding behaviors: Toward and integrative framework. *Aggression and Violent Behavior, 23*, 75–86. IF: 3.06

Fabes, R. A., Eisenberg, N., Jones, S., Smith, M., Guthrie, I., Poulin, R., … Friedman, J. (1999). Regulation, emotionality, and preschooler's socially competent peer interactions. *Child Development, 70*, 432–442.

Fink, E., Begeer, S., Peterson, C. C., Slaughter, V., & de Rosnay, M. (2015). Friendlessness and theory of mind: A prospective longitudinal study. *British Journal of Developmental Psychology, 33*, 1–17.

Finnie, V., & Russell, A. (1988). Preschool children's social status and their mother's behavior and knowledge in the supervisory role. *Developmental Psychology, 24*, 789–801.

Gresham, F. M., Elliott, S. N., & Kettler, R. J. (2010). Base rates of social skills acquisition/performance deficits, strengths and problem behaviors: An analysis of the Social Skills Improvement System-Rating Scales. *Psychological Assessment, 22*(4), 809–815.

Heilbron, N., & Prinstein, M. J. (2010). Adolescent peer victimization, peer status, suicidal ideation, and nonsuicidal self-injury: Examining concurrent and longitudinal associations. *Merrill-Palmer Quarterly, 56*, 388–419.

Hinde, R. A., Titmus, G., Easton, D., & Tamplin, A. (1985). Incidence of "friendship" and behavior toward strong associates versus nonassociates in preschoolers. *Child Development, 56*, 234–245.

Hodges, E. V. E., Malone, M. J., & Perry, D. (1997). Individual risk and social risk as interacting determinants of victimization in the peer group. *Developmental Psychology, 33*, 1032–1039.

Hodges, E. V. E., & Perry, D. G. (1999). Personal and interpersonal antecedents and consequences of victimization by peers. *Journal of Personality and Social Psychology, 76*, 677–685.

Howes, C. (1983). Patterns of friendship. *Child Development, 54*, 1041–1053.

Howes, C. (1988). Peer interaction of young children. *Monographs of the Society for Research in Child Development, 53*(1, Serial No. 217), i–92.

Howes, C., & Phillipsen, L. C. (1992). Gender and friendship: Relationships within peer groups of young children. *Social Development, 1*, 231–242.

Hubbard, J. A. (2001). Emotion expression processes in children's peer interaction: The role of peer rejection, aggression, and gender. *Child Development, 72*, 1426–1438.

Humphrey, N., & Wigelsworth, M. (2016). Making the case for universal school-based mental health screening. *Emotional and Behavioral Difficulties, 21*(1), 22–42.

Kochenderfer, B. J., & Ladd, G. W. (1996). Peer victimization: Cause or consequence of school maladjustment? *Child Development, 67*, 1305–1317.

Kochenderfer-Ladd, B., & Ladd, G. W. (2001). Variations in peer victimization: Relations to children's maladjustment. In J. Juvonen & S. Graham (Eds.), *Peer harassment in school: The plight of the vulnerable and victimized* (pp. 25–48). New York, NY: Guilford Press.

Kochenderfer-Ladd, B., & Ladd, G. W. (2016). Integrating academic and social-emotional learning in classroom interactions. In K. Wentzel & G. Ramani (Eds.), *Handbook of social influences in school contexts: Social-emotional, motivation and cognitive outcomes* (pp. 349–366). New York, NY: Routledge.

Kochenderfer-Ladd, B., & Wardrop, J. (2001). Chronicity and instability in children's peer victimization experiences as predictors of loneliness and social satisfaction trajectories. *Child Development, 72*, 134–151.

Ladd, G. W. (1990). Having friends, keeping friends, making friends, and being liked by peers in the classroom: Predictors of children's early school adjustment? *Child Development, 61*, 1081–1100.

Ladd, G. W. (2005). *Children's peer relationships and social competence: A century of progress*. New Haven, CT: Yale University Press.

Ladd, G. W. (2006). Peer rejection, aggressive or withdrawn behavior, and psychological maladjustment from ages 5 to 12: An examination of four predictive models. *Child Development, 77*, 822–846.

Ladd, G. W. (2008). Social competence and peer relations: Significance for young children and their service providers. *Early Childhood Services, 2*, 129–148.

Ladd, G. W., Birch, S. H., & Buhs, E. (1999). Children's social and scholastic lives in kindergarten: Related Spheres of Influence? *Child Development, 70*, 1373–1400.

Ladd, G. W., Ettekal, I., & Kochenderfer-Ladd, B. (2019). Longitudinal changes in victimized youth's social anxiety and solitary behavior. In H. Gazelle & K. Rubin (Guest Editors), Social withdrawal and anxiety in childhood and adolescence: Interaction between individual tendencies and interpersonal learning mechanisms in development. *Journal of Abnormal Child Psychology, 47*(7), 1211–1223.

Ladd, G. W., Ettekal, I., & Kochenderfer-Ladd, B. (2017). Peer victimization trajectories from kindergarten through high school: Differential pathways for children's school engagement and achievement? *Journal of Educational Psychology, 109*(6), 826–841.

Ladd, G. W., & Golter, B. S. (1988). Parents' initiation and monitoring of children's peer contacts: Predictive of children's peer relations in nonschool and school settings? *Developmental Psychology, 24*, 109–117.

Ladd, G. W., & Hart, C. H. (1992). Creating informal play opportunities: Are parents and preschooler's initiations related to children's competence with peers? *Developmental Psychology, 28*, 1179–1187.

Ladd, G. W., Herald, S. L., & Kochel, K. P. (2006). School readiness: Are there social prerequisites? *Early Education and Development, 17*, 115–150.

Ladd, G. W., Herald-Brown, S. L., & Reiser, M. (2008). Does chronic classroom peer rejection predict the development of children's classroom participation during the grade school years? *Child Development, 79*(4), 1001–1015.

Ladd, G. W., & Kochenderfer, B. J. (1996). Linkages between friendship and adjustment during early school transitions. In W. M. Bukowski, A. F. Newcomb, & W. W. Hartup (Eds.), *The company they keep: Friendship in childhood and adolescence* (pp. 322–345). New York, NY: Cambridge University Press.

Ladd, G. W., & Kochenderfer-Ladd, B. J. (2002). Identifying victims of peer aggression from early to middle childhood: Analysis of cross-informant data for concordance, estimation of relational adjustment, prevalence of victimization, and characteristics of identified victims. *Psychological Assessment, 14*, 74–96.

Ladd, G. W., Kochenderfer, B. J., & Coleman, C. C. (1996). Friendship quality as a predictor of young children's early school adjustment. *Child Development, 67*, 1103–1118.

Ladd, G. W., Kochenderfer, B. J., & Coleman, C. C. (1997). Classroom peer acceptance, friendship, and victimization: Distinct relational systems that contribute uniquely to children's school adjustment? *Child Development, 68*, 1181–1197.

Ladd, G. W., Kochenderfer-Ladd, B., Ettekal, I., Cortes, K., Sechler, C. M., & Visconti, K. J. (2014). The 4R-SUCCESS program: Promoting children's social and scholastic skills in dyadic classroom activities. Gruppendynamik & Organisationsberatung (*Group Dynamics and Organizational Consulting), 45*, 25–44. doi:10.1007/s11612-013-0231-1

Ladd, G. W., Kochenderfer-Ladd, B., & Sechler, C. M. (2014). Classroom peer relations as a context for social and scholastic development. In S. H. Landry & C. L. Cooper's (Eds.), *Wellbeing in children and families: Wellbeing: A complete reference guide* (Vol. 1, pp. 243–271). Oxford: England: Wiley-Blackwell. doi:10.1002/ 9781118539415.wbwell12

Ladd, G. W., Kochenderfer-Ladd, B., Visconti, K., Ettekal, I, Sechler, C., & Cortes, K. I. (2014). Grade-school children's social collaborative skills: Links with partner preference and achievement. *American Educational Research Journal, 51*, 152–183. doi:10.3102/0002831213507327

Ladd, G. W., & Price, J. M. (1987). Predicting children's social and school adjustment following the transition from preschool to kindergarten. *Child Development, 58*, 1168–1189.

Ladd, G. W., & Price, J. M. (1993). Playstyles of peer-accepted and peer-rejected children on the playground. In C. H. Hart (Eds.), *Children on playgrounds: Research perspectives and applications* (pp. 130–183). Albany, NY: State University of New York Press.

Ladd, G. W., Price, J. M., & Hart, C. H. (1990). Preschoolers' behavioral orientations and patterns of peer contact: Predictive of peer status? In S. R. Asher & J. D. Coie (Eds.), *Peer rejection in childhood* (pp. 90–115). New York, NY: Cambridge University Press.

McDougall, P., Hymel, S., Vaillancourt, T., & Mercer, L. (2001). The consequences of childhood peer rejection. In M. R. Leary (Ed.), *Interpersonal rejection* (pp. 213–247). Oxford, UK: Oxford University Press.

McKown, C., & Taylor, J. (2018). Introduction to the special issue on social-emotional assessment guide to educational practice. *Journal of Applied Developmental Psychology, 55*, 1–3.

Medford, E., & McGeown, S. P. (2016). Social, emotional, and behavioral influences on young children's pre-reading and word reading development. *Journal of Applied Developmental Psychology, 43*, 54–61.

Nakamoto, J., & Schwartz, D. (2010). Is peer victimization associated with academic achievement? A meta-analytic review. *Social Development, 19*, 221–242.

Nix, R. L., Bierman, K. L., Heinrichs, B. S., Gest, S. D., Welsh, J. A., & Domitrovich, C. E. (2016). The randomized-controlled trial of Head Start REDI: Sustained effects on developmental trajectories of social-emotional functioning. *Journal of Consulting and Clinical Psychology, 84*(4), 310–322.

Nylund, K., Bellmore, A., Nishina, A., & Graham, S. (2007). Subtypes, severity, and structural stability of peer victimization: What does latent class analysis say? *Child Development, 78*, 1706–1722.

Parker, J. G., & Asher, S. R. (1993). Friendship and friendship quality in middle childhood: Links with peer group acceptance and feelings of loneliness and social dissatisfaction. *Developmental Psychology, 29*, 611–621.

Parker, J. G., & Gottman, J. M. (1989). Social and emotional development in a relational context: Friendship interaction from early childhood to adolescence. In T. J. Berndt & G. W. Ladd (Eds.), *Peer relationships in child development* (pp. 95–131). New York, NY: John Wiley and Sons.

Perry, D. G., Hodges, E. V., & Egan, S. (2001). Determinants of chronic victimization by peers: A review and new model of family influence. In J. Juvonen & S. Graham (Eds.), *Peer harassment in school: The plight of the vulnerable and victimized* (pp. 73–104). New York, NY: Guilford Press.

Perry, D. G., Kusel, S. J., & Perry, L. C. (1988). Victims of peer aggression. *Developmental Psychology, 24*, 807–814.

Price, J. M., & Ladd, G. W. (1986). Assessment of children's friendships: Implications for social competence and social adjustment. In R. Prinz (Ed.), *Advances in behavioral assessment of children and families* (Vol. 2, pp. 121–149). Greenwich, CT: JAI Press.

Putallaz, M. (1983). Predicting children's sociometric status from their behavior. *Child Development, 54*, 1417–1426.

Reavis, R. D., Keane, S. P., & Calkins, S. D. (2010). Trajectories of peer victimization: The role of multiple relationships. *Merrill-Palmer Quarterly, 56*, 303–332.

Romano, E., Babshiskin, L., Pagani, L. S., & Kohen, D. (2010). School readiness, and later achievement: Replication and extension using a nationwide Canadian survey. *Developmental Psychology, 46*, 995–1007.

Rubin, K. H., & Krasnor L. (1986). Social-cognitive and social behavioral perspectives on problem solving. In M. Perlmutter (Ed.), *The Minnesota symposium on child psychology* (Vol. 18, pp. 1–68). Hillsdale, MI: Erlbaum.

Rudolph, K. D., Troop-Gordon, W., Hessel, E. T., & Schmidt, J. D. (2011). A latent growth curve analysis of early and increasing peer victimization as predictors of mental health across elementary school.

Journal of Clinical Child and Adolescent Psychology, 40, 111–122. doi:10.1080/1534416.2011.533413

Torres, M. M., Domitrovich, D. E., & Bierman, K. L. (2015). Preschool interpersonal relationships predict kindergarten achievement: Mediated by gains in emotion knowledge. *Journal of Applied Developmental Psychology, 39*, 44–52.

Troop-Gordon, W., & Ladd, G. W. (2005). Trajectories of peer victimization and perceptions of the self and schoolmates: Precursors to internalizing and externalizing problems. *Child Development, 76*, 1072–1091.

Vlachou, M., Botsoglou, K., & Andreou, E. (2013). Assessing bully/victim problems in preschool children: A multimethod approach. *Journal of Criminology*, doi:10.1155/2013/301658

Watson, A. C., Nixon, C. L., Wilson, A., & Capage, L. (1999). Social interaction skills and theory of mind in young children. *Developmental Psychology, 35*, 386–391.

Webster-Stratton, C. (2016). *Benefits of using the incredible years home coaching parent programs: Assuring success.* Article Retrieved from: http://www.incredibleyears.com/article/benefits-of-using-the-incredible-years-home-coaching-parent-programs-assuring-success/

Webster-Stratton, C., Reid, M. J., & Stoolmiller, M. (2008). Preventing conduct problems and improving school readiness: An evaluation of the Incredible Years Teacher and Child Training Program in high risk schools. *Journal of Child Psychology and Psychiatry, 49*(5), 471–488.

Weissberg, R. P., Durlak, J. A., Domitrovich, C. E., & Gullotta, T. P. (2015). Social and emotional learning: Past, present, and future. In *Handbook of social and emotional learning: Research and practice* (pp. 3–19). New York, NY: Guilford Press.

Zins, J. E., Bloodworth, M. R., Weissberg, R. P., & Walberg, H. J. (2007). The scientific base linking social and emotional learning to school success. *Journal of Educational and Psychological Consultation, 17*, 191–210.

3

The Emotional Basis of Learning and Development in Early Childhood Education

Susanne A. Denham and Kristi H. Liverette

Petey runs, darts, and jumps with a ball clenched tightly in his arms. He yells an invitation to play at another boy but cannot restrain his desire to keep the ball. He pulls it away from another boy, angrily shoving him and screaming insults.

Sean speaks hesitantly, often echoing others' communications, as if practicing. He is always last to attempt a task, never asserting ideas or desires. He is quiet, sometimes looking quite sad on the sidelines, seeking the comfort of his thumb.

Jeremy plays and interacts with peers fairly well, but has difficulty allowing others to lead activities or reject his ideas and is very upset when he makes a mistake.

Petey, Sean, and Jeremy's experiences illustrate that their emotional development requires careful nurturing. They must learn to send and receive emotional messages, to use emotion knowledge and emotion regulation to negotiate social exchanges, form relationships, and maintain curiosity and enthusiasm (Halberstadt, Denham, & Dunsmore, 2001; Saarni, 1999).

The components of emotional competence help to ensure effective social interactions built upon listening, cooperating, appropriate help seeking, joining interactions, and negotiating. Young children also utilize emotional competence to facilitate learning alongside and in collaboration with teachers and peers (Denham, Brown, & Domitrovich, 2010). Emotional competence thus supports early school success (i.e., positive attitudes toward learning, persistence, and adjustment to classroom routines, and the growth of even later academic competence; Denham, Bassett, Mincic, et al., 2012; Romano, Babchishin, Pagani, & Kohen, 2010). Children who understand and regulate emotions and are more emotionally positive when they enter school are more likely to develop positive and supportive relationships with peers and teachers, participate and achieve at higher levels throughout their early years in school (Garner & Waajid, 2008; Graziano, Reavis, Keane, & Calkins, 2007; Izard et al., 2001; Leerkes, Paradise, O'Brien, Calkins, & Lange, 2008). Conversely, children who enter school with fewer emotional competence skills are more often rejected by peers, develop less supportive relationships with teachers, participate in and enjoy school less, achieve at lower levels, and are at risk for later behavior problems and school difficulties (Denham, Bassett, Mincic, et al., 2012; Denham, Bassett, Thayer, et al., 2012; Herndon, Bailey, Shewark, Denham, & Bassett, 2013). Aspects of these skills are even uniquely associated with adult education, employment, mental health, and avoidance of crime and substance use (Jones, Greenberg, & Crowley, 2015). In short, emotional competence greases the cogs of a successful early school experience, with potentially long-lasting effects. We now turn to more detailed consideration of the nature and manifestations of preschoolers' emotional competence.

What Is Emotional Competence?

The social-emotional skills that preschoolers normally develop are quite impressive. Not everyone looks like Petey, Sean, or Jeremy. Consider the following example:

Four-year-olds Darrell and Jessica are pretending Paw Patrol®. They have drawn up a playground rescue scenario. Both have their "tools" ready to save the day. They are having fun! But then things get complicated, changing fast, as interaction often does. They are trying to decide who gets to use the shovel and pail to save the birds on the playground. Jessica suddenly decides that she should be Ryder, and that she doesn't want to do a playground rescue; she wants to do an underwater dolphin rescue instead. Darrell shouts, "No way, you have to be Skye!" After a second he added, with a smile, "Anyway, I wanted to use the shovel and pail to save the dolphins – they're your favorite, too!"

Now Jimmy, who had been nearby, runs over, whining to join them. No way!! Darrell, still concentrating on Jessica's demands, doesn't want Jimmy to join them – he's too much of a baby. Almost simultaneously, Jessica hurts her hand with the shovel, and starts to cry. And Tomas, the class bully, approaches, laughing at 4-year-olds making believe and crying.

This was much more than a simple playtime. Imagine the skills of emotional competence that are needed to successfully negotiate these interactions! Within a five-minute play period, a variety of emotional competencies are called for if the social interaction is to succeed. For example, Darrell has to know how to handle Jessica's emotions and his own during their disagreement, react to Jimmy's whining without hurting his feelings, and "handle" Tomas safely. Darrell needs to learn how to express his emotions in socially appropriate ways, handle provocation without getting too mad or too scared, engage with others positively, and build emotional relationships. Taken together, these abilities are vital for how Darrell gets along with others, understands himself, and feels good in his world, with himself and with others.

Defining Emotional Competence

We define emotional competence as *emotional effectiveness*, by which a child can reach short- and long-term goals, during or after emotion-eliciting encounters (Saarni, 1999). Emotionally competent young children begin to: (1) experience and purposefully express a broad variety of emotions, without incapacitating intensity or duration; (2) regulate their emotion whenever its experience is "too much" or "too little" for themselves, or when its expression is "too much" or "too little" to meet others' expectations; and (3) understand their own and others' emotions. It is important to view this development within children's key emotional tasks. During the early childhood years, emotional competence skills are organized around developmental tasks of maintaining positive emotional engagement with the physical and social world, making and maintaining relationships with other children and adults, while managing emotional arousal in the context of social interaction and cognitive demands. These skills are not easy ones for children just entering the peer arena, and the new classroom context can tax children's abilities. Children need to sit still, attend, follow directions, approach group play, complete preacademic tasks, and get along with others, in ways that challenge their nascent abilities. The emotional competence skills that develop dramatically during early childhood can assist with these hurdles.

Emotions, inherently social and functional, are ubiquitous in early childhood classrooms. As much as emotional competence skills affect interpersonal relations, interpersonal interactions guide development of these skills (Halberstadt et al., 2001). Thus, although the components of emotional competence are often viewed as individual differences, we emphasize their social roots, informed by both social constructivist and functionalist perspectives. The social constructivist approach focuses on emotions as social products. Their meaning and expression vary markedly across social contexts, and are affected by socialization according to cultural values and norms; for example, one culture's values about empathic emotions may differ from another's. Successful emotional competence skills also depend on a situation's social context (Saarni, 2001) – peer relationships, family, community activities, teacher relationships, preschool/childcare, culture, gender. For example, emotional expressiveness that renders Sammy a sought-after peer makes it difficult for his teacher to teach him important concepts.

Many emotion theorists also take a functionalist view: emotional expressiveness is important information for oneself *and* for others– others' behaviors often constitute antecedent conditions for one's emotions, and vice versa. Importantly, expression of emotion signals whether the child or other people need to modify or continue goal-directed behavior (Saarni, 2001; Walle & Campos, 2012). For example, if a girl experiences anger while playing at the puzzle activity table with another child, she may try to avoid the other child the next day, and even tell her mother "I don't want *her* to come to my birthday party." The experience of anger gave her information that affects her subsequent behavior. Her anger also gives information to others that affects their behavior – witnesses to her anger may seek to avoid her until she is calm.

Based on these precepts, the major goals of this chapter are to fully describe: (a) breadth and depth about the separate components of emotional competence – emotional experience and expressiveness, emotion knowledge, and emotion regulation – as they emerge for typically developing children through early childhood; and (b) research on these facets' direct and indirect contributions to successful social development and school success. After these descriptions, we summarize promotion of emotional competence by parents and teachers, and consider the roles of gender and culture in this socialization. Finally, the role of early childhood education is considered, along with ideas for future research and applied considerations.

Aspects of Emotional Competence: Emotional Experience and Expressiveness

This aspect of emotional competence includes identifying and expressing one's own emotions. Preschoolers understand and can report upon emotional experience more reliably than previously assumed (Durbin, 2010). Along with such awareness, they begin to use emotions to express nonverbal messages about a social situation or relationship (e.g., stamping feet or giving a hug). They also develop empathic involvement in others' emotions (e.g., patting a classmate who fell off the swings). Further, they appropriately display social and self-conscious emotions, such as guilt, pride, shame, and contempt (Denham, 1998). But what affective message should be sent, for successful interaction during early childhood, to facilitate specific goals? Jimmy learns that his whiny voice, downcast face, and averted posture do not promote successful entry into play. Young children also learn appropriate affective messages that work for a specific setting or playmate; if Jimmy needs to defend himself, an angry scowl may get Tomas to back off.

Emotional Expression, Emotional Experience, and School Success

Preschoolers' expression of specific emotions, especially their enduring patterns of expressiveness, relates to their overall success in interacting with peers and to their teachers' evaluation of their friendliness and aggression. Children who show relatively more happy than angry emotions, or more positive emotions in general: (a) are rated higher by teachers on friendliness and assertiveness, and lower on aggressiveness and sadness; (b) respond more prosocially to peers' emotions; and (c) are seen as more likable by their peers (Garner & Waajid, 2008; Hernández, Eisenberg, Valiente, Diaz, et al., 2017; Hernández, Eisenberg, Valiente, Spinrad, et al., 2017; Shin et al., 2011). Such findings extend across time. Observed happiness predicted children's positive social behavior six months later (Morgan, Izard, & Hyde, 2014); those sharing positive emotion with peers were better liked one year later (Lindsey, 2017).

Conversely, negative emotion (particularly anger) indexes concurrent social difficulty. Hernández et al. (Hernández, Eisenberg, Valiente, Diaz, et al., 2017; Hernández, Eisenberg, Valiente, Spinrad, et al., 2017) found that kindergarten girls' negative emotion was related to lessened peer acceptance and conflict with teachers, and anger intensity was related to poor relationships with teachers (see also Diaz et al., 2017). Anger's contextual appropriateness may be especially important; context-inappropriate anger was related to preschoolers' self-rejection and loneliness, and negative peer and teacher social competence nominations (Locke, Davidson, Kalin, & Goldsmith, 2009). Deleterious outcomes of anger can also extend across time (e.g., from toddlerhood anger to gradeschool lack of social competence; Taylor, Eisenberg, Van Schyndel, Eggum-Wilkins, & Spinrad, 2014). In short, enduring negative expressiveness can fuel a cascade of poor social outcomes, and sometimes behavior problems. For example, children's dysregulated anger during a disappointing gift task was both concurrently and predictively associated with externalizing behavior problems (Morris, Silk, Steinberg, Terranova, & Kithakye, 2010). Sadness or fear, whether observed in the classroom or in interaction with mother, is also related to withdrawal and internalizing difficulties (Rydell, Berlin, & Bohlin, 2003).

Emotional expressiveness styles are also related to school success. Positive emotion may, for example, support and direct attention, facilitate information processing, and enhance both motivation and resilience (Pekrun & Linnenbrink-Garcia, 2012). In one study, emotionally positive engagement with an examiner was related to pre-literacy (Denham, Bassett, Sirotkin, & Zinsser, 2013). Positive emotional experience and expressiveness with adults signal enjoyment and motivation to learn about self and others. Hernández et al. (2016) found that positive emotions were positively related to concurrent academic success (i.e., literacy skills, achievement, and/or school engagement), either directly or via positive relationships with teachers and peers.

Conversely, Herndon et al. (2013) found that preschoolers' *negative* emotionality was related to teachers' later reports of less positive engagement and independent motivation in learning. Preschoolers' negativity was also related to poorer current and later school adjustment, and kindergarten academic success (Denham, Bassett, Thayer, et al., 2012; see also Diaz et al., 2017; Hernández et al., 2016).

Summary of Outcomes of Emotional Expressiveness

In sum, preschoolers' expression of emotions, especially a positive emotional style, appears central to young children's concurrent and later positive outcomes in both social and academic realms. Educators could work to promote students' positive emotion and ability to deal with negative emotions and their source.

Aspects of Emotional Competence: Emotion Regulation

Beginning to attend preschool or childcare is an important transition that taxes children's emotion regulatory skills. Initiating, maintaining, and negotiating play, earning acceptance, resolving conflicts, and taking turns require preschoolers to "keep the lid on." Newly important peers are not very able to aid others' emotion regulation; social costs of emotional dysregulation are high with teachers and peers. Some organized emotional gatekeeper must be cultivated.

Emotion regulation includes monitoring feelings, and modifying them when necessary, so that they aid rather than impede the child's coping in varying situations, to meet intrapersonal, interpersonal, and cognitive goals (Gross & Thompson, 2007). When intensity, duration, or other parameters of the experience and expression of emotion are "too much" or "too little" to meet goals and expectations of the child and/or social partners, emotion regulation is needed (Cole, Martin, & Dennis, 2004). Emotions needing regulation include those that are aversive or distressing and those that are positive but overwhelming, as well as those that need to be amplified, for either intra- or interpersonally strategic reasons (e.g., crying to elicit help).

To succeed at emotion regulation, several abilities are key (Halberstadt et al., 2001). One must experience clear rather than diffused feelings, to know what to regulate. As preschoolers become more aware of emotions, one can also use emotions to facilitate communication and achieve a goal. They learn to retain or enhance emotions that are relevant and helpful (e.g., happiness attracts playmates). Even anger can be helpful; a boy hurt when falling, also mad at himself because others are watching, can "use" anger to spur a quick, albeit hobbling, recovery.

Young children begin to realize that one may feel a certain way "on the inside," but show a different outward demeanor (Denham, 1998). They especially learn that expressions of socially disapproved feelings may be controlled, in favor of more socially appropriate ones; sometimes real affective messages are inappropriate, "false" messages must be managed, and one must consider constraints of self-protective and prosocial display rules (Misailidi, 2006). For example, disappointment and even rage at being reprimanded may be relevant when an adult has blocked the child's goal, but such anger is usually imprudent to express. Further, Darrell controlled his fear when Tomas approached, instead showing a neutral expression that masked his internal shakiness; this tactic kept him safe. Anxiety when playing a new game is probably irrelevant to the goal of having fun, and needs to be dampened. In sum, emotion regulation helps children maintain genuine and satisfying relationships with others and pay attention to preacademic tasks.

How Does Emotion Regulation Develop?   Preschoolers often need external support to become skilled at such regulation. Adults assist them in cognitive coping strategies children will eventually use themselves (e.g., purposely redeploying attention). They also use language to help children regulate emotion by identifying and construing their feelings (e.g., "this will hurt only a little"), and to process causal associations between events and emotions. They demonstrate behavioral coping strategies, structuring the environment to facilitate regulation (e.g., avoiding situations that will frighten a daughter) or problem-solving emotional situations.

Over time, preschoolers become more able to make their own independent emotion regulation attempts. With their increasing cognitive ability and control of both attention and emotionality, preschoolers' awareness of the need for, and their use of, emotion regulation strategies increases. First, the experience of emotion (i.e., sensory input and physiological arousal) may need to be diminished or modulated. A child may modulate the emotional experience via self-soothing. Or, she may even alter the emotion being expressed; a child feeling anxious during group times at preschool may smile to convince herself and others that she is happy. Others may avoid situations, or try to change them, to avoid over-arousal.

Perceptual and cognitive management of emotion is also possible; a child may relinquish a goal, choose a substitute goal, or think through new causal attributions, to help herself feel more comfortable in her world. For example, a preschooler who is angry about being punished may say to herself, "I didn't want that cookie anyway." Refocusing attention is a perceptual means of managing the emotional experience. When trying to join Jessica and Darrell, Jimmy may focus on the game's "props" rather than the peers whose higher social status makes him nervous. Reasoning can also be particularly useful as a regulatory coping strategy. When Darrell becomes irritated with Jessica, he may suggest a successful compromise. Finally, children also *do* things to cope with the experience of emotion: fix the problem, look for support from adults, lash out aggressively, or cry even harder to vent emotion. Thus, they begin to use very specific coping strategies for regulation: problem-solving, support seeking, distancing, distraction, internalizing, externalizing, reframing or redefining the problem, cognitive "blunting," and denial.

Preschoolers begin to see connections between using these emotion regulation strategies and changes in their feelings, and become more flexible in choosing optimal ways of coping in specific contexts; such understanding of regulatory strategies often predicts their usage (Cole, Dennis, Smith-Simon, & Cohen, 2009). Many such strategies are useful for emotion regulation; they are sequentially associated with decreased anger (Gilliom, Shaw, Beck, Schonberg, & Lukon, 2002). In short, preschoolers are slowly moving from reliance upon other regulation of emotions to self-regulation of their feelings, although they still prefer less sophisticated emotion regulatory strategies (López-Pérez, Gummerum, Wilson, & Dellaria, 2017). Accordingly, the behavioral disorganization resulting from strong emotion decreases dramatically by school age.

Emotion Regulation and School Success.   Effective emotion regulatory coping is associated with preschool social success (Denham, Blair, Schmidt, & DeMulder, 2002; Di Maggio, Zappulla, & Pace, 2016; Orta, Çorapçi, Yagmurlu, & Aksan, 2013; Ren, Wyver, Rattanasone, & Demuth, 2016; Son & Chang, 2018; Spritz, Sandberg, Maher, & Zajdel, 2010). In fact, there are cascading and reciprocal relations between emotion regulation and social competence from age five to ten (Blair et al., 2015). Further, five-year-olds' active, not passive or disruptive, emotion regulation when faced with a disappointing gift predicted seven-year-olds' competent peer play (Penela, Walker, Degnan, Fox, & Henderson, 2015); similarly, positive reactions to a disappointing gift predicted older preschoolers' peer status (Nakamichi, 2017).

Despite growth demonstrated in these studies, emotion regulatory failure still occurs through the preschool period; such emotion dysregulation or lack of positive emotion regulatory strategy usage is often associated with young children's conadcurrent or later difficulties with aggression, other externalizing behavior and internalizing behavior, and compromised social competence (Chang, Shelleby, Cheong, & Shaw, 2012; Crespo, Trentacosta, Aikins, & Wargo-Aikins, 2017; Di Maggio et al., 2016; Lugo-Candelas, Flegenheimer, McDermott, & Harvey, 2017; Miller, Gouley, Seifer, Dickstein, & Shields, 2004; Ren et al., 2016; Yeo, Frydenberg, Northam, & Deans, 2014). Moreover, examining longitudinal change, Cohen and Mendez (2009) found emotional lability was associated with consistently maladaptive and declining social competence. Clearly emotional dysregulation, variously considered, already constitutes a risk factor.

Emotion regulation is also related to preschoolers' classroom adjustment and academic success (Bierman et al., 2008; Brophy-Herb, Zajicek-Farber, Bocknek, McKelvey, & Stansbury, 2013). Children less able to deal with emotions may not have resources to remain engaged with classroom tasks, cooperate, create relationships with teachers, enjoy school, or progress academically (Denham et al., 2013; Graziano et al., 2007; Herndon et al., 2013; Miller, Seifer, Stroud, Sheinkopf, & Dickstein, 2006; Trentacosta & Izard, 2007).

Summary of Outcomes for Emotion Regulation Along with and closely related to emotional expressiveness (Cole et al., 2004), this aspect of emotional competence should be a central focus of adults' support. Educators could promote emotion regulation, in the service of social competence, amelioration of problem behaviors, and school success.

Aspects of Emotional Competence: Emotion Knowledge

Children are constantly attempting to understand their own and others' behavior, and emotions convey crucial interpersonal information that can guide. Inability to interpret others' emotions can make the classroom a confusing, overwhelming place for children. How does emotion knowledge develop? Once perceived, affective messages must be interpreted accurately. Errors can lead to both intrapersonal and social difficulties. Preschoolers begin to (a) label emotional expressions both verbally and nonverbally; (b) identify emotion-eliciting situations; and (c) infer the causes of emotion-eliciting situations, and the consequences of specific emotions (Bassett, Denham, Mincic, & Graling, 2012; Fernández-Sánchez, Quintanilla, & Giménez-Dasí, 2015; Pons, Harris, & deRosnay, 2004; Sette, Bassett, Baumgartner, & Denham, 2015). They first distinguish between being happy and not being happy, feeling good versus bad. Early recognition of happy expressions is greater than recognition of negative emotions, with understanding anger and fear slowly emerging from the "not happy/sad" emotion category.

However, simply understanding expressions of emotion is not always sufficient to comprehend one's own or others' emotions; situational cues can be very important, especially when expressions may be masked or dissembled. Understanding the events that can elicit emotion, as well as accompanying expressions, increases preschoolers' flexibility in interpreting emotional signals. For example, Jessica may note, "When we don't listen, our teacher feels bad," and then adjust her behavior, even if her teacher's negative expressions are very muted.

As with expressions, preschoolers initially tend to understand happy situations better than negative ones. They gradually learn to differentiate among negative emotions (e.g., realizing that one feels more sad than angry when getting a "time out" from one's preschool teacher; Denham, 1998). They slowly separate angry situations from sad; fear situations present the most difficulty. Preschoolers also increasingly use emotion language to describe emotional situations (e.g., reminiscing about sadness when a pet died; Harris, 2008; Lagattuta & Wellman, 2002). Young preschoolers' emotion categories are broad, often including peripheral concepts, especially for negative emotions, but their emotion concepts gradually narrow (Widen & Russell, 2008, 2010).

Young children go further than just recognizing expressions and eliciting situations for discrete emotions. Using everyday experiences to create theories about causes of happiness, sadness, and anger, older preschoolers cite causes that are similar to ones given by adults (Fabes, Eisenberg, Nyman, & Michealieu, 1991; Lagattuta & Wellman, 2002). Jessica notes that her brother gets mad because he doesn't want to go to school, but that Daddy is happy to go to work.

Through their increased social sensitivity and experience, older preschoolers also develop strategies for appraising others' emotions when available cues are less salient and consensual. Five-year-olds are more likely than three- and four-year-olds to focus their explanations of emotions on personal dispositions as opposed to goal states (e.g., "She had a bad day" instead of "She didn't want Billy to play with her"). Thus, to more accurately interpret emotional information, data specific to a particular person or a particular situation may be needed.

Although this aspect of emotion knowledge is very important, it can be quite difficult to acquire and use. In a series of thought-provoking inquiries, Gnepp and colleagues (e.g., Gnepp, 1989; Gnepp & Gould, 1985; Gnepp, McKee, & Domanic, 1987; see also Lagattuta, 2007) described how children develop the ability to use various types of information to determine others' emotions. Important elements of emotional information are whether (a) the situation is equivocal (i.e., could elicit more than one emotion), (b) there are conflicting cues in the person's expressive patterns and the situation, and (c) person-specific information is needed.

Regarding *equivocality*, different people feel different emotions during some emotion-eliciting events. One child is happy to encounter a large dog, "smiling" with mouth open; another child is terrified. Preschoolers begin to recognize the equivocality of some emotion situations, and can identify it spontaneously if supportive methodologies are used (Denham, 1998). Even if a situation is not emotionally equivocal, preschoolers may struggle to discern a person's feelings. The person experiencing the event may react *atypically*, such as smiling while a spider drops into the room on its web. Resolving expressive and situational conflicts rather than relying on one cue isn't easy; preschoolers usually still prefer simple, script-based emotion knowledge. Over time they start to assess expressive and situational sources of information separately and strategically.

It is somewhat easier for preschoolers to use *unique normative information*, such as, "Sarah lives in Green Valley, where all people are friendly with tigers and play games with them all the time" (Gnepp, Klayman, & Trabasso, 1982). When asked how Sarah would feel about tigers, preschoolers used unique information to modify their responses to a normally unequivocal situation. Other *person-specific information*, such as behavioral dispositions, modifying normally strong emotion-event associations (e.g., "Mark eats grass whenever he can... Mother says they're having grass for dinner"). Older preschoolers utilized such information, with responses reflecting the unique perspective of the character in the story. Preschoolers are also becoming aware that categories such as age and gender moderate emotions for differing situations. Learning complex causal parameters about emotions is thus emerging for older preschoolers; knowing abstract causes for emotion is useful in interaction with friends (Fabes et al., 1991).

Sometimes one must also understand consequences of emotion, distinguishing them from causes; such knowledge can help a child know what to do when experiencing or witnessing emotion. Preschoolers build solid conceptions of consequences of emotions for self and others; for example, Maddie knows that her mother will comfort her when she is upset. Four- and five-year-olds also attribute plausible, nonrandom parental reactions to their own emotions (Denham, 1997); for example, happy fathers dance, sad mothers lay in their bed, and angry fathers give spankings. Knowing why an emotion is expressed, and its likely aftermath, aids one in regulating behavior or emotion, and in reacting to others' emotions (Morgan, Izard, & King, 2010).

Learning about Display Rules, Mixed Emotions, and Complex Emotions. It is tricky to interpret false emotional signals while interacting with others. One must be able to ignore them if it benefits one's goals, or to accept them as real if that is advantageous. One must also: (a) pick up real, relevant, helpful messages; (b) ignore real but irrelevant messages; and (c) somehow deal with real and relevant but not helpful messages. Perhaps Kristin's droopy eyebrows and down-turned lips look sad naturally; her playmates need to know this and not try to comfort or avoid her. Darrell needs to ignore Tomas' low intensity glares while playing with him.

Young children understand hiding or masking emotion as soon as they realize that they can pose expression voluntarily – prior to understanding and using familial/cultural display rules for minimizing or substituting one emotion for another. Understanding when and when not to show emotions is very valuable in maintaining social relations; this knowledge continues to develop through gradeschool (Gross & Harris, 1988; Wu, Wang, & Liu, 2017).

Understanding specific cultural or personal display rules, whether prosocial or self-protective, is emerging during early childhood (Misailidi, 2006), even though children already modify expressiveness to fit such rules. Half the preschool children in Gnepp and Hess' (1986) study cited at least verbal, if not emotional, rules for regulating emotion (i.e., verbal masking: "I don't care that I lost this silly contest"). Developmentally appropriate methods show that children begin to understand display rules as they use them (Banerjee, 1997; Josephs, 1994), beginning with emotions subject to socialization pressure (i.e., when children are urged not to show anger, they not only stop expressing it, but also know the "not showing anger" rule; Feito, 1997).

Along with display rules, mixed emotions are important to understand. They are not uncommon, as when three-year-old Maddie is amused at her baby brother's antics, lurching to grab her Dora™ backpack, but also annoyed when he tries to bite it. Young children begin to experience simultaneous emotions and ambivalence, and to understand them on a limited basis (Wintre & Vallance, 1994). Asking questions via age-appropriate methodologies again reveals preschoolers knowledge may be greater than previously assumed (Kestenbaum & Gelman, 1995; Peng, Johnson, Pollock, Glasspool, & Harris, 1992); the ability to spontaneously recognize conflicting emotions, especially their own, is just emerging (Larson, Yen, & Fireman, 2007).

Another emotion knowledge accomplishment is understanding sociomoral emotions such as guilt and shame, and self- and other-referent emotions such as pride, embarrassment, and empathy. Because young children are beginning to express complex emotions, they have some understanding of them, but it is limited and acquired slowly. Although four-year-olds understand valence and arousal levels associated with pride, gratitude, shame, worry, and jealousy, they cannot accurately explain their causes (Russell & Paris, 1994). Preschoolers are similarly unable to name feelings of pride, guilt, or shame accompanying success, failure, and transgression – pride at a gymnastic feat or resisting temptation, or guilt for stealing coins from a parent's wallet – until at least age six (Berti, Garattoni, & Venturini, 2000). They report simpler emotions, making important errors (e.g., that a transgressor would feel happy). Partial concepts of these emotions predominate (see Chobhthaigh & Wilson, 2015), in part because of children's incomplete appreciation of societal rules and obligations that evoke them (Harris, 2008).

Emotion Knowledge and School Success. Because social interactions or relationships are guided, even defined, by emotional transactions, emotion knowledge figures prominently in social success. It allows a preschooler to react appropriately to others, whether calmly or sympathetically. Interactions with an emotionally knowledgeable peer would likely be viewed as satisfying, rendering one more likable. For example, if a preschooler sees one peer bickering with another, and deduces that the peer suddenly experiences sadness, rather than intensified anger, she may comfort her friend rather than retreat or enter the fray. The youngster who understands emotions should interact more successfully when a friend gets angry with them, and can be more empathic when a peer gets hurt on the playground; talking about one's emotions can facilitate negotiating disputes. Similarly, teachers notice evidence of emotion knowledge – use of emotion language, sympathetic reactions – and evaluate it positively. Accordingly, preschoolers who apply their emotion knowledge have concurrent and later advantages in peer interaction; they are more prosocially responsive to their peers, and seen as more socially skilled and more likable (Alonso-Alberca, Vergara, Fernández-Berrocal, Johnson, & Izard, 2012; Castro, Halberstadt, & Garrett-Peters, 2016; Deneault & Ricard, 2013; Denham et al., 2003; Garner & Waajid, 2008, 2012; Izard et al., 2001; Parker, Mathis, & Kupersmidt, 2013; Sette et al., 2015; Torres, Domitrovich, & Bierman, 2015).

More specifically, dyad members' emotion knowledge and child-friend emotion conversation are involved in conflict resolution, positive play, and cooperative shared pretend

(Brown, Donelan-McCall, & Dunn, 1996; Dunn, Cutting, & Fisher, 2002; Liao, Li, & Su, 2014). Preschoolers' spontaneous use of emotion language is also related to peer acceptance (Fabes, Eisenberg, Hanish, & Spinrad, 2001). Their emotion knowledge is related to reasoned argument with, and caregiving of, siblings, and defending peers against bullies (Camodeca & Coppola, 2016). Further, preschool emotion knowledge is *negatively* related to nonconstructive anger during peer play (Garner & Estep, 2001). Kindergarten mixed emotion knowledge is related to understanding friends, and expecting teachers' benign reactions to mistakes (Dunn et al., 2002).

Lack of emotion knowledge is associated with behavior problems; preschoolers with identified aggression, peer problems, or attention deficit hyperactivity disorder (ADHD) show deficits in emotion expression and situation knowledge, both concurrently and predictively (Denham, Caverly et al., 2002; Di Maggio et al., 2016; Lugo-Candelas et al., 2017; Parker et al., 2013; Ren et al., 2016; Rodrigo-Ruiz, Perez-Gonzalez, & Cejudo, 2017; Woods, Menna, & McAndrew, 2017). Errors in emotion knowledge are related to risk for aggression problems; over-attributions of anger, similar to older children's hostile attribution, are related to preschool aggression and peer rejection (Schultz, Izard, & Ackerman, 2000). Internalizing issues, such as shyness, loneliness, and peer victimization, are also related to emotion knowledge deficits (Di Maggio et al., 2016; Heinze, Miller, Seifer, Dickstein, & Locke, 2015; Sette, Baumgartner, Laghi, & Coplan, 2016).

In terms of school success, understanding the barrage of one's own and others' emotions can make the many socially centered tasks encountered in the classroom easier; interactions are smoother so that more personal resources are left to focus on more cognitive tasks. Increasingly, researchers are confirming a link between school success and young children's emotion knowledge (Blankson et al., 2017; Garner & Waajid, 2008, 2012; Izard et al., 2001; Leerkes et al., 2008; Torres et al., 2009). In fact, a recent series of meta-analyses (Voltmer & von Salisch, 2017) shows that preschoolers' emotion knowledge is related to their academic achievement and school adjustment. Emotion knowledge also predicts later preschool and kindergarten school adjustment and academic success, both directly and indirectly (Bassett et al., 2012; Curby, Brown, Bassett, & Denham, 2015; Denham, Bassett, Mincic, et al., 2012; Denham, Bassett, Thayer, et al., 2012). Notably, emotion knowledge *growth* predicted later reading achievement and school engagement (Nix, Bierman, Domitrovich, & Gill, 2013; Torres et al., 2015).

Preschool emotion knowledge's contribution to school success extends even further in time. For example, preschool emotion knowledge predicted first grade academic achievement, mediated by kindergarten attentional abilities (Rhoades, Warren, Domitrovich, & Greenberg, 2011). Similarly, Izard and colleagues have found evidence of a link between emotion knowledge and later academic success in elementary school (Izard, 2002; Izard et al., 2001).

Summary of Outcomes of Emotion Knowledge. Taken together, these findings suggest that emotion knowledge facilitates positive social interactions, as well as school success, and that deficits can contribute to behavioral and learning problems. Trentacosta and Fine's (2010) meta-analysis showed remarkably consistent findings across numerous potential child, community, and methodological moderators. Such effects are also found cross-nationally (e.g., Eoh, Jeong, & Park, 2017). These links highlight needs to assess and boost emotion knowledge before school entry. Ascertaining difficulties could facilitate intervention before problems become entrenched.

Connecting the Pieces of Emotional Competence

As important as these relations are between each component of emotional competence and social competence or school success, they are also likely to support one another as an interrelated network (Eisenberg, Sadovsky, & Spinrad, 2005). As Cole et al. (2004) theorized and Denham Bassett, Mincic, et al. (2012) demonstrated, emotion expressiveness and regulation often operate in concert. Also, emotion knowledge plays an important role in children's expressive patterns and emotion regulation (Schultz, Izard, Ackerman, & Youngstrom, 2001). When a child knows that her playmate is delighted to have heaved the tricycle upright at last, she no longer is distressed herself, trying to figure out what to do with an angry friend. She can focus attention on other aspects of the situation. Lindsey (2017) also noted relations between young children's mutual positive affect and emotion knowledge; Hudson and Jacques (2014) showed that display rule knowledge contributed to five- to seven-year-olds' emotion regulation during a disappointing gift task.

Further, children experiencing intense, unregulated negative emotions are especially likely to suffer social difficulties (Contreras, Kerns, Weimer, Gentzler, & Tomich, 2000; Herndon et al., 2013). These co-deficits can promote other difficulties; children who showed much unregulated anger were seen by teachers oppositional two years later, at the end of kindergarten (Denham et al., 2003; Denham, Blair, et al., 2002). In fact, all aspects of emotional competence work together to promote children's school success (Denham, Bassett, Mincic, et al., 2012).

In contrast, even children high in negative emotionality are buffered from peer status problems by emotion regulation skills that parents and caregivers can teach them. Emotion knowledge may also support positive, regulated emotional expressiveness, in predicting social competence and school success (Denham, Bassett, Thayer, et al., 2012; Denham, Caverly, et al., 2002; Di Maggio et al., 2016). Further, in Denham, Bassett, and Wyatt (2014) emotion knowledge was related to observed emotion regulation and thence to classroom adjustment.

Summary of Relations among Components of Emotional Competence. Emotional competence components do not operate in isolation. Peers and adults experience children's

emotional competence skills working together during interaction and as supports for learning. Furthermore, emotional
competence components are also related in a variable-
centered manner. Knowing how skills of emotional competence work together can aid early childhood educators in
refining social-emotional curricula. Now we turn to means of
promoting this "total package."

What Fuels the Development of Emotional Competence?

Intrapersonal Contributors

Children's abilities and attributes can promote or hinder emotional competence. Some children are blessed with cognitive and
language skills that allow them to better understand their social
world, its emotions, and to better communicate their feelings,
wishes, desires, and goals for social interactions and relationships (Cutting & Dunn, 1999). A preschooler who can reason
flexibly may more readily perceive how another person might
emotionally react differently to a situation than s/he would –
though they delight *me,* others may fear swimming pools.

Language skill serves both emotion regulation, helping children codify a menu of goal-related emotion regulation strategies. With these, children can successfully ask
for help, for example; children with better language skill
as toddlers expressed less intense anger as four-year-olds
(Roben, Cole, & Armstrong, 2013). Language also supports
young children's emotion knowledge acquisition (Martin,
Williamson, Kurtz-Nelson, & Boekamp, 2015; Martins,
Osório, Veríssimo, & Martins, 2016; Seidenfeld, Johnson,
Cavadel, & Izard, 2014). "Children who present with ...
language difficulties, may be particularly vulnerable to emotion processing errors, as well as to missed opportunities
to engage in social interactions and conversations" (Martin
et al., 2016; p. 33). More verbal children can ask better questions about their and others' emotions, and understand the
answers, giving them an advantage in dealing with emotions.

Children with different emotional dispositions (i.e., temperaments) may be well- or ill-equipped to develop emotional competence (Calkins & Mackler, 2011). An especially
negative child may find she has a greater need for emotion
regulation, even though this is difficult for her. In contrast, a
child whose temperament allows him to shift attention from a
distressing situation to focus on comforting actions, objects,
or thoughts is better able to regulate.

Interpersonal Contributors: Parents' Socialization of Emotional Competence

Children come to their preschool years with these intrapersonal factors well in place, as either foundations of or road-
blocks to emotional and social competence. Caring adults are
faced with such children daily. What differences do our efforts make? How do we foster these emotional competencies
in children as they move into their school years? Much of the

individual variation in components of children's emotional
competence derives from experiences within the family and
classroom (Denham, 1998). Important adults have crucial
roles in its development.

Socialization of emotions is ubiquitous in children's everyday contact with parents, teachers, caregivers, and peers. All
people who interact with children exhibit a variety of emotions which the children observe. Further, children's emotions often require some kind of reaction, and some adults
consider instructing children about the world of emotions to
be an important area of teaching (Engle & McElwain, 2011).
Three mechanisms describe socialization of emotion: modeling emotional expressiveness, reacting to children's emotions, and teaching about emotion (Denham, 1998; Denham
et al., 2014; Eisenberg, Cumberland, & Spinrad, 1998). Each
mechanism can influence children's emotional expression,
knowledge, and regulation. Overall, parents' generally positive emotional expression, "safe" expression of negative
emotions, encouraging reactions to children's emotions, and
openness to and expertise in emotion talk, children become
emotionally competent. Each aspect is considered here.

Beliefs about emotions are also recognized as important to socialization of emotions (particularly acceptance of/
attention to emotions and the value of emotions and their
regulation; Meyer, Raikes, Virmani, Waters, & Thompson,
2014). Beliefs are related to actual enactment of socialization
of emotion (Halberstadt, Thompson, Parker, & Dunsmore,
2008; Halberstadt et al., 2013; Wong, Diener, & Isabella,
2008; Wong, McElwain, & Halberstadt, 2009).

Another important consideration is the reciprocity of
parent-child emotional transactions; children's emotionality undoubtedly affects parental socialization of emotion.
For example, mothers' positive emotion during a waiting
task, administered between 18 and 48 months, increased
more over time *if* their children were less angry, more content, or used more positive emotion regulation strategies
(Cole, LeDonne, & Tan, 2013; Fields-Olivieri, Cole, &
Maggi, 2017). Mothers' negative emotion decreased less
when children were angrier than agemates.

Most of the extant research on the socialization of social
and emotional competence involves young children and their
parents. Of course, parents are not the only socializers of
emotional competence. In the following, results regarding
young children's interactions with their parents are reported
first, followed by an emerging literature on teacher socialization of emotions. Sparse information on siblings and peers is
not included for space considerations.

Parents' Modeling Emotional Expressiveness. Children
observe adults' emotions and incorporate their observations into their expressive behavior. They vicariously learn
how to exhibit emotional expressions, and *which* to express
when, in what context (Denham & Grout, 1993; Denham,
Mitchell-Copeland, Strandberg, Auerbach, & Blair, 1997).
Specifically, parents' and children's positive emotional
expression are related (Davis, Suveg, & Shaffer, 2015).

Parents' emotional displays also foster children's emotion knowledge, by showing the emotional significance of events, behaviors accompanying differing emotions, and others' likely reactions. Moderately expressive parents give children information about emotions' expression, likely eliciting situations, and more personalized causes (Denham & Grout, 1993; Denham et al., 1997; Denham, Zoller, & Couchoud, 1994; Liew et al., 2003; Nixon & Watson, 2001).

Mothers' expressiveness also facilitates preschoolers' emotion regulation. For example, maternal positivity (supported by positive beliefs about children's emotions) contributes to Korean children's emotion regulation (Cho & Lee, 2015). When children have experience with clear but not overpowering parental emotions, they may also have more experience with empathic involvement with others' emotions (Martin, Clements, & Crnic, 2002; Valiente, 2004).

Hence, clear and mostly positive emotional environments are associated with positive outcomes in young children's emotional expressiveness, emotion knowledge, and emotion regulation. Conversely, parental expressiveness can make it more difficult for young children to address issues of emotion altogether. In particular, exposure to negative emotions expressed by adults can be problematic for young children; when mothers are often angry and tense with them, young children are angrier and less emotionally positive (Newland & Crnic, 2011). It is easy to imagine the confusion and pain of children relentlessly exposed to parents' negative emotions. In their aftermath, children whose mothers self-report more frequent anger and tension are angrier themselves, less prosocial, and less well liked than children of more positive mothers (Eisenberg et al., 2003; Garner & Spears, 2000). Although exposure to *well-modulated* negative emotion can be positively related to emotion knowledge, parents' frequent and intense negative emotions may upset children, as well as discourage self-reflection, so that little is learned about emotions, other than how to express negativity (Denham, 1998). In extreme cases, such as neglect and abuse, children make fewer, skewed distinctions among emotions (Pollak, Cicchetti, Hornung, & Reed, 2000; Sullivan, Bennett, Carpenter, & Lewis, 2008); their emotion knowledge is impaired.

As well, the trajectory from age two aggressiveness to age four externalizing problems is clearest for toddlers who experience high levels of maternal negative expressiveness (Rubin, Burgess, Dwyer, & Hastings, 2003). Thus, it may be that exposure to higher levels of negativity over-arouses the young child who cannot yet regulate emotions well, and represents a hostile-aggressive template for children to follow in their reactions to people and events.

Parental emotion regulation (as modeled regulated or dysregulated emotion) is also an important contributor to aspects of children's emotional competence. Thus, parental dysregulation also contributes to children's emotion regulation and behavior problems, often in concert with aspects of family emotional expressiveness. For example, Are and Shaffer (2016) found that preschoolers' mothers reporting emotion dysregulation also reported less positive family expressiveness and more negative expressiveness. Maternal dysregulation directly predicted children's emotion regulation or negativity/lability, and indirectly predicted children's emotion regulation via lack of positive expressiveness (see also Ulrich & Petermann, 2017). In contrast, where maternal dysregulation was low, and children's own positive emotion was high, preschoolers' behavioral adjustment was facilitated (Davis et al., 2015).

Specifically, parental emotion regulatory strategies can assist children in regulating emotions themselves. When mothers used attention refocusing, cognitive reframing, and comforting strategies during a disappointing gift task, their preschoolers also did. Further, mothers' joint attention refocusing and cognitive reframing were related to children's lessened sadness and anger afterward (Morris et al., 2011).

Contingent Reactions to Children's Emotions. Adults' contingent reactions to children's behaviors and emotional displays are also linked to young children's emotional competence. Contingent reactions include behavioral and emotional encouragement or discouragement of specific behaviors and emotions. More specifically, adults may react nonsupportively, punishing children's experience and expression of emotions, or showing dismissive attitudes toward the world of emotions, by ignoring the child's emotions in a perhaps well-meaning effort to "make it better" (Denham et al., 1994). Children who experience such adult reactions have more to be upset about – not only the emotion's elicitor, but also adults' reactions (Eisenberg et al., 1999).

Positive, supportive reactions (e.g., accepting, empathizing with, validating, and even encouraging children's experiences and expression of emotions, comforting or helping to solve the problem) convey a very different message, that emotions are manageable, even useful. Emotional moments are seen as opportunities for intimacy (Denham & Kochanoff, 2003; Eisenberg, Fabes, & Murphy, 1996). Such supportive reactions to emotions are related to preschoolers' expressiveness of positive emotions (Fabes, Poulin, Eisenberg, & Madden-Derdich, 2003) and emotion regulation (e.g., Meyer et al., 2014). When mothers are supportive, children show less distress and more sympathetic concern to the distress of others. They have guides to follow in responding to others' distress (Denham & Grout, 1993). Parents' supportive reactions may also help the child differentiate emotions (Denham & Kochanoff, 2003; Denham et al., 1994; Fabes et al., 2003). In contrast, parents using unsupportive reactions to emotions are more likely to have sadder, more fearful children (Berlin & Cassidy, 2003), often with compromised emotion regulation (Luebbe, Kiel, & Buss, 2011; Woods et al., 2017).

As also true with modeling, children's emotion regulation often mediates relations between parents' reactions to emotions and behavior problems. Children's dysregulated emotion mediated relations between mothers' nonsupportiveness and preschooler aggression (Woods et al., 2017).

Teaching about Emotions. This aspect of emotion socialization is the most direct. What parents and other adults say, or intentionally convey through other means, can impact their children's emotion knowledge. Teaching about emotions often consists of explaining an emotion and its relation to an observed event or expression. It may also include directing attention to salient emotional cues, helping children understand and manage their own responses, and segmenting social interactions into manageable emotional components. Adults who are aware of emotions, especially negative ones, and talk about them in a differentiated manner (e.g., clarifying, explaining, noting the child's responsibility for others' feelings, but not "preaching") assist children in expressing, experiencing, identifying, and regulating their own emotions. Dismissing adults may protectively refrain from talking too much about children's emotions.

Parents' tendencies to discuss emotions, if nested within a warm relationship, help children acquire all aspects of emotional competence (Harris, 2008). Discussing emotions helps children to separate impulses from behavior, giving them reflective distance from feeling states, and helps direct their attention to salient emotional cues with which to interpret and evaluate their feelings and to reflect upon causes and consequences (Mirabile, Scaramella, Sohr-Preston, & Robison, 2009). Verbal give-and-take about emotional experience while chatting with an adult helps the child to formulate coherent knowledge about emotional expressions, situations, and causes, fostering both emotion knowledge and regulation (Denham et al., 1994; Dunn, Brown, & Beardsall, 1991). Such conversations also coach children to perceive social consequences of their actions (e.g., "Johnny will be mad and not want to play with you, if you take his toys") and to empathize or consider another's viewpoint (e.g., "That hurt Toby's feelings – look, he feels sad"). When parents discuss and explain their and others' emotions, children show more empathy to peers (Denham et al., 1994; Garner, Jones, Gaddy, & Rennie, 1997).

The benefits of such teaching begin early; co-action of parent and child may be crucial. When parents elicited toddlers' labels and causes for emotions in a storybook task, children helped and shared more quickly and more often in later tasks (Brownell, Svetlova, Anderson, Nichols, & Drummond, 2013; see also Drummond, Paul, Whitney, Hammond, & Brownell, 2014). Further, questions can be important in emotion teaching's promotion of preschoolers' emotion knowledge (Bailey, Denham, & Curby, 2013), pushing children to formulate thoughts about the conversation's emotional content, practice using challenging language, and put emotional memories and experiences into words (Salmon & Reese, 2016). Thus, parents who can engage children in emotional conversation, and co-construct emotional meaning, can promote children's emotion knowledge (Brownell et al., 2013; Laible, Panfile Murphy, & Augustine, 2013).

Summary: How Parents Socialize Emotional Competence. In sum, there is a growing body of knowledge regarding the positive contributions of adults' socialization of emotion to young children's emotional competence. Its elements will be useful not only in parenting, but also in building adult roles in any successful social-emotional programming for young children.

Interpersonal Contributors: Teachers' Socialization of Emotion

It follows that *teachers'* socialization of emotional competence will also promote social-emotional and even academic success in school. What is known so far from a sparse literature is reviewed here, along with ideas of how to assist teachers in becoming better socializers of emotion (ideas that could potentially be useful to parents, as well).

During preschool, contexts outside the family become important for children's development. The classroom is rich in emotional experiences, and children learn about emotions through participating in and observing daily interactions with teachers and peers. Early childhood teachers and caregivers often intuitively believe that children need emotional closeness with teachers, and learn about emotions and expressing them acceptably from seeing how adults behave (Zembylas, 2007; Zinsser, Denham, Curby, & Shewark, 2015; Zinsser, Shewark, Denham, & Curby, 2014). But preservice teachers report little training on promoting emotional competence or managing their own feelings and displays of emotion (Garner, 2010; Schonert-Reichl, Kitil, & Hanson-Peterson, 2017). Unsurprisingly, individual differences exist in teachers' enactment of best practice in this area (Zinsser et al., 2014, 2015).

Encouraging emerging research, however, suggests that emotional competence concepts can be successfully infused in undergraduate curriculum and instruction courses (Waajid, Garner, & Owen, 2013). Greater understanding of teacher socialization of emotion could lead toward needed developments in early childhood teacher preservice/inservice training. Such change would be very useful; early childhood educators quickly recognize the emotional needs of children when these are pointed out, like turning on a faucet of understanding. When emotional competence is highlighted, appropriate handling of emotions in the classroom becomes a great concern to teachers, commensurate with their focus on children's behavior.

Recent research follows up on these ideas, specifying preschool teachers as pivotal facilitators of children's emotional competence (Denham, Bassett, & Zinsser, 2012). High levels of teacher emotional support and positive emotional tone in the classroom are related to better social-emotional outcomes for children (Curby, Brock, & Hamre, 2013; Spivak & Farran, 2016). Increasing research shows that preschool teachers also engage in a wide variety of more specific emotion socialization behaviors in the classroom, parallel to parental behaviors (Ahn & Stifter, 2006): teachers show emotions and react to children's emotions in ways like parents (Denham et al., 2012). They also use emotion language in the classroom, although relatively infrequently (Yelinek & Grady, 2017); they explain and question during teacher-led activities and use socializing and guiding language during free play (e.g., "we smile when we say hello," "you can pound these blocks if you're mad"), especially when it is aggressive.

Teachers' socialization behaviors are likely to send different messages about specific emotions and emotion-related behaviors to children in the classroom, just as they do in the home. Teachers' modeling, reacting, and teaching are likely to contribute to young children's emotional competence, and directly and indirectly (via children's emotional competence) to children's early school success. Recalling findings on parents' emotion regulation, teachers' own emotional competence also is likely to be key. What evidence is mounting on these probabilities?

Teachers' Own Emotional Competence. The ways in which teachers deal with their own emotional lives – perceiving emotions of self and others, using emotions to facilitate cognition and action, understanding emotions, and managing them – undoubtedly contribute to their socialization of pupils' emotional competence (Brackett & Katulak, 2006). For example, preschool teachers' emotional competence is related to their reactions to children's emotions; preschool teachers with low awareness of their own emotions were less likely to self-report that they would help children label and regulate their emotions, or to try to help solve the problem (Ersay, 2015). They also often ignored children's emotions, and less often comforted children's negative emotions or matched their positive emotions. Further, their negative emotional intensity was associated with punishing children's emotions, and lack of attention to their own emotions was related to their greater minimization of children's emotions.

Given such circumstances, and because teaching can be emotionally draining and unpredictable (Jeon, Hur, & Buettner, 2016), it would be beneficial to help teachers to become more emotionally competent themselves. Promotion of teachers' own emotional competence could also be useful for their modeling, increasing their abilities to accurately express emotions, generate positivity, reflect on, and manage emotions. Mindfulness techniques can help teachers maintain positivity, and reflective supervision could help teachers gain access to and understand their own emotions (Jennings & Greenberg, 2009; Kemeny et al., 2012).

Teacher Socialization of Emotion: Modeling. It is expected that teachers' positive emotionality helps children express and experience calmer, more regulated positivity themselves, and render them receptive to learning about emotions. In contrast, intense teacher negativity would create an atmosphere where regulation is difficult. Mild teacher negativity might help children learn about emotions; inexpressive teachers would not provide a welcoming platform for such learning. Despite predictions, very little research has yet targeted expressive modeling by teachers. Recent work suggested that teachers' negative expressiveness was negatively related to older preschoolers' positivity with peers (Morris, Denham, Bassett, and Curby, 2013). Emotionally negative preschool classroom environments also have been linked to displays of later aggressive, disruptive peer behavior, especially boys' (Howes, 2000). Further, when teachers in the USA and Italy show predominantly positive emotions, so do the children they teach (Denham et al., 2016). To promote children's emotional competence, teacher training could focus on helping teachers to be willing to show emotions, remain generally emotionally positive despite challenges, and modulate understandable negative emotions (Zinsser et al., 2014, 2015).

Teacher Socialization of Emotion: Reactions. Young children notice teachers' reactions to their emotions (Dunn, 1994). Encouraging responses from teachers could assist children in tolerating and regulating emotions, teaching them that emotions are moments for sharing, manageable, and even useful. Supportive reactions would help children "stay in the moment" to learn more about emotions, and also support their social and school success. Preschool teachers do react to children's emotions (Ahn & Stifter, 2006). They encourage positive expressiveness; after negative emotional expressions, they show empathy, comfort, distraction, problem-solving, ignoring, or negative responses such as restriction, threatening, ridicule, or minimization.

Teacher responses to child emotions do differ by child age. More socialization reactions are targeted at younger preschoolers (Kiliç, 2015). Toddlers' teachers are more encouraging, and use physical comfort and distraction in response to children's negative emotions more often than preschool teachers, who rely more on verbal mediation (Ahn, 2005; Ahn & Stifter, 2006). Further, early childhood teachers do not often validate children's negative emotions – a major tenet of positive socialization of emotion. When they do, children's more frequent positive emotion and prosocial behaviors are observed (Karalus, Herndon, Bassett, & Denham, 2016). Early childhood teachers are also very focused on their students developing independent emotion regulation (Ahn, 2005, Ahn & Stifter 2006; Karalus et al., 2016).

Building on these descriptions, Bassett and colleagues (2017) found that teachers' supportive, nonsupportive, and validating reactions to preschoolers' emotions contributed to children's negativity and emotion regulation, in expected directions, but particularly for those with low surgent temperaments. Morris et al. (2013) also showed that teachers' dismissing reactions were negatively related to older preschoolers' positive expressivity and emotion knowledge. Finally, accepting beliefs about children's emotions and perspective-taking ability promoted teachers' supportive reactions to children's emotions (Swartz & McElwain, 2012).

Training could focus on ways to assist teachers in valuing their supportive role concerning children's emotions and provide specific strategies to use in reacting to children's emotions (e.g., anger, fear, sadness, even over-excitement). Promoting teachers' own emotional competence would likely assist them in utilizing emotional encounters more advantageously. Stress reduction could bolster their expression of supportive reactions to children's emotions.

Teacher Socialization of Emotion: Teaching about Emotions. It is expected that teachers who discuss emotions give children tools to use in expressing/regulating emotions. Via such direct, not misleading or idiosyncratic, tutelage, teachers could help children learn about emotions. Ahn (2005) noted that emotion-related discussions in preschool classrooms (as opposed to toddlers') helped children infer causes of their negative emotions and taught them constructive ways of expressing negative emotion. Preschool teachers who value teaching children about emotions also promote children's more adaptive emotion regulation patterns (Denham, Grant, & Hamada, 2002).

These values and propensities for emotion talk can translate into classroom and parenting practice. Several picturebook-reading styles of preschool teachers have been identified, which relate positively to children's emotion knowledge. For example, children whose teacher used more questions for explaining causes and consequences of characters' emotions (e.g., "Do you think she is sad because the ball fell in the river?") showed greater growth in emotion knowledge than those whose teachers did not (Bassett, Denham, Mohtasham, & Austin, 2016).

Promoting teachers' own emotional competence could also improve their ability to perceive emotions accurately, so that they could usefully talk about them with children. Use of reflective supervision could also aid teachers in giving them access to emotion vocabulary and increasing their ease in discussing feelings. Further teacher training could focus on ways of helping teachers to value teacher-child emotion conversations and sustain interchanges about emotions in classroom activities and dialogues about ongoing classroom interactions.

Summary and Looking Forward: Teacher Socialization of Emotion. These initial research efforts require extension. Knowing more about how teachers' discrete emotion socialization behaviors, *and* more molar classroom emotional support, relate to children's developing emotional competence could be very useful for teacher training. Further, continued study is called for on aspects of teachers' lives that could promote their abilities as socializers of emotional competence: well-being (e.g., the balance of their job resources and demands, wages, and perception of being able to pay for their basic expenses; Cassidy, King, Wang, Lower, & Kintner-Duffy, 2017; Denham, Bassett, & Miller, 2017; King et al., 2016), their own emotional competence (e.g., Swartz & McElwain, 2012), and experience (Denham et al., 2017). As already noted, pre- and inservice training also

need to be improved, especially regarding evidence-based practices and leadership support (Buettner, Hur, Jeon, & Andrews, 2016; Steed & Roach, 2017).

The Roles of Gender and Culture in Early Childhood Emotional Competence

The aspects of emotional competence and their socialization already outlined here hold true in a general sense for all children and their socializers. But as already noted, the ways in which emotional competence is expressed and the ways that it is taught may differ between girls and boys, mothers and fathers, and across disparate cultures. Thus, although a full treatment of these important matters is beyond the scope of this chapter, an outline may be sketched.

Gender of Child and Parent

First, regarding modeling emotion, parents sometime differ in the emotions that they express around their children. Garner, Robertson, and Smith (1997) found that preschoolers' mothers reported showing more positive emotion (especially to daughters) and more sadness, than fathers (see also Denham, Bassett, & Wyatt., 2010). Parents of sons, especially fathers, reported showing more anger. Fathers' positivity, however, made an additional contribution to explained variance in children's own positivity during a challenging peer play session. As well, fathers hold more punitive ideas about how they should react to children's emotions, compared to mothers (Denham, Bassett, & Wyatt, 2010).

Although not all findings converge, and fathers' emotion conversations are not as deeply studied as mothers', we know that mothers, more than fathers, value teaching their children about emotions (Denham, Bassett, & Wyatt, 2010). Further, parents often talk more to their preschool-aged daughters about emotions, especially specific ones such as sadness; mothers and fathers also may differ in emotion talk to sons and daughters (Fivush, Berlin, Sales, Mennuti-Washburn, & Cassidy, 2003; Fivush, Brotman, Buckner, & Goodman, 2000). Mothers stress the interpersonal nature of emotions (Flannagan & Perese, 1998), and fathers sometimes appear *not* to view family conversations as opportunities to discuss emotions (Chance & Fiese, 1999).

There seems to be more difference in mothers' and fathers' socialization of emotion than in their treatment of sons and daughters, but evidence for gender-specific contributions of parental socialization to emotional competence does exist (e.g., Engle & McElwain, 2011). In Denham and colleagues (1997), girls' ability to regulate negative emotions was especially vulnerable to the detrimental effects of parental negative emotions and antisocial reactions to child emotions, and to the positive effects of their parents' own happiness relative to their anger. The greater salience of the family context for girls' behavior, and girls' greater sensitivity to parental influences need to be studied more explicitly in the realm of emotional competence.

Other findings on how maternal and paternal socialization of emotion variously contribute to young children's emotional competence are complex, but it is clear that inclusion fathers is important in fleshing out the entire picture of preschool socialization of emotion. Studying only maternal socialization of emotion would yield an incomplete understanding of the socialization of young children's emotional competence. At times maternal and paternal contributions to emotional competence seem to complement one another, as when mild maternal negativity along with paternal positive expressiveness predicted preschoolers' emotion knowledge (Denham, Bassett, & Wyat., 2010). Mothers' more frequent, gender-expected, negative expressiveness may be part of their "emotional gatekeeper" role in the family, with fathers acting as loving playmates. How these issues play out in the female-dominated world of early childhood education is an area lacking in research – how do boys fare in this environment, for example? Are girls still more susceptible to emotion socialization messages? The gendered world of emotion reminds us that attention to context is netcessary to our fullest understanding of young children's emotional competence.

Culture

All beliefs and practices associated with emotions are created and interpreted within cultural and historical, socially embedded, contexts, such as the situational ecologies in which emotions and interactions occur, and the criteria for interpreting social-emotional events (De Leersnyder, Boiger, & Mesquita, 2015). Thus, socialization of emotion is situated within every culture's narrative regarding the child outcomes that are most valued, and the best ways to reach these outcomes. One would expect qualitative differences between cultures in emotions modeled, reactions to emotions, and teaching about emotions. One might even expect subtle differences in how young children display emotional competence, and its developmental course.

Friedlmeier, Çorapçı, and Cole (2011) have put forward clear descriptions of how and why preferred modes of socialization of emotion will differ across cultures valuing individualistic or relational emotional competence (whether based on nationality or ethnicity). The Western, individualistic, cultural values described in most research permeate the very conceptions and expected outcomes of socialization of emotion already described here (e.g., being supportive in reactions to children's emotions, discussing emotions, being aware of children's emotions, being mostly emotionally positive, using care when expressing negative emotions). In contrast, within relational cultures, socialization of emotion is often informed by the need to consider the interpersonal group and its needs, rather than the individual child's. Such values may emphasize *not* encouraging emotional expressiveness – in fact, punishing it; negative expressiveness may be used more liberally to inform children of their need to refrain from their own expressiveness. Emotions may not be discussed because they need to be suppressed. Finally,

child outcomes of such socialization of emotion messages may be positive where Western thinking would predict them to be negative. For any cultural narrative, it is imperative to understand *what matters*.

We use Japanese culture as an example to examine these principles, given its clear differences from Western culture and relative abundance of pertinent research (see also Denham, Mason, Kochanoff, Neal, & Hamada, 2003). Regarding socialization of emotional expression, emotions of friendliness, calmness, and connectedness would be most available for observation by Japanese children, given their culture's relational values. Non-Western, relational cultures may value a less expressive presentation of self, given the goal of group harmony (e.g., Louie, Wang, Fung, & Lau, 2015). Anger, regarded as an extremely negative disturbance of interdependence, would be modeled less frequently (Denham, Caal, Bassett, Benga, & Geangu, 2004).

Japanese parents' reactions to children's emotions sometimes also differ from US parents' (Kanaya, Nakamura, & Miyake, 1989). In general, US parents see expression of emotions as legitimate, part of healthy self-assertion. In contrast, obedience, cooperation, interacting empathically, and acquisition of good manners are typical Japanese parenting goals (Ujiie, 1997). Thus, Japanese parents react most positively to children's suppression of emotion and demonstration of empathy; Zahn-Waxler and colleagues (1996) note that Japanese mothers encouraged emotional expression less than their American counterparts.

Research suggests that Japanese mothers do talk to their preschoolers about emotions (Kojima, 2000). They use emotion language for similar reasons as American mothers – to instruct their children about emotional meanings, to negotiate, to explain the feelings of one sibling to another (Watanabe, 2015). What differs is the content of their conversations, which may focus more on behavior, and on aspects of emotion relevant for Japanese culture (Doan & Wang, 2010). This teaching does contribute to emotion knowledge (Watanabe, 2015).

Relational and individualistic cultures' emotion socialization behaviors are often (but not always) similar in predicting children's emotional competence (Friedlmeier et al., 2011). Given the differences between these two cultures, especially in emotions emphasized by socializers, differences in emotional expressiveness would be expected. Japanese preschoolers show less anger and distress in conflict situations than US children, but do not differ in conflict *behaviors* (Zahn-Waxler et al., 1996). These differences fit the taboo on public expression of negative emotions (Nakamura, Buck, & Kenny, 1990). In contrast, the trajectory of developing competent emotion knowledge seems similar for Japanese and Western children. For example, even two-year-olds use some emotion language, and by the end of the preschool period, their understanding of emotion language appropriate to their culture is acute, including knowledge of dissemblance (Sawada, 1997). Furthermore, the trajectory of emotion regulation – from other-dependent toward independent – is similar in Japanese and Western preschoolers (Kanamaru & Muto, 2004).

Thus, many important differences exist between the exemplar cultures in socialization of emotion and in early childhood emotional competence itself. However, it is important to point out that many aspects are very similar across cultures – including general appraisals of the origins of parental emotions, such as happiness, sadness, and anger resulting from enjoying their children, loss, and child disobedience (Denham et al., 2004). Parents in more relational cultures, like their individualistic counterparts, may also endorse reactions attuned to children's individual needs (e.g., comforting toddlers' fear and helping them solve problems related to anger; Çorapçı, Friedlmeier, Benga, Strauss, Pitica, & Susa, 2018). Some goals may be universal.

Conceptualizing optimal socialization of emotion is culturally relative; care needs to be taken to know cultures' perspectives on socialization goals. Teachers must consider socialization messages pupils absorb at home, to integrate these emotional meanings in the classroom.

Educating for Emotional Competence in the Early Childhood Classroom

The material covered here show emotions matter – there is a clear connection between emotional competence and both social and school success. This point is especially true for those at risk due to poverty, community violence, family stress, maltreatment, or family life changes. The development of these inextricably intertwined competencies must not be left to chance.

Knowing the importance of children's emotional competence and the contributions of adults' socialization, we must discuss how successfully this is dealt with in schools (both programming and assessment), as well as support for parents. First, an integrated system of educational practice is recommended; Denham (2015) has described such a system. As already noted, (a) age-appropriate developmental *tasks* are the substrate upon which specific emotional competence *skills* are demonstrated and developed; (b) given these tasks as foundation, *standards* are created emanating from these important competencies as road maps of what skills to look for, expect, and teach; (c) standards inform choice of *assessment* tools, and vice versa; (d) both standards and assessment are useful in that they lead to *instruction* (which often leads to the need for further, regular assessment and revised standards, and can be supported by both professional development for teachers as emotion socializers, as well as curriculum or less structured programming; see Humphrey, 2013); and (e) finally, children's emotional competence develops. In this chapter, instructional programming and assessment are briefly considered.

Effective Emotional Competence Programming

There is a need for primary and secondary prevention programs targeted at preschoolers' emotional competence, to ensure their smooth transition to kindergarten. Several meta-analyses have noted the efficacy of programming for social-emotional learning (which includes the components of emotional competence; e.g., Durlak, Weissberg, Dymnicki, Taylor, & Schellinger, 2011; Taylor, Oberle, Durlak, & Weissberg, 2017). Durlak et al. showed that the reviewed programs showed improvement compared to control groups in social-emotional skills, behavior problems, and academic performance. Benefits of programming held true from kindergarten through high school, and across urban/suburban/rural contexts. Taylor et al. (2011) gave evidence that benefits were significant at follow-up periods from 6 months to 18 years, and did not vary by students' race, socioeconomic status (SES) or geographical location. Thus, crucial emotional competence skills can be promoted.

There are several criteria for quality programming in emotional competence. Durlak et al. (2011) summarize these by the acronym SAFE: (a) **S**equenced – lessons are connected and coordinated, consistent in providing clear objectives and activities, contributing to overall program goals; (b) **A**ctive – active learning approaches rather than lecture or other passive modes of learning are used; (c) **F**ocused – any useful program involves at least one of the emotional competence components considered important here; and (d) **E**xplicit – lessons are explicit in terms of the component skill that is their goal. For the most positive, long-lasting results, infusing emotional competence throughout all teaching and creating opportunities for skill application throughout the day would be crucial (see also McClelland, Tominey, Schmitt, & Duncan, 2017), as well as having all the adults and all the environments, both proximal and distal, in a child's life involved in emotional competence programming. These goals require school-wide coordination, and ultimately school-family and school-community partnerships (see Denham & Bassett, 2018, for more details). Further, McClelland et al. note that effective programming in early childhood education requires specialized training and professional development, and McLeod and colleagues (2017) specify numerous important practice elements with which educators support the growth of emotional competence during early childhood.

Much evidence-based programming, varying in emphasis on emotional expressiveness and utilization, emotion knowledge, and emotion regulation, has been tested and found efficacious in early childhood education (Denham & Burton, 1996, 2003; Domitrovich, Cortes, & Greenberg, 2007; Izard et al., 2008; Joseph & Strain, 2003; Kramer, Caldarella, Christensen, & Shatzer, 2010; Webster-Stratton & Reid, 2003, 2004, 2007). Many of these programs are delivered universally to all children in specific classrooms. Programming has also profitably incorporated literacy components with emotional competence (Bierman et al., 2008).

Several researchers have also noted that even toddlers can benefit from very simple programming aimed at teaching them emotion terms (Grazzani, Ornaghi, Agliati, & Brazzelli, 2016; Ornaghi, Grazzani, Cherubin, Conte, & Piralli, 2015; see also Fernández-Sánchez et al., 2015). After reading with their teacher books including an enriched emotional lexicon, and then conversing about them, children showed emotion knowledge and prosocial growth. The simplicity of this programming, and the young age of children benefitting from it are of interest.

Some programs feature work with parents, ranging from training parents on awareness, acceptance, and understanding of children's emotions and helping children to use words to describe how they feel (Havighurst, Wilson, Harley, Prior, & Kehoe, 2010), or using videotapes to stimulate group discussion, role-plays, and problem-solving, along with practice, rehearsal, and homework assignments (Webster-Stratton & Reid, 2007). Parents in Havighurst et al.'s intervention reported significant improvements in their own emotion awareness and regulation, increases in emotion teaching and emotion talk, and decreases in emotionally dismissive beliefs and behaviors. Child emotion knowledge improved, with reductions in behavior problems. Such programming has been extended to toddlers' parents (Lauw, Havighurst, Wilson, Harley, & Northam, 2014) and fathers (Wilson, Havighurst, & Harley, 2014). McClelland et al. (2017) call parent involvement a requirement, to involve multiple socializers of emotional competence.

Assessment of Emotional Competence

Given good programming, teachers will want to know where students stand on emotional competencies (Steed & Roach, 2017). Emotional competence assessment can highlight specific programming needs of children and classrooms, and show overall effects of programming (Denham, Ji, & Hamre, 2010). But any measure must meet certain standards (for details see Denham & Bassett, 2018; Kendziora, Weissberg, & Dusenbury, 2011). Finally, there needs to be a good reason *why* children are assessed, and there needs to be a system in place to *use* the resultant information. A data-based system could inform teachers how effective are their efforts in facilitating the social-emotional outcomes of their students (Steed & Roach, 2017). Useful emotional competence assessment tools can be found in Denham (2015), Denham, Ji, and Hamre (2010), and Humphrey et al. (2011). However, much work needs to be done to make assessments useful to educators and parents (McKown, 2017). The Collaborative for Academic, Social, and Emotional Learning Assessment Work Group has this goal.

Conclusions and Looking to the Future

Thus, continued research centering on preschoolers' emotional competence in the classroom is sorely needed. In particular, we need to extend the research on parents to the contributions made by early childhood teachers' socialization of emotion behaviors and attitudes. Further, beyond providing teachers with evidence-based tools to foster children's social and emotional development, we need to know how: (1) teachers' own emotional competence and beliefs about emotions vary, and why; (2) how classroom practices vary with teachers' emotion-related beliefs and emotional competence; (3) what kind of preservice/inservice experiences help teachers attend to their own emotional competence and cultivate positive attitudes toward an active role in socialization of emotion (Jennings & Greenberg, 2009). With greater understanding of teachers' mechanisms of emotion socialization, as well as maximization of teachers' own emotional competence, we could better promote children's optimal emotional competence development within early childhood education. As well, there are several higher-order needs that early childhood educators and applied developmental psychologists may help meet:

- To increase policy makers' awareness of research linking emotional competence and later social and school success. One promising effort is the Every Student Succeeds Act which is a federal effort to support social emotional learning through:
  - Increase funding for research and evidence-based practices
  - Expanding evidence-based practices to support innovation in policy and practice
  - Providing a broader approach to professional development and learning
  - Including supportive personnel in state and district school improvement plans
- Advocate for monetary resources for emotional competence-focused assessment and programming that are associated with the adaption and sustained use of strategies
- See that early childhood standards, curricula, and assessment tools incorporate developmentally appropriate attention to emotional competence
- Continue evaluating extant emotional competence programming for acceptability by families and teachers, treatment fidelity and maintenance, generalization and social validity of outcomes, and replication across investigators, early childhood education groups and settings, and across ethnic/ racially diverse groups (Joseph & Strain, 2003).

Moving in these directions will help to ensure that our efforts in this area will be efficacious. Working together, we can make sure that Darrell continues from his early excellent footing in emotional competence, to successfully meet the challenges of learning to read, write, calculate, problem solve, and sustain more complex relationships with others. We can help Jimmy, Tomas, and even Jessica to find better ways to interact so that their well-regulated behaviors support their social, emotional, and academic pursuits throughout their lives.

References

Ahn, H. J. (2005). Teachers' discussions of emotion in child care centers. *Early Childhood Education Journal, 32,* 237–242. doi:10.1007/s10643-004-1424-6

Ahn, H., & Stifter, C. (2006). Child care teachers' response to children's emotional expression. *Early Education and Development, 17,* 253–270. doi:10.1207/s15566935eed1702_3

Alonso-Alberca, N., Vergara, A. I., Fernández-Berrocal, P., Johnson, S. R., & Izard, C. E. (2012). The adaptation and validation of the emotion matching task for preschool children in Spain. *International Journal of Behavioral Development, 36*, 489–494. doi:10.1177/0165025412462154

Are, F., & Shaffer, A. (2016). Family emotion expressiveness mediates the relations between maternal emotion regulation and child emotion regulation. *Child Psychiatry & Human Development, 47*, 708–715. doi:10.1007/s10578-015-0605-4

Bailey, C. S., Denham, S. A., & Curby, T. W. (2013). Questioning as a component of scaffolding in predicting emotion knowledge in preschoolers. *Early Child Development and Care, 183*(2), 265–279. doi:10.1080/03004430.2012.671815

Banerjee, M. (1997). Hidden emotions: Preschoolers' knowledge of appearance-reality and emotion display rules. *Social Development, 15*, 107–132.

Bassett, H. H., Denham, S. A., Fettig, N. B., Curby, T. W., Mohtasham, M., & Austin, N. (2017). Temperament in the classroom: Children low in surgency are more sensitive to teachers' reactions to emotions. *International Journal of Behavioral Development, 41*, 4–14. doi:10.1177/0165025416644077

Bassett, H. H., Denham, S., Mincic, M., & Graling, K. (2012). The structure of preschoolers' emotion knowledge: Model equivalence and validity using a structural equation modeling approach. *Early Education & Development, 23*, 259–279. doi:10.1080/10409289.2012.630825

Bassett, H. H., Denham, S. A., Mohtasham, M., & Austin, N. (2016). *Teachers' book-reading styles and development of preschoolers' emotion knowledge: Validation of Book Readings for an Affective Classroom Education (BRACE) coding system.* Unpublished manuscript. Fairfax, VA: George Mason University.

Berlin, L. J., & Cassidy, J. (2003). Mothers' self-reported control of their preschool children's emotional expressiveness: A longitudinal study of associations with infant–mother attachment and children's emotion regulation. *Social Development, 12*, 478–495. doi:10.1111/1467-9507.00244

Berti, A. E., Garattoni, C., & Venturini, B. A. (2000). The understanding of sadness, guilt, and shame in 5-, 7-, and 9-year-old children. *Genetic, Social, and General Psychology Monographs, 126*, 293–318.

Bierman, K., Domitrovich, C., Nix, R., Gest, S., Welsh, J., Greenberg, M., ... & Gill, S. (2008). Promoting academic and social-emotional school readiness: The Head Start REDI program. *Child Development, 79*(6), 1802–1817. doi:10.1111/j.1467-8624.2008.01227.x

Blair, B. L., Perry, N. B., O'Brien, M., Calkins, S. D., Keane, S. P., & Shanahan, L. (2015). Identifying developmental cascades among differentiated dimensions of social competence and emotion regulation. *Developmental Psychology, 51*, 1062–1073. doi:10.1037/a0039472

Blankson, A. N., Weaver, J. M., Leerkes, E. M., O'Brien, M., Calkins, S. D., & Marcovitch, S. (2017). Cognitive and emotional processes as predictors of a successful transition into school. *Early Education and Development, 28*, 1–20. doi:10.1080/10409289.2016.1183434

Brackett, M. A., & Katulak, N. A. (2006). Emotional intelligence in the classroom: Skill-based training for teachers and students. In J. Ciarrochi & J. D. Mayer (Eds.), *Improving emotional intelligence: A practitioner's guide* (pp. 1–27). New York, NY: Taylor & Francis.

Brophy-Herb, H. E., Zajicek-Farber, M. L., Bocknek, E. L., McKelvey, L. M., & Stansbury, K. (2013). Longitudinal connections of maternal supportiveness and early emotion regulation to children's school readiness in low-income families. *Journal of the Society for Social Work and Research, 4*(1), 2–19. doi:10.5243/jsswr.2013.1

Brown, J. R., Donelan-McCall, N., & Dunn, J. (1996). Why talk about mental states? The significance of children's conversations with friends, siblings, and mothers. *Child Development, 67*, 836–849. doi:10.2307/1131864

Brownell, C. A., Svetlova, M., Anderson, R., Nichols, S. R., & Drummond, J. (2013). Socialization of early prosocial behavior: Parents' talk about emotions is associated with sharing and helping in toddlers. *Infancy, 18*, 91–119. doi:10.1111/j.1532-7078.2012.00125.x

Buettner, C. K., Hur, E. Y., Jeon, L., & Andrews, D. W. (2016). What are we teaching the teachers? Child development curricula in US higher education. *Child & Youth Care Forum, 45*, 155–175. doi:10.1007/s10566-015-9323-0

Calkins, S. D., & Mackler, J. S. (2011). Temperament, emotion regulation, and social development. In M. K. Underwood & L. H. Rosen (Eds.), *Social development: Relationships in infancy, childhood, and adolescence* (pp. 44–70). New York, NY: Guilford Press.

Camodeca, M., & Coppola, G. (2016). Bullying, empathic concern, and internalization of rules among preschool children: The role of emotion understanding. *International Journal of Behavioral Development, 40*, 459–465. doi:10.1177/0165025415607086

Cassidy, D. J., King, E. K., Wang, Y. C., Lower, J. K., & Kintner-Duffy, V. L. (2017). Teacher work environments are toddler learning environments: Teacher professional well-being, classroom emotional support, and toddlers' emotional expressions and behaviours. *Early Child Development and Care, 187*, 1666–1678. doi:10.1080/03004430.2016.1180516

Castro, V. L., Halberstadt, A. G., & Garrett-Peters, P. (2016). A three-factor structure of emotion understanding in third-grade children. *Social Development, 25*, 602–622. doi:10.1111/sode.12162

Chance, C., & Fiese, B. H. (1999). Gender-stereotyped lessons about emotion in family narratives. -*Narrative Inquiry, 9*, 243–255.

Chang, H., Shelleby, E. C., Cheong, J., & Shaw, D. S. (2012). Cumulative risk, negative emotionality, and emotion regulation as predictors of social competence in transition to school: A mediated moderation model. *Social Development, 21*, 780–800. doi:10.1111/j.1467-9507.2011.00648.x

Cho, H. J., & Lee, D-g. (2015). The mediating effect of mothers' emotional expressiveness in the relationship between their beliefs about children's emotion and the children's emotional regulation as it is perceived by their mothers. *Korean Journal of Child Studies, 36*(3), 1–18. doi:10.5723/KJCS.2015.36.3.1

Chobhthaigh, S. N., & Wilson, C. (2015). Children's understanding of embarrassment: Integrating mental time travel and mental state information. *British Journal of Developmental Psychology, 33*(3), 324–339. http://dx.doi.org.mutex.gmu.edu/10.1111/bjdp.12094

Cohen, J. S., & Mendez, J. L. (2009). Emotion regulation, language ability, and the stability of preschool children's peer play behavior. *Early Education and Development, 20*, 1016–1037. doi:10.1080/10409280903305716

Cole, P. M., Dennis, T. A., Smith-Simon, K. E., Cohen, L. H. (2009). Preschoolers' emotion regulation strategy understanding: Relations with emotion socialization and child self-regulation. *Social Development, 18*, 324–352. doi:10.1111/j.1467-9507.2008.00503.x

Cole, P. M., LeDonne, E. N., & Tan, P. Z. (2013). A longitudinal examination of maternal emotions in relation to young children's developing self-regulation. *Parenting, 13*, 113–132. doi:10.1080/15295192.2012.709152

Cole, P. M., Martin, S. E., & Dennis, T. A. (2004). Emotion regulation as a scientific construct: Methodological challenges and directions for child development research. *Child Development, 75*, 317–333. doi:10.1111/j.1467–8624.2004.00673.x

Çorapçı, F., Friedlmeier, W., Benga, O., Strauss, C., Pitica, I., & Susa, G. (2018). Cultural socialization of toddlers in emotionally charged situations. *Social Development*. Online only.

Crespo, L. M., Trentacosta, C. J., Aikins, D., & Wargo-Aikins, J. (2017). Maternal emotion regulation and children's behavior problems: The mediating role of child emotion regulation. *Journal of Child and Family Studies, 26*, 2797–2809. doi:10.1007/s10826-017-0791-8

Curby, T. W., Brock, L. L., & Hamre, B. K. (2013). Teachers' emotional support consistency predicts children's achievement gains and social skills. *Early Education & Development, 24*, 292–309. doi:10.1080/10409289.2012.665760

Curby, T. W., Brown, C. A., Bassett, H. H., & Denham, S. A. (2015). Associations between preschoolers' social-emotional competence and pre-literacy skills. *Infant and Child Development, 24*, 549–570. https://doi.org./10.1002/icd.1899

Cutting, A. L., & Dunn, J. (1999). Theory of mind, emotion understanding, language, and family background: Individual differences and interrelations. *Child Development, 70*, 853–865. doi:10.1111/1467–8624.00061

Davis, M., Suveg, C., & Shaffer, A. (2015). Maternal positive affect mediates the link between family risk and preschoolers' positive affect. *Child Psychiatry & Human Development, 46*, 167–175. doi:10.1007/s10578-014-0516-9

De Leersnyder, J., Boiger, M., & Mesquita, B. (2015). Cultural differences in emotions. *Emerging Trends in the Social and Behavioral Sciences: An Interdisciplinary, Searchable, and Linkable Resource.*

Deneault, J., & Ricard, M. (2013). Are emotion and mind understanding differently linked to young children's social adjustment? Relationships between behavioral consequences of emotions, false belief, and SCBE. *The Journal of Genetic Psychology: Research and Theory on Human Development, 174,* 88–116. doi:10.1080/00221325.2011.642028

Denham, S. A. (1997). "When I have a bad dream, Mommy holds me": Preschoolers' consequential thinking about emotions and social competence. *International Journal of Behavioral Development, 20,* 301–319.

Denham, S. A. (1998). *Emotional development in young children.* New York. NY: Guilford.

Denham, S. A. (2015). Assessment of social-emotional learning in educational contexts. In J. Durlak, C. E. Domitrovich, R. W. Weissberg, and T. P. Gullotta (Eds.), *The handbook of social and emotional learning* (pp. 285–300). New York: Guilford Press.

Denham, S. A., Bassett, H. H. (2018). Implications of preschooler's emotional competence in the classroom. In K. Keefer, J. D. A. Saklofske, and D. H. Parker (Eds.). *The Handbook of Emotional Intelligence in Education.* New York: Springer.

Denham, S. A., Bassett, H. H., & Miller, S. (2017). Early childhood teachers' socialization of emotion: Contextual and individual contributors. *Child and Youth Care Forum, 46,* 805–824. doi:10.1007/s10566-017-9409-y

Denham, S. A. Bassett, H. H., Mincic, M. M., Kalb, S. C., Way, E., Wyatt, T., & Segal, Y. (2012). Social-emotional learning profiles of preschoolers' early school success: A person-centered approach. *Learning and Individual Differences, 22,* 178–189. doi:10.1016/j.lindif.2011.05.001

Denham, S. A., & Bassett, H. H., Silva, R., Mortari, L., Plourde, S., Herndon, K., & Zinsser, K. (2016, July). *Preschool teachers' emotion socialization and child social-emotional behavior in two countries.* Poster presentation at the 24th Biennial Meeting of the International Society for the Study of Behavioral Development, Vilnius, Lithuania.

Denham, S. A., Bassett, H. H., Sirotkin, Y., & Zinsser, K. (2013). Head Start preschoolers' emotional positivity and emotion regulation predict their social-emotion behavior, classroom adjustment, and early school success. *National Head Start Association Dialog, 16*(2). Online.

Denham, S. A., Bassett, H. H., Thayer, S. K., Mincic, M., Sirotkin, Y. S., & Zinsser, K. (2012). Observing preschoolers' social-emotional behavior: Structure, foundations, and prediction of early school success. *Journal of Genetic Psychology, 173,* 246–278. doi:10.1080/00221325.2011.597457

Denham, S. A., Bassett, H. H., & Wyatt, T. (2010). Gender differences in the socialization of preschoolers' emotional competence. In A. Kennedy Root & S. A. Denham (Eds.), *The role of parent and child gender in the socialization of emotional competence* (pp. 29–50). *New Directions for Child and Adolescent Development.* San Francisco, CA: Jossey-Bass.

Denham, S. A., Bassett, H. H., & Wyatt, T. (2014). The socialization of emotional competence. In J. Grusec & P. Hastings (Eds.), *The handbook of socialization* (2nd ed., pp. 590–613). New York, NY: Guilford Press.

Denham, S. A., Bassett, H. H., & Zinsser, K. (2012). Early childhood teachers as socializers of young children's emotional competence. *Early Childhood Education Journal, 40,* 137–143. doi:10.1007/s10643-012-0504-2

Denham, S. A., Blair, K. A., DeMulder, E., Levitas, J., Sawyer, K. S., Auerbach-Major, S. T., et al. (2003). Preschoolers' emotional competence: Pathway to mental health? *Child Development, 74,* 238–256. doi:10.1111/1467-8624.00533

Denham, S. A., Blair, K. A., Schmidt, M. S., & DeMulder, E. (2002). Compromised emotional competence: Seeds of violence sown early? *American Journal of Orthopsychiatry, 72,* 70–82. doi:10.1037/0002-9432.72.1.70

Denham, S. A., Brown, C. A., & Domitrovich, C. (2010). "Plays nice with others": Social-emotional learning and academic success. In special issue, H. Teglasi (Ed.), *Overlaps between socio-emotional and academic development, Early Education and Development, 21,* 652–680.doi:10.10 80/10409289.2010.497450

Denham, S. A., & Burton, R. (1996). A social-emotional intervention for at-risk 4-year-olds. *Journal of School Psychology, 34,* 225–245. doi:10.1016/0022-4405(96)00013-1

Denham, S. A., & Burton, R. (2003). *Social and emotional prevention and intervention programming for preschoolers.* New York, NY: Kluwer-Plenum.

Denham, S. A., Caal, S., Bassett, H. H., Benga, O., & Geangu, E. (2004). Listening to parents: Cultural variations in the meaning of emotions and emotion socialization. *Cognitie Creier Comportament, 8,* 321–350.

Denham, S. A., Caverly, S., Schmidt, M., Blair, K., DeMulder, E., Caal, S., et al. (2002). Preschool understanding of emotions: Contributions to classroom anger and aggression. *Journal of Child Psychology and Psychiatry, 43,* 901–916. doi:10.1111/1469–7610.00139

Denham, S. A., Grant, S., & Hamada, H. A. (2002, June). *"I have two 1st teachers": Mother and teacher socialization of preschoolers' emotional and social competence.* Paper presented at the 7th Head Start Research Conference, Washington, DC.

Denham, S. A., & Grout, L. (1993). Socialization of emotion: Pathway to preschoolers' affect regulation. *Journal of Nonverbal Behavior, 17,* 215–227.doi:10.1007/BF00986120

Denham, S. A., Ji, P., & Hamre, B. (2010). *Compendium of social-emotional learning and associated assessment measures.* Chicago, IL: Collaborative for Academic, Social, and Emotional Learning.

Denham, S. A., & Kochanoff, A. T. (2003). Parental contributions to preschoolers' understanding of emotion. *Marriage & Family Review, 34*(3/4), 311–345.doi:10.1300/J002v34n03_06

Denham, S. A., Mason, T., Kochanoff, A., Neal, K., & Hamada, H. (2003). Emotional development. In Dawn Cavalieri, (Ed.), *International Encyclopedia of Marriage and Family Relationships, 2nd Edition* (pp. 419–426). New York: Macmillan.

Denham, S. A., Mitchell-Copeland, J., Strandberg, K., Auerbach, S., & Blair, K. (1997). Parental contributions to preschoolers' emotional competence: Direct and indirect effects. *Motivation and Emotion, 27,* 65–86. doi:10.1023/A:1024426431247

Denham, S. A., Zoller, D., & Couchoud, E. A. (1994). Socialization of preschoolers' understanding of emotion. *Developmental Psychology, 30,* 928–936. doi:10.1037/0012–1649.30.6.928

Di Maggio, R., Zappulla, C., & Pace, U. (2016). The relationship between emotion knowledge, emotion regulation and adjustment in preschoolers: A mediation model. *Journal of Child and Family Studies, 25,* 2626–2635. doi:10.1007/s10826-016-0409-6

Diaz, A., Eisenberg, N., Valiente, C., VanSchyndel, S., Spinrad, T. L., Berger, R. … & Southworth, J. (2017). Relations of positive and negative expressivity and effortful control to kindergarteners' student-teacher relationship, academic engagement, and externalizing problems at school. *Journal of Research in Personality, 67,* 3–14. https://doi.org/10.1016/j.jrp.2015.11.002

Doan, S. N., & Wang, Q. (2010). Maternal discussions of mental states and behaviors: Relations to emotion situation knowledge in European American and immigrant Chinese children. *Child Development, 81,* 1490–1503. doi:10.1111/j.1467–8624.2010.01487.x

Domitrovich, C. E., Cortes, R. C., & Greenberg, M. T. (2007). Improving young children's social and emotional competence: A randomized trial of the preschool "PATHS" curriculum. *The Journal of Primary Prevention, 28,* 67–91. doi:10.1007/s10935-007-0081-0

Drummond, J., Paul, E. F., Whitney, E. W., Hammond, S. I., & Brownell, C. A. (2014). "Here, there and everywhere:" Emotion and mental state talk in different social contexts predicts empathic helping in toddlers. *Frontiers in Psychology 5,* 361. doi:10.3389/fpsyg.2014.00361

Dunn, J. (1994). Understanding others and the social world: Current issues in developmental research and their relation to preschool experiences and practice. *Journal of Applied Developmental Psychology, 15,* 571–583. doi:10.1016/0193–3973(94)90023-X

Dunn, J., Brown, J. R., & Beardsall, L. A. (1991). Family talk about emotions, and children's later understanding of others' emotions. *Developmental Psychology, 27,* 448–455. doi:10.1037/0012–1649.27.3.448

Dunn, J., Cutting, A. L., & Fisher, N. (2002). Old friends, new friends: Predictors of children's perspective on their friends at school. *Child Development, 73*(2), 621–635. doi:10.1111/1467–9507.00091

Durbin, C. E. (2010). Validity of young children's self-reports of their emotion in response to structured laboratory tasks. *Emotion, 10,* 519–535. doi:10.1037/a0019008

Durlak, J. A., Weissberg, R. P., Dymnicki, A. B., Taylor, R. D., & Schellinger, K. B. (2011). The impact of enhancing students' social and emotional learning: A meta-analysis of school-based universal interventions. *Child Development, 82*, 405–432. doi:10.1111/j.1467-8624.2010.01564.x

Eisenberg, N., Cumberland, A., & Spinrad, T. L. (1998). Parental socialization of emotion. *Psychological Inquiry, 9*, 241–273. doi:10.1207/s15327965pli0904_1

Eisenberg, N., Fabes, R. A., & Murphy, B. C. (1996). Parents' reactions to children's negative emotions: Relations to children's social competence and comforting behavior. *Child Development, 67(5)*, 2227–2247. doi:10.2307/1131620

Eisenberg, N., Fabes, R. A., Shepard, S. A., Guthrie, I., Murphy, B. C., & Reiser, M. (1999). Parental reactions to children's negative emotions: Longitudinal relations to quality of children's social functioning. *Child Development, 70*, 513–534. doi:10.1111/1467–8624.00037

Eisenberg, N., Sadovsky, A., & Spinrad, T. L. (2005). Associations of emotion-related regulation with language skills, emotion knowledge, and academic outcomes. *New Directions for Child & Adolescent Development, 109*, 103–118. doi:10.1002/cd.143

Eisenberg, N., Valiente, C., Morris, A. S., Fabes, R. A., Cumberland, A., Reiser, M., … Losoya, S. (2003). Longitudinal relations among parental emotional expressivity, children's regulation, and quality of socioemotional function. *Developmental Psychology, 39(1)*, 3–19. doi:10.1037/0012–1649.39.1.3

Engle, J. M., & McElwain, N. L. (2011). Parental reactions to toddlers' negative emotions and child negative emotionality as correlates of problem behavior at the age of three. *Social Development, 20*, 251–271. doi:10.1111/j.1467–9507.2010.00583.x

Ersay, E. (2015). Preschool teachers' emotional awareness levels and their responses to children's negative emotions. *Procedia-Social and Behavioral Sciences, 191*, 1833–1837. doi:10.1016/j.sbspro.2015.04.220

Fabes, R., Eisenberg, N., Hanish, L. D., & Spinrad, T. L. (2001). Preschoolers' spontaneous emotion vocabulary: Relations to likeability. *Early Education and Development, 12(1)*, 11–28. doi:10.1207/s15566935eed1201_2

Fabes, R. A., Eisenberg, N., Nyman, M., & Michealieu, Q. (1991). Young children's appraisal of others spontaneous emotional reactions. *Developmental Psychology, 27*, 858–866. doi:10.1037/0012-1649.27.5.858

Fabes, R. A., Poulin, R. E., Eisenberg, N., & Madden-Derdich, D. A. (2003). The Coping with Children's Negative Emotions Scale (CCNES): Psychometric properties and relations with children's emotional competence. *Marriage & Family Review, 34(3/4)*, 285–310. doi:10.1300/J002v34n03_05

Feito, J. A. (1997). Children's beliefs about the social consequences of emotional expression. *Dissertation Abstracts International, 59(03B)*, 1411.

Fernández-Sánchez, M., Quintanilla, L., & Giménez-Dasí, M. (2015). Thinking emotions with two-year-old children: An educational programme to improve emotional knowledge in young preschoolers. *Cultura y Educación, 27*, 802–838. doi:10.1080/11356405.2015.1089385

Fields-Olivieri, M. A., Cole, P. M., & Maggi, M. C. (2017). Toddler emotional states, temperamental traits, and their interaction: Associations with mothers' and fathers' parenting. *Journal of Research in Personality, 67*, 106–119. doi:10.1016/j.jrp.2016.05.007

Fivush, R., Berlin, L. J., Sales, J. M., Mennuti-Washburn, J., & Cassidy, J. (2003). Functions of parent-child reminiscing about emotionally negative events. *Memory, 11*, 179–192. doi:10.1080/741938209

Fivush, R., Brotman, M. A., Buckner, J. P., & Goodman, S. H. (2000). Gender differences in parent-child emotion narratives. *Sex Roles, 42*, 233–253. doi:10.1023/A:1007091207068

Flannagan, D., & Perese, S. (1998). Emotional references in mother-daughter and mother-son dyads' conversations about school. *Sex Roles, 39*, 353–367. doi:10.1023/A:1018866908472

Friedlmeier, W., Çorapçi, F., & Cole, P. M. (2011). Emotion socialization in cross-cultural perspective. *Social and Personality Psychology Compass, 5*, 410–427. doi:10.1111/j.1751-9004.2011.00362.x

Garner, P. W. (2010). Emotional competence and its influences on teaching and learning. *Educational Psychology Review, 22*, 297–321. doi:10.1007/s10648-010-9129-4 doi:10.1007/s10648-010-9129-4

Garner, P. W., & Estep, K. M. (2001). Emotional competence, emotion socialization, and young children's peer-related social competence. *Early Education and Development, 12(1)*, 29–48. doi:10.1207/s15566935eed1201_3

Garner, P. W., Jones, D. C., Gaddy, G., & Rennie, K. (1997). Low income mothers' conversations about emotions and their children's emotional competence. *Social Development, 6*, 37–52. doi:10.1111/j.1467–9507.1997.tb00093.x

Garner, P. W., Robertson, S., & Smith, G. (1997). Preschool children's emotional expressions with peers: The roles of gender and emotion socialization. *Sex Roles: A Journal of Research, 36*, 675–691. doi:10.1023/A:1025601104859

Garner, P. W., & Spears, F. M. (2000). Emotion regulation in low-income preschoolers. *Social Development, 9*, 246–264. doi:10.1111/1467–9507.00122

Garner, P. W., & Waajid, B. (2008). The associations of emotion knowledge and teacher-child relationships to preschool children's school-related developmental competence. *Journal of Applied Developmental Psychology, 29(2)*, 89–100. doi:10.1016/j.appdev.2007.12.001

Garner, P. W., & Waajid, B. (2012). Emotion knowledge and self-regulation as predictors of preschoolers' cognitive ability, classroom behavior, and social competence. *Journal of Psychoeducational Assessment, 30*, 330–343. doi:10.1177/0734282912449441

Gilliom, M., Shaw, D. S., Beck, J. E., Schonberg, M. A., & Lukon, J. L. (2002). Anger regulation in disadvantaged preschool boys: Strategies, antecedents, and the development of self-control. *Developmental Psychology, 38(2)*, 222–235. doi:10.1037/0012–1649.38.2.222

Gnepp, J. (1989). Personalized inferences of emotions and appraisals: Component processes and correlates. *Developmental Psychology, 25*, 277–288. doi:10.1037/0012–1649.25.2.277

Gnepp, J., & Gould, M. E. (1985). The development of personalized inferences: Understanding other people's emotional reactions in light of their prior experiences. *Child Development, 56*, 1455–1464. doi:10.2307/1130465

Gnepp, J., & Hess, D. L. (1986). Children's understanding of verbal and facial display rules. *Developmental Psychology, 22(1)*, 103–108. doi:10.1037/0012–1649.22.1.103

Gnepp, J., Klayman, J., & Trabasso, T. (1982). A hierarchy of information sources for inferring emotional reactions. *Journal of Experimental Child Psychology, 33*, 111–123. doi:10.1016/0022–0965(82)90009-1

Gnepp, J., McKee, E., & Domanic, J. A. (1987). Children's use of situational information to infer emotion: Understanding emotionally equivocal situations. *Developmental Psychology, 23*, 114–123. doi:10.1037/0012–1649.23.1.114

Graziano, P. A., Reavis, R. D., Keane, S. P., & Calkins, S. D. (2007). The role of emotion regulation in children's early academic success. *Journal of School Psychology, 45(1)*, 3–19. doi:10.1016/j.jsp.2006.09.002

Grazzani, I., Ornaghi, V., Agliati, A., & Brazzelli, E. (2016). How to foster toddlers' mental-state talk, emotion understanding, and prosocial behavior: A conversation-based intervention at nursery school. *Infancy, 21*, 199–227. doi:10.1111/infa.12107

Gross, D., & Harris, P. (1988). Understanding false beliefs about emotion. *International Journal of Behavioral Development, 11*, 475–488.

Gross, J. J., & Thompson, R. A. (2007). Emotion regulation: Conceptual foundations. In J. J. Gross (Ed.), *Handbook of emotion regulation* (pp. 3–24). New York, NY: Guilford Press.

Halberstadt, A. G., Denham, S. A., & Dunsmore, J. (2001). Affective social competence. *Social Development, 10*, 79–119. doi:10.1111/1467–9507.00150

Halberstadt, A. G., Dunsmore, J. C., Bryant Jr., A., Parker, A. E., Beale, K. S., & Thompson, J. A. (2013). Development and validation of the Parents' Beliefs About Children's Emotions Questionnaire. *Psychological Assessment, 25*, 1195–1210.

Halberstadt, A. G., Thompson, J. A., Parker, A. E., & Dunsmore, J. C. (2008). Parents' emotion-related beliefs and behaviours in relation to children's coping with the 11 September 2001 terrorist attacks. *Infant and Child Development, 17*, 557–580. doi:10.1002/icd.569

Harris, P. (2008). Children's understanding of emotions. In M. Lewis, J. M. Haviland-Jones, & L. F. Barrett (Eds.), *Handbook of emotions* (pp. 320–331). New York City, NY: Guilford Press.

Havighurst, S. S., Wilson, K. R., Harley, A. E., Prior, M. R., & Kehoe, C. (2010).Tuning in to kids: Improving emotion socialization practices in parents of preschool children-findings from a community trial. *Journal of Child Psychology and Psychiatry, 51*, 1342–1350. doi:10.1111/j.1469–7610.2010.02303.x

Heinze, J. E., Miller, A. L., Seifer, R., Dickstein, S., & Locke, R. L. (2015). Emotion knowledge, loneliness, negative social experiences, and internalizing symptoms among low-income preschoolers. *Social Development, 24*, 240–265. doi:10.1111/sode.12083

Hernández, M. M., Eisenberg, N., Valiente, C., Diaz, A., VanSchyndel, S. K., Berger, R. H., ... & Southworth, J. (2017). Concurrent and longitudinal associations of peers' acceptance with emotion and effortful control in kindergarten. *International journal of behavioral development, 41*, 30–40. doi:10.1177/0165025415608519

Hernández, M. M., Eisenberg, N., Valiente, C., Spinrad, T. L., VanSchyndel, S. K., Diaz, A., ... & Southworth, J. (2017). Observed emotions as predictors of quality of kindergartners' social relationships. *Social Development, 26*, 21–39. doi:10.1111/sode.12179

Hernández, M. M., Eisenberg, N., Valiente, C., VanSchyndel, S. K., Spinrad, T. L., Silva, K. M., ... & Southworth, J. (2016). Emotional expression in school context, social relationships, and academic adjustment in kindergarten. *Emotion, 16*, 553–566. doi:10.1037/emo0000147

Herndon, K. J., Bailey, C. S., Shewark, E. A., Denham, S. A., & Bassett, H. H. (2013). Preschoolers' emotion expression and regulation: Relations with school adjustment. The *Journal of Genetic Psychology, 174*, 642–663. doi:10.1080/00221325.2012.759525

Howes, C. (2000). Social-emotional classroom climate in child care child-teacher relationships and children's second grade peer relations. *Social Development, 9*, 191–204. doi:10.1111/1467–9507.00119

Hudson, A., & Jacques, S. (2014). Put on a happy face! Inhibitory control and socioemotional knowledge predict emotion regulation in 5-to 7-year-olds. *Journal of Experimental Child Psychology, 123*, 36–52. doi:10.1016/j.jecp.2014.01.012

Humphrey, N. (2013). *Social and emotional learning: A critical appraisal.* London: Sage. doi:10.4135/9781446288603

Humphrey, N., Kalambouka, A., Wigelsworth, M., Lendrum, A., Deighton, J., & Wolpert, M. (2011). Measures of social and emotional skills for children and young people: A systematic review. *Educational and Psychological Measurement, 71*, 617–637. doi:10.1177/0013164410382896

Izard, C. E. (2002). Emotion knowledge and emotion utilization facilitate school readiness. *SRCD Social Policy Report, XVI*(3), 8.

Izard, C. E., Fine, S., Schultz, D., Mostow, A., Ackerman, B., & Youngstrom, E. (2001). Emotions knowledge as a predictor of social behavior and academic competence in children at risk. *Psychological Science, 12*, 18–23. doi:10.1111/1467–9280.00304

Izard, C. E., King, K. A., Trentacosta, C. J., Morgan, J. K., Laurenceau, J., Krauthamer-Ewing, E. S., & Finlon, K. J. (2008). Accelerating the development of emotion competence in head start children: Effects on adaptive and maladaptive behavior. *Development and Psychopathology, 20*, 369–397. doi:10.1017/S0954579408000175

Jennings, P. A., & Greenberg, M. T. (2009). The prosocial classroom: Teacher social and emotional competence in relation to student and classroom outcomes. *Review of Educational Research, 79*(1), 491–525. doi:10.3102/0034654308325693

Jeon, L., Hur, E., & Buettner, C. K. (2016). Child-care chaos and teachers' responsiveness: The indirect associations through teachers' emotion regulation and coping. *Journal of School Psychology, 59*, 83–96. doi:10.1016/j.jsp.2016.09.006

Jones, D. E., Greenberg, M., & Crowley, M. (2015). Early social-emotional functioning and public health: The relationship between kindergarten social competence and future wellness. *American Journal of Public Health, 105*, 2283–2290. doi:10.2105/AJPH.2015.302630

Joseph, G. E., & Strain, P. S. (2003). Comprehensive evidence-based social-emotional curricula for young children: An analysis of efficacious

adoption potential. *Topics in Early Childhood Special Education, 23*(2), 65–76. doi:10.1177/02711214030230020201

Josephs, I. (1994). Display rule behavior and understanding in preschool children. *Journal of Nonverbal Behavior, 18*, 301–326. doi:10.1007/BF02172291

Kanamaru, T., & Muto, T. (2004). Individual differences in emotional regulation of two-year old children during interactions with mothers. *Japanese Journal of Developmental Psychology, 15*, 183–194.

Kanaya, Y., Nakamura, C., & Miyake, K. (1989). Cross-cultural study of expressive behavior of mothers in response to their 5-month-old infants' different emotion expression. *Research and Clinical Center for Child Development, 11*, 25–31.

Karalus, S. P., Herndon, K., Bassett, H. H., & Denham, S. A. (2016). *Child-care teachers' socialization practices and beliefs on children's social emotional competence and the moderating contribution of classroom age.* Unpublished manuscript. Fairfax, VA: George Mason University.

Kemeny, M. E., Foltz, C., Cavanagh, J. F., Cullen, M., Giese-Davis, J., Jennings, P., ... & Ekman, P. (2012). Contemplative/emotion training reduces negative emotional behavior and promotes prosocial responses. *Emotion, 12*, 338–350. doi:10.1037/a0026118

Kendziora, K., Weissberg, R. P., Ji, P., & Dusenbury, L. A. (2011). *Strategies for social and emotional learning: Preschool and elementary grade student learning standards and assessment.* Newton, MA: National Center for Mental Health Promotion and Youth Violence Prevention, Education Development Center, Inc.

Kestenbaum, R., & Gelman, S. (1995). Preschool children's identification and understanding of mixed emotions. *Cognitive Development, 10*, 443–458. doi:10.1016/0885–2014(95)90006-3

Kiliç, S. (2015). Emotional competence and emotion socialization in preschoolers: The viewpoint of preschool teachers. *Educational Sciences: Theory and Practice, 15*, 1007–1020. doi:10.12738/estp.2015.4.2529

King, E. K., Johnson, A. V., Cassidy, D. J., Wang, Y. C., Lower, J. K., & Kintner-Duffy, V. L. (2016). Preschool teachers' financial well-being and work time supports: Associations with children's emotional expressions and behaviors in classrooms. *Early Childhood Education Journal, 44*, 545–553. doi:10.1007/s10643-015-0744-z

Kojima, Y. (2000). Maternal regulation of sibling interactions in the preschool years: Observational study of Japanese families. *Child Development, 71*, 1640–1647.

Kramer, T. J., Calderella, P., Christenson, L., & Shatzer, R. H. (2010). Social and emotional learning in the kindergarten classroom: Evaluation of the *Strong Start* curriculum. *Early Childhood Education Journal, 37*, 303–309. doi:10.1007/s10643-009-0354-8

Lagattuta, K. (2007). Thinking about the future because of the past: Young children's knowledge about the causes of worry and preventative decisions. *Child Development, 78*(5), 1492–1509. doi:10.1111/j.1467–8624.2007.01079.x

Lagattuta, K., & Wellman, H. (2002). Differences in early parent-child conversations about negative versus positive emotions: Implications for the development of psychological understanding. *Developmental Psychology, 38*(4), 564–580. doi:10.1037/0012–1649.38.4.564

Laible, D., Panfile Murphy, T., & Augustine, M. (2013). Constructing emotional and relational understanding: The role of mother–child reminiscing about negatively valenced events. *Social Development, 22*, 300–318. doi:10.1111/sode.12022

Larson, J., Yen, M., & Fireman, G. (2007). Children's understanding and experience of mixed emotions. *Psychological Science, 18*(2), 186–191 doi:10.1111/j.1467–9280.2007.01870.x

Lauw, M. S., Havighurst, S. S., Wilson, K. R., Harley, A. E., & Northam, E. A. (2014). Improving parenting of toddlers' emotions using an emotion coaching parenting program: A pilot study of tuning in to toddlers. *Journal of Community Psychology, 42*(2), 169–175. doi:10.1002/jcop.21602

Leerkes, E., Paradise, M., O'Brien, M., Calkins, S., & Lange, G. (2008). Emotion and cognition processes in preschool children. *Merrill-Palmer Quarterly, 54*(1), 102–124. doi:10.1353/mpq.2008.0009

Liao, Z., Li, Y., & Su, Y. (2014). Emotion understanding and reconciliation in overt and relational conflict scenarios among preschoolers.

International Journal of Behavioral Development, 38, 111–117. doi:10.1177/0165025413512064

Liew, J., Eisenberg, N., Losoya, S. H., Fabes, R. A., Guthrie, I. K., & Murphy, B. C. (2003). Children's physiological indices of empathy and their socioemotional adjustment: Does caregivers' expressivity matter? *Journal of Family Psychology, 17*(4), 584–597. doi:10.1037/0893–3200.17.4.584

Lindsey, E. W. (2017). Mutual positive emotion with peers, emotion knowledge, and preschoolers' peer acceptance. *Social Development, 26*, 349–366. doi:10.1111/sode.12201

Locke, R. L., Davidson, R. J., Kalin, N. H., & Goldsmith, H. H. (2009). Children's context inappropriate anger and salivary cortisol. *Developmental Psychology, 45*, 1284–1297. doi:10.1037/a0015975

López-Pérez, B., Gummerum, M., Wilson, E., & Dellaria, G. (2017). Studying children's intrapersonal emotion regulation strategies from the process model of emotion regulation. *The Journal of Genetic Psychology, 178*, 73–88. doi:10.1080/00221325.2016.1230085

Louie, J. Y., Wang, S. W., Fung, J., & Lau, A. (2015). Children's emotional expressivity and teacher perceptions of social competence: A cross-cultural comparison. *International Journal of Behavioral Development, 39*, 497–507. doi:10.1177/0165025414548775

Luebbe, A. M., Kiel, E. J., & Buss, K. A. (2011). Toddlers' context-varying emotions, maternal responses to emotions, and internalizing behaviors. *Emotion, 11*, 697–703. doi:10.1037/a0022994

Lugo-Candelas, C., Flegenheimer, C., McDermott, J. M., & Harvey, E. (2017). Emotional understanding, reactivity, and regulation in young children with ADHD symptoms. *Journal of Abnormal Child Psychology, 45*, 1297–1310. doi:10.1007/s10802-016-0244-7

Martin, S., Clements, M., & Crnic, K. (2002). Maternal emotions during mother-toddler interaction: Parenting in affective context. *Parenting, 2*(2), 105–126. doi:10.1207/S15327922PAR0202_02

Martin, S. E., Williamson, L. R., Kurtz-Nelson, E. C., & Boekamp, J. R. (2015). Emotion understanding (and misunderstanding) in clinically referred preschoolers: The role of child language and maternal depressive symptoms. *Journal of Child and Family Studies, 24*, 24–37. doi:10.1007/s10826-013-9810-6

Martins, E. C., Osório, A., Veríssimo, M., & Martins, C. (2016). Emotion understanding in preschool children: The role of executive functions. *International Journal of Behavioral Development, 40*, 1–10. doi:10.1177/0165025414556096

McClelland, M. M., Tominey, S. L., Schmitt, S. A., & Duncan, R. (2017). SEL interventions in early childhood. *The Future of Children, 27*, 33–47.

McKown, C. (2017). Social-emotional assessment, performance, and standards. *The Future of Children, 27*, 157–178.

McLeod, B. D., Sutherland, K. S., Martinez, R. G., Conroy, M. A., Snyder, P. A., & Southam-Gerow, M. A. (2017). Identifying common practice elements to improve social, emotional, and behavioral outcomes of young children in early childhood classrooms. *Prevention Science, 18*(2), 204–213.

Meyer, S., Raikes, H. A., Virmani, E. A., Waters, S., & Thompson, R. A. (2014). Parent emotion representations and the socialization of emotion regulation in the family. *International Journal of Behavioral Development, 38*, 164–173. doi:10.1177/0165025413519014

Miller, A. L., Gouley, K. K., Seifer, R., Dickstein, S., & Shields, A. (2004). Emotions and behaviors in the Head Start classroom: Associations among observed dysregulation, social competence, and preschool adjustment. *Early Education and Development, 15*, 147–165. doi:10.1207/s15566935eed1502_2

Miller, A. L., Seifer, R., Stroud, L., Sheinkopf, S. J., & Dickstein, S. (2006). Biobehavioral indices of emotion regulation relate to school attitudes, motivation, and behavior problems in a low-income preschool sample. *Annals of the New York Academy of Science, 1094*, 325–329. doi:10.1196/annals.1376.043

Mirabile, S. P., Scaramella, L. V., Sohr-Preston, S. L., & Robison, S. D. (2009). Mothers' socialization of emotion regulation: The moderating role of children's negative emotional reactivity. *Child & youth care forum, 38*(1), 19–37. doi:10.1007/s10566-008-9063–5

Misailidi, P. (2006). Young children's display rule knowledge: Understanding the distinction between apparent and real emotions and the motives

underlying the use of display rules. *Social Behavior and Personality, 34*, 1285–1296. doi:10.2224/sbp.2006.34.10.1285

Morgan, J. K., Izard, C. E., & Hyde, C. (2014). Emotional reactivity and regulation in Head Start children: Links to ecologically valid behaviors and internalizing problems. *Social Development, 23*(2), 250–266. doi:10.1111/sode.12049

Morgan, J. K., Izard, C. E., & King, K. A. (2010). Construct validity of the emotion matching task: Preliminary evidence for convergent and criterion validity of a new emotion knowledge measure for young children. *Social Development, 19*, 52–70. doi:10.1111/j.1467–9507.2008.00529.x

Morris, A. S., Silk, J. S., Morris, M. D., Steinberg, L., Aucoin, K. J., & Keyes, A. W. (2011). The influence of mother-child emotion regulation strategies on children's expression of anger and sadness. *Developmental Psychology, 47*, 213–225. doi:10.1037/a0021021

Morris, A. S., Silk, J. S., Steinberg, L., Terranova, A. M., & Kithakye, M. (2010). Concurrent and longitudinal links between children's externalizing behavior in school and observed anger regulation in the mother-child dyad. *Journal of Psychopathology and Behavioral Assessment, 32*, 48–56. doi:10.1007/s10862-009-9166-9

Morris, C. S., Denham, S. A., Bassett, H. H., & Curby, T. (2013). Relations among teachers' emotion socialization beliefs and practices, and preschoolers' emotional competence. *Early Education and Development, 24*, 979–999. doi:10.1080/10409289.2013.825186

Nakamichi, K. (2017). Differences in young children's peer preference by inhibitory control and emotion regulation. *Psychological Reports, 120*(5), 805–823.

Nakamura, M., Buck, R., & Kenny, D. A. (1990). Relative contributions of expression behavior and contextual information to the judgment of the emotional state of another. *Journal of Personality and Social Psychology, 59*, 1032–1039. doi:10.1037/0022–3514.59.5.1032

Newland, R. P., & Crnic, K. A. (2011). Mother–child affect and emotion socialization processes across the late preschool period: Predictions of emerging behaviour problems. *Infant and Child Development, 20*, 371–388. doi:10.1002/icd.729

Nix, R. L., Bierman, K. L., Domitrovich, C. E., & Gill, S. (2013). Promoting children's social-emotional skills in preschool can enhance academic and behavioral functioning in kindergarten: Findings from Head Start REDI. *Early Education & Development, 24*, 1000–1019. doi:10.1080/10409289.2013.825565

Ornaghi, V., Grazzani, I., Cherubin, E., Conte, E., & Piralli, F. (2015). 'Let's talk about emotions!'. The effect of conversational training on preschoolers' emotion comprehension and prosocial orientation. *Social Development, 24*, 166–183. doi:10.1111/sode.12091

Orta, I. M., Çorapçı, F., Yagmurlu, B., & Aksan, N. (2013). The mediational role of effortful control and emotional dysregulation in the link between maternal responsiveness and Turkish preschoolers' social competency and externalizing symptoms. *Infant and Child Development, 22*, 459–479. doi:10.1002/icd.1806

Parker, A. E., Mathis, E. T., & Kupersmidt, J. B. (2013). How is this child feeling? Preschool-aged children's ability to recognize emotion in faces and body poses. *Early Education & Development, 24*, 188–211. doi:10.1080/10409289.2012.657536

Pekrun, R., & Linnenbrink-Garcia, L. (2012). Academic emotions and student engagement. In S. L. Christenson, A. L. Reschly & C. Wylie (Eds.), *Handbook of research on student engagement* (pp. 259–282). Boston, MA: Springer.

Penela, E. C., Walker, O. L., Degnan, K. A., Fox, N. A., & Henderson, H. A. (2015). Early behavioral inhibition and emotion regu.altion: Pathways toward social competence in middle childhood. *Child Development, 86*, 1227–1240. doi:10.1111/cdev.12384

Peng, M., Johnson, C. N., Pollock, J., Glasspool, R., & Harris, P. L. (1992). Training young children to acknowledge mixed emotions. *Cognition and Emotion, 6*, 387–401. doi:10.1080/02699939208409693

Pollak, S. D., Cicchetti, D., Hornung, K., & Reed, A. (2000). Recognizing emotion in faces: Developmental effects of child abuse and neglect. *Developmental Psychology, 36*, 679–688. doi:10.1037/0012–1649.36.5.679

Pons, F., Harris, P. L., & de Rosnay, M. (2004). Emotion comprehension between 3 and 11 years: Developmental periods and hierarchical organization. *European Journal of Developmental Psychology, 1*, 127–152. doi:10.1080/17405620344000022

Ren, Y., Wyver, S., Xu Rattanasone, N., & Demuth, K. (2016). Social competence and language skills in Mandarin–English bilingual preschoolers: The moderation effect of emotion regulation. *Early Education and Development, 27*(3), 303–317.

Roben, C. K., Cole, P. M., & Armstrong, L. M. (2013). Longitudinal relations among language skills, anger expression, and regulatory strategies in early childhood. *Child Development, 84*, 891–905. doi:10.1111/cdev.12027

Romano, E., Babchishin, L., Pagani, L. S., & Kohen, D. (2010). School readiness and later achievement: Replication and extension using a nationwide Canadian survey. *Developmental Psychology, 46*, 995–1007. doi:10.1037/a0018880

Rubin, K. H., Burgess, K. B., Dwyer, K. M., & Hastings, P. (2003). Predicting preschoolers' externalizing behaviors from toddler temperament, conflict, and maternal negativity. *Developmental Psychology, 39*(1), 164–176. doi:10.1037/0012–1649.39.1.164

Russell, J. A., & Paris, F. A. (1994). Do children acquire concepts for complex emotions abruptly? *International Journal of Behavioral Development, 17*(2), 349–365. doi:10.1177/016502549401700207

Rydell, A.-M., Berlin, L., & Bohlin, G. (2003). Emotionality, emotion regulation, and adaptation among 5- to 8-year-old children. *Emotion, 3*(1), 30–47. doi:10.1037/1528–3542.3.1.30

Saarni, C. (1999). *Children's emotional competence*. New York, NY: Guilford Press.

Saarni, C. (2001). Epilogue: Emotion communication and relationship context. *International Journal of Behavioral Development, 25*, 354–356.

Salmon, K., & Reese, E. (2016). The benefits of reminiscing with young children. *Current Directions in Psychological Science, 25*, 233–238. doi:10.1177/0963721416655100

Sawada, T. (1997). Development of children's understanding of emotional dissemblance in another person. *Japanese Journal of Educational Psychology, 45*, 50–59.

Schonert-Reichl, K. A., Kitil, M. J., & Hanson-Peterson, J. (2017). *To reach the students, teach the teachers: A national scan of teacher preparation and social and emotional learning. A report prepared for the Collaborative for Academic, Social, and Emotional Learning (CASEL)*. Vancouver, BC: University of British Columbia.

Schultz, D., Izard, C. E., & Ackerman, B. P. (2000). Children's anger attribution bias: Relations to family environment and social adjustment. *Social Development, 9*, 284–301. doi:10.1111/1467–9507.00126

Schultz, D., Izard, C. E., Ackerman, B. P., & Youngstrom, E. A. (2001). Emotion knowledge in economically disadvantaged children: Self-regulatory antecedents and relations to social difficulties and withdrawal. *Development & Psychopathology, 13*, 53–67. doi:10.1017/S0954579401001043

Seidenfeld, A. M., Johnson, S. R., Cavadel, E. W., & Izard, C. E. (2014). Theory of mind predicts emotion knowledge development in Head Start children. *Early Education and Development, 25*, 933–948. doi:10.1080/10409289.2014.883587

Sette, S., Bassett, H. H., Baumgardner, E., & Denham, S. A. (2015). Structure and validity of affect knowledge test in a sample of Italian preschoolers. *Journal of Genetic Psychology, 176*, 330–347. doi:10.1080/00221325.2015.1075466

Sette, S., Baumgartner, E., Laghi, F., & Coplan, R. J. (2016). The role of emotion knowledge in the links between shyness and children's socioemotional functioning at preschool. *British Journal of Developmental Psychology, 34*, 471–488. doi:10.1111/bjdp.12144

Shin, N., Vaughn, B. E., Akers, V., Kim, M., Stevens, S., Krzysik, L., … Korth, B. (2011). Are happy children socially successful? Testing a central premise of positive psychology in a sample of preschool children. *The Journal of Positive Psychology, 6*, 355–367. doi:10.1080/17439760.2011.584549

Son, S. H. C., & Chang, Y. E. (2018). Childcare experiences and early school outcomes: The mediating role of executive functions and emotionality. *Infant and Child Development, 27*(4), e2087. doi:10.1002/icd.2087

Spivak, A. L., & Farran, D. C. (2016). Predicting first graders' social competence from their preschool classroom interpersonal context. *Early Education and Development, 27*, 735–750. doi:10.1080/10409289.2016.1138825

Spritz, B. L., Sandberg, E. H., Maher, E., & Zajdel, R. T. (2010). Models of emotion skills and social competence in the Head Start classroom. *Early Education and Development, 21*, 495–516. doi:10.1080/10409280902895097

Steed, E. A., & Roach, A. T. (2017). Childcare Providers' use of practices to promote young children's social–emotional competence. *Infants & Young Children, 30*(2), 162–171. doi:10.1097/IYC.0000000000000092

Sullivan, M. W., Bennett, D. S., Carpenter, K., & Lewis, M. (2008). Emotion knowledge in young neglected children. *Child Maltreatment, 13*, 301–306. doi:10.1177/1077559507313725

Swartz, R. A., & McElwain, N. L. (2012). Preservice teachers' emotion-related regulation and cognition: Associations with teachers' responses to children's emotions in early childhood classrooms. *Early Education & Development, 23*, 202–226. doi:10.1080/10409289.2012.619392

Taylor, R. D., Oberle, E., Durlak, J. A., & Weissberg, R. P. (2017). Promoting positive youth development through school-based social and emotional learning interventions: A meta-analysis of follow-up effects. *Child Development, 88*, 1156–1171. doi:10.1111/cdev.12864

Taylor, Z. E., Eisenberg, N., VanSchyndel, S. K., Eggum-Wilkens, N. D., & Spinrad, T. L. (2014). Children's negative emotions and ego-resiliency: Longitudinal relations with social competence. *Emotion, 14*, 397–406. doi:10.1037/a0035079

Torres, M. M., Domitrovich, C. E., & Bierman, K. L. (2015). Preschool interpersonal relationships predict kindergarten achievement: Mediated by gains in emotion knowledge. *Journal of Applied Developmental Psychology, 39*, 44–52. doi:10.1016/j.appdev.2015.04.008

Trentacosta, C., & Izard, C. (2007). Kindergarten children's emotion competence as a predictor of their academic competence in first grade. *Emotion, 7*(1), 77–88. doi:10.1037/1528–3542.7.1.77

Ujiie, T. (1997). How do Japanese mothers treat children's negativism? *Journal of Applied Developmental Psychology, 18*, 467–483. doi:10.1016/S0193–3973(97)90022-8

Ulrich, F., & Petermann, F. (2017). Parental emotion dysregulation as a risk factor for child development. *Kindheit und Entwicklung, 26*(3), 133–146. doi:10.1026/0942-5403/a000225

Valiente, C. (2004). The relations of mothers' negative expressivity to children's experience and expression of negative emotion. *Journal of Applied Developmental Psychology, 25*(2), 215–235. doi:10.1016/j.appdev.2004.02.006

Voltmer, K., & von Salisch, M. (2017). Three meta-analyses of children's emotion knowledge and their school success. *Learning and Individual Differences, 59*, 107–118. doi:10.1016/j.lindif.2017.08.006

Waajid, B., Garner, P. W., & Owen, J. E. (2013). Infusing social emotional learning into the teacher education curriculum. *The International Journal of Emotional Education, 5*, 31–48.

Walle, E. A., & Campos, J. J. (2012). Interpersonal responding to discrete emotions: A functionalist approach to the development of affect specificity. *Emotion Review, 4*, 413–422. doi:10.1177/1754073912445812

Watanabe, N. (2015). *Parental socialization of emotion in Japan: Contribution to preschoolers' emotion knowledge* (Doctoral dissertation). George Mason University, Fairfax, VA.

Webster-Stratton, C., & Reid, M. J. (2003). Treating conduct problems and strengthening social and emotional competence in young children: The Dina Dinosaur Program. *Journal of Emotional and Behavioral Disorders, 2*, 130–143. doi:10.1177/106342660301100030101

Webster-Stratton, C., & Reid, M. J. (2004). Strengthening social and emotional competence in young children – The foundation for early school readiness and success: Incredible Years Classroom Social Skills and Problem-Solving Curriculum. *Infants and Young Children, 17*, 96–113. doi:10.1097/00001163–200404000-00002

Webster-Stratton, C., & Reid, M. J. (2007). Incredible Years parents and teachers training series: A head start partnership to promote social competence and prevent conduct problems. In P. Tolan, J. Szapocznik, & S. Sambrano,

Soledad (Eds.), *Preventing youth substance abuse: Science-based programs for children and adolescents* (pp. 67–88). Washington, DC: American Psychological Association. doi:10.1037/11488-003

Widen, S. C., & Russell, J. A. (2008). Children acquire emotion categories gradually. *Cognitive Development, 23,* 291–312. doi:10.1016/j.cogdev.2008.01.002

Widen, S. C., & Russell, J. A. (2010). Differentiation in preschooler's categories of emotion. *Emotion, 10,* 651–661. doi:10.1037/a0019005

Wilson, K. R., Havighurst, S. S., & Harley, A. E. (2014). Dads tuning in to kids: Piloting a new parenting program targeting fathers' emotion coaching skills. *Journal of Community Psychology, 42,* 162–168. doi:10.1002/jcop.21601

Wintre, M., & Vallance, D. D. (1994). A developmental sequence in the comprehension of emotions: Multiple emotions, intensity and valence. *Developmental Psychology, 30,* 509–514. doi:10.1037/0012–1649.30.4.509

Woods, S. E., Menna, R., & McAndrew, A. J. (2017). The mediating role of emotional control in the link between parenting and young children's physical aggression. *Early Child Development and Care, 187,* 1157–1169. doi:10.1080/03004430.2016.1159204

Wong, M. S., Diener, M. L., & Isabella, R. A. (2008). Parents' emotion related beliefs and behaviors and child grade: Associations with children's perceptions of peer competence. *Journal of Applied Developmental Psychology, 29,* 175–186. doi:10.1016/j.appdev.2008.02.003

Wong, M. S., McElwain, N. L., & Halberstadt, A. G. (2009). Parent, family, and child characteristics: Associations with mother-and father-reported emotion socialization practices. *Journal of Family Psychology, 23,* 452–463. doi:10.1037/a0015552

Wu, X., Wang, Y., & Liu, A. (2017). Maternal emotional expressiveness affects preschool children's development of knowledge of display rules. *Social Behavior and Personality: An International Journal, 45*(1), 93–103. doi:10.2224/sbp.5783

Yelinek, J., & Grady, J. S. (2017). 'Show me your mad faces!' Preschool teachers' emotion talk in the classroom. *Early Child Development and Care,* Online First. doi:10.1080/03004430.2017.1363740

Yeo, K., Frydenberg, E., Northam, E., & Deans, J. (2014). Coping with stress among preschool children and associations with anxiety level and controllability of situations. *Australian Journal of Psychology, 66,* 93–101. doi:10.1111/ajpy.12047

Zahn-Waxler, C., Friedman, R. J., Cole, P. M., Mizuta, I., & Hiruma, N. (1996). Japanese and United States preschool children's responses to conflict and distress. *Child Development, 67,* 2462–2477. doi:10.2307/1131634

Zembylas, M. (2007). Emotional ecology: The intersection of emotional knowledge and pedagogical content knowledge in teaching. *Teaching and Teacher Education, 23,* 355–367. doi:10.1016/j.tate.2006.12.002

Zinsser, K. M., Denham, S. A., Curby, T. W., & Shewark, E. A. (2015). "Practice What You Preach": Teachers' perceptions of emotional competence and emotionally supportive classroom practices. *Early Education and Development, 26,* 899–919. doi:10.1080/10409289.2015.1009320

Zinsser, K. M., Shewark, E. A., Denham, S. A., & Curby, T. W. (2014). A mixed-method examination of preschool teacher beliefs about social–emotional learning and relations to observed emotional support. *Infant and Child Development, 23,* 471–493. doi:10.1002/icd.1843

4

Promoting Motor Development and Early Years Physical Literacy in Young Children

JACQUELINE D. GOODWAY, RURI FAMELIA, ALI BRIAN, JOHN C. OZMUN, AND DAVID L. GALLAHUE

A group of preschoolers spill out into the playground running and squealing with the joy of being outside. Two little girls hold hands and start skipping around the playground together while a couple of boys start throwing a ball back and forth between them. It seems like a typical day on the playground. However, what many people do not see are the large developmental differences in the performance of these basic skills by children. We often assume that young children naturally learn these motor skills of childhood, and that all children look alike in the patterns of movement they demonstrate; but, this is not so. For those children who are less proficient in their motor skill performance there are significant concerns about their future physical activity levels and their physical literacy journey (Cairney, Bedard, Dudley, & Kriellaars, 2016; Robinson et al., 2015; Stodden et al., 2008). So how do young children learn motor skills? What factors influence their motor development, physical activity behaviors, and ultimately their lifelong physical literacy journey?

This chapter will first provide a brief overview of an emerging concept of physical literacy, define motor development, and discuss principles of motor development. We will go on to describe and contrast popular models of motor development and the emergence of key fundamental motor skills (FMSs). A summary of gender differences in motor skills will be provided, along with developmental delays in FMS of young children. We will conclude with a summary of the literature seeking to improve motor skills and physical activity behaviors via intervention, along with implications for promoting an active start in young children.

Importance and Definitions of Physical Literacy

Physical literacy is a concept that is gaining global attention and many countries are beginning to develop physical literacy policies and programs that have implications for early childhood professionals, as well as the future health of our young children (Dudley, Cairney, Wainwright, Kriellaars, & Mitchell, 2017; Jurbala, 2015). The International Physical Literacy Association (IPLA) defines physical literacy as the "motivation, confidence, physical competence, knowledge and understanding to value and take responsibility for engagement in physical activities for life" (IPLA, 2017). Since this initial definition was first created (e.g., Higgs et al., 2005; Whitehead, 2001, 2010), countries such as Canada (Sport for Life, 2015) and later Australia (Australian Sports Commission, 2018) have developed different physical literacy definitions. However, all include the core constructs of: (1) development of motor competence, (2) the motivation and confidence to engage in physical activities, (3) knowledge and understanding of the how, why, and when we move, (4) a commitment to inclusive physical activities nurtured across the lifespan, and (5) that each person's physical literacy journey is unique to them.

A recent paper by Dudley and colleagues (Dudley et al., 2017) suggested that if we are to develop effective physical literacy policies within the education, sport, and public health sectors there are four core ingredients. The first is the development of *movement competence*, especially in the early childhood years. The second is that children have access to *movement environments* and *evidenced-based movement programs* in a variety of different contexts. The third key ingredient is *individual physical literacy journeys* that change across the lifespan. Finally, the fourth reflects the *power structures of movement*, that is, ensuring there is equal access to physical activities across gender, disability, race/ethnicity, religion, and poverty. Overall, Dudley et al. (2017) suggest we need to look carefully at our communities and examine the ways in which we can develop effective physical literacy policies and programs for children (and adults). Of these four pillars of physical literacy, we believe that the development of motor competence in the early childhood years is most important and early childhood centers need to provide evidenced-based motor skill programming. Before we review the literature on early motor skill interventions we will define motor development, and provide a brief overview of how motor skills emerge during the early childhood years.

Definition of Motor Development

Motor development may be defined as "the changes in motor behavior over the lifespan and the processes which underlie these changes" (Clark & Whitall, 1989, p. 194). As such, motor development is studied both as a product and as a process. Knowledge of the *products* (i.e., the outcomes) and the *processes* (i.e., the underlying mechanisms) of changes in motor behavior over time provide us with information that is vital to understanding individual pathways in motor development, especially during a time of rapid developmental change such as the period of early childhood.

A "product" perspective on motor development consists of understanding: (a) what are the typical phases and stages of motor development during early childhood? (b) What are the approximate age periods associated with typical markers of motor behavior in young children? (c) What do we know about predictable patterns of change in motor behavior that are typically seen in normally developing children compared to those who may be either developmentally delayed, or developmentally advanced? Answers to these questions are critical because they can help distinguish between "age-dependent" changes and "age-related" changes. Age-dependent changes suggest that all children of a certain age perform a motor skill in a specific way. However, age-related changes suggest that *some* children of the same age will show the similar movement skills but others may vary both in the rate and sequence of development. That is, children raised in different ecological and cultural settings or children with disabilities may be significantly ahead or behind their same aged peers in terms of motor development. By understanding what lies ahead in terms of anticipated change, we can be better informed to implement developmentally appropriate instruction and curricula decisions.

A "process" approach to motor development of young children helps us address the mechanisms that underlie developmental change. As such we gain information about the "how" and "why" of development. Namely: (a) how does change occur as documented? (b) Why is developmental change a nonlinear, self-organizing dynamic process? (c) How do heredity and the environment interact with the requirements of the motor task as one strives for greater motor control and movement competence? By understanding the mechanisms of change we can be better equipped to intervene and assist children in developing age-appropriate motor skills. There are certain principles of motor development that can help guide us as we seek to understand both the *product* and *process* of motor development.

Principles of Motor Development

Motor development looks at the changes in motor behavior across the lifespan. It is important to remember that these changes do not occur just because we get older, they require accompanying experiences. The following principles are valuable as we consider changes in motor behavior:

- *Change is qualitatively different and sequential* – As children "develop" motorically one can see qualitatively different patterns of movement (Gallahue, Ozmun, & Goodway, 2012; Haywood & Getchell, 2014). Later under developmental sequences we will describe how initial movement patterns are often crude, inconsistent, and inefficient but more developed patterns are mechanically efficient and able to be applied across multiple contexts (Gallahue et al., 2012). However, while the sequence of development through FMS will be similar for children, it is the age and rate of development through the sequence that varies (Gallahue et al., 2012). These common developmental sequences will be discussed later in the chapter.

- *Change is cumulative and directional* – Developmental change is built on previous capabilities. Early behaviors serve as the building blocks for later emerging skills. In the early childhood years, it is important that children develop competency in FMS such as throwing, skipping, and catching (Gallahue et al., 2012). FMSs are made up of *locomotor skills* that propel or transfer the body through space or from one point to another (e.g., run, gallop, skip, hop, jump, slide), and *manipulation skills* in which a child manipulates an object with the hands, feet, or other body parts (e.g., catch, throw, kick, strike, dribble, and roll: Gallahue et al., 2012). The FMS competence refers to the ability of individual to perform common FMSs at proficient level (Stodden et al., 2008). These FMSs are built upon the reflexes, reactions, and rudimentary skills acquired in infancy. Development also has direction to the change; that is, it is "going somewhere" toward some end goal that may advance or decline the motor performance. Thus, knowing a child's goal in movement is important in understanding his/her motor performance.

- *Change is multi-factorial based upon the interaction between the learner, the environment, and the task* – Changes in motor development are influenced by interaction of factors from the learner (child), the environment, and the task (Newell, 1984, 1986). In the playground throwing example above where boys were throwing a ball with each other, the task may have been to throw the ball as far as possible. The potential learner factors influencing the pattern of movement may be things like balance, strength, and the ability to demonstrate a contralateral (arm-leg opposition) pattern. The interaction of these factors results in the skill pattern demonstrated by the children. Knowledge of constraints that underlie a skill is critical for the teacher to understand as later we will show how this information can be used in instructing motor skills.

- *Change is variable between children* – This principle highlights the individuality in all learning. The sequence of progression through the developmental sequences is generally fairly consistent for most children. The rate, however, may vary considerably, depending on a combination of both environmental and biological factors (Malina, Bouchard, & Bar-Or, 2004; Saccani, Valentini, Pereira, Müller, & Gabbard, 2013; Venetsanou & Kambas, 2010). Whether a child reaches the proficient stage depends primarily on the ecological context of the environment including factors such as instruction, encouragement, and opportunities for practice, and biological factors such as perceptual-motor maturity and various anatomical and physiological considerations. It is in this principle we often see differences between our low-income children who have had little opportunities to move and their more affluent peers who may have been involved in a lot of different sports and activities (Goodway & Smith, 2005; Hardy, Reinten-Reynolds, Espinel, Zask, & Okely, 2012).

Overall, these principles offer insight into the products and processes of motor development. Additionally, three models of motor development offer insight into the sequential nature of motor development during early childhood.

Models of Motor Development

Three models of motor development share commonalities in the importance of the emergence of motor skills across childhood; but each model offers a slightly unique perspective on this process. We will briefly summarize these models with respect to the most pertinent parts of the model for early childhood. From a theoretical perspective the Gallahue (1982) and Seefeldt (1980) models emerged around the same timeframe during a more maturational focused era of development, with the Clark and Metcalfe (2002) model coming much later under the auspices of dynamic systems theory. However, all of these models suggest how children's physical literacy journeys may emerge from the standpoint of the construct of physical competence.

Sequential Progression in the Achievement of Motor Proficiency

Seefeldt (1980) proposed one of the earliest models in motor development shaped like a pyramid. At the base of this model are the "*Reflexes and Reactions*" of infancy. Built upon this foundation the young child begins to develop "*Fundamental Motor Skills*" including *locomotor* skills such as running and skipping and *manipulation* skills such as catching and throwing. The unique part to this model is the "*Proficiency Barrier*" after FMS. Seefeldt suggested that developing FMS competence is a prerequisite for future sports and games and that FMS to sports and games are the movement equivalent of the alphabets to reading and writing competence. Inherent in this idea is that a child who is not competent in FMS is unlikely to engage successfully in sports where these skills are needed and applied. Seefeldt believed the development of FMS competence in early childhood years was necessary if the child were to move to the last two phases of the

model, "*Transitional Skills*" (e.g., lead up soccer, t-ball) and "*Specific Sports Skills and Dances*" of middle childhood and adolescence. Thus, at the heart of this model is the importance of the early childhood years in developing the FMS competency necessary for lifelong participation in sports and other physical activities.

Hourglass Model of Motor Development

Around the same time Gallahue (Gallahue, 1982; Gallahue et al., 2012) used an "hourglass" to describe the processes of motor development. The falling sands into the hourglass represent the development of motor skills as influenced by both heredity and environment. As the sands land in the bottom of the hourglass, they build the phases and stages of motor development across the lifespan. The *reflexive movement phase* starts prenatally and develops well into the first year of life. Primitive reflexes such as the Moro reflex, as well as postural reflexes such as the body righting reflex, are inhibited (disappear) on a universally predictable schedule in typically developing infants. Next comes the *rudimentary movement phase* where the infant develops a variety of basic movement patterns such as control of the head, neck, and trunk (body stability), controlled reaching, grasping, and releasing (object manipulation), and proficiency in creeping and crawling (purposeful locomotion).

During the early childhood and primary school years children can be seen in what Gallahue (1982) called the "*fundamental movement phase*" (the same as FMS) of motor development. This is where children experiment and explore their movement potential in a variety of critical FMS that form the building blocks for later movement and physical literacy. In the subsequent *specialized movement skill phase*, more complex movement skills such as those in sports and games are refined and mastered. Overall, variability in the rate and extent of skill acquisition is determined by a wide variety of environmental as well as biological factors (see Gallahue et al., 2012 for a more detailed discussion of this model).

Mountain of Motor Development

Almost 20 years later, Clark and Metcalfe (2002) developed one of the most recent models of motor development, a six-phase "*Mountain of Motor Development*" model as a metaphorical way to understand the development of motor skills across the lifespan. Their model is based on the dynamical systems framework of multiply developing systems that self-organize in nonlinear ways. Clark and Metcalfe proposed that progression up the mountain was specific to an individual's experiences and the constraints they experienced along the route. Similar to the Gallahue (1982) and Seefeldt (1980) models, the first phase of this model is the "*Reflexive*" period and subsequently the "*Preadapted*" period, ending in the onset of independent walking and self-feeding behaviors. Similar to all other models, the *"fundamental movement"* (the same as FMS) phase that comes next is considered to be the "base camp" of the mountain of motor development and provides the basis for later "motor skillfulness" (p. 17). Further up the mountain children begin to apply FMS to *"Context Specific"* environments of sports and games and with appropriate experiences, children may develop *"Skillfulness"* (the top of the mountain). Unlike other models, and in line with the construct of physical literacy, Clark and Metcalfe recognize that no individual becomes skillful across a broad variety of activities. For example, a highly proficient gymnast may not be a good volleyball player. Thus, the mountain has different "peaks" (different sports or activities) with each peak being of a different height, reflecting that individuals will have varying levels of skillfulness across different activities. The biological and environmental constraints operating on an individual influence progression up the mountain range and ultimately a specific mountain peak. Clark and Metcalfe highlight the importance of early childhood in developing a broad base of FMS by about age of seven years. If these skills are developed, children are well positioned from their "base camp" on the mountain of motor development to navigate many different mountain peaks (sports and physical activities) given sufficient and appropriate experiences.

In summary, all three models of motor development highlight the importance of FMS. Gallahue's Triangulated Hourglass Model (Gallahue, 1982; Gallahue et al., 2012) emphasizes the interaction between biological factors (genetics) and external factors (tasks and environment) will influence the rate of FMS development. The Seefeldt model (1980) signifies the importance of young children becoming proficient at FMS in order to be able to apply these skills to perform more advanced sports skills. Clark and Metcalfe's (2002) model supports and reinforces that there is intra-individual and inter-individual factors that influence the rate of skill development within and between individuals. Interactions of intra- and inter-individual factors result in an individual who may be more skilled in certain skills than other skills, and who may have greater proficiency. In relation to physical literacy, Clark and Metcalfe's model captures that the concept of physical literacy journey is a lifelong process and unique for every individual with different individuals visiting different mountain peaks. However, all three models highlight to early childhood educators and parents the importance of FMS development during the early childhood years and how FMS competence is critical to lifelong engagement in physical activity.

Acquisition of FMSs

One of the core constructs of physical literacy is the development of physical competence. For young children in the early childhood years, what is most important to develop is FMS competence. This section will hope to answer the questions of how do these FMS develop and what can we do to promote motor competence in FMS?

As children approach their second birthdays, most have mastered the rudimentary movement abilities of infancy. From here, children begin to develop and refine the FMS of early childhood and the specialized movement skills of later childhood and beyond. FMSs are made up of *locomotor skills* that propel or transfer the body through space or from one point to another (e.g., run, gallop, skip, hop, jump, slide), and *manipulation skills* in which a child manipulates an object with the hands, feet, or other body parts (e.g., catch, throw, kick, strike, dribble, and roll; Gallahue et al., 2012). However, these skills do not naturally "emerge" during early childhood; rather, they result from many factors influencing the child's motor skill development (Newell, 1984, 1986). Therefore, movement experiences early in one's life play a substantial role in acquisition of FMS (Seefeldt, 1980; Stodden et al., 2008; Zask et al., 2012) and are seminal within one's journey toward being physically literate (Cairney et al., 2016).

Developmental Sequences of FMS

Developmental sequences provide researchers and practitioners with a way to understand the emergence of FMS. A developmental sequence is a series of highly predictable movements that are qualitatively different from each other and hierarchically placed in order (Roberton, 1978). There are two kinds of developmental sequences: *inter-skill* sequences are between skill sequences (e.g., first we learn to stand, then walk, and then run) whereas *intra-skill* sequences consist of "with-in" skill sequences (sequences for emergence of a specific skill). These intra-skill sequences consist of describing common patterns of movement seen for a specific skill like catching, and then placing those patterns in a "developmental sequence" going from more crude and inefficient patterns of movement to more sophisticated and biomechanically efficient patterns of movement (Roberton, 1978). It is valuable for the early childhood educator to understand both inter-skill and intra-skill sequences.

The *Total Body Approach* to developmental sequences was developed by Seefeldt, Haubenstricker, Branta and colleagues (see chapters 12 and 13 of Gallahue et al., 2012 for a more detailed description). Total body sequences describe the performance of the entire body and range from a three-stage (skip, gallop), to four-stage (kick, strike, punt, run, jump, hop), or five-stage (throw, catch) sequences. However, another approach to developmental sequences is the *Segmental or Component Approach* (see Gallahue et al., 2012). Researchers using the component approach conceptualized sequences slightly differently by determining developmental sequences for various body segments within a skill (Langendorfer & Roberton, 2002). In this method, specific stage characteristics are determined for each body segment and those stages can be combined in various ways across the total body. The component approach provides rich detail in describing how specific body segments change over time and how one body segment may be linked to another one, but it can be more challenging to see in real-world movement contexts (e.g., the gymnasium, playground, and/or during authentic assessment contexts that are not set up for research).

All of these different sequential approaches provide excellent information on skill patterns readily identified as children acquire and refine their motor skills. In some cases, such as in research and the elite level sport, the component approach may be the best way to examine performance. However, we believe that the total body approach may be more readily accessible and easily used for the early childhood educator.

Summary of Total Body Developmental Sequences for Locomotor and Manipulation Skills

Table 4.1 provides a description of the developmental stages for five locomotor skills (run, gallop, skip, hop, jump) and Table 4.2 for five manipulation skills (catch, throw, kick,

punt, strike). More detail and pictures surrounding these stages can be found in chapters 12 and 13 of Gallahue et al. (2012). Knowledge of these developmental sequences can assist early childhood educators in identifying the correct developmental level of the child, and knowing what will come next in the developmental sequence; thus being able to plan more effectively to move the child to the next level of development.

While developmental sequences provide useful information on skill development, two weaknesses need to be addressed. First, these linear models do not account for the varied performance we often see within a young child from trial to trail. Second, these models do not explain the processes underlying why children vary their performance. Dynamical systems research (Thelen, 1995) has expanded our understanding of motor development patterns and provides a conceptual framework to examine the underlying systems that affect pattern shifts. Initial review of developmental

Table 4.1   Summary of Locomotor Developmental Sequences

Fundamental Motor Skill	Stage 1	Stage 2	Stage 3	Stage 4
Gallahue, Ozmun and Goodway (2012)	Initial Stage	Emerging Stages		Proficient Stage
Run	*Run – Arms Above Head* Arms are high at head height. Flat-footed contact. Short, wide stride. Feet shoulder width apart.	*Run – Arms Mid Trunk* Arms at mid-trunk level. Vertical component of run still great. Legs near full extension.	*Heel-Toe Run – Arms Extended* Arms below waist. Arm-leg opposition with elbows nearly extended. Heel-toe contact.	*Run – Pumping Arms* Heel-toe contact (sometimes toe-heel when sprinting). Arm-leg opposition. Heel recovery close to buttocks. Elbow bent at 90 degrees.
Gallop	*Choppy Run – Gallop* Resembles rhythmically uneven run. Back leg crosses in front of lead leg during airborne phase and remains in front at touch down.	*Gallop – Stiff Back Leg* Slow-moderate tempo, choppy rhythm. Black leg is stiff. Hips often turned sideways. Vertical component exaggerated.	*Gallop – Smooth Rhythmical* Smooth, rhythmical pattern with moderate tempo. Feet remain close to ground. Hips facing forward.	
Skip	*Broken Skip* Broken skip pattern or irregular rhythm. Slow, deliberate movement. Ineffective arm action.	*Skip – High Arms and Legs* Rhythmical skip pattern. Arms swing high and provide body lift. Excessive vertical component.	*Rhythmical Skip* Arm action reduced/hands below shoulders. Easy, rhythmical movement. Support foot near surface on hop.	
Hop	*Hop – Free Foot in Front* Non-support (free) foot in front of base leg with thigh parallel to floor. Body upright and hands shoulder height.	*Hop – Free Foot by Support Leg* Non-support knee flexed with knee in front and foot beside support leg. Slight body lean forward. Both arms move together.	*Hop – Free Foot Behind Support Leg* Non-support thigh alongside base support leg with free foot behind support leg, knee flexed. More body lean forward. Arms swing forward together.	*Hop – Free Leg Pumps* Non-support leg is bent and knee pumps forward and back in a pendular action. Forward body lean. Arm opposition with swing leg.
Long Jump	*Short Jump – Braking Arms* Arms act as "brakes" moving forward then toward trunk on jump. Large vertical component. Legs not extended.	*Short Jump – Winging Arms* Arms act as "wings" to side of body. Vertical component still great. Legs near full extension.	*Longer Jump – Arms Swing to Head* Arms move forward/elbows in front of trunk at take-off. Hands swing to head height. Take-off angle still above 45 degrees. Legs often fully extended.	*Long Jump – Full Body Extension* Complete arm and leg extension at take-off. Take-off near 45 degree angle. Thighs parallel to surface when feet contact for landing.

Table 4.2 Summary of Manipulative Developmental Sequences

Fundamental Motor Skill	Stage 1	Stage 2	Stage 3	Stage 4	Stage 5
Gallahue, Ozmun and Goodway (2012)	**Initial Stage**		**Emerging Stages**		**Proficient Stage**
Throw	*Front – Chop Throw* Feet stationary. Front facing. Arm "chop throws" from ear. No spinal rotation.	*Sideways – Sling Shot* Body turned sideways. Horizontal wind. "Sling shot throw" with block rotation of trunk. Arm swings across body.	*Step Same Arm – Leg* High wind up of arm. Ipsilateral (same arm-leg) step. Little spinal rotation. Follow-through across body.	*Step Opposite Arm – Leg* High wind up of arm. Contralateral (opposite arm-leg) step. Little spinal rotation. Follow-through across body.	*Arm Wind Up* Arm swings downward and back. Contralateral step. Segmented body rotation. Arm-leg follow-through.
Two-Handed Catch	*Delayed Reaction* Delayed arm action to ball. Arms straight in front until ball contact, then scooping action to chest. Feet stationary. Head often turns to side.	*Hugging* Arms encircle ball as it approaches. Ball is "hugged" to chest. Feet are stationary or may take one step.	*Scooping* Arms out and scoop ball to chest. Arms "scoop" under ball to trap it to chest. Single step may be used to step into the ball flight.	*Hand Catch* Initial contact with ball is with hands only. Hand catch only if tossed to trunk. Feet stationary or limited to one step. Would not catch a ball tossed to side of body.	*Move to Ball* Tracks flight of ball and moves body under ball flight. Catch with hands only. Fine adjustment of fingers to ball position as ball is caught.
Kick	*Stationary – Push* Stationary position. Little/no leg wind up. Foot "pushes" ball. Often step backward after kick or poor balance.	*Stationary – Leg Swing* Stationary position. Free leg winds-up behind base leg. Opposition of arms and legs.	*Moving Approach* Moving approach to ball (one step or several steps). Foot travels in a low arc. Arm/leg opposition. Steps past/beside ball on follow-through.	*Leap-Kick-Hop* Rapid approach to ball. Leaps before kick. Backward trunk lean during wind-up. Kicks hard. Hops after kick.	
Punt (Drop ball and kick it)	*Stationary –Yoke and Push* Stationary position. No leg wind-up. Ball toss erratic "yoking." Push ball and often step back.	*Stationary Leg Swing* Stationary position. Free leg wind-up to rear. Yoking toss. Forceful kick attempt.	*Moving Approach* Moving approach to ball. Some arm/leg yoking. Ball is tossed or dropped. Often steps beyond ball after kick.	*Leap-Punt-Hop* Rapid approach to the ball. Controlled drop of ball. Leap before ball contact. Hop after ball contact.	
Strike (Bat a ball)	*Chop Strike* Hand position on bat variable. "Chopping" downward strike pattern. Feet stationary.	*Pushing* Horizontal push/ swing of bat. Block rotation of trunk. Feet stationary or stepping.	*Ipsilateral Step* Sideways orientation at start. Ipsilateral step. Diagonal downward swing of bat.	*Contralateral Step* Sideways orientation at start. Contralateral step. Segmented body rotation Wrist rollover on follow-through.	

sequences as opposed to a dynamical systems method of research often concludes that the two approaches are antithetical to each other. However, we contend that much can be gained by combining the two approaches. Newell (1984, 1986) suggests that FMS emerge within a dynamic system consisting of a specific task, performed by a learner with given characteristics, in a particular environment. In this dynamic systems theory perspective, factors (subsystems) within the learner will influence motor skill development. For example, motivation, strength, and neurological development are just a few of these many learner factors that may influence the performance. In addition, environmental considerations such as equipment used (e.g., size of the ball), previous experience,

and instruction may influence motor development. Both of these two factors (learner and environment) are specific to the task being asked of the performer (Newell, 1984, 1986).

A dynamical systems approach suggests that FMS development occurs in a nonlinear manner. That means that pattern shifts are not thought of in linear terms such as immature to mature (stage 1 to 2 to 3); rather shifts result in individuals performing in a variety of states commonly called *behavioral attractors*. Attractors are common forms of movement seen in specific situations and are typically comfortable ways of moving to which individuals gravitate as they practice moving. For example, an early attractor in catching is to "hug" the ball with the arms (stage 2 – see Table 4.2) before a child moves to a more complex attractor of catching the ball with the hands (stage 4). Shifts from one attractor to another may occur in any direction (more advanced or regression) dependent upon all impinging factors that affect that skill. For example, if a child is tossed a large ball they may "hug" the ball into their arms. However, if tossed a bean bag they may hand catch. Strong attractors are ones that are so embedded that it is difficult to shift that person out of that state. Weak attractors are patterns of movement we may see occasionally, but they are not as stable as strong attractors and can more readily be changed by environmental and learner constraints. We believe the total body stages in Tables 4.1 and 4.2 reflect the most common and most strong *attractors*.

Re-conceptualizing stages of developmental sequences into the concept of various attractors provides a better interpretation of what we see as we watch young children perform motor skills. This dynamic approach also places power in the hands of the teachers and parents as it supports the idea that teachers and parents can manipulate environmental and task constraints to help move children into new attractors that are more beneficial to the demands of a specific task. Thus, under a dynamic systems paradigm, children choose from an array of movement patterns (the developmental stages) to select the most appropriate pattern to achieve the task at hand. Our job as teachers and parents is to assist children in developing a large array of movement patterns from which they can select. In doing so, we begin to promote not only children's FMS proficiency but start them off on their physical literacy journeys. Thus, we need to provide children with access to *movement environments* and *evidenced-based movement programs* in different contexts (Dudley et al., 2017). Therefore, it is important for practitioners to consider not only the task, but other constraints, when identifying what pattern should be employed to execute a skill. Teachers and parents can manipulate constraints such as the equipment used (i.e., movement environment) and task selected to assist children in developing more proficient patterns of FMS.

Instructional Application of FMSs

Now that we have a better conceptual understanding of how FMSs develop, it may be valuable to understand how developmental sequences and behavioral attractors can be used instructionally. Let us use throwing as an example. Table 4.2 describes the five stages of throwing a ball starting with an inefficient "chop throw" (stage 1) and ending in a mechanically efficient throwing pattern with arm-leg opposition and wind-up and follow-through (stage 5). From a dynamic systems perspective each of these five different patterns of throwing are movement options for a child assuming they can perform all five (this will not usually be true for younger children). If a child is asked to throw for distance and force they would most likely select stage 5 from the movement options (if capable) as this pattern of throwing is most biomechanically efficient. However, if you placed a child five feet from a wall and asked him/her to hit it with a ball, they would most likely choose from stages 1 to 3 as little force is required to achieve the stated task, and arm-leg opposition (stage 4 or 5) is not necessary. Thus, one of the first things a teacher must understand is that the movement option selected by the child will be driven, in part, by the nature of the task given. When trying to promote a specific pattern of performance, the teacher needs to carefully design tasks that will promote the desired movement outcome. For example, to promote a stage 5 throw you might hang a sheet with bells on it, put a sticker on the opposite foot and hand, place a child further from the target, and encourage them to "step onto a footprint and throw hard" and make the bells jingle loudly.

Teachers should undertake a five-step process in developing movement activities for young children: (1) observe and evaluate the developmental level of the child – e.g., stage 2 catch "hugging"; (2) identify the desired performance (attractor) for the child to perform – e.g., stage 4, "catching with the hands"; (3) consider what learner factors might be influencing the child – e.g., poor fine motor control, inability to track the ball in flight, fear of being hit in the face by the ball; (4) consider how to manipulate aspects of the environment to promote hand catching – e.g., have a large, squishy ball, place the tosser close to the child, toss slowly, cue the child "hands out, reach for the ball," and (5) watch the child perform the task and modify it to make it more difficult or easier based upon your observations.

As can be seen from the above example, understanding the emergence of FMS is valuable to the early childhood teacher in being able to observe the pattern of the child's performance, identify what comes next in the developmental sequence, and develop engaging and developmentally appropriate learning experiences for the child. There are many good resources to assist the early childhood teacher in providing developmentally appropriate instructional activities and many national physical education and physical activity organizations within respective countries have excellent resources such as lesson plans and activity ideas. In reviewing such resources for quality, we encourage the early childhood educator to consider: (1) do the resources promote FMS development? (2) Do they consider the uniqueness of the individual child and suggest how to manipulate equipment and tasks to accommodate for individual differences? (3) Do activities engage all learners in moving rather than large groups sharing equipment such as relay games? (4) Do activities promote moderate to vigorous physical activity (MVPA) in at least part of the lesson? (5) Do the activities utilize different pedagogical approaches that are child centered? (6) Are the activities scaffolded in a way that there are not big jumps between the difficulty level of each activity? (7) Do the activities have specific goals to promote a particular aspect of movement or physical activity? (8) Are there various entry points and an array of task difficulty so that all children can experience regular success in performing the tasks?

In summary, during the early childhood years the key element is to develop basic competency and efficient body mechanics in a wide variety of FMS (Stodden et al., 2008). The locomotor and manipulation patterns identified in Tables 4.1 and 4.2 are examples of FMS movement abilities first mastered separately by the child. These basic skills are then gradually combined and enhanced in a variety of ways to become more complex and specialized movement skills used in daily living, recreational, and sport activities (Seefeldt & Haubenstricker, 1982; Stodden et al., 2008). Although most typically developing children have the potential to develop the most proficient stage in most FMS, it is critically important that they have ample opportunities for practice and quality instruction in a caring and nurturing environment. As such evidenced-based programs should be implemented in our preschools and school physical education programs as a central component of children's early education. Children who are skillful movers have the basic FMS building blocks necessary for an active life that maximizes their individual potential in terms of physical fitness and regular participation in physical activity (Gallahue et al., 2012; Robinson et al., 2015; Stodden et al., 2008).

Gender Differences in FMSs and Physical Activity

Like other academic skills, gender differences exist in FMS development with boys demonstrating superior skills to girls in some areas and these gender differences have persisted over three decades (Barnett et al., 2016a; Seefeldt & Haubenstricker, 1982; Thomas & French, 1985). Gender differences are important to understand as teachers, parents, and sport coaches plan movement experiences for children. Gender differences exist as early as three years of age and increase with age, favoring males (Thomas & French, 1985). Specific skills like throwing, striking, and kicking show particularly strong gender differences with boys being better than girls (Barnett, Hinkley, Okley, & Salmon, 2013; Barnett, van Beurden, Morgan, Brooks, & Beard, 2010; Ehl, Roberton, & Langendorfer, 2005; Garcia & Garcia, 2002; Hardy et al., 2012; Spessato, Gabbard, Valentini, & Rudisill, 2013). A number of studies have suggested that biological factors such as muscular strength, joint diameters, shoulder/hip ratio, and percent body fat may account for these gender differences (Butterfield, Angell, & Mason, 2012; Thomas & French, 1985). Others suggest environmental sources such as practice opportunities, the cultural context of sport, and socio-cultural factors like a male in the home influence gender differences (Cools, Martelaers, Samaey, & Andries, 2011; Iivonen & Sääkslahti, 2013). However, for the younger child (3–6 years) it has been reported there are minimal sex differences in strength (Beunen & Thomas, 2000) whereas others (Armstrong & Welsman, 2000; Blimke & Sale, 1998; Oja & Jurimae, 1998) indicate sex-related differences favoring boys as young as three years of age. Barnett et al. (2013) report that age was the only significant predictor of locomotor skills but swim lessons and home equipment were positively associated. For object control skills age was a significant predictor again, along with MVPA% and interestingly a lack

of dance classes. They (Barnett et al., 2013) concluded that motor skill correlates differed by skill type with child level factors appearing more important. Overall, there is much systematic work to be done in this area as many of the studies were not designed to answer the question around why there are gender differences between males and females.

A variety of data on the FMS of young children both within the USA and from across the globe has found differential gender effects between locomotor and manipulative skills. Within the USA there are gender differences across ethnicity and region (Goodway, Robinson, & Crowe, 2010; Robinson & Goodway, 2009). Goodway and her colleagues have consistently found there were no gender differences in locomotor skills but boys had significantly better manipulation skills than girls (Goodway & Branta, 2003; Goodway, Crowe, & Ward, 2003; Goodway et al., 2010; Robinson & Goodway, 2009).

Similar trends have been found internationally for Australia (Barnett et al., 2018; Barnett, van Beurden, Morgan, Brooks, & Beard, 2010; Okely & Booth, 2004; Zask et al., 2012a; Zask, Adams, Brooks, & Hughes, 2012b), Belgium (Brian et al., 2018), Brazil (Spessato et al., 2013; Valentini, Logan, Spessato, Pereira, & Rudisill, 2016), Indonesia (Famelia, Tsuda, Bakhtiar, & Goodway, 2018), and Iran (Kordi, Nourian, Ghayour, Kordi, & Younesian, 2012). It is not clear from the research literature why this is so, but for the past two decades gender differences have remained consistent across geographic region and ethnicity. Locomotor skills are considered to be more phylogenetic (based upon neurological/genetic factors) and do not require equipment to practice (Goodway, Famelia, & Bakhtiar, 2014); thus girls and boys may have similar opportunities to practice these skills. In contrast, potential explanations as to gender differences in manipulation skills may be factors such as biological differences between gender, differential access to equipment, role models, and motivation (Barnett et al., 2010; Brian et al., 2018; Cools et al., 2011; Iivonen & Sääkslahti, 2013). In a comparison between Belgium and US preschoolers, Belgium preschoolers outperformed US preschoolers in both locomotor and manipulation skills; however, both groups performed significantly worse on FMS when compared with the USA reference group (Brian et al., 2018). Boys have been reported to come to the testing environment with a greater familiarity of the vocabulary and equipment associated with manipulation skills than girls, perhaps suggesting prior experience plays a role in these findings (Goodway et al., 2010). Other alternative explanations for gender differences in FMS may be that girls tend to be driven by more social factors (e.g., pleasing the teacher, receiving verbal encouragement, and smiles) in the learning environment; while boys are more motivated by competition and the product of the performance (Garcia, 1994; Garcia & Garcia, 2002). Brian et al. (2018) suggest that physical education provided to preschoolers in Belgium from the age of three years may, in part, account for the superior FMS of these children compared to those in the USA.

Overall, these data suggest that teachers need to recognize girls and boys may have different developmental needs in the instructional environment, specifically in the area of manipulative skills. The findings from gender difference speak to Dudley et al.'s (2017) suggestion that we must consider the *power structures of* physical literacy if we are to have equitable access to develop physical literacy across the lifespan. In spite of the many opportunities to engage in movement programs for both boys and girls, girls remain significantly behind their male counterparts in manipulation skills. There is a need to ensure that girls do not get disadvantaged in movement environments and future research is needed to ensure that everybody has access to physical activity regardless of their gender.

Developmental Delay in Disadvantaged Preschoolers

Children whose families' income fall below the poverty guideline are identified as disadvantaged and being at risk for delay in demonstrating (or developing) the requisite academic and social skills for future educational success (IDEA, 2004). Many programs have been developed to serve this population. One of the largest in the USA is Head Start, which is a government-funded program that started in 1965 to promote school readiness of children ages birth to five years from low-income families by supporting the development of the whole child (Office of Head Start, 2019). Similar to other academic areas like literacy, disadvantaged preschool children who were enrolled in Head Start programs demonstrate developmental delays in their FMS (Goodway & Branta, 2003; Goodway et al., 2003, 2010; Robinson & Goodway, 2009), the foundational skills necessary for engagement in lifelong physical activity. Typically, developmentally delay is identified when a child is below the 25th percentile (Ulrich, 2000) or 30th percentile (IDEA, 2004) for same-aged peers with children between the 25th and 75th percentile considered typically developing. Children with such developmental delays require intervention to remediate those skills (Goodway et al., 2010; Ulrich, 2000).

A fairly large-scale study of the FMS of 275 preschool children enrolled in Head Start found that preschoolers were between the 10th and 17th percentile for locomotor skills and around the 16th percentile for manipulative skills (Goodway et al., 2010). Furthermore, 85% of the African American Midwestern preschoolers were developmentally delayed in manipulative skills (92% of girls and 78% of boys). For the locomotor data, 88% of Midwestern participants were delayed (90% of girls and 87% of boys). Similar findings were true for Southwestern Hispanic participants with 84% of participants being delayed in manipulative development (95% of girls and 72% of boys) and 91% in locomotor skills (92% of girls and 89% of boys). From these data, clearly a sizeable number of preschool children in Head Start were delayed in manipulative and locomotor skill development. Similar to the findings for gender above, the patterns found in the current study have remained fairly consistent for both African American and Hispanic populations, across regions, cities within the same region, and time (Goodway & Branta, 2003; Goodway et al., 2003; Robinson &

Goodway, 2009). Based on this evidence, young children served by Head Start require motor skill intervention to remediate the developmental delays found in FMS. Developmental delays in FMS have also been found in other developed countries, such as Israel (Golos, Sarid, Weill, & Weintraub, 2011) and Australia (Piek et al., 2013), and in developing countries such as Indonesia (Famelia, Tsuda, Bakhiar, & Goodway, 2018), Brazil (Spessato et al., 2013), and South Africa (Draper, Achmat, Forbes, & Lambert, 2012).

Further research should attempt to gain a better understanding of the underlying mechanisms influencing the FMS of these children if motor interventions are to be successful. There have been no empirical data to explain the underlying mechanisms accounting for these delays, but clearly constraints are operating that are consistent across populations. Perhaps one of the most consistent and powerful constraints is that the child is being reared in a financially impoverished environment. It has also been hypothesized that disadvantaged preschool children are exposed to a variety of other environmental constraints that influence their motor development negatively (Goodway & Branta, 2003; Goodway et al., 2003; Goodway & Smith, 2005). For example, lack of safe places to play and be active in the community, limited activity role models (especially for females), lack of access to motor skill programs; thus, no instruction or feedback on their motor skills may all contribute to these delays (Branta & Goodway, 1996; Goodway & Smith, 2005). Biological factors that stem from infancy such as poor prenatal care, small for gestational age at birth, and prematurity could be other constraints influencing children (Aylward, 2014; Pitchik et al., 2018). But why are developmental delays in FMS of particular long-term concern for this population of children? The delays reported above suggest that these populations of young children do not demonstrate the requisite competency in FMS to be able to break through hypothetical proficiency barrier discussed under the Sequential Progression in the Achievement of Motor Proficiency section above. That is, delays in FMS are a limiting factor in supporting children's success in ongoing sport and physical activity behaviors. Although the proficiency barrier is an old concept, the idea of the necessary level of competence needed in order to sustain physical activity and movement behaviors across the lifespan has become an important topic in the world of motor development (De Meester et al., 2018; Stodden, True, Langendorfer, & Gao, 2013). If we are to intervene in the FMS competence of young children, we need to understand the requisite level of FMS competence children must develop in order to support their physical literacy journey and acquire or sustain age-appropriate levels of physical activity. Therefore, the next section will provide information on motor skill intervention to promote children's FMS competence.

Motor Skill Intervention in Disadvantaged Preschoolers

An emerging body of evidence from different countries around the world has begun to examine the influence of motor skill intervention on the FMS of young children (Logan, Robinson, Wilson, & Lucas, 2012; Morgan et al., 2013; Veldman, Jones, & Okely, 2016). These studies show that when motorically delayed preschool children receive well-designed motor skill instruction, they can remediate these delays in FMS compared to children in the control group who received preschool curricula without well-designed motor skill intervention (Alhassan et al., 2012; Bellows, Davies, Anderson, & Kennedy, 2013; Bonvin et al., 2013; Brian, Goodway, Logan, & Sutherland, 2017a, 2017b; Deli, Bakle, & Zachopoulou, 2006; Golos et al., 2011; Goodway et al., 2003; Hardy, King, Kelly, Farrell, & Howlett, 2010; Jones et al., 2011; Robinson & Goodway, 2009; Tsapakidou, Stefanidou, & Tsompanaki, 2014; Zask et al., 2012b). A wide variety of motor skill interventions have been implemented in the literature and we will attempt to summarize the key findings in this section.

The instructional "dose" for motor skill interventions ranges from six weeks (Brian et al., 2017a, 2017b) to ten months (Bonvin et al., 2013). These motor skill intervention studies delivered the program either as the sole focus of the intervention or as a part of a larger intervention program combined with a nutrition program. The majority of the interventions were delivered using *direct instruction* and *mastery motivational climate* instructional approaches, which were implemented by motor development experts, early childhood teachers, or parents.

Direct instruction in motor skills involves a teacher-oriented approach to teaching motor skills where the teacher clearly describes and demonstrates the task to be performed and the children respond accordingly (Graham, Holt-Hale, & Parker, 2007). In this setting the children have few choices to select a task or equipment and the teacher instructs each element of the lesson (Graham et al., 2007). During direct instruction the teacher leads the children through a series of developmental tasks. For example, first the children may catch a self-tossed beach ball, then a self-tossed bean bag; then shift to catching a partner-tossed beach ball from five feet and then eight feet with the teacher attempting to move the child to higher stages of catching (see Table 4.2). In this instance, the teacher would demonstrate the skills and lead the children through each task when the teacher believed the children were ready to move on. While there may be some differences in when individual children move from one task to another, overall the children are performing the same series of tasks (Draper et al., 2012; Golos et al., 2011; Logan, Robinson, Webster, & Barber, 2013; Martin, Rudisill, & Hastie, 2009; Piek et al., 2013; Robinson & Goodway, 2009; Monsalves-Alvarez, Castro Sepúlveda, Zapata Lamana, Rosales Soto, & Salazar, 2015). The advantage to this approach is that the teacher knows which tasks the students have performed.

On the other hand, the *mastery motivational climate* approach is a more student-centered instructional pedagogy in which children have high autonomy to complete tasks and activities based on their preferences. A mastery motivation climate is developed by manipulating six "TARGET" structures within the lesson where the acronym TARGET stands for: Task, Authority, Grouping, Evaluation, and Time. During the intervention, activities with several levels of challenge are incorporated into the instruction (i.e., Task). Children are encouraged to make their own choice where to play (i.e., Authority), and with whom to play (i.e., Group), and how long to engage with the task (i.e., Time). Children are evaluated and recognized based on the self-reference and efforts (i.e., Evaluation and Recognition) during the intervention (Logan et al., 2013; Robinson, 2011). An advantage of this more student-oriented approach is that students learn how to regulate their own pace of learning and often develop stronger motivation to engage in the tasks (Logan et al., 2013; Martin et al., 2009; Robinson, 2011; Robinson & Goodway, 2009; Robinson, Webster, Logan, Lucas, & Barber, 2012). However, a disadvantage of this approach is that it is harder for the teacher to determine where the child has been in the skill centers (i.e., what skills the child chose to do) and how much instructional time the child got on specific tasks and skills.

In a direct instruction approach, a typical lesson might include: (1) 3–5 minute vigorous game or music warm up, (2) transition through two skills stations (e.g., kick and throw), each involving 10–12 minutes of instruction; and (3) concluding with a 3–5 minute cool down and debrief (Goodway & Branta, 2003; Goodway & Robinson, 2006, Brian et al., 2017a, 2017b). In contrast, a mastery motivational climate lesson might involve the teacher organizing two skill stations (e.g., kick, throw) but at each skill station there would be 3–5 levels of tasks that vary in difficulty (e.g., in catching different size balls, different distances). The child performs a 3–5 minute warm up as above, but then is free to go to any station, select any task, and work with any child while the teacher acts as a facilitator providing feedback, suggesting new tasks and encouraging children to attempt tasks most appropriate to a child's level. The lesson would conclude with a debrief and final feedback (Logan et al., 2013; Robinson et al., 2012; Robinson & Goodway, 2009). A study by Robinson and Goodway (2009) found that both direct and mastery approaches to teaching FMS resulted in similar gains across the intervention. They concluded that good instruction and tasks, regardless of pedagogical approach, resulted in significant improvements in FMS compared to the children who received their typical preschool program.

In addition to instructional approaches, motor skill interventions can be classified as those delivered by: (1) *motor development experts* who were motor development researchers and had been trained to deliver FMS interventions (Logan et al., 2012; Robinson, 2011; Robinson & Goodway, 2009), (2) *early childhood teachers* (Brian et al., 2017a, 2017b; Jones et al., 2011; Kordi et al., 2012; Piek et al., 2013; Zask et al., 2012a), and (3) *parents as teachers*

(Bonvin et al., 2013; Hamilton, Goodway, & Haubenstricker, 1999; Zask et al., 2012b).

The majority of the motor skill intervention in the past decade was delivered by motor development experts (e.g., those with masters or doctoral degrees in motor development, motor behavior, and/or physical education; Goodway & Branta, 2003; Riethmuller, Jones, & Okely, 2009; Robinson, 2011; Robinson & Goodway, 2009; Valentini & Rudisill, 2004). This approach was essential in the beginning phase of the motor skill intervention literature to ensure effective fidelity of the motor skill program (internal validity) and demonstrate that when delivered as intended, children's FMSs were enhanced (Hulleman, Rim-Kaufman, & Abry, 2013). However, one of the major shortcomings of this work was the authenticity of delivery as few early childhood settings have experts in motor development. Thus, the next phase of the early intervention literature was ecological shift to training early childhood teachers how to deliver evidenced-based programs.

A number of studies have been conducted with early childhood teachers in educational settings to establish the effectiveness of delivering motor skill programs in real-world settings in order to demonstrate the usability and translation of these programs (Adamo et al., 2015; Adams, Zask, & Dietrich, 2009; Brian et al., 2017a, 2017b; Jones et al., 2011; Kordi et al., 2012; Piek et al., 2013; Zask et al., 2012b). Early childhood teachers were trained on curriculum material designed by the researchers, prior to the delivering motor skill intervention. Then the teachers delivered the motor skill program as part of their regular preschool curriculum. It is notable that trained early childhood teachers can bring about significant (p <0.001) changes in their children's FMS in as little as twice a week for 30 minutes over a six-week period (Adamo et al., 2015; Brian et al., 2017a, 2017b; Jones et al., 2011; Kordi et al., 2012; Piek et al., 2013; Venetsanou & Kambas, 2004; Zask et al., 2012b). Although the effect sizes for teachers $-\eta^2 = 0.18$ (Zask et al., 2012b) to 0.59 (Adamo et al., 2015) – are not as great as those delivered by experts – $\eta^2 = 0.87$ (Apache, 2005) to 0.96 (Logan et al., 2013) – there is powerful translational evidence that confirms teachers can deliver strong motor development outcomes for their children. Interestingly, these early childhood teachers preferred and were more effective with direct approaches of instruction in motor skills compared to mastery motivational climate (Brian & Taunton, 2018). In addition, studies showed evidence that the effect of motor skill intervention was maintained a long period after the intervention (Barnett, Zask, Rose, Hughes, & Adams, 2015; Zask et al., 2012a).

Other studies have recognized the important role of parents as the first teachers of their children and studied parent-assisted instruction where parents along with teachers or motor development experts delivered the motor skill program (Bonvin et al., 2013; Reilly et al., 2006; Zask et al., 2012b). Parent-assisted instruction utilizes "parents" (i.e., mother, father, or primary caregiver) as the primary or secondary instructors of their children. Parents undergo parent training to learn about motor skill development and ways in which to work with their child. A lead teacher develops the lesson plans (which are similar to direct instruction above), and acts as a primary instructor and facilitator to parents who directly instruct their child. The lead teacher facilitates and makes sure the parent-child are performing the activities according to the lesson plan and may step in and model appropriate instruction for parents when necessary.

All the motor skill intervention approaches identified above have been successful in significantly impacting the FMS development of preschoolers who were delayed in their FMS competence compared to the control group who did not receive the intervention. Children who received motor skill intervention significantly increased (p <0.001) their locomotor skills and manipulative skills (Logan et al., 2012; Morgan et al., 2013; Veldman et al., 2016). The results, particularly for manipulative skills, showed large effect sizes ranging from $\eta^2 = 0.18$ (Zask et al., 2012b) to $\eta^2 = 0.96$ (Logan, et al., 2013). In all of these interventions, maximum opportunities to respond were provided, and as much as possible children had their own piece of equipment and tasks were individualized to each child's developmental needs.

Some general conclusions may be drawn from the studies identified above: (1) many children are delayed in their motor skills, and those children need motor skill intervention; (2) when provided with developmentally appropriate motor instruction in programs, these children can make significant and often large gains in their motor skills remediating their prior delays; (3) early childhood teachers were effective in promoting the FMS of their children using evidenced-based curriculum after initial training; and (4) the children in the control groups who received the typical preschool curricula where physical activity opportunities were often non-facilitated and play-based resulted in no improvements to FMS development (Logan et al., 2012). The latter point is particularly important as it suggests that play-based approaches to promoting motor skills in preschools across the country are unlikely to yield any positive effects. That is, just providing children with opportunities to play on the playground (even with motor equipment such as balls and bats) does not change the children's motor development (Logan et al., 2012). Like any other academic skill, if motor skills are to be improved, the following must occur: (1) thoughtful planning of motor skill development with an understanding of how these FMSs emerge (see Tables 4.1 and 4.2); (2) selection of a variety of good tasks aligned with the developmental level of the children; (3) many opportunities to practice a wide range of skills with maximum opportunities to respond; (4) teacher facilitation and demonstration of skills; (5) individual feedback on performance; and (6) reward structures and/or other motivational techniques (National Association for Sport and Physical Education, 2009). It is also helpful when children are allowed to make choices within the instructional environment, self-monitor, and engage in self-assessment. In other words, without this kind of facilitated approach to motor development, in many children motor skills will not naturally emerge. Given the importance of the early childhood time-frame to develop FMS competence and start on a positive physical literacy journey, it is important that young children receive evidenced-based FMS interventions.

Physical Activity Levels and Physical Activity Guidelines in Early Childhood

In the sections above, we have documented the importance of promoting motor competence, specifically FMS competence in young children. A well-cited model by Stodden et al. (2008) supports this view suggesting that there is a synergistic relationship between motor competence, especially FMS competence, and physical activity. Furthermore, this model suggests the interactions among the variables in the model will drive individuals toward a healthy or unhealthy weight status. Stodden and colleagues (2008) suggest during early childhood, opportunities to engage in physical activity drive the development of motor competence (in this case FMS competence). The relationship between motor competence and physical activity is mediated by perceived motor competence and physical fitness (Figure 4.1).

The conceptual model by Stodden and colleagues has been supported by a growing body of evidence and suggests that children need to develop motor competence in FMS in order to be physically active across the lifespan (Van Capelle, Broderick, van Doorn, Ward, & Parmenter, 2017; Barnett et al., 2009; Engel, Broderick, van Doorn, Parameter, & Hardy, 2018; Figueroa & An, 2017; Lopes, Stodden, Bianchi, Maia, & Rodrigues, 2012; Robinson et al., 2015). A young child who is less active physically will have less opportunity to improve FMS competence. Later, this child is more likely to opt out of physical activity when given a chance (e.g., in recess), which will further compound their low motor competence. Ultimately, they will also develop low perceived motor competence (self-judgment around one's ability to perform motor skills) and low physical fitness levels. All of these relationships strengthen from early childhood to adolescence resulting in a child who is inactive and overweight/obese. Early childhood is the timeframe in which to develop FMS competence to set children on a positive spiral of engagement in physical activity and a healthy developmental trajectory of physical literacy (Engel et al., 2018; Figueroa & An, 2017; Robinson et al., 2015; Van Capelle et al., 2017).

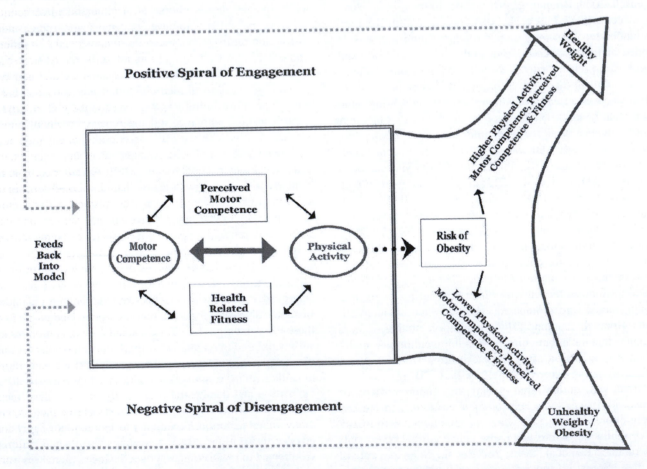

Figure 4.1 Developmental mechanisms influencing physical activity trajectories of children. Reprinted from "A Developmental Perspective on the Role of Physical Competence in Physical Activity: An Emergent Relationship" by Stodden et al., 2008, *Quest, 60*, p. 290–306. Copyright 2008 National Association for Kinesiology and Physical Education in Higher Education.

In line with findings on older children, there has been a significant rise in the obesity levels of young children (Cyril, Nicholson, Agho, Polonsky, & Renzaho, 2017; Lobstein & Jackson-Leach, 2016; Mihrshahi, Drayton, Bauman, & Hardy, 2018; Skinner, Ravanbakht, Skelton, Perrin, & Armstrong, 2018). In fact, children ages two to five years showed the sharpest increase in prevalence of overweight/obesity than any other time period (Skinner et al., 2018). Correspondingly, scholars have begun to focus attention on the physical activity levels of young children and the factors associated with physical activity (Guo, Schenkelberg, O'Neill, Dowda, & Pate, 2018; Pate, O'Neill, & Mitchell, 2010; Reilly, 2010; Schmutz et al., 2017; Ward, Vaughn, McWilliams, & Hales, 2010).

Known correlates of childhood and adolescent physical activity levels include FMS competence (Barnett et al., 2016a; Figueroa & An, 2017; Guo et al., 2018; Robinson et al., 2015). Yet, despite the importance of FMS with physical activity, most associational and predictive studies involving physical activity data on young children rarely include FMS in their analyses (less than 4% of studies according to a systematic review and meta-analysis by Schmutz et al., 2017). Indeed, attention seems to be shifting toward how physical activity associates with social-emotional behavior, executive function, cognitive development, and socio-ecological factors, and less on FMS competence in spite of its importance (Schmutz et al., 2017). Thus, the importance of FMSs needs to be disseminated across multiple fields so that it can be more widely recognized. Moreover, there is still much to be learned about the role motor competence plays in supporting physical activity behaviors from early childhood to adolescence and beyond. This certainly represents an area of future research. But how much activity, including time where children learn FMS as well as time in free play, is recommended for children in early childhood?

Physical Activity Guidelines for Early Childhood

In 2009 the National Association of Sport and Physical Education (NASPE) revised "Active Start," a set of national physical activity guidelines within the USA for children aged 0–5 years. Overall, NASPE recommend that: "All children birth to age 5 should engage in daily physical activity that promotes movement skillfulness and foundations of health-related fitness." These initial guidelines reflect what many other countries have subsequently developed.

The guidelines are different for infants (0–1 years), toddlers (1–3 years), and preschoolers (3–5 years). In each age category five guidelines are identified dealing with structured activity, unstructured activity, development of motor skills, safe places to be active, and education of caregivers. For the preschool population, the Active Start (NASPE, 2009) guidelines suggest: (1) accumulate at least 60 minutes of structured physical activity per day; (2) engage in at least 60 minutes and up to several hours of unstructured physical activity per day, and should not be sedentary for more than 60 minutes at a time except when sleeping; (3) develop

FMS competence as these skills are the building blocks for future physical activities and skillfulness; (4) have indoor and outdoor areas that meet or exceed recommended safety standards for performing large muscle activities; and (5) have caregivers who understand the importance of physical activity and promote movement skills by providing opportunities for structured and unstructured physical activity. The guidelines are much more comprehensive than the synthesis above. We encourage people to read the entire document as many different ideas are provided under each of the guidelines that promote choices for children and lots of different movement contexts allowing children and teachers to co-create movement across the day.

Since the adoption of the Active Start Guidelines in the USA, other countries have penned their own version. Guidelines of countries such as Australia ("Move and Play Every Day") (Australian Government, Department of Health, 2014) and the UK ("Start Active, Stay Active") (Department of Health, United Kingdom Government, 2011) recommend children younger than five years old should be encouraged to be physically active at a moderate intensity, at least three hours spread throughout the day, and time spent in sedentary behaviors be limited. Many countries are beginning to conceptualize guidelines for the young child within a 24-hour timeframe and how much time should be spent in sleep, physical activity, or sedentary behavior. The Canadian guidelines highlight that children should spend 180 minutes of total physical activity at any intensity spread across the day with activities that promote movement skills, are conducted in different environments, and hopefully achieve at least 60 minutes of energetic play (Tremblay et al., 2017). Collectively, these guidelines suggest that preschool children be physically active for at least 60 minutes per day with bouts of MVPA, have limited time spent in sedentary behavior, and have opportunities to develop FMS in safe places. It is not possible within the limits of this chapter to summarize in detail the literature on early childhood physical activity. However, three recent reviews of the literature capture the major findings in this area and will point the reader to other relevant readings.

Truelove et al. (2018) conducted a review (26 articles) of objectively and subjectively measured physical activity and sedentary behavior in 3–6-year-olds during the child care day. He concluded that children in child care settings spend 1.54 minutes per hour in MVPA and up to 40.64 minutes per hour in sedentary time. Thus, according to Truelove et al., children still fail to meet physical activity guidelines during child care settings. Hesketh, Lakshman, and van Sluijs (2017) review suggested that skill level, child enjoyment of physical activity, structured activity time, parents as role models, and many other factors are barriers and facilitators of physical activity across populations and settings in child care settings. However, both within and between studies there was variability in physical activity levels, depending upon assessment type. Hesketh et al. (2017) as well as others such as True et al. (2017) and Ward and colleagues (2010) suggested that future studies should attempt to intervene upon these modifiable features in the child care environment that might promote higher levels of physical activity.

Ward and colleagues (2010) reviewed the literature ($N = 19$ articles) surrounding interventions for increasing physical activity in child care settings. The majority of intervention studies produced positive outcomes tied to increasing physical activity (Ward et al., 2010). Twelve of the original 19 studies used a formal curriculum to increase daily total physical activity, motor skill development, or some other activity-related outcome. However, the majority of these studies were short term and lacked follow-up data to support their longitudinal effectiveness.

Fortunately, an emergent literature base now shows results from long-term follow-ups from physical activity and FMS interventions (e.g., Lai et al., 2014; Zask et al., 2012a). All concurred that improving FMS was a promising strategy for sustaining physical activity behaviors and FMS development. Interestingly, programs that were more successful in increasing physical activity provided more frequency and duration of structured physical activity (Ward et al., 2010) and also included FMS as a central focus of the intervention (Lai et al., 2014). Despite this, in the studies with higher amounts of structured physical activity, the amount of physical activity was still below the NASPE "Active Start" (2009) recommendations for preschoolers.

The Lai et al. review concluded that policy should be developed to require a focus on learning FMS during the preschool years to increase the likelihood of sustained physical activity behaviors. The findings from these review studies not only align with recommendations for promoting the movement competence construct of physical literacy (e.g., Dudley et al., 2017), but provide further support for the hypothesized relationships within the Stodden et al. (2008) model. However, few early childhood centers have policies and structured programs that would promote FMS competence (Brian, Pennell, Schenkelburg, & Sacko, 2019; McWilliams et al., 2009). Not only do few early childhood centers require structured physical activity time, most preschool teachers feel ill-equipped to lead such programming (Brian et al., 2019). Ideally, early childhood centers would have a licensed physical educator to meet the motor and physical activity needs of their children. However, this is highly unrealistic. Thus, preservice teacher training programs need to incorporate an early year's motor development/physical activity class to help classroom teachers meet the motor and physical activity needs of their children.

Recommendations for Promoting Early Childhood Motor Competence and Physical Activity

We believe that the early years are critical to the lifelong health and physical activity of this nation's children. The area of motor skills is so often misunderstood with the common misconception that if we let them out to play, FMS will naturally develop during the early childhood years. In this chapter, we have reviewed the theoretical and empirical support on the emergence of FMS, how FMS may not emerge in a timely sequence in some populations, and the variety of factors that affect motor skill development. In addition, we have reviewed the developmental sequences of FMS, early childhood motor skill interventions, along with a summary of the physical activity levels of young children. We also hope that we have provided motivation to design facilitated motor skill programming to promote FMS competence during early childhood. We believe that one marker of a high-quality early childhood program is one where children receive regular *structured* (facilitated) motor skill instruction along with many opportunities to engage in *unstructured* physical activity experiences throughout the day (NASPE, 2009; Tremblay et al., 2017) along with limiting time spent in sedentary behaviors. Also, that the teachers of this program are knowledgeable about motor skill development and become important role models to their children in this important and often ignored area of development. Most importantly, we believe that FMS development is too important to be left to chance if we are truly concerned about increasing young children's levels of physical activity and giving all young children a positive start to their physical literacy journeys.

Based on the literature reviewed, there are a number of recommendations:

1. Many young children, especially those from disadvantaged environments, demonstrate significant delays in FMS and need motor skill intervention.
2. Both girls and boys are delayed in FMS, but girls are significantly lower in manipulative skills than boys. There are no differences between gender in locomotor skills. Thus, we need to make sure that FMS interventions particularly meet the needs of girls who are delayed in their manipulative skills.
3. The business as usual control groups in the intervention studies typically showed no improvement in their FMS and were essentially "flatliners." Thus, what is typically delivered in our early childhood settings is not adequate to help children develop the necessary levels of motor competence to be physically active. We need to enact policy in our early childhood settings ensuring that all children receive evidenced-based programming to promote their motor competence.
4. Studies conducted by experts had larger effect sizes than studies delivered by teachers. However, teachers can be trained to deliver motor skill programs effectively resulting in positive outcomes for children. This approach is a cost-effective way to promote FMS development and physical activity in young children and has translational power.
5. The dose of motor skill interventions ranged from 360 minutes to 7,680 minutes. Motor skill interventions with a minimum of 360 minutes of instructional time have shown

significant improvement in children's motor competence, and up to large effect sizes (Brian et al., 2017a, 2017b). In essence, the amount of time needed to be devoted to these programs is minimal and feasible in early childhood settings.

In conclusion, early motor skill interventions need to be delivered within our child care settings to promote the motor competence of young children, especially those from disadvantaged communities. These programs are essential to help our children get an active start and begin a positive physical literacy journey across the lifespan.

References

Adamo, K. B., Wilson, S., Harvey, A. J., Grattan, K. P., Naylor, P., Temple, V. A., & Goldfield, G. S. (2015). Does intervening in childcare settings impact fundamental movement skill development? *Medicine & Science in Sports & Exercise, 48*(5), 926–932.

Adams, J., Zask, A., & Dietrich, U. (2009). Tooty Fruity Vegie in preschools: An obesity prevention intervention in preschools targeting children's movement skills and eating behaviours. *Health Promotion Journal of Australia, 20*(2), 112–119.

Alhassan, S., Nwaokelemeh, O., Ghazarian, M., Roberts, J., Mendoza, A., & Shitole, S. (2012). Effects of locomotor skill program on minority preschoolers' physical activity levels. *Pediatric Exercise Science, 24*(3), 435–449.

Apache, R. G. (2005). Activity-based intervention in motor skill development. *Perceptual and Motor Skills, 100*(3_suppl), 1011–1020.

Armstrong, N., & Welsman, J. R. (2000). Development of aerobic fitness during childhood and adolescence. *Pediatric Exercise Science, 12*, 128–149.

Australian Government, Department of Health. (2014). *Move and play every day*. Retrieved March 2, 2018 from: https://www.health.gov.au/internet/main/publishing.nsf/content/ F01F92328EDADA5BCA257B-F0001E720D/$File/Move%20and%20play%20every%20day%20 0-5yrs.PDF

Aylward, G. P. (2014). Neurodevelopmental outcomes of infants born prematurely. *Journal of Developmental & Behavioral Pediatrics, 35*(6), 394–407.

Barnett, L., Hinkley, T., Okely, A. D., & Salmon, J. (2013). Child, family and environmental correlates of children's motor skill proficiency. *Journal of Science & Medicine in Sport, 16*(4), 332–336.

Barnett, L. M., Lai, S. K., Veldman, S. L. C., Hardy, L. L., Cliff, D. P., Morgan, P. J., ... Rush, E. (2016a). Correlates of gross motor competence in children and adolescents: A systematic review and meta-analysis. *Sports Medicine, 46*(11), 1663–1688. doi:10.1007/s40279-016-0495-z

Barnett, L. M., Telford, R. M., Strugnell, C., Rudd, J., Olive, L. S., & Telford, R. D. (2018). Impact of cultural background on fundamental movement skill and its correlates. *Journal of Sports Sciences, 37*(5), 492–499. doi:10.1080/02640414.2018.1508399

Barnett, L., van Beurden, E., Morgan, P., Brooks, L., & Beard, J. (2009). Childhood motor skill proficiency as a predictor of adolescent physical activity. *Journal of Adolescent Health, 44*, 252–259.

Barnett, L. M., van Beurden, E., Morgan, P. J., Brooks, L. O., & Beard, J. R. (2010). Gender differences in motor skill proficiency from childhood to adolescence: A longitudinal study. *Research Quarterly for Exercise and Sport, 81*(2), 162–170.

Barnett, L. M., Zask, A., Rose, L., Hughes, D., & Adams, J. (2015). Three-year follow-up of an early childhood intervention: What about physical activity and weight status? *Journal of Physical Activity & Health, 12*(3), 319–321.

Bellows, L. L., Davies, P. L., Anderson, J., & Kennedy, C. (2013). Effectiveness of a physical activity intervention for Head Start preschoolers: A randomized intervention study. *American Journal of Occupational Therapy, 67*(1), 28–36.

Beunen, G., & Thomis, M. (2000). Muscular strength development in children and adolescents. *Pediatric Exercise Science, 12*, 174–197.

Blimkie, C. J. R., & Sale, D. G. (1998). Strength development and trainability during childhood. In E. Van Praagh (Ed.), *Pediatric anaerobic performance* (pp. 193–224). Champaign, IL: Human Kinetics.

Bonvin, A., Barral, J., Kakebeeke, T. H., Kriemler, S., Longchamp, A., Schindler, C., ... Puder, J. J. (2013). Effect of a governmentally-led physical activity program on motor skills in young children attending child care centers: A cluster randomized controlled trial. *International Journal of Behavioral Nutrition & Physical Activity, 10*, 90. doi:10.1186/1479-5868-10-90

Brian, A., Bardid, F., Barnett, L. M., Deconinck, F. J., Lenoir, M., & Goodway, J. D. (2018). Actual and perceived motor competence levels of Belgian and United States preschool children. *Journal of Motor Learning and Development, 6*(S2), S320–S336.

Brian, A., Goodway, J. D., Logan, J. A., & Sutherland, S. (2017a). SKIPing with teachers: An early years motor skill intervention. *Physical Education and Sport Pedagogy, 22*(3), 270–282.

Brian, A., Goodway, J. D., Logan, J. A., & Sutherland, S. (2017b). SKIPing with Head Start teachers: Influence of T-SKIP on object-control skills. *Research Quarterly for Exercise and Sport, 88*(4), 479–491.

Brian, A., Pennell, A., Schenkelburg, M., & Sacko, R. (2019). Preschool teachers' confidence with and facilitation of the active start guidelines for physical activity. *Journal of Motor Learning and Development, 6*(2), 333–344.

Brian, A., & Taunton, S. (2018). Effectiveness of intervention varies on instructor and pedagogical strategy. *Physical Education and Sport Pedagogy, 23*(2), 222–233.

Butterfield, S. A., Angell, R. M., & Mason, C. A. (2012). Age and sex differences in object control skills by children ages 5 to 14. *Perceptual and Motor Skills, 114*(1), 261–274.

Cairney, J., Bedard, C., Dudley, D., & Kriellaars, D. (2016). Towards a physical literacy framework to guide the design, implementation and evaluation of early childhood movement-based interventions targeting cognitive development. *Annual Reviews of Sports Medicine, 3*(4), 1073.

Clark, J. E., & Metcalfe, J. S. (2002). The mountain of motor development: A metaphor. In. J. E. Clark & J. H. Humphrey (Eds.), *Motor development: Research and review* (Vol. 2, pp. 62–95). Reston, VA: National Association for Sport and Physical Education (NASPE) Publications.

Clark, J. E., & Whitall, J. (1989). What is motor development: The lessons of history. *Quest, 41*, 183–202.

Cools, W., Martelaer, K., D., Samaey, C., & Andries, C. (2011). Fundamental movement skill performance of preschool children in relation to family context. *Journal of Sports Sciences, 29*, 649–660. doi:10.1080/0264 0414.2010.551540

Cyril, S., Nicholson, J. M., Agho, K., Polonsky, M., & Renzaho, A. M. (2017). Barriers and facilitators to childhood obesity prevention among culturally and linguistically diverse (CALD) communities in Victoria, Australia. *Australian and New Zealand Journal of Public Health, 41*(3), 287–293.

De Meester, A., Stodden, D., Goodway, J., True, L., Brian, A., Ferkel, R., & Haerens, L. (2018). Identifying a motor proficiency barrier for meeting physical activity guidelines in children. *Journal of Science and Medicine in Sport, 21*(1), 58–62.

Deli, E., Bakle, I., & Zachopoulou, E. (2006). Implementing intervention movement programs for kindergarten children. *Journal of Early Childhood Research, 4*(1), 5–18.

Department of Health, United Kingdom Government. (2011). *Start active, stay active*. Retrieved from: https://www.gov.uk/government/publications/start-active-stay-active-a-report-on-physical-activity-from-the-four-home-countries-chief-medical-officers

Draper, C. E., Achmat, M., Forbes, J., & Lambert, E. V. (2012). Impact of a community-based programme for motor development on gross motor skills and cognitive function in preschool children from disadvantaged settings. *Early Child Development and Care, 182*(1), 137–152.

Dudley, D., Cairney, J., Wainwright, N., Kriellaars, D., & Mitchell, D. (2017). Critical considerations for physical literacy policy in public health, recreation, sport, and education agencies. *Quest, 69*(4), 436–452.

Ehl, T., Roberton, M. A., & Langendorfer, S. J. (2005). Does the throwing "gender gap" occur in Germany? *Research Quarterly for Exercise and Sport, 76*, 488–493.

Engel, A. C., Broderick, C. R., van Doorn, N., Parmenter, B. J., & Hardy, L. L. (2018). Exploring the relationship between fundamental motor skill interventions and physical activity levels in children: A systematic review and meta-analysis. *Sports Medicine, 48*(8), 1845–1857. doi:10.1007/s40279-018-0923-3

Famelia, R., Tsuda, E., Bakhiar, S., & Goodway, J. D. (2018). Relationships among perceived and actual motor skill competence and physical activity in Indonesian preschoolers. *Journal of Motor Learning and Development. 6*(S2), S403–S423.

Figueroa, R., & An, R. (2017). Motor skill competence and physical activity in preschoolers: A review. *Maternal and Child Health Journal, 21*(1), 136–146. doi:10.1007/s10995

Gallahue, D. L. (1982). *Understanding motor development in children.* Hoboken, NJ: John Wiley & Sons.

Gallahue, D. L., Ozmun, J. C., & Goodway, J. D. (2012). *Understanding motor development: Infants, children, adolescents, adults* (7th ed.). New York, NY: McGraw Hill.

Garcia, C. (1994). Gender differences in young children's interaction when learning fundamental motor skills. *Research Quarterly for Exercise and Sport, 65*(3), 213–225.

Garcia, C., & Garcia, L. (2002). Examining developmental changes in throwing. In J. E. Clark & J. H. Humphrey (Eds.), *Motor development: Research and review* (Vol. 2, pp. 62–95). Reston, VA: National Association for Sport and Physical Education (NASPE) Publications.

Golos, A., Sarid, M., Weill, M., & Weintraub, N. (2011). Efficacy of an early intervention program for at-risk preschool boys: A two-group control study. *American Journal of Occupational Therapy, 65*(4), 400–408.

Goodway, J. D., & Branta, C. F. (2003). Influence of a motor skill intervention on fundamental motor skill development of disadvantaged preschool children. *Research Quarterly for Exercise and Sport, 74*(1), 36–47.

Goodway, J. D., Crowe, H., & Ward, P. (2003). Effects of motor skill instruction on fundamental motor skill development. *Adapted Physical Activity Quarterly, 20*(3), 298–314.

Goodway, J. D., Famelia, R., & Bakhtiar, S. (2014). Future directions in physical education & sport: Developing fundamental motor competence in the early years is paramount to lifelong physical activity. *Asian Social Science, 10*(5), 44. doi:10.5539/ass.v10n5p44

Goodway, J. D., & Robinson, L. E. (2006). SKIPing toward an active start: Promoting physical activity in preschoolers. *Beyond the Journal: Young Children, 61*(3), 1–6.

Goodway, J. D., Robinson, L. E., & Crowe, H (2010). Developmental delays in fundamental motor skill development of ethnically diverse and disadvantaged preschoolers. *Research Quarterly for Exercise and Sport, 81*(1), 17–25.

Goodway, J. D., & Smith, D. W. (2005). Keeping all children healthy: Challenges to leading an active lifestyle for preschool children qualifying for at-risk programs. *Family & Community Health, 28*, 142–155.

Graham, G., Holt-Hale, S. A., & Parker, M. (2007). *Children moving: A reflective approach to teaching physical education* (5th ed.). Mountain View, CA: Mayfield.

Guo, H., Schenkelberg, M. A., O'Neill, J. R., Dowda, M., & Pate, R. R. (2018). How does the relationship between motor skill performance and body mass index impact physical activity in preschool children? *Pediatric Exercise Science, 30*(2), 266–272.

Hamilton, M., Goodway, J. D., & Haubenstricker, J. (1999). Parent-assisted instruction in a motor skill program for at-risk preschool children. *Adapted Physical Activity Quarterly, 16*(4), 415–426.

Hardy, L. L., King, L., Kelly, B., Farrell, L., & Howlett, S. (2010). Munch and move: Evaluation of a preschool healthy eating and movement skill program. *International Journal of Behavioral Nutrition and Physical Activity, 7*(1), 80.

Hardy, L. L., Reinten-Reynolds, T., Espinel, P., Zask, A., & Okely, A. D. (2012). Prevalence and correlates of low fundamental movement skill competency in children. *Pediatrics, 130*(2), e390–e398.

Haywood, K. M., & Getchell, N. (2014). *Lifespan motor development* (6th ed.). Champaign, IL: Human Kinetics.

Hesketh, K. R., Lakshman, R., & van Sluijs, E. M. F. (2017). Barriers and facilitators to young children's physical activity and sedentary behaviour: A systematic review and synthesis of qualitative literature. *Obesity Reviews, 18*(9), 987–1017.

Higgs, C., Balyi, I., Way, R., Cardinal, C., Norris, S., & Bluechart, M. (2005). *Developing physical literacy: A guide for parents of children ages 0 to 12.* Vancouver, Canada: Canadian Sport Centres.

Hulleman, C. S., Rimm-Kaufman, S. E., & Abry, T. (2013). Innovative methodologies to explore implementation. Whole-part-whole: Construct validity, measurement, and analytical issues for fidelity assessment in education research. In T. G. Halle, A. J. Metz, & I. Martinez-Beck (Eds.), *Applying implementation science in early childhood programs and systems* (pp. 65–93). Baltimore, MD: Paul H. Brookes Publishing Co.

Iivonen, S., & Sääkslahti, A. K. (2013). Preschool children's fundamental motor skills: A review of significant determinants. *Early Child Development and Care, 184*(7), 1107–1126. doi:10.1080/03004430.2013.837897

Individuals with Disabilities Education Act (IDEA). (2004). 20 U.S.C. § 1400.

IPLA (International Physical Literacy Association). (2017). The definition of physical literacy. Retrieved July 30, 2019 from http://www.physical-literacy.org.uk/

Jones, R. A., Riethmuller, A., Hesketh, K., Trezise, J., Batterham, M., & Okely, A. D. (2011). Promoting fundamental movement skill development and physical activity in early childhood settings: A cluster randomized controlled trial. *Pediatric Exercise Science, 23*(4), 600–615.

Jurbala, P. (2015). What is physical literacy. *Quest, 67*(4), 367–383. doi:10.1080/00336297.2015.1084341

Kordi, R., Nourian, R., Ghayour, M., Kordi, M., & Younesian, A. (2012). Development and evaluation of a basic physical and sports activity program for preschool children in nursery schools in Iran: An interventional study. *Iranian Journal of Pediatrics, 22*(3), 357–363.

Langendorfer, S. J., & Roberton, M. A. (2002). Developmental profiles in overarm throwing: Searching for "attractors", "stages", and "constraints." In J. E. Clark & J. H. Humphrey (Eds.). *Motor development: Research and review: Vol. 2* (pp. 1–25). Reston, VA: National Association for Sport and Physical Education (NASPE) Publications.

Lai, S. K., Costigan, S. A., Morgan, P. J., Lubans, D. R., Stodden, D. F., Salmon, J., & Barnett, L. M. (2014). Do school-based interventions focusing on physical activity, fitness, or fundamental movement skill competency produce a sustained impact in these outcomes in children and adolescents? A systematic review of follow-up studies. *Sports Medicine, 44*(1), 67–79.

Lobstein, T., & Jackson-Leach, R. (2016). Planning for the worst: Estimates of obesity and comorbidities in school-age children in 2025. *Pediatric Obesity, 11*(5), 321–325.

Logan, S., Robinson, L., Webster, E. K., & Barber, L. (2013). Exploring preschoolers' engagement and perceived physical competence in an autonomy-based object control skill intervention: A preliminary study. *European Physical Education Review, 19*(3), 302–314.

Logan, S. W., Robinson, L. E., Wilson, A. E., & Lucas, W. A. (2012). Getting the fundamentals of movement: A meta-analysis of the effectiveness of motor skill interventions in children. *Child: Care, Health and Development, 38*(3), 305–315.

Lopes, V. P., Stodden, D. F., Bianchi, M. M., Maia, J. A., & Rodrigues, L. P. (2012). Correlation between BMI and motor coordination in children. *Journal of Science and Medicine in Sport, 15*(1), 38–43.

Malina, R. M., Bouchard, C. L., & Bar-Or, O. (2004). *Growth, maturation, and physical activity* (2nd ed.). Champaign, IL: Human Kinetics.

Martin, E. H., Rudisill, M. E., & Hastie, P., (2009). The effectiveness of a mastery motivational climate motor skill intervention in a naturalistic physical education setting. *Physical Education and Sport Pedagogy, 14*, 227–240.

McWilliams, C., Ball, S. C., Benjamin, S. E., Hales, D., Vaughn, A., & Ward, D. S. (2009). Best-practice guidelines for physical activity at child care. *Pediatrics, 124*(6), 1650–1659.

Mihrshahi, S., Drayton, B. A., Bauman, A. E., & Hardy, L. L. (2018). Associations between childhood overweight, obesity, abdominal obesity and obesogenic behaviors and practices in Australian homes. *BMC public health, 18*(1), 44.

Monsalves Álvarez, M., Castro Sepúlveda, M., Zapata Lamana, R., Rosales Soto, G., & Salazar, G. (2015). Motor skills and nutritional status outcomes from a physical activity intervention in short breaks on preschool children conducted by their educators: A pilot study. *Nutricion Hospitalaria, 32*(4), 1576–1581.

Morgan, P. J., Barnett, L. M., Cliff, D. P., Okely, A. D., Scott, H. A., Cohen, K. E., & Lubans, D. R. (2013). Fundamental movement skill interventions in youth: A systematic review and meta-analysis. *Pediatrics, 132*(5), e1361–e1383.

National Association for Sport and Physical Education. (2009). *Active start: A statement of physical activity guidelines for children birth to five years,* (2nd ed.). Oxon Hill, MD: AAHPERD Publications.

Newell, K. M. (1984). Physical constraints to development of motor skills. In J. Thomas (Ed.), *Motor development during preschool and elementary years* (pp. 105–120). Minneapolis, MI: Burgess.

Newell, K. M. (1986). Constraints on the development of coordination. In M. G. Wade & H. T. Whiting (Eds.), *Motor development in children: Aspects of coordination and control* (pp. 341–360). Dordrecht, The Netherlands: Nijhoff.

Office of Head Start. (2019). *Head Start Programs.* Retrieved from: https://www.acf.hhs.gov/ohs/about/head-start

Oja, L., & Jurimae, T. (1998). Relationship between physical activity, motor ability, and anthropometric variables in 6-year-old Estonian children. In J. Parizkova & A. P. Hills (Eds.). *Physical fitness and nutrition during growth* (pp. 68–78). Basel, Belgium: Karger.

Okely, A. D., & Booth, M. L. (2004). Mastery of fundamental movement skills among children in New South Wales: Prevalence and sociodemographic distribution. *Journal of Science and Medicine in Sport, 7*(3), 358–372.

Pate, R. R., O'Neill, J. R., & Mitchell, J. (2010). Measurement of physical activity in preschool children. *Medicine & Science in Sports & Exercise, 42*, 508–512.

Piek, J. P., McLaren, S., Kane, R., Jensen, L., Dender, A., Roberts, C., ... Straker, L. (2013). Does the Animal Fun program improve motor performance in children aged 4–6 years? *Human Movement Science, 32*(5), 1086–1096.

Pitchik, H. O., Fawzi, W. W., McCoy, D. C., Darling, A. M., Abioye, A. I., Tesha, F., ... Sudfeld, C. R. (2018). Prenatal nutrition, stimulation, and exposure to punishment are associated with early child motor, cognitive, language, and socioemotional development in Dar es Salaam, Tanzania. *Child: Care, Health and Development, 44*(6), 841–849.

Reilly, J. J. (2010). Low levels of objectively measured physical activity in preschoolers in child care. *Medicine & Science in Sports & Exercise, 42*, 502–507.

Reilly, J. J., Kelly, L., Montgomery, C., Williamson, A., Fisher, A., McColl, J. H., ... Grant, S. (2006). Physical activity to prevent obesity in young children: Cluster randomised controlled trial. *BMJ: British Medical Journal (International Edition), 333*(7577), 1041–1043.

Riethmuller, A. M., Jones, R. A., & Okely, A. D. (2009). Efficacy of interventions to improve motor development in young children: A systematic review. *Pediatrics, 124*(4), e782–e792.

Roberton, M. A. (1978). Stages in motor development. In M. V. Ridenour (Ed.). *Motor development: Issues and applications* (pp. 63–81). Princeton, NJ: Princeton Book Company.

Robinson, L. E. (2011). Effect of a mastery climate motor program on object control skills and perceived physical competence in preschoolers. *Research Quarterly for Exercise and Sport, 82*(2), 355–359.

Robinson, L. E., & Goodway, J. D. (2009). Instructional climates in preschool children who are at risk. Part I: Object control skill development. *Research Quarterly for Exercise and Sport, 80*(3), 533–542.

Robinson, L. E., Stodden, D. F., Barnett, L. M., Lopes, V. P., Logan, S. W., Rodrigues, L. P., & D'Hondt, E. (2015). Motor competence and its effect on positive developmental trajectories of health. *Sports Medicine, 45*(9), 1273–1284.

Robinson, L. E., Webster, E. K., Logan, S. W., Lucas, W. A., & Barber, L. T. (2012). Teaching practices that promote motor skills in early childhood settings. *Early Childhood Education Journal, 40*(2), 79–86.

Saccani, R., Valentini, N. C., Pereira, K. R., Müller, A. B., & Gabbard, C. (2013). Associations of biological factors and affordances in the home with infant motor development. *Pediatrics International, 55*(2), 197–203.

Schmutz, E. A., Leeger-Aschmann, C. S., Radtke, T., Muff, S., Kakebeeke, T. H., Zysset, A. E., ... Munsch, S. (2017). Correlates of preschool children's objectively measured physical activity and sedentary behavior: A cross-sectional analysis of the SPLASHY study. *International Journal of Behavioral Nutrition and Physical Activity, 14*(1), 1.

Seefeldt, V. (1980). The concepts of readiness applied to motor skill acquisition. In R. A. Magill, M. J. Ash, & F. L. Smoll (Eds.), *Children in sport* (pp. 335–348). Champaign, IL: Human Kinetics.

Seefeldt, V., & Haubenstricker, J. (1982). Patterns, phases, or stages: An analytic model for the study of developmental movement. In J. A. S. Kelso & J. E. Clark (Eds.). *The development of movement control and co-ordination* (pp. 309–318). New York, NY: Wiley.

Skinner, A. C., Ravanbakht, S. N., Skelton, J. A., Perrin, E. M., & Armstrong, S. C. (2018). Prevalence of obesity and severe obesity in US children, 1999–2016. *Pediatrics, 141*(3), e20173459.

Spessato, B. C., Gabbard, C., Valentini, N., & Rudisill, M. (2013). Gender differences in Brazilian children's fundamental movement skill performance. *Early Child Development and Care, 183*(7), 916–923.

Sport for Life et al. (2015). Canada's physical literacy consensus statement. Retrieved September 9, 2019 from https://sportforlife.ca/wp-content/uploads/2016/06/Consensus-Handout.pdf

Stodden, D. F., Goodway, J. D., Langendorfer, S. J., Roberton, M. A., Rudisill, M. E, Garcia, C., & Garcia, L. E. (2008). A Developmental perspective on the role of motor skill competence in physical activity: An emergent relationship. *Quest, 60*, 290–306.

Stodden, D. F., True, L., K., Langendorfer, S. J., & Gao, Z. (2013). Associations among selected motor skills and health-related fitness: Indirect evidence for Seefeldt's proficiency barrier in young adults. *Research Quarterly for Exercise and Sport, 84*(3), 397–403.

Thelen, E. (1995). Motor development: A new synthesis. *American Psychologist, 50*, 79–95.

Thomas, J. R., & French, K. E. (1985). Gender differences across age in motor performance: A meta-analysis. *Psychological Bulletin, 98*, 260–282.

Tremblay, M. S., Chaput, J. P., Adamo, K. B., Aubert, S., Barnes, J. D., Choquette, L., ..., Gruber, R. (2017). Canadian 24-hour movement guidelines for the early years (0–4 years): An integration of physical activity, sedentary behaviour, and sleep. *BMC Public Health, 17*(5), 874.

True, L., Pfeiffer, K. A., Dowda, M., Williams, H. G., Brown, W. H., O'Neill, J. R., & Pate, R. R. (2017). Motor competence and characteristics within the preschool environment. *Journal of Science and Medicine in Sport, 20*(8), 751–755.

Truelove, S., Bruijns, B. A., Vanderloo, L. M., O'Brien, K. T., Johnson, A. M., & Tucker, P. (2018). Physical activity and sedentary time during childcare outdoor play sessions: A systematic review and meta-analysis. *Preventive Medicine, 108*, 74–85.

Tsapakidou, A., Stefanidou, S., & Tsompanaki, E. (2014). Locomotor development of children aged 3.5 to 5 years in nursery schools in Greece. *Review of European Studies, 6*(2), 1.

Ulrich, D. (2000). *Test of Gross Motor Development-2.* Austin, TX: Pro-Ed.

Valentini, N. C., Logan, S. W., Spessato, B. C., de Souza, M. S., Pereira, K. G., & Rudisill, M. E. (2016). Fundamental motor skills across childhood: Age, sex, and competence outcomes of Brazilian children. *Journal of Motor Learning and Development, 4*(1), 16–36.

Valentini, N. C., & Rudisill, M. E., (2004). An inclusive mastery climate intervention and the motor skill development of children with and without disabilities. *Adapted Physical Activity Quarterly, 21*(3), 330–347.

Van Capelle, A., Broderick, C. R., van Doorn, N., Ward, R. E., & Parmenter, B. J. (2017). Review: Interventions to improve fundamental motor skills in pre-school aged children: A systematic review and meta-analysis. [Review Article]. *Journal of Science and Medicine in Sport, 20*, 658–666.

Veldman, S. L. C., Jones, R. A., & Okely, A. D. (2016). Efficacy of gross motor skill interventions in young children: An updated systematic review. *BMJ Open Sport & Exercise Medicine, 2*(1). doi:10.1136/bmjsem-2015–000067

Venetsanou, F., & Kambas, A. (2004). How can a traditional Greek dances programme affect the motor proficiency of pre-school children? *Research in Dance Education, 5*(2), 127–138.

Venetsanou, F., & Kambas, A. (2010). Environmental factors affecting pre-schoolers' motor development. *Early Childhood Education Journal, 37*(4), 319–327.

Ward, D. S., Vaughn, A., McWilliams, C., & Hales, D. (2010). Interventions for increasing physical activity at child care. *Medicine & Science in Sports & Exercise, 42*, 526–534.

Whitehead, M. (2001). The concept of physical literacy. *European Journal of Physical Education, 6*(2), 127–138.

Whitehead, M. (Ed.). (2010). *Physical literacy: Throughout the lifecourse.* London, UK: Routledge.

Winter, S. M., & Sass, D. A. (2011). Healthy & ready to learn: Examining the efficacy of an early approach to obesity prevention and school readiness. *Journal of Research in Childhood Education, 25*(3), 304–325.

Zask, A., Adams, J. K., Brooks, L. O., & Hughes, D. F. (2012b). Tooty Fruity Vegie: An obesity prevention intervention evaluation in Australian pre-schools. *Health Promotion Journal of Australia, 23*(1), 10–15.

Zask, A., Barnett, L. M., Rose, L., Brooks, L. O., Molyneux, M., Hughes, D., … Salmon, J. (2012a). Three year follow-up of an early childhood intervention: Is movement skill sustained? *International Journal of Behavioral Nutrition & Physical Activity, 9*, 127. doi:10.1186/1479-5868-9-127.

Part II

Early Childhood Educational Curriculum and Instruction

5

Print and Digital Picture Books in the Service of Young Children's Mathematics Learning

HERBERT P. GINSBURG, COLLEEN USCIANOWSKI, CRISTINA CARRAZZA, AND SUSAN C. LEVINE

Introduction

In the last edition of this *Handbook*, the chapter on Views and Issues in Children's Literature (Saracho, 2012) covered such topics as the history of children's literature, literary criticism, narrative theory, and research from a literary perspective, but did not include a discussion of math picture books. The same was true of another Handbook chapter on Children's Literature (Galda, Ash, & Cullinan, 2000).

Given this, the focus of this chapter may seem unusual for a review of young children's literature. For one thing, our main topic is "math" picture books, although, as we shall see, this narrow topic is more expansive and inclusive than it might first seem. But even so, why an exclusive focus on math? Surely this kind of book represents only a small fraction of children's literature, and, some might believe, not the most interesting. We focus on math picture books for several reasons, the main one being that they can serve as a friendly and meaningful introduction to math for both child and adult. Our focus on math does not imply that we devalue other kinds of picture books or that we want to turn the magical world of picture book reading into dull drill, the procedure that all too many associate with math education in our schools.

A second focus of our chapter is on digital books (e-books, interactive books), that is, books that adult and child "read" and with which they engage on an electronic device. For some, this kind of reading raises red flags: does the e-book promote active reading or passive entertainment? Do not children already spend too much time tethered (electronically) to screens? Some preschools have a zero-tolerance policy with regard to touch screen tablets and computers. We think this approach is mistaken. Digital devices in themselves are not harmful. The real issue is the value of the experiences that children can have in interacting with them. Exactly the same can be said about paper books. We should not ban e-books because some are terrible.

Finally, we note that our perspective derives in good measure from developmental psychology and cognitive science.

We think that science-based ideas about children's thinking and development can contribute to the understanding and betterment of children's literature and its uses. At the same time, we believe that this scientific perspective is not antithetical to a humanistic approach to children's literature. Indeed, one of our goals is to show how math picture books can and should fall squarely within the tradition of rich literature that stimulates children's thought, enjoyment, wonder, curiosity, and love of reading.

The first section deals with the effectiveness of paper picture books, with either implicit or explicit math content, in promoting children's math learning. The section then considers issues of quality and design.

The second section focuses on the potential for e-books to have a positive impact on children's learning and engagement, particularly relating to early math concepts and language. This section also concludes with a discussion of quality and design issues.

We conclude with a discussion of how the importance of math picture books for early math education in the home, school, and library requires promoting their use, improving their writing and design, and conducting further research.

Math Picture Book Reading

Parents often engage in learning activities with their young children, but these early interactions are more likely to support children's language and literacy skills than their math skills. In fact, parents believe math education is not their responsibility but rather should be in the hands of the school (Cannon & Ginsburg, 2008). This assumption is concerning because the math-related talk and activities parents engage in with their children before they start formal schooling, such as counting or labeling amounts, are predictive of their number knowledge and scaffold the development of foundational math concepts, such as understanding the "cardinal" meaning of the number words. The child needs to understand that the number words each refer to a quantity, a set size, so that the child can not only count to "three" but also understand what "three" *means* (Gunderson & Levine, 2011; Levine, Suriyakham, Rowe, Huttenlocher, & Gunderson, 2010). Furthermore, children's math knowledge at this age is one of the most important predictors of their future academic achievement, in mathematics as well as more broadly (Claessens & Engel, 2013; Duncan et al., 2007). Because parents tend to embrace language and literacy in the home, math picture books are potentially powerful tools that can be used to support young children's math learning.

There are two main types of books that can afford rich math input. The first type is children's print picture books explicitly designed to teach mathematics concepts and skills. These "explicit math books" include counting books, shape books, and storybooks that usually have a reference to math content in their title or covers. The second type of children's math books includes those that implicitly support numerical or spatial learning. These "implicit math books"—e.g., *Goldilocks and the Three Bears*—are usually storybooks containing rich math content that is not the primary focus of the story. Both types of picture books (implicit and explicit, non-fiction and fiction) have the potential to afford rich math input. In the implicit math books, math concepts such as number, shapes, or spatial relations can be represented and talked about through the illustrations and the text. For example, in *Goldilocks and the Three Bears* there is one-to-one correspondence between the number of bears and the number of beds. Children can also grasp concepts of spatial relations and relative size, as they realize that as the bears increase in size, their beds increase in size. Even though this story is not designed to teach math explicitly, it still introduces important math concepts.

Evidence from observational studies suggests that parents are able to attend to the math content in storybooks when reading to their young children. A study with four-year-old children and their parents found that most parents engaged in math-related talk when reading a storybook with no explicit math focus (Anderson, Anderson, & Shapiro, 2004). While the pages did not include direct prompts to count, the illustrations afforded the opportunity for math talk by featuring multiple characters of varied number, size, and shape. Results suggest, however, that there is considerable variation in both the amount and content of their math talk. Parents were most likely to focus on size and different aspects of number, while paying little attention to shapes (Anderson et al., 2004). Another study with four-year-olds and their parents found a strong relationship between the frequency of parent number talk during storybook reading and parent socioeconomic status. Higher income parents were more likely to engage in talk related to counting, quantity, or size during the activity than an ethnically diverse group of lower income parents (Vandermass-Peeler, Nelson, Bumpass, & Sassine, 2009).

Math Picture Book Reading Intervention Studies

One important type of picture book is the storybook (as opposed, for example, to a counting book or shape book).

Few studies have explored *what* children learn from reading math storybooks, yet evidence from classroom interventions suggests they can be a powerful tool to increase children's math knowledge. A study by Casey, Erkut, Ceder, and Young (2008) found that kindergarteners showed greater learning from a geometry lesson that incorporated a story-telling context compared to a lesson that focused on the spatial content alone. Hassinger-Das, Jordan, and Dyson (2015) showed that kindergartners with early math difficulties who read a storybook that featured mathematical vocabulary performed better on a relevant mathematics task than students who received a number sense intervention aimed at improving children's counting, number relations, and operations. This result is striking considering that the storybooks incorporating the math vocabulary were not specifically designed to teach the concepts to which the vocabulary referred. Finally, math learning through stories impacts not only children's knowledge, but also their attitudes about math. A study with kindergartners from Korea showed that children's interest in math activities significantly increased after a math storybook intervention compared to a reading control (Hong, 1996).

While most of these studies have been conducted in classrooms, there is reason to believe that the benefit of storybooks on children's math learning also extends to the home environment. An experimental study with first-graders assessed the effectiveness of a math app that delivered nightly short numerical story problems followed by math-related word problems for parents and children to solve together (Berkowitz et al., 2015). These story problems dealt with a variety of topics of interest to children, often tied to a timely event, such as Halloween. One example involved the increase in volume when cream is whipped due to the inclusion of air; another involved the number of toes that different kinds of elephants have. Following each story problem, math questions ranged in difficulty from the preschool level to questions that would be appropriate for children in fifth grade and beyond. Children of math-anxious parents who were assigned to the math app intervention learned more math over the school year than children of math-anxious parents randomly assigned to a reading control group. This result suggests that scripting math input through a storybook or app not only supports children's math learning but is also a powerful tool to help those parents who may be less comfortable supporting their children's math development in other ways (Maloney, Converse, Gibbs, Levine, & Beilock, 2015).

Most research related to math picture books has explored how children's math learning benefits from reading books with implicit or explicit math content compared to control groups. However, few studies have assessed how learning may vary depending on the content of the math books themselves. The importance of thinking about the math content of number books is highlighted by experimental findings showing that certain kinds of content support children's learning of foundational math concepts such as cardinality. In an important training study, children either heard an experimenter only count the sets on the page, only label the cardinal value of sets, alternate between counting and labeling, or label the cardinal value immediately followed by counting (Mix, Sandhofer, Moore, & Russell, 2012). Children showed significant gains in their understanding of the cardinal meaning of number words only when they heard an experimenter label the set's cardinal value and then count the set, showing that the label was correct and also that counting determines the total set size (Mix et al., 2012). This kind of evidence can benefit picture book writers—and the children they reach—as they create picture books that are both engaging and that support children's math learning.

In commercially available math picture books, there is significant variation in the way math information is conveyed. A review of research on commercial counting books found that they present number information in a variety of ways, some of which may not be conducive to promoting young children's understanding (Ward, Mazzocco, Bock, & Prokes, 2017). Potentially detrimental features include showing distractors in the illustrations along with the to-be-counted set or not labeling the cardinal value of a set (the number of items in the set). While there is no direct evidence that these inconsistencies affect children's learning, it is reasonable to assume they would guide the reading interaction as parents mainly stick to the text when reading a counting book (Mix et al., 2012) and that their math talk is prompted by the illustrations (Anderson et al., 2004).

Research also suggests that it is important to consider how the nature of the book interacts with the child's prior knowledge level in terms of supporting learning. A recent experimental study has directly tested how variations in content affect children's number learning, depending on children's prior knowledge. Gibson, Gunderson, and Levine (in press) gave parents experimenter-created books to read with their three-year-olds at home for four weeks. Some parents, the experimental groups, received and read with their children a number book that either focused on small numbers (1–3) or large numbers (4–6), while other parents, the control group, received and read a book that replaced all number-relevant information with adjectives. Results showed that children whose parents read number books learned more about the cardinal value of number words than children whose parents were given adjective books that contained no number-related text or illustrations. This finding provides direct evidence that picture books can be an effective tool to promote young children's number understanding. Furthermore, children who were at the earlier stages of number development benefited most from reading the small number books with their parents. In contrast, children with more number word understanding benefitted from reading either the small or large number books. This result suggests that the effectiveness of the book content in supporting learning depends on the child's prior knowledge and that tailoring the content to the child's level is important, at least at the early stages of number word understanding. Once children's knowledge advances, based on repeated reading of "easier" books, parents should be encouraged to move on to books that hold the potential to extend this knowledge.

In brief, picture books—fiction and non-fiction—can be a powerful tool to promote children's math learning. Yet, it is important to keep in mind that not all types of books may be equally effective. Variations in both math content in the book and the child's knowledge level may affect what children learn from the reading interaction. Thus, it is important for picture book writers to consider these research findings as they create text and illustrations for children's picture books. The next section elaborates on the analysis of picture book quality and design.

Quality and Design of Children's Math Books

How should we evaluate children's explicit and implicit math picture books? Parents, teachers, librarians, and other adults (like publishers) want to be able to identify high-quality picture books for children. We propose two different, but not mutually exclusive, types of quality guidelines. One set examines the books as literature and deals with such issues as narrative quality and cultural and gender stereotypes. These guidelines should be especially useful for math educators, who typically have little experience with picture books and seldom consider them as vehicles for math learning. At the same time, early childhood educators may find these guidelines quite obvious. The second set of guidelines, based on developmental and cognitive principles, involves analysis of the picture book from the point of view of math learning. These guidelines may be quite new to early childhood educators, who often do not focus on math learning in the context of children's literature.

Picture Books as Literature

A picture book, math-related or not, needs first of all to be, in the eyes of children and adults, a book worth reading. Children should enjoy it and want to read it, often more than once. Adults should feel the same way. A high-quality picture book—including dictionaries, storybooks, alphabet books, wordless books, counting books, and shape books—has several characteristics that are based mostly on aesthetics and values.

Literary Merit. The first and essential principle is literary merit. A children's book is not a controlled scientific experiment or a scientific product. It is a form of art, so that judgment of the book is based as much on aesthetic principles (Austin, 1998; Hellwig, Monroe, & Jacobs, 2000; Jalongo, 2004; Wilburne, Keat, & Napoli, 2011) as on psychological or educational ideas or research. Picture books, fiction and non-fiction, should be captivating and enjoyable. Characters should be attractive (or scary) and grab attention. The text should comprise rich and expressive language. The illustrations should be beautiful as well as meaningful. The story, if there is one, should be compelling. The non-fiction books should cover important phenomena.

Child Appropriateness. Children's books should obviously be appropriate for the general age range they are designed to reach. Stories for children, some of which date back to old fairy tales, involve topics often central to children's lives, like independence, fear, sharing, and conflict. Non-fiction books often involve animals, vehicles, and children. Creating age-appropriate books is difficult to achieve unless the writer has some understanding of children's emotional life, intellectual abilities, and interests, and considers how the child will interpret and understand the material. The writer of math books needs to make vigilant efforts to take the *child*, and not only the content, into consideration.

Opening Eyes. A central feature of books is that they can open children's—and adults'—eyes to a larger world beyond theirs, whether it be the world of animals, trucks, numbers, shapes, feelings, or the developmentally appropriate equivalent of *Crime and Punishment* (perhaps *Striking Classmate and Time-Out*). Books can stimulate wonder and curiosity, introducing the child to new and surprising ideas.

Humor and Word Play. Many children's books strive to be funny, and some succeed. For example, in *Click, Clack, Moo: Cows That Type* (Cronin, 2000), Farmer Brown has some cows that type (on an old-fashioned typewriter!). In fact, they drive him to a frenzy when they send him a note requesting electric blankets because the barn is cold. Strife ensues, and also a labor strike, and in the end… *One Big Pair of Underwear* (Gehl & Lichtenheld, 2014), which certainly has a funny title, uses rhymes, repetition, rhythm, and alliteration to amuse (Ginsburg, 2018). For example, among the characters are "THREE young yaks with black backpacks" that contain "salty snacks." Message for adults: let your hair down (an odd, antic expression) and join the playful reading.

Illustrations. Illustrations play a major and useful role in children's books (Carney & Levin, 2002). Illustrations can even comprise the entirety of a book—no words needed. But most picture books have words, and illustrations allow young children to see what the words say, provide information that the text does not, set the tone for a page (for example, creepy or cheerful). Kiefer (1993) stresses that "…the visual expression of meaning and the resulting emotional experiences made possible by that expression should be paramount in evaluating picture books" (p. 88). Because young children look mostly at the illustrations, and not the text as it is being read (Evans & Saint-Aubin, 2005), the quality and clarity of the illustrations are essential (Sipe, 2012). Unfortunately, and too frequently, the text and illustrations may not work together to produce a meaningful book (Austin, 1998; Hunsader, 2004). Clearly the two should not clash.

Peril Alert. Unfortunately, gender (Ladd, 2011) and cultural (Mendoza & Reese, 2001) stereotypes still appear in children's books, which may also fail to include characters from a range of ethnic and racial groups (Pescosolido, Grauerholz, & Milkie, 1997). The writer needs to be sensitive to these problems and avoid them. The reader needs to be able to help the child understand the problems when they are encountered in the course of book reading.

Children's Math Books

Explicit Math Books. All of the features and principles already discussed apply to this species of children's book. Like any other children's books, explicit math books involve telling stories with literary merit, using humor, creating useful illustrations, considering the child's point of view, and all the rest. Math books also need to avoid the various perils described above.

At the same time, creation of children's math books requires consideration of special features and design principles, the analysis of which is rare, with a few notable exceptions (Ward et al., 2017), and also requires dealing with a new set of perils associated with cultural misconceptions specific to math.

Features of Explicit Math Books. The first special feature is the deliberate goal of helping children to learn several mathematical topics appropriate for young children.

- Number (counting, the meaning of equivalent numbers, more/less/same)
- Operations on number (addition, subtraction, division, 1–1 correspondence)
- Shape (the basic ideas of shape, for example, the difference between scalene and right triangle)
- Space (the relation of objects in space, for example, a bear can be both in front of a truck yet behind a lemon)
- Pattern (the ideas of a steadily growing series of numbers like 2, 4, 6, 8… or a repeating sequence like blue, yellow, blue, yellow…)
- Measurement (including use of a common unit like a shoe or a centimeter)

The second special feature, even if it is not necessarily present in all explicit math books, is written symbolism, including common written numerals like 1, 2, 3 and the +, −, =, <, and > symbols. Written symbols of this type occupy a special place in children's math books, although they may appear usually incidentally (for example, numbers on a clock or on money) in some implicit math or non-math books as well.

Quality Principles for Explicit Math Books. What principles can we use to evaluate the quality of math picture books? We draw upon and supplement the work of Austin (1998),

Flevares and Schiff (2014), Hellwig et al. (2000), Hunsader, (2004), Marston, (2010), Marston and Mulligan (2012), Schiro (1997), van den Heuvel-Panhuizen and Elia (2012), and Ward et al. (2017).

ACCURATE MATH

It is obvious that books designed to promote math learning should have accurate math. Unfortunately, this is not always the case. Sometimes books promote, either directly or indirectly, incorrect math ideas: "… 76% of books [reviewed] had at least 1 explicit inaccuracy of 2-dimensional shapes" (Nurnberger-Haag, 2017, p. 415).

MATH IDEAS

The books need to deal with significant math ideas, not just pedestrian material (like memorizing number facts or learning the names of common shapes) that is not at the heart of math and not sufficiently challenging for young children. Children (and adults) need to learn that math is not simply and getting right answers, memorizing facts, and naming shapes. Instead it is a set of ideas that are interesting, useful, and even amusing (for example, how is it possible that two elephants are equivalent to two ants?).

MATH LANGUAGE

Math picture books should help children learn to understand basic math language (Jennings, Jennings, Richey, & Dixon-Krauss, 1992), like *fewer*, *pattern*, and *rectangle*. Also, *doing* substantive math requires that children learn to describe their math thinking, to explain it, to defend it, and understand math language when someone else uses it. For all these reasons, designers need to ensure that the story involves accurate math language.

EMBEDDED MATH THINKING

It is possible to embed in the text, material that encourages, models, describes, and explains math thinking (Ward et al., 2017). For example, when a story character needs to count a set of objects, the character can *model* a method of solution (pointing to the objects one at time during the count), *describe* the solution ("I need to count each one of these slithery snakes"), *explain* the solution ("I don't want to miss any snakes or count any of them twice"), and *involve* the child ("How would you figure this out?"). Note that all of these guidelines involve use of math language.

ILLUSTRATIONS

These are as crucial for math books as for picture books in general. Shape books need images of shapes to describe and analyze and number books need pictures of things to count and to relate to abstract concepts. The following example shows how an illustration can buttress an important idea

Figure 5.1 Illustration from *Circus Shapes*.

about shape, namely that a square is still a square even when it is rotated as shown, or when it is small or large, or yellow, red, blue, and green (Murphy, 1997) (Figure 5.1).

Unfortunately, many math books do not use accurate illustrations. For example,

> … in 48% of [counting] books, numerals or number words referred to a different numerosity than what was pictured…
> (Ward et al., 2017, p. 60)

SYNTHESIS BETWEEN FORMAL AND INFORMAL

The final principle is perhaps the most important. Before entrance to school, even preschool, young children already have many everyday or informal math ideas. For example, there is a sense in which young children already understand basic ideas of adding (give me more!) and subtracting (you took them away!). But they need to learn much more: formal mathematics is superior in many respects (e.g., power and clarity) to everyday math. A key educational principle, drawing on Vygotsky's (1986) theory, is that children's everyday knowledge can benefit from exposure to formal math, and that their understanding of formal math can benefit from the "body and vitality" (p. 193), of their everyday math. The key is creating a synthesis of the two. For example, the child (like almost all children and indeed babies) who has an intuitive idea of "more than" needs to learn to connect it to the > symbol. The child may learn to understand, not in so many words:

> Oh, that [the > symbol] means *more than* because I can *see* that there are many cats on this side and fewer on this side. Now I can use > to show that there are more of any objects here than there, no matter what they are.

And eventually the child will learn that a > b can be true of *any* numbers that are not the same.

Math books are at risk of the same kind of perils as picture books generally. As noted above, gender (Ladd, 2011), cultural (Mendoza & Reese, 2001), and ethnic (Pescosolido et al., 1997) stereotypes are all too common in picture books. In the case of math picture books, some tend to portray girls as less likely to succeed in math than boys. Girls may be shown as not liking math and not having the ability to do it well (Picker & Berry, 2000). Math picture books need to avoid this stereotype, as well as the others.

Implicit Math Books.   Implicit math books utilize the same features as do children's books generally, and do not include written symbolism, except for the ordinary spoken and written counting numbers (like numerals on clocks or house numbers), and perhaps a few common shapes. The best advice to potential authors of implicit math books is to ignore this entire section on design principles. Just write the book as an attractive, high-quality book. By definition, implicit math books do not intentionally rely on features and principles of explicit math books.

Electronic Picture Books

The term "children's book" likely elicits an image of a traditional paper book that entails words and static images and comes encased in a hard or soft cover. Indeed, the majority of books read with children are paper books and the majority of research on picture book reading involves the use of these printed books. However, just as technological innovations have changed the way children play games and watch television, they have changed the way children can access stories. Stories are no longer limited to paper and can exist in a digital format that is read on a tablet device, smartphone, or computer screen. Young children have increasing access to these touch-screen devices and computers at home (Livingstone, Marsh, Plowman, Ottovordemgentschenfelde, & Fletcher-Watson, 2014; Ofcom, 2014). Although reading high-quality print books can confer important math benefits, it is also important to understand the ways in which children can learn from stories presented in a digital format. In this section, we discuss research on how children can learn from electronic books (e-books) and present design principles for e-books created for the purpose of teaching math. Although the focus of this chapter is math learning, there have been few studies specific to math e-book reading with young children. Therefore, we begin by providing a general overview of how the technological aspects of e-books can benefit children's learning and engagement and how this has implications for math learning. Then we will review studies on math e-book reading before concluding with a description of the features and design principles that should be considered when creating and using math e-books.

Although digital technologies can have negative effects on young children's lives (Guernsey & Levine, 2015), here we focus on the potential for e-books to have a positive impact on children's learning and engagement, particularly relating to early math concepts and language. At the same time, we acknowledge that parents and practitioners may have worries about the effects of reading on a digital platform. We echo the sentiment of others (Guernsey & Levine, 2015), that content and context matter when considering whether to read e-books with young children and deciding how long to limit children's screen time. As we describe in more detail later in the chapter, the content should be well designed, with features appropriate for children's developing minds. Furthermore, e-books should be read jointly with an adult who can guide children's experience on the digital device. Organizations such as the National Association for the Education of Young Children, the Fred Rogers Center for Early Learning and Children's Media (2012), and Zero to Three (Barr, McClure, & Parlakian, 2018) have produced excellent guidelines to help parents (and teachers) make informed decisions about the use of digital technologies with young children.

E-books combine elements of traditional print books and technological features that enable the story to be presented using multimedia enhancements. Such technological affordances allow for the text to be highlighted and narrated aloud as it scrolls across the screen. Animated characters can act out the story on screen, accompanied by sound effects and music. The reader can activate hotspots with a screen touch or mouse click. For instance, when a reader clicks on a difficult vocabulary word, the definition will appear on screen, where it is read aloud and depicted in a brief animation. However, there is a surprising lack of uniformity in the amount and type of features provided across different e-books (de Jong & Bus, 2003; Korat & Shamir, 2004). While some e-books closely resemble printed books merely presented on a digital screen instead of on paper, other e-books have an array of interactive features and more closely resemble a game or an app than a traditional book. Parents today have many choices of book formats, ranging from print books to highly interactive e-books, and research comparing these various formats can help families choose a type of book that best supports their children's learning and development.

What Children Can Learn from E-Book Reading

The changing technological landscape means that children experience stories in a different manner than previous generations, and these new technologies warrant new research into children's reading. As discussed earlier, shared reading with print books confers many benefits to young children. E-books need not replace print books but can complement them (for readers beginning at around four years of age) and offer unique affordances that only technological enhancements can provide, such as animation that can improve children's comprehension of the plot or of ideas of transformation (for example, evil witches turning into toads). Recent research is beginning to reveal the ways in which e-books can (and cannot) help young children learn novel words, improve their comprehension of the story, and become engaged readers. While these are general outcomes of reading e-books, we believe they have implications for math learning, as well. As we describe each of these three potential outcomes, we draw conclusions about how the findings can be extended to understand the effects of e-books on children's math learning.

Vocabulary Knowledge. Studies suggest that e-books, like print books, can improve children's language skills, including vocabulary knowledge, phonological awareness, concepts of print, and text comprehension. In particular, gains in word knowledge as a result of e-book reading have been well documented in the literature. For example, Korat, Shamir, and Heibal (2013) instructed parents to read either a print book or an e-book with their children five times over the course of two weeks. Children in both groups demonstrated significantly higher comprehension of novel vocabulary terms from the story than did a control group of children who were not exposed to either book condition, demonstrating that e-books can be as effective as print books in helping children develop vocabulary knowledge. Furthermore, Korat and colleagues' (2013) findings suggest that even a brief reading experience with either type of book can significantly improve children's word knowledge; a lengthy time commitment is not required. In another study, children demonstrated the greatest growth in word knowledge when reading a highly interactive e-book that included animation, background music, sounds, and hotspots that defined tricky words in contrast to reading a basic e-book with static images and text (Smeets & Bus, 2015), which is essentially equivalent to a print book.

Instead of comparing e-books and print books, other studies have examined various formats of e-books to determine the particular features most likely to enrich word knowledge. The results show that several features are effective in promoting word comprehension. Children can learn the meaning of novel words through either an e-book dictionary mode providing a definition or through use of contextual clues and animation (Korat & Shamir, 2008). Smeets and Bus (2012) found that both multiple-choice questions requiring children to select an image that best represents the meaning of a textual word, and software-based feedback on the accuracy of responses promote enhanced receptive and expressive word knowledge. Furthermore, e-books with a feature that allows the reader to select a word and hear the onset phoneme read aloud can help improve children's phonological awareness (Chera & Wood, 2003). Similarly, Korat and colleagues (2013) found positive results using an e-book that can segment each syllable in a word and slowly pronounce the phonemes in each syllable, helping children

learn how to read words by segmenting and blending their constituent sounds.

In addition to general vocabulary words, e-books have the potential to expose children to specific math language. Words associated with math concepts are content-specific, complex, and often abstract (Harmon, Hedrick, & Wood, 2005). Therefore, math words should be explicitly taught to children in meaningful contexts that connect to their informal language and knowledge (Riccomini, Smith, Hughes, & Fries, 2015). Prior work has shown that young children's receptive and expressive knowledge of math language is related to their numeracy abilities. For example, Purpura and Reid (2016) found that children's knowledge of quantitative and spatial terms was a significant predictor of their performance on a numeracy assessment above and beyond their knowledge of general vocabulary terms. Other studies have demonstrated that the quantity of number words that children hear at home (Levine et al., 2010; Susperreguy & Davis-Kean, 2016) and the quality of math input (Gunderson & Levine, 2011; Ramani, Rowe, Eason, & Leech, 2015) are positive predictors of their early number knowledge and performance on numeracy tasks. Children as young as three and four years old have been shown to possess a mathematical lexicon (Purpura & Reid, 2016) and can increase it through the use of e-books. They can click on a math word in the story and hear its pronunciation and definition. In the next section we demonstrate how words in e-books can be portrayed with animation, which can further contribute to children's understanding of novel math language and comprehension of mathematical concepts.

Story Comprehension. Animation is another feature of e-books that has the potential to aid in children's literacy and math development. Animated visuals bring the text to life by acting out the story on each page or scene, which may help children develop comprehension skills. Korat (2010) demonstrated that use of animations improved both kindergarten and first-grade children's reading comprehension and ability to retell the plot of the story, although the effect was stronger for the older children. Animation presented simultaneously with the text can help facilitate children's understanding of the plot and interpretation of difficult phrases, such as "giving the cold shoulder." Moreover, e-books can highlight or zoom in on key aspects of the animation, which serves to draw children's attention to details that aid in their understanding of the scene. Paivio's (1986) dual coding theory suggests that information processed concurrently by both the visual and auditory channels is processed more deeply than when it is presented alone in either channel. E-books can afford this deep level of processing through the use of congruent animation and audio, which may strengthen children's text comprehension and recall of the story (Mayer, 2001). Similarly, animation and audio enhancements can bolster children's comprehension of early math concepts. For example, important early numeracy ideas such as counting and comparing quantities, ordinal relations, and basic computation can be animated and narrated as the plot unfolds. Touch-screen capabilities allow children to interact with the on-screen characters and help them to count or order amounts of things. Studies on math software for young children suggest that manipulating on-screen objects using gestures can be at least as beneficial for math learning as manipulating physical objects (Clements & Sarama, 2007; Sarama & Clements, 2003) and likely adds to e-books' engaging quality.

Engagement and Attention. Several studies show that e-books can foster engagement, measured by children exhibiting positive affect, as well as the presence of an emotional bond between adult and child during the shared book reading (Lauricella, Barr, & Calvert, 2014; Moody, Justice, & Cabell, 2010; Ross, Pye, & Randell, 2016; Strouse & Ganea, 2017). When children are engaged in reading and enjoy stories, they are motivated to continue reading, which builds their literacy skills (McGeown et al., 2015; Petscher, 2010) and has the potential to build their math skills as well. Ross et al. (2016) measured the emotional expressions of parents and seven-year-old children while reading print and e-books. Both children and their parents displayed longer durations of positive emotional expressions, such as laughing and smiling, when reading the highly interactive e-book compared to the print book. Few negative emotions were observed in either condition. Similarly, Strouse and Ganea (2017) found that children presented more positive affective behaviors when reading e-books than when reading print books. Furthermore, children in their study were more attentive to the story when it was presented on a touch-screen device and made more comments during reading, demonstrating their interest in discussing the story (Strouse & Ganea, 2017). E-books may not only have the effect of creating enthusiastic readers but may also elicit greater persistence and focus than print books (Moody et al., 2010). Although most studies measure children's affect and attention, parents also demonstrate higher levels of interest during e-book reading. Parents were more likely to actively engage their children in reading by initiating interaction and drawing the child's attention to parts of the story during joint e-book reading than during joint print book reading (Lauricella et al., 2014). Focused and sustained attention to a story that includes math content and longer parent-child interactions about the math content of the e-book can increase the likelihood that children will gain math knowledge while reading.

Interestingly, self-report data indicate a different pattern of results regarding interest and engagement in e-book reading. Strouse and Ganea (2017) surveyed caregivers, who reported that their children prefer to read print books and demonstrate higher levels of attention when reading print books than e-books. These divergent findings may be explained, in part, by the lack of large-scale studies on e-book reading. Many of the observational studies on engagement and attention during e-book reading have a small number of participants. Larger studies with a diverse sample of families and a diverse sample of e-books are needed to further explore parent and child interaction with e-books and generalize findings to the population. Furthermore, parents and children may display high levels of engagement due to the novelty of reading on a touch-screen device, which is still relatively infrequent among parents and young children (Strouse & Ganea, 2017). Longitudinal studies allow for the novelty to diminish and can reveal whether engagement and attention while reading e-books persist over time.

The Conditions Conducive to Learning from E-books

Although key features of technology-enhanced e-books have the potential to help children gain academic skills and become engaged readers, research suggests that not all e-book reading interactions are equally effective for all children. Children's outcomes are influenced by their initial skill level and the role that the adult assumes in the reading interaction. Children at risk for language delays, including those from economically disadvantaged or immigrant families and those who score low on measures of language ability, may gain the most from practicing their literacy skills on a digital platform. Conversely, young learners with strong emergent literacy skills and a solid grasp of foundational reading principles may not need the level of support and guidance provided by multimedia enhancements. Studies have demonstrated that children with the weakest language skills at pretest exhibited the greatest degree of improvement in literacy skills at posttest (e.g., Korat & Shamir, 2008; Korat et al., 2013; Takacs, Swart, & Bus, 2015). E-books have also been found to have a particularly positive effect on children from low socio-economic groups (Korat et al., 2013; Verhallen & Bus, 2010) and children at risk for learning disabilities (Shamir, Korat, & Fellah, 2012; Shamir & Shlafer, 2011). Taken together, the studies cited above demonstrate the potential of well-designed e-books to improve the literacy skills of low-SES children, children with weak language, and children at risk for learning disabilities. Similarly, we believe that well-designed e-books can have a particularly large positive impact on the math skills of these groups.

As noted, e-books must be well designed to produce positive and avoid negative outcomes. Labbo and Kuhn (2000) presented a detailed case study of five-year-old Roberto reading two e-books: one with multimedia features congruent with the plot and the other with extraneous multimedia features incongruent with the plot. The authors conclude that the presence of confusing, extraneous features in the latter kind of e-book can cause children like Roberto to become passive readers who stop trying to make sense of the story and disengage from the cognitive processes that develop into good reading skills. Similarly, Smeets, van Dijken, and Bus (2014) tested the use of e-books with kindergarten children with severe language impairment and found that background sounds and music interfered with their ability to learn new words in the story. Willoughby, Evans, and Nowak (2015) similarly found that children who read e-books spent more time activating animation hotspots that were unrelated to literacy skills, while children who read print alphabet books spent more time on-task, labeling objects in the illustrations and naming letters. It is clear that not all e-books are equally as effective in promoting children's learning and engagement and particular design features can affect the books' usefulness as a learning tool. As more studies evaluate e-book reading, researchers, authors, and publishers can acquire a better understanding of how to create effective e-books containing productive uses of multimedia enhancements and avoid unproductive enhancements. Later in this section we describe the design of an e-book that was created with careful consideration of how the various features can improve young children's math knowledge.

The potential of e-books to promote learning does not only relate to the design of the book and the characteristics of the learner but is also associated with the quality of the parent-child interaction during reading. A recent study by Dore and colleagues (2018) assessed how well children comprehend a story after either reading an e-book with a parent, seeing the e-book story independently with an integrated audio narration, or seeing the e-book pictures without narration. Results showed that while children were able to comprehend some of the content with the audio narration and significantly more than with the pictures alone, they recalled the most information about the story after reading it with a parent. This study suggests that simply exposing children to the input in storybooks might not be enough. Parental involvement is necessary to make the most out of the experience.

Math E-Books

Just as research on print math books has been rare, very few empirical studies have been conducted on e-books created with the intention of fostering young children's mathematical knowledge. We were only able to identify only three experimental studies of this type (Segal-Drori, Kalmanovich, & Shamir, 2018; Shamir & Baruch, 2012; Shamir & Lifshitz, 2013). All three studies involved the use of the same e-book, *Grandfather's Minibus*, which tells the story of a boy being driven to school by his grandfather and the friends and animals that board the minibus along the way. Readers can choose to experience the book in one of three modes: *Read Story Only, Dictionary Mode* (in which clicking on or touching a word produces its definition), or *Read with Hotspots*, which when clicked or touched cause a cloud to appear and explain the relevant math through visual and verbal explanations. Children at risk for learning disabilities demonstrated

improved knowledge of addition and ordinality (order, sequence) after reading the e-book in all three modes compared to a business-as-usual control group (Shamir & Baruch, 2012; Shamir & Lifshitz, 2013). Furthermore, Segal-Drori et al. (2018) found that reading *Grandfather's Minibus* had a positive impact on the addition and ordinality skills of both kindergartners at risk for learning disabilities and typically developing children, although the latter group demonstrated greater growth in math skills.

In a series of observational case studies, Ginsburg, Uscianowski, and Almeda (2018) and Uscianowski, Almeda, and Ginsburg (2018) investigated young children's reading of several e-books that were specially developed to help children learn number ideas and strategies. The design of the books emphasized the integration of math principles in an engaging plot that unravels naturally throughout the story. Children engage in problem-solving scenarios alongside the friendly monsters as they help them pack instruments or plan a surprise birthday party. The hypothesis was that technologically enhanced features built into our e-books—such as animation, sound effects, touch-screen capabilities, and immediate feedback—can help young children develop their mathematical knowledge and skills. The observational studies found that the math e-books gave children practice with important early numeracy concepts, such as subitizing (seeing the number of a group of objects quickly and without counting), cardinality, addition strategies, and symbolic representation of numbers (for example, representing 3 as three dots or the numeral 3), and seemed to result in significant learning. Furthermore, children exhibited high levels of motivation, engagement, and attention when reading the math e-books.

In brief, e-books can benefit children's learning and engagement in ways that equal, and in some ways exceed, those of general and math print picture books. However, the quality of the e-book, the quality of the print book, and the quality of the adult support all matter. Reading, whether with print or electronic books, can be, but is not necessarily, a pleasurable and profitable learning experience for both adult and child. To understand the variations in quality and to produce improved print and e-book stories, the next section discusses book features and design principles underlying effective e-books.

Evaluating the Quality of Children's Digital Math Books

As digital books are becoming increasingly popular (Bus, Takacs, & Kegel, 2014), there is a need to deepen our understanding of their features and design (Smeets & Bus, 2013; Takacs et al., 2015).

These books take several forms. One is a simple digital version of ordinary books with text and illustrations. The adult or child reads the text and sees the illustrations on a digital device, just as she would read a paper book.

A second form is a digital book that involves illustrations and also the audible reading of text. As the texts scrolls on the page, a voice reads each word, which is usually highlighted as it is read. If the reader touches a word, it speaks its verbal equivalent.

A third form offers audible reading, but most importantly includes video of the story. For example, if the text describes a monkey jumping off a bed, a video shows that event, providing a supplement to the spoken text. Think of this as a kind of television show with subtitles.

A fourth form offers another feature—strong interactivity—that can be used on touch-screen devices. The child can use a finger to touch and move objects on the screen for various purposes. The child can also touch to indicate answers, to get feedback, and much more.

Most principles of design already reviewed apply to digital math books as well as to print books: accurate math; not only memorized facts or procedures, but also concepts and ideas; stimulating math language; embedded thinking; and synthesis between formal math and everyday math knowledge. But digital books offer several unique affordances that lead to important principles, which we illustrate through the following extended example.

In Monster Birthday Surprise (Ginsburg, in preparation) the purple protagonist Oona wants to get presents for her sister Neenee's ninth birthday. As shown in this picture, Oona is shopping to get bags of monster mix for the party. She says (as indicated in accompanying text scrolling on the bottom), "Help me put this many in the cart," as she holds up a picture of four dots. "I drew a dot for each bag we need. Put the same number of bags in this cart. Toot this party horn when you are done." At this point, the child can tap on each of the bags to make it go into the cart. As this description shows, the first principle of the interactive book is the inclusion of meaningful child problem-solving activity tied to a clear explanation of the problem, in this case dot representation of number (Figure 5.2).

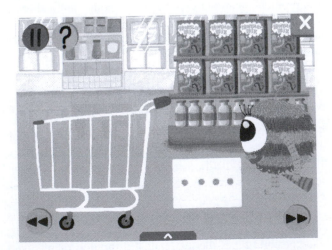

Figure 5.2 Illustration from *Monster Birthday Surprise*.

After the child toots the horn to indicate that he has put into the cart as many bags as the dots indicated, Oona checks the result. As she counts, the boxes light up in a special way. When she says "one" the first box on the left lights up; when she says "two" both the first and second boxes light up; and so on until all four are lit. This feedback sequence shows that each number word indicates the cardinal number—the total—*up to that point*. By contrast, if the child puts in the cart too many bags, Oona says, "Oopsie, we have more bags than dots. We need to put some back on the shelf." If the child puts in too few, Oona says, "That doesn't look like enough. When in doubt check the list [of dots]."

This example illustrates a second principle, namely feedback contingent on the individual child's activity: Oona checks a correct answer as a visual display shows the idea behind the counting—cardinal number. Oona responds to an incorrect answer by explaining the problem and suggesting a solution.

The same example also illustrates a third principle, dynamic representation. The boxes light up to illustrate Oona's count. This dynamic representation vividly shows the method of counting and the meaning of cardinal number. It may be easier to think about dynamic representation with another example, simple subtraction. Dynamic representation can show objects leaving a set as the remainder changes each time. Indeed, this little episode exploring one simple type of written representation involves child activity, contingent feedback, explanation, checking, and dynamic representation. Many other features of digital books could be described as well.

In brief, it is vital to understand key features of picture books—conventional and math-oriented, paper and electronic—in order to analyze, evaluate, recommend, and produce engaging, appropriate, and effective picture books. The design principles begin with art—literary merit, which cannot be produced by research alone. The principles also stress sound mathematics (for math-oriented books), child appropriateness, as well as coherent relations between text and illustrations and between children's everyday knowledge and formal math. All of these principles and more should govern the creation of e-books, which at their best can be designed to involve and encourage meaningful and dynamic formal representation, contingent feedback, explanation, checking, and thinking.

Conclusions

We have learned that picture books—implicit/explicit, and print/digital—can indeed promote young children's mathematics learning, as well as other aspects of their development, for example, their language. Math picture books should be an integral part of early education, at home, in school, and in the library. We consider next promoting their use, improving their writing and design, and conducting further research.

Promoting the Use of Picture Books

Given the demonstrated value of early picture book reading, we need to help adults to share math picture books in effective and sensitive ways. Several types of assistance are necessary. One is to help those adults with low levels of literacy to share math picture books (and picture books more generally) with their young children. Another is to help math-anxious parents become enthusiastic readers/sharers of math picture books. Further, it is important to help adults—teachers, parents, and librarians—understand their children as readers. Many adults truly do not understand that children see the world, including picture books, in distinctive ways, so that children may "see" a page differently from how adults do. Helping adults overcome their egocentrism in relation to their children is the first step in helping children learn more from math picture books and develop as readers more generally. Finally, it may be useful to provide adults with explicit guidance in reading individual math picture books and math picture books in general.

Just as we need to help parents use math print books, we must also help them effectively select and read high-quality e-books. Should they choose to read the e-book with hot spots imbedded throughout the story, or will that distract their child? Furthermore, parents may struggle to find their role among the sound effects, music, animation, and hot spots in the e-book. When should they pause the story to clarify a tricky word or ask their child a question? We have already learned enough from the existing research to make a start at designing materials and workshops that can help adults deal with these issues.

Finally, we need materials for leaders in early childhood education, particularly those who train prospective or practicing teachers. The leaders need to learn about the role of math learning in reading, and in early childhood education generally. Several organizations, including DREME (http://prek-math-te.stanford.edu) and the Erikson Institute (Brownell et al., 2014), are producing materials that can be useful for the leaders as they promote professional development. But clearly, a great deal more work needs to be done in this very promising area.

Producing Books

Many math picture books contain errors or challenges of one type or another. Publishers and writers can use some help too. One exciting opportunity for cognitive/math education experts and writers of math picture books is to form collaborations that will result in the production of engaging math picture books that incorporate design principles likely to foster children's math learning.

As picture books evolve into interactive, multimedia experiences, we must ensure that they are helping and not hindering children's learning. A well-designed e-book can define difficult vocabulary, use animation strategically to help the child understand the math ideas, and include interactive elements that children can manipulate to practice math skills. However, a poorly designed e-book can prevent learning. For example, hotspots that allow children to play a game mid-story may well interfere with children's learning. E-book designers and authors should examine current and future studies on children's learning from digital media to guide their use of multimedia enhancements in stories.

Research

Although we have learned that picture books can be effective tools of math education, there is a good deal we still need to investigate. One major issue is repeated reading. Often children like to read and then re-read some books, but little is known about what appears to be an important aspect of reading. How does the adult reader respond to repeated reading? How does the child's attention vary depending on different book qualities? How does the child's math learning change over time? Another important issue for research is adults' methods for choosing books to read. Parents, teachers, and librarians all select picture books for children. What criteria do they use? What sources do they rely upon to guide the selection? A third issue is the question of appropriate math picture books for bilingual children, particularly Spanish speakers, some of whose parents cannot read English. Should the children learn from books in English or Spanish or both? How can the non-English reading parents be involved in helping their children to learn to read? These are only some of the important issues that need to be addressed by both research and development.

The End

So this is the end of our story about storybooks and other picture books. But no doubt the story is not complete and the end is still out of sight.

References

Anderson, A., Anderson, J., & Shapiro, J. (2004). Mathematical discourse in shared storybook reading. *Journal for Research in Mathematics Education, 35*(1), 5–33. doi:10.2307/30034801

Austin, P. (1998). Math books as literature: Which ones measure up? The role of literature. *The New Advocate, 11*(2), 119–133.

Barr, R., McClure, E., & Parlakian, R. (2018). *What the research says about the impact of media on children aged 0–3 years old*. Washington, DC: Zero to Three.

Berkowitz, T., Schaeffer, M. W., Maloney, E. A., Peterson, L., Gregor, C., Levine, S. C., & Beilock, S. L. (2015). Math at home adds up to achievement in school. *Science, 350*(6257), 196–198. doi:10.1126/science.aac7427

Brownell, J. O., Chen, J.-Q., Ginet, L., Hynes-Berry, M., Itzkowich, R., Johnson, D., & McCray, J. (2014). *Big ideas of early mathematics: What teachers of young children need to know*. Upper Saddle River, NJ: Pearson Education.

Bus, A. G., Takacs, Z. K., & Kegel, C. A. T. (2014). Affordances and limitations of electronic storybooks for young children's emergent literacy. *Developmental Review, 35*, 79–97. doi:10.1016/j.dr.2014.12.004

Cannon, J., & Ginsburg, H. P. (2008). "Doing the math": Maternal beliefs about early mathematics versus language learning. *Early Education and Development, 19*(2), 238–260. doi:10.1080/10409280801963913

Carney, R. N., & Levin, J. R. (2002). Pictorial illustrations still improve students' learning from text. *Educational Psychology Review, 14*(1), 5–26. doi:10.1023/A:1013176309260

Casey, M. B., Erkut, S., Ceder, I., & Young, J. M. (2008). Use of storytelling context to improve girls' and boys' geometry skills in kindergarten. *Journal of Applied Developmental Psychology, 29*, 29–48. doi:10.1016/j.appdev.2007.10.005

Chera, P., & Wood, C. (2003). Animated multimedia 'talking books' can promote phonological awareness in children beginning to read. *Learning and Instruction, 13*, 33–52. doi:10.1016/S0959-4752(01)00035-4

Claessens, A., & Engel, M. (2013). How important is where you start? Early mathematics knowledge and later school success. *Teachers College Record, 115*(6), 1–29.

Clements, D. H., & Sarama, J. (2007). Effects of a preschool mathematics curriculum: Summative research on the building blocks project. *Journal for Research in Mathematics Education, 38*(2), 136–163.

Cronin, D. (2000). *Click, clack, moo: Cows that type.* New York, NY: Simon & Schuster.

de Jong, M. T., & Bus, A. G. (2003). How well suited are electronic books to supporting literacy? *Journal of Early Childhood Literacy, 3*, 147–164. doi:10.1177/14687984030032002

Dore, R. A., Hassinger-Das, B., Brezack, N., Valladares, T. L., Paller, A., Vu, L., … Hirsh-Pasek, K. (2018). The parent advantage in fostering children's e-book comprehension. *Early Childhood Research Quarterly, 44*, 24–33. doi:10.1016/j.ecresq.2018.02.002

Duncan, G. J., Dowsett, C. J., Claessens, A., Magnuson, K., Huston, A. C., Klebanov, P., … Sexton, H. (2007). School readiness and later achievement. *Developmental Psychology, 43*(6), 1428–1446.

Evans, M. A., & Saint-Aubin, J. (2005). What children are looking at during shared storybook reading: Evidence from eye movement monitoring. *Psychological Science, 16*(11), 913–920. doi:10.1111/j.1467-9280.2005.01636.x

Flevares, L. M., & Schiff, J. R. (2014). Learning mathematics in two dimensions: A review and look ahead at teaching and learning early childhood mathematics with children's literature. *Frontiers in Psychology, 5*, 1–13. doi:10.3389/fpsyg.2014.00459

Galda, L, Ash, G. E., & Cullinan, B. E. (2000). Children's literature. In P. D. Pearson, R. Barr, & M. L. Kamil (Eds.), *Handbook of reading research* (pp. 361–379). Mahwah, NJ: Routledge.

Gehl, L., & Lichtenheld, T. (2014). *One big pair of underwear.* New York, NY: Beach Lane Books.

Gibson, D. J., Gunderson, E. A., & Levine, S. C. (in press). Effects of general and specific number input on children's number learning.

Ginsburg, H. P. (2018) Review of *One Big Pair of Underwear.* Retrieved from https://medium.com/@DREMEmath/mathical-prize-winning-math-storybooks-for-young-children-2af02d508eec

Ginsburg, H. P. (in preparation). *Monster Birthday Surprise.* [application software].

Ginsburg, H. P., Uscianowski, C., & Almeda, M. (2018). Interactive math storybooks and their friends. In I. Elia, J. Mulligan, A. Anderson, A. Baccaglini-Frank, & C. Benz (Eds.), *Contemporary research and perspectives on early childhood mathematics education* (pp. 245–263). New York, NY: Springer.

Guernsey, L., & Levine, M. H. (2015). *Tap, click, read: Growing readers in a world of screens.* San Francisco, CA: Jossey-Bass & Pfeiffer Imprints, Wiley.

Gunderson, E. A., & Levine, S. C. (2011). Some types of parent number talk count more than others: Relations between parents' input and children's cardinal-number knowledge. *Developmental Science, 14*(5), 1021–1032. doi:10.1111/j.1467-7687.2011.01050.x

Harmon, J. M., Hedrick, W. B., & Wood, K. D. (2005). Research on vocabulary instruction in the content areas: Implications for struggling readers. *Reading & Writing Quarterly, 21,* 261–280. doi:10.1080/10573560590949377

Hassinger-Das, B., Jordan, N. C., & Dyson, N. (2015). Reading stories to learn math: Mathematics vocabulary instruction for children with early numeracy difficulties. *The Elementary School Journal, 116,* 242–264. doi:10.1086/683986

Hellwig, S. J., Monroe, E. E., & Jacobs, J. S. (2000). Making informed choices: Selecting children's trade books for mathematics instruction. *Teaching Children Mathematics, 7*(3), 138–143.

Hong, H. (1996). Effects of mathematics learning through children's literature on math achievement, and dispositional outcomes. *Early Childhood Research Quarterly, 11,* 477–494. doi:10.1016/S0885-2006(96)90018-6

Hunsader, P. D. (2004). Mathematics trade books: Establishing their value and assessing their quality. *The Reading Teacher, 57*(7), 618–629.

Jalongo, M. R. (2004). *Young children and picture books* (2nd ed.). Washington, DC: National Association for the Education of Young Children.

Jennings, C. M., Jennings, J. E., Richey, J., & Dixon-Krauss, L. (1992). Increasing interest and achievement in mathematics through children's literature. *Early Childhood Research Quarterly, 7*(2), 263–276. doi:10.1016/0885-2006(92)90008-M

Kiefer, B. (1993). Visual criticism and children's literature. In B. Hearne & R. Sutton (Eds.), *Evaluating children's books: Aesthetic, social, and political aspects of analyzing and using children's books* (pp. 73–91). Urbana, IL: Graduate School of Library and Information Services.

Korat, O. (2010). Reading electronic books as a support for vocabulary, story comprehension and word reading in kindergarten and first grade. *Computers and Education, 55*(1), 24–31. doi:10.1016/j.compedu.2009.11.014

Korat, O., & Shamir, A. (2004). Do Hebrew electronic books differ from Dutch electronic books? A replication of a Dutch content analysis. *Journal of Computer Assisted Learning, 20*(4), 257–268. doi:10.1111/j.1365-2729.2004.00078.x

Korat, O., & Shamir, A. (2008). The educational electronic book as a tool for supporting children's emergent literacy in low versus middle SES groups. *Computers and Education, 50*(1), 110–124. doi:10.1016/j.compedu.2006.04.002

Korat, O., Shamir, A., & Heibal, S. (2013). Expanding the boundaries of shared book reading: E-books and printed books in parent-child reading as support for children's language. *First Language, 33*(5), 504. doi:10.1177/0142723713503148

Labbo, L. D., & Kuhn, M. R. (2000). Weaving chains of affect and cognition: A young child's understanding of CD-ROM talking books. *Journal of Literacy Research, 32,* 187–210. doi:10.1080/10862960009548073

Ladd, P. R. (2011). A study on gendered portrayals in children's picture books with mathematical content. *International Journal of Knowledge Content Development & Technology, 1*(2), 5–14. doi:10.5865/IJKCT.2011.1.2.005

Lauricella, A. R., Barr, R., & Calvert, S. L. (2014). Parent-child interactions during traditional and computer storybook reading for children's comprehension: Implications for electronic storybook design. *International Journal of Child-Computer Interaction, 2*(1), 17–25. doi:10.1016/j.ijcci.2014.07.001

Levine, S. C., Suriyakham, L. W., Rowe, M. L., Huttenlocher, J., & Gunderson, E. A. (2010). What counts in the development of young children's number knowledge? *Developmental Psychology, 46*(5), 1309–1319. doi:10.1037/a0019671

Livingstone, S., Marsh, J., Plowman, L., Ottovordemgentschenfelde, S., & Fletcher-Watson, B. (2014). *Young children (0–8) and digital technology: A qualitative exploratory study national report – UK.* Luxembourg: Joint research Centre, European Commission. Retrieved from http://eprints.lse.ac.uk/60799/

Maloney, E. A., Converse, B. A., Gibbs, C. R., Levine, S. C., & Beilock, S. L. (2015). Jump-starting early childhood education at home: Early learning, parent motivation, and public policy. *Psychological Science, 10*(6), 727–732. doi:10.1177/1745691615607064

Marston, J. L. (2010). Developing a framework for the selection of picture books to promote early mathematical development. In L. Sparrow, B. Kissane, & C. Hurst (Eds.), *Shaping the future of mathematics education: Proceedings of the 33rd annual conference of the mathematics education research group of Australasia incorporated* (Vol. 2, pp. 383–390). Fremantle, WA: MERGA.

Marston, J., & Mulligan, J. (2012). Using picture books to integrate mathematics in early learning. In P. Whiteman & K. De Gioia (Eds.), *Children and childhoods 1: Perspectives, places and practices* (pp. 209–225). Newcastle upon Tyne, UK: Cambridge Scholars Publishing.

Mayer, R. E. (2001). *Multimedia learning*. Cambridge, UK: Cambridge University Press.

McGeown, S. P., Johnston, R. S., Walker, J., Howatson, K., Stockburn, A., & Dufton, P. (2015). The relationship between young children's enjoyment of learning to read, reading attitudes, confidence and attainment. *Educational Research, 57*(4), 389. doi:10.1080/00131881.2015.1091234

Mendoza, J., & Reese, D. (2001). Examining multicultural picture books for the early childhood classroom: Possibilities and pitfalls. *Early Childhood Research & Practice, 3*(2), 1–38.

Mix, K. S., Sandhofer, C. M., Moore, J. A., & Russell, C. (2012). Acquisition of the cardinal word principle: The role of input. *Early Childhood Research Quarterly, 27*, 274–283. doi:10.1016/j.ecresq.2011.10.003

Moody, A. K., Justice, L. M., & Cabell, S. Q. (2010). Electronic versus traditional storybooks: Relative influence on preschool children's engagement and communication. *Journal of Early Childhood Literacy, 10*(3), 294–313. doi:10.1177/1468798410372162

Murphy, S. J. (1997). *Circus shapes*. New York, NY: HarperCollins Publishers.

National Association for the Education of Young Children and the Fred Rogers Center. (2012). *Technology and interactive media as tools in early childhood programs serving children from birth through age 8.* Washington, DC: National Association for the Education of Young Children and the Fred Rogers Center.

Nurnberger-Haag, J. (2017). A cautionary tale: How children's books (mis)teach shapes. *Early Education and Development, 28*(4), 415–440. doi:10.1080/10409289.2016.1242993

Ofcom. (2014). *Children and parents: Media use and attitudes report.* London, UK: Office of Communications. Retrieved from http://stake holders.ofcom.org.uk/binaries/research/ media-literacy/media-use-attitudes-14/Childrens_2014_Report.pdf

Paivio, A. (1986). *Mental representations: A dual coding approach*. Oxford, UK: Oxford University Press.

Pescosolido, B. A., Grauerholz, E., & Milkie, M. A. (1997). Culture and conflict: The portrayal of blacks in U.S. children's picture books through the mid- and late-twentieth century. *American Sociological Review, 62*(3), 443–464.

Petscher, Y. (2010). A meta-analysis of the relationship between student attitudes towards reading and achievement in reading. *Journal of Research in Reading, 33*(4), 335. doi:10.1111/j.1467-9817.2009.01418.x

Picker, S. H., & Berry, J. S. (2000). Investigating pupils' images of mathematicians. *Educational Studies in Mathematics, 43*(1), 65–94.

Purpura, D. J., & Reid, E. E. (2016). Mathematics and language: Individual and group differences in mathematical language skills in young children. *Early Childhood Research Quarterly, 36*, 259–268. doi:10.1037/dev000005510.1016/j.ecresq.2015.12.020

Ramani, G. B., Rowe, M. L., Eason, S. H., & Leech, K. A. (2015). Math talk during informal learning activities in Head Start families. *Cognitive Development, 35*, 15–33. doi:10.1016/j.cogdev.2014.11.002

Riccomini, P. J., Smith, G. W., Hughes, E. M., & Fries, K. M. (2015). The language of mathematics: The importance of teaching and learning mathematical vocabulary. *Reading & Writing Quarterly, 31*(3), 235–252. doi:10.1080/10573569.2015.1030995

Ross, K. M., Pye, R. E., & Randell, J. (2016). Reading touch screen storybooks with mothers negatively affects 7-year-old readers' comprehension but enriches emotional engagement. *Frontiers in Psychology, 7*, 1–17. doi:10.3389/fpsyg.2016.01728

Saracho, O. N. (2012). Views and issues in children's literature. In O. N. Saracho & B. Spodek (Eds.), *Handbook of research on the education of young children* (3rd ed., pp. 135–146). London, UK: Routledge.

Sarama, J., & Clements, D. H. (2003). Building blocks of early childhood mathematics. *Teaching Children Mathematics, 9*(8), 480–484.

Schiro, M. (1997). *Integrating children's literature and mathematics in the classroom: Children as meaning makers, problem solvers, and literary critics.* New York, NY: Teachers College Press.

Segal-Drori, O., Kalmanovich, L. B. H., & Shamir, A. (2018). Electronic book for promoting emergent math: A comparison between kindergarteners at risk for learning disabilities and with typical development. *Journal of Educational Computing Research*, 073563311876945. doi:10.1177/0735633118769459

Shamir, A., & Baruch, D. (2012). Educational e-books: A support for vocabulary and early math for children at risk for learning disabilities. *Educational Media International, 49*(1), 33–47. doi:10.1080/09523987.2012.662623

Shamir, A., Korat, O., & Fellah, R. (2012). Promoting vocabulary, phonological awareness and concept about print among children at risk for learning disability: Can e-books help? *Reading and Writing, 25*(1), 45–69. doi:10.1007/s11145-010-9247-x

Shamir, A., & Lifshitz, I. (2013). E-Books for supporting the emergent literacy and emergent math of children at risk for learning disabilities: Can metacognitive guidance make a difference? *European Journal of Special Needs Education, 28*(1), 33–48. doi:10.1080/08856257.2012.742746

Shamir, A., & Shlafer, I. (2011). E-books effectiveness in promoting phonological awareness and concept about print: A comparison between children at risk for learning disabilities and typically developing kindergarteners. *Computers and Education, 57*(3), 1989–1997. doi:10.1016/j.compedu.2011.05.001

Sipe, L. R. (2012). Revisiting the relationships between text and pictures. *Children's Literature in Education, 43*(1), 4–21. doi:10.1007/s10583-011-9153-0

Smeets, D. J. H., & Bus, A. G. (2012). Interactive electronic storybooks for kindergartners to promote vocabulary growth. *Journal of Experimental Child Psychology, 112*(1), 36–55. doi:10.1016/j.jecp.2011.12.003

Smeets, D. J. H., & Bus, A. G. (2013). Picture storybooks go digital: Pros and cons. In S. B. Neuman, L. B. Gambrell, & C. Massey (Eds.), *Reading instruction in the age of common core standards* (pp. 176–189). Newark, DE: International Reading Association.

Smeets, D. J. H., & Bus, A. G. (2015). The interactive animated e-book as a word learning device for kindergartners. *Applied Psycholinguistics, 36*(4), 899–920. doi:10.1017/S0142716413000556

Smeets, D. J. H., van Dijken, M. J., & Bus, A. G. (2014). Using electronic storybooks to support word learning in children with severe language impairments. *Journal of Learning Disabilities, 47*(5), 435–449. doi:10.1177/0022219412467069

Strouse, G. A., & Ganea, P. A. (2017). A print book preference: Caregivers report higher child enjoyment and more adult-child interactions when reading print than electronic books. *International Journal of Child-Computer Interaction.* doi:10.1016/j.ijcci.2017.02.001

Susperreguy, M. I., & Davis-Kean, P. E. (2016). Maternal math talk in the home and math skills in preschool children. *Early Education and Development, 27*(6), 841–857. doi:10.1080/10409289.2016.1148480

Takacs, Z. K., Swart, E. K., & Bus, A. G. (2015). Benefits and pitfalls of multimedia and interactive features in technology-enhanced storybooks: A meta-analysis. *Review of Educational Research, 85*(4), 698–739. doi:10.3102/0034654314566989

Uscianowski, C., Almeda, M, & Ginsburg, H. (2018). Interactive digital storybooks and the role of parents in supporting young children's math development. In M. Caspe, T. A. Woods, & J. Kennedy (Eds.), *Promising practices for engaging families in STEM Learning* (pp. 115–133). Charlotte, NC: Information Age Publishing.

van den Heuvel-Panhuizen, M., & Elia, I. (2012). Developing a framework for the evaluation of picture books that support kindergartners' learning of mathematics. *Research in Mathematics Education, 14*(1), 17–47. doi: 10.1080/14794802.2012.657437

Vandermaas-Peeler, M., Nelson, J., Bumpass, C., & Sassine, B. (2009). Numeracy-related exchanges in joint storybook reading and play. *International Journal of Early Years Education, 17*(1), 67–84. doi:10.1080/09669760802699910

Verhallen, M. J. A. J., & Bus, A. G. (2010). Low-income immigrant pupils learning vocabulary through digital picture storybooks. *Journal of Educational Psychology, 102*(1), 54–61. doi:10.1037/a0017133

Vygotsky, L. S. (1986). *Thought and language.* Cambridge, MA: MIT Press.

Ward, J. M., Mazzocco, M. M., Bock, A. M., & Prokes, N. A. (2017). Are content and structural features of counting books aligned with research on numeracy development? *Early Childhood Research Quarterly, 39,* 47–63. doi:10.1016/j.ecresq.2016.10.002

Wilburne, J. M., Keat, J. B., & Napoli, M. P. (2011). *Cowboys count, monkeys measure, and princesses problem solve: Building early math skills through storybooks.* Baltimore, MD: Brookes Publishing Company.

Willoughby, D., Evans, M. A., & Nowak, S. (2015). Do ABC eBooks boost engagement and learning in preschoolers? An experimental study comparing eBooks with paper ABC and storybook controls. *Computers & Education, 82,* 107–117. doi:10.1016/j.compedu.201

6

Expanding the Focus of Early Years Mathematics Education

Statistics and Probability

AISLING M. LEAVY AND MAIRÉAD HOURIGAN

Background

Mathematics education in the early twentieth century focused on school age children with the concomitant neglect of the formative years of birth to age eight. Instead, early years' education was devoted to the development of social and literacy skills and intentional teaching of mathematics was delayed until elementary school (Balfanz, 1999). This delay was due, in large part, to the view that children were not intellectually capable of the types of thinking and reasoning necessary to support mathematical thinking; a viewpoint informed by early theories of Thorndike (1922) and Piaget and Szeminska (1952) whose research concluded that abstract and logical thinking was not possible until the concrete-operational stage. Subsequently this deficit view of young children's mathematical ability was challenged by a substantial body of research contending that young children have a well-developed understanding of informal mathematics (Gelman, 1972; Ginsburg, Klein, & Starkey, 1998) and can engage in complex intuitive mathematical thinking before the commencement of formal education (Clements & Sarama, 2007). Therefore the focus shifted from '…what young children could not do to what they *could* do' (Hachey, 2013, p. 420). This recent surge in attention to young children's mathematical capacities has been referred to as both 'a revolution' by Hachey (2013, p. 419) and 'not a revolution but rather a potentially important step in the evolution of work that began at least a half century ago' by Stipek (2013, p. 431). Regardless of the perspective taken, agreement exists that there is growing momentum and energy around the need to provide mathematically rich foundational learning opportunities for young children.

Research exploring the efficacy of mathematics curriculums designed for young children has shown that high-quality mathematics programmes produce learning gains for young children in their number and geometrical understandings (Arnold, Fisher, Doctoroff, & Dobbs, 2002; Clements & Sarama, 2007; Clements, Sarama, Spitler, Lange, & Wolfe, 2011; Klein, Starkey, Clements, Sarama, & Iyer, 2008; Presser, Clements, Ginsburg, & Ertle, 2015; Sophian, 2004). Furthermore, the finding that specific numerical knowledge developed prior to entry to elementary school is a strong predictor of later achievement (National Mathematics Advisory Panel, 2008; National Research Council, 2009), even in areas beyond mathematics itself (Duncan et al., 2007; Lerkkanen, Rasku-Puttonen, Aunola, & Nurmi, 2005), has resulted in growing support for an emphasis on early number. While the importance of focusing on number in early childhood is undisputed, a recent systematic review of the literature and evaluation of the quality of existing research culminated in Frye et al. (2013) making five recommendations designed to support young children as they learn mathematics. A common theme running through these recommendations was that 'there is much more to early math than understanding number and operations' (p. 8). Moreover, Lehrer and Lesh (2003, p. 384) argue that dedication of our energies solely on number may lead to the neglect of 'realms of mathematics that may well provide foundations for a mathematics education'.

Keeping in mind the reported gains in learning arising from the intentional teaching within these mathematics programmes, alongside the recommendation by Frye et al. (2013) to broaden the early years' mathematics curriculum and the caution of Lehrer and Lesh (2003), we argue that there is a need to expand our perspective on what content should constitute the focus of early mathematics. In particular, we propose that consideration is given to the provision of experiences in statistics and probability. In 2009, Sarama and Clements referred to the dearth of research on children's learning of statistics and probability in the early years. The past decade, however, has seen a mounting interest in the promotion of young children's statistical and probabilistic reasoning. Moreover, we have a remit to prepare children for changing societal needs and literacies. Young children live in an ever increasing data-driven society. They engage with online media and technologies at younger ages thus exposing them to an abundance of information presented in new and innovative forms.

These experiences are changing the landscape of early childhood and consequently we need to consider how we can best prepare young children for this data-laden and technological age. Indeed it could be argued that this is the day referred to by H.G. Wells in his statement 'Statistical thinking will one day be as necessary for efficient citizenship as the ability to read and write' (cited in Huff, 1954).

Research on Statistical and Probabilistic Understandings in the Early Years

In the following sections we identify some of the big ideas in statistics and probability that are accessible to young children. Big ideas have been described as 'overarching clusters and concepts and skills that are mathematically central and coherent, consistent with children's thinking, and generative for future learning' (Sarama & Clements, 2009, pp. 16–17). Rather than present these ideas discretely, we report on research which helps us interpret young students' understandings of the big ideas in probability in addition to studies which utilise frameworks that help unpack young students' understandings of statistics as they are immersed within the practices and activities of statisticians.

Statistical Thinking Frameworks and Data Modelling

In 1999, Wild and Pfannkuch outlined a statistical thinking framework for empirical enquiry which consisted of four dimensions: an investigative cycle, types of thinking, an interrogative cycle and dispositions. The investigative cycle, termed the PPDAC (Problem, Plan, Data, Analysis, Conclusion) cycle, has gained considerable traction in statistics education. This cycle incorporates attention to 'the way one acts and what one thinks about during the course of a statistical investigation' (p. 225) and was informed by and modelled on the practices of statisticians. Unfortunately, while some statistics has been taught in the early years, it has been procedural in nature and focuses efforts on exploring pre-made questions such as identification of favourite colours or modes of transport to school. School statistics education has traditionally placed an inordinate focused on the DAC part of the PPDAC cycle, and Shaughnessy (2007) argues that greater attention is warranted on the PP components allowing a much needed focus on the problem formulation, problem design and data production components of statistical investigation:

> If students are given only pre-packaged statistics problems, in which the tough decisions of problem formulation, design and data production have already been made for them, they will encounter an impoverished, three-phase investigative cycle and will be ill-quipped to deal with statistics problems in their early formulation stages.
>
> (Shaughnessy, 2007, p. 963)

Another means to address the shortcomings of approaches to teaching school statistics is the adoption of a modelling perspective. A central tenet of the modelling perspective is that some of the 'big ideas' in primary mathematics are, in fact, models that make sense of mathematically significant situations. Within statistics, data modelling is what statisticians and others do when they reason statistically and try to make sense of real situations. Thus a data modelling approach is a process that involves 'posing questions; developing attributes of phenomena; measuring and structuring these attributes; and then composing, refining, and displaying models of their relations' (Lehrer & Schauble, 2000, p. 51). Eliciting the desirable statistical ideas and processes that we wish young learners to engage with when participating in data modelling relies heavily on the design of tasks, or problem situations that are embedded in meaningful contexts. Research concludes that, when appropriate supports are provided, data modelling can be used successfully to promote statistical reasoning in the early years. In the sections that follow, we outline some of the research relating to young children's engagement with components of statistical thinking frameworks and data modelling approaches.

The PPDAC cycle and data modelling perspectives facilitate young children to interact with big statistical ideas within age appropriate learning environments (English, 2010, 2012; Fielding-Wells, 2018; Kinnear, 2013; Kinnear & Clarke, 2016; Leavy & Hourigan, 2018; Makar, 2018; Makar, Bakker, & Ben-Zvi, 2011). These environments provide sufficient supports and scaffolds for young learners to engage in statistical reasoning and to see how statistical concepts are related to each other and how they contribute to statistical problem solving. In doing so, these approaches shift attention away from heretofore disjointed approaches that disconnect and isolate core statistical ideas from the rich contexts and situations within which they are usually embedded.

The Important Role of Context

Within the area of statistical enquiry, familiarity with the context of the statistical problem, frequently referred to as the data context, is particularly critical to support learners in seeking and explaining patterns revealed in the data (Shaughnessy & Pfannkuch, 2002; Wild & Pfannkuch, 1999). Several studies have identified familiarity with the data context as a critical component which supports the development of statistical understandings of young children (Leavy & Hourigan, 2016; Watson, 2018). This particular function of context within statistics is highlighted by Cobb and Moore (1997) in their statement 'statistics requires a different kind of thinking because *data are not just numbers, they are numbers with a context*' (p. 801) and furthermore that 'in data analysis, context provides meaning' (p. 803). Facilitating access to the data context has been carried out successfully with young children through several means, most notably, the use of children's literature, the use of statistical investigations and data modelling environments. Children's literature is an increasingly common didactical tool in mathematics education which provides children with an appealing context. Optimum engagement with the context, Elia, Van den Heuvel-Panhuizen, and Georgiou (2010) contend, adds meaning to the mathematical situations being presented. Indeed, the critical role played by picture books in initiating interest in the data context and task context was identified by Kinnear (2018) in her exploration of a number of picture story books. Such picture books, when used as part of data modelling and statistical investigations, have been shown to contribute to the emerging understandings of big statistical ideas (English, 2010, 2012; Hourigan & Leavy, 2016; Kinnear, 2013; Watson, 2018).

Young Children's Understandings of the Big Ideas in Statistics

Representing and Structuring Data. Inscriptions have long been recognised as mediators of mathematical and scientific activity. Perkins and Ungers (1994) define representations to mean 'symbols in any symbol system (formal notations, language, picturing, etc.) that serve to denote or exemplify' (p. 2). However, Worthington and Carruthers (2003) contend that the mathematical underpinnings and communicative function of early representations are often overlooked resulting in a missed opportunity for harnessing and promoting young children's emerging mathematical potential. Support for this viewpoint is reflected in a statement by van Oers (2010) when he cautions that 'not paying attention to these events (related to children's graphical markings) means that educators may neglect important and stimulating early events for the promotion of mathematical thinking' (p. 32).

Inscriptions and representations are fundamental components of statistical inquiry and research has emphasised the need for the provision of classroom experiences that provide children the opportunity to structure and represent the data in the ways *they* choose (English, 2010; Hourigan & Leavy, 2016; Makar, 2018; Watson, 2006). Research into young children's ability to structure and represent data, while still scant, suggests that young children have the ability to communicate data in appropriate representational forms. Leavy and Hourigan (2018) investigated the inscriptional capabilities of 26 children aged five to six years as part of a four-day data modelling investigation involving decision making about the design of a zoo. Children were shown a purpose-made video of a zoo keeper where he requested that children help identify the friendliest animals in his zoo by tracking the appearance of animals as they engaged in a virtual walk through the zoo. Children were invited to 'make a mark' of their choosing whenever they noted the appearance of a pre-designated animal. Categorisation of inscriptions, using the Worthington and Carruthers (2003) taxonomy of mathematical graphics, revealed a variety of meaningful representations and approaches to index and describe the data. Children's justifications for their invented inscriptions ranged from aesthetic considerations, ease and simplicity, to contextually driven decision-making and approaches

motivated by efficiency. Their efforts to distinguish between repeated data values and different instances of the same attribute led Leavy and Hourigan to conclude that the 'representations were more than a record of frequencies and served in some cases as cognitive tools' (p. 104). The authors identified the high task interest and familiarity with the data context as important contributing factors that supported young children's inscriptional capacities.

The creation of inscriptions is also evident in the efforts of young children to structure and organise data. There is some evidence presented by Lehrer and Schauble (2007) that children show a lack of awareness of the viewer by their selection of novel and esoteric design features of representations and the concomitant neglect of design features that communicate meaning more clearly. It may be argued, however, that this study focusing primarily on classification as opposed to an investigative cycle may not have provided sufficient scaffolds for young learners in the provision of a contextually rich environment to support their statistical reasoning. In contrast, studies with young children in carefully designed data modelling environments reveal the heretofore unharnessed potential of young children in the area of representations (English, 2010, 2012; Makar, 2018). Stability in the construction of pictographs to communicate aspects of the data was reported by English (2010, 2012) arising from a study of the data modelling processes of six-year-olds. In this study, an environmental theme was developed by reading two storybooks called *Fun with Michael Recycle* and *Litterbug Doug*. Arising from the *Fun with Michael Recycle* story, children explored the classroom to identify reusable/recyclable and waste items that had been hidden. They were then asked to discuss the attributes of the items and organise, analyse and represent their data using any method of their own choice. While pictographs remained the dominant representation to structure and represent data; when requested to consider whether, in an effort to help *Michael Recycle*, their attributes and representations could be presented in a different way, most children made one or more changes to their pictographs. Changes involved making modifications to inscriptions, using a mix of names and drawings or making changes to paper orientation, attributes and orientation of column/row data on the pictogram. Such demonstrated flexibility in modifying representations may indicate the development of meta-representational competence and knowledge relating to representations (diSessa, 2004; diSessa, Hammer, Sherin, & Kolpakowski, 1991; Lehrer & Lesh, 2003). Support may be found in a study by Estrella (2018) where she also reported on the meta-representational competence of three five-year-old preschool children when engaged in a statistical investigation exploring their favourite sports activities. Children classified the class's favourite sports into six activities by type (jumping, running, skating, bike-riding, playing basketball and playing football). They provided a count for each category (i.e. the frequency of the variable) and wrote this number on the representation. Thus they used transnumeration techniques as they ordered and grouped data and engaged in analysis of a subset of the data. Furthermore when explaining their representation they made connections between the frequency and context by identifying the favourite sport. Estrella reports on the observed invention and learning of children as they created, modified and became aware of their own understanding of the representation they constructed. The findings from these studies appear to suggest that when young children are placed in carefully designed environments where they have familiarity with the context, what may emerge are relatively sophisticated approaches to data inscription and representation arising from young children's efforts to make sense of and communicate statistical situations.

Generating and Selecting Attributes.   Classification is a procedure that enables the individual to assign all the elements of a collection to a category according to some dimension that they share. Classification plays an important role in the development of mathematical reasoning (Kamii, Rummelsburg, & Kari, 2005) and there is some evidence indicating that children experiencing difficulties in classifying lag behind their peers in mathematics in later years (Pasnak et al., 1987). Great advances have been made in identifying children's classification skills and a comprehensive overview of this research is available in Sarama and Clements (2009). Although classification has long been regarded as a powerful and important concept, these understandings have historically been considered as having primacy and importance in the domain of early number. However, these concepts have been framed in more recent years as a critical entry route into the teaching and learning of early statistics. Sorting and classifying underpin core statistical activity because data need to be sorted and classified in order to make meaning. Viewed within the structures of a statistical thinking framework such as that proposed by Wild and Pfannkuch (1999), classification is necessary once data are collected ('Data' phase of the PPDAC cycle) in order to organise and prepare it for representation ('Analysis' phase of the PPDAC cycle). Many of the skills involved in classification, when carried out within the context of statistical inquiry, take the form of identification and selection of attributes.

When presented with a set of objects, selecting attributes requires that the child attend to the qualities of items rather than the items themselves. For example, when presented with a set of model animals a child might describe them as land and sea animals as opposed to a fish, a horse, a shark and a cow. There is evidence to indicate that when selecting attributes to focus upon that the young child can override the reliance on perceptual similarities in favour of more taxonomically relevant features such as function (Blair & Somerville, 2009; Gelman & Markman, 1986). However, this task of deciding what is 'worthy of attention' (Hanner, James, & Rohlfing, 2002, p. 100) has been shown to be challenging in several earlier studies with young children. In these studies, there was evidence that children overly depended on the perceptual similarity between objects when selecting attributes to

categorise objects (Gentner & Namy, 1999). In addition, studies by Hanner, James and Rohlfing (2002) and Lehrer and Schauble (2000) revealed young children's difficulties in communicating selected attributes were evidenced in their use of imprecise descriptors and the selection of descriptors that could not be evaluated by examination of the objects.

The findings arising from these studies have informed the ways in which we think about the design of opportunities for young children to engage with data. Consequently, recent studies explicitly attend to providing the supporting conditions considered necessary to aid young learners when selecting attributes. Ownership, competence and expertise (knowledge of the subject matter or data context), for example, have been identified as important factors that support engagement (DiSessa et al., 1991) and inform decisions when selecting attributes. Over the past decade, studies which incorporate careful attention to the aforementioned design features within data modelling environments reveal that children as young as four to six years old can switch attention to a selected attribute and avoid or eliminate attention to other attributes that may be visually compelling (English, 2010, 2012; Kinnear, 2013; Leavy & Hourigan, 2018). Children's expertise and knowledge of the contexts used in these studies informed the selection of attributes. Children were presented with messy, complex, multi-attribute data that were not clearly defined and did not possess readily discernible features that were shared among the group. Children's knowledge and expertise in relation to these data contexts supported them in identifying attributes and categorising objects. While the initial attributes selected focused on perceptual attributes such as in the selection of material (plastic, paper and cardboard) in the recycling contexts (English, 2010, 2012) and a focus on the appearance of animals (colour, size and texture) in the zoo context (Leavy & Hourigan, 2018); when asked to consider the problem situation (recycling or grouping of animals for the purpose of designing a zoo), children showed the ability to revise, extend or even discard these initial models in favour of models that were perceived to address the problem better. Hence, of particular interest in these studies is the fluidity of the initial models constructed by children. This demonstrated ability to 'switch their attention from one item feature to another' (English, 2012, p. 27) was evidenced when children shifted attention from the perceptual and towards consideration of more imperceptible attributes that responded to and addressed aspects of the problem situation. A similar fluidity was observed by Kinnear (2013) wherein she ascribed children's keen awareness of the variation between attributes as contributing to and informing their classifications. This awareness of variation between attributes was also evident in the study by Leavy and Hourigan (2018) where children demonstrated the ability to respond to situations where objects possessed more than one of the selected attribute. One example was when a group of children were classifying the data (i.e. zoo animals) according to the attributes *good/bad*. While some in the group classified the horse as 'good' and wanted to place it with good animals such as the seal and pelican, others wanted to place it with bad animals such as the lion because 'it will knock you over and make you fall on the ground'. These five- to six-year-olds discussed the situation and negotiated a solution by constructing a new and more encompassing category 'sometimes good and sometimes bad' to address these situations where an object possessed more than one attribute.

Making Predictions and Informal Inferences about Data. Inference is a central activity in statistics. Statistical inference involves drawing conclusions about the world, conclusions that extend beyond a given set of data. Formal statistical inference may involve inferring properties of a population based on a random sample selected from that population, or using inferential statistics to ascertain whether differences between groups are due to some systematic influence other than chance. While the challenges of teaching and understanding formal inference are widely acknowledged, there is a convincing argument that developing younger student's informal statistical inference lays the foundations to support rich statistical learnings and develops readiness for more formal statistical ideas at a later stage (Ben-Zvi, 2006; English, 2010, 2012; Makar & Rubin, 2009; Makar et al., 2011; Paparistodemou & Meletiou-Mavrotheris, 2008).

Studies examining the ability of young children to engage in informal inferential reasoning have used a variety of approaches and stimuli that support the use of informal inference. In an exploration of children's understandings of data, variation and expectation, Watson (2018) reports on the outcomes of interviews with seven six-year-olds as they engaged with four meaningful tasks: taking a lollipop from a container of 100 lollipops (50 red, 20 yellow, 30 green), representing books children had read using cut-out images of books, examining a bar chart of four different means of transport to school and speculating about the maximum daily temperature in their city. Watson found that children's predictions involving tasks that began with variation (reading books, transport to school) were generally not based on the data presented and drew from imaginary situations. She concluded that while recognising and discussing variation was natural to the children, their ability to deal with variation generally develops before the ability to express meaningful expectation related to that variation.

Data modelling environments appear to have been more successful in promoting informal inferential reasoning by either utilising picture books to support inferences (English, 2010, 2012; Kinnear, 2013; Kinnear & Clarke, 2016) or presenting contextually rich problem situations which require the construction of inferences to inform decision-making (Leavy & Hourigan, 2018). Similarly, inquiry-based learning environments (Makar, Bakker, & Ben-Zvi, 2015) and data visualisation environments utilising innovative technologies (Ben-Zvi, 2006; Paparistodemou & Meletiou-Mavrotheris, 2008) have also been shown to support informal inference by engaging young children in solving ill-structured problems using mathematics as evidence.

A study of the data modelling approaches of six-year-olds (English, 2012) indicated that young children were able to make informal inferences about data presented. Children were presented with a table of data representing the different types of litter (apples and newspapers, for example) collected by *Litterbug Doug* from Monday to Wednesday in the park and were asked to predict how many of each type of litter he would collect on Thursday. Children recognised patterns and trends in the data (amounts of litter collected on Monday, Tuesday and Wednesday) and made predictions and informal inferences about the situations presented (litter collected on Thursday). Many children focused on the values of particular cases (*case value lens*) and others demonstrated the ability to consider the frequency of cases with a particular value (*classifier lens*). There was also evidence of what English (2012) terms a *pre-aggregate lens* which included approaches that considered all the data, compared the frequencies and had some attention to overall trends. While not as sophisticated as an *aggregate lens*, which involves consideration of the entire distribution as an entity in itself (Konold, Higgins, Russell, & Khalil, 2014), the presence of this pre-aggregate lens is a strong indicator of the nascent potential of young children to engage in informal inference. A study by Leavy (2017) provides support for the findings of studies by both English and Kinnear and presents evidence that five- to six-year-olds, when engaged in a rich data modelling activity, possess some of the building blocks of informal inference most notably in the approaches that point to a pre-aggregate view of data. In this study, children were presented with a table of data illustrating the number of animals born in a zoo across four years. Children made predictions about the number of animals born the following year (year five). Evidence of the use of a pre-aggregate lens was visible in children's awareness of and attention to patterns in the data when making predictions and also in those strategies that coordinated an awareness of trends in the data (i.e. animal births increasing and decreasing in alternative years) with understandings of the context (i.e. the number of babies a particular animal could have) to inform predictions. Similarly, Kinnear (2013) presents evidence of six-year-old children demonstrating some elements of aggregate reasoning when drawing on knowledge of a story book to make inferences from the data. When making predictions, children generalised beyond the data and used the data to support their generalisations. These predictions demonstrated understanding 'or intuitive knowledge of reasonable distributional variation and the ability to draw inferences from it' (p. 241).

Similar to the finding reported by Watson (2018), Kinnear (2013) also reports on the use of abductive reasoning in situations where children based their predictions on the context but not on the data presented, more specifically drawing on their knowledge of the plot in a storybook to explain data values presented in a table of data. Makar and Rubin (2009) refer to abductive reasoning as a form of data-based reasoning employed by young children when observing patterns in data. In the case of young children who have limited life experiences to draw from, the reasoning is usually contextually based.

While not as accurate as the predictions arising from the studies of English (2010, 2012), the use of abductive reasoning can be considered as inferential as it represents an effort to provide explanations for data based on informed guesses arising from an individual's knowledge base. While Watson (2018) identifies some instances of abductive reasoning in her study of six-year-olds (e.g. when presenting general characteristics of seasons when exploring weather data and drawing on familiarity of bus routes in discussions of the transport data), she also reports on responses that arose entirely from the imagination and not from context (e.g. choosing numbers they like). Watson suggests that there is a progression in such reasoning which starts with imaginary reasoning outside of the context, to abductive reasoning which draws on the presented contexts and ultimately to informal inferential reasoning which uses the data within the context when making decisions.

Interestingly, there is evidence that the use of scaffolds such as technology can advance inferential reasoning. Paparistodemou and Meletiou-Mavrotheris (2008) highlighted the affordances of *Tinkerplots* in supporting eight-year-old children as they formulated and evaluated data-based inferences. The authors describe the demonstrated abilities of children to engage in data-based argumentation and draw conclusions about data they had collected, to make generalisations about data and use the data to draw inferences about a larger population. All of these abilities alongside using the data to draw inferences about an unknown population by articulating uncertainty were reported to indicate the presence of the 'seeds of inferential reasoning' (p. 93).

Makar (2016) carried out a series of teaching experiments extending across a six-month-long period in an effort to explore the emergence of statistical inference with a class of five- to six-year-olds. Mathematics lessons were built around experiences involving the use of storybooks, data-handling activities and patterns. Drawing from her observations of the emerging practices of informal statistical inference, Makar identified a number of foundational skills that are important for supporting young students in engaging in informal statistical inference. The skills include the ability to articulate and predict from observations, to record and organise data, to use invented methods (to make sense of, and record and organise data), to work with aggregates and speculate about and explore variability.

These studies with young children emphasise the critical role played by interesting and meaningful contexts and purposeful driving questions in providing affordances and supports when making inferences about statistical situations. Indeed, in their discussion of the role of *generalisation* in informal statistical inference, Makar and Rubin (2009) emphasise the important role of context and driving questions in supporting children in thinking inferentially about data. They argue that 'in working to "look beyond the data", it is not just making a conclusion *about data* that provides the conceptual muscle to draw inferences, but a conclusion *about the situation* which the data is meant to represent or signify' (p. 91).

Implications of Research for Early Years' Education

The previous sections emphasises the critical role played by meaningful contexts, inquiry, and investigative and data modelling experiences. An implication of engaging young children in any of these approaches is the careful teacher scaffolding and support required to focus children on the inquiry process and the statistical content. A study by Fielding-Wells (2018) of five- to six-year-olds involved in data investigation identified that the predominant support that was beneficial to children was teacher scaffolding which came in the form of questioning and feedback provided by the teacher. Such scaffolding drew on teachers' knowledge of the context, knowledge of statistical and mathematical content and knowledge of statistical inquiry. The critical role of the teacher in supporting young children's emerging statistical reasoning is also evidenced in a classroom study carried out by Makar (2018) of four- to five-year-olds engaged in statistical enquiry. Makar revealed these young children's capacity to reason about a statistical context in ways that paralleled more formal statistical thinking. The classroom teacher, who was very experienced in teaching using an inquiry approach, asked questions that drew from children's ideas and emphasised the desired statistical content. As a result, children demonstrated recognition of the need to collect data in order to answer a statistical question, the benefit of both recording, representing and the subsequent analysing of data. Arising from the research, Makar provides a framework, utilising what she terms as 'statistical-context structures', which allows teachers and instructional designers to identify elements of the problem context that scaffold children's thinking about statistical concepts, representations and processes. These statistical context structures may represent a way to make accessible many of the big ideas identified as key structural elements in statistics such as data, variability, aggregate and population, and may be useful supports for early years' educators when engaging in intentional teaching of statistical concepts.

The Place of Probability in Early Years' Education

For some time, there has been consensus that all students should study probability. An understanding of probability is necessary in order to make informed decisions across various aspects of everyday and professional life (Gal, 2005; Liu & Thompson, 2007). It is particularly important for children, as most of the games they engage in involve the idea of chance (Paparistodemou & Meletiou-Mavrotheris, 2018; Tatsis, Kafoussi, & Skoumpourdi, 2008).

Despite this, there has been less agreement regarding when the formal study of probability should begin. Probability is a relative latecomer to mathematics education curricula and for much time it has struggled to acquire a minor place within secondary school curricula. However, there was a belief that rather than reserving exposure to secondary school, the foundations should be laid in the very early years of life. In response to ongoing proposals that younger children should be exposed to probability, in the late 1980s probability (alongside statistics) was introduced to primary curriculum internationally (Bryant & Nunes, 2012; Jones, Langrall, & Mooney, 2007). In the meantime, probability education has become a contested area, with curriculum authorities in some countries (e.g. USA, UK) recently suspending its introduction until the post-primary years (CCSI, 2010; DoE, 2013). In other countries (e.g. Australia) however, children as young as six to seven years are introduced to informal probability concepts (ACARA, 2014). Support for inclusion of probability education within early years' education comes from those who justify this on the basis that in their everyday interactions with the world, young children need to make sense of probabilistic situations in determining what is likely, or possible (Yurovsky, Boyer, Smith, & Yu, 2013). In light of the conflicting viewpoints and practices, a critical analysis of the relevant research is both timely and informative.

Theories of probability have developed over many decades. The various perspectives on the quantification of uncertainty have developed incrementally as a reaction to each other. That is, historically each interpretation has evolved in a bid to address perceived flaws in previous definitions of probability (Konold et al., 2011). The three main perspectives are termed the classical, frequentist and subjective interpretations of probability. The classical interpretation of probability refers to the ratio between the number of favourable cases in an event and the total number of equally likely cases. This ratio is also called theoretical probability and is determined through analysis of a sample space (list of all possible outcomes). The frequentist interpretation (also called experimental probability) is the probability of an event based on the relative frequency of favourable outcomes in a large sample of trials and is achieved by completing an experiment or simulation. Subjective probability refers to a personal degree of belief and is determined by subjective judgement and information available (Batanero, Chernoff, Engel, Lee, & Sánchez, 2016; Jones et al., 2007).

Research on Young Children's Understandings of Probability

Relative to other content areas, research focusing on probability is limited. In addition to this, within the research which has been carried out, studies examining early years' learners are much fewer than those in other age profiles in particular secondary school and adult learners. Despite this, over the last decade there is growing interest in exploring young children's probabilistic thinking (Nikiforidou, 2018). The research which does exist provides insights and recommendations critical to the development of practice in the area.

Research regarding the probabilistic capacities of children in the early years is evident since the late twentieth century. Piaget and Inhelder (1975) explored the development of probabilistic thinking, focusing on the role of intellectual ability. This work characterised children who were in the first pre-operational stage of thinking (before the age of seven to eight) as demonstrating pre-logical thinking and demonstrating limited capacity to understand relevant probabilistic concepts. They argued that the ability to relate the part (favourable outcome) to the whole (all possible outcomes) was necessary for probabilistic understanding. Fischbein (1975), in his study which focused on the role of intuition, reported that before the ages six to seven children can demonstrate a capacity to evaluate chance and estimate the odds probabilistically in certain conditions (e.g. where the problem was clear, the number of possibilities small, incentives were given for correct answers).

Building on previous research on the characteristics of young children's understandings of probability, Jones, Langrall and Thornton (1997) developed a framework for evaluating children's probabilistic thinking. The framework examined understandings within four probability concepts: sample space, probability of an event, probability comparisons and conditional probability. After extensive observation and interview at different ages, they proposed four levels of probabilistic thinking (Level 1: Subjective level, Level 2: Transitional level, Level 3: Informal Quantitative level, Level 4: Numerical level). Level 1 reflects subjective thinking where the child makes intuitive decisions based on their personal preferences (See Table 6.1). Level 2 reflects transitional thinking between subjective thinking (Level 1) and naïve quantitative thinking (Level 3). At this level children make limited attempts to quantify probabilities. Level 3 thinking involves children using more formal quantitative thinking, for example using more logical generative strategies when listing outcomes of a two-stage experiment (e.g. throwing two dice). Level 4 incorporates numerical thinking and students use numerical measures to justify their responses (Jones et al., 2007). Nikiforidou (2018) suggests that Level 1 is the level aligned with early years' education.

These previous studies have laid the foundations for subsequent research on young children's probabilistic thinking.

Table 6.1 Jones et al.'s (1997) Framework for Assessing Probabilistic Thinking (Level 1)

Concept	Level 1
Sample space	Incomplete list of outcomes for one-stage experiments
Probability of an event	Predicts most/least likely event based on subjective judgements Distinguishes 'certain', 'impossible', possible events in a limited way
Probability comparison	Compares the probability of an event in two different sample spaces, usually based on subjective or numeric judgements
Conditional probability	Following a particular outcome, predicts that it will occur the next time, or alternatively that it will not occur again (overgeneralises)

Information obtained from Figure 1 in Jones et al. (1997). A framework for nurturing young children's thinking in probability. *Educational Studies in Mathematics, 32,* 101–125.

Overall, they report limited understandings of probability among children in the early years. The remainder of this section examines insights from more recent studies in supporting or challenging these beliefs and which explore young children's understandings of the big ideas in probability. Relevant studies explicitly examine the probabilistic capacities of children in the early years which include infants and toddlers as well as pre-schoolers and children of primary school age.

Language of Chance

Comprehension and use of chance language is important given its use in everyday decision-making as well as in statistical analysis. Despite this, there is a lack of research examining children's facility in evaluating and using chance phrases (Watson & Moritz, 2003). The few relevant studies which were carried out in the late twentieth century revealed that older children demonstrated greater facility in interpreting chance language (Jones et al., 2007). For example, Hoffner, Cantor and Badzinski (1990) reported that younger children (pre-K-grade 1) were less able to differentiate between similar probabilistic terms such as probable and definite than their older peers (grade 4). Fischbein, Nello and Marino (1991) also uncovered difficulties with the terms 'impossible', 'possible' and 'certain', for example equating 'rare' with 'impossible'. However, Nascarato and Grando's (2014) study suggests that confusions regarding chance language persist among older children. They found that 10 to 12 year olds used the term 'less probable' to describe impossible events and 'improbable' to describe events which occur frequently. Interestingly, a study by Watson (2005) revealed that children equated equal likelihood with the presence of uncertainty. While a study by Kazak and Leavy (2018) presents evidence of a small number of seven to eight year olds demonstrating the difficulties outlined by Fischbein et al. (1991) and Nascarato and Grando (2014), on the whole the authors reported seven to eight year olds used chance language relatively accurately to describe the likelihood of chance events. There is much potential for further study within the context of early years' learners.

Random Phenomena

Jones et al. (2007, p. 918) characterise random phenomena as 'having short-term unpredictability and long-term stability'. The research which exists in this area suggests young children have difficulty in making rational judgements about this construct. Piaget and Indelder (1975), in their study of 4 to 12 year olds' understanding of the movement of red and white beads (originally arranged in two separate groups) on a tray which was tilted over and back, found that many younger children, particularly those aged four to seven years, predicted that the distinct colours would stay separate. Subsequently, Kuzmak and Gelman (1986) claimed that their study (involving two different dispenser mechanisms: one

where balls were lined up in a straight line and could be seen, the other a series of complex moving tubes designed to eject a ball in a random fashion) suggests that children aged four to seven years could accurately identify whether they could predict the outcome. Bryant and Nunes (2012) suggest that this claim may be hasty given that children could have simply judged that it was harder to be sure what would happen rather than make a judgement directly related to randomness. In a more recent study, Nikifordou and Pange (2010) tested four to six year old children's notion of randomness in a task examining how they graphically represent items on a grid. The children's preference for uniform distribution of items suggests a minimal understanding of randomness. However, more positive findings regarding young children's understandings of randomisation were evident within a study that used a computer microworld to gauge five to eight year olds' understandings of randomisation. In order to succeed in the game, it was necessary for children to arrange balls of two distinct colours in a random arrangement (Paparistodemou, Noss, & Pratt, 2008). While the majority did not adopt this strategy at the start and instead opted for symmetrical arrangements, upon engaging with the game nearly half of the children tried out a random arrangement and several gave reasonably coherent explanations for why. The relative success of these young children compared to the findings of the other studies may be linked with the extended time spent on the problem (approximately 2½ hours), opportunities provided to consider and trial different strategies and the benefit of experience of similar games.

Chiesi and Primi (2009) compared eight-year-olds', 10-year-olds' and college students' conceptions of randomness in terms of sequences of outcomes. Participants were presented with 15 green and 15 blue balls. They were told that when four balls were selected in a row, all four balls drawn were blue and asked to predict the next draw and given three choices: next ball more likely to be blue than green (positive recency), next ball drawn more likely to be green than blue (negative recency), the two colours were equally likely (correct response). The study reported that none of eight-year olds responded correctly and they made twice as many positive recency than negative recency choices.

Quantifying Probability

While determining the likelihood of an event (theoretical probability) requires analysis of the sample space, studies focusing on young children generally examined their ability to identify the most or least likely outcome. In the last decade there has been an increased interest in the probabilistic capacities of infants in determining the likelihood of various events. For example in Teglas, Girotto and Gonzalez's (2007) study, one-year-olds were presented two different experiments consisting of three identical items and one unique item. On analysing the findings of the two experiments, the authors reported that the infants responded on the basis of probability (the likelihood of events) as opposed to familiarity, with infants looking for longer when they observed less likely events than they did when witnessing more likely events (Teglas et al., 2011). Xu and Garcia's (2008) study of eight-month olds also reports that infants looked longer at improbable events than probable ones. These studies provide the basis for additional research to explore the strengths and limitations of very young children's probabilistic understandings.

Studies examining older children's capacities in this regard reported positive findings. For example, Teglas et al. (2007) found that from age four, children demonstrated an ability to predict events defined by a simple property. Nikifordou and Pange (2010) also reported that four to six year olds could correctly infer the most likely outcome in picture card tasks. Nikifordou, Pange and Chadjipadelis (2013) reported that four to six year olds (working in pairs) demonstrated stable understandings in their ability to predict which outcome was most likely across all spinner tasks. Kazak and Leavy (2018) used an alternative approach when examining seven to eight year old children's ability to determine the likelihood of an event. They adopted Acredolo, O'Connor, Banks and Horobin's (1989) Jelly Bean task alongside a non-numerical scale (happy face scale) which would facilitate deeper insights into these young children's estimates of likelihood. The study also explored the impact of experiment and simulation on children's predictions. While there was overall evidence that children made appropriate predictions, there was some evidence of the influence of everyday interpretations of chance language. For example the tendency to equate rare and impossible outcomes was evident in situations where some students marked zero on the scale to represent the chance of pulling a green jellybean from a bag containing one green and seven purple jellybeans. While the majority of children were able to identify equally likely events prior to experiment, also of interest were situations where some children marked the neutral position on the scale when unsure of the possibility of an event occurring – these findings reflect previous research (Konold, 1989). In some cases, the experiment using small samples (24 trials) was found to be misleading for children.

Following a series of three studies of 4 to 10 year olds, Girotto and Gonzalez (2008) concluded that children from six years were able to solve more difficult problems in which they updated their judgement in light of additional information (posterior probability). For example if children were presented with five yellow chips (four square and one round) and three blue chips (all round), while they initially predict§1ed that a yellow chip was more likely, when advised that the chip which had been drawn was round, they predicted it was more likely to be a blue chip.

Comparing Probabilities

Probability comparison involves determining which of two probability situations is more likely or whether both are equally likely to occur. Piaget and Inhelder (1975) reported that six to eight year olds struggled to compare two probabilities using different sample spaces. Falk, Falk and Leving (1980), in their study of four to seven year olds, asked children to select the roulette type wheel which was more likely to stop on a particular colour. The wheels were of different sizes and the areas and numbers of sections varied. While many six to seven year olds used proportional reasoning to solve the task, it proved particularly challenging for the younger children who tended to pick the wheel with the larger number of sections. Falk and Wilkening (1998) engaged 6 to 13 year olds in an adjustment task, where children were presented with two urns (Urn 1: two different coloured beads, Urn 2: beads of one colour). Children were informed that the urns would be part of a lottery game. While the experimenter would select a bead from one of the urns, the child would draw one from the other. One colour was identified the winning colour. The task required children to complete the contents of Urn 2 by putting in beads of the missing colour so there was the same chance of getting the winning colour in each urn. In contrast to the previous study, six to seven year olds in this study did not demonstrate proportional reasoning but rather placed the same number of coloured beads as that in the complete urn without considering the other colour. The required proportional reasoning was only evident among children from age 11 in this study. Generally younger children focused on the quantity of one of the colours only. However, subsequently, various research studies have reported more positive findings in this regard. Remarkably, Denison and Xu (2010) found that infants (10–14 months) demonstrated an ability to evaluate chances in choice tasks. Materials which were considered more desirable (e.g. lollipops covered in purple paper with stars decorations) were used alongside less attractive versions (lollipops covered in black plain paper). Children were presented with two jars (Jar 1: 40 desirable objects, 10 undesirable objects; Jar 2: 10 desirable objects, 40 undesirable objects). After observing the contents of each jar, an object was taken from each jar and hidden in two distinct spaces. The infants did not see the objects selected. The study found that infants would make an optimal choice, searching in the place where the preferred outcome was more likely. While the authors acknowledge that in their initial research (Denison & Xu, 2010) children could have relied on simple comparison of absolute quantities as opposed to proportions to succeed in these tasks, Denison and Xu (2014) subsequently completed four studies to thoroughly examine infant's abilities to compare probabilities. The findings demonstrate that infants (12–14 months) made optimal choices even when the totals were not the same (e.g. Jar 1: 16 desirable, 4 undesirable; Jar 2: 24 desirable, 96 undesirable) so they had to consider proportions.

It is interesting to find that on using the same tasks as those used by Denison and Xu (2010, 2014) in a comprehensive study of three to five year olds, Girotto, Fontanari, Gonzalez, Vallortigara and Blaye (2016) found that only five-year olds made optimal choices. Toddlers aged three to four years did not demonstrate equivalent probabilistic ability but instead performed randomly, even on the simpler tasks. Girotto et al. (2016) consider the reasons for this 'gap' in children's probabilistic ability. They question whether infant's probabilistic abilities have been overestimated or that the development of this ability may not follow a linear trajectory. They also question the potential impact of the protocol demands (explanations and instructions) on toddler's ability to attend fully to the tasks. These contrasting findings require further examination.

Girotto et al.'s (2016) findings that five-year-olds demonstrated a capacity to compare probabilities reflect the findings of other recent studies. For example, Girotto and Gonzalez (2008) reported that in a choice task where children had to compare the chance of two competing outcomes, children aged five years and older predicted correctly. Falk, Yudilevich-Assouline and Elstein (2012) carried out a comprehensive study to examine strategies used by 6 to 11 year olds when choosing the urn with the higher winning probability. Reflecting Falk and Wilkening (1998), the findings suggest that the younger children were more likely to focus on just one element (predominantly the winning element) rather than consider the relationship between the elements.

Combinatorial Reasoning

Combinatorial reasoning involves the ability to work out all the possible combinations in the sample space. Piaget and Inhelder (1975) used an experiment where they presented children with a set of counters of four different colours (15 yellow, 10 red, 7 green, 3 blue). These sets were then placed in a sack and shaken thoroughly. Children were asked to draw out a pair of counters and make a prediction first of the colours of each counter in the pair. As the counters were not returned to the sack, the probability of possible pairs varied constantly. Given the complexity of this activity, it is not surprising to find that five to seven year olds demonstrated no sign of systematic analysis of the probability of drawing the different colours and often did not even take account of the different number of each colour. Gonzalez and Goritto (2011) used three experiments to examine 5 to 10 year olds children's understandings of combinations. The findings suggest that children from age six years were able to predict the occurrence of a relation on the basis of its probability. While these findings seem to contradict previous findings, unlike the Piagetian test, the tasks did not require children to count the possible outcomes but to provide an approximate comparison.

Consistency of Research Findings

It may appear that the respective studies on young children's probabilistic understandings are reporting conflicting findings. However, in reality discrepancies in findings across studies could be attributed to the influence of task characteristics particularly in relation to suitability of the context, materials, difficulty and expectations (Falk et al., 2012; Nikifordou et al., 2013; Skoumpourdi, Kafoussim, & Tatsis, 2009). In general, more recent studies use a relevant-involvement method with minimal dependence on verbal ability which means that children's abilities to demonstrate relevant probabilistic concepts are tested without requiring them to provide explicit enumerations of the possibilities (Falk et al., 2012; Gonzalez & Goritto, 2011). However, this does not suggest less rigour as such research has reached conclusions based on the findings of quite comprehensive projects consisting of three to four studies.

Implications of Research for Early Years' Education

In light of the findings, we question decisions to delay the formal introduction of probability until post-primary education. Such decisions may result in students' experiencing additional difficulties due to the development of faulty intuitions and overgeneralisations arising from a lack of formal critique of everyday interactions with uncertainty. For example, in the case of the language of probability, there is an acknowledgement that the delayed treatment of probability will make it more difficult for children to incorporate the probabilistic meaning of various terms (e.g. certain) that have been interpreted differently for an extended period in everyday interactions (Groth, 2018). This proposal that probability be positioned within early years' curricula reflects Bruner's (1960) notion of spiral curriculum, where the foundations are laid as early as possible in a form compatible with the child's levels of readiness thus facilitating the revisiting and redevelopment of understandings throughout formal education.

There is also some direction regarding appropriate educational practice and learning environments conducive to fostering young children's probabilistic understandings (Falk et al., 2012; Skoumpourdi et al., 2009). An active approach is recommended where learners engage with meaningful contexts and tasks. The importance of the nature and the structure of the probability task has been emphasised repeatedly (Falk et al., 2012; Skoumpourdi et al., 2009). Although Kafoussi (2004) used stories in puppet shows, role play and games and Kazak and Leavy (2018) used a 'jelly bean task' to promote interest and engagement, Nikiforidou (2018) also suggests the use of picture story books as a potential source. The teaching sequence recommended by Sharma (2014) consists of introducing the task within a meaningful context, making predictions, informally playing the game, whole class sharing and discussion, group data collection, recording and analysis prior to further exploration involving representing the outcomes.

It is considered essential that children have ample opportunities to engage with relevant manipulatives and/or appropriate technology in order to make and test predictions. The place of technology within probability education is shifting, in light of the central place of technology in children's everyday lives (Batanero et al., 2016). As witnessed in Paparistodemou et al.'s (2008) study, technological tools and software can potentially offer graphically attractive and game-like experiences of probabilistic concepts (Nikiforidou, 2018). Technology software also has the potential to provide insights into a large sample of the phenomenon being explored. Kazak and Leavy (2018) reported that children aged seven to eight years used visual proportions from *Tinkerplots* to make more informed probability estimations.

Similar to the teaching of statistics discussed earlier in the chapter, the teacher plays a central role in teaching probability by posing open-ended questions and selecting tasks that promote thinking and reasoning. The use of sentence beginners is also recommended to support children in communicating their ideas (Nikiforidou, 2018; Sharma, 2014). Thus, engaging children in appropriate probability education from early years facilitates continuously revisiting concepts through a spiral curriculum in order to develop probability literate adults into the future who have 'the ability to access, use, interpret and communicate probability-related information and ideas in order to engage and effectively manage the demands of real-world roles and tasks involving uncertainty and risk' (Gal, 2012, p. 4).

Summary and Conclusion

Our review of the literature suggests that young children's understandings of various statistical and probabilistic concepts are more sophisticated than initially conceived. Early years' learners show a capacity to engage in various statistical processes as well as a sensitivity to uncertain situations (English, 2012; Girotto et al., 2016; Nikifordou et al., 2013). In respect to probability, many of the studies suggest the presence of probabilistic thinking beyond that associated with Jones et al.'s (1997) Level 1 (see Table 6.1). Similarly, young children display relatively sophisticated understandings of the foundational components of data modelling and statistical inquiry. The findings also suggest that these understandings may not be dependent on previous experiences or formal instruction (Gonzalez & Girotto, 2011; Leavy & Hourigan, 2018). Consequently, it is necessary to consider how such informal and intuitive understandings can be fostered and developed within early years' education. Prior knowledge and intuitions should provide the starting point for constructing conceptual understandings (Garfield & Ben-Zvi, 2009; Jones, Langrall, & Thornton, 1999; Nikiforidou, 2018; Sharma, 2014). The research outlined in this chapter also provides guidance regarding appropriate educational practice and learning environments conducive to fostering young children's statistical and probabilistic understandings (Falk et al., 2012, Kinnear, 2013; Makar, 2018; Skoumpourdi et al., 2009). Such environments factor the interests and prior experiences of the young children in task design. In addition, they require active engagement in reasoning and responding to the context, thus promoting meaningful inquiry and in the process revealing their emerging statistical and probabilistic understandings. These interactive and collaborative learning environments are central to appropriate practice, where

young children are given opportunities to share and discuss observations, ideas, justifications and reflections. Therefore, we support the view of Falk et al. (2012) that young children are capable of engaging in probability (and statistics) in playful ways.

Although the research outlined provides impressive accounts of children's statistical and probabilistic learning, in order to more effectively develop robust understandings we need to rely on more than the natural and spontaneous learning that may occur from informal play experiences in early childhood settings. We need to design and evaluate intentional teaching experiences and sequences that provide opportunities for young children to encounter statistical and probabilistic concepts in a progressive and developmentally appropriate fashion. While much of the recent research involving young children in statistical inquiry and data modelling activities has advanced our understandings considerably, there remains a relative paucity of research examining the impact of particular child-centred approaches in developing children's probabilistic literacy (Nikifordou et al., 2013). Therefore, we recommend a focus on how practices in early years' education settings influence young children's emerging understandings (Gal, 2012; Kafoussi, 2004).

If statistics and probability are to be included in any meaningful way in early years' curricula, it is essential that early years' educators are supported in facilitating the various elements of the envisaged child-centred practices. Optimising the mathematical development and understandings of young children requires 'intentional teaching that supports learning experiences that expose them to mathematical concepts in a progressive and developmental fashion' (Presser et al., 2015, p. 402). Consequently, early years' teachers require opportunities to develop appropriate mathematical knowledge for teaching (Ball, Thames, & Phelps, 2008). Paparistodemou and Meletiou-Mavrotheris (2018) report that this has been overlooked as there is a common perception that the content in the early childhood years is simple and playful. Indeed, research examining both prospective and qualified primary teachers' knowledge of specific statistical and probability concepts reports difficulties and misconceptions (Dollard, 2011; Gómez-Torres, Batanero, Diaz, & Contreras, 2016; Hourigan & Leavy, 2019; Leavy, 2010). While beyond the remit of this chapter, this knowledge development is critical in promoting appropriate practice and experiences in the early years' settings.

References

Acredolo, C., O'Connor, J., Banks, L., & Horobin, K. (1989). Children's ability to make probability estimates: Skills revealed through application of Anderson's functional measurement methodology. *Child Development, 60*, 933–945.

Arnold, D., Fisher, P. H., Doctoroff, G. L., & Dobbs, J. (2002). Accelerating math development in Head Start classrooms. *Journal of Educational Psychology, 94*(4), 762–770.

Australian Curriculum, Assessment and Reporting Authority (ACARA). (2014). *Foundation to year 10 curriculum: Statistics and probability.*

Retrieved from http://www.australiancurriculum.edu.au/mathematics/curriculum/f-10?layout=1

Balfanz, R. (1999). Why do we teach children so little mathematics? Some historical considerations. In J. V. Copley (Ed.), *Mathematics in the early years* (pp. 3–10). Reston, VA: National Council of Teachers of Mathematics.

Ball, D. L., Thames, M. H., & Phelps, G. (2008). Content knowledge for teaching: What makes it special? *Journal of Teacher Education, 59,* 389–407.

Baroody, A. J., Lai, M.-L., & Mix, K. S. (2006). The development of young children's number and operation sense and its implications for early childhood education. In B. Spodek & O. Saracho (Eds.), *Handbook of research on the education of young children* (pp. 187–221). Mahwah, NJ: Erlbaum.

Batanero, C., Chernoff, E. J., Engel, J., Lee, H. S., & Sánchez, E. (2016). *Research on teaching and learning probability.* ICME-13 Topical Surveys. Cham: Springer.

Ben-Zvi, D. (2006). Scaffolding students' informal inference and argumentation. In A. Rossman and B. Chance (Eds.), *Proceedings of the seventh international conference on teaching statistics.* Voorburg, The Netherlands: International Statistical Institute.

Blair, M., & Somerville, S. C. (2009). The importance of differentiation in young children's acquisition of expertise. *Cognition, 112,* 259–280.

Bruner, J. (1960). *The process of education.* Cambridge, MA: Harvard University Press.

Bryant, P., & Nunes, T. (2012). *Children's understanding of probability: A literature review.* London, UK: Nuffield Foundation.

Chiesi, F., & Primi, C. (2009). Recency effects in primary-age children and college students. *International Electronic Journal of Mathematics Education, 4*(3), 259–274.

Ciancio, D. S., Rojas, A. C., McMahon, K., & Pasnak, R. (2001). Teaching oddity and insertion to Head Start children: An economical cognitive intervention. *Journal of Applied Developmental Psychology, 22,* 603–621.

Clements, D. H., & Sarama, J. (2007). Effects of a preschool mathematics curriculum: Summative research on the building blocks project. *Journal for Research in Mathematics Education, 38*(2), 136–163.

Clements, D. H., Sarama, J., Spitler, M. E., Lange, A. A., & Wolfe, C. B. (2011). Mathematics learned by young children in an intervention based on learning trajectories: A large-scale cluster randomized trial. *Journal for Research in Mathematics Education, 42*(2), 126–177.

Cobb, G. W., & Moore, D. S. (1997). Mathematics, statistics, and teaching. *The American Mathematical Monthly, 104*(9), 801–823. doi:10.2307/2975286

Common Core Standards Initiative (CCSI). (2010). Common Core State Standards for Mathematics. Retrieved from http://www.corestandards.org

Cross, T. C., Woods, T. A., & Schweingruber, H. (Eds.). (2009). *Mathematics learning in early childhood: Paths towards excellence and equity.* Washington, DC: National Academies Press.

Denison, S., & Xu, F. (2010). Twelve- to fourteen-month-old infants can predict single-event probability with large set sizes. *Developmental Science, 13,* 798–803.

Denison, S., & Xu, F. (2014). The origins of probabilistic inference in human infants. *Cognition, 130,* 335–347.

Department of Education (DoE). (2013). *The national curriculum in England: Key stages 3 and 4 framework document.* Retrieved from http://www.gov.uk/government/publicatons/national-curriculum-in-england-secondary-curriculum

diSessa, A. A. (2004). Metarepresentation: Native competence and targets for instruction. *Cognition and Instruction, 22*(3), 291–292.

DiSessa, A., Hammer, D., Sherin, B., & Kolpakowski, T. (1991). Inventing graphing: Metarepresentational expertise in children. *Journal of Mathematical Behavior, 10*(1), 117–160.

Dollard, C. (2011). Preservice elementary teachers and the fundamentals of probability. *Statistics Education Research Journal, 10*(2), 27–47.

Duncan, G. J., Dowsett, C. J., Claessens, A., Magnuson, K., Huston, A. C., Klebanov, P., … Japel, C. (2007). School readiness and later achievement.

Developmental Psychology, 43(6), 1428–1446. doi:10.1037/0012-1649.43.6.1428

Elia, I., van den Heuvel-Panhuizen, M., & Georgiou, A. (2010). The role of pictures in picture books on children's cognitive engagement with mathematics. *European Early Childhood Research Journal, 18*(3), 275–297. doi:10.1080/1350293X.2010.500054

English, L. D. (2010). Young children's early modelling with data. *Mathematics Education Research Journal, 22*(2), 24–47.

English, L. D. (2012). Data modelling with first-grade students. *Educational Studies in Mathematics, 81,* 15–30.

Epstein, A. S. (2003). How planning and reflection develop young children's thinking skills. *Young Children, 58*(5), 28–36.

Epstein, A. S. (2007). *The intentional teacher: Choosing the best strategies for young children's learning.* Washington, DC: National Association for the Education of Young Children.

Estrella, S. (2018). Data representations in early statistics: Data sense, meta-representational competence and transnumeration. In A. M. Leavy, M. Meletiou-Mavrotheris, & E. Paparistodemou (Eds.), *Statistics in early childhood and primary education: Supporting early statistical and probabilistic thinking.* Singapore: Springer Nature. doi:10.1007/978-981-13-1044-7_3

Falk, R., Falk, R., & Levin, I. (1980). A potential for learning probability in young children. *Educational Studies in Mathematics, 11,* 181–204.

Falk, R., & Wilkening, F. (1998). Children's construction of fair chances: Adjusting probabilities. *Developmental Psychology, 34*(6), 1340–1357.

Falk, R., Yudilevich- Assouline, P., & Elstein, A. (2012). Children's concept of probability as inferred from their binary choices- revisited. *Educational Studies in Mathematics, 81,* 207–233.

Fielding-Wells, J. (2018). Scaffolding statistical inquiries for young children. In A. M. Leavy, M. Meletiou-Mavrotheris, & E. Paparistodemou (Eds.), *Statistics in early childhood and primary education: Supporting early statistical and probabilistic thinking.* Singapore: Springer Nature. doi:10.1007/978–981-13–1044–7_3

Fischbein, E. (1975). *The intuitive sources of probabilistic thinking in children.* Boston, MA: D. Reidel Publishing Company.

Fischbein, E., Nello, M. S., & Marino, M. S. (1991). Factors affecting probabilistic judgments in children and adolescents. *Educational Studies in Mathematics, 22,* 523–549.

Frye, D., Baroody, A. J., Burchinal, M., Carver, S. M., Jordan, N. C., & McDowell, J. (2013). *Teaching math to young children: A practice guide* (NCEE 2014-4005). Washington, DC: National Center for Education Evaluation and Regional Assistance (NCEE). Retrieved from http://whatworks.ed.gov

Gal, I. (2005). Towards "probability literacy" for all citizens: Building blocks and instructional dilemma. In G. A. Jones (Ed.), *Exploring probability in school: Challenges for teaching and learning* (pp. 39–63). Dordrecht, the Netherlands: Kluwer.

Gal, I. (2012). Developing probability literacy: Needs and pressures stemming from frameworks of adult competencies and mathematics curricula. *Proceedings of the 12th international congress on mathematical education* (pp. 1–7). Seoul, Korea.

Garfield, J. B., & Ben-Zvi, D. (2009). Helping students develop statistical reasoning: Implementing a statistical reasoning learning environment. *Teaching Statistics, 31*(3), 72–77.

Gelman, R. (1972). Logical capacity of very young children: Number invariance rules. *Child Development, 43,* 75–90.

Gelman, S. A., & Markman, E. M. (1986). Categories and induction in young children. *Cognition, 23,* 183–209.

Gentner, D., & Namy, L. L. (1999). Comparison in the development of categories. *Cognitive Development, 14,* 487–513.

Ginsburg, H. P., Klein, A., & Starkey, P. (1998). The development of children's mathematical thinking: Connecting research with practice. In I. Sigel & A. Renninger (Eds.), *Handbook of child psychology, Volume 4: Child psychology and practice* (5th ed., pp. 401–476). New York, NY: Wiley.

Girotto, V., & Gonzalez, M. (2008). Children's understanding of posterior probability. *Cognition, 106*(1), 325–344.

Girotto, V., Fontanari, L., Gonzalez, M., Vallortigara, G., & Blaye, A. (2016). Young children do not succeed in choice tasks that imply evaluating chances. *Cognition, 152*, 32–39.

Gómez-Torres, E., Batanero, C., Diaz, C., & Contreras, J. M. (2016). Developing a questionnaire to assess the probability content knowledge of prospective primary school teachers. *Statistics Education Research Journal, 15*(2), 197–215.

Gonzalez, M., & Goritto, V. (2011). Combinatorics and probability: Six- to ten-year-olds reliably predict whether a relation will occur. *Cognition, 120*, 372–379.

Groth, R. E., 2018. Unpacking implicit disagreements among early childhood standards for statistics and probability. In A. Leavy, M. Meleltiou-Mavrotheris, & E. Paparistodemou (Eds.), *Statistics in early childhood and primary education: Supporting early statistical and probabilistic thinking* (pp. 149–162). Singapore: Springer.

Hachey, A. C. (2013). The early childhood mathematics education revolution. *Early Education and Development, 24*(4), 419–430. doi:10.1080/10409289.2012.756223

Hanner, S., James, E., & Rohlfing, M. (2002). Classification models across grades. In R. Lehrer & L. Schauble (Eds.), *Investigating real data in the classroom* (pp. 99–117). New York, NY: Teachers College.

Hoffner, C., Cantor, J., & Badzinski, D. M. (1990). Children's understanding of adverbs denoting degree of likelihood. *Journal of Child Language, 17*(1), 217–231.

Hourigan, M., & Leavy, A. M. (2016). Practical problems: Introducing statistics to kindergarteners. *Teaching Children Mathematics, 22*(5), 283–291.

Hourigan, M., & Leavy, A. M. (2019, Online First). Pre-service teachers' understanding of probabilistic fairness: Analysis of decisions around task design. *International Journal for Mathematical Education in Science and Technology.* doi:10.1080/0020739X.2019.1648891

Huff, D. (1954). *How to lie with statistics.* New York, NY: Norton.

Jones, G. A., Langrall, C. W., & Mooney, E. S. (2007). Research in probability: Responding to classroom realities. In F. K. Lester Jr. (Ed.), *The second handbook of research on mathematics teaching and learning: A project of the national council of teachers of mathematics* (pp. 909–955). Charlotte, NC: Information Age Publishing.

Jones, G. A., Langrall, C. W., Thornton, C. A., & Mogill, A. T. (1997). A framework for nurturing young children's thinking in probability. *Educational Studies in Mathematics, 32*, 101–125.

Jones, G. A., Langrall, C. W., Thornton, C. A., & Mogill, A. T. (1999). Students' probabilistic thinking in instruction. *Educational Studies in Mathematics, 30*(5), 487–519.

Kafoussi, S. (2004). Can kindergarten children be successfully involved in probabilistic tasks? *Statistics Education Research Journal, 3*(1), 29–39.

Kamii, C., Rummelsburg, J., & Kari, A. R. (2005). Teaching arithmetic to low-performing, low SES first graders. *Journal of Mathematical Behavior, 24*, 39–50.

Kazak, S., & Leavy, A. (2018). Emergent reasoning about uncertainty in primary school children with a focus on subjective probability. In A. M. Leavy, M. Meleltiou-Mavrotheris, & E. Paparistodemou (Eds.), *Statistics in early childhood and primary education: Supporting early statistical and probabilistic thinking* (pp. 37–54). Singapore: Springer Nature. doi:10.1007/978-981-13-1044-7_3

Klein, A., Starkey, P., Clements, D., Sarama, J., & Iyer, R. (2008). Effects of a pre- kindergarten mathematics intervention: A randomized experiment. *Journal of Research on Educational Effectiveness, 1*(3), 155–178.

Kinnear, V. (2013). *Young children's statistical reasoning: A tale of two contexts.* Unpublished PhD dissertation, Queensland University of Technology.

Kinnear, V. (2018). Initiating interest in statistical problems: The role of picture story books. In A. M. Leavy, M. Meleltiou-Mavrotheris, & E. Paparistodemou (Eds.), *Statistics in early childhood and primary education: Supporting early statistical and probabilistic thinking* (pp. 183–199). Singapore: Springer Nature. doi:10.1007/978-981-13-1044-7_3

Kinnear, V., & Clarke, J. (2016). Young children's abductive reasoning about data. In *Proceedings of the 13th international congress on mathematical education.* Hamburg, July 24–31. http://icme13.org/files/ICME13-Programme356_low36.pdf

Konold, C. (1989). Informal conceptions of probability. *Cognition and Instruction, 6*, 59–98.

Konold, C., Higgins, T., Russell, S. J., & Khalil, K. (2014). Data seen through different lenses. *Educational Studies in Mathematics, 88*(3), 305–325.

Konold, C., Madden, S., Pollatsek, A., Pfannkuch, M., Wild, C., Ziedins, W., … Kazak, S. (2011). Conceptual challenges in co-ordinating theoretical and data-centred estimates of probability. *Mathematical Thinking and Learning, 13*(1–2), 68–86.

Kuzmak, S. D., & Gelman, R. (1986). Young children's understanding of random phenomena. *Child Development, 57*(3), 559–566.

Leavy, A. M. (2008). An examination of the role of statistical investigation in supporting the development of young children's statistical reasoning. In O. Saracho & B. Spodek (Eds.), *Contemporary perspectives on mathematics education in early childhood* (pp. 215–232). Charlotte, NC: Information Age Publishing.

Leavy, A. M. (2010). The challenge of preparing preservice teachers to teach informal inferential reasoning. *Statistics Education Research Journal, 9*(1), 46–67.

Leavy, A. M. (2017). Insights into the approaches of young children when making informal inferences about data. In T. Dooley & G. Gueudet (Eds.), *Proceedings of the tenth Congress of the European Society for Research in Mathematics Education* (CERME10, February 1–5, 2017). Dublin, Ireland: DCU Institute of Education and ERME.

Leavy, A. M., & Hourigan, M. (2016). Crime scenes and mystery players! Using interesting contexts and driving questions to support the development of statistical literacy. *Teaching Statistics, 38*(1), 29–35. doi:10.1111/test.12088

Leavy, A. M., & Hourigan, M. (2018). The role of perceptual similarity, data context and task context when selecting attributes: Examination of considerations made by 5–6 year olds in data modelling environments. *Educational Studies in Mathematics, 97*(2), 163–183. doi:10.1007/s10649-017-9791-2

Leavy, A. M., & Hourigan, M. (2018). Inscriptional capacities of young children engaged in statistical investigations. In A. M. Leavy, M. Meleltiou-Mavrotheris, & E. Paparistodemou (Eds.), *Statistics in early childhood and primary education: Supporting early statistical and probabilistic thinking.* Singapore: Springer Nature. doi:10.1007/978-981-13-1044-7

Lehrer, R., & Lesh, R. (2003). Mathematical learning. In W. Reynolds & G. Miller (Eds.), *Comprehensive handbook of psychology* (Vol. 7., pp. 357–390). New York, NY: John Wiley.

Lehrer, R., & Schauble, L. (2000). Inventing data structures for representational purposes: Elementary grade students' classification models. *Mathematical Thinking and Learning, 21*(1&2), 51–74.

Lehrer, R., & Schauble, L. (2007). Contrasting emerging conceptions of distribution in contexts of error and natural variation. In M. C. Lovett & P. Shah (Eds.), *Thinking with data* (pp. 149–176). New York, NY: Taylor & Francis.

Lerkkanen, M. K., Rasku-Puttonen, H., Aunola, K., & Nurmi, J. E. (2005). Mathematical performance predicts progress in reading comprehension among 7-year-olds. *European Journal of Psychology of Education, 20*(2), 121–137.

Liu, Y., & Thompson, P. W. (2007). Teachers' understandings of probability. *Cognition and Instruction, 25*(2), 113–160.

Makar, K. (2016). Developing young children's emergent inferential practices in statistics. *Mathematical Thinking and Learning, 18*(1), 1–24.

Makar, K. (2018). Theorising links between context and structure to introduce powerful statistical ideas in the early years. In A. M. Leavy, M. Meleltiou-Mavrotheris, & E. Paparistodemou (Eds.), *Statistics in early childhood and primary education: Supporting early statistical and probabilistic thinking* (pp. 3–20). Singapore: Springer Nature. doi:10.1007/978-981-13-1044-7_3

Makar, K., Bakker, A., & Ben-Zvi, D. (2011). The reasoning behind informal statistical inference. *Mathematical Thinking and Learning, 13*(1–2), 152–173. doi:10.1080/10986065.2011.538301

Makar, K., Bakker, A., & Ben-Zvi, D. (2015). Scaffolding norms of argumentation-based inquiry in a primary mathematics classroom. *ZDM – The International Journal on Mathematics Education.* http://link.springer.com/article/10.1007/s11858-015-0732-1

Makar, K., & Rubin, A. (2009). A framework for thinking about informal statistical inference. *Statistics Education Research Journal, 8*(1), 82–105. [Online: http://www.stat.auckland.ac.nz/~iase/serj/SERJ8(1)_Makar_Rubin.pdf]

Nascarato, A. M., & Grando, R. C. (2014). The role of language in building probabilistic thinking. *Statistics Education Research Journal, 13*(2), 93–103.

National Association for the Education of Young Children. (2009). *Developmentally appropriate practice in early childhood programs serving children from birth through age 8: A position statement of the National Association for the Education of Young Children.* Retrieved from http://www.naeyc.org/files/naeyc/file/positions/position%20statement%20Web.pdf

National Council of Teachers of Mathematics. (2000). *Principles and standards for school mathematics.* Reston, VA: Author.

National Mathematics Advisory Panel. (2008). *Foundations for success: The final report of the National Mathematics Advisory Panel.* Washington, DC: U.S. Department of Education, Office of Planning, Evaluation and Policy Development.

National Research Council. (2009). *Mathematics learning in early childhood: Paths toward excellence and equity.* Washington, DC: National Academy Press.

Nikiforidou, Z. (2018). Probabilistic thinking and young children: theory and pedagogy. In A. M. Leavy, M. Meletiou-Mavrotheris, & E. Paparistodemou (Eds.), *Statistics in early childhood and primary education: Supporting early statistical and probabilistic thinking* (pp. 21–36). Singapore: Springer Nature. doi:10.1007/978-981-13-1044-7_3

Nikiforidou, Z., & Pange, J. (2010). The notions of chance and probabilities in preschoolers, *Early Childhood Education Journal, 38,* 305–311.

Nikiforidou, Z., Pange, J., & Chadjipadelis, T. (2013). Intuitive and informal knowledge in preschoolers' development of probabilistic thinking. *International Journal of Early Childhood, 45*(3), 347–357.

Paparistodemou, E., & Meletiou-Mavrotheris, M. (2008). Enhancing reasoning about statistical inference in 8 year-old students. *Statistics Education Research Journal, 7*(2), 83–106.

Paparistodemou, E., & Meletiou-Mavrotheris, M. (2018). Teacher's reflections on challenges for teaching probability in the early years. In A. M. Leavy, M. Meletiou-Mavrotheris, & E. Paparistodemou (Eds.), *Statistics in early childhood and primary education: Supporting early statistical and probabilistic thinking* (pp. 201–217). Singapore: Springer Nature. doi:10.1007/978–981–13–1044–7_3

Paparistodemou, E., Noss, R., & Pratt, D. (2008). The interplay between fairness and randomness in a spatial computer game. *International Journal for Computer Mathematics Learning, 13,* 89–110.

Pasnak, R., Brown, K., Kurkjian, M., Mattran., K., Triana., E., & Yamamoto, N (1987). Cognitive gains through training in classification, seriation, conservation. *Genetic, Social, and General Psychology Monographs, 113,* 295–321.

Perkins, D. N., & Unger, C. (1994). A new look in representations for mathematics and science learning. *Instructional Science, 22,* 1–37.

Piaget, J., & Inhelder, B. (1975). *The origin of the idea of chance in children.* (L. Leake, Jr., P. Burrell, & H. Fischbein, Trans). New York, NY: Norton (original work published 1951).

Piaget, J., & Szeminska, A. (1952). *The child's conception of number.* London, UK: Routledge and Kegan Paul.

Presser, A. L., Clements, M., Ginsburg, H., & Ertle, B. (2015). Big math for little kids: The effectiveness of a preschool and kindergarten mathematics curriculum. *Early Education and Development, 26*(3), 399–426. doi:10.1080/10409289.2015.994451

Sarama, J., & Clements, D. H. (2004). Building blocks for early childhood mathematics. *Early Childhood Research Quarterly, 19,* 181–189.

Sarama, J., & Clements, D. H. (2009). *Early childhood mathematics education research: Learning trajectories for young children.* New York, NY: Routledge.

Sharma, S. (2014). Teaching probability: A socio-constructivist perspective. *Teaching Statistics, 37*(3), 78–84.

Shaughnessy, J. M. (2007). Research on statistics learning and reasoning. In F. K. Lester Jr (Ed.), *Handbook of research on mathematics teaching and learning* (2nd ed., pp. 957–1009). Greenwich, CT: Information Age.

Shaughnessy, M., & Pfannkuch, M. (2002). How faithful is old faithful? Statistical thinking: A story of variation and prediction. *Mathematics Teacher, 95*(4), 252–259.

Skoumpourdi, C., Kafoussim S., & Tatsis, K. (2009). Designing Probabilistic tasks for kindergartners. *Journal of Early Childhood Research, 7*(2), 153–172.

Sophian, C. (2004). Mathematics for the future: Developing a Head Start curriculum to support mathematics learning. *Early Childhood Research Quarterly, 19,* 59–81.

Stipek, D. (2013). Mathematics in early childhood education: Revolution or evolution? *Early Education and Development, 24*(4), 431–435. doi:10.1080/10409289.2013.777285

Tatsis, K., Kafoussi, S., & Skoumpourdi, C. (2008). Kindergarten children discussing the fairness of probabilistic games: The creation of a primary discursive community. *Early Childhood Education Journal, 36,* 221–226.

Teglas, E., Girotto, V., Gonzalez, M., & Bonatti, L. L. (2007). Intuitions of probabilities shape expectations about the future at 12 months and beyond. *Proceedings of the National Academy of Sciences, 104,* 19156–19159.

Teglas, E., Vul, E., Girotto, V., Gonzalez, M., Tenenbaum, J. B., & Bonatti, L. L. (2011). Pure reasoning in 12-month-old infants as probabilistic inference. *Science, 332,* 1054–1058.

Thorndike, E. L. (1922). *The psychology of arithmetic.* New York, NY: Macmillan.

van Oers, B. (2010). Emergent mathematical thinking in the context of play. *Educational Studies in Mathematics, 74*(1), 23–37.

Watson, J. M. (2005). The probabilistic reasoning of middle school students. In G. A. Jones (Ed.), *Exploring probability in school: Challenges for teaching and learning* (pp. 145–168). New York, NY: Springer.

Watson, J. M. (2006). *Statistical literacy at school: growth and goals.* Mahwah, NJ: Lawrence Erlbaum.

Watson, J. M. (2018). Variation and expectation for six-year-olds. In A. M. Leavy, M. Meletiou-Mavrotheris, & E. Paparistodemou (Eds.), *Statistics in early childhood and primary education: Supporting early statistical and probabilistic thinking* (pp. 55–73). Springer Nature: Singapore. doi:10.1007/978–981–13–1044–7_3

Watson, J. M., & Moritz, J. B. (2003). Fairness in dice: A longitudinal study of students' beliefs and strategies for making judgements. *Journal for Research in Mathematics Education, 34,* 270–304.

Wild, C., & Pfannkuch, M. (1999). Statistical thinking in empirical enquiry. *International Statistical Review, 67*(3), 223–265.

Worthington, M., & Carruthers, E. (2003). *Children's mathematics: Making marks, making meaning.* London, UK: Paul Chapman Publishing.

Xu, F., & Garcia, V. (2008). Intuitive statistics by 8-month-old infants. *Proceedings of the National Academy of Sciences of the United States of America, 105,* 5012–5015.

Yurovsky, D., Boyer, T, Smith, L. B., & Yu, C. (2013). Probabilistic cue combination: Less is more. *Developmental Science, 16*(2), 149–158.

7

Early Literacy

A Multimodal Process

SUSAN E. HILL

Over the past decade, shifts in policy and practice have led to increased research attention on young children's language and literacy development (Pelatti, Piasta, Justice, & O'Connell, 2014). In an extensive review of quantitative and qualitative early literacy research, Teale, Whittingham and Hoffman (2018) identified four patterns in early literacy: accretion or a gradual growth in knowledge, the influence of 'scientifically valid' research, limited response to the increasingly diversified student populations and a greater focus on very young children. There is a more academic focus within preschools and the early years of school, and D'Agostino and Rodgers (2017) claim that kindergarten is now the new first grade.

The definition of early literacy has been extended by social views about the nature of mature literate competence in the twenty-first century. That is, a view of the future adult and how he or she will read, write and communicate has reached down to shape the education system's approach to inculcating young children into literacy and, consequently, parents' understandings of how to prepare their children for literacy instruction. *The National Council of Teachers of English* (2013) definition of literacy states 'Because technology has increased the intensity and complexity of literate environments, the 21st century demands that a literate person possess a wide range of abilities and competencies, many literacies'.

In this view of literacy, reading and writing is necessary and also important for active, successful participants of society to be proficient and fluent with technology, cross-cultural connections, and analysis and synthesis of multiple streams of information, and to create, critique, analyse and evaluate multimedia texts.

Early literacy research today requires a continual retrospective and prospective revisioning of literacy development to deal with this dynamic situation. As researchers try to anticipate the skills children will need, they also look back to reconsider whether concepts of literacy prevailing at earlier stages can be relevant. This is leading to a reconsideration of the notion of early literacy.

Research into literacy in early childhood is increasingly exploring how the digital world is changing and 'current trends suggest examinations of young children's digital literacies will likely yield the freshest and most provocative insights to our knowledge' (Teale et al., 2018, p. 39). More recently, studies investigating the impact of communication technologies on early literacy have developed methodologies for exploring multimodality, collaborative interactions and children's use of play artefacts (Wohlwend, Peppler, Keune, & Thompson, 2017).

Perspectives on Early Literacy

The current perspectives on early literacy embody a diverse range of theories and practices and at their core there are different values and beliefs about the nature of literacy and the process of literacy learning. These theoretical orientations may be viewed on a historical continuum. However, owing to the additive nature of educational knowledge (old theories are rarely completely discarded as new entrants arrive) currently many theories seeking to explain children's acquisition of literacy simultaneously contest the field of knowledge. This chapter begins by briefly looking back on some familiar understandings of early literacy and considering the strengths and limitations of each for conceptualizing young children's literacy acquisition in these times. The seminal work of Crawford (1995) is useful in summarizing and analysing these separate positions and her work informs the discussion below. The focus of the chapter then turns to the semiotic, multimodal perspective, which holds considerable promise to enrich theorizations of a changing view of literacy that encompasses developments in digital technologies and new textual practices. Selected studies that examine aspects of literacy from this perspective are then reviewed including research on multimodality, digital literacies and multi-bilinguality.

Developmentalism and the Concept of Emergent Literacy

From a maturationist developmental perspective, all children pass through a series of invariant stages that cannot be hurried (Gesell, 1940). Maturation occurs as a result of a biological process of neural ripening, a little like ripening fruit or a blossoming. In the allied developmental readiness view of literacy, the key idea is that children must be *ready* before they can learn how to read. However, in tension with this, yet embraced by the developmental view, is the idea that nurturance can influence development by accelerating the rate at which children pass through stages. From a literacy perspective, this means that children's readiness for formal literacy learning can be influenced by preparatory activities facilitated by a caring adult, for example sound and letter recognition. This view is linked to the connectionist perspective where knowledge of some complex phenomenon (for example, reading) is achieved by first learning the pieces and then putting them together (Crawford, 1995). The developmental readiness and connectionist perspectives focus on elements or skills which may be predictive of future literacy achievement. For example, learning the sounds and letters of the alphabet using a synthetic phonic approach is viewed essential in the simple view of reading (Vaughn, 2018).

Importantly however, researchers Snow and Matthews (2016) and Paris (2005) point out that letter knowledge is 'constrained' to a small set of knowledge that is mastered in relatively brief periods of development. In comparison, vocabulary and world knowledge is 'unconstrained' and develops over the duration of learning. Prescriptions to teach 'constrained' skills like letter knowledge usually only lead to temporary gains and only in skills aligned with the 'constrained' skill. Snow and Matthews (2016) state:

> Researchers and educators widely acknowledge that language skills and world knowledge are important for success with literacy. Yet many prekindergarten through third-grade classrooms, particularly those serving low-income children, still focus on constrained skills, which are easy to teach and easy to test. Ensuring that teachers pay appropriate attention to unconstrained skills in early childhood and primary classrooms is a serious challenge.
>
> (p. 59)

There is evidence that the large reviews of scientific evidence in early literacy in the National Early Literacy Panel (NELP) (2008) led to a focus on developing early literacy skills particularly letter knowledge and phonemic awareness. D'Agostino and Rodgers (2017) claim that over a 12-year period there has been an increased achievement in basic skills but there is an ever increasing gap between high and low achieving students in the actual reading of connected and whole texts.

The 'emergent literacy' perspective proposed by Clay (1975) was influenced by cognitive and developmental psychology: literacy learning was not viewed as the acquisition of a series of reading skills but rather as a dynamic, ongoing process that begins long before children commence formalized schooling (Teale & Sulzby, 1986). In the emergent literacy perspective, oral language was provided as a model for the development of print-related literacy. Teachers immerse children in a print-rich environment with real books and encouraged writing original texts. Children develop as readers and writers through immersion in print-rich environments and from experiences with print that encourage engagement, experimentation and risk taking. Invented spellings and approximations were accepted as part of the learner's ongoing process of making sense and gaining control over literacy. Developmentally appropriate practices guided both the curriculum and the structure of class activities (Copple & Bredekamp, 2009). Formal direct instruction, particularly the teaching of isolated skills and worksheets, was seen as inappropriate for young children.

Defining the boundaries of the emergent stage, McGee and Purcell-Gates (1997) limit the period of emergent literacy from birth to when literacy independence at a conventional level is in evidence. They suggest that there are two time periods (0–5 and 5–independence). The context for the first period is the home and community and perhaps preschool and religious school, and for the second period the formal school instructional context and the home and community. The transition from home to school settings is a central issue and continuity between these settings is seen as the ideal situation.

Literacy in Social Contexts

The social constructivist perspective, influenced by Vygotsky (1978), views children as competent and capable users of oral and written language within their cultural group of families and communities. This perspective argues that formal literacy education should build upon these competencies (Crawford, 1995). The child's family context is understood in a broader sociocultural context of the community which makes particular kinds of communication practices, or 'funds of knowledge' important and provides opportunities for their practice (Llopart & Esteban-Guitart, 2018; Moll, Amanti, Neff, & González, 1992). From this perspective, the differences between the processes of young readers and more proficient language users are understood to be a matter of sophistication, practice and experience, not a particular stage of psychological development (Heath, 1983). In the social constructivist perspective, the early literacy curriculum scaffolds literacy learning and builds on the cultural and social language and literacy experiences children have before formal schooling. A key challenge in bringing the sociocultural perspective of literacy into the contemporary early literacy field is that while touch-screen technologies are prominent in homes in many educational districts and classrooms there is a dominant focus on print-based alphabetic skills (Flewitt, Messer, & Kucirkova, 2015). In a study into children's use of apps to learn alphabet letters, Neumann (2018) calls for more research into how teachers can capitalise on children's home and community digital experiences with mobile devices and integrate tablets and literacy apps into early childhood classrooms.

Critical perspectives are concerned with exploring unequal power within different social and political contexts and also with social action (Gee, 2002; Rogers & Labadie, 2016). A critical perspective contends that social practices, including literacy practices and literacy teaching practices, are set up to meet the interests and help maintain the privileged positions of those within the dominant culture (Orellana & D'Warte, 2010). Despite an increasing emphasis in literacy education on critical pedagogies, currently there is minimal scholarship focusing on the implications of critical literacy with picture books in preschool (Pre-K) and kindergarten classrooms (Kim, 2016). One study by Vasquez (2010) recommends the use of podcasting and new technologies for young children to engage in critical literacy and social action projects about everyday events. In order for young children to develop critical perspectives on issues related to racial/cultural diversity and equality, to pose questions and share different opinions, teachers need to foster a very supportive literacy environment in which young children are encouraged to provide a vocal multiplicity of responses rather than limiting children by presenting a pre-determined and single answer (Kim, 2016). Young children's socially situated identities are important within a critical perspective. Gee (2002) writes of the importance of teachers finding associational 'bridges' between a child's primary Discourse and the school-based language and literacy practices if schools are to resonate with the child's experiences of the world and initial sense of self. A child's primary Discourse with a big 'D' is similar to an 'identity kit' and includes 'ways of talking, listening, writing, reading, acting, interacting, feeling, believing, valuing, and feeling (and using various objects, symbols, images, tools and technologies) in the service of enacting meaningful socially situated identities and activities' (Gee, 2002, p. 35).

Semiotic Perspectives on Young Children's Use of Multimodal Signs and Symbols

A semiotic perspective focuses on different modes of communication and it can be argued that young children's speech, drawing, reading and writing is essentially a multimodal process (Worthington & van Oers, 2017). The modes (forms of communication), materiality and affordances are significant aspects of multimodality. According to Bezemer and Kress (2008), a mode is 'a socially and culturally shaped resource for meaning making' (p. 171). Modes can be speaking, writing, gesture and various visual forms. Each mode has affordances, or different potentials and constraints to express meanings. Materiality refers to the 'stuff' chosen to make particular meanings (paper, plastic, sticks, pens).

A semiotic perspective explores how individuals and groups use print on paper to make meanings as well as how meanings are made and goals accomplished using other 'semiotic resources' such as oral language, bodies through gesture, visual imagery, numerical symbols and sound effects or music (Wohlwend et al., 2017). More than a decade ago, the New London Group (1996) predicted that children would be increasingly exposed to communication tools and situations that are multimodal rather than exclusively linguistic. In the twenty-first century, young children are increasingly making meaning by drawing on multiple sign systems and multimedia symbol systems, and these electronic symbol-making systems may be best understood from a semiotic perspective (Flewitt et al., 2015; Labbo & Ryan, 2010). The dynamic changes in literacy and the complexity of texts that young children engage with requires educators to go beyond what can be described and given value through the lens of traditional literacy (Hill, 2010). Early literacy within a social semiotic perspective considers different genres as socially constructed language practices, reflecting community norms and expectations. These norms are not static but change to reflect changing sociocultural needs and contexts (Purcell-Gates, Duke, & Martineau, 2007). Increasingly, young children are drawing on multiple sign systems and multimedia symbol systems and even in technologically restricted classrooms, in pretend play, children create their own props to use as cell phones, iPads and video games (Wohlwend, 2009).

The semiotic approach does not replace older definitions of literacy. Rather, it is inclusive of, and adds to, both the traditional print-oriented and the more recent language-oriented communications model. Figure 7.1 illustrates this:

The inner circle represents the traditional print-oriented definition of literacy. Here, there is an emphasis on encoding and decoding print. The middle circle in Figure 7.1 represents a language-oriented definition of literacy, which includes print but extends the range of representational resources to include oral language. Oral language is foundational to social as well as conceptual learning and it is how

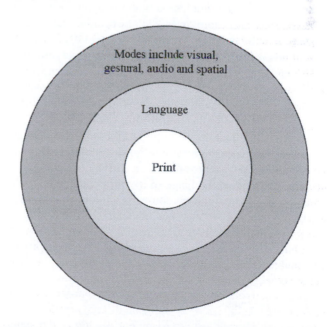

Figure 7.1 A semiotic perspective of literacy. Adapted from Hill, S., & Nichols, S. (2006). Emergent literacy: Symbols at work. In B. Spodek & O. N. Saracho (Eds.), *Handbook of research on the education of young children* (2nd ed., pp. 153–165). Mahwah, NJ: Lawrence Erlbaum Associates.

children are socialized into the cultural practices of their communities (Malec, Peterson, & Elshereif, 2017). In the preschool years, children's oral language vocabulary, preschool teachers' analytic talk about books and early support in the home for literacy predicted fourth-grade vocabulary and comprehension (Dickinson & Porche, 2011). Preschool and early school experiences are mediated by oral language as this is how children learn about school, how to participate in and attend learning in groups and forming relationships. While there are heated debates about the 'word gap' research by Hart and Risley (1995), it is clear that building on all children's verbal strengths is paramount for learning to read and write (Sperry, Sperry, & Miller, 2018). Both oral and written forms of language are important and different ways of knowing and different oral language functions allow students to think and access knowledge in different ways (Halliday, 1975). Moving to the outer circle, literacy from a semiotic perspective encompasses not only print and language but also broader range of representational resources, or modalities. For example in multimedia, print is combined with sound, movement and visual imagery to create complex texts that require the 'reader' to process in multiple modes simultaneously (Bearne, 2009).

Kress and Van Leeuwen (2001) developed a semiotic framework for the analysis of multimodal texts and communication practices which incorporate four 'domains of practice' (p. 4): discourse, design, production and distribution/reproduction. An example of this approach applied at the level of a young child's literacy practices might be to consider how a child may create an illustration by using elements from different domains such as media narratives, personal observations as well as playground rituals and how this text may be distributed to audiences both immediate and distant using production technologies such as printing, texting and uploading to the internet. Kervin and Mantei (2017) describe how children can create multimodal stories using resources, including the children's own drawings, images from Google Maps and the Puppet Pals Director's Pass app, to leverage children's experiences in their school and community contexts for a meaningful and authentic literacy learning opportunity. The children use both paper-based materials and digital technologies to create multimodal stories.

A semiotic perspective builds on earlier sociocultural research by extending the range of meaning-making resources that young children can use. In early childhood education, a semiotic perspective enriches our analysis of the early literacy by considering how discourse, design, production and distribution/reproduction may impact on texts, their production and their reception.

Digital Literacies

Digital literacies incorporate a semiotic, multimodal perspective on early literacy. Over the past decades, developments in digital technologies have profoundly affected the field of literacy, spurring the redefining of literacy itself (NCTE, 2013)

and impacting the home environments of young children as well as the materials and methods used for literacy instruction in early education settings (Wohlwend et al., 2017). In this section of the chapter research into digital literacies explores the recent themes of: young children's use of technology related to literacy, the use of multimodal technology to support reading and importantly young children's reading of paper books and e-books.

There has been a rapid proliferation of story and game apps aimed at the early years and the iPad is a popular device for family entertainment and informal education. It is often claimed that iPads and other touch-screen devices place sophisticated media in the hands of users. Moreover, some have argued that the iPad is particularly appealing for young children because of its weight, portability and intuitive touch-screen interface. Merchant (2015) critically appraises the claims of weight, portability and the intuitive touch-screen interface in a close analysis of young children (14–22 months) in two story-app sharing interactions with an adult. An analysis of the material affordances of the iPad and apps was developed and highlighted important issues for practitioners, but it also suggested that the interface, and the story apps used, may not be quite as intuitive and easy to use as has been suggested. More research is required on how adults and young children engage, interact and power share with apps and iPads.

In a study of new technologies and home-school communication, Snell, Hindman and Waskic (2018) explored how texting might enhance family-school engagement in early childhood settings. Using focus groups and surveys of teachers in an urban early childhood programme, they examined the nature of current communication (including texting) between school and home, openness among teachers and families to the idea of sending or receiving home-school communication via text, and beliefs among teachers and families about how texting can support various aspects of family-school engagement. Results suggest that many teachers and millennial generation families are enthusiastic about using texting and view texting as a tool to further family-school engagement and communication and to enhance child outcomes.

Digital composing tools can support the two-way travel of content between home and school – an exchange that is particularly important for schools serving culturally and linguistically diverse populations. In a study by Rowe and Miller (2016), children developed multilingual e-books with translations by bilingual adults known to the children. Beginning early in the school year, these e-books were publicly shared in large group activities. The emergent bilingual/biliterate children created dual-language recordings for their e-books, integrating photographs and voice recordings with print.

To explore the use of iPads across different age levels, Flewitt et al. (2015) explored the use of iPads in a Children's Centre nursery (three- to four-year-olds), a primary school reception class (four- to five-year-olds) and a Special School (7- to 13-year-olds), discussed their potential uses with staff in pre- and post-interviews and observed how they were integrated into practice over a two-month period. They found variability in the ways iPads were used across the settings. One commonality was that well-planned, iPad-based literacy activities stimulated children's motivation and concentration. iPads also offered rich opportunities for communication, collaborative interaction and independent learning, and for children to achieve high levels of accomplishment. In some cases, this led teachers favourably to re-evaluate the children's literacy competence, and enabled children to construct positive images of themselves in the literacy classroom.

Research with increasingly young infants and toddlers using tablets and smartphones differs from book experiences, in that they offer a haptic touch-screen interface which modifies the narrative experience, changes how text is navigated and shared, and impacts the creation of meaning, as literacy moves beyond printed text and into an increasingly connected world (Harrison & McTavish, 2016; Merchant, 2015). Hourcade, Mascher, Wu and Pantoja (2015) analysed 208 YouTube videos of infants and toddlers interacting with tablets. Just as there is predictable progression in print book-handling skills, children seem to acquire skills in screen navigation in a consistent developmental manner. These type of screen skills included transitioning from whole hand or multiple fingers to a single finger to manipulate a tablet, then learning to swipe and drag the screen to access content (Hourcade et al., 2015). Additionally, toddlers handled tablets the same as holding books, often with the tablet in the child's lap and being held with the child's hands (Hourcade et al., 2015; Merchant, 2015).

There are cautions though regarding young children's use of handheld devices. Merchant (2015) claimed that the novelty value and accessibility of current apps for very young children needs further careful research. Sosa (2016) found that, when interacting with young toddlers, age 10–16 months old, mothers said fewer words, and there were fewer conversational turns, parental responses and productions of content-specific words when playing with an electronic toy compared with playing with traditional toys and books. Children also vocalized less when interacting with parents in the electronic toy condition.

In a meta-analysis of research into toddler and preschoolers' use of e-books, Reich, Yau and Warschauer (2016) suggested that time away from screens was most beneficial for infants/toddlers as the bulk of research reviewed indicated that face-to-face interaction for very young children was superior for learning than screen time. However, results from studies were mixed when preschoolers and e-books were considered. Some studies indicated increased parent-child conversation during print, whereas others noted increased speech during e-book reading. They recommended that any e-books for preschoolers should be designed to support and scaffold learning (compared with including games and sounds irrelevant to the story) and that e-books have the most impact when mediated and shared with an adult (Reich et al., 2016).

Seminal research into adult-child interactions with *e-books and traditional books* was investigated by Kim and Anderson (2008). This research compared mother-child interactions in three contexts: *shared reading* with a *book* in a traditional print format, with an *electronic book* in a CD-ROM and PDF format and with an *electronic book* with hyperlinks to a video clip format. The adult-child interactions involved mother-child interactions with three-year-old and seven-year-old children and compared children's extra-textual talk during the *shared* readings. The results indicated mother-child interactions differed in the contexts, with more complex talk evident with *electronic* texts. Children's extra-textual talk differed depending on their ages, and the talk seemed to be context specific. Moody, Justice and Cabell (2010) explored children's engagement with e-books versus traditional storybooks and found that e-storybooks afforded benefits to children's reading engagement and communicative participation. The authors found that both computerized and traditional storybooks can influence children's literacy and oral language; however, both book forms demand supportive interactions with an adult. It should be noted that, often, the conversations around e-books centred on how to 'work' the book by pushing buttons or swiping versus focusing on the story itself (Reich et al., 2016).

E-books, the digital equivalent of the storybook, have quickly become popular and are widely available. Scaffolds in e-books include search capability, hyperlinks, audio and visual enhancements and, in some cases, hotspot pop-up definitions for words. The digital scaffolds found in e-books provide additional opportunities for independent practice and interactive exploration of a text, available even when an adult is not present to read with a child (Smeets & Bus, 2012). Research by Wright, Fugett and Caputa (2013), comparing print and electronic books, found that Grade 2 students were more inclined to use reading resources when digital text was the medium rather than conventional print. E-books have also been shown to motivate children to be active readers. When using e-books, children tend to more naturally investigate words, images and interactivities – such as user-controlled animations, tap-to-hear word pronunciations, built-in dictionaries, definitions, games and puzzles – in the reading environment. Larson (2010) explored the use of ereaders, like kindles, in a second-grade classroom and found the children adjusted the font size, accessed the built-in dictionary to look up meanings of words, reviewed the phonetic spelling of words to help 'sound out' text and also activated the text-to-speech feature to listen to words that they found difficult or to reread text passages. The children also made notes on the ereader in response to the e-books and were able to use the ereader to go online to search for additional information.

While digital literacies in early childhood remains the focus of this section, research into traditional forms of book reading continues to be important. Young children response to books has been the focus of a large body of research over several decades (Elster, 1994; Sulzby, 1985). More recent research has explored young children's multimodal responses to picture books (Pantaleo, 2017). However, Sulzby's (1985) early research remains seminal because it described early reading behaviours that developed from preschool image or picture-governed reading to print-governed reading. This earlier research revealed categories of early reading behaviours moving from non-narrative to narrative language, from an oral-like to a written-like narrative register, and from picture-dominated to print-dominated reading. Similarly, Elster (1994) found that early readings of preschoolers were a sequence of reading and talk episodes. Children combine visual cues from pictures; they drew on their memories, experiences and knowledge base, and on the social interactions with a listener long before beginning to attend to print. The features of the book being read, including the salience of the illustrations, predictable language patterns and changing print formats, influenced the strategies used by the early readers. The adult listeners were used as a resource as the preschool children moved from dialogue to monologue and from non-narrative to narrative language. Elster (1994) pointed out that early readers use multiple sources of information concurrently: pictures, print, social interaction, memory of teacher-led discussions, attention to text language and understanding of oral and written language conventions. Elster (1994) found, through microanalysis of children's reading and talk about particular books, that these different sources of information were chosen and combined situationally by readers in response to the book, the child's memory and social interaction.

Digital devices may be found in 99% of homes, but young children may be merely passive receivers of content. The challenge for educators is to use digital devices in play settings to generate rich oral language interactions and for young children to produce and create meaning.

Writing and Multimodal Meaning Making

Studies exploring writing from sociocultural and semiotic theories support a view of writing as a meaning-making practice undertaken in specific social contexts. This chapter includes studies of early writing that focus on the significance of social context and on the place of writing within a complex repertoire of representational practices. This includes studies of the mark-making that is one of the first indicators of very young children's understanding of symbolic significance. Studies of early writing are contributing much to our understanding of the complex interrelationships between different representational practices and their contexts. These interrelationships have been explored in a range of studies.

Worthington and van Oers (2017) employed cultural-historical and multimodal, social semiotic theories to explore the ways in which children make meanings through symbolic tools and their use of their literacies to communicate meanings in the social context of their spontaneous pretend play. In one example, they documented how a child and his dad recently swiped a plastic card through an electronic card reader in a city car park. Isaac connected this concept with

the business cards his dad used for work. The child's own interest in technologies, electricity and security measures, and his considerable knowledge of environmental signage were also evident in his play in the early childhood centre when the child announced:

> '….you need to have a business card to get in here. I'm fixing the gate so it has electric. You have to have a business card to swipe. I don't need one - I use my hands.' Isaac gave a piece of paper to Oliver, 'Here's your business card.' Then, writing more marks on a label, he announced, 'This says 'Swipe here with your special code card'.'
>
> (Worthington & van Oers, 2017, p. 160)

Yang and Noel (2006) analysed the drawings of 17 four- to five-year-old children and found that the development of children's functional literacy can be facilitated by encouraging them to use drawing as the starting point for name writing and/or letter reproduction. Adults can also use children's drawing as a 'communicative act' to initiate 'dialogue' between children and adults. Drawing can be viewed not only as a medium of representing meanings but also as a tool for learning. Young children often explore diverse modes of graphic representations incorporating the semiotic representations embedded in the social-cultural environment. Adults can embrace children's diverse modes of symbolic representations by encouraging children's free exploration of all types of scribbles and placement patterns.

Dyson (2001) focused on six-year-old children undertaking a classroom task, that of writing a factual report. Here also, the semiotic and sociocultural perspective enabled a rich description of the complex relationships of meaning making involved in the production of a specific text, in this case a written report on the topic 'Space'. Dyson (2001) described one child, Noah, in the process of producing the text 'Space Case says there was a space ship' (Space Case is a television adventure). The production of this text involved the coordination of writing, drawing, oral language and symbolic sounds. Noah began by vocalizing each word in the text as he wrote it. However, half way through the word 'there', he stopped writing and began drawing a space ship. At the same time, he began to narrate a scene from a space adventure in a dramatic voice complete with sound effects. Noah's meaning making, his complete text, was multimodal and dynamic. It did not reside only in the piece of paper which held his marks.

Young children use a wide variety of materials in their representational practices, not all of them are conventional literacy materials such as paper and pencil. Pahl (2002, p. 146) uses the term 'artefactual' to designate the practice of making texts out of objects. One example, from her ethnographic study of three boys at home and school, was of a child Fatih making a map out of beads on the carpet at home. This study brought to light the ephemeral and often invisible early literacy practices which are embedded in children's and families' activities. A few minutes before Fatih made the bead map, he had been praying with the beads according to his family's religious practice, and shortly after its production the map was cleared away to make room for other activities. Pahl (2002) calls these ephemeral products 'momentary texts' (p. 160). This concept of the momentary text is particularly useful in thinking about literacy in the context of new technologies that enable children to rapidly create, destroy and transform textual products.

Rich descriptions such as those discussed above have been a hallmark of early literacy research for decades. However, they are assuming a different kind of significance in relation to current debates about the meaning of literacy, and of literacy acquisition for young children. In the past, young children's use of a combination of linguistic and non-linguistic resources for making meaning has been understood as a characteristic of an emergent stage prior to the achievement of literate competence. This view rested on a definition of literate competence as competence in the consumption and production of print (reading and writing).

Current redefinitions of what it means to be fully literate with new digital technology are changing the way we understand early writing and mark-making (Worthington & van Oers, 2017). The ability to simultaneously coordinate multiple linguistic and non-linguistic elements has become understood as a quality of literate competence. Children's composition of complex multimodal texts goes beyond what can be described and given value through the lens of traditional print-based literacy.

Being Bilingual in an Ever Changing World

In this chapter, it is argued that literacy, even when print language based, requires the mastery of multiple modes of representation and practices of communication. The picture becomes even more complex when considering the multiple languages that are available within our communities. In countries with one official language, to be literate is understood in relation to that dominant language. Families with a different first language (L1) take on the official language as their second (L2). Entry into the school system is often the point at which immersion in the L2 begins. So at the same time as 'minority' children are encountering school literacy, many of them are acquiring a second language and moving from monolinguality in L1 to bilinguality. In early literacy development English is viewed as the official language and is referred to as L1 and L2 for minority language speakers. Others argue that the forms of competence acquired by bi- and multilingual children challenge normative views of literacy development on which the concept of early literacy has been based (Orellana & D'warte, 2010).

Chan and Sylva (2014) reviewed the literature on the emergent literacy of native English speakers and a discussion of the general effects of bilingualism and cross-linguistic transfer. Research suggests that *child* L1 and L2 acquisition patterns and rates may be very similar overall and that the same general processes are at the very centre of all language acquisition. Models and principles derived from L1 research

could be cautiously adopted as a theoretical framework for analysing L2 phenomena.

A study of bilingual and biliterate, dual language learners (DLLs) by Wagner (2017) provides evidence that DLLs are actively constructing ideas about reading, bilingualism/biliteracy and whom they are as readers as they learn to read. Framing early reading in an identity perspective presents opportunities to look more holistically at the language and reading practices of DLLs as they learn to read and navigate two or more languages at home and school. Researchers often focus on prominent language groups, most notably English-Spanish bilinguals, without giving attention to more diverse bilingual populations. Paying attention to the diversity and diverse needs of DLLs is still much needed in order to understand and support the unique reading and identity paths of these children.

When considering early literacy in situations where more than one language is in use, it is useful to distinguish between different features of language. Some language features are specific to a particular language or group of languages, so in order to become fully competent in these languages one must acquire knowledge of and facility with these features. Other language features may cross linguistic boundaries. The concept of language register is useful here. Following Halliday (1994), a language register can be viewed as a 'configuration of semantic resources that the member of a culture typically associates with a situation type' (p. 26). What is referred to as literate language is a register that can be expressed not only in English but in many languages.

Another important language register that children acquire at school is the pedagogic register, that is, the pattern of language used in interactions around teaching and learning. For bilingual children, this represents an additional challenge at a time when they are just beginning to build L2 or English competence. As with literate language, children's understanding of pedagogic registers may not be visible, because of their reticence in using their L2. This is demonstrated in a case study by Drury (reported in Parke, Drury, Kenner, & Robertson, 2002). Samia, a four-year-old girl whose first language is Pahari, attended a nursery school where there was a settled routine to facilitate children's learning. Every session, each child selected and planned an activity, indicating this by registering their name on a white board. After carrying out the activity, they reported on their learning to the whole group. The pedagogic register here was characterized by self-regulatory and explanatory language on the part of children and facilitative language on the part of adults. Samia was observed to carry out the planning and the activities competently though with minimal interaction with peers or adults. At reporting time, she was extremely reticent, having only her limited L2 available for communication with the whole group.

To investigate bilingual children's ability to make connections between languages and language practices from different domains in their lives, one study set up a series of peer-teaching activities (Kenner & Kress, 2003). Young children from three different L1 backgrounds (Arabic, Spanish and Chinese) were first observed in home, school and community settings. They were then invited to teach an English-speaking monolingual partner some of the basics of writing in the focus child's first language. In this way, researchers were able to discover children's understanding of pedagogic registers in literacy teaching and learning, as well as their competence in written language production.

One case focused on Selina, a Chinese background girl who attended a community school each Saturday morning. At this school, she learned to write characters by building up a sequence of strokes. Each page of her books was ruled into a grid and each character was written in the centre of a grid square. The learning routine consisted of teacher modelling with minimal explanation followed by sustained, silent writing of many repetitions of a single character. The researchers noted that many Western teachers 'would not expect a five-year-old to be capable of such physical control over the act of writing' (Kenner & Kress, 2003, p. 186). Selina demonstrated her understanding of the pedagogic register of her L1 teaching when she acted as peer teacher. She demonstrated how to write the character and instructed her peer to 'do it like this one'. However, when her peer was unable to reproduce the character with sufficient accuracy, Selina showed that she had also grasped the pedagogic register of her mainstream educational setting. She increased her verbal feedback and suggested to her peer 'pretend you're in Year 1 in Chinese school'.

Many children from linguistic minority backgrounds have considerable experience with digital tools that their families use for entertainment, transnational net-working and viewing multilingual content (Kenner & Ruby, 2013). Rowe and Miller (2016) suggest that children's familiarity with the technologies used in their homes and communities can become resources for school learning and points of connection between home and school. Therefore, for children from language minority backgrounds, access to digital technologies in schools is a matter of equity as well as an opportunity to connect home and school language and literacy practices.

In the Rowe and Miller's (2016) study, children with adult support used child-friendly, digital cameras and iPads equipped with writing, drawing and bookmaking apps to compose multimodal, multilingual e-books containing photos, child-produced drawings, writing and voice recordings. Children took digital cameras home, and home photos were loaded onto the iPads for bookmaking. The results showed that all emergent bilingual/biliterate children created dual-language recordings for their e-books. The researchers concluded that: (a) the ability to integrate photos and voice recordings with print and drawings provided new opportunities for learning and teaching not available in page-based composing; (b) the affordances of iPads for children's learning were shaped by local language and literacy practices. Interestingly, the dual-language recordings were in English and Spanish and minority languages such as Burmese, Nepalese and Kurdish.

Sending digital cameras home and inviting children and families to take photos of their experiences increased the two-way travel of culturally relevant content between home and school. Children's home photos depicted many different aspects of their lives outside of school, providing them with opportunities to compose texts about people, places and objects that were personally and culturally significant. For children learning English as a new language, the creation of e-books to talk about photos of familiar classroom activities provided an opportunity to use English vocabulary they were learning at school. Photos provided a shared visual referent that both children and adults could touch and point to in order to build common ground for conversations that included both English and the child's heritage language. Photos also provided common ground that helped adults interpret children's emergent writing.

Kenner and Kress's study (2003) shows the advantage of taking a semiotic perspective to early literacy when considering the experiences of bilingual children for the reason that different language codes have different semiotic properties. The spatial arrangement of symbols on the field of the page is different in Arabic, for instance, than in English. Different perceptual and physical competencies are involved in producing and interpreting texts written using different language systems. Rather than seeing this as disadvantageous, new literacies will require a broader repertoire of representational practices: therefore bi- and multilingual children should be better positioned for multi-literate futures. This can only be the case, however, if their competencies are made visible and valued within the mainstream and if the complexities of their double emergence into L1 and L2 literacy are understood.

Orellana and D'Warte (2010) argue that bilingual children's special forms of competence should be recognized and capitalized on or they may even be lost as the children grow older. These researchers studied how bilingual children draw on their knowledge of home and dominant languages to interpret texts and communicate in ways responsive to the conditions of different social situations. Current teaching and assessment practices do not adequately value such linguistic flexibility and border crossing which, in conditions of increasing global flows of information and populations, may well become an element in mature literate competence. It is in recognizing this, that studies of bilingual literacy acquisition from a semiotic perspective challenge models of literacy development premised on a notion of mature literacy competence that was adequate for past times.

Summary

Much research into early literacy has been of a scientific predictive nature to find discrete elements of literacy which may be a precursor or predictor for future development. While the strengthening of the relationship between research and practice in the field of early literacy is welcome, Burnett (2017) argues that in many ways, the fixed linear logic associated with 'hard evidence' is at odds with complex understandings of young learners and learning. From a multimodal perspective, a major issue is the changing meaning of mature literacy competence and the likelihood that today's children face futures of continually evolving new technologies for text production, new kinds of texts and new practices of reading. While print literacy is central, the ability to operate across multiple modalities, value and understand different languages, and use visuals and various text types is becoming the hallmark of an effective literate citizen, making both the search for predictors and the drive to disaggregate literacy into components, of questionable relevance.

There is much is to be gained by defining literacy more broadly from a semiotic position to include linguistic and non-linguistic forms of communication. Literacy is changing and children are increasingly exposed to communication tools and situations that are multimodal rather than exclusively linguistic. Research is required into how young children engage in critical literacy, posing questions from different points of view and sharing different opinions while engaging in social action projects. More research is required into multimodal digital literacies and to do this it is necessary to broaden the base of what we know about early literacy to better understand how children are making meaning with these new forms in various social contexts.

References

Bearne, E. (2009). Multimodality, literacy and texts: Developing a discourse. *Journal of Early Childhood Literacy, 9*(2), 156–187. doi:10.1177/1468798409105585

Bezemer, J., & Kress, G. (2008). Writing in multimodal texts: A social semiotic account of designs for learning. *Written Communication, 25*(2), 166–195. doi:10.1177/0741088307313177

Burnett, C. (2017). Acknowledging and interrogating multiplicities: Towards a generous approach in evaluations of early literacy innovation and intervention. *Journal of Early Childhood Literacy, 17*(4), 522–550. doi:10.1177/1468798416645851

Chan, L., & Sylva, K. (2014). Exploring emergent literacy development in a second language: A selective literature review and conceptual framework for research. *Journal of Early Childhood Literacy, 15*(1), 3–36. doi:10.1177/1468798414522824

Clay, M. M. (1975). *What did I write? Beginning writing behaviour.* Auckland, New Zealand: Heinemann.

Copple, C., & Bredekamp, S. (Eds.). (2009). *Developmentally appropriate practice in early childhood programs serving children from birth through age 8* (3rd ed.). Washington, DC: National Association for the Education of Young Children.

Crawford, P. A. (1995). Early literacy: Emerging perspectives. *Journal of Research in Childhood Education, 10*(1), 71–86. doi:10.1080/02568549509594689

D'Agostino, J., & Rodgers, E. (2017). Literacy achievement trends at entry to first grade. *Educational Researcher, 46*(2), 78–89. doi:10.3102/0013189X17697274

Dickinson, D. K., & Porche, M. V. (2011). Relation between language experiences in preschool classrooms and children's kindergarten and fourth-grade language and reading abilities. *Child Development, 82*(3), 870–886. doi:10.1111/j.1467–8624.2011.01576.x

Dyson, A. H. (2001). Where are the childhoods in childhood literacy? An exploration in outer (school) space. *Journal of Early Childhood Literacy, 1*(1), 9–39. doi:10.1177/14687984010011002

Elster, C. (1994). Patterns within preschoolers' emergent readings. *Reading Research Quarterly, 29*(4), 402–418. doi:10.2307/747787

Flewitt, R., Messer, D., & Kucirkova, N. (2015). New directions for early literacy in a digital age: The iPad. *Journal of Early Childhood Literacy, 15*(3), 289–310. doi:10.1177/1468798414533560

Gee, J. (2002). A sociocultural perspective on early literacy development. In S. Neuman & D. Dickinson (Eds.), *Handbook of early literacy research* (pp. 30–42). New York, NY: Guildford Press.

Gesell, A. (1940). *The first five years of life.* New York, NY: Harper & Bros.

Halliday, M. A. K. (1975). *Learning how to mean: Explorations in the development of language.* London, UK: Edward Arnold.

Halliday, M. A. K. (1994). Language as social semiotic. In J. Maybin (Ed.), *Language and literacy in social practice* (pp. 11–22). Clevedon, UK: Multilingual Matters Ltd.

Harrison, E., & McTavish, M. (2016). 'i'Babies: Infants' and toddlers' emergent language and literacy in a digital culture of iDevices. *Journal of Early Childhood Literacy, 18*(2), 163–188. doi:10.1177/1468798416653175

Hart, B., & Risley, T. R. (1995). *Meaningful differences in the everyday experience of young American children.* Baltimore, MD: Brookes.

Heath, S. (1983). *Ways with words: Language, life and work in communities and classrooms.* Retrieved from Cambridge University Press. doi:10.1017/CBO9780511841057

Hill, S. (2010). The millennium generation: Teacher-researchers exploring new forms of literacy. *Journal of Early Childhood Literacy, 10*(3), 314–340. doi:10.1177/1468798410372820

Hill, S., & Nichols, S. (2006). Emergent literacy: Symbols at work. In B. Spodek & O. N. Saracho (Eds.), *Handbook of research on the education of young children* (2nd ed., pp. 153–165). Mahwah, NJ: Lawrence Erlbaum Associates.

Hourcade, J. B., Mascher, S. L., Wu, D., & Pantoja, L. (2015, April 18–23). *Look, my baby is using an iPad! An analysis of YouTube videos of infants and toddlers using tablets.* Paper presented at the 33rd Annual ACM Conference on Human Factors in Computing Systems, Seoul, Republic of Korea. doi:10.1145/2702123.2702266

Kenner, C., & Kress, G. (2003). The multisemiotic resources of biliterate children. *Journal of Early Childhood Literacy, 3*(2), 179–202. doi:10.1177/14687984030032004

Kenner, C., & Ruby, M. (2013). Connecting children's worlds: Creating a multilingual syncretic curriculum through partnerships between complementary and main-stream schools. *Journal of Early Childhood Literacy, 13*(3), 395–417. doi:10.1177/1468798412466404

Kervin, L., & Mantei, J. (2017). Children creating multimodal stories about a familiar environment. *The Reading Teacher, 70*(6), 721–728. doi:10.1002/trtr.1556

Kim, J., & Anderson, J. (2008). Mother-child shared reading with print and digital texts. *Journal of Early Childhood Literacy, 8*(2), 213–245. doi:10.1177/1468798409357387

Kim, S. J. (2016). Opening up spaces for early critical literacy: Korean kindergarteners exploring diversity through multicultural picture books. *Australian Journal of Language & Literacy, 39*(2), 176–187.

Kress, G., & Van Leeuwen, T. (2001). *Multimodal discourse: The modes and media of contemporary communication.* London, UK: Arnold.

Labbo, L., & Ryan, T. (2010). Traversing the 'Literacies' landscape: A semiotic perspective on early literacy acquisition and digital literacies instruction. In E. Baker (Ed.), *The new literacies: Multiple perspectives on research and practice* (pp. 88–105). New York, NY: The Guilford Press.

Larson, L. C. (2010). Digital readers: The next chapter in e-book reading and response. *The Reading Teacher, 64*(1), 15–22. doi:10.1598/RT.64.1.2

Llopart, M., & Esteban-Guitart, M. (2018). Funds of knowledge in 21st century societies: Inclusive educational practices for under-represented students. A literature review. *Journal of Curriculum Studies, 50*(2), 145–161. doi:10.1080/00220272.2016.1247913

Malec, A., Peterson, S. S., & Elshereif, H. (2017). Assessing young children's oral language: Recommendations for classroom practice and policy. *Canadian Journal of Education, 40*(3), 362–392.

Merchant, G. (2015). Keep taking the tablets: iPads, story apps and early literacy. *Australian Journal of Language & Literacy, 38*(1), 3–11.

McGee, L., & Purcell-Gates, V. (1997). Conversations: So what's going on in research in emergent literacy? *Reading Research Quarterly, 32*(3), 310–319. doi:10.1598/RRQ.32.3.5

Moll, L. C., Amanti, C., Neff, D., & González, N. (1992). Funds of knowledge for teaching: Using a qualitative approach to connect homes and classrooms. *Theory into Practice, 31*(2), 132–141. doi:10.1080/00405849209543534

Moody, A., Justice, L., & Cabell, S. (2010). Electronic versus traditional storybooks: Relative influence on preschool children's engagement and communication. *Journal of Early Childhood Literacy, 10*(3), 294–313. doi:10.1177/1468798410372162

National Council of Teachers of English. (2013). *The NCTE definition of 21st century literacies*. Retrieved 12 September, from http://www2.ncte.org/statement/21stcentdefinition/

National Early Literacy Panel. (2008). *Developing early literacy: A scientific synthesis of early literacy development and implications for intervention* (Maryland ED Pubs, National Institute for Literacy). Retrieved from https://lincs.ed.gov/publications/pdf/NELPReport09.pdf

Neumann, M. (2018). Using tablets and apps to enhance emergent literacy skills in young children. *Early Childhood Research Quarterly, 42*(1), 239–246. doi:10.1016/J.ECRESQ.2017.10.006

New London Group. (1996). A pedagogy of multiliteracies: Designing social futures. *Harvard Educational Review, 66*(1), 60–92. doi:10.17763/haer.66.1.17370n67v22j160u

Orellana, M., & D'warte, J. (2010). Recognizing different kinds of 'Head Starts'. *Educational Researcher, 39*(4), 295–300. doi:10.3102/0013189X10369829

Pahl, K. (2002). Ephemera, mess and miscellaneous piles: Texts and practices in families. *Journal of Early Childhood Literacy, 2*(2), 145–166. doi:10.1177/14687984020022002

Pantaleo, S. (2017). Exploring the artwork of young students' multimodal compositions. *Education 3–13, 45*(1), 17–35. doi:10.1080/03004279.2015.1033438

Paris, S. (2005). Reinterpreting the development of reading skills. *Reading Research Quarterly, 40*(2), 184–202. doi:10.1598/RRQ.40.2.3

Parke, T., Drury, R., Kenner, C., & Robertson, L. H. (2002). Revealing invisible worlds: Connecting the mainstream with bilingual children's home and community learning. *Journal of Early Childhood Literacy, 2*(2), 195–220. doi:10.1177/14687984020022004

Pelatti, C. Y., Piasta, S. B., Justice, L. M., & O'Connell, A. (2014). Language- and literacy-learning opportunities in early childhood classrooms: Children's typical experiences and within-classroom variability. *Early Childhood Research Quarterly, 29*(4), 445–456. doi:10.1016/j.ecresq.2014.05.004

Purcell-Gates, V., Duke, N., & Martineau, J. (2007). Learning to read and write genre-specific text: Roles of authentic experience and explicit teaching. *Reading Research Quarterly, 42*(1), 8–45. doi:10.1598/RRQ.42.1.1

Reich, S., Yau, J., & Warschauer, M. (2016). Tablet-based eBooks for young children: what does the research say? *Journal of Developmental & Behavioral Pediatrics, 37*(7), 585–586.

Rogers, R., & Labadie, M. (2016). Rereading assent in critical literacy research with young children. *Journal of Early Childhood Literacy, 18*(3), 396–427. doi:10.1177/1468798416675503

Rowe, D. W., & Miller, M. E. (2016). Designing for diverse classrooms: Using iPads and digital cameras to compose eBooks with emergent bilingual/biliterate four-year-olds. *Journal of Early Childhood Literacy, 16*(4), 425–472. doi:10.1177/1468798415593622

Smeets, D., & Bus, A. (2012). Interactive electronic storybooks for kindergartners to promote vocabulary growth. *Journal of Experimental Psychology, 112*(1), 36–55.

Snell, E., Hindman, A., & Wasik, B. (2018). Exploring the use of texting to support family-school engagement in early childhood settings: Teacher and family perspectives. *Early Child Development and Care*. doi:10.1080/03004430.2018.1479401

Snow, C., & Matthews, T. (2016). Reading and language in the early grades reading and language in the early grades. *Future of Children, 26*(1), 57–74.

Sosa, A. V. (2016). Association of the type of toy used during play with the quantity and quality of parent-infant communication. *JAMA Pediatrics, 170*(2), 132–137. doi:10.1001/jamapediatrics.2015.3753

Sperry, D. E., Sperry, L. L., & Miller, P. J. (2018). Language does matter: But there is more to language than vocabulary and directed speech. *Child Dev*. doi:10.1111/cdev.13125

Sulzby, E. (1985). Children's emergent reading of favourite story books: A developmental study. *Reading Research Quarterly, 20*(4), 458–481.

Teale, W., & Sulzby, E. (1986). *Emergent literacy: Writing and reading*. Norwood, NJ: Ablex Publishing Corporation.

Teale, W. H., Whittingham, C. E., & Hoffman, E. B. (2018). Early literacy research, 2006–2015: A decade of measured progress. *Journal of Early Childhood Literacy*. doi:10.1177/1468798418754939

Vasquez, V. (2010). Critical literacy isn't just for books anymore. *Reading Teacher, 63*(7), 614–616.

Vaughn, S. (2018). Introduction to the special issue on the simple view of reading from pre-K to Grade 12. *Remedial and Special Education, 39*(5), 259.

Wagner, C. J. (2017). Being bilingual, being a reader: Prekindergarten dual language learners' reading identities. *Journal of Early Childhood Literacy, 18*(1), 5–37. doi:10.1177/1468798417739668

Wright, S., Fugett, A., & Caputa, F. (2013). Using e-readers and internet resources to support comprehension. *Educational Technology & Society, 16*(1), 367–379.

Wohlwend, K. (2009). Early adopters: Playing new literacies and pretending new technologies in print-centric classrooms. *Journal of Early Childhood Literacy, 9*(2), 117–140. doi:10.1177/1468798409105583

Wohlwend, K. E., Peppler, K. A., Keune, A., & Thompson, N. (2017). Making sense and nonsense: Comparing mediated discourse and agential realist approaches to materiality in a preschool makerspace. *Journal of Early Childhood Literacy, 17*(3), 444–462. doi:10.1177/1468798417712066

Worthington, M., & van Oers, B. (2017). Children's social literacies: Meaning making and the emergence of graphical signs and texts in pretence. *Journal of Early Childhood Literacy, 17*(2), 147–175. doi:10.1177/1468798415618534

Yang, H., & Noel, A. (2006). The developmental characteristics of four- and five-year-old pre-schoolers' drawing: An analysis of scribbles, placement patterns, emergent writing, and name writing in archived spontaneous drawing samples. *Journal of Early Childhood Literacy, 6*(2), 145–162. doi:10.1177/1468798406066442

8

Educating for Democratic Citizenship in Early Childhood

Stacy DeZutter

From its inception, early childhood education has been viewed as a venue for preparing children to become engaged participants in democratic society. Foundational thinkers like John Dewey, Frederick Froebel, and Maria Montessori emphasized the importance of citizenship preparation in the education of young children (Saracho & Spodek, 2007). Following from this charge, this chapter examines the questions recently taken up by researchers committed to citizenship education in early childhood, focusing on research since 2010.

"Citizenship education" has been defined by the United Nations Educational, Scientific, and Cultural Organization (UNESCO) as "educating children, from early childhood, to become clear-thinking and enlightened citizens who participate in decisions concerning society" (UNESCO, 2010). UNESCO further defines three objectives for citizenship education:

- educating people in citizenship and human rights through an understanding of the principles and institutions [which govern a state or nation];
- learning to exercise one's judgement and critical faculty; and
- acquiring a sense of individual and community responsibilities.

(UNESCO, 2010)

Inherent to the idea of citizenship education is the idea of democracy, which UNESCO defines as a political system that provides

- The separation of the legislative, executive and judiciary powers;
- Free elections;
- Pluralism of political parties; and
- Acceptance by the state of the general principles of law and human rights as defined by the international community.

(UNESCO, 2010)

UNESCO (2010) emphasizes that democracy must be understood as a "practice" or a "way of acting," rather than simply a set of institutions, and this in turn means that citizenship education will not just aim to advance knowledge about democratic society, but will seek to produce disposition toward the practices that constitute democracy.

In formal, Western early childhood education, that is, education for young children up to age eight, citizenship education has traditionally been the purview of social studies, and has focused on the first of UNESCO's (2010) goals, "educating people in citizenship and human rights through an understanding of the principles and institutions [which govern a state or nation]." However, the conversation that unfolds in this review is not confined to discussions specifically about social studies. Rather, following UNESCO's (2010) mandate for citizenship education that focuses on democratic practice, I have taken a broader approach, asking how recent research might inform the education of young children for participatory citizenship in a democratic society. I have structured the chapter according to the three most prominent areas of inquiry I found among recent studies. The first area of work includes research that aims to position young children as citizens in their own classrooms, which aligns with the second of UNESCO's (2010) goals, "learning to exercise one's judgement and critical faculty," by giving children experiences in which they must form views and make decisions. This work explores two interrelated themes: honoring children's perspectives on issues that affect them within the classroom and beyond and discovering ways to engage children as active participants in their classroom communities. Also included in this "positioning" theme is a small set of studies examining how early childhood teachers might best support the development of pro-social views on diversity and race, which is recognized as an essential element of developing competent citizens in an increasingly multicultural society. The second area of research looks at specific teaching methods and lessons that aim to advance citizenship preparation through the use of the arts and service learning. This work aligns with UNESCO's (2010) goal that children should "acquir[e] a sense of individual and community responsibilities" by giving children the opportunity to do meaningful work in their local communities and beyond. Research on social studies is the third area of research. Recent work on social studies in early childhood education focuses on how social studies teachers can respond effectively to the mandates of the Common Core standards, focusing on content area literacy instruction.

Minding the Gaps

This chapter would not give an adequate view of early childhood citizenship education research if I did not as well consider the serious gaps in research as of this writing. In this respect, there has been little movement since the publication of the previous version of this chapter, in the third edition of the *Handbook of Research on the Education of Young Children* in 2012. In that chapter, Kelly and I reviewed research in three areas of "social competence education," including social studies, democratic classrooms, and social skills programs. We bemoaned the lack of serious research attention to social studies and democratic competence education in early childhood, noting that our review of social studies journals from 2007 to 2010 yielded numerous non-empirical articles offering advocacy, recommendations, and simple lesson descriptions but very few articles presenting systematic research (DeZutter & Kelly, 2012). We looked back to Levstik and Tyson's (2008) lament for the paltry research base on social studies at all levels of education in their *Handbook of Research on Social Studies Education.* Despite these authors' optimism about an uptick in research in the future, little had changed in 2012, and little has changed now.

For the present chapter, I searched for English-language peer-reviewed research articles, from 2011 to the present (spring 2018), defining a "research article" as one that describes a systematic collection and analysis of data in enough detail that the study could be replicated. I used the following search strategies in EBSCOhost's multi-database academic search engine, "Big Search," limiting results to peer-reviewed journals.

- Search for any combination of "early childhood" with "social studies," "civic," "citizen," or "democracy"
- Search all indexed peer-reviewed research journals related to social studies or civic learning for "early childhood"
- Search all indexed peer-reviewed journals on early childhood education research for "social studies," "civic," "citizen," or "democracy."

These searches yielded surprisingly few peer-reviewed research studies, and for this reason, I have elected to include studies from relatively low-impact journals when those studies have the potential to advance the research conversation on educating young children for democratic citizenship.

Children as Citizens in Classrooms

It is necessary for everyone, including children, to experience the realization of citizenship and democratic values in their everyday lives, participate in democratic processes and practices or otherwise democracy itself might be under threat.

(Joubert, 2012, p. 450)

In keeping with Joubert's (2012) urging, the largest body of work I explore here takes on the question of how to position young children as active citizens within early childhood classrooms and what happens when we do. The central idea is that children are not merely citizens-to-be, in formation for a time in the future when they reach the age of majority and become voters. Instead, children are viewed as citizens already, with rights to be heard, to exert influence, and to engage in social action. It is therefore necessary for young children to learn not just *about* democratic citizenship but rather "*how* democratic citizenship is enacted in daily experiences" (Zachrisen, 2016, p. 181, emphasis in original). On this view, early childhood citizenship education must focus on ways to acknowledge and engage children as active agents in their own social worlds.

Interestingly, nearly all of this group of studies come from outside the United States (with the exceptions of Husband, 2015; Kim, Wee, & Lee, 2016; Sunal, Kelley, Minear, & Sunal, 2011) and nearly all of them name the UN's Convention on the Rights of the Child as providing impetus at least in part for their work (Dockett, Kearney, & Perry, 2012; Grindheim, 2014; Hammond, Hesterman, & Knaus, 2015; Joubert, 2012; Phillips 2011; Theobald & Kultti, 2012; Tholin, 2012; Twigg, Pendergast, & Twigg, 2015). In addition, several nations, such as Australia, South Africa, and Norway, have recently passed legislation mandating that early childhood education includes opportunities for young children to have experiences as active participants in democratic processes. The studies selected for review here have implications beyond their local or national contexts and will be valuable to democratic educators worldwide because they are driven by certain widely agreed upon components of democratic citizenship, including a sense of community, respect for all voices, and active participation. A third influence on this work, cited by several researchers (e.g., Dockett et al., 2012; Hammond et al., 2015; Joubert, 2012), is the "new sociology of childhood" with its focus on childhood as a social construction and on children as active co-constructors of their lives.

Honoring Children's Perspectives

For some researchers, a first step in positioning children as active classroom citizens is to honor their voices. In part, this means finding out what children think and understand about democratic concepts, rather than making assumptions or working from received wisdom. This work follows from the child conceptions research reported in DeZutter and Kelly (2012), with a key difference that for the most part it is not explicitly situated within the field of social studies. In 2012, we noted that research on social studies in early childhood has focused on examining the development of children's thinking in the areas of history, geography, and economics, including children's conceptions of historical time; nested relationships such as neighborhood, city, state, and nation; and basic economic concepts such as shelter, work and income, and trade. The research reported here likewise seeks to understand children's conceptions, but there is a noticeable shift in the tenor of this work. These newer studies are emphatically interested in civic learning through democratic experience, rather than in laying the foundations for the later study of the disciplines that are included in social studies. This recent work seeks to understand children as citizens of the worlds they currently inhabit rather than as citizens-in-the-making (Joubert, 2012).

Consistent with this view, the newer studies seek deeper, more emic understandings of children and their worlds, and this leads researchers to adopt ethnographic research methods. In fact, many offer their research studies as proof of concept that children can and should function as co-researchers. For example, several studies in this section (Dockett et al., 2012; Hammond et al., 2015; Joubert, 2012; also Theobald & Kultti, 2012, in the next section) use variations of a research method known as participatory rights-based research (PRBR), in which all stakeholders in the research collaborate on every step of the process, together determining research questions, research design, analytical approach, findings, and interpretation. The method arises out of a concern for research participants to be positioned as subjects rather than objects; to ensure their voices are heard and their agency is honored. In PRBR, "the power in the research process is transferred from the researchers to the researched" (Joubert, 2012, p. 454). PRBR is consistent with these researchers' aim to supplant a view of children as powerless with "a perspective of them as competent, capable, and active citizens" (Hammond et al., 2015, p. 371).

One of the most compelling studies of this kind is by Dockett et al. (2012) who are interested in how children understand the concept of community and how they think about their local communities. Working with children aged two to six and their teachers in several Australian schools, Dockett et al. found that all five educators in the study reported that "community" was too abstract a concept for children to comprehend, but the children themselves were able to articulate not only concrete ideas about community but broader conceptions as well. Dockett and colleagues observed that among educators who saw children's competence and experience as limited, children's participation was not prioritized or taken seriously; however, when educators invited children's contributions without seeking to limit them, children expressed a breadth of knowledge about their local community as well as aspirations for its improvement. This study illustrates why research on young children's conceptions is central to the aim of positioning them as active citizens in the present; it will be important to demonstrate to teachers that children are capable of much more than may have been assumed, so that teachers afford children opportunities to fully engage in citizenship practices within classrooms.

Other recent studies designed to bring children's understandings of citizenship concepts into the spotlight include Hammond et al. (2015), Sunal et al. (2011), Joubert (2012), Twigg et al. (2015), and Phillips (2011, 2012). Each of these studies reveals both the competence and the limitations in children's thinking, a topic to which I will return later in the chapter. For example, Hammond et al. (2015) aimed to document Australian five- and six-year-olds' understandings of poverty. In their study using a multi-week photo elicitation process, they found both robust and problematic understandings among the children who participated. Sunal et al. (2011) asked, "'Which classroom experiences do K-6 students associate with, and identify as, democratic citizenship?' and 'What does this tell us about their current understanding of this concept?'" (p. 192). Study participants were asked to photograph citizenship activities that occur at school and create captions for the photos. Content analysis reveals that, across all grades, the common themes in children's work were shared decision making, student choice, equal opportunity, and community involvement. At the same time, the researchers worry that children across all grades seemed to have underdeveloped notions of democratic citizenship.

In addition to understanding children's points of view on various aspects of citizenship, research that views children as citizens rather than citizens-to-be emphasizes the value in understanding and highlighting young children's lived experiences as citizens of their local worlds. Joubert (2012), working with eight-year-olds in South Africa, asserts that classrooms can provide children with lived experience as citizens, including experience exercising their right to be heard. Using an elicitation process involving digital photography and verbal reflection, Joubert found that the children have clear likes and dislikes about their local community and that they desire to change the things they disliked, concluding that children "are capable of intervening and giving meaning to their world" (p. 462). Twigg et al. (2015) used in-depth interviewing to better understand Australian three- and four-year-olds' lived experience as global citizens, finding that young children make thoughtful decisions about friendship, are aware of differences and commonalities of people in other countries, are technologically savvy, and make informed judgments about sharing resources. For her study, Phillips (2012) created a classroom forum for Australian five- and six-year-olds to engage in open dialogue about social justice issues, which she sees as an essential practice to active citizenship. Her analysis of video and audio data from this program identified ways in which young children enact their agency as citizens, revealing themes of resistance and rebellion in the face of injustice and constrained choice. Phillips asserts the importance of listening to what children's underlying desires might be, rather than attempting to suppress resistance and rebellion as undesirable forms of social behavior in the classroom. She sees her research as "a shift from pedagogical and research emphases on adults endeavoring to support and enable children's agency to adults being alert to how, when, and where children seize their agency" (p. 155). In an earlier piece, Phillips (2011) asked how five- and six-year-olds' active citizenship can be "provoked through a practice of social justice storytelling" (p. 779). Phillip's (2011) ethnographic study yielded a range of insights (discussed further in the "Methods and Lessons Research" section, below), among them that educators' views of children influence the ways in which they open or interfere with young children's opportunities to exercise agency, a similar finding to Dockett et al. (2012), above.

Phillips (2012) offers the methods used in her research as not just data-gathering devices but as tools that might be used by teachers. Indeed, several of the researchers in this group of studies suggest that their research methods might also serve as teaching tools, an assertion that makes sense given that ethnographic elicitation techniques and student-centered teaching methods both aim to unearth participants' current understandings and assumptions, and make those available for reflection. Hammond et al. (2015) suggest that the tools of their research, photographs comparing the contents of full and nearly empty refrigerators to prompt discussion about the causes and experiences of poverty, could be used as a teaching tool to disrupt some of the problematic beliefs children hold (e.g., people are poor because they are lazy), as a step toward enabling children to become agents for change who seek to address social inequities in their own worlds. Like Hammond et al. (2015), Joubert (2012) suggests that her photograph-and-reflection method could be fruitfully used as a teaching tool. This would give young children an opportunity to define their world and "get acquainted with the practice of citizenship" while "provid[ing] adults with an opportunity to listen to children as citizens" (p. 462).

One critique that might be rendered toward this group of studies is that, in attempting to make the argument that children have voices worth hearing and competence worth acknowledging, they sometimes state their cases too strongly. For example, Joubert (2012) asserts that through the digital photography project, six- and seven-year-olds "showed their capability of acting as agents for transforming their home environment" (p. 449) but, in fact, the data presented included only one idea about making change ("I do not like smoke. Will ask my father to call a meeting to tell people not to smoke." p. 460) and were otherwise only a listing of opinions. It is not clear how Joubert's (2012) data show children to be capable of acting for change. Similarly, Hammond et al. (2015) assert that their study "revealed children's sense of agency as global citizens to affect social justice and the advancement of human rights" (p. 381). This assertion seems to derive from the fact that children had suggestions on how to alleviate poverty (e.g., "sell old toys that you want to chuck away then you could get lots of money," p. 379), but nothing in the data as presented points to children perceiving themselves as having agency to make social change. In fact, the authors point out that the children saw poverty as distant and not relevant to their own lives, which makes it seem even less likely that they felt empowered to work to change it. Phillips (2012) asserts that adults must "use their greater access to resources to bring

young children's initiatives on humanitarian issues into the public sphere" (p. 791), despite offering no indication that the five- and six-year-olds in her study formulated any viable humanitarian initiatives. These overstatements point to an underlying tension that arises when we aim to position children as citizens-in-the-present: even as we characterize children as capable and competent citizens in their own, circumscribed worlds, we must attend to the limitations in their agency and in their ability to conceptualize social action on a grander scale. I will revisit this topic later in the chapter.

Democratic Classroom Culture

In pointing out that teachers' conceptions of children shape how effectively they engage children in citizenship practices, Dockett et al. (2012) and Phillips (2012) point to the importance of the next line of research. Several researchers examine the ways in which classroom norms and interactions support or inhibit children's participation in various democratic practices. This is closely related to what Kelly and I discussed in our 2012 chapter as the "democratic classroom" model, although this phrase is no longer ubiquitous in search results. Instead, I found studies that examine what some scholars refer to as "classroom culture," the patterns of interaction and norms for behavior that are taken for granted by participants but that may align more or less fruitfully with a vision of children as active citizens of a participatory community. As with the studies in the previous section, these studies use ethnographic methods to build extensive, nuanced descriptions of the classroom cultures under study.

Grindheim (2014) conducted an ethnographic study in a Norwegian kindergarten, asking how anger is validated or suppressed in the course of participation among adults and children as well as participation among peers. She found that children's anger over disrespect or injustice was interpreted by adults as a need for emotional control. Grindheim argues that "Given children's right to participate and express their will, it would be more appropriate to develop ways of solving the conflicts and listening to the message of the child rather than trying to modify their anger" (p. 316). Similarly, Johansson and Emilson (2016), working in Sweden, studied four preschool classrooms (ages one to three), attending to interpersonal conflicts as sites of resistance. Echoing the Phillips (2012) study discussed above, Johansson and Emilson assert that children's conflicts may be a potent site for democracy learning because they allow children to exercise resistance, including "argumentation, distraction, hesitation, ignoring, persistence, and by showing courage, solidarity, and playfulness" (p. 31). Conflicts also allow children to experience plurality based in respect. The researchers assert, "early experiences with resistance are necessary for children to become responsible citizens with the ability to criticize and resist authorities and injustice that children may encounter in the future" (p. 20). However, similar to Grindheim (2014), this study found that teachers' desire to maintain order suppressed opportunities for children to work through conflict. Johanssan and Emilson advocate allowing children space for disagreement and for teachers to manage the class not by asserting dominance but by responding to children's perspectives. They also call for more research on how teachers can support children to use friendly conflicts and resistance as sites for democratic learning.

Several studies examine participation structures in classrooms, identifying those that support democratic behaviors and those that do not. "Participation structures" are norms for turn taking and interaction, including whether or not a child must have permission from a teacher to speak and whether children's speech is directed to the teacher or to classmates. As one example of this type of work, Zachrisen (2016) conducted an ethnographic study on the participation structures of classroom play among children ages one to three in Norway, looking for connections between interaction patterns and the communication of democratic values. Zachrisen is especially interested in how play interactions can contribute to children's sense of belonging, asserting that when structured appropriately, classroom play can be an opportunity for children to experience elements of democratic participation including mutual relations, contributing to a larger collective, and responsibility to a group. Such opportunities occur, however, only when the teacher is on the sidelines or plays as an equal peer. Play time that is teacher-directed tends to include only dyadic interactions between the teacher and each individual student, which does not serve to develop the communal characteristics found with the other participation structures.

Theobald and Kultti (2012) looked at participation structures in a PreK/K classroom in Australia. They sought to identify ways in which teachers include children as participants in conversations throughout the school day, finding many examples of ways the teacher afforded children agency and influence within conversations, but also many examples in which the teacher adhered to traditional norms of schooling that conflict with democratic classroom practices, including a concern with content coverage and behavioral control. Similarly focused on classroom conversation, Tholin (2012) collaborated with a preschool teacher in Norway to develop a series of planned classroom discussions during project-based learning, examining which linguistic strategies achieve the democratic aim of inviting children into a participatory community via conversation around project-based work. Tholin found that certain approaches accomplish this better than others. The use of topics that are interesting to all students is essential, because the aim is for all students to participate. The use of open-ended questioning strategies is preferable to the ubiquitous initiation-response-feedback format, which focuses on correct responses rather than offering space for children to express their ideas and perspectives. Like Theobald and Kultti (2012), Tholin notes the tension between participatory talk in the classroom and the teacher's "formal pedagogical mandate" to cover the curriculum (p. 45). Tholin advocates for more playful and improvisational approaches to classroom conversation and for collaboration with children as to what should be talked about.

Multiculturalism and Race

Teaching multiculturalism and racial justice is increasingly recognized as an essential element of preparing children for citizenship in a diverse and ever more globalized society. A few researchers have recently examined approaches to addressing racial and cross-cultural issues with young children. For example, Kim et al. (2016) examined Korean Kindergarteners' bias against Africans and African Americans before and after their teacher engaged them in a multi-week unit using multicultural literature. As a part of the unit, the teacher used a range of methods to help the children make personal connections to the texts. When the unit began, stereotypes against Africans and African Americans as impoverished, dirty, and lacking clothing were common; by end, children no longer exhibited such stereotypes. The unit also helped children develop a vocabulary that was used at school and at home to talk about racial issues. Kim et al. emphasize the role of classroom social interactions around the books in engendering these changes and the importance of creating a space where children can freely share their views. Additionally, they urge teachers to help young children explore a variety of perspectives to prevent developing or reinforcing bias.

Husband (2015) notes the absence of research on how young children think about race and respond to discussions of racism. He "seeks to develop an oppositional consciousness of race and racism" among his first grade students and to "help children begin to identify how racial injustice exists and operates in the larger society" (p. 2). He developed nine lessons on African America history, then used a content analysis to examine children's written responses. Responses fell into three categories: ignoring oppression altogether ("repressive responses"), non-combative resistance, and retaliatory resistance. Husband concludes that teachers need to teach children how to question racial injustice as a way to help them move beyond "repressive" responses and prevent students from becoming adults who passively accept racism. Like Kim et al. (2016), Husband suggests teachers present children with a wide range of options for confronting social injustice; he also calls for teachers to help children complicate and nuance their understandings of race and racism. Husband suspects that the dearth of scholarly work on teaching racial issues in early childhood may be because this is thought to be cognitively out of reach for young children, or simply too harsh a topic, although his study suggests neither assumption is accurate.

Attending to classroom conversational norms in a way that parallels the democratic classroom culture research above, Loveridge, Rosewarne, Shuker, Barker, and Nager (2012) examined how diversity is depicted through classroom practices and statements in two New Zealand early childhood education centers. They found that each classroom had a differing approach, with one focused more on addressing diversity among individual children but ignoring larger social justice issues, resulting in concepts of diversity being decontextualized from larger social forces. The other classroom pushed deeper into issues of complexity and contention without aiming for pat solutions, acknowledging inequalities of power and that diversity is inextricably linked with issues of social justice. Loveridge et al. affirm the latter, despite the greater challenges involved, as better serving the aims of democratic citizenship education.

The Slave Master and Other Dilemmas

As I have already noted, there is an unavoidable tension that runs through the work in this section: the tension between researchers' desire to position young children as competent, agentic citizens and the traditional understanding of children as dependent and "in formation" (cf. Zachrisen, 2016). Indeed, several studies run into this head on, when results revealed limitations in children's ability to think in pro-democratic ways. An especially troubling example can be found in an early study by Husband (2010), in which children preferred to identify with the slave master in a story rather than the slaves, because the slave master was not suffering and was not the victim (see also Hammond et al., 2015; Joubert, 2012; Twigg et al., 2015).

The researchers highlighted in this chapter seek to redress a long history of underestimating young children's competence as well as deeply institutionalized practices that suppress children's voices and autonomy. At the same time, it cannot be ignored that young children have less experience in the world, are less developed cognitively, and require protection from harm. Indeed, the UN Convention on the Rights of the Child (1989), which serves as an inspiration for much of this work, asserts these issues emphatically. It is therefore imperative that researchers working to position children as citizens in the present do not disregard the fact that children are nonetheless traveling along a developmental trajectory. We must not assert children's civic competence so strongly that we overlook the need to deal with the "slave master" problem and others that arise as a result of children's developmentally situated ways of thinking and feeling. In addition, as researchers endeavor to engage children's agency as democratic actors, we must be careful not to communicate to children that they have more agency than they actually have. Proclamations that young children can change the world (e.g., Hammond et al., 2015, p. 381; Joubert, 2012, p. 453) are inspiring, but also hyperbolic. As Phillips (2011) reminds us, children do not have the same level of control over their lives as adults, they have a limited scope for participation, and they are physical and economically dependent on adults. In Phillips's (2011) view, this makes it all the more important that educators notice the social actions young children initiate within the worlds they do inhabit and make "well-considered responses that sustain rather than constrain agency" (p. 791).

It will also be important for researchers committed to identifying and promoting characteristics of democratic classroom culture to grapple with the reality that classrooms can never be pure democracies. While there are several fronts on which progress might be made – Theobald and Kullti (2012),

for example, list the emphasis on outcomes over process, the challenge of time allocations, the need for routines to manage large groups of children, and institutional codes of behavior for "teacher" and "student" as barriers to be overcome – ultimately, teachers are responsible for the care and safety of the children in their classrooms, placing teachers necessarily in positions of power and authority. This fact will unavoidably intrude on the democratic culture of a classroom (cf. Grindheim, 2014; Johanssen and Emilson, 2015).

Methods and Lessons Research

A second type of research on citizenship education is studies that aim to assess the effectiveness of specific classroom methods or lessons. Recent work of this type clusters around two themes, the use of the arts and the use of service learning projects. As with the work already reported, the studies in this section identify as studies in support of citizenship education.

According to Montgomery, Miller, Foss, Tallakson, and Howard (2017), the arts allow children to tap simultaneously into their imaginations and feelings, allowing the child to experience empathy and envision social change, which is perhaps one reason why methods and lessons research for citizenship education includes numerous arts-based projects. In addition to some of the studies already discussed (Joubert, 2012; Phillips, 2012; Sunal et al., 2011), the following studies document the use of various art forms as catalysts for democratic behavior and civic learning. Branscombe, Chandler, and Little (2015) analyzed a Kenyan drum project as a means to teach children about multimodal communication as well as certain cultural universals. Branscombe et al. (2015) suggest their project might serve as an exemplar solution for teachers who struggle to find instructional time for the arts and for social studies in an increasingly narrowed curriculum. Serriere (2010) used children's digital photographs as discussion starters to explore "everyday democracy" in children's lives, finding this technique effective in helping children envision possibilities for social change in their everyday world. Dunkerly-Bean, Sunday, and Summers (2017) observed while a teacher led her class through drawing and creative play activities around global justice issues. Dunkerly-Bean et al. found that the children's responses were problematically individualistic (cf. Hammond et al., 2015), and posited that the teacher's framing of the issue may have drawn attention to individual responsibility more than larger justice issues.

Phillips's (2011) study, also described in the classroom culture section above, used storytelling, drawing, sculpture, and dance to explore issues of social justice with five- and six-year-olds. As a result of this exploration, children formulated plans for local actions and, with the help of adults, implemented their plans in their local community. Another arts-focused study, Montgomery et al. (2017), analyzed a project on human rights in which kindergarteners created fabric banners as a fundraiser for a partner school in El Salvador, finding that children were able to recognize injustice and privilege when it was connected to their sense of fairness. Silva (2016), in a case study of a unit on social justice seen through the lives of artists, found that first graders not only engaged deeply in discussion but formed viable action plans to address local problems related to their discussions. Echoing the concerns about child agency described above, Silva cautions readers that in doing this type of work, care is needed to guide children toward feasible projects; it will be important to steer children away from attempting social justice work that extends beyond the limits of their agency.

Three studies above, Phillips (2011), Montgomery et al. (2017), and Silva (2016), also contribute to the second cluster of methods and lesson research, which involves analysis of service learning projects. Service learning has long been understood as a powerful pedagogical tool for citizenship education. While many authors decry the lack of research, or any type of professional discussion, on service learning with young children, those cited here may serve to open the conversation.

Fair and Delaplane (2015) examined the quality of written reflections over several months as second graders made weekly visits to a retirement home. They observed that children were able to take multiple perspectives in their writing and to reflect on the reciprocal nature of relationships. Scott and Graham (2015) administered the Civic Responsibility Survey to first, second, and fifth graders before and after their engagement in inquiry-driven service learning projects, finding that the projects yielded significant changes in scores on empathy, connection to community, and civic awareness scales. However, civic efficacy scores only increased for fifth graders, perhaps because linking the immediate service learning experience to a sense of one's civic efficacy more generally involves more abstraction than the younger participants are prepared to do (Scott & Graham, 2015).

One further caution about doing service learning work with children comes from Phillips (2011), who warns that because children have limited or no access to the public sphere and must rely on adults to bring their initiatives to fruition, there is a danger that adults will fall into the role of "enablers," thereby masking children's agency. She advocates that educators embrace the possibility of "two-way learning" (p. 792), so that adults not only support children's efforts but also aim to learn from children's own insights and democratic practices.

Content Area Literacy in Social Studies

The final group of studies in this chapter is focused on the issue of content area literacy within social studies. While this set of studies is far from a substantial body of work, I include it to draw attention to the evolution of an ongoing concern voiced often in early childhood education literature, the marginalization of social studies within the curriculum. In 2012, Kelly and I cited a 2007 NCES report for grades 1 through 4 that found that elementary social studies receives an average of 2.5 hours of instruction per week, compared to 11.3 hours of literacy and 5.4 hours of math (Morton & Dalton, 2007). Levstik and Tyson note that the early grades are "the most fragile portion of the social studies curriculum" (2008, p. 7); social studies is often set aside in favor of literacy and mathematics. "Indeed, scholars have bemoaned the marginalization of social studies for quite some time," we wrote, "although the problem seems to have intensified in the wake of No Child Left Behind and high stakes testing" (DeZutter & Kelly, 2012, p. 208). Since that writing, we in the United States have witnessed the implementation of the Common Core State Standards (CCSS) in the majority of states, along with the passage of the Every Student Succeeds Act (ESSA) in place of No Child Left Behind. These developments have done little to address the narrowing of the curriculum. As Connor et al. (2017) note, ESSA departs from No Child Left Behind (NCLB) in some important ways but none that suggest a larger role for social studies in the early grades. The Common Core standards focus on literacy and mathematics, and include attention to content area literacy skills, which can be addressed using social studies content. It should be noted that while the CCSS extend only down to kindergarten, the National Association for the Education of Young Children has raised concern about the "downward mapping" (2009, p. 4) of standards, which results in pre-kindergarten programs shaping their curricula around preparing children to succeed in the standards-based settings they will encounter beginning in kindergarten.

I found only four empirical studies related to content area literacy in early childhood social studies that met the parameters of my search. Three of these can be summarized briefly, as follows. Connor et al. (2017) examine the effectiveness of an individualized content area literacy program for kindergarten through fourth grade, finding that the intervention improved social studies content knowledge and could be feasibly used within a literacy block without decrement to progress in reading. Gonzalez et al. (2010) found that when social studies and science vocabulary is strategically integrated into shared book reading with low-income preschoolers, it has positive effects on both expressive and receptive vocabulary. Strachan (2015) finds that interactive read-alouds of informational texts with kindergarteners yield significant gains in both social studies concepts and content area literacy. These studies share little with the work discussed in the previous sections of this chapter; there is no explicit concern for citizenship learning or democratic participation. Instead the concern is on children's ability to learn social studies terms and concepts in decontextualized ways, primarily, from informational texts. Given this, and the fact that so many of the studies in earlier sections of the chapter purport to serve the aims of citizenship education but do not categorize themselves as research in social studies, one must wonder whether social studies research – and by extension, social studies in schools – has become unmoored from its original purpose, and is proceeding without a sense of the mandate that early childhood education founders endowed it with.

Recognizing this problem as it plays out in social studies instruction, Shiveley (2014) proposes that social studies teachers at all levels of schooling adopt a guiding question for their practice: "Am I teaching in a manner that promotes vital democratic citizenship traits, skills, and dispositions?" (2014, p. 85). Shively does not address how this might be done in the face of pressures from content- and literacy-driven standards, perhaps because we do not have a base of empirical work to guide us through this challenge.

The fourth study, Falkner (2018), does a bit more than the others to hold social studies to its promise of citizenship development while acknowledging the realities of how social studies is typically taught in the United States. Falkner (2018) rues the inadequate attention to race and racism in schools, including within social studies, agreeing with Husband (2015) that this is likely due to a belief that the topic is too complex or too sensitive for young children. Falkner would also like to redress the haphazard way that social studies is integrated into language arts, calling educators to interrogate the materials used in classrooms so teachers may better engage with topics around racism. She analyzes books by Ezra Jack Keats, finding that Keats's books disrupt the dominant narrative of the delinquent black boy while complicating issues of inequity in urban environments. She offers Keats's work as an example of a resource early grade teachers can use to critically examine depictions of race within the curriculum, within the context of teaching social studies in conjunction with literacy.

Recommendations: Where Do We Go from Here?

Some clear "next steps" for research on citizenship education in early childhood flow from the discussions above. The researchers highlighted in this chapter are intent on bringing about a turn in early childhood citizenship education research, moving from an assumption that early childhood education is preparing future citizens toward a focus on the ways in which children live and act as citizens in the present. But this work is still in its infancy, asking the most introductory questions, such as "what happens if we view children this way, what do we see?" and "what are the basic characteristics of classroom interactions that align with an understanding of children as democratic participants?" Additionally, there seems to be little cross-conversation as yet; almost none of the researchers reviewed here seem to be aware of each other's work. In the years to come, I would hope that researchers interested in the implications of understanding young children as citizens of their classrooms, communities, and the world come together to define a research agenda. A robust and cohesive body of work from this perspective has the potential to motivate a large-scale transformation in how democratic citizenship education in early childhood is approached worldwide.

The idea of children as global citizens emerges in a few of the studies reported here including Hammond et al. (2015), Twigg et al. (2015), and Zachrisen (2016), and those that aim to promote multiculturalism. Given the speed at which democratic societies are becoming globalized, a great deal more work on understanding and teaching children for global citizenship is needed. In addition, digital citizenship is becoming more and more intertwined with global citizenship, yet the idea of digital citizenship receives almost no mention in the work reviewed here (with the exception of Twigg et al., 2015). Considering the pervasiveness of technology in early childhood classrooms and the young age at which children begin to encounter digital life, there is an urgent need for research on supporting young children as digital citizens.

The specter of social studies marginalization points to another major area of research that is sorely lacking. We need a much clearer, empirically based current picture of not only how much social studies is happening in early childhood education, but what is the nature and quality of those endeavors. Since, as this chapter has shown, citizenship education does not neatly map on to the discipline of social studies, the same is needed for efforts in citizenship education: we need a big picture understanding about how much attention citizenship education receives in early childhood educational settings, in what ways, and how effectively.

With regard to social studies, more than ever there is a need for researchers to address how early childhood educators can navigate the current educational climate while being true to the civic purposes the field was built on. But there is perhaps an even more pressing need. Research is needed to support the long-standing claims of the value of social studies to young children and to democratic society. In fact, as Kelly and I noted in 2012, we might conclude that social studies in early childhood has not been a research priority because it has not been a curricular priority, but might the converse also be true? Perhaps social studies is easily pushed from the curriculum because we lack a research-based argument for its inclusion.

The Reach of Citizenship Education

Educating for democratic participation by its nature assumes at least some outcomes that reach beyond the classroom and beyond the present moment; it is doubtful that the authors represented here embrace active citizenship for individuals *only* when they are very young. Indeed, the National Council for Social Studies (NCSS) in its position statement, *Early childhood in the social studies context*, asserts

> The social studies in the early childhood/elementary years are crucial if we expect the young people of this nation to become active, responsible citizens for maintaining the democratic values upon which this nation was established. Unless children acquire the foundations of knowledge, attitudes, and skills in social studies in the important elementary years, it is unlikely that teachers in the junior and senior high schools will be successful in preparing effective citizens for the 21st century.
> (Berson & Villotti, 2019)

Yet, it is far from clear that early childhood social studies programs, even when fervently implemented, accomplish either of the goals named here. The social studies research literature is silent on the issue of how early childhood programs affect later social studies learning; the same is true regarding the discipline's impact beyond the K-12 classroom. This issue extends to other citizenship education endeavors as well, whether they identify as part of "social studies" or not. There is some research on older children that suggests that participation in classrooms that exhibit certain democratic characteristics, such as an open environment for discussions and the use of active learning pedagogies, fosters civic engagement as well as democratic thinking (Hahn & Alviar-Martin, 2008), but this research does not include young children, and it is not clear what these findings mean for life beyond school.

The challenge of demonstrating the value of early childhood citizenship education beyond its immediate moment will be considerable. Young children have few opportunities beyond their classrooms to participate in civic life; their participation in larger society is for the most part distant in time, and a great deal of further education will come in between. There is a need for carefully designed longitudinal studies to test claims that early childhood citizenship education indeed has an effect on civic competence and participation later in life. Further, it will be necessary not only to investigate whether civic competence developed (or acknowledged and engaged) in early childhood extends to life beyond school, but to ask how and why this happens (or doesn't), and to understand what factors influence the process.

Focusing on the Present

On the other hand, as the majority of studies cited in this chapter assert, citizenship education holds demonstrated value within the early childhood classroom itself. Classroom practices informed by democratic ideals affirm children's agency and competence, potentially make school a more positive experience, and help children to be better members of the school community. Researchers who wish to contribute to the argument in favor of citizenship education in early childhood will need to bring into high relief the benefits of citizenship education that accrue within early childhood classrooms.

Life-Wide Research

Research in math, science, and literacy has revealed that children learn to think in ways valued by these disciplines through participation in a wide range of non-school activities, including "informal" educational contexts such as museums, extracurricular activities, clubs, and enrichment classes, as well as everyday activities within their families and communities (Bransford et al., 2006). Such research has proven a potent source of insight for school-based educators, because it allows them to work in tandem with, rather than against, the understandings that children bring with them from other contexts in which they participate. Early childhood citizenship education would certainly benefit from this sort of "life-wide" approach (Bransford et al., 2006).

A few studies in this chapter acknowledge the concept of life-wide learning. Hammond et al. (2015) assert that attending to children's lived experiences includes attending to their life beyond school, and find that young students can explore a wide range of perspectives when "learning experiences are derived from home and community experiences" (p. 372). Joubert (2012) asks "How could eight-year-old children's experiences of their home environment assist educators to improve these children's citizenship practice?" (p. 450). Kim et al. (2016) included interviews with parents in their data set and found that children employed what they had learned about race and diversity at home with their families.

Research will need to delve deeper into the relationships between the various contexts in which young children participate, for example, by examining interactions between the forms of democratic behavior children encounter in their families, religious communities, and elsewhere, and the forms being promoted at school or by investigating the ways young children move between multiple contexts for citizenship learning, and how they negotiate points of discontinuity among these contexts.

Conclusion

My guiding question for this chapter is "what research is being done about the education of young children for life in a democratic society?" Searches for research literature since 2010 revealed work relating to three themes: positioning children as citizens in classrooms, use of the arts and service learning, and content-area literacy in social studies. Researchers around the world have taken up the mantle of children as present-moment citizens of their classrooms, their local communities, and the world. Driven by a commitment to children's rights and a desire to acknowledge children's competence and agency as social actors, scholars have examined, primarily through ethnographic and often highly participatory means, classroom norms, practices, and interventions that support democratic behaviors and sensibilities as well as children's lived experiences as active citizens. Those focused on specific teaching methods have found promise in the arts and service learning as means to connect children to civic engagement and social justice concerns. Meanwhile, for better or worse, research on social studies – originally designated as a focal site for civic learning in early childhood – has responded to the current standards- and literacy-driven climate by shifting its emphasis to text-based learning that aligns with literacy standards.

In all of the areas examined in this chapter, there is much work to be done, beginning with research that can guide future decision making about whether and how best to include citizenship education and social studies in early childhood education. In addition, the recent turn to focus on children as citizens in the present, rather than in-formation, offers both challenges and exciting avenues for research. A strong research base from this perspective could potentially transform how democracy education is conceptualized in early childhood settings in the future and around the globe.

References

Berson, I., & Villotti, K. (2019). *Early childhood in the social studies context*. Position Statement of the National Council for the Social Studies (NCSS). Retrieved from https://www.socialstudies.org/early-childhood-social-studies-context

Branscombe, A., Chandler, P. T., & Little, S. L. (2017). Students drum life stories: The role of cultural universals in project work. *The Journal of Social Studies Research, 41*(1), 53–62. doi:10.1016/j.jssr.2015.10.004

Bransford, J., Vye, N., Stevens, R., Kuhl, P., Schwartz, D., & Bell, P. (2006). Learning theories and education: Toward a decade of synergy. In P. Alexander & P. Winne (Eds.), *Handbook of educational psychology* (2nd ed., pp. 209–244). Mahwah, NJ: Erlbaum.

Connor, C. M., Dombek, J., Crowe, E. C., Spencer, M., Tighe, E. L., Coffinger, S., … Petscher, Y. (2017). Acquiring science and social studies knowledge in kindergarten through fourth grade: Conceptualization, design, implementation, and efficacy testing of content-area literacy instruction (CALI). *Journal of Educational Psychology, 109*(3), 301–320. doi:10.1037/edu0000128

DeZutter, S. L., & Kelly, M. (2012). Social competence education in early childhood: A sociocultural perspective. In O. Saracho & B. Spodek (Eds.), *Handbook of research on the education of young children* (3rd ed., pp. 206–218). New York, NY: Routledge.

Dockett, S., Kearney, E., & Perry, B. (2012). Recognising young children's understandings and experiences of community. *International Journal of Early Childhood, 44*(3), 287–305. doi:10.1007/s13158-012-0073-y

Fair, C. D., & Delaplane, E. (2015). "It is good to spend time with older adults. You can teach them, they can teach you": Second grade students reflect on intergenerational service learning. *Early Childhood Education Journal, 43*(1), 19–26. doi:10.1007/s10643-014-0634-9

Falkner, A. (2018). Racialized space and discourse in the picture books of Ezra Jack Keats. *The Journal of Social Studies Research, 42*(2), 171–184. doi:10.1016/j.jssr.2017.05.006

Gonzalez, J. E., Pollard-Durodola, S., Simmons, D. C., Taylor, A. B., Davis, M. J., Kim, M., & Simmons, L. (2010). Developing low-income preschoolers' social studies and science vocabulary knowledge through content-focused shared book reading. *Journal of Research on Educational Effectiveness, 4*(1), 25–52. doi:10.1080/19345747.2010.487927

Grindheim, L. T. (2014). 'I am not angry in the kindergarten!' Interruptive anger as democratic participation in Norwegian kindergartens. *Contemporary Issues in Early Childhood, 15*(4), 308–318. doi:10.2304/ciec.2014.15.4.308

Hahn, C. L., & Alviar-Martin, T. (2008). International political socialization research. In L. S. Levstik & C. A. Tyson (Eds.), *Handbook of research in social studies education* (pp. 81–108). New York, NY: Routledge.

Hammond, L. L., Hesterman, S., & Knaus, M. (2015). What's in your refrigerator? Children's views on equality, work, money and access to food. *International Journal of Early Childhood, 47*(3), 367–384. doi:10.1007/s13158-015-0150-0

Husband, T. (2010). He's too young to learn about that stuff: Anti-racist pedagogy and early childhood social studies. *Social Studies Research & Practice, 5*(2), 61–75.

Husband, T. (2015). "Please stop whipping me": Writing about race and racism in an early childhood social studies classroom. *Inquiry in Education, 6*(1), http://digitalcommons.nl.edu/ie/vol6/iss1/2

Johansson, E., & Emilson, A. (2016). Conflicts and resistance: Potentials for democracy learning in preschool. *International Journal of Early Years Education, 24*(1), 19–35. doi:10.1080/09669760.2015.1133073

Joubert, I. (2012). Children as photographers: Life experiences and the right to be listened to. *South African Journal of Education, 32*(4), 449–464. doi:10.15700/saje.v32n4a677

Kim, S. J., Wee, S. J., & Lee, Y. M. (2016). Teaching kindergartners racial diversity through multicultural literature: A case study in a kindergarten classroom in Korea. *Early Education and Development, 27*(3), 402–420. doi:10.1080/10409289.2015.1069110

Levstik, L. S., & Tyson, C. A. (2008). Introduction. In L. S. Levstik & C. A. Tyson (Eds.), *Handbook of research in social studies education* (pp. 1–14). New York, NY: Routledge.

Loveridge, J., Rosewarne, S., Shuker, M. J., Barker, A., & Nager, J. (2012). Responding to diversity: Statements and practices in two early childhood education contexts. *European Early Childhood Education Research Journal, 20*(1), 99–113. doi:10.1080/1350293X.2011.634998

Montgomery, S. E., Miller, W., Foss, P., Tallakson, D., & Howard, M. (2017). Banners for books: "Mighty-hearted" Kindergartners take action through arts-based service learning. *Early Childhood Education Journal, 45*(1), 1–14. doi:10.1007/s10643-015-0765-7

Morton, B. A., & Dalton, B. (2007). *Changes in instructional hours in four subjects by public school teachers of grades 1 through 4*. Washington, DC: NCES.

Phillips, L. (2011). Possibilities and quandaries for young children's active citizenship. *Early Education & Development, 22*(5), 778–794. doi:10.1080/10409289.2011.597375

Phillips, L. G. (2012). Retribution and rebellion: Children's meaning making of justice through storytelling. *International Journal of Early Childhood, 44*(2), 141–156. doi:10.1007/s13158-012-0053-2

Saracho, O. N., & Spodek, B. (2007). Social learning as the basis for early childhood education. In O. N. Saracho & B. Spodek (Eds.), *Contemporary perspectives on social learning in early childhood education* (pp. 303–310). Charlotte, NC: Information Age Publishing Inc.

Serriere, S. C. (2010). Carpet-time democracy: Digital photography and social consciousness in the early childhood classroom. *The Social Studies, 101*(2), 60–68. doi:10.1080/00377990903285481

Shiveley, J. (2014). Teaching for democratic citizenship: Arriving at a guiding question for pedagogical practice. *Social Studies Research & Practice, 9*(3), 81–87.

Silva, J. M. (2016). Reading, writing, and revolution: Facilitating social activism in first grade. *The Social Studies, 107*(5), 1–8. doi:10.1080/00377996.2016.1192095

Scott, K. E., & Graham, J. A. (2015). Service-learning: Implications for empathy and community engagement in elementary school children. *Journal of Experiential Education, 38*(4), 354–372. doi:10.1177/1053825915592889

Strachan, S. L. (2015). Kindergarten students' social studies and content literacy learning from interactive read-alouds. *The Journal of Social Studies Research, 39*(4), 207–223. doi:10.1016/j.jssr.2015.08.003

Sunal, C. S., Kelley, L. A., Minear, A. K., & Sunal, D. W. (2011). Elementary students represent classroom democratic citizenship experiences via photos. *Journal of Social Studies Research, 35*(2), 191–216.

Theobald, M., & Kultti, A. (2012). Investigating child participation in the everyday talk of a teacher and children in a preparatory year. *Contemporary Issues in Early Childhood, 13*(3), 210–225. doi:10.2304/ciec.2012.13.3.210

Tholin, K. R. (2012). Something to talk about: Does the language use of preschool teachers invite children to participate in democratic conversation? *European Early Childhood Education Research Journal, 20*(1), 35–46. doi:10.1080/1350293x.2012.650010

Twigg, D., Pendergast, D., & Twigg, J. (2015). Growing global citizens: Young children's lived experiences with the development of their own social world. *International Research in Early Childhood Education, 6*(1), 79–91.

UNESCO. (2010). Citizenship Education for the 21st Century. Retrieved from http://www.unesco.org/education/tlsf/mods/theme_b/interact/mod07task03/appendix.htm

Zachrisen, B. (2016). The contribution of different patterns of teachers' interactions to young children's experiences of democratic values during play. *International Journal of Early Childhood, 48*(2), 179–192. doi:10.1007/s13158-016-0166-0

9

Repositioning the Visual Arts in Early Childhood Education

Continuing Reconsideration

CHRISTINE MARMÉ THOMPSON AND CHRISTOPHER M. SCHULTE

With his head slightly turned and eyes peeking toward the large window behind him, Andy informed me of his dilemma: "I can't make the dump truck," he said. It wasn't only that Andy desired to make a dump truck, as if any old dump truck would do the trick. Rather, the issue was that Andy wanted to make *the* dump truck, the one that was recently – a few moments before, in fact – idling outside of his classroom window, just down the street. But the existence of this particular dump truck was fleeting, having a presence that quickly blurred the moment the stop light turned green. "It's not there no more." Andy noted. Then, after a few seconds of contemplation, with his left hand holding the paper firmly in place, he proceeded to make a series of lines, adding a large circular shape on each end. Pointing to the circular form that now appeared to his right, Andy declared: "That's the dump truck. See it? It's right there." "Yes, I see it," I responded. "It even has the same big wheels, just like the dump truck we saw outside in the street." Andy seemed to be quite pleased with my observation, as he flashed a big smile at me. "Oh yeah, the dump truck has really *really REALLY* big tires." Then, after reaching for and grabbing the orange marker from the cup in the center of the table, Andy proceeded to add a set of oval-like shapes, which formed a larger ring around the existing circular form he'd placed on the left side of the drawing. Before I could ask what was happening though Andy began to inform me that the lines he had just drawn were, in actuality, "roads" that the dump truck used to "drive around the work site." In the moments that followed, Andy continued to look out the window, checking to see if the dump truck would again appear, giving him the opportunity he so desired, to observe in greater detail the truck's complexities. As he waited, Andy continued to draw, dabbing forcefully at his paper, a repeated gesture that rendered an excessive number of "dots" (just shy of 80, to be precise). As we began to laugh about the number of dots he was rapidly accumulating, Andy did a double-take. Having turned his head and body toward the window, his eyes were now steadily fixed on the intersection just outside. "There it is!" He said. "It's the dump truck!"

Indeed, there it was, the same red dump truck. However, this time, the dump truck presented something new for Andy to consider. It was now carrying a full load; its massive bucket filled to the brim with concrete and rocks. "Look at the rocks!" Andy yelled, ecstatic about the development. When the truck finally lurched forward, pulling away from the intersection, Andy returned slowly to his seat, attending once again to his drawing. "Actually... You know what?" Andy asked me. "What's that?" I said in return. Pointing to the dots that he had previously drawn on his paper, he remarked: "These aren't dots anymore. They're rocks."[1]

In many respects, this was a small and ordinary incident of classroom life, readily recognizable as the type of fleeting interaction that occurs at drawing tables or art centers, as children produce visual narratives that respond to the issues and intrigues to which they are most committed at the time, often in the company of peers and interested adults. Once, not so very long ago, researchers concerned with children's art would have focused exclusively on Andy himself, the solitary artist in dialogue with his work (Brooks, 2005, 2009; Dyson, 1989; Schulte, 2015a, 2015b, 2015c; Sunday, 2012, 2018; Wood & Hall, 2011). The presence of others, their comments and questions, their critical or appreciative responses, and the broader context of this drawing event would have been reduced to background noise or erased entirely (Atkinson, 2002; Matthews, 1999). As Pearson (2001) suggests, the act of drawing might have passed without remark, in favor of an analysis of the drawing itself, for children's artworks have often been granted greater significance than the work that produced them. Even when advice to teachers continued to insist upon the primacy of process over product, researchers focused attention all but exclusively on the residue of that process.

In recent years, researchers concerned with the education of young children have devoted considerable energy to the serious critique of the research and theory upon which practice in early childhood art has been based. Stimulated by a renewed sense of responsibility for early childhood education, and more direct involvement with young children and their teachers, art educators in museums, schools, and universities have joined in questioning many of their shared assumptions about young children and their encounters with art. This reconceptualization draws upon sources overlooked or lightly used in the past, when developmental psychology structured thinking about young children and their art, and radically child-centered approaches to early art education were widely accepted as exemplary practice. Almost 30 years ago, Jeffers (1993) reported that the art educators she surveyed emphasized developmental issues in the methods classes they offered to university students majoring in early childhood and elementary education, identifying development as one of three major concerns addressed in such courses. This finding was somewhat surprising in an era in which a discipline-based approach to art education prevailed, and, to an extent unprecedented in the history of North American art education, developmental issues vanished from ongoing conversations within and beyond that field.

This discipline-based perspective evolved further in the decade that followed, expanding toward a focus on visual culture, broadly defined (see, e.g., Duncum, 2003; Wilson, 2004), but leaving in its wake an enduring commitment among art educators to the study of images and objects in their aesthetic, critical, historical, social, and political contexts. There has also been a marked resurgence of interest in the art experience of contemporary children and adolescents, and in the development of curricular theory and instructional approaches that are responsive to that experience (see, e.g., Cinquemani, 2014, 2018; Davies, 2014; Kind, 2018; Nutbrown, 2013; Theil, 2018; Thompson, 2015, 2016; Trafi-Prats, 2014, 2018).

Jeffers' (1993) reading of the content of preservice education of teachers suggests an arrhythmia in the field, a lack of syncopation between what beginning teachers are taught, and what researchers and theorists recommend (Richards, 2007). McArdle and Piscatelli (2002) suggest that early childhood art education is best viewed as a "palimpsest," where old and new ideas from multiple informing disciplines persist and coexist, even when they may be deeply incompatible. The developmental stage theories that served as the foundation of early art education throughout much of the twentieth century are undeniably appealing to prospective teachers, providing a measure of predictability in a curricular area that many classroom teachers approach with considerable uncertainty and apprehension. Developmental stages supply a structure that is comprehensible and comprehensive, an approach to early art education that can be reproduced in any classroom, if children's experiences with art are structured in a particular way that accords well with the child-centered traditions of early childhood practice. At the same time, researchers and theorists who focus on early art education question the "hegemony of developmental psychology on our understanding of children" (Tarr, 2003, p. 7) and the traditional structure of universal stages with their tendency to "decontextualize child and children" (p. 7).

Art education research, necessarily interdisciplinary in focus, has become increasingly attuned to larger cultural issues. A pervasive reconceptualization of the "image of the child" (Malaguzzi, 1995; see also, Kaplan, 2014; McClure, 2009, 2011a) can be seen in the emergence of the new sociology of childhood (James, Jenks, & Prout, 1998) and studies of children's culture (Dyson, 2003; Jenkins, 1998; Sunday, 2015; Thompson, 2017), and exemplified in the practice of preschool education in Reggio Emilia (New, 2007; Parnell, 2011; Pohio, 2009; Rinaldi, 2006). The most dramatic changes that have occurred in research on early childhood art and art education involve changes of perspective or theoretical orientation. As our understanding of young children and of the content and contexts of art education have continued to evolve, different forms and emphases have emerged as priorities in art education research.

Art education's relationship to early childhood practice is historically close and often beset by difficulty. Art educators seldom teach young children directly, although the establishment of preschool programs in public schools, and interest in the role of the *atelierista* (Vecchi, 1998), has changed this situation to some extent, in some communities. Indeed, many of the art educators who have worked most closely with young children, and who have written about those experiences, entered early childhood classrooms as researchers, often simultaneously working with those who are actually doing the teaching (see, e.g., Schulte, 2011; Sunday, 2017; Tarr, 1995; Taunton & Colbert, 2000; Thompson, 1999, 2002, 2003; Thompson & Bales, 1991; Trafi-Prats, 2012). Art education in early childhood classrooms continues to depend primarily on early childhood specialists (Baker, 1994), who sometimes rely on advice provided by art educators through publication or teaching. This means, among many other things, that art educators are often outside observers in the early childhood settings where their research takes place, and seldom in a position to submit their ideas directly to the test of practice. This may account for a tendency, apparent in research on children's art from the beginning of its history, to wrap descriptions of child art in prescriptions for practice, to offer educational advice extrapolated from psychological study (see, e.g., Kellogg, 1970; Luquet, 1927/2001; Matthews, 2002). This advice was frequently motivated by a desire to preserve children's art in the most unadulterated state possible. Fortunately, this tendency seems to be muted as researchers enter classrooms with the intention of viewing children's art making and response as "social practice" (Pearson, 2001) in action, and confront the urgency of formulating advice for teachers that is sound, practical, and clearly articulated.

> As Wilson (1997) points out, Child "art" is a product of the modernist era. To the modernist art educator and psychologist, artistic development was essentially a natural unfolding process that led to individual expression. This belief was not unlike the preferred modernist view of the artist as an individual with the obligation, perhaps the moral imperative, to develop a unique style of expression unconstrained by artistic convention.
>
> (p. 82)

But, Wilson continues, child art, like all art, is an "open concept" (Weitz, 1959, pp. 145–156), defined and redefined in response to changing conditions: "objects and events become child art when they are so interpreted" (Wilson, 1997, p. 81). The boundaries of art continually expand, as new media, new experiences, and new technologies and understandings become available. The emergence of photography projects for children (Ewald & Lightfoot, 2001; Kelly, 2014; McClure, 2018; Tarr & Kind, 2016; Wiseman, Makinen, & Kupiainen, 2016) and video as a medium for telling stories in (and about) the classroom (Brooks, 2006; Clark, 2011; Eckhoff, 2015; Grace & Tobin, 2002; McClure, 2010, 2011a, 2013; Robson, 2011; Trafi-Prats, 2012) are examples of approaches to art making that fundamentally alter the circumstances in which children experience themselves as artists. As new approaches continue to emerge and circumstances evolve, it is important to continually think in new ways about the child's interests and interactions, and of the complexities of knowing, being, and working together in the world (Knight, 2018; Mangen, 2010; McClure & Sweeny, 2015; Sakr, 2017b; Schulte & Thompson, 2018; Terreni, 2011). Wilson acknowledges that understanding child art inevitably requires interpretation, and that, this phenomenon, historically and persistently of interest to so many different constituencies, cannot help but mean different things to different people: "When individuals with different sets of interests and values interpret children's objects differently, those objects are transformed into very different things, things that are sometimes works of art and sometimes not" (Wilson, 1997, p. 82). The world of art, the world of education, and the world of the child provide distinct perspectives on the same phenomenon, and each perspective, on its own, may well conceal as much as it reveals.

The attitudes we hold toward children's art and art experience are inevitably conditioned by prevailing cultural beliefs about art and childhood (Korzenik, 1981; Leeds, 1989; Wilson, 1997), beliefs that are shaped by things seen and discussions heard through the media, in our daily conversations with colleagues and service station attendants and our children's teachers, or in the more rarified conversations that occur in the "official" art worlds of galleries, museums, and critical reviews, and the equally heady realms of educational research and theory. At one time, in the middle of the twentieth century, the lush easel paintings produced by preschool children were prized, both by artists who saw in them an enviable freedom of gesture and a complete indifference to the task of representing tangible objects and scenes, and by psychologists and educators who saw them as evidence of a healthy confidence and exuberant well-being. More recently, interest in the narrative dimensions of children's art emerged among artists and critics, coinciding with increased attention among educators to the role of drawing in the "prehistory" of writing (Vygotsky, 1962; see also, Chang & Cress, 2013; Mackenzie & Veresov, 2013; McArdle & Wright, 2014) and in the process of meaning making in which young children

are constantly engaged (Wilson & Wilson, 1982/2009). These values, absorbed from our culture in the process of living, affect the kinds of experience teachers provide for children, and the interests researchers bring to the classrooms where these experiences are pursued. Neither childhood nor art is a simple or static concept: Neither is amenable to stable or enduring definition in a manner that will stand the test of time or transfer, intact, from one context to another. In the early decades of the twenty-first century, the primary focus of research in early art education, defined in the broadest possible terms, is the process through which children learn to represent and to read the world by means of visual images. As it has been throughout its history, early childhood art remains an object of scholarly attention for psychologists, art educators, and early childhood specialists, artists, and art historians, and has an immediate practical interest for parents and teachers. These multiple perspectives, diverse as they often are, converge in three broad, overlapping categories – development, context, and curriculum (Bresler & Thompson, 2002) – that provide organization to the remainder of this discussion.

Development: Questioning Traditional Views

For much of the twentieth century, a model of "natural development" prevailed in discussions of child art, describing an innate and universal process with children "located in one of several stages, which are internally consistent, formally logical and intellectually revealing" (Freedman, 1997, p. 95). These stages of artistic development, as outlined by Luquet (1927; Costall, 2001), Lowenfeld (1957), and others (see, e.g., Kerschensteiner, 1905; Ricci, 1894), were supported by psychobiological explanations. Based upon the "presupposition of innate ability" (Atkinson, 2002, p. 7), stage theory encouraged the belief that artistic competence unfolds predictably from within the individual child, given the most minimal encouragement. Landmarks along the path of artistic development were labeled differently and sometimes described in terms that varied, if only slightly, from one researcher to the next. Puzzling detours and derailments of the process in its later stages were noted. However, the journey's destination remained constant: Children were developing toward the capacity to draw realistically, to capture visual likeness on the drawing page, to create convincing two-dimensional versions of a three-dimensional world.

Two assumptions underlying the traditional model of artistic development have come into question since the 1980s. Doubts initially raised by Wilson and Wilson (1982), Wolf and Perry (1988), and others about two elements of developmental theory – (1) the idea that representational accuracy is the sole or universal endpoint of the process of artistic development, and (2) the belief that benign neglect was the most favorable ground in which this process would unfold – have been confirmed by subsequent research (Bentley, 2011; Knight, 2013a; Sakr, 2017b).

Questioning the Standard of Realism

Although few researchers in art education overtly acknowledge their debt to Piaget, the research and theory of artistic development, from Lowenfeld to the present day, has emerged in dialogue with Piagetian assumptions (Atkinson, 2002; Brooks, 2003), as informed by the work of French theorist Georges Luquet (1913, 1927). Though Piaget rarely wrote directly about artistic development, in his occasional statements on the matter, he admitted how puzzling he found children's drawings, in their defiance of the expected trajectory of skills developing toward increased refinement in middle childhood, and in their deviations from realistic representation.

The aspects of child art that provoked Piaget continue to puzzle researchers, leading to questions concerning both the validity of the original developmental descriptions, and their continued viability in contemporary culture (see, e.g., Kindler & Darras, 1997; Thompson, 2003; Walsh, 2002; Wilson, 1997; Wilson & Wilson, 1977, 1982; Wolf & Perry, 1988). These critiques frequently penetrate to the most basic assumptions of developmental theory. Kindler and Darras (1997), for example, point out that stage theories of artistic development define art too narrowly, focusing primarily on children's drawings, and excluding or ignoring large swaths of behavior that are considered artistic in contemporary practice, including many of the art works that children make for their own purposes and pleasure. They argue that stage theories of artistic development are too linear and monofocal to account for the multiple symbolic languages that children accumulate as they grow. They suggest instead that it is the distinctive "repertoires" (Wolf & Perry, 1988) that children acquire that allow them to choose between different styles of drawing as the occasion warrants (Bremmer & Moore, 1984; Kindler, 1999, 2010).

Particularly problematic is the traditional emphasis on realistic representation as the single, desirable end-point of artistic development (Barrett & Light, 1976; Golomb, 2002, 1992/2004; Willats, 1997). This assumption is questionable from the standpoint of both Western and world art where expression and narrative frequently surpass realistic rendering as the primary concerns of visual representation. As psychologist Claire Golomb (1992) remarks, in elevating photorealistic likeness to the pinnacle of artistic achievement, "we mistake a style valued by our culture for an intrinsic phase of human development" (p. 46).

Young children fare badly in the face of "a hypothesized standard of realism," when their efforts to represent some aspect of their experience in the world, presumably intended to be realistic, are, almost inevitably, "declared... deficient". When research begins with this perspective on the nature of representation, deviations from reality are seen as evidence of conceptual immaturity. Golomb suggests that this notion has been adopted rather uncritically by Piagetians, neo-Piagetians, and the British school of researchers (e.g., Cox, 1992; Freeman, 1980; Freeman & Cox, 1985) who examine task demands and production deficits in children's drawings.

Yet these researchers examined issues of graphic representation in ways that acknowledged the complexity of factors contributing to that process. For example, Cox (1992, 1993, 1997; Freeman & Cox, 1985) offers a variation of the "production deficit hypothesis" (Golomb, 2002, p. 13) originally proposed by Freeman (1980; Freeman & Cox, 1985), a theory that looks to children's inexperience in drawing, rather than their conceptual deficits, to explain the problems they encounter when they attempt to compose a drawing. Attempting to explain why children's drawings of the same object may vary according to the task proposed to them, the intentions the child brings to the task, and the child's engagement in the process, Cox suggests that the child's internal mental model mediates between immediate perception, prior knowledge of the object, and the drawing currently appearing on the page. This conclusion is compatible with a theory of drawing developed by Wilson and Wilson (1977), which substitutes the notion that children develop and choose among multiple "drawing programs" for Lowenfeld's proposal that young children slowly develop and gradually modify schemas for each of the objects they draw and for the arrangement of those objects within the space of a drawing (Freedman, 1997, p. 101). While Wilson and Wilson recognize the importance of small incremental changes in children's drawings, and the potential of simultaneously developing drawing programs, repertoires, and end-points (Wolf & Perry, 1988), however, Cox continues to regard the realistic vantage of the "view-centered" representation as the more advanced, and hence desirable, destination for children's drawing (Cooke, Griffin, & Cox, 1998).

Matthews (1999) raises the question, "What does it mean to talk about 'the way things really look'? What is the true shape of a cat or a cloud?" (p. 5). Influenced by the theoretical perspective of Arnheim, Golomb offers a perspective on children's artistic experience as a gradual process of differentiation, in which structures acquire greater fluidity, complexity, and detail as the intentions children bring to drawings change and the range of graphic strategies at their disposal expands. She adopts an inclusive definition of representation in order to acknowledge the centrality and the difficulty of the task children undertake in drawing and other symbolic activities:

> Representation is a constructive mental activity; it is not a literal or exact imitation or copy of the object, although the perceiver may, at times, find a resemblance striking or even deceptive. Representation in this sense is a major biological, psychological, and cultural achievement.
>
> (Golomb, 2002, p. 5)

Atkinson (2002) ponders the extent to which the "natural attitude" (p. 34) toward representation is perpetuated and enforced through teaching practice at all educational levels. As he notes, this presumption creates a self-fulfilling prophecy in art education: "in valuing particular traditions of practice it attempts to reproduce them and thus perpetuate a particular cultural hegemony towards practice and understanding in art education" (p. 35).

Following this significant period of unrest in terms of understanding children's artistic development, there emerged an increasing attraction to a "sociological perspective on development" (Freedman, 1997). This period was marked by an interest in retaining the sense that children's actions have "an internal structure and systematicity" (Matthews, 1999, p. 6), while acknowledging those factors in each child's environment and experience that may alter that internal structure and modify its systems of operation in ways that distinguish the artistry of a particular child (Thompson, 1999).

Sociocultural Perspectives: Development as Learning

Despite the caution they introduce about reliance on traditional stage theories of development, Kindler and Darras (1997) remark that existing descriptions of the earliest stages of children's art making, particularly the prerepresentational phase typically referred to as the "scribbling stage," seem to be relatively reliable. They note that stage theories tend to become increasingly unstable as children reach the middle school years and descend into the trough of the U-curve described by Gardner (1982) and others (Davis, 1997). At the same time, there is growing evidence that preschool art, even in these earliest moments, is culturally conditioned and socially influenced (Alland, 1983; Deans & Brown, 2008; Kukkonen & Chang-Kredl, 2018; Matthews, 1999; Robinson, 2001; Wood & Hall, 2011). The most basic configurations of marks made on paper often reflect the prevailing aesthetic of a child's cultural surround. As Kindler and Darras (1997) observe, this recognition of the malleability of the artistic process renders reliance on stage theories problematic, since "Stage theories are founded on a culture-free assumption and either neglect to consider the implications of the cultural and social context, or view any extraneous influences as detrimental to the natural, biologically defined process of development" (p. 19). The significance of sociocultural factors, recognized by many researchers engaged in cross-cultural study of children's drawings early in the twentieth century (cf. Paget, 1932, for example), was downplayed by researchers intent on emphasizing the universality of child art (Golomb, 1992; Kellogg, 1970). However, as Kindler and Darras (1997) point out, those who are reluctant to admit exceptions to the rules of a universal language of child art are forced to minimize and discount obvious cultural and individual differences in children's drawings. In a manner congruent with a more general post-Piagetian perspective (Inagaki, 1992), the existence and significance of these individual and cultural variations are increasingly recognized and addressed in art education research (Kindler, 1994; Thompson & Bales, 1991; Wilson & Wilson, 1977, 1982, 1984, 1985).

Interest in social, cultural, and individual variations on the themes of artistic development has existed from the beginning of the study of child art. In the introduction to his translation of Luquet's *Le Dessin Enfantin* (1927), Costall (2001) emphasizes Luquet's recognition that children make choices in the act of drawing: "The young child chooses intellectual realism… Intellectual realism is not something the child 'undergoes' as a preliminary to visual realism. It reflects a 'reasonable' commitment to an alternative *ideal* of what a drawing should be" (pp. xvii–xviii), and persists as "a serious and enduring option" (p. xix) for image making throughout life. Following what Costall (2001) describes as an initial "frenzy for amassing vast collections of drawings, usually with the help of school teachers, but [with] the researchers seldom [having] anything to do with the children themselves" (pp. vii–viii), the study of child art has gravitated toward studies that are smaller in scale, often taking the form of longitudinal case studies, or, more recently, observations of classrooms and children working within them (see, e.g., Edens & Potter, 2004; Karlsson, 2011; Kendrick & McKay, 2004; Richards, 2009; Tan & Gibson, 2017; Thompson, 2009; Wright, 2014; Yamada-Rice, 2010). There has been substantial interest at certain historical moments in children's responses to works of art and other visual phenomena, topics that have also been studied both through formal experimentation and informal methods of observation (Acer & Omerroolu, 2008; Argent, 2016; Baroutsis, Kervin, Woods, & Comber, 2017; Dockett, Main, & Kell, 2011; Eckhoff, 2008; Kisidaa, Bowenb, & Greene, 2017; Kocamanoglu & Acer, 2015). Although traditional experimental designs are still employed, particularly in psychological approaches to the study of child art (Bland, 2012; Brown, Garnett, Velasquez-Martin, & Mellor, 2017; Kim & Jung, 2017; Sonter & Jones, 2018), qualitative approaches to research in early childhood art education have become increasingly prevalent.

Context

Much of the impetus for these changes in thinking about early art education derives &&from the unavoidable recognition of changes in the circumstances of young children's lives, which has, in many and complex ways, brought the education of young children back into the realm of art educators' responsibility. As increasing numbers of young children began to spend their days in the company of unrelated adults and peers, in preschools and daycare settings, the opportunities for art educators and researchers to work directly with young children or with their teachers multiplied rapidly. As a direct result, researchers concerned with early childhood art have begun to look at children in context (Hope, 2018; Hsiao, 2010; Kinnunen & Einarsdottir, 2013; Soundy & Drucker, 2010), learning to draw and to make sense of images in classrooms (Cabral, 2018; Kim, 2018; Pramling Samuelsson, Sheridan, & Hansen, 2013), homes, and neighborhoods (e.g., Richards, 2014, 2018; Trafi-Prats, 2008, 2012, 2017, 2018), with the help of other children and teachers as well as parents. The domesticated childhood, and the solitude of early artistic ventures that were assumed in earlier studies can no longer be considered the norm for young children in North America nor much of the world.

Young children's formal introductions to art experience frequently occur in contexts that are structured, social and school-like, making early art education an issue of equal importance to teachers and to parents. As art educators' contact with young children has increased, it has also become apparent that even the youngest among them bring prior aesthetic experiences and values to school, preferences developed through interactions with friends and family, established attachments to certain images and objects, and constant exposure to visual culture, including "art for children" (Blank, 2012; Bresler, 2002; Gibson & Mcallister, 2005; Lin & Thomas, 2002; Walsh, 2002).

With this recognition of the fluidity of demographic and sociological patterns has come an understanding that contemporary children and circumstances "no longer fit the existing explanations" (Graue & Walsh, 1998, p. 33). James et al. (1998) note that the conceptions of childhood that inform educational thought and practice are subject to rapid and radical change within a culture, as they are to marked variations among cultures. Many of the assumptions we hold dear about young children, the conventional wisdom we exchange in daily conversations and professional discourse, do not withstand close scrutiny, as Jenkins (1998) observes:

> Our grown-up fantasies of childhood as a simple space crumble when we recognize the complexity of forces shaping our children's lives and defining who they will be, how they will behave, and how they will understand their place in the world.
>
> (p. 4)

As Duncum (2002) suggests, "children never were what they were" (p. 97). And child art, like childhood itself, is, was, and always will be an interpreted phenomenon, a construction of adult understanding. Recognizing this, we are obliged to become conscious of the interests that accompany us when we watch children making art, and to attempt to look more closely both at the child and the context in which he or she works: "If we are to understand child art we must look at what the child has represented and expressed, the conditions under which child art is made, and ourselves and others in the act of studying it" (Wilson, 1997, p. 83).

Among the most dramatic effects of this attention to the contexts of early art experience has been the recognition that much that was accepted as established knowledge about child art may no longer pertain to children's art when it is understood as a "social practice" (Pearson, 2001, p. 348). Previous research concentrated primarily upon analysis of the products or "artifactual residue" of the art-making process, and often involved experimental procedures, designed quite deliberately to require children to grapple with problems that they would not attempt in their spontaneous drawings (e.g., Freeman & Janikoun, 1972; Willats, 1977). Matthews (1999) points out that "Studies of children's art and drawing based solely upon experimental data always distort descriptions of development" (p. 3) for this reason. Matthews' own research relies heavily on naturalistic observational work, both with his own children at home and in classrooms in London and Singapore. He notes, however, that some experimental studies are useful in illuminating issues that are difficult to observe in naturalistic settings. Costall (2001) indicates that Luquet, working early in the twentieth century, shared this conviction that direct observation was a far more appropriate and informative method for the study of children's art than formal experimentation.

Pearson, among others (Einarsdottir, Dockett, & Perry, 2009; Leeds, 1986; Schulte, 2013, 2015a, 2015b, 2015c, 2016; Soundy, 2012; Thompson, 1997; Thompson & Bales, 1991), argues that children's reasons for making art can and should be distinguished from the products of that activity. The collection and analysis of children's drawings is an engrossing pursuit: Children's works, treated as archeological artifacts, can and do yield intriguing information. Not only does analysis of drawings inform us about the construction of visual images, but, approached from a more postmodern perspective (see, e.g., Gamradt & Staples, 1994; Rogers, 2018; Schulte, 2018a, 2018b, 2018c; Wangmo, 2018), it also promises insight into children's interests and concerns. As Pearson points out, however, children's drawings have typically been used in attempts to understand something that is not "children drawing," whether that is the nature of their experience at school or at home, or the ways in which they conceptualize and represent hierarchies of value or relationships among objects arrayed in space. Pearson's critique articulates a shift in thinking more profound, even, than the movement toward direct observation of drawing events, a trend that recognizes the layers of information that become available when researchers witness a drawing being made and the contextual influences that are enfolded in the final product. He points toward a movement beyond the consideration of children's drawings as developmental evidence, toward research that attempts to document the child's lived experience of making images, often within the mediated social space of a classroom or peer culture. The timeworn adage that advises teachers of young children to focus on the art process, rather than the product, applies to this more contextualized approach to research, with the qualification that the products of children's activity are frequently important as the documentation and embodiment of that process (Knight, 2013a; Schulte, 2011; Wilson & Thompson, 2007; Wright, 2003, 2005, 2007).

Pearson suggests further that traditional research, by insisting that drawing is a universal activity among young children, has failed to recognize the indisputable fact that some children, and many adults, do not draw. Pearson suggests that the reasons children choose to draw, or not to draw, are complex and heavily reliant on context:

> Whatever value drawing has for children is bound to the context in which it takes place, and as the context shifts so does the value. This is why drawing can be play activity,

narrative activity, a measured strategy for social approval, or the equally measured pursuit of the inductively grasped competence appropriate to given representation systems. Drawing is also a strategy for coping with boredom, with isolation. It can be a retreat from violent social relations. It can be the means for pursuing a passionate interest in horses or trains which at the same time achieves some or all of the above ends.

(pp. 357–358)

Pearson suggests that research on children drawing should move away from examinations of the documents that result from that process toward the individual and situational factors that prompt children to make the choice to engage in that activity in the first place. Walsh (2002) cautions that children are unable to create "artistic selves" in the absence of opportunity, the availability of materials and models and the time to explore them, and the encouragement to do so. Pearson suggests that, when these conditions are in place, we may learn a great deal about the nature of art experience and its role in "good human functioning" (Arnheim, 1997, p. 11) by studying those children who do not take advantage of these opportunities as closely as those who do.

The concept that there are "varieties of visual experience" (Feldman, 1992) in which children participate is by no means new. Lark-Horovitz, Lewis, and Luca (1973) articulated subtle but significant differences in the content, form, and agency involved in spontaneous, voluntary, directed, and copied or to-be-completed works fifty years ago, and discussions of the characteristics and relative merits of school art and spontaneous children's art that begin with Wilson (1974) and Efland (1976, 1983) continue today (Anderson & Milbrandt, 1998; Bresler, 1992, 1994, 2002; Hamblen, 2002). Contemporary research concentrates both on children's "directed" work, made in response to an adult request, usually with a topic specified (Chang, 2012; MacDonald, 2013; Ulker, 2012), and on their independent or "voluntary" drawings (Thompson, 1997, 2015). Research has identified clear differences between "spontaneous and scaffolded" (Boyatzis, 2000, p. 15) drawings, leading Boyatzis to recommend that both the actual developmental level demonstrated in "spontaneous" drawings and the proximal developmental level attained in drawings made with instruction should be considered in evaluations of a child's developmental level:

perhaps artistic skill level ought to be conceived not only in terms of either the modal (functional) drawing level or the highest (optimal) level. Rather artistic skill may be better conceptualized as that range of symbolic flexibility between the two.

(p. 15)

Drawing Together: Social Context and Child Art

As early as 1979, Cocking and Copple noted that the "exposure to others" that occurs as children draw together expands children's conceptions of what is possible in drawing. For many years, partially due to the limited opportunities

available to art educators to study young children in groups, the implications of this observation remained unexplored. Still operating under the deeply ingrained cultural wisdom that defines artistic practice in general, and early artistic practice in particular, as highly individualized, unpredictable, and immune to influence, researchers frequently treated as extraneous any interactions that did occur in the classrooms they were studying. "Many accounts of the development of children's drawing seem to assume that some of the children's actions…are simply irrelevant to drawing proper" (Matthews, 1999, p. 5). Now, as Boyatzis and Watson (2002) suggest, there is a growing tendency to see "social and symbolic processes" (p. 1) entwined in early artistic experiences.

The movement toward adoption of a Vygotskian perspective in both art education practice and research during the latter part of the twentieth century supplanted more clearly Piagetian approaches used in earlier research (Brooks, 2003, 2005, 2009; Newton & Kantner, 1997; Thompson & Bales, 1991) and teaching. As Atkinson (2002) points out, a still more radical post-structural perspective views both the nature and culture positions as discourses which create particular versions of the child: "From a post-structural perspective, the Piagetian or Vygotskian child is not to be viewed as a natural or social entity but as an ideological product of particular discourses in which the child is constructed accordingly" (p. 6). No matter what its prospects for longevity of influence may be, the Vygotskian perspective is especially fruitful for art education research, particularly in regard to the attention it has drawn to peer learning as an almost inevitable, and desirable, fixture of classrooms in which children make art together (Zurmuehlen, 1990). Boyatzis and Albertini (2000) believe that peer influence reaches its maximum strength in middle childhood, when gender segregation, conformity, and criticality reach their peaks. However, the effects they describe are by no means absent from early childhood classrooms:

Many young children are inclined to accompany their actions with running commentaries that may be taken as conversational overtures, even when they are not intentionally addressed to another person (Anning & Ring, 2004; Mulcahy, 2002; Rech, 2018; Schulte, 2013; Thompson, 2002, 2009; Thompson & Bales, 1991). When children draw in the presence of peers, such private speech is frequently mistaken as a form of address that elicits an answer from another child. Many of the resulting comments, which may or may not evolve into conversations, tend to be evaluative, with one child offering an (often unsolicited) evaluation of the other's work or of the thought that is impelling that work forward. Cunningham (1997) observed that seven-year-olds tend to offer positive comments in situations such as this, and these unsolicited evaluations often lead to revisions. Teachers may be squeamish about the sometimes brutal honesty of the critical comments children exchange. Boyatzis and Albertini (2000) suggest that there is more good than harm to be found in such exchanges which they consider a primary benefit of children drawing together in the social space of the classroom:

> This image of artistic development as socially embedded is consistent with a Vygotskian model of development rather than one that characterizes the child as a solitary graphic problem solver. …Children surely draw alone, make stylistic choices independently, and undergo endogenous symbolic development. But our observations…point toward the value of conceptualizing children's drawing and artistic development as occurring within sociocognitive contexts that may function as a zone of proximal development in which the interpsychological is internalized… Surely children often draw alone, but even then they may benefit from hearing the internalized questions, evaluations, and suggestions of peers echoing from actual dyadic and group interaction.
>
> (pp. 45–46)

In line with contemporary reassessments of the developmental process in early art education, unprecedented attention has been paid to the necessity of adults and peers in structuring and supporting the process of learning to create and to respond to visual forms (Cutcher & Boyd, 2018; Eckhoff, 2013; Frisch, 2006; Kindler, 1995; Knight, 2013b; Thompson, 1995, 1997, 2009; Zurmuehlen, 1990). In spite of this increased attention to the desirable influence of teachers and peers in the emergence of early childhood art, few studies have focused on the role of parents as children's first art teachers. Exceptions include studies by Knight (2009), Braswell (2002), and Yamagata (1997).

Curriculum

It would not be surprising to find that neither the operational curriculum nor instructional practices in early childhood art education have kept pace with recommendations drawn from research and theory in recent years. What research would now suggest departs abruptly from the traditional wisdom long accepted as appropriate art education practice in early childhood settings. Art experiences are cherished by elementary and early childhood teachers as the last bastion of creative freedom in the schools (Bresler, 2002), a freedom threatened by art educators' recent insistence that art is a process which must be structured and scaffolded if it is to satisfy children's expectations, much less fulfill its educational potential.

Katz (1998) remarked that one of the lessons she had learned from her many visits to the preschools of Reggio Emilia was that young children can use graphic languages – drawing, painting, collage, construction – "to record their ideas, observations, memories, and so forth…to explore understandings, to reconstruct previous ones, and to co-construct revisited understandings of the topics investigated" (p. 20). This understanding of "art as epistemology" (Gallas, 1994, p. 130), as a way of "enabling children to know what they know," allows us to recognize and employ art in the classroom as a "method for examining his[her/their] world as well as his[her/their] means of externalizing what he[she/they]

was learning for others to share" (Gallas, 1994, p. 135). This interest in "drawing to learn" (Anning, 1999, p. 166) disrupts many strongly held beliefs about the young child as natural artist, and the role of the teacher in preserving that artistry untarnished by adult manipulation. It suggests not only that topics for drawings and painting can be assigned, but that experiences with art materials can, and perhaps should, be structured with both expressive and communicative purposes in mind. This approach to art as a symbolic language, the subject of considerable discussion in the waning decades of the last century, emphasizes the possibility of teachers helping children to develop facility in "the hundred languages" (Malaguzzi, 1998, p. 3) available to them, to master an expanded range of the tools and symbol systems (Vygotsky, 1978) that are used in their culture.

Equally as influential as the accumulating consensus of research and theory in affecting this radical shift in thinking about the nature of curriculum and instruction in early childhood art has been the example of Reggio Emilia. Although serious and sustained research on the theory and practice of art education in the preschools of Reggio Emilia continues to accumulate (see, e.g., Danko-McGhee & Slutsky, 2003; Fernández Santín & Feliu Torruella, 2017; Lindsay, 2015; Swann, 2008; Wexler & Cardinal, 2009), the work routinely produced by the children who benefit from that practice demonstrates unequivocally the possibility of exceptional sophistication in teaching and learning, and the range of artistic expression that is possible for young children who are encouraged to explore challenging content through visual forms.

The influence of Reggio Emilia is extensive, the questions it raises for early art education are profound and challenging. Pitri (2003) observed a university-based preschool in order to document the conceptual problem solving that occurred during art activities. She found that some conceptual problems were teacher-generated, in situations in which the teacher asked children to plan and to make choices. Child-generated conceptual problems emerged in response to interpersonal or practical challenges, e.g., in attempts to join an ongoing activity or negotiations about the sharing of art materials. Other problems were more substantive, "caused by children's representational or expressive challenges" (p. 20). Drawing upon previous research on the definition of problems during art activities, Pitri concluded that "Problem finding is related to being receptive to ideas and responding to changes in the environment" (p. 21). She noted that this approach is exemplified in the practice of Reggio Emilia (see, also, discussion of problem finding in Olsson, 2009).

Tarr (2003) sees in the "image of the child" maintained in the theory and practice of Reggio Emilia an opportunity to question the image that guides curriculum development and instructional practice in North American early art education:

> What images of children do we hold when we plan curriculum that follows accepted practices of studio, criticism and art history? Do we plan a different delivery system where

children individually recreate the art culture(s) they are in? When they have a discussion about a work of art, are they consuming culture or actively constructing understanding about the work that is unique to each child and to each group? Do we celebrate this construction, or do we try to replace it with cultural replication?

(p. 10)

This discussion occurs, however, within earshot of continuing debates regarding the relative merits of "unfolding or teaching" (Gardner, 1976) in early art education.

While this debate may no longer rest upon the question of whether adults should influence child art, as it once did, differences of opinion remain in regard to the nature and extent of that influence. Even this is a dramatic departure from the emphasis on "spontaneous self-instruction" (Froebel, in Kellogg, 1970, p. 62; see also McLennan, 2010) that long characterized understandings of "best practices" in early art education.

Kindler (1995) states, "Adult intervention may not only be useful, but essential to children's artistic learning" (p. 11), and others readily agree (Boyatzis, 2000; Chapman, 1978; Davies, 2014; Davis & Gardner, 1993; Frisch, 2006; Golomb, 1992; Reggio Children & Project Zero, 2001; Ring, 2006; Schulte, 2011; Thompson, 2009; Wilson, 2004, 2007). Even researchers long associated with traditional interpretations of the developmental process now advocate a more contextual approach to the understanding of art experience in childhood (Boyatzis, 2000; Gardner, 2017).

With this recognition of the importance of adult influence and the scaffolding of early artistic learning has come a conviction that direct instruction of young children is not only possible but desirable, as an element within a curriculum that is constructed to preserve independent exploration. This balance between teacher direction and children's agency, between "voluntary" and "directed" work (Lark-Horovitz et al., 1973), has been achieved in a number of programs and projects documented in recent literature (Grace & Tobin, 2002; Tarr, 2003), most notably in the educational programs originating in Reggio Emilia. And yet the concept remains controversial, both among teachers for whom the concept of directing young children's work with art materials defies the doctrine they were taught and have come to accept, and among researchers whose recommendations for teaching are more often appended as opinions than offered as corollaries of research (see, e.g., Matthews, 1999; Winner, 1989).

Several authors have pointed to the dangers inherent in these recommendations that teachers' involvement in early artistic learning increase. The difficulty of preserving children's choices, of reserving a space for the expression of ideas and experiences that matter most deeply to children, must be acknowledged (Tobin, 1995; Thompson, 2003). Writing about primary art education in the UK, Anning (1999) comments:

Though the technicalities and styles of learning how to draw are left to serendipity, the content of drawings in schools is clearly prescribed by teachers. Children learn that their drawings in schools must reflect teachers' views of 'childhood innocence' – nothing violent or unseemly – safe and sanitized portraits of 'people who help us' or observational drawings of pot plants or stuffed animals in glass cases borrowed from museums. In most primary classroom settings, as the children grapple with the conventions of 'school art,' their unofficial drawing about what really interests them goes underground.

(p. 170)

The conflict of values that underlies the situation Anning describes has to do with teachers' understanding of art and of children, as well as their sense of what may be appropriate (or comfortable) to discuss in an educational context. It also suggests that, after decades of insisting upon its disciplinary status, art remains on the margins of educational thought and practice, conceived as something other than the sturdy fabric of education, a decorative element that may enhance the garment but is in no way essential to its function. Although researchers involved with child art have long insisted that art is far more tightly interwoven in the fabric of human learning than contemporary Western culture tends to admit, the complex sociocultural and historical reasons for the peripheral position of art in North American schools and preschools remain to be fully explicated, widely understood, and revised in action.

Egan and Ling (2002) draw on Vygotsky to formulate an argument for the centrality of art education in early childhood learning. Its current marginalization, they suggest, is based upon acceptance of "a set of basic educational ideas that are mistaken" (p. 93), those ideas about young children that are so often taken for granted in casual conversation, including the presumption that children are egocentric and easily distracted. They point to the ways in which these shared understandings pervade research and pedagogy, as well, citing in particular the tenacity of the belief that intellectual development follows a path much like biological development, climbing continually onward toward greater complexity and facility. Continued reliance upon these unquestioned assumptions results in "a devaluation of both the preschool child's state of knowing and the cognitive area of artistic expression" (Davis, 1997, p. 54). Egan and Ling propose instead that some important intellectual capacities reach their peak in the early years of life and decline thereafter, a possibility recognized by Piaget and others who have speculated on U-shaped developmental trajectories in children's drawing. Identifying those things that young children do more easily than they will at any other time in their lives, Egan and Ling refer specifically to the ability to think imaginatively.

Arnheim (1997) suggests that

Child art, then, profits from being recognized as an inseparable aspect of good human functioning. No society can afford to ignore the fact that the capacity for behaving artistically is inherent in every human being and cannot be neglected without detriment to the individual and to society as a whole.

(11)

There is a growing recognition of the arts as intrinsically interdisciplinary. Goldberg (1997) suggests the limitations of an art-for-arts-sake model, which emphasizes the disciplinary integrity of the subject at the expense of severing its ties to other aspects of children's learning: "Students can learn about the arts, learn with the arts, and learn through the arts. The most familiar, most common, and least integrated experience students have with the arts is learning about them" (p. ix). Gallas (1994) suggests three ways to move the arts to a central position in the curriculum, by considering them as (1) methodologies for acquiring knowledge, (2) subjects of study, and (3) an array of expressive opportunities for communicating with others. She demonstrates these possibilities ably in her accounts of learning in her classrooms. Increasing interest in the role of the visual arts in/as components of "mulitliteracies" or "visual literacies" (McArdle, 2008, p. 273; see also Binder, 2011; Duncum, 2004; Narey, 2009; The New London Group, 1996; Ryan & Healy, 2008) builds upon the recognition of art and visual culture as potent but under-utilized languages in which young children may be particularly fluent. The wide "pictorial turn" occasioned by new modes of communication and information technologies in contemporary life, the acknowledged role of art making and visual imagery in early learning, and the intrinsic relationships among verbal, written, and graphic symbolic languages contribute to this growing interest in art as a form of learning (see, e.g., Bautista, Moreno-Nunez, Bull, Amsah, & Koh, 2018; DeFauw, 2016; Heydon, 2012; Souto-Manning & James, 2008). Several such studies focus on the role of the arts in educating young children challenged by poverty or life circumstances (e.g., Brown, Benedett, & Armistead, 2010; Hancock & Wright, 2018), while others consider the contributions of art experience to children's understandings of math, science, environmentalism, and other topics central to early childhood learning (e.g., Eckhoff, 2017, 2018; Ceppi, 2014). While these developments may offer the arts a more central and integrated presence in early childhood education, the possibility of relegating the visual to a supporting role in the transition to forms of literacy traditionally sanctioned by formal schooling persists. As McArdle (2008) observes, all too often, "Words like multiliteracies and visual literacies have replaced the word 'arts'" (p. 273).

Conclusion: Unanswered Questions and Emerging Issues

In the last decade, building on the work of scholars in cultural studies, the arts and humanities, and the social sciences more broadly, researchers in early art education and early childhood education have embraced the influence of the posthuman turn (e.g., Clark, 2014; Kind, 2010, 2015; Murris, 2016; Nxumalo, 2016; Pacini-Ketchabaw & Kummen, 2016; Trafi-Prats, 2017) – a theoretical orientation that recognizes matter as animated and agential, a move that both widens and diversifies considerably the picture of reality used to think children's lives and everyday practices. In taking this turn, researchers have continued to expose the "limiting pressures" (McClure, 2011a) of the developmental paradigm and its selective ways of framing the early art experiences of children (e.g., Craw, 2015; Osgood & Sakr, 2019; Schulte, 2017; Schulte & Thompson, 2018). But these spaces of critique have also given way to new questions and different forms of ethical practice, helping researchers to address the often-inarticulable ways that materials and young children – in early childhood spaces – transform each other (e.g., Kind, 2010, 2015; Pacini-Ketchabaw, Kind, & Kocher, 2016). Despite this and other shifts in perspective, which continue to pose challenges to some of the most basic assumptions that have underpinned modernist conceptions of childhood art, many of the perennial questions facing early art educators remain unresolved, even as new issues emerge. As in the past, these concerns also reflect changes in art worlds and cultural life, as well as changing viewpoints on childhood and education. One such issue, still largely unexamined in the research literature (but see Matthews, 1999), is the future of drawing and other traditional forms of artistic practice in an age of digital media. As Atkinson (2002) poses the question, "The contemporary explosion of new forms of visual expression and visual production in a variety of media almost begs the question how is it possible to understand or theorise art practice today, what does this term mean?" (p. 13). Future research in early childhood art must address these issues in an age in which imagery is arguably more ubiquitous and insistent than ever before. Closely related to this concern is the question of how early childhood education will, or should, be affected by the movement in art education toward the study of visual culture and, increasingly, digital visual culture and the aesthetics of children's "digital playscapes" (McClure, 2018) (see also, e.g., Knight, 2018; McClure, 2010; Mustola, 2018; Mustola, Koivula, Turja, & Laakso, 2018).

In much the same way that young children were neither seen nor heard in discussions of the discipline-based proposals of the 1980s and 1990s, early childhood education has been represented in ongoing discussions of visual culture primarily in the form of theory and proposals for practice. In research conducted thus far, the entry of popular media culture into the classroom has been a dominant concern. Thompson (2003, 2006) traces changes in the subject matter of children's voluntary drawings as they are increasingly influenced by visual culture – especially media and peer culture – producing idiosyncratic developmental trajectories quite different from those that describe the kinds of drawings we recognize as child art classics. Grace and Tobin (2002) describe a classroom video production, in which the unofficial interests of children shift to center stage, and document the choices children make as they begin to consider the sensibilities of their audience. Recent studies by Matthews and Seow (2009) and McClure (2007, 2009) suggest that young children readily adopt digital media as means of expression, finding that these tools and processes expand their thinking in ways that mirror and supplement more traditional media and materials (Swann, 2005). Interest in the application of digital technologies to research with young children is increasingly apparent, as researchers attempt to amplify children's role in the research process and the voices that are heard in research products (Kind, 2013; McClure, 2011b; Pink, 2001; Richards, 2009; Sakr, Connelly, & Wild, 2016; Thompson, 2009).

At the end of this period devoted to reconsideration and reconceptualization of the assumptions that have guided educators and researchers concerned with art experience in the early childhood years, the time for focused research activity, addressing issues of development, context, and curriculum, has arrived. There is a clear consensus in this large and loosely organized field that traditional answers no longer tell us much about contemporary childhood, that art itself has changed in ways that must be reflected, even in the preschool classroom. There is a need for increasingly situated studies of children making art and interpreting visual images in the company of other children and adults, in the contexts where significant learning about art occurs, in classrooms and community-based programs, families, and neighborhoods.

Note

1. Importantly, the dots that became rocks, eventually became eyes, which was the result of a conversation relating to how a Ninja Turtle's eyes peek out from the mask.

References

Acer, D., & Ömeroðlu, E. (2008). A study on the effect of aesthetic education on the development of aesthetic judgment of six-year-old children. *Early Childhood Education Journal, 35*(4), 335–334.

Alland, A., Jr. (1983). *Playing with form: Children draw in six cultures.* New York, NY: Columbia University Press.

Anderson, T., & Milbrandt, M. (1998). Authentic instruction in art: Why and how to dump the school art styles. *Visual Arts Research, 24*(1), 13–20.

Anning, A. (1999). Learning to draw and drawing to learn. *Journal of Art and Design Education, 18*(2), 163–172.

Anning, A., & Ring, K. (2004). *Making sense of children's drawings.* Berkshire, UK: Open University Press.

Arnheim, R. (1997). A look at a century of growth. In A. M. Kindler (Ed.), *Child development in art* (pp. 9–16). Reston, VA: National Art Education Association.

Atkinson, D. (2002). *Art in education: Identity and practice.* Boston, MA: Kluwer Academic Press.

Baker, D. (1994). Toward a sensible art education: Inquiring into the role of visual arts in early childhood education. *Visual Arts Research, 20*(2), 92–104.

Baroutsis, A., Kervin, L., Woods, A., & Comber, B. (2017). Understanding children's perspectives of classroom writing practices through drawings. *Contemporary Issues in Early Childhood.* doi:10.1177/146394 9117741743

Barrett, M. D., & Light, P. H. (1976). Symbolism and intellectual realism in children's drawings. *British Journal of Educational Psychology, 46*(2), 198–202. doi:10.1177%2F146394911774174

Bautista, A., Moreno-Núnez, A., Bull, R., Amsah, F., & Swee-Fuan, K. (2018). Arts-related pedagogies in preschool education: An Asian perspective. *Early Childhood Research Quarterly, 45*, 277–288.

Bentley, D. F. (2011). "I smile with my mind": Reconceptualizing artistic practice in early childhood. *Journal of Research in Childhood Education, 25*(2), 160–176.

Binder, M. (2011). Contextual worlds of child art: Experiencing multiple literacies through images. *Contemporary Issues in Early Childhood, 12*(4), 367–380.

Bland, D. (2012). Analysing children's drawings: Applied imagination. *International Journal of Research & Method in Education, 35*(3), 235–242.

Blank, J. (2012). Aesthetic education in the early years: Exploring familiar and unfamiliar personal-cultural landscapes. *Contemporary Issues in Early Childhood, 13*(1), 50–62.

Boyatzis, C. J. (2000). The artistic evolution of Mommy: A longitudinal case study of symbolic and social processes. In C. Boyatzis & M. W. Watson (Eds.), *Symbolic and social constraints on the development of children's artistic style* (pp. 5–30). San Francisco, CA: Jossey-Bass.

Boyatzis, C. J., & Albertini, G. (2000). A naturalistic observation of children drawing: Peer collaboration processes and influences in child art. In C. Boyatzis & M. W. Watson (Eds.), *Symbolic and social constraints on the development of children's artistic style* (pp. 31–48). San Francisco, CA: Jossey-Bass.

Boyatzis, C. J., & Watson, M. W. (Eds.). (2002). *Symbolic and social constraints on the development of children's artistic style.* San Francisco, CA: Jossey-Bass.

Braswell, G. (2001). Collaborative drawing during early mother-child interactions. *Visual Arts Research, 27*(2), 27–39.

Bresler, L. (1992). Visual art in the primary grades: A portrait and analysis. *Early Childhood Research Quarterly, 7*, 397–414.

Bresler, L. (1999). The hybridization and homogenization of school art: Institutional contexts for elementary art students. *Visual Arts Research, 25*(2), 25–37.

Bresler, L. (2002). School art as a hybrid genre: Institutional contexts for art curriculum. In L. Bresler & C. M. Thompson (Eds.), *The arts in children's lives: Context, culture, and curriculum* (pp. 169–183). Boston, MA: Kluwer Academic Press.

Bresler, L., & Thompson, C. M. (Eds.). (2002). *The arts in children's lives: Context, culture, and curriculum.* Boston, MA: Kluwer Academic Press.

Brooks, M. (2003). Drawing, thinking, meaning. *Tracey.* Retrieved from http://www.lboro.ac.uk/departments/ac/tracey/thin/brooks.html

Brooks, M. (2005). Drawing as a unique mental development tool for young children: Interpersonal and intrapersonal dialogues. *Contemporary Issues in Early Childhood, 6*(1), 8–91.

Brooks, M. (2006). Visual ethnography in the primary classroom. *Journal of Australian Research in Early Childhood Education, 13*(2), 67–80.

Brooks, M. (2009). What Vygotsky can teach us about young children's drawing. *International Art in Early Childhood Research Journal, 1*(1), 1–13.

Brown, E. D., Benedett, B., & Armistead, M. E. (2010). Arts enrichment and school readiness for children at risk. *Early Childhood Research Quarterly, 25*(1), 112–124.

Brown, E. D., Garnett, M. L., Velasquez-Martin, B. M., & Mellor, T. L. (2017). The art of Head Start: Intensive arts integration associated with advantage in school readiness for economically disadvantaged children. *Early Childhood Research Quarterly, 45*, 204–214.

Cabral, M. (2018). Fighting the Mad King: Play, art, and adventure in an early childhood art studio. In C. Schulte & C. Thompson (Eds.), *Communities of practice: Art, play, and aesthetics in early childhood* (pp. 77–91). Boston, MA: Springer.

Ceppi, G. (2014). A "widespread atelier" for exploring energy: "From wave to wave", a unique place where science, art, and design intersect and converge in an open and dynamic way. *Bank Street Occasional Paper Series, 2014*(31). Retrieved from https://educate.bankstreet.edu/occasional-paper-series/vol2014/iss31/7

Chang, N. (2012). What are the roles that children's drawings play in inquiry of science concepts? *Early Child Development and Care, 182*(5), 621–637.

Chang, N., & Cress, S. (2013). Conversations about visual arts: Facilitating oral language. *Early Childhood Education Journal, 42*(6), 415–422.

Chapman, L. (1978). *Approaches to art in education.* New York, NY: Harcourt Brace Jovanovich.

Cinquemani, S. (2014). Entering the secret hideout: Fostering newness and space for art and play. *Bank Street Occasional Paper Series, 2014*(31).

Retrieved from https://educate.bankstreet.edu/occasional-paper-series/vol2014/iss31/2

Cinquemani, S. (2018). Artistic encounters: Ethical collaborations between children and adults. In C. M. Schulte & C. M. Thompson (Eds.), *Communities of practice: Art, play, and aesthetics in early childhood* (pp. 61–76). Cham, Switzerland: Springer.

Clark, A. (2011). Breaking methodological boundaries? Exploring visual, participatory methods with adults and young children. *European Early Childhood Education Research Journal, 19*(3), 321–330.

Clark, V. (2014). Entanglements of neoliberal capitalism, whiteness, and technoculture in early childhood art encounters. *Power and Education, 6*(3), 318–326.

Cocking, R. R., & Copple, C. E. (1979). Change through exposure to others: A study of children's verbalizations as they draw. In M. K. Poulsen & G. I. Lubin (Eds.), *Piagetian theory and its implications for the helping professions (Proceedings, Eighth Interdisciplinary Conference, Vol. II)* (pp. 124–132). University Park: University of Southern California Press.

Cooke, G., Griffin, D., & Cox, M. (1998). *Teaching young children to draw.* Bristol, PA: Falmer Press.

Costall, A. (2001). Introduction. In G.-H. Luquet (Ed.), *Children's drawings (Le dessin enfantin)* (Trans. with introduction, by A. Costall) (pp. vii–xxiv). New York, NY: Free Association Books.

Cox, M. (1992). *Children's drawings.* New York, NY: Penguin Books.

Cox, M. (1993). *Children's drawings of the human figure.* Hove, UK: Lawrence Erlbaum.

Cox, M. (1997). *Drawings of people by the under-fives.* London, UK: Falmer.

Craw, J. (2015). Making art-matterings: Engaging with art in early childhood education, in Aotearoa New Zealand. *Journal of Pedagogy, 6*(2), 133–153.

Cunningham, A. (1997). Criteria and processes used by seven-year-old children in appraising art work of their peers. *Visual Arts Research, 23*(1), 41–48.

Cutcher, A., & Boyd, W. (2018). Preschool children, painting and palimpsest: Collaboration as pedagogy, practice and learning. *International Journal of Art & Design Education, 37*(1), 53–64.

Danko-McGhee, K., & Slutsky, R. (2003, July). Preparing early childhood teachers to use art in the classroom: Inspirations from Reggio Emilia. *Art Education, 60*(3), 12–18.

Davies, B. (2014). The affective flows of art-making. *Bank Street Occasional Paper Series, 2014*(31). Retrieved from https://educate.bankstreet.edu/occasional-paper-series/vol2014/iss31/3

Davis, J. (1997). The "U" and the wheel of "C": Development and devaluation of graphic symbolization and the cognitive approach at Harvard Project Zero. In A. M. Kindler (Ed.), *Child development in art* (pp. 45–58). Reston, VA: National Education Association.

Davis, J., & Gardner, H. (1993). The arts and early childhood education: A cognitive developmental portrait of the young child as artist. In B. Spodek (Ed.), *Handbook of research in early childhood education* (2nd ed.). New York, NY: Macmillan, pp. 191–206.

Deans, J., & Brown, R. (2008). Reflection, renewal and relationships: An ongoing journey in early childhood arts education. *Contemporary Issues in Early Childhood, 9*(4), 339–353.

DeFauw, D. L. (2016). Drawing children into reading: A qualitative case study of a preschool drawing curriculum. *Early Child Development and Care, 186*(4), 624–641.

Dockett, S., Main, S., & Kell, L. (2011). Consulting young children: Experiences from a museum. *Visitor Studies, 14*(1), 13–33.

Duncum, P. (2002). Children never were what they were: Perspectives on childhood. In Y. Gaudelius & P. Speiers (Eds.), *Contemporary issues in art education* (pp. 97–106). Upper Saddle River, NJ: Prentice-Hall.

Duncum, P. (2003). Theorising everyday aesthetic experience with contemporary visual culture. *Visual Arts Research, 28*(2), 4–15.

Duncum, P. (2004). Visual culture isn't just visual: Multiliteracy, multimodality, and meaning. *Studies in Art Education, 45*(3), 252–264.

Dyson, A. H. (1989). *Multiple worlds of child writers: Friends learning to write.* New York, NY: Teachers College Press.

Dyson, A. H. (2003). "Welcome to the jam". Popular culture, school literacy, and the making of childhoods. *Harvard Educational Review, 73*(3), 328–361. doi:10.17763/haer.73.3.d262234083374665. Retrieved from http://www.edreview.org/harvard03/fa03/f03dyson/htm

Eckhoff, A. (2008). The importance of art viewing experiences in early childhood visual arts: The exploration of a master art teacher's strategies for meaningful early arts. *Early Childhood Education Journal, 35*(5), 463–472.

Eckhoff, A. (2013). Conversational pedagogy: Exploring interactions between a teaching artist and young learners during visual arts. *Early Childhood Education Journal, 41*(5), 365–372.

Eckhoff, A. (2015). Ethical considerations of children's digital image-making and image-audiencing in early childhood environments. *Early Child Development and Care, 185*(10), 1617–1628.

Eckhoff, A. (2017). *Creative investigations in early mathematics.* Lewisville, NC: Gryphon House, Inc.

Edens, K., & Potter, E. (2004). "Yes, it's a good picture": Preschoolers' evaluation of their pictures. *Arts and Learning Research Journal, 20*(1), 85–109.

Efland, A. D. (1976). School art style: A functional analysis. *Studies in Art Education, 17*(2), 37–44.

Efland, A. D. (1983). School art and its social origin. *Studies in Art Education, 24*, 49–57.

Egan, K., & Ling, M. (2002). We begin as poets: Conceptual tools and the arts in early childhood. In L. Bresler & C. M. Thompson (Eds.), *The arts in children's lives: Context, culture, and curriculum* (pp. 93–100). Boston, MA: Kluwer Academic Press.

Einarsdottir, J., Dockett, S., & Perry, B. (2009). Making meaning: Children's perspectives expressed through drawings. *Early Child Development and Care, 179*(2), 217–232.

Ewald, W., & Lightfoot, A. (2001). *I wanna take me a picture: Teaching photography and writing to children.* Boston, MA: Beacon Press.

Feldman, E. B. (1992). *Varieties of visual experience.* Englewood Cliffs, NJ: Prentice Hall.

Fernández Santín, M., & Feliu Torruella, M. (2017). Reggio Emilia: An essential tool to develop critical thinking in early childhood. *Journal of New Approaches in Educational Research, 6*(1), 50–56.

Freedman, K. (1997). Artistic development and curriculum: Sociocultural learning considerations. In A. M. Kindler (Ed.), *Child development in art* (pp. 95–106). Reston, VA: National Art Education Association.

Freeman, N. H. (1980). *Strategies of representation in young children.* London, UK: Academic Press.

Freeman, N. H., & Cox, M. (1985). *Visual order.* London, UK: Academic Press.

Freeman, N. H., & Janikoun, R. (1972). Intellectual realism in children's drawings of a familiar object with distinctive features. *Child Development, 43*, 1116–1121.

Frisch, N. S. (2006). Drawing in preschools: A didactic experience. *International Journal of Art & Design Education, 25*(1), 74–85.

Gallas, K. (1994). *The languages of learning.* New York, NY: Teachers College Press.

Gamradt, J., & Staples, C. (1994). My school and me: Children's drawings in postmodern educational research and evaluation. *Visual Arts Research, 20*(1), 36–49.

Gardner, H. (1976). Unfolding or teaching? On the optimal training of artistic skills. In E. W. Eisner (Ed.), *The arts, human development, and education* (pp. 5–18). Berkeley, CA: McCutchan.

Gardner, H. (1982). *Art, mind, and brain.* New York, NY: Basic Books.

Gardner, H. (2017). Reflections on artful scribbles: The significance of children's drawings. *Studies in Art Education, 58*(2), 155–158. doi:10.1080/00393541.2017.1292388

Gibson, M., & Mcallister, N. (2005). BIG ART *small viewer*: A collaborative community project. *Contemporary Issues in Early Childhood, 6*(2), 204–208.

Goldberg, M. (1997). *Arts and learning.* New York, NY: Longman.

Golomb, C. (1992/2004). *The child's creation of a pictorial world*. Berkeley: University of California Press (2nd ed.) London, UK: Lawrence Erlbaum.

Golomb, C. (2002). *Child art in context: A cultural and comparative perspective*. Washington, DC: American Psychological Association.

Grace, D. J., & Tobin, J. (2002). Pleasure, creativity, and the carnivalesque in children's video production. In L. Bresler & C. M. Thompson (Eds.), *The arts in children's lives: Context, culture, and curriculum* (pp. 195–214). Boston, MA: Kluwer Academic Press.

Graue, M. E., & Walsh, D. J. (1998). *Studying children in context: Theories, methods and ethics*. Thousand Oaks, CA: Sage Publications.

Hamblen, K. (2002). Children's contextual art knowledge: Local art and school art context comparisons. In L. Bresler & C. M. Thompson (Eds.), *The arts in children's lives: Context, culture, and curriculum* (pp. 15–27). Boston, MA: Kluwer Academic Press.

Hancock, D. R., Wright, S. W. (2018). Enhancing early childhood development through arts integration in economically disadvantaged learning environments. *The Urban Review, 50*(3), 430–446.

Heydon, R. M. (2012). Multimodal communication and identities options in an intergenerational art class. *Journal of Early Childhood Research, 10*(1), 51–69.

Hope, A. (2018). Young children as curators. *International Journal of Art & Design Education, 37*(1), 29–40.

Hsiao, C-Y. (2010). Enhancing children's artistic and creative thinking and drawing performance through appreciating picture books. *International Journal of Art & Design Education, 29*(2), 143–152.

Inagaki, K. (1992). Piagetian and post-Piagetian conceptions of development and their implications for science education in early childhood. *Early Childhood Research Quarterly, 7*, 115–133.

James, A., Jenks, C., & Prout, A. (1998). *Theorizing childhood*. New York, NY: Teachers College Press.

Jeffers, C. (1993). A survey of instructors of art methods classes for pre-service elementary teachers. *Studies in Art Education, 34*(4), 233–243.

Jenkins, H. (Ed.). (1998). *The children's culture reader*. New York: New York University Press.

Kaplan, H. (2014). Visualizing spaces of childhood. *Bank Street Occasional Paper Series, 2014*(31). Retrieved from https://educate.bankstreet.edu/occasional-paper-series/vol2014/iss31/6

Karlsson, M. B. (2011). Pictures of spring: Aesthetic learning and pedagogical dilemmas in visual arts. In N. Pramling & I. P. Samuelsson (Eds.), *Educational encounters: Nordic studies in early childhood didactics* (pp. 85–104) (International perspectives on early childhood education and development, Vol. 4). Dordrecht, the Netherlands: Springer.

Katz, L. G. (1998). What can we learn from Reggio Emilia? In C. Edwards, L. Gandini, & G. Forman (Eds.), *The hundred languages of children: The Reggio Emilia approach– advanced reflections* (2nd ed., pp. 27–45). Westport, CT: Ablex Publishing.

Kellogg, R. (1970). *Analyzing children's art*. Palo Alto, CA: Mayfield Publishing Co.

Kelly, J. (2014). "See what I see": Photography as a window to children's meaning making. *Art in Early Childhood Research Journal*, (1), 1–18. Retrieved from http://artinearlychildhood.org/

Kendrick, M., & McKay, R. (2004). Drawings as an alternative way of understanding young children's constructions of literacy. *Journal of Early Childhood Literacy, 4*(1), 109–127.

Kerschensteiner, G. (1905). *Die Entwicklung der Zeichnerischen Begabung* [The development of drawing talent]. Munich, Germany: Carl Greber.

Kim, H. (2018).Towards a dialogic understanding of children's art-making process. *International Journal of Art & Design Education, 37*(1), 101–112.

Kim, K., & Jung, H. (2017). Effect of integrated art curriculum of exploration, expression and appreciation for young children on teaching efficacy of pre-service early childhood teachers. *International Information Institute (Tokyo) Information, 20*(4B), 2705–2718.

Kind, S. (2010). Art encounters: Movements in the visual arts and early childhood education. In V. Pacini-Ketchabaw (Ed.), *Flows, rhythms, and intensities of early childhood education curriculum* (pp. 113–131). New York, NY: Peter Lang.

Kind, S. (2013). Lively entanglements: The doings, movements and enactments of photography. *Global Studies of Childhood, 3*(4), 427–441.

Kind, S. (2015). Material encounters. *International Journal of Child, Youth and Family Studies 5*(4/2), 865–877.

Kind, S. (2018). Collective improvisations: The emergence of the early childhood studio as an event-full place. In C. M. Schulte & C. M. Thompson (Eds.), *Communities of practice: Art, play, and aesthetics in early childhood* (pp. 5–21). Cham, Switzerland: Springer.

Kindler, A. M. (1994). Artistic learning in early childhood: A study of social interactions. *Canadian Review of Art Education, 21*(2), 91–106.

Kindler, A. M. (1995). Significance of adult input in early artistic development. In C. M. Thompson (Ed.), *The visual arts and early childhood learning* (pp. 10–14). Reston, VA: National Art Education Association.

Kindler, A. M. (1999). "From endpoints to repertoires": A challenge to art education. *Studies in Art Education, 40*(4), 330–349.

Kindler, A. M. (2010). Art and art in early childhood: What can young children learn from "a/Art activities?" *Art in early childhood, 2*(1), 1–14.

Kindler, A. M., & Darras, B. (1997). Map of artistic development. In A. M. Kindler (Ed.), *Child development in art* (pp. 17–44). Reston, VA: National Art Education Association.

Kinnunen, S., & Einarsdottir, J. (2013). Feeling, wondering, sharing and constructing life: Aesthetic experience and life changes in young children's drawing stories. *International Journal of Early Childhood, 45*(3), 359–385.

Kisidaa, B., Bowenb, D. H., & Greene, J. P. (2017). Cultivating interest in art: Causal effects of arts exposure during early childhood. *Early Childhood Research Quarterly, 45*(4), 197–203. doi:10.1016/j.ecresq.2017.12.003

Knight, L. (2009). Mother and child sharing through drawing: Intergenerational collaborative processes for making artworks. *International Art in Early Childhood Research Journal, 1*(1), 1–12.

Knight, L. (2013a). Not as it seems: Using Deleuzian concepts of the imaginary to rethink children's drawings. *Global Studies of Childhood, 3*(3), 254–264.

Knight, L. (2013b). Small acts of resistance: The role of intergenerational collaborative drawing in early childhood teaching and learning. In F. McArdle & G. Boldt (Eds.), *Young children, pedagogy and the arts* (pp. 21–33). New York, NY: Routledge.

Knight, L. (2018). Digital aesthetics and multidimensional play in early childhood. In C. Schulte & C. Thompson (Eds.), *Communities of practice: Art, play, and aesthetics in early childhood* (pp. 133–151). (Landscapes: the arts, aesthetics, and education, Vol. 21). Dordrecht, The Netherlands: Springer.

Kocamanoglu, D. O., & Acer, D. (2015). Examining children's art products and determining their aesthetic judgment in a preschool classroom. *Journal of Education and Future, 7*, 1–16.

Korzenik, D. (1981, September). Is children's work art? Some historical view. *Art Education, 34*(5), 20–24.

Kukkonen, T., & Chang-Kredl, S. (2018). Drawing as social play: Shared meaning-making in young children's collective drawing activities. *International Journal of Art & Design Education, 37*(1), 74–87.

Lark-Horovitz, B., Lewis, H., & Luca, M. (1973). *Understanding children's art for better teaching* (2nd ed.). Columbus, OH: Charles E. Merrill.

Leeds, J. A. (1986). Teaching and the reasons for making art. *Art Education, 39*(7), 17–21.

Leeds, J. A. (1989). The history of attitudes toward child art. *Studies in Art Education, 30*(2), 93–103.

Lin, S. F., & Thomas, G. V. (2002). Development of understanding of popular graphic art: A study of everyday aesthetics in children, adolescents and young adults. *International Journal of Behavioral Development, 26*(3), 278–287.

Lindsay, G. (2015). Reflections in the mirror of Reggio Emilia's soul: John Dewey's foundational influence on pedagogy in the Italian educational project. *Early Childhood Education Journal, 43*(6), 447–457.

Lowenfeld, V. (1957). *Creative and mental growth* (3rd ed.). New York, NY: Macmillan.

Luquet, G. H. (1927). *Le dessin enfantin (The childish drawing)*. Paris, France: Alcan.

Luquet, G. H. (1927/2001). *Children's drawings* (Trans, with intro, by A. Costall). London, UK: Free Association Books.

MacDonald, A. (2013). Using children's representations to investigate meaning-making in mathematics. *Australasian Journal of Early Childhood, 38*(2), 65–73.

Mackenzie, N., & Veresov, N. (2013). How drawing can support writing acquisition: Text construction in early writing from a Vygotskian perspective. *Australasian Journal of Early Childhood, 38*(4), 22–29.

McArdle, F. (2008). Editorial. *Contemporary issues in early childhood, 9*(4), 273–274.

McArdle, F., & Piscatelli, B. (2002). Early childhood art education: A palimpsest. *Australian Art Education, 25*(1), 11–15.

McArdle, F., & Wright, S. (2014). First literacies: Art, creativity, play, constructive meaning-making. In G. M. Barton (Ed.), *Literacy in the arts: Retheorising learning and teaching* (pp. 21–38). Cham, Switzerland: Springer International Publishing.

McClure, M. (2007) Play as process: Choice, translation, reconfiguration, and the process of culture. *Visual Arts Research, 33*(65), 63–70.

McClure, M. (2009). Spectral childhoods and educational consequences of images of children. *Visual Arts Research, 35*(2), 91–104.

McClure, M. (2010). Digital visual childhood: Little kids, video, and the blogosphere. In R. Sweeny (Ed.), *Inter/actions/inter/sections: Art education in a digital visual culture* (pp. 20–29). Reston, VA: National Art Education Association.

McClure, M. (2011a). Child as totem: Redressing the myth of inherent creativity in early childhood. *Studies in Art Education, 52*(2), 127–141.

McClure, M. (2011b). ¡Pendejo! Preschoolers' profane play: Why children make art. *Journal of Social Theory in Art Education, 31*(1/25). Retrieved from https://scholarscompass.vcu.edu/jstae/vol31/iss1/6/

McClure, M. (2013). The Monster and Lover-Girl: Mapping complex relations in preschool children's digital video productions. *Studies in Art Education, 55*(1), 18–34. doi:10.1080/00393541.2013.11518914

McClure, M. (2018). Beyond screen time: Aesthetics of digital playscapes for young children. In C. M. Schulte & C. M. Thompson (Eds.), *Communities of practice: Art, play, and aesthetics in early childhood* (pp. 153–163). Dordrecht, The Netherlands: Springer.

McClure, M., & Sweeny, R. (2015). Participatory youth culture: Young children as media and MOC makers in a post-millennial mode. In K. L. Heider & M. R. Jalongo (Eds.), *Young children and families in the information age* (pp. 245–254). (*Advances in theory and research, implications for practice*, Vol. 10). Dordrecht, The Netherlands: Springer.

McLennan, D. M. P. (2010). Process or product? The argument for aesthetic exploration in the early years. *Early Childhood Education Journal, 38*(2), 81–85.

Malaguzzi, L. (1995, May). Your image of the child: Where teaching begins. *Child Care Information Exchange,* (96), 52–61.

Malaguzzi, L. (1998). No way: The hundred is there. In C. Edwards, L. Gandini, & G. Forman (Eds.), *The hundred languages of children: The Reggio Emilia approach – advanced reflections* (p. 3). Westport, CT: Ablex Publishing.

Mangen, A. (2010). Point and click: Theoretical and phenomenological reflections on the digitization of early childhood education. *Contemporary Issues in Early Childhood, 11*(4), 415–431.

Matthews, J. (1999). *The art of childhood and adolescence: The construction of meaning*. Philadelphia, PA: Falmer Press.

Matthews, J. (2002). Infancy. In E. Eisner & M. Day (Eds.), *Handbook of research in art education* (pp. 253–298). Mahwah, NJ: Lawrence Erlbaum Associates.

Matthews, J., & Seow, P. (2009). Electronic paint: Understanding children's representation through their interactions with digital paint. In S. Herne, S. Cox, & R. Watts (Eds.), *Readings in primary art education* (pp. 269–286). Bristol, UK: Intellect Books.

Mulcahy, C. (2002). Talking about art: Understanding children's perspectives. *Arts and Learning Research Journal, 18*(1), 19–35.

Murris, K. (2016). *The posthuman child: Educational transformation through philosophy and picturebooks*. New York, NY: Routledge.

Mustola, M. (2018). Children's play and art practices with agentic objects. In C. M. Schulte & C. M. Thompson (Eds.), *Communities of practice: Art, play, and aesthetics in early childhood* (pp. 117–131). Cham, Switzerland: Springer.

Mustola, M., Koivula, M., Turja, L., & Laakso, M. L. (2018). Reconsidering passivity and activity in children's digital play. *New Media & Society, 20*(1), 237–254.

Narey, M. (Ed.). (2009). *Making meaning: Constructing multimodal perspectives of language, literacy, and learning through arts-based early childhood education*. New York, NY: Springer.

New, R. (2007). Reggio Emilia as cultural activity: Theory in practice. *Theory into Practice, 46*(1), 5–13.

The New London Group. (1996). A pedagogy of multiliteracies: Designing social futures. *Harvard Educational Review, 66*(1), 60–92.

Newton, C., & Kantner, L. (1997). Cross-cultural research in aesthetic development: A review. In A. M. Kindler (Ed.), *Child development in art* (pp. 165–182). Reston, VA: National Art Education Association.

Nutbrown, C. (2013). Conceptualising arts-based learning in the early years. *Research Papers in Education, 28*(2), 239–263.

Nxumalo, F. (2016). Storying practices of witnessing: Refiguring quality in everyday pedagogical encounters. *Contemporary Issues in Early Childhood, 17*(1), 39–53.

Olsson, L-M. (2009). *Movement and experimentation in young children's learning: Deleuze and Guattari in early childhood education*. New York, NY: Routledge.

Osgood, J., & Sakr, M. (2019). *Postdevelopmental approaches to childhood art*. London, UK: Bloomsbury.

Pacini-Ketchabaw, V., Kind, S., & Kocher, L. (2016). *Encountering materials in early childhood education*. New York, NY: Routledge.

Pacini-Ketchabaw, V., & Kummen, K. (2016). Shifting temporal frames in children's common worlds in the Anthropocene. *Contemporary Issues in Early Childhood, 17*(4), 431–441.

Paget, G. W. (1932). Some drawings of men and women made by children of certain non-European races. *Journal of the Royal Anthropological Institute, 62*, 127–144.

Parnell, W. (2011). Revealing the experience of children and teachers even in their absence: Documenting in the early childhood studio. *Journal of Early Childhood Research, 9*(3), 291–309.

Pearson, P. (2001). Towards a theory of children's drawing as social practice. *Studies in Art Education, 42*(4), 348–365.

Pink, S. (2001). *Doing visual ethnography: Image, media and representation in research*. London, UK: Sage Publications.

Pitri, E. (2003). Conceptual problem solving during artistic representation. *Art Education, 56*(4), 19–23.

Pohio, L. (2009). Reggio Emilia pedagogy in early childhood education: How can this approach enhance visual arts experiences in New Zealand. *He Kupu, 2*(2), 10–18.

Pramling Samuelsson, I., Sheridan, S., & Hansen, M. (2013). Young children's experience of aesthetics in preschool. *Tidsskrift for Nordisk Barnehageforskning* (Nordic early childhood education research), *6*. doi:10.7577/nbf.457

Rech, L. (2018) "Now we all look like Rapunzels": Drawing in a Kindergarten writing journal. In C. Schulte & C. Thompson (Eds.), *Communities of practice: Art, play, and aesthetics in early childhood* (pp. 39–59). Cham, Switzerland: Springer.

Reggio Children & Project Zero. (2001). *Making learning visible: Children as individual and group learners*. Reggio Emilia, Italy: Reggio Children.

Ricci, C. (1894). L' Arte dei bambini. *Pedagogical Seminary, 3*, 302–307.

Richards, R. (2014). The private and public worlds of children's spontaneous art. *Studies in Art Education, 55*(2), 143–156.

Richards, R. (2018). Sensitive and supportive interactions: Tuning into children's requests for help during art-making. In C. Schulte & C. Thompson (Eds.), *Communities of practice: Art, play, and aesthetics in early childhood* (pp. 93–113). Cham, Switzerland: Springer.

Richards, R. D. (2007). Outdated relics on hallowed ground: Unearthing attitudes and beliefs about young children's art. *Australian Journal of Early Childhood Education, 32*(4), 22–30.

Richards, R. D. (2009). Young visual ethnographers: Children's use of visual ethnography to record, share and extend their art experiences. *International Art in Early Childhood Research Journal, 1*(1). Retrieved from http://artinearlychildhood.org/artec/images/article/ARTEC_2009_Research_Journal_1_Article_3.pdf

Rinaldi, C. (2006). *In dialogue with Reggio Emilia: Listening, researching and learning.* New York, NY: Routledge.

Ring, K. (2006). Supporting young children drawing: Developing a role. *International Journal of Education through Art, 2*(3), 195–209.

Robinson, K. (2001). *Out of our minds: Learning to be creative.* Oxford, UK: Capstone Publishing.

Robson, S. (2011). Producing and using video data in the early years: Ethical questions and practical consequences in research with young children. *Children & Society, 25*(3), 179–189.

Rogers, M. (2018). Listening to children's voices through art: Communication experiences and understandings in Mosaic research. *Art in Early Childhood, 2018*(1), 157–266.

Ryan, M. E., & Healy, A. H. (2008) 'Art'efacts of knowing: Multiliteracies and the arts. In A. H. Healy (Ed.), *Multiliteracies and diversity: New pedagogies for expanding landscapes* (pp. 82–101). South Melbourne, Australia: Oxford University Press.

Sakr, M. (2017a). *Digital technologies in early childhood art: Enabling playful experiences.* London, UK: Bloomsbury.

Sakr, M. (2017b). 'We're just gonna scribble it': The affective and social work of destruction in children's art-making with different semiotic resources. *Contemporary Issues in Early Childhood, 18*(2), pp. 227–239.

Sakr, M., Connelly, V., & Wild, M. (2016). "Evil Cats" and "Jelly Floods": Young children's collective constructions of digital art making in the early years. *Journal of Research in Childhood Education, 30*(1), 128–141.

Schulte, C. M. (2011). Verbalization in children's drawing performances: Toward a metaphorical continuum of inscription, extension, and re-inscription. *Studies in Art Education, 53*(1), 20–34.

Schulte, C. M. (2013). Being there and becoming-unfaithful. *International Journal of Education & the Arts, 14*(SI 1/5). Retrieved from http://www.ijea.org/v14si1/

Schulte, C. M. (2015a). Intergalactic encounters: Desire and the political immediacy of children's drawing. *Studies in Art Education, 56*(3), 241–256.

Schulte, C. M. (2015b). Lines of deterritorialization: The becoming-minor of Carter's drawing. *Studies in Art Education, 56*(2), 142–155.

Schulte, C. M. (2015c). Researching Anna's drawing: The pedagogical composition of concern. *Qualitative Inquiry, 21*(6), 546–553.

Schulte, C.M. (2016). Possible worlds: Deleuzian ontology and the project of listening in children's drawing. *Cultural Studies-Critical methodologies, 16*(2), 141–150.

Schulte, C. M. (2017). Possible worlds: Deleuzian ontology and the project of listening in children's drawing. *Cultural Studies? Critical Methodologies, 16*(2), 141–150.

Schulte, C. M. (2018a). Entering the milieus of children's drawing: Complicated proximities. *International Journal of Education & the Arts, 19*(SI 1.4). Retrieved from doi:10.18113/P8ijea19si04

Schulte, C. M. (2018b). The untimely death of a bird: A posthuman tale. In C. R. Kuby, K. Spector, & J. Johnson Thiel (Eds.), *Posthumanism and literacy education* (pp. 71–81). New York, NY: Routledge.

Schulte, C. M. (2018c). The will-to-research children's drawing. In C. Schulte & C. Thompson (Eds.), *Communities of practice: Art, play, and aesthetics in early childhood* (pp. 213–228). (Landscapes: The arts, aesthetics, and education, Vol. 21). Cham, SUI: Springer.

Schulte, C. M., & Thompson, C. M. (Eds.). (2018). *Communities of practice: Art, play, and aesthetics in early childhood.* Cham, Switzerland: Springer.

Sonter, L. J., & Jones, D. J. (2018). Drawing as a tool to support children's executive function in play. *Art in Early Childhood Research Journal, 2018*(1). Retrieved from http://artinearlychildhood.org/journals/2018/ARTEC_2018_Research_Journal_1_Article_6_Sonter.pdf

Soundy, C. S. (2012).Searching for deeper meaning in children's drawings. *Childhood Education, 88*(1), 45–51.

Soundy, C. S., & Drucker, M. F. (2010). Picture partners: A co-creative journey into visual Literacy. *Early Childhood Education Journal, 37*(6), 447–460.

Souto-Manning, M., & James, N. (2008). A multi-arts approach to early literacy and learning. *Journal of Research in Childhood Education, 23*(1), 82–95.

Sunday, K. E. (2012). "I'm going to have to draw it to find out": Children's drawing performances, knowing, and the formation of egocentric speech. *Art in Early Childhood Research Journal, 2012*(1). Retrieved from http://artinearlychildhood.org/journals/2012/ARTEC_2012_Research_Journal_1_Article_3_Sunday.pdf

Sunday, K. E. (2015). Relational making: Re/Imagining theories of child art. *Studies in Art Education, 56*(3), 228–240.

Sunday, K. E. (2017). Drawing as a relational event: Making meaning through talk, collaboration, and image production. In M. Narey (Ed.), *Multimodal perspectives of language, literacy, and learning in early childhood* (pp. 87–105). *Educating the young child (Advances in theory and research, implications for practice,* Vol. 12). Cham, Switzerland: Springer.

Sunday, K. E. (2018). Drawing and storytelling as political action: Difference, plurality and coming into presence in the early childhood classroom. *International Journal of Art & Design Education, 37*(1), 6–17.

Swann, A. (2005, July). The role of media and emerging representation in early childhood. *Art Education, 58*(3), 41–47.

Swann, A. (2008). Children, objects, and relations: Constructivist foundations in the Reggio Emilia approach. *Studies in Art Education, 50*(1), 36–50.

Tan, M., & Gibson, R. (2017). 'You feel like you're an artist. Like Leonardo da Vinci': Capturing young children's voices and attitudes towards visual arts. *International Journal of Education through Art, 13*(3), 295–315.

Tarr, P. (1995). Preschool children's socialization through art experiences. In C. M. Thompson (Ed.), *The visual arts and early childhood learning* (pp. 23–27). Reston, VA: National Art Education Association.

Tarr, P. (2003). Reflections on the image of the child: Reproducer or creator of culture. *Art Education, 56*(4), 6–11.

Tarr, P., & Kind, S. (2016). The gaze and the gift: Ethical issues when young children are photographers. In J. Moss & B. Pini (Eds.), *Visual research methods in educational Research* (pp. 251–266). London, UK: Palgrave Macmillan.

Taunton, M., & Colbert, C. (2000). Art in the early childhood classroom: Authentic experiences and extended dialogues. In N. J. Yelland (Ed.), *Promoting meaningful learning: Innovations in educating early childhood professionals* (pp. 67–76). Washington, DC: National Association for the Education of Young Children.

Terreni, L. (2011). Interactive whiteboards, art and young children. *Computers in New Zealand Schools: Learning, Teaching, Technology, 23*(1), 78–100.

Theil, J. J. (2018). 'A cool place where we make stuff': Co-curating relational spaces of muchness. In C. Schulte & C. Thompson (Eds.), *Communities of practice: Art, play, and aesthetics in early childhood* (pp. 23–37). Dordrecht, The Netherlands: Springer.

Thompson, C., & Bales. S. (1991). "Michael doesn't like my dinosaurs:" Conversations in a preschool art class. *Studies in Art Education, 33*(1), 43–55.

Thompson, C. M. (Ed.). (1995). *The visual arts and early childhood learning.* Reston, VA: National Art Education Association.

Thompson, C. M. (1997). Transforming curriculum in the visual arts. In S. Bredekamp & T. Rosegrant (Eds.), *Reaching potentials: Transforming early childhood curriculum and assessment* (pp. 81–98). Washington, DC: National Association for the Education of Young Children.

Thompson, C. M. (1999). Action, autobiography and aesthetics in young children's self-initiated drawings. *International Journal of Art & Design Education, 18*(2), 155–161.

Thompson, C. M. (2002). Drawing together: Peer influence in preschool-kindergarten art classes. In L. Bresler & C. M. Thompson (Eds.), *The arts in children's lives: Context, culture, and curriculum* (pp. 129–138). Boston, MA: Kluwer Academic Press.

Thompson, C. M. (2003). Kinderculture in the art classroom: Early childhood art and the mediation of culture. *Studies in Art Education, 44*(2), 135–146.

Thompson, C. M. (2006). The "ket aesthetic": Visual culture in childhood. In J. Fineberg (Ed.), *When we were young: New perspectives on the art of the child* (pp. 31–43). Berkeley: University of California Press.

Thompson, C. M. (2009). Mira! Looking, listening, and lingering in research with children. *Visual Arts Research, 35*(1), 24–34.

Thompson, C. M. (2015). Prosthetic imaginings and pedagogies of early childhood art. *Qualitative Inquiry, 21*(6), 554–561.

Thompson, C. M. (2016). The spaces between: Children, teachers, researchers, artists. *Visual Inquiry, 5*(1), 115–121.

Thompson, C. M. (2017). Listening for stories: Childhood studies and art education. *Studies in Art Education, 58*(1), 7–16.

Tobin, J. (1995, May). The irony of self-expression. *American Journal of Education, 103*, 233–258.

Trafi-Prats, L. (2008). A visual culture art education curriculum for early childhood teacher education: Re-constructing the family album. *International Journal of Art & Design Education, 27*(1), 53–62.

Trafí-Prats, L. (2012). Urban children and intellectual emancipation: Video narratives of self and place in the city of Milwaukee. *Studies in Art Education, 53*(2), 125–138. doi:10.1080/00393541.2012.11518857

Trafí-Prats, L. (2014). The existential territories of global childhoods: Resingularizing subjectivity through ecologies. *Bank Street Occasional Paper Series, 2014*(31). Retrieved from https://educate.bankstreet.edu/occasional-paper-series/vol2014/iss31/5

Trafí-Prats, L. (2017). Learning with children, trees, and art: For a compositionist visual art-based research. *Studies in Art Education, 58*(4), 325–334. doi:10.1080/00393541.2017.1368292

Trafí-Prats, L. (2018). Mothering as a feminist aesthetics of existence. In C. M. Schulte & C. M. Thompson (Eds.), *Communities of practice: Art, play, and aesthetics in early childhood* (pp. 197–211). (*Landscapes: The arts, aesthetics, and education*, Vol. 21). Cham, Switzerland: Springer.

Ulker, R. (2012). Turkish children's drawing of nature in a certain way: Range of mountains in the back, the sun, couple of clouds, a river rising from the mountains. *Educational Sciences: Theory and Practice, 12*(4), 3173–3180.

Vecchi, V. (1998). The role of the *atelierista*: An interview with Lella Gandini. In C. Edwards, L. Gandini, & G. Forman (Eds.), *The hundred languages of children: The Reggio Emilia approach–advanced reflections* (2nd ed., pp. 139–148). Westport, CT: Ablex Publishing.

Vygotsky, L. S. (1962). *Thought and language* (E. Hanfmann & G. Vakar, Trans. & eds.). Cambridge, MA: Harvard University Press.

Vygotsky, L. S. (1978). *Mind in society*. Cambridge, MA: Harvard University Press.

Walsh, D. (2002). Constructing an artistic self: A cultural perspective. In L. Bresler & C. M. Thompson (Eds.), *The arts in children's lives: Context, culture, and curriculum* (pp. 101–111). Boston, MA: Kluwer Academic Press.

Wangmo, T. (2018). Between the lines and beyond the pages: Through the art of a child. *Art in Early Childhood, 2018*(7). Retrieved August 24, 2018 from http://artinearlychildhood.org/journals/2018/ARTEC_2018_Research_Journal_1_Article_7_Wangmo.pdf

Weitz, M. (1959). The role of theory in aesthetics. In M. Weitz (Ed.), *Problems in aesthetics: An introductory book of readings* (pp. 145–159). New York, NY: Macmillan.

Wexler, A. J., & Cardinal, R. (2009). *Art and disability: The social and political struggles facing education*. New York, NY: Macmillan.

Willats, J. (1977). How children learn to draw realistic pictures. *Quarterly Journal of Experimental Psychology, 29*, 367–382.

Willats, J. (1997). Children's drawing development. *Art and representation: New principles in the analysis of pictures* (pp. 287–319). Princeton, NJ: Princeton University Press.

Wilson, B. (1974). The superheroes of J. C. Holz. *Art Education, 27*(8), 2–9.

Wilson, B. (1997). Child art, multiple interpretations, and conflicts of interest. In A. M. Kindler (Ed.), *Child development in art* (pp. 81–94). Reston, VA: National Art Education Association.

Wilson, B. (2004). Child art after modernism: Visual culture and new narratives. In E. W. Eisner & M. D. Day (Eds.), *Handbook of research and policy in art education* (pp. 299–328). Mahwah, NJ: Lawrence Erlbaum Associates.

Wilson, B. (2007). Art, visual culture, and child/adult collaborative images: Recognizing the other-than. *Visual Arts Research, 33*(65), 6–20.

Wilson, B., & Thompson, C. M. (2007). Pedagogy and the visual culture of childhood and youth. *Visual Arts Research, 33*(65), 1–5.

Wilson, B., & Wilson, M. (1977). An iconoclastic view of the imagery sources in the drawings of young people. *Art Education, 30*(1), 5–11.

Wilson, B., & Wilson, M. (1982/2009). *Teaching children to draw: A guide for parents and teachers*. Englewood Cliffs, NJ: Prentice-Hall.

Wilson, B., & Wilson, M. (1984). Children's drawings in Egypt: Cultural style acquisition as graphic development. *Visual Arts Research, 10*(1), 13–26.

Wilson, B., & Wilson, M. (1985). The artistic tower of Babel: Inextricable links between culture and graphic development. *Visual Arts Research, 11*(1), 90–104.

Winner, E. (1989). How can Chinese children draw so well? *Journal of Aesthetic Education, 23*(1), 41–63.

Wiseman, A. M., Mäkinen, M., & Kupiainen, R. (2016). Literacy through photography: Multimodal and visual literacy in a third grade classroom. *Early Childhood Education Journal, 44*(5), 537–544.

Wolf, D. P., & Perry, M. D. (1988). From endpoint to repertoires: Some new conclusions about drawing development. *Journal of Aesthetic Education, 22*(1), 17–34.

Wood, E., & Hall, E. (2011). Drawings as spaces for intellectual play. *International Journal of Early Years Education, 19*(3–4), 267–281.

Wright, S. (2003). *The arts, young children and learning*. Boston, MA: Allyn and Bacon.

Wright, S. (2005). Children's multi-modal meaning-making thru drawing and storytelling. *Teachers College Record*. ID Number: 12175. Retrieved from http://www.tcrecord.org

Wright, S. (2007). Graphic-narrative play: Young children's authoring through drawing and telling. *International Journal of Education and the Arts, 8*(8). Retrieved December 23, 2010 from http://ijea.asu.edu/v8n8/

Wright, S. (2014). 'I mean, the queen's fierce and the king's not': Gendered embodiment in children's drawings. *International Journal of Early Childhood, 46*(3), 391–406. doi:10.1007/s13158-014-0124-7

Yamada-Rice, D. (2010). Beyond words: An enquiry into children's home visual communication Practices. *Journal of early childhood literacy, 10*(3), 341–363.

Yamagata, K. (1997). Representational activity during mother-child interaction: The scribbling stage of drawing. *British Journal of Development, 15*, 355–366.

Zurmuehlen, M. (1990). *Studio art: Praxis, symbol, presence*. Reston, VA: National Art Education Association.

10

Musical Experiences and Learning in Early Childhood

Susan Young

Introduction

In a baby music class in Reykjavik, Iceland a mother sings a traditional Icelandic lullaby, and her baby gazes into her face listening attentively. In a village compound in Bengland45, Sub-Saharan Africa, a mixed-age group of young children playing together on the village compound tap gourd bowls to make rhythmical percussion music to entertain two toddlers they are minding. In a well-equipped, college-based music room in New York, a group of four-year-olds attending a private music class are highly engaged in finding their own spontaneous dance moves to a jazz song recording. In a rural English market town, a five-year-old girl spends after school time singing along and dancing to a Disney karaoke app on her touchscreen tablet. The ways in which babies, toddlers and young children engage with music and learn in their first years from birth to five are so various that the task of providing a balanced and up-to-date survey of research and scholarship across this field is daunting. The main development of the last 10–15 years, with which this chapter is mainly concerned, has been a considerable broadening of scope, from micro research into specific, tiny electrical impulses in the music-active brain of infants to consideration of macro cultural and political issues in diverse international contexts and how they impact on children's musical experiences. And between such extremes of scale and scope are complex interplays of social, material, technological, environmental and cultural influences that constitute young children's musical experiences and their learning.

The disciplines of psychology and education continue to dominate the field of early childhood music education—and this chapter reflects their predominance—but the prominent position of these disciplines, although persisting, has shifted in recent years to include a wider range of disciplinary perspectives. Indeed, this shift represents one of the defining characteristics of the most recent developments in early childhood music education research (see Young, 2018). Disciplinary perspectives from anthropology, sociology, cultural/media studies and the critical theories have become increasingly influential. Scholars working within these areas, who often align with the umbrella field of Childhood Studies, have sought to understand and theorize significant recent changes in children's everyday lives and how childhood is conceptualized (Young, 2018).

While it is mostly children in the minority world who have been the subjects of the research and recipients of the education activities under consideration in this chapter, increased awareness of childhoods globally, in the majority world, has resulted in greater sensitivity to the specific and culturally defined—and in many respects privileged—childhoods experienced by children in the minority world. However, it should be said that although many scholars in the wider field of early childhood education are alert to these contemporary issues and theoretical challenges that accompany them, these important issues are only just beginning to be taken up in early childhood music education research and practice.

Paradigm Shifts

Broadly speaking, there have been two major paradigm shifts in research into young children's music that have occurred during the last 10–15 years (Young, 2016). The first has been a shift in how infancy and the first three years of childhood are viewed (Young, 2003a, 2005). The 'competent' infant who is capable and skillful and is attuned and responsive to her environment has eclipsed the incompetent infant of behaviorism (Tronick, 2007). The revised view of the 'competent' infant has resulted in a considerable expansion of research into musical aptitudes, abilities, experience and activity in the birth to three years age phase (see Trainor & Hannon, 2013 for review; also Adachi & Trehub, 2018) greatly facilitated by tools, methods and technologies, mainly laboratory based, that have been developed to examine early infant behavior (e.g. Trehub, 2015). As a result of these advances in research, the infant in her first year is now understood to possess and to use core musical competences, to attune and engage with her world socially, and for cognitive development. Moreover, via these theories of musical engagement, the infant is understood to be not merely the passive receiver of experience, but an active participant, intrinsically influencing her own developmental pathway (Trevarthen & Malloch, 2018). In recent years there have been considerable advances in our knowledge of inherent musical proclivities and how they impact on infant and toddler musical behaviors (Trainor & Hannon, 2013) and of how infants perceive music and their preferences (ibid). There have been advances in our understanding of adult-infant musical exchanges (e.g. Street, 2006) and musical lives and parenting in the earliest years (e.g. Custodero, 2006).

It is important to be aware, however, that research with infants is more plentiful than with children in the one to three years age phase. The reasons for this difference are largely methodological and practical but also hint at the underlying motivations for the infant musical research. Once they have mastered walking, toddlers are mobile, not very biddable, and have limited languages skills to understand instructions. So designing experimental research tasks for toddlers presents particular challenges. There is, therefore, what I have referred to elsewhere as a 'toddler gap' in research and in our understanding of young children's musicality (Young, 2016). There are some signs that the increased presence of toddlers in daycare settings is leading to research with a music focus based on observational, play-based and adult-child interactive approaches that are appropriate in these settings and more suited to the characteristics of young children (Arculus, 2013; Gudmundsdottir & Trehub, 2018; Nome, 2016). But this work is still in short supply. I referred also to the underlying motivations for research into the musical abilities of infants which tend to be driven more by a curiosity to reveal what musical capacities might be innate, with the aim of contributing to the larger picture of human musicality (see e.g. Trehub, 2015), than first and foremost an interest and concern for the specific musical experiences and lives of babies and toddlers.

This expanded research-based interest in the birth to three years age phase has its parallel in increased provision for music across this age phase. This increase reflects growing demands in minority-world countries for out-of-home care as more parents with very young children return to work. In addition, the shift to the 'competent' infant has brought about changing conceptions of upbringing. Parenting and caring is no longer concerned simply with providing physical care and comfort for under 3s but concerned also with cognitive stimulation and entertainment (Lareau, 2003). As a result, the provision of music for under 3s has burgeoned in recent years, not only within child care settings but also provided by a plethora of private, entrepreneurs offering 'mommy and me' music classes. These classes have become a commodified product designed to appeal largely to the middle-class mothers who have the resources to access them (Ilari, Moura, & Bourscheidt, 2011).

The second paradigm shift has been a move away from viewing 'the child' as self-contained and detached from context to a wide-angled view that recognizes children as embedded in socio-cultural environments, and their musical experiences to be context contingent (e.g. Barrett, 2010). This paradigm shift reflects broad changes away from the study of individual behavior in mainly education-derived activities, toward understanding how musical experiences, thinking and skills are acquired and performed within wider socio-cultural contexts. Researchers realized that children's musical lives are lived through and in the complexity of their everyday lives and that focusing on the educational context alone, or children's responses to experimental tasks, is far too narrow. To study children's lives in context has required a turn to ethnographic and interpretive methods that are best suited to collecting and analyzing data from naturalistic settings such as the home and (mainly outdoor) play spaces. Observations of spaces where young children free-play with peers (easier-to-access environments than the home) have provided some very informative observational studies of music play among peers that have been very influential in shifting conceptions of young children's musicality and how they learn musically by highlighting their musical competences and self-initiated modes of music-making (Campbell, 2010; Marsh, 2008; Minks, 2013). Most notably there has been a significant increase in research into music at home and in family life; a closed and more difficult-to-access environment for research (e.g. Gingras, 2012). Due to the challenges, initially, researchers mainly gave accounts of their own children's musical home lives (e.g. de Vries, 2005; Forrester, 2010). However, increasingly researchers have found innovative methods for gathering data from the home that include parent diaries (Tafuri, 2008; Wu, 2018), whole day video recording (Young & Gillen, 2010), children acting as participant researchers (Gingras, 2012), 'show and tell' visits (Ilari & Young, 2016) and children wearing digital recording devices (Dean, 2017). This work is now moving into the finer detail of children's everyday domestic lives, to study children's music-making in the car (Koops, 2014), making music solitarily at home (Dean, 2018) and in relationship with siblings (Koops & Kuebel, 2019) and music play with new technologies (Young, 2012; Young & Wu, 2019).

The burgeoning interest in children's everyday lives at home, looking inward to the small scale and family related, has been accompanied by a growth of studies interested in children within communities, looking outward. Much valuable work is arriving from scholars exploring children's musical experiences in internationally dispersed communities (Andang'o, 2016; Campbell, 2006, 2007, 2010; Ilari, 2007; Ilari & Young, 2016; Koops, 2010; Kreutzer, 2001; Lew, 2005; Lum, 2008, 2009, 2012; Marsh, 2008). Some, although less, research and literature is now starting to explore and be sensitive to how variations in social environment and culture impact on aspects of musicality, for example in relation to musical perception and preference (Soley & Sebastián-Gallés, 2015), to singing and cultural identity (Ilari, Chen-Hafteck, & Crawford, 2013), to the formation of musical identity (Barrett, 2011; Ilari, 2017), to the interactive rhythms between mothers and infants (Gratier, 1999), and in educational provision (e.g. Adachi, 2013). Viewed collectively this rich vein of work into children's musical lives both in families and in communities endeavors to take account of the resources and opportunities for music made available to young children in varied socio-cultural environments and the values, expectations and aspirations held by the adults and culture surrounding them (Lum, 2012; Young, 2009; 2012).

Most recently those who adopt more psychologically orientated viewpoints and methods are also turning their attention to the wider contexts and environments for music with an interest on how they impact on musical behaviors, for example, developing rating scales to study the home environment (Politimou, Stewart, Müllensiefen, & Franco, 2018), evaluating home-based musical behaviors according to developmental criteria (e.g. Wu, 2018) or carrying out comparative studies of music perception between infants and young children immersed in different musical cultures (Soley, 2019). Soley's fascinating corpus of work, for example, reveals that through exposure, children become sensitive to the structures in the musical system of their culture, and they lose sensitivity to structures not found in their native musical system (ibid; also Soley & Spelke, 2016). These studies also suggest that infants, early in their lives, become sensitive to musical features that are common across musical systems such as the ability to discriminate what is consonant or dissonant within that musical style and how the beat is defined and the typical rhythms parsed.

However, as understanding of the richness and diversity of children's everyday musical lives (and how much their musical learning is enhanced and shaped by these experiences) has increased, this research is starting to reveal the gaps between what young children bring with them into the educational encounter and what is offered to them by educators. Studies with even quite young children are beginning to suggest that conventional pedagogies based on longstanding developmental models may be seriously underestimating young children's musical capabilities (notably Gudmundsdottir & Trehub, 2018), implying that children are acquiring more musical skills and knowledge in everyday life than hitherto anticipated. In addition, as children's lives at home become increasingly immersed and entangled with new technologies, particularly touchscreen technologies that are portable and accessible, there may be another gap between the technology-enabled music and musical experiences of home and those of the educational setting (Young & Wu, 2019). This awareness of possible gaps is coupled with a children's rights perspective that recognizes the importance of respecting and valuing children's own cultural identity and heritage. As populations become more diverse, educational settings may offer musical experiences that do not connect with—may even deny or at worst suppress—children's own musical identity and heritage (e.g. Gluschankof, 2019; Love, 2015). So a growing awareness of these 'gaps' is presenting educational researchers with a new set of dilemmas that are starting to be explored, often in practical projects based on

action research principles and the preparation of new teaching approaches and materials (e.g. Pieridou Skoutella, 2019; Gluschankof, 2019).

Although not a paradigm shift as such, but a very significant expansion, neuroscience research into diverse aspects of musicality has burgeoned in recent years and is widely referred to in academic, professional and popular literatures. The expansion has been driven not only by increasingly advanced, available and affordable brain imaging technology and analysis software, but also by a growing interest in musical behaviors within the wider disciplines of neuroscience and psychology (see Altenmüller et al., 2012; Miendlarzewska & Trost, 2014; Schlaug, 2015 for reviews). The discovery that engaging in regular and consistent musical activity, in particular learning to play an instrument, may result in lasting changes to brain structure among adults (Hyde et al., 2009; Miendlarzewska & Trost, 2014; Wan & Schlaug, 2010) has prompted much excited speculation about the potential value of music learning in the early years when brain development is plastic. The changes to brain structure may have beneficial consequences for intelligence and academic performance (Costa-Giomi, 2014; Schellenberg, 2011, 2016), executive functions (Palleson et al., 2010), speech perception (e.g. Strait, Hornickel, & Kraus, 2011) and literacy (e.g. Moreno, 2009; Moreno et al., 2009).

In the flurry of enthusiasm for the potential benefits of music learning, some urge a more cautious approach (Young, 2018). It stands to reason, after all, that musical training can induce domain-specific gains in terms of improved sensorimotor and auditory abilities (Kraus & Chandrasekaran, 2010) and that music, therefore, makes an important contribution to a well-rounded early education (Uibel, 2012). However, what remains to be determined is whether or not training in the musical domain might enhance performance in an untrained domain (see Benz, Sellaro, Hommel, & Colzato, 2015 for useful overview). Almost nothing is known about the mechanisms that could, or may, mediate any transfer of training. While it may appear from popular reporting that this field of research has made a number of significant, firm discoveries, headlines can be misleading. Returning to the original research reports, they typically testify to the very limited, provisional and tentative status of many findings (Ilari & Cho, 2019; Vandenbroeck, 2014; Young, 2018). Because of the complex and costly nature of the research, sample sizes are typically small, replication is rare and the ethical restrictions on neuroscientific studies with the very young means that most discussion of music's brain enhancing potentials is based on extrapolations from research with animals or adults. Moreover, as Vandenbroeck emphasizes (2014), it is important to recognize the political context within which these findings are often being adopted for advocacy purposes. The move toward a narrow curriculum prioritizing the core learning of numeracy and literacy in many countries leads to the neglect of music education, and claims of music's wider 'brain-enhancing' benefits make convincing advocacy statements in the effort to secure music's rightful place in the curriculum. Moreover, most of the neuroscientific findings have explored the effects of formal instrumental training, rather than the wider range of musical activities that would normally constitute a preschool curriculum and there is concern that neuroscientific findings endorse a limited and conservative view of music learning based on training in skills drawn from Western art music. Undeniably the search for infant musical competences and the implications for human biological capacities that ensue are one important contributing dimension to a more holistic picture of music learning and plasticity, and may help to inform and tailor music-based, enriching programs designed to provide all-round perceptual and cognitive benefits. But it is important to be wary of exaggerated claims and not to reduce the valuable contribution of music to children's all round education and allow it to become merely the servant to a narrow, core-skills curriculum.

Musical Development

Developmental accounts of children's musical progress, often now calling up neuroscience findings for further endorsement, still play a very prominent role in early childhood music education (e.g. Lamont, 2016), particularly in curriculum- and practice-based materials. This prominent role persists in spite of critiques and reservations about developmentalism raised by many academics (Young, 2018). It is important, therefore, to approach musical development from a position that keeps in mind certain caveats: primarily that the underpinning research has been carried out almost exclusively with white, middle-class children who have been acculturated to Western music. In spite of this ethnocentrism, the descriptions have been presented as if widely applicable to all children, irrespective of class, race, gender, religion or ethnicity. Sociology of childhood scholars emphasizes the heterogeneity of childhood, contrasting this with psychology's tendency to homogenize (Burman, 2008; Kehily, 2004). In the global movements of people leading to very diverse school populations that characterize contemporary times, versions of children's musical competences and development derived from mono-cultural research are no longer applicable—or indeed acceptable on grounds of social justice. Such post-development perspectives are widespread in general early childhood educational theory (see, for example, Wood & Hedges, 2016) and are starting to arise in early childhood music education research and practice (see Gluschankof, 2019; Pieridou-Skoutella, 2019). Interest in intercultural approaches in practice is starting to emerge, such as the integration of immigrant communities through age-appropriate musical activities (Marsh & Dieckmann, 2016; Young, 2017).

Notwithstanding contemporary critiques of developmentalism, its principles, concepts and assumptions continue to occupy a central place in music education practice and so, in order to fulfill this chapter's aim of providing an overview, I offer a resume of research into musical development and introduce the main models. In the 1960s through to the 1980s

there was a surge of interest in general child development. This motivated a search for a theory of chronological musical development comparable to the general theories of development, most notably that of Piaget. Hargreaves's key text on musical development was published in 1986 and in the same year two influential models of musical development were presented in journal articles: a general model of musical development by Swanwick and Tillman (1986; widely known as the Swanwick and Tillman spiral), and a model of singing development by Welch (1986; later revised in 1998; see also Welch, 2016). For a period of time interest in musical development gave form and direction to music education research and framed discussion around key conceptual ideas from psychology such as the formation of concepts, intuitive and formal learning, stages or phases of learning—and the interpretation of these conceptual ideas for and in music learning contexts (see Hargreaves, 1986). Music psychologists have been extending this field of research ever since, mainly probing very specific behaviors supported by the advancement of cleverly designed methods for eliciting and assessing the responses of even quite young babies to musical stimuli. Trainor, a lead researcher in this field, provides a very valuable contemporary overview (Trainor & Hannon, 2013).

There are some over-arching issues and questions in relation to musical development to hold in mind. Broadly speaking, information gathered about children's musicality birth to five years is in short supply and patchy (cf. the 'toddler gap' I mentioned earlier). Most of the research and the developmental models it gives rise to have focused on the middle years of childhood, giving only limited indicators for early childhood or dipping into the preschool years but no younger. The available information has usually been derived from relatively small samples of children and, as emphasized earlier, mainly from one narrow demographic. Musical activity, and so likewise musical development, incorporates many different dimensions—singing, playing instruments, movement and listening/perception. So developmental models have either aimed for generality, and thereby risked neglecting the detail of different types of musical behavior, or aimed to include different types of musical behavior, and risked over-complexity. An example of the first is the 'Swanwick and Tillman spiral' that has offered a general model of musical growth but gives a very limited, general account of musicality in early childhood (Swanwick & Tillman, 1986). An example of the second is the recently designed 'Sounds of Intent' framework (Voyajolu & Ockelford, 2016). While this model encompasses the detail of children's observable musical behaving from birth and beyond, including the social dimension, the result is highly complex; a feature that has proved off-putting for its use in practice. To avoid both pitfalls, some models have focused on specific areas, most notably on singing development, although there have been some valuable attempts to arrive at models of development in other domains such as, for example, movement to music (e.g. Chen-Haftek, 2004), rhythm (e.g. Upitis, 1985) and listening and musical preference (see Phelps III, 2014).

Much of the subsequent work that has been interested in developmental trajectories takes the original 1980s/1990s studies as a stepping-off point, particularly in relation to singing development—challenging, revising and proposing modifications to these original models. The next section looks first and briefly at the most well-known generic model of musical development, the Swanwick and Tillman spiral, and then continues by giving attention to singing development—attention that is justified because the performance of songs is the mainstay of early childhood music education practice.

General Models of Musical Development

The Swanwick and Tillman model, strongly influenced by Piagetian theory, offers a domain-general model of musical development. The first stages of children's musical activity are characterized as a period of indeterminate sensory-motor activity, a pre-stage of finding out what sounds can be produced vocally or with sound-makers. This characterization of young children musically in somewhat deficit terms has been challenged by a number of subsequent studies. It is fair to say that the Swanwick and Tillman model has now largely been superseded by more refined and domain-specific understandings of musical development. The challenges to the spiral model arose from research into young children engaged in self-initiated and self-guided musical play that revealed the competences that they exhibit in their earliest musical explorations (Barrett, 1998; Cohen, 1980; Delalande, 2015; Glover, 2000; Gluschankof, 2002; Young, 2000a). All these researchers have argued that analysis of young children's musical activity reveals forms of structuring, implying intention and meaning (Sundin, 1998), thus refuting what they suggest is the impoverished version offered by Swanwick and Tillman. The method of research therefore plays an important role in studies purporting to identify developmental pathways because the method either can allow children to reveal their capabilities, or, conversely, can obscure them.

Singing and Singing Development

Young children's singing, encompassing the first vocal explorations of babies, spontaneous forms of singing and the singing performance of pre-composed songs, is a strong and enduring strand of both research and practice in early childhood music. Two major studies in the 1990s, one in the USA and the other in the UK, have drawn on developmental theories to propose models of singing development (Rutkowski, 1997; Welch, 1998; also Welch, Sergeant, & White, 1996). Both models are based on children's reproduction of songs in their first educational experiences when they enter preschool or elementary school around the age of four and upward. It is important to note, therefore, that they did not draw their conclusions from data drawn from younger children, but plotted a developmental pathway from the varied responses of the children taking part in their study. Both models were evolved by their authors from considerable bodies of data, viewed and reviewed across periods of time. Rutkowski's nine phase *Singing Voice Development Measure* (Rutkowski, 1997; also Rutkowski & Miller, 2003) suggests that children move from speech-like chanting of the song text, to singing within a limited range ('speaking range singer') to the demonstration of an expanded vocal pitch range that is associated with the child's increased competency in vocal pitch matching. Welch's original model of 1986 was revised in 1998 following a substantial longitudinal study of children in their first years of schooling in London, UK (four years upward). His revised model of vocal pitch-matching development suggests that the words of the song appear to be the initial center of interest rather than the melody with singing often 'chant like'. This leads to a second phase in which there is growing awareness of the ability to change pitch and match it to a model. A third phase is characterized by mostly accurate melodic shape and intervals but changes in tonality may occur to a final phase of almost complete accuracy of simple songs.

Stadler Elmer (2000, 2011; Stadler Elmer & Elmer, 2000) based her research not only on children's reproduction of songs, as Welch and Rutkowski had done, but also on children's inventing of new songs either spontaneously or prompted by request. She suggests that it is helpful to distinguish two different types of 'singing rules': the invention of new songs by setting one's own rules, and the reproduction of songs by accepting given rules. Musical development as manifested in singing, Stadler Elmer proposes, may be best understood as a continuous process of simultaneous imitation and playful exploration. She argues that this process is fostered by a musically stimulating environment that supports children's creative, playful engagement with music.

In more recent years, work into children's singing (and pre-singing vocalization) has expanded in directions identified at the start of the chapter, with an increase in activity focusing on the years before preschool from birth through to three, and in wider socio-cultural contexts including the home, community settings and variations in cultural background. Among infants much attention has been given to emerging vocal activity in the directions of both language and music (e.g. Imberty, 1996). This work in the field of psycholinguistics, music psychology and increasingly adopting neuroscientific methods has provided ample information about children's first vocalizations and raised interesting questions concerning definitions of singing and speech, the confluence or divergence of music and language (Patel, 2012), whether infants can distinguish singing from speech, the functions of different vocal modes and their development. This important area of work has been enriched by studies into the interactive dimension of children with caregivers and understandings of the role that vocalization plays in these interactions, particularly to convey emotion and intention (Trevarthen & Malloch, 2018) and to foster sociality (Mehr, Song, & Spelke, 2016). A later section will return to adult-infant interaction in more detail; for now I continue the focus on singing.

Studies have moved into the wider contexts of home (Addessi, 2009; Barrett, 2005, 2010; de Vries, 2009; Sole, 2017; Street, 2006), between family members and as part of parenting practices (Custodero, 2006; Custodero, Britto, & Brooks-Gunn, 2003; Custodero & Johnson-Green, 2008; de Vries, 2005) and beyond into varied community and socio-cultural contexts (Dzansi, 2004; Emberly, 2009; Marsh, 2008). Looking more closely at some influential studies, Tafuri (2008) and Barrett (2010) both carried out studies with younger children and included the home context. Located in Bologna, Italy, Tafuri recruited mothers in the final trimester of pregnancy to commit to a longitudinal research project that would continue until the children reached school age. Parents and their children attended regular music sessions at which data were collected and they completed pre-structured parent diaries documenting their children's musical activity in their everyday lives outside the sessions. Tafuri's work offers valuable longitudinal information that plots many dimensions of musical activity among a relatively large group, although singing was a focus. Most significantly the children in Tafuri's group acquired singing competences—in particular learning to sing in tune—at an age earlier than might have been formerly implied by theories of singing development. This advancement Tafuri attributes to the enriched musical environment of home and positive expectations on the part of parents.

Gudmundsdottir and Trehub (2018) have recently taken home recordings uploaded onto YouTube and have also applied age-appropriate methods for evaluating singing proficiency in toddlers through play-based activities. Findings from both methods have suggested, adding confirmation to Tafuri's finding, that singing skills may be more advanced in early childhood than previously suggested in the literature. Gudmundsdottir argues convincingly (2018), in line with Stadler Elmer, that by avoiding the test-song method of the earlier studies by Welch and Rutkowski, children can reveal their true capabilities. This point echoes the argument made earlier in relation to studies of children's self-initiated music-making with instruments, that their self-assigned musical play revealed capabilities that researcher-assigned tasks obscured.

Other studies have focused less on the acquisition of singing skills per se and more on how children use songs in everyday life and the meaning and purposes of song singing for young children, from their perspective (e.g. Barrett, 2011, 2017). Barrett (2010) recruited 18 parent-child pairs aged between 18 and 54 months attending music sessions and daycare to study song-making, of both invented and known songs, in order to study the 'extent, purpose and use' of song-making in the children's lives. Barrett's findings suggest that young children use song-making in varied contexts in their daily lives and for a range of purposes, reflecting their capacity to adopt and adapt the musical features of their environment in their music-making (also Knudsen, 2008). Song-making, according to Barrett, provides a means 'by which young children practice and elaborate on the musical forms of their cultural settings' (Barrett, 2010), and provides a rich repertoire of activity that underpins musical development and the

formation of musical identity. Barrett describes her important corpus of work as offering a cultural ecological model of early musical development.

Accessing the home even more directly, Dean (2018) equipped three- and four-year-old children with a wearable recording device (tucked in a T-shirt pocket) which collected their vocalizations, including singing, across a whole day of children's home life. This method enabled Dean to collect the children's vocalizations when they were alone, away from family interactions. From these collections she not only revealed the quantity of self-initiated singing during a day of home life—a surprising quantity in many instances—but, in keeping with Barrett, also identified children's many purposes for their singing that were interwoven with the patterns and routines of daily life, developing a theme of musical agency.

Hand in hand with this period of focus on children's processes of learning to sing has been discussion challenging familiar Western conceptions of singing ability and musicality as an innate capacity upon which learning can have little influence (e.g. Welch, 2016). The 1990s saw an important strand of writing in music psychology, strongly influenced by ethnomusicology, around the theme of musicality not as genetically determined and unsusceptible to experience therefore, but as a common human ability that all possess and that can be improved with experience. The commonly held view among practitioners is that only a very few children are genuinely 'musical'. As a result singing is thought to be an activity that children do 'naturally' but their singing ability is not modifiable and does not require any pedagogical input or special guidance. Conversely, among researchers and music education specialists, there is recognition that singing is a learnt activity that progresses in ways that can be identified—even if there are some strong differences of opinion about how singing develops and what constitutes the most effective pedagogical approaches. Nevertheless, there is general agreement among music education specialists that improving as a singer requires a singing-rich, supportive environment in which appropriate songs are modeled and well-designed pedagogical strategies employed. Interview studies with practitioners reveal the persistence of these culturally embedded beliefs in musicality as a gift possessed by only a small minority, rather than a capacity possessed by all (e.g. Wassrin, 2016). These studies suggest that much work still needs to be done to shift beliefs around children's musicality, and singing specifically, before practice will change.

The development of young children's accuracy as singers, and the relative contribution of educational experience in supporting children's singing learning, is a central issue for both researchers and practitioners (Demorest, Nichols, & Pfordresher, 2017; Hedden, 2012; Rutkowski, 2018). There have been several valuable reviews of singing studies that summarize findings to make them more readily applicable to practice (e.g. Hedden, 2012). Based on studies of singing pedagogy (Hedden, 2012), taken collectively the findings suggest that effective teachers adopt certain, identifiable approaches. They use particular activities with initial singers to help them hear their voices and learn to control the vocal mechanism. They structure singing tasks by encouraging children to learn to match one note, then short patterns, before progressing to songs. They recognize that the vocal ranges of the children should determine their choice of songs and that vocal modeling should be carefully done to assist in helping children match pitch and timbre. However, the most important, overall, element to arise from the corpus of singing pedagogy research is that the quantity and variety of singing experience and appropriate pedagogical input can definitely improve the accuracy of children's singing.

Some studies have revealed differences in singing according to gender and ethnic background. The longitudinal study led by Welch had identified gender differences with boys making less progress at singing complete songs over time than girls. This difference may be attributed to gender stereotyping with singing perceived as being a more 'feminine' activity. A few studies have explored cross-cultural comparisons (e.g. Rutkowski, Chen-Haftek, & Gluschankof, 2002) and sought to identify cultural variations in children's singing acquisition and to develop more localized, culturally sensitive understandings of young children's singing activity. For example, children speaking Cantonese, a tonal language, achieve singing mastery earlier than English counterparts (Mang, 2006) which suggests that children's native language may affect how children use their voices in singing (Rutkowski & Trollinger, 2005). There are studies of young children's music in diverse cultural contexts that adopt an ethnomusicological perspective (Marsh, 2008; Minks, 2013). To date these socio-culturally nuanced studies specifically of singing are few and far between and, moreover, the majority focus on children in their first school years.

There are some early indicators that changes in the home musical environment brought about by the arrival of new technologies, notably touchscreen technologies that are becoming widespread and very accessible to young children, facilitate singing at home, particularly sing-along activities to song performances designed for children (Young & Wu, 2019). This suggests that the nature of singing and singing experiences in early childhood are changing. In viewing YouTube clips of young children singing the popular 'Frozen' theme song from the Disney film, it is notable that a wide vocal range and challenging melodic contour, outside the range and contour normally prescribed by developmentally appropriate practice, can be achieved when a recorded song provides a means to learn through self-guided, self-motivated rehearsal. A small number, but a growing number of studies are starting to explore the influence of media (Marsh, 2008; Vestad, 2010) and new technologies on children's singing activity and musical learning (Bickford, 2013; Young, 2009).

Musical Play

A broad interest in children's self-initiated musical play has occupied a longstanding but thin strand of research activity running alongside other more prolific and dominating areas of research. Studies of musical play are often initiated by practitioner-researchers who have first-hand experience of children's musical engagements. The Pillsbury Nursery studies, although carried out as long ago as the late 1930s, still stand as a historical landmark (Moorhead & Pond, 1941/1978; Pond, 1981). The Pillsbury Nursery, in California, USA, was an experimental nursery established for the purpose of studying young children's innate musicality. Donald Pond, a trained musician and composer, was appointed to observe, document and analyze the children's self-initiated musical activity. The booklets giving notated examples of children's music-making that include song, movement and music made with instruments, and Pond's descriptions, collected from a wide age span of children over the extended life of the nursery, remain a valuable source of insight (ibid). The images of children underlying the Pillsbury study are based on the belief that children possess an innate musicality that lies close to the historical origins of music in its simplicity and purity. Pond likened their music-making to ancient chants and traditional music. He believed that in a conducive environment children can manifest their inner musicality.

In the late 1990s, early 2000s the rationale for the educational value of musical play had to be established in the face of longstanding traditions of adult-led, music-as-performance, models of practice. The main tenet of this argument was that general early childhood practice recognizes play as the medium through which children learn in self-motivated activity and just the same principles could—indeed should—apply to children's learning in music. This argument now seems to have been widely accepted, at least in much of the early childhood music education literature, even if still somewhat neglected in practice (see Soccio, 2013 for useful review). Building on earlier core work which observed, documented and described musical play (e.g. Littleton, 1998) more recent work has progressed to focus on spontaneously made music in more nuanced situations, with younger children (Delalande, 2015), from particular curricular perspectives (Trinick & Pohio, 2018) in particular types of environment such as playgrounds and junk-play areas (Zur, 2017), the home (Tafuri, 2008) among siblings (Koops & Kuebel, 2019) and among children in cultures where playing outdoors in friendship groups is common (Minks, 2013). The child-centered, progressive conceptions of children that were originally framed by Pond in the Pillsbury studies continue in approaches to early childhood music today, although reframed by contemporary theoretical and pedagogical influences. For example, in early childhood practice today the philosophy and approaches developed in the North Italian nurseries of Reggio Emilia offer a model of child-centered, democratic practice based on exploratory play that is internationally emulated and has been adapted for music pedagogy (e.g. Hanna, 2017; Nyland, Acker, Ferris, & Deans, 2015; O'Hagin, 2007).

Singing Play

Looking at self-initiated singing play first, the earlier studies took place in early childhood settings. The Pillsbury studies offer a booklet discussing notated examples of children's self-made songs that remains a valuable source if they are read mindful of the conceptions of children and music that underlie them (Moorhead & Pond, 1941/1978). Björkvold's (1989) study and writing on young children's spontaneous song in Scandinavian nursery settings is also informative for its connections between song and play. Young (2002) carried out an observational study of children between the ages of two and three years, and from a synthesis of earlier studies and this new data she identified different forms of spontaneous singing, tying these into multi-modal and environmental factors and calling for broad definitions of children's expressive vocal play that could encompass the variety that she observed (Young, 2002, 2006). This study identified singing that blended with the children's movements, with their concentrated play with objects, with dramatic, enactive play with toys, with vocal play to represent vehicle and animal sounds in play with toys, and singing as part of dramatic play with peers and other adults. Both Young and Marsh have pointed out that little room is made for children's self-generated and expressive vocal music-making in pedagogical practice and that careful listening and documenting of this activity reveals competences that traditional pedagogical approaches to young children's singing often underestimate and rarely connect with or build on (Marsh & Young, 2016).

Musical Play with Instruments

In the 1980s, the documentation from the Pillsbury Nursery study that had languished for many years was rediscovered and gave impetus to a number of studies in the USA that followed his lead (e.g. Cohen, 1980). In the UK new educational directions in the 1970s and 1980s emphasized children as makers of their own music rather than reproducers of adult music and prompted Glover to study young children's self-made music in an educational context. She offered analyses that demonstrated the children's structured musical thinking that underpinned their improvisations and compositions (Glover, 2000). Delalande has maintained a long fascination with children's own music-making with instruments, carrying out studies with two- and three-year-olds both in his native France and in collaborative work with pedagogues working in Northern Italian daycare (2015). In his work he adopts a Piagetian perspective in which he proposes that the sounds the child produces become a sound object for exploration and experimentation (ibid). Young (2000a, 2000b, 2003b), taking up the research baton from Cohen, Glover and Delalande, looked in more detail at children's spontaneous play with instruments and identified forms of organization not only arising from the child's body movement but also from the material and social environment, thus reflecting both of the paradigmatic shifts ('competence' and 'context') mentioned in the introduction. Children playing independently would find forms of organization from the structure of the instrument (also Dansereau, 2015), and children playing with an adult play partner would find forms of organization from

social interaction patterns of turn-taking or synchronizing. A study by Gluschankof of children attending a kindergarten in Israel found that young children of Palestinian heritage living in Israel recreated culturally stylistic modes of playing educational percussion (2002). With increasingly diverse populations of children, such studies point to the need to increase our knowledge of how children are enculturated into musical styles of their own heritage and how educational practice can accommodate that musical diversity.

In summarizing this small but important group of studies that have focused on children's spontaneous music-making with instruments and sound-producing objects, collectively they have proposed that children's music-making should be studied as a complex process involving multi-modal engagement and spatial, social and material factors. Importance is given to the ways in which adults hear and respond children's musical play, with expectations of its value and meaning for the children. Valuing musical play as 'musical' on children's terms calls for definitions of music that are broad and generous. Many are calling up the ethnomusicologist Small's concept of 'musicking' (1977) to denote an act of making music that is integrated into its environmental surroundings, social, cultural and material. Adopting a competence-based view and taking the child's perspective are all part of a general movement toward methodological innovations, inspired by Childhood Studies scholars, which attempt to treat children respectfully, not as the objects of research studies but as co-participants (Kellett, 2010).

Musical Engagement

Children's learning to be singers has taken a lead position in early childhood music education research, reflecting its importance to very young children as an accessible and meaningful mode of music-making and its leading role in early childhood music education practice. Music-making with instruments also occupies an important, if secondary, position. Hence the lion's share of this chapter has been given to these active, performative domains of music-making. There are other important areas of young children's musical experiences that have also received attention, although less prominently. Children engage as listeners with music (recorded or live) or music-like communications made by others (e.g. Lamont, 2008; Sims & Nolker, 2002) and show their responses through movement, facial expressions and vocalizing (e.g. Metz, 1986). Again, research is influenced by the paradigm shifts mentioned at the start of the chapter, with earlier studies focused mainly on preschoolers in educational settings, and later work focusing more on younger children (Kida & Adachi, 2008) and more diverse contexts at home (Chen-Haftek, 2004), attending daycare or participating in private baby/toddler music classes (Retra, 2010). We can also see how studies framed by ethnomusicological thinking challenge Westernized images of children's participation in music by drawing attention to their limitations. Mans (2002) provides an interesting description and discussion of modes of participation among young Namibian children where they may be included on the fringes of community music and dance occasions and their encouragement to participate is seen as an important aspect of socialization (Mans, 2002).

More recent work focused on embodied engagement with music, reflecting the expansive interest in infant musical proclivities, has been interested in what is termed 'entrainment'—meaning, the ability of even very young children to move to music and often keep in time with the music (depending on the pace and rhythmic characteristics of the music and their movement vocabulary). The fact that moving together to music is commonly a social activity has intrigued researchers who have been exploring the group social dynamics of entrainment and its link with social bonding and the sharing of social goals (e.g. Kirschner & Ilari, 2014; Kirschner & Tomasello, 2010). For example, in one study, children as young as 14 months were found to be more helpful toward an adult when they have been bounced in time, synchronously with them, in comparison with when they were bounced out of time (Cirelli, Wan, & Trainor, 2016). This finding could suggest that in daycare and preschool settings, group rhythmic activity where children move in time with one another could improve their feelings of helpfulness and cooperation toward others in their group.

Entrainment is closely linked with an influential strand of research into infant musicality that has focused on the way early adult-infant interaction is sustained by music-like features, broadly termed *communicative musicality* by Malloch (2000) working with Trevarthen (2009). Communicative musicality has proved to be a very fruitful theory for early childhood music education providing an interpretive frame for many different dimensions of young children's musical activity, particularly among babies and toddlers. While interest in adult-infant interaction has evolved since the 1970s (e.g. Brazelton & Tronick, 1980; Trevarthen, 1977), the realization of its musical qualities arose initially in work by Papousek (1996), basing their study on their own experiences of parenting, and more recently by Malloch with Trevarthen (Malloch, 2000; Malloch & Trevarthen, 2009). From the moment of birth, close observational studies of infants in interaction with their immediate caregivers, usually their mothers, have revealed their ability to make eye contact, to gaze at faces, to listen intently to vocalizations (Nakata & Trehub, 2004) and to make reciprocating gestures. As their vocal and movement abilities develop, these vocalizations and gestures increasingly convey meaning and intention. Careful analysis of video-recorded interactions has revealed the music-like features and qualities that underpin successful infant-adult interactions: rhythmic synchronization, well-timed reciprocal contributions, expressively contoured pitch variations and carefully graduated and matching dynamic qualities (Malloch & Trevarthen, 2009; Trevarthen, 2000). Moreover, interactions are sustained by a careful balance of repetition of the same to generate predictability and to support sharing, and the introduction of novelty to stimulate interest and to raise or moderate the emotional tenor (Shenfield, Trehub, &

Nakata, 2003; Young, 2003a. This fundamental characteristic of time-based interactions (Young, 2011) has been proposed as a generative source in improvisations (Young, 2003b) that might be played out on instruments (Young, 2005), in singing-play (Yennari, 2010) and playful, responsive pedagogical approaches (Custodero, 2008). In one respect this understanding of sociable infant behavior connects and leads on from the studies that explore perceptual and processing skills in detail, demonstrating their function in enabling young children to engage, to entrain and to communicate with those immediately around them. What is also fascinating is that the findings emerging from brain studies begin to identify processes that enable anticipation in time, so essential to communicative musical participation (Trainor & Zatorre, 2009). These neural processes seem to entail encoding what has just gone, predicting what might just happen and then adjusting if the prediction is not fulfilled.

The theory of communicative musicality has proved fruitful to practitioners in observing, analyzing, indentifying and conceptualizing the characteristics of play among babies and toddlers in child care (Nome, 2016) and in suggesting how child care workers can engage with, interact with and extend their play (Nyland, 2019). However, again, the proviso of cultural variation should be raised. It is suggested that parents throughout the world interact with their babies and very young children with vocalizing and moving their bodies rhythmically (Trehub, 2004, 2015) both to soothe and animate—and that this fundamental behavior represents a universal musical parenting strategy that is a generative source of creativity (Dissanayake, 2000). However, there are variations in style that seem to be culturally determined (Young, 2018). Careful observations of a group of Somali-born women now resident in Bristol revealed a different style of infant interaction to the norm that was built into and anticipated by the music education worker. Instead of being interested to participate with their babies in animated, interactive, playful ways, they preferred to remain passive and watch the music worker (Young, 2017). While, as another example, parents in the USA may adopt an animated style of interaction with their children, mothers from other cultural backgrounds may prefer a style that aims to soothe and quiet their children (see DeLoache & Gottlieb, 2000).

Pedagogy and Learning

Although many points have arisen in the preceding sections which relate research to pedagogical practice, this next section looks more closely at some specific aspects. The design of pedagogical approaches can be considerably assisted by information offered by early childhood music research in its many different theoretical perspectives. However, the pathway from research to practice is not always direct and smooth, with criticisms levied at both researchers and educators for failures relating to the oft-quoted practice/theory divide. A study by Wassrin (2016) explores pedagogues' socially constructed representations of children as musical, their conceptions of musicality, and serves as a valuable reminder that beliefs and images of musical childhoods held by practitioners will profoundly influence how research information is received and implemented. If, for example, as mentioned earlier in relation to singing, educators hold strong beliefs of singing ability as innate, natural, easy and fixed, they are unlikely to be receptive to research findings around effective methods for supporting children's learning as singing. Note that unhelpful assumptions are held only by educators; researchers too may hold certain beliefs that shape their research priorities or hinder their ability to relate their work to applied, real-world pedagogical contexts.

Perhaps the greater rapprochement between research and practice has occurred and still continues in the area of musical development. The increasing quantity of scientific information, including neuroscience, accumulating from the studies of musical competences in infancy, could be a valuable source of influence on practice, but to date, its influence is less apparent. The primary area of influence is seen in the formulating of general rationales and advocacy statements by educators, politicians, commercial music providers and policy makers. The messages of potential general cognitive gains accruing from participation in music and brain plasticity are highly appealing. However, the strong belief that an early start to formalized learning in music is a good start is not born out by research as Trehub (2015) emphasizes.

Research by educators has also focused on the application of theories of engagement and learning to early childhood music. There has, in recent years, been a broad trend to develop more relational, interactive models of practice inspired by readings of Vygotskian theory and concomitant interest in the role of the adult (e.g. Hsee & Rutkowski, 2006). Custodero, in a very important corpus of research, has applied Csikszentmihaly's theory of flow to young children's participation in music classes, providing thereby a pedagogical model which balances the challenge and enjoyment of participation in educationally framed musical activities with skill level. Custodero's work places importance on the child's opportunities to 'self-assign' in music sessions and the supportive role of the adult (Custodero, 2002, 2005). Holgersen, adopting a theoretical perspective of phenomenology (2002), studied children aged one to five taking part in a music group and identified movement and social interaction as key dimensions of the children's participation. While the methods, theoretical framing and contexts for studies into music pedagogy may vary, when viewed collectively with other similar contemporary work (reviewed in Young, 2008) some commonalities emerge that characterize contemporary, theory-based approaches to pedagogy. These common features are the contribution of embodied and play-based approaches to children's music learning and the important role of the adult not as didactic instructor, but as interactive and responsive to children's contributions in order to value and understand—or at least endeavor to—the musical intentions and meaning underlying the children's actions.

There are individual examples of the application of other principles and theories to early childhood music education. The principles of multi-cultural education have influenced project studies by Chen-Haftek (2007) and intercultural approaches have informed the work of Pieridou-Skoutella (2019). Culturally responsive practice, particularly with children of color, is explored by Robinson (2016) and some interpretations of critical pedagogy underpinned a project study by Young and Street (2009).

Other researchers have taken a different angle, starting with the need to develop models of practice appropriate to a widening range of adults working with young children. For example with generalist early childhood practitioners, particularly in daycare settings (e.g. Suthers, 2004), music performers from orchestras or community groups (Smith, 2010) and with parents to develop music practice in the home (Young, Street, & Davies, 2007). Suthers stated in 2004 that the need for research into effective training approaches for adults has become more pressing in recent years as the range of provision for under 3s has increased and with the increase, a need to promote quality practice. Many years on, her statement still stands. Suthers argued that programs for children under three are notably different in content and approach from those for older children, requiring, therefore, qualitatively different approaches to how music might be integrated. Her work in devising integrated musical activity in child care arrived at three dimensions: music as part of caregiving routines, music as play and sociable music experiences (Suthers, 2004).

The need to expand models of practice so that they are appropriate to the cultural, social and political climates within their own countries is also pressing for a group of researchers and educators working outside the dominant USA and North West European countries; for example, in developing countries such as Kenya (Andang'o & Mugo, 2007), Brazil, (Ilari, 2007), in post-colonial locations such as Singapore (Lum, 2008, 2009, 2012), post-communist countries such as Estonia, (Kiilu, 2010) and post-apartheid South Africa (Woodward, 2007) and for researchers cognizant of the increasing diversity of communities within their own countries as a consequence of immigration (Robinson, 2006; Young, 2008).

As Young and Wu (2019) have argued, children's musical lives outside of educational settings are being altered through the arrival of new technologies, particularly touchscreen technologies which are portable and easy to use, even for very young children. Yet there is a little activity exploring the use of new technology or digital music content in educational settings. There can even be antipathy, with educators considering music technology either unnecessary or inappropriate. What studies there are have tended to have adopt conventional musical content, for example Carnival of the Animals (e.g. Burton & Pearsall, 2016; Tu, Cslovjecsek, Pérez, Blakey, & Shappard, 2014), or to have viewed children's activity through a conventional developmental lens (e.g. Brooks, 2015).

Pedagogical Approaches: The 'Methods'

Early childhood music education is characterized by the presence of some distinctive pedagogical approaches, typically and commonly referred to as 'methods'. These practice-based approaches, usually known by the name of their originator as for example Kodaly, Orff, Dalcroze, Gordon and Suzuki (see Campbell & Scott-Kassner, 2009 for descriptions of these approaches), still assume a strong position in early childhood music education practice with educators adopting and then often identifying strongly with one approach. On account of this strong position, I cannot ignore them in this chapter, concerned as it is to give a current and representative overview of early childhood music education and research. However in respect of their relationship to research and scholarship the pedagogical approaches are problematic. They have crystallized in to specific pedagogies often underpinned with sets of ideas that are accorded the status of theory but have usually emerged from the consensual versions of what counts as good practice rather than empirical study. They represent philosophies and approaches conceived by their originators at particular times and in particular socio-cultural contexts that embody broad assumptions and ideals concerning childhood and music. These pedagogical approaches perpetuate and are perpetuated through canonized texts and authorized practices that discourage reflective, truly open-minded appraisal of their approaches and are rarely open to external influence or new information from research.

Conclusion

In this chapter I have presented my account of an up-to-date picture of research into the musical experiences of very young children and relate these to educational practice. I have explained recent developments as expanding on two fronts—namely the birth to three age phase, and into wider social and cultural contexts—and hopefully conveyed some of the valuable and interesting extensions to our understanding and knowledge of young children's musicality and their musical learning. The work which has attracted the greatest attention in recent years has no doubt been the music psychology and neuroscientific investigations into infant musical capabilities and processing. But I have, however, tried to keep in fair balance the interplay between biological, social, material and cultural dimensions of young children's early musical experiences and to resist the pull of positivist research that continues to dominate. The activity exploring and expanding our understandings of musical childhoods in real-life domestic contexts, in daycare centers and in culturally diverse situations has received less attention, been subject to fewer citings and collective reviews, and is, perhaps by its very nature, more fragmented and diffuse. Moreover, there is a difference in value and status accorded to scientific, laboratory-based studies, often large scale and well funded, in comparison with naturalistic, every day, practice-based studies that are typically small scale and poorly funded. Yet it is through this more mundane, practice-orientated, 'real life', fragmented research that we develop our understandings of how children learn musically and then consider how pedagogy might be modified in response.

At this present time, with research expanding in these new directions, early childhood music educators, from my viewpoint, are experiencing difficulty in identifying a framework within which to accommodate and conceptualize contemporary work. The period of time when an interest in developmental models predominated may have represented a 'heyday' when research and practice united around common themes and enterprises. The sector as a whole is marked by a number of challenges that impinge significantly on music educators: low levels of funding, poor pay and employment opportunities; increasing privatization; and the squeezing out of arts subjects as the curriculum prioritizes basic skills. As a result much early childhood music provision has, of necessity, become privatized and increasingly marketized resulting in music as a commodified product that must give precedence to purchaser appeal over appropriateness for young children, and secure a market niche through branding and franchising (Young, 2017). Research also becomes drawn into market processes and can be viewed as useful only if it can increase purchasing power. In such a climate I have proposed a notion of 'musical childhoods' drawing strongly from Childhood Studies as a possible frame within which to theorize and also critique this new range and diversity of activity (Young, 2018). 'Musical childhoods' could accommodate multi-perspectival and multi-dimensional activity within a post-development perspective that would introduce thinking tools from critical theory to discuss and examine assumptions, methods and strategies that underpin research and practice with more vigor than I suggest is currently the case.

Since I set out to offer an overview, there are omissions and gaps that should be mentioned. A couple of small areas I have deliberately left out: children's emergent notations and drawings to music and first formal instrumental lessons. Both areas involve children at the older end of early childhood and are relatively distinct and specific areas of activity. Other areas have received less attention because they have received disappointingly little attention: namely variations according to gender, ethnicity, religion or class. Nevertheless, I have endeavored to include mentions of research that widen the inclusiveness. At risk of repetition, there is a pressing need to extend the scope of research to non-Western musical domains and to engage in investigating musical learning in all its cultural diversity. While contemporary childhoods are changing dramatically as technological developments and fields such as literacy education are actively researching and theorizing these changes, there has been very little response from early childhood music education.

In offering a concluding summary on an optimistic note, we may confidently say that adults and infants throughout the world interact by vocalizing and moving rhythmically in ways that are intrinsically musical and expressive. We know that infants and small children possess sophisticated aural perceptual skills, that their bodies and minds are 'pre-wired' for music and that musical experience seems to influence how brain connections form. Infants enculturated to specific musical styles can parse the music they hear in ways that are conventional to that musical style. Very young children take great interest in sounds and are highly motivated to explore them and make music in ways that have forms of coherence. Small children engage in spontaneous forms of musical play with their voices, creating expressive vocalizations and songs, with their bodies in rhythmic movement, with objects and instruments and increasingly sophisticated forms of technology available to them. Young children live in environments in which there is a wide range of forms of musical engagement and participation for them, ranging from the highly designed and formal, to those in which children are peripheral participants. Finally, we know that adults are highly motivated to try to understand young children's musical worlds and how best to engender and enhance their musical experiences and learning.

References

Adachi, M. (2013). The nature of music nurturing in Japanese preschools. In P. Campbell & T. Wiggins (Eds.), *The Oxford handbook of children's musical cultures* (pp. 449–465). Oxford, UK: Oxford University Press.

Adachi, M., & Trehub, S. E. (2018). Musical lives of infants. In G. McPherson & G. Welch (Eds.), *The Oxford handbook of music education* (Vol. 2, pp. 5–25). Oxford, UK: Oxford University Press.

Addessi, A. R. (2009). The musical dimension of daily routines with under-four children during diaper change, bedtime and free-play. *Early Child Development and Care, 179*(6), 747–768.

Altenmüller, E., Demorest, S. M., Fujioka, T., Halpern, A. R., Hannon, E. E., Loui, P., … Zatorre, R. J. (2012). Introduction to the neurosciences and music IV: Learning and memory. *Annals of the New York Academy of Sciences, 1252*(1), 1–16. doi:10.1111/j.1749-6632.2012.06474.x

Andang'o, E. (2016). *Young Kenyan children's multifaceted musical identities: In school, at home and in places of worship. Proceedings of the 17th international seminar of the ISME commission on early childhood music education*, Gehrels Music Education & Akoesticum, Ede, The Netherlands, 17–22 July.

Andang'o, E., & Mugo, J. (2007). Early childhood music education in Kenya: Between broad national policies and local issues. *Arts Education Policy Review, 109*(2), 45–53.

Arculus, C. (2013). *What is the nature of communication between two-year-olds in a musical free play environment?* (Unpublished Master's thesis). University of Central England, Birmingham, UK.

Barrett, M. (1998). Researching children's compositional processes and products: Connections to music education practice? In B. Sundin, G. E. McPherson, & G. Folkestad (Eds.), *Children composing: Research in music education 1998: 1* (pp. 10–34). Lund, Sweden: Malmo Academy of Music, Lund University.

Barrett, M. (2005). Musical communication and children's communities of musical practice. In D. Miell, R. Macdonald, & D. J. Hargreaves (Eds.), *Musical communication* (pp. 261–280). Oxford, UK: Oxford University Press.

Barrett, M. (2010). Young children's song-making: An analysis of patterns of use and development. In S. M. Demorest, S. J. Morrison, & P. S. Campbell (Eds.), *Proceedings of the 11th International Conference on Music Perception and Cognition (ICMPC)* (p. 74). Seattle, Washington, DC, August 23–27, 2010.

Barrett, M. S. (2011). Musical narratives: A study of a young child's identity work in and through music-making. *Psychology of Music, 39*(4), 403–423.

Barrett, M. S. (2017). From small stories. In R. MacDonald, D. J. Hargreaves, & D. Miell (Eds.), *Handbook of musical identities* (pp. 63–78). Oxford, UK: Oxford University Press.

Benz, S., Sellaro, R., Hommel, B., & Colzato, L. S. (2015). Music makes the world go round: The impact of musical training on non-musical cognitive functions—A review. *Frontiers in Psychology, 6*, 2023.

Bickford, T. (2013). Tinkering and tethering: Children's MP3 players as material culture. In P. S. Campbell & T. Wiggins (Eds.), *The Oxford handbook of children's musical cultures* (pp. 527–542). Oxford, UK: Oxford University Press.

Björkvold, J. (1989). *The muse within: Creativity and communication, song and play from childhood through maturity* (W. H. Halverson, Trans.). New York, NY: Harper Collins.

Brazelton, T. B., & Tronick, E. (1980). Preverbal communication between mothers and infants. In D. R. Olson (Ed.), *The social foundations of language and thought* (pp. 299–315). New York, NY: Norton.

Brooks, W. L. (2015). Music in infant-directed digital video discs: A content analysis. *Music Education Research, 17*(2), 141–161.

Burman, E. (2008). *Deconstructing developmental psychology* (2nd ed., revised). London, UK: Brunner-Routledge.

Burton, S. L., & Pearsall, A. (2016). Music-based iPad app preferences of young children. *Research Studies in Music Education, 38*(1), 75–91.

Campbell, P. S. (2006). Global practices. In G. McPherson (Ed.), *The child as musician: A handbook of musical development* (pp. 415–437). New York, NY: Oxford University Press.

Campbell, P. S. (2007). Musical meaning in children's cultures. In L. Bresler (Ed.), *Inter-national handbook of research in arts education* (pp. 881–894). Dordrecht, The Netherlands: Springer.

Campbell, P. S. (2010). *Songs in their heads: Music and its meaning in children's lives* (2nd ed.). Oxford, UK: Oxford University Press.

Campbell, P. S., & Scott-Kassner, C. (2009). *Music in childhood: From preschool through the elementary grades* (3rd ed., Enhanced Edition). New York, NY: Thompson/Schirmer.

Chen-Haftek, L. (2004). Music and movement from zero to three: A window to children's musicality. In L. Custodero (Ed.), *Proceedings of the 11th international conference of the ISME early childhood commission, Barcelona, Spain: Escola Superior de Musica de Catalunya. 5–9 July, 2004* (pp. 45–54). New York, NY: Harper & Row.

Chen-Haftek, L. (2007). Contextual analyses of children's responses to an integrated Chinese music and culture experience. *Music Education Research, 9*(3), 337–353.

Cirelli, L. K., Wan, S. J., & Trainor, L. J. (2016). Social effects of movement synchrony: Increased infant helpfulness only transfers to affiliates of synchronously moving partners. *Infancy, 21*(6), 807–821.

Cohen, V. (1980). *The emergence of musical gestures in kindergarten children* (Unpublished Doctoral dissertation). University of Illinois, Urbana.

Costa-Giomi, E. (2014). The long-term effects of childhood music instruction on intelligence and general cognitive abilities, *Update: Applications of Research in Music Education, 33*(2), 20–26.

Custodero, L. A. (2002). Seeking challenge, finding skill: Flow experience in music education. *Arts Education and Policy Review, 103*(3), 3–9.

Custodero, L. A. (2005). Observable indicators of flow experience: A developmental perspective on musical engagement in young children from infancy to school age. *Music Education Research, 7*(2), 185–209.

Custodero, L. A. (2006). Singing practices in 10 families with young children. *Journal of Research in Music Education, 54*(1), 37–56.

Custodero, L. A. (2008). Living jazz, learning jazz: Thoughts on a responsive pedagogy of early childhood music. *General Music Today, 22*(5), 24–29.

Custodero, L. A., Britto, P. R., & Brooks-Gunn, J. (2003). Musical lives: A collective portrait of American parents and their young children. *Applied Developmental Psychology, 24*, 553–572.

Custodero, L. A., & Johnson-Green, E. A. (2008). Caregiving in counterpoint: Reciprocal influences in the musical parenting of younger and older infants. *Early Child Development and Care, 178*(1), 15–39.

Dansereau, D. R. (2015). Young children's interactions with sound-producing objects. *Journal of Research in Music Education, 63*(1), 28–46.

Dean, B. (2017). *A Hidden World of Song: Singing in the everyday home lives of 3–5-year-old children* (Unpublished PhD thesis). School of Education, University of Exeter, Exeter, UK.

Delalande, F. (2015). *Naissance de la musique: Les explorations sonores de la première enfance* [The Birth of Music: Sounds Explorations in Early Childhood]. Rennes, France: Presses Universitaires de Rennes.

DeLoache, J., & Gottlieb, A. (Eds.). (2000). *A world of babies: Imagined childcare guides for seven societies*. Cambridge, UK: Cambridge University Press.

Demorest, S. M., Nichols, B., & Pfordresher, P. Q. (2017). The effect of focused instruction on young children's singing accuracy. *Psychology of Music, 46*(4), 311–330.

de Vries, P. (2005). Lessons from home: Scaffolding vocal improvisation and song acquisition with a 2-year-old. *Early Childhood Education Journal, 32*(5), 307–312.

de Vries, P. (2009). Music at home with the under fives: What is happening? *Early Child Development and Care, 179*(4), 395–405.

Dissanayake, E. (2000). *Art and intimacy: How the arts began*. Seattle and London, UK: University of Washington Press.

Dzansi, M. (2004). Playground music pedagogy of Ghanaian children. *Research Studies in Music Education, 22*(1), 83–92.

Emberly, A. (2009). *"Mandela went to China… and India too": Musical cultures of childhood in South Africa* (Unpublished Doctoral dissertation). University of Washington, Seattle.

Forrester, M. A. (2010). Emerging musicality during the pre-school years: A case study of one child. *Psychology of Music, 38*(2), 131–158.

Glover, J. (2000). *Children composing 4–14*. London, UK: RoutledgeFalmer.

Gingras, P. (2012). *Music at home: A portrait of family music-making* (Unpublished doctoral dissertation). University of Rochester, Rochester, NY.

Gluschankof, C. (2002). The local musical style of kindergarten children: A description and analysis of its natural variables. *Music Education Research, 4*(1), 37–49.

Gluschankof, C. (2019). Self-initiated musicking in kindergarten as instances of emancipation: The case of Arabic speaking young children in Israel. In S. Young & B. Ilari (Eds.), *Music in Early Childhood: Multi-disciplinary perspectives and inter-disciplinary exchanges* (pp. 173–186). New York, NY: Springer.

Gratier, M. (1999). Expressions of belonging: The effect of acculturation on the rhythm and harmony of mother-infant vocal interaction. *Musicae Scientiae Special Issue 1999–2000, 3*(1), 93–122. doi:10.1177/10298649000030S107

Gudmundsdottir, H., & Trehub, S. (2018). Adults recognise toddlers' song renditions. *Psychology of Music, 46*(2), 281–291.

Hanna, W. (2017). *The children's music studio: A Reggio-inspired approach*. New York, NY: Oxford University Press.

Hargreaves, D. J. (1986). *The developmental psychology of music*. London, UK and New York, NY: Cambridge University Press.

Hedden, D. (2012). An overview of existing research about children's singing and the implications for teaching children to sing. *Update: Applications of Research in Music Education, 30*(2), 52–62.

Holgersen, S.-E. (2002). *Mening og Deltagelse. Iagttagelse af 1–5 årige børns deltagelse i musikundervisning*. Ph.d.-afhandling. København: Danmarks Pædagogiske Universitet. [*Meaning and participation. Observation of 1-to-5-year-old children's participation in music teaching.*] (Unpublished doctoral Dissertation). The Danish University of Education, Copenhagen, Denmark.

Hsee, Y., & Rutkowski, J. (2006). Early musical experience in touch with general human development: An investigation of Vygotsky's scaffolding in music lessons for preschoolers. In L. Suthers (Ed.), *Touched by musical discovery, disciplinary and cultural perspectives: Proceedings of the ISME early childhood music education commission seminar, July 9–14* (pp. 112–120). Taiwan: Chinese Cultural University Taipei.

Hyde, K. L., Lerch, J., Norton, A., Forgeard, M., Winner, E., Evans, A. C., & Schlaug, G. (2009). Musical training shapes structural brain development. *The Journal of Neuroscience, 29*(10), 3019–3025.

Ilari, B. (2007). Music and early childhood in the Tristes Tropiques: The Brazilian experience. *Arts Education Policy Review, 109*(2), 7–18.

Ilari, B. (2017). Children's ethnic identities, cultural diversity and music education. In R. MacDonald, D. J. Hargreaves, & D. Miell (Eds.), *Handbook of musical identities* (pp. 527–542). Oxford, UK: Oxford University Press.

Ilari, B., Chen-Hafteck, L., & Crawford, L. (2013). Singing and cultural understanding: A music education perspective. *International Journal of Music Education, 31*(2), 202–216.

Ilari, B., & Cho, E. (2019). Neuromusical research and young children: Harmonious relationship or discordant notes? In B. Ilari & S. Young (Eds.), *Music in early childhood: Multi-disciplinary perspectives and inter-disciplinary exchanges* (pp. 119–137). New York, NY: Springer.

Ilari, B., Moura, A., & Bourscheidt, L. (2011). Between interactions and commodities: Musical parenting of infants and toddlers in Brazil. *Music Education Research, 13*(1), 51–68.

Ilari, B., & Young, S. (2016). *Children's home musical experiences across the world*. Bloomington: Indiana University Press.

Imberty, M. (1996). Linguistic and musical development in preschool and school-age children. In I. Deliège & J. Sloboda (Eds.), *Musical beginnings: Origins and development of musical competence* (pp. 191–213). New York, NY: Oxford.

Kehily, M. J. (2004). *An introduction to childhood studies*. Oxford, UK: Open University Press.

Kellett, M. (2010). *Rethinking children and research*. London, UK: Continuum Publishing.

Kida, I., & Adachi, M. (2008). The role of the musical environment at home in the infant's development – Part 2: Exploring effects of early musical experiences on the infant's physical and motor development during the first 2 years. In M. Adachi (Ed.), *Proceedings of the 10th International Conference on Music Perception and Cognition (ICMPC 10)*, Sapporo, Japan, 25th–29th August.

Kiilu, K. (2010). *The development of the concept of music education in Estonian kindergartens, 1905–2008: A historical-critical overview* (Unpublished research report: Department of Teacher Education). University of Helsinki, Helsinki, Finland.

Kirschner, S., & Ilari, B. (2014). Joint drumming in Brazilian and German preschool children: Cultural differences in rhythmic entrainment, but no prosocial effects. *Journal of Cross-Cultural Psychology, 45*(1), 137–166.

Kirschner, S., & Tomasello, M. (2010). Joint music making promotes prosocial behavior in 4-year-old children. *Evolution and Human Behavior, 31*(5), 354–364.

Knudsen, J. S. (2008). Children's improvised vocalisations: Learning, communication and technology of the self. *Contemporary Issues in Early Childhood, 9*(4), 287–296.

Koops, L. H. (2010). Learning in The Gambia "Deñuy jàngal seen bopp" (They teach themselves). *Journal of Research in Music Education, 58*(1), 20–36.

Koops, L. H. (2014). Songs from the car seat: Exploring the early childhood music-making place of the family vehicle. *Journal of Research in Music Education, 62*(1), 52–65.

Koops, L. H., & Kuebel, C. (2019). Probing the dynamics of sibling interactions in relation to musical development. In B. Ilari & S. Young (Eds.), *Music in early childhood: Multi-disciplinary perspectives and inter-disciplinary exchanges* (pp. 39–58). New York, NY: Springer.

Kraus, N., & Chandrasekaran, B. (2010). Music training for the development of auditory skills. *Nature Reviews: Neuroscience, 11*, 599–605.

Kreutzer, N. J. (2001). Song acquisition among rural Shona-speaking Zimbabwean children from birth to 7 years. *Journal of Research in Music Education, 49*, 198–211.

Lamont, A. (2008). Young children's musical worlds: Musical engagement in 3–5-year-olds. *Journal of Early Childhood Research, 6*(3), 247–261.

Lamont, A. (2016). Musical development from the early years onwards. In S. Hallam, I. Cross, & M. Thaut (Eds.), *The Oxford handbook of music psychology* (2nd ed., pp. 399–414). Oxford, UK: Oxford University Press.

Lareau, A. (2003). *Unequal childhoods: Class, race and family life*. Berkeley: University of California Press.

Lew, C.-T. (2005). *The musical lives of young Malaysian children: In school and at home* (Unpublished doctoral dissertation). University of Washington, Seattle.

Littleton, D. (1998). Music learning and child's play. *General Music Today, 12*(1), 8–15.

Love, B. L. (2015). What is hip hop-based education doing in *nice* fields like early childhood and elementary education? *Urban Education, 50*(1), 106–131.

Lum, C.-H. (2008). Home musical environment of children in Singapore: On globalization, technology, and media. *Journal of Research in Music Education, 56*(2), 101–117.

Lum, C.-H. (2009). Musical memories: Snapshots of a Chinese family in Singapore. *Early Child Development and Care: Special Issue, 179*(6), 707–716.

Lum, C.-H. (2012). Hanging out with Britney and Raihan: The colorful musical lives of Malay/Muslim children in Singapore. In C.-H. Lum & P. Whiteman (Eds.), *Musical childhoods in Asia and the Pacific* (pp. 57–74). New York, NY: Information Age Publishing.

Malloch, S. (2000). Mothers and infants and communicative musicality. *Musicae Scientiae, Special Issue, 1999–2000*, 29–57.

Malloch, S., & Trevarthen, C. (Eds.). (2009). *Communicative musicality. Exploring the basis of human companionship.* Oxford, UK: Oxford University Press.

Mang, E. (2006). The effects of age, gender and language on children's singing competency. *British Journal of Music Education, 23*(2), 161–174.

Mans, M. (2002). Playing the music: Comparing children's song and dance in Namibian education. In L. Bresler & C. M. Thompson (Eds.), *The arts in children's lives: Context, culture and curriculum* (pp. 71–86). Dordrecht, The Netherlands: Kluwer Academic Publishers.

Marsh, K. (2008). *The musical playground: Global tradition and change in children's songs and games.* New York, NY: Oxford University Press.

Marsh, K., & Dieckmann, S. (2016). Interculturality in the playground and playgroup: Music as shared space for young immigrant children and their mothers. In P. Burnard, E. Mackinlay, & K. Powell (Eds.), *The Routledge international handbook of intercultural arts research* (pp. 358–368). London, UK: Routledge.

Marsh, K., & Young, S. (2016). Musical play. In G. McPherson (Ed.), *The child as musician: A handbook of musical development* (2nd ed., pp. 462–484). New York, NY: Oxford University Press.

Mehr, S. A., Song, L. A., & Spelke, E. S. (2016). For 5-month-old infants, melodies are social. *Psychological Science, 27*(4), 486–501.

Metz, E. (1986). *Movement as a musical response among pre-school children* (Unpublished Doctoral dissertation). Arizona State University, Tempe.

Miendlarzewska, E. A., & Trost, W. J. (2014). How musical training affects cognitive development: Rhythm, reward and other modulating variable. *Frontiers in Neuroscience, 7*, 294.

Minks, A. (2013). *Voices of play: Miskitu children's speech and song on the Atlantic coast of Nicaragua.* Tucson: University of Arizona Press.

Moorhead, G. E., & Pond, D. (1941, reprinted 1978). *Pillsbury foundation studies: Music of young children.* Santa Barbara, CA: Pillsbury Foundation for Advancement of Music Education.

Moreno, S. (2009). Can music influence language and cognition? *Contemporary Music Review, 28*(3), 329–345.

Moreno, S., Marques, C., Santos, A., Santos, M., Castro, S. L., & Besson, M. (2009). Musical training influences linguistic abilities in 8-year-old children: More evidence for brain plasticity. *Cerebral Cortex, 19*, 712–723.

Nakata, T., & Trehub, S. E. (2004). Infants' responsiveness to maternal speech and singing. *Infant Behavior & Development, 27*, 455–464.

Nome, D. (2016). The sound of the children: Social life among toddlers in kindergarten as a song and a dance. Paper presented at the 26th EECERA Annual Conference. *Happiness, relationships, emotion and deep-level learning.* Dublin, Ireland, August 31st–September 3rd.

Nyland, B. (2019). The art of listening: Infants and toddlers in education and care group settings. In S. Young & B. Ilari (Eds.), *Music in early childhood: Multi-disciplinary perspectives and inter-disciplinary exchanges* (pp. 59–71). New York, NY: Springer.

Nyland, B., Acker, A., Ferris, J., & Deans, J. (2015). *Musical childhoods: Explorations in the preschool years.* London, UK: Routledge.

O'Hagin, I. B. (2007). Musical learning and the Reggio Emilia approach. In K. Smithrim & R. Upitis (Eds.), *Listen to their voices: Research and practice in early childhood music* (pp. 196–210). Waterloo, ON: Canadian Music Educators' Association.

Palleson, K. J., Brattico, E., Bailey, C. J., Korvenoja, A., Koivisto, J., Gjedde, A., & Carlson, S. (2010). Cognitive control in auditory working memory is enhanced in musicians. *PLoS ONE, 5*(6), e11120.

Papousek, H. (1996). Musicality in infancy research: Biological and cultural origins of early musicality. In I. Deliège & J. Sloboda (Eds.), *Musical beginnings* (pp. 37–55). Oxford, UK: Oxford University Press.

Patel, A. D. (2012). Language, music, and the brain: A resource-sharing framework. In P. Rebuschat, M. Rohrmeier, J. Hawkins, & I. Cross (Eds.), *Language and music as cognitive systems* (pp. 204–223). Oxford, UK: Oxford University Press.

Phelps III, R. P. (2014). *Development of musical preference: A comparison of perceived influences* (Unpublished Master's thesis). Florida State University College of Music, Tallahassee, Florida.

Pieridou Skoutella, A. (2019). Interculturalism in early childhood music education and the training of educators: An anthropological framework from the Mediterranean. In S. Young & B. Ilari (Eds.), *Music in early childhood: Multi-disciplinary perspectives and inter-disciplinary exchanges* (pp. 155–172). New York, NY: Springer.

Politimou, N., Stewart, L., Müllensiefen, D., & Franco, F. (2018). Music@ Home: A novel instrument to assess the home musical environment in the early years. *PLoS ONE, 13*(4), e0193819.

Pond, D. (1981). A composer's study of young children's innate musicality. *Bulletin: Council for Research in Music Education, 68*, 1–12.

Retra, J. (2010). *Music is movement: A study into developmental aspects of movement representation of musical activities among preschool children in a Dutch music education setting* (Unpublished PhD thesis). University of Exeter, Exeter, UK.

Robinson, K. (2006). White teacher, students of color: Culturally responsive pedagogy for elementary general music in communities of color. In C. Frierson-Campbell (Ed.), *Teaching music in the urban classroom, Vol. 1: A guide to survival, success, and reform* (pp. 35–53). Lanham, MD: Rowman and Littlefield Publishers, Inc.

Rutkowski, J. (1997). The nature of children's singing voices: Characteristics and assessment. In B. A. Roberts (Ed.), *The phenomenon of singing* (pp. 201–209). St John's, NF: Memorial University Press.

Rutkowski, J. (2018). Development and pedagogy of children's singing. In A. Reynolds & S. Burton (Eds.), *Engaging musical practices: A sourcebook for elementary general music* (pp. 33–50). Lantham, MD: Rowman & Littlefield.

Rutkowski, J., Chen-Haftek, L., & Gluschankof, C. (2002). Children's vocal connections: A cross-cultural study of the relationship between first graders' use of singing voice and their speaking ranges. In *Proceedings of the 10th international conference of the ISME early childhood Commission* (pp. 39–50). Copenhagen, Danish University of Education.

Rutkowski, J., & Miller, M. S. (2003). A longitudinal study of elementary children's acquisition of their singing voices. *Update: Applications of Research in Music Education, 22*(1), 5–14.

Rutkowski, J., & Trollinger, V. L. (2005). Experiences: Singing. In J. W. Flohr (Ed.), *The musical lives of young children* (pp. 78–97). Upper Saddle River, NJ: Prentice Hall.

Schellenberg, S. (2011). Examining the association between music lessons and intelligence. *British Journal of Psychology, 102*(2), 283–302.

Schellenberg, S. (2016). Music and non-musical abilities. In G. E. McPherson (Ed.), *The child as musician: A handbook of musical development* (2nd ed., pp. 149–176). Oxford, UK: Oxford University Press.

Schlaug, G. (2015). Musicians and music making as a model for the study of brain plasticity. In E. Altenmüller, S. Finger, & F. Boller (Eds.), *Music, neurology, and neuroscience: Evolution, the musical brain, medical conditions, and therapies, Vol. 217* (pp. 27–55). Amsterdam, The Netherlands: Elsevier.

Shenfield, T., Trehub, S. E., & Nakata, T. (2003). Maternal singing modulates infant arousal. *Psychology of Music, 31*, 365–375.

Sims, W. L., & Nolker, D. B. (2002). Individual differences in music listening responses of kindergarten children. *Journal of Research in Music Listening, 50*(4), 292–300.

Small, C. (1977). *Music, society and education.* Middletown, CO: Wesleyan University Press.

Smith, T. F. (2010). Presenting chamber music to young children. *General Music Today, 24*(2), 9–16.

Soccio, A. (2013). The relation of culture and musical play: A literature review. *Update: Applications of research in music education, 32*(1), 52–58.

Sole, M. (2017). Crib song: Insights into functions of toddlers' private spontaneous singing. *Psychology of Music, 45*(2), 172–192.

Soley, G. (2019). The social meaning of shared musical experiences in infancy and early childhood. In B. Ilari & S. Young (Eds.), *Music in early childhood: Multi-disciplinary perspectives and inter-disciplinary exchanges* (pp. 73–86). New York, NY: Springer.

Soley, G., & Sebastián-Gallés, N. (2015). Infants prefer tunes previously introduced by speakers of their native language. *Child Development, 86*(6), 1685–1692.

Soley, G., & Spelke, E. S. (2016). Shared cultural knowledge: Effects of music on young children's social preferences. *Cognition, 148*, 106–116.

Stadler Elmer, S. (2000). *Spiel und Nachahmung. Über die Entwicklung der elementaren musikalischen Aktivitäten.* Aarau, Switzerland: Nepomuk.

Stadler Elmer, S. (2011). Human singing: Towards a developmental theory. *Psychomusicology, 21*, 13–30.

Stadler Elmer, S., & Elmer, F.-J. (2000). A new method for analyzing and representing singing. *Psychology of Music, 28*(1), 23–42.

Strait, D. L., Hornickel, J., & Kraus, N. (2011). Subcortical processing of speech regularities underlies reading and music aptitude in children. *Behavioral and Brain Function, 7*(1), 44.

Street, A. (2006). *The role of singing within mother-infant interactions* (Unpublished PhD thesis). University of Surrey, Guildford, UK.

Sundin, B. (1998). Musical creativity in the first six years. In B. Sundin, G. E. McPherson, & G. Folkestad (Eds.), *Children composing: Research in music education 1998: 1* (pp. 35–56). Lund, Sweden: Malmo Academy of Music, Lund University.

Suthers, L. (2004). Music experiences for toddlers in day care centres. *Australian Journal of Early Childhood, 29*, 45–50.

Swanwick, K., & Tillman, J. (1986). The sequence of musical development. *British Journal of Music Education, 3*(3), 305–339.

Tafuri, J. (2008). *Infant musicality: New research for educators and parents.* Aldershot, UK: Ashgate.

Trainor, L. J., & Hannon, E. E. (2013). Musical development. In D. Deutsch (Ed.), *The psychology of music* (3rd ed., pp. 423–498). London, UK: Elsevier Inc.

Trainor, L. J., & Zatorre, R. J. (2009). The neurobiological basis of musical expectations. In S. Hallam, I. Cross, & M. Thaut (Eds.), *Oxford handbook of music psychology* (pp. 171–183). Oxford, UK: Oxford University Press.

Trehub, S. E. (2004). Music in infancy. In J. Flohr (Ed.), *Musical lives of young children* (pp. 24–29). Englewood Cliffs, NJ: Prentice Hall.

Trehub, S. E. (2015). Infant musicality. In S. Hallam, I. Cross, & M. Thaut (Eds.), *The Oxford handbook of music psychology* (2nd ed.). Oxford, UK: Oxford University Press.

Trevarthen, C. (1977). Descriptive analyses of infant communication behaviour. In H. R. Schaffer (Ed.), *Studies in mother-infant interaction: The Loch Lomond symposium* (pp. 227–270). London, UK: Academic Press.

Trevarthen, C. (2000). Musicality and the intrinsic motive pulse: Evidence from human psychobiology and infant communication. *Musicae Scientiae Special issue, 1999–2000*, 155–215.

Trevarthen, C., & Malloch, S. (2018). Musicality and musical culture: Sharing narratives of sound from early childhood. In G. E. McPherson & G. F. Welch (Eds.), *The Oxford handbook of music education* (Vol. 2, pp. 26–39). Oxford, UK: Oxford University Press.

Trinick, R., & Pohio, L. (2018). The "serious business" of musical play in the New Zealand early childhood curriculum. *Music Educators Journal, 104*(4), 20–24.

Tronick, E. (2007). *The neurobehavioral and socio-emotional development of infants and children.* London, UK: Norton Publishing.

Tu, C., Cslovjecsek, M., Pérez, J., Blakey, J., & Shappard, E. (2014). Assessing the interactivity of 3-year-old children with an iPad app: The Carnival of the Animals. *Perspectives: Journal of the Early Childhood Music and Movement Association, 9*(3), 15–18.

Uibel, S. (2012). Education through music – The model of the Musikkindergarten Berlin. *The Neurosciences and Music IV: Learning and Memory, 1252*(1), 51–55.

Upitis, R. (1985). *Children's understanding of rhythm: The relationship between development and musical training* (Unpublished doctoral dissertation). Harvard University, Cambridge, MA.

Vandenbroeck, M. (2014). The brainification of early childhood education and other challenges to academic rigour. *European Early Childhood Education Research Journal, 22*(1), 1–3.

Vestad, I. L. (2010). To play a soundtrack: How children use recorded music in their everyday lives. *Music Education Research, 12*(3), 243–255.

Voyajolu, A., & Ockelford, A. (2016). Sounds of intent in the early years: A proposed framework of young children's musical development. *Research Studies in Music Education, 38*(1), 93–113.

Wan, C. Y., & Schlaug, G. (2010). Music making as a tool for promoting brain plasticity across the life span. *The Neuroscientist : A Review Journal Bringing Neurobiology, Neurology and Psychiatry, 16*(5), 566–577.

Wassrin, M. (2016). *Towards Musicking in a Public Sphere: 1–3 year olds and music pedagogues negotiating a music didactic identity in a Swedish preschool* (Doctoral dissertation). Stockholm University, Stockholm, Sweden.

Welch, G. (2016). Singing and vocal development. In G. MacPherson (Ed.), *The child as musician: A handbook of musical development* (2nd ed., pp. 441–461). Oxford, UK: Oxford University Press.

Welch, G. F. (1986). A developmental view of children's singing. *British Journal of Music Education, 3*(3), 295–303.

Welch, G. F. (1998). Early childhood musical development. *Research Studies in Music Education, 11*, 27–41.

Welch, G. F., Sergeant, D. C., & White, P. (1996). The singing competences of five-year-old developing singers. *Bulletin of the Council for Research in Music Education, 127*, 155–162.

Wood, E., & Hedges, H. (2016). Curriculum in early childhood education: Critical questions about content, coherence, and control. *The Curriculum Journal, 27*(3), 387–405.

Woodward, S. C. (2007). Nation building—one child at a time: Early childhood music education in South Africa. *Arts Education Policy Review November/December, 109*(2), 43–53.

Wu, Y.-T. (2018). *The musical development of young children of the Chinese diaspora in London* (Unpublished PhD thesis). University College London, Institute of Education, London, UK.

Yennari, M. (2010). First attempts at singing of young deaf children using cochlear implants: The song they move, the song they feel, the song they share. *Music Education Research, 12*(3), 281–297.

Young, S. (2000a). *Young children's spontaneous instrumental music-making in nursery settings* (Unpublished PhD Thesis). University of Surrey, Guildford, UK.

Young, S. (2000b). The interpersonal dimension: A potential source of creativity for young children? *Musicae Scientiae special issue, 1999–2000*, 165–179.

Young, S. (2002). Young children's spontaneous vocalisations in free-play: Observations of two- to three-year-olds in a day-care setting. *Bulletin of the Council for Research in Music Education, 152*, 43–53.

Young, S. (2003a). *Music with the under fours.* London, UK: Routledge Falmer.

Young, S. (2003b). Time-space structuring in spontaneous play on educational percussion instruments among three- and four-year-olds. *British Journal of Music Education, 20*(1), 45–59.

Young, S. (2005). Changing tune: Reconceptualising music with the under-threes. *International Journal of Early Years Education, 13*(3), 289–303.

Young, S. (2006). Seen but not heard: Young children's improvised singing. *Contemporary Issues in Early Childhood, 7*(3), 270–280.

Young, S. (2008). *Music 3–5*. London, UK: RoutledgeFalmer.

Young, S. (2009). Towards constructions of musical childhoods: Diversity and digital technologies. *Early Child Development and Care, 179*(6), 695–705.

Young, S. (2011). Children's creativity with time, space and intensity: Foundations for the temporal arts. In D. Faulkner & E. Coates (Eds.), *Exploring children's creative narratives* (pp. 82–104). Abingdon, UK: Routledge.

Young, S. (2012). Theorizing musical childhoods with illustrations from a study of girls' karaoke use at home. *Research Studies in Music Education, 34*(2), 113–127.

Young, S. (2016). Early childhood music education research: An overview. *Research Studies in Music Education, 34*(1), 29–44.

Young, S. (2017). Diverse parenting goals and community music in early childhood. *International Journal of Community Music, 10*(3), 261–272.

Young, S. (2018). *Critical new perspectives on early childhood music*. London, UK: Routledge.

Young, S., & Gillen, J. (2010). Musicality. In J. Gillen & C. A. Cameron (Eds.), *International perspectives on early childhood research: A day in the life* (pp. 27–36). Basingstoke, UK: Palgrave Macmillan.

Young, S., & Street, A. (2009) Time to play: Developing inter-culturally sensitive approaches to music in children's centres serving predominantly Muslim communities. In A. R. Addessi & S. Young (Eds.), *Proceedings of the 4th conference of the European network of music educations and research of young children*, 22nd–25th July, Bologna Italy (pp. 32–39). Bologna, Italy, Bononia University Press.

Young, S., Street, A., & Davies, E. (2007). The music one-to-one project: Developing approaches to music with parents and under-two-year-olds. *European Early Childhood Education Research Journal, 15*(2), 253–267.

Young, S., & Wu, Y.-T. (2019). Music at their finger-tips: Musical experiences via touchscreen technologies in the everyday lives of young children. In B. Ilari & S. Young (Eds.), *Music in early childhood: Multi-disciplinary perspectives and inter-disciplinary exchanges* (pp. 235–252). New York, NY: Springer.

Zur, S. S. (2017). Musical creativity in Israel's "junkyard" playgrounds. *Proceedings of the 8th conference of the European network of music educators and researchers of young children*, June 20–24, 2017, Cambridge, UK.

11

Play in Early Childhood Education

James E. Johnson, Serap Sevimli-Celik, Monirah A. Al-Mansour, Tuğçe Burcu Arda Tunçdemir, and Pool Ip Dong

Professional and public interest in children's play is increasing and appears unstoppable. Cambridge University's first "Professor of Play" David Whitebread calls play "in fashion" academically and clinically; "the new renaissance" is reflected in current academic journals such as *The International Journal of Play* and many recent books (Whitebread, 2018). At the level of application, this new enthusiasm is shown by heightened media attention, community "Play Days," conferences, and other indicators. In early childhood education (ECE), which covers from birth to eight years according to the National Association for the Education of Young Children (NAEYC), play is arguably the most researched topic, with results often useful for practice and policy. Keeping up with research on play is very challenging because of the sheer volume of studies on numerous topics including the ones that follow. An attempt is made in this chapter to refer to research within the areas of expertise of the co-authors while offering selected coverage of general play concepts, issues, and applications to practice and policy.

Historically, play has been regarded as a cornerstone of early learning (e.g., Montessori, 1912/1964), with critics offering alternative perspectives (e.g., Kuschner, 2012). Education institutions within the USA have been impacted by the learning standards movement (Christie & Roskos, 2007). One consequence are data that kindergarten is becoming the new first grade (Bassok, Latham, & Rorem, 2016). Importance of play to ECE has been questioned. Challenges or questions as to its significance can be answered by reference to literature on: (a) concepts and definitions of play, (b) the importance of play, and (c) play pedagogy.

Concepts and Definitions of Play

Play is mental or physical activity with notable attributes. Included are: (a) positive affect, (b) freely chosen, (c) under the control of the young child, (d) motivated by the play process per se, (e) meaning determined by the young child, (f) transformational and dynamic, (g) play actions and play thoughts build on one another. Compiling this list has been influenced by play scholars such as Roger Callios who in *Man, Play and Games* (1961/1958) identified vertigo, competition, mimicry, and chance and discussed these play forms and a gradient continuum from more free (*paidia*) to more controlled (*ludus*) play. Play is uncertain, rule-bound, fictive, unproductive, free, and separated from reality. Johan Huizinga explained in *Homo Ludens* (Huizinga, 1955) that play is voluntary, not serious; play is or can be very absorbing; and without material gain, play is also rule-bound, conducive to social belongingness and framed from reality. Gordon Burghardt in *The Genesis of Animal Play* (2005) informs that play occurs when the organism is relaxed and safe and without extreme wants, play is *autolectic* (i.e., spontaneous, voluntary, intentional, and often pleasurable or rewarding), repeated behaviors are often seen in play, having some purpose play is nevertheless not entirely functional in the context expressed, and play is often exaggerated in expression and incomplete as final functional elements are dropped. Burghardt writes play from a biological perspective centered on animal play, yet his attributes resemble ones stated and deemed useful in ECE.

Young children play with their bodies, objects, symbols, and others as considered in observational systems used by researchers and teachers to account for it. One commonly employed assesses play as solitary, parallel, or socially interactive and nested with play types such as physical, functional, constructive, dramatics, or games with rules (Rubin, Maioni, & Hornung, 1976). This nested approach accounts for both the sociality of play and its cognitive form. Block and puzzle play (constructive), simply using toys (functional), or enactments with dolls, puppets, or in dress-up clothes (dramatic) can occur when young children are alone (solitary), near other children playing similarly (parallel), or in social commerce (interactive, which can be merely associating or, on a higher level, cooperating with peers).

Play development is a central background concern in teaching young children. Briefly, infants engage in much exploratory play and imitative play with objects – solitarily, socially with peers, or with caring parents or teachers. Toddlers like face-to-face playing with objects, doing finger-plays, singing, and the like; they are growing up and are exploring a wider world and showing increasing autonomy in their play behavior. During the preschool years children are seen often building with blocks, or using icons and numbers and letters in computer play, performing social pretense is common and theoretically important as a leading mental activity from three to six years old (El'Konin, 1978). Kindergarteners and primary grade children play games with rules, invent imaginary worlds, and have developing new interests seen in various forms of creative and intellectual play, often displayed in collaborations with peers.

Educational play, another key concept, is play that is initiated, controlled, paced, terminated, and assessed by the teacher for its educational merit; it is a planned part of the ECE curriculum expressed in setting up and allowing for and guiding child-initiated activities in more teacher-directed play. Educational play differs from children's ordinary play in contexts outside teachers' influence. Spodek (1974) emphasized that teacher involvement is the central ingredient in educational play, but he also stressed that in order for the activity to stay play, the activity has to remain player-centered. Contemporary thinking holds that educational play has a social foundation stemming from the child's relationships and negotiations with the teacher and classmates. Genuine play states therefore are experienced in educational play as in ordinary play, provided that teachers do not disrupt the play by taking over. Pedagogies of play rest on this understanding. Educational play brings the teacher's and children's agendas together, teachers have educational aims and children bring their playing to the teacher.

Play and Learning

Play and play-related behaviors such as exploration and imitation are important learning processes during the early years. Seen as adaptive behaviors, and viewed along the Piagetian assimilation-accommodation continuum, play as assimilation is bending reality to fit pre-existing cognitive schemata in complement to accommodation (i.e., modifying cognitive schemata in response to incoming information). Both processes work in tandem to achieve adaptation. Accommodation generates new learning, while assimilation integrates and makes it more meaningful. In the classroom when the child is imitating or exploring he or she is engaged more in accommodative than assimilative behaviors. These actions are stimulus-oriented, while playing is more response-oriented with the playing child seemingly asking "what can I do with this?" Often these behaviors form a pattern as the child examines, re-examines, transforms, imagines, and creates.

Examining newer forms, such as digital play, researchers Bird and Edwards (2015) continue to usefully distinguish epistemic play (investigative behaviors) and ludic play (pretense). Still, play is a dynamic state and seldom are children exclusively playing in a certain "classified" way for an extended period of time; mixes occur in kinds of play and non-play or play-like behaviors, such as imitation or investigation. Various behaviors occur in complementary and dynamic ways. Play can become work, and work can become play for the child who is playing and learning.

Making a related point DeVries (2001) recommended that much of what children do in ECE classrooms should be called "work activities," which would include construction, exploring, investigating, problem solving, and experimenting. Pretending, physical and bodily activities and group games remain the primary play forms. She recommended that teachers include in the curriculum high-quality, intellectually challenging projects that stimulate social, emotional, moral, and intellectual development.

Typically, a child's behaviors can be described as a mixture or a sequencing of "work" and "play," but the two states should not be lumped together or viewed as opposites. Play and work function together in serving the child in adapting to and learning from experiences; play is one type of meaning making and a response to an experience of meaning making (DeLisi, 2015). This nuanced understanding of play and learning is not always appreciated but is prerequisite to developing and employing sound pedagogy of play in the field. It is important, for example, in distinguishing play as an educative process from rituals and routines as educative processes (Johnson, 2016).

Play Assessment

Teachers usually think about play on the basis of what is known about contexts, children's actions, and inferred mental states (Johnson, Al-Mansour, & Sevimli-Celik, 2014). A useful distinction to make is between play frame or context (surrounding the play episode) and play script or text (within the play episode). One can then keep separate meta-play negotiations or play disruptions (e.g., teacher intrusions or children's conflict that snap the play frame) from enactments occurring during play episodes. Observing and understanding play requires recognizing its multilayered qualities and synthesizing information about person, object, space, time, and situational factors.

Evaluation of levels of play is important, needed to judge whether a child is playing in a developmentally expected manner. For example, Smilansky (1968) used two criteria for differentiating sociodramatic play from dramatic play: social interaction and verbal communication. Both dramatic play and sociodramatic play included role play with respect to self and others, object and situation transformations, and persistence (at least ten minutes). Bodrova (2008) operationalized with more evaluative language mature versus immature play, with indicators including: (a) ability to sustain a specific role by consistently engaging in actions, speech, and interactions that fit the character enacted, (b) ability to use substitute or pretend objects, (c) ability to follow rules associated with the make-believe scenario, and (d) ability to integrate many themes and ideas and sustain play over time spans of several days or weeks. Immature play is when a child plays like a younger child, for instance, a four-year-old playing like a two-year-old. Immature play in this example could be characterized by one or more of these attributes: play that is repetitive, dependent on concrete props, lacking in role enactment, including the presence of peer conflicts, not following implicit or explicit play rules, and simple or unelaborated content in play episodes of short duration.

Play evaluation gauges what children are doing so that teachers can guide them toward developmentally enriching play. Play records should retain action sequences and contextual information. Deliberate attention must be paid to children's goals, means for reaching them, and their understanding. With play evaluation, the teacher is better prepared for deciding on appropriate interventions (Johnson, Christie, & Wardle, 2005; Van Hoorn, Nourot, Scales, & Alward, 2015).

Importance of Play

Self-Regulation

Self-regulation is exercising control over one's emotions, cognitions, impulses, and actions. Mature play entails self-regulation and uses the executive functions (EF) of cognitive flexibility, inhibitory control, and working memory in the service of organizing, sequencing, switching, and planning play actions and intentions. Mature play uses and strengthens self-regulation when children create an imaginary situation, take on and act out roles, and follow rules implicit in the play scenario. However, although social pretense as a means of developing self-regulation has received the most attention in the literature (Bodrova, 2008), mature constructive, physical, and games-with-rules play forms also have been noted as instrumental to its development (Bodrova & Leong, 2007; Riley, San Juan, Klinkner, & Ramminger, 2008).

Mature play stimulates the maturation of EF (i.e., working memory, inhibitory control, and cognitive flexibility) occurring in the prefrontal cortex of the brain (Diamond, Barnett, Thomas, & Munro, 2007; Yogman, Garner, Hutchinson, Hirsh-Pasek, & Golinkoff, 2018). Play can foster a sense of control and self-regulation of one's own learning. During play children set their own challenges and determine their own focus of attention and planning. These cognitive mechanisms can contribute to effortful, intentional use of imagination, creativity, and problem solving. Children create their own zone of proximal development and are self-scaffolding in play; during play children transcend the concrete here and now and use abstract thought and build symbolic competence (Vygotsky, 1978). Research suggests that there is co-development or relations among play, self-regulation, and EF during the early years.

For example, Whitebread (2010) found that self-regulatory skills could be facilitated in three- to five-year-old children through a variety of playful activities designed by 32 teachers in England. These activities included constructing a model, dressing a doll, and playing board and card games, either with peers or adults. Play actions were rated as higher in metacognitive or self-regulatory quality when they happened in a social context characterized by extensive collaboration and talk. Analysis of 582 play episodes showed that adult questioning had a slightly positive impact on what children could say about their own learning, but this greatly depressed children's self-regulation and motivation. Supporting play in educational settings to achieve self-regulation requires a mix of adult emotional support, children's initiation and feelings of control, cognitive challenges in the play activities, and private speech and collaborative talk to bring about learning and metacognitive awareness. In another important study, Diamond et al. (2007) tested 147 pre-kindergarteners in state-funded programs and found that the Tools of the Mind curriculum, based on 40 activities that promoted executive functioning (including mature dramatic play), led to improved cognitive control at the end of the second year of the program using the Dots and Flanker tasks, Stroop-type measures of EF.

Social Competence

Quality play crafts "social brains" (Panksepp, 2010; Pellis, Pellis, & Bell, 2010). Evolutionary neuroscience research on animals has helped bring understanding of the great importance of early play for regulation and learning to function with others. Deprivation of play opportunities for an organism results in serious disruptions in normal patterns of social interaction. Although most of this research has generated objective data on animal play, there are strong implications for ECE. The consequences of play deprivation for early brain development and subsequent social and emotional development cannot be overstated.

Both social competence and early learning of academic content hinge upon the ability to be focused and maintain self-control, which themselves are strengthened by mature or age-appropriate play. Social competence is reflected in ability and willingness to engage in socially responsible behaviors and positive social play with peers. This involves emotional regulation and perspective taking, as suggested by research. For instance, Elias and Berk (2002) found that middle-class three- and four-year-olds who engaged in more mature sociodramatic play were more cooperative during circle and clean-up times than were children with lower scores on the play measures, controlling for verbal ability and initial self-control scores. High impulse children as scored at the beginning of the school year, who engaged in complex sociodramatic play, improved the most in "clean-up time" performance over the course of the year.

Peer interactions in open-ended play also benefit social skill learning, cooperation, and building confidence in dealing with other children. Broadhead, Howard, and Wood (2010) reported that when play is that thematically driven by young children, or said differently they are able to follow their own interests and plans, then there is more likely to be higher levels of cooperation, richer language, better problem solving, and reciprocity. The Social Play Continuum (associative, social, highly social, and cooperative) observation tool was used by teachers and researchers to quantify and also to locate and to reflect upon peer play in the classroom setting. Broadhead et al. (2010) also studied teacher-initiated and teacher-directed activities where children were shown that their play was valued. For example, if less mature social play was performed by older children, the teacher would wait until after the play is finished before engaging in discussions with them about it. This collaborative approach to play observation, intervention, and reflection aimed to help teachers create a more harmonious classroom atmosphere where quality play can flourish.

Broadhead and colleagues' sensitive child-centered approach to social play and building and respecting classroom community is similar to the approach used by Rogers and Evans (2008). The latter study used child focus groups to capture the child's or an "insider's" view of role play. Rogers and Evans found that the children's reasons for entering a play center often was reported to be with or near a friend with a friend, unlike the teachers' reasons for the play centers. Both these investigations gesture toward the value of trying to obtain multiple perspectives on play or a co-constructed pedagogy of play. There is potential educational value in teachers and children discussing the play. In addition, it seems clear that both child-initiated and adult-guided play and other related activities are helpful for building in young children self-regulation and social-emotional competence; mature play which is related to these two important attributes is therefore correctly regarded as a means to prepare children for school and academic achievement and future life success in general.

Play that strengthens self-regulation and increases social competence in young children helps them in attaining school readiness and subsequent classroom success. Play of this kind is important because it makes it more likely that children with this play background will be able to demonstrate social and emotional skills necessary for performing the student role. Taking turns, following directions, and other basics of school life depend on having these general skills. Play also is valuable during the preschool years for its benefits to emerging literacy and numeracy; well-developed play bodes well for a child's later academic performance in these areas (Hirsh-Pasek, Golinkoff, Berk, & Singer, 2009).

Literacy

Research supports the importance of mature play for language and early learning (Christie, 2010; Roskos & Christie, 2004). Literacy rests on language and representational competence. Play benefits these foundations and literacy in the areas of alphabet knowledge, concepts about print, oral language, comprehension, and phonological awareness. Roskos and Christie (2004) reviewed research and concluded that play promotes literacy because play uses language and symbols and aids in children's making connections between oral and written media. Studies include Dickinson and Tabors (2001) who followed 74 low-income family three-year-olds over several years, and reported significant associations between children's talk during play and their later literacy scores. Studies attest to the close affinity between play and various indices of early literacy including oral vocabulary, writing, and comprehending stories (McNamee, 2015).

Numeracy

The play-math connection is well studied. Young children encounter many opportunities to acquire knowledge and develop math skills in their play activities. Ginsburg (2006) noted the potential for reading and book use to help children learn about perspectives, angles, covariation (e.g., the Three Bears and their bed sizes corresponding to their body sizes), numbers, and so forth. Block play invites considerable opportunities to develop spatial knowledge; play with small objects encourages counting, patterning, and grouping. Ginsberg's *Everyday Math* curriculum for young children uses materials and physical actions, and balances play with more direct instruction that can be playful. A range of instructional methods can promote playful learning in math.

Play is associated with emerging spatial and quantitative concepts in young children. Child-initiated play and adult-guided play are both valuable. Gelman (2006) showed the motivating power of play; children learn and use math skills when they are embedded in a game more than when they are not. Ramani and Siegler (2008) showed that playing the game "Chutes & Ladders" promoted preschoolers' number line estimation ability, knowing the numerals, counting, and concepts about quantity. Worthington (2010) reported that during play young children invent math symbols and develop their imaginations and mathematical graphics, such as gestures to stand for the "take away" sign. Fisher, Hirsh-Pasek, Golinkoff, and Newcombe (2013) reported four- to five-year-olds benefitted from play guided by adults in terms of their acquiring geometric knowledge (learning shapes), compared with children in free play or direct instruction conditions.

Physical Well-Being

Play promotes the development of physical skills and fosters active and healthy lifestyles necessary in fighting childhood obesity. Opportunities for children to play and move during the early years also contribute to their intellectual and social-emotional development and academic performance. More specifically, investigators have reported the effects of physical activity on EF, attention, and academic achievement (Aadland et al., 2017; Dalziell, Boyle, & Mutrie, 2015). For example, one study investigated the relation of active play during recess time with preschool children's self-regulation and early academic skills. Significant positive correlations were reported between the levels of active play and indices of self-regulation and early math and literacy skills of preschoolers (Becker, McClelland, Loprinzi, & Trost, 2014). Studies have also examined the relationship of physical activity participation with mental health, with results suggesting that children who participate in more physical activity have better social and emotional health, higher self-esteem, and fewer emotional problems (Vella, Cliff, Magee, & Okely, 2015).

Moreover, studies indicate that support from teachers predicts young children's maintaining physically active lifestyles (Guldager, Andersen, Seelen, & Leppin, 2018). Teachers' encouragement of physical play is important (Copeland, Kendeigh, Saelens, Kalkwarf, & Sherman, 2012), and this is shown by their setting up classroom opportunities for children to engage in recommended levels of physical activity, and also by how they go about arranging environments for various movement activities to increase overall physical activity and to decrease sedentary time (Neshteruk, Mazzucca, Østbye, & Ward, 2018).

Early childhood research also suggests a connection between time spent outdoors and children's well-being. For example, Largo-Wight, Guardino, Wludyka, Hall, Wight, and Merten (2018) followed kindergartners for six weeks and found that contact with nature improved student's behavior; along with fewer teacher interventions, students exhibited less off task behaviors. Ulset, Vitaro, Brendgen, Bekkus, and Borge (2017) found a positive correlation between the time spent outdoors and children's attention skills. Outdoor challenges of overcoming natural obstacles and children's deciding on risky behaviors happen in social interaction and engagement with peers, with these experiences supporting the development of confidence in children (McClain & Vandermaas-Peeler, 2015).

Educators need to find ways for maximizing outdoor time, appreciating and using the outdoors as an extension of the indoor curriculum. Research shows that teacher beliefs and practices are important predictors of the quality of outdoor play time. When teachers acknowledge and support outdoor play, children engage in play that is active, fun, risky, and challenging (Sandseter, 2012). Maynard, Waters, and Clement (2013), interestingly, found that teachers were also more likely to use open questions when outside; they seemed more relaxed and less commanding in their interactions with children. Similarly, Blanchet-Cohen and Elliot (2011) reported that teachers endorsed the idea of being outside with children because of the improved quality of their relationships with them. Compared to being indoors, spending time outside encourages teachers to be more exploratory, flexible, and imaginative due to the unknown directions of children's discoveries. Recognizing the benefits of outdoor play, motivating teachers to provide time for it, and creating environments where both teachers and children appreciate being outside, all are recommended to promote the general health and well-being of both children and teachers alike.

Creative Expression

Creativity in play is often difficult to define. Play expression varies and is more likely to approach being creative when its conditions are free, spontaneous, and unstructured – with many possible outcomes. Pretend and constructive play can encourage creative thinking and spark imagination. The question whether play is linked to general child attributes of being creative or imaginative has not been answered definitively. Mottweiler and Taylor (2014) assessed 75 four- to five-year-old children's engagement in elaborated role play through an interview and parental questionnaire. The study found that children who engaged in more elaborate role play scored significantly higher for creativity in their narratives than did children who exhibited less elaborate role play. Wallace and Russ (2015) examined how pretend play predicted the creativity of 31 girls over a four-year period, from when the girls were between five and ten years old to when they were between 9 and 14 years old. The study found that children who were more imaginative and organized in their pretend play at the start of the study scored higher on the creative test four years later. In pretend play children perform transformational operations that may be linked with creative thought (Mellou, 1995). Nevertheless, the use of imagination in pretend play is recognized as a form of creativity (Russ, 1993).

Constructive play too can become creative with the right circumstances: materials which invite open-ended play with multiple outcomes. Celebi-Oncu and Unluer (2010) examined creativity in children's play and use of play materials. Results showed that most of the children were not able to express creativity with different kinds of play materials; in their play children greatly preferred to use toys as play materials. In a second study, Celebi-Oncu and Unluer (2010) also found that most of the children were not able to use real objects as creatively as play materials. Although play may lead to more creative, innovative ways of thinking and problem solving, this does not automatically happen, and assuredly evidence of causal relations is lacking (Whitebread et al., 2017).

Play Pedagogy

Play pedagogies strive for playful learning in which play emanates from the children and educational aims come from the teachers targeting domains ranging from physical-motor, social-emotional, moral-ethical to cognitive linguistic. Activities are often networked to different curricular areas. For instance, play pedagogy for the literacy learning is teachers' planning structured learning of academic content (e.g., alphabet knowledge and letter sounds) with appropriate play activities. These typically include language and literacy-enhanced play props, such as phones and phone books, and pads and pencils for pretend writing which often involves invented spelling – an expression of phonemic awareness. Inscriptions, logos, signs, and other forms of environmental print are present that are thematically related to topics being taught or introduced elsewhere in the curriculum. For example, pretend play about a car repair garage would be linked to a storybook and art/drawing experiences about a mechanics shop, and even to drill and practice activities for learning vocabulary and basic concepts about machines, tools, and repair.

A continuum of teaching strategies is employed from low-structure free or teacher-guided play activities, to moderate structure such as play planning for small groups, to high-structure teacher-directed play pedagogy. Tiered activities and individualized teaching using play techniques are recommended in order to meet the needs and interests of all children. An important issue is degree and type of adult involvement needed for quality child-governed play to occur (Johnson et al., 2005; Van Hoorn et al., 2015).

Ugaste (2007) following Vygotsky (1978) notes the need to use actual experiences the children have had in the play so that the play contains a "personal" idea – one that is affect-laden and motivating for the children. Play pedagogy, then, is much more than simply the teachers playing with the children or observing them play. An integrated approach combines: (a) providing children with real-world experiences to set up motivation, a personal idea for play or a particular interest a child has, with knowledge about play content, (b) preparing the play environment with various props and materials, and (c) the teacher's role in scaffolding the play (Novosyolova et al., 1989). Methods using the integrated approach include imaginative, sociodramatic, and thematic-fantasy play training procedures (e.g., Saltz & Johnson, 1974; Singer, 1973; Smilansky, 1968), as well as other techniques related to learning and play that can serve classroom teachers.

Narrative Approach

Vivian Paley's narrative approach is influential in ECE (McNamee, 2015). Paley's story-telling/story-acting methods are designed to generate social, multimodal literacy through play. Her techniques focus attention on promoting children's literacy-making behaviors that support the development of a classroom narrative culture. Nicolopoulou, McDowell, and Brockmeyer (2006) have extended this method to include journal writing (scribbling to pictorial depictions to pseudo-writing using invented spelling) agreeing with Paley that fantasy play is the social glue that holds all the curricular components together and builds community.

McNamee (2015) reported that Head Start preschoolers produced stories that sometimes reflected ideas and content introduced by the teachers during other activities such as "read-a-louds," songs, and reciting and gesturing nursery rhymes. Children's own play and dramatizations and their general experiences blended together. Children shared experiences and valued others' ideas, play pedagogy brought together teacher's and children's agendas, and this was a meaningful and caring curriculum.

Paley's (2004) story-telling and story-acting method aims to advance literacy, narrative competence, and community building. This method involves children going to a story table to tell their story. Child-authored stories are later enacted with one's peers on a classroom "stage." Children benefit from an improved social-emotional climate in the classroom, and from more sensitivity and meaningfulness in the curriculum.

Play pedagogies combining child-initiated free play with teacher-guided play and teacher-directed play are recommended. Paley used free play with teacher guidance together with teacher-directed play (i.e., child story-telling with dramatization, and teacher telling a story to the classroom of children encouraging fantasy and play). Play experiences are relationally created among the children with the teacher. It is challenging and worthwhile to combine effectively child-initiated, teacher-guided, and teacher-directed play. Play over-all is a blending of play and learning (Wood, 2015).

Creative Drama

Creative drama often means that teachers and children play together, support each other and gain experiences about being someone or something other than themselves. They can continue to be who they are, but they are also not totally constrained by who they are during performing (Lobman, 2011). Creative drama helps children and teachers reorganize their cognitive patterns regarding an experience, an event, an idea, or behavior in a group setting through the use of theater or drama techniques such as role playing or improvisation (San, 2003). In creative drama, interactive and positive learning occurs in an environment which enhances social relationships and knowledge construction (Heathcote, 1984). Properly done children are encouraged to take risks themselves and to challenge others to do likewise (Holzman, 2000). Teachers lead the children nudging them to take roles and responsibilities all the while maintaining fictional worlds where they explore together roles and issues of import (O'Neill, 2008).

Collaboration happens in three stages: (1) preparation – warming up, (2) improvisation, and (3) evaluation. In the first stage participants' bodies and senses are used intensively. Games and movement activities are implemented in order to create group dynamics. Teachers lead and join in, priming the pump for everyone's engagement. Then the improvisation stage begins marked by the emergence of purpose, an idea sparking improvisation and role playing on the basis of the experiences of group members (Adiguzel, 2013). Now teachers help children take responsibilities of their roles, encouraging them to share their experiences while creating with the help of music, pictures, and colorful costumes. In the third stage teachers and children evaluate and discuss the outcomes – the significance and qualities of the activities as well as students' feelings and opinions

During improvisation and evaluation stages various creative drama strategies are used to foster participants' inquiry, creative thinking and collaboration skills, as well as scene understanding. These strategies also provide opportunities to increase character development and story-telling which are components of performance skills. Creative drama strategies include: conscience alley, flashbacks and flash forwards, forum theatre, mantle of the expert, role play, still images and freeze frames, story-telling, tableaux, and teacher in role. Effective creative drama as a play pedagogy requires teacher mastery and use of these strategies; teachers must also model and give appropriate responses and adapt expectations based on individual children's abilities and interests or needs.

Studies have found that creative drama programs enhance both children and teachers' skills and abilities. For example, Yaser and Aral (2012) reported increases in children's self-awareness and creative thinking and expression. In Lobman's (2005) study, teachers reported that their students' interactions and their skills of creativity, taking risks, and listening and accepting ideas were improved. Furthermore, creative drama may help teachers to construct their own identities (Wales, 2009). Understanding self and others teachers need to not only understand children's skills and abilities, but also improve their leadership skills by using imaginations (McCaslin, 2006) and considering children's opinions (Wee, 2009). Creative drama also enhances pre-service teachers' oral communication skills, critical thinking, creativity, and self-confidence (Athiemoolam, 2013) as well as writing skills and attitudes toward writing (Erdogan, 2013). Moreover, learning drama techniques helped teachers to respond better to children's ideas and thoughts and build self-esteem (Lee, Cawthon, & Dawson, 2013). Additionally, drama-based training has a positive effect on delivering equality and diversity training for pre-service teachers (Hayat & Walton, 2013) and offers an experience that enables pre-service teachers to rehearse difficult conversations, explore ethical dilemmas, model and explore how they want to be (Hogan, 2014). In sum, creative drama enhances pre-service and in-service teachers' communication, interaction and reasoning skills, as well as creativity.

Open-Ended Activities

Young children entering the workforce in 2030 will be facing the twenty-first century challenges which call for building knowledge, dispositions and skills for creative thinking, problem solving, and communication. How can ECE help children maximize their potential? Useful is remembering that Einstein said that imagination is more important than knowledge. Through imaginative and creative play children learn to understand the world around them. In this vein ECE in general and play pedagogy in particular should be based on a realization that children most likely employ creative thinking when they are given chances to do open-ended activities and manipulate open-ended materials freely. These opportunities advance quality play while furthering overall development. Resnick (2017) argued that optimal learning during the early years is through imagining, creating, playing, sharing, reflecting, and again imagining. People of all ages, in fact, should think and act creatively to thrive in today's changing world, and this way of thinking known for many years is ideally suited to the needs of the twenty-first century.

Piaget (1936) asserted that children actively construct knowledge through their everyday interactions with people and objects. Children seek knowledge by constantly creating, revising, and testing their own theories as they play with things around them. According to Piaget, children do not get ideas; they make them because they are active builders of knowledge, not passive recipients. Children are born with creative potential. An important ECE challenge is cultivating this understanding with only partial knowledge of the dynamics of creative work.

Some education professionals in today's practice unfortunately respond poorly to this challenge, teaching children literacy and math skills in isolation. They overlook what is even more important than learning to read and write, the exposure to the beauty of discovering numbers and letters. In *Creative Schools: The Grassroots Revolution That's Transforming Education*, Sir Kenneth Robinson (2015) highlighted that focusing on skills in isolation can kill interest in any discipline. The real drive for creative expression is the motivation and passion for discovery. Educators realize that when children are motivated in their work and play they will acquire or practice academic skills automatically, and creative mastery will grow as will their habits of the mind or dispositions to be enthused and engaged learners, makers, and players.

Quality pedagogies of play include making situational arrangements or setting the stage for using open-ended materials or loose parts (Nicholson, 1970), and doing activities that permit discovery, curiosity, exploration, imagination, and play (Al-Mansour, 2014). Creative play does not require expensive and fancy materials to flourish. Research suggests that even in the poorest country in the world, children are capable of playing creatively despite their poverty (Berinstein & Magalhaes, 2009).

A noteworthy example of using reusable, discarded, and open-ended materials is REMIDA, the creative recycling center in Reggio Emilia, Italy. Here discarded materials become resources and here unsold or rejected stock from shops is collected so that they can be reused for a different purpose. REMIDA is where you can make the most of waste materials, using them to create a new product that shows respect for the environment (Ferrari & Giacopini, 2005). Both materials from nature and those that are man-made are used by children to shape small worlds of their own, thereby enriching their imaginations. Encouraging reusable, discarded, and open-ended materials brings the old-fashioned play back on track, and helps foster creativity with its components, such as playfulness, humor, curiosity, flexibility, and originality. Such activity is fun, perhaps especially so because it is without a set of specific goals or predetermined outcomes. Working with open-ended materials is particularly effective when children are attempting to solve problems. Open-ended materials can encourage creative and divergent thinking.

Electronic Technology

Technology and media have spurred new social and cultural changes for young children's play and teachers' pedagogy. Young children's engagement with digital technology called "digital play" has led to new pedagogy aiming for multimodal learning, where children actively make their meanings and express their voices. Digital play in recreational and educational forms is a current burgeoning area of ECE research (Stephen & Edwards, 2018). Digital play refers to young children's interaction with digital technologies in a play-based manner (Marsh, Plowman, Yamada-Rice, Bishop, & Scott, 2016). Examples include taking pictures of their favorite toys with digital cameras, playing digital games and applications (apps) with iPads, shooting videos of siblings, and watching YouTube clips.

Digital play as a new curricular tool in ECE (Donohue, 2015) is growing along with its being something children like to do on their own. Modern technological inventions create new play affordances. Features of the most advanced technology (e.g., ease of use, fast reactivity, visual record, and flexibility) facilitate young children's creative play by allowing them to express their ideas and imagination visually. Active interactions among technologies, people (peers, parents, and educators), and local/global cultures empower young children's voices and perspectives, thereby enabling educators to listen to and understand children's thoughts.

Digital play can be integrated in to various play-based pedagogies (Edwards, 2013), and children's strong desire and motivation to play with digital technologies can maximize benefits of new digital media, promoting young children's persistence and ability to deal with limits. Recent studies have suggested educational potentials of children's use of or play with digital technology, such as fostering children's communication (Fleer, 2014), collaborative interaction, and independent learning (Flewitt, Messer, & Kucirkova, 2015), as well as group play with story-telling (Wohlwend, 2015), emergent literacy (Neumann & Neumann, 2017), social-emotional development (Sharapan, 2015), and communication with parents and community (Cotto, 2015).

Qualities and consequences of digital play vary depending on the kinds of digital devices and other materials children use; how, when, where, and with whom children play; and what social and cultural contexts children have. Children's engagement and learning with digital technology should be considered with different research methods and contextualized views. Recently, Guernsey (2012) and Fred Rogers Center (2012) urge consideration of the 3Cs: *Content*, *Context*, and the individual *Child*. Better digital play in ECE settings can be expected when educators operate with simultaneous attention to (1) the contents of digital play, (2) the diverse social and cultural contexts, and (3) each individual child's roles, interests, needs, and abilities. To reach this, educators need technology skills, hands-on experiences, digital literacy, teaching tools and methods, knowledge of relevant empirical research, and examples of digital play (Donohue & Schomburg, 2015). Above all, teachers should enjoy working and playing with their children using digital technology.

Summary and Conclusion

This chapter has discussed research organized in three sections: (1) definitions and concepts, including content pertaining to play and learning and play and assessment; (2) importance of play, including subsections for self-regulation, social competence, literacy, numeracy, physical well-being, and creative expression; and (3) play pedagogy, including sections on narrative approach, creative drama, the use of open-ended objects and activities, and the use of electronic technology. Content covered is important to the field and in line with the co-authors' interests. As noted in the introduction, the literature in the area is voluminous and selections had to be made. In conclusions, a few observations are offered.

With nuanced understanding of play concepts, with knowing the importance of play in child development, professionals in the field are better positioned to articulate and implement pedagogies of play, thereby stemming the tide of academic take-over of ECE. Pedagogies of play as presented in this chapter include ones requiring appropriate adult guidance and direction. That free play (i.e., child-initiated) is of paramount value (Gray, 2013) does not contradict this assertion. Both free play and adult involvement in play are important; they complement each other. Playful communities of learning in ECE settings gain strength by the dynamic tension. Play that is spontaneous or planned, child- or teacher-initiated, teacher -guided or -directed, all are important to have. Required is a binocular view adjusting one lens for getting what is meaningful to the child and the other for getting what is meaningful to the teacher(s).

Play pedagogy is successful when teachers have good relations with their children and have mastered play-based assessment and communication techniques for individual children and the group. Recently, research attention has been given to systematic evaluation group-centered teaching as an indicator of classroom quality (van Schaik, Leseman, & de Haan, 2018). More studies are needed to inform educators of young children about group processes and teacher sensitivity to group processes. In particular, this topic must be examined in relation to children's collaborative play, whether adult curated or not.

Certainly, group goals and not just individual child goals are behind the rationale for play in the ECE programs. Play in ECE programs needs further study, and especially in ones serving heterogeneous groups of young children. Teachers must know different ways to implement pedagogies of play. Some research already informs more differentiated approaches. Extended time frames and the use of open-ended materials, such as blocks for complex constructive play, have been reported to enable better social commerce between minority and majority group children, even children who do not know each other's languages (Ong, 2005). Bringing children together and having them share play experiences promotes education that is multicultural and inclusive. Paley's narrative curriculum gives children voices, and a chance to relate to each other's lives outside the walls of the school; this can be a wonderful medium of expression, kindness, and sharing – crucial to schooling and development of the mind and the human spirit (McNamee, 2005).

More focus on age-mixed play seems warranted. Its value is recognized (Katz, Evangelou, & Hartman, 1990), an indicator of quality programs by The World Organization for Early Childhood Education(*OMEP* – Organisation Mondiale pour l' Education Prescolaire). Compared to same-age social play, interactions with younger and older peers have special benefits. Older peers have opportunities to develop empathy and teaching skills while playing with younger children, and younger children learn from older role models. Given current population trends and immigration, ECE teachers need to learn more about culturally and linguistically diverse same- and mixed-age play. Research results can help ECE tap this special kind of social play's potential for facilitating learning and well-being of every child in varied ECE contexts.

References

Aadland, K., Moe, V., Aadland, E., Anderssen, S., Resaland, G., & Ommundsen, Y. (2017). Relationships between physical activity, sedentary time, aerobic fitness, motor skills and executive function and academic performance in children. *Mental Health and Physical Activity, 12*, 10–18.

Adiguzel, H. Ö. (2013). The progress and current situation of creative drama in the Turkish education system. *Journal of Education and Future, 1*(3), 97–103.

Al-Mansour, M. A. (2014). *Young children journey into a world of play with open-ended materials: A case study of the creative play club* (Unpublished doctoral dissertation). The Pennsylvania State University, University Park, Pennsylvania. Retrieved from https://etda.libraries.psu.edu/files/final_submissions/10080

Athiemoolam, L. (2013). Using drama-in-education to facilitate active participation and the enhancement of oral communication skills among first year pre-service teachers. *Scenario: Journal for Drama and Theatre in Foreign and Second Language Education, 7*(2), 22–36. Retrieved from http://research.ucc.ie/scenario/2013/02/Athiemoolam/04/en#toc

Bassok, D., Latham, S., & Rorem, A. (2016). Is kindergarten the new first grade? *AERA Open, 1*(4), 1–31. doi:10.1177/2332858415616358

Becker, D. R., McClelland, M. M., Loprinzi, P., & Trost, S. G. (2014). Physical activity, self-regulation, and early academic achievement in preschool children. *Early Education and Development, 25*(1), 56–70.

Berinstein, S., & Magalhaes, L. (2009). A study of the essence of play experience to children living in Zanzibar, Tanzania. *Occupational Therapy International, 16*(2), 89–106. doi:10.1002/oti.270

Bird, J., & Edwards, S. (2015). Children learning to use technologies through play: A digital play framework. *British Journal of Educational Technology, 46*(6), 1149–1160.

Blanchet-Cohen, N., & Elliot, E. (2011). Young children and educators engagement and learning outdoors: A basis for rights-based programming. *Early Education and Development, 22*, 757–777.

Bodrova, E. (2008). Make-believe play versus academic skills: A Vygotskian approach to today's dilemma of early childhood education. *European Early Childhood Education Research Journal, 16*(3), 357–369.

Bodrova, E., & Leong, D. (2007). *Tools of the mind* (2nd ed.). Upper Saddle River, NJ: Merrill/Pearson.

Broadhead, P., Howard, J., & Wood, E. (Eds.). (2010). *Play and learning in the early years: From research to practice*. Los Angeles, CA: SAGE Publications LTD.

Burghardt, G. (2005). *The genesis of animal play: Testing the limits*. Cambridge, MA: MIT Press.

Caillois, R. (1961). *Man, play, and games*. New York, NY: The Free Press, original work published in 1958.

Celebi-Oncu, E., & Unluer, E. (2010). Preschool children's using of play materials creatively. *Procedia Social and Behavioral Sciences, 2*, 4457–4461.

Christie, J. (2010). *Integrating dramatic play into skills-based early literacy programs*. Paper presented at a meeting of the International Council for Children's Play, Lisbon, Portugal.

Christie, J., & Roskos, K. (2007). Play in an era of early childhood standards. In T. Jambor & J. Gils (Eds.), *Several perspectives on children's play: Scientific reflections for practitioners* (pp. 133–145). Philadelphia, PA: Garant.

Copeland, K. A., Kendeigh, C. A., Saelens, B. E., Kalkwarf, H. J., & Sherman, S. N. (2012). Physical activity in child-care centers: Do teachers hold the key to the playground? *Health Education Research, 27*, 81–100.

Cotto, L. M. (2015). Technology as a tool to strengthen the community. In C. Donohue (Ed.), *Technology and digital media in the early years: Tools for teaching and learning* (pp. 218–234). New York, NY: Taylor & Francis.

Dalziell, A., Boyle, J., & Mutrie, N. (2015). Better movers and thinkers (BMT): An exploratory study of an innovative approach to physical education. *Europe's Journal of Psychology, 11*, 722–741.

DeLisi, R. (2015). Piaget's sympathetic but unromantic account of children's play. In J. Johnson, S. Eberle, T. Henricks, & D. Kuschner (Eds.), *The handbook of the study of play* (pp. 227–238). Lanham, MD: Rowan & Littlefield.

DeVries, R. (2001). Transforming the "play-oriented curriculum" and work in constructivist early education. In A. Goncu & E. Klein (Eds.), *Children in play, story, and school* (pp. 72–106). New York, NY: Guilford.

Diamond, A., Barnett, S., Thomas, J., & Munro, S. (2007). Executive function can be improved in preschoolers by regular classroom teachers. *Science, 318*, 1387–1388.

Dickinson, D., & Tabors, P. (Eds.). (2001). *Beginning literacy with language: Young children learning at home and school*. Baltimore, MD: Brookes.

Donohue, C. (2015). Technology and digital media as tools for teaching and learning in the digital age. In C. Donohue (Ed.), *Technology and digital media in the early yours: Tools for teaching and learning* (pp. 21–35). New York, NY: Routledge.

Donohue, C., & Schomburg, R. (2015). Teaching with technology: Preparing early childhood educators for the digital age. In C. Donohue (Ed.), *Technology and digital media in the early yours: Tools for teaching and learning* (pp. 36–53). New York, NY: Routledge.

Edwards, S. (2013). Digital play in the early years: A contextual response to the problem of integrating technologies and play-based pedagogies in the early childhood curriculum. *European Early Childhood Education Research Journal, 21*(2), 199–212.

Elias, C., & Berk, L. (2002). Self-regulation in young children: Is there a role for sociodramatic play? *Early Childhood Research Quarterly, 17*, 216–238.

El'konin, D. B. (1978). Psikhologiya igry [Psychology of play]. Moscow, Russia: Pedagogika.

Erdogan, T. (2013). The effect of creative drama method on pre-service classroom teachers' writing skills and attitudes towards writing. *Australian Journal of Teacher Education, 38*(1), 45–61.

Ferrari, A., & Giacopini, E. (2005). *Remida day*. Reggio Emilia, Italy: Reggio Children Publisher.

Fisher, K. R., Hirsh-Pasek, K., Golinkoff, R. M., & Newcombe, N. (2013). Taking shape: Supporting preschoolers' acquisition of geometric knowledge through guided play. *Child Development, 84*(6), 1872–1878.

Fleer, M. (2014). The demands and motives afforded through digital play in early childhood activity settings. *Learning, Culture and Social Interaction, 3*(3), 202–209.

Flewitt, R., Messer, D., & Kucirkova, N. (2015). New directions for early literacy in a digital age: The iPad. *Journal of Early Childhood Literacy, 15*(3), 289–310.

Fred Rogers Center for Early Learning and Children's Media at Saint Vincent College. (2012). *A framework for quality in digital media for children: Considerations for parents, educators, and media creators*. Latrobe, PA: Author.

Gelman, R. (2006). Young natural-number arithmeticians. *Current Directions in Psychological Science, 15*, 193–197.

Ginsburg, H. (2006). Mathematical play and playful mathematics: A guide to early education. In D. Singer, R. Michnick Golinkoff, & K. Hirsh-Pasek (Eds.), *Play-learning: How play motivates and enhances children's cognitive and social-emotional growth* (pp. 145–165). New York, NY: Oxford University Press.

Gray, P. (2013). *Free to learn: Why unleasing the instinct to play will make our children happier, more self-reliant, and better students for life.* New York, NY: Basic Books

Guernsey, L. (2012). *Screen time: How electronic media from baby videos to educational software affects your young child.* New York, NY: Basic Books.

Guldager, D. J., Andersen, P. T., von Seelen, J., & Leppin, A. (2018). Physical activity school intervention: Context matters. *Health Education Research, 33*(3), 232–242.

Hayat, K., & Walton, S. (2013). Delivering equality and diversity training within a university setting through Drama-Based training. *Journal of Psychological Issues in Organizational Culture, 3*(S1), 290–305. doi:10.1002/jpoc.21096

Heathcote, D. (1984). From the particular to the universal. In L. Johnson & C. O' Neill (Eds.), *Collected writings on education and drama* (pp. 103–110). London, UK: Hutchinson.

Hirsh-Pasek, K., Roberta, M. G., Berk, L. R., & Singer, D. (2009). *A mandate for playful learning in preschool.* New York, NY: Oxford University Press.

Hogan, S. (2014). Being ethical: Process drama and professional ethics education for pre- service drama teachers. *N J The Drama Australia Journal, 38*(1), 74–87.

Holzman, L. (2000). Performative psychology: An untapped resource for educators. *Educational and Child Psychology, 17*(3), 86–103.

Huizinga, J. (1955). *Humo Ludens: A study of the play-element in civilization.* Boston, MA: Beacon.

Johnson, J. (2016). Play, definition of. In C. Couchenour & K. Chrisman (Eds.), The SAGE *encyclopedia of contemporary early childhood education,* Volume 3 (pp. 1011–1014). Thousand Oaks, CA: SAGE Publications LTD.

Johnson, J., Al-Mansour, M., & Sevimli-Celik, S. (2014). Researching play in early childhood. In O. N. Saracho (Ed.), *Handbook of research methods in early childhood education: Review of research methodologies,* Volume II (pp. 473–507). Charlotte, NC: Information Age Publishing.

Johnson, J., Christie, J., & Wardle, F. (2005). *Play, development, and early education.* Boston, MA: Allyn & Bacon.

Katz, L., Evangelou, D., & Hartman, J. (1990). *The case for mixed-age groupings in early education.* Washington, DC: National Association for the Education of Young Children.

Kuschner, D. (2012). Play is natural to childhood but school is not, The problem of integrating play into the curriculum. *International Journal of Play, 1*(3), 242–249.

Largo-Wight, E., Guardino, C., Wludyka, P. S., Hall, K. W., Wight, J. T., & Merten, J. W. (2018). Nature contact at school: The impact of an outdoor classroom on children's well-being. *International Journal of Environmental Health Research, 28*(6), 653–666. doi:10.1080/09603123.2018.1502415

Lee, B., Cawthon, S., & Dawson, K. (2013). Elementary and secondary teacher self-efficacy for teaching and pedagogical conceptual change in a drama-based professional development program. *Teaching and Teacher Education, 30,* 84–98.

Lobman, C. (2005). "Yes and": The uses of improvisation for early childhood professional development. *Journal of Early Childhood Teacher Education, 26*(3), 305–319.

Lobman, C. (2011). Democracy and development: The role of outside-of-school experiences in preparing young people to be active citizens. *Democracy and Education, 19*(1), Article 5.

Marsh, J., Plowman, L., Yamada-Rice, D., Bishop, J., & Scott, F. (2016). Digital play: A new classification. *Early Years, 36*(3), 242–253.

Maynard, T., Waters, J., & Clement, J. (2013). Moving outdoors: Further explorations of 'child-initiated' learning in the outdoor environment. *Education, 41*(3), 282–299.

McCaslin, N. (2006). *Creative drama in the classroom and beyond* (8th ed.). Boston, MA: Allyn & Bacon.

McClain, C., & Vandermaas-Peeler, M. (2015). Social contexts of development in natural outdoor environments: Children's motor activities, personal challenges and peer interactions at the river and the creek. *Journal of Adventure Education and Outdoor Learning, 16*(1), 31–48.

McNamee, G. (2005). "The one who gathers children": The work of Vivian Gussin Paley and current debates about how we educate young children. *Journal of Early Childhood Teacher Education, 25,* 275–296.

McNamee, G. (2015). *The high-performing preschool, Story acting in Head Start classrooms.* Chicago, IL: University of Chicago Press.

Mellou, E. (1995). Review of the relationship between dramatic play and creativity in young children. *Early Child Development and Care, 112,* 85–107.

Montessori, M. (1964). *The Montessori method.* New York, NY: Schocken Publishers (Original work published, 1912).

Mottweiler, C. M., & Taylor, M. (2014). Elaborated role play and creativity in preschool age children. *Psychology of Aesthetics, Creativity, and the Arts, 8*(3), 277–286. doi:10.1037/a0036083

Neshteruk, C. D., Mazzucca, S., Østbye, T., & Ward, D. S. (2018). The physical environment in family childcare homes and children's physical activity. *Child Care Health Development, 44,* 746–752.

Neumann, M. M., & Neumann, D. L. (2017). The use of touch-screen tablets at home and pre-school to foster emergent literacy. *Journal of Early Childhood Literacy, 17*(2), 203–220.

Nicholson, S. (1970). "What do playgrounds teach?" *The planning and design of the recreation environment.* Davis, CA: University of California-Davis Publishers.

Nicolopoulou, A., McDowell, J., & Brockmeyer, C. (2006). Narrative play and emergent literacy: Storytelling and story-acting meet journal writing. In D. Singer, R. Michnick Golinkoff, & K. Hirsh-Pasek (Eds.), *Play-learning: How play motivates and enhances children's cognitive and social-emotional growth* (pp. 124–144). New York, NY: Oxford University Press.

Novosyolova, S., Zvorygina, E., Ivankova, R., Kondratova, V., Saar, A., & Grinjaviciene, N. (1989). The integral method of play facilitation at the preschool age. In S. Novosyolova (Ed.), *Igra doshkol'nika [Child's play at preschool age]* (pp. 70–94). Moscow, Russia: Pedaogika.

O'Neill, B. (2008). *Storytelling and creative drama: A dynamic approach to inclusive early childhood education* (Unpublished doctoral dissertation). Teachers College, Columbia University, New York, NY.

Ong, N. (2005). *Cultural diversity in education.* Paper presented at "Block building: Fostering cognitive, linguistic, and social competence session" National Association for the Education of Young Children, Washington, DC.

Paley, V. (2004). *A child's work: The importance of fantasy play.* Chicago, IL: University of Chicago Press.

Panksepp, J. (2010). Science of the brain as a gateway to understanding play: An interview with Jaak Panksepp. *American Journal of Play, 2*(3), 245–277.

Pellis, S., Pellis, V., & Bell, H. (2010). The function of play in the development of the social brain. *American Journal of Play, 2*(3), 278–296.

Piaget, J. (1936). *Origins of intelligence in the child.* London, UK: Routledge & Kegan Paul.

Ramani, G., & Siegler, R. (2008). Promoting broad and stable improvements in low-income children's numerical knowledge through playing board games. *Child Development, 79*(2), 375–394.

Resnick, M. (2017). *Lifelong kindergarten: Cultivating creativity through projects, passion, peers, and play.* Cambridge, MA. The MIT Press.

Riley, D., San Juan, R., Klinkner, J., & Ramminger, A. (2008). *Social and emotional development: Connecting science and practice in early childhood settings.* St. Paul, MN: Redleaf Press.

Robinson, K. (2015). *Creative schools: The grassroots revolution that's transforming education.* New York, NY: Penguin Publishing Group.

Rogers, S., & Evan, J. (2008). *Inside role-play in early childhood education: Researching young children's perspectives.* New York, NY: Routledge.

Roskos, K., & Christie, J. (2004). Examining the play-literacy interface: A critical review and future directions. In E. F. Zigler, D. Singer, &

S. Bishop-Josef (Eds.), *Children's play: Roots of reading* (pp. 95–123). Washington, DC: Zero to Three.

Rubin, K., Maioni, T., & Hornung, M. (1976). Free play behaviors in middle- and lower- class children: Parten and Piaget revisited. *Child Development, 47*, 414–419.

Russ, S. W. (1993). *Affect and creativity: The role of affect and play in the creative process*. Hillsdale, NJ: Erlbaum.

Saltz, E., & Johnson, J. (1974). Training for thematic-fantasy play in culturally disadvantaged children: Preliminary results. *Journal of Educational Psychology, 66*, 623–630.

San, I. (2003). Dramada Temel Kavramlar. [Creative drama in education] In A. Öztürk (Ed.), Çocukta Yaratıcılık ve Drama. Eskişehir: Anadolu Üniversitesi Yayınları Nu: 1488 [*Creativity and drama in childhood*]. Ankara, Turkey: Anadolu University Publications.

Sandseter, E. B. H. (2012). Restrictive safety or unsafe freedom? Norwegian ECEC practitioners' perceptions and practices concerning children's risky play. *Child Care in Practice, 18*(1), 83–101.

Sharapan, H. (2015). Technology as a tool for social-emotional development: What we can learn from fred rogers' approach. In C. Donohue (Ed.), *Technology and digital media in the early yours: Tools for teaching and learning* (pp. 12–20). New York, NY: Routledge.

Singer, J. (1973). *The child's world of make-believe: Experimental studies of imaginative play*. New York, NY: Academic Press.

Smilansky, S. (1968). *The effects of socio-dramatic play on disadvantaged preschool children*. New York, NY: Wiley.

Spodek, B. (1974). The problem of play: Educational or recreational. In D. Sponseller (Ed.), *Play as a learning medium* (pp. 7–28). Washington, DC: National Association for the Education of Young Children.

Stephen, C., & Edwards, S. (2018). *Young children playing and learning in a digital age: A cultural and critical perspective*. New York, NY: Routledge.

Ugaste, A. (2007). The cultural-historical approach to play in the kindergarten context. In T. Jambor & J. Gils (Eds.), *Several perspectives on children's play: Scientific reflections for practitioners* (pp. 105–118). Philadelphia, PA: Garant.

Ulset, V., Vitaro, F., Brendgen, M., Bekkus, M., & Borge, A. (2017). Time spent outdoors during preschool: Links with children's cognitive and behavioral development. *Journal of Environmental Psychology, 52*, 69–80.

Van Hoorn, J., Nourot, P., Scales, B., & Alward, K. (2015). *Play at the center of the curriculum* (6th ed.). Columbus, OH: Pearson Merrill Prentice Hall.

Van Schaik, S., Leseman, P., & de Haan, M. (2018). Using a group-centered approach to observe interactions in early childhood education. *Child Development, 89*(3), 897–913.

Vella, S. A., Cliff, D. P., Magee, C. A., & Okely, A. D. (2015). Associations between sports participation and psychological difficulties during childhood: A two-year follow up. *Journal of Science and Medicine in Sport, 18*(3), 304–309.

Vygotsky, L. (1978). *Mind in society: The development of higher psychological processes*. Cambridge, MA: Harvard University Press.

Wales, P. (2009). Positioning the drama teacher: Exploring the power of identity in teaching practices. Research in drama education. *The Journal of Applied Theatre and Performance, 14*(2), 261–278.

Wallace, C. E., & Russ, S. W. (2015). Pretend play, divergent thinking, and math achievement in girls: A longitudinal study. *Psychology of Aesthetics, Creativity, and the Arts, 9*(3), 296–305. doi:10.1037/a0039006

Wee, S. J. (2009). A case study of drama education curriculum for young children in early childhood programs. *Journal of Research in Childhood Education, 23*(4), 489–501.

Whitebread, D. (2010). Play, metacognition and self-regulation. In P. Broadhead, J. Howard, & E. Wood (Eds.), *Play and learning in the early years* (pp. 161–176). Los Angeles, CA: SAGE Publications LTD.

Whitebread, D. (2018). Play: The new renaissance. *International Journal of Play, 7*(3), 237–243.

Whitebread, D., Neale, D., Jensen, H., Liu, C., Solis, S. L., Hopkins, E., … Zosh, J. M. (2017). *The role of play in children's development: A review of the evidence* (research summary). The LEGO Foundation, DK. Retrieved from https://www.legofoundation.com/media/1065/play-types-_-development-review_web.pdf

Wohlwend, K. E. (2015). One screen, many fingers: Young children's collaborative literacy play with digital puppetry apps and touchscreen technologies. *Theory into Practice, 54*(2), 154–162.

Wood, E. (2015). The play-pedagogy interface in contemporary debates. In L. Brooker, M. Blaise, & S. Edwards (Eds.), *The SAGE Handbook of play and learning in early childhood* (pp. 145–156). Los Angeles, CA: SAGE Publications LTD.

Worthington, M. (2010). Play is a complex landscape: Imagination and symbolic meanings. In P. Broadhead, J. Howard, & E. Wood (Eds.), *Play and learning in the early years* (pp. 127–144). Los Angeles, CA: SAGE Publications LTD.

Yaser, M. C. & Aral, N. (2012). Drama education on the creative thinking skills of 61–72 months old pre-school children. *US-China Education Review A, 6*, 568–577.

Yogman, M., Garner, A., Hutchinson, J., Hirsh-Pasek, K., & Golinkoff, R. M. (2018). The power of play: A pediatric role in enhancing development in young children. *Pediatrics, 142*(3), e20182058.

12

The Landscape of Outdoor Play

John A. Sutterby

When one considers the landscape of outdoor play, generally people consider the playground equipment available and its arrangement. Perhaps the green scaping around the equipment might also be considered as part of the environment. The real landscape is a bit more complicated; there are elements beyond playground equipment that should be considered conceptualizing the landscape. As an expanded concept of the landscape of play, additional elements will be included like the historical precedents of play, the attitudes of adults toward the outdoors, the governmental policies which regulate play and alternatives to traditional play environments.

The landscape of play is not static. The types of materials available for play change over time. The players themselves are also changing. The culture of play is changing. The outdoor play of traditional games is being replaced by indoor cyber activities. Outdoor play is being changed because of adult anxiety, which is limiting the types of activities that children can do without close adult supervision. Finally, academic anxiety is changing the landscape of play in that rather than engaging in free unsupervised play, children are instead in structured play activities outdoors such as sports leagues (Frost, 2012).

The purpose of this chapter is to examine some of the less visible elements of the landscape of play as well as how they have changed and adapted over time. In addition, this chapter will describe some of the current elements of the landscape that will help better understand why play spaces look the way they do and what play they might find in the current context.

History of Outdoor Environments and Play

Understanding the history surrounding outdoor environments gives a better understanding on how outdoor play spaces have evolved over time and how each era influences the following. The ideal of the outdoors and attitudes toward the outdoors are not a static experience. Early colonials had a great distrust toward the outdoors. They saw themselves as acting on God's will to eradicate the wilderness. The wilderness was considered dangerous and people who lived in the wilderness, especially Native Americans, were looked upon with suspicion. The goal of these early settlers was to reshape the landscape into one resembling the English countryside (Pluymers, 2011). Play in the outdoors was discouraged for children during this era as play was seen as a sinful waste of time. Native American children at this time on the other hand spent a great deal of time in the outdoors engaged in play and exploration (Frost, 2010).

Romantic and Democratic Ideals for Play

The Romantic period of the early nineteenth century began to challenge attitudes toward the wilderness. Henry David Thoreau for example lived a simple life in his experience at Waldon Pond. He advocated for a slower pace of life, as he spent his time hiking and observing nature. The rapid urbanization and industrialization of that period encouraged resistance that led to back to nature movements. Thoreau traveled deep into nature and found there a spiritual experience. Humans in industrialized society were seen as lacking part of their human identity (Lifton, 1998).

One of the most significant members of the Romantic Movement in relation to the landscape of play was Frederick Froebel, the father of kindergarten. His experience as a forest agent and his work in a mineral museum led him to see that nature itself was the center and foundation of knowledge. He created an early childhood curriculum based on experiences in nature such as gardening and hiking along with experiences with materials such as blocks to lead children to understand the significance of nature and the environment. Many play elements of Froebel's kindergartens remain today in modern preschools such as fingerplays, block play, outdoor circle games and nature excursions (Brosterman, 1997).

The concept of the public park grew out of these romantic ideals. Frederick Law Olmsted was somewhat of a product of the romantic nature movement encouraged by Thoreau and Emerson among others. He was tasked to develop a great park in the center of Manhattan Island in New York City.

The significant people in New York City wanted a park as they saw unregulated building across the island. These people wanted to preserve a part of Manhattan as a natural preserve. Central Park project became one of the first places where play and recreation would be seen as important and protected (Sutterby, 2017a).

Olmsted and his colleague Calvert Vaux were hired to design and build a park like none other in the world. This park, Central Park, became the first major park in a major city open to the public. The park itself is completely designed by Olmsted, the first of the landscape architects. Streams, tree plantings and rolling hills are all man-made creations designed to look like native environments. Second, the park itself is designed to be open to all. Efforts to wall off parts of the park for wealthy patrons are discouraged in order to allow all citizens of New York the opportunity for leisure in nature. Olmsted also wanted the parks to encourage people to come together and not isolate themselves in their neighborhoods (Menard, 2010; Roper, 1973).

These larger park designs spread across the country. Olmsted went on to champion other public park developments such as the Prospect Park in New York, Emerald Neckless Parks in Boston and the Yosemite Park in California to preserve these spaces for everyone not just the very wealthy (Kosnoski, 2011; Sutterby, 2017b). Increasing attention to leisure for adults also began to foster an interest in opportunities for children to play safely in environments designed specifically for play.

The Playground Movement

The idea of the playground for building for democracy was also seen with the beginnings of the Playground Movement. The Playground Movement was an undercurrent of the Progressive Movement of the late nineteenth and early twentieth centuries. Immigrants from Europe were coming to the United States in large numbers. Making these immigrants conform to US values was a concern to Progressive leaders. Many large cities decided to concentrate on the Americanization of children as a way to change these immigrant communities. The Playground Movement was seen as one way to do this. Playgrounds were built in mostly urban settings to teach American games such as baseball, physical fitness and orderliness (Frost, 2010).

The inclusion of places for children to play spread across the United States until nearly every large city included playgrounds for children to play on as well as playgrounds as part of the school landscape. The increasing urbanization of the United States during this time period was a factor in the development of these playgrounds. These original playgrounds were often very large manufactured pieces of equipment often installed over hard surfaces. These spaces provided great risk to the children who played in them, but they also were a sheltered space away from the streets and increasing automobile traffic (Frost, 1991).

Playground and Recreational Segregation

It is important to note that the democratic ideals behind the movement to build parks and playgrounds have not been shared equally with all US citizens. Although the Playground Movement tried to develop play facilities, these facilities were often segregated by race. Playground segregation was part of Jim Crow Law in the South as well as de facto segregation of play facilities in other parts of the country. 'Parks' boards' often would only create parks and playgrounds in White areas of cities and create parks for Black citizens on a smaller scale and with inferior facilities. Black citizens often created private parks for recreational purposes as they were not allowed to use White-only facilities (McQueeney, 2015).

National parks were also segregated depending on local custom. National parks in the South, for example the National Park at Hot Springs, Arkansas, did not allow African American Patrons, although they did have African American attendants. While parks such as Shenandoah National Park provided segregated facilities for Black and White patrons, most national parks in the South remained segregated until the beginning of World War II when the park service began to desegregate facilities (Shumaker, 2005).

In 1954 Brown vs. The Board of Education struck down laws allowing for segregation of school facilities. It required many years more and the Civil Rights Movement to officially end segregation in public facilities such as parks and playgrounds. Unfortunately, de facto segregation of play facilities continues as communities create private facilities or exclude persons based on financial requirements. In many places schools have been resegregated through the use of attendance zones that create schools that are 100% children of color (Hannah-Jones, 2014).

Currently, there is still a difference in opportunities to access play environments in many areas based on race and ethnicity. Children of color are more likely to attend schools without recess. They also live in areas which have inferior play environments (Jarrett, Sutterby, DeMarie, & Stenhouse, 2015). Research on playgrounds in St. Louis for example found that Black children were more likely to live farther away from a safe playground than White children (Arroyo-Johnson et al., 2016). In New York City, playground evaluations showed a difference between White and Black participants when considering playground maintenance, cleanliness and safety (Silver, Giorgio, & Mijanovich, 2014).

National parks are also still experiencing segregation. Hispanics and African Americans make up a smaller proportion of park visitors in relation to their percentage of the population as a whole in the United States. Hispanics and African Americans were less likely to express knowledge of parks and are more likely to feel unsafe in national parks. Economic segregation at national parks may also become more of a concern as increasing entrance fees will keep low-income families from visiting national parks (Taylor, Grandjean, & Gramann, 2011).

Community-Based Playgrounds

World War II spawned a renewed interest in play and democratic ideals. One forerunner of the Community-Based Playgrounds Movement, Aldo Van Eyck, set out to build play into the urban landscape of post-war Amsterdam. Using simple materials such as sand and concrete and climbers, Van Eyck set out to bring children's play into the center of the community. He worked with city leaders as well as neighborhoods in a collaborative fashion. He eventually designed and oversaw the construction of over 700 play spaces in the city (Lefaivre, Roode, & Fuchs, 2002).

Another forerunner for the Community-Based Playground Movement was the Adventure Playground Movement which was popular in Europe. The Adventure Playground Movement started in Denmark toward the end of World War II. These playgrounds had little if any equipment, but instead building materials such as bricks, ropes and boards. The children built the play structures themselves under the supervision of adult play leaders (Bengtsson, 1972). Adventure playgrounds never really caught on in the United States as they do not generally fit American sensibilities (Frost, 2010).

"Let's build a playground!" was a phrase heard often in the decades of the 1970s and 1980s. This time period for playground development has been called the Community-Based Playground era (Sutterby, 2017b). As communities set out to build their own playgrounds, they often turned to playground design leaders who wrote texts on how to organize and build a playground with few resources. This usually involved using scrap lumber, tires, cable spools, ropes and other cast-off materials.

The Community-Based Playground Movement was seen as a democratic effort to get the users of the playground to participate in the creation of the playground. They espoused a community-centered ethic that people who built their own playgrounds would have ownership of it and would be more likely to take care of it.

> I used to think I wanted to built (sic) playgrounds for people; then I thought that I would build playgrounds with people; but now I see that by far the best-though most difficult-way is to encourage people to build for themselves.
>
> (Hogan, 1974, p. xi)

The Community-Built Playground Movement began to lose steam in the 1990s. The materials like wood and ropes used to build the playgrounds deteriorated and had to be replaced or removed. New playground regulations like the Consumer Product Safety Commission Handbook of Playground Safety and the Americans with Disabilities Act limited what playgrounds could contain. In addition, improved manufacturing practices such as injection molded play components lead to the end of this era (Frost & Sutterby, 2017; Sutterby, 2017b).

Current Play Environments

An analysis of the current landscape of play shows a movement away from the community and democratic ideals that were prevalent in previous playground movements and into a more bureaucratic and controlled context. The type of playground and playground equipment available today for children's play at public parks and schools has become standardized to a great extent. Playground equipment is expected to require little or no maintenance. A handful of types of equipment are generally found such as slides, climbers, some overhead equipment, panels and sometimes swings. The decks and many of the climbers are made out of steel or aluminum and the slides and panels are made from pressure molding.

Playground companies which used to emphasize fun now must find ways to include curricular activities or emphasize the fitness benefits of playground equipment in order to sell it to schools and public parks. Playground surfacing tends to rotate around either poured rubber surfacing, shredded rubber or shredded bark mulch. Shade structures which were relatively unknown 25 years ago are now ubiquitous. Unfortunately, the standardization of playground equipment has also lead to playgrounds which pretty much look the same no matter what context they are in (Frost, Wortham, & Reifel, 2012; Sutterby, 2017a).

As we examine this changing landscape for play, a number of forces have begun to exert themselves on the play environment. The main forces shaping what play spaces look like and how children play in these spaces are a growing culture of fear by adults for children's unsupervised play, an emphasis on playground safety, the influence of public policies on play environments and the requirements of the Americans with Disabilities Act on play and recreational environments.

Adult Attitudes toward Outdoor Play
Nothing sells newspapers as quickly as fear.

(Engle, 2018, p. 32)

Adult Fear and Supervision

One of the dramatic changes to the landscape of children's play over the last couple of decades is the idea that children cannot be left unsupervised by an adult at any time (Brooks, 2018). This has an impact on children in that their opportunities for recreation are reduced. An issue discussed in popular culture is the idea that adults need to be constantly supervising children. There are often stories in the news about a parent who leaves their child in a car or at home, or allows them to walk the dog alone, who is then charged with criminal child endangerment or neglect. Adult fear for children's safety has become a serious concern as it reduces the opportunities of children to play and explore their own world.

This fear is expressed as a fear of stranger danger and the idea that everything possible should be done to keep children from any physical risk at all. Research indicates that these risks are less than they are perceived to be and that they are overblown by the media. Because this fear is so pervasive it is leading people to report to law enforcement for children in activities such as walking a dog, sitting in a car and playing in a public park. Although directed at parents, it is more typically mothers who are blamed and shamed for not providing what the reporter believes to be sufficient supervision (Brooks, 2018).

Allowing children to be unsupervised was once considered the purview of parents, increasingly law enforcement is being used to coerce parents into not allowing their children freedom from supervision. Laws meant to deter child abuse and neglect are now being used when parents have encouraged children to play in a park or explore their neighborhood. Some states are beginning to codify how much supervision children require and at what age. The application of these laws however is often left to local prosecutors who have widely different beliefs about supervision (Brooks, 2018; Sullivan, 2015).

The idea that supervision should be constant is becoming more pervasive in child safety literature. Inadequate supervision on playgrounds by parents and caregivers according to Huynh, Demeter, Burke and Upperman (2017) leads to increases in playground injuries. Although parents and caregivers in the study claimed to be supervising, they were also distracted either with electronic devices or talking to other adults. Parents and caregivers also perceived the playground as a safe place to play so their requirements for supervision are less.

Adult fear has led to the shrinking of children's play worlds often limited to indoor spaces. The consequence of this is the lack of physical activity children get and the increased incidence of diabetes and obesity in children. Lack of outdoor activity can also have negative effects onchildren's well-being as exposure to natural environments has been shown to improve health outcomes (Sharma-Brymer & Bland, 2016).

This emphasis on supervision of outdoor play also applies to school contexts. Schwebel (2006) describes a playground scenario where playground monitors supervise about 150 children. He asks, "Are the children on our imagined playground safe? Clearly not" (p. 142). The suggestion that children are not safe on a playground even when supervised is part of this culture of fear spread by experts on safety. Schwebel suggests that adult supervisors should spend more time reinforcing rules, limiting children's activities and impulsive behaviors and model safe behaviors. Increased adult supervision is recommended without considering what the consequences might be for children's free play.

There is a movement that is resisting the idea that children should be treated as incompetent and unable to function without supervision. Originally called the "free range" children's movement it is now going under the title "Let Grow." The idea is based on the work of Lenore Skenazy (2010) who let her child ride on the subway unsupervised. This movement encourages parents to let their children explore their outdoor environment so that they will become competent and confident. As a backlash against punishing parents for letting their children explore, Utah has passed the first free range law allowing for parents to decide how much supervision their children require (De la Cruz, 2018).

Playground Safety

One aspect of the landscape which has been based on adult fear is the emphasis on playground safety. Since the publication of the Consumer Product Safety Commission guidelines in 1981, the *Public Playground Safety Handbook* (CPSC, 2015) has been used as the primary standard for safety for playgrounds in the United States. In an effort to meet the requirements of the handbook and to help recognize equipment that meets these guidelines, the International Playground Equipment Manufacturers Association has developed a certification program for playground equipment manufacturers and for manufacturers of playground surfacing.

In order to meet the standards for certification, playground equipment manufacturers have had to develop designs which are fairly limited in scope. There is not much difference between different climbers, slides have to be done in a particular way and swings are standardized as well. The reliance on these standards has led to many types of equipment being eliminated from most playgrounds. For example, merry-go-rounds have generally disappeared from playgrounds. There is a variety of spinning equipment still available, but it is generally not in the form of the traditional merry-go-round. Teeter totters or see saws also have been mostly eliminated from playgrounds.

The cost of the equipment and the large space requirements are two factors that have led to the elimination of this equipment from playgrounds. Another factor is adult perception of risk. Many adults associate danger with equipment such as merry-go-rounds and teeter totters as they may associate them with earlier versions from their childhoods. Another frequent victim of lack of space and perception of risk on the playground are swings. Although they are almost always listed as one of the most popular pieces of playground equipment, they do require a great deal of space and often are perceived as dangerous.

Changing Policies

> The playground at Maple Street Elementary School is quiet these days. The only movements on the swing sets are a result of a strong west wind edging the swings back and forth.
> (Henley, McBride, Milligan, & Nichols, 2007, p. 56)

The landscape of outdoor play is not only the physical environment but also the policies that shape these environments and how children are allowed to interact with these environments.

One major change to the landscape for play has been the increased emphasis on academics in public schooling through the Accountability Movement. The Accountability Movement has been around for a long time. Over the years, it has been noted that children's opportunities to play have been reduced. Henley et al. (2007) discuss how the passage of the No Child Left Behind Act impeded children's opportunities for outdoor play. They suggest children's childhoods are being robbed because they no longer have the opportunity to act like children. This also leaves playgrounds empty as children no longer have time for outdoor play.

More recently the trend to reduced hours of free play time continues to be noted. Jarrett (2016) describes how recess has been eliminated for many young children as test preparation takes up more and more time in the classroom. Thacher (2010) also describes how morning recess was eliminated from the schedule so children can spend more time on academics. Although there are many benefits of recess for children, eliminating recess often seems like an easy solution for schools that underperform on state exams.

The Accountability Movement is also impacting children's opportunities for outdoor play after school. Teachers seeking to increase test scores along with parents wanting their children to succeed academically have encouraged the increase in homework which children are expected to complete. Children, especially elementary age children, have seen steady increases in the amount of time required for homework and the number of days of homework, leaving less unstructured time after the school day (Jacobson, 2008; Loveless, 2014).

Americans with Disabilities Act

The final rule for the children's playgrounds was published by the US Access Board in 2004 (McGovern, 2015). These rules apply to new construction and reconstruction of playgrounds. This rule requires several elements to be included in new playground construction, including accessibility of different types of play components, ways to access elevated components like ramps and transfer platforms as well as a route to the playground and requirements that safety surfacing also be accessible (U.S. Access Board, 2005).

The purpose of these rules is to allow children and adults with mobility issues the opportunity to engage with their peers during a free play experience. Ripat and Becker (2012) suggest that inclusivity is one of the most important factors for children with disabilities. Although children with mobility issues cannot participate in all activities on a playground, being in the middle of the action is considered to be a major source of enjoyment. Another significant factor that impacts children with disabilities on the playground is the importance of having similar playground experiences as children without mobility issues. Participating in swinging, reaching a height or engaging in pretend play within the playground are all experiences that children with disabilities are able to enjoy when the playground is accessible.

Unfortunately, the new rules do not apply to grandfathered playgrounds, so many playgrounds remain inaccessible for children with disabilities. In these cases, children either do not participate in play or have to resort to relying on adults to carry them onto playground equipment. Shade is also another important issue for some children with disabilities, so facilities that do not provide shade are avoided (Ripat & Becker, 2012).

One suggestion for increasing the use of playgrounds by people with disabilities is to include them in the actual design process of the play space. Many playground designers are unaware of how to design a space to make it more accessible. The guidelines provided by the Americans with Disabilities Act give regulations, but may not realize how children actually use the space. Also there has not been much thought to how children with other disabilities play, for example, children with sensory issues or autism may not have spaces designed for them (Woolley, 2013).

New Landscapes for Outdoor Play

Although the current landscape for play has become more controlled and standardized, there are members of the community who are working to return to the more democratic ideals of previous generations. The landscape for outdoor play has often centered around built environments such as parks, playgrounds and schools. More recently, alternative spaces for play have been developed that expand the notion of what a play space should be. Traditionally, especially in rural America, play spaces were informal, natural and spontaneous. Schoolyards had little if any playground equipment so children used natural materials and elements as the focus of play (Frost, 2010, 2012). Some of the new landscapes for play include unschooling programs and nature preschools.

Unschooling

Home schooling and unschooling present new opportunities for children to engage in outdoor play environments. Unschooling programs encourage children to engage in their own academic pursuits which often allows for more unstructured time during the day. Unschooling and home schooling environments do not limit children to only indoor environments and also encourage play across age groups. They encourage exploration and play rather than structured curriculum and structured schedules (Gray, 2016).

Summer programs are unschooling environments in that they are often able to step out from traditional academics as they are often less academically focused. Because of this freedom they can include more innovative types of outdoor activities. Kinard, Gainer and Soto Huerta (2018) describe one such program at an early childhood center. In this program, the children are not confined to any particular space during the school day; instead, they can move from classroom to classroom or from the classroom to the outdoors. Because it is a summer program there is no intent to turn outdoor play into a contrived learning experience. The environment and the players themselves provide the learning experience.

Nature Preschools

Following the release of Louv's *Last child in the woods* (2008), there has been renewed interest in getting children to experience the outdoors in a natural space rather than a build space. Modeled after European forest kindergartens which have children spend virtually the entire day outdoors in any type of weather. These less structured programs usually have little academic content and rely on nature itself as the focus of learning. The number of these schools in the United States has increased dramatically over the last decade (Bailie, 2012; NAAEE, 2017).

The importance of natural environments for children has been documented by research over several decades. Outdoor play provides mental health benefits like reducing anxiety and depression. Vegetation cover for example has been linked to reducing mild and moderate depression (Cox et al., 2017). Young children who are more connected to nature, even in urban environments, have better social and emotional well-being (Sobko, Jia, & Brown, 2018). Acknowledging the robust impact of nature on children's health should serve as an important incentive for the continued spread of nature preschools.

Conclusions

This chapter has examined the current landscape of play in the context of historical touchpoints rooted in outreach and segregation. Adult attitudes toward play and play environments have also been examined and how these shape the types of activities children can engage in. Administrative policies shape the types of play spaces which are available, when they are available and to whom they are available. Finally, alternatives to traditional environments are examined to see where play environments might be going next.

Creating environments for play is always situated in a particular context. In this case the current environment is one where there is a situation where efforts to create a safe place to play are being challenged by an effort to bring back the ideals of play occurring within a community. An ideal of the play environment as a place where people from all walks of life play and recreate together is something that has long been part of the fabric of American life. Focusing on that ideal will help communities continue to plan for play and enhance the lives of children and their families.

References

Arroyo-Johnson, C., Woodward, K., Milam, L., Ackermann, N., Komaie, G., Goodman, M., & Hipp, J. (2016). Still separate, still unequal: Social determinants of playground safety and proximity disparities in St. Louis. *Urban Health: Bulletin of the New York Academy of Medicine, 93*(4), 627–638. doi:10.1007/s11524-016-0063-8

Bailie, P. E. (2012). *Connecting children to nature: A multiple case study of nature center preschools* (Doctoral dissertation). University of Nebraska – Lincoln. Available from ProQuest Dissertations and Theses database (Order No: 3546594).

Bengtsson, A. (1972). *Adventure playgrounds*. New York, NY: Praeger.

Brooks, K. (2018). *Small animals: Parenthood in the age of fear*. New York, NY: Flatiron Books.

Brosterman, N. (1997). *Inventing kindergarten*. New York, NY: Harry N. Abrams.

Consumer, Product Safety Commission. (2015). *Public playground safety handbook*. Bethesda, MA: Consumer Product Safety Commission.

Cox, D., Shanahan, D., Hudson, H., Plummer, K., Siriwardena, G., Fuller, R., … Gaston, K. (2017). Doses of neighborhood nature: The benefits for mental health of living with nature. *BioScience, 67*, 147–155. doi:10.1093/biosci/biw173

De la Cruz, D. (March 29, 2018). Utah passes 'free range' parents law. *New York Times*, Retrieved from https://www.nytimes.com/2018/03/29/well/family/utah-passes-free-range-parenting-law.html

Engle, M. (2018). *Jazz owls: A novel of the Zoot Suit riots*. New York, NY: Simon and Schuster.

Frost, J. (1991). *Play and playscapes*. Belmont, CA: Wadsworth Publishing.

Frost, J. (2010). *History of children's play and play environments*. New York, NY: Routledge.

Frost, J. (2012). The changing culture of play. *International Journal of Play, 1*(2), 117–130.

Frost, J., & Sutterby, J. (2017). Outdoor play is essential to whole child development. *Young Children, 72*(3), 82–85.

Frost, J., Wortham, S., & Reifel, S. (2012). *Play and Child Development* (4th ed.). New York, NY: Pearson.

Gray, P. (2016). Children's natural ways of educating themselves still work: Even for the three Rs. In D. Geary & D. Berch (Eds.), *Evolutionary perspectives on child development and education. Evolutionary psychology* (pp. 67–93). New York, NY: Springer. doi:10.1007/978-3-319–29986-0_3

Hannah-Jones, N. (2014). Segregation now. *Propublica*. https://www.propublica.org/article/segregation-now-full-text

Henley, J., McBride, J., Milligan, J., & Nichols, J. (2007). Robbing elementary students of their childhood: The perils of no child left behind. *Education, 128*(1), 56–63.

Hogan, P. (1974). *Playgrounds for free: The utilization of used and surplus materials in playground construction*. Cambridge, MA: The MIT Press.

Huynh, H., Demeter, N., Burke, R., & Upperman, J. (2017). The role of adult perceptions and supervision behavior in preventing child injury. *Journal of Community Health, 42*, 649–655. doi:10.1007/s10900-016-0300–9

Jacobson, L. (2008). Children's lack of playtime seen as troubling health, school issue. *Education Week, 28*(14), 1–15.

Jarrett, O. (2016). The state of play in the USA: Concerns and hopeful trends. *International Journal of Play, 5*(1), 4–7.

Jarrett, O., Sutterby, J., DeMarie, D., & Stenhouse, V. (2015). Children's play opportunities are not equitable: Access to quality play experiences as a social justice issue. *In Supporting Children's Play*. Washington, DC: NAEYC.

Kinard, T., Gainer, J., & Huerta, M. (2018). *Power play: Explorando y empujando fronteras en una escuela en Texas through a multilingual play-based early learning curriculum*. New York, NY: Peter Lang.

Kosnoski, J. (2011). Democratic vistas: Frederick Law Olmsted's parks as spatial meditation of urban diversity. *Space and Culture, 14*(1), 51–66. doi:10.1177/1206331210389268

Lefaivre, L., Roode, I., & Fuchs, R. (2002). *Aldo Van Eyck: The playgrounds in the city*. Amsterdam, The Netherlands: Stedelijk Museum.

Lifton, F. (1998). Henry Thoreau's cult(ivation) of nature: American landscape and American self in 'Ktaadn' and 'Walking.' *ATQ, 12*(1), 67.

Louv, R. (2008). *Last child in the woods*. Chapel Hill, NC: Algonquin Books of Chapel Hill.

Loveless, T. (2014). *How well are American students learning? With sections on the PISA-Shanghai controversy, homework, and the common core*. Washington, DC: The Brookings Institution.

McGovern, J. (2015). ADA requirements for playgrounds: Made simple. *Playground Professionals*. Retrieved from https://www.playground-professionals.com/playground/accessibility/ada-requirements-playgrounds-made-simple106

McQueeney, K. (2015). *Playing with Jim Crow: African American private parks in early twentieth century New Orleans* (Unpublished Master's Thesis). University of New Orleans, New Orleans, LA.

Menard, A. (2010). The enlarged freedom of Frederick Law Olmsted. *The New England Quarterly, 83*(3), 508–538.

North American Association for Environmental Education (NAAEE). (2017). *Nature preschools and forest kindergartens: 2017 national survey*. Washington, DC: Author.

Pluymers, K. (2011). Taming the wilderness in sixteenth- and seventeenth-century Ireland and Virginia. *Environmental History, 16,* 610–632. doi:10.1093/envhis/emr056

Roper, L. (1973). *FLO, a biography of Frederik Law Olmsted.* Baltimore, MD: Johns Hopkins Paperbacks.

Ripat, J., & Becker, P. (2012). Playground usability: What do playground users say? *Occupational Therapy International, 19,* 144–153.

Schwebel, D. (2006). Safety on the playground: Mechanisms through which adult supervision might prevent child playground injury. *Journal of Clinical Psychology in Medical Settings, 13*(2), 141–149. doi:10.1007/s10880-006-9018-7

Sharma-Brymer, V., & Bland, D. (2016). Bringing nature to schools to promote physical activity. *Sports Medicine, 46,* 955–962. doi:10.1007/s40279-016-0487-z

Silver, D., Giorgio, M., & MIjanovich, T. (2014). Utilization patterns and perceptions of playground users in New York City. *Journal of Community Health, 39,* 363–371. doi:10.1007/s10900-013-9771-0

Shumaker, S. (2005). *Untold stories from America's national parks: Segregation in the national parks. PBS.* Retrieved from http://www.pbs.org/nationalparks/about/untold-stories

Skenazy, L. (2010). *Free-Range kids: How to raise safe, self-reliant children (Without going nuts with worry).* New York, NY: Jossey Bass.

Sobko, T., Jia, Z., & Brown, G. (2018). Measuring connectedness to nature in preschool children in an urban setting and its relation to psychological functioning. *PLoS ONE, 13*(11), 1–17. doi:10.1371/journal.pone.0207057

Sullivan, B. (2015). 'Free-range' parents encourage kids to broaden their horizons: The law, not so much. *American Bar Association Journal.* Retrieved from http://www.abajournal.com/magazine/article/free_range_parents_encourage_kids_to_broaden_their_horizons_the_law_not_so/

Sutterby, J. (2017a). *The democratic playground.* Paper presented at the Annual Meeting of The Association for the Study of Play. Rochester, NY.

Sutterby, J. (2017b). From the park to the playground: Building for democracy. In M. Moore & C. Sabo-Risley (Eds.), *Play in American life* (pp. 155–165). Bloomington, IN: Archway Publishing.

Taylor, P., Grandjean, B., & Gramann, J. (2011). *Racial and ethnic diversity of national park system visitors and non-visitors.* Laramie: Wyoming Survey & Analysis Center.

Thacher, N. (2010). No recess. *Education Week, 30*(12), 26–27.

U.S. Access Board. (2005). *Accessible play areas: A summary of accessibility guidelines for play areas.* Retrieved from https://www.access-board.gov/attachments/article/1369/play-guide.pdf

Woolley, H. (2014). Now being social: The barrier of designing outdoor play spaces for disabled children. *Children and Society, 27,* 448–458. doi:10.1111/j.1099–0860.2012.00464.x

13

Technology in Early Childhood Education

Julie Sarama and Douglas H. Clements

More than two decades ago, we believed that the research and high-quality educational practice agreed that "we no longer need to ask whether the use of technology is 'appropriate'" in early childhood education (Clements & Swaminathan, 1995, p. 275) and since then others have agreed (Hsin, Li, & Tsai, 2014; Sigdel, 2017). The research remains convincing, but social/political currents undulate, and there are still organizations firmly opposed to young children's technology use. This is important, because some teachers retain a bias against technology (Lee & Ginsburg, 2007; Sargent, 2017) that in at least some ways contradicts research evidence (Herodotou, 2018b; Hsin et al., 2014; Lindahl & Folkesson, 2012; Reeves, Gunter, & Lacey, 2017) and because anti-technology polemics can be used to justify positions that lack empirical support. We and others have refuted such criticisms, while accepting that not all uses are beneficial (Clements & Sarama, 2003; Lentz, Seo, & Gruner, 2014; Sarama & Clements, in press). Research continues to accumulate that, for example, homes with more technology better support mathematics learning (e.g., Li, Atkins, & Stanton, 2006; Navarro et al., 2012), and this is particularly so for certain children (e.g., African-American children, Judge, 2005). However, garnering benefits and avoiding misuses depend on the *way* technologies are used.

Debates regarding how technology *should* be used in improving learning often involve false dichotomies. For example, some educators focus solely on drills—an approach that if used *alone* can be ineffective and even mis-educative (Dewey, 1938/1997). Other educators tolerate only "open-ended" or (narrowly defined) developmentally appropriate technology applications. Let us see what the evidence says for key domains: social-emotional development, literacy and language, and STEM (science, technology, engineering, and mathematics) subjects. Because there are hundreds of studies old and new but limited space, we cite illustrative recent studies and, with a few exceptions for seminal studies, summarize findings from earlier research reviews without citing individual studies that these articles document (for details, see Clements, 1987; Clements & Nastasi, 1993; Clements &

Sarama, 2003; Cuban, 2001; Roblyer, 1985; Watson, Nida, & Shade, 1986).

Social-Emotional Development

Perhaps the criticism that is oldest and most resistant to research evidence is that educational technology is developmentally inappropriate for young children (see Clements, 1987) and thus could hurt children's learning and social-emotional development. One argument is that such technology inappropriately demands abstract thinking. Such criticisms are based on discredited interpretations of Piagetian theory. Others argue that they will lead to stress and isolationism (e.g., Barnes & Hill, 1983).

In contrast to these concerns, children, at least in well-designed educational environments, display positive emotions when using technology (Kumtepe, 2006). They show higher positive affect and interest when they work together (e.g., Couse & Chen, 2010) and prefer to work with a peer rather than alone. Kindergartners' peer conversations when using technology display self-confidence, perspective-taking skills, and reflective self-assessment (Hyun, 2005). Kindergartners who use technology well demonstrate fewer problem behaviors and better social skills (Kumtepe, 2006). Further, working on technology can instigate new instances and forms of collaborative work such as helping or instructing, and discussing and building upon each other's ideas. Children develop a different sense of social relations, assisting each other and cooperating to solve problems and complete tasks. These positive effects are not limited to certain types or approaches to the use of technology, but rather seem to be a result of children engaging with interactive environments. Some research indicates that these effects may depend on children's proficiency with computer use, so educators may wish toward ensuring all children are proficient (Kumtepe, 2006).

However, some games are designed specifically to develop young children's social-emotional competence. The digital game Emotion Detectives was designed to promote children's acquisition of emotional knowledge skills, such as recognizing, appreciating, and understanding emotions and their expressions; prosocial behaviors, such as helping, sharing, comforting, and showing concern for others; and problem-solving abilities (Koivula, Huttunen, Mustola, Lipponen, & Laakso, 2016). For example, children match facial expressions that display the same emotion. Later, they solve social-emotional problems for characters in the software. They recognize emotions, identify the reason for the emotions, and, then, select the best solution to the conflict and resolve it in both thoughts and concrete action. Observations of five- and six-year-olds indicated that children learned social-emotional skills through playing the game and their interactions with their peers (Koivula et al., 2016).

The addition of a technology center does not disrupt ongoing play, but does facilitate extensive positive social interaction, cooperation, and helping behaviors (Clements & Sarama, 2003; Zaranis & Synodi, 2017). Even in the preschool classroom, a technology center fosters a positive climate characterized by praise and encouragement of peers and creation of new friendships. Technologically based activity is more effective in stimulating vocalization than toys and also evokes higher levels of social play. Also encouraging, technology activities facilitate social interaction between children with Individualized Educational Plans (IEPs) and their peers without IEPs. Preschoolers with special needs gain substantially and significantly in social-emotional development from their work with technology (Clements & Sarama, 2003).

Thus, *high-quality* technology experiences facilitate positive social-emotional development. A review of 87 studies concluded that most showed that technology use enhances children's collaboration and interaction with others and their development of multiculturalism (Hsin et al., 2014).

Language and Literacy

Technology-facilitated increases in social interaction help generate increased use of language. Preschoolers' language activity, measured as words spoken per minute, is about twice as high at computers as at any of the other activities, including playdough, blocks, art, or games (Clements & Sarama, 2003). In general, classroom technology is a valuable resource in facilitating language use, particularly interactional language functions (Clements & Sarama, 2003). Children's conversations reveal thinking, questioning, and talking that is purposeful, reflective, exploratory, and autonomous (Hyun & Davis, 2005). Children in a nursery setting tell longer and more structured stories following a digital graphics presentation than following a static presentation. Similarly, preschoolers dictated significantly more about digital than hand-drawn pictures. They used a developmentally appropriate version of computer programming language, Logo, with which children direct an on-screen "turtle" to draw pictures. Logo use engenders interaction and language rich with emotion, humor, and imagination. Logo also facilitates language-impaired preschooler's perceptual-language skills and increases first

graders' scores on assessments of visual-motor development, vocabulary, and listening comprehension, addressing concerns that technology will diminish play, fantasy, and the corresponding rich use of language. When children are in control, they create fantasy that goes beyond what developers and teachers expected (Clements & Sarama, 2003).

Technology-Assisted Instruction (TAI)

TAI involves using technology as a teaching machine. The technology presents information and tasks, whereupon the child responds, and the technology evaluates the response and gives feedback. This may be in a tutorial, drill and practice, game, or other context. TAI may be as or more cost-effective than traditional instruction and other instructional interventions, such as peer tutoring and reducing class size (see Clements, 1987). This approach has been successful with all children (Shin, Sutherland, Norris, & Soloway, 2012), with substantial gains reported for children from low-resource communities (McManis & McManis, 2016; Sarama & Clements, in press).

Unique capabilities of TAI include careful and patient presentation of information or tasks, immediate feedback, visual displays, animated graphics and speech, ability to keep a variety of records, and individualization. This allows it to be a useful tool; for example, first graders learned vocabulary using iPads independently as effectively as they did from their teacher (Dennis, Whalon, Kraut, & Herron, 2016). Similarly, when these capabilities are used, drill-and-practice TAI increases preschool and primary-grade children's prereading or reading skills. For example, graphical representations of words enhances word recognition and recall in early reading and increases phonological awareness (Clements & Sarama, 2003). Likewise, preschoolers and kindergartners can develop such emergent reading abilities as phonological awareness, visual discrimination and letter naming, sound knowledge, print concepts, listening comprehension, and name writing (Bauserman, Cassady, Smith, & Stroud, 2005; McKenzie, Spence, & Nicholas, 2018; Neumann, 2018; Segers & Verhoeven, 2005). A review of 42 studies found an effect size of about 0.20 standard deviations, a small but significant benefit (Blok, Oostdam, Otter, & Overmaat, 2002). Large rigorous study of one program, ABRACADABRA, found positive results for multiple early reading skills (Piquette, Savage, & Abrami, 2014; Savage et al., 2013), and a review of seven studies of ABRA found average effects of 0.19 overall and 0.15 for phonics, 0.09 for reading comprehension, and 0.43 for listening comprehension (Abrami, Borohkovski, & Lysenko, 2015).

Newer technologies can broaden the types of activities that are possible. For example, one program increased preschoolers' phonological skills via kinesthetic practice using a playful virtual environment with a cartoon avatar controlled by gestures (Goffredo et al., 2016). Web-based games increased eight of 12 early literacy skills in preschoolers and kindergartners (Schmitt, Hurwitz, Sheridan Duel, & Nichols

Linebarger, 2018), and games led to consistent reading gains (Homer et al., 2014; Kyle, Kujala, Richardson, Lyytinen, & Goswami, 2013). Interactive robots have also increased reading ability of preschoolers (Hsiao, Chang, Lin, & Hsu, 2015).

The amount of practice can be important. A small number of sessions with simple readiness software, such as drills that teach letter matching and recognition or phonemic awareness, may have little or no effect (Goodwin, Goodwin, Nansel, & Helm, 1986; Mathes, Torgesen, & Allor, 2001). In contrast, placing computers in kindergartners' classrooms for several months significantly increases reading readiness skills; placing them in the home as well yields greater gains. About ten minutes' work with TAI per day can significantly benefit primary-grade children's reading skill development (Clements & Sarama, 2003).

TAI approaches have also addressed equity concerns. A technological intervention including enhancement of oral reading fluency and comprehension led to positive effects on both practiced and novel passages and an increased growth rate for second-grade African-American urban students (Bennett, Gardner, Cartledge, Ramnath, & Council, 2017). First graders who are Dual Language Learners (DLLs) who used TAI to address specific, critical literacy needs demonstrated greater gains than control students in the domains of vocabulary, phonics, phonological awareness, and text comprehension (Cassady, Smith, & Thomas, 2018; see also Macaruso & Rodman, 2011a). Moreover, children who are second and third language learners and dyslexic made gains in multiple competencies with TAI (Pfenninger, 2015). In brief, TAI has:

- improved reading skills of children with autism spectrum disorder, although only when they had the ability to attend (Hill & Flores, 2015);
- taught young children with developmental delays to identify initial phonemes and to maintain and generalize these skills (Chai, Vail, & Ayres, 2015);
- helped students with learning disabilities master letter sounds (Campbell & Mechling, 2009) and improved reading fluency (Özbek & Girli, 2017);
- taught listening and reading comprehension to less-skilled second graders (Potocki, Ecalle, & Magnan, 2013); and
- rapidly improved early skill deficits in phonological sensitivity (Lonigan et al., 2003; Macaruso & Rodman, 2011b), phonics (Volpe, Burns, DuBois, & Zaslofsky, 2011), and decoding (DuBois, Volpe, & Hemphill, 2014; Gorp, Segers, & Verhoeven, 2017; Van der Kooy-Hofland, Bus, & Roskos, 2012).

Note though that all characteristics of children are important to consider; for example, in one study, TAI was effective except for children with low executive function and low computer skills, which might need to be addressed first (Kegel, 2009, however, notes that other programs have improved both executive function and literacy, Reeves et al., 2017; van de Sande, Segers, & Verhoeven, 2016). In another,

an early-intervention TAI program boosted phonological skills of four- to six-year-olds with literacy difficulties, but less so if these difficulties were linked to phonological working memory deficits (O'Callaghan, McIvor, McVeigh, & Rushe, 2016).

TAI also helps struggling readers from low-resource communities to read (Amendum, Vernon-Feagans, & Ginsberg, 2011) and comprehend what they read (Schechter, Macaruso, Kazakoff, & Brooke, 2015). Given the lack of resources, though, does relatively expensive technology make sense for them? It may, because even in low-income families, toddlers and preschoolers are using smartphones and touchscreen tablets on a regular basis (American Academy of Pediatrics Council on Communications and Media, 2013). From 85% to 90% of families living below the poverty line have a tablet or smartphone (Rideout & Katz, 2016). We need to help these populations use technology wisely, however, as access is not enough. In one study, families from low- and high-resource communities had equivalent library technology resources, but adults from low-resource communities lacked the opportunities to learn how to use them effectively with their children (Neuman & Celano, 2012). There are successful home TAI programs (Watson & Hempenstall, 2008) to overcome this barrier and also new tools available for helping families guide their children in planning their technology-based playtime, which may also build self-regulation competencies (Hiniker, Lee, Sobel, & Choe, 2017).

Of course, software that is high quality is more likely to lead to gains. Unfortunately, many of the great number of apps for preschoolers do not include sound teaching strategies (including those for literacy and mathematics, Callaghan & Reich, 2018). Among the biggest problems the researchers identified: missing instructions, poor feedback (correctness only, not informative), ineffective guidance and modeling as to how to solve a problem that children could not solve, and lack of responsiveness to children's individual skill levels. Missing even one important characteristic, such as individualizing to children's needs, has resulted in a lack of any gains from a TAI program in literacy for at-risk children (Kreskey & Truscott, 2016).

Literacy Tools

E-Books. Other approaches include technologically based interactive storybooks, which can help close the gap between children who are "well-read-to" at home and those who are not (Talley, Lancy, & Lee, 1997). As a large component of a technologically based literacy program for preschoolers, such software significantly and positively affected a wide range of emergent literacy skills and knowledge, including specific print concepts, oral communication, retelling stories, recognizing letters, "reading" books, predicting and sequencing, making judgments, and listening (Korat & Segal-Drori, 2016).

Most e-books include multimodal text; that is, they combine text, still and animated images, sounds, and music and may include narratives in which children can carry out actions of book's characters in a game-like format (Kankaanranta, Koivula, Laakso, & Mustola, 2017). However, some only encourage children to click on pictures to see animation, which appears less effective than paper books for literacy education (although animations do not interfere with benefits in some studies, de Jong & Bus, 2004). Animation that enhances the story can help children gain knowledge of implied elements of stories referring to characters' motives and expand children's vocabulary and syntax (Verhallen, Bus, & de Jong, 2006). Similarly, focused hotspots can help children learn vocabulary, but irrelevant ones might lead to disengagement with the text. And text to speech can support autonomous learning, but too much for too long could become a substitute for children reading on their own (Miller & Warschauer, 2014). E-books with relevant features such as dictionary and related play may be particularly beneficial (Korat & Shamir, 2008). Augmented reality picture books can increase preschool children's cognition and listening skills (Yilmaz, Kucuk, & Goktas, 2017). Other features are possible, such as presenting a common story such as Goldilocks, but allowing readers to experience the story in two different ways. Click on Goldilocks, and you experience the story from her point of view; click on the bears, and you view it from theirs. You can also flip back and forth from the bears' scene to Goldilocks' (Guernsey & Levine, 2016). These are potentially rich language and literacy explorations.

Addressing equity, e-books appear to help children from low-resource communities learn word meanings, understand stories, and remember linguistic information (Korat & Shamir, 2008; Verhallen et al., 2006), and help at-risk preschoolers with embedded instruction for oral language (Greenwood et al., 2016). E-books benefit those at risk for learning disabilities as well (Shamir, Korat, & Shlafer, 2011). Most studies show that children learn more from and are more engaged with well-designed e-books (e.g., Ciampa, 2012; Richter & Courage, 2017; Roskos, Brueck, & Widman, 2009) than print books in competencies such as concepts of print, vocabulary, and word reading (Ihmeideh, 2014; Karemaker, Pitchford, & O'Malley, 2010; Segal-Drori, Korat, Shamir, & Klein, 2010; Smeets & Bus, 2015; Zipke, 2017), including DLLs (Leacox & Jackson, 2014), who have successfully made their own e-books (Richter & Courage, 2017). More difficult technologically is speech *recognition*. Some studies exploring this feature found that it is beneficial to first graders who are struggling to write (Baker, 2017).

Using the books well improves outcomes. For example, children learn more using the e-books with peers (Shamir, Korat, & Barbi, 2008) or with adults (Segal-Drori et al., 2010). Because some researchers report limitations in adult-child interaction (Kozminsky & Asher-Sadon, 2013), it is important that adults do not let "bells and whistles" of e-books distract them from the text (Krcmar & Cingel, 2014;

Richter & Courage, 2017), especially for children with language delays (Smeets, van Dijken, & Bus, 2014).

Writing in Light. Another approach to early literacy is having children write and publish on technology (e.g., word processors), which can encourage a fluid idea of the written word and free young children from mechanical concerns. Children using technology tend to write more, have fewer fine motor control problems, worry less about making mistakes, and make fewer mechanical errors. They discuss their writing more when using technology, collaborate on writing, and, when shown how, even edit their writing. They improve their style using more descriptive phrases and also create better plots with climaxes and character descriptions (Clements & Sarama, 2003). They have more positive attitudes toward writing and are more motivated to write (Beam & Williams, 2015). However, holistic ratings of quality of technology versus traditional media are mixed. Quality increases if children are encouraged to use the word processor to edit their text in substantive ways (Beam & Williams, 2015; Clements & Sarama, 2003). Importantly, some studies show the benefits of handwriting compared to typing (Kiefer et al., 2015), so exclusive use of technology may not be optimal for writing.

Voice-aided word processing can act as a scaffold for young children's writing by promoting the acquisition of several components of preschool literacy, developing an "inner voice" for constructing and editing text subvocally. However, teachers need to use digital speech wisely and assess children's readiness for voice-aided instruction. For example, if children are inventing their spelling, text to speech may not be helpful.

Again, technology can be especially helpful for children who are disadvantaged or have disabilities. For instance, it can help children who are deaf or hard of hearing to learn phonological awareness and speech production (Smith & Wang, 2010) and writing (Williams, 2011). Children who write using technology at home have higher print awareness, print knowledge, and sound knowledge (Neumann, 2016). Although this is only correlational, it suggests a way to address entering skills of at-risk children.

There are other approaches to technology that show promise as well. Third-grade children engaged in digital storytelling, which increased their ideas, organization, word choice, sentence fluency, story elements, and word count conventions in their writing (Yamac & Ulusoy, 2016). In a photo journal project, preschoolers were motivated to read others' notes and to respond using invented spellings (Pelletier, Reeve, & Halewood, 2006).

Thus, from TAI to e-books to word processing to other creative uses, educational technology, *used well*, appears to have the potential to make positive contributions to young children's learning of language and literacy. Indeed, it may open up new types of literacies.

New Literacies. Technology, including apps and games, also offers multiple literacies, including technological competencies, procedural literacy, and use of multiple forms of media and representational forms, and multimodalities. Digital environments can be a deliverer of literacy, a site for interaction around texts, and a medium for meaning-making (Burnett, 2010). There may be new opportunities for informal learning, for different kinds of play, and for creativity, and previously unseen competencies and strengths can emerge (Siegel, Kontovourki, Schmier, & Enriquez, 2008). Researchers and teachers might well be constantly open to new uses and new visions of multiple literacies and multiple uses of multimedia. And, more prosaically, just *using* a computer at home is associated with increased literacy development, such as letter knowledge (Castles et al., 2013).

Research is clear that to achieve full literacy children need skills *and* knowledge (IOM (Institute of Medicine) and NRC (National Research Council), 2012). STEM helps build that knowledge. So do other uses of technology that emphasizes art, history, literature, and different cultures (Guernsey & Levine, 2016). Let us examine the STEM fields next.

STEM

Being the "T" in STEM, it is unsurprising that computer technology (there are many other types) can help children learn these fields. From the earliest days to the present, more research has been conducted in math, and, to the lesser extent, technology, so the following review is dominated by those fields (not because they are more important).

Technology-Assisted Instruction (TAI)

Even children as young as two or three years of age can benefit from technology-assisted instruction (TAI) to develop mathematical skills and concepts. One review of rigorous studies indicated that TAI applications that are well designed and implemented could have a positive impact on mathematics performance (National Mathematics Advisory Panel, 2008), and recent studies support this conclusion (Foster, Anthony, Clements, & Sarama, 2016; Moradmand, Datta, & Oakley, 2013; Nusir, Alsmadi, Al-Kabi, & Sharadgah, 2013; Outhwaite, Faulder, Gulliford, & Pitchford, 2018; Schacter & Jo, 2016; Thompson & Davis, 2014). Another recent review concluded that there are positive effects, although they are modest (e.g., effect size of +0.15 standard deviations, Cheung & Slavin, 2013). This review also suggested differences due to the model of TAI used. Supplemental TAI had the largest effect, at a size of +0.18. The other two interventions, technology-management learning and comprehensive programs, which integrated TAI and traditional instruction, had a smaller effect size, +0.08 and +0.07, respectively. However, another meta-analysis of educational technology for early mathematics found a moderate effect size of 0.48 (0.53 for number sense, 0.42 for operations, 0.57 for word problems, and 0.59 for geometry and measurement) (Harskamp, 2015). Individual research-based programs, however, have shown high effect sizes, including

more than 1 SD (Aragón-Mendizábal, Aguilar-Villagrán, Navarro-Guzmán, & Howell, 2017).

Practice. A common use of TAI is to provide practice; for example, TAI has produced significant increases in skills such as sorting and counting for children as young as three years (Clements & Nastasi, 1993), as well as addition facts and computational estimation (Fuchs et al., 2006, 2008; Salminen, Koponen, Räsänen, & Aro, 2015). Indeed, some reviewers claim that the largest gains in the use of TAI have been in practicing mathematics for lower-primary-grade students (Fletcher-Flinn & Gravatt, 1995), especially in compensatory education programs (Clements & Nastasi, 1993). About ten minutes per day proved to be sufficient time for significant gains; 20 minutes was even better (note that research suggests short repeated sessions, so for young children, 5–15 minutes in a session is suggested). Another program showed good effects in arithmetic fluency for a first grader who practiced for 15 minutes three times per week for four months (Smith, Marchand-Martella, & Martella, 2011). Similarly, first-grade students improved their learning of whole-number concepts in skills working with TAI for 48 15-minute sessions (Fien et al., 2016). Preschoolers using Math Shelf as a supplement to their regular curriculum for 15 weeks made sizable gains (> 1 SD) compared to control children (Schacter & Jo, 2016). Kindergarteners learned more mathematics than their peers using the Building Blocks software for 21 weeks (Foster et al., 2016). Geometry and spatial reasoning via TAI is also more effective than traditional approaches in school (Lin & Chen, 2016; Lin & Hou, 2016; Zaranis & Synodi, 2017) and home (Silander et al., 2016).

The practical goal of most of these studies was to address equity issues, that is, to close early learning opportunity gaps, such as those experienced by young children from low-resource communities. Others have addressed similar equity problems with different populations, and again there are many advantages of technology if used well (Clements & Sarama, 2017; Fien et al., 2016). Children with special needs also benefit from TAI, more so than other approaches (Cascales-Martínez, Martínez-Segura, Pérez-López, & Contero, 2017). For instance, technology practice can be especially helpful for children who have mathematical difficulties or mathematical learning disabilities (Harskamp, 2015; Mohd Syah, Hamzaid, Murphy, & Lim, 2016). However, this must come at the right point in the learning trajectory (see below) and it should be the right kind of practice. For example, "bare bones" practice, such as repeated, speed-based, *drill* in arithmetic "facts," does not help children who are at the level of more immature counting strategies. Instead, research suggests practice that helps them understand concepts and learn arithmetic facts before any time-pressured drills (Clements & Sarama, 2017). Also, practice that teaches fluency and cognitive strategies is more effective than either alone, especially for boys (Carr, Taasoobshirazi, Stroud, & Royer, 2011). After 40- to 30-minute sessions, the combination of these was most effective (effect size, 0.53 compared to the control group). However, boys seemed to benefit more on their use of the strategies and on fluency. Girls tended to continue to use simple counting; they improved, but did not use more sophisticated strategies, perhaps because the boys had more number sense at pretest (Carr et al., 2011). Both technology and non-technology approaches may need to better support girls development.

Research has shown that technology applications, not even necessarily designed for this purpose, can help children with Attention Deficit Hyperactivity Disorder (ADHD). One study showed a substantial improvement in first graders' logic, mathematical and concentration skills, problem solving, and sometimes even the stoppage of involuntary tics (Zaretsky, 2017). There are promising findings also for children who are DLLs (Lysenko et al., 2016). Technology use for mathematics was associated with a reduced gap in math achievement between native English-speaking and DLL students (Kim & Chang, 2010). Use of Building Blocks software (Clements & Sarama, 2007/2018) as a supplement significantly improved the mathematics competencies of Hispanic DLLs from low-income backgrounds (Foster et al., 2016).

A caveat is that drills should be used carefully and usually in moderation, especially with the youngest children whose creativity may be harmed by a consistent diet of drills (Haugland, 1992). Some students may be less motivated to perform academic work or less creative following a steady diet of only drills (Clements & Nastasi, 1993). There is also a possibility that children will be less motivated to perform academic work following drills and that drills on computers alone may not generalize as well as paper-and-pencil work (Clements & Nastasi, 1993; Duhon, House, & Stinnett, 2012). Having children practice about 20% of the time on paper and pencil seems to solve that generalization limitation (Rich, Duhon, & Reynolds, 2017). In contrast, practice that encourages the development and use of strategies provides different contexts (supporting generalization), and promotes problem solving that may be more appropriate than drills, or may be best used in combination with it. To be effective, all types of practice must follow and be consistent with Phase 1 and Phase 2 instruction and appropriate for the children's culture.

Practice does not have to be restricted to routine drills. Deliberate practice that is more intentional, involving thinking, problem solving, and reflection for analyzing, conceptualizing, and cultivating one's strategies and understandings (Lehtinen, Hannula-Sormunen, McMullen, & Gruber, 2017). TAI can include such deliberate practice. For example, the Number Navigation Game (NNG) is based on research on adaptive arithmetic strategies and principles of deliberate practice (Lehtinen et al., 2015). Children create their own calculation strategies to progress, with the tasks and constraints becoming gradually more demanding, requiring more and more advanced numerical strategies. The game provides strategic scaffolding and continuous feedback (Lehtinen et al., 2015). NNG achieves its goals and, with teacher support, can be transferred to pre-algebraic skills (Lehtinen et al., 2017). We return to the use of games in the following section, "Games and Environments." Another example is the use of Realistic Mathematics Education with learning trajectories, a well-established approach, to teach arithmetic by using stories that present arithmetic problems (Zaranis, 2017). Kindergartners engaged in this approach, which combined non-computer contexts as introductions followed by similar work on computers, learned substantially more arithmetic than children who followed the regular school program (including some simple software).

Other TAI models include and often combine approaches that also go beyond simple practice. In one study, combinations of problem solving, stories, and practice taught preschoolers number concepts and natural science (solubility and recycling). Further, measurement concepts provided through use of tutorials or video models have taught length to preschoolers (Aladé, Lauricella, Beaudoin-Ryan, & Wartella, 2016) and area to primary-grade students (Clements et al., 2018).

Successes have been reported for other research-based programs. For example, TAI, even with minimal scaffolding, has been found to be a feasible means of helping at-risk first graders discover the add-1 rule (adding one is the same as "counting one more") by way of pattern detection (Baroody, Purpura, Eiland, & Reid, 2015). The software might pose, "What number comes after three when we count?" and then was immediately followed by answering a related addition question, "3+1=?" Also, an "add-zero" item and an addition item (with both addends greater than one) served as non-examples of the add-1 rule to discourage overgeneralizing this rule. A similar technology program that combined fluency and cognitive strategy use helped second graders, especially boys, improve their arithmetic achievement (Carr et al., 2011).

Different types and different ways of using TAI can achieve different goals. For example, all kindergartners working in multimedia environments improved their mathematical skills more than those not working with any technology environment. Further, those working individually performed at the highest level, while those working cooperatively increased their positive attitude about cooperative learning (Weiss, Kramarski, & Talis, 2006). Finally, longer tutorials are rare in early mathematics, but some programs are developing new approaches. One program used collaborative multimedia environments with problems that children (four to seven years old) solved cooperatively with feedback (Kramarski & Weiss, 2007). These children outperformed those who worked collaboratively but without the multimedia environment. In another approach, children created digital images that represented a person or character and used that character to share thoughts and ideas through typed text or the computer microphone (Cicconi, 2014).

Games and Environments. Properly chosen, *technology games* may also be effective, facilitating both greater skills and conceptual change (Ketamo & Kiili, 2010). Second graders with an average of one hour of interaction with a technology game over a two-week period responded correctly to twice as many items on an addition facts speed test as did students in a control group (Kraus, 1981). Even younger children benefit from a wide variety of technology-based as well as nontechnology games (Clements & Sarama, 2008b). For example, in one simple game, young children place finger combinations on an iPad to play a game of recognizing and representing numbers before time runs out. Early pilot work with this novel interface, which also promotes use of children's most accessible manipulative, their fingers, is promising (Barendregt, Lindström, Rietz-Leppänen, Holgersson, & Ottosson, 2012). Even a popular game, Angry Birds, has been shown to help four- and five-year-olds learn science concepts such as projectile motion (Herodotou, 2018a). Interactive 3D visualization helps second graders learn about the Earth-Sun-Moon system by allowing them to observe the space objects move in the virtual space. This technology provided a hands-on experience that may support young children's ability to view phenomena that could typically demand direct, long-term observations in outer space (Isik-Ercan, Zeynep Inan, Nowak, & Kim, 2014).

Game-based learning also shows promise for children with disabilities, as well as migrant children, because they attract children with imaginary worlds, interesting stories, and shared experiences with peers. They also may offer a variety of new affordances to explore and play with (Kankaanranta et al., 2017). Moreover, well-designed games can facilitate the development of a wide range of skills such as phonological awareness, memory enhancement strategies, motor skills and coordination, and logical and mathematical competencies (Peirce, 2013).

Newer technology games can take quite different forms and can target different areas of a child's learning. For example, the robot Nao can be used to promote engagement, social interaction, and geometry learning by engaging children in social games and activities (Keren & Fridin, 2014). The robot pictured on a screen identifies a shape and asks children to find and touch the same shape on the physical robot. Evaluations revealed that these experiences improved both geometric thinking and meta-cognitive tasks in kindergartners (Keren & Fridin, 2014). Geometry education benefits from technology in many ways, providing technological supports on visualization, manipulation, cognitive tools, discourse promoters, and ways of thinking (Crompton, Grant, & Shraim, 2018). Thus, games and exploratory environments, again *of high quality*, can make unique contributions to STEM learning, and a greater variety are sure to be invented. The following sections discuss other approaches to educational technology.

STEM Tools

Digital Manipulatives for STEM. Digital manipulatives are technology-based version of physical manipulatives from counters to shapes and beyond. A recent meta-analysis of 66 studies found positive effects for the use of digital manipulatives (Moyer-Packenham & Westenskow, 2013). Such benefits of digital manipulatives use include: bringing mathematical ideas and processes to conscious awareness; encouraging and facilitating complete, precise explanations; supporting mental actions on objects; changing the very nature of the manipulative; symbolizing mathematical concepts; linking the concrete and the symbolic with feedback; and recording and replaying students' actions (see also Moyer-Packenham & Westenskow, 2013; Sarama & Clements, 2009a; for details, see Sarama, Clements, & Vukelic, 1996). Additionally, digital manipulatives may often be more manageable, flexible, and extensible than physical ones for young children (Sarama & Clements, 2016). In one study, third graders working with digital manipulatives made statistically significant gains learning fractional concepts (Reimer & Moyer, 2004). The digital manipulatives were easier and faster to use than physical manipulatives and provided immediate and specific feedback. Another study found that a technology manipulative program helped second graders learn multiplication (Paek, Hoffman, Saravanos, Black, & Kinzer, 2011). Kindergartners' work on digital manipulatives has substantiated the developmental progressions for several learning trajectories, showing that they also have power to assess children and thus enlighten teachers and researchers (Tucker, Lommatsch, Moyer-Packenham, Anderson-Pence, & Symanzik, 2017). Digital manipulatives can take many forms. Some support explorations, such as a probability "microworld" that has successfully taught kindergartners probability concepts (Fesakis, Kafoussi, & Malisiova, 2011). Others may be embedded within tutorial or practice TAI programs.

Digital manipulatives may also play an important role for children with disabilities. Teachers of students with special needs indicated significant student accessibility barriers; for example, 75% of special needs teachers had students with tactile defensiveness or lack of gross motor skills, 85% had students with weak to no fine motor skills, and 83% had students who lost track of the math objectives while manipulating materials. These barriers made use of physical manipulatives difficult or impossible. Because 94% of the teachers agreed that the use of manipulatives is valuable, and how the teachers overwhelmingly noted their student engagement with technology, students' use of digital manipulatives is particularly promising (Jimenez & Stanger, 2017).

Technology can also support children's own manipulatives—their fingers. Several apps build understanding of cardinality (Sedaghatjou & Campbell, 2017) and arithmetic (Barendregt et al., 2012) by giving young children tasks (and feedback) in which they must place a given number of fingers on a tablet.

Recall that many of the apps for young children do not include sound teaching strategies (Callaghan & Reich, 2018) so software selection is critical, as always. Among the weaknesses, in mathematics, a key problem is the lack of responsiveness to children's individual levels of thinking. The criticality of that in the highly sequential and hierarchical domain of mathematics is why we and others develop software along research-based learning trajectories, to which we turn.

Learning Trajectories. *Learning trajectories* are a device for constructive-based learning and teaching. Each learning trajectory has three parts: (a) a goal, (b) a developmental progression, and (c) instructional activities. To attain a certain mathematical competence in a given topic or domain (the goal), students learn each successive level (the developmental progression), aided by tasks (instructional activities) designed to build the mental actions on objects that enable thinking at each higher level (Clements & Sarama, 2014; Sarama & Clements, 2009b). Teaching strategies include early exploratory work (or play) and a range of techniques from problem solving to a variety of explicit instructional strategies such as brief tutorials and practice. As an illustration, consider a learning trajectory for composing geometric shapes (Clements & Sarama, 2007/2013). The *goal* is to learn geometric composition—using problem-solving abilities to put shapes together to make other shapes. The *developmental progression* indicates that children with an initial lack of competence in composing geometric shapes gain the ability to combine shapes—initially through trial and error and gradually by attributes—into pictures, and finally synthesize combinations of shapes into new shapes. Instructional tasks include a series of activities including solving geometric puzzles and open-ended creation of designs and pictures that build through the developmental progression. After initially solving outline puzzles with physical manipulatives, children enjoy playing and solve problems with digital manipulatives "snap" and stay together accurately (see LearningTrajectories.org). More importantly, they use the program's tools to perform actions on the shapes. Because they have to figure out how to move the blocks and *choose* a motion such as slide or turn, they are more conscious of these geometric motions. Four-year-old Juanita initially referred to the "spinning" tools, but later called them the "turn shapes" tools, and after several months was describing directions and quantities, such as "OK, get *this* [right or clockwise] turn tool and turn it three times!" Such choices also encourage children to be more *deliberate*. They "think ahead" and talk to each other about what shape and action to choose next. In these ways, the technology slows down their actions and increases their reflection. Just as important, using the motion tools deliberately helps children become familiar with seeing shapes in different orientations and realizing that changing the orientation does not affect the shape's name or class. In a related activity, children are challenged to build a picture or design with physical blocks and copy it into the program. Again, this requires the use of specific tools for the geometric motions of slide, flip, and turn and encourages children to reflect on the orientation of the shapes. Note that tool-type interfaces are needed to gain this benefit even though direct manipulation is possible. Multiple studies have supported the effectiveness of this learning trajectory (Clements & Sarama, 2007, 2008a;

Clements, Sarama, Spitler, Lange, & Wolfe, 2011). The software combines the tasks (motivating puzzles) and tools (geometric motion tools) with introductions and brief hints and then tutorials if children make several consecutive mistakes.

Science Tools. Digital tools also show promise for the teaching and learning of science. For example, photobook technology can document science exploration, engendering conversations both at school and home, and thus repeatedly triggering memories that reinforce the "me, as scientist" viewpoint (Katz, 2011). Primary-grade students who engaged in guided experimentation activities using handheld computers connected to temperature sensors to measure change in temperature given different types of insulation materials learned about thermodynamics systems (Varma, 2014). In another study, children as young as three to five years have used stop-motion animation to model and thus learn about science concepts. Animations are played slowly, two frames per second, enabling the creators to narrate the slow-moving images to explain a science concept or tell a story (Fleer & Hoban, 2012). The animation can include enhancements such as narration, music, photos, diagrams, 2D and 3D models, labels, static images, repetitions, and characters, which can be co-created by teachers and children. For example, a preschooler interested in playground spinner was helped by her teachers to use toys to take photographs that then were combined in an animation that promoted discussion of informal and scientific concepts (such as the harder you push, the faster it spin, Fleer & Hoban, 2012). Incorporating the use of a variety of technologies helps children engage in integrated STEM activities, from recording information on computers to using search engines to learn more (Kermani & Aldemir, 2015; see also Ok & Kim, 2017). The authors emphasize that such integration of intentional math and science learning supported with technology in early childhood programs serving children from disadvantaged socio-economic backgrounds can make a real and significant improvement in their STEM learning (Kermani & Aldemir, 2015). A review of research concluded that iPads and iPods can be used in many ways for STEM education and can be effective for enhancing both academic performance and engagement of students with disabilities (Ok & Kim, 2017).

Programming, Coding, and Robotics. STEM as an integrated discipline is perhaps most evident in programming, especially programming robots. Programming, or coding—instructing a computer to follow a set of commands, is possible for children as young as preschoolers, with the proper technology environment and guidance from teachers (Gedĭk, Çetĭn, & Koca, 2017). Lower-primary-grade children have shown greater explicit awareness of the properties of shapes and the meaning of measurements after programming a robotic turtle to move and draw shapes with Logo. They learn about the measurement of length and angle (Sarama, Clements, Swaminathan, McMillen, & González Gómez, 2003) and competencies such as sequencing (Kazakoff, Sullivan, &

Bers, 2013). Especially now with new versions of computer languages, such as Scratch Jr. (Flannery et al., 2013; Portelance, Strawhacker, & Bers, 2016), young children can learn related language and can transfer their knowledge to other tasks, such as map reading and interpreting the right and left rotation of objects. For example, first-grader Ryan wanted to turn the turtle to point into his rectangle. He asked the teacher, "What's half of 90?" After she responded, he typed RT 45 (for "right turn 45°"). When the turtle said nothing, Ryan said, "Oh, I went the wrong way," while keeping his eyes on the screen. "Try LEFT 90," he said at last. This inverse operation produced exactly the desired effect. These effects are not limited to small studies. A major evaluation of a coding-based geometry curriculum included 1,624 students and their teachers (Clements, Battista, & Sarama, 2001b).

The original Logo turtle was a robot that moved about on the floor. Computer coding of more modern robotics environments such as Nao (Keren & Fridin, 2014) or Lego-Logo has even stronger focus on engineering. In Lego-Logo, children create Lego structures, including lights, sensors, motors, gears, and pulleys, and they control their structures through computer codes. Another study shows how students five to seven years of age learned modeling, exploring, and evaluating building and programming Lego robots in Australia (McDonald & Howell, 2012). Such studies show that technological and hands-on learning environments complement each other. For example, second graders who acted out programming commands with their bodies demonstrated better problem-solving skills than a group who planned only with paper and pencil (Sung, Ahn, Kai, & Black, 2017), one more validation of Papert's notion of "body synchrony" (see also Clements, Battista, & Sarama, 2001a; Sarama & Clements, 2016). Such experiences can positively affect mathematics and science achievement and competencies in higher-order thinking skills (Sarama & Clements, in press), especially for students at risk for academic failure (Day, 2002). This approach addresses equity concerns in other ways as well. If started as young as kindergarten, few differences appear between boys and girls, and both benefit from work with robots (Sullivan & Bers, 2013). Younger children can meaningfully and joyfully play with programmable digital toys such as Beebot, but explicit scaffolding may be important to have them think about the sequencing that defines "programming" (Newhouse, Cooper, & Cordery, 2017). From directing robots to carry, push, and/or sort recyclable materials found in the classroom (Sullivan, Kazakoff, & Bers, 2013) to learning more advanced geometry, programming and robotics are accessible, engaging, and beneficial for young children.

Creative Thinking

Contrary to the concern that computers may limit children's creativity, most studies show that certain environments we have mentioned—drawing, programming, word processing, challenging problem solving, and so forth—*engender*

creativity (for reviews, see Burnett, 2010; Clements & Sarama, 2003; Kankaanranta et al., 2017; Mustola, Koivula, Turja, & Laakso, 2016). One critical component of creativity, originality, has been consistently and positively affected. These results provide further evidence that high-quality technological environments enhance higher-order processes, such as problem-solving skills, decision-making ability, understanding of cause and effect, and longer attention spans (Clements & Sarama, 2003; Sarama & Clements, in press).

Other Important Issues

Space constraints prevent discussion of many other important issues. We simply mention three here. First, both families and teachers need guidance in using technology. Just finding high-quality software is a challenge, as even popular search processes do not produce high-quality software that develops knowledge as well as skills (Guernsey & Levine, 2016). However, there are effective, engaging alternatives such as the resources provided here (e.g., Clements & Sarama, 2007/2018, 2017/2019; Guernsey & Levine, 2016, and others reviewed here).

Second, it is important to note that studies of educational technology too often use designs that lack rigor and correct statistical procedures (e.g., comparing two classes, but ignoring the embeddedness of children in the statistical computations), although this review includes many fine exceptions (e.g., Amendum et al., 2011; Foster et al., 2016; Outhwaite et al., 2018; Piquette et al., 2014; Savage et al., 2013; Van der Kooy-Hofland et al., 2012). Therefore, reported effects may not be accurate, and more rigorous, larger scale research is needed.

Third, different models of educational technology, and combinations of them, can be effective, but only if teachers receive adequate professional development and support. It is encouraged that teachers and those who supervise and teach them review the provided resources to further understand critical issues such as managing the technology environment (Sarama & Clements, 2006) and effective strategies for teaching with technology (Bourbour, Vigmo, & Samuelsson, 2015; Clements & Sarama, 2008b, 2010; Sarama & Clements, in press). Note that sometimes teachers discontinue use of even successful TAI due to a misfit between their beliefs about learning and the TAI's approach (D'Agostino, Rodgers, Harmey, & Brownfield, 2016), so professional development must be comprehensive.

Summary of Guidelines and Cautions

This third issue, that teaching support and professional development in using high-quality education technology, is just one of several cautions woven throughout this review. Especially because technology can be expensive and can have a high overhead in terms of teacher time and effort, it is important to reiterate considerations of positive guidelines and caveats from research and the wisdom of expert practice, the purpose of Table 13.1.

Table 13.1 Highlights of Positive Guidelines and Cautions from Research on Educational Technology

Issue	Educative Guidelines	Cautions
Social-emotional development	Ensure children's proficiency with technology. Arrange settings to encourage collaboration (e.g., two chairs in front of a computer, one to the side for an adult). Model and teach children to collaborate with and help each other.	Too few computers (e.g., one) can engender competition. Provide adequate access and plan rotating use.
Time on computers	Productive use of educational technology can be accomplished (depending on the activity) in 10–20 minutes sessions each day, or a couple of days per week.	Although time children spent can vary with the type of program (e.g., many children can create artwork or program (code) productively for a considerable time), overall screen time should not exceed an hour (Kabali et al., 2015). Sedentary screen time at home is usually the most pernicious influence, so communication with families is important.
TAI	Check that software is empirically validated or at least research-based. Ensure that software is consistent with the goals and values of the educational program. Consider software that encourages collaborative problem solving as well as learning of content.	Ensure children have the executive function and computer skills to meaningfully and successfully interact with the educational technology. The benefits of educational technology described here are from high-quality software, *most easily available software is not of high quality* (see Callaghan & Reich, 2018).
Interactivity and language	Many types of software generate language, but those such as story creation, programming (coding), and other open-ended software that puts children in control should be a special focus for engendering right language experiences.	Children will even discuss their work on drill-oriented TAI software (as long as they are seated near each other in the classroom—isolating children in separate booths in a computer lab is not recommended), but the discussions may not be as rich.
TAI drill and practice	Ensure software conforms to research on practice. Also consider software that allows playful approaches, uses graphics, uses robots, and so forth.	Avoid overusing drill software, especially with the youngest children. Ensure children understand underlying concepts first. A steady diet of only drill software can have negative effects.
"Bells and Whistles"	Dynamic graphics, video, robotics, and other technological characteristics can enhance motivation, engagement, and learning *if* they are designed in accordance with research-based pedagogy to reach educational goals.	Such technological "enhancements" can distract teachers and children from the content and concepts that are to be learned if they are, indeed, only "bells and whistles" without educational purpose.
STEM	Because mathematics is more sequential and hierarchical than most other subjects, research-based TAI can make a substantive contribution, especially if it follows research-validated learning trajectories. Careful attention to the needs of all children, especially those with special needs, is critical. Consider the use of STEM tools (e.g., digital manipulatives, sensors, robotics).	Because many educators think of mathematics as "just skills," an imbalance of drill software may limit children's development of concepts and problem solving—creative mathematics.
Inservice and preservice education	Provide extensive, comprehensive, and ongoing professional development and resources to teachers.	Less than ten hours of education on technology is actually counterproductive (Ryan, 1991).

Final Words

In conclusion, used in a supportive, interactive, research-validated educational context, high-quality technology can make substantial contributions to early childhood education. Benefits may be especially promising for children with disabilities (Ok & Kim, 2017). Unfortunately, reality often falls short of realizing this promise. To be effective, policies and practices need to be based on research and the wisdom of expert practice. Teachers can use mobile computers (iPads) in a variety of ways that improve teaching and learning (Milman, Carlson-Bancroft, & Vanden Boogart, 2014). In many contexts, however, simply providing hardware is not likely to increase learning (Ortiz & Cristia, 2014). Further, even if used well, technology alone cannot be expected to have more than a moderate effect (Cheung & Slavin, 2013). Throughout this chapter, we draw implications from what we have learned from research regarding selecting models of educational technology, using effective teaching strategies, and providing professional development.

Acknowledgments

This chapter was supported in part by the Bill & Melinda Gates Foundation, Grant #OPP1118932; Heising-Simons Foundation, Grants #2013-79 and #2015-157; National Science Foundation, Grant #DRL-1222944; and the Institute of Education Sciences through Grant R305A150243. Any opinions, findings, and conclusions or recommendations expressed in this material are those of the authors and do not necessarily reflect the views of these foundations. We express our appreciation to Becky Chance for assistance with literature searches and to Julia Ratchford for proofreading.

References

Abrami, P. C., Borohkovski, E., & Lysenko, L. (2015). The effects of AB-RACADABRA on reading outcomes: A meta-analysis of applied field research. *Journal of Interactive Learning Research, 26*(4), 337–367.

Aladé, F., Lauricella, A. R., Beaudoin-Ryan, L., & Wartella, E. (2016). Measuring with Murray: Touchscreen technology and preschoolers' STEM learning. *Computers in Human Behavior, 62,* 433–441. doi:10.1016/j.chb.2016.03.080

Amendum, S. J., Vernon-Feagans, L., & Ginsberg, M. C. (2011). The effectiveness of a technologically facilitated classroom-based early reading intervention. *The Elementary School Journal, 112*(1), 107–131. doi:10.1086/660684

American Academy of Pediatrics Council on Communications and Media. (2013). Children, adolescents, and the media. *Pediatrics, 132,* 958–961.

Aragón-Mendizábal, E., Aguilar-Villagrán, M., Navarro-Guzmán, J. I., & Howell, R. (2017). Improving number sense in kindergarten children with low achievement in mathematics. *Anales de Psicología, 33*(2), 311–318. doi:10.6018/analesps.33.2.239391

Baker, E. A. (2017). Apps, iPads, and literacy: Examining the feasibility of speech recognition in a first-grade classroom. *Reading Research Quarterly, 52*(3), 291–310.

Barendregt, W., Lindström, B., Rietz-Leppänen, E., Holgersson, I., & Ottosson, T. (2012). *Development and evaluation of Fingu: A mathematics iPad game using multi-touch interaction.* Paper presented at the Proceedings of the 11th International Conference on Interaction Design and Children, Bremen, Germany, June 12 to June 15, 2012.

Barnes, B. J., & Hill, S. (1983, May). Should young children work with microcomputers—Logo before Lego™? *The Computing Teacher, 10,* 11–14.

Baroody, A. J., Purpura, D. J., Eiland, M. D., & Reid, E. E. (2015). The impact of highly and minimally guided discovery instruction on promoting the learning of reasoning strategies for basic add-1 and doubles combinations. *Early Childhood Research Quarterly, 30, Part A*(0), 93–105. doi:10.1016/j.ecresq.2014.09.003

Bauserman, K. L., Cassady, J. C., Smith, L. L., & Stroud, J. C. (2005). Kindergarten literacy achievement: The effects of the PLATO integrated learning system. *Reading Research and Instruction, 44*(4), 49–60.

Beam, S., & Williams, C. (2015). Technology-mediated writing instruction in the early literacy program: Perils, procedures, and possibilities. *Computers in the Schools, 32*(3), 18.

Bennett, J. G., Gardner, R., Cartledge, G., Ramnath, R., & Council, M. R. (2017). Second-grade urban learners: Preliminary findings for a computer-assisted, culturally relevant, repeated reading intervention. *Education and Treatment of Children, 40*(2), 145–186.

Blok, H., Oostdam, R., Otter, M. E., & Overmaat, M. (2002). Computer-assisted instruction in support of beginning reading instruction: A review. *Review of Educational Research, 72*(1), 101–130. doi:10.3102/00346543072001101

Bourbour, M., Vigmo, S., & Samuelsson, I. P. (2015). Integration of interactive whiteboard in Swedish preschool practices. *Early Child Development & Care, 185*(1), 100–120. doi:10.1080/03004430.2014.908865

Burnett, C. (2010). Technology and literacy in early childhood educational settings: A review of research. *Journal of Early Childhood Literacy, 10*(3), 247–270. doi:10.1177/1468798410372154

Callaghan, M. N., & Reich, S. M. (2018). Are educational preschool apps designed to teach? An analysis of the app market. *Learning, Media and Technology, 43*(3), 280–293. doi:10.1080/17439884.2018.1498355

Campbell, M. L., & Mechling, L. C. (2009). Small group computer-assisted instruction with SMART board technology: An investigation of observational and incidental learning of nontarget information. *Remedial and Special Education, 30*(1), 47–57.

Carr, M., Taasoobshirazi, G., Stroud, R., & Royer, M. (2011). Combined fluency and cognitive strategies instruction improves mathematics achievement in early elementary school. *Contemporary Educational Psychology, 36,* 323–333.

Cascales-Martínez, A., Martínez-Segura, M.-J., Pérez-López, D., & Contero, M. (2017). Using an augmented reality enhanced tabletop system to promote learning of mathematics: A case study with students with special educational needs. *EURASIA Journal of Mathematics, Science & Technology Education, 13*(2), 355–380.

Cassady, J. C., Smith, L. L., & Thomas, C. L. (2018). Supporting emergent literacy for English language learners with computer-assisted instruction. *Journal of Research in Reading, 41*(2), 350–369. doi:10.1111/1467–9817.12110

Castles, A., McLean, G. M. T., Bavin, E., Bretherton, L., Carlin, J., Prior, M., … Reilly, S. (2013). Computer use and letter knowledge in pre-school children: A population-based study. *Journal of Paediatrics and Child Health, 49*(3), 193–198. doi:10.1111/jpc.12126

Chai, Z., Vail, C. O., & Ayres, K. M. (2015). Using an iPad application to promote early literacy development in young children with disabilities. *Journal of Special Education, 48*(4), 268–278.

Cheung, A. C. K., & Slavin, R. E. (2013). The effectiveness of educational technology applications for enhancing mathematics achievement in K-12 classrooms: A meta-analysis. *Educational Research Review, 9*(1), 88–113. doi:10.1016/j.edurev.2013.01.001

Ciampa, K. (2012). ICANREAD: The effects of an online reading program on grade 1 students' engagement and comprehension strategy use. *Journal of Research on Technology in Education, 45*(1), 27–59.

Cicconi, M. (2014). Vygotsky meets technology: A reinvention of collaboration in the early childhood mathematics classroom. *Early Childhood Education Journal, 42*(1), 57–65. doi:10.1007/s10643-013-0582-9

Clements, D. H. (1987). Computers and young children: A review of the research. *Young Children, 43*(1), 34–44.

Clements, D. H., Battista, M. T., & Sarama, J. (2001a). *Logo and geometry.* Reston, VA: National Council of Teachers of Mathematics.

Clements, D. H., Battista, M. T., & Sarama, J. (2001b). Logo and geometry. *Journal for Research in Mathematics Education, 10,* monograph series. Reston, VA: National Council of Teachers of Mathematics. doi:10.2307/749924

Clements, D. H., & Nastasi, B. K. (1993). Electronic media and early childhood education. In B. Spodek (Ed.), *Handbook of research on the education of young children* (pp. 251–275). New York, NY: Macmillan.

Clements, D. H., & Sarama, J. (2003). Strip mining for gold: Research and policy in educational technology—A response to "Fool's Gold". *Educational Technology Review, 11*(1), 7–69.

Clements, D. H., & Sarama, J. (2007). Effects of a preschool mathematics curriculum: Summative research on the *Building Blocks* project. *Journal for Research in Mathematics Education, 38*(2), 136–163.

Clements, D. H., & Sarama, J. (2007/2013). *Building blocks, Volumes 1 and 2.* Columbus, OH: McGraw-Hill Education.

Clements, D. H., & Sarama, J. (2007/2018). *Building blocks software [Computer software].* Columbus, OH: McGraw-Hill Education.

Clements, D. H., & Sarama, J. (2008a). Experimental evaluation of the effects of a research-based preschool mathematics curriculum. *American Educational Research Journal, 45*(2), 443–494. doi:10.3102/0002831207312908

Clements, D. H., & Sarama, J. (2008b). Mathematics and technology: Supporting learning for students and teachers. In O. N. Saracho & B. Spodek (Eds.), *Contemporary perspectives on science and technology in early childhood education* (pp. 127–147). Charlotte, NC: Information Age.

Clements, D. H., & Sarama, J. (2010). Technology. In V. Washington & J. Andrews (Eds.), *Children of 2020: Creating a better tomorrow* (pp. 119–123). Washington, DC: Council for Professional Recognition/National Association for the Education of Young Children.

Clements, D. H., & Sarama, J. (2014). *Learning and teaching early math: The learning trajectories approach* (2nd ed.). New York, NY: Routledge.

Clements, D. H., & Sarama, J. (2017). Valid issues but limited scope: A response to Kitchen and Berk's research commentary on educational technology. *Journal for Research in Mathematics Education, 48*(5), 474–482.

Clements, D. H., & Sarama, J. (2017/2019). Learning and teaching with learning trajectories ([LT]²). Retrieved from Marsico Institute,

Morgridge College of Education, University of Denver, www.learning-trajectories.org

Clements, D. H., Sarama, J., Barrett, J. E., Van Dine, D. W., Cullen, C. J., Hudyma, A., ... Eames, C. L. (2018). Evaluation of three interventions teaching area measurement as spatial structuring to young children. *The Journal of Mathematical Behavior, 50*, 23–41. doi:10.1016/j.jmathb.2017.12.004

Clements, D. H., Sarama, J., Spitler, M. E., Lange, A. A., & Wolfe, C. B. (2011). Mathematics learned by young children in an intervention based on learning trajectories: A large-scale cluster randomized trial. *Journal for Research in Mathematics Education, 42*(2), 127–166. doi:10.5951/jresematheduc.42.2.0127

Clements, D. H., & Swaminathan, S. (1995). Technology and school change: New lamps for old? *Childhood Education, 71*, 275–281.

Couse, L. J., & Chen, D. W. (2010). A tablet computer for young children? Exploring its viability for early childhood education. *Journal of Research on Technology in Education, 43*(1), 75–98.

Crompton, H., Grant, M. R., & Shraim, K. Y. H. (2018). Technologies to enhance and extend children's understanding of geometry: A configurative thematic synthesis of the literature. *Educational Technology & Society, 21*(1), 59–69.

Cuban, L. (2001). *Oversold and underused.* Cambridge, MA: Harvard University Press.

D'Agostino, J. V., Rodgers, E., Harmey, S., & Brownfield, K. (2016). Introducing an iPad app into literacy instruction for struggling readers: Teacher perceptions and student outcomes. *Journal of Early Childhood Literacy, 16*(4), 522–548.

Day, S. L. (2002). Real kids, real risks: Effective instruction of students at risk of failure. *Bulletin, 86*(682). doi:10.1177/019263650208663203

de Jong, M. T., & Bus, A. G. (2004). The efficacy of electronic books in fostering kindergarten children's emergent story understanding. *Reading Research Quarterly, 39*(4), 378–393.

Dennis, L. R., Whalon, K., Kraut, L., & Herron, D. (2016). Effects of a teacher versus iPad-facilitated intervention on the vocabulary of at-risk preschool children. *Journal of Early Intervention, 38*(3), 170–186.

Dewey, J. (1938/1997). *Experience and education.* New York, NY: Simon & Schuster.

DuBois, M. R., Volpe, R. J., & Hemphill, E. M. (2014). A randomized trial of a computer-assisted tutoring program targeting letter-sound expression. *School Psychology Review, 43*(2), 210–221.

Duhon, G. J., House, S. H., & Stinnett, T. A. (2012). Evaluating the generalization of math fact fluency gains across paper and computer performance modalities. *Journal of School Psychology, 50*, 335–345. doi:10.1016/j.jsp.2012.01.003

Fesakis, G., Kafoussi, S., & Malisiova, E. (2011). Intuitive conceptions of kindergarten children about the total of two dice problem, through the use of a microworld. *International Journal for Technology in Mathematics Education, 18*(2), 61–70.

Fien, H., Doabler, C. T., Nelson, N. J., Kosty, D. B., Clarke, B., & Baker, S. K. (2016). An examination of the promise of the Numbershire level 1 gaming intervention for improving student mathematics outcomes. *Journal of Research on Educational Effectiveness, 9*(4), 635–661. doi:10.1080/19345747.2015.1119229

Flannery, L. P., Silverman, B., Kazakoff, E. R., Bers, M. U., Bonta, P., & Resnick, M. (2013). *Designing ScratchJr: Support for early childhood learning through computer programming.* Paper presented at the Proceedings of the 12th International Conference on Interaction Design and Children, New York, NY. Retrieved from http://dl.acm.org/citation.cfm?id=2485785

Fleer, M., & Hoban, G. (2012). Using "slowmation" for intentional teaching in early childhood centres: Possibilities and imaginings. *Australasian Journal of Early Childhood, 37*(3), 61–70.

Fletcher-Flinn, C. M., & Gravatt, B. (1995). The efficacy of computer assisted instruction (CAI): A meta-analysis. *Journal of Educational Computing Research, 12*(3), 219–242. doi:10.2190/51D4-F6L3-JQHU-9M31

Foster, M. E., Anthony, J. L., Clements, D. H., & Sarama, J. (2016). Improving mathematics learning of kindergarten students through computer

assisted instruction. *Journal for Research in Mathematics Education, 47*(3), 206–232. doi:10.5951/jresematheduc.47.3.0206

Fuchs, L. S., Fuchs, D., Hamlett, C. L., Powell, S. R., Capizzi, A. M., & Seethaler, P. M. (2006). The effects of computer-assisted instruction on number combination skill in at-risk first graders. *Journal of Learning Disabilities, 39*, 467–475.

Fuchs, L. S., Powell, S. R., Hamlett, C. L., Fuchs, D., Cirino, P. T., & Fletcher, J. M. (2008). Remediating computational deficits at third grade: A randomized field trial. *Journal of Research on Educational Effectiveness, 1*, 2–32.

Gedik, N., Çetin, M., & Koca, C. (2017). Examining the experiences of preschoolers on programming via tablet computers. *Mediterranean Journal of Humanities, 7*(1), 193–203. doi:10.13114/mjh.2017.330

Goffredo, M., Bernabucci, I., Lucarelli, C., Conforto, S., Schmid, M., Nera, M. M., ... Grasselli, B. (2016). Evaluation of a motion-based platform for practicing phonological awareness of preschool children. *Journal of Educational Computing Research, 54*(5), 595–618.

Goodwin, L. D., Goodwin, W. L., Nansel, A., & Helm, C. P. (1986). Cognitive and affective effects of various types of microcomputer use by preschoolers. *American Educational Research Journal, 23*, 348–356.

Gorp, K., Segers, E., & Verhoeven, L. (2017). Enhancing decoding efficiency in poor readers via a word identification game. *Reading Research Quarterly, 52*(1), 105–123.

Greenwood, C. R., Carta, J. J., Kelley, E. S., Guerrero, G., Kong, N. Y., Atwater, J., & Goldstein, H. (2016). Systematic replication of the effects of a supplementary, technology-assisted, storybook intervention for preschool children with weak vocabulary and comprehension skills. *The Elementary School Journal, 116*(4), 574–599. doi:10.1086/686223

Guernsey, L., & Levine, M. H. (2016). Nurturing young readers: How digital media can promote literacy instead of undermining it. *American Educator, 40*(3), 23–28, 44.

Harskamp, E. (2015). The effects of computer technology on primary school students' mathematics achievement: A meta-analysis. In S. Chinn (Ed.), *The Routledge international handbook of dyscalculia* (pp. 383–392). Abingdon, Oxon, UK: Routledge.

Haugland, S. W. (1992). Effects of computer software on preschool children's developmental gains. *Journal of Computing in Childhood Education, 3*(1), 15–30.

Herodotou, C. (2018a). Mobile games and science learning: A comparative study of 4 and 5 years old playing the game angry birds. *British Journal of Educational Technology, 49*(1), 6–16.

Herodotou, C. (2018b). Young children and tablets: A systematic review of effects on learning and development. *Journal of Computer Assisted Learning, 34*(1), 1–9.

Hill, D. A., & Flores, M. M. (2015). A preliminary investigation of the benefits of computer-aided instruction in reading decoding for students with autism spectrum disorder and other developmental disabilities. *Journal of the American Academy of Special Education Professionals, 72*, 82.

Hiniker, A., Lee, B., Sobel, K., & Choe, E. K. (2017). *Plan & play: Supporting intentional media use in early childhood.* Paper presented at the Proceedings of the 2017 Conference on Interaction Design and Children. doi:10.1145/3078072.3079752

Homer, B. D., Kinzer, C. K., Plass, J. L., Letourneau, S. M., Hoffman, D., Bromley, M., ... Kornak, Y. (2014). Moved to learn: The effects of interactivity in a Kinect-based literacy game for beginning readers. *Computers & Education, 74*, 37–49. doi:10.1016/j.compedu.2014.01.007

Hsiao, H.-S., Chang, C.-S., Lin, C.-Y., & Hsu, H.-L. (2015). "iRobiQ": The influence of bidirectional interaction on kindergarteners' reading motivation, literacy, and behavior. *Interactive Learning Environments, 23*(3), 269–292.

Hsin, C.-T., Li, M.-C., & Tsai, C.-C. (2014). The influence of young children's use of technology on their learning: A review. *Educational Technology & Society, 17*(4), 85–99.

Hyun, E. (2005). A study of 5- to 6-year-old children's peer dynamics and dialectical learning in a computer-based technology-rich classroom environment. *Computers and Education, 44*(1), 69–91.

Hyun, E., & Davis, G. (2005). Kindergartners' conversations in a computer-based technology classroom. *Communication Education, 54*(2), 118–135. doi:10.1080/03634520500213397

Ihmeideh, F. M. (2014). The effect of electronic books on enhancing emergent literacy skills of pre-school children. *Computers & Education, 79*, 40–48. doi:10.1016/j.compedu.2014.07.008

IOM (Institute of Medicine) and NRC (National Research Council). (2012). *The early childhood care and education workforce: Challenges and opportunities: A workshop report*. Washington, DC: The National Academies Press.

Isik-Ercan, Z., Zeynep Inan, H., Nowak, J. A., & Kim, B. (2014). "We put on the glasses and moon comes closer!" Urban second graders exploring the earth, the sun and moon through 3d technologies in a science and literacy unit. *International Journal of Science Education, 36*(1), 129–156.

Jimenez, B. A., & Stanger, C. (2017). Math manipulatives for students with severe intellectual disability: A survey of special education teachers. *Physical Disabilities: Education and Related Services, 36*(1), 1–12. doi:10.14434/pders.v36i1.22172

Judge, S. (2005). Impact of computer technology on academic achievement of young African American children. *Journal of Research in Childhood Education, 20*(2), 91–101. doi:10.1080/02568540509594554

Kabali, H. K., Irigoyen, M. M., Nunez-Davis, R., Budacki, J. G., Mohanty, S. H., Leister, K. P., & Bonner, R. L. (2015). Exposure and use of mobile media devices by young children. *Pediatrics, 136*(6), 2015–2151.

Kankaanranta, M., Koivula, M., Laakso, M.-L., & Mustola, M. (2017). Digital games in early childhood: Broadening definitions of learning, literacy, and play. In M. Ma & A. Oikonomou (Eds.), *Serious games and edutainment applications: Volume II* (pp. 349–367). Cham, Switzerland: Springer International Publishing. doi:10.1007/978-3-319–51645-5_16

Karemaker, A., Pitchford, N. J., & O'Malley, C. (2010). Enhanced recognition of written words and enjoyment of reading in struggling beginner readers through whole-word multimedia software. *Computers & Education, 54*(1), 199–208.

Katz, P. (2011). A case study of the use of internet photobook technology to enhance early childhood "scientist" identity. *Journal of Science Education and Technology, 20*(5), 525–536.

Kazakoff, E., Sullivan, A., & Bers, M. (2013). The effect of a classroom-based intensive robotics and programming workshop on sequencing ability in early childhood. *Early Childhood Education Journal, 41*(4), 245–255. doi:10.1007/s10643-012-0554–5

Kegel, C. A. T., van der Kooy-Hofland, V. A. C., & Bus, A. G. (2009). Improving early phoneme skills with a computer program: Differential effects of regulatory skills. *Learning and Individual Differences, 19*(4), 549–554. doi:10.1016/j.lindif.2009.07.002

Keren, G., & Fridin, M. (2014). Kindergarten social assistive robot (KindSAR) for children's geometric thinking and metacognitive development in preschool education: A pilot study. *Computers in Human Behavior, 35*, 400–412. doi:10.1016/j.chb.2014.03.009

Kermani, H., & Aldemir, J. (2015). Preparing children for success: Integrating science, math, and technology in early childhood classroom. *Early Child Development and Care, 185*(9), 1504–1527. doi:10.1080/03004430.2015.1007371

Ketamo, H., & Kiili, K. (2010). Conceptual change takes time: Game based learning cannot be only supplementary amusement. *Journal of Educational Multimedia and Hypermedia, 19*(4), 399–419.

Kiefer, M., Schuler, S., Mayer, C., Trumpp, N. M., Hille, K., & Sachse, S. (2015). Handwriting or typewriting? The influence of pen or keyboard-based writing training on reading and writing performance in preschool children. *Advances in Cognitive Psychology, 11*(4), 136–146. doi:10.5709/acp-0178-7

Kim, S., & Chang, M. (2010). Does computer use promote the mathematical proficiency of ELL students? *Journal of Educational Computing Research, 42*, 285–305.

Koivula, M., Huttunen, K., Mustola, M., Lipponen, S., & Laakso, M.-L. (2016). The emotion detectives game: Supporting the social-emotional competence of young children. In M. Ma & A. Oikonomou (Eds.), *Serious games and edutainment applications: Volume II*

(pp. 29–53). Cham, Switzerland: Springer International Publishing. doi:10.1007/978-3-319–51645-5_2

Korat, O., & Segal-Drori, O. (2016). E-book and printed book reading in different contexts as emergent literacy facilitator. *Early Education and Development, 27*(4), 532–550.

Korat, O., & Shamir, A. (2008). The educational electronic book as a tool for supporting children's emergent literacy in low versus middle SES groups. *Computers & Education, 50*(1), 110–124. doi:10.1016/j.compedu.2006.04.002

Kozminsky, E., & Asher-Sadon, R. (2013). Media type influences preschooler's literacy development: E-book versus printed book reading. *Interdisciplinary Journal of E-Learning and Learning Objects, 9*, 233–247.

Kramarski, B., & Weiss, I. (2007). Investigating preschool children's mathematical engagement in a multimedia collaborative environment. *Journal of Cognitive Education and Psychology, 6*, 411–432.

Kraus, W. H. (1981). Using a computer game to reinforce skills in addition basic facts in second grade. *Journal for Research in Mathematics Education, 12*, 152–155.

Krcmar, M., & Cingel, D. P. (2014). Parent–child joint reading in traditional and electronic formats. *Media Psychology, 17*(3), 262–281. doi:10.1080/15213269.2013.840243

Kreskey, D. D., & Truscott, S. D. (2016). Is computer-aided instruction an effective tier-one intervention for kindergarten students at risk for reading failure in an applied setting? *Contemporary School Psychology, 20*(2), 142–151.

Kumtepe, A. T. (2006). The effects of computers on kindergarten children's social skills. *Turkish Online Journal of Educational Technology – TOJET, 5*(4), 6.

Kyle, F., Kujala, J., Richardson, U., Lyytinen, H., & Goswami, U. (2013). Assessing the effectiveness of two theoretically motivated computer-assisted reading interventions in the United Kingdom: GG Rime and GG Phoneme. *Reading Research Quarterly, 48*(1), 61–76.

Leacox, L., & Jackson, C. W. (2014). Spanish vocabulary-bridging technology-enhanced instruction for young English language learners' word learning. *Journal of Early Childhood Literacy, 14*(2), 175–197.

Lee, J. S., & Ginsburg, H. P. (2007). Preschool teachers' beliefs about appropriate early literacy and mathematics education for low- and middle-socioeconomic status children. *Early Education and Development, 18*(1), 111–143.

Lehtinen, E., Brezovszky, B., Rodríguez-Aflecht, G., Lehtinen, H., Hannula-Sormunen, M. M., McMullen, J., … Jaakkola, T. (2015). Number navigation game (NNG): Design principles and game description. *Describing and studying domain-specific serious games* (pp. 45–61). doi:10.1007/978-3-319–20276-1_4

Lehtinen, E., Hannula-Sormunen, M. M., McMullen, J., & Gruber, H. (2017). Cultivating mathematical skills: From drill-and-practice to deliberate practice. *ZDM Mathematics Education.* doi:10.1007/s11858-017-0856-6

Lentz, C. L., Seo, K. K.-J., & Gruner, B. (2014). Revisiting the early use of technology: A critical shift from "how young is too young?" to "how much is 'just right'?". *Dimensions of Early Childhood, 42*(1), 15–23.

Li, X., Atkins, M. S., & Stanton, B. (2006). Effects of home and school computer use on school readiness and cognitive development among Head Start children: A randomized controlled pilot trial. *Merrill-Palmer Quarterly, 52*(2), 239–263. doi:10.1353/mpq.2006.0010

Lin, C.-H., & Chen, C.-M. (2016). Developing spatial visualization and mental rotation with a digital puzzle game at primary school level. *Computers in Human Behavior, 57*, 23–30. doi:10.1016/j.chb.2015.12.026

Lin, Y.-H., & Hou, H.-T. (2016). Exploring young children's performance on and acceptance of an educational scenario-based digital game for teaching route-planning strategies: A case study. *Interactive Learning Environments, 24*(8), 1967–1980.

Lindahl, M. G., & Folkesson, A.-M. (2012). ICT in preschool: Friend or foe? The significance of norms in a changing practice. *International Journal of Early Years Education, 20*(4), 422–436. doi:10.1080/09669760.2012.743876

Lonigan, C. J., Driscoll, K., Phillips, B. M., Cantor, B. G., Anthony, J. L., & Goldstein, H. (2003). A computer-assisted instruction phonological sensitivity program for preschool children at-risk for reading problems. *Journal of Early Intervention, 25*(4), 248–262. doi:10.1177/105381510302500402

Lysenko, L., Rosenfield, S., Dedic, H., Savard, A., Idan, E., Abrami, P. C., … Naffi, N. (2016). Using interactive software to teach foundational mathematical skills. *Journal of Information Technology Education: Innovations in Practice, 15*, 19–34.

Macaruso, P., & Rodman, A. (2011a). Benefits of computer-assisted instruction to support reading acquisition in English language learners. *Bilingual Research Journal, 34*(3), 301–315.

Macaruso, P., & Rodman, A. (2011b). Efficacy of computer-assisted instruction for the development of early literacy skills in young children. *Reading Psychology, 32*(2), 172–196.

Mathes, P. G., Torgesen, J. K., & Allor, J. H. (2001). The effects of peer-assisted literacy strategies for first-grade readers with and without additional computer-assisted instruction in phonological awareness. *American Educational Research Journal, 38*, 371–410.

McDonald, S., & Howell, J. (2012). Watching, creating and achieving: Creative technologies as a conduit for learning in the early years. *British Journal of Educational Technology, 43*(4), 641–651. doi:10.1111/j.1467–8535.2011.01231.x

McKenzie, S., Spence, A., & Nicholas, M. (2018). Going on Safari: The design and development of an early years literacy iPad application to support letter-sound learning. *Electronic Journal of e-Learning, 16*(1), 16–29.

McManis, M. H., & McManis, L. D. (2016). Using a touch-based, computer-assisted learning system to promote literacy and math skills for low-income preschoolers. *Journal of Information Technology Education: Research, 15*, 409–429.

Miller, E. B., & Warschauer, M. (2014). Young children and e-reading: Research to date and questions for the future. *Learning, Media and Technology, 39*(3), 283–305. doi:10.1080/17439884.2013.867868

Milman, N. B., Carlson-Bancroft, A., & Vanden Boogart, A. (2014). Examining differentiation and utilization of iPads across content areas in an independent, preK-4th grade elementary school. *Computers in the Schools, 31*(3), 119–133. doi:10.1080/07380569.2014.931776

Mohd Syah, N. E., Hamzaid, N. A., Murphy, B. P., & Lim, E. (2016). Development of computer play pedagogy intervention for children with low conceptual understanding in basic mathematics operation using the dyscalculia feature approach. *Interactive Learning Environments, 24*(7), 1477–1496. doi:10.1080/10494820.2015.1023205

Moradmand, N., Datta, A., & Oakley, G. (2013). *My maths story: An application of a computer-assisted framework for teaching mathematics in the lower primary years*. Paper presented at the Society for Information Technology & Teacher Education International Conference 2013, New Orleans, LA. Conference paper. Retrieved from http://www.editlib.org/p/48603

Moyer-Packenham, P. S., & Westenskow, A. (2013). Effects of virtual manipulatives on student achievement and mathematics learning. *International Journal of Virtual and Personal Learning Environments, 4*(3), 35–50. doi:10.4018/jvple.2013070103

Mustola, M., Koivula, M., Turja, L., & Laakso, M.-L. (2016). Reconsidering passivity and activity in children's digital play. *New Media & Society, 20*(1), 237–254. doi:10.1177/1461444816661550

National Mathematics Advisory Panel. (2008). *Foundations for success: The final report of the National Mathematics Advisory Panel*. Washington, DC: U.S. Department of Education, Office of Planning, Evaluation and Policy Development.

Navarro, J. I., Aguilar, M., Marchena, E., Ruiz, G., Menacho, I., & Van Luit, J. E. H. (2012). Longitudinal study of low and high achievers in early mathematics. *British Journal of Educational Psychology, 82*(1), 28–41. doi:10.1111/j.2044–8279.2011.02043.x

Neuman, S. B., & Celano, D. C. (2012, Fall). Worlds apart: One city, two libraries, and ten years of watching inequality grow. *American Educator, 36*(3), 13–23.

Neumann, M. M. (2016). Young children's use of touch screen tablets for writing and reading at home: Relationships with emergent literacy. *Computers & Education, 97*, 61–68. doi:10.1016/j.compedu.2016.02.013

Neumann, M. M. (2018). Using tablets and apps to enhance emergent literacy skills in young children. *Early Childhood Research Quarterly, 42*, 239–246. doi:10.1016/j.ecresq.2017.10.006

Newhouse, C. P., Cooper, M., & Cordery, Z. (2017). Programmable toys and free play in early childhood classrooms. *Australian Educational Computing, 32*(1), 14.

Nusir, S., Alsmadi, I., Al-Kabi, M., & Sharadgah, F. (2013). Studying the impact of using multimedia interactive programs on children's ability to learn basic math skills. *E-Learning and Digital Media, 10*(3), 305–319.

O'Callaghan, P., McIvor, A., McVeigh, C., & Rushe, T. (2016). A randomized controlled trial of an early-intervention, computer-based literacy program to boost phonological skills in 4- to 6-year-old children. *British Journal of Educational Psychology, 86*(4), 546–558.

Ok, M. W., & Kim, W. (2017). Use of iPads and iPods for academic performance and engagement of prek-12 students with disabilities: A research synthesis. *Exceptionality, 25*(1), 54–75.

Ortiz, E. A., & Cristia, J. (2014). *The IDB and technology in education: How to promote effective programs? Technical note 670*. Washington, DC: Inter-American Development Bank.

Outhwaite, L. A., Faulder, M., Gulliford, A., & Pitchford, N. J. (2018). Raising early achievement in math with interactive apps: A randomized control trial. *Journal of Educational Psychology*. doi:10.1037/edu0000286

Özbek, A. B., & Girli, A. (2017). The effectiveness of a tablet computer-aided intervention program for improving reading fluency. *Universal Journal of Educational Research, 5*(5), 757–764.

Paek, S., Hoffman, D., Saravanos, A., Black, J., & Kinzer, C. (2011). *The role of modality in virtual manipulative design*. Paper presented at the CHI '11 Extended Abstracts on Human Factors in Computing Systems, Vancouver, BC, Canada.

Peirce, N. (2013). *Digital game-based learning for early childhood*. Retrieved from Learnovate Centre website http://www.learnovatecentre.org/wp-content/uploads/2013/05/Digital_Game-based_Learning_for_Early_Childhood_Report_FINAL.pdf

Pelletier, J., Reeve, R., & Halewood, C. (2006). Young children's knowledge building and literacy development through knowledge forum[r]. *Early Education and Development, 17*(3), 323–346.

Pfenninger, S. E. (2015). MSL in the digital ages: Effects and effectiveness of computer-mediated intervention for FL learners with dyslexia. *Studies in Second Language Learning and Teaching, 5*(1), 109–133.

Piquette, N. A., Savage, R. S., & Abrami, P. C. (2014). A cluster randomized control field trial of the ABRACADABRA web-based reading technology: Replication and extension of basic findings. *Frontiers in Psychology, 5*, 1413.

Portelance, D. J., Strawhacker, A. L., & Bers, M. U. (2016). Constructing the ScratchJr programming language in the early childhood classroom. *International Journal of Technology and Design Education, 26*(4), 489–504.

Potocki, A., Ecalle, J., & Magnan, A. (2013). Effects of computer-assisted comprehension training in less skilled comprehenders in second grade: A one-year follow-up study. *Computers & Education, 63*, 131–140.

Reeves, J. L., Gunter, G. A., & Lacey, C. (2017). Mobile learning in prekindergarten: Using student feedback to inform practice. *Educational Technology & Society, 20*(1), 37–44.

Reimer, K., & Moyer, P. S. (2004, April). *A classroom study of third-graders' use of virtual manipulatives to learn about fractions*. Paper presented at the American Educational Research Association, San Diego, CA.

Rich, S. E., Duhon, G. J., & Reynolds, J. (2017). Improving the generalization of computer-based math fluency building through the use of sufficient stimulus exemplars. *Journal of Behavioral Education, 26*(2), 123–136.

Richter, A., & Courage, M. L. (2017). Comparing electronic and paper storybooks for preschoolers: Attention, engagement, and recall. *Journal of Applied Developmental Psychology, 48*, 92–102. doi:10.1016/j.appdev.2017.01.002

Rideout, V., & Katz, V. S. (2016). *Opportunity for all? Technology and learning in lower-income families*. New York, NY: The Joan Ganz Cooney Center at Sesame Workshop.

Roblyer, M. (1985). *Measuring the impact of computers in instruction: A non-technical review of recent research for educators*. Washington, DC: Association for Educational Data Systems.

Roskos, K., Brueck, J., & Widman, S. (2009). Investigating analytic tools for e-book design in early literacy learning. *Journal of Interactive Online Learning, 8*(3), 218–240.

Ryan, A. W. (1991). Meta-analysis of achievement effects of microcomputer applications in elementary schools. *Educational Administration Quarterly, 27*(2), 161–184.

Salminen, J., Koponen, T., Räsänen, P., & Aro, M. (2015). Preventive support for kindergarteners most at-risk for mathematics difficulties: Computer-assisted intervention. *Mathematical Thinking and Learning, 17*(4), 273–295. doi:10.1080/10986065.2015.1083837

Sarama, J., & Clements, D. H. (2006). Mathematics, young students, and computers: Software, teaching strategies and professional development. *The Mathematics Educator, 9*(2), 112–134.

Sarama, J., & Clements, D. H. (2009a). "Concrete" computer manipulatives in mathematics education. *Child Development Perspectives, 3*(3), 145–150.

Sarama, J., & Clements, D. H. (2009b). *Early childhood mathematics education research: Learning trajectories for young children*. New York, NY: Routledge.

Sarama, J., & Clements, D. H. (2016). Physical and virtual manipulatives: What is "concrete"? In P. S. Moyer-Packenham (Ed.), *International perspectives on teaching and learning mathematics with virtual manipulatives* (Vol. 3, pp. 71–93). Cham, Switzerland: Springer International Publishing. doi:10.1007/978-3-319-32718-1_4

Sarama, J., & Clements, D. H. (in press). Promoting a good start: Technology in early childhood mathematics. In E. Arias, J. Cristia, & S. Cueto (Eds.), *Promising models to improve primary mathematics learning in Latin America and the Caribbean using technology*. Washington, DC: Inter-American Development Bank.

Sarama, J., Clements, D. H., Swaminathan, S., McMillen, S., & González Gómez, R. M. (2003). Development of mathematical concepts of two-dimensional space in grid environments: An exploratory study. *Cognition and Instruction, 21*, 285–324.

Sarama, J., Clements, D. H., & Vukelic, E. B. (1996). The role of a computer manipulative in fostering specific psychological/mathematical processes. In E. Jakubowski, D. Watkins, & H. Biske (Eds.), *Proceedings of the 18th annual meeting of the North America chapter of the international group for the psychology of mathematics education* (Vol. 2, pp. 567–572). Columbus, OH: ERIC Clearinghouse for Science, Mathematics, and Environmental Education.

Sargent, A. R. (2017). *Urban preschool teachers' instructional technology integration perceptions and practices* (Doctoral Dissertation). Hampton University, Hampton, VA.

Savage, R., Abrami, P. C., Piquette, N., Wood, E., Deleveaux, G., Sanghera-Sidhu, S., & Burgos, G. (2013). A (Pan-Canadian) cluster randomized control effectiveness trial of the ABRACADABRA web-based literacy program. *Journal of Educational Psychology, 105*(2), 310–328.

Schacter, J., & Jo, B. (2016). Improving low-income preschoolers mathematics achievement with Math Shelf, a preschool tablet computer curriculum. *Computers in Human Behavior, 55*(A), 223–229. doi:10.1016/j.chb.2015.09.013

Schechter, R., Macaruso, P., Kazakoff, E. R., & Brooke, E. (2015). Exploration of a blended learning approach to reading instruction for low SES students in early elementary grades. *Computers in the Schools, 32*(3), 18.

Schmitt, K. L., Hurwitz, L. B., Sheridan Duel, L., & Nichols Linebarger, D. L. (2018). Learning through play: The impact of web-based games on early literacy development. *Computers in Human Behavior, 81*, 378–389. doi:10.1016/j.chb.2017.12.036

Sedaghatjou, M., & Campbell, S. R. (2017). Exploring cardinality in the era of touchscreen-based technology. *International Journal of Mathematical Education in Science and Technology, 48*(8), 1225–1239.

Segal-Drori, O., Korat, O., Shamir, A., & Klein, P. S. (2010). Reading electronic and printed books with and without adult instruction: Effects on emergent reading. *Reading and Writing: An Interdisciplinary Journal, 23*(8), 913–930.

Segers, E., & Verhoeven, L. (2005). Long-term effects of computer training of phonological awareness in kindergarten. *Journal of Computer Assisted Learning, 21*(1), 17–27. doi:10.1111/j.1365–2729.2005.00107.x

Shamir, A., Korat, O., & Barbi, N. (2008). The effects of CD-ROM storybook reading on low SES kindergarteners' emergent literacy as a function of learning context. *Computers & Education, 51*(1), 354–367.

Shamir, A., Korat, O., & Shlafer, I. (2011). The effect of activity with e-book on vocabulary and story comprehension: A comparison between kindergarteners at risk of learning disabilities and typically developing kindergarteners. *European Journal of Special Needs Education, 26*(3), 311–322.

Shin, N., Sutherland, L. M., Norris, C. A., & Soloway, E. (2012). Effects of game technology on elementary student learning in mathematics. *British Journal of Educational Technology, 43*(4), 540–560. doi:10.1111/j.1467-8535.2011.01197.x

Siegel, M., Kontovourki, S., Schmier, S., & Enriquez, G. (2008). Literacy in motion: A case study of a shape-shifting kindergartener. *Language Arts, 86*(2), 89–98.

Sigdel, S. (2017). *Technology and learning capacity of children: A positive impact of technology in early childhood* (MBA Student Scholarship). Johnson & Wales University, Providence, RI.

Silander, M., Moorthy, S., Dominguez, X., Hupert, N., Pasnik, S., & Llorente, C. (2016). *Using digital media at home to promote young children's mathematics learning: Results of a randomized controlled trial*. Retrieved from Society for Research on Educational Effectiveness. 2040 Sheridan Road, Evanston, IL 60208. Retrieved from https://search.proquest.com/docview/1871568227?accountid=14608

Smeets, D. J. H., & Bus, A. G. (2015). The interactive animated e-book as a word learning device for kindergartners. *Applied Psycholinguistics, 36*(4), 899–920. doi:10.1017/S0142716413000556

Smeets, D. J. H., van Dijken, M. J., & Bus, A. G. (2014). Using electronic storybooks to support word learning in children with severe language impairments. *Journal of Learning Disabilities, 47*(5), 435–449. doi:10.1177/0022219412467069

Smith, A., & Wang, Y. (2010). The impact of visual phonics on the phonological awareness and speech production of a student who is deaf: A case study. *American Annals of the Deaf, 155*(2), 124–130.

Smith, C. R., Marchand-Martella, N. E., & Martella, R. C. (2011). Assessing the effects of the *Rocket Math* program with a primary elementary school student at risk for school failure: A case study. *Education and Treatment of Children, 34*, 247–258.

Sullivan, A., & Bers, M. (2013). Gender differences in kindergarteners' robotics and programming achievement. *International Journal of Technology & Design Education, 23*(3), 691–702. doi:10.1007/s10798-012-9210-z

Sullivan, A., Kazakoff, E. R., & Bers, M. U. (2013). The wheels on the bot go round and round: Robotics curriculum in pre-kindergarten. *Journal of Information Technology Education: Innovations in Practice, 12*, 203–219.

Sung, W., Ahn, J.-H., Kai, S. M., & Black, J. (2017). *Effective planning strategy in robotics education: An embodied approach*. Paper presented at the Society for Information Technology & Teacher Education International Conference 2017, Austin, TX, United States. Retrieved from https://www.learntechlib.org/p/177387

Talley, S., Lancy, D. F., & Lee, T. R. (1997). Children, storybooks, and computers. *Reading Horizons, 38*(2), 116–128.

Thompson, C. J., & Davis, S. B. (2014). Classroom observation data and instruction in primary mathematics education: Improving design and rigour. *Mathematics Education Research Journal, 26*(2), 301–323. doi:10.1007/s13394-013-0099-y

Tucker, S. I., Lommatsch, C. W., Moyer-Packenham, P. S., Anderson-Pence, K. L., & Symanzik, J. (2017). Kindergarten children's interactions with touchscreen mathematics virtual manipulatives: An innovative mixed methods analysis. *International Journal of Research in Education and Science, 3*(2), 646–665.

van de Sande, E., Segers, E., & Verhoeven, L. (2016). Supporting executive functions during children's preliteracy learning with the computer. *Journal of Computer Assisted Learning, 32*(5), 468–480. doi:10.1111/jcal.12147

Van der Kooy-Hofland, V. A. C., Bus, A. G., & Roskos, K. (2012). Effects of a brief but intensive remedial computer intervention in a sub-sample of kindergartners with early literacy delays. *Reading and Writing, 25*(7), 1479–1497. doi:10.1007/s11145-011-9328-5

Varma, K. (2014). Supporting scientific experimentation and reasoning in young elementary school students. *Journal of Science Education and Technology, 23*(3), 381–397.

Verhallen, M. J., Bus, A. G., & de Jong, M. T. (2006). The promise of multimedia stories for kindergarten children at risk. *Journal of Educational Psychology, 98*(2), 410–419.

Volpe, R. J., Burns, M. K., DuBois, M., & Zaslofsky, A. F. (2011). Computer-assisted tutoring: Teaching letter sounds to kindergarten students using incremental rehearsal. *Psychology in the Schools, 48*(4), 332–342. doi:10.1002/pits.20557

Watson, J. A., Nida, R. E., & Shade, D. D. (1986). Educational issues concerning young children and microcomputers: Lego with Logo? *Early Child Development and Care, 23*, 299–316.

Watson, T., & Hempenstall, K. (2008). Effects of a computer based beginning reading program on young children. *Australasian Journal of Educational Technology, 24*(3), 258–274.

Weiss, I., Kramarski, B., & Talis, S. (2006). Effects of multimedia environments on kindergarten children's mathematical achievements and style of learning. *Educational Media International, 43*(1), 3–17. doi:10.1080/09523980500490513

Williams, C. (2011). Adapted interactive writing instruction with kindergarten children who are deaf or hard of hearing. *American Annals of the Deaf, 156*(1), 23–34.

Yamac, A., & Ulusoy, M. (2016). The effect of digital storytelling in improving the third graders' writing skills. *International Electronic Journal of Elementary Education, 9*(1), 59–86.

Yilmaz, R. M., Kucuk, S., & Goktas, Y. (2017). Are augmented reality picture books magic or real for preschool children aged five to six? *British Journal of Educational Technology, 48*(3), 824–841. doi:10.1111/bjet.12452

Zaranis, N. (2017). Does the use of information and communication technology through the use of Realistic Mathematics Education help kindergarten students to enhance their effectiveness in addition and subtraction? *Preschool & Primary Education, 5*(1), 46–62. doi:10.12681/ppej.9058

Zaranis, N., & Synodi, E. (2017). A comparative study on the effectiveness of the computer assisted method and the interactionist approach to teaching geometry shapes to young children. *Education and Information Technologies, 22*(4), 1377–1393.

Zaretsky, E. (2017). The impact of using logic patterns on achievements in mathematics through application-games. In J. Horne (Ed.), *Philosophical Perceptions on Logic and Order* (p. 73). doi:10.4018/978-1-5225-2443-4ch002

Zipke, M. (2017). Preschoolers explore interactive storybook apps: The effect on word recognition and story comprehension. *Education and Information Technologies, 22*(4), 1695–1712.

14

Media Exposure in Early Childhood and Infancy

Examining Traditional Media (TV) and Mobile Digital Technologies

Domenica De Pasquale, Karin Archer, and Eileen Wood

In today's society, screen media technologies are seamlessly woven into everyday life for the vast majority of children, and increasingly so for infants. Screen media technologies include television and a wide array of digital devices (e.g., laptops, tablets, mobile phones, etc.). Much of the extant literature examines the prevalence, use and impact of these two technologies independently. Distinctions between television and other digital devices may be relevant in some cases but in others distinctions may be artificial. For example, television, as typically depicted in the literature, refers to a stationary device with little to no interactivity, whereas a defining feature of digital devices is their potential for high levels of interactivity combined with design features that are responsive to learner actions (Aliagas & Margallo, 2017; Chambers et al., 2008; Lysenko & Abrami, 2014; Savage et al., 2013; Willoughby & Wood, 2008). It is important that broad generalizations regarding differences in these types of screen media should not be overgeneralized. Specifically, today, videos and television shows are easily streamed on portable digital devices such as tablets and mobile phones, while computer games and other types of software are often accessed and used through television consoles. These interchangeable functions caution against overly simplistic categorizations of different types of screen media. Instead, considerations must assess not only how much these different types of screen media are being used but also for what purpose they are being used in order to understand their potential impact on early development. In the following chapter, we will explore the ubiquitous nature of technologies in the lives of young children, toddlers and infants today. In addition to reporting prevalence, we will examine the function these technologies serve for parents and children as well as summarize outcomes associated with their use. The chapter will consider the unique literatures available for television and mobile computer technologies independently, as well as issues relevant to screen media in general.

Initial Introductions to Screen Media and Their Prevalence

Almost two decades ago, guidelines regarding the introduction and use of screen media recommended that children under two years of age should not be exposed to screens at all (American Academy of Pediatrics, 1999, 2001). More recently, the American Academy of Pediatrics (2016) revised this guideline and recommended that children younger than 18 months of age should not be exposed to screen media with the exception of video chatting. Despite these long-standing recommendations prohibiting screen media exposure for children under the age of two (American Academy of Pediatrics, 1999, 2001), both television viewing and use of digital devices by young children, toddlers and infants have been common (Rideout, 2013). Introduction to television now occurs early in infancy with children as young as three months of age being identified as the youngest age for first exposure, with nine months of age being the average age for first exposure (Zimmerman, Christakis, & Meltzoff, 2007a). The presence of televisions in children's bedrooms has increased access to television for many children. Specifically, by 2013 16% of children under two years of age and 37% of children aged two to four years had a television in their bedroom (Rideout, 2013). By age two, 90% of children are regularly watching television for an average of 40–44 minutes per day (Rideout, 2013; Zimmerman et al., 2007a). This rises to just over an hour (64 minutes) per day among two- to four-year-olds (Rideout, 2013). More recently, among Canadian parents, the average age of introduction for television was reported to be 8.3 months, with over 95% of infants having been exposed to television by the time they were two years old (Archer, 2017; Archer, Dodds, & Wood, 2016). Together, these data indicate that early introduction to television is now common.

Similar to the observed increase in television exposure, the prevalence of digital screen technologies has seen a rapid increase over the past decade. Data from a few years ago indicated that children as young as two to four years of age were engaged with 'computers' for approximately 8.4 minutes per day (Carson, Tremblay, Spence, Timmons, & Janssen, 2013). While the amount of time on 'computers' remained low at five minutes per day by 2017, the amount of time on mobile screen technologies was approximately 58 minutes per day for two- to four-year-olds (Common Sense Media, 2017). It is important to note that there are disparities across countries regarding engagement with digital screen technologies. For example, a cross-country summary indicated that 78% of Dutch toddlers, 70% of Swedish three- to four-year-olds, a third of British three- to four-year-olds and 25% of three- to four-year-olds in the United States accessed online activities (for a review see Holloway, Green, & Livingston, 2013). Despite these differences among countries, the common message is that young children and infants around the world are coming into increasing contact and use of digital screen technologies.

Early introduction to mobile digital screen technologies today means introduction in infancy. For example, from 2011 to 2013 parent surveys revealed an increase from 10% to 38% in the percentage of infants using mobile digital devices (Rideout, 2013). By 2015, parents were reporting that 89% of two-year-olds had touched or scrolled the screen of a mobile digital device, 95% had watched television on a mobile digital device and 77% had used apps (Kabali et al., 2015). By 2017, 80% of parents reported introducing mobile digital devices to their infants with an average age of introduction of 13 months (Archer, 2017; Archer et al., 2016).

Earlier exposure to mobile screen media technologies is associated with a corresponding increase in the amount of time or number of opportunities in a day that infants and young children use digital screen technologies. For example, recent research indicates that 14% of children in the United States use mobile digital devices at least an hour a day by one year of age (Kabali et al., 2015). These findings confirm a growing trend for younger children and even infants to become regular users of mobile digital screen technologies.

Challenges Reporting Screen Media Prevalence

Prevalence statistics provide an important cue to media exposure; however, reports of screen media use may need to be interpreted with some caution. Asking parents to identify whether or not their child has been introduced to mobile screen media technology can be a problematic question. For example, in one study, although 80% of parents responded to survey questions describing how frequently their child was *using* a mobile digital screen technology, only 65% of these parents indicated in the affirmative that their child had been *introduced* to mobile digital screen technology (Archer, 2017). This discrepancy may reflect some hesitation on the part of parents to acknowledge introducing technology to very young children and infants. However, when questions ask directly about use, which perhaps bypasses any perceived judgment regarding use, parents are willing to provide

information. Awareness of this discrepancy presents an interesting concern when attempting to acquire accurate reports of children's early introduction to technology in both research and applied contexts. Accurate reports in both contexts may be best served by asking parents how much children use screen media technology rather than asking whether their child uses screen media technology or not.

A second challenge parents face when asked to report technology use is averaging or estimating usage time when use may vary dramatically from day to day and across children of differing ages (Rideout, 2013; Rideout & Hamel, 2006). For example, in one study of children between two and six years of age, engagement with digital technologies within a given week ranged from 0 hours to 80 hours (De Pasquale, 2018; De Pasquale, Wood, & Petkovski, 2016). The variability indicates that although parents are generally introducing screen media earlier, exposure time is much less uniform with some families exhibiting much more restrictive access and use of digital screen technologies than others (Lauricella, Wartella, & Rideout, 2015; Plowman, Stevenson, Stephen, & McPake, 2012). In addition, it is often difficult for parents to accurately report use of technology because children have access outside the home (Ko, 2002; Stephen & Plowman, 2008; Wang & Hoot, 2006; Wood, 2001). Further, in many homes screen media are 'on' constantly during a day with programs of varying types running in the background while other activities are taking place. 'Background screen media' makes it difficult to estimate exposure as it is constantly on and available (Anderson & Subrahmanyam, 2017; Pempek, Kirkorian, & Anderson, 2014). Awareness of earlier exposure and increasing amounts of exposure are important indicator statistics; however, given challenges parents face in quantifying precisely how much time children are exposed to technology, estimates of exposure time need to be considered with some caution. It may be more useful to consider exposure to screen media not as a number but rather in terms of what children are engaged with when using the technology.

Introduction to Technology: Accident or Intention

Is the trend toward increasingly earlier exposure to screen media accidental or intentional? In a recent Canadian study (Wood et al., 2016) nearly 45% of parents supported the introduction of screen media between the ages of 1½ and 2½ years, while 60.6% of parents indicated they would introduce screen media before 2.5 years of age, 71.4% before the age of 3 and 81.2% support the introduction of screen media before the age of 3.5 (De Pasquale, 2018; Wood et al., 2016). Another recent study indicated that just over 50% of parents intentionally initiated their child's introduction to mobile screen media (Archer et al., 2016). Thus, it appears that for approximately half of the young children and infants introduced to screen media technologies, exposure is intentional while the introduction of screen media technologies for the remaining half of the children appeared to be unplanned.

Two environmental contributors to unplanned and early exposure include exposure outside of the home by others and the presence of siblings. As noted earlier, many children have access to screen media through various venues outside of the home including daycare/child-care, baby-sitters, family and friends of children (De Pasquale, 2018; Ko, 2002; Stephen & Plowman, 2008; Wang & Hoot, 2006; Wood, 2001). Interestingly, birth order is related to age of first exposure. Older siblings have a significant impact on the age of introduction to screen media for younger siblings. This cohort difference may be a function of family context. Specifically, infants may be exposed to screen media earlier in contexts where an older sibling is present and presumably using screen media (De Pasquale, 2018; McHale, Updegraff, & Whiteman, 2012; Plowman, McPake, & Stephen, 2008; Plowman et al., 2012). Overall, the influence of others whether within the family or beyond is an important factor when studying exposure and use of screen media.

Concerns with Early Screen Exposure

One of the most common and persistent concerns regarding screen media technologies is that time involving screen media technologies displaces time that could be spent more fruitfully in other more beneficial activities. Much of the extant literature examining negative outcomes or 'screen effects' is based on research involving television viewing. Indeed, a significant and consistent body of literature demonstrates negative impacts in all areas of development including cognitive, language and social development associated with passive television viewing (Barr, Lauricella, Zack, & Clavert, 2010; Christakis, Zimmerman, DiGiuseppe, & McCarty, 2004; Conners-Burrow, McKelvey, & Fussell, 2011; Lin, Cherng, Chen, Chen, & Yang, 2015). Among young children in particular, considerable research focuses on the negative impact television viewing has on language development. Results consistently indicate a strong relationship between increased levels of viewing television and delays in vocabulary development (Lin et al., 2015; Nathanson & Rasmussen, 2011; Zimmerman Christakis, & Meltzoff, 2007b). The presence of background television has also been associated with reductions in the quantity and quality of parental language directed toward children (Anderson & Subrahmanyam, 2017; Pempek et al., 2014).

A second concern regarding screen media involves negative emotional and behavioral outcomes. Again, much of the extant research involves television exposure. For example, increased television exposure for infants and young children has been associated with emotional reactivity and aggression (e.g., Domingues-Montanari, 2017). These negative effects may be tied to the content of the programming watched by infants and toddlers. For example, Barr and colleagues (2010) found that infants with a high level of exposure to adult-directed television demonstrated poor executive functioning skills, specifically inhibitory self-control and emergent metacognition skills; these results were not found in infants exposed only to age-appropriate content. Similarly, increased hyperactivity and aggression have been found among children who watched inappropriate content for their age (Conners-Burrow et al., 2011) while increased attention problems were noted among children who watched violent and entertainment-focused programs, but not for children who watched programs listed as educational (Zimmerman & Christakis, 2007). Although these findings make clear that television viewing can be detrimental across many aspects of development, they also highlight the need to examine what is being viewed as negative outcomes may not be a necessary outcome from television viewing.

Are the 'screen effects' observed with television use replicated when mobile screen media are used? As of yet the literature regarding infant and early childhood use of screen media is not sufficiently developed to answer this question. However, if screen media technologies are used in the same manner as has been demonstrated for television (i.e., viewing adult, violent or inappropriate content), it would be expected that similar negative outcomes would follow. However, the inherent capabilities afforded by screen media technologies may yield more positive outcomes. For example, although screen media typically fail to provide many cues that support learning during social interactions (Kirkorian, 2018; Krcmar, 2010; Kuhl, 2007), when these social cues are incorporated into screen media using video chat with a person, transfer is enhanced (Kirkorian, 2018; Myers, LeWitt, Gallo, & Maselli, 2017; Nielsen, Simcock, & Jenkins, 2008; Roseberry, Hirsh-Pasek, & Golinkoff, 2014; Troseth, Saylor, & Archer, 2006). Although these are promising findings that suggest the increased interactivity available with computer-based digital devices, they may yield different outcomes than are typically observed in television contexts; much more research is needed before such conclusions could be made. In the interim, both television and screen media must be used cautiously and with attention paid to the type of programming introduced.

Advantages Associated with Screen Media Use Early in Development

Negative outcomes are not a *necessary* product of screen media use. Parents report that television can be an important tool for promoting learning and many seek to provide their children with educational programming. For example, among infants up to one year of age, parents reported that their children 'sometimes' or 'often' watched educational shows (40%) followed by children's entertainment shows (20%) and only 14% reported providing general audience or adult shows (Rideout, 2013). Considerable research has demonstrated that well-designed, pedagogically sound and child-appropriate programming is associated with learning gains. For example, a recent meta-analysis demonstrated gains in literacy and numeracy skill development and social reasoning for children across 15 countries following exposure to Sesame Street (Mares & Pan, 2013). Social, emotional and cognitive gains from viewing television can be bolstered when parents co-view and interact with their children while viewing television (e.g., Connell, Lauricella, & Wartella, 2015; Schaan & Melzer, 2015; Strouse, Troseth, O'Doherty, & Saylor, 2018). Co-viewing allows parents to clarify, make connections and evaluations of content, and to reiterate key ideas. Co-viewing also provides an opportunity for parent-child interactions. The positive effects of co-viewing, however, are only evident when parents regularly watch television with the child – which research indicates is not typically the case (Kirkorian, Pempek, Murphy, Schmidt, & Anderson, 2009). Thus, encouraging parents to share television time and engage in co-viewing is an important activity to promote in the early years.

Digital screen media technologies offer the potential for enhanced instruction. Learning gains have been evident across many domains including science, math and reading (e.g., Jamshidifarsani, Garbaya, Lim, Blazevic, & Ritchie, 2019; Kafai, 2010; Tamim, Bernard, Borokhovski, Abrami, & Schmid, 2011) and across a diverse array of activities (e.g., creating presentations, gathering information, gaming, using digital cameras, listening to music and watching television: Burnett, 2013; Gronn, Scott, Edwards, & Henderson, 2014). Affordances inherent in intuitive devices such as tablets and smartphones provide a context where children can now use and learn from screen media at increasingly younger ages. The interactive multimedia capabilities of many tablet and mobile phone technologies can stimulate visual, auditory, tactile and kinaesthetic sensory systems and the response to children's input is instant, providing immediate feedback (Cooper, 2005; Tahnk, 2011). Multimedia formats present information through more than one modality. As a result, users can experience information verbally, visually and through touch, and this can occur using one, or all modalities simultaneously. The redundancy of information that is typically provided through these differing modalities (especially redundancy of verbal and visual information) can enhance learning (Takacs, Swart, & Bus, 2015). In addition, many software programs are designed with differing levels allowing children to move from easier to more challenging activities. These leveled activities reflect hierarchically arranged sub-goals which organize and structure the learning experience. These instructional design features enable even very young or inexperienced users to quickly learn to use the technology and explore new things, learn new skills and gain knowledge (McManis & Gunnewig, 2012). In addition to design features, the pedagogical and content quality contributes to effective use of screen media. Several recent evaluations regarding the comprehensiveness of software programs suggest that many may not include the full taxonomy of skills that underlie competencies in areas such as mathematics and literacy skills (e.g., Grant et al., 2012; Larkin, 2016; Lee, Douglas, Wood, & Andrade, 2017). However, many programs are well designed and even those that target limited skill sets can deliver experiences in these specific areas as well (Wood, Specht, Willoughby, & Mueller, 2008). Overall,

digitally delivered instruction has the promise to attract and engage learners. In addition, well-conceived and designed programs offer the potential to facilitate learning.

Parents tend to endorse the use of digital screen media specifically to support their child's learning and to provide opportunities to gain experiences and skills which are viewed to be essential to their child's future education and employment (Davies, 2011; Wood et al., 2016). One study (Michael Cohen Group, 2011) explained the increased engagement of touch-screen technology as it caters to a variety of ages and skills allowing for independent exploration. Children as young as two to three years of age, and younger, are able to use touch-screen technology to perform simple tasks such as matching and counting, and motor skills such as learning hand-eye coordination to target, press or drag. Four- to five-year-olds demonstrated more directed and advanced motor skills such as initial press, drag and swipe. Finally, six- to eight-year-olds recognize and master the skills needed to operate games (Michael Cohen Group, 2011). Overall, touch-screen technologies allow for an easier to use and more intuitive interface for children (McManis & Gunnewig, 2012).

Recent research supports the intuitive nature of mobile touch-screen technologies and how these technologies can facilitate different learning experiences for very young children. For example, parent-child interactions during play serve an important function in promoting development. Consistent with Vygotsky's (1978) socio-cultural theory, more knowledgeable adults can guide and scaffold young children to bridge the gap between what young children and infants can do on their own and what they can achieve with assistance. Do traditional three-dimensional play contexts elicit different kinds of parent-child interactions than the two-dimensional displays afforded through digital touch-screen technologies? Early research suggests this might be the case. A recent study of parent-child interactions with young children, Ho and colleagues (2018), found that the two types of play contexts yielded different types of spatial talk by parents. Specifically, they found that spatial words generated by parents did not differ in overall quantity across the two contexts but did differ in terms of the types of words elicited. The researchers suggested that the two play contexts may be complementary in promoting more diverse spatial talk. Understanding that digital screen media, and screen media in general, can serve a unique but complementary learning function for very young learners contributes to our understanding of best practice. Screen media technologies may be best used in conjunction with other types of play or instruction (e.g., Ho et al., 2018; Slavin, Lake, Chambers, Cheung, & Davis, 2009).

What We Know and Where We Need to Go

Considerable research has examined the use of television as a source of entertainment, education and child-care for young children (e.g., Rideout & Hamel, 2006; Rideout, Vandewater, & Wartella, 2003; Wartella, Richert, &

Robb, 2010; Zimmerman et al., 2007a). Although there is a long-standing, well-developed research base regarding television in childhood covering the preschool years and beyond, much less is known about early exposure in infancy and the early toddler years. Our understanding of the impact of digital media technologies in the earliest years of life is even more limited. Much of our current research with infants involves parent reports gathered through surveys, some observations conducted in home or lab contexts and a limited but growing number of empirical studies. In part, the delay in empirical findings with our youngest children, especially infants, is a product of long-standing concern regarding potential negative effects from screen media exposure early in life. With the knowledge that so many infants and toddlers are exposed to screen media and that this exposure is not infrequent, there is a need to more thoroughly explore these technologies across multiple contexts, and areas of development (i.e., cognitive, social and physical) both for immediate and long-term impact.

Screen media (both television and mobile digital technologies) are already a seamless part of infants and young children's early experiences. Television has been an important influence in the lives of children since its introduction and it continues to be an important screen media device for young children and infants today due to its familiarity, its promise for educational gains and its use as a form of entertainment. The flexibility of mobile screen media permits parents and children to access the Internet anywhere, anytime (Chen & Kinshuk, 2005; Evans & Johri, 2008; Hoppe, Joiner, Milrad, & Sharples, 2003; Mueller, Wood, De Pasquale, & Archer, 2011; Norris & Soloway, 2008), which allows technology to become more fully integrated into a variety of contexts in everyday life, for example, while travelling in the car, shopping or visiting. Both forms of screen media offer opportunities for children to learn (Bus & Neuman, 2009; Korat, 2009, 2010; Korat & Blau, 2010); however, passive use, exposure to inappropriate content or excessive use of screen media are concerns that may defeat anticipated learning gains (Vandewater, Bickham, & Lee, 2006). Establishing guidelines that parents and child-care providers can use regarding optimal or 'best-practice' use of screen media technologies is needed.

Guidelines for best practice depend on the quality of available programming and parental involvement. Distinguishing programming quality can be difficult for both parents and early childhood educators. In some countries programming content is evaluated only in terms of appropriate language (e.g., swearing), adult content (i.e., nudity and relationships involved) and level of violence but not in terms of educational value. In countries such as the United States, legislation (i.e., the Children's Television Act) was developed to identify programs deemed educational and informative for children with the notation 'E/I' to indicate that the program is suitable and has educational value (Federal Communications Commission, n.d.). Even when programs are identified as educational or informative, however, parents and childhood educators must determine for themselves what concepts are being taught in the program and how well concepts are being presented.

This is a significant challenge. Currently, no mechanism exists for parents, educators or child-care providers to be able to evaluate the educational content of software programs or apps. Addressing this shortcoming is necessary to facilitate optimal use of all types of screen media, but is especially important for digital screen media given the burgeoning market of apps and software programs being developed for young children. Sporadic but growing research attention is focusing on the systematic evaluation of children's software for both skills taught and developmental appropriateness (e.g., Grant et al., 2012; Papadakis & Kalogiannakis, 2017). To date, translation of research findings into media accessible for parents and children is sparse (e.g., Wood et al., 2012). Going forward, there is a need for more of this systematic evaluation research as well as development of mechanisms for translation to parents and educators.

Research indicates that parental involvement while using screen media technologies should be advocated as a means to maximize benefits (Flanagan, 2013; Flynn & Richert, 2015; Kirkorian, et al., 2009). Parental involvement includes scaffolding children to better enable them to understand the media as well as content being presented. Interaction of parents with their young children and infants while engaged with screen media expands children's social, emotional and cognitive understandings and provides children with critical time with parents.

In summary, research regarding screen media use by infants, and even by toddlers, is in its infancy—much more work is needed to build a comprehensive picture. However, extant research suggests that screen media is now, and will be, an important influence in the lives of young children and there is a growing body of literature that identifies how we can maximize the positive influences of screen media exposure.

References

Aliagas, C., & Margallo, A. M. (2017). Children's responses to the interactivity of storybook apps in family shared reading events involving the iPad. *Literacy, 51*(1), 44–52. doi:10.1111/lit.12089

American Academy of Pediatrics. (1999). Media education. *Pediatrics, 104*, 341–342.

American Academy of Pediatrics. (2001). Media violence. *Pediatrics, 108*, 1222–1226.

American Academy of Pediatrics, Council on Communications and Media. (2016). Media and young minds. *Pediatrics, 138*(5), e20162591. doi: 10.1542/peds.2016-2591

Anderson, D. R., & Subrahmanyam, K. (2017). Digital screen media and cognitive development. *Pediatrics, 140*(5), S57–S61. doi:10.1542/peds.2016-1758C

Archer, K. (2017). Infants, toddlers and mobile technology: Examining parental choices and the impact of early technology introduction on cognitive and motor development. *Theses and Dissertations (Comprehensive)*. 1925. https://scholars.wlu.ca/etd/1925

Archer, K., Dodds, M., & Wood, E. (2016). *Parental views on early introduction and use of mobile technology by infants and toddlers.* Poster presented at the 24th Biennial Meeting of the International Society for the Study of Behavioural Development, Vilnius, Lithuania.

Barr, R., Lauricella, A., Zack, E., & Calvert, S. L. (2010). Infant and early childhood exposure to adult-directed and child-directed television programming: Relations with cognitive skills at age four. *Merrill-Palmer Quarterly, 56*(1), 21–48. doi:10.1353/mpq.0.0038

Burnett, C. (2013). Investigating children's interactions around digital texts in classrooms: How are these framed and what counts? *Education 3–13, 43*(2), 197–208.

Bus, A. G., & Neuman, S. B. (2009). *Multimedia and literacy development.* New York, NY: Routledge.

Carson, V., Tremblay, M. S., Spence, J. C., Timmons, B. W., & Janssen, I. (2013). The Canadian sedentary behaviour guidelines for the early years (zero to four years of age) and screen time among children from Kingston, Ontario. *Paediatrics & Child Health, 18*(1), 25–28.

Chambers, B., Slavin, R. E., Madden, N. A., Abrami, P. C., Tucker, B. J., Cheung, A., & Gifford, R. (2008). Technology infusion in success for all: Reading outcomes for first graders. *The Elementary School Journal, 109*(1), 1–15. doi:10.1086/592364

Chen, J., & Kinshuk (2005). Mobile technology in educational services. *Journal of Educational Multimedia and Hypermedia, 14*(1), 91–109.

Christakis, D. A., Zimmerman, F. J., Digiuseppe, D. L., & McCarty, C. A. (2004). Early television exposure and subsequent attentional problems in children. *Pediatrics, 113*(4), 708–713. doi:10.1542/peds.113.4.708

Common Sense Media. (2017). The Common Sense Consensus: Media Use by Kids Age Zero to Eight, Common Sense Media, San Francisco, CA. Retrieved from https://www.commonsensemedia.org/sites/default/files/uploads/research/csm_zerotoeight_fullreport_release_2.pdf

Connell, S. L., Lauricella, A. R., & Wartella, E. (2015). Parental co-use of media technology with their young children in the USA. *Journal of Children and Media, 9*(1), 5–21.

Conners-Burrow, N. A., Mckelvey, L. M., & Fussell, J. J. (2011). Social outcomes associated with media viewing habits of low-income preschool children. *Early Education & Development, 22*(2), 256–273. doi:10.1080/10409289.2011.550844

Cooper, L. Z. (2005). Developmentally appropriate digital environments for young children. *Library Trends, 54*, 286–302. doi:10.1353/lib.2006.0014

Davies, C. (2011). Digitally strategic: How young people respond to parental views about the use of technology for learning in the home. *Journal of Computer Assisted Learning, 27*(4), 324–335. doi:10.1111/j.1365-2729.2011.00427.x

De Pasquale, D. (2018). Examining parental scaffolding in computer based contexts as a function of task difficulty and mobility of computer device. *Theses and Dissertations (Comprehensive).* 2033. https://scholars.wlu.ca/etd/2033

De Pasquale, D., Wood, E., & Petkovski, M. (2016, July). *Parent-child interactions during shared computer use* (Poster presentation at ISSBD). Vilnius, Lithuania.

Domingues-Montanari, S. (2017). Clinical and psychological effects of excessive screen time on children. *Journal of Paediatrics and Child Health, 53*(4), 333–338. doi:10.1111/jpc.13462

Evans, M. A., & Johri, A. (2008). Facilitation guided participation through mobile technologies: Designing creative learning environments for self and others. *Journal of Computing in Higher Education, 20*(2), 92–105.

Federal Communications Commission. (n.d.). *Children's educational television.* Retrieved from https://www.fcc.gov/consumers/guides/childrens-educational-television

Flanagan, R. (2013). Effects of learning from interaction with physical or mediated devices. *Cognitive Processes, 14*, 213–215.

Flynn, R. M., & Richert, R. A. (2015). Parents support preschoolers' use of a novel interactive device. *Infant and Child Development, 24*(6), 624–642. doi:10.1002/icd.1911

Grant, A., Wood, E., Gottardo, A., Evans, M. A., Phillips, L., & Savage, R. (2012). Assessing the content and quality of commercially available reading software programs: Do they have the fundamental structures to promote the development of early reading skills in children? *NHSA Dialog, 15*(4), 319–342. doi:10.1080/15240754.2012.725487

Gronn, D., Scott, A., Edwards, S., & Henderson, M. (2014). 'Technological me': Young children's use of technology across their home and school contexts. *Technology, Pedagogy and Education, 23*(4), 439–454.

Ho, A., Lee, J., Wood, E., Kassies, S., & Heinbuck, C. (2018). Tap, swipe, and build: Parental spatial input during iPad ® and toy play. *Infant and Child Development, 27*(1), doi:10.1002/icd.2061

Holloway, D., Green, L., & Livingstone, S. (2013). *Zero to eight: Young children and their internet use.* Report LSE, London, UK: EU Kids Online.

Hoppe, H. U., Joiner, R., Milrad, M., & Sharples, M. (2003). Guest editorial: Wireless and mobile technologies in education. *Journal of Computer Assisted Learning, 19*(3), 255–259.

Jamshidifarsani, H., Garbaya, S., Lim, T., Blazevic, P., & Ritchie, J. M. (2019). Technology-based reading intervention programs for elementary grades: An analytical review. *Computers & Education, 128*, 427–445.

Kabali, H. K., Irigoyen, M. M., Nunez-Davis, R., Budacki, J. G., Mohanty, S. H., Leister, K. P., & Bonner, R. L. (2015). Exposure and use of mobile media devices by young children. *Pediatrics, 136*(6), 1044–1050. doi:10.1542/peds.2015-2151

Kafai, Y. B. (2010). World of whyville: An introduction to tween virtual life. *Games and Culture: A Journal of Interactive Media, 5*(1), 3–22. doi:10.1177/1555412009351264

Kirkorian, H. L. (2018). When and how do interactive digital media help children connect what they see on and off the screen? *Child Development Perspectives, 12*(3), 210–214. doi:10.1111/cdep.12290

Kirkorian, H. L., Pempek, T. A., Murphy, L. A., Schmidt, M. E., & Anderson, D. R. (2009). The impact of background television on parent-child interaction. *Child Development, 80*(5), 1350–1359. doi:10.1111/j.1467-8624.2009.01337.x

Krcmar, M. (2010). Assessing the research on media, cognitive development, and infants. *Journal of Children and Media, 4*, 119–134. doi:10.1080/17482791003629586

Ko, S. (2002). An empirical analysis of children's thinking and learning in a computer game context. *Educational Psychology, 22*(2), 219–233. doi:10.1080/01443410120115274

Korat, O. (2009). The effects of CD-ROM storybook reading on Israeli children's early literacy as a function of age group and repeated reading. *Education Information Technology, 14*(1), 39–53.

Korat, O. (2010). Reading electronic books as a support for vocabulary, story comprehension and word reading in kindergarten and first grade. *Computers & Education, 55*(1), 24–31.

Korat, O., & Blau, H. (2010). Repeated reading of CD-ROM storybook as a support for emergent literacy: A developmental perspective in two SES groups. *Journal of Educational Computing Research, 43*(4), 443–462.

Kuhl, P. K. (2007). Is speech learning "gated" by the social brain? *Developmental Science, 10*, 110–120. doi:10.1111/j.1467-7687.2007.00572.x

Larkin, K. (2016). Mathematics education and manipulatives: Which, when, how? *ERIC, 21*, 12–17.

Lauricella, A. R., Wartella, E., & Rideout, V. J. (2015). Young children's screen time: The complex role of parent and child factors. *Journal of Applied Developmental Psychology, 36*, 11–17. doi:10.1016/j.appdev.2014.12.001

Lee, J., Douglas, E., Wood, E., & Andrade, S. (2017). *How educational are math apps for preschoolers?* Poster presented at the 2017 Society for Research in Child Development Biennial Meeting, Austin, TX.

Lin, L., Cherng, R., Chen, Y., Chen, Y., & Yang, H. (2015). Effects of television exposure on developmental skills among young children. *Infant Behavior and Development, 38*, 20–26. doi:10.1016/j.infbeh.2014.12.005

Lysenko, L. V., & Abrami, P. C. (2014). Promoting reading comprehension with the use of technology. *Computers & Education, 75*, 162–172. doi:10.1016/j.compedu.2014.01.010

Mares, M., & Pan, Z. (2013). Effects of Sesame Street: A meta-analysis of children's learning in 15 countries. *Journal of Applied Developmental Psychology, 34*(3), 140–151.

McHale, S. M., Updegraff, K. A., & Whiteman, S. D. (2012). Sibling relationships and influences in childhood and adolescence. *Journal of Marriage and Family, 74*(5), 913–930. doi:10.1111/j.1741-3737.2012.01011.x

McManis, L. D., & Gunnewig, S. B. (2012). Finding the education in educational technology with early learners. *Young Child, 67*, 14–24.

Michael Cohen Group & USDOE [US Department of Education]. (2011). Young children, apps and iPad. New York, NY: Michael Cohen Group. Retrieved from http://mcgrc.com/wp-content/uploads/2012/06/ipad-study-cover-page-report-mcg-info_new-online.pdf

Mueller, J., Wood, E., De Pasquale, D., & Archer, K. (2011). Students learning with mobile technologies in and out of the classroom. In A. Méndez-Vilas (Ed.), *Education in a technological world: Communicating current and emerging research and technological efforts* (pp. 414–420). Badajoz, Spain: Formatex Research Center.

Myers, L. J., LeWitt, R. B., Gallo, R. E., & Maselli, N. M. (2017). Baby FaceTime: Can toddlers learn from online video chat? *Developmental Science, 20*, 1–15. doi:10.1111/desc.12430

Nathanson, A. I., & Rasmussen, E. E. (2011). TV viewing compared to book reading and toy playing reduces responsive maternal communication with toddlers and preschoolers. *Human Communication Research, 37*(4), 465–487. doi:10.1111/j.1468–2958.2011.01413.x

Nielsen, M., Simcock, G., & Jenkins, L. (2008). The effect of social engagement on 24-month-olds' imitation from live and televised models. *Developmental Science, 11*, 722–731. doi:10.1111/j.1467–7687.2008.00722.x

Norris, C., & Soloway, E. (2008). Getting mobile handhelds help bring K-12 classrooms into the 21st century. *District Administration*, 21–24. Retrieved from https://www.thefreelibrary.com/Getting+mobile%3a+handheld+computers+bring+K12+classrooms+into+the+21st...-a0181752787

Papadakis, S., & Kalogiannakis, M. (2017). Mobile educational applications for children. What educators and parents need to know. *International Journal of Mobile Learning and Organisation, 11*(2), 256–277. doi:10.1504/IJMLO.2017.085338

Pempek, T. A., Kirkorian, H. L., & Anderson, D. R. (2014). The effects of background television on the quantity and quality of child-directed speech by parents. *Journal of Children and Media, 8*(3), 211–222. doi:10.1080/17482798.2014.920715

Plowman, L., McPake, J., & Stephen, C. (2008). Just picking it up? Young children learning with technology at home. *Cambridge Journal of Education, 38*(3), 303–319. doi:10.1080/03057640802287564

Plowman, L., Stevenson, O., Stephen, C., & McPake, J. (2012). Preschool children's learning with technology at home. *Computers & Education, 59*(1), 30–37. doi:10.1016/j.compedu.2011.11.014

Rideout, V. (2013, October 28). *Zero to eight: Children's media use in America 2013* (Rep.). Retrieved from https://www.commonsensemedia.org/research/zero-to-eight-childrens-media-use-in-america-2013

Rideout, V., & Hamel, E. (2006, May). *The media family: Electronic media in the lives of infants, toddlers, preschoolers and their parents* (Rep.). Retrieved from https://kaiserfamilyfoundation.files.wordpress.com/2013/01/7500.pdf

Rideout, V. J., Vandewater, E. A., & Wartella, E. A. (2003). *Zero to six: Electronic media in the lives of infants, toddlers and preschoolers*. Henry J, Kaiser Family Foundation, 2400 Sand Hill Road, Menlo Park, CA. Retrieved from https://libproxy.wlu.ca/login?url=https://search-proquest-com.libproxy.wlu.ca/docview/62170647?accountid=15090

Roseberry, S., Hirsh-Pasek, K., & Golinkoff, R. M. (2014). Skype me! Socially contingent interactions help toddlers learn language. *Child Development, 85*, 956–970. doi:10.1111/cdev.12166

Schaan, V., & Melzer, A. (2015). Parental mediation of children's television and video game use in Germany: Active and embedded in family processes. *Journal of Children and Media, 9*(1), 58–76.

Slavin, R., Lake, C., Chambers, B., Cheung, A., & Davis, S. (2009). Effective reading programs for the elementary grades: A best-evidence synthesis. *Review of Educational Research, 79*(4), 1391–1466. doi:10.3102/0034654309341374

Savage, R., Abrami, P., Piquette, N., Wood, E., Deleveaux, G., Sangher-Sidhu, S., & Burgo, G. (2013). A (Pan-Canadian) cluster randomized control effectiveness trial of the ABRACADABRA web-based literacy program. *Journal of Educational Psychology, 105*(2), 310–328. doi:10.1037/a0031025

Stephen, C., & Plowman, L. (2008). Enhancing learning with information and communication technologies in pre-school. *Early Child Development and Care, 178*(6), 637–654.

Strouse, G. A., Troseth, G. L., O'Doherty, K. D., & Saylor, M. M. (2018). Co-viewing supports toddlers' word learning from contingent and noncontingent video. *Journal of Experimental Child Psychology, 166*, 310–326.

Takacs, Z., Swart, E., & Bus (2015). A benefits and pitfalls of multimedia and interactive features in technology-enhanced story books: A meta-analysis. *Review of Educational Research, 85*(4), 698–739.

Tahnk, J. (2011). Digital milestones: Raising a tech-savvy kid. *Parenting Early Years, 25*, 78–84.

Tamim, R. M., Bernard, R. M., Borokhovski, E., Abrami, P. C., & Schmid, R. F. (2011). What forty years of research says about the impact of technology on learning: A second-order meta-analysis and validation study. *Review of Educational Research, 81*(1), 4–28. doi:10.3102/0034654310393361

Troseth, G. L., Saylor, M. M., & Archer, A. H. (2006). Young children's use of video as a source of socially relevant information. *Child Development, 77*, 786–799. doi:10.1111/j.1467-8624.2006.00903.x

Vandewater, E. A., Bickham, D. S., & Lee, J. H. (2006). Time well spent? Relating television use to children's free-time activities. *Pediatrics, 117*(2), 181–191.

Vygotsky, L. (1978). *Mind in society: The development of higher psychological processes*. Cambridge, MA: Harvard University Press.

Wang, X. C., & Hoot, J. L. (2006). Information and communication technology in early childhood education. *Early Education and Development, 17*(3), 317–322.

Wartella, E., Richert, R. A., & Robb, M. B. (2010). Babies, televisions and videos: How do we get here? *Development Review, 30*, 116–127.

Willoughby, T., & Wood, E. (2008). *Children's learning in a digital world*. Malden, MA: Blackwell Publishing.

Wood, E., Gottardo, A., Grant, A., Evans, M. A., Phillips, L., & Savage, R. (2012). Developing tools for assessing and using commercially available reading software programs to promote the development of early reading skills in children. *NHSA Dialog, 15*(4), 350–354.

Wood, E., Petkovski, M., De Pasquale, D., Gottardo, A., Evans, M. A., & Savage, R. (2016). Parent scaffolding of young children when engaging with mobile technology. *Frontiers in Psychology, 7*, 1–11. doi:10.3389/fpsyg.2016.00690

Wood, E., Specht, J., Willoughby, T., & Mueller, J. (2008). Integrating computer technology in early childhood education environments: Issues raised by early childhood educators. *Alberta Journal of Educational Research, 54*(2), 210–226. Retrieved from http://search.proquest.com/docview/622155958?accountid=15090

Wood, J. (2001). Can software support children's vocabulary development? *Language Learning & Technology, 5*(1), 166–201.

Zimmerman, F. J., & Christakis, D. A. (2007). Associations between content types of early media exposure and subsequent attentional problems. *Pediatrics, 120*(5), 986–992. doi:10.1542/peds.2006-3322

Zimmerman, F. J., Christakis, D. A., & Meltzoff, A. N. (2007a). Television and DVD/video viewing in children younger than 2 years. *Archives of Pediatrics & Adolescent Medicine, 161*(5), 473–479. doi:10.1001/archpedi.161.5.473

Zimmerman, F. J., Christakis, D. A., & Meltzoff, A. N. (2007b). Associations between media viewing and language development in children under age 2 years. *The Journal of Pediatrics, 151*(4), 364–368.

Part III

Foundations of Early Childhood Educational Policy

15

Low-Income and Young Children

TIANA MOORE, REBECCA M. RYAN, REBECCA C. FAUTH, AND JEANNE BROOKS-GUNN

Young children in the United States are at a higher risk to live in poverty than any other age group. In 2017, about one in five of all children under age six in the United States lived in families with incomes below the poverty threshold (Fontenot, Semega, & Kollar, 2018).[1] Furthermore, another one-fifth of children under age six live in near-poor households, defined by a household income just above the poverty threshold (between 100% and 200% of the poverty threshold). Families who are poor and near-poor (often termed "low-income") have difficulty making their income cover expenses each month (Edin & Kefalas, 2011). Children in poor and near-poor households not only lack basic financial resources, but also are likely to experience hardships that often accompany low-income, such as inadequate food, clothing, housing, and health care (Haveman, Blank, Moffitt, Smeeding, & Wallace, 2015).

Children under age six are more likely to live in low-income households than older children, adolescents, and adults (in part because their parents are young and earning less). Compared to White children, Black and Hispanic children are more likely to live in low-income households and as a result, they are disproportionately vulnerable to the adversities associated with low-income during early life. These inequities are significant—68% of Black children and 63% of Hispanic children lived in low-income households in 2015, compared to approximately 33% of White children (Jiang, Granja, & Koball, 2017; Pac, Nam, Waldfogel, & Wimer, 2017). Growing up in poverty is associated with lower levels of well-being for children across a range of developmental domains. Differences between children living in poor and non-poor families, particularly in the cognitive domain, tend to appear between 18 and 24 months of age and are of equal or greater size by age five (Duncan & Murnane, 2011). Young children who grow up in poor households are likely to enter kindergarten with lower levels of early math, reading, and language skills than their non-poor peers. Differences between poor and non-poor children's achievement have increased over the past 75 years. Comparing children born between 1943 and 2001, children who were in the bottom 10% of the income distribution saw their differences in standardized achievement test scores move from about 0.60 of a standard deviation to 1.25 of a standard deviation less than children who were in the top 90% of the income distribution (based on family income) (Reardon, 2011). These early gaps remain when children enter elementary school, where children living in poor families exhibit lower school achievement than children in non-poor families (Duncan & Brooks-Gunn, 1997; Reardon, 2011), and these differences are still apparent in high school, where children living in poverty have higher rates of special education placement, grade retention, teenage pregnancy, and school dropout than their counterparts (Duncan, Yeung, Brooks-Gunn, & Smith, 1998; Votruba-Drzal, 2006). Not only are these early differences sustained into adolescence, but poverty experienced during the first five years is more strongly associated with deleterious outcomes than poverty experienced in later childhood and adolescence (Duncan, Magnuson, Kalil, & Ziol-Guest, 2012; Duncan et al., 1998; Duncan, Ziol-Guest, & Kalil, 2010).

This chapter covers four topics. First, the complexities in measuring poverty and identifying links to child development are explored. Second, potential pathways through which poverty may influence child development are considered. Here, two perspectives frame the discussion, one emphasizing the role of familial relationships and parenting (Conger & Elder, 1994; McLoyd, 1990) and another stressing the impact of parental investments in resources for children (Becker, 1991; Haveman & Wolfe, 1994). This section focuses on a variety of family and neighborhood pathways. The third section describes eight different federal programs and policies that provide money as well as food, housing, and health care to poor and near-poor families with the aim of reducing poverty (i.e., bringing families in deep poverty closer to the poverty threshold or moving families above the threshold) or its impact on children. These programs include income enhancement (Temporary Assistance for Needy Families [TANF] and the Earned Income Tax Credit [EITC]), food assistance (Women, Infants, and Children [WIC] and Supplemental Nutritional

Assistance Program [SNAP]), child care assistance (subsidies for mothers who are employed), early childhood educational programs (Early Head Start [EHS] and Head Start [HS]), housing assistance programs (public housing and Section 8 Housing Choice Vouchers), and home visiting services (Mother, Infant, and Early Childhood Home Visiting [MIECHV] Program). Child health insurance is another major program whose receipt is linked to family income, but is not discussed given space constraints (all poor children are eligible for Medicaid, as are many near-poor children, who also qualify for the Children's Health Insurance Program [CHIP]). Federally funded services for young children with disabilities are considered in Chapter 19 (in this volume); these programs for the most part are not income tested. The fourth section is a brief conclusion.

The Consequences of Growing Up in a Poor Family

Complexities in Measuring Poverty and Its Effects

Children growing up in poverty live in families whose incomes are at or below the poverty threshold, the official federal poverty measure in the United States. This threshold, which was originally developed in 1959, is based on expected food expenditures (a thrifty food budget) for families of varying sizes and varying ages and is adjusted annually for the Consumer Price Index (cost of living). The original definition took the cost for a thrifty food budget as defined by the Department of Agriculture and multiplied it by three (the assumption being that food accounted for one-third of families' expenses at that time). It is an absolute threshold, linked to family expenditures regardless of whether the median household income changes over time (and obviously it has since 1959, even adjusted for cost of living). The poverty threshold is used for statistical purposes to demarcate families according to whether they are above or below the threshold. Each family's income may also be calculated as a percentage of the poverty threshold (i.e., if a family of one parent and two children is at the poverty threshold, their income would be $19,749 in 2017; if at 50% of the threshold, our hypothetical family's income would be $9,875; and if at 150% of the threshold, it would be $29,624). The poverty threshold and its variants are commonly used to calculate the number of years a family has lived in poverty (which reflects the *persistence* of family poverty), as well as the ages of a particular child when their family experiences poverty (which indicates the *timing* of poverty).

The extant poverty threshold measure has been criticized for myriad reasons, most notably for underestimating the type and degree of expenditures families must outlay from month to month, ignoring regional differences in living costs, overestimating the amount spent on food, and excluding alternative sources (such as food stamps and housing subsidies) for income that were specifically designed for low-income families, such as food stamps and housing subsidies (Citro & Michael, 1995). Since 2011, a Supplemental Poverty Measure (SPM) aimed at redressing many of these criticisms has been used as a complement to the existing threshold. The SPM calibrates the threshold based on the average expenditures of families living below the median income, and includes in its calculation not only food costs, but also the costs of clothing, medical expenses, utilities, and regional differences in housing costs. Federal in-kind benefits are also included in families' income calculations. The SPM is a relative measure, calculating a family's poverty status by comparing their resources relative to those of the average family (based on median family income). Given this, a family's poverty status can change depending on the rise and fall of median income, even if the family's income is relatively stable over time. The New York City Longitudinal Study of Wellbeing, also known as the Poverty Tracker, is a survey of New York City residents that assesses the dynamic nature of economic disadvantage over time (Neckerman, Garfinkel, Teitler, Waldfogel, & Wimer, 2016). Findings from the study suggest that the SPM is an improved measure of poverty, but it may not fully capture the landscape of disadvantage for families. Non-monetary indicators of disadvantage (such as food insecurity or housing insecurity) are not reflected in the SPM (nor in the original poverty threshold). At the moment, the SPM and the original poverty measure are both used to describe the proportion and distribution of families who are poor. In part, the original poverty measure is useful in that data are available since 1960 to the present. The SPM is estimated using specific information that is obtained for each family (by taking into account the receipt of certain federal programs as well as employment status and regional housing costs), or in some cases, imputing many of these parameters. Estimates also have been made by anchoring the SPM threshold to a particular year, making it more comparable to an absolute poverty threshold (Pac et al., 2017). (The original poverty threshold only takes into account income, size, and age of those in a household.) And, importantly for our discussion, the original poverty threshold is used to determine eligibility for the programs and policies discussed in the third section of this chapter.

Another methodological issue in studying low-income and children is establishing that family income (and not factors associated with family income) drives the reported associations between income and child development. Not only does family income status covary with other environmental disadvantages that could negatively affect children's development, but poor parents may differ from more affluent parents in terms of preferences, characteristics, and motivations in ways that simultaneously influence their allocation of resources to children (Mayer, 1997). Chief among those correlated risk factors are family characteristics such as low maternal education, single parenthood, and young parenthood, which relate to children's outcomes as well as family income status (Cooper, McLanahan, Meadows, Brooks-Gunn, & Johnson, 2009; Magnuson, 2007; Waldfogel, Craigie, &

Brooks-Gunn, 2010). Indeed, some researchers have capitalized on this dependence by jointly exploring the links between combinations of demographic risk factors and child outcomes. The premise is that cumulative risks might be a better predictor of outcomes than individual risks, such as maternal education or income alone.[2] While the demographic cumulative risk approach is useful for illustrating that family circumstances are often bundled, our aim is to explore the independent associations between income poverty and young children's outcomes. Therefore, all studies presented in this chapter control for potentially confounding characteristics such as teenage parenthood, low maternal education, and single parenthood when estimating the association between poverty and child outcomes. At the same time, some confounding factors may be unmeasured, which means that what we want to label an "income effect" on children's outcomes may result from other family or environmental factors. Thus, we will also review studies that have attempted to remedy this problem using more sophisticated research designs and analytic techniques such as fixed effects models that compare related children or use repeated observations of the same children over time (to control for unobserved family of child characteristics), or natural experiments whereby changes in families' income resulting from externally derived conditions such as receipt of tax credits are tracked and monitored (e.g., Dahl & Lochner, 2009; Dearing, McCartney, & Taylor, 2006; Duncan, Kalil, & Ziol-Guest, 2017; Votruba-Drzal, 2006). The goal of these studies is to obtain estimates of the potential impact of family income on young children, in part, to answer the question, "If a family received more income or in-kind benefits that reduced income demands (i.e., assistance in purchasing food), would young children's outcomes be positively affected?"

Poverty's Potential Impact on Young Children

Since the 1990s, researchers have had access to a number of large nationally representative longitudinal studies of child development including the National Longitudinal Survey of Youth 1979 (NLSY79-CD), the Panel Study of Income Dynamics Child Development Supplement (PSID-CDS), and the three Early Childhood Longitudinal Studies (Kindergarten Class of 1998–1999, ECLS-K; Kindergarten Class 2010–2011, ECLS-K: 2011; and Birth Cohort, ECLS-B). The PSID has followed all members of the initial cohort recruited 50 years ago (births, marriages, divorces), yielding multiple generations of family members. A series of child development supplements have added information about children's behavior, relationships, cognitive, linguistic, and school functioning. The NLSY79-CD supplement follows children born to women of the NLSY79 cohort (children of men in the NLSY79 survey were not followed), who gave birth at various times after 1979. The ECLS comprises three longitudinal studies that follow cohorts of children over time, gathering data on development and early school experiences.[3] Another birth cohort, the Fragile Families and Child

Well-Being Study, is a multi-stage, nationally representative sample of births in large cities (200,000 or over) at the turn of the century. These families have been seen six times (a seventh wave, when the children are 22, is being initiated).

Each of these studies includes large sample sizes (i.e., at least 3,000), robust assessments of children's developmental outcomes over time, and detailed information on families' economic status and related characteristics including maternal education, maternal IQ, maternal mental health, family structure, and, in some instances, neighborhood residence (Brooks-Gunn, Berlin, & Fuligni, 2000). Research on the links between family income and young children's development, including children's cognitive, linguistic, social, and emotional outcomes, is reviewed below. The aforementioned studies are prioritized, rather than smaller-scale, non-representative studies with limited outcome and economic data, because they offer more generalizable findings.

Cognitive, Linguistic, and Achievement Outcomes

Measures of cognitive development include young children's IQ scores, early math, early literacy, and verbal skills, and, for school-aged children, achievement. Full-scale intelligence tests, numeracy and problem-solving assessments, expressive and receptive language assessments, and tests of learning competence may be employed. Negative associations between poverty and children's cognitive outcomes tend to emerge between 18 and 24 months of age (Klebanov, Brooks-Gunn, McCarton, & McCormick, 1998; Smith, Brooks-Gunn, & Klebanov, 1997). When examining the links between family poverty (defined as a family income of 150% of the poverty threshold or less) and children's IQ scores measured at one, two, and three years in the Infant Health and Development Program, low maternal education was negatively associated with IQ at age one, while income was at age two.

Earlier effects of poverty are being found using more neurodevelopmental measures. Additionally, associations between families' socioeconomic status and both brain structure and function are reported (Brito & Noble, 2014; Kim et al., 2013; Luby et al., 2013; Stevens, Lauinger, & Neville, 2009). Associations are particularly strong in regions of the brain that support language and executive functioning (Noble et al., 2015). Working memory and selective attention have been associated with childhood socioeconomic status (Evans & Schamberg, 2009; Stevens et al., 2009).

The negative associations between poverty and children's cognitive outcomes that emerge during toddlerhood, and perhaps earlier, continue throughout early childhood. For instance, income-related differences in children's IQ and vocabulary scores increased nearly two points from age two to three years (Klebanov et al., 1998). In other studies, variation in IQ, Peabody Picture Vocabulary Test (PPVT, a receptive language measure), and reading recognition scores by income remained stable over time with children living in non-poor families scoring around four points or higher than children living in poor families at ages two, three, and five (Duncan, Brooks-Gunn, & Klebanov, 1994; Smith et al., 1997). Taken together, young children reared in poverty generally scored between 15% and 40% of a standard deviation lower on standardized cognitive assessments compared with their peers living in non-poor families. To interpret the magnitude of these differences, consider that a typical IQ test has a mean of 100 and a standard deviation of 15 points. Young children in poor families score between two and six points lower than those in non-poor families according to these studies.

Research has also addressed unmeasured variables that might be correlated with family income and child outcomes. One estimation technique increases the number of family factors controlled in regressions, such as maternal IQ, and another technique compares siblings within families. Associations between family income and young children's cognitive outcomes are smaller using these techniques (Blau, 1999; Duncan et al., 1998; Yeung, Linver, & Brooks-Gunn, 2002).

Although the average associations with income may be modest, they are far larger for families at the lower end of the income distribution. For example, increases in income between one and three years of age were positively associated with cognitive outcomes measured at three years for children living in poor families only (NICHD-SECCYD; Dearing, McCartney, & Taylor, 2001). Specifically, children living in poverty whose families experienced an increase in income-to-needs of at least one standard deviation above the mean scored on par with their non-poor counterparts on all cognitive outcomes measured. Similar findings using data from the PSID have been reported (Duncan et al., 2010). Specifically, modest increases in income for families earning below $25,000 during the first five years of children's lives led to significant increases in hours worked and earnings in adulthood, associations not found for children in higher income families. Other studies that compared children's outcomes at different poverty levels have found the largest cognitive deficits (in some studies up to 8–12 points) for young children living in deep poverty (i.e., 50% of the poverty threshold, Korenman, Miller, & Sjaastad, 1995; Smith et al., 1997). Taken together, these suggest that the development of children living in poor families may be more sensitive to changes in income than development among children living in non-poor families.

Social and Emotional Outcomes

Young children's social and emotional development is typically measured using parent-report assessments of children's behavior, such as levels of friendliness, cooperation, and engagement as well as instances of temper tantrums, defiance, and aggression; children's responses to staged vignettes; or children's behavior during parent-child interactions. Children living in poor families report more emotional or behavioral problems than children living in non-poor families from early childhood onward (Pagani, Boulerice, & Tremblay, 1997; Yoshikawa, Aber, & Beardslee, 2012). Typically, however,

more modest income associations are found for children's behavior than for cognitive outcomes (Dearing et al., 2001; Duncan et al., 1994). Stronger associations with behavioral outcomes are found when duration of poverty is considered. For example, five-year-olds who lived in persistently poor families exhibited more internalizing and externalizing problems than children who experienced short-term poverty as well as those whose families had never been poor (Duncan et al., 1994).

As with cognitive outcomes, changes in family income have a much larger association with children's behavioral outcomes among children living in poor than in non-poor families. An increase in family income-to-needs is associated with improvements in children's behavior problems and pro-social skills either more strongly or only for children living in poor relative to non-poor families (NICHD-SECCYD; Dearing et al., 2001; Taylor, Dearing, & McCartney, 2004). A $10,000 increase in family income among children living in never-poor families reduced externalizing behaviors by less than 1% of a standard deviation, whereas the same change produced a 15% decrease of a standard deviation in externalizing behaviors among children living in chronically poor families (Dearing et al., 2006). These findings reveal how young children from the poorest families may be at a particular disadvantage upon entering school in terms of their ability to attend in class, regulate their behavior, and form relationships with peers and teachers.

As mentioned previously, unmeasured factors may bias associations between family income and children's cognitive outcomes. Yet, studies using more conservative estimation techniques than controlling for family background variables have found small but significant income associations with children's behavior problems (for example, models comparing siblings and cousins, see Blau, 1999). Costello, Compton, Keeler, and Angold (2003) capitalized on the opening of a casino on a Native American reservation to assess the impact of income on White and Native American children's behavioral problems. (The casino opened in the middle of a longitudinal study of families in the Smokey Mountains.) Native American families who were lifted out of poverty by the casino opening (which granted a share of the profits to all reservation families) experienced a reduction in externalizing symptoms that put them on par with children living in non-poor families; their internalizing symptoms, however, were unaffected by the income change.

Summary

Although the association between income poverty and child outcomes may be small after other factors correlated with poverty are controlled, the preponderance of evidence suggests that differences between poor and non-poor children are present during early childhood and that these differences persist. Moreover, associations between poverty and child development are much larger when poverty is deep (less than 50% of the poverty threshold), long term, and present early in the child's life. This pattern also means, however, that increases in income can enhance the outcomes of children living in poor families much more than children in non-poor families.

Pathways through Which Poverty Impacts Young Children's Development

Pathways through which poverty operates to influence child development are factors related to both income and child outcomes that link the two. Pathways are often divided into those concerned with family stress and those concerned with family investment. The first perspective focuses on associations between poverty and relationships within families. In this view, exemplified by the family stress model (Conger & Elder, 1994; Elder, 1999), financial pressure or deprivation undermines parents' psychological and emotional resources, disrupting parenting styles, parent-child interactions, and child development as a result (Conger & Conger, 2000). The second perspective emphasizes that income allows parents to purchase materials, experiences, and services to foster children's skills and abilities. These goods and services include stimulating learning materials, nutritious food, safe living conditions, and quality child care. According to this investment perspective, children living in poverty have fewer opportunities to build their skills because their parents cannot afford to make the necessary time and money investments (Haveman & Wolfe, 1994; Linver, Brooks-Gunn, & Kohen, 2002). Figure 15.1 illustrates potential pathways related to the family stress and investment perspectives and research on these perspectives is reviewed here. Of course, because they

may operate in tandem, the lines between the two perspectives can blur; however, in the sections below, we aim to distinguish them and are explicit when studies have examined the two in combination.

Recently, several other perspectives have been conceptualized. One perspective differentiates between the experiences of threat and deprivation (McLaughlin, Sheridan, & Lambert, 2014). Threat refers to adverse events that have the potential to cause harm (e.g., child abuse, witnessing violence in the home or neighborhood). Deprivation refers to the absence of environmental inputs (e.g., food insecurity, housing insecurity, child neglect). It is hypothesized that high levels of threat will result in dysregulation of the Hypothalamic-Pituitary-Adrenal (HPA) Axis, the system by which the body's stress response is regulated. Activation of this system can result in the secretion of the stress hormone cortisol. Dysregulation of HPA functioning could result in heightening awareness and reactivity to the environment (often measured by either resting cortisol levels or changes in cortisol in relation to stressful tasks or experiments). Research is just beginning to explore this model. Another perspective considers household instability, or what Evans and colleagues (2005) have called a "context of chaos." Experiences such as multiple moves to different housing, turnover in who is living in a household, domestic violence, and lack of routines are measured. Such experiences result in stress, for both the parent and the child, possibly leading to changes in the child's regulatory systems; additionally, parents in such households may find it difficult to help their children regulate their responses to stressful situations (Lupien, McEwen, Gunnar, & Heim, 2009).

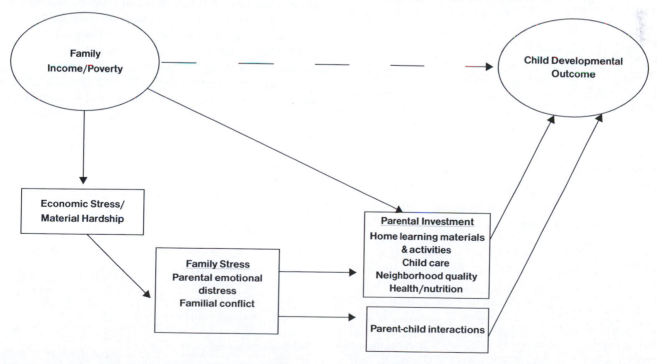

Figure 15.1 Theoretical model depicting pathways through which poverty impacts children's school readiness: the family stress model and the investment perspective.

The Family Stress Perspective

Economic stress includes poverty, unstable work, income loss, and unemployment. These conditions cause financial strain that frequently make it necessary for families to cut back on consumption of goods and services, seek public assistance, live in undesirable and unsafe neighborhoods, or assume additional employment to make ends meet (Edin & Lein, 1997). According to the family stress model, these hardships can lead to emotional distress in parents, such as increased levels of depression and anxiety. Decreases in income have been associated with increases in mothers' depressive symptoms and the probability of clinical depression, with these increases particularly pronounced for mothers at the lowest income levels (Dearing et al., 2006). Emotional instability as a result of economic strain can also trigger familial conflict. For example, parental job loss, particularly when experienced by the father, has been associated with increases in marital conflict and interpersonal violence (Garfinkel, Wimer, & McLanahan, 2016; Kalil & Wightman, 2010).

These psychosocial stressors, in turn, can hinder a parent's ability to be supportive, sensitive, and consistent with children (McLoyd, 1990). Parenting characterized by high levels of warmth, cognitive stimulation, and clear limit setting has been consistently associated with favorable cognitive, emotional, and behavioral outcomes for children (Baumrind, 1966; Belsky, 1999; Brooks-Gunn & Markman, 2005; McLoyd, 1998). By contrast, parenting characterized by harsh, arbitrary discipline, or emotional detachment has been linked to development of negative emotional and cognitive outcomes (Ispa, et al., 2004; Shonkoff & Phillips, 2000). These associations—from financial strain, to parental depression and anxiety, to marital discord and disrupted parenting, and finally to negative child outcomes—represent the crux of the family stress perspective (see Figure 15.1).

The family stress perspective is primarily used to explain how financial loss impacts child behavior (Conger, Rueter, & Conger, 2000). Research on financial loss is distinct from poverty studies in that the former examines how declines in income alter family dynamics, rather than how persistent poverty shapes lives. In his classic work on the Great Depression, Elder (1999) found that parental emotional distress caused by income loss led to marital conflict and punitive parenting, particularly by fathers. However, researchers have extended the family stress model to explain the associations between poverty and child functioning. McLoyd (1990) hypothesizes that like income loss, living in poverty imposes extraordinary burdens on parents, such as struggling to afford basic food and clothing, living in low-quality housing conditions, and residing in unsafe neighborhoods. These burdens and the stress that they cause adversely affect parent mental health and, subsequently, parenting practices. Specifically, maternal emotional distress and depression have been repeatedly associated with harsh discipline, low supportiveness, and parent emotional detachment, as well as higher conflict between parents and children (Petterson &

Albers, 2001). Some studies suggest that the impact of this dynamic is more pronounced among disadvantaged families (Yeung et al., 2002).

In some studies, the family stress perspective has been applied specifically to families with young children (Barajas, Philipsen, & Brooks-Gunn, 2007; Duncan et al., 1994; Gershoff, Aber, Raver, & Lennon, 2007; Linver et al., 2002; Yeung et al., 2002). Family income impacts young children's social and emotional competence (social skills, self-regulation, and internalizing and externalizing behavior), in part, because poverty is linked to elevated levels of material hardship (e.g., food security and housing stability) and levels of parenting stress, which, consequently, decrease parental warmth and cognitive stimulation (Gershoff et al., 2007). Links are weaker for young children's cognitive outcomes (Guo & Harris, 2000; Hanson, McLanahan, & Thomson, 1997; Jackson, Brooks-Gunn, Huang, & Glassman, 2000; Linver, Brooks-Gunn, & Kohen, 1999, 2002; Yeung et al., 2002). This finding suggests distinct pathways through which income impacts children's emotional and cognitive development, with emotional outcomes perhaps responding more strongly to family stress.

It is important to recognize that just as parental emotional distress and punitive parenting can disrupt early behavioral development, responsive parenting can buffer young children against the negative effects of growing up in poverty. Supportive parenting behaviors can significantly reduce the risks associated with growing up in poverty (Apfel & Seitz, 1997; Ispa et al., 2004; McLoyd, 1990; Werner & Smith, 1992). Factors that can help foster emotional health and positive parenting for low-income mothers include various forms of social support. Mothers who have stable emotional support, such as a confidant or some companionship, are less likely than mothers without social ties to report parenting anxiety or to parent in coercive and punitive ways (Crnic & Greenberg, 1987). Similarly, the availability of parenting support including other adults in the household to help with child care and household tasks has been shown to increase mothers' responsiveness and sensitivity to infants (Crockenberg, 1987). It is perhaps for this reason that higher levels of social support among low-income mothers are linked to better behavioral and health outcomes among preschool-aged children (Leininger, Ryan, & Kalil, 2009; Ryan, Kalil, & Leininger, 2009).

The Investment Perspective

While the family stress perspective focuses on the links between economic deprivation and the emotional environments in which children live, the investment perspective emphasizes the links between poverty and the resources available to children. Without sufficient income, parents cannot buy the materials, experiences, and services that facilitate children's positive development (Duncan & Murnane, 2016). Variation in cognitive and, to a lesser extent, behavioral outcomes between children living in poor and non-poor families is linked to this disparity in parental investments. Economists frame these investments in terms of both money (i.e., purchasing of goods and services) and time (i.e., providing stimulating experiences; Becker, 1991). Poor parents have fewer money and time resources to invest in children (see McLanahan, 2004), not only because their earnings are low, but also because their work schedules are less flexible and more often nonstandard (Presser, 2003). Moreover, a disproportionate number of single parents shoulder both breadwinning and caregiving responsibilities, which limits time available for children (Han, Hetzner, & Brooks-Gunn, 2019; Kendig & Bianchi, 2008). In addition to poverty, the material hardship that so often accompanies it may also undermine parental investments. As parents struggling to make ends meet, they may not be able to purchase developmental supports for their children if it means foregoing necessary goods (Gershoff et al., 2007). The following section focuses on a selection of resources, activities, and environments that parents provide to their young children, and links between these investments and children's development.

Home Environment

Many aspects of the home environment are relevant to children's development including the availability of learning materials, parents' stimulation of children's learning, the physical condition of the home (e.g., crowding, cleanliness), and the stability of the home (moves to new residences, moves of individuals in and out of households). The most commonly used measure of the home learning environment is the Home Observation for Measurement of the Environment (HOME) (Caldwell & Bradley, 1984), which includes items assessing the availability of learning materials, such as the number of books, puzzles, and educational toys; items gauging the physical conditions of the home, such as whether the home is cluttered, cramped, dirty, or unsafe; and parents' provision of out-of-home experiences for their children including visits to the library or zoo and extracurricular activities. Numerous studies have demonstrated links between low HOME scores and children's outcomes including developmental delay, growth stunting, poor school performance, and later IQ scores (Bradley & Corwyn, 2002; Garrett, Ng'andu, & Ferron, 1994; Klebanov et al., 1998).

Given that the HOME emphasizes aspects of the home environment that can be bought by parents (although they do not have to be), it should come as no surprise that HOME scores significantly vary according to families' income. A comprehensive descriptive study using the NLSY79-CD data revealed that children living in non-poor families had greater access to stimulating materials in the home and were more likely to go on enriching trips (e.g., to a museum) than their counterparts living in poor families (Bradley, Corwyn, Pipes McAdoo, & Garcia Coll, 2001). Relative to children living in poor families, parents of children living in non-poor families were twice as likely to read to their children several times a week; were more likely to teach their children letters, colors,

shapes, and sizes; and had homes that were safer, cleaner, and less cluttered. The impact of family income on parents' ability to provide stimulating home environments was much stronger for parents at the low end of income distribution than further up (Dearing & Taylor, 2007).

The quality of the home environment accounts for a sizable proportion of the link between income and young children's outcomes, especially in the cognitive domain (Duncan et al., 1994; Gershoff et al., 2007; Linver et al., 2002; Yeung et al., 2002). HOME scores mediated the unfavorable associations between shifts in family income over the first three years of children's lives and their school readiness, language development, and prosocial behavior (NICHD-SECCYD; Dearing et al., 2001). Overall, HOME scores have been found to attenuate the associations between income and children's cognitive outcomes by up to one-half (Bradley, 1995; Brooks-Gunn & Markman, 2005; Duncan et al., 1994; Korenman et al., 1995). Children's early home learning environments may have long-lasting influences on their development. Poor families' early involvement in their kindergarten children's education (i.e., reading to children, attending school meetings, communication with schools) was positively linked to children's later literacy performance in elementary school, particularly for children whose mothers had low educational attainment, suggesting that reading to children and related activities can override the potentially deleterious combination of low-income and low maternal education on children's development (Dearing, McCartney, Weiss, Kreider, & Simpkins, 2004).

Links between home environment quality and children's behavioral outcomes are found, although they are often less strong than those for cognitive outcomes (Dearing et al., 2001; Linver et al., 2002; Yeung et al., 2002). These associations may represent a joining of the family stress and investment models. That is, parents who experience high levels of depression and anxiety may be less likely than a parent with stable emotional health not only to interact positively with their children, but also to provide stimulating experiences. Figure 15.1 depicts this combination, as family stress not only predicts parenting behavior but also predicts parental investments. Supporting this model, HOME scores were associated with children's behavior problem scores via their influence on maternal emotional distress as well as parenting practices (PSID; Yeung et al., 2002). In this way, the family stress and investment models may operate in tandem, with family stress impacting parents' ability and motivation to invest material and time resources in children's development.

Neighborhoods

Although poor parents face a limited set of choices about where to raise their children, the neighborhoods they live in represent another investment that parents make in their children's development. It is in neighborhoods that young children receive child care, visit medical centers, attend school, and develop social relationships. The 1990s saw an explosion in research focusing on links between neighborhood characteristics including income or socioeconomic status (SES; i.e., percent poor, on public assistance, unemployed, professionals, college-educated, and female-headed households in a given geographic area) and children's outcomes, controlling for family-level income and other characteristics. For example, positive associations between neighborhood affluence and preschool-aged children's IQ and vocabulary scores have been reported in numerous data sets (Brooks-Gunn, Duncan, Klebanov, & Sealand, 1993; Chase-Lansdale, Gordon, Brooks-Gunn, & Klebanov, 1997; Kohen, Brooks-Gunn, Leventhal, & Hertzman, 2002). By the age of five years, children's IQ scores increased by 2.2 points for each year that they resided in an affluent neighborhood (Leventhal & Brooks-Gunn, 2001). Neighborhood characteristics, such as low average SES, high male unemployment, and low percentage of managerial or professional workers, have also been unfavorably linked to young children's behavior (Brooks-Gunn et al., 1993; Chase-Lansdale et al., 1997; Duncan et al., 1994). It is perhaps for these reasons that, more recently, Chetty, Hendren, and Katz (2016) found that children under age 13 whose families were randomly assigned to move from high-poverty to low-poverty neighborhoods had substantially higher rates of college attendance and higher earnings in adulthood than their peers who remained in high-poverty neighborhoods.

Specific neighborhood processes such as social cohesion, disorder, and safety seem to underlie links between neighborhood characteristics and children's outcomes. Studies have found inverse associations between neighborhood cohesion and children's behavior problems (Curtis, Dooley, & Phipps, 2004; Xue, Leventhal, Brooks-Gunn, & Earls, 2005), verbal ability (Kohen et al., 2002), and problem-solving skills (Caughy & O'Campo, 2006), and these links may be particularly strong among children living in very disadvantaged neighborhoods (Caughy, Nettles, & O'Campo, 2008). Neighborhood disorder is also associated with young children's cognitive outcomes (Kohen et al., 2002) and their internalizing problems (Caughy, Nettles, & O'Campo, 2008). Neighborhood influences on parents' well-being represent another pathway by which neighborhoods may indirectly influence children's development. For example, one study reported that neighborhood disadvantage was linked to low levels of neighborhood cohesion, which was in turn linked to poor family functioning and maternal depression, which in turn was linked to fewer literacy activities and more parental harshness. These parenting behaviors, in turn, were linked to children's verbal ability and problem behavior at age five (Kohen, Leventhal, Dahinten, & McIntosh, 2008).

Child Care

Along with aspects of the home environment and neighborhood, parents make investments in their children by placing them in nonmaternal child care and preschool programs. Although home environment and parenting quality are more

powerful predictors of children's outcomes than are child care characteristics, most research suggests that experiences in child care do independently influence cognitive and emotional development. The size and direction of these associations are dependent on age of entry into care, time spent in child care, child care quality, and family income level.

Links between child care and behaviors such as aggression and noncompliance have been reported for children, primarily those who enter care in the first year of life and remain in full-time child care throughout early childhood (Baydar & Brooks-Gunn, 1991; NICHD-ECCYN & Duncan, 2003). These links are found after controlling for other child care characteristics including quality, as well as family background and maternal sensitivity (NICHD-ECCYN & Duncan, 2003). The link between quantity and externalizing behaviors was seen in sixth grade (Belsky et al., 2007) and in high school (risk-taking and impulsive behaviors, Vandell et al., 2010).

Similar results were found looking at mothers' return to work in the first months of life (Brooks-Gunn, Han, & Waldfogel, 2010). Full-time maternal employment before children reached nine months was associated with poorer child cognitive outcomes by age three for white children (Brooks-Gunn, Han, & Waldfogel, 2002), which remained at 4.5 years and first grade; however, these negative associations were attenuated by use of center-based child care and maternal sensitivity by age 4.5 years (Brooks-Gunn et al., 2010). Hours in center-based child care may be differently associated with behavioral and cognitive outcomes, leading to less optimal behavioral outcomes but better cognitive ones by school entry. The whole of these findings suggest that the links between early child care and children's outcomes are not simple, may vary by developmental domain, and need to take into account a range of factors that influence children's development (Han et al., 2019).

Child care quality is a key factor that affects associations between early child care and children's outcomes. In high-quality child care environments, children have access to a range of materials that stimulate emergent literacy, language development, logical reasoning, and social skills, and have caregivers who engage them in cognitively stimulating activities, initiate and respond to their verbalizations, and have frequent positive interactions with them that include smiling, touching, and holding, among many other socially and cognitively enhancing behaviors. Utilization of high-quality (vs. low-quality) care predicts more favorable cognitive outcomes for children during their early years that continue well into the school age years (Belsky et al., 2007; Burchinal et al., 2000; Love et al., 2003; NICHD-SECCYN, 2002). Positive but modest associations between early child care quality and children's achievement in high school have also been reported (Vandell et al., 2010).[4] Modest associations between child care quality and child outcomes might be due to the fact that the effect of child care quality is nonlinear: that is, quality may be more strongly associated when it reaches a certain threshold of caregiver–child stimulation and sensitivity than it does throughout the quality continuum (Burchinal, Vandergrift, Pianta, & Mashburn, 2009). Thus, quality may need to be quite high—or improve by a substantial margin—to meaningfully enhance children's cognitive and behavioral outcomes.

Studies have also examined links between child care and outcomes specifically for low-income children, yielding mixed results, with some reporting favorable associations between provider responsiveness and warmth and children's early literacy skills and social behavior (Loeb, Fuller, Kagan, & Carroll, 2004) and others finding small associations between child care quality and young children's behavior and no direct links to children's achievement (Votruba-Drzal, Coley, & Chase-Lansdale, 2004). However, studies that compared the correlation between child care quality and higher versus lower income status tend to find that quality matters more for those with less (McCartney, Dearing, Taylor, & Bub, 2007; Pianta, Barnett, Burchinal, & Thornburg, 2009). Child care quality assessed through the preschool years may moderate the association between family income-to-needs and children's achievement during middle childhood, in part, because early child care quality boosted the school readiness of preschoolers living in poor families (Dearing, McCartney, & Taylor, 2009).

Yet, while high-quality child care may serve as a protective factor for children living in poor families, low-quality child care may compound other risks. Studies not specifically addressing children living in poor families found that low-quality care, particularly if initiated within the first year, is unfavorably associated with a range of developmental outcomes (NICHD-SECCYD, 1997, 1998). The combination of poor-quality child care and under-stimulating home environments was linked to greater externalizing behaviors in a sample of low-income children (Votruba-Drzal et al., 2004), such that low-quality child care may serve to further undermine the development of children living in poor families. Access to high-quality child care is particularly limited in low-income communities (Loeb et al., 2004), suggesting many children in low-income and poor families may be at risk of this double jeopardy.

Child Health and Nutrition

Another type of parental investment important for children's well-being is the provision of medical care (including prenatal care), nutrition, and screening for disabilities. Research has long documented an SES-health gradient, in which the most affluent members of society have significantly better health outcomes than the less affluent, particularly people who are living in poverty (Adler et al., 1994; Deaton, 2002). Research has also found that, while stronger in adulthood, this gradient has its origins in childhood, particularly in terms of the onset and development of chronic conditions such as asthma, and is not explained by maternal education or availability of health insurance (Case, Lubotsky, & Paxson, 2002). Health problems and nutritional deficits are also more likely among

children living in poor than non-poor families, which may be a pathway through which poverty affects children's cognitive and school-related outcomes.

Disparities in child health outcomes by poverty status begin very early in life. Children living in poor families are more likely to be born with low birth weight than other children (Collins, Wambach, David, & Rankin, 2009), which is strongly related to a number of later difficulties including poorer development in math, motor, and spatial skills, language, and memory, as well as increased likelihood of grade repetition and special education placements relative to normal birth-weight infants (Klebanov, Brooks-Gunn, & McCormick, 1994; McCormick, Brooks-Gunn, Workman-Daniels, Turner, & Peckham, 1992). Studies that have examined long-term outcomes of low birth-weight children have found that they are still at risk for adverse outcomes as adolescents and possibly into adulthood (Conley & Bennett, 2000).

Nutrition and food insecurity, which focuses on families' limited or uncertain ability to acquire nutritionally adequate and safe foods due to monetary constraints, are also important. Several studies have demonstrated that poverty and its correlates are predictors of food insecurity (Hernandez & Jacknowitz, 2009; Skalicky et al., 2006); immigrant status also seems to be important, with the risk of food insecurity particularly high in households headed by foreign-born mothers (Chilton et al., 2009; Kalil & Chen, 2008).

Links between food insecurity and young children's health are commonly reported (Chilton et al., 2009; Rose-Jacobs et al., 2008; Skalicky et al., 2006); however, associations between food insecurity and young children's cognitive and emotional development are less frequently studied. A nutritionally adequate diet is essential to key skills associated with school readiness (Carlson, Rosenbaum, Keith-Jennings, & Nchako, 2016). Food insecurity experienced at school entry may have some longer lasting influences on children's mathematics and social outcomes in elementary school (Cook & Frank, 2008).

Finally, young children's well-being is influenced by residence in low-quality housing, which tends to elevate children's potential exposure to environmental toxins. Specifically, children living in poor families are more likely to be exposed to lead paint within the home compared to non-poor children (Brody et al., 1994). Exposure to lead, even at relatively low levels, is associated with childhood problems in cognition, attention, aggression, impulse control, as well as growth and other physical impairments (Bellinger, 2004; Needleman, 1979). Childhood lead exposure can lead to adverse outcomes that persist well into adulthood: one study found that early exposure was linked to decreased gray matter in certain areas of the adult brain affiliated with attention, executive functions, and decision making (Cecil et al., 2008). In addition to risk of lead poisoning, poor children have greater exposure to toxic environmental conditions resulting from residential proximity to waste incinerators or air pollution (Currie & Almond, 2011; Evans, 2001).

Summary

To understand the association between poverty and children's cognitive and emotional outcomes, the pathways through which poverty affects child development must be considered. Two broad perspectives characterize this literature, the family stress model and the investment model. Because the family stress model hinges on parenting and parent–child relationships, it is more closely related to child emotional and behavioral outcomes, although cognitive development is inextricably linked to these processes as well. The investment model implicates the monetary limitations poor parents face in raising their children. Regardless of parenting quality, children living in poor families are most likely to lack the materials, services, and resources at home, child care, and in their neighborhoods that children living in non-poor families enjoy. Although the quality of these environments relates more strongly to children's cognitive outcomes, children's emotional and physical health outcomes have also been linked to these investments. In the next section, we address how public policies can improve the quality of children's environments and alleviate family stress.

Federally Funded Programs for Poor Families

Federal and state governments employ a range of social policy initiatives to alleviate poverty that have the potential to improve family functioning, relieve material hardship, and enhance children's development. Federal policies are presented here (keep in mind that states manage many policies and have latitude in their implementation). Overall, these antipoverty policies can be grouped into three overall types of programs (Currie, 2006): cash assistance with work requirements, such as welfare and tax credits; in-kind benefit programs, such as child care subsidies, food assistance, and housing; and early childhood education programs. Cash assistance increases families' economic resources and self-sufficiency, in doing so, can influence the pathways through which poverty impacts children, yet facilitating child development is not necessarily a stated goal of these programs. In-kind programs offer subsidies for housing, food, and child care. Presumably, these programs, while not providing cash, offset the costs of basic necessities (child care for working mothers is arguably a necessity, as the United States has no universal child care system in place). By contrast, the third program type aims explicitly to alleviate poverty's impacts on children through child- and parent-focused educational services. The following section describes eight federally funded programs that target poor and sometimes near-poor families with young children.

Earned Income Tax Credit (EITC) and Child Tax Credit (CTC)

Enacted in 1975, the EITC is the country's largest cash antipoverty program. The EITC grants tax credits to low-income families based on their household composition and earnings.

The program has expanded greatly since its beginnings. At its inception in 1975, the EITC represented a relatively modest (10%) earning subsidy for low-income families. Over 40 years later, the amount of the credit has increased fourfold for families with at least one child (Bastian & Michelmore, 2018). The maximum credit amount has also drastically increased since EITC's start. The mid-1990s proved to be a period of rapid expansion of EITC, with the maximum refundable credit increasing for all, but the most dramatic increase seen in families with two or more children (Hoynes & Patel, 2015). Eighty percent of filers eligible for the credit claim it, translating to 28 million people receiving the EITC credit in 2012, a dramatic increase from the 12.5 million people who filed for the credit in 1990 (Hoynes, 2014).

EITC's structure incentivizes work by increasing the tax credit as a worker's income rises, at a rate determined by family composition and tax filing status. While the credit advantages low-income households with children the most, low-income households without children are also eligible for the credit, though the maximum credit that can be received is comparatively low. The credit is calculated as a percentage of a worker's earnings until the credit reaches its maximum allowance, at which point the credit begins to gradually phase out (Figure 15.2).

Figure 15.2 highlights the way in which the tax credit is calculated for single households with no children, a family with one child, a family with two children, and a family with three or more children. For example, in 2018, a taxpayer with three or more children and a household income between $14,290 and $18,660 could earn the maximum credit during that year ($6,431). If the household had earnings above $18,660, the amount of that household's credit begins to decrease, until eventually phasing out completely once that family hits annual earnings of $49,194 or more. The credit is refundable, so if a filer's tax liability is smaller than the amount of the credit, the difference is refunded to the household.

The EITC is heralded as one of the most effective antipoverty initiatives of the present day—an initiative that both supplements the income of working families and incentivizes work. Indeed, in 2016 it was estimated that the tax credit lifted approximately 5.8 million people out of poverty, three million of whom were children (Center on Budget and Policy Priorities, 2018). The credit effectively raises wages for low-income workers, with the most substantial credits received by working parents with dependent children. According to some estimates, the EITC increases family income by over 20% for those living in poverty (Dahl & Lochner, 2009; Kim, 2001). In 2012, eligible families with children received an average credit of $2,970 per household (Hoynes & Patel, 2015). This increase in income, in turn, may enhance child outcomes, particularly in the cognitive domain. Dahl and Lochner (2009) estimated that a $1,000 increase in family income derived from the EITC produced a 6% increase in children's math and reading test scores, with poor and minority families receiving the most benefit. However, as with welfare-based earning supplements, these improvements seem to fade out over time.

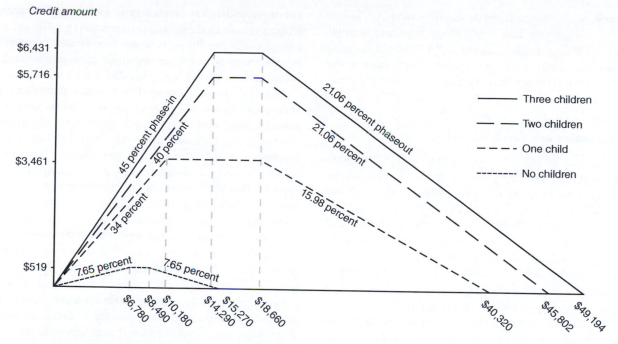

Figure 15.2 Earned income tax credit 2018.

Source: Urban-Brookings Tax Policy Center (2018). Internal Revenue Service.

Notes: Assumes all income comes from earnings. Amounts are of taxpayers filing a single or head-of-household tax return. For married couples filing a joint tax return, the credit begins to phase out at income $5,690 higher than shown.

Timing of a child's exposure to cash transfer programs such as EITC has been of interest to researchers and policymakers alike in recent years. Yet, the evidence is equivocal on the benefits of EITC receipt during children's early years and their outcomes. For example, Bastian and Michelmore's (2018) analysis of the EITC's long-term reach examined associations between EITC receipt and educational outcomes. They found no significant relation between exposure to EITC prior to age 13 and educational attainment. Further research on timing and receipt of cash transfers is needed to inform current policy discourse.

The CTC is refundable tax credit that is designated for those who file with a dependent under the age of 17. Unlike EITC, it is not inflation-adjusted and as a result, the maximum credit amount ($1,000) has remained the same since 2003 (Maag & Isaacs, 2017). To supplement the existing CTC, policymakers and researchers have discussed the potential benefits of a Young CTC. Such a policy proposal would provide families with children under the age of five an additional, refundable tax credit in addition to the CTC already in place. Such an income supplement would support families during a crucial period in a child's development.

Supplemental Nutrition Assistance Program (SNAP)

The SNAP is a mean-tested federal program that provides nutritional assistance to millions of low-income individuals. The program originated in 1961 as a pilot and became a permanent federal program in 1975. Recent figures place expenditures for the program at approximately $31 billion annually. In 2017, SNAP helped approximately 40 million Americans; nearly 70% of those participants were families with children (Carlson et al., 2016). Households receive an average monthly benefit of $255 (Hoynes & Schanzenbach, 2018); however, the benefit amount is largely dependent upon family composition.

Participation in SNAP is high, with nearly 85% of individuals eligible for the program receiving benefits (U.S. Department of Agriculture, 2018). SNAP is an entitlement program with funding to support all eligible households with incomes below 130% of the federal poverty line. Time limits for SNAP receipt and work requirements are also considered when determining eligibility, although families with children under 18 are not subject to restrictions regarding length of SNAP use (U.S. Department of Agriculture, 2016). While SNAP is federally funded, each state manages its own application process and is allowed some autonomy in determining additional eligibility requirements. States are allowed to add additional work or job training requirements and, in some states, consider previous criminal convictions in determination of eligibility.

SNAP has proven to be an essential program in the lives of many low-income children and families. In 2015, the program is estimated to have reduced the number of children living in poverty by 3.8 million (Hoynes & Schanzenbach, 2018; Wheaton & Tran, 2018). Research on other program effects on children is limited; however, SNAP has been associated with lowered incidence of low birth weight births for low-income Black and White families (Almond, Hoynes, & Schanzenbach, 2011). SNAP receipt in early childhood may confer health advantages in both adolescence and adulthood (Hoynes & Schanzenbach, 2018; Hoynes, Schanzenbach, & Almond, 2016).

Women, Infants, and Children (WIC)

Following a period of increased focus on domestic malnutrition and hunger in the 1960s and 1970s, the Special Supplemental Nutrition Program for WIC was developed (Oliveira et al., 2002). The program originated as a two-year pilot program in 1972, modeled after a food voucher program which served the Baltimore area, run by Johns Hopkins University. During the pilot phase, WIC provided services to children up to age four and breastfeeding mothers. In 1975, WIC became a permanent federal program, expanding both coverage and the types of services provided to participants.

Today, WIC has three primary functions: nutritional assistance, educational support for mothers, and resource referral (Oliveira et al., 2002). Participants receive nutritional assistance through vouchers or checks that can be redeemed for a prespecified set of items that fall under their nutritional package category. In contrast to other nutritional assistance efforts, WIC has detailed guidelines concerning both the type and quantity of foods that can be purchased by participants. Food items in nutritional packages are determined by the category, age, and breastfeeding status of the participant, and participants are limited to only purchases of WIC-approved items at retail locations. Education services including nutritional counseling and breastfeeding support are provided to mothers at local WIC agencies following the birth of their children. Lastly, local WIC agencies provide resources and referrals services, and often offer basic on-site health services and screenings.

In 2014, federal expenditures for WIC were just over $6 billion. Each state receives an allocation of federal funding for the program and, though not required, many states opt to supplement their federal allocation with state funds. While WIC is not an entitlement program, most families that meet categorical (i.e., pregnant, postpartum, or breastfeeding mothers; infants under age one; children under age five), residential, income, and nutritional status eligibility requirements are able to enroll in the program without the need for lengthy waitlists. Compared to other means-tested food and nutrition programs, WIC has a higher income cut-off allowing the program to cover both poor and near-poor families: participants' household incomes must be below 185% of the federal poverty line (Hoynes & Schanzenbach, 2015).

In 2014, WIC served approximately eight million people, approximately half of all individuals who were eligible for the program that year (U.S. Department of Agriculture, 2017). Eighty percent of all infants eligible for the program are covered; however, this number drops to approximately 68% after infancy and continues to fall until children age

out of eligibility. Approximately half of all eligible pregnant women are covered. Significant variation in coverage levels exists by state, and by participant category with mothers with infants enrolling at higher rates than pregnant mothers and older children who are also eligible for the program.

The association between WIC and child outcomes has been studied for decades. Several studies have found associations between WIC participation and improved birth outcomes (Currie, 2008; Devaney, Ellwood, & Love, 1997). Lower incidences of preterm birth, low birth weight, and very low birth weight are all associated with WIC participation status. Additionally, WIC receipt is associated with having at least four well-child visits during infancy (Chatterji & Brooks-Gunn, 2004). A growing number of studies have linked WIC receipt with a range of health outcomes including lower rates of anemia, failure to thrive, and childhood obesity (Currie & Bitler, 2004; Kowalski-Jones & Duncan, 2002; Lee & Mackey-Bilaver, 2007). While decades of research has provided evidence for an association between WIC participation and short-term positive outcomes for infants and mothers, more recent research has explored associations between WIC participation and outcome for older children. WIC participation was associated with fewer diagnoses of ADHD and lower likelihood of grade repetition for older children, suggesting that the benefits of WIC may extend beyond just the period of program eligibility (Chorniy, Currie, & Sonchak, 2018).

Temporary Assistance for Needy Families (TANF)

The cash assistance program TANF replaced the entitlement program Aid to Families with Dependent Children with time-limited, work-based assistance as of 1996 (Moffitt, 2003). The reach of this non-entitlement program is limited, only providing assistance for 23% of families with children below the poverty line in 2017 (Floyd, Burnside, & Schott, 2018). This percentage has been on a steady decline since TANF was first created.

Several pre-TANF welfare-to-work experiments illuminate the likely impacts of various TANF provisions including work mandates, income supplements, noncompliance sanctions, and time limits on family income as well as children's outcomes. Collectively, these studies suggest not only that work-oriented policies increase family income and decrease poverty rates (Schoeni & Blank, 2003), but that only programs that supplement parents' earnings with cash actually increase family income net of the decreases in welfare payments (Morris, Gennetian, & Duncan, 2005). Perhaps for this reason, a study of 13 welfare-to-work programs found that those providing earnings supplements increased children's cognitive test scores and achievement outcomes by approximately 7% of a standard deviation (Morris, Duncan, & Clark-Kaufman, 2005), whereas programs offering only work supports had no consistent correlation. However, even the most comprehensive of these earning supplement programs produced only short-term impacts on young children's academic skills and test scores, with gains disappearing after the program ended (Huston et al., 2005).

These results suggest that programs work best if they raise family income rather than encourage parental employment alone. This finding should come as no surprise when one considers the direct associations between poverty and child development, as well as the benefits associated with even small upward shifts in income, particularly for children living in deep and entrenched poverty. These increases in income must be substantial enough to lift families out of poverty if the objective is to improve children's developmental outcomes. This parallels the literature suggesting income changes must be substantial and permanent to meaningfully alter children's developmental trajectories (Blau, 1999).

Public Housing and Housing Choice Vouchers

With housing costs outpacing the growth of wages for low-income workers, many families find it difficult to afford housing. The two primary types of housing assistance currently available to low-income families are public housing and the Housing Choice Voucher Program (commonly referred to as Section 8). Both programs are funded through the US Department of Housing and Urban Development (HUD). Subsidized housing is not an entitlement: of the low-income households that were income-eligible for housing assistance, only one in four received some form of housing assistance, leaving millions of eligible renters vulnerable to an increasingly unaffordable housing market.

Public housing as we know it today has roots in the New Deal era, a time in which the federal government began constructing subsidized housing for poor families (Turner & Kingsley, 2008). Geographic variation exists for income eligibility for public housing and local median income is considered in those calculations; however, the federal government provides general guidelines for income eligibility. Rent is determined by a household's annual gross income as well as household composition, with deductions from the total tenant payment afforded to families with dependent children (U.S. Department of Housing and Urban Development, 2019). Approximately 1.2 million public housing units exist in the United States, managed by over 3,000 local housing authorities. Households with children represent 40% of residents of public housing residents (Kingsley, 2017).

The Section 8 Housing Choice Voucher program was first authorized by Congress in 1974. Currently, it is the largest federal assistance program providing direct support to tenants, representing over two million housing units. Eligible families receive a voucher that they can use in the private market, allowing families some degree of choice in where to live. The amount of the voucher varies by family composition and size. Families are advised on the size of the unit they are approved for by their local housing authority and are expected to contribute 30% of their adjusted gross income to rent and utilities of the unit. Additionally, if the unit that a family selects has rent that is higher than the amount of the voucher the family receives (i.e., the payment standard), the family must pay the difference (U.S. Department of Housing and Urban Development, 2019). While Section 8 Housing Choice Vouchers are intended to give families some autonomy in selecting a rental unit, choices are constrained. Significant geographic variation in landlord acceptance rates of vouchers exists (U.S. Department of Housing and Urban Development, 2018a). Landlords in high-rent neighborhoods, which are often areas with access to better schools and jobs, were found to deny vouchers at a higher rate than landlords in relatively low-rent neighborhoods. Challenges in finding housing that accepts vouchers, in addition to the requirement that families pay rent above the payment standard, often limits choice for low-income families.

Public housing is widely underfunded, forcing many local housing authorities to forego necessary updates and repairs to existing units. As a response to a public housing stock in need of repair and improvement, HUD developed Rental Assistance Demonstration (RAD) in 2012. The program allows local housing authorities to leverage private resources as a means to update public housing in need of critical repairs. While housing assistance traditionally seeks to improve affordability for housing, this housing demonstration centers on improving quality in parallel. Housing that undergoes a RAD conversion transitions from traditional public housing to a Section 8 Housing Choice Voucher platform, with mechanisms in place to ensure that families do not lose housing eligibility during the conversion. As of 2018, over 100,000 housing units have undergone RAD conversion (U.S. Department of Housing and Urban Development, 2018b).

Previous research has examined associations between child outcomes and receipt of housing assistance, most often comparing outcomes of children whose families received some form of assistance to those whose families did not. Notably, children in families receiving housing assistance were found to be less likely to be underweight than children in families who did not (Aratani, Lazzeroni, Brooks-Gunn, & Hernandez, 2018; Meyers et al., 2005). Long-term outcomes of housing assistance receipt have also been studied. Newman and Harkness (2002) found that living in public housing during childhood is associated with increased employment rates and reduced welfare receipt later in life. Additionally, another study found that living in public housing was positively associated with housing quality and academic achievement of children (Currie & Yelowitz, 2000). Given that some research on housing and neighborhoods has suggested that benefits conferred by housing assistance are age-dependent (Chetty et al., 2016), it is important to note that the aforementioned studies examined outcomes of children who were residents of public housing after age six. While some studies have found nil effects of public housing across a variety of cognitive domains (ABT Associates, 2006), more nuanced analyses have found differential impacts of housing on child outcomes. A study primarily using longitudinal data from the Panel Study of Income Dynamics (PSID) found that children with fewer behavioral problems and better cognitive performance benefit the most from household use of housing assistance (Newman & Holupka, 2017).

The constrained nature of choice in using Section 8 vouchers and the placement of public housing units means that most low-income families typically live in high-poverty neighborhoods. A demonstration was designed in the 1990s to help poor families in public housing move via the Section 8 voucher. Families were randomly assigned to one of three groups: one group that remained in public housing, one group that received Section 8 vouchers to be used in any geographic area, and one group that received special vouchers which had to be used in low-poverty neighborhoods. The goal was to see if outcomes would be improved by families moving out of public housing, and if so, if outcomes would be further improved by moving into low-poverty neighborhoods via the special voucher. Several findings are noteworthy. First, many families in the special voucher group did not use their vouchers as they were unable to find rental units in low-poverty neighborhoods. Second, families who did manage to move to low-poverty neighborhoods frequently returned to higher poverty neighborhoods. Third, given the low take-up and high returns to high-poverty neighborhoods, few short-term effects were found. Fewer depressive symptoms reported by parents and children who moved to low-poverty neighborhoods were the most notable short-term effects observed (Leventhal & Brooks-Gunn, 2003). Fourth, while no short- or medium-term school outcomes were seen, there is evidence for longer-term outcomes. Recent analyses have shown higher college attendance and earnings were observed for children whose families received the special voucher and moved prior to the child's age of 13, suggesting that young children may benefit the most from programs that incentivize transitions from high-poverty to lower-poverty neighborhoods (Chetty et al., 2016).

Child Care Subsidies

The Child Care and Development Fund (CCDF) assists low-income families in providing care for their children, allowing mothers to work while also easing the financial burden of child care costs. It is a federally funded, but state-administered program that is authorized through the Child Care and Development Block Grant. State-level administration of CCDF allows states to tailor the program to meet their population's specific child care needs and goals. States are permitted to use CCDF funds for child care subsidies and also for activities that promote quality and availability of child care in their state (U.S. Government Accountability Office, 2016).

In 2015, the federal government spent 8.5 billion dollars on CCDF (Hill, Gennetian, & Mendez, 2019). CCDF is funded through a variety of funding streams, including federal discretionary funding as well as mandatory and state matching funds (Johnson, Martin, & Brooks-Gunn, 2011). Disbursement of the subsidies comes in the form of vouchers given to parents, which can be used at most child care providers, or as subsidized slots in some child care settings (Johnson, Ryan, & Brooks-Gunn, 2012). These subsidies can be used for a variety of care options, including licensed child care facilities, family child care homes, and informal care settings with family or friends, allowing families' autonomy in deciding which care arrangement is best for their children.

Each month, the CCDF funds child care for 1.4 million children under the age of 13 (Administration for Children and Families, 2019). Eligibility for the program is contingent on a range of factors, including mother's participation in work or workforce training activities, age of child (i.e., infancy to age 13), and a household income of less than 85% of the state median income. Broad eligibility criteria for the subsidies are set by the federal government; however, states can tailor their application process to some degree. States can set their own requirements on number of hours parents must work and also modify the income eligibility threshold (Enchautegui, Chien, Burgess, & Ghertner, 2016). While 14.2 million children meet federal eligibility criteria for CCDF, additional state-level eligibility criteria lowers the eligibility figure to 8.2 million children (Hill et al., 2018). Since CCDF subsidies are not an entitlement, many states identify priority groups that receive funding before others that are eligible, yet do not fall into one of the identified categories. Many states include TANF recipients, children with special needs, homeless families, and children in foster care as priority groups for the subsidy (Tran, Minton, Haldar, & Giannarelli, 2016).

While, in concept, the program is designed to support low-income mothers in their efforts to work and achieve financial stability, issues arise with regard to implementation. Most states require subsidy receipt to be redetermined every 12 months; however, seven states and federal territories require families to undergo the process every six months (Tran et al., 2016). Stringent recertification requirements can lead to lapses in subsidy coverage for some families, posing a risk to the continuity of care for the child.

Child care subsidies may be crucial to low-income families' economic well-being and low-income mothers' ability to work. Theoretically, subsides could indirectly improve child outcomes by promoting maternal employment and elevating family income, or by enabling families to purchase higher quality child care than they could otherwise afford. Using data from the 1999 National Survey of American Families, Blau and Tekin (2007) found that child care subsidies did increase employment among single mothers by as much as 33 percentage points. However, the few studies that have examined the association between subsidies and children's child care quality have found that subsidy users choose lower quality child care environments than those provided by Head Start or public school-based preschools, but higher quality care than those in unsubsidized care (Ryan, Johnson, Rigby, & Brooks-Gunn, 2011). These mixed results might explain why studies that examine subsidies and child outcomes are either neutral or negative (Datta Gupta & Simonsen, 2010; Herbst & Tekin, 2009; Johnson, Martin, & Brooks-Gunn, 2013). Additionally, studies that attempt to compare outcomes between families who receive child care subsidies and families who were eligible, but did not receive a subsidy often encounter issues around selection given the issues surrounding program uptake. Child care subsidy recipients tend to be more advantaged than non-recipients (Johnson et al., 2011).

Head Start

Head Start was first conceptualized in the fall of 1964 as a War on Poverty-era educational program designed to prepare young, poor children for school. Head Start officially began in 1965 and was designed as an eight-week summer program for four-year-olds, focusing on children's physical and mental health, nutrition, social and emotional development, services for children's families, and community and parental involvement. The Head Start model reflected a "whole child approach" that located children's health and development in a variety of child, family, and community contexts. The program was expanded in August 1965 to a school-year program and eligibility was expanded to children between the ages of three and five whose household incomes fall at or below the federal poverty line. The Department of Health and Human Services currently runs Head Start, serving 720,000 three- and four-year-olds, about 8% of all preschoolers in the country and just under 40% of all eligible children (Friedman-Krauss et al., 2018). The program is federally funded; however, control over program administration is delegated to local agencies.

Head Start recognizes the importance of early identification of childhood impairments or disabilities as a threshold step toward the delivery of effective intervention services and resource referrals. Children enrolled in Head Start were found to have greater access to hearing and vision diagnostic services compared to their counterparts not enrolled in Head Start (Puma, Bell, Cook, & Heid, 2010). Additionally, to meet the needs of all children, Head Start programs were mandated to set aside at least 10% of their enrollment for preschool children with special needs in 1972.

After initial screening, Head Start's referral services support continuity of care for children. Children who are identified as requiring additional services are typically referred by Head Start to other social service providers to ensure that appropriate support is provided. Head Start brokers partnerships with community organizations and providers to ensure seamless provision of services to families with children who require additional support. Additionally, Head Start often links these families to other public programs that also serve low-income families, such as Medicaid and State Children's Health Insurance Programs (S-CHIP).

One of the earliest studies of Head Start's association with outcomes for poor children was the Educational Testing Service Head Start Longitudinal Study. Researchers extensively canvassed largely low-income neighborhoods to recruit families with three-year-olds and assessed the children's emotional, cognitive, and language skills prior to age eligibility for Head Start. Follow-up took place a year later and children were then categorized, based on family choice rather than experimental means, into one of three groups: children enrolled in Head Start, children enrolled in non-Head Start preschool programs, and children not enrolled in any formal preschool program. Significant baseline demographic, cognitive, and linguistic differences were found across the three groups, with children enrolled in Head Start being most disadvantaged across all measures—evidence that Head Start serves the poorest of the poor in their communities. The study also found that participation in Head Start was related to the greatest gains on developmental assessments (Lee, Brooks-Gunn, & Schnur, 1988; Lee, Brooks-Gunn, Schnur, & Liaw, 1990).

In the program's earliest days, efforts were made to encourage the poorest communities of the country to develop Head Start programs. The Office of Economic Opportunity (OEO), which at the time ran the Head Start program, offered technical grant-writing assistance to the nation's poorest counties as they developed Head Start grant proposals. OEO sent staff to these counties to identify potential service providers for Head Start programs and, once identified, help those service providers develop competitive grant proposals for Head Start funding. Longitudinal data from these counties allowed researchers to conduct a regression discontinuity design to determine if differences in OEO's offer of technical assistance across counties were linked to subsequent differences in county-level mortality and educational achievement between 1970 and 2000, which then could be inferred to be due to Head Start. Ultimately, OEO's technical assistance for the poorest counties was associated with higher rates of high school completion and college enrollment (Ludwig & Miller, 2005).

A series of studies have compared sibling pairs in which one attended Head Start while the other either did not attend a preschool program or attend a non-Head Start program. Head Start siblings have been found to fare better across a number of outcomes (Currie & Thomas, 1995; Deming, 2009).

While several assessments of Head Start's association with outcomes for children have taken place, only in 1998 did a legislative mandate to determine the program's impact occur. This gave rise to Head Start's only national randomized experiment, the Head Start Impact Study (HSIS). The study sampled 5,000 HSST enrollees from 84 HSST agencies nationwide and children were randomized into either a group that enrolled in Head Start or a control group that did not. Furthermore, to investigate if there were differential effects by age, two cohorts were studied in parallel—those who entered HSST at age three and those who entered at age four. HSIS examined Head Start impacts across four domains: cognitive development, social-emotional development, health status, and parenting practices. For the four-year-old cohort, Head Start had an effect on their receptive vocabulary, spelling, and parent-reported literacy compared to the control group. For the three-year-old cohort, children in the Head Start program group scored higher on receptive vocabulary measures, showed lower levels of hyperactive behavior, and showed better health status compared to the control group. Both cohorts experienced an increase in access to dental care. However, these effects were mostly not sustained into elementary school (Puma et al., 2010).

More nuanced analyses suggest that Head Start's impact may be larger for some groups over others. Zhai, Brooks-Gunn, and Waldfogel (2014) found that effects of Head Start participation on child outcomes were largely dependent upon the alternative care arrangement for a child. Specifically, effects were strongest when comparing Head Start children to children in matched comparison groups who received either informal child care (provided by family, relatives, or non-relatives) or no care. These findings suggest that children who otherwise would not attend preschool benefit the most from Head Start.

Quality of Head Start programs has garnered attention in recent years. Head Start has extensive performance standards for all aspects of program as a means to ensure that quality is maintained across all Head Start sites. Revised in 2016, these standards include increased program time, increased emphasis on family partnerships and goal setting, and a requirement that programs implement a research-based curriculum (Administration for Children and Families, 2016). While programs may use a range of preschool curricula, the most commonly used is the Creative Curriculum (Hulsey et al., 2011). Head Start has also seen an increase in the number of teachers with bachelor's and master's degrees in the classroom. Currently, 73% of all Head Start teachers have at least a bachelor's degree, a significant jump from 47% a decade before (DeParle, 2019). Performance standards additionally require teachers to receive ongoing and individualized professional development (Administration for Children and Families, 2016). Head Start programs that fall short of these performance standards are required to recompete for federal funding in a process known as the designation renewal system (National Institute for Early Education Research, 2017). A proportion of programs whose performance is low will lose their HSST grant and the contract will be put out for bid (DeParle, 2019).

Early Head Start (EHS)

Recognizing the needs of pregnant women and the importance of the first three years of life, the OEO opened Parent Child Centers in 1967 to offer services to low-income pregnant women, infants, and toddlers. Almost 30 years later in 1995, the federal government launched a more ambitious program, Early Head Start (EHS), a comprehensive, two-generation program focused on promoting the development and well-being of expectant mothers and children up to age three with incomes below the federal poverty line (Barnett & Friedman-Krauss, 2016). EHS programs may offer a variety of services, including home visits, center-based educational child care, case management, parenting education, health care and referrals, and family support. Compared to Head Start, EHS is a much smaller program, only reaching fewer than 5% of eligible participants (Barnett &

Friedman-Krauss, 2016). Communities receiving EHS funds can choose the modes of service delivery that meet their particular needs. The Survey of Early Head Start revealed that nearly 60% of programs offered multiple options to families, whereas only 17% of EHS programs were exclusively home-based, and 23% were exclusively center-based (Love, Chazan-Cohen, Raikes, & Brooks-Gunn, 2013).

Recognizing the need for evaluation early on in the program's history, the federal government funded the Early Head Start Research and Evaluation Project a year after EHS was first implemented. Approximately 3,000 EHS eligible families in 17 sites across the country either were randomly assigned to receive EHS services or were assigned to the non-EHS control group. Child and family assessments were conducted at 14, 24, 36, and 54 months; third- and fifth-grade follow-ups were also conducted. The EHS study examined effects across a wide range of outcomes, including cognitive and language outcomes, social-emotional skills, quality of the home environment, and family health and well-being. Child aggression was lower and intelligence scores were higher at ages two and three. More positive parenting behaviors were observed for EHS families, beginning at age two and sustained through age three, with EHS mothers showing increased sensitivity in their interactions. The impact of EHS was modest in all domains, with effect sizes ranging from 0.10 to 0.20. EHS also had an effect on continuity of care, with EHS impacting whether or not the child enrolled in formal care, Head Start, or otherwise, after the end of the program (Love et al., 2013).

The age five follow-up demonstrated the sustained impact of EHS in some domains. Relative to the control group participants, EHS participants showed better approaches to learning, lower behavior problems, and better attention at age five; however, program participants did not differ from control groups with regard to early academics. Effects at age five were larger for some groups of EHS participants though. While cognitive effects were not sustained for the sample of children overall, these effects were sustained for African-American children and Hispanic children who were Spanish speakers. With regard to parenting at age five, mothers of EHS participants had lower depressive scores (Love et al., 2013).

Non-experimental findings also provided additional insight into associations with child outcomes over time. Overall, children who participated in both EHS and Head Start fared better than children who participated in only one program or no program at all (Love et al., 2013). Those who participated in both programs scored higher on a measure that assesses positive approaches to learning and had home environments that were more stimulating—parents were more likely to read more to their children, there were a larger number of books in the home, and parent teaching behaviors were observed more frequently (Love et al., 2013). For dual-language learners, findings suggest that EHS and HS participation was beneficial for their receptive vocabulary skills. These findings provide evidence in support of the benefit of continuity of services from birth to age five.

The Baby Family and Child Experiences Survey (FACES), a longitudinal study of 89 EHS programs launched in 2009 that described EHS program services and staff, changes in program enrollees over time, and associations between services provided and child and family outcomes (Vogel & Boller, 2015), found high exit rates from EHS by age three, which may account for the modest effects of EHS observed. This was consistent with findings from the randomized trial, in which a substantial number of children exited the program prior to age three as well.

Head Start performance standards are wide-ranging and comprehensive, including detailed information about which services should be provided and intensity of such services; however, EHS sites included in the randomized trial differed on how well they were able to implement these performance standards at their respective sites. This variability was linked to outcomes at age three for EHS participants. Additionally, EHS program sites did not utilize a standardized curriculum across program sites or even within program type (Love & Brooks-Gunn, 2010; Love et al., 2013).

Mother, Infant, and Early Childhood Home Visiting (MIECHV) Program

Home visiting has a long history of supporting the well-being of mothers and children through improving parenting practices. One of the earliest models of home visitation dates back to the late nineteenth century through private charity organizations. During this time, more than 4,000 women volunteered to serve as "friendly visitors," providing moral and behavioral guidance to poor families (Weiss, 1993). These home visits focused on correcting perceived character flaws of poor families rather than providing material or social supports and largely disappeared in response to such criticism. In the 1960s, a resurgence of home visiting occurred as part of the War on Poverty. This renewed effort on family support programs also marked a new focus on comprehensive approaches to address parental and child well-being during visits (Duggan et al., 2013; Sweet & Applebaum, 2004).

Despite its lengthy history, funding for home visiting has largely been piecemeal in nature. In the 1990s, the Social Security Act included some funding for family support programs. These programs were funded with the goal of increasing the stability of the family unit through a variety of community-based services (Layzer, Goodson, Bernstein, & Price, 2001). Nearly 50% of the programs employed home visitation as their primary service delivery method and nearly all of the programs had the goal of improving parenting practices. Two decades later, the Patient Protection and Affordable Care Act was passed and established Maternal, Infant, and Early Child Home Visiting (MIECHV), a program administered by the Maternal Child Health Bureau within the Department of Health and Human Services. This program represented an expansion of funding for home visiting programs at the federal level. In 2017, the program served nearly 80,000 expectant mothers or families

with young children, with most support going to children and families deemed to be at risk (compared to approximately 975,000 children served annually by Head Start and EHS combined). Nearly 75% of participating families were at or below 100% of the federal poverty line and over half of participants had a high school diploma or less (Maternal and Child Health Bureau, 2016). The initial MIECHV authorization provided $1.5 billion to be spent across the first five years of the program (Michalopoulos et al., 2015). In the most recent fiscal year, MIECHV allocated approximately $340 million in funding to states, territories, and tribal lands in the United States in support of home visiting programs. MIECHV requires that 75% of funding be used by states to develop home visiting programs that the federal government has deemed effective, including Nurse-Family Partnership, Healthy Families America, Parents as Teachers, and Early Head Start Home-Based Option. The remaining quarter of funding be used by states for "promising" approaches, which will require evaluation to determine efficacy. Many states leverage other funding sources, such as Medicaid and TANF, to supplement MIECHV funds, given the relatively low number of families that MIECHV can fund (Witgert, Giles, & Richardson, 2012).

Home visiting refers to a service-delivery method rather than a universal set of program components. Programs differ across a variety of domains—the ages of children served, frequency and intensity of the intervention, staffing (e.g., paraprofessional, nurse), content of the curriculum, and programmatic scope (e.g., whether the program is designed for high-risk populations or if administered universally). Several home visiting models for expectant mothers and families with young children have emerged over the years, each with unique program features and goals.

Decades of research has informed the home visiting evidence base, although not all programs have been shown to be effective (Howard & Brooks-Gunn, 2009; Sweet & Applebaum, 2004). Both parent-centered outcomes (e.g., parenting behaviors, maternal depression and stress, parenting sensitivity) and child-centered outcomes (e.g., child health, cognitive development, behavior problems) have been examined. Evaluations of home visiting programs have yielded mixed results, with many studies showing favorable, albeit modest, impacts on family outcomes, and others showing no effects (see, e.g., Avellar & Supplee, 2013; Chen & Chan, 2016; Filene, Kaminski, Valle, & Cachat, 2013). Research evaluates program models as a whole, and it is unclear which program components are most effective (Howard & Brooks-Gunn, 2009; Sweet & Applebaum, 2004).

To ensure that MIECHV-funded programs draw upon the robust research base on home visiting, the Department of Health and Human Services launched the Home Visiting Evidence of Effectiveness (HomVEE) review. HomVEE provides research-backed guidance to state grantees when adapting and implementing home visiting programs in their respective states. Of the 45 models reviewed, only 20 met the rigorous standards set by HomVEE for effectiveness (Office of Planning, Research, and Evaluation, 2017). MIECHV grantees may choose from these 20 home visiting models when developing their individual plans, using a database that contains details of home visiting programs, outcomes measured by each program, as well as evidence for efficacy of such programs to help them select a program that is aligned with the needs of their residents. HomVEE also supports states in implementation by providing profiles that detail estimated costs, staff training requirements, and other prerequisites required to initiate a particular program in their respective states. In addition to HomVEE, the Home Visiting Research Network (HVRN) was established along with MIECHV. This research group brings together interdisciplinary leaders to fill gaps in home visiting research as well as increase focus on implementation science related to policy (Duggan et al., 2013). Jointly, both HomVEE and HVRN reflect MIECHV's commitment to program improvement through prioritizing research efforts.

Building off of this commitment to evidence-based early childhood interventions, at the time of MIECHV passage, the Department of Health and Human Services funded a legislatively mandated randomized trial of over 4,000 families to evaluate the effectiveness of MIECHV. Families were recruited and randomly assigned to one of four home visiting programs (Early Head Start [Home-Based Option], Healthy Families America, Nurse-Family Partnership, and Parents as Teachers) or a control group. Preliminary analyses have been conducted and show few main effects when children were of 15 months. Notably, children had fewer emergency room visits, and mothers were found to have fewer depressive symptoms and higher rates of health insurance coverage (Michalopoulos et al., 2019). However, these modest effects may in part be attributed to the issues with regard to implementation of home visiting programs. Home visiting programs often have difficulty enrolling families, and once enrolled, participant attrition before the recommended program duration and number of home visits is common (Duggan et al., 2018; Hernandez et al., 2019; O'Brien et al., 2012; Olds, 2003).

Enhancing the Development of Poor Children

What does the foregoing research tell us about how to enhance cognitive, social, and emotional outcomes of children growing up in poverty? Countless studies have demonstrated that, to varying degrees, poverty influences children's development across key domains. In short, income matters. However, the question remains how best to provide poor families the means to purchase necessities—food, housing, child care, and health care—as well as how to reduce material hardship more generally.

This chapter reviewed three categories of benefits available to low-income families: cash benefits (i.e., TANF), tax credits (i.e., EITC and CTC), and in-kind benefits (i.e., WIC, SNAP, child care subsidies, and housing subsidies). These programs reduce the number of families who are poor and for those still below the poverty threshold, these programs provide food, cash (if parents are working), tax credits (some of which are universal and some of which are predicated on parental work), and, for the lucky few, subsidized housing. Child care subsidies represent another crucial in-kind benefit for poor families.

The landscape of benefits available to low-income families has changed over time. As a proportion of all benefits available for low-income families with young children, cash assistance has greatly decreased over time, representing from around 90% of the benefits available to families in 1968 to only about 40% in 2013 (Pac et al., 2017). Conversely, tax credits available to families have increased as a proportion of benefits available since first introduced in the 1970s. Credits comprised 30%–35% of benefits received in 2013. In-kind benefits increased from about 10% in 1968 to 20% by the late 1980s and have roughly remained constant since then. While the distribution of benefits available to families has changed over time, the average benefit received by low-income households with children has remained quite consistent over time. The average value of assistance received by low-income families with young children has remained roughly between $8,000 and $10,000 since 1968 (these calculations do not include federal early childhood education programs). What is different is the increase in tax credits predicated on work and the decrease in direct cash transfers.

These programs do not reach all poor families and most are not entitlement programs. As parents with young children are no longer eligible to receive cash assistance without work or time limits of cash receipt, child care is necessary for virtually all poor families with young children (about 70% of all poor mothers are working during their child's infancy). Since no federal universal paid family leave policy exists, mothers with low-income and little to no savings often have little choice to take time off in the first months of their child's life (about two-thirds of adults in the United States favored universal paid family leave when this chapter was written). Child care subsidies are available to poor mothers who work; however, they do little to ensure quality of care and they are not an entitlement. Widely available full-day high-quality early education could remove a barrier to consistent, full-time employment—one of the goals of welfare reform and a necessity for families to leave poverty—while also improving child well-being. Federally funded early childhood education programs, like Head Start and Early Head Start, serve poor children; however, the majority of eligible children are served by neither program.

While these programs may not be perfect, they do make a difference in lives of low-income families with young children. In the absence of the many of these programs, research has projected that the child poverty rate would increase by a substantial margin. The National Academy of Sciences, Engineering, and Medicine released a report in the winter of 2019, entitled *A Roadmap to Reducing Child Poverty*. This report estimates the percentage of children who are poor, using the SPM discussed earlier. Using this measure, the current rate

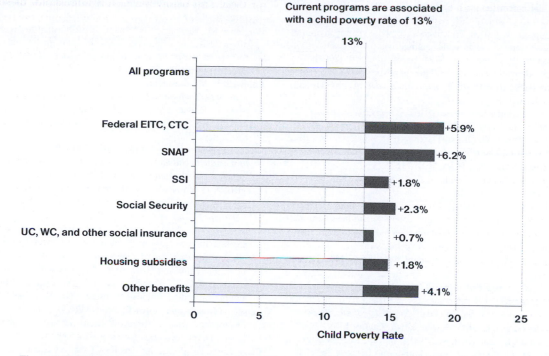

Figure 15.3 Changes in child poverty rates if each current income support program were eliminated.

is 13%. It would be over 20% higher if the benefits discussed in this chapter did not exist (their accounting also includes Social Security, Social Security Income, and other social insurance programs). From the report, Figure 15.3 outlines these reductions by type of program.

The EITC and CTC reduced the number of children in poverty by almost 6%, while SNAP reduced this rate by another 5%. The poverty rates could be further reduced by an expansion of programs serving the poor. Young children, when poor or near-poor, need these supports in order to flourish. Research suggests that we invest more resources in programs that work best, work to improve quality and implementation of programs that show mixed results, and generally integrate these programs for low-income families and children across the board.

Notes

1. Defined as a before-tax household income at or below the federal poverty line. In 2017, this threshold was $16,895 for a single parent household with one child, $19,749 for a single parent with two children, $24,858 for a two-parent household with two children. The poverty threshold is recalculated each year using the Consumer Price Index and is absolute, not relative. A relative threshold is based on a percentage of the household median income in a county in a given year. Therefore, it changes if nation-wide incomes rise or fall. Most Organisation for Economic Cooperation and Development (OECD) countries, an organization comprised of 36 high-income economy member countries, use a relative, not an absolute threshold.

2. Another tradition in social science adds other risks, such as parental depression, low cognitive ability, little social support, and no cognitively stimulating materials in the home into the cumulative risk score (Liaw & Brooks-Gunn, 1994; Sameroff, Seifer, Baldwin, & Baldwin, 1993). However, for this chapter, these more social, cognitive, and emotional inputs are conceptualized as possible pathways through which poverty might influence children.

3. Two other valuable resources are the National Institute of Child Health and Human Development and Study of Early Child Care and Youth Development (NICHD-SECCYD), which recruited mothers in ten hospitals throughout the country and followed these families through the child's 15th birthday, and the Infant Health and Development Program (IHDP), which followed low birth weight babies born in eight hospitals through age 15. These studies each follow approximately 1,000 families.

4. Determining the association between quality and children's outcomes is analytically challenging as it requires disentangling the obvious, but likely unmeasured, overlap between parental characteristics and choice of child care settings.

References

ABT Associates. (2006). *Effects of housing vouchers on welfare families*. U.S. Department of Housing and Urban Development, Washington, DC.

Adler, N. E., Boyce, T., Chesney, M. A., Cohen, S., Folkman, S., Kahn, R. L., & Syme, S. L. (1994). Socioeconomic status and health. The challenge of the gradient. *The American Psychologist, 49*(1), 15–24.

Administration for Children and Families. (2016). *Introducing the New Head Start Performance Standards: Final Rule*. Office of Head Start.

Administration for Children and Families. (2019). *What Is the Child Care and Development Fund (CCDF)?* Retrieved from https://www.acf.hhs.gov/archive/occ/faq/what-is-the-child-care-and-development-fund-ccdf

Almond, D., Hoynes, H. W., & Schanzenbach, D. W. (2011). Inside the war on poverty: The impact of food stamps on birth outcomes. *Review of Economics and Statistics, 93*(2), 387–403.

Apfel, N., & Seitz, V. (1997). The firstborn sons of African American teenage mothers: Perspectives on risk and resilience. In S. S. Luthar, J. A. Burack, Ciccetti, D., & Weisz, J. R. (Eds.), *Developmental psychopathology: Perspectives on adjustment, risk, and disorder* (pp. 486–506). New York, NY: Cambridge University Press.

Aratani, Y., Lazzeroni, S., Brooks-Gunn, J., & Hernandez, D. (2018). Housing subsidies and early childhood development: A comprehensive review of policies and demonstration projects. *Housing Policy Debate, 29*(2), 319–342.

Avellar, S., & Supplee, L. (2013). Effectiveness of home visiting in improving child health and reducing child maltreatment. *Pediatrics, 132*(2), S90–S99.Barajas, R. J., Philipsen, N., & Brooks-Gunn, J. (2007). Cognitive and emotional outcomes for children in poverty. In D. R. Crane & T. B. Heaton (Eds.), *Handbook of families and poverty* (pp. 311–333). Thousand Oaks, CA: Sage.

Barnett, W. S., & Friedman-Krauss, A. (2016). *State(s) of Head Start*. The National Institute for Early Education Research.

Bastian, J., & Michelmore, K. (2018). The long-term impact of the earned income tax credit on children's education and employment outcomes. *Journal of Labor Economics, 36*(4), 1127–1163.

Baumrind, D. (1966). Effects of authoritative control on child behavior. *Child Development, 37*, 887–907.

Baydar, N., & Brooks-Gunn, J. (1991). Effects of maternal employment and child-care arrangements on preschoolers' cognitive and behavioral outcomes: Evidence from the Children of the National Longitudinal Survey of Youth. *Developmental Psychology, 27*(6), 932–945.

Becker, G. S. (1991). *A treatise on the family*. Cambridge, MA: Harvard University Press.

Bellinger, D. C. (2004). Lead. *Pediatrics, 113*(Supplement 3), 1016 LP–1022.

Belsky, J. (1999). Interactional and contextual determinants of attachment security. In J. Cassidy & P. Shaver (Eds.), *Handbook of attachment theory and research* (pp. 249–264). New York, NY: Guilford.

Belsky, J., Vandell, D. L., Burchinal, M., Clarke-Stewart, K. A., Mccartney, K., & Owen, M. T. (2007). Are there long-term effects of early child care? *Child Development, 78*(2), 681–701.

Blau, D. M. (1999). The effect of income on child development. *Review of Economics and Statistics, 81*(2), 261–276.

Blau, D., & Tekin, E. (2007). The determinants and consequences of child care subsidies for single mothers in the USA. *Journal of Population Economics, 20*, 719–741.

Bradley, R. H. (1995). Environment and parenting. In M. H. Bornstein (Ed.), *Handbook of parenting: Vol. 2. Biology and ecology of parenting* (pp. 235–261). Mahwah, NJ: Erlbaum.

Bradley, R. H., & Corwyn, R. F. (2002). Socioeconomic status and child development. *Annual Review of Psychology, 53*, 371–399.

Bradley, R. H., Corwyn, R. F., McAdoo, H. P., & Garcia Coll, C. (2001). The home environments of children in the United States part I: Variations by age, ethnicity, and poverty status. *Child Development, 72*(6), 1844–1867.

Brito, N. H., & Noble, K. G. (2014). Socioeconomic status and structural brain development. *Frontiers in Neuroscience, 8*, 276.

Brody, D. J., Pirkle, J. L., Kramer, R. A., Flegel, K. M., Matte, T. D., Gunter, E. W., … Paschal, D. C. (1994). Blood lead levels in the U.S. population: Phase 1 of the Third National Health and Nutrition Examination Survey (NHANES III, 1988–1991). *Journal of the American Medical Association, 272*, 277–283.

Brooks-Gunn, J., Berlin, L. J., & Fuligni, A. S. (2000). Early childhood intervention programs: What about the family? In J. P. Shonkoff & S. J. Meisels (Eds.), *Handbook of early childhood intervention* (2nd ed., pp. 549–588). New York, NY: Cambridge University Press.

Brooks-Gunn, J., Duncan, G. J., Klebanov, P., & Sealand, N. (1993). Do neighborhoods influence child and adolescent development? *American Journal of Sociology, 99*, 353–395.

Brooks-Gunn, J., Han, W. J., & Waldfogel, J. (2002). Maternal employment and child cognitive outcomes in the first three years of life: The NICHD Study of Early Child Care. *Child Development, 73*(4), 1052–1072.

Brooks-Gunn, J., Han, W. J., & Waldfogel, J. (2010). First-year maternal employment and child development in the first 7 years. *Monographs of the Society for Research in Child Development, Serial 296, 75*(2), 7–9.

Brooks-Gunn, J., & Markman, L. (2005). The contribution of parenting to ethnic and racial gaps in school readiness. *The Future of Children, 15*, 139–168.

Burchinal, M. R., Roberts, J. E., Riggins, R., Jr., Zeisel, S. A., Neebe, E., & Bryant, D. (2000). Relating quality of center-based child care to early cognitive and language development longitudinally. *Child Development, 71*(2), 339–357.

Burchinal, M., Vandergrift, N., Pianta, R., & Mashburn, A., (2009). Threshold analysis of association between child care quality and child outcomes for low-income children in pre-kindergarten programs. *Early Childhood Research Quarterly, 25*, 166–176.

Caldwell, B. M., & Bradley, R. H. (1984). *Home observation for measurement of the environment*. Little Rock, AR: University of Arkansas.

Carlson, S., Rosenbaum, D., Keith-Jennings, B., & Nchako, C. (2016). *SNAP works for America's children*. Washington, DC: Center on Budget and Policy Priorities.

Case, A., Lubotsky, D., & Paxson, C. (2002, February). *Economic status and health in childhood: The origins of the gradient*. Princeton, NJ: The Center for Health and Wellbeing, Princeton University.

Caughy, M. O. B., Nettles, S. M., & O'Campo, P. J. (2008). The effect of residential neighborhood on child behavior problems in first grade. *American Journal of Community Psychology, 42*(1–2), 39–50.

Caughy, M. O. B., & O'Campo, P. J. (2006). Neighborhood poverty, social capital, and the cognitive development of African American preschoolers. *American Journal of Community Psychology, 37*(1–2), 141–154.

Cecil, K. M., Brubaker, C. J., Adler, C. M., Dietrich, K. N., Altaye, M., Egelhoff, J. C., … Lanphear, B. P. (2008). Decreased brain volume in adults with child- hood lead exposure. *PLoS Medicine, 5*(5), 741–750.

Center on Budget and Policy Priorities. (2018). *Policy basics: The earned income tax credit*. Retrieved from https://www.cbpp.org/research/federal-tax/policy-basics-the-earned-income-tax-credit

Chase-Lansdale, P. L., Gordon, R. A., Brooks-Gunn, J., & Klebanov, P. (1997). Neighborhood and family influences on the intellectual and behavioral competence of preschool and early school-age children. In J. Brooks-Gunn, G. J. Duncan, & J. L. Aber (Eds.), *Neighborhood poverty: Vol. 1. Context and consequences for children* (pp. 79–118). New York, NY: Russell Sage Foundation.

Chatterji, P., & Brooks-Gunn, J. (2004). WIC participation, breastfeeding practices, and well-child care among unmarried, low-income mothers. *American Journal of Public Health, 94*(8), 1324–1327.

Chen, M., & Chan, K. L. (2016). Effects of parenting programs on child maltreatment prevention: A meta-analysis. *Trauma, Violence, & Abuse, 17*(1), 88–104.

Chetty, R., Hendren, N., & Katz, L. (2016). The effects of exposure to better neighborhoods on children: New evidence from the moving to opportunity project. *American Economic Review, 106*(4), 855–902.

Chilton, M., Black, M. M., Casey, P. H., Cook, J., Cutts, D., Jacobs, R. R., … Frank, D. A. (2009). Food insecurity and risk of poor health among US-born children of immigrants. *American Journal of Public Health, 99*(3), 556–562.

Chorniy, A., Currie, J., & Sonchak, L. (2018). *Does prenatal WIC participation improve child outcomes* (Working Paper No. 24691). Cambridge, MA: National Bureau of Economic Research.

Citro, C. F., & Michael, R. T. (Eds.). (1995). *Measuring poverty: A new approach*. Washington, DC: National Academy Press.

Collins, James, W., Jr, Wambach, J., David, R. J., & Rankin, K. M. (2009). Women's lifelong exposure to neighborhood poverty and low birth weight: A population-based study. *Maternal and Child Health Journal, 13*(3), 326–33.

Conger, R. D., & Conger, K. J. (2000). Resilience in midwestern families: Selected findings from the first decade of a prospective longitudinal study. *Journal of Marriage & Family, 64*, 361–373.

Conger, R. D., & Elder, G. H. (1994). *Families in troubled times: Adapting to change in rural America*. New York, NY: Aldine de Gruyter.

Conger, K. J., Rueter, M. A., & Conger, R. D. (2000). The role of economic pressure in the lives of parents and their adolescents: The family stress model. In L. J. Crockett & R. K. Silbereisen (Eds.), *Negotiating adolescence in times of social change* (pp. 201–223). New York, NY: Cambridge University Press.

Conley, D., & Bennett, N. G. (2000). Is biology destiny? Birth weight and life chances. *American Sociological Review, 65*, 458–467.

Cook, J. T., & Frank, D. A. (2008). Food insecurity, poverty, and human development in the United States. *Annals of the New York Academy of Sciences, 1136*, 193–209.

Cooper, C., McLanahan, S., Meadows, S., Brooks-Gunn, J., & Johnson, D. (2009). Family structure transitions and maternal parenting stress. *Journal of Marriage and Family, 71*(3), 558–574. Retrieved from http://www.jstor.org/stable/40262902

Costello, E. J., Compton, S. N., Keeler, G., & Angold, A. (2003). Relationships between poverty and psychopathology: A natural experiment. *Journal of the American Medical Association, 290*(15), 2023–2029.

Crnic, K., & Greenberg, M. (1987). Maternal stress, social support, and coping: Influences on the early mother–infant relationship. In C. F. Z. Boukydis (Ed.), *Research on support for parents and infants in the postnatal period* (pp. 25–40). Norwood, NJ: Ablex.

Crockenberg, S. (1987). Predictors and correlates of anger toward and punitive control of toddlers by adolescent mothers. *Child Development, 58*(4), 964–975.

Currie, J. M. (2006). *The invisible safety net: Protecting the nation's poor children and families*. Princeton, NJ: Princeton University Press.

Currie, J. M. (2008). Feeding the hungry: Food stamps, school nutrition programs, and WIC. In *The invisible safety net: Protecting the nation's poor children and families* (pp. 61–89). Princeton, NJ: Princeton University Press.

Currie, J., & Almond, D. (2011). Human capital development before age five. In D. Card & O. Ashenfelter (Eds.), *Handbook of labor economics* (Vol. 4, Part B, pp. 1315–1486). Amsterdam, Netherlands: Elsevier.

Currie, J. M., & Bitler, M. (2004). Does WIC work? The effect of WIC on pregnancy and birth outcomes. *Journal of Policy Analysis and Management, 23*, 73–91.

Currie, J. M., & Thomas, D. (1995). Does Head Start make a difference? *The American Economic Review, 85*(3), 341–364.

Currie, J., & Yelowitz, A. (2000). Are public housing projects good for kids? *Journal of Public Economics, 75*(1), 99–124.

Curtis, L., Dooley, M., & Phipps, S. (2004). Child well-being and neighbourhood quality: Evidence from the Canadian National Longitudinal Survey of Children and Youth. *Social Science and Medicine, 58*(10), 1917–1927.

Dahl, G., & Lochner, L. (2009). *The impact of family income on child achievement: Evidence from the Earned Income Tax Credit* (Working Paper No. 14599). Cambridge, MA: National Bureau of Economic Research. Retrieved from http://www.nber.org/papers/w14599.pdf

Datta Gupta, N., & Simonson, M. (2010). Noncognitive child outcomes and universal high-quality child care. *Journal of Public Economics, 94*, 30–43.

Dearing, E., McCartney, K., & Taylor, B. A. (2001). Change in family income-to-needs matters more for children with less. *Child Development, 72*(6), 1779–1793.

Dearing, E., McCartney, K., & Taylor, B. A. (2006). Within-child association between family income and externalizing and internalizing problems. *Developmental Psychology, 42*(2), 237–252.

Dearing, E., McCartney, K., & Taylor, B. (2009). Does higher quality early child care promote low income children's math and reading achievement in middle childhood? *Child Development, 80*, 1329–1349.

Dearing, E., McCartney, K., Weiss, H. B., Kreider, H., & Simpkins, S. (2004). The promotive effects of family educational involvement for low-income children's literacy. *Journal of School Psychology, 42*(6), 445–460.

Dearing, E., & Taylor, B. A. (2007). Home improvements: Within-family associations between income and the quality of children's home environments. *Journal of Applied Developmental Psychology, 28*(5–6), 427–444.

Deaton, A. (2002). Policy implications of the gradient of health and wealth. *Health Affairs, 21*(2), 13–30.

Deming, D. (2009). Early childhood intervention and life-cycle skill development: Evidence from Head Start. *American Economic Journal: Applied Economics, 1*(3), 111–134.DeParle, J. (2019, February 4). Cleaner classrooms and rising test scores: With tighter oversight, head start shows gains. *The New York Times*.

Devaney, B. L., Ellwood, M. R., & Love, J. M. (1997). Programs that mitigate the effects of poverty on children. *The Future of Children, 7*(2), 88–112.

Duggan, A., Minkovitz, C. S., Chaffin, M., Korfmacher, J., Brooks-Gunn, J., Crowne, S., … Harwood, R. (2013). Creating a national home visiting research network. *Pediatrics, 132*(Supplement), S82–S89.

Duggan, A., Portilla, X., Filene, J., Crowne, S., Hill, C., Lee, H., & Knox, V. (2018). *Implementation of evidence-based early childhood home visiting: Results from the mother and infant home visiting program evaluation*. OPRE Report 2018–76A. Washington, DC: Office of Planning, Research, and Evaluation, Administration for Children and Families, U.S. Department of Health and Human Services.

Duncan, G. J., & Brooks-Gunn, J. (Eds.). (1997). *Consequences of growing up poor*. New York, NY: Russell Sage Foundation Press.

Duncan, G. J., Brooks-Gunn, J., & Klebanov, P. (1994). Economic deprivation and early-childhood development. *Child Development, 65*, 296–318.

Duncan, G. J., Kalil, A., & Ziol-Guest, K. (2017). Increasing inequality in parent incomes and children's schooling. *Demography, 54*(5), 1603–1626.

Duncan, G., Magnuson, K., Kalil, A., & Ziol-Guest, K. (2012). The importance of early childhood poverty. *Social Indicators Research, 108*(1), 87–98.

Duncan, G. J., & Murnane, R. J. (2014). Introduction: The American dream, then and now. In G. J. Duncan & R. J. Murnane (Eds.), *Whither opportunity? Rising inequality, schools, and children's life chances* (pp. 3–26). New York, NY: Russell Sage Foundation.

Duncan, G. J., & Murnane, R. J. (2016). Rising inequality in family incomes and children's educational outcomes. *RSF: The Russell Sage Foundation Journal of the Social Sciences, 2*(2), 142–158.

Duncan, G. J., Yeung, W. J., Brooks-Gunn, J., & Smith, J. R. (1998). How much does childhood poverty affect the life chances of children? *American Sociological Review, 63*, 406–423.

Duncan, G. J., Ziol-Guest, K. M., & Kalil, A. (2010). Early-childhood poverty and adult attainment, behavior, and health. *Child Development, 81*(1), 306–325.

Edin, K., & Kefalas, M. (2011). *Promises I can keep: Why poor women put motherhood before marriage*. Berkeley: University of California Press.

Edin, K., & Lein, L. (1997). *Making ends meet: How single mothers survive welfare and low-wage work*. New York, NY: Russell Sage Foundation.

Elder, G. H. (1999). *Children of the great depression: Social change in life experience*. Boulder, CO: Westview Press.

Enchautegui, M., Chien, N., Burgess, K., & Ghertner, R. (2016). *Effects of the CCDF subsidy program on the employment outcomes of low income mothers*. U.S. Department of Health and Human Services, Office of the Assistant Secretary for Planning and Evaluation.

Evans, G. W. (2001). Environmental stress and health. In A. Baum, T. A. Revenson, & J. E. Singer (Eds.), *Handbook of health psychology* (pp. 365–385). Mahwah, NJ: Erlbaum.

Evans, G., Gonnella, C., Marcynyszyn, L., Gentile, L., & Salpekar, N. (2005). The role of chaos in poverty and children's socioemotional adjustment. *Psychological Science, 16*(7), 560–565.

Evans, G. W., & Schamberg, M. A. (2009). Childhood poverty, chronic stress, and adult working memory. *Proceedings of the National Academy of Sciences, 106*(16), 6545–6549.

Filene, J., Kaminski, J., Valle, L., & Cachat, P. (2013). Components associated with home visiting outcomes: A meta-analysis. *Pediatrics, 132*(2), S100–S109.

Floyd, I., Burnside, A., & Schott, L. (2018). *TANF reaching few poor families*. Washington, DC: Center on Budget and Policy Priorities.

Fontenot, K., Semega, J., & Kollar, M. (2018). *U.S. Census Bureau Current Population Reports, Income and Poverty in the United States: 2017*. Washington, DC: U.S. Government Printing Office.

Friedman-Krauss, A., Barnett, W. S., Weisenfeld, G., Kasmin, R., DiCrecchio, N., & Horowitz, M. (2018). *The state of preschool 2017: State preschool yearbook.* New Brunswick NJ: National Institute for Early Education Research.

Garfinkel, I., McLanahan, S., & Wimer, C. (2016). Introduction. In I. Garfinkel, S. McLanahan, & C. Wimer (Eds.), *Children of the great recession* (pp. 1–30). New York, NY: Russell Sage Foundation.

Garrett, P., Ng'andu, N., & Ferron, J. (1994). Poverty experiences of young children and the quality of their home environments. *Child Development, 65*(2), 331–345.

Gershoff, E. T., Aber, J. L., Raver, C. C., & Lennon, M. C. (2007). Income is not enough: Incorporating material hardship into models of income associations with parenting and child development. *Child Development, 78*(1), 70–95.

Guo, G., & Harris, K. M. (2000). The mechanisms mediating the effects of poverty on children's intellectual development. *Demography, 37,* 431–448.

Han, W-J., Hetzner, N. P., & Brooks-Gunn, J. (2019). Employment and parenting. In M. Bornstein (Ed.), *The handbook of parenting* (3rd ed.). Mahwah, NJ: Lawrence Erlbaum.

Hanson, T. L., McLanahan, S., & Thomson, E. (1997). Economic resources, parental practices, and children's well-being. In G. J. Duncan & J. Brooks-Gunn (Eds.), *Consequences of growing up poor* (pp. 190–238). New York, NY: Russell Sage Foundation.

Haveman, R., Blank, R., Moffitt, R., Smeeding, T., & Wallace, G. (2015). The war on poverty: Measurement, trends, and policy. *Journal of Policy Analysis & Management, 34*(3), 593–638. doi:10.1002/pam.21846

Haveman, R., & Wolfe, B. (1994). *Succeeding generations: On the effects of investments in children.* New York, NY: Russell Sage Foundation.

Herbst, C., & Tekin, E. (2009). *Child care subsidies and child development* (Working paper 15007). Cambridge, MA: National Bureau of Economic Research.

Hernandez, D. C., & Jacknowitz, A. (2009). Transient, but not persistent adult food insecurity influences toddler development. *Journal of Nutrition, 139*(8), 1517–1524.

Hernandez, D., Topping, A., Hutchinson, C. L., Martin, A., Brooks-Gunn, J., & Petitclerc, A. (2019). Client attrition in the Nurse Family Partnership: Revisiting metrics of impact in a home visitation program in the United States. *Health and Social Care in the Community, 27*(4), 483–493.

Hill, Z., Gennetian, L. A., & Mendez, J. (2019). A descriptive profile of state Child Care and Development Fund policies in states with high populations of low-income Hispanic children. *Early Childhood Research Quarterly, 47,* 111–123.

Hoynes, H. (2014). A revolution in poverty policy: The earned income tax credit and the well-being of American families. *Pathways,* Summer, 23–27.

Hoynes, H., & Patel, A. (2015). Effective policy for reducing inequality? The earned income tax credit and the distribution of income (Working Paper No. 21340). Cambridge, MA: National Bureau of Economic Research.

Hoynes, H., & Schanzenbach, D. W. (2015). *U.S. Food and Nutrition Programs* (Working Paper No. 21057). Cambridge, MA: National Bureau of Economic Research.

Hoynes, H., & Schanzenbach, D. W. (2018, Spring). Safety net investments in children. *Brookings Papers on Economic Activity, 1,* 89–150.

Hoynes, H., Schanzenbach, D., & Almond, D. (2016). Long-run impacts of childhood access to the safety net. *The American Economic Review, 106*(4), 903–934.

Howard, K., & Brooks-Gunn, J. (2009). The role of home visiting programs in preventing child abuse and neglect. *Future of Children, 19*(2), 119–146.

Hulsey, L. K., Aikens, N., Kopack, A., West, J., Moiduddin, E., & Tarullo, L. B. (2011). *Head Start children, families, and programs: Present and past data from FACES* (OPRE Report 2011–33a). Washington, DC: Office of Planning, Research and Evaluation, Administration for Children and Families, U.S. Department of Health and Human Services.

Huston, A., Duncan, G., McLoyd, V., Crosby, D., Ripke, M., Weisner, T., & Eldred, C. (2005). Impacts on children of a policy to promote employment and reduce poverty for low-income parents: New Hope after five years. *Developmental Psychology, 41,* 902–918.

Ispa, J., Fine, M., Halgunseth, L., Harper, S., Robinson, J., Boyce, L., ... Brady-Smith, C. (2004). Maternal intrusiveness, maternal warmth, and mother-toddler relationship outcomes: Variations across low-income ethnic and acculturation groups. *Child Development, 75*(6), 1613–1631.

Jackson, A. P., Brooks-Gunn, J., Huang, C.-C., & Glassman, M. (2000). Single mothers in low-wage jobs: Financial strain, parenting, and preschoolers' outcomes. *Child Development, 71*(5), 1409–1423.

Jiang, Y., Granja, M. R., Koball, H. (2017, January). *Basic facts about low-income children: Children under 6 years.* New York, NY: National Center for Children in Poverty.

Johnson, A., Martin, A., & Brooks-Gunn, J. (2011). Child-care subsidies and school readiness in Kindergarten. *Child Development, 84*(5), 1806–1822.

Johnson, A., Martin, A., & Brooks-Gunn, J. (2013). Who uses child care subsidies? Comparing recipients to eligible non-recipients on family background characteristics and child care preferences. *Children and Youth Services Review, 33*(7), 1072–1083.

Johnson, A., Ryan, R., & Brooks-Gunn, J. (2012). Child-care subsidies: Do they impact the quality of care children experience? *Child Development, 83*(4), 1444–1461.

Kalil, A., & Chen, J. (2008). Family citizenship status and food insecurity among low-income children of immigrants. *New Directions in Child and Adolescent Development, 121,* 43–62.

Kalil, A., & Wightman, P. (July, 2010). *Parental job loss and family conflict* (Working Paper Series No. WP-10–07). Washington, DC: National Center for Family and Marriage Research.

Kendig, S., & Bianchi, S. M. (2008). Family structure differences in maternal time with children. *Journal of Marriage and Family, 70*(5), 1228–1240.

Kim, R. Y. (2001). The effects of the Earned Income Tax Credit on children's income and poverty: Who fares better? *Journal of Poverty, 5*(1), 1–22.

Kim, P., Evans, G., Angstadt, M., Ho, S., Sripada, C., Swain, J., ... Phan, K. (2013). Effects of childhood poverty and chronic stress on emotion regulatory brain function in adulthood. *Proceedings of the National Academy of Sciences of the United States of America, 110*(46), 18442–18447.

Kingsley, W. T. (2017). *Trends in housing problems and federal housing assistance.* Washington, DC: Urban Institute.

Klebanov, P. K., Brooks-Gunn, J., McCarton, C., & McCormick, M. C. (1998). The contribution of neighborhood and family income to developmental test scores over the first three years of life. *Child Development, 69,* 1420–1436.

Klebanov, P. K., Brooks-Gunn, J., & McCormick, M. C. (1994). School achievement and failure in very low birth weight children. *Journal of Developmental and Behavioral Pediatrics, 15,* 248–256.

Kohen, D., Brooks-Gunn, J., Leventhal, T., & Hertzman, C. (2002). Neighborhood income and physical and social disorder in Canada: Associations with young children's competencies. *Child Development, 73*(6), 1844–1860.

Kohen, D., Leventhal, T., Dahinten, S., & McIntosh, C. (2008). Neighborhood disadvantage: Pathways of effects for young children. *Child Development, 79*(1), 156–169.

Korenman, S., Miller, J. E., & Sjaastad, J. E. (1995). Long-term poverty and child development in the United States: Results from the NLSY. *Children and Youth Services Review, 17,* 127–155.

Kowalski-Jones, L., & Duncan, G. (2002). Effects of participation in the WIC program on birthweight: Evidence from the National Longitudinal Survey of Youth. *American Journal of Public Health, 92*(5), 799–804.

Layzer, J. I., Goodson, B. D., Bernstein, L., & Price, C. (2001). *National Evaluation of Family Support Programs Volume A: The meta-analysis.* Cambridge, MA: ABT Associates.

Lee, V., Brooks-Gunn, J., Schnur, E., & Liaw, F. (1990). Are Head Start effects sustained? A longitudinal follow-up comparison of disadvantaged children attending Head Start, no preschool, and other preschool programs. *Child Development, 61*(2), 495–507.

Lee, V. E., Brooks-Gunn, J., & Schnur, E. (1988). Does Head Start work? A 1-year follow-up comparison of disadvantaged children attending Head Start, no preschool, and other preschool programs. *Developmental Psychology, 24*(2), 210–222.

Lee, B. J., & Mackey-Bilaver, L. (2007). Effects of WIC and food stamp program participation on child outcomes. *Children and Youth Services Review, 29*(4), 501–517.

Leininger, L. J., Ryan, R. M., & Kalil, A. (2009). Low-income mothers'social support and children's injuries. *Social Science and Medicine, 68*(12), 2113–2121.

Leventhal, T., & Brooks-Gunn, J. (2001). Changing neighborhoods and child well-being: Understanding how children may be affected in the coming century. *Advances in Life Course Research, 6*, 263–301.

Leventhal, T., & Brooks-Gunn, J. (2003). Moving to opportunity: An experimental study of neighborhood effects on mental health. *American Journal of Public Health, 93*(9), 1576–1582.

Liaw, F.-R., & Brooks-Gunn, J. (1994). Cumulative familial risks and low-birthweight children's cognitive and behavioral development. *Journal of Clinical Child Psychology, 23*(4), 360–372.

Linver, M. R., Brooks-Gunn, J., & Kohen, D. E. (1999). Parenting behavior and emotional health as mediators of family poverty effects upon young low-birthweight children's cognitive ability. *Annals of the New York Academy of Sciences, 896*, 376–378.

Linver, M. R., Brooks-Gunn, J., & Kohen, D. E. (2002). Family processes as pathways from income to young children's development. *Developmental Psychology, 38*(5), 719–734.

Loeb, S., Fuller, B., Kagan, S. L., & Carroll, B. (2004). Child care in poor communities: Early learning effects of type, quality, and stability. *Child Development, 75*, 47–65.

Love, J. M., & Brooks-Gunn, J. (2010). Getting the most out of Early Head Start: What has been accomplished and what needs to be done. In R. Haskins & W. S. Barnett (Eds.), *Investing in young children: New directions in federal preschool and early childhood policy* (pp. 29–37). Washington, DC: Brookings Institute.

Love, J., Chazan-Cohen, R., Raikes, H., & Brooks-Gunn, J. (2013). What makes a difference? Early Head Start Evaluation findings in a developmental context. *Monographs of the Society for Research in Child Development, 78*, 1–173.

Love, J. M., Harrison, L., Sagi-Schwartz, A., Van IJzendoorn, M. H., Ross, C., & Ungerer, J. A. (2003). Child care quality matters: How conclusions may vary with context. *Child Development, 74*(4), 1021–1033.

Luby, J., Belden, A., Botteron, K., Marrus, N., Harms, M. P., Babb, C., ... Barch, D. (2013). The effects of poverty on childhood brain development. *JAMA Pediatrics, 167*(12), 1135.

Ludwig, J., & Miller, D. L. (2007). Does Head Start improve children's life chances? Evidence from a regression-discontinuity design. *Quarterly Journal of Economics, 122*(1), 159–208.

Lupien, S. J., McEwen, B. S., Gunnar, M. R., & Heim, C. (2009). Effects of stress throughout the lifespan on the brain, behaviour, and cognition. *Nature Reviews Neuroscience, 10*(6), 434–445.

Maag, E., & Isaacs, J. (2017). *Analysis of a young child tax credit: Providing an additional tax credit for children under 5*. The Urban Institute.

Magnuson, K. (2007). Maternal education and children's academic achievement during middle childhood. *Developmental Psychology, 43*(6), 1497–1512.

Maternal and Child Health Bureau. (2016). *Demonstrating improvement in the maternal, infant, and early childhood home visiting program: A report to congress*. Washington, DC: Health Resources and Services Administration, U.S. Department of Health and Human Services.

Mayer, S. E. (1997). *What money can't buy: Family income and children's life chances*. Cambridge, MA: Harvard University Press.

McCartney, K., Dearing, E., Taylor, B. A., & Bub, K. L. (2007). Quality child care supports the achievement of low-income children: Direct and indirect pathways through caregiving and the home environment. *Journal of Applied Developmental Psychology, 28*(5–6), 411–426.

McCormick, M. C., Brooks-Gunn, J., Workman-Daniels, K., Turner, J., & Peckham, G. (1992). The health and developmental status of very low birth weight children at school age. *Journal of the American Medical Association, 267*, 2204–2208.

McLanahan, S. S. (2004). Diverting destinies: How children are faring under the second demographic transition. *Demography, 41*, 607–627.

McLaughlin, K. A., Sheridan, M. A., & Lambert, H. K. (2014). Childhood adversity and neural development: Deprivation and threat as distinct dimensions of early experience. *Neuroscience & Biobehavioral Reviews, 47*, 578–591.

McLoyd, V. C. (1990). The impact of economic hardship on black families and children: Psychological distress, parenting, and socioemotional development. *Child Development, 61*, 311–346.

McLoyd, V. C. (1998). Socioeconomic disadvantage and child development. *American Psychologist, 53*(2), 185.

Meyers, A., Cutts, D., Frank, D., Levenson, S., Skalicky, A., Heeren, T., ... Zaldivar, N. (2005). Subsidized housing and children's nutritional status: Data from a multisite surveillance study. *Archive of Pediatric Adolescent Medicine, 159*(6), 551–556.

Michalopoulos, C., Crowne, S., Portilla, X., Lee, H., Filene, J., Duggan, A., & Knox, V. (2019). *A summary of results from the MIHOPE and MIHOPE-strong start studies of evidence-based home visiting*. OPRE Report 2019-09. Washington, DC: Office of Planning, Research, and Evaluation, Administration for Children and Families, U.S. Department of Health and Human Services.

Michalopoulos, C., Lee, H., Duggan, A., Lundquist, E., Tso, A., Crowne, S., ... Knox, (2015, January). *The mother and infant home visiting program evaluation: Early findings on the maternal, infant, and early childhood home visiting program. A report to congress*. OPRE Report 2015-11. Administration for Children & Families.

Moffitt, R. (2003). The temporary assistance for needy families program. In R. Moffitt (Ed.), *Means-tested transfer programs in the United States* (pp. 291–364). Cambridge, MA: National Bureau of Economic Research.

Morris, P., Duncan, G., & Clark-Kaufman, E. (2005). Child well-being in an era of welfare reform: The sensitivity of transitions in development to policy change. *Developmental Psychology, 41*, 919–932.

Morris, P. A., Gennetian, L. A., & Duncan, G. J. (2005). Effects of welfare and employment policies on young children: New findings on policy experiments conducted in the early 1990s. *Social Policy Report Society for Research in Child Development, 19*(2), 3–17.

National Academies of Sciences, Engineering, and Medicine. (2019). *A roadmap to reducing child poverty*. Washington, DC: The National Academies Press.

National Institute for Early Education Research. (2017). *Head Start considering changes to create 'less burdensome' competition process*. Retrieved from http://nieer.org/news/head-start-considering-changes-create-less-burdensome-competition-process

National Institute of Child Health and Development (NICHD), Early Child Care Research Network. (2002). Structure, process, outcome: Direct and indirect effects of caregiving quality on young children's development. *Psychological Science, 13*, 199–206.

National Institute of Child Health and Development (NICHD), Early Child Care Research Network. (1997). The effects of infant child care on infant–mother attachment security: Results of the NICHD Study of Early Child Care. *Child Development, 68*(5), 860–879.

National Institute of Child Health and Development (NICHD), Early Child Care Research Network. (1998). Early child care and self-control, compliance, and problem behavior at 24 and 36 months. *Child Development, 69*, 1145–1170.

National Institute of Child Health and Development (NICHD), Early Child Care Research Network, & Duncan, G. J. (2003). Modeling the impacts of child care quality on children's preschool cognitive development. *Child Development, 74*(5), 1454–1475.

Neckerman, K. M., Garfinkely, I., Teitler, J. O., Waldfogel, J., & Wimer, C. (2016). Beyond income poverty: Measuring disadvantage in terms of material hardship and health. *Academy of Pediatrics, 16*(3), S52–S59.

Needleman, H. L. (1979). Lead levels and children's psychologic performance. *New England Journal of Medicine, 301*(3), 163.

Newman, S., & Harkness, J. (2002). The long-term effects of public housing on self-sufficiency. *Journal of Policy Analysis and Management, 21*(1), 21–43.

Newman, S., & Holupka, C. S. (2017). The effects of assisted housing on child well-being. *American Journal of Community Psychology, 60*(1), 66.

Noble, K. G., Houston, S. M., Brito, N. H., Bartsch, H., Kan, E., Kuperman, J. M., … Rowell, E. R. (2015). Family income, parental education and brain structure in children and adolescents. *Nature Neuroscience, 18*(5), 773–778.

O'Brien, R. A., Moritz, P., Luckey, D. W., Mcclatchey, M. W., Ingoldsby, E. M., & Olds, D. L. (2012). Mixed methods analysis of participant attrition in the nurse-family partnership. *Prevention Science, 13*(3), 219–228.

Office of Planning, Research, and Evaluation. (2017). *Home visiting: Reviewing evidence of effectiveness.* Retrieved from: https://homvee. acf.hhs.gov/homevee_executive_summary_brief_august_2017_508_ compliant.pdf

Olds, D. (2003). Reducing program attrition in home visiting: What do we need to know? *Child Abuse & Neglect, 27*(4), 359–361.

Oliveira, V., Racine, E., Olmsted, J., Ghelfi, L. (2002). *The WIC program: Background, trends, and issues* (Food Assistance and Nutrition Research Report 27). United States Department of Agriculture.

Pac, J., Nam, J., Waldfogel, J., & Wimer, C. (2017). Young child poverty in the United States: Analyzing trends in poverty and the role of anti-poverty programs using the Supplemental Poverty Measure. *Children and Youth Services Review, 74*, 35–49.

Puma, M., Bell, S., Cook, R., & Heid, C. (2010). *Head Start impact study: Final report.* Washington, DC: U.S. Department of Health and Human Services, Administration for Children and Families.

Pagani, L., Boulerice, B., & Tremblay, R. E. (1997). The influence of poverty on children's classroom placement and behavior problems. In G. J. Duncan & J. Brooks-Gunn (Eds.), *Consequences of growing up poor* (pp. 311–339). New York, NY: Russell Sage Foundation.

Petterson, S. M., & Albers, A. B. (2001). Effects of poverty and maternal depression on early child development. *Child Development, 72*(6), 1794–1813.

Pianta, R. C., Barnett, W. S., Burchinal, M., & Thornburg, K. R. (2009). The effects of preschool education: What we know, how public policy is or is not aligned with the evidence base, and what we need to know. *Psychological Science in the Public Interest, 10*(2), 49–88.

Presser, H. B. (2003). *Working in a 24/7 economy: Challenges for American families.* New York, NY: Russell Sage Foundation.

Reardon, S. F. (2011). The widening academic achievement gap between the rich and the poor: New evidence and possible explanations. In R. Murnane & G. Duncan (Eds.), *Wither opportunity? Rising 5 inequality and the uncertain life chances of low-income children.* New York, NY: Russell Sage Foundation Press.

Rose-Jacobs, R. Black, M. M., Casey, P. H., Cook, J. T., Cutts, D. B., Chilton, M., … Frank, D. A. (2008). Household food insecurity: Associations with at-risk infant and toddler development. *Pediatrics, 121*(2), 65–72.

Ryan, R. M., Kalil, A., & Leininger, L. (2009). Low-income mothers' private safety nets and children's socioemotional well-being. *Journal of Marriage and Family, 71*(2), 278–297.

Ryan, R. M., Johnson, A., Rigby, E., & Brooks-Gunn, J. (2011). The impact of child care subsidy use on child care quality. *Early Childhood Research Quarterly, 26*(3), 320–331.

Sameroff, A. J., Seifer, R., Baldwin, A., & Baldwin, C. (1993). Stability of intelligence from preschool to adolescence: The influence of social and family risk factors. *Child Development, 64*(1), 80–97.

Schoeni, R. F., & Blank, R. M. (2003). *What has welfare reform accomplished? Impacts on welfare participation, employment, income, poverty, and family structure* (PSC Research Report No. 03–544).

Shonkoff, J. P., & Phillips, D. A. (Eds.). (2000). *From neurons to neighborhoods: The science of early child development.* Washington, DC: National Academy of Sciences.

Skalicky, A., Meyers, A. F., Adams, W. G., Yang, Z., Cook, J. T., & Frank, D. A. (2006). Child food insecurity and iron deficiency anemia in low-income infants and toddlers in the United States. *Maternal and Child Health Journal, 10*(2), 177–185.

Smith, J. R., Brooks-Gunn, J., & Klebanov, P. (1997). Consequences of living in poverty for young children's cognitive and verbal ability and early

school achievement. In G. J. Duncan & J. Brooks-Gunn (Eds.), *Consequences of growing up poor* (pp. 132–189). New York, NY: Russell Sage Foundation.

Stevens, C., Lauinger, B., & Neville, H. (2009). "Differences in the neural mechanisms of selective attention in children from different socioeconomic backgrounds: An event-related brain potential study. *Developmental Science, 12*(4), 634–646.

Sweet, M., & Appelbaum, M. (2004). Is home visiting an effective strategy? A meta-analytic review of home visiting programs for families with young children. *Child Development, 75*(5), 1435–1456.

Taylor, B. A., Dearing, E., & McCartney, K. (2004). Incomes and outcomes in early childhood. *Journal of Human Resources, 39*, 980–1007.

Tran, V., Minton, S., Haldar, S., & Giannarelli, L. (2016). *Child care subsidies under the CCDF program: An overview of policy differences across states and territories as of October 1, 2016.* Washington, DC: The Urban Institute.

Turner, M., & Kingsley, W. T. (2008). *Federal programs for addressing low-income housing needs: A policy primer.* Washington, DC: Urban Institute.

Urban-Brookings Tax Policy Center. (2018). *What is the earned income tax credit?* Retrieved from https://www.taxpolicycenter.org/briefing-book/ what-earned-income-tax-credit

U.S. Department of Agriculture. (2016). *Supplemental Nutrition Assistance Program (SNAP) employment and training best practices study: Final report.*

U.S. Department of Agriculture. (2017). *National and State-Level Estimates of Special Supplemental Nutrition Program for Women, Infants, and Children (WIC) Eligibles and Program Reach in 2014, and Updated Estimates for 2005–2013* (Summary).

U.S. Department of Agriculture. (2018). *Trends in Supplemental Nutrition Assistance Program Participation Rates: Fiscal Year 2010 to Fiscal Year 2016* (Summary).

U.S. Department of Housing and Urban Development. (2018a). *A pilot study of landlord acceptance of Housing Choice Vouchers.* Washington, DC: Office of Policy Development and Research.

U.S. Department of Housing and Urban Development. (2018b). *Rental Assistance Demonstration (RAD).* Retrieved from https://www.hud.gov/ RAD

U.S. Department of Housing and Urban Development. (2019). *HUD's Public Housing Program.* Retrieved from https://www.hud.gov/topics/ rental_assistance/phprog

U.S. Government Accountability Office. (2016). *Child care: Access to subsidies and strategies to manage demand vary across states.* Retrieved from https://www.gao.gov/products/GAO-17-60

Vandell, D. L., Belsky, J., Burchinal, M., Steinberg, L., Vandergrift, N., & NICHD ECCRN. (2010). Do effects of early child care extend to age 15 years? Results from the NICHD study of early child care and youth development. *Child Development, 81*(3), 737–756.

Vogel, C., & Boller, K. (2015). *Early head start family and child experiences survey (Baby FACES) spring 2009-spring 2012.* Ann Arbor, MI: Inter-University Consortium for Political and Social Research.

Votruba-Drzal, E. (2006). Economic disparities in middle childhood: Does income matter? *Developmental Psychology, 42*(6), 1154–1167.

Votruba-Drzal, E., Coley, R. L., & Chase-Lansdale, P. L. (2004). Child care and low-income children's development: Direct and moderated effects. *Child Development, 75*, 296–312.

Waldfogel, J., Craigie, T., & Brooks-Gunn, J. (2010). Fragile families and child wellbeing. *The Future of Children, 20*(2), 87–112.

Weiss, H. (1993). Home visits: Necessary but not sufficient. *The Future of Children, 3*(3), 113–128.

Werner, E. E., & Smith, R. S. (1992). *Overcoming the odds: High risk children from birth to adulthood.* Ithaca, NY: Cornell University Press.

Wheaton, L., & Tran, V., (2018). *The anti-poverty effects of the supplemental nutrition assistance program.* Washington, DC: The Urban Institute.

Witgert, K., Giles, B., & Richardson, A. (2012). *Medicaid financing of early childhood home visiting programs: Options, opportunities, and challenges.* Washington, DC: The Pew Center on the States and the National Academy for State Health Policy.

Xue, Y., Leventhal, T., Brooks-Gunn, J., & Earls, F. (2005). Neighborhood residence and mental health problems of 5- to 11-year-olds. *Archives of General Psychiatry, 62,* 554–563.

Yeung, J., Linver, M., & Brooks-Gunn, J. (2002). How money matters for young children's development: Parental investment and family processes. *Child Development, 73,* 1861–1879.

Yoshikawa, H., Aber, J. L., & Beardslee, W. R. (2012). The effects of poverty on the mental, emotional, and behavioral health of children and youth: Implications for prevention. *American Psychologist, 67*(4), 272–284.

Zhai, F., Brooks-Gunn, J., & Waldfogel, J. (2014). Head Start's impact is contingent on alternative type of care in comparison group. *Developmental Psychology, 50*(12), 2572–2586.

16

The Education of Young Emergent Bilingual Children

An Update and Call for Action

DAVID B. YADEN, JR., MILEIDIS GORT, CAMILLE C. MARTINEZ, AND ROBERT RUEDA

Introduction

The primary focus of this chapter is on the education of young emergent bilingual (EB) learners in the United States between birth and eight years of age. One notable change during the past five years since an earlier chapter (Rueda & Yaden, 2013) in the third edition of this *Handbook* was published is the appearance of numerous summary reports of research from government sources, non-profit organizations, and researchers regarding the education of Pre-K students and students commonly designated as *dual language learners* (DLLs) in particular (e.g., Carnock, 2018; Castro, García, & Markos, 2013; Child Trends, 2014; Espinosa, 2013; Guzman-Orth, Lopez, & Tolentino, 2017; National Institute for Early Education Research [NIEER], 2017; Takanishi & Le Menestrel, 2017; United States Department of Education [USDOE], 2015; Weiland, 2016; Yoshikawa et al., 2013). These and additional reports spell out in great detail several issues and challenges related to the academic achievement of young emergent bilinguals (e.g., Mulligan, Haesdt, & McCarroll, 2012; Mulligan, McCarroll, Flanagan, & Potter, 2018; Rathbun & Zhang, 2016) such as the fragmentation and undereducation of the early childhood workforce (Institute of Medicine [IOM], 2015; Whitebook, McLean, Austin, & Edwards, 2018); inconsistencies in the identification and classification of Pre-K emergent bilingual children within extant programs (Williams, 2014); spotty and incomplete data gathering about the nature of the young emergent bilingual population among states (NIEER, 2017); limited assessment instrumentation in languages other than English (Barrueco, López, Ong, & Lozano, 2012; Guzman-Orth, Lopez, & Tolentino, 2017; USDOE, 2015) as well as the continued prejudice in U.S. schools against bilingual programs in general. Thus, despite repeated analyses indicating the history of academic achievement in bilingual programs (e.g., Collier & Thomas, 2017; Lindholm-Leary & Genesee, 2014; Ramirez, 1992; Thomas & Collier, 2003), the robust economic advantages of having a bilingual workforce (cf. Gandara & Acevedo, 2016), and the well-proven financial impact of participating in early childhood education overall (cf. Elango, Garcia, Heckmann, & Hojman, 2015; Garcia, Heckmann, Leaf, & Prados, 2018) for underserved children speaking languages other than English and for the communities in which they live, purposeful resistance to and failure to fully support young emergent bilingual children, are still very much a reality.

The Benefits of Bilingualism

Given the level of specificity—and converging perspectives and findings—between many of these research syntheses of the emergent bilingual population in terms of demographic statistics, enrollment figures for Pre-K, and lower achievement scores, in this chapter we will only highlight select findings as they provide information about the young emergent bilingual population itself. In addition, we will focus specifically on the system of early education in the country that is struggling to meet the needs of this very vulnerable population. Second, given that the overwhelming consensus of the neuroscience research related to bilingual development in early childhood stresses the cognitive, metacognitive, and social-emotional benefits of learning more than one language (see Ferjan Ramirez & Kuhl, 2017; Halle et al., 2014; Li, Legault, & Litcofsky, 2014; Marian & Shook, 2012; Stocco & Prat, 2014; Takanishi & Le Menestrel, 2017), we will take the stance that the persistent gap in academic performance between young EBs and their monolingual, English-speaking peers, although decreasing slightly (see Reardon & Portillo, 2016), is more of a function of pedagogical, programmatic, and/or policy issues at the state and local institutional levels rather than an inherent limitation of bilingual development itself. The position we take is supported by two recent national reports by the National Academies of Sciences (cf. Takanishi & Le Menestrel, 2017) and the recent joint statement of the Departments of Health and Human Services and Education (DHHS/DOE, 2017) that make it clear that bilingualism not only is a natural outcome of growing up in a multilingual environment, but, in terms of a policy option, should be a national goal to be vigorously pursued:

> Over half of the world's population is estimated to be bilingual or multilingual. Research indicates that supporting bilingualism from early ages can have wide ranging benefits, from providing children cognitive and social advantages early in life, to long term employment opportunities and competitiveness in the workplace later in life. At the same time, data indicate that children who are DLLs in the U.S., on average, lag behind their monolingual English-speaking peers in academic achievement. *These patterns may suggest that there is a mismatch between the learning experiences these children need to meet their potential, and the quality of experiences they are currently receiving* [italics added]. Given the growing number of young children who are DLLs and the sizable proportion of the workforce they will make up in the coming years, ensuring they are prepared for school and do well once they arrive is an economic imperative that will directly influence the competitiveness of the U.S. in an evolving global economy.
>
> (DHHS/DOE, 2017, pp. 1–2)

In earlier versions of this chapter (Rueda & Yaden, 2006, 2013), we focused most heavily on national studies and research that highlighted the gaps in readiness ability and academic performance of young EBs. While these gaps for the most part have stubbornly remained during the past five years, a growing body of brain research on bilingual development in early childhood (e.g., Ferjan Ramirez & Kuhl, 2017; Klein, Mok, Chen, & Watkins, 2014; Marian & Shook, 2012; Ramírez-Esparza, Garcia-Síerra, & Kuhl, 2017) indicates strongly that learning more than one language is something the brain is "hard-wired" to do quite well under supportive conditions in both the home and the school (cf. Takanishi & Le Menestrel, 2017).

Therefore, in this chapter, we will not repeat the already widely published findings of the achievement gaps between emergent bilingual populations, but rather attempt to highlight more of the structural inequities in the Pre-K education system which contribute to these ongoing gaps between monolingual English-speaking and EB populations, all the while failing to capitalize on the language and learning abilities of young EB children (cf. Bauer & Gort, 2012; Escamilla et al., 2013 for similar arguments).

Emergent Bilingual Learners and Other Terminological Distinctions

Finally, we prefer and use throughout this chapter the term *emergent bilingual* (EB) *learner* in place of the label *dual language learner* (DLL). We recognize that the latter terminology appears widely in the literature and in recent definitions by the National Academy of Sciences (Takanishi & Le Menestrel, 2017) and the United States Departments of Health and Human Services and Education (DHHS/DOE,

2017), where the designation DLL primarily refers to young children, birth to five years of age, who are defined as "learning two (or more) languages at the same time, or learning a second language while continuing to develop their first language" (DHHS/DOE, 2017, pp. 2–3). However, occurrence of overlapping definitions of terms is, unfortunately, frequent. For example, in the DHHS/DOE policy statement (2017), children between the ages of 5 and 21 are designated as *English learners* (EL); in the National Academy of Sciences report, Takanishi and Le Menestrel (2017) designate children, ages three to five, as both DLL and EL (English learner), whereas persons after age five learning English are termed as EL. In addition, DLL has often been used to designate children, ages three to eight, as well (cf. Espinosa, 2013).

Nevertheless, our preference in this chapter is to use the term *emergent bilingual* (EB) to cover the age span of children from birth through age five as well as to refer to the larger population of K-12 students, age five to 21 (cf. Takanishi & Le Menestrel, 2017)—our rationale being as follows. In an earlier chapter (Rueda & Yaden, 2013), we pointed out that the term DLL overlaps and is often used interchangeably with the designations of *Limited English Proficient* (LEP), *Languages Other Than English* (LOTE), or *English Learner* (EL). One issue with these latter designations is that they fail to capture the sense of language learning as a *dynamic, developmental and incremental process*. Moreover, they tend to define students along a single dimension, specifically proficiency in English, to the exclusion of the natural language environments they encounter outside of school and to the exclusion of their own daily language practices. Therefore, in the prior edition of this *Handbook*, Rueda and Yaden (2013) purposely used the term *Dual Language Learner* (DLL) to more accurately designate the actual language environments and practices of students.

While we still believe that DLL is a much more asset-oriented term than those used in the past, it still masks, sometimes silences, and, at worst, erases children's current bilingualism-in-process and their potential for developing more advanced bilingualism with continued support, exposure, and experiences (cf. Bauer & Gort, 2012; Garcia & Kleifgen, 2018; Gort & Harris, 2018, for similar arguments). Another unfavorable connotation of the term DLL is that it infers (perhaps unintentionally) a "fractional" view of bilinguals, constructing them as having two discrete language systems that have to be developed separately, when, in fact, bilinguals develop one complex linguistic system (see Cummins, 1991; Grosjean, 2010) that they use at all times to navigate the world and to learn.

That said, we realize that DLL has also been adopted by Head Start (DHHS/DOE, 2017) and the Dual Language Learners National Work Group (Williams, 2015), among others, to refer to young learners, age eight and under, who are learning English in school while continuing to develop basic proficiency in their home/community language. However, the designation DLL ignores the large and growing number of young children entering early childhood educational settings and preschools who are *simultaneous bilinguals*, being raised in bilingual and multilingual homes and in communities where more than one language is spoken and heard. That is, the way in which the DLL label has been constructed around very young children leaves out the recognition of the complex bilingualism of those who grow up bilingual from the early years, who also need development and expansion of their entire language repertoire, and not just "dual" languages as if they were two autonomous entities. Thus, the term *emergent bilingual* (EB) most accurately indexes, both theoretically and practically, the type of language learner who is the object of our attention in this chapter—those young children whose bilingualism is still emerging and will be for years to come.

In the remainder of the chapter, we examine recent work on young EBs particularly synthesizing research on the classification of the population within Pre-K settings as well as assessment and programmatic issues across states. First, we begin by providing some recent data on characteristics of and changes in the profiles of the U.S. population of emergent bilinguals overall, then of school-aged students, and, finally, of young EB children primarily under the age of five. Next, following this survey of recent demographics, in the second and third major sections we summarize some of persistent academic achievement differences between EB and other populations and the prevalence of multilingualism in much of the modern world outside the United States. Our fourth major section speaks directly and primarily to the structural inequities in primarily programmatic and policy issues at the state level and ongoing negative attitudes and prejudices against bilingualism in general. In concluding this chapter, our final two sections set out a "prospective" vision for future research based upon more nuanced research designs based upon intersectionality approaches and a usage-based theory (cf. Tomasello, 2010) of language acquisition which celebrates the language learning capability of human beings and children in particular. Throughout the chapter, we will include characteristics of the broader population of older emergent bilinguals when data regarding the Pre-K years are less consistent. We also on occasion will use the designation DLL or EL if the source we are referencing uses those terms.

A Demographic Overview of the Emergent Bilingual Population

As in the previous two iterations of this chapter (Rueda & Yaden, 2006, 2013), changing demographics in the country continue to be a major factor to consider in the education of all children, but particularly those speaking languages other than English at home. In this section, to provide a broad demographic context, we provide a brief look at the EB population in the nation as a whole, then with school-aged populations, followed by Pre-K enrollment, and, finally, with the early EB Pre-K subgroup.

Languages Spoken at Home in the United States

According to the most recent Census Bureau reports (U.S. Census Bureau, 2015) compiled between 2009 and 2013, nearly 380 different languages are spoken in U.S. homes by the population of persons over five years of age (total est. 291,484,482) with English being spoken by 79%; Spanish by 13%; other Indo-European languages by 3.6%; Asian and Pacific Island languages by 3.3%; and all other languages, including Native American and African, by approximately 1%. Thus, slightly over one in five persons (21%) in the school-aged and adult population (est. 60,361,574) speak a language at home other than English, with Spanish by far being the most predominant with 37,458,470 speakers (62%), comprising nearly two-thirds of the non-English languages spoken at home. The next eight most frequently spoken languages in U.S. homes with between one and three million speakers are Chinese (Cantonese, Mandarin), French, Tagalog, Vietnamese, Korean, German, Arabic, and Russian, together comprising about 20% of languages other than English spoken in U.S. households (World Atlas, 2018).

While it is impossible to tell from these population statistics the levels and proficiency of bilingualism (e.g., English/language X) in the United States, the language question (#14) in the *American Community Survey* (ACS, 2016) includes "How well does this person speak English?" after the identification of the non-English language with the choices of answers being "very well," "well," "not well," and "not at all." Responses to this portion of the question reveal that of the 21% of persons speaking a language other than English at home 8.5% indicate that they cannot speak English "very well," however, implying then that over half (12.5%/21% = 59.5%) of bilingual persons in the United States have a fair amount of bilingualism. The ACS (2016) also provides specific information from Spanish bilinguals who indicate that 5.4% of the 13.1% of Spanish speakers report that they cannot speak English "very well." In addition, of other Indo-European, Asian, Pacific Islander, and Native American languages—all with less than 4% of speakers—roughly one-third of language speakers in each category indicate that they cannot speak English "very well," suggesting, in turn, that some two-thirds of bilingual speakers do speak English at least "well."

In summary then, the overall picture of 21% of persons five-years-old and older in the United States who speak a language other than English is that some six of ten of them speak English "well" or "very well" in addition to their home language. Thus, U.S. schools operate in a societal context where bilingualism has been steadily on the rise.

The K-12 Population of EBs Who Are English Learners

According to the Department of Education, *English learners* (EL, designated as EBs in this report) are defined as

> students who enter school speaking a language other than English . . . whose difficulties in speaking, reading, writing, or understanding the English language may be

sufficient to deny the individual the ability to successfully achieve in classrooms where the language of instruction is English.

(USDOE, p. 43)

While the average percentage of designated EBs in public K-12 classrooms across the nation currently stands at 9.5% (McFarland et al., 2018, p. 70), the variation across states is enormous, from a low of 1% in Virginia to a high of 21% in California. The eight states where school-aged EB students are mostly concentrated at 10% or higher include California (21%), Texas (16.4%), Nevada (16.4%), New Mexico (15.7%), Colorado (11.6%), Alaska (11.5%), Kansas (10.6%), and Washington (10.4%). In general, however, the percentage of EB students has increased in a majority of the states (36 of 50) over the past 15 years (McFarland et al., 2018, p. 71).

Not surprisingly, as of fall 2015, Latino EB students constituted over three quarters (77.7%) of EB student enrollment (see Table 16.1). Arabic and Asian students were the next largest racial/ethnic group, constituting 2.4% and 2.1%, respectively. And, as might be expected, geographically the EB population primarily resides in urban/suburban areas according to census designations (see Figure 16.1).

Finally, as can be seen in Figure 16.2, the K-12 EB population as of 2015 was heavily concentrated in kindergarten (16.3% of all students), first grade (16.5%), and second grade (16.0%), dropping by half (8.2%) at sixth grade and approximately by half again (3.9%) by grade 12 (McFarland et al., 2018, p. 72). However, although accurate counts particularly for Latino EBs are more difficult to come by due to various logistical challenges in data gathering (cf. O'Hare, Mayol-Garcia, Wildsmith, & Torres, 2016), the numbers of EB students, ages three to five, appear to be much larger.

Total Pre-K Enrollment

There have been steadily increasing numbers of Pre-K children enrolled in outside-the-home preschool arrangements over the past five decades (cf. also Paschall, 2019). However, depending upon how data categories are combined by researchers from various census reports, the numbers of young EBs enrolled in the preschool years cannot be specified precisely. In terms of total Pre-K enrollment, the number of three- to five-year-old children participating in preprimary programs has nearly doubled from 1970 to 2016, from just over four million (est. 4,104,000) to nearly eight million (est. 7,776,000), constituting 65% of the total population (est. 12,032,000) of three- to five-year-olds who are enrolled in some public or private preschool arrangement (see Table 16.2).

It is important to note as well that the percentages of enrollment numbers vary by both age and parent educational attainment (often used as a proxy for socioeconomic status). For example, in 2016 more five-year-olds (86%) were enrolled than four-year-olds (66%) than were three-year-olds (42%). In turn, 54% of children, ages three to five, had parents or caregivers with graduate or professional degrees compared to 41% with bachelor's degrees, 35%–37% with associate degrees or some college, and 30%–33% with less than a high diploma or high school/GED (McFarland et al., 2018). Thus, the socioeconomic status of the family and education level of caregivers play major roles in whether children can take advantage of the affordances of high-quality preschool.

Finally, in 2016, the percentage of three- to five-year-olds enrolled in preschool programs was 35% for Black children, 34% for Latino children, 45% for children of Asian race/ethnicity, and 42% for White children. The preschool

Table 16.1 Number and Percentage Distribution of English Language Learner (ELL) Students and Number of ELL Students as a Percent of Total Enrollment, by the Most 11 Most Commonly Reported Home Languages of ELL Students: Fall 2015

Home Language	Number of ELL Students	Percentage Distribution of ELL Students[1]	Number of ELL Students as a Percent of Total Enrollment
Spanish, Castilian	3,741,066	77.1	7.6
Arabic	114,371	2.4	0.2
Chinese	101,347	2.1	0.2
Vietnamese	81,157	1.7	0.2
English[2]	80,333	1.7	0.2
Somali	34,813	0.7	0.1
Hmong	34,813	0.7	0.1
Russian	33,057	0.7	0.1
Haitian, Haitian Creole	30,231	0.6	0.1
Tagalog	27,277	0.6	0.1
Korean	27,268	0.6	0,1

[1] Detail does not sum to 100% because not all categories are reported.

[2] Examples of situations in which English might be reported as an ELL student's home language include students who live in multilingual households and students adopted from other countries who speak English at home but also have been raised speaking another language.

Source: U.S. Department of Education. National Center for Education Statistics, ED*Facts* file 141, Data Group 678, extracted July 21, 2017; and Common Core of Data (CCD), "State Nonfiscal Survey of Public Elementary and Secondary Education," 2015–2016. See *Digest of Education Statistics 2017*, table 204.27. Retrieved from https://nces.ed.gov/pubs2018/2018144.pdf.

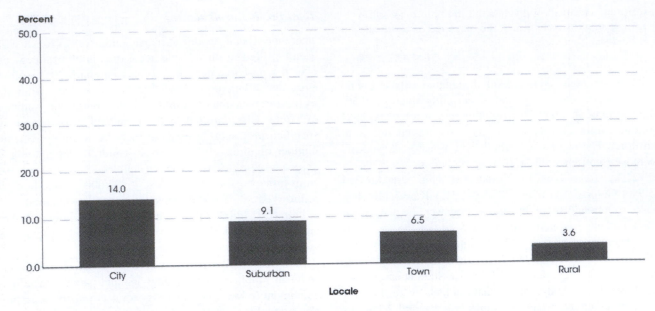

Figure 16.1 Percentage of public school students who were English language learners, by locale: Fall 2015.

Source: U.S. Department of Education, National Center for Education Statistics, Common Core of Data (CCD), "Local Education Agency Universe Survey," 2015–2016, See *Digest of Education Statistics 2017*, table 214.40. Retrieved from https://nces.ed.gov/pubs2018/2018144.pdf

Note: Data are based on locales of school districts.

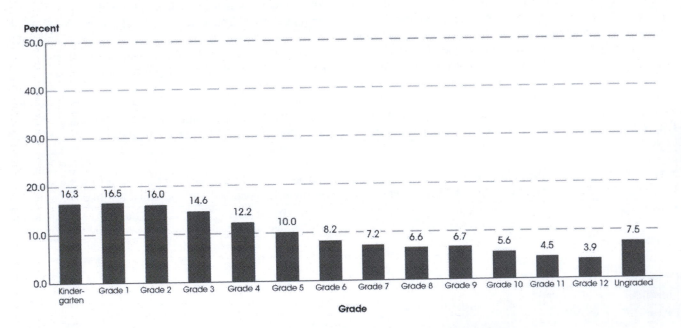

Figure 16.2 Percentage of public K-12 students who were English language learners, by grade level: Fall 2015.

Source: U.S. Department of Education, National Center for Education Statistics, ED*Facts* file 141, Data Group 678, extracted July 21,2017; and Common Core of Data (CCD), "State Nonfiscal Survey of Public Elementary and Secondary Education," 2015–2016. See *Digest of Education Statistics 2017*, table 204.27. Retrieved from https://nces.ed.gov/pubs2018/2018144.pdf

enrollment rates of three- to five-year-olds who were Pacific Islander (40%), American Indian/Alaska Native (41%), and of two or more races (41%) were not measurably different from the preschool enrollment rates of children from other racial/ethnic groups (McFarland et al., 2018).

It is of interest as well that the United States is ranked 30th of 33 countries making up the Organization for Economic Cooperation and Development (OECD) with 54% of three- and five-year-olds enrolled in Pre-K compared to 100% of children in the United Kingdom, Israel, and France (McFarland et al., 2018). The OECD average is 80%; the United States is only ranked higher than Canada (25% of threes and fours enrolled), Switzerland (25%), and Turkey (21%).

Table 16.2 Enrollment of Three-, Four-, and Five-Year-Old Children in Preprimary Programs, by Age of Child, Level of Program, and Attendance Status: Selected Years, 1970 through 2016

[Standard errors appear in parentheses]

Age of child, level and control of program, and attendance status	1970	1980	1990	1995[1]	2000[1]	2003[1]	2005[1]	2010[1,2]	2014[1,2]	2015[1,2]	2016[1,2]
1	2	3	4	5	6	7	8	9	10	11	12
3 to 5 years old[3]											
Total population (in thousands)	10,949 (131.4)	9,284 (121.0)	11,207 (145.5)	12,518 (153.7)	11,858 (155.3)	12,204 (149.6)	12,134 (149.1)	12,949 (80.4)	12,191 (79.1)	11,958 (79.8)	12,032 (113.7)
Enrollment of three- to five-year-olds (in thousands)											
Total	4,104 (78.9)	4,878 (75.0)	6,659 (88.8)	7,739 (86.4)	7,592 (86.2)	7,921 (82.6)	7,801 (82.7)	8,246 (107.3)	7,890 (99.9)	7,681 (107.3)	7,776 (103.5)
Level and attendance status											
Preschool	1,094 (48.9)	1,981 (61.5)	3,379 (83.0)	4,331 (84.7)	4,326 (86.5)	4,859 (84.7)	4,529 (83.4)	4,797 (94.5)	4,658 (94.0)	4,475 (96.9)	4,701 (116.0)
Full-day	291 (26.2)	681 (39.1)	1,150 (54.9)	1,951 (64.5)	2,049 (67.9)	2,479 (69.6)	2,275 (67.3)	2,297 (81.4)	2,288 (76.9)	2,264 (73.0)	2,544 (91.0)
Part-day	803 (42.5)	1,301 (52.1)	2,229 (72.2)	2,381 (69.8)	2,277 (70.8)	2,380 (68.5)	2,255 (67.1)	2,500 (75.4)	2,370 (77.1)	2,211 (81.3)	2,157 (86.7)
Kindergarten	3,010 (72.8)	2,897 (69.6)	3,280 (82.3)	3,408 (79.2)	3,266 (80.3)	3,062 (75.0)	3,272 (76.6)	3,449 (75.9)	3,233 (75.0)	3,207 (84.3)	3,075 (92.9)
Full-day	407 (30.9)	870 (43.8)	1,428 (60.3)	1,738 (61.5)	1,959 (66.7)	1,950 (63.4)	2,274 (67.3)	2,516 (69.7)	2,576 (72.2)	2,613 (77.3)	2,494 (86.7)
Part-day	2,603 (69.4)	2,026 (62.0)	1,853 (67.2)	1,670 (60.5)	1,307 (56.3)	1,112 (49.8)	998 (47.4)	932 (53.4)	657 (42.9)	594 (42.3)	581 (44.8)
Control											
Public	2,830 (71.4)	3,066 (70.6)	3,971 (86.5)	4,750 (86.3)	4,847 (88.3)	5,051 (85.2)	5,213 (85.4)	5,829 (105.5)	5,543 (93.9)	5,426 (95.6)	5,586 (98.7)
Private	1,274 (52.3)	1,812 (59.5)	2,688 (77.2)	2,989 (75.8)	2,745 (75.8)	2,870 (73.4)	2,588 (70.7)	2,417 (77.1)	2,348 (76.5)	2,255 (70.5)	2,190 (83.4)
Attendance status											
Full-day	698 (39.8)	1,551 (56.0)	2,577 (76.1)	3,689 (81.1)	4,008 (85.0)	4,429 (83.2)	4,548 (83.5)	4,813 (98.5)	4,864 (100.4)	4,877 (101.5)	5,038 (105.0)
Part-day	3,406 (75.5)	3,327 (72.0)	4,082 (87.0)	4,051 (83.2)	3,584 (82.5)	3,492 (78.2)	3,253 (76.4)	3,432 (88.5)	3,027 (79.1)	2,804 (91.6)	2,738 (87.7)
Percent of three- to five-year-olds enrolled											
Total	37.5 (0.72)	52.5 (0.81)	59.4 (0.79)	61.8 (0.69)	64.0 (0.73)	64.9 (0.68)	64.3 (0.68)	63.7 (0.66)	64.7 (0.70)	64.2 (0.79)	64.6 (0.81)
Full-day as a percent of total enrollment	17.0 (0.91)	31.8 (1.04)	38.7 (1.02)	47.7 (0.90)	52.8 (0.95)	55.9 (0.87)	58.3 (0.87)	58.4 (0.92)	61.6 (0.93)	63.5 (1.04)	64.8 (1.03)
Full-day preschool as a percent of total preschool enrollment	26.6 (2.08)	34.3 (1.66)	34.0 (1.39)	45.0 (1.20)	47.4 (1.25)	51.0 (1.12)	50.2 (1.16)	47.9 (1.31)	49.1 (1.32)	50.6 (1.34)	54.1 (1.45)
Full-day kindergarten as a percent of total kindergarten enrollment	13.5 (0.97)	30.0 (1.33)	43.5 (1.48)	51.0 (1.36)	60.0 (1.41)	63.7 (1.36)	69.5 (1.26)	73.0 (1.38)	79.7 (1.24)	81.5 (1.21)	81.1 (1.34)

[1] Beginning in 1994, preprimary enrollment data were collected using new procedures. Data may not be comparable to figures for earlier years.

[2] Beginning in 2010, standard errors were computed using replicate weights, which produced more precise values than the generalized variance function methodology used in prior years.

[3] Enrollment data for five-year-olds include only those students in preprimary programs and do not include those enrolled in primary programs.

Note: Preprimary programs include kindergarten and preschool (or nursery school) programs. "Preschool," which was referred to as "nursery school" in previous versions of this table, is defined as a group or class that is organized to provide educational experiences for children during the year or years preceding kindergarten. Data are based on sample surveys of the civilian noninstitutionalized population, which excludes persons living in institutions (e.g., prisons or nursing facilities). Detail may not sum to totals because of rounding.

Source: U.S. Department of Commerce, Census Bureau, Current Population Survey (CPS), October, 1970 through 2016. (This table was prepared August 2017.) Retrieved from https://nces.ed.gov/pubs2017/2017094.pdf

The EB Early Childhood Population

In addition to the various techniques researchers employ in using census databases which generate different figures for EB categories as mentioned above, another barrier to getting accurate data on the EB population in preschool is the fact that, according to the National Institute of Early Education Research (NIEER), only 24 states actually collect information about home language in state-funded preschool programs (NIEER, 2017). According to NIEER's analysis, in the 24 states where data are collected, the EB average enrollment is 29%, whereas in state-funded preschools nationwide nearly one out of four (23%) young Pre-K students is an EB. The Migration Policy Institute, on the other hand, calculates that the general population of EB students (birth to age eight) in the country is almost a third (32%) with somewhat less than half of that portion (41.5%) of children three to four years of age in an out-of-the home preschool arrangement either half or full day (Park, O'Toole, & Katsiaficas, 2017, p. 3). Head Start (ACF, 2017), on the other hand, reports a slightly lower percentage (29% vs. 32%) of children speaking languages other than English at home. Additionally, Park et al. (2017) list the top five home languages of the parents of the EB population nationwide as being Spanish (59%) and Chinese (3.3%) with Tagalog, Vietnamese, and Arabic being all at 1.9%. However, of the 29% of EB students in Head Start, some 80% (79.3%) of that population speaks Spanish as the primary language at home (ACF, 2017).

Thus, depending upon how the calculation is made, it is probably safe to say that at least between one-fourth and one-third of the nation's children between the ages of three and five who are enrolled in preschool or preprimary programs in the United States can be classified as emergent bilinguals and that between 60% and 75% of young EBs have Spanish as a home language (Baker & Páez, 2018). However, there is no doubt that in some urban areas higher concentrations of young emergent bilingual children will be found in local Pre-K settings and that variations in home language exist as well.

Academic Achievement of the Elementary and Preschool EB Populations

Unfortunately, the incidence of reading failure in English among EB populations as indexed by national measures remains high particularly within low-income families, ethnic minority groups, and students who have been designated as English learners across the nation through the primary grades. While we will raise questions later in the chapter about the explanatory and theoretical nature of such findings as tied to these traditional categories, their ubiquity remains in the literature.

Score Differences between EBs and Non-EBs by Fourth Grade

For example, NAEP data for fourth grade in 2015 show that the scaled scores of the population of EBs compared to their non-EB peers is on average 37 points lower in reading (189 vs. 226) and 25 points lower in math (218 vs. 243; Park et al., 2017). Similar findings come from the fourth-grade round of the Early Childhood Longitudinal Study tracking children who began kindergarten in 2011 and finished fourth grade in 2015. Scaled scores for students from families where English was not the home language scored lower in reading (119.1 vs. 124.6), math (106.4 vs. 111.6), and science (61.2 vs. 67.7) (Mulligan et al., 2018). In addition, White and Asian non-Hispanic fourth-grade students scored higher in all subjects than their Black (non-Hispanic), Latino, AIAN, and Pacific Island peers.

Score Differences between EBs and Non-EBs Beginning Kindergarten

Perhaps as disturbing as the differences are at mid-elementary for children designated as EBs is the fact that similar disparities between ethnicity/race and language appear at the beginning of kindergarten also and fail to be ameliorated by additional time in formal education (cf. Rathbun & Zhang, 2016). Many of these differences detected early on reflect variations in childcare arrangements, level of education, and the income of caregivers—gaps which grow rather than diminish under the influence of subsequent schooling. Findings from reports of national studies (see Mulligan et al., 2012; Rathbun & Zhang, 2016) of the achievement as measured in English of first-time kindergartners in the ECLS-K:2011 longitudinal study indicate that in the areas of reading, mathematics, executive functioning, and approaches to learning the following patterns can be observed:

- Asian first-time kindergartners had higher reading and math scores than first-time kindergartners of other race/ethnicities.
- White first-time kindergartners had higher reading and math scores than Black, Latino, Native Hawaiian/Pacific Islander, and American Indian/Alaska Native students.
- Black students scored higher than Latino students on the reading assessment.
- Native Hawaiian/Pacific Islanders had higher math scores than Latinos.
- First-time kindergartners with a primary home language of English scored higher in reading and math than those coming from homes with a primary home language other than English. (Mulligan et al., 2012, p. 3)

In a second, more detailed analysis (Rathbun & Zhang, 2016) of these first-time kindergarten data from the ECLS-K:2011 multiple regression techniques were used to control several demographic variables at a time. Findings revealed that the gaps between English speakers and EBs were, nonetheless, significant, favoring the English speakers across performances in reading, mathematics, and cognitive flexibility or executive functioning. These differences in achievement were also correlated with the childcare arrangement the year before kindergarten with children in center-based care outperforming children in all other childcare arrangements whether home-based relative- or nonrelative care (Rathbun & Zhang, 2016, p. 17).

What is apparent from the multivariate analyses (cf. Rathbun & Zhang, 2016) of the ECLS-K:2011 study is that the three- to four-year-old EB population—which is primarily Latino—has been characterized by the standard statistical categories in which score performances are typically suppressed—limited center-based care before kindergarten, non-English home language, income below 200% of the federal poverty level and non-White race/ethnicity. Interestingly, as Rathbun and Zhang (2016) have pointed out, for many of these categories, particularly childcare arrangements, the percentages of participating children have not changed appreciably between 1995 and 2012, according to the National Household Education Surveys (Mamedova & Redford, 2019), with the exception that slightly more Latino children have entered center-based care, although the more prevalent trend is for low-income Latino families to choose relative care (cf. Mendez & Crosby, 2018).

The score differences recently reported by Mulligan et al. (2012, 2018) and Rathbun and Zhang (2016) particularly between Latino EBs and their White/Asian English-speaking counterparts at the beginning of kindergarten have been a consistent finding with every prior analysis of the series of Early Childhood Longitudinal Studies, including ECLS-K:1998–1999 and ECLS-B:2001–2002, results that were reported in our previous chapter (Rueda & Yaden, 2013) in this volume and will not be repeated here. Interestingly, in their further detailed analysis of ECLS-K:1998–1999 data, Reardon and Galindo (2009) point out that the Latino/White gap narrows most quickly in the early elementary grades before flattening out by fifth grade, suggesting that as young Latino EBs learn English early on their academic performance initially increases during the first few primary grades. However, since the development of English for academic purposes is slow and complex, developing over four to seven years according to research (cf. Espinosa, 2013), opportunities for enriched language support and exposure to more sophisticated content are reduced due to diminished programmatic affordances and, in some cases, policies which restrict the use of primary languages altogether. Since the overwhelming consensus of research (DHHS/DOE, 2017) is that high-quality first- and second-language support and programming results in increased dual language proficiency and intellectual gains in academic content, we turn now to a discussion of extant barriers primarily at the state and local levels which impede overcoming the persistent, but, we believe, ameliorable achievement gaps.

International Multilingualism as Public Health and Economic Issues

On the larger world stage, it is clear that multilingualism is viewed not only as a scholarly interest, but also as an international necessity for peace and global health. For example, the World Health Organization (WHO) in its 2008 resolution "Multilingualism: A plan of action" stated that "In order to work effectively, WHO needs to exchange information and communicate in multiple languages. Language should not be a barrier to fulfilling its mandate: to address the health needs of Member States. A multilingual WHO is better equipped to communicate health messages, to produce and disseminate health information, and to generate, share, and use knowledge about health in an equitable manner (WHO, 2008)." In addition, organizations like the International Association of Bilingualism with its juried outlet the *International Journal of Multilingualism* provide a global forum for discussing both the most pressing theoretical and applied issues in the learning of more than one language.

In order to better understand the inequities faced by emergent bilinguals in U.S. Pre-K educational settings, it is important to invoke this wider context of language learning outside the United States—both to provide a comparison of scientific findings regarding bilingualism as and to understand the current capacity of U.S. schooling to meet the often- and currently stated goal of American business that "a strong education system is crucial to preparing people for good jobs and bright futures and sustaining a 21st century workforce that can compete in the global economy" (U.S. Chamber of Commerce, 2019). If "globally competitive" includes being bilingual, then the United States remains far behind with an average percentage of 21% (U.S. Census Bureau, 2015) of persons speaking a language other than English whereas the average percentage across the 28 countries of the European Union (EU) who are highly proficient in at least two languages is nearly six of ten persons (59%, Eurostat, 2015) with an additional 89% who self-report that they feel comfortable conversing in a language other than their mother tongue (Eurostat, 2015).

These percentages are important since they cast doubt on the unfounded notion among some researchers and educators that learning more than one language is "burdensome" (cf. Takanishi & Le Menestrel, 2017, p. 2), a view most prevalent in studies of bilingualism during the first half of the century (see Grosjean, 2010, 2011 for an analysis). In stark opposition to this belief, a contrasting view emerges from the substantial body of recent language research since then that supports the current joint policy statement by the U.S. Departments of Health and Human Services and Education (2017) that "there is no scientific research that suggests that learning multiple languages—or being bilingual—can lead to a developmental delay for children" (p. 6). Further, it is all the more important to realize that while being exposed early in life to a second language is preferred, 68% of respondents to a survey by the EU indicated that they learned their second language while in school (Eurostat, 2015).

Thus, from our point of view, there is no justifiable, scientific, or instructional reason for why the achievement gap between emergent bilingual students and monolingual, English-speaking students in U.S. schools remains as large as it is—particularly if the schooling system portends to be more than simply an enabler of the initial differences in socioeconomic status, parent education, or Pre-K experience at the outset.

We now turn to a discussion of some of the hypothesized reasons why the current educational system remains stagnant in educating its increasing population of emergent bilingual learners, including the lack of purposeful data gathering on the bilingual population; limited approaches to assessment and failure to understand the language strengths of emergent bilingual students; poorly designed instructional programs; an undereducated and overwhelmingly English monolingual workforce; and prejudice against the largest group of emergent bilingual students in schools—Spanish speakers (cf. DHHS/DOE, 2017).

Challenges and Barriers to Improved Education for Young Emergent Bilingual Children

Inconsistent Data Gathering in Programs Serving Young EBs

If it can be assumed that good data are one of the first requirements for making sound educational decisions, then it is little wonder that decision-making is hampered by the relative lack of information on very young emergent bilingual children which is difficult to come by. In the second year of their reporting on the status of EB students in state-funded preschools in the *State Preschool Yearbook*, the National Institute for Early Education Research (Friedman-Krauss et al., 2017) found that only 24 states report specific statistics on the home languages of emergent bilinguals at the preschool level—even though there are some 60 state-funded Pre-K programs in the country (cf. also Carnock, 2018). The inconsistencies among states regarding explicit support policies—note the "none" in Table 16.3—for young emergent bilinguals as well as workforce requirements and training, instruction in the home language, and bilingual assessment procedures are dramatically illustrated in Table 16.3. Thus, over half of the states in the nation that have a federally funded Pre-K program fail to provide explicit information as to how those programs support the nearly one-third of children who would be designated as emergent bilinguals.

In addition, despite current, forward-looking federal policies on early bilingual development and teaching (DHHS/DOE, 2017)—born of a half century or more of painful discrimination against non-English speaking families and their children—state policies (or lack thereof) and inadequate programming for language supports still pose the greatest impediment to overall systemic change. As seen in Figure 16.3 from the *2018 Early Childhood Workforce Index* published by the Center for the Study of Childcare Employment (Whitebook et al., 2018), of the five major dimensions in the study of the early childhood workforce—compensation, workforce data, qualifications, financial resources, and workforce environment—44 of 50 states are deemed "stalled" on compensation, one of the key cornerstones in fostering significant change in the early education system (see also Allen & Backes, 2018). Only mechanisms for collecting better data about the workforce itself are "making headway," but only in slightly less than half of the states.

Limited Bilingual Assessment in Languages Other than English

While it has been a consistent recommendation from professional bodies (Takanishi & Le Menestrel, 2017), researchers (e.g., Halle, Hair, Wandner, McNamera, & Chien, 2012), and federal agencies (DHHS/DOE, 2017; Office of Head Start, 2015) that emergent bilingual children be assessed in both their home and second language, this seldom seems to be the practice, particularly at the Pre-K level, despite the fact that there has been a dramatic increase in the availability of assessments in languages other than English, particularly in Spanish (Barrueco et al., 2012; Mahoney, 2017; Stefanakis, 1999). Some of the reasons for this dearth of bilingual assessment practices include inadequate translations from English to another language and the subsequent psychometric issues which arise (Barrueco et al., 2012), lack of training in standardized test interpretation (Espinosa & Garcia, 2012), and what Barrueco et al. (2012) have termed *rater effects* or "a systematic source of variability in ratings or assessment scores that is attributable to the person conducting the assessment and not to the child's actual performance or behavior" (p. 8), a variability most associated with the administration of "authentic" or informal measures.

Whatever these reasons, the human consequences of misdiagnosing a child due to the failure of assessing them in their home language at the beginning of school are poignantly and tragically represented by the case of "Robby," as detailed in the National Academy of Sciences volume *Promoting the educational success of children and youth learning English: Promising futures* (Takanishi & Le Menestrel, 2017, pp. 394–400). Erroneously classified as an English-speaking child at the beginning of kindergarten, his eventual trajectory into special education was only realized to be mistaken at the beginning of middle school. A brief excerpt, worth quoting in some length, from the report appears below:

> Finally, with the help of an attorney, Robby's parents were able to schedule another IEP meeting. At this meeting, current and former teachers, psychologists, speech therapists, counselors, special education administrators, resource teachers, and specialists lined up to present arguments for the need to place Robby in an [Non-Severely Handicapped/Special Day Class] NSH/SDC school. As part of the opposition, Robby's parents prepared a statement, in Spanish, presenting their objections. Then, Robby's advocates presented his case. *First, Robby knew no English when he started school, and Proposition 227 notwithstanding, under the Supreme Court's ruling in Lau v. Nichols, the school had an obligation to help him overcome the language barrier between him and the school's curriculum* [italics added]. Second, despite the

Table 16.3 Policy Requirements Related to Serving Preschool DLLs

State/Program	Approved Written Plan for Supporting DLLs Is Required	Extra Funding Allocated for Serving DLLs	Bilingual Instruction is Permitted	Monitoring Focused on the Quality of Bilingual Instruction	Children are Screened in Their Home Language	Children are Assessed in Their Home Language	DLLs are Placed in Classes with Other Children with Same Home Language	Polices to Support Families of Preschool DLLs	Staff have Training/ Qualifications Related to Working with DLLs	Total Policy Supports for Preschool DLLs
Alabama*	✓		✓		✓	✓	✓	✓		6
Alaska										None
Arizona										None
Arkansas*										None
California SPP*		✓	✓		✓	✓				4
California TK	✓	✓	✓	✓				✓	✓	6
Colorado			✓					✓		2
Connecticut CDCC										None
Connecticut SR										None
Connecticut Smart Start*										None
Delaware			✓	✓	✓	✓		✓		5
District of Columbia		✓	✓		✓	✓		✓		5
Florida										None
Georgia*			✓					✓		2
Hawaii*			✓					✓		2
Illinois*			✓	✓	✓	✓				4
Indiana*					✓	✓		✓	✓	4
Iowa Shared Visions	✓		✓		✓	✓		✓		5
Iowa SWVPP*	✓		✓		✓	✓		✓		5
Kansas Preschool	✓	✓	✓	✓	✓	✓		✓		7
Kansas State Pre-K	✓	✓	✓	✓	✓	✓	✓	✓		8
Kentucky*										None

(Continued)

Table 16.3 (Continued)

State/Program	Approved Written Plan for Supporting DLLs Is Required	Extra Funding Allocated for Serving DLLs	Bilingual Instruction is Permitted	Monitoring Focused on the Quality of Bilingual Instruction	Children are Screened in Their Home Language	Children are Assessed in Their Home Language	DLLs are Placed in Classes with Other Children with Same Home Language	Policies to Support Families of Preschool DLLs	Staff have Training/Qualifications Related to Working with DLLs	Total Policy Supports for Preschool DLLs
Louisiana 8(g)										None
Louisiana LA 4										None
Louisiana NSECD										None
Maine*	✓	✓	✓	✓	✓	✓	✓	✓	✓	9
Maryland										None
Massachusetts IPLE*										None
Massachusetts UPK			✓					✓		2
Michigan			✓							1
Minnesota HdSt	✓		✓	✓	✓	✓		✓	✓	7
Minnesota VPK		✓	✓					✓	✓	4
Mississippi										None
Missouri*										None
Nebraska			✓		✓					2
Nevada*		✓	✓	✓	✓	✓	✓	✓		7
New Jersey Abbott*	✓		✓	✓	✓			✓		5
New Jersey ECPA	✓		✓	✓	✓			✓		5
New Jersey ELLI	✓		✓	✓	✓			✓		5
New Mexico*			✓		✓	✓		✓		4
New York	✓		✓	✓	✓	✓		✓		6
North Carolina	✓		✓		✓			✓		4
Ohio										None

State/Program	Approved Written Plan for Supporting DLLs Is Required	Extra Funding Allocated for Serving DLLs	Bilingual Instruction is Permitted	Monitoring Focused on the Quality of Bilingual Instruction	Children are Screened in Their Home Language	Children are Assessed in Their Home Language	DLLs are Placed in Classes with Other Children with Same Home Language	Polices to Support Families of Preschool DLLs	Staff have Training/Qualifications Related to Working with DLLs	Total Policy Supports for Preschool DLLs
Oklahoma*		✓	✓					✓	✓	4
Oregon HdSt*			✓		✓	✓		✓		4
Oregon Preschool Promise*										None
Pennsylvania RTL										None
Pennsylvania HSSAP										None
Pennsylvania K4 & SBPK										None
Pennsylvania PKC			✓							2
Rhode Island*	✓	✓	✓		✓	✓		✓		6
South Carolina*	✓		✓		✓	✓		✓		5
Tennessee			✓					✓		2
Texas*	✓	✓	✓	✓	✓	✓		✓	✓	8
Vermont*										None
Virginia										None
Washington*			✓					✓		2
West Virginia*	✓	✓	✓	✓	✓	✓		✓		6
Wisconsin 4K										None
Wisconsin HdSt										None
Total	17	11	35	14	21	19	4	33	7	
Guam										None

* State preschool programs reported enrollment by home language or DLL status.

Source: NIEER State of the preschool, p. 32, DLL Table 2: Policy requirements related to serving preschool DLLs. Retrieved from http://nieer.org/wp-content/uploads/2018/04/YB2017_DLL-Special-Report.pdf

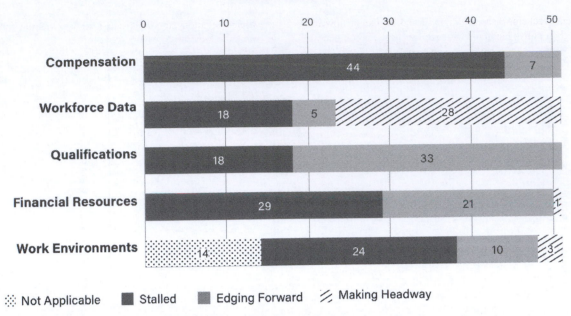

Figure 16.3 State assessments for early childhood workforce policies.

Source: Early Childhood Workforce Index 2018, Figure 1.3, p. 8. Retrieved from https://cscce.berkeley.edu/early-childhood-workforce-2018-index/

Note: The 14 states identified as "not applicable" under the Work Environments category could not be assessed due to a lack of data in the QRIS compendium. Not all of these states lack a QRIS. For more information, see Work Environments, p. 81.

evidence presented of "language deficiencies and severe linguistic disorders," Robby's language development had been normal until he started school. Third, the results of the psychoeducational testing appeared to be flawed: even disregarding the questionable use of tests normed on native speakers of English with a child who was clearly an EL, it appeared that the district's school psychologist based her finding on two subtests that came at the end of the testing session—the only two parts in which Robby's performance fell below the cut-off score. When another psychologist tested Robby again, he performed above the cut-off on equivalent tests.

(pp. 399–400)

Despite the fact that the school psychologist who originally tested Robby apologized for the initial misdiagnosis in kindergarten, and that Robby was able to enroll in another middle school in which he made the honor roll in junior high, maintained a solid B average through high school, and was in college when this story was published (Takanishi & Le Menestrel, 2017), the trauma to both Robby and his family which was entirely of the school's making as a result of improper assessment practices and the policies which supported it is unacceptable and avoidable. That it took nearly half of Robby's school life before he was recognized as a bilingual child and legal pressure to bring the school officials to the table is an egregious miscarriage of educational professionalism to be sure. Still the overall absence of sufficiently reliable assessment instruments has prompted this statement from the Departments of Health and Human Services and Education:

> Valid and reliable developmental and behavioral screening tools and assessment that measure children's progress in learning across domains are critical for providing high-quality, individualized early learning experiences. . . . [However,] most

tools are not normed and have not been validated for use with children who are DLLs and their families, and most are not translated into the many languages America's children speak at home. Additionally, in instances where valid and reliable tools are available – such as tools in Spanish – staff may not have the capacity to interpret and communicate the findings in a meaningful way.

(DHHS/DOE, 2017, p. 12)

Under-Resourced Early Childhood Curriculum and Reclassification Policy Conflicts

Even though the extensive analysis of the early childhood workforce carried out by the Institute of Medicine and the National Research Council (see Allen & Kelly, 2015) resulted in a recommendation that educators working with young children—including emergent bilinguals—have the "ability to advance the learning and development of children who are dual language learners" (Chapter 12, Box 12.2, p. 9), designing better programs with more knowledgeable teachers of young emergent bilinguals has been an ongoing theme for the past two decades in earlier volumes of research syntheses of early childhood research, development, and education by the National Academies of Sciences, Engineering and Medicine and the National Research Council (NRC) (e.g., Bowman, Donovan, & Burns, 2000; Shonkoff & Phillips, 2000; Snow, Burns, & Griffin, 1998). For example, in one of the most widely cited of these NRC reports, Snow et al. (1998) wrote 20 years ago that

> If language-minority children arrive at school with no proficiency in English but speaking a language for which there are instructional guides, learning materials, and locally available

proficient teachers, these children should be taught how to read in their native language while acquiring oral proficiency in English and subsequently taught to extend their skills to reading in English.

(Snow et al., 1998, p. 325)

These authors also recommended that young English learners be assessed in their most dominant language to ensure that their full language proficiency across languages was recognized. However, this recommendation—made again in recent reports (cf. Barrueco et al., 2012; DHHS/DOE, 2017)—for the most part has failed to be taken up in any large scale in the majority of early childhood programs.

It is a discouraging fact as well that discussions of the "fragmentation" of the early childhood workforce have remained constant over two decades. In their seminal report on early childhood development, *Neurons to neighborhoods*, Shonkoff and Phillips (2000) wrote the following:

Early childhood policies and practices are highly fragmented, with complex and confusing points of entry that are particularly problematic for underserved segments of the population and those with special needs. This lack of an integrative early childhood infrastructure makes it difficult to advance prevention-oriented initiatives for all children and to coordinate services for those with complex problems.

(p. 12)

This observation, however, has been nearly repeated verbatim in the recent analyses of the "chaos" of the early childhood education system. As Williams (2015) has observed:

This policy chaos translates into widespread confusion for how DLLs experience public education. In most cases, reclassification standards seem arbitrary; they appear to be completely detached from states' other DLL policies as well as the most recent research on what these students need. In addition, given that DLLs' families appear to be especially likely to move during their children's schooling, diverse reclassification standards can seriously disrupt these students' educations.

(p. 2)

Three recent reports, however (see Allen & Backes, 2018; Allen & Kelly, 2015; Whitebook et al., 2018), have directly confronted the fact that there has been very little success in improving either the skills of the early childhood workforce or the inadequate, unsystematic financing structure of the Pre-K educational system overall—both of which have direct impacts on the quality and programming for young emergent bilingual children.

English Monolingualism in the ECE Workforce

Further complicating the education of young emergent bilinguals is the fact that two-thirds to three-quarters of the staff in center-based early childhood settings (Whitebook et al, 2018) speak only English (see Figure 16.4). The general English monolingualism of center-based preschool staff in the nation stands in contrast to Head Start figures, for example, where of the one out of three enrolled preschool students speaking a language other than English, some 80% are Spanish speakers (Administration for Children and Families (ACF), 2017).

Thus, it becomes a perplexing dilemma as to just how any of the recommendations of several of the national studies (e.g., Allen & Backes, 2018; Takanishi & Le Menestrel, 2017) regarding emergent bilinguals such as those from Institute of Medicine (Allen & Kelly, 2015) will actually get implemented.

Professionals need to be able to support diverse populations. Care and education professionals, with the support of the systems in which they practice, need to be able to respectfully, effectively, and equitably serve children from backgrounds that are diverse with respect to family structure, socioeconomic status, race, ethnicity, culture, language, and ability.

(p. 494)

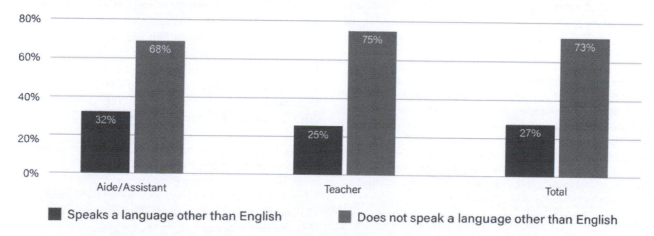

Figure 16.4 Languages spoken by center-based staff by job role: national.

Source: *Early Childhood Workforce Index 2018*, Figure 2.1, p. 22. Retrieved from https://cscce.berkeley.edu/early-childhood-workforce-2018-index/

Note: The NSECE asked center-based teaching staff, "Do you speak a language other than English?": thus, from the available data, we cannot distinguish those who speak English and another language from those who only speak a language other than English.

Ongoing Prejudice and Deficit-Oriented Research Approaches

In our view, the recommendations directly above will have little "teeth," as it were, particularly in view of the outright and frequent prejudice against non-English speakers as described in the recent joint DHHS/DOE (2017) statement regarding challenges and barriers in improving the education system for young bilingual students and their families. In discussing the "implicit and explicit biases" against emergent bilingual children, the joint statement reads:

> Families who are limited in their English proficiency, immigrant families, children of color, and children who are EBs often face explicit and implicit bias and discrimination across many societal institutions, including early learning and education institutions. This may manifest itself through institutional policies and through practices and uneven power dynamics at the individual level. In both cases, these dynamics stand in the way of attending to the developmental and learning needs of these populations.
>
> (p. 10)

Another pernicious barrier, we believe, that is impeding a better understanding of the dynamics of becoming bi- and/or multilingual is the view that young bilingual learners face a "word" or "vocabulary gap"—a highly contested issue (see Adair, Sanchez-Suzuki Colgrove, & McManus, 2017; Avineri et al., 2015; Baugh, 2017; Duran, 2017; Dudley-Marling & Lucas, 2009; Johnson, Avineri, & Johnson, 2017 for arguments) originally derived from the Hart and Risley (1995) study which posited a 20-million "word gap" between white-collar and working-class children in America based upon the lack of conversation in homes of the latter. However, the results of this study are improperly generalized to EB populations and used to ignore the languaging abilities that EBs bring to the task of becoming bilingual, framing them into a never-ending deficit orientation (e.g., Hindman, Wasik, & Snell, 2016; Neuman, Neuman, Dwyer, 2011). However, as Anders, Yaden, Da Silva Iddings, Katz, and Rogers (2016) have stated, much of the discussion of the achievement gaps of children in poverty—many of whom are emergent bilinguals—is

> unfortunately abetted by research in the field which fails to search for linguistic and cognitive strengths in less economically situated communities. As scholars in the field, instead of focusing literacy research on the need for increasing the word banks for children who struggle academically, we propose redirecting this scholarship to focus on the ways students and families from culturally and linguistically diverse backgrounds can uniquely contribute to this conversation with their own richness of language resources.

The "proof," if it needs to be reiterated again, that learning multiple languages is a uniquely human capacity accomplished worldwide by two-thirds of the speakers of the planet's some 7,000 languages (Ethnologue, 2018) under all kinds of conditions is further supported by the body of extensive empirical bilingual/second language research which has been liberally documented in the literature (Escamilla et al., 2013; Gort, 2015, 2018, 2019; Gort & Reyes, 2016).

Adopting a Prospective and Intersectionality Approach to Language Learning

In summary, what we are calling for is an epistemological shift in researchers' thinking about standard research categories which balkanize linguistic abilities into siloed social and racialized groups (e.g., ethnicity, race, income, education, etc.) *as if* those categories were causal and not simply correlational. In short, we are suggesting a research orientation for early childhood and emergent bilingual study similar to what the *intersectionality* perspective (Cho, Crenshaw, & McCall, 2013; Crenshaw, 1991) has brought to legal, gender, and cultural studies as well as disability research (cf. Artiles, 2013; Hernández-Saca, Kahn, & Cannon, 2018) in forcing a theoretical reframing of many traditional designations—interrogating those descriptions from a sociohistorical perspective (Hernández-Saca et al., 2018) as to who is included, left out, stigmatized, oppressed, and, in some cases, denied social or health services beyond what is summarily indexed by the general census categories of age, ethnicity, marital status, household size, income, occupation, etc.

Further, just as Hernández-Saca et al. (2018) identified a "special education symbolism" or stereotype that is evoked about individuals with various "dis/ability" labels which marginalize them compared to populations without those labels, we suspect there is also an *emergent bilingual or DLL symbolism* or mindset that is evoked about these young second- or multi-language learners in schools or research settings, creating at the outset an overall negative ideology about their performance outcomes—that they lack sufficient vocabulary to be successful, that their parents or single parent lacks interest in their education, that their home life is dangerous for a child, or that few people in the home may be literate enough in either the home language or English to help the child with school work. That these tendentious myths are nonetheless operative and damaging to families and children is directly supported by the well-substantiated overrepresentation of EB students in the special education population (e.g., see Artiles, Rueda, Salazar, & Higareda, 2002, 2005; Guzmán & Fernandez, 2014; Klingner et al., 2005; Linn & Hemmer, 2011; MacSwan & Rolstad, 2006; Sullivan, 2011 for detailed discussions).

While there is a comprehensive list of recommendations for research reporting in chapter 13 of the National Academies of Sciences volume *Promoting the educational success of children and youth learning English: Promising futures* (Takanishi & Le Menestrel, 2017), including a finer delineation of many research categories, for example:

- disaggregate panethnic and ethnic group categories, such as Latin American, Latino, Asian American and Pacific Islander, and African;

- disaggregate data by age group, including infants from birth to two years, pre-K (ages 3–5), elementary school (ages 6–12), and middle to high school (ages 13–18);

the gathering of data in many of the standard categories is still emphasized:

- stratify data by families' socioeconomic status;
- identify EB/ELs by country of origin and immigration status; and
- provide information about the participants' competence in English and their home language(s), including both oral and written language skills.

Unfortunately, researchers take these demographic categories for granted without any real grounded theoretical basis as to whether they themselves have any explanatory power in language learning. Most likely they are opaque proxies for other more subtle contextual, relational, or deeper factors related to language learning more difficult to identify and incorporate into language learning frameworks.

As mentioned earlier, we suggest that researchers reorient their conceptual frameworks by beginning with the general assumption—since all research is based upon "presuppositions" (Bateson, 1979, p. 27; cf. also Gould, 2003; Kuhn, 2010; Lakatos & Feyerabend, 1999; Vygotsky, 1997)—that *multilingualism is the natural language learning state given a minimum set of optimal conditions*. The research goal then becomes identifying in any educational setting how those optimal conditions can be put into place. We see optimal conditions as being those where regardless of race, class, gender, sexuality, ethnicity, age, ability, etc., children's efforts at language learning are supported and not circumscribed or discriminated against by such visible identity markers (see also Collins, 2015).

Summary, Conclusions, and Contrapuntal Readings

In this chapter, we have tried to highlight a few of the forces driving research with young emergent bilingual children. Certainly, one of the most consistent pressures has been the steady and rapid shift in the United States from a homogenous to heterogenous Pre-K-12 population. In the past two decades, for example, the overall average percentage of children speaking languages other than English across all grades has increased to one out of ten students (9.5%, cf. McFarland et al., 2018) with the numbers of preschool emergent bilinguals approaching one out of every three children. Thus, we have found it encouraging that major research syntheses (e.g., Allen & Backes, 2018; Allen & Kelly, 2015; DHHS/DOE, 2017; Takanishi & Le Menestrel, 2017) of the language development and learning of emergent bilingual children and the capacities of the early childhood workforce also incorporate extensive recommendations for policy, professional development, research, and practice at both local and state levels.

Nonetheless, we have also emphasized that in spite of a significant increase in recent national policy statements aimed at language diversity much of the research on emergent bilinguals still emanates from a deficit perspective (cf. Hindman et al., 2016). Therefore, while more recent research and theory has adopted an asset-based approach (e.g., Gort, 2006, 2012, 2015), this asset-based approach has not similarly characterized extant policies and practices particularly in the states (cf. NIEER, 2017) as can be seen by the fact that many of the achievement outcomes for EB/EL students have not improved. We have, however, advanced the hypothesis that a strong case can be made that the reasons for lower performance are less likely to be due to learner-based deficits and more likely to be a result of discriminatory policy, programmatic, and instructional factors particularly at state levels.

Thus, we have suggested to language researchers that not only an asset-based research approach is needed, but also a reconceptualizing of our traditional research categories or "buckets," as it were, into which we conveniently segregate our participants and define their performance. Quite frankly, these categories are socially constructed and descriptive, and not theoretical or explanatory in terms of language learning. Given that many of the recommendations for improving the educational outcomes for emergent bilingual students are decades old, it might be surmised that our taken-for-granted experimental or quasi-experimental research designs—the "gold standard," as it were—are less insightful into understanding improved language and academic performance as are similarly state and local policies which severely circumscribe what instructional supports and educational opportunities are available to students. While certainly only a beginning, we offer two alternative routes for researchers to take in studying issues surrounding the development of young emergent bilingual learners.

First, in his discussions of categorizations in race and disability research, Artiles (2013) has called for a "contrapuntal analytic stance" that "enables us to discern hybrid patterns in intersectional analysis and warns us about the need for strengthening theoretical clarity and its concomitant methodological implications" (p. 341). A *contrapuntal reading*, first given force and substance by the late Palestinian literary critic and postcolonial scholar, Edward Said, in his classic *Culture and imperialism* (1993), in essence, is a type of reading which not only pushes against a dominant narrative established by those in power, but also re-envisions and re-interprets those traditional accounts with the voices and histories of those who tend to be muted or silenced in the official view (see also Chowdhry, 2007). In that same vein, special education researchers as Artiles (2013) and Hernández-Saca et al. (2018) have reinterpreted the special education literature to demonstrate how race, ethnicity, gender, and sexual orientation, for example, interact with various designations of exceptionality—often resulting in discrimination and poor service delivery based upon other factors than the disability itself.

We also believe that adopting such a "contrapuntal" approach by researchers studying young emergent bilinguals would reveal stereotypical attitudes, lack of political will, and inflexible research approaches which continue to support language policies and instructional solutions which have never worked and impede the language development of bilingual children so that their full potential will never be reached and their potential for academic success never maximized. Rather than, as mentioned, automatically assuming that a single-parent home, an income so many percentage points above or below the poverty line, or the presence of a non-English language in the home is a "risk factor" with inevitable consequences, taking a strength-based approach by appreciating the marvelous ability of young children to learn more than one language and carefully studying the interaction of those abilities with personal, familial, neighborhood, and schooling variables may result in insights which will break the current impasse in young EBs' school success.

Second, and finally, more useful approaches to researching the language learning of young EBs, for example, might come from hypothesizing a usage-based theory of language acquisition (see Tomasello, 2009, 2010) that examines how the youngest of the human species become both "experts at mind-reading" in terms of understanding intention, and "experts at culture" in relation to collaborating and interacting from birth (Tomasello, Carpenter, Call, Behne, & Moll, 2005). Therefore, adopting a "prospective" assumption of language learning rather than looking for a "lack of" would redirect researchers' attentions to the complexities of just how young children and young EBs in particular sort out the cognitive and social distinctions necessary to not only develop facility in one language, but rather two or even three in many cases. Focusing upon how these early language abilities develop in the Pre-K years and can be supported by early education offers a much more hopeful and richer field of exploration than the one currently pursued which casts young EBs as inevitably and inexorably behind from their very earliest years of life. As educators and researchers of emergent bilingualism in young children, we have much to learn and a pressing responsibility to dig deeper into the phenomenon with more theoretical perspicacity and greater methodological sophistication.

References

Adair, J. K., Sanchez-Suzuki Colgrove, K., & McManus, M. E. (2017). How the word gap argument negatively impacts young children of Latinx immigrants' conceptualizations of learning. *Harvard Educational Review, 87*(3), 309–334.

Administration of Children and Families. (2017). *Head Start program facts: Fiscal Year 2017*. Retrieved from https://eclkc.ohs.acf.hhs.gov/sites/default/files/pdf/hs-program-fact-sheet-2017_0.pdf

Allen, L., & Backes, E. (Eds.). (2018). *Transforming the financing of early care and education* [A Consensus Study Report of the Committee on Financing Early Care and Education with a Highly Qualified Workforce, National Academies of Sciences, Engineering, and Medicine]. Washington, DC: The National Academies Press. doi:10.17226/24984

Allen, L., & Kelly, B. B. (Eds.). (2015). *Transforming the workforce for children birth through age 8: A unifying foundation* [Report of the Institute of Medicine (IOM) and National Research Council]. Washington, DC: The National Academies Press.

American Community Survey. (2016). *Why we ask: Language spoken at home*. Washington, DC: United States Census Bureau.

Anders, P. L., Yaden, D. B., Jr., Da Silva Iddings, C. A., Katz, L., & Rogers, T. (2016). More words for the poor? Problematizing the "language gap." *Journal of Literacy Research, 48*(2), 131–133.

Artiles, A. J. (2013). Untangling the racialization of disabilities: An intersectionality critique across disability models. *Du Bois Review: Social Science Research on Race, 10*(2), 329–347.

Artiles, A. J., Rueda, R., Salazar, J. J., & Higareda, I. (2002). English-language learner representation in special education in California urban school districts. In D. J. Losen & G. Orfield (Eds.), *Racial inequality in special education* (pp. 265–284). Boston, MA: Harvard Education Press.

Artiles, A. J., Rueda, R., Salazar, J. J., & Higareda, I. (2005). Within-group diversity in minority disproportionate representation: English Language Learners in urban school districts. *Council for Exceptional Children, 71*(3), 283–300.

Avineri, N., Johnson, E., Brice-Heath, S., McCarty, T., Ochs, E., Kremer-Sadlik, T., … Paris, D. (2015). Invited forum: Bridging the "language gap." *Journal of Linguistic Anthropology, 25*(1), 66–86.

Baker, M., & Páez, M. (2018). *The language of the classroom: Dual language learners in Head Start, public Pre-K and private preschool programs*. Washington, DC: Migration Policy Institute.

Barrueco, S., López, M., Ong, C., & Lozano, P. (2012). *Assessing Spanish-English bilingual preschoolers: A guide to best approaches and measures*. Baltimore, MD: Paul Brookes.

Bateson, G. (1979). *Mind and nature: A necessary unity*. New York, NY: Hampton Press.

Bauer, E. B., & Gort, M. (Eds.). (2012). *Early biliteracy development: Exploring young learners' use of their linguistic resources*. Abingdon, UK: Routledge.

Baugh, J. (2017). Meaning-less differences: Exposing fallacies and flaws in "the word gap" hypothesis that conceal a dangerous "language trap" for low-income American families and their children. *International Multilingual Research Journal, 11*(1), 39–51.

Bowman, B. T., Donovan, M. S., & Burns, M. S. (Eds.). (2000). *Eager to learn: Educating our preschoolers* [Report of the Committee on Early Childhood Pedagogy, National Research Council, Commission on Behavioral and Social Sciences and Education]. Washington, DC: National Academy Press. Retrieved from https://www.nap.edu/download/9745

Carnock, J. T. (2018). *Dual language learner data gaps: The need for better policies in the early years*. Washington, DC: New America.

Castro, D. C., García, E. E., & Markos, A. M. (2013). *Dual language learners: Research informing policy*. Chapel Hill: The University of North Carolina, Frank Porter Graham Child Development Institute, Center for Early Care and Education—Dual Language Learners.

Child Trends. (2014). *Dual language learners: Indicators of child and youth well-being*. Bethesda, MD: Child Trends.

Cho, S., Crenshaw, K. W., & McCall, L. (2013). Toward a field of intersectionality studies: Theory, applications, and praxis. *Signs: Journal of Women in Culture and Society, 38*(4), 785–810.

Chowdhry, G. (2007). Edward Said and contrapuntal reading: Implications for critical interventions in international relations. *Millennium, 36*(1), 101–116.

Collier, V. P., & Thomas, W. P. (2017). Validating the power of bilingual schooling: Thirty-two years of large-scale, longitudinal research. *Annual Review of Applied Linguistics, 37*, 203–217.

Collins, P. H. (2015). Intersectionality's definitional dilemmas. *Annual Review of Sociology, 41*, 1–20.

Crenshaw, K. (1991). Mapping the margins: Intersectionality, identity politics, and violence against women of color. *Stanford Law Review, 43*, 1241–1299.

Cummins, J. (1991). Interdependence of first- and second-language proficiency in bilingual children. In E. Bialystok (Ed.), *Language processing in bilingual children* (pp. 70–89). New York, NY: Cambridge University Press.

Dudley-Marling, C., & Lucas, K. (2009). Pathologizing the language and culture of poor children. *Language Arts, 86*(5), 362.

Duran, L. (2017). The truth about the word gap [*OZY: Opinion*]. Retrieved from https://www.ozy.com/opinion/the-truth-about-the-word-gap/75658.

Elango, S., García, J. L., Heckman, J. J., & Hojman, A. (2015). *Early childhood education* [IZA Discussion Papers, No. 9476]. Bonn, DEU: Institute for the Study of Labor (IZA). Retrieved from https://www.econstor.eu/bitstream/10419/124985/1/dp9476.pdf

Escamilla, K., Hopewell, S., Butvilofsky, S., Sparrow, W., Soltero-González, L., Ruiz-Figueroa, O., & Escamilla, M. (2013). *Biliteracy from the start: Literacy squared in action*. Philadelphia, PA: Caslon.

Espinosa, L. M. (2013). *Pre-K-3rd: Challenging common myths about dual language learners: An update to the seminal 2008 report*. New York, NY: Foundation for Child Development.

Espinosa, L. M., & Garcia, E. (2012). *Developmental assessment of young dual language learners with a focus on kindergarten entry assessments: Implications for state policies* [Working paper No.1, Center for Early Care and Education Research—Dual Language Learners (CECER-DLL)]. Chapel Hill: The University of North Carolina, Frank Porter Graham Child Development Institute.

Ethnologue. (2018). *Languages of the world*. Retrieved from https://www.ethnologue.com

Eurostat. (2015). *Foreign language learning in the EU*. Retrieved from https://ec.europa.eu/eurostat/statistics-explained/index.php?title=File:-Foreign_language_learning_cut-01.jpg

Ferjan Ramirez, N., & Kuhl, P. K. (2017). The brain science of bilingualism. *Young Children, 72*, 38–44.

Friedman-Krauss, A. H., Barnett, W. S., Weisenfeld, G. G., Kasmin, R., DiCrecchio, N., & Horowitz, M. (2017). *State of preschool 2017: State preschool yearbook*. New Brunswick, NJ: Rutgers University, Graduate School of Education, National Institute for Early Education Research.

Gandara, P., & Acevedo, S. (2016). *Realizing the economic advantages of a bilingual workforce*. Retrieved from https://www.civilrightsproject.ucla.edu/research/k-12-education/language-minority-students/realizing-the-economic-advantages-of-a-multilingual-workforce

Garcia, J. L., Heckmann, J. J., Leaf, D. E., & Prados, M. J. (2018). *Quantifying the life-cycle benefits of a prototypical early childhood program* [NBER Working Paper No. 23479]. Retrieved from http://www.nber.org/papers/w23479.pdf

García, O., & Kleifgen, J. A. (2018). *Educating emergent bilinguals: Policies, programs, and practices for English language learners* (2nd ed.). New York, NY: Teachers College Press.

Gort, M. (2006). Strategic codeswitching, interliteracy, and other phenomena of emergent bilingual writing: Lessons from first-grade dual language classrooms. *Journal of Early Childhood Literacy, 6*(3), 323–354.

Gort, M. (2012). Codeswitching patterns in the writing-related talk of young emergent bilinguals. *Journal of Literacy Research, 44*(1), 45–75.

Gort, M. (Ed.). (2015). Translanguaging [Special issue]. *International Multilingual Research Journal, 9*(1).

Gort, M. (Ed.). (2018). *The complex and dynamic languaging practices of emergent bilinguals: Translanguaging across diverse education and community contexts*. New York, NY: Taylor & Francis. ISBN-13: 978–1138827417

Gort, M. (2019). Developing bilingualism and biliteracy in early and middle childhood. *Language Arts, 96*(2), 229–243.

Gort, M., & Harris, P. (Eds.). (2018). Emergent biliteracy in early childhood. Special theme issue of *Journal of Early Childhood Literacy, 18*(1), 3–4.

Gort, M., & Reyes, I. (Eds.). (2016). Biliteracy development in schools and communities [Special issue]. *Language Arts, 93*(5).

Gould, S. J. (2003). *The hedgehog, the fox, and the magister's pox: Mending the gap between the science and humanities*. Cambridge, MA: The Belknap Press.

Grosjean, F. (2010). *Bilingual: Life and reality*. Cambridge, MA: Harvard University Press.

Grosjean, F. (2011, June 16). What are the effects of bilingualism? The consequences of bilingualism as seen by studies over time [Web log comment]. Retrieved from https://www.psychologytoday.com/us/blog/life-bilingual/201106/what-are-the-effects-bilingualism

Guzmán, N. A., & Fernandez, M. R. (2014). Rates of representation of culturally and linguistically diverse students in South Texas. *Journal of Case Studies in Education, 6*, 1–17.

Guzman-Orth, D., Lopez, A. A., & Tolentino, T. (2017). *A framework for the dual language assessment of young dual language learners in the United States* [ETS Research Report No. RR-17–37]. Princeton, NJ: Educational Testing Service.

Halle, T. G., Hair, E., Wandner, L., McNamera, M., & Chien, N. (2012). Predictors and outcomes of early vs. later English language proficiency among English language learners. *Early Childhood Research Quarterly, 27*, 1–20.

Halle, T. G., Whittaker, J. V., Zepeda, M., Rothenberg, L., Anderson, R., Daneri, P., & Buysse, V. (2014). The social–emotional development of dual language learners: Looking back at existing research and moving forward with purpose. *Early Childhood Research Quarterly, 29*(4), 734–749.

Hart, B., & Risley, T. R. (1995). *Meaningful differences in the everyday experience of young American children*. Baltimore, MD: Paul H Brookes Publishing.

Hernández-Saca, D. I., Kahn, L. G., & Cannon, M. A. (2018). Intersectionality dis/ability research: How dis/ability research in education engages intersectionality to uncover the multidimensional construction of dis/abled experiences. *Review of Research in Education, 42*, 286–311.

Hindman, A. H., Wasik, B. A., & Snell, E. K. (2016). Closing the 30-million word gap: Next steps in designing research to inform practice. *Child Development Perspectives, 10*(2), 134–139.

Institute of Medicine and the National Research Council. (2015). *Transforming the workforce for children birth through age eight*. Washington, DC: The Institute of Medicine and the National Research Council.

Johnson, E. J., Avineri, N., & Johnson, D. C. (2017). Exposing gaps in/between discourses of linguistic deficits. *International Multilingual Research Journal, 11*(1), 5–22. doi:10.1080/19313152.2016.1258185

Klein, D., Mok, K., Chen, J. K., & Watkins, K. E. (2014). Age of language learning shapes brain structure: A cortical thickness study of bilingual and monolingual individuals. *Brain & Language, 131*, 20–24.

Klingner, J. K., Artiles, A. J., Kozleski, E., Harry, B., Zion, S., Tate, W., … Riley, D. (2005). Addressing the disproportionate representation of culturally and linguistically diverse students in special education through culturally responsive educational systems. *Education Policy Analysis Archives, 13*(38), 1–40.

Kuhn, T. S. (2010). Afterwards. In P. Horwich (Ed.), *World changes: Thomas Kuhn and the nature of science*. Pittsburg, PA: University of Pittsburgh Press.

Lakatos, I., & Feyerabend, P. (1999). *For and against method*. Chicago, IL: University of Chicago Press.

Li, P., Legault, J., & Litcofsky, K. A. (2014). Neuroplasticity as a function of second language learning: Anatomical changes in the human brain. *Cortex, 58*, 301–324.

Lindholm-Leary, K., & Genesee, F. (2014). Student outcomes in one-way, two-way, and indigenous language immersion education. *Journal of Immersion and Content-Based Language Education, 2*(2), 165–180.

Linn, D., & Hemmer, L. (2011). English language learner disproportionality in special education: Implications for the scholar-practitioner. *Journal of Educational Research and Practice, 1*(1), 70–80.

MacSwan, J., & Rolstad, K. (2006). How language proficiency tests mislead us about ability: Implications for English Language Learner placement in special education. *Teachers College Record, 108*(11), 2304–2328.

Mahoney, K. (2017). *The assessment of emergent bilinguals: Supporting English language learners*. Bristol, UK: Multilingual Matters.

Mamedova, S., & Redford, J. (2019). *Early childhood program participation, from the National Household Education Surveys Program of 2012* (NCES 2013-029.REV2). Washington, DC: National Center for Education Statistics, Institute of Education Sciences, U.S. Department of Education. Retrieved from https://nces.ed.gov/pubsearch

Marian, V., & Shook, A. (2012). The cognitive benefits of being bilingual. *Cerebrum: The Dana Forum on Brain Science*, 1–12. Retrieved from https://www.ncbi.nlm.nih.gov/pmc/articles/PMC3583091/

McFarland, J., Hussar, B., Wang, X., Zhang, J., Wang, K., Rathbun, A., ... Bullock Mann, F. (2018). *The condition of education 2018* [NCES 2018–144]. U.S. Department of Education. Washington, DC: National Center for Education Statistics. Retrieved September 7, 2018 from https://nces.ed.gov/pubsearch/pubsinfo.asp?pubid=2018144

Mendez, J., & Crosby, D. (2018). *Why and how do low-income Hispanic families search for early care and education.* Bethesda, MD: The National Center for Research on Hispanic Families & Children.

Mulligan, G. M., Hastedt, S., & McCarroll, J. C. (2012). *First-time kindergartners in 2010–11: First findings from the kindergarten rounds of the early childhood longitudinal study, kindergarten class of 2010–11* [ECLS-K:2011; NCES 2012–049]. U.S. Department of Education. Washington, DC: National Center for Education Statistics. Retrieved from http://nces.ed.gov/pubsearch

Mulligan, G. M., McCarroll, J. C., Flanagan, K. D., & Potter, D. (2018). *Findings from the fourth-grade round of the early childhood longitudinal study, kindergarten class of 2010–11* [ECLS-K:2011; NCES 2018–094]. U.S. Department of Education, Washington, DC: National Center for Education Statistics. Retrieved from http://nces.ed.gov/pubsearch

National Institute for Early Education Research. (2017). *Special report: Supporting dual language learners in state-funded preschool: State of the preschool yearbook, 2018.* New Brunswick: National Institute for Early Education Research (NIEER), Graduate School of Education at Rutgers, The State University of New Jersey.

Neuman, S. B., Newman, E. H., & Dwyer, J. (2011). Educational effects of a vocabulary intervention on preschoolers' word knowledge and conceptual development: A cluster-randomized trial. *Reading Research Quarterly, 46*(3), 249–272.

Office of Head Start. (2015). *Head Start early learning outcomes framework: Birth to five.* Washington, DC: U.S. Department of Health and Human Services, Administration for Children and Families.

O'Hare, W. P., Mayol-Garcia, Y., Wildsmith, E., & Torres, A. (2016). *The invisible ones: How Latino children are left out of our nation's census count.* Bethesda, MD: Child Trends Hispanic Institute and the National Association of Latino Elected and Appointed Officials Education Fund.

Park, M., O'Toole, A., & Katsiaficas, C. (2017). *Dual language learners: A national demographic and policy profile* [Fact Sheet]. Washington, DC: Migration Policy Institute. Retrieved from https://www.migrationpolicy.org/research/dual-language-learners-national-demographic-and-policy-profile.

Paschall, K. (2019). *Nearly 30% of infants and toddlers attend home-based child care as their primary arrangement* [Child Trends Report]. Retrieved from https://www.childtrends.org/nearly-30-percent-of-infants-and-toddlers-attend-home-based-child-care-as-their-primary-arrangement.

Ramirez, J. D. (1992). Executive summary. *Bilingual Research Journal, 16*(1–2), 1–62.

Ramírez-Esparza, N., García-Sierra, A., & Kuhl, P. K. (2017). The impact of early social interactions on later language development in Spanish–English bilingual infants. *Child Development, 88*(4), 1216–1234.

Rathbun, A., & Zhang, A. (2016). *Primary early care and education arrangements and achievement at kindergarten entry* [NCES 2016–070]. Washington, DC: National Center for Education Statistics, U.S. Department of Education.

Reardon, S. F., & Galindo, C. (2009). The Hispanic-White achievement gap in math and reading at the elementary grades. *American Educational Research Journal, 46*(3), 853–891.

Reardon, S. F., & Portilla, X. A. (2016). Recent trends in income, racial, and ethnic school readiness gaps at kindergarten entry. *AERA Open, 2*(3), 1–18. doi:10.1177/2332858416657343

Rueda, R., & Yaden, D. (2006). The literacy education of linguistically and culturally diverse young children: An overview of outcomes, assessment, and large-scale interventions. In B. Spodek & O. N. Saracho (Eds.), *Handbook of research on the education of young children* (2nd ed., pp. 167–186). Mahwah, NF: Lawrence Erlbaum.

Rueda, R., & Yaden, D. B., Jr. (2013). The education of young dual-language learners: An overview. In O. Saracho & B. Spodek (Eds.), *Handbook of research on the education of young children* (3rd ed., pp. 157–168). New York, NY: Routledge.

Said, E. W. (1993). *Culture and imperialism.* New York, NY: Knopf.

Shonkoff, J. P., & Phillips, D. A. (Eds.). (2000). *From neurons to neighborhoods: The science of early childhood development* [A Report of the Committee on Integrating the Science of Early Childhood Development, Board on Children, Youth, and Families, Commission on Behavioral and Social Sciences and Education, National Research Council and Institute of Medicine]. Washington, DC: National Academy Press.

Snow, C. E., Burns, M. S., & Griffin, P. (1998). *Preventing reading difficulties.* Washington, DC: National Academy Press.

Stefanakis, E. (1999). *Whose judgment counts? Assessing bilingual children.* Portsmouth, NH: Heinemann.

Stocco, A., & Prat, C. S. (2014). Bilingualism trains specific brain circuits involved in flexible rule selection and application. *Brain and language, 137*, 50–61.

Sullivan, A. (2011). Disproportionality in special education identification and placement of English language learners. *Exceptional Children, 77*(3), 317–334.

Takanishi, R., & Le Menestrel, S. (Eds.). (2017). *Promoting the educational success of children and youth learning English: Promising futures* [A Consensus Study Report of the National Academies of Sciences, Engineering, & Medicine]. Washington, DC: The National Academies Press. doi:10.17226/24677

Thomas, W. P., & Collier, V. P. (2003). The multiple benefits of dual language: Dual language programs educate both English learners and native English speakers without incurring extra costs. *Educational Leadership, 61*(2), 61–64.

Tomasello, M. (2009). *The cultural origins of human cognition.* Cambridge, MA: Harvard university press.

Tomasello, M. (2010). *Origins of human communication.* Cambridge, MA: MIT press.

Tomasello, M., Carpenter, M., Call, J., Behne, T., & Moll, H. (2005). Understanding and sharing intentions: The origins of cultural cognition. *Behavioral and brain sciences, 28*(5), 675–691.

U.S. Chamber of Commerce (2019). *Education* [Mission statement]. Retrieved from https://www.uschamber.com/education.

U.S. Department of Education, Office of English Language Acquisition. (2015). *Dual language education programs: Current state policies and practices.* Washington, DC: U. S. Department of Education.

U.S. Department of Health and Human Services, Administration for Children and Families & U.S. Department of Education. (2017). *Policy statement on supporting the children who are dual language learners in early childhood programs.* Washington, DC: U.S. Department of Health and Human Services.

United States Census Bureau. (2015). *Table 1. Detailed languages spoken at home and ability to speak English for the population 5 years and over for United States: 2009–2013.* Washington, DC: United States Census Bureau.

Vygotsky, L. S. (1997). *Cognition and language. The collected works of L. S. Vygotsky, Vol. 3. Problems of the theory and history of psychology* (R. W. Rieber & J. Wollock, Eds., R. van der Veer, Trans.). New York, NY: Plenum Press.

Weiland, C. (2016). Launching preschool 2.0: A road map to high quality public programs at scale. *Behavioral Science & Policy, 2*(1), 37–46.

Whitebook, M., McLean, C., Austin, L. J. E., & Edwards, B. (2018). *Early childhood workforce index – 2018.* Berkeley, CA: Center for the Study of Child Care Employment, University of California, Berkeley. Retrieved from http://cscce.berkeley.edu/topic/early-childhood-workforce-index/2018/

World Health Organization. (2007, April). Multilingualism: A plan of action (A Report of the Executive Board, 121st Session, Agenda Item 6.3). Retrieved from http://apps.who.int/gb/archive/pdf_files/EB121/B121_6-en.pdf?ua=1

Williams, C. P. (2014). *Chaos for dual language learners: An examination of state policies for exiting children from language services in the Prek-3rd grades.* Bethesda, MD: New America.

Williams, C. P. (2015). *New American's dual language learners national workgroup sets up shop*. Retrieved from https://www.newamerica.org/education-policy/edcentral/dllworkgrouplaunch/

World Atlas. (2018). *The most spoken languages in America*. Retrieved from https://www.worldatlas.com/articles/the-most-spoken-languages-in-america.html

Yoshikawa, H., Wieland, C., Brooks-Gunn, J., Burchinal, M. R., Espinosa, L. M., Gormley, W. T., ... Zaslow, M. J. (2013). *Investing in our future: The evidence base on preschool education*. Retrieved from https://www.fcd-us.org/assets/2016/04/Evidence-Base-on-Preschool-Education-FINAL

17

Educational Policy in the United States Regarding Bilinguals in Early Childhood Education

Ann-Marie Wiese, Delis Cuéllar, and Eugene E. García

Introduction

The population of children in the United States with at least one parent who speaks a language other than English at home has increased by 24% since 2000. In fact, young dual language learners (DLLs) now make up close to one third of all young children (ages birth to eight) in the United States (Park, O'Toole, & Katsiaficas, 2017). At the same time, this population has traditionally been underserved by the educational system and has not kept pace with their monolingual English-speaking peers (Takanishi & Le Menestrel, 2017). Maximizing opportunities for DLLs requires an understanding that language development is interdependent with multiple factors and an array of other institutional conditions and cultural practices (García & Ozturk, 2017), including educational policy and practice. The conceptual framework shown in Figure 17.1 illustrates this multitude of variables that come into play when addressing the learning and development of DLLs. The framework is based on a report of the National Academies of Sciences, Engineering, and Medicine, which provides the most comprehensive and authoritative collection of theoretical and empirical information on young DLLs to date (Takanishi & Le Menestrel, 2017).

Given the role educational policy plays in shaping the challenges and opportunities faced by DLLs and English learners (ELs) (Takanishi & Le Menestrel, 2017), this chapter summarizes past and present federal legislation and provides an overview of state-level policies that guide the education of these learners, with an emphasis on preschool age children. The active track record of policy action has not left a clear path and is still being negotiated (Wiese & García, 2006). Therefore, this chapter aims to inform not only policymakers but also service providers by addressing this complex collage of policy and practice and by making research-based recommendations for the early childhood education (ECE)

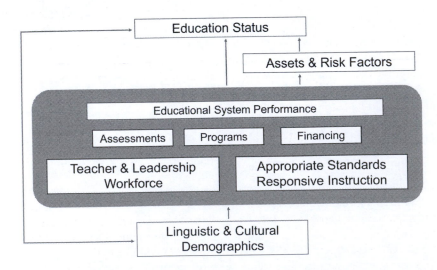

Figure 17.1 Conceptual framework for dual language learner and English learner educational success.

field, particularly in the areas of program policy, classroom practice, and assessment. The chapter covers the following topics:

- description of the DLL population, including a discussion of the heterogeneity of this population and specific cultural and linguistic assets;
- federal policy, including a summary of how reauthorizations of the Elementary and Secondary Education Act (ESEA) have addressed ELs;
- state policy, including a survey of recent state efforts to address DLLs in preschool and particularly California's efforts, as an exemplar, to shift from an English-only stance to one that values development of both the home language and English; and
- implications for ECE programs, including recommendations related to the assessment of DLLs and programmatic and classroom-level practices.

Description of the Dual Language Learner Population

While the term *English learner* (EL) is used to refer to children enrolled in the pre-K-12 educational system, the term *dual language learner* (DLL) is used to refer to children under the age of five who are exposed to more than one language in family, home, and primary care circumstances. The population of DLLs is a heterogeneous one, with hundreds of languages represented and three in four DLLs speaking Spanish (Capps et al., 2005). Moreover, linguistic background is not the only early developmental context relevant to DLLs: DLLs and their families vary widely in terms of race, ethnicity, socioeconomic status, immigrant generation, religion, country of origin, legal status, integration, social networks, and so on. Each of these factors, though not mutually exclusive, interacts with children's development.

Whereas nine out of ten DLLs are born in the United States, most live with immigrant families in which at least one parent was born outside the United States. Thus, the early development of DLLs is inextricably related to the type of immigrant experiences their family has (Tobin, Adair, & Arzubiaga, 2013). For example, DLLs with an undocumented parent, a situation that affects two in five of all DLLs, tend to face more precarious hardships than those with two documented parents (Bean, Brown, Leach, Bachmeier, & Van Hook, 2013; Jensen & Bachmeier, 2015). A parent's undocumented status is associated with greater poverty, lower rates of preschool enrollment, less support from social programs, and higher levels of family uncertainty (Yoshikawa, 2011; Yoshikawa & Kholoptseva, 2013).

The cultures, languages, and experiences of ELs and DLLs are highly diverse; moreover, they grow up in contexts that expose them to a number of risk factors (e.g., low levels of parental education, low family income, refugee status, homelessness) that can have a negative impact on their school success, especially when these disadvantages are compounded. However, this same population possesses significant assets, including bilingual skills, positive attitudes toward education and educators, and many come from two-parent families with strong extended-family support.

We know from the existing science on multilingualism that young children can attain proficiency in more than one language (Bialystok, 2010; Genesee, 2010; Takanishi & Le Menestrel, 2017; Unsworth, 2016), and dual language programs in the early years can produce positive outcomes across multiple domains (García & Frede, 2010; Li, Edwards, & Gunderson, 2010; Reyes & Kleyn, 2010). Indeed, Cheung and Slavin (2012) found that English reading outcomes for Spanish-dominant DLLs were stronger for those in bilingual programs than for those in English-only programs. More specifically, Cheung and Slavin (2012) reported a small but practically meaningful and replicable effect size of 0.21 in the results of their systematic review.

Valentino and Reardon (2015) studied language proficiency and academic achievement outcomes of Latino elementary-grade ELs in different types of dual language programs (transitional, developmental, two-way, and English mainstream) in California. Of importance, the study controlled for parental choice—all parents in both the control (English instruction) and treatment (dual language instruction) groups requested dual language instruction for their children. Similar to Cheung and Slavin's (2012) results, the findings indicated that ELs in bilingual or dual language programs, relative to ELs in English-only programs, were more likely to meet an English language arts threshold and to be reclassified as English proficient. Furthermore, Valentino and Reardon (2015) found that, by seventh grade, ELs in dual immersion/two-way and transitional bilingual programs had much higher English language arts scores than those in English-only instruction classrooms and that other academic test scores of ELs in dual immersion/two-way programs far outpaced those of ELs in other programs. Although research shows benefits of multilingualism, federal policy related to language learners has tended to emphasize English learning at the expense of home language development.

Federal Legislation: The Elementary and Secondary Education Act and English Learners

Educational policy matters because it sets assumptions and expectations for what and how ELs should learn in schools. Over the past 50 years, federal policies in particular have sought to support EL academic learning outcomes by addressing the reality that students with limited English proficiency face a significant barrier to mastery of subject matter content taught in English.

Recent ECE expansion has generated related policy-to-practice assumptions and expectations for DLLs. Figure 17.2 summarizes the historical policy attention generated by federal court litigation and federal legislative actions related

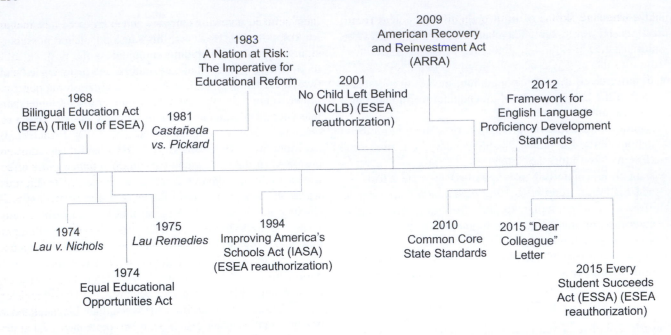

ESEA = Elementary and Secondary Education Act

Figure 17.2 Timeline of English learner policies.

directly to those children and students who do not speak English as they enter formal educational environments in the United States.[1] As Figure 17.2 indicates, policy attention to this population has been continuous since 1968 into the present.

Although the courts have been the primary vehicle to address non-English-speaking students' civil rights as relevant to equal educational opportunity (Jiménez-Castellanos & García, 2017), federal policy articulation related to equal educational opportunity has been most prominent via the ESEA. ELs have been addressed beginning with Title VII of the ESEA: the Bilingual Education Act (BEA) of 1968 and continuing through to the English Language Acquisition, Language Enhancement, and Academic Achievement Act, Title III of the most recent reauthorization of the ESEA, the Every Student Succeeds Act (ESSA) of 2015.[2]

The Bilingual Education Act, 1968–1994: Native Language Instruction and English Learners

Since its inception in 1968 through its final reauthorization in 1994,[3] the BEA stood as the US primary federal legislative effort to provide equal educational opportunity to language-minority students. Like *Lau v. Nichols*, the initial Title VII legislation emanated from the Civil Rights Act of 1964 as part of the "war on poverty." The legislation was primarily a "crisis intervention," or a political strategy to funnel poverty funds to the second largest minority group in the Southwest: Mexican Americans (Casanova, 1991; García & Gonzalez, 1995).

Intended as a remedial effort, the BEA aimed at meeting the educational needs of low-income bilingual children by addressing the children's "language deficiencies" and, as such, responding to the call for equal educational opportunity (Navarro, 1990). No particular program of instruction was recommended—local education agencies (LEAs) would receive financial assistance "to develop and carry out new and imaginative … programs" (BEA, 1968, §702). Among the approved activities were the following programs: bilingual education, history and culture, ECE, and adult education for parents.

The 1974 reauthorization provided the following definition of bilingual education: "instruction given in, and study of, English, and, to the extent necessary to allow a child to progress effectively through the educational system, the native language" (§703(a)(4)(A)(i)). While the BEA acknowledged the role native language could play in supporting a transition to English, it did not promote bilingual education as an enrichment program in which the native language was maintained. Other significant changes in terms of eligibility included the elimination of poverty as a requirement, the inclusion of Native American children as an eligible population, and a provision for English-speaking children to enroll in bilingual education programs to "acquire an understanding of the cultural heritage of the children of limited English-speaking ability" (§703 (a)(4)(B)).

Subsequent reauthorizations of the BEA until 1994 shifted the focus to English acquisition as the primary goal of education for bilingual children. The final reauthorization of the BEA took place in 1994 and still included among its goals "developing the English skills and to the extent possible, the native-language skills" of limited English proficient (LEP) students. However, the 2001 reauthorization of the ESEA, known as the No Child Left Behind Act (NCLB), introduced Title III: Language Instruction for Limited English Proficient and Immigrant Students.

Language Instruction for Limited English Proficient and Immigrant Students Act of 2001: From Bilingual Education to English Only

The ESEA was reauthorized in 2001 as NCLB. The Language Instruction for Limited English Proficient and Immigrant Students Act, Title III of NCLB, marked a shift away from developing bilingual capacities to English language proficiency, which is reflected in many areas including purpose, programs, allocation of funds, and accountability and assessment. In fact, the word *bilingual* was completely eliminated from the law and any government office affiliated with the law.

As part of Title III, federally administered competitive grants to bilingual and immigrant education programs were consolidated; resources were allocated primarily through a state formula program for language instruction educational programs (LIEPs) "based on scientifically based research" (U.S. Department of Education, 2002).[4] A LIEP was defined as

> an instruction course in which LEP students are placed for the purpose of developing and attaining English proficiency, while meeting challenging state and academic content and student academic achievement standards; a LIEP may make use of both English and a child's native language to enable the child to develop and attain English proficiency.
> (U.S. Department of Education, 2003, p. 20)

The formula grants were to be distributed to each state based on their enrollments of LEP and immigrant students. Finally, because each state had to then allocate 95% of the funds to individual LEAs, federal legislation played a diminished role in promoting quality programs that served as guiding lights to the nation's bilingual student population.

Elementary and Secondary Education Act Reauthorization of 2015: Every Student Succeeds Act

The most recent reauthorization, in 2015, of the ESEA, known more prominently as the ESSA, went into effect on July 1, 2017. While the 2015 reauthorization replaced the term *limited English proficient* with *English learner*,[5] the state formulary grant structure introduced in the 2001 legislation remains the primary vehicle by which federal funds are allocated to support English Learners (ELs), including the stipulation that 95% of the state award must flow to LEAs. However, the 5% reserved for state-level funding can be used to address a new requirement to establish and implement

standardized statewide entrance and exit procedures, including assessing children who may be ELs within 30 days of enrollment (ESEA Section 3111(b)(2)(A)).[6]

In terms of local-level activities, LEAs receiving Title III funds must still provide a LIEP and professional development to teachers. While the 2001 legislation required that the LIEPs be "scientifically based," the 2015 legislation requires that the LIEPs be "effective" (ESEA Sections 3115(a), 3115(c)(1), 3113(b)(3)(E), and 3116(b)(1)). In addition, LEAs must also use Title III funds to provide other effective activities and strategies to enhance LIEPs,[7] which must include parent, family, and community engagement (ESEA Section 3115(c)(1)–(3)). These activities can include community participation programs, family literacy services, parent and family outreach and training, and training to ELs and their families (ESEA Section 3115(d)(6)).

Title III Provisions Moved to Title I. A significant revision in the 2015 reauthorization is that many provisions related to ELs moved from Title III to Title I of the ESEA, which targets funds for programs that support socioeconomically disadvantaged children (U.S. Department of Education, 2016). However, states and LEAs can still use Title III funds for EL-related activities that were previously required under Title III and are now required under Title I.

Accountability for how a child performs on English proficiency assessments is among the provisions that formerly fell under Title III. Title I now addresses the inclusion of ELs in academic content assessments in reading/language arts, mathematics, and science; English language proficiency assessments; accountability measures; and school improvement initiatives. For example, the state English language proficiency standards must align with state academic content standards in reading/language arts, mathematics, science, and other subject areas (ESEA Section 1111(b)(1)(F); Section 1111(b)(2)(G)(ii)). At the local level, Title I LEA activities include notifying EL parents about LIEPs (ESEA Section 1112(e)(3)), establishing effective outreach to families of ELs (ESEA Section 1112(e)(3)(C)), and reporting to the state on ELs achieving English language proficiency (ESEA Section 1111(h)(2)).[8] The inclusion of activities such as these makes it exceedingly clear that ELs are a critical part of Title I.

Early Learning. Although previous reauthorizations of the ESEA in general permitted the use of Title III funds for ELs as young as three years old, ESSA takes it a step further and provides specific guidelines for addressing younger ELs in the following ways:

- The purpose section specifically calls out preschool teachers (ESEA Section 3102 [reauthorized as ESSA]).
- The section on subgrants to LEAs for ELs calls out "early childhood education programs" and "effective preschool ... language instruction educational programs" (ESEA Section 3115 [reauthorized as ESSA]).

- Funds for professional development may be used with teachers of ELs in publicly funded preschool programs (U.S. Department of Education, 2016, p. 32).
- The section on requirements for local plans addresses the coordination of activities and data sharing among Head Start, Early Head Start, and other ECE providers (ESEA Section 3116 [reauthorized as ESSA]).[9]

In fact, LEAs are encouraged to take into consideration the unique needs of preschool age ELs:

> An LEA that uses Title III subgrant funds to support preschool-aged ELs should ensure that its language instruction and other services are developmentally appropriate for young ELs, culturally responsive, and reflective of the latest research on effective instruction for ELs in early learning programs and supportive of all ELs' needs. An LEA should consider the developmental and language needs of children when determining which students may be served using Title III funds.
>
> (U.S. Department of Education, 2016, p. 33)

Furthermore, the ESEA reauthorization includes several key features that relate to ELs (adapted from Takanishi & Le Menestrel, 2017, slides 24–25):

- replaces the term *limited English proficient* with *English learner*;
- acknowledges the heterogeneity of the EL population including recently arrived ELs, long-term ELs, and ELs with disabilities;
- directs states to develop policies designed to forge closer connections between early learning programs and K-12 education, specifically K-3;
- shifts the locus of decision-making authority for accountability to states and localities and limits federal authority in allowing exceptions;
- expects states to administer and report academic assessments that are intended to identify schools (not districts) that are in need of comprehensive or targeted assistance;
- encourages states to be more innovative in their assessment and accountability systems, including using a variety of readiness and engagement indicators;
- holds schools rather than districts accountable for ELs' progress toward English language proficiency;
- requires states to describe their rules for how student progress toward English proficiency is to be accomplished;
- requires states to develop standardized entry and exit procedures for determining whether a student is an EL that are consistent across districts within the state;
- expects districts to provide supports to schools in need of assistance and be the policy unit from which much of the improvement work will be carried out;
- allows states to include students formerly classified as ELs in the EL subgroup for academic assessment

purposes for a period of up to four years (as opposed to two years); and
- includes requirements for family engagement under Titles I, III, and IV.

Overall, federal policy has emphasized a shift away from developing bilingual capacities and toward a focus on English language acquisition. Still, through reauthorizations of the ESEA, federal legislation continues to provide guidance as it relates to ELs and in 2015 specifically promoted a focus on young ELs (or DLLs) in preschool.

State Policy: Addressing Dual Language Learners in Preschool

In recent years, increased attention has been given to how state policy articulates guidance regarding DLLs in preschool, prior to their entry into the K-12 system. In fact, beginning in 2014–2015, the National Institute for Early Education Research (NIEER) State of Preschool Survey included supplemental questions to develop a better understanding of state policies to support DLLs in a state-funded preschool for the first time. The NIEER report from the most recent survey in 2017 that 35 states have specific policies to support DLLs in state preschool; however, they vary widely across the states (see Table 17.1).[10]

Overall, six states with a high population of DLLs and high DLL enrollment in preschool—California, Illinois, Nevada, New Jersey, New Mexico, and Texas—have policies to support DLLs; yet many of the other states with high populations of DLLs, including New York and Florida, do not even have a process in place to identify children's home language(s), which is a crucial first step in determining the best approach to support their learning and development.

Table 17.1 Policy Requirements Related to Dual Language Learners in State Preschool

Specific Policy	Total Number of States
Approved written plan for supporting DLLs is required	13
Extra funding allocated for serving DLLs	10
Bilingual instruction is permitted	29
Monitoring focused on the quality of bilingual instruction	11
Children are screened in their home language	18
Children are assessed in their home language	17
DLLs are placed in classes with other children with the same home language	4
Policies to support families of preschool DLLs	27
Staff have training or qualifications related to working with DLLs	6

Adapted from Friedman-Krauss et al. (2018, p. 34).

To provide quality early childhood learning experiences for the increasing population of young DLLs, it is important to understand how states address DLLs in their early learning and development standards and guidelines (ELDG)—that is, how the ELDG delineate expectations for young children's learning and development across domains, specify curricular and instructional approaches to be implemented, and provide guidance for child and program assessment. The ELDG set the expectations and directly affect the day-to-day experiences of DLLs in preschool; as we know from research, effective practices for DLLs require enhancements to better meet these students' unique strengths and needs (Takanishi & Le Menestrel, 2017).

A recent review of a subset of states' ELDG classified 21 states and the District of Columbia[11] as adopting one of three approaches to serving DLLs (Espinosa & Calderon, 2015):

- Dual language approach: state explicitly promotes bilingualism and includes the goal of becoming bilingual and biliterate throughout the ECE system (one state).
- English language development approach: states recognize the benefit of acquiring English during the preschool years while continuing to develop the home language, frequently offer targeted instructional enhancements, and recommend specific strategies to support DLLs' acquisition of English and comprehension of activities and instruction conducted in English (16 states).
- English immersion approach: states emphasize English, without attention to home language maintenance, and are often focused on DLLs acquiring English as rapidly as possible, without specific strategies to support English acquisition and comprehension of activities and instruction conducted in English (District of Columbia and four states).

It is not surprising that a vast majority of states took the English language development approach—most ECE programs do not have the capacity to offer dual language approaches for DLLs given a host of reasons including but not limited to lack of staff who speak the home languages of the children, diversity of home languages in a given preschool program, and family and community preference. This is the case despite research that indicates that instruction in the home language as a complement to English instruction does not delay children's learning of English (Takanishi & Le Menestrel, 2017). Nevertheless, it is important to consider that to date there is no consensus on what English language proficiency looks like in preschool age children (Zepeda, 2017) and that learning English is a complex task that takes children years to reach full proficiency. Consequently, young children's exposure to all of their languages, and what language(s) they use most successfully to communicate, are important factors in understanding and supporting children's development and language learning trajectories.

As similarly found in the NIEER survey results, Espinosa and Calderon (2015) conclude that ELDG represent highly

Table 17.2 Program Criteria for Serving Dual Language Learners in Preschool

Program Criteria Specific to DLLs	Number of States, *including District of Columbia*
Statement of philosophy	13
Identification procedures	3
Separate standards domain	3
Addressed in standards domain for language and literacy	15
Addressed in standards domain for social-emotional development	6
Family engagement approaches	7
Teacher qualifications	5
Teaching practices and strategies	12
Assessment recommendations	7

variable approaches to the education of DLLs along a series of program criteria for best practices when serving DLLs in preschool (see Table 17.2).

The current state of ECE policy related to DLLs is situated within the landscape of language policy, which often is the focus for English learners in the K-12 educational system. The following section highlights California as an example of a state with recent policy shifts in support of ELs with implications for supporting DLLs in preschool.

California as an Exemplar: From an English-Only Language Policy to English Plus Home Language

California's Proposition 227 passed in 1998, and for almost 20 years it required all children to be placed in "English language classrooms" and ELs to be provided, for up to one year, specialized support to learn English through a prescribed methodology identified as "structured English immersion" or "sheltered English immersion." After one year, ELs would be placed in a regular classroom. Proposition 227's restrictive language policy allowed home and native language instruction only through an exclusionary and complicated process requiring annual parental waivers and extended beyond current federal law, which neither requires nor prohibits the use of native language (Wiley, Lee, & Rumberger, 2009). In 2016, Proposition 58 reversed Proposition 227, allowing "language acquisition programs" that "lead to grade level proficiency and academic achievement in both English and another language" (Zepeda, 2017).

Just a year later in 2017, the English Learner Roadmap issued by the California Department of Education (CDE) stating that

English learners fully and meaningfully access and participate in a 21st century education, from early childhood through grade twelve that results in their attaining high levels of English proficiency, mastery of grade level standards, and opportunities to develop proficiency in multiple languages.

(Hakuta, 2018, p. 36)

To this end, the language policy removes barriers to bilingual instruction; four principles support the vision and provide the foundation of California's English Learner Roadmap: (a) assets-oriented and needs-responsive schools, (b) intellectual quality of instruction and meaningful access, (c) system conditions that support effectiveness, and (d) alignment and articulation within and across systems.

These recent developments complement California's current approach to DLLs as represented in the state's ELDG, which provide an integrated set of research- and evidence-based resources that support early learning and development through best practices in early education and consist of five components: (a) early learning foundations (standards), (b) curriculum frameworks, (c) assessment of children's progress, (d) program guidelines and related resources, and (e) professional development. Each component in the system provides resources that focus on different aspects of supporting the efforts of early care and education teachers, including a focus on DLLs throughout. The remainder of this section describes how DLLs are addressed in California's ELDG.

Early Learning Foundations, Curriculum Frameworks, and Professional Development. The early learning and development standards, known as foundations[12] in California, describe knowledge and skills that young children typically develop when provided with developmentally, culturally, and linguistically appropriate high-quality learning experiences (California Department of Education, 2008, 2010a, 2012). In other words, the foundations describe what all young children typically learn with appropriate support.

The support individual young children need to attain the competencies varies from child to child. Given its high proportion of young DLLs, California has developed standards in a separate domain to address English language development for preschool age children. Furthermore, the accompanying curriculum frameworks dedicate a stand-alone chapter to English language development that provides guidance on how to support DLLs through the environment, interactions, and activities (California Department of Education, 2010b, 2011, 2013a). Throughout the chapters on other domains of learning and development, such as social–emotional development or mathematics, the curriculum frameworks address specific considerations when working with DLLs and their families.

California's Early Childhood Educator Competencies describe the knowledge, skills, and dispositions that current and pre-service early childhood educators should have and include a dual language development competency area. An online interactive self-reflective assessment tool provides a summary, videos, and activities to guide self-reflection as teachers deepen their understanding of each competency area. To support teachers in state-funded preschool programs, the California Department of Education has developed an online learning portal with modules that address foundations, frameworks, assessment, and other state-approved content.[13] Both the self-reflective assessment tool and the online learning portal provide teachers some, if not all, content in Spanish.

Preschool Program Guidelines. California's current preschool program guidelines articulate elements of high-quality preschool programs (California Department of Education, 2015). They provide guidance relevant to culturally and linguistically diverse children and families on specific topics such as the role of the preschool teacher, assessment, and family engagement. In addition, a chapter is dedicated to best practices for DLLs, including guiding principles, programmatic approaches, and teaching strategies to support home language development while also promoting English language development.

Approach to Assessment. California's approach to assessment endeavors alignment with the National Association for the Education of Young Children's (NAEYC) guidance in the supplement to its position statement on early childhood curriculum, assessment, and program evaluation: "All young children have the right to be assessed in ways that support their learning and development. For children whose home language is not English, this means being assessed in culturally and linguistically responsive ways" (NAEYC, 2009, p. 1). For DLLs, such guidance calls for assessment of their learning and development in the home language and English to gain an accurate sense of their knowledge and skills. In fact, the revised *Head Start Early Learning Outcomes Framework* calls for DLLs to be assessed in both languages (Office of Head Start, 2015) because using English-only assessments will underestimate children's true abilities (Takanishi & Le Menestrel, 2017). As such, California's early learning and development system provides guidance for all state-funded preschool programs to complete assessments in the child's home language and English. To this end, the California Department of Education's (2013b) Desired Results Developmental Profile (DRDP [2015])[14] represents a significant effort to assess young DLLs in a culturally and linguistically appropriate manner.

The DRDP (2015) is a standardized observational assessment aligned with early learning and development standards and kindergarten standards. Throughout the development of the DRDP (2015), special consideration was taken to address the needs of young DLLs, particularly the call to assess their knowledge and skills in both the home language and English (WestEd Center for Child and Family Studies, 2018).

The DRDP (2015) addresses the assessment of young DLLs in the home language and English in two primary ways:

- From early infancy through kindergarten, teachers observe and document children's behavior in both the home (or first) language and English to obtain a more accurate profile of the children's knowledge and skills across developmental domains. If the teacher does not speak the child's home language, he or she draws upon teachers and staff who speak the child's language and know the child. The teacher should also be collaborating with families to collect documentation in the home language.

- Beginning in preschool, teachers rate children's progress on two language and literacy development domains. The Language and Literacy Development domain assesses all children's progress in developing foundational language and literacy skills. The English-Language Development domain assesses current knowledge and skills and progress in learning to communicate in English.

Implications for Early Childhood Education Programs

Assessment

Current research demonstrates that, more and more, early care and education programs are "superdiverse," meaning they have classrooms in which educators and children speak English in addition to various languages other than English (Hurwitz & Olsen, 2018). Nevertheless, language data for young children ages birth to five who are exposed to multiple languages are difficult to obtain because standardized identification measures and comprehensive data repositories to inform the public about young multilingual children are nonexistent (Mathews, 2011). Although, during the enrollment process, school districts require parents to fill out a home language survey to identify ELs, current national data demonstrate that most state preschool programs do not collect information on the languages spoken in children's homes (Friedman-Krauss et al., 2018).

Systematic, early, and accurate identification of children who are exposed to multiple languages is an important first step for the assessment of young DLLs. Early childhood and education programs should have in place data-gathering methods to identify children's language histories. This identification process can involve direct observation of the child's language use and language information reported by the child's family. For DLLs ages birth to five, essential documentation consists of (a) all of the languages the child is exposed to; (b) languages spoken in the child's home and community, by whom and since when; (c) whether the child developed his or her languages simultaneously or is doing so consecutively; and (d) language goals and aspirations that families have for the child (Cuéllar, 2016; Espinosa & Gutiérrez-Clellen, 2013; Michael-Luna, 2015). Observing children's use of language and collecting information on their exposure to all of their languages can help early childhood practitioners determine in which language the child can express himself or herself best or, in other words, assess the child's language dominance. Knowing the language that a child uses to best express himself or herself allows adults to properly scaffold interactions in the language and maximize a child's learning and development.

Once DLLs are identified and their language dominance is determined, preschool assessment approaches that accurately depict and measure what DLLs know must be implemented. Attaining accurate information of DLLs' knowledge requires assessments to be conducted in the child's home language and in English because children's general knowledge is heavily influenced by language exposure (Peña & Bedore, 2011; Zepeda, 2017). For instance, a multilingual child might have knowledge regarding math or literacy concepts and be able to express said knowledge more easily using the home language instead of English or be able to more accurately show what he or she knows by using the languages known in combination rather than any one language alone. Allowing bilingual children to respond to assessment items in either of their languages is a promising practice to attain more accurate assessment results (Peña & Bedore, 2011).

As mentioned previously, there is no consensus on what English language proficiency looks like in preschool age children, in this case particularly in DLLs (Zepeda, 2017). It is therefore important for assessment results to be considered alongside children's developmental level in the English language acquisition process and for results to be used mainly for instructional improvements and for accurately identifying children who may have language delays (Espinosa & García, 2012; Espinosa & Gutiérrez-Clellen, 2013). Figure 17.3 shows the developmental stages of English language acquisition and includes important implications for instructional improvements and accurate identification of children with special language needs (Espinosa & Gutiérrez-Clellen, 2013).

In short, the assessment process for young DLLs (Figure 17.3) includes the timely identification of the languages that children are exposed to at home and the evaluation of their abilities in their home language and English that at the same time account for their stage of English language acquisition. The current state of knowledge about DLLs' language development suggests that we should cautiously make sense of standardized measures and that no single assessment can determine if a DLL is proficient in the English language. Evaluation results of assessments conducted in English and the language of the home are best used to provide children with better instruction (i.e., scaffolded language learning opportunities) or to initiate referral for further evaluation.

Early Learning Approaches

First and foremost, to promote effective development for DLLs, early care and education settings must be programmatically prepared to offer DLLs developmentally appropriate interactions and activities that support their learning (Espinosa & Calderon, 2015; Takanishi & Le Menestrel, 2017). A recent report from the National Academies of Sciences, Engineering, and Medicine focusing on the education of DLLs suggests that, for infants and toddlers,

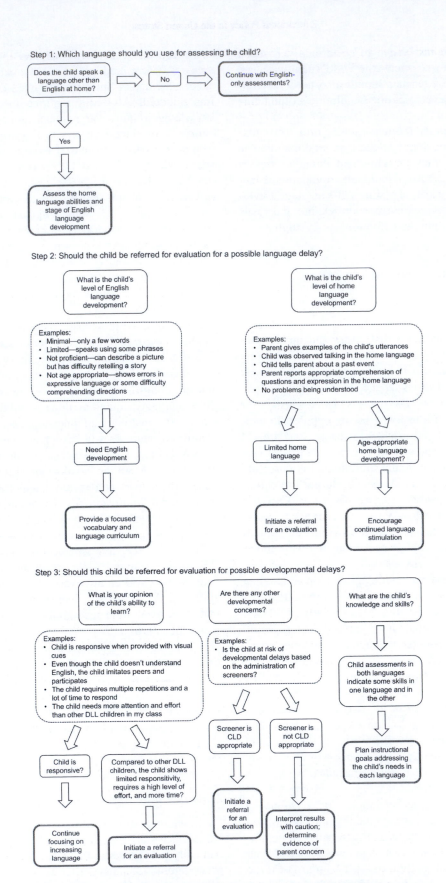

Figure 17.3 Assessment process. Adapted from "Assessment of Young Dual Language Learners in Preschool," by L. M. Espinosa and V. F. Gutiérrez-Clellen, 2013, *California's Best Practices for Young Dual Language Learners: Research Overview Papers*, pp. 202–204. Copyright 2013 by the State Advisory Council on Early Learning and Care.

caregivers need to be responsive to children's verbalizations, use language to scaffold children's self-regulation skills, and encourage young children's play and exploration to support the development of their burgeoning linguistic, emotional, and cognitive abilities (Takanishi & Le Menestrel, 2017).

For older DLLs (ages three to five), rather than didactically teaching specific skills or knowledge, developmentally appropriate care and education must emphasize communication, children's language development, and play as well as seek to scaffold the underlying social dispositions and cognitive capabilities that will allow children to become self-directed learners (Bodrova & Leong, 2005, 2007, 2015; Cohen, Kramer-Vida, Frye, & Andreou, 2014; Copple & Bredekamp, 2009; Riojas-Cortez, 2001). Unfortunately, DLLs may experience preschool programming that primarily focuses on the development of discrete skills, such as phonics instruction, which highlights children's ability to memorize decontextualized letter sounds and mainly concentrates on their English language development (Cuéllar & García, 2012; García, 2011; Song, 2016).

To better serve the needs of DLLs, in addition to implementing generally conceived developmentally appropriate practice that aligns with early learning standards, early care and education programs must provide DLL-specific supports (American Institutes for Research, 2010; Espinosa & Calderon, 2015; Office of Head Start, 2015; Peisner-Feinberg et al., 2014). From a review of the academic literature, three themes emerge that preschool programs can address for improving the quality of education for DLLs: valuing diversity, language development, and family engagement (Baquedano-López, Alexander, & Hernandez, 2013; Barrueco, Smith, & Stephens, 2015; California Department of Education, 2015; Cuéllar, 2016; Espinosa & Calderon,

2015; Freedson, Figueras, & Frede, 2008; Goldenberg, Nemeth, Hicks, Zepeda, & Cardona, 2013; Jensen & García, in press; Michael-Luna, 2015; Office of Head Start, 2015; Park & McHugh, 2014; Park, McHugh, Batalova, & Zong, 2015; Reyes, Da Silva Iddings, & Feller, 2016; Zepeda, 2017). Although we discuss these three themes separately, they in fact overlap in meaningful ways, affect each other, and work in tandem.

Valuing Diversity. Table 17.3 shows procedures and activities that program leaders and educators can engage in to set a positive, affirming, educational environment for DLLs from a diversity perspective. For instance, program directors can implement a program philosophy that values diversity by providing educators with anti-bias professional learning opportunities (Derman-Sparks, LecKeenan, & Nimmo, 2015) and by encouraging educators to learn about the diverse experiences that children have outside the program and integrate these into their lesson planning and with children's interactions (Jensen & García, in press; Rogoff, Mejia-Arauz, & Correa-Chavez, 2015).

Language Development. Table 17.4 shows program-wide and classroom-level language considerations that have the potential to meaningfully improve the education that DLLs receive. DLL-specific program improvement goals can be determined using the Classroom Assessment of Supports for Emergent Bilingual Acquisition (CASEBA)—a validated assessment instrument that rates the quality of the supports offered by teachers to preschool multilingual children (American Institutes for Research, 2010; Freedson et al., 2008). At the classroom level, to the extent possible, educators should support DLLs' home language development along with their English language development. For example, educators can

Table 17.3   Diversity Approaches That Support Dual Language Learners

Program-wide strategies	Classroom strategies
Establish a program philosophy or mission and vision statement that values diversity in all of its variations including ethnicity, cultural background, language, and family structure.	Create an environment where children's ethnic and cultural diversity is present in positive ways, such as framed family photos and art pieces from various countries.
Systematically collect data on the diversity of the staff, children, families, and their communities.	Incorporate diversity in your classroom by reading books or telling stories that feature culturally diverse characters in a positive light throughout the school year.
When possible, hire staff members who match the ethnic, cultural, and linguistic diversity of the children in the program and the residents in their community.	Discuss how children in various communities and cultures are alike and different and promote the idea that everyone is deserving of fair treatment and respect.
Take steps to increase the racial, cultural, ethnic, and linguistic diversity of the children and families whom your program serves.	Incorporate children's diverse ways of learning when planning lessons, activities, and routines.
Make partnerships with community agencies, colleges, and universities to build professional pathways for candidates with a background in social justice, racial and ethnic equity, and multicultural education.	Integrate authentic props, music, and activities in your instructional practice from diverse countries throughout the year so that children can build a positive self-awareness, confidence, and family pride.
Provide professional development on anti-bias for all staff and set up clear standards and procedures to address discriminatory attitudes and behaviors that are biased against any group, child, family, or staff member.	Learn about the diverse life experiences that children have outside of school and incorporate them into your interactions with children.

Sources: Barrueco, Smith, and Stephens (2015); California Department of Education (2015); Derman-Sparks, LeeKeenan, and Nimmo (2015); Jensen and García (in press); Park and McHugh (2014); Park, McHugh, Batalova, and Zong (2015); and Rogoff, Mejia-Arauz, and Correa-Chavez (2015).

Table 17.4 Language Considerations That Support Dual Language Learners

Program-wide strategies	Classroom strategies
Establish a philosophy that explicitly values all levels of multilingualism across all program members (e.g., program director, teachers, children, assistants, family liaisons).	Encourage children to use any language that they want, including translanguaging (i.e., the use of multiple languages in combination), to ensure they can communicate their needs and don't feel inhibited by having to speak a particular language.
Systematically support children's development of their home language while also promoting their English language development.	Incorporate children's home language(s) and English into the physical environment (e.g., print and post bilingual labels).
Systematically collect data on the languages of the children and families that your program serves and also those of their communities.	Expose children to multiple languages even when you don't speak a foreign language (e.g., show YouTube video of greetings, lead songs in multiple languages, invite multilingual adults to the class).
When possible, hire qualified multilingual staff members at all levels of your organization, or fund initiatives to help staff learn needed additional languages.	Have a literacy-rich environment that includes age-appropriate multilingual books written in languages that use letters and characters that are written left to right, right to left, and up and down (i.e., in columns).
Provide staff with professional development on how to support children's dual language development, the stages of second language acquisition, and the effects of language ideologies and language policies on children's development.	Show interest in the language experiences that children have outside your classroom (e.g., in which language do your students dream?).
Provide staff with professional development opportunities that tie together early learning standards and guidelines with children's English language development and home language development.	Point to the similarities and differences between languages and, if possible, connect the home language to English (e.g., cognates) to expand children's comprehension.
Establish procedures that allow children to be assessed in their home language and in English.	Explicitly teach vocabulary and, if possible, use the children's home language to further explain or use vocabulary in context.
Use research-based measures to set DLL-specific program improvement goals (e.g., CASEBA*) and provide professional development to meet said goals.	Have high-quality conversations about stories and books (dialogic reading) in the home language and in English.

* *Classroom Assessment of Supports for Emergent Bilingual Acquisition* (Freedson, Figueras, & Frede, 2008).

Sources: California Department of Education (2015); Castro, Espinosa, and Paez (2011); Cuéllar and Blanco (2018); Cuéllar and García (2012); Espinosa and Calderon (2015); Espinosa and Gutierrez-Clellen (2013); Freedson, Figueras, and Frede (2008); Goldenberg, Nemeth, Hicks, Zepeda, and Cardona (2013); Tabors and Snow (1994); Takanishi and Le Menestrel (2017).

Table 17.5 Developmentally Appropriate Learning and Language Use via Dramatic Play for Dual Language Learners in Preschool

Question 1	Question 2	Question 3	Question 4
How can I plan the dramatic-play area?	What's the expected purpose of language use?	How do I expect adult and child to interact in this activity?	What language supports can be used to scaffold further development in this activity?
Sociocultural Context Incorporate children's home culture, tradition, and language.	**Plan** Children will be attracted to items they are familiar with from home. **Key Uses** Express self and recount.	**Child** • Retells a familiar story related to a toy in the dramatic-play area. • Shares his or her own ideas. **Adult** Asks open-ended questions.	**Language Supports** • Value and create space for the use of all languages. • Add more culturally affirming dramatic-play props. • Use gestures. • Engage in one-on-one interactions.

Adapted from "Develop English Language Skills by Considering How Young Children Use Language," by D. Cuéllar and P. Blanco, 2018, *ASCD Express*, 13(17), pp. 1–2. Copyright 2018 by ASCD. Retrieved from http://www.ascd.org/ascd-express/vol13/1317-cuellar.aspx

support children's languages by making sure that assessments occur in both English and the home language and by encouraging children to use any language that they want or even engage in translanguaging (i.e., the use of multiple languages in combination).

For DLLs, classroom activities should be guided by early learning standards, support social interactions in all of their languages, and concentrate on the main purposes for which children use language (Cuéllar & Blanco, 2018). Table 17.5 provides a framework with four guiding questions to represent how educators could consider language use in their interactions while incorporating play-based, developmentally appropriate activities for DLLs.

Family Engagement. The development and education of DLLs is greatly enhanced when early care and education staff engage with families of DLLs in a respectful, affirming, language-focused manner that emphasizes their funds of knowledge (Barrueco et al., 2015; Cuéllar, 2016; Moll, Amanti, Neff, & Gonzalez, 1992; Nieto, 2012, 2017). Table 17.6 outlines different ways to partner with families of DLLs from a programmatic and classroom perspective.

Table 17.6 Considerations for the Engagement of Families of Dual Language Learners

Program-wide strategies	Classroom strategies
Set a mechanism for families and school staff to access interpreters or translators as needed.	Encourage families to interact with their children in the language that they are most comfortable speaking, and explain that learning two languages does not cause delays or confusion for young children.
Ensure that families have a voice in establishing the programmatic vision for family engagement so that issues that matter to them are addressed.	Have conversations with families about DLLs' propensity to show a preference for speaking English and a reluctance to continue speaking the home language when exposed to English during preschool. Encourage families to make plans regarding this possibility.
Notify program staff that the positive, respectful, ongoing engagement of children's parents and/or extended family members is a core duty of the teaching and caring of young children.	Learn about families' daily routines and find ways to incorporate their daily experiences in your developmentally appropriate interactions with children.
Provide staff with professional development opportunities to learn about affirming, assets-based ways of working with families that emphasize advocacy and families' funds of knowledge.	To individualize care and instruction, ask families to teach you about the language history of their children including interlocutors, estimated skill levels, and timing of exposure to each language.
Provide staff with guidelines on systematic exploration of the children's families' aspirations regarding their children's language, cultural, and identity development.	Invite family members to sing, read, or tell stories to the children in your class in their home language even if only one child speaks a language other than English at home.
Use lay language to meaningfully communicate with families about your program's goals and how these relate to the families' language aspirations for their children.	Create spaces in your classroom for families and parents that share a language and cultural background to explore their commitment to home language and culture maintenance.
Implement a family engagement program that is linguistically and culturally affirming, and supports families in advocating for their children.	

Sources: Barrueco, Smith, and Stephens (2015); Cuéllar (2016); Cuéllar and García (2012); Hurwitz and Olsen (2018); Jensen and García (in press); Michael-Luna (2015); Nieto (2012); Office of Head Start (2015); Park and McHugh (2014); Song (2016); WIDA (2016b).

Conclusion: Preparing Dual Language Learners in the United States for the Future

The growing population of DLLs serves as a call to action to educators and policymakers beginning in preschool and continuing through elementary and secondary education. The aim is to foster DLLs' long term academic success through the development, implementation and promotion of culturally and linguistically competent policies and practices. This chapter has attempted to further contextualize our understanding of education for DLLs and ELs through the discussion of policy. For this population in the United States, policy counts (García & García, 2012; Takanishi & Le Menestrel, 2017).

To this end, the search for general principles of learning that will work for all students must be redirected, particularly in policy venues. This redirection should consider particular implementations of general and non-general principles of teaching and learning that serve a diverse set of environments in and out of school. This mission requires an understanding of how individuals with diverse sets of experiences, packaged individually into cultures, make meaning, communicate that meaning, and extend that meaning, particularly in social contexts we call schools. Such a mission requires in-depth treatment of the processes associated with producing diversity and of the issues of socialization in and out of schools, coupled with a clear examination of how such understanding is actually transformed into educational practices.

What does the future hold for DLL students and American society in general? As recent research indicates, one could predict that as more DLLs enter high-quality, culturally and linguistically responsive early learning settings, barriers to their academic, social, and economic success and mobility will fall. Within a knowledge-driven, responsive, and engaging learning environment, previous knowledge (e.g., the home language, cultural background) is seen as a tool for acquiring and using new knowledge. When diversity is perceived and acted on as a resource for teaching and learning instead of a problem, a focus on what students bring to the process generates an asset-oriented approach rather than a deficit-oriented approach. Consequently, this asset-oriented approach sets the stage for educational success for all children, particularly DLLs, in early childhood and beyond.

Notes

1. For a discussion of the historical role of federal courts in establishing the legal rights of ELs, see Gándara (2015).
2. The BEA is also known as Title VII of the ESEA. The ESEA was reauthorized on several occassions since 1968 and until 2001, when it was reauthorized as the No Child Left Behind Act (NCLB). The most recent reauthorization of the ESEA occurred in 2015 when ESSA replaced NCLB.
3. The legislation was reauthorized on five occasions (1974, 1978, 1984, 1988, and 1994).
4. In addition to the state formulary grants, the 2001 reauthorization allocated funding for discretionary competitive grants for LIEPs that served LEP children from Native American, Alaska Native, Native Hawaiian, and Pacific Islander backgrounds as well as discretionary competitive grants for professional development to institutions of higher education. Of importance is a change in how professional development programs and activities are described; instead of using the term *high quality*, the 2015 legislation uses the term *effective*, and this applies to state-level and local-level activities funded by Title III (see https://www2.ed.gov/programs/nfdp/faq.html#1 for further information on the National Professional Development Program and ESEA Sections 3111(b)(2)(B) and 3115(c)(2)).

5. The legislation acknowledges the diversity of the EL population by calling out long-term ELs, immigrant ELs, and ELs with disabilities in reporting requirements.

6. The 2001 legislation specified that the 5% reserved for state-level activities could be used for planning, evaluation, administration, and interagency coordination; technical assistance to subgrantees; and recognition of subgrantees. This policy is also true for the 2015 legislation, which specifies that the technical assistance to subgrantees can be used for family engagement. The 2015 legislation also allows for state-level professional development to improve the teaching of ELs and state-level planning and direct administrative costs.

7. Other enhancements might include services to ELs with disabilities, such as acquiring educational technology.

8. For further explanation of provisions that have moved from Title III to Title I, refer to U.S. Department of Education (2016, pp. 13–14).

9. For further guidance regarding early learning programs and Title III, refer to U.S. Department of Education (2016, pp. 32–35).

10. The report surveyed 60 state preschool programs nationwide, which means that some states have more than one program represented. For example, California included its State Preschool Program (CSPP) with oversight provided by the California Department of Education's Early Education and Support Division (renamed recently to Early Learning and Care Division) and Transitional Kindergarten with oversight provided by the Elementary and Secondary Education Division. For the purposes of this summary, results are counted and reported at the state level, not by individual state preschool program type.

11. The report included the District of Columbia and states with high proportions of DLL populations and that are part of the North Carolina-led K-3 Assessment Consortium: Alaska, Arizona, California, Delaware, Georgia, Hawaii, Illinois, Iowa, Maine, Maryland, Massachusetts, New Jersey, New York, North Carolina, North Dakota, Oregon, Rhode Island, South Carolina, Texas, Washington, Wisconsin, and the District of Columbia.

12. In California the term *foundations* is used rather than *standards*, emphasizing that the learning and development that happens in the early years of life is foundational to children's lifelong achievement, both in and out of school. The early learning and development foundations are aligned to the Common Core State Standards and include social–emotional development.

13. A complete listing of available modules can be found at https://www.caearlychildhoodonline.org/Modules%20Available_English_033017.pdf.

14. The *DRDP (2015): A Developmental Continuum from Early Infancy to Kindergarten Entry* was developed by the California Department of Education (2013b). Two divisions of the California Department of Education jointly developed the DRDP (2015): The Early Education and Support Division (recently renamed to the Early Learning and Care Division) and the Special Education Division. Lead agencies that participated in the development of the instrument include WestEd's Center for Child and Family Studies, the Desired Results Access Project at the Napa County Office of Education, and the Berkeley Evaluation and Assessment Research (BEAR) Center at the University of California, Berkeley. The *Desired Results Developmental Profile-Kindergarten* was developed by the California Department of Education in collaboration with the BEAR Center at the University of California, Berkeley with additional enhancements created in collaboration with the Illinois State Board of Education.

References

American Institutes for Research. (2010). *Evaluation of preschool for all (PFA) implementation in San Francisco county: Year 5 report.* San Francisco, CA: First 5 San Francisco.

Baquedano-López, P., Alexander, R. A., & Hernández, S. J. (2013). Equity issues in parental and community involvement in schools: What teacher educators need to know. *Review of Research in Education, 37*, 141–182.

Barrueco, S., Smith, S., & Stephens, S. (2015). *Supporting parent engagement in linguistically diverse families to promote young children's learning: Implications for early care and education policy.* New York, NY: Child Care & Early Education Research Connections.

Bean, F. D., Brown, S. K., Leach, M. A., Bachmeier, J. D., & Van Hook, J. (2013). *Unauthorized Mexican migration and the socioeconomic integration of Mexican Americans.* Retrieved from https://www.russellsage.org/research/reports/unauthorized-immigrants

Bialystok, E. (2010). Global–local and trail-making tasks by monolingual and bilingual children: Beyond inhibition. *Developmental Psychology, 46*(1), 93–105.

Bilingual Education Act (BEA), Pub. L. No. (90–247), 81 Stat. 816 (1968).

Bilingual Education Act (BEA), Pub. L. No. (93–380), 88 Stat. 503 (1974).

Bodrova, E., & Leong, D. J. (2005). High quality preschool programs: What would Vygotsky say? *Early Education and Development, 16*(4), 435–444.

Bodrova, E., & Leong, D. J. (2007). *Tools of the mind: The Vygotskian approach to early childhood education.* Saddle Rock, NJ: Pearson.

Bodrova, E., & Leong, D. J. (2015). Vygotskian and post-Vygotskian views on children's play. *American Journal of Play, 7*(3), 371–388.

California Department of Education. (2008). *California preschool learning foundations, Volume 1.* Sacramento, CA: CDE Press.

California Department of Education. (2010a). *California preschool learning foundations, Volume 2.* Sacramento, CA: CDE Press.

California Department of Education. (2010b). *California preschool curriculum framework, Volume 1.* Sacramento, CA: CDE Press.

California Department of Education. (2011). *California preschool curriculum framework, Volume 2.* Sacramento, CA: CDE Press.

California Department of Education. (2012). *California preschool learning foundations, Volume 3.* Sacramento, CA: CDE Press.

California Department of Education. (2013a). *California preschool curriculum framework, Volume 3.* Sacramento, CA: CDE Press.

California Department of Education. (2013b). *DRDP (2015): A developmental continuum from early infancy to kindergarten entry.* Sacramento, CA: CDE Press.

California Department of Education. (2015). *California preschool program guidelines.* Sacramento, CA: CDE Press. Retrieved from https://www.cde.ca.gov/sp/cd/re/documents/preschoolproggdlns2015.pdf

Capps, R., Fix, M., Murray, J., Ost, J., Passel, J. S., & Hrwantoro, S. (2005). *The new demography of America's schools: Immigration and the No Child Left Behind Act.* Washington, DC: The Urban Institute.

Casanova, U. (1991). Bilingual education: Politics or pedagogy. In O. García (Ed.), *Bilingual education* (Vol. 1, pp. 167–182). Amsterdam, The Netherlands: John Benjamins Publishing Company.

Cheung, A. C., & Slavin, R. E. (2012). Effective reading programs for Spanish-dominant English language learners (ELLs) in the elementary grades: A synthesis of research. *Review of Educational Research, 82*(4), 351–395.

Cohen, L. E., Kramer-Vida, L., Frye, N., & Andreou, M. (2014). The effect of bilingual instruction and play on preschoolers' English proficiency. *International Journal of Play, 3*(1), 36–52.

Copple, C., & Bredekamp, S. (2009). *Developmentally appropriate practice in early childhood programs serving children from birth to age 8* (3rd ed.). Washington, DC: National Association for the Education of Young Children.

Cuéllar, D. (2016). *WIDA focus on bulletin: The early years: Assets-based, language-focused family engagement for dual language learners.* Madison, WI: Board of Regents of the University of Wisconsin System. Retrieved from https://www.wida.us/get.aspx?id=2072

Cuéllar, D., & Blanco, P. (2018). Develop English language skills by considering how young children use language. *ASCD Express, 13*(17), 1–2. Retrieved from http://www.ascd.org/ascd-express/vol13/1317-cuellar.aspx

Cuéllar, D., & García, E. E. (2012). Working with Latino preschoolers: The literacy and language goals of teachers and mothers. In B. Falk (Ed.), *Defending childhood: Keeping the promise of early education* (pp. 114–132). New York, NY: Teachers College Press.

Derman-Sparks, L., LeeKeenan, D., & Nimmo, J. (2015). *Leading anti-bias early childhood programs: A guide for change.* New York, NY: Teachers College Press.

Espinosa, L. M., & Calderon, M. (2015). *State early learning and development standards/guidelines, policies and related practices*. Boston, MA: Build Initiative. Retrieved from http://buildinitiative.org/Portals/0/Uploads/Documents/BuildDLLReport2015.pdf

Espinosa, L. M., & García, E. E. (2012). *Developmental assessment of young dual language learners with a focus on kindergarten entry assessments: Implications for state policies (Working Paper #1)*. Chapel Hill: The University of North Carolina, Frank Porter Graham Child Development Institute; Center for Early Care and Education Research-Dual Language Learners (CECER-DLL).

Espinosa, L. M., & Gutiérrez-Clellen, V. F. (2013). Assessment of young dual language learners in preschool. In *California's best practices for young dual language learners: Research overview papers* (pp. 172–208). Sacramento, CA: California Department of Education, pp. 202–204. Retrieved from https://www.cde.ca.gov/sp/cd/ce/documents/dllresearchpapers.pdf

Freedson, M., Figueras, A., & Frede, E. (2008). *Classroom assessment of supports for emergent bilingual education*. New Brunswick: National Institute for Early Education Research, Rutgers, The State University of New Jersey.

Friedman-Krauss, A. H., Barnett, S. W., Weisenfeld, G. G., Kasmin, R., DiCrecchio, N., & Horowitz, M. (2018). *The state of preschool 2017: State preschool yearbook*. New Brunswick, NJ: National Institute for Early Education Research.

Gándara, P. (2015). Charting the relationship of English learners and the ESEA: One step forward, two steps back. *RSF: The Russel Sage Foundation Journal of Social Sciences, 1*(3), 112–128. Retrieved from https://muse.jhu.edu/article/605403

García, E. E. (2011). ¡Ya Basta!: Challenging restrictions on English language learners. *Dissent, 58*(4), 47–50.

García, E. E., & Frede, E. C. (2010). *Young English language learners: Current research and emerging directions for practice and policy*. New York, NY: Teachers College Press.

García, E. E., & García, E. H. (2012). *Understanding the language development and early education of Hispanic children*. New York, NY: Teachers College Press.

Garcia, E. E., & Gonzalez, R. (1995). Issues in systemic reform for culturally and linguistically diverse students. *Teachers College Record, 96*(3), 418–431.

García, E. E., & Ozturk, M. (2017). *An asset-based approach to Latino education in the United States*. New York, NY: Routledge.

Genesee, F. (2010). Dual language development in preschool children. In E. E. García & E. C. Frede (Eds.), *Young English language learners* (pp. 59–79). New York, NY: Teachers College Press.

Goldenberg, C., Nemeth, K., Hicks, J., Zepeda, M., & Cardona, L. M. (2013). *Paper 3: Program elements and teaching practices to support young dual language learners*. Sacramento, CA: Governor's State Advisory Council on Early Learning and Care.

Hakuta, K. (2018). *California English learner roadmap: Strengthening comprehensive educational policies, programs, and practices for English learners*. Sacramento, CA: California Department of Education.

Hurwitz, A., & Olsen, L. (2018). *Supporting dual language learner success in superdiverse preK-3 classrooms: The Sobrato early academic language model*. Washington, DC: Migration Policy Institute.

Jensen, B., & Bachmeier, J. (2015). *A portrait of U.S. children of Central American origins and their educational opportunity*. Washington, DC: MacArthur Foundation.

Jensen, B., & García, E. (in press). Fostering equitable developmental opportunities for dual language learners in early education settings. In V. L. Gadsden, B. Graue, F. J. Levine, & S. K. Ryan (Eds.), *Diversity issues in early education*. Washington, DC: American Educational Research Association.

Jiménez-Castellanos, O., & García, E. (2017). Intersection of language, class, ethnicity, and policy: Toward disrupting inequality for English language learners. *Review of Research in Education, 41*(1), 428–452. doi:10.3102/0091732X16688623

Li, G., Edwards, P. A., & Gunderson, L. (2010). *Best practices in ELL instruction*. New York, NY: The Guilford Press.

Mathews, H. (2011). *Meeting the early learning challenge: Supporting English language learners*. Washington, DC: CLASP.

Michael-Luna, S. (2015). What parents have to teach us about their dual language children. *Young Children, 70*(5), 42–47.

Moll, L. C., Amanti, C., Neff, D., & Gonzalez, N. (1992). Funds of knowledge for teaching: Using a qualitative approach to connect homes and classrooms. *Theory into Practice, 31*(2), 132–141.

National Association for the Education of Young Children (NAEYC). (2009). *Where we stand: On assessing young English language learners*. Washington, DC: Author. Retrieved from http://www.naeyc.org/files/naeyc/file/positions/WWSEnglishLanguageLearnersWeb.pdf

Navarro, R. A. (1990). The problems of language, education, and society: Who decides. In E. E. García & R. V. Padilla (Eds.), *Advances in bilingual education research* (pp. 289–313). Tucson: University of Arizona Press.

Nieto, S. (2012). Honoring the lives of all children: Identity, culture and language. In B. Falk (Ed.), *Defending childhood: Keeping the promise of early education* (pp. 48–62). New York, NY: Teachers College Press.

Nieto, S. (2017). Becoming sociocultural mediators: What all educators can learn from bilingual and ESL teachers. *Issues in Teacher Education, 26*(2), 129–141.

Office of Head Start. (2015). *Head Start early learning outcomes framework: Ages birth to five*. Washington, DC: U.S. Department of Health and Human Services, Administration for Children and Families.

Park, M., & McHugh, M. (2014). *Immigrant parents and early childhood programs: Addressing barriers of literacy, culture and systems knowledge*. Washington, DC: Migration Policy Institute.

Park, M., McHugh, M., Batalova, J., & Zong, J. (2015). *Immigrant and refugee workers in the early childhood field: Taking a closer look*. Washington, DC: Migration Policy Institute.

Park, M., O'Toole, A., & Katsiaficas, C. (2017). *Dual language learners: A national demographic and policy profile*. Washington, DC: Migration Policy Institute.

Peisner-Feinberg, E., Buysse, V., Fuligni, A., Burchinal, M., Espinosa, L., Halle, T., & Castro, D. C. (2014). Using early care and education quality measures with dual language learners: A review of the research. *Early Childhood Research Quarterly, 29*, 786–803.

Peña, E. D., & Bedore, L. M. (2011). It takes two: Improving assessment accuracy in bilingual children. *The ASHA Leader, 16*(13), 20–22.

Reyes, I., Da Silva Iddings, A. C., & Feller, N. (2016). Building relationships with diverse students and families: A funds of knowledge perspective. *Journal of Early Childhood Literacy, 16*(1), 8–33.

Reyes, S. A., & Kleyn, T. (2010). *Teaching in two languages: A guide for K-12 bilingual educators*. Thousand Oaks, CA: Corwin Press.

Riojas-Cortez, M. (2001). Preschoolers funds of knowledge displayed through sociodramatic play episodes in a bilingual classroom. *Early Childhood Education Journal, 29*(1), 35–40.

Rogoff, B., Mejia-Arauz, R., & Correa-Chavez, M. (2015). A cultural paradigm—Learning by observing and pitching in. *Advances in Child Development and Behavior, 49*, 1–22.

Song, K. (2016). "No one speaks Korean at school!": Ideological discourses on language in a Korean family. *Bilingual Research Journal, 39*(1), 4–19.

Takanishi, R., & Le Menestrel, S. (2017). *Promoting the educational success of children and youth learning English: Promising futures* (Report of the National Academies of Sciences, Engineering, and Medicine). Washington, DC: The National Academies Press. doi:10.17226/24677

Tobin, J., Adair, J. K., & Arzubiaga, A. (2013). *Children crossing borders: Immigrant parent and teacher perspectives on preschool for children of immigrants*. New York, NY: Russell Sage Foundation.

U.S. Department of Education. (2016). *Non-regulatory guidance: English learners and Title III of the Elementary and Secondary Education Act (ESEA), as amended by the Every Student Succeeds Act (ESSA)*. Washington, DC: Author. Retrieved from https://www2.ed.gov/policy/elsec/leg/essa/essatitleiiiguidenglishlearners92016.pdf

U.S. Department of Education, Office of Elementary and Secondary Education. (2002). *Outline of programs and selected changes in the No Child Left Behind Act of 2001*. Washington, DC: Author.

U.S. Department of Education, Office of English Language Acquisition, Language Enhancement, and Academic Achievement for Limited English Proficient Students. (2003). *Non-regulatory guidance on the Title III state formula grant program*. Washington, DC: Author.

Unsworth, S. (2016). Quantity and quality of language input in bilingual language development. In E. Nicoladis & S. Montanari (Eds.), *Lifespan perspectives on bilingualism* (pp. 136–196). Washington, DC: American Psychological Association.

Valentino, R. A., & Reardon, S. F. (2015). Effectiveness of four instructional programs designed to serve English learners: Variation by ethnicity and initial English proficiency. *Educational Evaluation and Policy Analysis, 37*(4), 612–637. Retrieved from https://ies.ed.gov/ncee/wwc/Study/82341

WestEd Center for Child and Family Studies. (2018). *The desired results developmental profile (2015): A strengths-based approach to assessing young dual language learners* (Unpublished research brief). WestEd, Sausalito, CA.

Wiese, A., & Garcia, E. E. (2006). Educational policy in the United States regarding bilinguals in early childhood education. In B. Spodek & O. N. Saracho (Eds.), *Handbook of research on the education of young children* (2nd ed., pp. 361–374). Mahwah, NJ: Lawrence Erlbaum Associates.

Wiley, T. G., Lee, J. S., & Rumberger, R. W. (2009). *The education of language minority immigrants in the United States*. Buffalo, NY: Multilingual Matters.

Yoshikawa, H. (2011). *Immigrants raising citizens: Undocumented parents and their children*. New York, NY: Russell Sage Foundation.

Yoshikawa, H., & Kholoptseva, J. (2013). *Unauthorized immigrant parents and their children's development*. Washington, DC: Migration Policy Institute.

Zepeda, M. (2017). *California's gold: An advocacy framework for young dual language learners*. Los Altos, CA: Heising-Simons Foundation.

18

Early Childhood Multicultural Education

Esther Elena López-Mulnix

The perspective presented here reflects years of experience in education and the mental health field. It is also one that values interdisciplinary and multigenerational collaboration, as well as the ubiquitous characteristic of individuals' culture.

The multicultural field is sometimes difficult to discern, and it can become an overwhelming task. Where does one begin? How does one go about becoming multiculturally effective? The author hopes these pages will facilitate and support teachers' journeys to discover, learn, and practice multicultural teaching skills.

Cross cultural communication occurs constantly. Countries' geographical boundaries do not stop individuals from different cultures from communicating with each other. There is constant international travel, and internet communication is an intricate, familiar part of people's daily experience. Children, in most places, live in a world where immediate virtual responses with Twitter, Instagram, Facebook, FaceTime, Skype, WhatsApp, etc., are seconds away from their small screens. The importance of becoming effective multicultural early childhood educators (ECEs) seems even more urgent when the physical "real" world in which children currently live is very diverse. For the purpose of this chapter the words "effective multicultural skills" are used to indicate the educator's ability (awareness, sensitivity, and skill) to produce a desired effect, i.e., educational engagement in children with different cultural attributes.

Literature Review

Supporting literature and research is weaved throughout the chapter. There are two major content areas: multicultural teaching effectiveness, and recommendations for policy and practice. The area of multicultural teaching effectiveness is composed of three sections: multicultural awareness, cultural values, and power and privilege of intersecting groups of reference. The second area is that of conclusions and recommendations for policy and practice. This area is composed of three sections: practical suggestions to develop early

educators multicultural model; use of reflection in action, and dialogic pedagogy in the classroom; and policy applications of the California early childhood educator (ECE) competencies. The competency on culture, diversity, and equity if implemented can foster education of all children with equity, and life-long educational engagement that begins in headstart and pre-kindergarten classrooms.

In the USA, early elementary school classrooms reflect the following demographics: 49% of children are identified as White, 26% as Hispanic, 14% as Black, 5% as Asian, 4.6% as two or more races, 1.2% as American Indian or Alaska Native, and 0.4% as Pacific Islander (nces.ed.gov National Center for Education Statistics, February 2018). Thus, now more than ever, it is imperative for educators to learn effective multicultural teaching skills.

The above elementary school demographics in the USA underscore the diversity of the students in early elementary school classrooms. In addition to students' diversity, prospective teachers in the USA are increasingly homogenous. Preservice teachers tend to be female, White, and middle class. The great diversity of students and the homogeneity of teachers underscore the need for teachers to learn multicultural skills. Individuals are socialized into the norms that their groups of reference aspire to and are not familiar or meaningfully engaged cross culturally (Hardy, 2004; Howard, 2006; Kozol, 2005; Orfield & Lee, 2004). Further, there is a "... pervasiveness of institutions to privilege one set of racial experiences over another" (Gonzalez & Morrison, 2016). Thus, cultural differences among teachers and students make it necessary for prospective teachers to develop multicultural skills.

Effective multicultural teaching skills are based on multicultural awareness and knowledge; without these, teachers will not be prepared to appreciate students who aspire to values different from their own. The literature and research support the importance of positive student-adult relationships in school. These relationships are deemed central to student academic success (Pianta, Stuhlman, & Hamre, 2002; Rodríguez, 2008; Stanton-Salazar, 2001; Valenzuela, 1999).

Culture is defined here as the world view of an individual, which is supported by assumptions, values, biases, preconceived notions, and personal limitations (Sue & Sue, 2008) based on reference group markers, such as race, ethnicity, religion, gender, socioeconomic status, sexual orientation, physical and mental abilities. Thus, culture is anchored in the intersectionality of those reference groups. Furthermore, culture here is explored from an advantage not a disadvantage or deficit perspective (Thompson, 2014). In other words, cultural values are understood from a desirable, beneficial perspective.

Multicultural Teaching Effectiveness

Multicultural Awareness. Educators become multiculturally proficient by developing multicultural awareness, knowledge, and skill (López & Mulnix, 2004). Prospective teachers can find a space here to examine the need for young children's voices to be actively engaged and integrated in the curriculum content. It is the integration of all voices that makes a classroom multiculturally effective.

Educators will discover and appreciate the values that children from differing cultural groups aspire to attain. These values might be quite different from those the educators might hold, and yet, they are just as desirable. Niesz (2010) reviewed research about teacher education programs and suggested teachers' perceptions and attitudes about their prospective students were driving forces for advocating for their students and for the instruction decisions they made in the classroom (Ladson-Billings, 1999).

Developing cultural awareness can begin with the identification of values. Individuals pursue values based on their groups of reference. Groups of reference are organized around personal attributes, such as race, ethnicity, gender, socioeconomic status, sexual orientation, religion, mental and physical abilities. Some personal attributes are easily understood, but others are complex or intertwined. For example, race has been used to describe physical characteristics (skin color, hair texture and color, etc.), and ethnicity is used to encompass cultural traditions such as language, culinary customs, etc. Other group markers do not seem to need a particular definition, such as gender, socioeconomic status, religion, sexual orientation, and physical or mental abilities.

Multicultural scholars (Sue & Sue, 2008) organized personal attributes in the USA in two categories: those of majority individuals who also have power and those of minority individuals who tend to be oppressed by those in power. In the USA, there is a majority/dominant American world view. This view confers power to individuals or groups with the following personal attributes: White race, European or US ethnicity with English as the native language, Christian, male, heterosexual, of high socioeconomic status, able minded and bodied (Katz, 1985; Sue & Sue, 2008). Minority individuals in the USA tend to have personal attributes such as being a person of color, female, non-Christian, of low socioeconomic status, homosexual, and having a disabled mind and/or body.

However, the above categories coexist and intersect. Individuals possess multiple personal attributes. These attributes play pivotal and socially significant roles in people's lives and help shape their identity and determine their value system. It is these aspects of people's identity that inform how they see themselves and the world, how others see them, and how they relate to each other (https://www.psychologytoday.com/us/basics/race-and-ethnicity, July 5, 2018).

Cultural Values. One way to continue this multicultural journey is to learn the values supported by different groups of people. Cultural values have been organized by Hofstede, Hofstede, and Minkov (2010) and Sue and Sue (2008) and were identified by Stewart (1971), Pedersen (1988), Wehrly (1995), and others. There are patterns of cultural assumptions and values that can be used to understand (awareness and knowledge) and develop multicultural proficiency. Once teacher educators are multiculturally proficient, they can provide prospective early childhood educators with a guided pluralistic and practical view of the world.

People stress or define cultural assumptions or values differently based on the cultural attributes or group markers (race, ethnicity, gender, religion, socioeconomic status, sexual orientation, mind and body ability) they possess. Hofstede et al. (2010) offered six cultural dimensions depicting continua of cultural values. These continua hold values that can be considered important (high) or not (low) by a particular group of people. The first continuum was labeled *power distance* or strong hierarchy. Power distance was the extent to which the less powerful members of a group expect and experience the distribution of power unequally. The second continuum was labeled *individualism/collectivism*. This was the degree of interdependence (collectivism) or independence (individualism) a group maintains among its members. The third continuum was labeled *masculinity/femininity*. A masculine group's motivation was competition, winning was considered success, as well as wanting to be the best. Femininity in a group was motivated by quality of life, liking what was done, and not standing out were considered success. The fourth continuum was *uncertainty avoidance*. This was the extent to which members of a group feel threatened by ambiguous or unknown situations and have created beliefs and groups that try to avoid the unknown. The fifth continuum was *long-term orientation*. This was the degree to which group members maintained a link with the group's own past while dealing with challenges of present and future. The sixth was *indulgence/restraint*. This was the degree to which people tried to control their desires and impulses.

Following Hofstede's six cultural dimensions, the values considered by the majority or dominant values in the USA are: low power distance or no hierarchy, high individualism or independence, high masculinity or competition, high uncertainty avoidance, low long-term orientation, and high indulgence. However, many minority individuals in the USA consider their values to be at a different end of some continua.

For example, most experiences of minority individuals support a high power distance. This is to say, women, people of color, disabled individuals, etc., often experience discrimination and feel treated as "less competent or second class" individuals. In addition, other continua, such as collectivism, more accurately depict their aspirations or personal reality. Further, women are socialized into behaving in a nurturing manner and taking care of others (usually children, students, etc.); thus, in order for women to be perceived as successful, they are expected to collaborate and not to stand out.

There are several combinations of group markers a child's environment (immediate and extended family) might represent. In addition, there is at least one more cultural issue to consider: the *saliency* of a particular group marker in a particular context or the intersectionality of the different group markers in the child's particular family or environment situation. This is to say, the saliency or importance of a particular group marker intersects with the other group markers. Thus, importance changes according to the context. For example, for a female child in a classroom composed of females of different socioeconomic class, gender might have less saliency than socioeconomic class. This has also been called intersectionality and "living culture," as Bennett, Cochrane, Mohan, and Neal wrote in 2016. This is to say, there are several group markers, and they coexist within the individual's identity, where they intersect.

Solorzano and Delgado Bernal (2001) defined "LatCrit as a theory that elucidates Latinas/Latinos' multidimensional identities and can address the intersectionality of racism, sexism, classism and other forms of oppression" (p. 312). This theory can be applied to other groups of people who experience oppression based on different cultural attributes (religion, gender, etc.). Rodríguez (2008), reflecting on prior research (Solorzano & Delgado Bernal, 2001), stated that the basic foundations of student-teacher relationships in school are forged with trust based on recognition, inspiration, motivation, and support (Rodríguez & Wasserberg, 2010).

It would be a good exercise to develop multicultural teaching skills to become aware of the values a teacher holds, then identify the values of her/his students, and get to know them to appreciate them and support their values. Furthermore, a society might be at its best when it recognizes and uses different values in different situations. Thus, a child who experiences an effective multicultural environment might learn to use competition and collaboration selectively, as well as individualism and collectivism, etc. Values would be used strategically and they would complement each other.

Power and Privilege. Culture was defined as the ubiquitous intersectionality of attributes such as gender, race, ethnicity, social class, physical and mental abilities, and sexual orientation that people draw from their daily living to communicate, develop, negotiate, and learn (Bennett, Cochrane, Mohan, & Neal, 2015; Gonzalez & Morrison, 2016; López Bernstein, 1997; Noble, 2013; Sennet, 2012; Wilson, 2011, 2014; Wise, 2009). Nevertheless, sometimes it is difficult to separate some personal attributes. Race and ethnicity represent different constructs. However, race and ethnicity are terms often used interchangeably and sometimes with complementarity. For example, the US Census Bureau, in its population tables, uses the term "Hispanic" to refer to persons of any race whose birth or ancestry is from Mexico, Puerto Rico, and Cuba, and more recently, it has also included Central America. However, it does not include persons with ancestry or birth in Spain or Portugal (https://www.census.gov/data.html, July 2018). Thus, sometimes it becomes difficult to discern or separate the constructs of race and ethnicity.

Once the advantages of multicultural experiences are understood, the appreciation of differing values becomes natural. Teachers learn and welcome or reinforce the use of different values like individualism and collectivism, competition and collaboration, etc. Thus, classrooms stop replicating only majority values—those held by individuals with power and privilege, and become places where children learn to appreciate and integrate minority values. They learn from each other. They become multiculturally skilled. Educating multiculturally skilled children necessitates that their multicultural interactions be guided from an advantage perspective in a positive inclusive manner to develop their multicultural awareness, knowledge, and skill (López & Mulnix, 2004). Individuals draw upon interpersonal resources and techniques as they craft the skills involved in negotiating place and others (Bennett et al., 2015, p. 2307; Noble, 2013; Sennet, 2012; Wilson, 2011, 2014; Wise, 2009).

It was stated in the preceding section that children are socialized into becoming *aware* of their own group markers (gender, race, ethnicity, religion, sexual orientation, socioeconomic class, physical and mental abilities), the values those markers support, and who they are becoming (identity). Multicultural early childhood education (ECE) aims to expand children's developing multicultural awareness. This development of multicultural awareness can support diverse values based on different group markers. The process of developing multicultural awareness can help children become multiculturally knowledgeable. Children can then demonstrate appreciation for the values of other children who are different from them. If this is done successfully, this multiculturally skilled behavior would expand the center to include both majority and minority individuals.

Conclusion and Recommendations for Policy and Practice

Early childhood educators can model multicultural skills in the classroom by listening and including differing voices, giving those dissenting voices the freedom to disagree or be in conflict (Elkader, 2016). For example, in a kindergarten class, children were asked to complete a story by adding an ending. The children's endings seemed to reflect their cultural experiences (Saracho, 2003).

López-Mulnix recently (López-Mulnix, personal communication February, 2018) replicated the "complete a story" experience with children age four to six years old. This story began by describing a lively large family (grandparents, mother, father, children) getting together to plan the celebration of a birthday. They planned to go to the park for a couple of hours during the weekend and bring balloons, food, and drinks. However, the grandmother stated she will not be able to join them. After this incomplete story was told, the children were asked to finish the story. The children's endings to the story seemed to fall into two categories: one focusing on the grandmother and another focusing on the birthday celebration. Children who expressed concern for the grandmother assumed she was sick or needed help and directed the family to assist her; children who were concerned about the birthday party concentrated on the birthday celebration.

Thus, the results seemed to reflect one of the values within the cultural continuum of individualistic/collectivistic behaviors. This is to say, children identified by their parents as of Hispanic or Arabic ethnicity ended the story with reference to the grandmother. This ending seemed to illustrate a collectivistic value. One in which there is a high degree of interdependence among the members of these children's families. On the other hand, children identified by their parents as belonging to a White ethnic group of reference ended the story with the birthday, its preparation, and not ruining it. This ending seemed to illustrate the degree of independence these children's families maintain among their members. Indeed Saracho's (2003) conclusion that the children's endings reflected their cultural experience seemed replicated in the results of López-Mulnix (2018).

Prospective early childhood educators, when using storytelling, are encouraged to (1) become *aware* of the ending they anticipate (which would be culturally congruent to the curriculum and their value system), (2) listen *sensitively* to gain *knowledge* from children's diverse contributions (which would be grounded in the children's culture), and (3) incorporate *skillfully* those different perspectives in the curriculum without rejecting or not attending to them, even if they are initially perceived as inadequate (Gonzalez-Mena, 2013; López & Mulnix, 2004). In this way, educators can assist all the children in the classroom to value culturally congruent behavior and develop literacy readiness in a multiculturally sensitive manner. This can help children to be inclusive and accept as desirable values that are different from those they aspire to and have been socialized to acquire.

Educators' Multicultural Development Model

Teaching early educators to use well-developed multicultural skills (López-Bernstein, 1997; López & Mulnix, 2004) can be addressed using López-Bernstein model. Once prospective teachers have developed effective multicultural skills, it is suggested here that they demonstrate those skills with reflection in action (Schön, 1987) and the use of dialogic pedagogy (ElKader, 2016) in early education classrooms.

Children develop their cultural identity throughout their lives. Education can facilitate this development. Children are socialized in the classroom, and classrooms can replicate society or mindfully offer an alternative inclusive perspective in which all students' voices are heard. The educator in the latter classroom embraces dissension and differences of view point. This acceptance can expand the educator's and the children's multicultural awareness, knowledge, and multicultural effectiveness.

López-Bernstein (1997) delineated a pathway for effective multicultural educators. The pathway presented three areas of multicultural development: (1) construction of the self, (2) personal working method, and (3) integration of personal experiences of discrimination and marginalization. López-Bernstein's (1997) research investigated how prospective educators developed their multicultural competency. She discovered three major areas that participants seemed to be using to develop their multicultural effectiveness.

The first area of multicultural development was the *construction of the self.* This area represented how prospective educators used the perception of themselves and their students. The construction of the self evolved in three levels—from least to most developed. The first level was when educators perceived their self as being separate from their culture. The second level was when educators perceived themselves in a process of negotiating self and culture. Finally, the third level in this area was when educators achieved the perception of an encultured self.

The second area of multicultural development was the educators' *working method.* This second area represented how prospective educators evolved in their work with their students. The working method had three levels—from least to most developed. The first level was when educators avoided cultural issues. The second level was when educators found themselves labeling or sorting cultural attributes or personal group markers. Finally, the third level in the working method area was when educators were in a process of accommodating culture.

The third area of multicultural development was represented by the educators' *integration of personal experiences* of discrimination and marginalization in themselves and others. This was the process of how prospective educators integrated episodes of discrimination and/or marginalization experiences into their lives and/or those of their students. The integration of cultural personal experiences had three levels—from least to most developed. The first level of the integration of personal experiences was labeled ethical closure. Educators in this first level were narrowly interpreting experiences of discrimination and marginalization. The second level of the integration of personal experiences was described as one of discovering and struggling. Finally, the most developed level of the integration of personal experiences was that in which educators seem to be choosing where to stand. In this level educators were choosing to use their experiences with oppression (oppressed or oppressor) to become more sensitive to others' experiences and more skilled multiculturally. All three themes seem to show an evolutionary process that prospective educators in multicultural training underwent. In her research, the participants represented in the third level of each theme had, in most instances, progressed through the first two levels.

López-Bernstein's multicultural pathway can be used to examine educators' multicultural journeys, locate the level of development attained, and seek opportunities to continue developing multicultural teaching skills during their training. The pathway seems to suggest that teacher educators can model for early childhood prospective teachers how to facilitate positive cultural identity development. In addition, prospective early childhood educators will aid in the formation of multicultural perspectives for students in their classrooms. Children will then learn that other children might have a different, but just as valuable, view of the world. This needs to take place from a "win-win" or advantage perspective for all children, keeping in mind the ubiquitous nature of intersecting cultural attributes or reference group markers because they will support different values. All students need to be engaged and mentored by their teachers in order to expand the socialization process and to permit all voices to be heard (Rodríguez & Oseguera, 2015).

Reflection in Action and Dialogic Pedagogy

Early educators need to look for an advantage perspective of differing values to teach students to appreciate different values, to see different values as complementary. The perception of positive personal values would include both individualistic and collectivistic perspectives. Achievement would be a product of both competition and collaboration. There will be praise for those who "do" and those who "contemplate." Speaking more than one language will be considered a true asset. Using rhythm or chanting to learn facts (another language, multiplication tables) will be considered another way of learning.

There is a continuous need for reflective thinkers (Shor, 1993) that can only be fulfilled if children learn to think critically, and this cannot be achieved without engaging them. Donald Schön (1983) wrote about encouraging educators to reflect in the moment of action (teaching) in a way that is similar to how students are invited to reflect on their learning. In 1987, he challenged teachers to "… move into the center of the learning situation, into the center of their own doubts" (p. 83). Children who are culturally different from the teacher elicit doubts when the teacher considers their dissenting voice. Further, Bakhtin (1991) suggested that a true educational project could not take place without an amalgam of voices that coexist and that have the freedom to disagree or be in conflict (Elkader, 2016). However, to be open and ready to integrate students' contributions to the curriculum, educators need to be aware of their cultural values, be sensitive to differing values, and consider students equal in their rights to express their voices. This multicultural skill has been called "dialogic pedagogy" by Elkader (2016).

Saracho and Martínez-Hancock (2004), paraphrasing Sheets (2002), stated that

> it is important in the schools to apply sets of values, attitudes, and beliefs that resemble those held by both students and teachers … multicultural education for pre-service early education teachers … [is] key … to develop … prospective teachers' cultural sensitivity.

A dialogic pedagogy seems to demonstrate multicultural awareness, knowledge, and skill. Dialogic pedagogy refers to conversations taking place among equal subjects, providing a safe, unoppressive, and potentially transformative learning environment to all students (Elkader, 2016).

However, most instructional dialogue is a monologic approach to education because it ignores the students' agency in their own learning. Matusov (2011) maintained that an authentic dialogic project allows students to be authors of their own learning, which can only happen if the instructor seeks an answer from the student without imposing her/his own convictions [cultural values]. The instructor needs to listen openly and develop an appreciation for those differing values.

Almost 50 years ago, Freire (1970), discussing liberatory pedagogy, said teachers needed to "reinvent" themselves to develop meaningful relationships with their students. The author argues here that one way to reinvent oneself is to become multicultural. This is to say, open to diverse values, and integrate them into one's repertoire. This is not a simple process, and sometimes, it is difficult to attain. Using another voice from the USA rich educational past, an example of the perception of majority superiority is conveyed by Maya Angelou (1981) when she recounted the paternalistic attitude of a White individual who stated: "Some of my best friends are [Black]…" (p. 284).

No country has citizens to spare. It is in the best interest of all citizens that early education engages all students and their families. In particular those students at risk of school attrition. One important factor that can contribute to school attrition seems to be the replication of oppression in the classroom. Oppression occurs in a classroom where students are not heard and are not positively rewarded because they hold different values from those of the adult in the classroom. It is time for prospective teachers to develop their multicultural teaching skills and stop replicating a discriminatory socialization where only majority values are embraced.

This chapter began by outlining the importance of multicultural early education. This education can stop replicating discrimination and oppression and affirm all children. Multicultural education begins with teachers' multicultural education by developing prospective teachers' cultural identities. Facilitating prospective teachers' multicultural journeys through awareness, knowledge, and skill. Prospective teachers will develop an enculturated self that accommodates culture and integrates cultural experiences of power and privilege. They will become aware of their own values and learn to appreciate the values that some children in their classroom might have because of their groups of reference (race, ethnicity, religion, gender, etc.). Only then will prospective teachers be ready to practice a critical pedagogy, as they present an open and inclusive curriculum that engages the experiences of all of their students.

Early Childhood Education Policy

Currently, federal policy for Early Childhood Education (ECE) is broad and calls on each state to make applicable rules. Thus, some states are more specific and have dedicated resources to facilitate the implementation of the policies. One state that has done extensive work on multicultural competencies for ECE is California. The author recommends early childhood educators to become familiar with California's example and advocate its replication in the rest of the United States of America. California has developed a comprehensive approach to developing Early Childhood Education and promotes and supports prospective teachers in their development. The Early Childhood Educator Competencies from the state of California can be found at https://www.cde.ca.gov/sp/cd/re/ececomps.asp._It describes and provides specific topics and best practices on 12 overlapping areas. Area number two is: Culture, Diversity, and Equity. This competency has three major sections: key concepts, dispositions, and performance areas. There are four performance areas that are indispensable to develop multicultural competencies and align well with López-Bernstein's model of multicultural development for educators. These performance areas are: respect for all differences and similarities, culturally responsive approaches, culture and language development and learning, and culturally inclusive learning environments. ECE will find specific attitudinal and behavioral examples to develop culture, diversity, and equity in the early childhood education classroom.

References

Angelou, M. (1981). *The heart of a woman*. New York: New York Bantam Books.

Bakhtin, M. M. (1991). *Dialogic imagination: Four essays by M. M. Bakhtin*. Austin: University of Texas Press.

Bennett, K., Cochrane, A., Mohan, G., & Neal, S. (2015). Listening. *Emotion, Space and Society, 17*, 7–14.

Bennett, K., Cochrane, A., Mohan, G., & Neal, S. (2017). Negotiating the educational spaces of urban multiculture: Skills, competencies and college life. *Urban Studies, 54*(10), 2305–2321.

California Department of Education. (2018, November 15). California early childhood educator competencies. *Culture, Diversity & Equity*. Retrieved from https://www.cde.ca.gov/sp/cd/re/ececomps.asp

ElKader, N. A. (2016). Dialogic pedagogy and educating preservice teachers for critical multiculturalism. *SAGE Open, 6*, 1–13. doi:10.1177/2158244016628592

Freire, P. (1970). *Pedgogy of the Oppressed*. Translated by Myra Bergman Ramos. New York: Bloomsbury.

Gonzalez, R. G., & Morrison, J. (2016). Culture or no culture? A Latino critical research analysis of Latino persistence research. *Journal of Hispanic Higher Education, 15*(1), 87–108.

Gonzalez-Mena. (2013). *Child, family, and community: Family centered early care education* (7th ed.). Boston, MA: Pearson.

Hardy, R. D. (2004). The new diversity: Demographic shifts since Brown are changing the face of America's racial and ethnic landscape. *American School Board Journal, 191*, 40–44.

Hofstede, G., Hofstede, G. J., & Minkov, M. (2010). *Cultures and organizations: Software of the mind* (3rd ed.). New York, NY: McGraw Hill.

Howard, G. R. (2006). We can't teach what we don't know: White teachers, multiracial schools (2nd ed.). New York, NY: Teachers College Press.

Katz, J. H. (1985). The sociopolitical nature of counseling. *The Counseling Psychologist, 13*, 615–624.

Kozol, J. (2005). *The shame of the nation: The restoration of Apartheid schooling in America*. New York, NY: Crown.

Ladson-Billings, G., & Tate, W. F. (2016). Toward a critical race theory of education. *The Teachers College Record Journal, 97*(1), 47–68.

López-Bernstein, E. E. (1997). *Realms of culture: Therapists' perspectives on self and others* (Doctoral dissertation Syracuse University 1997/1998). UMI Dissertation Abstracts Data. Base UMI-98194-45.

López, E. E., & Mulnix, M. W. (2004). Educating the next generation: Culture centered teaching for school-aged children. In O. N. Saracho & B. Spodek (Eds.), *Contemporary perspectives on language policy and literacy instruction in early childhood education* (pp. 259–280). Charlotte, NC: Information Age Publishing.

Matusov, E. (2011). Authorial teaching and learning. In E. J. White & M. Peters (Eds.), *Bakhtinian pedagogy: Opportunities and challenges for research, policy and practice in education across the globe* (pp. 21–46). New York, NY: Peter Lang Publishers.

Niesz, T. (2010). Beneath the surface: Teacher subjectivities and the appropriation of critical pedagogies. *Equity and Excellence in Education, 39*, 335–344.

Noble, G. (2013). Cosmopolitan habits: The capacities and habits of intercultural conviviality. *Body and Society, 19*, 162–185.

Orfield, G., & Lee, C. (2004). *Brown at 50: King's dream or Plessy's nightmare?* Cambridge, MA: Civil Rights Project at Harvard University.

Pedersen, P. B. (1988). *A handbook for developing multicultural awareness*. Alexandria, VA: American Association for Counseling and Development.

Pianta, R. C., Stuhlman, M. W., & Hamre, B. K. (2002). How schools can do better: Fostering stronger connections between teachers and students. *New Directions for Youth Development, 93*, 91–107.

Rodríguez, L. F. (2008). Struggling to recognize their existence: Student-adult relationships in the urban high school context. *The Urban Review, 40*(5), 436–453.

Rodríguez, L. F., & Oseguera, L. (2015). Our deliberate success: Recognizing what works for Latina/o students across the educational pipeline. *Journal of Hispanic Higher Education, 14*(2), 128–150.

Rodríguez, L. F., & Wasserberg, M. (2010). From the classroom to the country: Project POWER engages Miami's youth in action research initiatives for educational rights. *The Journal of Urban Education: Focus on Enrichment, 7*(30), 103–107.

Saracho, O. N. (2003). Teachers' roles: Literacy-related play of kindergarten Spanish-speaking students. *Journal of Hispanic Higher Education, 2*(4), 358–376.

Saracho, O. N., & Martínez-Hancock, F. (2004). The culture of Mexican Americans: Its importance for early educators. *Journal of Hispanic Higher Education, 3*(3), 254–269.

Schön, D. (1983). *The reflective practitioner: How professionals think in action*. New York, NY: Basic Books.

Schön, D. (1987). *Educating the reflective practitioner: Toward a new design for teaching and learning in the professions*. San Francisco, CA: Jossey-Bass.

Sennet, R. (2012). *Together: The rituals, pleasures and politics of cooperation*. London, UK: Allan Lane.

Sheets, R. H. (2002). "You're just a kid that's there"—Chicano perception of disciplinary events. *Journal of Latinos and Education, 2*(1), 105–122.

Shor, I. (1993). Education is politics: Paulo Freire's critical pedagogy. In P. McLaren & P. Leonard (Eds.), *Paulo Freire: A critical encounter* (pp. 24–35). New York, NY: Routledge.

Solorzano, D., & Delgado Bernal, D. (2001). Critical race theory, transformational resistance and social justice: Chicana and Chicano students in an urban context. *Urban Education, 36*, 308–342.

Stanton-Salazar, R. D. (2001). *Manufacturing hope and despair: The school and kin support networks of U.S.-Mexican youth*. New York, NY: Teachers College Press.

Stewart, E. C. (1971). *American cultural patterns: A cross-cultural perspective*. Pittsburgh, PA: Regional Council for International Understanding.

Sue, D. W., & Sue, D. (2008). Counseling the culturally diverse: Theory and practice (5th ed.). Hoboken, NJ: John Wiley & Sons, Inc.

Thompson, F. T. (2014). Effective multicultural instruction: A non-color-blind perspective. *SAGE Open, 4*(1), 1–15. doi:10.1177/2158244014522070

Valenzuela, A. (1999). *Subtractive schooling: U.S.-Mexican youth and the politics of caring*. Albany: State University of New York Press.

Wehrly, B. (1995). *Pathways to multicultural counseling competence*. Pacific Grove, CA: Brooks Cole.

Wilson, H. (2011). Passing propinquities in the multicultural city: The every encounters of bus passengering. *Environment and Planning A, 43*, 634–649.

Wilson, H. (2014). Multicultural learning: Parent encounters with difference in a Birmingham primary school. *Transactions of the Institute of British Geographers, 39*(1), 102–114.

Wise, A. (2009). Everyday multiculturalism: Transversal crossings and working class cosmopolitans. In A. Wise & S. Velayutham (Eds.), *Everyday multiculturalism* (pp. 21–45). Basingstoke, UK: Palgrave Macmillan. Retrieved from https://www.psychologytoday.com/us/basics/race-and-ethnicity, July 5, 2018.

19

Quality Inclusive Practices for Preschoolers with Disabilities

Providing Access, Opportunities for Participation, and Supports

Bernadette M. Laumann, Michaelene M. Ostrosky, and Wu-Ying Hsieh

Inclusive education for young children with disabilities has been promoted for more than 30 years (Guralnick & Bruder, 2016; Odom, Buysse, & Soukakou, 2011). In 1986 Public Law 99-457 (Education of the Handicapped Act Amendments of 1986, now known as the Individuals with Disabilities Education Act [IDEA]) mandated the free and appropriate public education of preschool children (ages three to five) with disabilities, thus expanding opportunities for younger children with special needs to be educated in the least restrictive environment. This federal legislation directs states and local school districts to provide special services to preschoolers with disabilities in educational settings (e.g., Head Start, child care centers, public pre-kindergarten (pre-k) classrooms, and community playgroups) where they can fully participate in developmentally, individually, and culturally appropriate activities and routines with their typically developing peers.

The field of early intervention/early childhood special education (EI/ECSE) draws upon the research literature and recommended practices from both early childhood education (EC) and special education. EC practices focus on the development and learning of children without disabilities. They include a high-quality classroom environment with warm, nurturing teacher/child relationships, meaningful instruction, and attention to daily organization that facilitates young children's feelings of safety and security (Copple & Bredekamp, 2009). For most young children with disabilities a high-quality EC setting is an optimal learning environment. In addition to a developmentally appropriate setting and curriculum, teachers, caregivers, and therapists must intentionally provide individualized supports for children with disabilities in order to meet their unique learning needs (Division for Early Childhood, 2014).

In response to legislation and research on the benefits of inclusion for young children with disabilities (Odom, Schwartz, & ECRII Investigators, 2002) the two largest professional EC organizations, the National Association for the Education of Young Children (NAEYC; represents EC professionals) and the Division for Early Childhood of the Council for Exceptional Children (DEC; represents EI/ECSE

professionals), developed a joint position statement on EC inclusion (DEC/NAEYC, 2009). This statement provides the fields with a consensus definition of inclusion:

> "Early childhood inclusion embodies the values, policies, and practices that support the right of every infant and young child and his or her family, regardless of ability, to participate in a broad range of activities and contexts as full members of families, communities, and society. The desired results of inclusive experiences for children with and without disabilities and their families include a sense of belonging and membership, positive social relationships and friendships, and development and learning to reach their full potential."
>
> (DEC/NAEYC, 2009, p. 1)

This position statement demonstrates the value that both professional organizations place on inclusive experiences for *all* young children. The statement also provides focus for the two fields to collaborate with families toward creating high-quality inclusive environments where young children with and without disabilities can participate together as a result of individualized supports.

An even more important and detailed policy statement in support of inclusion for young children with disabilities was disseminated in 2015 when the U.S. Department of Health and Human Services (DHHS) and the U.S. Department of Education (DOE) released a Policy Statement on Inclusion of Children with Disabilities in Early Childhood Programs (U.S. DHHS & U.S. DOE, 2015). This policy statement specifies tasks that will create high-quality inclusion for young children with disabilities and their families; it provides directives with examples that states and local communities may use to plan and implement inclusion. While Child Care of America (formerly NACCRR) does not have a separate or co-authored inclusion statement, this organization has begun to align its work with the DEC/NAEYC and the DHHS/DOE statements (c.f., Bires, Berman, Kenefick, & Rausch, 2017).

Over the past 30 years research has documented the benefits of inclusion for students with and without disabilities including: enhanced educational outcomes, improved social interactions and friendships, increased independence, social skill acquisition, and positive attitudes towards one another (Barton & Smith, 2014). However, high-quality inclusion does not occur automatically. It requires awareness of all aspects of a child's world, including attention to social inclusion and a sense of belonging and acceptance (Yu, Meyer, & Ostrosky, 2013). In this chapter we focus on preschool inclusion by describing recent research and practices that promote inclusion for young children with disabilities. We build upon the work of ECSE researchers (c.f., Barton & Smith, 2015) by organizing our discussion around the critical areas of access, participation, and supports for young children with disabilities in high-quality inclusive settings.

Access: A Defining Feature of High-Quality EC Inclusion

All young children should have *access* to a variety of learning opportunities (e.g., child care centers, recreation programs, and public and private preschool programs). Eliminating physical and other structural barriers is a key element to providing access for all children and their families. "The goal is to ensure that all children have access to effective learning environments; typical routines, activities, and settings, and general education curricula" (Barton, & Joseph, 2015, p. 35).

Each year the U.S. Department of Education Office of Special Education and Rehabilitative Services (OSERS) reports on the implementation of IDEA. This report highlights the numbers of students receiving early intervention or special education services in the U.S. The most recent report, the 40th Annual Report to Congress, indicates that in 2016, a total of 6.4% of all young children ages three to five years were receiving some special education and related services. The report states that 66.8% were in a regular early childhood program for *some amount* of their time in school. Of that 66.8%, only 39.9% attended *a regular early childhood program for at least ten hours per week* where they received special education and related services. Those receiving special education and related services in a separate classroom (i.e., all children enrolled in the class have an identified disability) accounted for 22.7% of preschool children served under IDEA (OSERS, 2018). These statistics demonstrate that we have much more work to do to increase access to inclusive classrooms for young children with disabilities, as recent reports describe minimal increases over the years in the number of children with disabilities who have access to inclusive classroom placements (Barton & Smith, 2014; Odom et al., 2011; U.S. DHHS & U.S. DOE, 2015).

Access: Welcoming All Children

Providing access to a broad range of learning opportunities, activities, and settings is a defining feature of high-quality early childhood inclusion. Universal design for learning (UDL) (CAST, 2018) is a framework that borrows from the field of architecture where physical spaces are designed so people with a variety of needs can access them (e.g., ramps or curb cuts to make the street more manageable for those with physical disabilities). UDL provides *access to learning* for *all* children (i.e., children with and without disabilities, dual language learners), for it is intentionally built into the planning and design of not only the physical spaces (furniture, bathrooms, shelving) in early care and education programs, but encompasses the developmentally and individually appropriate, evidence-based curriculum, authentic assessment, and evaluation processes. Conn-Powers, Cross, Traub, and Hutter-Pishgahi (2006) describe three ways that the UDL principles can provide all children with access to learning:

- multiple means of representation to give learners various ways of acquiring information and knowledge,
- multiple means of expression to provide learners alternatives for demonstrating what they know, and
- multiple means of engagement to tap into learners' interests, offer appropriate challenges, and increase motivation (p. 4).

The removal of physical, curricular, and assessment barriers promotes *access* to learning for each child who steps into an early childhood setting.

In looking carefully at access to inclusive early childhood programs, there is national recognition that quality in early childhood programs is of critical concern to EC and ECSE professionals, administrators, families, and policy makers (Cate, Diefendorf, McCullough, Peters, & Whaley, 2010). Environmental rating scales are used in state Quality Rating and Improvement Systems (QRIS) to evaluate early care and education programs in the areas of physical materials/space, teacher/child interaction, safety and security for children, and opportunities for professional growth for staff (NAEYC, 2011). Environmental rating scales and assessments (e.g., Early Childhood Environmental Rating Scale-Revised [ECERS-R]; Classroom Assessment Scoring System [CLASS]) that address teacher and child relationships, meaningful instruction, and classroom organization (Harms, Clifford, & Cryer, 1998; Mashburn et al., 2008) have provided the field with quantitative measures that state licensing organizations and families use for guidance about EC program quality. However, most environmental rating scales give minimal attention to how the preschool environment meaningfully addresses the unique needs of children with disabilities (Odom et al., 2011). Early childhood classroom rating scale items rarely focus on how children with disabilities are fully welcomed as members of the classroom community. For example, when considering classroom environments, representation matters. Classroom materials (e.g., books, posters), should be carefully chosen to represent the children, families, and staff who are members of that classroom community. Completing a critical review of classroom materials can provide opportunities for teachers to examine the extent that they have included all children (Souto-Manning, Rabadi-Raol, Robinson, & Rerez, 2018).

More than two decades of research on disability representation in EC classrooms (e.g., seeing oneself represented in resources such as books that include positive role models with disabilities, posters displaying someone using sign language, or Braille labels on doors within a building) reveals that classroom materials related to fostering a sense of belonging are still not present in inclusive early childhood settings (Favazza, Ostrosky, Meyer, Yu, & Mouzourou, 2017). In fact, recent data show that 98% of targeted classrooms lacked materials to support a sense of belonging, which contributes to social emotional development (Favazza et al., 2017; Yu, Ostrosky, Favazza, & Meyer, 2016). Moreover, teachers reported a need for greater knowledge and skills to support social emotional outcomes, understand how attitudes develop, and create accepting classroom communities (Yu et al., 2016). This is consistent with other research indicating teachers' perceptions of their own competence in meeting the needs of children in inclusive classrooms (Baker-Ericzén, Mueggenborg, & Shea, 2008). Thus, high-quality EC inclusion remains as yet an unachieved goal in many places. However, a focus on environmental considerations such as disability representation, UDL strategies, and teacher education (Souto-Manning et al., 2018) can support access to high-quality inclusion.

Access to high-quality inclusive EC programs can also be facilitated through the intentional use of appropriate assistive technology (AT). "The term 'assistive technology device' means any item, piece of equipment, or product system, whether acquired commercially off the shelf, modified, or customized, that is used to increase, maintain, or improve functional capabilities of a child with a disability" (IDEA, 2004). AT refers to a continuum of low tech (e.g., Velcro enhanced books) to high tech (e.g., a laptop computer with a touchscreen or an iPad with communication apps) materials. The DEC Recommended Practices on Environments includes an Assistive Technology (AT) checklist (ECTA, 2017) that may be used to determine a child's need for AT to gain access to the learning environment and participate in daily routines and activities. Research has shown that young children with disabilities can learn to use assistive technology to increase their skills and more fully participate in activities (Campbell, Milbourne, Dugan, & Wilcox, 2006). According to a recent national survey, 85% of parents allow their young children under age six to use technology at home (Erikson Institute, 2016). Increasingly young children with and without disabilities and their families engage with technologies at home, in EC settings, and in the community. Due to the increased use of technology in early care and education settings, AT devices used by children with disabilities (e.g., iPad apps) may be viewed as typical educational materials that many children use. Coaching and training from therapists regarding the use of AT materials can provide teaching staff in inclusive EC programs with support in planning and implementing learning activities for children with disabilities (Rush & Shelden, 2011), thereby increasing access to classroom activities for these children.

Participation: Engaging Children in EC Inclusive Settings

In early childhood classrooms, it is not unusual to have a diverse group of students playing and learning together, including children with disabilities, children from different racial and ethnic backgrounds, children with language differences, and children from a variety of family structures (Cox-Petersen, 2011). Over the past two decades preschool settings are increasingly enrolling more children with disabilities. Nearly one-third of students with disabilities are included in EC settings with children without disabilities (Odom et al., 2011). However, negative attitudes toward and perceptions of individuals with disabilities have persisted and often result in limited participation in play and learning activities for children with special needs; in fact, this pervasiveness has garnered global attention, leading to the United Nations ratification of the Convention on the Rights of Persons with Disabilities (2006), and recently noted in UNICEF's report on the State of the World's Children: Children with Disabilities (2013).

Historically, researchers have asserted that successful and effective social interaction with peers leads to positive social emotional development (DEC/NAEYC, 2009). Research indicates that children who engage in successful peer interactions have stronger friendships and are more often included in classroom activities than children who lack these skills. This has importance for preschoolers in inclusive settings. Given the link between social emotional development and other developmental domains (Denham & Brown, 2010), supporting children's participation in play and peer interactions is important. Evidence suggests having close friendships may partially mediate the relationship between social competence and acceptance. Studies by Meyer and Ostrosky (2016) and Yu, Ostrosky, and Fowler (2015) align with research emphasizing the importance of individualizing classwide programs based on children's needs and supporting children's friendship formation to promote peer acceptance. Additionally, friendships in the early years provide a context for practicing social-emotional skills, and later on provide children with protective features that help guide their skills related to school readiness (Child Mental Health Foundations and Agencies Network, 2000).

While much attention has focused on bullying in the upper elementary and high school grades, many younger children with disabilities experience social emotional challenges that interfere with friendship formation and academic success, subsequently leading to negative learning outcomes, such as limited participation (e.g., Nyre, Vernberg, & Roberts, 2007). Thus, acceptance of human differences (i.e., when children with diverse abilities are served together in inclusive settings) requires careful attention to address children's social emotional needs and foster a sense of belonging and acceptance for everyone (Yu et al., 2013). While many EC teachers report that they support inclusion for children with disabilities (Muccio, Kidd, White, & Burns, 2014), and strive to help them participate in play and learning activities with peers, teachers' beliefs do not always match their ability to create accepting inclusive classrooms.

What Does Participation Look Like?

There are some children who need individualized accommodations and supports to access a range of learning opportunities, activities, and environments. Ideally their caregivers have the tools and strategies to approach children's development in ways that afford an equality of opportunities. Without these accommodations and supports children might not be able to fully participate in play and learning activities with their peers and caregivers. Over the past 30 years, the field of EI/ECSE has developed a robust evidence base of inclusive, family-based, and developmentally appropriate interventions and instructional practices (Division for Early Childhood, 2014). An important finding in recent years has to do with the direct impact children's social emotional development has on brain development and developmental outcomes (Center on the Developing Child, 2011). Specifically, EC caregivers must understand the importance of adult-child and peer-peer relationships, be responsive to the individualized developmental needs of children within the context of their families' priorities and concerns and be knowledgeable of how evidence-based practices can support healthy development.

Compared to their typically developing peers, children with disabilities are more likely to develop social emotional or mental health issues, or display challenging behaviors, interfering with their ability to learn and interact with others in a positive manner (Horner, Carr, Strain, Todd, & Reed, 2002). Furthermore, children who have social emotional needs are less likely to benefit from typical intervention strategies (e.g., ignoring, redirection). They need teachers with a repertoire of responsive intervention and instructional strategies, ranging from promotion and prevention strategies to individualized, intervention strategies in order to address their social emotional or behavioral issues; these are often referred to as a multi-tiered system of support (Ostrosky & Sandall, 2013). Research about different instructional approaches, recommended practices, and key components that are necessary for instruction to be effective for children and families from a variety of backgrounds and experiences continues to grow (Division for Early Childhood, 2014), thereby increasing the likelihood of young children's active participation in inclusive settings.

Additionally, children's attitude development plays a key role in mediating the social acceptance of children with disabilities and differences, for by age five children are already forming perceptions of, and attitudes toward children with disabilities (Gerber, 1977). In a review of the literature, Diamond and Innes (2001) describe the fundamental relationship between the acceptance of children with disabilities and their socialization and full membership or participation in inclusive programs, concluding that research on effective strategies to promote greater understanding and acceptance

of children with disabilities is necessary to more fully include children with disabilities. An attitude is a complex, multi-component construct that includes a cognitive component (i.e., ideas about people with disabilities), affective component (i.e., feelings associated with people with disabilities), and behavioral component (that predispose a child's behavior or actions toward the attitude referent such as a child with a disability) (Favazza et al., 2017). Attitudes are learned from *indirect experiences* (conversations, books), *direct experiences* (interactions with people with disabilities), and *the child's primary social group* (peers, family members) (Triandis, Adamopoulos, & Brinberg, 1984). Families are a children's first social group and play a critical role in attitude formation but as children age, this group expands to include peers and teachers (Yuker, 1988). Therefore, EC teachers and their teaching teams play an essential role during the critical time when children's attitudes of acceptance or rejection are developing. Yet many professionals note that they do not learn about attitude development or promoting acceptance in their pre-service programs, are not comfortable engaging in discussions about disabilities or differences with their students, and were unaware of strategies that support inclusion such as UDL and adapting the environment, materials, and activities so as to support socialization, peer interactions, and participation (Yu, Ostrosky, Favazza et al., 2016). As noted in DEC/NAEYC's joint position statement (2009), the desired goals for all children included in EC classrooms are: a sense of membership, positive social relationships and friendships, and support to maximize children's learning potential. Attention to children's participation in play and learning activities is critical and requires that early educators have a toolkit full of strategies and practices to provide accommodations and supports, as well as facilitate positive attitude development.

Supports: Providing an Infrastructure for Inclusive EC Settings

Supports for high-quality inclusive EC settings can be found in systems level priorities. These priorities may include pre-service and in-service professional development, incentives for inclusion and increased opportunities for communication and collaboration among families and professionals (DEC/NAEYC, 2009).

Pre-Service Teacher Education

High-quality inclusion in EC programs will only occur when teachers and therapists have positive attitudes and the necessary knowledge and skills to effectively teach *all* children. The CEC, DEC, and NAEYC pre-service teacher preparation standards have been aligned [The Early Childhood Personnel Center (ECPC), 2018] and can serve (along with state specific EC and ECSE personnel preparation standards) as the foundation for building unified or blended EC/ECSE preparation programs. Muller (2006) surveyed and then completed interviews with stakeholders at seven Institutions of Higher Education (IHEs) that offer a unified certificate for EC and ECSE teachers. The data revealed that offering teachers of young children a unified certificate resulted in promoting more inclusion at the classroom level. One state, Massachusetts noted that the ". . . percentage of children with disabilities in inclusive early childhood classrooms had grown from 20% to 90%" (p. 9).

In-Service Professional Development

Classroom embedded professional development experiences have intentionally included opportunities for EC and ECSE professionals to gain the knowledge, skills, and experiences to provide high-quality inclusive programs (National Professional Development Center on Inclusion, 2009). Professional development to support research and evidence-based practices is openly available to teachers, administrators, and families. In-service professional development can be accessed through multiple online resources (e.g., the Early Childhood Technical Assistance Center, Head Start Early Childhood Learning and Knowledge Center, Head Start Center for Inclusion, IRIS Center, and the National Center for Pyramid Model Innovations), which provide practical professional development that is grounded in research and evidence-based practices (c.f., https://challengingbehavior.cbcs.usf.edu/docs/A-classroom-wide-model-promoting-soical-emotional-dev-addressing-challenging-behavior-preschool.pdf).

Incentives for Inclusion

In addition to having informed EC program administrators, another system of support for inclusion is through state funding for pre-k programs where the elements of quality include support for English learners and children with disabilities (Wechsler, Melnick, Maier, & Bishop, 2016). As more states provide publicly funded pre-k programs, there will continue to be opportunities for communities to creatively combine funding and other resources to support high-quality inclusive programs (Cate & Peters, 2017).

Increased Communication and Collaboration among Families and Professionals

Communication and collaboration among families and professionals is an important part of the infrastructure needed to support high-quality inclusion. Administrative support at the local level for high-quality inclusion is critical to successful outcomes for children with disabilities and their families. Leaders can be local child care directors, EC coordinators, building principals, and special education directors (Division for Early Childhood, 2014). Early childhood program and school district administrators are key to creating a welcoming environment for all members of the community (Barton & Smith, 2015). They can arrange time and resources to promote collaborative relationships among professionals and families. They can work together with staff and families to

promote their program's vision for high-quality inclusion. In addition to knowledge and skills about special education laws and mandates, leaders of high-quality inclusive EC programs must provide adequate time for teachers and therapists to communicate about child and family goals, align schedules to support home visits to share specialized strategies with families, and develop meaningful partnerships with mental health and other community service providers to support critical needs of the program, families, children, and staff (Barton & Smith, 2015; U.S. DHHS & U.S. DOE, 2015).

Future Research Ideas and Implications for Practice

We need to prepare teachers who understand inclusion as educational equity, for equity is grounded in fairness and predicated on educational opportunities which foster success for all, by promoting access, participation, and appropriate supports. Pre- and in-service professional development activities are necessary components of successful inclusion. Guralnick and Bruder (2016) speak of the need to better prepare EC teachers at the pre-service level so that we have a "quality workforce that is able to effectively and collaboratively implement curricular and instructional modifications, adaptations, and instructional practices to benefit all children in EC classrooms, regardless of ability or needs" (p. 173). Professional development at the in-service level must focus on teaching teams, including teachers, teaching assistants, and support staff such as physical therapists and speech language clinicians. Topics addressed in both in-service and pre-service programs should include the following, which contribute to high-quality inclusive classrooms: (a) professionals' knowledge, dispositions, and skills, (b) evidence-based strategies that support inclusion, (c) the evaluation and adaptation of space, materials, and equipment, (d) adult guidance and support of children's activities and play, including peer interactions, (e) support for communication and conflict resolution, (f) relationships between adults and children, (g) adaptation of group activities (i.e., UDL), and (h) family professional partnerships (Favazza et al., 2017; Soukakou, Winton, West, Sideris, & Rucker, 2015).

Resources and materials are available to support the development of high-quality inclusive early childhood programs. For example, the Pyramid Model is a conceptual framework and a multi-tiered model addressing social and emotional development for all children that is focused on prevention, promotion, and intervention, all of which should be in place to address the needs of children within EC programs (Hemmeter, Fox, & Snyder, 2013). Program-wide implementation of the Pyramid Model follows a systems approach to ensure that appropriate policies and practices are in place (Fox, Lentini, & Binder, 2013). Quesenberry, Ostrosky, and Hemmeter (2011) reported that without clear policies, EC staff are less likely to consistently implement procedures to support children's social emotional development. Professional development has the potential to support improved outcomes for children and their families (c.f., Hemmeter et al., 2013).

Research studies and state Quality Rating and Improvement Systems (QRIS) that rely on environmental assessment tools (e.g., ECERS-R and CLASS) as measures of program quality also should include tools such as the Inclusive Classroom Profile (ICP) (Soukakou et al., 2015) that can inform the early care and education field about the quality of inclusive EC programs for children with disabilities and their families. Data from the ICP can help professionals further identify activities to enhance program quality (Soukakou, Winton, & West, 2012).

Future research initiatives need to more fully address federal, state, and local leadership practices that promote an increase in high-quality inclusive EC services that are available to families (U.S. DHHS & U.S. DOE, 2015). Case studies of specific leadership initiatives that support systems level changes to promote high-quality inclusive early care and education programs can begin to promote new ideas for collaboration across various EC programs (e.g., public pre-k, Head Start, child care centers, and family child care providers) to seamlessly address the delivery of special education services to children with disabilities and their families. Currently the Child Care Development Block Grant (CCDBG) Act (2014) ensures that states describe the coordination of any services provided under the Child Care and Development Fund (CCDF) with programs that serve children with disabilities (U.S. DHHS & U.S. DOE, 2015). The use of formal collaborative agreements should further the goal of providing better coordinated systems of services; however research is still needed to inform leaders about the types of cross-agency and program agreements that result in exemplary inclusive practices for children and families.

Conclusion

Practitioners, researchers, and advocates believe that *all* young children deserve to participate in high-quality early care and education experiences. More than 30 years of research on inclusive settings has shown that young children with and without disabilities benefit from high-quality inclusive preschool programs. Federal law (IDEA, 2004) states that children with disabilities should receive special education services and supports in the least restrictive environment (i.e., in settings where they would be enrolled if they did not have a disability). The DEC/NAEYC (2009) Joint Position Statement on Inclusion and the U.S. Department of Health and Human Services and the U.S. Department of Education (2015) Policy Statement on Inclusion have charged the EC and ECSE fields to create high-quality inclusive programs for children with disabilities and their families. Although federal law, EC and ECSE professional organizations, and federal policy strongly recommend high-quality inclusion for children with disabilities, work is still needed as consensus on inclusive program quality has not been reached across states (National Professional Development Center on Inclusion, 2009).

The *State of Preschool 2017: State Preschool Yearbook* reports that during the 2016–2017 school year 1.5 million young children in the U.S. were enrolled in publicly funded pre-k programs (Friedman-Krauss et al., 2018). Publicly funded programs (e.g., pre-k, Head Start) are often chosen by families to provide inclusive early education and care for young children with disabilities, yet research indicates that there is great variability in the quality of publicly funded early education programs (Chaudry & Datta, 2017). With 30 years of research, position and policy statements supporting high-quality inclusion, and a national focus on the quality of public EC programs, we believe this is a critical time for researchers, state education personnel, public pre-k, Head Start, and child care administrators to develop shared policies and advocate for the resources that will ensure *all* young children have access and the necessary supports to fully participate in high-quality inclusive EC education programs.

References

Baker-Ericzén, M. J., Mueggenborg, M. G., & Shea, M. M. (2008). Impact of trainings on child care providers' attitudes and perceived competence toward inclusion: What factors are associated with change? *Topics in Early Childhood Special Education, 28,* 196–208.

Barton, E. E., & Joseph, J. D. (2015). What is quality inclusion? In E. E. Barton & B. J. Smith (Eds.), *The preschool inclusion toolbox* (pp. 33–43). Baltimore, MD: Brookes.

Barton, E. E., & Smith, B. J. (2014). *Fact sheet on preschool inclusion.* Denver, CO: Pyramid Plus: The Colorado Center for Social Emotional Competence and Inclusion.

Barton, E. E., & Smith, B. J. (2015). Advancing high-quality preschool inclusion: A discussion and recommendations for the field. *Topics in Early Childhood Special Education, 35,* 69–78.

Bires, C., Berman, K., Kenefick, E., & Rausch, A. (2017). *Building inclusive state child care systems.* Retrieved from https://www.theounce.org/wp-content/uploads/2017/03/BuildingInclusiveStateChildCareSystems.pdf

Campbell, P. H., Milbourne, S., Dugan, L. M., & Wilcox, M. J. (2006). A review of evidence on practices for teaching young children to use assistive technology devices. *Topics in Early Childhood Special Education, 26*(1), 3–13.

CAST. (2018). *Universal design for learning guidelines version 2.2.* Retrieved from http://udlguidelines.cast.org

Cate, D., Diefendorf, M., McCullogh, K., Peters, M. L., & Whaley, K. (Eds.). (2010). *Quality indicators of inclusive early childhood programs/practices: A compilation of selected resources.* Chapel Hill: The University of North Carolina, FPG Child Development Institute, National Early Childhood Technical Assistance Center.

Cate, D., & Peters, M. (2017). *Preschool inclusion finance toolkit 2017.* Retrieved from https://fpg.unc.edu/sites/fpg.unc.edu/files/resources/reports-and-policy-briefs/preschool_inclusion_finance_toolkit_2017-07-07.pdf

Center on the Developing Child. (2011). *Enhancing and practicing executive function skills with children from infancy to adolescence.* Retrieved from https://children.wi.gov/Documents/Harvard%20Parenting%20Resource.pdf

Chaudry, A., & Datta, A. R. (2017). The current landscape for public pre-kindergarten programs. In D. A. Phillips, M. W. Lipsey, K. A. Dodge, R. Haskins, D. Bassok, M. R. Buchinal, G. J. Duncan, M. Dynarski, K. A. Magnuson, & C. Weiland (Eds.), *The current state of scientific knowledge on pre-kindergarten effects* (pp. 5–18). Durham, NC: Duke University Center for Child and Family Policy and Washington, DC: The Brookings Institute.

Child Mental Health Foundations and Agencies Network. (2000). *A good beginning: Sending America's children to school with the social and emotional competence they need to succeed.* Bethesda, MD: National

Institute of Mental Health. Retrieved from https://files.eric.ed.gov/fulltext/ED445810.pdf

Conn-Powers, M., Cross, A. F., Traub, E. K., & Hutter-Pishgahi, L. (2006). The universal design of early education: Moving forward for all children. *Beyond the Journal: Young Children on the Web*. Washington, DC: NAEYC. Retrieved from https://www.iidc.indiana.edu/styles/iidc/defiles/ECC/ECC_Universal_Design_Early_Education.pdf

Copple, C., & Bredekamp, S. (Eds.). (2009). *Developmentally appropriate practice in early childhood programs* (3rd ed.). Washington, DC: NAEYC.

Cox-Petersen, A. (2011). *Educational partnerships*. Los Angeles, CA: Sage.

DEC/NAEYC. (2009). *Early childhood inclusion: A joint position statement of the Division for Early Childhood (DEC) and the National Association for the Education of Young Children (NAEYC)*. Chapel Hill: The University of North Carolina, FPG Child Development Institute. Retrieved from https://www.decdocs.org/position-statement-inclusion

Denham, S. A., & Brown, C. (2010). "Plays nice with others": Social-emotional learning and academic success. *Early Education & Development, 21*, 652–680.

Diamond, K. E., & Innes, F. K. (2001). Young children's attitudes toward peers with disabilities. In M. Guralnick (Ed.), *Early childhood inclusion: Focus on change* (pp. 159–178). Baltimore, MD: Brookes.

Division for Early Childhood. (2014). *DEC recommended practices in early intervention/early childhood special education*. Retrieved from http://www.dec-sped.org/dec-recommended-practices

Early Childhood Technical Assistance Center (ECTA). (2017). *Assistive technology checklist*. Retrieved from http://ectacenter.org/~pdfs/decrp/ENV-5_Assistive_Tech_2017.pdf

Erikson Institute. (2016). *Technology and young children in the digital age: A report from the Erikson Institute*. Retrieved from https://www.erikson.edu/wp-content/uploads/2018/07/Erikson-Institute-Technology-and-Young-Children-Survey.pdf

Favazza, P. C., Ostrosky, M. M., Meyer, L., Yu, S., & Mouzourou, C. (2017). Limited representation of individuals with disabilities in early childhood classes: Alarming or status quo? *International Journal of Inclusive Education, 21*, 650–666.

Fox, L., Lentini, R., & Binder, D. (2013). Promoting the social-emotional competence of all children: Implementing the pyramid model program-wide. In M. M. Ostrosky & S. R. Sandall (Eds.), *Young exceptional children monograph series no. 15: Addressing young children's challenging behaviors* (pp. 14–18). Los Angeles, CA: DEC.

Friedman-Krauss, A. H., Barnett, W. S., Weisenfeld, G. G., Kasmin, R., DiCrecchio, N., & Horowitz, M. (2018). *The state of preschool 2017: State preschool yearbook*. New Brunswick, NJ: National Institute for Early Education Research.

Gerber, J. P. (1977). Awareness of handicapping conditions and sociometric status in an integrated pre-school setting. *Mental Retardation, 15*, 24–25.

Guralnick, M. J., & Bruder, M. B. (2016). Early childhood inclusion in the United States: Goals, current status, and future directions. *Infants & Young Children, 29*(3), 166–177.

Harms, T., Clifford, R. M., & Cryer, D. (1998). *The early childhood environment rating scale- Revised edition* (ECERS-R). New York, NY: Teachers College Press.

Hemmeter, M. L., Fox, L., & Snyder, P. (2013). A tiered model for promoting social-emotional competence and addressing behavior. In V. Buysse & E. Peisner-Feinberg (Eds.), *Handbook of response to intervention in early intervention* (pp. 85–102). Baltimore, MD: Brookes.

Horner, R. H., Carr, E. G., Strain, P. S., Todd, A. W., & Reed, H. K. (2002). Problem behavior interventions for young children with autism: A research synthesis. *Journal of Autism and Developmental Disabilities, 32*, 423–447.

Individuals with Disabilities Education Improvement Act (IDEA) of 2004, PL 108–446, 20 U.S.C. 1400 *et seq.*

Mashburn, A. J., Pianta, R. C., Hamre, B. K., Downer, J. T., Barbarin, O. A., Bryant, D, … Howes, C. (2008). Measures of classroom quality in prekindergarten and children's development of academic, language, and social skills. *Child Development, 79*(3), 732–749.

Meyer, L. E., & Ostrosky, M. M. (2016). Impact of an affective intervention on the friendships of kindergarteners with disabilities. *Topics in Early Childhood Special Education, 35*(4), 200–210.

Muccio, L. S., Kidd, J. K., White, C., & Burns, M. (2014). Head Start instructional professionals' inclusion perceptions and practices. *Topics in Early Childhood Special Education, 34*, 40–48.

Muller, E. (2006). *Unified early childhood and early childhood special education teacher certification: State approaches. Project forum*. Retrieved from www.nasde.org

National Association for the Education of Young Children (NAEYC). (2011). *NAEYC position on quality rating and improvement systems*. Retrieved from https://www.naeyc.org/sites/default/files/globally-shared/downloads/PDFs/our-work/public-policy-advocacy/2011_QRIS_Statement_0.pdf

National Professional Development Center on Inclusion. (2009, November). *Why program quality matters for early childhood inclusion: Recommendations for professional development*. Chapel Hill: The University of North Carolina, FPG Child Development Institute, Author.

Nyre, J. E., Vernberg, E. M., & Roberts, M. C. (2007). Serving the most severe of serious emotionally disturbed students in school settings. In M. D. Weist, S. W. Evans, & N. A. Lever (Eds.), *Handbook of school mental health: Advancing practice and research* (pp. 203–222). New York, NY: Kluwer Academic/Plenum Publishers.

Odom, S. L., Buysse, V., & Soukakou, E. (2011). Inclusion for young children with disabilities: A quarter century of research perspectives. *Journal of Early Intervention, 33*(4), 344–356.

Odom, S. L., Schwartz, I. S., & ECRII Investigators. (2002). So, what do we know from all this? Synthesis points of research on preschool inclusion. In S. L. Odom (Ed.), *Widening the circle: Including children with disabilities in preschool programs* (pp. 154–174). New York, NY: Teachers College Press.

Office of Special Education and Rehabilitative Services (OSERS). (2018). *40th annual report to congress implementation of the individuals with disabilities education act, 2018*. Washington, DC: Author.

Ostrosky, M. M., & Sandall, S. (Eds.). (2013). *Young exceptional children monograph series no. 15: Addressing young children's challenging behaviors*. Missoula, MT: DEC.

Quesenberry, A. C., Ostrosky, M. M., & Hemmeter, M. L. (2011). Addressing challenging behaviors in Head Start: A closer look at program policies and procedures. *Topics in Early Childhood Special Education, 30*, 209–220.

Rush, D. D., & Sheldon, M. L. (2011). *The early childhood coaching handbook*. Baltimore, MD: Brookes.

Soukakou, E., Winton, P., & West, T. (2012). *The Inclusive Classroom Profile (ICP): Report on preliminary findings of demonstration study in North Carolina*. Chapel Hill, NC: NPDCI, FPG Child Development Institute.

Soukakou, E. P., Winton, P. J., West, T. A., Sideris, J. H., & Rucker, L. M. (2015). Measuring the quality of inclusive practices: Findings from the inclusive classroom profile pilot. *Journal of Early Intervention, 36*(3), 223–240.

Souto-Manning, M., Rabadi-Raol, A., Robinson, D., & Rerez, A. (2018). What stories do my classroom and its materials tell? Preparing early childhood teachers to engage in equitable and inclusive teaching. *Young Exceptional Children*. doi:10.1177/1096250618811619

The Early Childhood Personnel Center (ECPC). (2018). *CEC, DEC, & NAEYC Personnel standards alignment*. Retrieved from https://ecpcta.org/cec-dec-naeyc-personnel-standards- alignment/

Triandis, H. C., Adamopoulos, J., & Brinberg, D. (1984). Perspectives and issues in the study of attitudes. In R. L. Jones (Ed.), *Attitudes and attitude change in special education: Theory and practice* (pp. 21–40). Reston, VA: Council for Exceptional Children.

UNICEF. (2013). *The state of the world's children 2013: Children with disabilities*. Retrieved from https://www.unicef.org/sowc2013/

United Nations. (2006). *Convention on the rights of persons with disabilities and optional protocol*. Retrieved from http://www.un.org/disabilities/documents/convention/convoptprot-e.pdf

U.S. Department of Health and Human Services, & U.S. Department of Education. (2015). *Policy statement on inclusion of children with disabilities in early childhood programs*. Retrieved from https://ed.gov/policy/speced/guid/earlylearning/joint-statement-full-text.pdf

Wechsler, M., Melnick, H., Maier, A., & Bishop, J. (2016). *The building blocks of high-quality early childhood education programs*. Palo Alto, CA: Learning Policy Institute. Retrieved from https://learningpolicyinstitute.org/product/building-blocks-high-quality-early-childhood-education-programs

Yu, S. Y., Meyer, L. E., & Ostrosky, M. M. (2013). Creating accepting classroom environments: Promoting positive attitudes toward peers with challenging behaviors. In M. M. Ostrosky & S. R. Sandall (Eds.), *Young exceptional children monograph series no. 15: Addressing young children's challenging behaviors* (pp. 14–28). Los Angeles, CA: DEC.

Yu, S. Y., Ostrosky, M. M., Favazza, P. C., & Meyer, L. E. (2016). "Where are the kids like me?" Classroom materials that help create a sense of belonging. In T. Caralino & L. E. Meyer (Eds.), *DEC recommended practices monograph no. 2 environment: Promoting meaningful access, participation, and inclusion* (pp. 115–126). Washington, DC: DEC.

Yu, S. Y., Ostrosky, M. M., & Fowler, S. A. (2015). The relationship between preschoolers' attitudes and play behaviors toward classmates with disabilities. *Topics in Early Childhood Special Education, 35*(1), 40–51.

Yu, S. Y., Ostrosky, M. M., Meyer, L. E., Favazza, P. C., Mouzourou, C., & Leboeuf, L. (2016). Using teacher impression journals to improve intervention effectiveness. *Topics in Early Childhood Special Education, 35*(4), 245–255.

Yuker, H. E. (Ed.). (1988). *Attitudes toward persons with disabilities*. New York, NY: Springer.

20

Family Context in Early Childhood Education

Barbara H. Fiese and Meghan Fisher

All children are raised in some form of family. But families take different forms in terms of number of adults in the household, contact with extended kin, and sheer size of the group. Families differ in the beliefs that they hold about trustworthiness of relationships and in their daily practices and routines. Families live in neighborhoods that reflect available resources for healthy foods, physical activity, social support, and quality of education. This chapter describes how families are dynamic systems with shared practices and beliefs that contribute to child well-being and preparedness to learn. These practices and beliefs are embedded in a socioeconomic context that includes cultural influences as well as neighborhood context. Thus, an ecological model (Bronfenbrenner & Morris, 1998) is proposed to situate the family in a larger developmental context.

In some cases, and at some times, families function in such a way that children's growth is fostered and there is optimal development. In other cases, however, individual and socioeconomic forces compromise the family's ability to provide a supportive environment for their children. Examples are provided of the effects of cumulative risk under high-risk child-raising conditions such as poverty or parental psychopathology that may derail positive family process and make children vulnerable to behavioral and learning problems. There is a reason for optimism, however, as protective factors may promote positive development through responsive parent-child interactions and structured home environments.

Family life is often marked by transitions: marriage, the birth of a child, going to school, leaving home, marriage of children, becoming grandparents are just a few of the transitions that members experience as part of normative changes (Walsh, 2003). Several transitions are apparent during early childhood: gaining autonomy through learning to walk, asserting opinions in learning to talk, and being poised to learn when transitioning from home to school. An important transition where characteristics of the child, family, social institutions, and culture transact is the transition to formal school. The family plays an important role in easing these transitions by establishing partnerships with childcare providers and

school personnel. However, this transition is moderated by available resources in the community and the cultural context in which education is provided. The third section of the chapter discusses family partnerships with early care providers and educators and transition to kindergarten as important settings for early learning. Further, the section highlights the importance of establishing partnerships between early care settings in light of increasing diversity in real life.

Family Ecologies

Ecological Models

Ecological models (Bronfenbrenner & Morris, 1998; Evans, 2004; Ferguson & Evans, 2019) propose that development is the result of multiple levels of influence including those that are the most proximal to the child's experience (parent-child interactions) and those that are more distal (cultural values and practices) (see Figure 20.1). At the core is the child herself,

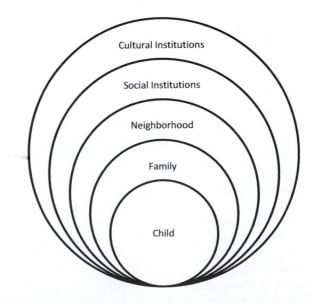

Figure 20.1 Ecological model.

processing herself, possessing her own temperament, style of engaging with others, and personality. The family context includes structural aspects of the family such as number of adults in the household, marital status, and number of people residing in the household. Variations in the number of adults in the household and stability in marital status have been found to be related to cognitive, social, and emotional outcomes for children (Amato, 2005). However, these outcomes are likely to be moderated by family economic status and neighborhood resources.

Parent-Child Interaction.   The family context also includes social interaction features such as parenting style, family belief systems, family routines and ritualism, and contact with extended kin. Over the past two decades, there has been consistent support for the importance of sensitive and responsive parent-child interaction in supporting healthy outcomes for children from youth (Cox & Paley, 1997). From an ecological systems perspective, parent-child interaction patterns are seen as embedded in the larger social system and sensitive to current strains in the marital relationship, economic conditions, and regulated by cultural norms. In turn, families and their routine and ritual practices are considered to be influenced by generational traditions and cultural context.

Considerable attention has been paid to the role that sensitive parent-child interaction patterns play in positive child development. Grusec and Davidov (2010) have proposed a multi-dimensional framework for how parenting extends across domains during early childhood to foster self-control, mastery of problem-solving, and emotion regulation. Consistent with this model, Leerkes and colleagues have found that parental responsivity to distress is a strong predictor of emotion regulation above and beyond parental warmth (Leerkes, Blankson, & O'Brien, 2009).

Equally important is the role of parents that provide scaffolding and emotional support during problem-solving tasks. During the early childhood years, when parents actively engage their children in book reading and build their vocabulary through child-directed conversations they are better prepared to enter school and demonstrate better executive function skills (Fay-Stammach, Hawes, & Meredith, 2014; Tamis-LeMonda et al., 2014). Further, how this support is delivered affects school readiness. Parents who provide emotional support during problem-solving tasks are more likely to have children ready to enter school than parents who just provide cognitive support and information (Leerkes, Blankson, O'Brien, Calkins, & Marcovitch, 2011).

Interparental Relationships.   Interparental relationships can also have a profound effect on children during early development. Although relationship instability can have a negative effect on children's socioemotional development (Sbarra, Bourassa, & Manvelian, 2019), children's exposure to conflict and violent relationships can have detrimental effects. Children who are exposed to high levels of interparental hostility and disengagement are more likely to exhibit behavioral and emotional problems (Cummings & Davies, 2010) as well as increase conflict between parent and child (Sherrill, Lochman, DeCoster, & Stromeyer, 2017).

Extended Kin.   Extended kin, particularly grandparents, can play a pivotal role in the lives of young children. Many grandparents play an active role in raising their grandchildren and may reside in the same household (Margolis, 2016). Indeed, three out of four grandparents provide some sort of care for their grandchildren on a weekly basis (Luo, LaPierre, Hughes, & Waite, 2012). There is some evidence to suggest that grandparent involvement provides a protective role under conditions of poverty and stressful child raising conditions such that children are provided emotional and instrumental support (Uhlenberg & Cheuk, 2010; Wood & Liossis, 2007). Grandparents may provide stability when parenting is disrupted through divorce or other challenges such as drug abuse or interpersonal violence (Dolbin-McNab, 2019).

Neighborhood.   The neighborhood level is important for child development because it provides not only the geography where children live but also the broader economic context that houses business and institutions such as childcare sites, schools, and places of worship (Leventhal & Brooks-Gunn, 2000). Neighborhoods may influence the effects of family processes on child outcomes through relational support, collective self-efficacy, and tangible resources related to positive development. For example, children raised in more affluent neighborhoods are consistently better prepared to enter kindergarten (Chase-Landsdale & Gordon, 1996) and have better access to quality child care than children raised in lower income neighborhoods (Burchinal, Nelson, Carlson, & Brooks-Gunn, 2008). Research supports the role that neighborhood resources may play in early cognitive development. Children who move from high-poverty neighborhoods to low-poverty neighborhoods have been found to increase their self-regulation (Roy, Mccoy, & Raver, 2014). These effects extend into academic and behavioral indicators from kindergarten and early elementary school years with children raised in disadvantaged neighborhoods performing poorer on academic tests (Morrissey & Vinopal, 2018).

Country.   Support for institutions such as child care, schools, and social support programs can also influence child outcomes through family processes. For example, providing balanced nutrition during the early childhood years is essential for optimal brain development. However, for some families limited economic resources may restrict their ability to adequately feed their children and thus they rely on federally supported programs such as the Supplemental Nutrition Assistance Program (SNAP) or the Women, Infants, and Children (WIC) program administered by the U.S. Department of Agriculture (USDA). Particularly for very young children, being raised in food insecure households may place them at risk for neurocognitive and developmental difficulties (Cook & Frank 2008), poor health, child hospitalizations, and admissions to the ED (Cook et al., 2013).

Culture. Most distal to the child's experience are cultural institutions. Certainly, cultural values and traditions affect child development through family practices and beliefs. For example, immigrant families are less likely to enroll their children in center-based child care than nonimmigrant families (Brandon, 2004) and children from Latino families are less likely to receive out-of-home care prior to entering kindergarten (Buysse, Castro, West, & Skinner, 2005). While an ecological approach provides an appreciation of the complexity of child development, in and of itself it does not allude to the process by which individual children develop well or poorly in particular contexts. In order to understand the mechanisms linking different ecologies to child outcome, it is important to consider how risk may operate across contexts and how different processes may mediate or moderate the effects of risk.

Cumulative Risk

Ecological models emphasize the complexity of child development. To take into account this complexity, it is important to recognize that a child's current state is rarely the result of a single factor, but instead is the result of multiple factors that accumulate over time. In terms of the family context, this means that family functioning at any point in time will be the result of several factors including the child's current state, family of origin factors such as mental health history of the parents and grandparents, current economic conditions, and cumulative history of family stability. Take for example the effects of family instability on children's social and emotional development. Children have the opportunity to thrive when there is stability in their lives including predictable routines, regular schedules, and a safe place to call home. When a family moves there is the chance that friendships are lost, there is a transition to a new school, and routines are disrupted. Household moves are often the result of relationship breakup by the mother (Adam & Chase-Landsdale, 2002). Thus, family instability also indicates a change in relationships in the family and potential for increased levels of family conflict. Family instability has been defined as a number of residential moves, relationship disruptions, and job loss. This index of family instability has been found to be related to teacher and parent report of children's behavior problems (Ackerman, Kogos, Youngstrom, Schoff, & Izard, 1999). However, the effects were moderated by child temperament in that children with more difficult temperaments were more susceptible to family instability and this was expressed through higher levels of internalizing behavior problems. Children who

experience family instability earlier in life and over longer periods of time were at the greatest risk for internalizing problems. However, the likelihood for externalizing behavior and academic problems were just as great if the child had recently experienced family instability (Ackerman, Brown, & Izard, 2004).

Examining environmental risk factors such as family instability provides some insight into the cumulative indexes that may predict child outcomes at any given point in time. Although providing guidance in terms of identifying potential risk factors, it does not provide direction as to the process by which behavior is changed and the role that family organizational and belief systems may operate in promoting health and well-being in children. In order to specify the process by which families affect child outcome, it is important to provide a model of how behavior changes over time.

Transactions in Development

The transactional model as proposed by Sameroff and colleagues (Sameroff, 2010: Sameroff & Fiese, 2000) emphasizes the mutual effects between parent and child, embedded and regulated by cultural codes. In this model, child outcome is predictable neither by the state of the child alone nor by the environment in which she is being raised. Rather, it is a result of a series of transactions that evolve over time with the child responding to and altering the environment. Thus, to be able to predict how families influence children one must also ask how children influence families.

Let us take a very simple example of parents telling bedtime stories to their children and its connection to early literacy skills (Beals, 2001). Consider a situation where there are birth complications and the caregiver has recently moved due to a breakup with the child's father. Once the caregiver brings the infant home from the hospital, there may be residues of worry and anxiety about the child's health, anger about the father leaving her and the child at a time of great need, and concern about how to pay for continued care. The worry and concern may lead to inconsistent parenting patterns such that at times the child is responded to sensitively and at other times the caregiver's preoccupations with paying the bills, lost relationship, and adjusting to a new baby leave her irritable and inconsistent in her parenting practices. In an attempt to get the caregiver's attention, the child may develop some behaviors that can be interpreted as indicative of a difficult temperament (e.g., whining, difficulty in soothing, persistence). When bedtime arrives the caregiver may be exhausted by strained interactions throughout the day and prefer to leave the child with a bottle rather than reading a story. Over time, the child is not exposed to joint book reading and family routines are carried out in a perfunctory way rather than as an opportunity to set aside time to be together. When the child arrives at school she is ill-equipped to read and may not meet normative expectations for language development. The process is outlined in Figure 20.2.

Child

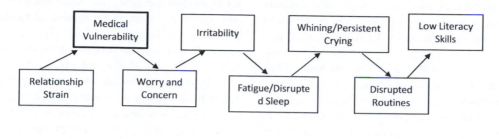

Parent

Figure 20.2 Transactional model of development.

What was the cause of this outcome? Did the mother's reasonable worry about a potentially medically vulnerable child lead to poor language skills? Did the recent breakup with the child's father and being a single parent cement the child's future in terms of school problems? Did the child's difficult temperament cause him or her not to read? Did the disruption of bedtime routines directly result in delays in language development? From a transactional perspective, poor literacy skills are not the result of any one factor but develop over a series of exchanges between child and caregiver in a given environment. For early childhood educators, the significance of this model resides in understanding both dynamic change processes and opportunities for intervention. If child outcome is the product of multiple influences then there are multiple avenues for implementing change. In this case, it may be possible to redefine the relationship between caregiver and child through interaction coaching and encouraging responsive parenting practices (McDonough, 2000). It may also be possible to educate caregivers about the significance of joint book reading and create a bedtime routine that involves caregiver and child.

The transactional model also highlights the importance of how parent-child interactions become part of parent belief systems that regulate child behavior over time. In order to better elucidate this process, it is important to consider how families as a group regulate behavior and how children contribute to family process.

Family Routines and Rituals

A distinction can be made between routines of daily living and rituals in family life that parallel aspects of the practicing and representing family (Fiese & Spagnola, 2007). Routines and rituals can be considered in terms of how they are communicated, time commitment, and continuity. In the case of routines, communication tends to be fairly instrumental with a focus on "this is what needs to be done." Routines typically involve a momentary commitment with little

thought being given to the activity once it is completed. They tend to be repeated over time in a similar manner. Rituals, on the other hand, are communicated through symbols and convey "this is who we are" as a group. There is an emotional commitment to rituals and they often evoke strong affect. Once the activity is over, there is a tendency to replay it in memory with particular attention to feelings of belonging and connection with others. Rituals provide continuity over time and are frequently passed down across generations. When routines are disrupted, it is a hassle. When rituals are disrupted, there is a threat to group identity.

Routines are closely associated with family practices and can be part of daily and weekly activities such as mealtime, bedtime, and getting ready for school. Rituals can also occur in these settings if there is a symbolic and emotional investment in the activity and may also extend to settings such as annual celebration (e.g., birthdays) and religious observances. During the child-raising years, maintaining routines and rituals is one way in which family tasks are carried out (Fiese, 2006). Indeed, there is reason to believe that the practice of family routines is sensitive to developmental transitions within the family. Families of infants are less likely to report the establishment of routines around mealtime, weekends, and special celebrations than parents of children of preschool age (Fiese, Hooker, Kotary, & Schwagler, 1993). However, once routines are established, mothers of infants feel more confident in their capacity to parent (Sprunger, Boyce, & Gaines, 1985). During the transition to kindergarten, parents who report more parenting stress also report declining family routines (DeCaro & Worthman, 2011).

Early childcare routines, such as sleep routines, provide structure for social interaction. Establishing early care routines around bedtime provides predictability and order and can soothe then infant as they go to sleep. Considerable research exists supporting the notion that a consistent set of predictable activities prior to bedtime is associated with better sleep hygiene, reduced parent stress, and better child self-regulation (Mindell & Williamson, 2018). Promoting positive bedtime routines may be one avenue for supporting healthy outcomes during the early childhood years.

During the preschool and early school years, predictability of mealtime and bedtime routines are also associated with more optimal child outcomes. For example, low frequency of family mealtimes for children in kindergarten is associated with greater risk of obesity, particularly if meals are accompanied by television viewing (Gable, Chang, & Krull, 2007; Jones, Fiese & the STRONG Kids Team, 2014). The emotional climate established during mealtimes has been found to be related to food consumption during the preschool years with the expression of more positive emotions associated with the consumption of healthier foods (Saltzman, Bost, Musaad, Fiese, & Wiley, 2018). How families interact during mealtimes is also associated with child mental health outcomes. Families who provide clear and direct communication, are responsive to the child's affect, and provide structure to the meal itself are less likely to have children with problematic behaviors and demonstrate a more positive mealtime emotional climate (Dickstein, St. Andre, Sameroff, Seifer, & Schiller, 1999; Fiese & Marjinsky, 1999; Saltzman et al., 2018).

Similarly, the establishment of regular bedtime routines during preschool and early childhood years is associated with better outcomes for young children. Preschool children who experience both regular mealtimes and bedtimes in their families are less likely to develop obesity (Andersen & Whitaker, 2010; Jones et al., 2014). During the preschool years, less sleep at night is related to increased odds for developing problematic behaviors, particularly externalizing problems (Lavigne et al., 1999). These behavioral problems may extend into later childhood and adolescence (Gregory & Sadeh, 2012). However, consistent with the ecological approach, the effects of mealtime and bedtime routines on child outcomes may not be direct but are also influenced by sociodemographic context.

Regularity of bedtimes and mealtimes varies by socioeconomic context. The likelihood that children between 4 and 35 months will have the same bedtime and mealtime every day varies by family income in one report using a national database. Less than 50% of the low-income households reported having the same bedtime and mealtime for their young children in comparison to 70% of higher income families (Child Trends, 2003). Children raised in lower income households were also observed to have later onset of sleep and shorter duration of sleep when sleep patterns were collected via actigraphs (deJong et al., 2016). Further, the type of bedtime routines that families practice with their young children varies by racial and ethnic background. White families are more likely to provide comfort objects or read to their child than non-White non-Latino families (Milan, Snow, & Belay, 2007). African American families are more likely to use bathing as part of a bedtime routine. Latino families are most likely to provide a bottle to their child as part of a bedtime routine.

The routines of daily living begin to shape children's behavior and expectations very early on. Infants and toddlers learn to sooth themselves during bedtime routines, expand their vocabulary during playtime routines, and become part of the social group during family mealtimes. What may appear on the surface to be mundane daily activities, in fact, form the child's early learning playground. The daily routines of early childhood prepare the child for more formalized learning on several levels. The repetition of routine activities may reinforce newly learned skills. The predictability of routines may aid in regulating behavior, providing a guide for what is acceptable and what is not. Routines that are flexible encourage children to become more active participants in family life, which in turn may lead to feelings of competence when approaching new and novel tasks. It is also likely that families who create organized households through regular routines also set the stage for optimal early literacy skills. For example, children's early literacy skills are associated with not only a parent's beliefs about the importance of developing such skills but also daily home routines such as dinnertime and sharing in family homework time (Serpell, Sonnenschein, Baker, & Ganapathy, 2002). Thus, families create a social environment where mundane activities are planned ahead, genuine interest in the day's events is communicated, and the repetitiveness of these events provides a sense of belongingness that can promote health and well-being for the child.

Daily routines are also be regulated by cultural expectations. For example, Caribbean immigrant families expect young children (prekindergarten and kindergarten age) to have homework and will organize approximately five hours per week in the family's routine to attend to the child's homework (Roopnarine, Bynoe, & Singh, 2004). Less frequent, but equally important in developing a sense of personal identity are cultural celebrations that remind family members of their origins and often involve opportunities for storytelling and cementing relationships through the preparation of different ethnic dishes (Falicov, 2003; Giray & Ferguson, 2018).

To summarize, routines are directly observable and provide predictability and order to family life. During early childhood, families are faced with the task of creating schedules around feeding, sleeping, and increasingly over time activities to connect the child to other institutions such as schools. There is the potential for these family-based practices to set the stage for the child's responsiveness to structure and order in the classroom. Children who have experienced regular routines in the home may have expectations for environmental orderliness that eases their transition to school where key educational tasks are embedded in structured and sequenced activities (Norton, 1993). Routines may assist children in developing self-regulation skills and cognitive abilities (Ferretti & Bub, 2014). Early childhood educators have the opportunity to partner with families to encourage regular routines in the home. One important example is preparation for the transition to kindergarten. Early childhood educators can play a pivotal role in preparing the child not only for her new role in more formal learning environments but also for assisting parents in what to expect. For example, in a survey of parents anticipating their child's transition to kindergarten there was a consistent lack of knowledge about what to expect about their child's daily routines in kindergarten and lack of preparedness at home (Wildenger, McIntyre, Fiese, & Ecker, 2008). Most parents anticipated that their children would need to go to bed close to an hour earlier, wake up 30 minutes earlier, and that mealtimes would need to be adjusted. However, the summer prior to entry into kindergarten no changes had been made. Early childhood educators have the opportunity to partner with parents to identify new schedules and plan for changes at home.

Whereas the routines of daily living may prepare children to respond to order, rituals in family life reflect the affective and emotional climate of relationships. Children who are raised in homes where collective gatherings are deliberately planned, eagerly anticipated, and hold symbolic significance are likely to feel that they belong to a valued group and in turn create a stronger sense of self (Fiese, 2006).

There is preliminary evidence to suggest that families who maintain meaningful family rituals across the transition from kindergarten to elementary school have children who perform better academically. In a longitudinal study of 70 families who were originally interviewed when their child was four and then again when their child was nine years of age, we found different patterns of family ritual stability. For some families, the meaning associated with family rituals remained relatively high over the five-year period, for others it remained relatively low. There were some families where the affective component declined over time. It was this later group where children experienced the most difficulty in the early school years and performed less well on tests of academic achievement (Fiese, 2002). We speculate that in instances where meaningful rituals are disrupted there are likely to be other stresses within the family. Children may be keenly aware of changes in routines and ritual involvement. Whereas young children may not be able to articulate the amount of stress present in the family environment they certainly notice when eagerly anticipated events are canceled or altered in a significant way. Rituals may signify to the child the relative health of family relationships. Thus, children who feel emotionally connected to their families may be less likely to develop internalizing and externalizing symptoms that can affect engaging in classroom activities (Brody & Flor, 1997; Fiese, 2000).

Family Risk and Protective Factors

We have emphasized the multiply determined nature of family process in relation to child development. Family process is not a unidimensional variable but one that operates in the realm of behavior and beliefs that are subject to stresses and conditions in the environment. Risk conditions do not operate in isolation either and are likely to cluster together and have cumulative rather than singular effects (Sameroff, 1995; Ferguson & Evans, 2019). Poverty has an overwhelming effect on child development (Evans, 2004; Ferguson & Evans, 2019). This section is dedicated to a discussion of the effects of poverty on family processes, with particular attention to neighborhood poverty and the potential for environmental chaos to act as a mediating factor.

Poverty and the Family

Approximately 14 million children in the United States lived in poverty in the first decade of the twenty-first century (Wight, Chau, & Aratani, 2010). Young children, those under nine years of age, are overrepresented in terms of being exposed to low-income and impoverished living conditions. Close to 44% of young children are raised in low-income households and 21% live in poor households (Koball & Jiang, 2018). What are the consequences of living in poverty for young children and what role does the family play in potentially protecting children from the harmful effects of poverty?

First, young children living in poverty often experience food insecurity. That is, they do not have adequate sources of food at all times or a variety of nutritious foods to lead a healthy life. Food insecurity disproportionally affects households with children. In 2016, the food insecurity rate for all U.S. households was 12.3% (Coleman-Jensen, Rabbitt, Gregory, & Signh, 2017). During 2016 the prevalence rate for households with children was 16.5%, for households with children under age six was 16.6%, and for households with children headed by a single woman was 31.6% (Coleman-Jensen et al., 2017). The consequences of inadequate sources of, and poor quality food in early childhood include a compromised immune system with preschool children having more colds (Alaimo, Olson, Frongillo, & Briefel, 2001), poorer health overall (Cook et al., 2004), performing less well in kindergarten (Winicki & Jemison, 2003), and being less prepared to enter kindergarten (Johnson & Markowitz, 2018).

How might the overlapping conditions of poverty and household food insecurity affect family processes known to affect child development? First, families who rely on supplemental food assistance programs to adequately feed their children spend more time shopping for and preparing food and less time eating together than higher income families (Andrews & Hamrick, 2009). Families in food insecure households may also experience more chaos in their daily lives and have more difficulty around mealtime planning (Fiese, Gundersen, Koester, & Jones, 2016). Lower income families experience more of a burden in carrying out daily routines (Fiese, Winter, & Botti, 2011; Roy, Tubbs, & Burton, 2004). This burden is often expressed through feelings of not being able to sufficiently balance caregiving tasks with added demands on time needed for transportation, finding child care, and oftentimes working more than one job (Roy et al., 2004). Further, parents with fewer economic resources also experience more stress in parenting, engaging in either harsh or nonresponsive parenting styles (Evans, 2004; Ferguson & Evans, 2019).

Children raised in poverty are often ill-equipped to make the transition from home to school (Rimm-Kaufmann, Pianta, & Cox, 2000). By the time they reach school age, children raised in low-income or poverty conditions are more likely than middle- or upper-middle-class children to experience multiple stressors in their immediate environment – overcrowding, poor quality of housing, and neighborhood violence, to name a few (Evans, 2004). Factors such as these have been linked to greater psychological distress in both urban and rural children (Duncan & Brooks-Gunn, 1997; Evans & English, 2002) and arguably have a negative impact on children's ability to explore new learning experiences and develop intellectually. Children who are more challenged psychologically by experiencing multiple stressors are in a less positive position to acquire new skills.

There are anecdotal examples of children who have succeeded despite any one of these stressors. One may call to mind a child who has thrived in school despite a background of poverty. If this child "made it," why can't another? Despite similarities in one or a few risk factors, it is important to consider that it is not the presence of any particular stressor or a specific combination of risk factors that is uniquely detrimental for children. Rather, it is the cumulative value of any combination of them (Sameroff, 2010; Sameroff & MacKenzie, 2003). Sameroff and colleagues have demonstrated that when parental education, employment status, parental psychopathology, parent-child interaction patterns, child temperament, and neighborhood conditions are considered simultaneously child intelligence levels can be predicted both concurrently and prospectively (Guttman, Sameroff, & Cole, 2003). What is of interest for our discussion is that neither a single risk variable nor even clusters of risk predicted child performance. Multiple risk factors acting in concert predict less optimal outcomes. For this reason, it is not possible to devise a simple formula identifying exactly which factors determine a negative outcome. Thus, it is not sufficient to state that being raised in poverty leads to poor outcomes for children. Rather, it is essential to consider which aspects of poverty, when, for whom, and under what conditions lead to compromised functioning. We consider how neighborhood factors, parental psychopathology, and family process may contribute to child outcome in these high-risk factors.

Neighborhood Risk Factors

Families live in neighborhoods, and neighborhood factors, particularly high concentrations of poverty within relatively small geographic areas, have been associated with poorer child performance on measures of mental health, verbal ability, IQ scores, and school achievement (Duncan, Magnuson, Kalil, & Ziol-Guest, 2012; Leventhal & Brooks-Gunn, 2000; Leventhal & Newman, 2010). Findings such as these are not exclusive to children in urban neighborhoods. Low-income and poverty status in children and families living in rural communities have been identified as a risk factor as well (Evans, 2004; Ferguson & Evans, 2019). Families who live in rural communities and experience poverty during the child's first two years of life demonstrate significantly lower cognitive, language, executive functioning, and social skills (Burchinal et al., 2018).

Neighborhoods vary in terms of the social capital that is made available to families. This capital ranges from the physical and built environment that includes locations for learning such as libraries, cultural enrichment such as performance centers, and places for physical activity such as parks and recreation facilities. Lower income neighborhoods are typically less well-resourced in terms of technologies that promote learning (Evans, 2004) and parks for physical activity (Gordon-Larsen, Nelson, Page, & Popkin, 2006). For young children, this means decreased opportunities to interact in environments that have up-to-date computing equipment similar to what will be used in schools. Further, lack of access to parks and recreation facilities places the child at risk for developing unhealthy weight and its associated health consequences (Grigsby-Toussaint, Chi, & Fiese, 2011).

Social capital in neighborhoods also includes the availability of social support and relationships with neighbors. Poorer neighborhoods are also characterized by poor lighting, poorly maintained streets and sidewalks, and high rates of unoccupied buildings (Evans, 2004). Opportunities to form relationships with neighbors and develop sources of support can be compromised when there is a need to keep doors locked and transience is common. Faced with increasing rates of violence, families may feel powerless in protecting their children from gangs and illegal activities (Brooks-Gunn, 1997). What may be considered adaptive and supportive behavior in middle-class neighborhoods may actually place children at greater risk in poorer neighborhoods. For example, maintaining distance from some neighbors and sacrificing employment to be able to monitor children's behavior more closely may be adaptive for some high-risk families (Burton & Jarrett, 2000).

There are several differences in early literacy skills and the home environments of children raised in poverty compared to those who are not. In a large study of nearly 30,000 children and their families using NLSY data files, Bradley and colleagues (Bradley, Corwyn, McAdoo, & Coll, 2001) employed the HOME inventory to assess different aspects of children's experiences in their homes, targeting specific comparisons between nonpoor and poor families, further broken down by race/ethnicity, comparing poor and nonpoor European American, African American, and Latino American families. For European American, African American, and Latino American families, it was observed that nonpoor parents were more likely to spontaneously speak to their children (excluding scolding) than poor parents. In addition, it was found that regardless of racial/ethnic group, poor families were more likely to have no books in the household and that regardless of race/ethnicity, poor parents were more likely than nonpoor parents to endorse that they never read to their children or only read to them a few times per year.

Poverty status had a greater impact on the availability of learning materials than did ethnicity. Generally, poor children were much less likely to have three or more children's books during infancy and early childhood than were nonpoor children. In addition, poor children were less likely to visit enriching places and events in the community. These differences were found across all ethnic groups and all age groups.

During infancy and childhood, and across all racial/ethnic groups, nonpoor mothers were twice as likely as were poor mothers to read to their children three or more times per week.

The results of the Bradley and colleagues study suggest that children raised in poorer environments are less likely to be exposed to routine book reading and that their verbal environment, overall, may be relatively impoverished. However, it is possible to affect literacy skills and qualities of the home environment related to the child's preparedness to learn.

Recall the role that elaborative reminiscing and family storytelling may play in creating a sense of family identity and socializing children. Reese and colleagues have developed an intervention for families participating in Head Start that encourages elaborative reminiscing as part of a program to promote early literacy skills (Reese, Leywa, Sparks, & Grolnick, 2010). Mothers of children enrolled in Head Start were visited in their home and trained either in a dialogic (question/answer) joint book reading style or in elaborative reminiscing. The elaborative reminiscing group was encouraged to discuss past events with their children on a daily basis and then elaborate with their children through open-ended questions and increasing their child's participation. At the end of the school year, children who had been exposed to the elaborative reminiscing practices in the home scored higher on an expressive vocabulary test, had better story comprehension, and produced narratives of higher quality than children exposed to the dialogic joint book reading intervention. This preliminary study suggests that home-based interventions that promote family storytelling about routine events may have a positive effect on early literacy skills for children raised in low-income environments.

Chaos as a Risk Factor in Low-Income Environments

Consistent with the ecological model, the effects of poverty on child development can be seen as part of the cumulative effect of exposure to adverse events in the neighborhood and family, and compromised social capital. However, a focus on the risk factors alone does not indicate the process by which poverty may affect the promotive factors known to positively affect child development. From a family systems perspective, it is particularly important to identify how families respond to and potentially counteract the harmful effects of high-risk environments in order to protect children and promote health and well-being. One framework that allows for an examination of process level factors and the intersection of family and neighborhood factors is an examination of family chaos.

Bronfenbrenner and Evans (2000) have offered a perspective on chaos in family life describing it as "frenetic activity, lack of structure, unpredictability in everyday activities, [and] high levels of ambient stimulation" (p. 21). There are several characteristics that are shared by chaotic environments, whether at home, in neighborhoods, or in schools. There is a high level of background noise, physical crowding; schedules are disrupted and plans have to be changed at the last minute; time is perceived to be out of one's control; and conversations are often interrupted (Bradley, 2004; Evans, Gonnella, Marcynyszyn, Gentile, & Salpekar, 2005; Fiese & Winter, 2010). Living in chaotic environments involves not only the disruption of daily activities but also the felt experience of an uncontrollable environment.

For families living in poverty, juggling time is an ever-present occupation. For parents with limited economic resources, daily routines of feeding, grooming, and dropping off children to multiple care providers is more than just hectic, report Roy and colleagues (Roy et al., 2004). There is a sense that time is out of control and daily routines are driven by those outside the family such as bus drivers, bosses, and a carillon of childcare providers.

Chaotic living conditions including high levels of background noise (e.g., the constant presence of television) and family instability (changes in residence and partners) affect young children's health and preparedness to learn. In a small pilot study of children enrolled in Head Start, it was found that children who lived in more chaotic households got less sleep and evidenced a sense of learned helplessness toward learning (Brown, & Low, 2008). Longitudinal studies also suggest that environmental chaos (noise, crowding, foot traffic) and home chaos (lack of routines, confusion) mediate the relation between poverty and child socioemotional development (Evans et al., 2005). Chaos has also been found to predict the likelihood of families experiencing food insecurity above and beyond family income (Fiese et al., 2016).

In addition to creating feelings of learned helplessness, chaotic environments may disrupt positive parenting practices. High levels of home chaos have been found to be related to higher levels of negative parenting and lower levels of positive parenting (Coldwell, Pike, & Dunn, 2006; Dumas et al., 2005). Further, parents in chaotic households are less likely to positively respond to their child's emotions, and that in turn is related to behavior problems (Valiente, Lemery-Chalfant, & Reiser, 2007). The pathway for these effects may be linked to increased risk for poor maternal executive functioning under high chaotic environments in low-income households (Deater-Deckard, Chen, Wang, & Bell, 2012).

Neighborhoods can also be characterized by relative degrees of chaos: housing density, physical disorder, instability of residents, neighborhood level routines (e.g., rhythm of daily life in terms of the number of residents leaving for work at the same time), and supervision and monitoring of children in the neighborhood (Brooks-Gunn, Johnson, & Leventhal, 2010; Roy, 2019). Unfortunately, the empirical base indicating the cumulative effects of neighborhood chaos factors on child development is scant. There is evidence to suggest, however, that living in noisy neighborhoods (e.g., those close to airports) increases risk for reading problems and lowers academic performance (Evans, 2006). Perhaps the strongest evidence linking neighborhood chaos and child outcomes is the role of neighborhood monitoring of children's activities and collective efficacy. When family members feel that they can trust their neighbors and have a sense that there is collective support in the neighborhood in contrast to chaotic and unpredictable relationships with neighbors, there is typically more monitoring of child and adolescent behavior. This type of collective monitoring is most closely associated with rates of violence in the neighborhood (Leventhal & Brooks-Gunn, 2000). Although most commonly studied in families with adolescents, neighborhood peer relationships in the preschool years are also important, and aggressive behaviors can be modeled from neighborhood peers as young as three years of age (Leventhal & Brooks-Gunn, 2000).

A Resiliency Framework for Early Childhood Educators

Whereas an examination of environmental chaos points to the multiple layers of influence on child development and an appreciation of the ecological foundations of early learning, it provides little direction in terms of active solutions for families in their daily lives. In order to more fully appreciate how families face daily challenges so that their children may thrive, a family resiliency framework is warranted. Researchers have identified a set of family-level characteristics that promote resiliency and increase the likelihood that children will be able to face and overcome adversity (Black & Lobo, 2008; Luthar, Cicchetti, & Becker, 2000; Masten, 2001; Patterson, 2002; Sigman-Grant, Hayes, VanBrackle, & Fiese, 2015). In general, families that are able to set aside time to be together, interact in a warm and supportive manner, communicate their thoughts and feelings in a direct manner, create regular and meaningful routines and rituals, and are flexible during normative and nonnormative transitions are more likely to protect their children from the harmful effects of risk. We have already discussed the important role of family routines in promoting health development for children. As a process for promoting resiliency, it is important to point out how routines and rituals that include supportive and positive forms of communication are more likely to be associated with positive outcomes for children (Dickstein, Brooks-Gunn, Yeung, & Smith, 1998; Fiese et al., 2011).

Consistent with the resiliency framework that has identified core elements at the family level that may serve as resources for children under high-risk conditions, there are parallel processes in early childhood settings that may serve similar functions. Yates and colleagues have proposed that early childhood education and care settings are provision resources that may moderate the effects of family-level adversity (Yates, Egeland, & Sroufe, 2003). Applying principles of developmental theory and evidence supporting the central role of attachment relationships during the early years, qualities of the early care and education environment can serve as a resource for resilience. Indeed, Hall and colleagues have demonstrated in a random sample of over 2,000 preschool age children, the moderating effects of teacher-child relationships on cognitive development in the context of family risk (e.g., low levels of maternal education, unemployment, number of nonparental caregivers: Hall et al., 2009).

Considering the strong influence of regular routines in family life, the power of strong relationships, and the importance of stability for young children, there are several opportunities where early childhood educators can serve as resources for families. Efforts to provide parents with educational materials about the importance of regular routines – information about how to overcome barriers to implementing routines, reinforcing regular storytelling, and providing connections between activities at home and school – appear to be warranted. Early childhood educators are uniquely poised to take their knowledge of the importance of building quality relationships to build these important parenting skills.

Summary

Household poverty places a major challenge in raising children prepared to learn. However, poverty is more than just a lack of economic resources. It affects nearly every aspect of daily living from place of residence, allocation of time, and creation of routines. Household poverty increases the risk that children will be raised in chaotic environments that include high levels of ambient noise, residential crowding, low levels of collective efficacy in neighborhoods, disruption of family routines such as mealtime and bedtime, and promotion of feelings of learned helplessness.

There is cause for optimism, however. A resiliency framework suggests that family-level processes that include a cohesive family unit, regular routines, and open communication can protect children from risk. Further, the quality of the preschool environment may further buffer children from adversity. Figure 20.3 outlines those factors that may protect

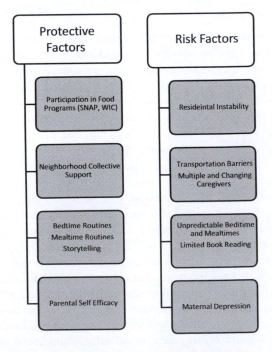

Figure 20.3 Risk and protective factors in chaotic households.

children from chaotic environments and those that will likely increase risk. A review of risk and resilience also points to the important role of connecting schools with families.

Connecting Schools with the Changing Face of Families

A child's early success in school will rely in part on how well connected the family is to the school and how aware of school practices. One of the single most important factors in bridging the gap between school and home is parent participation (Lambiase, 2014). Family-school partnerships emphasize the vital importance of open communication, healthy relationships, mutual respects, mutual participation, and genuine willingness to share power and responsibility between family and school (Henderson, Mapp, Johnson, & Davies, 2007; Semke & Sheridan, 2012). Families who form active partnerships with early childhood settings and in the early elementary school year have a positive impact on child outcomes (Epstein & Sanders, 2002). The research on promoting family-school partnerships is relatively extensive and consistent in supporting more parental involvement in the early school years (Arnold, Zeljo, Doctoroff, & Ortiz, 2008; Epstein & Sanders, 2002; Reynolds, 1992). A recent meta-analysis conducted by Ma, Shen, Krenn, Hu, and Yuan (2016) looked at the relationship between learning outcomes and parental involvement from the aspects of both the family and the school. From the role of parents (family involvement), the key to a strong relationship was behavioral involvement, home supervision, and home-school connection (Ma et al., 2016). In terms of the role of schools and community (partnership development), the meta-analysis suggests three key aspects for a strong relationship: (1) schools and social services gain more capacity to engage parents, (2) school and community leaders have respectful and effective relationships with families and children, and (3) authentic partnerships among families, schools, and communities are institutionalized in an organization's culture, practices, and programs (Ma et al., 2016). Several decades of research has shown the extensive benefits to parents taking an active role or at least being well informed in their child's educational experience.

Parent Involvement

The term "parent involvement" is used extensively in the literature, and has been defined in various ways. The traditional definition refers to parent involvement as a host of activities where parents engage not only in and support the education of their children, but also in the children's schools. One of the most widely used frameworks for parent involvement is the Epstein Model (Epstein et al., 2009). This framework is based on a six-item classification system typology of parental involvement including parenting, communication, volunteering, learning at home, decision-making, and collaborating with community (Epstein et al., 2009). Epstein's Model captures the traditional definitions by recognizing parents'

role in the home environment, while also acknowledging the responsibility of the school to support and encourage these activities through the establishment of collaborative relationships.

Parents can become involved in helping their children's learning through educationally enriching activities at home that could include reading books, visiting libraries, talking about the child's day at school, or playing games that consists of counting (Ramani, Rowe, Eason, & Leasch, 2015; Roberts, Jergens, & Burchinal, 2005; Schick, 2014). Research has shown that parents' increase in home involvement in early education has been associated with growth in children's communication and literacy ability (Hammer, Farkas, & Maczuga, 2010; Roberts et al., 2005; Schick, 2014), math skills (Ramani et al., 2015), and social emotional development (Sheridan, Knoche, Edwards, Bovaird, & Kupzyk, 2010). This allows parents to participate in fostering a child's skills and abilities at home, extending the learning environment beyond just the early childhood program.

Parental involvement also emphasizes the importance of the role parents play within their child's educational program. Parents can support their children's education by exchanging information with teachers regarding home life, attending functions and meetings at the educational program, as well as volunteer in the classroom. Parents who have an understanding of the school's expectations and how a school operates are better advocates of their children than those who are less knowledgeable (Delgado-Gaitan, 1991). Parents can also take on more active roles by participating in the decision-making process at the early childhood program by serving on committees or governance boards (Cotton & Wikelund, 1995). By engaging in these activities within a child's educational program, parents can potentially increase their social capital (Hill & Taylor, 2004; Lee & Bowen, 2006). This increase in networks can help leverage additional support or resources such as other enrichment opportunities that can be beneficial to the child (Bryan, Holcomb-McCoy, Day-Vines, & Moore-Thomas, 2011; Lee & Bowen, 2006). These added supports can be particularly helpful when a family is faced with a challenge, as a family has more resources to draw on to overcome hurdles along the way. Parent-school involvement has been shown to be related to children's social skills and math skills during the pre-kindergarten years (Powell, Son, File, & San Juan, 2010). When parents are working together with their child's teacher and early childhood program, they are able to strengthen the learning that occurs both at the program and at home.

A key component of effective early childhood programs is the ability to build collaborative relationships between school, families, and the community (Spagnola & Fiese, 2007), which can be developed through establishing parental involvement. Parents and schools can work together to identify educational needs and goals for children, which assists in developing understanding and expectations between each other, while promoting a collaborative relationship. Parent involvement in a child's early education can benefit the child's transition from early childhood program to elementary school. The positive fostering by early childhood programs on parent involvement can have the ability to influence sustained parental involvement.

Parent involvement can lead families to feeling empowered. Empowerment is an ongoing intentional process involving mutual respect, critical reflection, caring, and group participation (Delgado-Gaitan, 1991). However, traditional definitions of parent involvement used by the literature, as well as schools, are based on school cultures that are constructed from middle-class, European American cultural norms (Bower & Griffin, 2011; Fields-Smith, 2007; Freeman, 2010; Hill & Craft, 2003; Lee & Bowen, 2006). These definitions fail to taken into account other strategies that families might utilize, which can lead to frustration and misguided views of both parties.

Head Start Utilizes Parent Involvement

Families play a huge role in the contribution to their children's learning and development. Family involvement may be even more important for children residing in low-income households, where children face being at risk for academic and social challenges in school later on (Jeynes, 2005; Lee & Burkam, 2002). The beneficial ability of parental involvement is valued by Head Start, the nation's largest federally funded early childhood education program for low-income children and families. A cornerstone of the program is working with families to encourage their involvement in children's learning and education (Pizzo & Tufankjian, 2004; Weiss, Daring, Mayer, Kreider, & McCartney, 2005). Head Start's National Performance Standards require that programs support family participation in all aspects of their children's early education experiences, and foster parents' skills in promoting children's learning and development that extend beyond the classroom (Head Start Performance Standards, 2016). Not only does Head Start emphasize that parents engage with their children, but the program creates opportunities for parents to play an active role and work with staff toward the goals the family creates for themselves and their children (Ma et al., 2016). This creates an authentic partnership between the family and the program. Head Start programs are a prime example of a setting that aims to enhance family involvement on all levels. However, we do recognize that Head Start programs vary across sites and that family engagement is, in some cases, an aspirational policy.

Diverse Family Characteristics

Low-income families are presented with additional barriers that present challenges to participating in traditional forms of parent involvement. Working parents have been found to volunteer less frequently in their child's preschool classrooms (Castro, Bryant, Peisner-Feinberg, & Skinner, 2004), which is possibly due to work schedules and time scarcity that reduces time for involvement (Weiss et al., 2003). Parents

from low-income households might also be working in more than one job, perhaps less flexible jobs, to meet financial demands for their families. Research has also shown that families who receive financial support through governmental assistance programs are less likely to be involved with their child's transition from preschool to kindergarten (McIntyre, Eckert, Fiese, DiGennaro, & Wildenger, 2007). These parents were less likely to attend meetings, be active in communication with the preschool, or participate in visits to the kindergarten classroom. However, Freeman (2010) showed that low-income families often participate in less structured approaches, such as informal conversations or unscheduled visits, which sometimes are not valued by the school, and therefore efforts are not recognized. For low-income families, work schedules, lack of transportation, and lack of child care may prevent families from being as involved in the school (e.g., attending meetings, volunteering), but these families could be participating in other various ways that are difficult to measure or acknowledge.

Parental involvement should also consider race, ethnicity, and culture beliefs as research has demonstrated differences among these characteristics in families. Differing cultural beliefs and attitudes toward parental involvement could be misinterpreted as lack of interest. Research has suggested that Hispanic and African American communities often place considerable trust in teachers and consider their children's education as the school's responsibility (Seginer, 2006). Thus, there tends to be less family-initiated communication which is seen as a lack of involvement (Bowers & Griffin, 2011). Minority parents whose cultural backgrounds and social values differ from school administrators find it challenging to engage in the child's education (Henderson et al., 2007). However, Jeynes (2011) argues that parents of color and low-income status often participate more than what educators acknowledge. When the educational programs focus on a parent's participation in meetings or involvement solely at the school, the activities the parents engage in at home go unnoticed.

Variations exist between educators and parents regarding what constitutes "parent involvement." However, schools are cautioned on defining parental involvement and associating it with specific behaviors or activities (Bower & Griffin, 2011). Schools' definitions often fail to incorporate considerations for diverse families, and do not capture all aspects of parental involvement, which can leave families feeling disenfranchised and their efforts not going unrecognized (Freeman, 2010). Furthermore, some of the less structured approaches, such as unscheduled visits, can be seen as obtrusive (Fields-Smith, 2007) instead of a parent being active in a child's education. Parents might be apprehensive to speak to educators due to being discouraged in such interactions in the past. This discouragement can push parents even further away, which impacts these parents' participation in the future. Educational programs need to consider differences in cultural norms by race/ethnicity and socioeconomic status in order to capture all variations and use parent involvement as an effective strategy (Bowers & Griffin, 2011).

Changes in Family Living Arrangements

Family living arrangements are becoming increasingly complex, which affects the availability of resources for young children. The number of children being born to single parents has risen from 5% in 1960 to approximately 40% at the beginning of the twenty-first century (Kreider, 2007). This increase is due, primarily, to the increasing number of children being raised in households where cohabitation rather than marriage characterizes the family structure (Bumpass, 2000). About two-fifths of all children spend some time in a cohabiting family. This is important because cohabitation results in relationship instability for children. For example, Osborne and McLanahan (2007) have identified different forms of unmarried households to include cohabiting, households where there were "visiting" or dating relationships, and single mothers. Children living in these types of households experienced different levels of relationship transitions such that 30% of single parent, 20% of "visiting," and 10% of cohabiting households experienced three or more relationship transitions between birth and three years of age. In contrast, for children born in married households the rate of relationship transitions was approximately 2%.

Increase in Cohabitation

In the last several decades, children's family life has become progressively diverse. One of the most considerable changes in family structure is the increase in cohabitation. In 2015, there were more than eight million different sex couples cohabitating in the United States, which has been the largest amount reported in the past 20 years (United States Census Bureau, 2015). Cohabitation can take many forms, but the most common arrangement is a biological mother and male partner. In 2013, about 7% of children were living in cohabiting parent families (Payne, 2013), and by the age of 12, 40% had spent some time in a cohabiting household (Manning, 2015).

Cohabiting families are similar in the basic family structure to married parent families, wherein two adults are present in the home (Manning, 2015). However, a major distinction between the two types of families is stability of the parents' relationship. Overall, cohabiting relationships last an average of 18 months, resulting in only 33% of children born to cohabiting parents remaining in a stable family through age 12 compared to 75% of children born to married parents (Kennedy & Bumpass, 2008). Cohabitation is often an indicator of family instability, which has been shown to be strongly related to poorer outcomes of children, such as deficits in psychosocial well-being (Manning, 2015). Overall, children experience more issues related to emotional well-being, and an increase in behavioral and academic problems if they are living with biological cohabiting parents compared to children living with biological married parents (Berger & McLanahan, 2015).

The effects of relationship instability on early child development may be both direct and indirect. Relationship instability may indirectly affect child cognitive and social development by compromising parenting skills. Mothers who experience multiple relationship transitions during the early child raising years are more likely to experience stress and feel ill-equipped to meet the demands of parenting (Brown, 2010). This stress and ambiguity in relationship status may affect the child's sense of security. Single parents may also spend less time with their children (Sandberg & Hofferth, 2001), a known resource to protect children from adversity. Most notable is that the effects of relationship instability and transitions are most profound during the early childhood years. Young children are more sensitive to changes in relationships, the effects of residential moves, and economic hardships than those during middle childhood (Duncan, Brooks-Gunn, Yeung, & Smith, 1998; Shonkoff & Phillips, 2000). The consequences of early relationship disruptions and instability include poorer health, problematic behaviors, and poorer peer relationships (Brown, 2010; Cavanagh & Huston, 2008).

Cohabitating families often have fewer economic resources than families who have married parents (Brown, Manning, & Payne, 2017). Cohabiting parents are less likely to be employed than married parents, and their median household income is 50% lower than that of married parent households (Kalil & Ryan, 2010). This could be linked to the fact that both mothers and fathers in cohabitating relationships have lower levels of education than their married counterparts (Manning, 2015). Increased levels of education assists in providing not only economic resources, but also other formal and informal resources, social skills, and other types of support. These families tend to be poor, and poverty has shown to be a risk factor for children's overall well-being in many ways.

The solution, however, does not appear to be promoting marriage at any cost (Brown, 2010). The essential ingredients associated with outcomes during early childhood appear to be the quality of relationships and provision of resources. In this regard, there are several opportunities for early childhood educators to form positive partnerships with parents who may have the sole responsibility for raising their children. Parent involvement in early care and education has proven to predict later academic achievement and school competence above and beyond the influence of family background (Miedel & Reynolds, 1999; Reynolds, 2000). The key elements to promoting family involvement appear to be establishing a partnership of shared responsibility for the child's learning, involvement in early care and education activities, and establishing quality relationships between parents and educators (Weiss, Lopez, & Rosenberg, 2010). Common activities that would promote early learning in the home and school could be shared book reading and encouraging parents to attend meals and snacks in schools. This reinforcement of parallel activities in home and early care settings has the potential to benefit the child as well as model and reinforce self-efficacy for the parent.

Involving Fathers in Early Childhood Education

Although there has been an increasing appreciation of the important role that fathers play in child development (Lamb, 2012; Parke, 2004), fathers have not always been included in systematic ways in family-school partnership programs. This is somewhat surprising given the evidence that when fathers are involved in the educational process their children do better in school (National Center for Education Statistics [NCES], 1998). An innovative program has been developed by McBride and colleagues to promote father involvement in a prekindergarten program that serves children at risk for later school failure (McBride, Rane, & Bae, 2001). Involving fathers is set as a priority in the pre-K program, but by intervening directly with teachers, rather than with fathers. In-service sessions with teachers were conducted to provide information about the positive benefits of father involvement and set goals for father involvement. Activities were identified that would encourage father involvement such as bowling nights with children. After the 26-week program, the treatment group had significantly more family involvement overall with, and more father involvement than families served by a control group where teacher behavior was not altered.

McBride offers general principles of program development for early childhood educators that can promote more father involvement (McBride, Dyer, & Rane, 2008):

1. Develop a clear rationale. If an early childhood program desires to involve fathers more in its programming, it is important to clearly articulate the benefits of father involvement. This will be likely to include a deeper understanding of the family ecology including sociodemographic factors within the family and the role of the father in the family.
2. Acknowledge resistance. Not all teachers will embrace initiatives that focus on fathers. This may be particularly true when fathers are seen as "absent" partners and there is a question of directing limited resources to resistant players.
3. Clearly specify targets. This advice holds true for any program development. However, when launching a new initiative to promote father engagement it is important to clearly specify who in the family may be playing the role of the father. This may not be the biological father but may be an uncle or other male figure.
4. Do not reinvent the wheel. Educators should consider whether volunteer programs designed for mothers or other community members may fit well with initiatives to encourage father involvement.
5. Help women become facilitators. It is unlikely that early childhood programs will be fully staffed with enough men to launch an effort. Identifying women in the organization who can provide outreach and facilitate program development is important.

6. Involve mothers in developing the initiative. It is important to keep mothers involved in program development. Mothers are often the gatekeepers for access to their children (McBride, Schoppe-Sullivan, & Ho, 2005) and can make or break initiatives involving fathers if they feel that the mother's role is not also acknowledged.
7. Continue to meet mothers' needs. Consistent with the role of gatekeeper, it is important to keep mothers involved for a whole family approach.
8. Create a father/male friendly environment. Create a space for fathers including their own bulletin board, make sure there are adequate facilities for men, and tailor activities for men.
9. Acknowledge diversity. As has been noted in this chapter, family structures can change. It is important to keep track of the changes in family structure and whether changes in residence also mean changes in partnership.
10. Proceed slowly. Start slow in building father initiatives and do not get discouraged if it takes a while for the initiative to gain speed.
11. Provide training and support services. Seek out experts in your community on the benefits of father involvement and have them provide in-service sessions for staff members.
12. Evaluate and revise efforts. Programming should be an ongoing and evolving practice that takes into account successes as well as barriers to implementation.

Involving the whole family, including fathers, into early childhood programs has the potential to benefit children in several ways. There are opportunities for an enriched learning environment through added verbal stimulation as well as physical play. There is also the added benefit that fathers can provide support for mothers and become more fully engaged in the daily life of the child. Although it may take added effort to include fathers systematically in early childhood programs, they too are a part of the child's future.

Integrating Family Context and Early Childhood Education: Summary and Conclusions

Families are complex and dynamic systems. Families practice regular routines that organize daily life and can provide a sense of order and predictability for young children. Over time, families create beliefs about relationships based, in part, on repetitive interactions occurring in routine settings such as mealtime, bedtime, and preparing for school. Child functioning at any given point in time is the result of a series of transactions between parenting practices and beliefs about relationships. Children may be placed at risk for less than optimal outcomes when they are raised in chaotic environments. For early childhood educators, the take-home message is that families come to create definitions of who they are as a group. This family identity will shape how the child responds to classroom structure, her preparedness to engage in educational activities, and potentially in academic success.

There are multiple ways in which families create their identity. For some families, there are high expectations for child success and daily life is organized around supporting enriching activities. For other families, protecting children from harm is a priority and family-level efforts must be directed toward keeping the family safe. In either case, families typically work hard to ensure optimal development for their children given the context in which they live.

There are three lessons to consider when linking families and early childhood educators. First, it may be beneficial to capitalize on routines as a way to connect families and educators. Setting aside regular times to review newly learned skills at home and perhaps creating family night activities that support learning can become part of routine communications between parents and early childhood educators. Parents should be assured that what appears as a mundane task may afford opportunities for learning. Routine conversations at the dinner table, counting the silverware when putting away the dishes, and learning about bacteria when taking a walk to the pond are examples where daily practices are rich learning opportunities. Indeed, folding learning into these routine interactions will likely result in more sustained interest than presenting children with additional drill sheets during homework time. Early childhood educators have an opportunity to work with parents on establishing healthy home routines by emphasizing regular bedtime routines known to support cognitive and socioemotional development (Mindell & Williamson, 2018). Support of healthy routines can be offered through classroom curriculums (Fisher et al., 2019), parent newsletters, and online resources (see www.parenting247.org for an example).

Second, families are diverse. With the changing nature of family structure, it is important to remember that a child's family structure is not necessarily restricted to a mother or father. Extended family members, neighbors, and kinship ties outside the local area can be sources of support. Each family will create its own unique that can aid educators in better understanding the children under their charge. It is also important to include fathers or prominent male figures in early childhood programs. It is important to recognize that families also vary in terms of how much risk and stress that they experience. Prevention research on variations in family risk factors has identified that more distressed families may actually benefit more from early prevention programs such as the Family Check Up (Pelham, Dishion, Tein, Shaw, & Wilson, 2017). Thus, the cumulative effects of poverty, stress, and mental health issues should be taken into account and seen as both potential moderators and opportunities for prevention.

Third, by their very nature families change. Not only are there changes in membership through births, deaths, and dissolution of relationships, but there are also developmental changes that foster the child's growth. By being sensitive to the ways in which families negotiate transitions between developmental stages as well as prepare their children to transition from home to school settings, educators may become a valuable resource for families during these vulnerable periods.

Early care and education settings can play a pivotal role during transitions points such as the transition to kindergarten. Transition policies and practices have an effect on child academic outcomes and these effects are mediated by parent involvement (Schulting, Malone, & Dodge, 2005). Thus, there is an opportunity to create policies and practices that ease transitions from school to school and promote parent involvement.

Families and early childhood educators bear the responsibility of preparing future generations to become productive citizens and lifelong learners. Recognizing the complexity of family life is not an impossible challenge but one worthy of respect. Being aware of the potential chaos in a child's family life and creating opportunities for calm, organized, and meaningful exchanges between home and school places, early childhood educators play an important role in the health and well-being of all children.

References

Ackerman, B. P., Brown, E. D., & Izard, C. E. (2004). The relations between persistent poverty and contextual risk and children's behavior in elementary school. *Developmental Psychology, 40*, 367–377.

Ackerman, B. P., Kogos, J., Youngstrom, E., Schoff, K., & Izard, C. (1999). Family instability and the problem behaviors of children from economically disadvantaged families. *Developmental Psychology, 35*, 258–268.

Adain, E. K., & Chase-Landsdale, P. L. (2002). Home sweet home(s): Parental separations, residential moves, and adjustment problems in low-income adolescent girls. *Developmental Psychology, 38*, 792–805.

Alaimo, K., Olson, C. M., Frongillo, E. A., & Briefel, R. R. (2001). Food insufficiency, family income, and health in US preschool and school-aged children. *American Journal of Public Health, 91*, 781–786.

Amato, P. R. (2005). The impact of family formation change on the cognitive, social, and emotional well-being of the next generation. *Future of Children, 15*, 75–96.

Andersen, S. E., & Whitaker, R. C. (2010). Household routines and obesity in US preschool-aged children. *Pediatrics, 125*(3), 420–428.

Andrews, M., & Hamrick, K. (2009). *Shopping for, preparing, and eating food: Where does the time go?* Retrieved from http://www.ers.usda.gov/AmberWaves/December09/Findings/ShoppingFood.htm

Arnold. D. H., Zeljo, A., Doctoroff, G. L., & Ortiz. C. (2008). Parent involvement in preschool: Predictors and the relation of involvement to preliteracy development. *School Psychology Review, 37*, 74–90.

Beals, D. E. (2001). Eating and reading: Links between family conversations with preschoolers and later language and literacy. In D. K. Dickinson & P. O. Tabors (Eds.), *Beginning literacy with language: Young children at home and school* (pp. 75–92). Baltimore, MD: Brookes.

Berger, L. M., & McLanahan, S. S. (2015). Income, relationship quality, and parenting: Associations with child development in two-parent families. *Journal of Marriage and Family, 77*(4), 996–1015.

Black, K., & Lobo, M. (2008). A conceptual review of family resilience factors. *Journal of Family Nursing, 14*, 33–55.

Bower, H., & Griffin, D. (2011). Can the Epstein Model of parental involvement work in a high-minority, high-poverty, elementary school? A case study. *Professional School Counseling, 14*(2), 77–87.

Bradley, R. H. (2004). Chaos, culture, and covariance structures: A dynamic systems view of children in the United States. *Parenting: Science and Practice, 4*, 243–257.

Bradley, R. H., Corwyn, R. F., McAdoo, H. R., & Coll, C. G. (2001). The home environments of children in the United States. Part 1: Variations by age, ethnicity, and poverty status. *Child Development, 72*, 1844–1867.

Brandon, P. D. (2004). The child care arrangements of preschool-age children in immigrant families in the United States. *International Migration, 49*(42), 65–87.

Brody, G. H., & Flor, D. L. (1997). Maternal psychological functioning, family processes, and child adjustment in rural, single-parent, African American families. *Developmental Psychology, 33*, 1000–1011.

Bronfenbrenner, U., & Evans, G. W. (2000). Developmental science in the 21st century: Emerging questions, theoretical models, research designs, and empirical findings. *Social Development, 9*, 115–125.

Bronfenbrenner, U., & Morris, P. A. (1998). The ecology of developmental processes. In W. Damon & R. M. Lerner (Eds.), *Handbook of child psychology* (pp. 993–1028). Hoboken, NJ: Wiley.

Brooks-Gunn, J. (1997). Neighborhood poverty. In G. D. J. Brooks-Gunn & L. Aber (Eds.), *Neighborhood poverty: Context and consequences for children* (pp. 279–298). New York, NY: Russell Sage Foundation.

Brooks-Gunn, J., Johnson, A. D., & Leventhal, T. (2010). Disorder, turbulence, and resources in children's homes and neighborhoods. In G. W. Evans & T. D. Wachs (Eds.), *Chaos and its influence on children's development: An ecological perspective* (pp. 155–170). Washington, DC: American Psychological Association.

Brown, E. D., & Low, C. M. (2008). Chaotic living conditions and sleep problems associated with children's responses to academic challenges. *Journal of Family Psychology, 22*, 920–923.

Brown, S. L. (2010). Marriage and child well-being: Research and policy perspectives. *Journal of Marriage and Family, 72*, 1059–1077.

Brown, S. L., Manning, W. D., & Payne, K. K. (2017). Relationship quality among cohabiting versus married couples. *Journal of Family Issues, 38*(12), 1730–1753.

Bryan, J., Moore-Thomas, C., Day-Vines, N. L., & Holcomb-McCoy, C. (2011). School counselors as social capital: The effects of high school college counseling on college application rates. *Journal of Counseling & Development, 89*, 190–199.

Bumpass, L. L. H. (2000). Trends in cohabitation and implications for children's family context in the United States. *Population Studies, 54*, 29–41.

Burchinal, M., Carr, R. C., Vernon-Feagans, L., Blair, C., Cox, M., & The Family Life Project Key Investigators. (2018). Depth, persistence, and timing of poverty and the development of school readiness skills in rural low-income regions: Results from the family life project. *Early Childhood Research Quarterly, 45*, 115–130.

Burchinal, M., Nelson, L., Carlson, M., & Brooks-Gunn, J. (2008). Neighborhood characteristics and child care type and quality. *Early Education and Development, 19*, 702–725.

Burton, L. M., & Jarrett, R. L. (2000). In the mix, yet on the margins: The place of families in urban neighborhood and child development research. *Journal of Marriage and Family, 62*, 1114–1135.

Buysse, V., Castro, D. C., West, T., & Skinner, M. (2005). Addressing the needs of Latino children: A national survey of state administrators of early childhood programs. *Early Childhood Research Quarterly, 20*, 146–163.

Castro, D. C., Bryant, D. M., Peisner-Feinberg, E. S., & Skinner, M. L. (2004). Parent involvement in Head Start programs: The role of parent, teacher and classroom characteristics. *Early Childhood Research Quarterly, 19*(3), 413–430.

Cavanagh, S. E., & Huston, A. C. (2008). The timing of family instability and children's social development. *Journal of Marriage and Family, 70*, 1258–1269.

Chase-Landsdale, P. L., & Gordon, R. A. (1996). Economic hardship and the development of five- and six-year-olds: Neighborhoods and regional perspectives. *Child Development, 67*, 3338–3367.

Child Trends, C. (2003). *Regular bedtime and mealtime.* Retrieved from http://www.childtrendsdatabank.0rg/archivepgs/91.html

Coldwell, J., Pike, A., & Dunn, J. (2006). Household chaos-links with parenting and child behaviour. *Journal of Child Psychology and Psychiatry, 47*, 1116–1122.

Coleman-Jensen, A., Rabbitt, M. P., Gregory, C. A., & Singh, A. (2017). *Household food security in the United States in 2016.* Washington, DC: Economic Research Service, United States Department of Agriculture.

Cook, J. T., Black, M. M., Chilton, M., Cutts, D. B., Ettinger de Cuba, S., Heeren, T. C., ... Frank, D. A. (2013). Are food insecurity's health impacts underestimated in the U.S. population? Marginal food security also predicts adverse health outcomes in young U.S. children and mothers. *Advances in Nutrition, 4*, 51–61.

Cook, J. T., & Frank, D. A. (2008). Food security, poverty, and human development in the United States. *Annals of the New York Academy of Sciences, 1136*, 193–209. doi:10.1196/annals.1425.001

Cook, J. T., Frank, D. A., Berkowitz, C., Black, M. M., Casey, P. H., Cults, D. B., ... Heeren, T. (2004). Food insecurity is associated with adverse health outcomes among human infants and toddlers. *Journal of Nutrition, 134*, 1432–1438.

Cotton, K., & Wikelund, R. K. (1995). *Parent involvement in education.* Retrieved from https://educationnorthwest.org/sites/default/files/parent-involvement-in-education.pdf

Cox, M., & Paley, B. (1997). Families as systems. *Annual Review of Psychology, 48*, 243–267.

Cummings, E. M., & Davies, P. T. (2010). *Marital conflict and children: An emotional security perspective.* New York, NY: Guilford Press.

De Jong, D. M., Cremone, A., Kurdziel, L. B. F., Desrochers, P., LeBourgeois, M. K., Sayer, A., ... Spencer, R. M. C. (2016). Maternal depressive symptoms and household income in relation to sleep in early childhood. *Journal of Pediatric Psychology, 41*, 961–970.

Deater-Deckard, K., Chen, N., Wang, Z., & Bell, M. A., (2012). Socioeconomic risk moderates the link between household chaos and maternal executive function. *Journal of Family Psychology, 26*, 391–399.

DeCaro, J. A., & Worthman, C. M. (2011). Changing family routines at kindergarten predict biomarkers of parental stress. *International Journal of Behavioral Development, 35*, 441–448.

Delgado-Gaitan, C. (1991). Involving parents in the schools: A process of empowerment. *American Journal of Education, 100*(1), 20–46.

Dickstein, S., Seifer, R., Hayden, L. C., Schiller, M., Sameroff, A. J., Keitner. G. I., ... Magee, K. D. (1998). Levels of family assessment: II. Impact of maternal psychopathology on family functioning. *Journal of Family Psychology, 12*, 23–40.

Dickstein, S., St. Andre, M., Sameroff, A. A., Seifer, R., & Schiller, M. (1999). Maternal depression, family functioning, and child outcomes: A narrative assessment. In B. H. Fiese, A. J., Sameroff, H. D., Grotevant, F. S. Wamboldt, S. Dickstein, & D. L. Fravel (Eds.), *The stories that families tell: Narrative coherence, narrative interaction, and relationship beliefs. Monographs of the Society for Research in Child Development, 64*(2), Serial No. 257, 84–104.

Dolbin-McNab, L. (2019). Grandparenthood. In B. H. Fiese (Editor in Chief), *APA handbook of contemporary of family psychology, volume 1. Foundations, methods, and contemporary issues across the lifespan.* (pp. 557–574). Washington, DC: American Psychological Association.

Dumas, J. E., Nissley, J., Nordstrom, A., Smith, E. P., Prinz, R. J., & Levine, D. W. (2005). Home chaos: Sociodemographic, parenting, interactional, and child correlates. *Journal of Clinical Child and Adolescent Psychology, 34*, 93–104.

Duncan, G. J., & Brooks-Gunn, J. (1997). *Consequences of growing up poor.* New York, NY: Russell Sage Foundation.

Duncan, G. J., Brooks-Gunn, J., Yeung, W. J., & Smith, J. R. (1998). How much does childhood poverty affect the lives of children? *American Sociological Review, 63*, 406–423.

Duncan, G. J., Magnuson, K., Kalil, A., & Ziol-Guest, K. (2012). The importance of early childhood poverty. *Social Indicators Research, 108*, 87–98.

Epstein, J. L., & Sanders, M. G., (2002). Family, school, and community partnerships. In M. H. Bornstein (Ed.), *Handbook of parenting* (Vol. 5, pp. 407–437). Mahwah. NJ: Erlbaum.

Epstein, J. L., Sanders, M., Sheldon, S., Simon, B., Salinas, K., Jansorn, N., ... Williams, K. (2009). *School, family, and community partnerships: Your handbook for action* (3rd ed.). Thousand Oaks, CA: Corwin.

Evans, G. W. (2004). The environment of childhood poverty, *American Psychologist, 59*, 77–92.

Evans, G. W. (2006). Child development and the physical environment. *Annual Review of Psychology, 57*, 423–451.

Evans, G. W., & English, K. (2002). The environment of poverty: Multiple stressor exposure, psychophysiological stress, and socioemotional adjustment. *Child Development, 73*, 1238–1248.

Evans, G. W., Gonnella, C., Marcynyszyn, L. A., Gentile, L., & Salpekar, N. (2005). The role of chaos and poverty and children's socioemotional adjustment. *Psychological Science, 16*, 560–565.

Falicov, C. J. (2003). Immigrant family processes. In F. Walsh (Ed.), *Normal family processes* (3rd ed., pp. 280–300). New York, NY: Guilford.

Fay-Stammbach, T., Hawes, D. J., & Meredith, P. (2014). Parenting influences on executive function in early childhood: A review. *Child Development Perspectives, 8*, 258–264.

Ferguson, K. T., & Evans, G. W. (2019). Social ecological theory: Family systems and family psychology in bioecological and bioecocultural perspective. In B. H. Fiese (Editor in Chief), *APA handbook of contemporary of family psychology, volume 1. Foundations, methods, and contemporary issues across the lifespan* (pp. 143–161). Washington, DC: American Psychological Association.

Ferretti, L. K., & Bubb, K. L. (2014). The influence of family routines on the resilience of low-income preschoolers. *Journal of Applied Developmental Psychology, 35*, 168–180.

Fields-Smith, C. (2007). Social class and African-American parents involvement. In J. A. VanGalen & G. W. Noblit (Eds.), *Late to class: Social class and schooling in the new economy* (pp. 167–202). Albany, NY: State University of New York Press.

Fiese, B. H. (2000). Family matters: A systems view of family effects on children's cognitive health. In R. J. Sternberg & E. L. Grigorenko (Eds.), *Environmental effects on cognitive abilities* (pp. 39–57), Mahwah, NJ: Erlbaum.

Fiese, B. H. (2002). Routines of daily living and rituals in family life: A glimpse at stability and change during the early school years. *Zero to Three, 22*, 10–13.

Fiese, B. H. (2006). *Family routines and rituals.* New Haven, CT: Yale University Press.

Fiese, B. H., Gundersen, C., Koester, B., & Jones, B. (2016). Family Chaos and lack of mealtime planning is associated with food insecurity in low income households. *Journal of Economics and Human Behavior, 21*, 147–155. doi:10.1016/j.ehb.2016.01.004

Fiese, B. H., Hooker, K. A., Kotary, L., & Schwagler, J. (1993). Family rituals in the early stages of parenthood. *Journal of Marriage and the Family, 55*(3), 633–642.

Fiese, B. H., & Marjinsky, K. A. T. (1999). Dinnertime stories: Connecting relationship beliefs and child behavior. In B. H. Fiese, A. J., Sameroff, H. D. Grotevant, F. S. Wamboldt, S. Dickstein, & D. L. Fravel (Eds.), *The stories that families tell: Narrative coherence, narrative interaction, and relationship beliefs. Monographs of the Society for Research in Child Development, 64*(2), Serial No. 257, 52–68.

Fiese, B. H., & Spagnola, M. (2007). The interior life of the family: Looking from the inside out and outside in. In A. S. Masten (Ed.), *Multilevel dynamics in developmental psychopathology: Pathways to the future* (pp. 119–150). Mahwah, NJ: Erlbaum.

Fiese, B. H., & Winter, M. A. (2010). Family dynamics of chaos and its relation to children's socio-emotional wellbeing. In G. W. Evans & T. D. Wachs (Eds.). *Chaos and children's development: Levels of analysis and mechanisms* (pp. 49–66). Washington, DC: American Psychological Association Press.

Fiese, B. H., Winter, M. A., & Botti, J. C. (2011). The ABC's of family mealtimes: Observational lessons for promoting healthy outcomes for children with persistent asthma. *Child Development, 82*, 133–145.

Fisher, M., Villegas, E., Sutter, C. Musaad, S., Fiese, B., & Koester, B. (2019). Sprouts growing healthy habits: Curriculum development and exploratory study. *Frontiers in Psychology, 7*, 65–65.

Freeman, M. (2010). 'Knowledge is acting': Working-class parents' intentional acts of positioning within the discursive practice of involvement. *International Journal of Qualitative studies in education, 23*, 181–198.

Gable, S., Chang, Y., & Krull, J. L. (2007). Television watching and frequency of family meals are predictive of overweight onset and persistence in a national sample of school-age children. *Journal of the American Dietetic Association, 107*, 53–61.

Giray, C., & Ferguson, G. M. (2018). Say yes to "Sunday Dinner" and not to "Nyam and Scram": Family mealtimes, nutrition, and emotional health among adolescents and mothers in Jamaica. *Appetite, 128*, 129–137.

Gordon-Larsen, P., Nelson, M., Page, R., & Popkin, B. M. (2006). Inequality in the built environment underlies key health disparities in physical activity and obesity. *Pediatrics, 117*, 417–424.

Gregory, A. M., & Sadeh, A. (2012). Sleep, emotional and behavioral difficulties in children and adolescents. *Sleep Medicine Reviews, 16*, 129–136.

Grigsby, D. S., Chi. S., & Fiese, B. H. (2011). Where they live, how they play: Neighborhood greenness and outdoor physical activity among preschoolers. *International Journal of Health Geographics*, 10, 66.

Grusec, J. E., & Davidov, M. (2010). Integrating different perspectives on socialization theory and research: A domain-specific approach. *Child Development, 81*, 687–709.

Guttman, L. M., Sameroff, A. J., & Cole, R. (2003). Academic growth curve trajectories from 1st to 12th grade: Effects of multiple social risk factors and preschool child factors. *Developmental Psychology, 39*, 777–790.

Hall, J., Sylva, K., Melhuish, E., Sammons, P., Siraj-Blatchford, I., & Taggart, B. (2009). The role of pre-school quality in promoting resilience in the cognitive development of young children. *Oxford Review of Education, 35*, 331–352.

Hammer, C. S., Farkas, G., & Maczuga, S. (2010). The language and literacy development of Head Start children: A study using the family and child experiences survey database. *Language, Speech, and Hearing Services in Schools, 41*, 70–83.

Head Start Performance Standards, 45 C.F.R. Chapter XIII 1302.51 (2016).

Henderson, A. T., Mapp, K. L., Johnson, V. R., & Davies, D. (2007). *Beyond the bake sale: The essential guide to family-school partnerships.* New York, NY: New Press.

Hill, N. E., & Craft, S. A. (2003). Parent-school involvement and school performance: Mediated pathways among socioeconomically comparable African American and Euro-American families. *Journal of Educational Psychology, 95*, 74–83.

Hill, N. E., & Taylor, L. C. (2004). Parental school involvement and children's academic achievement: Pragmatics and Issues. *Current Directions in Psychological Science, 13*, 161–164.

Jeynes, W. H. (2005). A meta-analysis of the relation of parental involvement to urban elementary school student academic achievement. *Urban Education, 40*, 237–269.

Jeynes, W. H. (2011). *Parent involvement and academic success.* New York, NY: Routledge.

Johnson, A. D., & Markowitz, A. J. (2018). Associations between household food insecurity in early childhood and children's kindergarten skills. *Child Development, 89*, e1–e17.

Jones, B. L., Fiese, B. H., & the STRONG Kids Team. (2014). Parent routines, child routines, and family demographics associated with obesity in parents and preschool aged children. *Frontiers in Psychology, 5*, 1–10.

Kalil, A., & Ryan, R. M. (2010). Mothers' economic conditions and sources of support in fragile families. *The Future of Children, 20*(2), 39–61.

Kennedy, S., & Bumpass, L. (2008). Cohabitation and children's living arrangements: New estimates from the United States. *Demographic Research, 19*, 1663–1692.

Koball, H., & Jiang, Y. (2018). *Basic facts about low-income children: Children under 18 years, 2016.* New York, NY: National Center for Children in Poverty, Columbia University Mailman School of Public Health.

Kreider, R. M. (2007). *Living arrangements of children: 2004. Current populations report.* Washington, DC: U.S. Census Bureau.

Lamb, M. E. (2012). Mothers, fathers, families and circumstances: Factors affecting children's adjustment. *Applied Developmental Science, 16*, 98–111.

Lambiase, K. (2014). *The benefits of parent-school partnerships: A cooperative approach to increase student learning & achievement.* Retrieved from Sophia, the St. Catherine University Repository Website. https://sophia.stkate.edu/maed/48

Lavigne, J. V., Arend, R., Rosenblum, D., Smith, A., Weissbluth, M., Binns, H., & Christoffel, K. K. (1999). Sleep and behavior problems among preschoolers. *Journal of Developmental and Behavioral Pediatrics, 20*, 164–169.

Lee, J., & Bowen, N. K. (2006). Parent involvement, cultural capital, and the achievement gap among elementary school children. *American Education Research Journal, 43*, 193–218.

Lee, V. E., & Burkam, D. (2002). *Inequality at the starting gate: Social background differences in achievement as children begin school.* Washington, DC: Economic Policy Institute.

Leerkes, E. M., Blankson, A. N., & O'Brien, M. (2009). Differential effects of maternal sensitivity to infant distress and nondistress on social-emotional functioning. *Child Development, 80*, 762–775.

Leerkes, E. M., Blankson, A. N., O'Brien, M., Calkins, S. D., & Marcovitch, S. (2011). The relation of maternal emotional and cognitive support during problem solving to pre-academic skills in preschoolers. *Infant and Child Development, 20*, 353–370.

Leventhal, T., & Brooks-Gunn, J. (2000). The neighborhoods they live in: The effects of neighborhood residence on child and adolescent outcomes. *Psychological Bulletin, 126*, 309–337.

Leventhal, T., & Newman, S. (2010). Housing and child development. *Children and Youth Services Review, 32*, 1165–1174.

Luo, Y., LaPierre, T. A., Hughes, M. E., & Waite, L. J. (2012). Grandparents providing care to grandchildren: A population-based study of continuity and change. *Journal of Family Issues, 33*, 1143–1167.

Luthar, S. S., Cicchetti, D., & Becker, B. (2000). The construct of resilience: A critical evaluation and guidelines for future work. *Child Development, 71*, 543–562.

Ma, X., Shen, J., Krenn, H. Y., Hu, S., & Yuan, J. (2016). A meta-analysis of the relationship between learning outcomes and parental involvement during early childhood education and early elementary education. *Educational Psychology Review, 28*, 771–801.

Manning, W. D. (2015). Cohabitation and child wellbeing. *The Future of Children, 24*(2), 51–66.

Margolis, R. (2016). The changing demography of grandparenthood. *Journal of Marriage and Family, 78*, 610–622.

Masten, A. S. (2001). Ordinary magic: Resilience processes in development. *American Psychologist, 56*, 227–238.

McBride, B. A., Dyer, W. J., & Rane, T. R. (2008). Family partnerships in early childhood programs: Don't forget fathers/men. In M. M. Cornish (Ed.). *Promising practices for partnering with families in the early years* (pp. 41–57). Charlotte, NC: Information Age.

McBride, B. A., Rane, T. R., & Bae, J. (2001). Intervening with teachers to encourage father/male involvement in early childhood programs. *Early Childhood Research Quarterly, 16*, 77–93.

McBride, B. A., Schoppe-Sullivan, S. J., & Ho, M. (2005). The mediating role of fathers' school involvement on student achievement. *Journal of Applied Developmental Psychology, 26*, 201–216.

McDonough, S. C. (2000). Interaction guidance: An approach for difficult to engage families. In C. H. Zeenah (Ed.). *Handbook of infant mental health* (pp. 485–493). New York, NY: Guilford.

McIntyre, L. L., Eckert, T. L., Fiese, B. H., DiGennaro, F. D., & Wildenger, L. K. (2007). The transition to kindergarten: Family experiences and involvement. *Early Childhood Education Journal, 35*, 83–88.

Miedel, W. T., & Reynolds, A. J. (1999). Parent involvement in early intervention for disadvantaged children: Does it matter? *Journal of School Psychology, 37*, 379–402.

Milan, S., Snow, S., & Belay, S. (2007). The context of preschool children's sleep: Racial/Ethnic differences in sleep locations, routines, and concerns. *Journal of Family Psychology, 21*, 20–28.

Mindell, J. A., & Williamson, A. A. (2018). Benefits of a bedtime routine in young children: Sleep, development, and beyond. *Sleep Medicine Reviews, 40*, 93–108.

Morrissey, T. W., & Vinopal, K. M. (2018). Neighborhood poverty and children's academic skills and behavior in early elementary school. *Journal of Marriage and Family, 80*, 182–197.

National Center for Education Statistics (NCES). (1998). *Students do better when their fathers are involved in school.* Retrieved from http://www/nces.ed.gov/pubs98/98121.html

Norton. D. (1993). Diversity, early socialization, and temporal development: The dual perspective revisited. *Social Work, 38*, 82–90.

Osborne, C & McClanahan, S. (2007). Partnership instability and child well-being. *Journal of Marriage and Family, 69*, 1065–1083.

Parke, R. D. (2004). Development in the family. *Annual Review of Psychology, 55*, 365–399.

Patterson, J. M. (2002). Understanding family resilience. *Journal of Clinical Psychology, 7*, 233–246.

Payne, K. K. (2013). *Children's family structure.* Bowling Green, OH: National Center for Family and Marriage Research, Bowling Green State University.

Pelham, W. E., Dishion, T. J., Tein, J., Shaw, D. S., & Wilson, M. N. (2017). What doesn't work for whom? Exploring heterogeneity in responsiveness to the family check-up in early childhood using a mixture model approach. *Prevention Science, 18*, 911–922.

Pizzo, P. D., & Tufankjian, E. E. (2004). A persistent pattern of progress: Parent outcomes in longitudinal studies of Head Start children and families. In E. Zigler, & S. J. Styfco (Eds.), *The head start debates* (pp. 193–214). Baltimore, MD: Brookes Publishing.

Powell, D. R., Son, S., File, N., & San Juan, R. R. (2010). Parent-school relationships and children's academic and social outcomes in public school pre-kindergarten. *Journal of School Psychology, 48*, 269–292.

Ramani, G. B., Rowe, M. L., Eason, S. H., & Leech, K. A. (2015). Math talk during informal learning activities in head Start families. *Cognitive Development, 35*, 15–33.

Reese. E., Leywa, D., Sparks, A., & Grolnick, W. (2010). Maternal elaborative reminiscing increases low-income children's narrative skills relative to dialogic reading. *Early Education and Development, 21*, 318–342.

Reynolds, A. J. (1992). Comparing measures of parental involvement and their effects on academic achievement. *Early Childhood Research Quarterly, 7*, 441–462.

Reynolds, A. J. (2000). *Success in early intervention: The Chicago Child-Parent Centers,* Lincoln: University of Nebraska Press.

Rimm-Kaufmann, S. E., Pianta, R. C., & Cox, M. J. (2000). Teachers' judgments of problems in the transition to kindergarten. *Early Childhood Research Quarterly, 15*, 147–166.

Roberts, J., Jergens, J., & Burchinal, M. (2005). The role of home literacy practices in preschool children's language and emergent literacy skills. *Journal of Speech Language and Hearing Research, 48*, 345–359.

Roopnarine, J., Bynoe, P. F., & Singh, R. (2004). Factors tied to the schooling of children of English-speaking and Caribbean immigrants in the United States. In U. P. Gielen & J. Roopnarine (Eds.). *Childhood and adolescence: Cross-cultural perspectives and applications* (pp. 319–349). Westport, CT: Praeger.

Roy, A. L. (2019). Broadening perspectives on poverty: Implications for family well-being and children's development. In B. H. Fiese (Editor in Chief), *APA handbook of contemporary of family psychology, volume 1. Foundations, methods, and contemporary issues across the lifespan* (pp. 241–254). Washington, DC: American Psychological Association.

Roy, A. L., Mccoy, D., C., & Raver, C. C. (2014). Instability versus quality: Residential mobility, neighborhood poverty, and children's self-regulation. *Developmental Psychology, 50*, 1891–1896.

Roy, K. M., Tubbs, C. Y., & Burton, L. M. (2004). Don't have no time: Daily rhythms and the organization of time for low-income families. *Family Relations, 53*, 168–178.

Saltzman, J. A., Bost, K. K., Musaad, S. M. A., Fiese, B. H., & Wiley, A. R. (2018). Predictors and outcomes of mealtime emotional climate in families with preschoolers and the STRONG Kids Team. *Journal of Pediatric Psychology, 43*, 195–206.

Sameroff, A. J. (1995). General systems theories and developmental psychopathology. In D. Cicchetti & D. Cohen (Eds.), *Handbook of developmental psychopathology* (Vol. 1, pp. 659–695). New York, NY: Wiley.

Sameroff, A. J. (2010). A united theory of development: A dialectic integration of nature and nurture. *Child Development, 81*, 6–22.

Sameroff, A. J., & Fiese, B. H. (2000). Transactional regulation: The developmental ecology of early intervention. In S. J. Meisels & J. P. Shonkoff (Eds.), *Early intervention: A handbook of theory, practice, and analysis* (pp. 3–19). New York, NY: Cambridge University Press.

Sameroff, A. J., & MacKenzie, M. J. (2003). Research strategies for capturing transactional models of development: The limits of the possible. *Development and Psychopathology, 15*, 613–640.

Sandberg, J. F., & Hofferth, S. L. (2001). Changes in children's time with parents: United States, 1981–1997. *Demography, 38*, 423–436.

Sbarra, D. A., Bourassa, K. J., & Manvelian, A. (2019). Marital separation and divorce: Correlates and consequences. In B. H. Fiese (Editor in Chief), *APA handbook of contemporary of family psychology, volume 1. Foundations, methods, and contemporary issues across the lifespan* (pp. 687–705). Washington, DC: American Psychological Association.

Schick, A. R. (2014). Home-school literacy experiences of Latino preschoolers: Does continuity predict positive child outcomes? *Journal of Applied Developmental Psychology, 35*, 370–380.

Schulting, A. B., Malone, P. S., & Dodge, K. A. (2005). The effect of school-based kindergarten transition policies and practices on child academic outcomes. *Developmental Psychology, 41*, 860–871.

Seginer, R. (2006). Parents' educational involvement: A developmental ecology perspective. *Parenting: Science & Practice, 6*(1), 1–48.

Senke, C. A., & Sheridan, S. M. (2012). Family-school connections in rural educational setting: A systematic review of the empirical literature. *School Community Journal, 22*, 21–47.

Serpell, R., Sonnenschein, S., Baker, L., & Ganapathy, H. (2002). Intimate culture of families in the early socialization of literacy. *Journal of Family Psychology, 16*, 391–405.

Sheridan, S. M., Knoche, L. L., Edwards, C. P., Bovaird, J. A., & Kupzyk, K. A. (2010). Parental engagement and school readiness: Effects of the getting ready intervention on preschool children's social-emotional competencies. *Early Education and Development, 21*, 125–156.

Sherrill, R. B., Lochman, J. E., DeCoster, J., & Stromeyer, S. L., (2017). Spillover between interparental conflict and parent-child conflict within and across days. *Journal of Family Psychology, 31*, 900–909.

Sigman-Grant, M., Hayes, J., VanBrackle, A., & Fiese, B. (2015). Family resiliency: A neglected perspective in addressing obesity in young children. *Childhood Obesity, 11*, 1–10.

Spagnola, M., & Fiese, B. H. (2007). Family routines and rituals: A context for development in the lives of young children. *Infants & Young Children, 20*(4), 284–299.

Sprunger, L. W., Boyce, W. T., & Gaines, J. A. (1985). Family-infant congruence: Routines and rhythmicity in family adaptations to a young infant. *Child Development, 56*, 564–572.

Tamis-LeMonda, C. S., Song, L., Luo, R., Kuchirko, Y., Kahana-Kalman, R., Yoshikawa, H., & Raufman, J. (2014). Children's vocabulary growth in English and Spanish across early development and associations with school readiness skills. *Developmental Neuropsychology, 39*, 69–87.

Uhlenberg, P., & Cheuk, M. (2010). The significance of grandparents to grandchildren: An international perspective. In D. Dannefer & C. Phillipson (Eds.), *The Sage handbook of social gerontology* (pp. 447–458). Thousand Oaks, CA: Sage.

United States Census Bureau. (2015). Unmarried couples of the opposite sex. In UC-1-1 (Ed.). *United States Census Bureau: U.S. Department of Commerce Economics and Statistics Administration.* Washington, DC: U.S. Census Bureau.

Valiente, C., Lemery-Chalfant, K., & Reiser, M. (2007). Pathways to problem behaviors: Chaotic homes, parent and child effortful control, and parenting. *Social Development, 16*, 249–267.

Walsh, F. (2003). *Normal family processes* (3rd ed.). New York, NY: Guilford.

Weiss, H. B., Dearing, E., Mayer, E., Kreider, H., & McCartney, K. (2005). Family educational involvement: Who can afford it and what does it afford? In C. R. Cooper, C. Garcia Coll, W. T. Bartko, H. M. Davis, & C. Chatman (Eds.), *Developmental pathways through middle childhood* (pp. 17–39). Mahwah, NJ: Lawrence Erlbaum Associates.

Weiss, H. B., Mayer, E., Kreider, H., Vaughan, M., Dearing, E., Hencke, R., Pinto, K. (2003). Making it work: Low-income working mothers' involvement in their children's education. *American Educational Research Journal, 40*(4), 879–901.

Weiss, H. M., Lopez, E., & Rosenberg, H. (2010). *Beyond random acts: Family, school, and community engagement as an integral part of education reform.* Cambridge, MA: Harvard Family Research Project.

Wight, V. R., Chau, M., & Aratani, Y. (2010). *Who are America's poor children?* Retrieved from http://nccp.org/publications/pub_912.html

Wildenger, L. H., McIntyre, L. L., Fiese, B. H., & Eckert, T. L. (2008). Children's daily routines during kindergarten transition. *Early Childhood Education Journal, 36*, 69–74.

Winicki, J., & Jemison, K. (2003). Food security and hunger in the kindergarten classroom: Its effect on learning and growth. *Contemporary Economic Policy, 21*, 145–157.

Wood, S., & Liossis, P. (2007). Potentially stressful events and emotional closeness between parents and adult grandchildren. *Journal of Family Issues, 28*, 380–398.

Yates, T. M., Egeland, B., & Sroufe, L. A. (2003). Rethinking resilience: A developmental process perspective. In S. S. Luthar (Ed.), *Resilience and vulnerability: Adaptation in the context of childhood adversity* (pp. 243–265). Cambridge, UK: Cambridge University Press.

21

The Preparation of Early Childhood Educators

A Complex Landscape

Mary Harrill, Madelyn Gardner, Shyrelle Eubanks, Douglas Imig, and David Imig

Introduction

Preparing early childhood educators is complex work. It is complex because teachers of young children must respond to the cognitive, physical, social, and emotional needs of young children, which are intertwined and rapidly changing in their first years (Institute of Medicine & National Research Council, 2015). It is complex because early childhood education focuses on a large age span (birth through age eight) and includes a multitude of settings (e.g., family child care, Head Start, Early Head Start, private centers, elementary schools, and public pre-K). Early childhood educator preparation is complex because it occurs across all degree levels (with degrees at the associate and baccalaureate level often preparing individuals for the same role in the profession). Adding to that complexity is the variability of curriculum among preparation programs for early childhood education and the demand for greater inclusion of a far more diverse student population. It is complex because of the challenging working conditions that the early childhood workforce will encounter (Whitebook, McLean, Austin, & Edwards, 2018). And, it is complex because of a policy landscape that holds different expectations for those teaching in birth through age eight settings – primarily, by allowing individuals teaching in birth through age five settings to do so absent education credentials, beyond a high school diploma, and to operate in a system that offers few opportunities for advanced certification or professional development. On the other hand, states require those teaching in public pre-K-age eight settings to have a bachelor's degree and teaching license and they work within a system that has organized professional development opportunities and requirements. Thus, while the preparation of early childhood educators shares many of the commonalities in terms of features and challenges that face the preparation of K-12 teachers (Chen, 2018; Leachman, Masterson, & Figueroa, 2017; Litvinov, Alvarez, Long, & Walker, 2018), there are distinct constraints and challenges specific to early childhood preparation. This chapter provides a high-level exploration of the early childhood preparation landscape and its complexities as well as developments that can point the early childhood preparation profession forward.

It is important to first define the role of early childhood educator and their scope of responsibility. As defined by Power to the Profession (P2P) (National Association for the Education of Young Children [NAEYC], 2018), a national initiative to create a clear and cohesive framework for the early childhood profession, the early childhood educator is someone who "… cares for and promotes the learning, development and wellbeing of children birth through age eight to establish a foundation for lifelong learning and development." These individuals have seven core responsibilities which shape the focus of the programs that train them (NAEYC, 2018):

1. Planning and implementing intentional, developmentally appropriate learning experiences that promote the Social-Emotional Development, Physical Development and Health, Cognitive Development, and General Learning Competencies of each child served
2. Establishing and maintaining a safe, caring, inclusive, and healthy learning environment
3. Observing, documenting, and assessing children's learning and development using guidelines established by the profession
4. Developing reciprocal, culturally responsive relationships with families and communities
5. Advocating for the needs of children and their families
6. Advancing and advocating for an equitable, diverse, and effective early childhood education profession
7. Engaging in reflective practice and continuous learning

For purposes of this chapter, the focus will be primarily on the higher education programs that prepare beginning early childhood educators. The period of early childhood is broadly defined as spanning from birth through age eight. As a result, professional training of early childhood educators encompasses at least two sectors. The first, focused on children ages birth to three, is strongly dominated by a focus on care and development. The second, encompassing pre-kindergarten through grade three, falls under both the public education and private early childhood care and learning settings. The preparation landscape is further complicated by additional training programs designed to prepare specialists, administrators, and researchers in the early childhood field or that lead to advanced certification. There are also a variety of training programs that do not lead to a degree, and hundreds of classes and training organizations that offer professional development to early childhood educators prior to and during employment in early learning settings. We explore these components of the preparation landscape below.

There are multiple sets of professional standards within the profession and around which collegiate-based preparation programs can build their curriculum and field experiences.[1] The standards, though, that most commonly influence early childhood preparation programs, particularly higher education programs, are NAEYC's Standards for Professional Preparation. These standards outline what completers of preparation programs – associate through advanced early childhood degrees – should know and be able to do in order to fulfill their responsibilities as early childhood educators. These standards are the only ones that not only span the entire young child continuum (birth through age eight) and all early learning settings, but also serve as a frame for many states' early childhood competencies and professional development systems, for K-3 licensure requirements, and professional accountability systems through NAEYC's Accreditation of Early Childhood Higher Education Programs and NAEYC Recognition of programs through the Council for the Accreditation of Educator Preparation (CAEP) national recognition system. These standards will serve as the reference point for this chapter.

NAEYC Professional Preparation Standards are as follows:

- Promoting child development and learning – grounding students prepared in an early childhood degree program in a child development knowledge base;
- Building family and community relationships – enabling students prepared in early childhood degree program to understand that successful early childhood education depends on partnerships with children's families and communities;
- Observing, documenting, and assessing to support young children and families – facilitating students prepared in early childhood degree programs to understand that child observation, documentation, and other forms of assessment are central to the practice of all early childhood professionals;
- Using developmentally effective approaches to connect with children and families – helping students prepared in early childhood degree programs to understand that teaching and learning with young children is a complex enterprise that varies depending on children's ages, characteristics, and the settings within which teaching and learning occur;

- Using content knowledge to build meaningful curriculum – encouraging students prepared in early childhood degree programs to use their knowledge of academic disciplines to design, implement, and evaluate experiences that promote positive development and learning for each and every young child;
- Becoming a professional – ensuring that students prepared in early childhood degree programs identify and conduct themselves as members of the early childhood profession; and
- Providing early childhood field experiences *(this is a programmatic standard not a learner outcome standard for the individual early childhood educator)* – ensuring that students prepared in early childhood degree programs have experience in at least two of three early childhood age groups (0–3, 3–5, 5–8) and in at least two of three early learning settings (P-12 schools, childcare centers and homes, and Head Start).

The Need for High-Quality Early Childhood Educators

Those who prepare early childhood educators understand that children develop and learn rapidly in the first years of life. During this time, as many as one million new neural connections are formed each second in a young child's brain, producing essential circuitry that provides a basis for later learning and health (Center on the Developing Child at Harvard University [CDCHU], 2009). This rapid growth occurs across a number of interrelated domains, including children's physical, cognitive, linguistic, and self-regulatory and social-emotional skills (Institute of Medicine and National Research Council, 2015). While these stages are nearly universal, each child's developmental trajectory is unique. Children develop specific skills in each of these domains at different times and in different ways (Cantor, Osher, Berg, Steyer, & Rose, 2018).

Children's development and learning is substantially influenced by early experiences and relationships. Research from multiple fields has established several key factors that support optimal development. In particular, responsive and stable attachments with loving adults are a crucial ingredient in healthy development. These bonds provide the security, affection, and support children need to engage with other people and their environments in ways that advance their growth and learning (Cantor et al., 2018; Institute of Medicine, 2000). Opportunities for children and adults to engage in responsive and reciprocal interactions – sometimes referred to as "serve and return" interactions – shape children's early brain circuitry and lay the foundation for later language and social skills (CDCHU, 2016). Relationships with caring adults also shield young children from unhealthy levels of stress by creating secure environments that help them to effectively manage physiological stress responses. These buffering relationships are particularly important for children who experience sustained or severe stressors, such as violence, neglect, or the loss of a parent, which can otherwise have lasting effects on children's mental and physical health (CDCHU, 2016).

In the United States, close to half of children (45%) spend time in out-of-home care before age five (Laughlin, 2013)[2] and nearly all children enroll in formal schooling beginning in kindergarten (McFarland et al., 2018). The nature of these environments and the relationships that children form with their educators have an important influence on children's learning and development (CDCHU, 2016). Early childhood education programs aim to prepare early childhood educators who – in turn – will play a central role in crafting high-quality experiences that will prepare young children for school readiness and later success.

Early childhood teacher educators must prepare teachers to create supportive, engaging, and developmentally grounded learning environments and experiences. This is complex work. It requires educators to build meaningful relationships with children and their families, individualize instruction and support the specific needs of each child, and adopt intentional strategies for promoting whole child development (Darling-Hammond & Cook-Harvey, 2018). Research and professional standards provide insights about the specialized knowledge and competencies that early educators need to accomplish these aims. For example, in 2015 the Institute of Medicine and National Research Council released a report that, among other findings, articulated key early educator knowledge and competencies. The report was the product of extensive consideration by a national panel of experts in early childhood development, early care and education, social policy, and educator preparation (see Institute of Medicine and National Research Council [2015] for additional information about the effort). It grouped essential knowledge and competencies for early educators into four overarching areas:

- A core knowledge base around early childhood development and learning, developmentally appropriate assessments, and subject matter areas (e.g., mathematics, language and literacy, science, social studies, and the arts)
- Facility with practices to help children learn, including creating strong relationships, managing classroom environments, implementing appropriate curricula and assessments, and adapting instruction to support the needs of individual children
- Competency supporting the development and learning of diverse populations of children, including those who may live in low-income households or have special needs
- Skills to develop and use partnerships to respectfully engage with families, refer children and families to other support services, and continue educators' own learning as professionals

High-quality early education is delivered by educators with specialized knowledge about child and brain development and age-appropriate instructional strategies (Wechsler, Melnick, Maier, & Bishop, 2016). The challenge is for educator preparation programs to incorporate this knowledge and strategies into the fabric of their efforts.

Educator preparation is a core component of pre-K success. Pre-k programs with positive evaluations in terms of school readiness and later academic achievement employ educators with training specific to early childhood education – usually a bachelor's degree. This is a commonality among publicly funded pre-K programs in Tulsa, Oklahoma; Boston, Massachusetts; and across New Jersey. All of these programs require lead preschool teachers to have a four-year degree focused on early childhood (Wechsler et al., 2016). Head Start, meanwhile, mandates that at least half of lead classroom teachers have four-year degrees. Each of these programs also emphasizes the importance of continuing professional education after teachers enter the classroom, extending ongoing supports such as coaching from expert mentors and thoughtfully structured professional learning opportunities throughout educators' careers.

A Snapshot of the Early Care and Education Workforce

Overview and Context

Early care and education encompasses programs serving children from birth through age eight (or third grade). In the United States, early care and learning commonly takes place in a variety of settings, including public or private schools, private childcare centers or homes, community-based childcare or after school programs, and Head Start centers. Before kindergarten entry, the early care and education landscape is highly fragmented and spans a broad array of options, many of which require parents to pay for the provision of care. Once children enter kindergarten, the vast majority attend a public school (including charter schools), though private schools enroll preschool students as well (McFarland et al., 2018).

Nationwide, there are estimated to be two million paid early educators serving children before age five. About half of those educators teach in center-based programs, while the remainder work in homes (Whitebook et al., 2018). Likewise, approximately 1.9 million public school educators teach children in elementary school (McFarland et al., 2018).

One important strength of the early care and education workforce is its racial, ethnic, and linguistic diversity. This is especially true of the educator workforce serving children before kindergarten entry. Aside from gender – the early learning workforce serving children ages five and younger is overwhelmingly female – educators working in child care and preschool more closely mirror the demographic composition of the children they serve than do k-12 educators (Whitebook et al., 2018). Nationally, about 40% of early educators are people of color, compared to less than 20% of the public k-12 teacher workforce. Moreover, about one in four early educators speaks a language other than English (Whitebook et al.,

2018). At the same time, research has revealed that educators of color are disproportionately represented in lower-paid segments of the field, which also tend to require less education. This stratification suggests there remains important work to be done to create an equitable pipeline for the preparation of a diverse early educator workforce (Whitebook et al., 2018).

Further, it is impossible to separate conversations about the preparation of early educators from broader discussions of compensation, professional development, and other working conditions that affect educators. These conditions affect early childhood educators once they enter the classroom and play a significant role in educators' professional decisions. Across contexts and settings, early educators typically face common challenges related to their compensation and professional supports, though the extent and nature of these challenges varies across settings.

For example, in the United States, childcare workers rank in the 2nd percentile and preschool teachers in the 15th percentile of all workers with regard to annual earnings. Indeed, these early educators are typically paid about half of what elementary school teachers make, although school-based preschool teachers in some states and districts may earn wages similar to those of other k-12 teachers. As a result, more than half of all childcare providers rely on some form of public income assistance (Whitebook et al., 2018). Initially, these low compensation rates may seem at odds with the high cost of early care and education services – a cost that is often borne directly by the parents of young children. However, early care and education is labor intensive, requiring low educator-to-child ratios, and receives limited public investments. There is a gap between the cost to provide high-quality early care and education and what families can afford to pay, creating a dynamic where many early educators earn low wages even as families struggle to afford care (Workman, 2018).

This low compensation drives turnover in the field (Totenhagen, Hawkins, & Casper, 2016; Whitebook & Sakai, 2003). Especially as standards for early childhood educators rise and become more similar to those in higher-paying k-12 jobs, it may be difficult for early education programs to retain their highly educated staff without increasing wages. Low retention in the childcare workforce is a persistent challenge with rates as high as 30%, which is associated with negative outcomes for children, staff, and centers (Porter, 2012).

Moreover, professional supports that are common among k-12 educators, such as paid professional development days or opportunities for professional collaboration, are typically not provided for educators working in childcare centers, Head Start, or preschools (Whitebook, 2014). For example, a survey of early care and education site directors in Alameda County, California found that only half of their early childhood educators are paid for professional development time and only two-thirds receive regular planning time (Austin, Sakai, & Dhamija, 2016). It is not unusual for staff in childcare or preschool classrooms to pursue professional learning unpaid and in the evenings or on weekends. As with compensation, access to these sorts of professional supports varies within the early

childhood field; some preschool teachers in public schools may have supports commensurate with their k-12 peers, while others receive many fewer such opportunities. Without addressing these challenges, efforts to prepare a diverse pool of highly skilled educators will be ineffective.

Qualifications and Preparation

The 2015 Institute of Medicine and National Research Council recommended that states adopt aligned qualifications for educators of children from birth to age eight and specifically that lead teachers of children of all ages possess at least a bachelor's degree in early childhood (Institute of Medicine & National Research Council, 2015). No state has yet adopted such a requirement. Instead, most states have variable education standards for early learning teachers based on the setting or program in which educators work (Whitebook & McLean, 2017).

In every state, public teachers of kindergarten through 12th grade are required to possess a bachelor's degree and state certification or license appropriate for the grades that they teach (All Star Directories, 2018).[3] Public childcare and preschool programs serving children birth to age five have much more variable requirements. For example, Head Start lead teachers must hold at least an associate's degree in early childhood, and at least half of all Head Start teachers have at least a bachelor's degree in early childhood education (45 C.F.R. §1302, 2016).

Among state-funded preschool programs, about half (23 out of 43) require lead preschool teachers to hold a bachelor's degree whether they teach in a public school, childcare center, or other setting. However, some states do not require that the bachelor's degree be in early childhood or a related field. Still other states require a four-year degree for some, but not all, preschool teachers working in some state-subsidized programs. For example, teachers in school-based programs may be required to hold a bachelor's degree, while those teaching in childcare centers may need an associate's degree. In general, licensed childcare programs rarely require teachers to hold associate's or bachelor's degrees. Only ten states require lead teachers in center-based childcare programs to hold at least a Child Development Associate and most of the remaining states require only a high school degree for lead teachers (Whitebook & McLean, 2017).

These qualification standards establish a minimum level of education necessary to teach in a given program, and in practice many early educators possess preparation above and beyond this base. However, unlike in the k-12 workforce, there is no consistent source for high-quality national data about the qualifications and preparation experiences of early educators (Whitebook & McLean, 2017) and few, if any states, have the capacity to track such information (McLean, 2018).

Insights into the qualifications of the workforce are uneven. Data from Head Start indicate that about three-quarters of lead teachers hold a bachelor's degree (in 2015); that figure is almost 25 percentage points higher than is required by law and likely reflects the investments made by Head Start in supporting the preparation of its teachers (Kaplan & Mead, 2017). A study from North Carolina found that 62% of teachers in all licensed childcare centers held a bachelor's degree in some field, though only 38% possessed a degree focused on early childhood education or a related field (Child Care Services Association, 2015). Likewise, a study in Colorado found that over half (54%) of lead teachers held at least a bachelor's degree (Schaak & Le, 2017). However, only 17% of lead teachers held a bachelor's or graduate degree with a focus on early childhood education. Though many educators possess degrees above and beyond what may be required by law, data limitations often mean that program requirements for education credentials or degrees are the primary source of information about the type of preparation expected of educators.

A Snapshot of the Early Childhood Educator Preparation Landscape

Early childhood programs tend to differentiate themselves from K-12 preparation programs because of their stronger emphasis on child development and on family and community relationships. As noted above, these are the first two standards of NAEYC's Professional Preparation Standards. These two standards focus on the students' understanding and application of child development knowledge including the importance of building positive relationships with young children as well as understanding the importance of families' role in influencing children's development and building strong relationships with families and community partners to support children's growth and development.

The early childhood preparation landscape varies significantly depending on which sector of the early childhood workforce it is preparing (age range and/or early learning setting) and the state (and sometimes federal) regulations and legislation that set early childhood personnel qualifications. The authors have identified three categories of preparation pathways for beginning early childhood educators that are named in Power to the Profession (NAEYC, 2018):[4] professional training programs,[5] early childhood associate degree programs, and early childhood baccalaureate and initial master's degree programs. As noted previously, in most states, the education credentials needed to become an early childhood educator are minimal. Thus, the "preparation" of these individuals tends to be disconnected from professional standards and instead requires individuals to meet clock hours that are primarily related to health and safety practices, not content that is focused on the full responsibilities of an early childhood educator. For those seeking a non-degree education credential, like the CDA,[6] preparation might include completing a formal program with sequenced and scaffolded learning opportunities aligned to the CDA Competency Standards, but it is not required. They can choose to select professional development classes based on their self-identified areas of need or choose not to take any classes prior to the CDA exam.

Quantifying the number of professional training programs and early childhood degree programs can be challenging. While on the higher education side, the general number of early childhood degree programs can be identified – there are approximately 1,300 early childhood associate degree programs, 1,069 early childhood baccalaureate programs (these include degrees that lead to licensure as well as those that do not), 612 early childhood master's programs, and 84 early childhood doctorate programs – there is not a way to easily identify which of those programs lead to a teaching license. More challenging to identify are the number of early childhood professional training programs as they can be found both within and outside higher education, they do not lead to a uniform education credential such as an associate or baccalaureate degree, and they are not a defined category of professional development programs within state regulatory bodies, professional bodies, or the federal government.

Within higher education, early childhood education degree programs can be found in several places. Early childhood degree programs that lead to licensure are typically housed in the school, college, or department of education within institutions of higher education. These tend to be programs preparing individuals to work with children in pre-K-3 or K-3 settings. The content of these programs may have a heavier focus on teaching methodologies, than on child development and working with families and communities. Many more early childhood degree programs do not lead to licensure, and they are often housed elsewhere within institutions such as schools/colleges/departments of health, agriculture, child studies, professional studies, human environmental sciences. They tend to have a heavier focus on child development and a focus on working with children age birth to five.

Another challenge in creating a cohesive early childhood preparation system is the lack of agreement on what to call degree programs that prepare early childhood educators. At both the associate and baccalaureate levels there are over 60 names for early childhood degree programs, and this does not include the various tracks that can be found within programs (such as for administrators, special education, preschool). These names range from early childhood to child development to family studies to early education and care to early childhood development to preschool education, and so on. And, there are multiple degree types at each level as well (e.g., A.A., A.A.S., A.S., B.S.E., B.A., B.S., M.A., M.A.T.). Depending on the degree type, the proportion of credit hours are allocated to general education, early childhood education, and electives changes. This impacts significantly the opportunities for students to learn and practice early childhood competencies.

Persistent Challenges in Preparing Early Childhood Educators

Field Experiences

There is no data source that can quantify the average number of field experience hours across all early childhood degree programs; however, using programs[7] in NAEYC's accreditation system as a proxy, the average number of available field experience hours in an early childhood associate degree program is 262. For NAEYC nationally recognized programs[8] (baccalaureate and graduate degrees that lead to licensure), the approximate average number of field experience hours is 414.

At a more programmatic level, early childhood preparation programs share many of the same challenges found in K-12 teacher preparation programs (Sumrall et al., 2017), though some of these are more pronounced (Whitebook & Austin, 2015). As with their K-12 preparation program counterparts, field experiences[9] are embedded throughout early childhood preparation programs, and they are critical component of preparation allowing students to observe and practice the competencies established in NAEYC's Professional Preparation Standards. The quality of field sites and opportunities for field experiences across the young child age range and across early learning settings, though, varies greatly from program to program.

Part of this stems from a structural challenge. K-12 teacher preparation programs often have an advantage of developing partnerships with school districts which then opens access to multiple field sites (public schools) within the districts. This helps streamline the establishment of field sites in various schools and supports a more consistent implementation of expectations and practices of quality candidate mentoring across the field sites. For early childhood programs, there is rarely a central entity, such as a school district, with which a program can build a partnership. Thus, programs must then establish partnerships one by one with field sites. Given that early learning settings span family/home providers, private centers, Head Start programs, public pre-K, primary grades, and multiple age ranges, establishing partnerships with field sites is a time-consuming and daunting task for faculty who are already under-resourced.

Another challenge in the area of field experiences is that many students in early childhood programs are working either full- or part-time (often in early learning settings). This presents a practical dilemma for students whose employers do not provide them with paid time off so that they can complete their field experiences at other sites, thus forcing students to take unpaid leave or preventing them from completing their field experiences. For faculty, this often leaves them in a position of negotiating with their students' employers for their needed time off, working with students to find creative solutions to completing their field experience obligations, or in some cases, allowing students to complete the majority or all of their field experiences with their employer. The latter, though, limits the students' experiences with the diversity of early learning settings, and often times with the full age range of young children.

Other challenges include, as found in K-12 preparation, that the lexicon of field experiences varies greatly with and across degree levels (e.g., definitions of field experiences, clinical experiences, practica, student teaching, internships),

and the number of field experience hours and types of field experiences differ program to program. And, as always, the lack of resources (faculty, budget, etc.) within most higher education programs greatly impacts the ability for programs to develop quality field experiences.

Access to and Completion of Higher Education

While research shows that higher education impacts the quality of early childhood educators (Institute of Medicine & National Research Council, 2015; Manning, Garvis, Flemming, & Wong, 2017), as highlighted earlier in this chapter, much of the early childhood workforce does not hold a higher education credential. Ensuring that educators have access to and the necessary supports to complete early childhood degree programs is a particular challenge. In early childhood degree programs, the nontraditional student is often the traditional student (Limardo, Hill, Stadd, & Zimmer, 2016); thus, higher education programs must attend to providing supports that address barriers students may face.

Those preparing to become early childhood educators often present both advantages and challenges different from candidates preparing to teach in older grade levels. For example, students tend to be older, often bringing with them extensive work experience both inside and outside of early learning settings that contributes positively to their content knowledge and executive function skills. On the other hand, it may have been many years since the students were in an academic setting, and they may lack confidence in their ability to be successful in their studies and need extra academic supports, particularly for their general education courses. The early childhood candidate pool also benefits from being more racially and linguistically diverse than the K-12 workforce. Ultimately, this benefits all children, particularly young children of color and/or those who are English language learners (Gershenson, Hart, Lindsay, & Papageorge, 2017).

At the same time, many of these students in early childhood degree programs are working full- or part-time (often in a low-wage setting), have family responsibilities, may be first-generation college students, did not receive adequate secondary education, and face financial and housing insecurity as well as transportation challenges. The work the T.E.A.C.H. Early Childhood National Center has done over the years to help early childhood students pursuing higher education has led to identifying key supports that lead to their success: high-quality advice to guide students through their programs, to motivate them, and to connect them to resources addressing financial/housing/transportation challenges, etc.; financial aid that allows them to graduate debt-free; paid release time to allow them to take courses and complete field experiences; coursework that transfers; flexibility in the time and delivery mode of coursework; and an education credential that leads to increased pay and/or leadership with their employer.

Closely tied to being able to provide the necessary supports to students is the need for preparation programs to be adequately organized (e.g., clear conceptual frameworks, cohesive programs of study that sequence and build on learning opportunities related to the standards, qualified faculty, strong advising for students) and resourced. Unfortunately, there are few data sources available to analyze early childhood faculty to student ratios, faculty qualifications, degree program budgets, faculty teaching loads, etc. Preliminary analysis of data from NAEYC-accredited higher education programs indicates that the average number of full-time faculty in a program is three, though the median is two. Additionally, many programs at the associate's degree level have only one full-time faculty member. The average number of students enrolled in a program is 140 with the median number at 96. This represents a challenging faculty to student ratio, particularly for clinically based programs such as early childhood education. Data from the accreditation system also show that early childhood degree programs are typically less resourced than other similar clinically based programs on their campuses, such as nursing. The supply and demand chain for early childhood faculty are unknown, though presumably, much like in other disciplines, many early childhood faculty are approaching retirement. While much of the focus in early childhood preparation is on strengthening the pathways between the associate and baccalaureate degrees, attention also needs to be focused on building better pathways to the master's and doctoral levels in order to build a robust early childhood faculty pipeline.

Articulation and Transfer

One of the primary barriers to advancing the education credentials of the early childhood workforce is transfer and articulation. For those seeking a degree, the community college is often the first point of entry, and many of those who seek to continue onto a baccalaureate degree find that their early childhood credits do not transfer (in full or in part). This forces them to repeat classes, spend more dollars on tuition and books, and significantly extend their time in college while still balancing many of the challenges addressed in the above section. In addition, given that so many early childhood students, particularly at the associate degree level, attend college part-time, often taking one to two courses a semester, this negatively impacts the likelihood of their graduation and continuing on to a baccalaureate degree. Research has shown that when students take nine credits or more a semester, this increases their chances for completing their program and pursuing a baccalaureate degree (Jenkins & Cho, 2012). This is all the more reason to ensure that all credits transfer into the baccalaureate. Additional barriers to successful transfer and articulation include inadequate advising, perceptions about the quality of associate degree programs, general education requirements, and course numbering (Cassidy, 2015).

There are various models of early childhood articulation agreements ranging from "faculty to faculty," "course to course," and "program to program" (Loewenberg, 2018; Lutton, 2013). In the first model, faculty at partner institutions agree upon which courses and how many credits will transfer. This relies on a high degree of trust between faculty, making the articulation agreements vulnerable if there is faculty turnover. The latter two models can be implemented between two partners, within state systems, or in state policy. In the "course to course" model, participating institutions agree upon the course content and sometimes upon course titles and numbers to ensure consistency and enable the transfer of credit. If programs want to change a course, though, this can put the articulation agreement in jeopardy. The third model, "program-to-program," is most promising as it ensures that all credits transfer and relies on student performance outcome measures to ensure that students have mastered expected competencies. Often this can be demonstrated through a capstone portfolio or using NAEYC accreditation as an assurance that students are adequately prepared in the competencies. A challenge with this model, though, is that while all credits transfer, whether they transfer as general education credits, in the early childhood major, or as electives can vary depending on the agreement. Some examples of states utilizing the "course to course" and "program to program" models that are specific to early childhood degree transfer include North Carolina, Connecticut, Pennsylvania, South Carolina, Indiana, and Massachusetts.

Some institutions of higher education have invested in specialized advising for early childhood education students to remedy this mismatch. For example, two community colleges in San Mateo County, California fund full-time program service coordinators who understand ECE pathways and can provide tailored advice and guidance to early childhood education students (Melnick, Meloy, Gardner, Wechsler, & Maier, 2018). In California, PEACH – Partnerships for Education, Articulation, and Coordination through Higher Education – is working to strengthen educational pathways for early educators. Started in 2011, the initiative has convened diverse stakeholders from early childhood and institutes of higher education, including community colleges, state colleges and universities, and private institutions. From the start, one of PEACH's central goals was to strengthen articulation and alignment across institutions in the Los Angeles area to facilitate credit transfer and degree completion. To accomplish this, a PEACH working group that included both higher education faculty and campus articulation officers undertook the detail-oriented task of identifying gaps in alignment and articulation and then meeting one-on-one with campus representatives to explore possibilities for improvement. Likewise, regional meetings provided opportunities for broader-scale collaboration on the issue. In the years following this effort, colleges and universities around Los Angeles experienced a 20% average increase in the acceptance of transfer credits.

K-3 Challenges

This section will examine the challenges of adequately preparing early childhood educators working in the early elementary grades (K-3) and discuss examples of promising practices in state and districts.

Despite the results of a recent survey conducted by the National Association for the Education of Young Children (NAEYC) which found that a "strong majority" of participants working in kindergarten through third-grade classrooms consider themselves early childhood educators, there is not firm agreement on whether early childhood education actually includes kindergarten through third grade (NAEYC, 2018). Regardless of how the age groups are labeled, children in kindergarten through third grade (K-3) are still in the process of developing many foundational skills that require teachers equipped with a deep understanding of both child development and academic disciplines such as literacy and mathematics to facilitate their learning (NAEYC, 2009). The problem is that there is considerable variation in state policies related to the preparation and licensure (also known as certification) of teachers working in K-3 classrooms. For example, many states issue a K-5 license to teach in elementary schools and an early childhood license that allows teachers to teach both in pre-kindergarten (pre-K) and in the early grades of elementary schools. This overlap contributes to the disparate preparation for teachers in the early grades. For example, elementary licenses tend to focus more on subject area-matter content more appropriate for older children, while early childhood licenses tend to focus on incorporating play and exploration into learning experiences and how to engage families to support a child's development (Bornfreund, Cook, Lieberman, & Lowenburg, 2015). Few state licensure systems are set up to ensure that candidates possess the full range of knowledge and skills needed with overlapping licenses for the early grades (Institute of Medicine & National Research Council, 2015).

A 2016 examination of both NAEYC-accredited and the Association for Childhood Education (ACEI)-approved programs that prepare teachers to teach in grades pre-K-3 classrooms found that program standards for elementary education licensure (ELED) paid little attention to many essential principles of early instruction (Fowler, 2016). Specifically, ELED licensure standards did not adequately address early childhood assessment, child observation, play and learning, and self-regulation (Fowler, 2016). The same study also found, and recent anecdotal evidence supports, that neither early childhood education oriented (ECED) nor ELED licensure standards adequately address essential features of early literacy (Will, 2018). Unfortunately, little evidence is available on which licensure standards produce the most effective educators and the best outcomes for children across the pre-K-3 grade span (National Research Council, 2015).

There are promising policies in states and practices within districts education that seek to improve teacher preparation across the entire early childhood field. In the report (Bornfreund et al., 2015), it was stated:

> in order to significantly improve children's literacy development as well as learning and development in other areas such as early math, science, and social-emotional domains, federal, state, and local education agencies need to take a comprehensive, coordinated, and connected birth-through-third grade approach.

and identified the following policies related to teacher preparation and licensure as essential for supporting children's early literacy development:

- The state offers an early childhood educator license (pre-K-3 or birth-3);
- Kindergarten teachers are required to hold an ECE license;
- ELED candidates are required to have child development coursework and preparation in the science of reading; and
- ECED teacher candidates are required to pass a reading pedagogy test (Bornfreund et al., 2015).

Although the report was focused on policies to support literacy development and only five states (New York, Connecticut, Oklahoma, West Virginia, and Wisconsin) met the highest standard based on their progress toward 65 policy indicators in 2016 when the report was published, the case can be made that the proposed policies also support broader learning goals for children in the pre-K-3 education space. For example, both Oklahoma and West Virginia require pre-K teachers to have a bachelor's degree and specialization in early childhood education (Bornfreund et al., 2015). Oklahoma also requires kindergarten teachers to have an early childhood license and requires both early childhood and elementary teacher candidates to pass a ready pedagogy test (Bornfreund et al., 2015). In a continued examination of state and local efforts to support children's learning from birth through age eight, Cook and Bornfreund (2015) reported that Massachusetts is engaging school districts across the state in a coordinated effort to align programs, supports, and resources across the birth through third-grade continuum. A key component of this alignment includes strengthening the birth through third-grade workforce by creating a single, unified credentialing system that spans from birth through second grade.

Similarly, the State of California is also engaged in reviewing credentials given to early childhood educators both inside and outside public schools and reviewing program standards for the current P-12 credential to improve learning outcomes for children from birth through third grade (Jackson, 2015). Although these examples are too few in number, they provide a beacon of hope with regard to addressing the challenges of preparing teachers to work effectively in early kindergarten through third-grade classrooms.

Accountability for Professional Preparation

Accountability for the various sectors in the early childhood profession greatly influences how early childhood educators are prepared. For example, as described in the previous section, licensure, which is an accountability lever for the individual early childhood educator, has an impact on how preparation programs are designed. Accountability for early childhood professional preparation programs must address the same questions that K-12 educator preparation programs face. Accountable for what? To whom? By what measures? Currently, the answers to those questions vary across states and across the sectors within early childhood professional preparation. In short, accountability for early childhood preparation programs is disparate, often not connected to professional standards, and not easily visible to those within and outside the profession. This is particularly true for trainers and training organizations outside of the professional training program and degree-based preparation program pathways. For the latter, though, there are some long-standing accountability levers and promising developments.

For CDA professional training programs, a segment of the professional training program sector, the Council for Professional Recognition operates the CDA Gold Standard system to recognize high-quality programs that prepare individuals for the CDA. The system, launched in 2018, is open to CDA training programs both within and outside higher education institutions. The standards evaluate programs' ability to prepare program completers in professional competencies[10] as defined by standards for the CDA credential as well as evaluate the infrastructure of the training program to ensure it is sufficiently resourced and organized to prepare individuals for the CDA.

For higher education degree programs, there are multiple accountability levers; however the levers vary based on whether the program leads to licensure, the degree level of the program, and, to an extent, the age group for which the program is preparing individuals to work. Early childhood degree programs that lead to licensure are offered at the baccalaureate and initial master's degree levels. These programs are housed within an "Educator Preparation Provider" (EPP), the school, college, or department of education within the institution that has met state requirements for offering preparation programs. Some states require that the EPP be accredited by the Council for the Accreditation of Educator Preparation (CAEP). In addition, states that require CAEP accreditation may also stipulate that programs within the EPP be nationally recognized by the professional organization for that subject area. CAEP partners with professional organizations to operate the national recognition system. Since the 1980s, the National Association for the Education of Young Children (NAEYC) has served as the Specialty Professional Association (SPA) for early childhood education within CAEP. NAEYC recognizes the early childhood degree programs that meet NAEYC's Professional Preparation Standards. The primary focus of the review is on how well the programs' major assessments are aligned to the standards and on the use of student performance data generated from those assessments. Through this system, NAEYC recognizes approximately 20% of early childhood degree programs at the baccalaureate and graduate levels.[11]

However, the CAEP recognition system is only open to a subset of early childhood degree programs – those that lead to licensure and that are housed in a CAEP participating EPP. In addition, the recognition system is an electronic review of the early childhood degree program's alignment to NAEYC's standards, focused primarily on the program's assessment system. Given this, NAEYC and many in the early childhood preparation sector recognized a need to create an accountability system that was open to more early childhood degree programs and that provided a more extensive review of the content and structure of early childhood degree programs. In 2006, NAEYC launched the Early Childhood Associate Degree Accreditation (ECADA) system. It operates as a mechanism to support quality improvement in early childhood degree programs as well as to hold programs accountable for meeting the profession's expectations for preparing early childhood educators. While some states have incorporated NAEYC accreditation into their accountability policy landscape and/or committed significant resources toward supporting programs pursuing it, it remains a primarily voluntary system.

Using NAEYC's Professional Preparation Standards for Initial Programs as the standards for the system, programs undergo an extensive self-study process that examines every facet of the program –its mission and conceptual framework, the students and student supports it provides, faculty qualifications and responsibilities, program resources, organization and evaluation, curriculum, field experiences, assessment systems, and student performance data. Site visits are conducted by peer reviewers and the accreditation decision is made by a commission. Both peer reviewers and commissioners are early childhood faculty representing all degree levels and institutional types. In 2016, the system expanded to accredit programs at the baccalaureate and initial master's degree levels and now is known as NAEYC Accreditation of Early Childhood Higher Education Programs. Approximately 20% of early childhood associate degree programs are accredited by NAEYC. Several baccalaureate and master's degree programs are accredited, with more in the pipeline.

While most higher education programs utilize NAEYC's standards to influence their curriculum and field experiences, the reality is that a significant segment of the early childhood higher education preparation sector does not need to have professional accreditation, they do not need to have state program approval (as required for licensure programs), and they are not held accountable for preparing effective early childhood educators. This includes the majority of early childhood associate degree programs and non-licensure baccalaureate and master's degree programs.

A Vision for Moving Forward

A lack of clarity and cohesion within the preparation of early childhood educators is perhaps the most pressing issue facing early childhood preparation programs, impacting all areas of this sector and components of the programs. These areas include a lack of consensus on the standards that should guide preparation, the core content or curriculum that should be part of every early childhood preparation program, infrastructure to adequately support students in early childhood programs, transfer and articulation pathways between programs, and consistency in quality of field experiences.

In addition, a lack of data on the characteristics and outcomes of students in early childhood preparation programs, characteristics and outcomes of preparation programs, the impact of preparation on the quality of early childhood educators, and the impact of graduates of early childhood preparation programs on young children's learning and development hinders the profession's ability to fully understand the preparation landscape. To date, the research has been limited and findings, particularly related to the impact of preparation on early childhood educator quality, have been mixed. A major investment in a research agenda that can illuminate these areas will greatly advance the profession's capacity to address undergirding challenges to programs and anticipate future challenges.

The first step toward achieving a vision for a clear and cohesive preparation sector is establishing a unified acknowledgment that early childhood educators must have formal preparation in early childhood content prior to serving as educators of record with young children. This is not a question in K-12 education where all states require teachers to have a baccalaureate degree and, for the most part, specific preparation in teacher education (U.S. Department of Education, 2016). For early childhood education, though, there is extensive disagreement about whether and how much preparation early childhood educators should have. Closely related to this is realizing consensus on a unified set of professional competencies for early childhood educators. Other professions have core knowledge and skills that every individual must understand and demonstrate prior to entering the profession. The early childhood education profession lacks this consensus, and, as such, the content in preparation programs can vary greatly within different programs at the same institution, across institutions and across the country. Much of the disarray across the various preparation program pathways (non-degree and degree alike) stems from a lack of agreement on these foundational issues.

To address these challenges, Power to the Profession is underway to define the early childhood profession and build consensus around a set of professional guidelines that are driven by the profession and implemented across the country. Preparation programs are a key feature of every profession (Hargreaves & Fullan, 2012) and, as such, the framework generated by Power to the Profession elevates completing early childhood professional training programs and higher education degree programs as a requirement for individuals to be designated as early childhood educators. Through the framework, recommendations also distinguish between the levels of early childhood educators and associated expectations for knowledge and application of agreed upon professional competencies at each level. This will help preparation programs better understand the depth and the breadth to

which their students must master the professional competencies, will promote more consistency in the content of preparation programs and ensure programs are adequately focusing on young children, birth to age eight.

Clarity (about what early childhood educators need to know and be able to do), consensus (about the necessity for and key components of effective preparation), and cohesion (in a system that supports and prepares early childhood educators) will drive the profession forward and advance a high-quality preparation of early childhood educators.

Notes

1. Early Childhood Professional Standards include: Special Educator Professional Preparation Initial and Advanced Standards; the Early Childhood Special Education/Early Intervention Specialty Set (Early Intervention/Early Childhood Special Education) – owned by the Council for Exceptional Children; The Division for Early Childhood's (DEC) Recommended Practices for high-quality inclusive programs for all children birth to age eight); Council for Professional Recognition – Child Development Associate (CDA) Competency Standards owned by the Council for Professional Recognition; Early Childhood Generalist Standards (for teachers of students ages three to eight) owned by the National Board for Professional Teaching Standards; Critical Competencies for Infant-Toddler Educators – owned by Zero to Three.
2. Just over a third (33%) of children under five are regularly cared for by a non-relative and an additional 12% are regularly cared for by both a relative and non-relative.
3. Though private school teachers are often exempt from state licensing standards, those teachers still typically hold a four-year degree. Bureau of Labor Statistics, U.S. Department of Labor. (2018). *Occupational outlook handbook, kindergarten and elementary school teachers*. Retrieved from https://www.bls.gov/ooh/education-training-and-library/kindergarten-and-elementary-school-teachers.htm
4. See Decision Cycles 3, 4, and 5 of Power to the Profession.
5. Professional training programs normally require less than one year to complete. Completers may meet the educational requirements for industry-recognized national credentials and other portable credentials. These programs are a minimum of 120 clock hours (definition taken from Draft 1 of Decision Cycles 3, 4, and 5 of Power to the Profession).
6. The Child Development Associate (CDA) credential is issued by the Council for Professional Recognition.
7. Approximately 230 associate degree programs included in this number.
8. Approximately 249 programs included for this estimation.
9. "Includes formal and informal opportunities for field observations, field work, practica, student teaching and other clinical practice experiences such as home visiting."
10. The competencies are birth-age five focused.
11. In February 2020, NAEYC will conclude its role as a SPA in the CAEP system.

References

Austin, L. J. E., Sakai, L., & Dhamija, D. (2016). *2016 Alameda County early care and education workforce study*. Berkeley: Center for the Study of Child Care Employment, University of California, Berkeley.

Bornfreund, L. (2011). *Getting in sync: Revamping licensing and preparation for teachers in the pre-k, kindergarten and the early grades*. Washington, DC: New America Foundation.

Bornfreund, L., Cook, S., Lieberman, A., & Lowenberg, A. (2015). *From crawling to walking: ranking states on birth-3rd grade policies that support strong readers*. Retrieved from https://static.newamerica.org/

attachments/11902-from-crawling-to-walking/50-State Scan.fe1ae7082 db6418dabeb3eee29cea669.pdf

Cantor, P., Osher, D., Berg, J., Steyer, L., & Rose, T. (2018). Malleability, plasticity, and individuality: How children learn and develop in context. *Applied Developmental Science, 22*(2), 1–31.

Cassidy, D. (2015). *A perspective on early childhood education articulation.* Retrieved from https://earlyeducatorcentral.acf.hhs.gov/sites/default/files/public/documents/A%20Perspective%20on%20Ea 1y%20Childhood%20Education%20and%20Articulation.pdf

Center on the Developing Child at Harvard University. (2009). *Five numbers to remember about early childhood development (Brief).* Cambridge, MA: Author. Retrieved from https://developingchild.harvard.edu

Center on the Developing Child at Harvard University. (2016). *From best practices to breakthrough impacts: A science-based approach to building a more promising future for young children and families.* Cambridge, MA: Author. Retrieved from https://developingchild.harvard.edu/

Chen, G. (2018, November 12). 10 Major Challenges Facing Public Schools. *Public School Review.* [Web log post]. Retrieved from https://www.publicschoolreview.com/blog/10-major-challenges-facing-public-schools

Child Care Services Association. (2015). *The early care and education workforce in North Carolina: 2015 statewide fact sheet for early care and education centers.* Retrieved from https://www.childcareservices.org/wp-content/uploads/2017/11/statewide-factsheet-2015.pdf

Cook, S., & Bronfreund, L. (2015). *Starting young: Massachusetts birth through third grade policies that support literacy development.* Washington, DC: New America Foundation.

Darling-Hammond, L., & Cook-Harvey, C. M. (2018). *Educating the whole child: Improving school climate to support student success.* Palo Alto, CA: Learning Policy Institute.

Fowler, C. (2016). Grade-level overlap and standards mismatch between nationally recognized programs that prepare teachers for grade Pre-k-3. *Journal of Early Childhood Teacher Education, 37*(3), 203–215.

Gershenson, S., Hart, M. D. C., Lindsay, C. A., & Papageorge, N. W. (2017). *The long-run impacts of same race teachers* (IZA DP No. 10630). Retrieved from Institute on Labor Economics website http://ftp.iza.org/dp10630.pdf.

Hargreaves, A., & Fullan, M. (2012). *Professional capital: Transforming teaching in every school.* New York, NY: Teachers College Press.

Head Start Performance Standards, A Rule by the Children and Families Administration, U.S. Department of Health and Human Services. 45 C.F.R. §1302, *Federal Register*, September 6, 2016.

Institute of Medicine. (2000). *From neurons to neighborhoods: The science of early childhood development.* Washington, DC: The National Academies Press.

Institute of Medicine and National Research Council. (2015). *Transforming the workforce for children birth through age 8: A unifying foundation.* Washington, DC: The National Academies Press.

Jackson, S. (2015). *Not golden yet: Building a stronger workforce for young children in California.* Washington, DC: New American Foundation.

Jenkins, D., & Cho, S.-W. (2012). *Get with the program: Accelerating community college students' entry into and completion of programs of study* (CCRC Working Paper 32). New York, NY: College Research Center, Teachers College, Columbia University.

Kaplan, M., & Mead, S. (2017). *The best teachers for our littlest learners? Lesson from Head Start's last decade.* Washington, DC: Bellwether Education Partners.

Laughlin, L. (2013). *Who's minding the kids? Child care arrangements.* Washington, DC: United States Census Bureau.

Leachman, M., Masterson, K., & Figueroa, E. (2017). *A punishing decade for school funding.* Washington, DC: Center on Budget and Policy Priorities.

Limardo, C., Hill, S., Stadd, J., & Zimmer, T. (2016). *Accessing career pathways to education and training for early childhood professionals.* Retrieved from U. S. Department of Education website https://www2.ed.gov/programs/racetothetop-earlylearningchallenge/pathways/elcpi-accessibility-ada.pdf

Litvinov, B., Alvarez, B., Long, C., & Walker, T. (2018, August 3). Ten Challenges Facing Public Education Today [Web log post]. Retrieved from http://neatoday.org/2018/08/03/10-challenges-facing-public-education-today/

Loewenberg, A. (2018). *Ensuring a smooth pathway using articulation agreements to help early childhood educators pursue a BA.* Washington, DC: New America Foundation. Retrieved from https://www.newamerica.org/education-policy/reports/ensuring-smooth-pathway/ and articulation include Pennsylvania, Connecticut, Massachusetts, North Carolina, South Carolina, Indiana and Tennessee

Lutton, A. (2013, November). Advancing the early childhood profession: Supporting successful degree completion by early childhood professionals. *Young Children, 68*(5), 51–53.

Manning, M., Garvis, S., Fleming, C., & Wong, T. W. G. (2017). *The relationship between teacher qualification and the quality of the early childhood care and learning environment. A Campbell Systematic Review.* doi:10.4073/csr.2017.1

McFarland, J., Hussar, B., Wang, X., Zhang, J., Wang, K., Rathbun, A., ... Bullock Mann, F. (2018). *The condition of education 2018.* Washington, DC: Institute of Education Sciences, National Center for Education Statistics, U.S. Department of Education.

McLean, C. (2018, May 7). *Missing information hampers policymaking for young children* [Web log post]. Retrieved from http://cscce.berkeley.edu/missing-information-hampers-policymaking-for-young-children/

Melnick, H., Meloy, B., Gardner, M., Wechsler, M., & Maier, A. (2018). *Building an early learning system that works: Next steps for California.* Palo Alto, CA: Learning Policy Institute.

National Association for the Education of Young Children. (2009). *NAEYC standards for early childhood professional preparation.* Washington, DC: Author.

National Association for the Education of Young Children. (2018). Power to the profession decision Cycle 1: Professional identity and boundary. Retrieved from https://www.naeyc.org/sites/default/files/globally shared/downloads/PDFs/our-work/initiatives/consensus-draft-decision-cycle-1.pdf

National Association for the Education of Young Children. (2018). *One of us: K-3 teachers are early childhood educators.* Washington, DC: Author.

National Research Council, Committee on the Science of Children Birth to Age 8: Deepening and Broadening the Foundation for Success, Board on Children, Youth, and Families. (2015). *Transforming the workforce for children birth through age 8: A unifying foundation.* Retrieved from https://www.nap.edu/catalog/19401/transforming-the-workforce-for-children-birth-through-age-8-aPorter, N. (2012). *High turnover among early childhood educators in the United States.* Child Research Net. Retrieved from http://www.childresearch.net/projects/ecec/2012_04.html

Schaak, D. D., & Le, V. (2017). *Colorado early childhood workforce survey 2017: Who is Colorado's early educator workforce? Demographic and educational characteristics.* Denver, CO: Transforming the Early Childhood Workforce in Colorado.

Sumrall, T. C., Scott-Little, C., La Paro, K. M., Pianta, R. C., Burchinal, M., Hamre, B., ... Howes, C. (2017). Student teaching within early childhood preparation programs: An examination of key features across 2 and 4 year institutions. *Early Childhood Education Journal, 45*(6), 821–830.

Totenhagen, C. J., Hawkins, S. A., & Casper, D. M. (2016). Retaining early childhood education workers: A review of the empirical literature. *Journal of Research in Childhood Education, 30*(4), 585–599.

U.S. Department of Education. (2016). *Preparing and credentialing the nation's teachers: The Secretary's 10th report on teacher quality.* Washington, DC: Author.

Wechsler, M., Melnick, H., Maier, A., & Bishop, J. (2016). *The building blocks of high-quality early childhood education programs.* Palo Alto, CA: Learning Policy Institute.

Whitebook, M. (2014). *Building a skilled teacher workforce: Shared and divergent challenges in early care and education and in grades k–12.* Seattle, WA: Bill and Melinda Gates Foundation.

Whitebook, M., & Austin, L. J. E. (2015), *Taking stock across the states*. Berkeley: Center for the Study of Child Care Improvement, University of California, Berkeley.

Whitebook, M., & McLean, C. (2017). *Educator expectations, qualifications, and earnings: Shared challenges and divergent systems in ECE and k-12 (brief)*. Berkeley: Center for the Study of Child Care Employment, Institute for Research on Labor and Employment, University of California, Berkeley.

Whitebook, M., McLean, C., Austin, L. J. E., & Edwards, B. (2018). *Early childhood workforce index – 2018*. Berkeley: Center for the Study of Child Care Employment, University of California, Berkeley. Retrieved from http://cscce.berkeley.edu/topic/early-childhood-workforce-index/2018/

Whitebook, M., & Sakai, L. (2003). Turnover begets turnover: An examination of job and occupational instability among child care. *Early Childhood Research Quarterly, 18*(3), 273–293.

Will, M. (2018). Teachers criticize their colleges of ed for not adequately preparing them to teach reading. Education Week, *Teacher Beat*. October 24, 2018.

Workman, S. (2018). *Where does your child care dollar go? Understanding the true cost of quality early childhood education*. Washington, DC: Center for American Progress. Retrieved from https://www.americanprogress.org/issues/early-childhood/reports/2018/02/14/446330/child-care-dollar-go/

22

Promising Approaches to Professional Development for Early Childhood Educators

Douglas R. Powell and Karen E. Diamond

Currently there is considerable interest in professional development (PD) for in-service teachers as a tool for strengthening the impact of early childhood classrooms on children's learning and development. PD is a central feature of recent policy and programmatic initiatives aimed at improving the effects of programs for young children across a range of early childhood sectors, including child care, state-supported prekindergarten, and Head Start (Martinez-Beck & Zaslow, 2006).

Beginning in the early 2000s, the press for expansion of PD has been accompanied by a conceptualization of PD that emphasizes intensive and sustained opportunities for teacher learning, content focused on what teachers are expected to teach and on the realities of a teacher's classroom and larger context, and modes of participation that facilitate active learning and collaborative relationships with PD staff and/or teacher colleagues (e.g., Garet, Porter, Desimone, Birman, & Yoon, 2001; Hawley & Valli, 1999; Wayne, Yoon, Zhu, Cronen, & Garet, 2008). These emphases in PD reflect the view that adults learn most effectively through their own practice, reflections on their practice, and interactions with content experts over an extended period of time (Bransford, Brown, & Cocking, 1999).

Research has not kept pace with the growth of PD. Currently scholars are investigating the outcomes of specific PD strategies and different levels of intensity. Because short-term PD is widely viewed as an insufficient way to support improvements in teachers' practices, investigations generally focus on effects of programs at the upper end of the PD intensity continuum such as comprehensive interventions that combine coursework, individualized work with teachers in their classrooms, and the use of student progress monitoring tools (Landry, Anthony, Swank, & Monesque-Bailey, 2009).

This chapter examines three promising approaches to PD with early childhood educators. We describe professional learning communities employed to improve the quality of instruction and learning in early childhood classrooms. Collaborative group work with teachers and other experts is a core feature of this approach to PD. We also describe programs in which content experts (e.g., early literacy specialists)

provide individualized supports to teachers in the context of their classrooms. Terms used to describe this strategy of PD include coaching, consultation, and mentoring. Lastly, we consider technological innovations aimed at improving the efficiency and accessibility of PD. Attention is given to recent advances in the uses of technology in PD, specifically technologically mediated forms of individualized work with teachers.

The PD approaches examined in this chapter promote regular and active teacher engagement of an on-going PD activity, and view one-time workshops as limited in their ability to support significant change in teachers' actions in their classrooms. Each of the broad approaches to PD considered in this chapter adheres to a distinctive theory of change. In coaching, feedback from a content expert on a teacher's implementation of a new teaching practice in his or her classroom is among the presumed drivers of instructional change whereas the hypothesized active ingredients of a professional learning community are collaborative group work with colleagues on the development of lessons or activities and collective sharing of reflections on their uses in group participants' classrooms.

Regardless of format, there are important differences in the uses of PD vis-à-vis the targeted content and method of instruction. Specifically, some initiatives aimed at improving the quality of early childhood classrooms employ PD as a means of supporting teachers in the implementation of a new curriculum or supplementary curriculum resources (e.g., Bierman et al., 2008). Other instructional improvement efforts use PD to promote teachers' adoption of effective research-based instructional strategies within the context of a classroom's existing curriculum (e.g., Powell, Diamond, Burchinal, & Koehler, 2010). PD may also be used as a forum for teachers to generate lessons or activities, as noted earlier. Interventions that offer both PD and curriculum resources leave important questions unanswered about the relative contribution of the PD approach and new curriculum to student outcomes unless the PD and curriculum components are systematically varied to provide distinctive intervention conditions.

The chapter draws on studies of PD related to: early literacy and language development, a comprehensive early childhood curriculum, teachers' descriptive praise, and teacher-child interaction to illustrate PD approaches. Early literacy and language is a primary focus because this content area has been examined more frequently in early childhood PD research than other areas.

Professional Learning Communities

A professional learning community in the field of education typically consists of a small group of educators and perhaps other stakeholders who meet regularly to work collaboratively on instructional and/or curriculum changes aimed at improving student learning (Vescio, Ross, & Adams, 2008). Mutually supportive reflection on participants' descriptions of efforts to implement new or revised teaching practices is often a core element of a group's efforts. Several examples of using a professional learning community to improve student outcomes in early childhood education are described below.

A program known as Teacher Study Groups (TSG) has been in development for more than a decade (Dimino & Taylor, 2009), focused on improving instruction in vocabulary knowledge and comprehension in first-grade classrooms. A randomized controlled trial of the TSG found positive effects on teacher knowledge and observed teaching practice, and a promising impact on students' oral language (Gersten, Dimino, Jayanthi, Kim, & Santoro, 2010). In a recent large-scale replication study, significant impacts of the TSG were found for teacher knowledge and observed teaching practices, but not for student outcomes (Jayanthi et al., 2018). The TSG program involves ten teacher group meetings of two to seven members, held twice a month for six months and lasting for about 75 minutes. The groups use a relatively informal approach to discuss and collaborate on ways to teach words in depth, drawing on strategies for rich vocabulary instruction promoted by Beck, McKeown, and Kucan (2002) and others.

Three levels of a learning community were established to support Head Start teachers' implementation of a comprehensive early childhood curriculum known as the Evidence-based Program for the Integration of Curricula (EPIC), designed to promote skills in mathematics, language, literacy, and approaches to learning. The levels included the classroom teaching team (lead teacher and assistant), a small group comprised of five to six teaching teams and a mentor teacher who had experiences implementing the EPIC curriculum, and a large group comprised of all teaching teams plus the Head Start program's educational coordinator. The implementation plan called for each teaching team to meet weekly to review children's progress and plan for curriculum implementation in the upcoming week, the small group to meet monthly to reflect on a previous EPIC unit and prepare for a new curriculum unit, and the large group to meet quarterly to discuss implementation issues, share best practices, and review outcomes. Positive effects were found on children's mathematics and listening comprehension skills (Fantuzzo, Gadsden, & McDermott, 2011).

Research on outcomes of the learning community model of PD is often limited to teachers' reports of their experiences in learning communities. Independent observations of instructional practices, assessments of student learning, and use of experimental designs are uncommon (Vescio et al., 2008). Fortunately, effects of the TSG program and the EPIC curriculum were examined in rigorous random assignment studies that included assessments of fidelity of PD implementation, among other study design features. The large-scale replication study of the TSG model involved a sample of 182 first-grade teachers and their 1,811 students from 62 schools in 16 school districts in four states (Jayanthi et al., 2018). The study of the EPIC curriculum was conducted with a sample of 1,415 children in 70 Head Start classrooms in a large urban area (Fantuzzo et al., 2011).

The TSG and EPIC models of professional learning communities both focused on instructional practices deemed to be promising or effective in research. Their respective models differ from a "communities of practice" model in which a knowledge base on best practices is developed from teachers' collective experiences and collaborative actions with researchers (Buysse, Sparkman, & Wesley, 2003; Wesley & Buysse, 2006). For example, Perry and colleagues describe a community of practice PD effort in which teachers and researchers jointly developed early literacy activities and assessments (Perry, Walton, & Calder, 1999). In a variant of this model, a PD program aimed at improving the language and literacy outcomes of Latino dual language learners included community of practice meetings for teachers to create lessons around a commonly agreed upon goal within a scientifically based content framework (Buysse, Castro, & Peisner-Feinberg, 2010). In addition to creating lessons, community of practice meetings were used to provide feedback and reflection on teachers' implementation of lessons and generate a product for dissemination to other teachers. A random assignment study of the PD program, known as Nuestros Niños, found significant improvements in the quality of teachers' literacy and language instruction and gains in children's phonological awareness skills in their primary language (Buysse et al., 2010). Random assignment is a gold standard in research that ensures each participant in a study has the same opportunity to be assigned to one of the groups examined in an investigation (Myers & Dynarski, 2003).

Coaching

The format of coaching and similar forms of classroom-based work with a teacher or teaching team is highly conducive to individualizing the presentation of information on evidence-based practices and feedback on a teacher's efforts to implement recommended instruction (Powell & Diamond, 2011). Typically coaching is offered as part of a multi-component PD program that includes introductory (e.g., Powell et al., 2010) or concurrent (e.g., Raver et al., 2008) workshops, an ongoing course (e.g., Neuman & Wright, 2010), and/or web resources (Pianta, Mashburn, Downer, Hamre, & Justice, 2008; Powell et al., 2010) aimed at providing information on evidence-based practices related to the content of the PD. In some PD programs, coaches demonstrate or model the targeted practice in a teacher's classroom (Wasik, Bond, & Hindman, 2006). Coaching may be offered to strengthen teachers' implementation of a new curriculum (e.g., Bierman et al., 2008).

It is common for a coach or mentor to observe a teacher in his or her classroom and then meet individually with the teacher to provide and discuss feedback on the observation. (See a later section of this chapter for a description of technologically mediated approaches to conducting observations and providing feedback.) Usually feedback includes two basic types of information that is aligned with the PD program's content: an identification of appropriately implemented practices and recommendations for practice improvements. One PD program refers to these two forms of feedback as "glows" and "grows," respectively (Landry et al., 2009, p. 452). To help teachers reflect on their practices, some programs provide a teacher with records of his or her actions in the classroom via videotapes of the teacher's behaviors (Hamre, LoCasale-Crouch, & Pianta, 2008) or transcripts of audio-taped teacher interactions with children (Dickinson, Watson, & Farran, 2008).

The ExCELL program offered to Head Start teachers is illustrative of combining coaching with other forms of PD support to teachers (Wasik, 2010). ExCELL is designed to train teachers to implement evidence-based practices that promote children's literacy and language development. The PD content is organized into modules (e.g., interactive book reading, alphabet knowledge) that are the basis of three-hour group training sessions conducted monthly. In each group training session, a conceptual rationale for recommended practices is presented and specific teaching strategies are described and modeled by coaches. Teachers also have opportunities to test the strategies during group activities. A three-hour coaching session is offered weekly to each teacher. Each session includes observation and documentation of teaching practices related to targeted outcomes (e.g., emphasis on letters). In the week that follows a group training session, the coach models with children in each teacher's classroom the instructional strategies that were presented during the training. The teacher observes the coach's modeling by using an observation checklist that highlights key teaching behaviors. In addition to providing additional exposure to targeted instructional practices, a goal of the modeling is to demonstrate how the recommended practices can be used with children in the teacher's classroom. The teacher is given about one week to practice the targeted instruction prior to the coach observing the teacher implement the strategy in his or her classroom. The observation checklist used by the teacher to assess the coach's modeling of the practice is also used by the

coach to observe the teacher's implementation of the practice. The coach's completed checklist is used as a discussion springboard at a conference with the teacher immediately following the observation. Coach feedback includes positive aspects of the teacher's actions and recommendations for improvement. Videotaping of teachers' implementation of practices emphasized in ExCELL also occurs frequently as an additional tool to facilitate coach and teacher discussion of the teacher's practice. In addition, teachers receive theme guides, suggested daily lesson plans, and a variety of classroom materials such as books and picture/word cards of targeted vocabulary.

Results of an outcome study of the ExCELL program indicate that teachers provided higher-quality classrooms, including observed book reading sessions, than teachers in comparison classrooms. Children in ExCELL classrooms performed significantly better than their peers in comparison classrooms on measures of receptive vocabulary and phonological sensitivity, but not on letter knowledge (Wasik & Hindman, 2011).

Several research teams have examined the relative impact of coaching offered in combination with another method of PD. In a random assignment study, a literacy-focused workshops-plus-coaching combination was slightly more effective than workshops alone. Children of teachers who received workshops-plus-coaching had more consistently positive outcomes in oral language, phonological awareness, and print knowledge than children of teachers who received workshops only (Lonigan, Farver, Phillips, & Clancy-Menchetti, 2011). A quasi-experimental study by Neuman and Cunningham (2009) found that center- and family-based child care providers' participation in a 3-credit, 15-week course plus weekly coaching was associated with significant improvements in providers' language and literacy practices. Coursework alone had negligible effects on instructional quality. The lack of positive outcomes of the 15-week course is in contrast with findings from another quasi-experimental study that found a positive impact of a four-credit course, offered as two three-day intensive sessions, on classroom supports for early literacy (Dickinson & Caswell, 2007). The latter PD program, conducted with Head Start teachers, also provided training to teachers' on-site supervisors in how to support teachers' implementation of new practices. A subsequent study by Neuman and Wright (2010) sought to disentangle the three-credit course and coaching and provide an equal amount of support for both coaching and coursework PD conditions (i.e., three hours weekly across ten weeks). At the end of the PD program, classrooms of teachers who participated in coaching only, compared to classrooms of teachers who participated in a course only, had higher-quality book and writing areas plus literacy environments overall but not higher-quality teaching strategies.

In a large-scale study of a PD program that sequentially combined a semester-long course and coaching, teachers reported in the post-coaching year that children in their classrooms demonstrated greater levels of behavior control. There were no effects on directly assessed language or literacy skills. The PD program focused on effective teacher-child interactions (Pianta et al., 2017). The coaching program is My Teaching Partner. A separate, large-scale experimental study of a 14-week course on effective teacher-child interaction skills found positive effects on teachers' instructional interactions and one aspect of emotional interactions (regard for student perspectives) in the classroom. No effects were found for indicators of teachers' classroom organization skills such as behavior management, and for classroom climate and teacher sensitivity aspects of emotional support. Child outcomes were not examined (Hamre et al., 2012). A subsequent adaptation of the course was called "Making the Most of Classroom Interactions" and investigated in a study of PD offered in Georgia's Pre-K program. The Georgia study is described in a later section of this chapter (see Factors Associated with PD Implementation and Outcomes).

Technological Innovations

Technology holds great promise of extending the reach of PD, particularly to schools and teachers in rural and geographically remote communities where PD opportunities are limited. Technology also enables teachers to participate in PD on their own schedules. Teachers have pursued web-based learning, including accessing online courses and webinars, for a number of years (Amendum, Vernon-Feagans, & Ginsberg, 2011). Only recently has there been sufficient development of web-based technologies to provide teachers with individualized support and feedback integrated into their daily work teaching children in their classrooms, replacing or complementing traditional face-to-face real-time mentoring (Gentry, Denton, & Kurz, 2008).

Computer-based technology has been used to provide PD through a variety of means, including web conferencing (Amendum et al., 2011), electronic mail (Hemmeter, Snyder, Kinder, & Artman, 2011), webcams in classrooms (Pianta et al., 2008), and software that links a mentor/coach's feedback to videotaped segments of teachers' instruction (linked teaching-feedback; Powell et al., 2010). In each of these different approaches, teachers receive information about what they do well and areas for growth. In some approaches, technology is used to link teacher and mentor concurrently (e.g., webcams, web conferencing) whereas others use technology to provide feedback asynchronously (e.g., communications between teacher and mentor occur outside of real time through email or linked teaching-feedback). Advantages of mentoring experiences that occur asynchronously include more flexibility in scheduling and multiple opportunities for teachers to review feedback (Powell et al., 2010).

Technologically mediated mentoring or coaching has been used to support teachers' implementation of a specific curriculum and lessons (e.g., My Teaching Partner Language and Literacy Curriculum, Pianta et al., 2008) as well as to support teachers' use of targeted instructional strategies that are independent of a specific curriculum (e.g., Amendum et al., 2011; Hemmeter et al., 2011; Powell et al., 2010).

Amendum and colleagues (2011) used a webcam along with web conferencing to observe and support individual teachers. The intervention focused on teachers' implementation of Targeted Reading Strategies (TRI), a Tier 2 intervention within a Response-to-Intervention framework for kindergarten and first-grade students who were struggling to read. This intervention was independent of the reading curriculum used in the classroom. Literacy coaches located at a distance provided real-time coaching for the teacher to support implementation of these strategies. Coaching feedback was provided either during the TRI lesson, immediately following the lesson, or both, depending on the teacher's preferences; debriefing after the observation was included, if time permitted. Coaching "visits" via webcam occurred weekly and then biweekly as teachers implemented TRI strategies; additional web conferencing included weekly grade-level meetings about children's performance as well as occasional PD sessions. Thus, this PD intervention used technology for "real-time" mentoring through individual webcam consultations along with group web conferencing. The quality and frequency of teachers' implementation of TRI were assessed on a regular basis (as indicators of fidelity of implementation). Results suggested that kindergarten teachers implemented intervention strategies with higher fidelity than did first-grade teachers (Vernon-Feagans et al., 2010) and that there were significant effects of the intervention on kindergarten children's learning but not on the performance of first graders.

Hemmeter and colleagues (2011) have examined the impact of feedback delivered by email on preschool teachers' use of descriptive praise for children's positive behaviors during group instruction, a strategy designed to increase children's engagement and decrease challenging behaviors. Initial training was provided to teachers face-to-face and focused on the use of, and rationale for using, descriptive praise. Following the initial training, trainers (coaches) observed circle time activities in the classroom two to three times per week and sent teachers email feedback on their use of descriptive praise statements. Each email feedback message included an embedded link, directing a teacher to view a trainer/coach-selected video clip of a teacher using descriptive praise statements in a similar preschool context. Teachers replied to the email feedback to indicate that it had been received, but there was no way to determine the care with which feedback was reviewed. Unlike the TRI intervention described previously, trainers/coaches were physically present as teachers implemented the intervention but feedback was provided electronically, after the coach's observation. Advantages of providing feedback to teachers by email included the opportunity for teachers to review feedback at a convenient time (i.e., feedback to the teacher did not disrupt the classroom routine) and to include links to real-life video examples of other teachers implementing practices with which they were struggling. In this multiple probe, single-subject study, training, and feed-back were associated with increases in teachers' use of descriptive praise. Results indicated that children's challenging behaviors decreased somewhat, but inconsistently, across the four classrooms included in the study.

Powell and colleagues (2010) used individualized web-mediated feedback as part of a literacy-focused PD intervention with Head Start teachers. They used a randomized control-trial design to compare the effectiveness of two different approaches to providing PD (face-to-face or technologically mediated coaching). In the technologically mediated PD intervention, teachers videotaped their own instruction, sent the tape to their coach, and received feedback on a CD that they could review on their laptop computer. The coaching feedback included comments paired with specific segments of their videotaped practice, along with links to video exemplars of other teachers implementing similar instructional approaches. There were significant effects of the literacy-focused PD intervention on the broad classroom environment and on teachers' instruction of letters and sounds, along with significant effects on children's knowledge of letters and sounds. Importantly, there were no consistent differences in outcomes for either teachers or children across the two intervention approaches (Powell et al., 2010). The results of this study are particularly important in suggesting that benefits of technologically mediated PD interventions may be similar to those in which the same intervention content is provided in face-to-face interaction. In contrast, results of a study of face-to-face versus webcam literacy coaching of kindergarten and first-grade teachers pointed to greater benefits of webcam coaching regarding teacher practices (Vernon-Feagans, Bratsch-Hines, Varghese, Bean, & Hedrick, 2015).

Video libraries of effective instruction have been used in several recent studies of coaching interventions (cf., Hemmeter et al., 2011; Pianta et al., 2008; Powell et al., 2010). One form of a video library is a case-based hypermedia resource that provides teachers with video examples of evidence-based practices (cases) along with descriptive information that highlights specific aspects of instruction. Advantages of a case-based hypermedia resource include providing teachers with direct access to information related to specific teaching practices, along with opportunities to focus on specific instructional approaches that may be particularly challenging (Koehler, 2002). Powell, Diamond, and Koehler (2010) found that teachers in their intervention were most likely to use the hypermedia resource in the late afternoon and in the evening, suggesting that one of the advantages of this tool is that it can be used at a time that the teacher finds most convenient. Results of research by Pianta et al. (2008) suggest that providing teachers with access to video exemplars only, without coaching support, leads to quite modest improvements in teachers' instruction; individualized coaching feedback appears to add value to that provided by models or exemplars of evidence-based instruction.

Factors Associated with PD Implementation and Outcomes

Similar to the uses of curricula and other educational interventions, it is unusual for all components of a PD program to be implemented and engaged as intended. PD content areas may receive differential levels of emphasis (Powell, Steed, & Diamond, 2010), for example, and assigned readings may not be pursued in advance of a program session (Gersten et al., 2010). Available evidence points to considerable between-teacher variation in the amount of participation in PD programs. In the Raver et al.'s (2008) program to improve teachers' emotionally supportive classroom practices, approximately 37% of teachers participated in less than half of five Saturday trainings. Forty-nine of 173 teachers (28%) involved in the MTP study did not submit at least one videotape of their teaching during each of three time periods across the school year (Pianta et al., 2008). Twelve percent of teachers in the technologically mediated coaching condition of the Powell et al.'s (2010) study submitted fewer than six of the seven videotapes specified in the one-semester coaching protocol.

Teacher characteristics are plausible contributors to participation in and outcomes of a PD program, but associations are unclear. For example, some investigators (e.g., Downer, LoCasale-Crouch, Hamrey, & Pianta, 2009) but not others (e.g., Domitrovich, Gest, Gill, Jones, & DeRousie, 2009) have found teachers' professional characteristics (e.g., experience) to be predictive of engagement in a PD coaching program. Teachers may not fully engage in a PD program when a teaching practice recommended by the program is viewed as out of reach or inconsistent with current approaches (Powell & Diamond, 2011). For example, Dickinson and colleagues describe a teacher who was minimally engaged in a language-focused PD program presumably because the PD program's request that she initiate interactions with children during center time was at odds with her "preferred habit of standing back and observing children, and interacting only when problems arose" (Dickinson et al., 2008, p. 145).

There appear to be differences in the capacities of school districts and other organizational sponsors of early childhood education to implement a PD model with fidelity. For example, school district schedules and teacher release time policies in some schools led to 30-minute TSG sessions during teacher planning periods across multiple days whereas other school districts were able to provide a full 75-minute TSG meeting twice a month as specified in the program model. Also, the TSG model was implemented with a lower level of fidelity in school districts that did not use a core reading series, presumably because teachers did not have a common lesson for collaborative work. Further, TSG facilitators differed by school district in their skills in keeping group sessions on track (Gersten et al., 2010).

With regard to PD outcomes, increasingly there is interest in independent evaluations of PD models conducted at arm's length from their developers, and in real-world policy contexts that shape program implementation. Illustrative of this direction is a randomized controlled trial of My Teaching Partner and Making the Most of Classroom Interactions, two PD programs referenced earlier in this chapter (Early, Maxwell, Ponder, & Pan, 2017). Notable features of the study include the independent status of the investigators (who were not involved in developing the PD programs) and the PD coaches and instructors (who were not employed by organizational sponsors of the two PD programs). Also, the PD programs were implemented with all teachers in Georgia's Pre-K program, not only teachers who volunteered to participate. Both PD programs had modest positive effects on some targeted outcomes related to teacher-child interactions. Child outcomes were not investigated (Early et al., 2017).

A study of a language and literacy program for rural preschool children in the Appalachian region of the United States is another example of a PD-related investigation conducted with keen interest in real-world circumstances (Mashburn, Justice, McGinty, & Slocum, 2016). The study examined effects of Read It Again (Justice, McGinty, Sofka, Slocum, & Pentimonti, 2009), a curriculum designed through a collaborative process with West Virginia practitioners and policy-makers to be highly scalable with regard to cost (e.g., free, downloadable manual) and use (e.g., fit a range of program structures). Pertinent to the focus of the current chapter is the Mashburn et al. study's random assignment of teachers to one of two different forms of PD: (1) a full-day workshop prior to the start of the school year plus a technologically mediated 12-module self-study program or (2) a full-day workshop but no self-study modules. Both groups received classroom materials for the 30-week program. There were no differences between the two forms of PD across six child outcome variables. Overall, the curriculum had positive impacts on children's concepts of print, print knowledge, and alphabet knowledge, but not on language development (Mashburn et al., 2016).

A related line of investigation with regard to PD outcomes is the association between changes in teacher behaviors and children's outcomes. At a broad level, the PD theory of change posits that improvements in teachers' classroom practices will lead to improvements in children's outcomes. The Mashburn et al.'s (2016) study pertains to the question of how much PD is needed to promote meaningful change in children's skills. Their results suggest that more PD may not be necessary. Offering a 12-module study program and a full-day workshop was no more effective than offering a full-day workshop only. In contrast, a modest PD program for child care providers found that ten hours of PD annually (a state requirement) focused on early literacy was associated with improvements in teachers' literacy knowledge and practices, but not with gains in children's outcomes (Gerde, Duke, Moses, Spybrook, & Shedd, 2014). A meta-analysis of language- and literacy-focused early childhood PD studies found that although PD led to small-to-medium effects on phonological awareness and a small effect on children's alphabet knowledge, improvements in children's outcomes were not

predicted by gains in teachers' outcomes (Markussen-Brown et al., 2017).

Determining the threshold of dosage of PD needed for meaningful improvements in children's outcomes is of understandable interest to policy-makers. Perhaps equally important but less frequently investigated is the PD pedagogical strategy. Consider, for example, the outcomes of a small-scale, random assignment study of coaching with versus without coach demonstrations of evidence-based book-reading practices. Results suggest that demonstration and teachers' observational learning may contribute to significant change in teachers' practices (Gettinger & Stoiber, 2016).

Future Directions

Advances in the use of PD to improve the outcomes of early childhood programs require empirical evidence from well-designed studies of effects of varying approaches to PD. Random assignment studies and meta-analyses that compare outcomes of different PD methods, such as teacher study groups versus expert coaching with individual teachers, are especially needed. Research is also needed on thresholds of PD intensity and duration that yield meaningful change in children's learning. Nuanced understandings of how PD intensity and duration interact with teacher variables (e.g., initial quality of instruction) and other attributes of a PD program (e.g., complexity and novelty of the PD content) to produce improvements in teachers' instruction and student outcome gains may be particularly helpful in informing the design of future PD efforts. Findings of studies that disentangle features of comprehensive instructional improvement initiatives are essential to making prudent decisions about the active ingredients of educational reform efforts that include PD. More may not necessarily mean better.

The processes of teacher change warrant careful investigation (Sheridan, Edwards, Marvin, & Knoche, 2009). Little is known about mediators of improvements in teachers' instruction. For example, it is not clear whether and how teachers' increased knowledge of a content area leads to improvements in quality of instruction, and whether relations are linear.

Another needed line of research pertains to conditions that support or impede the implementation of PD. Our review of promising PD programs revealed some possible influences that warrant further investigation. The existence of a common curriculum appeared to be a factor in facilitating the work of teacher study groups (Gersten et al., 2010). Findings of other research also suggest that the lack of a core curriculum weakens the effects of teacher training (Fukkink & Lont, 2007). Our review also noted that organizational capacity to promote change in core practices may moderate the implementation and effects of PD programs. There is some evidence that effects of mentoring varied by the organizational auspice (e.g., Head Start, Title 1) of an early childhood program (Assel, Landry, Swank, & Gunnewig, 2007). The credentials and resourcefulness of PD staff seem obvious contributors to PD effects but, with few exceptions (e.g., Downer et al., 2009), PD outcome studies rarely examine staff variables. Because most PD studies lack an adequate sample of PD staff for analyses of outcomes by staff characteristics, research that analyzes pooled data from different PD studies may be a productive way to better understand staff contributions to PD outcomes.

The early childhood field's corpus of scientific knowledge about what works in supporting high-quality teaching is promising. Researchers have identified approaches to PD that are based on conceptually coherent frameworks and experimental evidence of effectiveness. To build on this progress, researchers need to replicate outcome studies in diverse settings and conduct investigations that inform efforts to take effective PD approaches to scale. This requires attention to the conditions under which PD takes hold and contributes to significant and sustained improvements in teacher practices and children's outcomes. Without this line of research, we run the risk of wasting teacher time and other resources on PD approaches that yield little or no benefit. With well-developed programs of research on PD, the field has a great opportunity to move closer to realizing the promise of early childhood education as a foundation of subsequent school success.

References

Amendum, S. J., Vernon-Feagans, L., & Ginsberg, M. C. (2011). The effectiveness of a technologically-facilitated classroom-based early reading intervention: The targeted reading intervention. *The Elementary School Journal, 48,* 763–794.

Assel, M. A., Landry, S. H., Swank, P. R., & Gunnewig, S. (2007). An evaluation of curriculum, setting, and mentoring on the performance of children enrolled in pre-kindergarten. *Reading and Writing, 20,* 463–494.

Beck, I. L., McKeown, M. G., & Kucan, L. (2002). *Bringing words to life: Robust vocabulary instruction.* New York, NY: Guilford.

Bierman, K. L., Domitrovich, C. E., Nix, R. L., Gest, S. D., Welsh, J. A., … Gill, S. (2008). Promoting academic and social-emotional school readiness: The Head Start REDI program. *Child Development, 79,* 1802–1817.

Bransford, J. D., Brown, A. L., & Cocking, R. R. (Eds.). (1999). *How people learn: Brain, mind, experience, and school.* Washington, DC: National Academy Press.

Buysse, V., Castro, D. C., & Peisner-Feinberg, E. (2010). Effects of a professional development program on classroom practices and outcomes for Latino dual language learners. *Early Childhood Research Quarterly, 25,* 194–206.

Buysse, V., Sparkman, K. L., & Wesley, P. W. (2003). Communities of practice: Connecting what we know with what we do. *Exceptional Children, 69,* 263–275.

Dickinson, D. K., & Caswell, L. (2007). Building support for language and early literacy in preschool classrooms through in-service professional development: Effects of the Literacy Environment Enrichment Program (LEEP). *Early Childhood Research Quarterly, 22,* 243–260.

Dickinson, D. K., Watson, B. G., & Farran, D. C. (2008). It's in the details: Approaches to describing and improving preschool classrooms. In L. M. Justice & C. Vukelich (Eds.), *Achieving excellence in preschool literacy instruction* (pp. 136–161). New York, NY: Guilford.

Dimino, J., & Taylor, M. J. (2009). *Learning how to improve vocabulary instruction through teacher study groups.* Baltimore, MD: Brookes Publishing.

Domitrovich, C. E., Gest, S. D., Gill, S., Jones, D., & DeRousie, R. S. (2009). Individual factors associated with PD training outcomes of the Head Start REDI program. *Early Education and Development, 20,* 402–430.

Downer, J. T., Locasale-Crouch, J., Hamre, B., & Pianta, R. (2009). Teacher characteristics associated with responsiveness and exposure to consultation and online PD resources. *Early Education and Development, 20,* 431–455.

Early, D. M., Maxwell, K. L., Ponder, B. D., & Pan, Y. (2017). Improving teacher-child interactions: A randomized controlled trial of making the most of classroom interactions and my teaching partner professional development models. *Early Childhood Research Quarterly, 38,* 57–70.

Fantuzzo, J. W., Gadsden, V. L., & McDermott, P. A. (2011). An integrated curriculum to improve mathematics, language, and literacy for Head Start children. *American Educational Research Journal, 48,* 763–794.

Fukkink, R. G., & Lont, A. (2007). Does training matter? A meta-analysis and review of caregiver training studies. *Early Childhood Research Quarterly, 22,* 294–311.

Garet, M. S., Porter, A. C., Desimone, L., Birman, B. F., & Yoon, K. S. (2001). What makes professional development effective? Results from a national sample of teachers. *American Educational Research Journal, 38,* 915–945.

Gentry, L. B., Denton, C. A., & Kurtz, T. (2008). Technologically-based mentoring provided to teachers: A synthesis of the literature. *Journal of Technology and Teacher Education, 16,* 339–373.

Gerde, H. K., Duke, N. K., Moses, A. M., Spybrook, J., & Shedd, M. K. (2014). How much for whom? Lessons from an efficacy study of modest professional development for child care providers. *Early Education and Development, 25,* 421–441.

Gersten, R., Dimino, J., Jayanthi, M., Kim, J. S., & Santoro, L. E. (2010). Teacher study group: Impact of the PD model on reading instruction and student outcomes in first grade classrooms. *American Educational Research Journal, 47,* 694–739.

Gettinger, M., & Stoiber, K. C. (2016). Coaching and demonstration of evidence-based book-reading practices: Effects on Head Start teachers' literacy-related behaviors and classroom environment. *Journal of Early Childhood Teacher Education, 37,* 117–141.

Hamre, B. K., LoCasale-Crouch, J., & Pianta, R. C. (2008). Formative assessment of classrooms: Using classroom observations to improve implementation quality. In L. M. Justice & C. Vukelich (Eds.), *Achieving excellence in preschool literacy instruction* (pp. 102–119). New York, NY: Guilford.

Hamre, B.K, Pianta, R. C., Burchinal, M., Field, S., LoCasale-Crouch, J. L., Downer, J. T., … Scott-Little, C. (2012). A course on effective teacher-child interactions: Effects on teacher beliefs, knowledge, and observe practice. *American Educational Research Journal, 49,* 88–123.

Hawley, W., & Valli, L. (1999). The essentials of effective professional development: A new consensus. In L. Darling-Hammond & G. Sykes (Eds.), *Teaching as the learning profession: Handbook of policy and practice* (pp. 127–150). San Francisco, CA: Jossey-Bass.

Hemmeter, M. L., Snyder, P., Kinder, K., & Artman, K. (2011). Impact of performance feedback delivered via electronic mail on preschool teachers' use of descriptive praise. *Early Childhood Research Quarterly, 26,* 96–110. Hindman, A. H., Snell, E. K., Wasik, B. A., Lewis, K. N., Hammer, C. S., & Iannone-Campbell, C. (2011). Research and practice partnerships for professional development in early childhood: Lessons from ExCEL-e. *Journal of Education for Students Placed at Risk, 20,* 12–28.

Jayanthi, M., Dimino, J., Gersten, R., Taylor, M. J., Haymond, K., Smolkowski, K., & Newman-Gonchar, R. (2018). The impact of teacher study groups in vocabulary on teaching practice, teacher knowledge, and student vocabulary knowledge: A large-scale replication study. *Journal of Research on Educational Effectiveness, 11,* 83–108.

Justice, L.M., McGinty, A., Sofka, A., Slocum, L., & Pentimonti, J.M. (2009). *Read it again PreK! Teachers self-study materials workbook.* Columbus, OH: The Ohio State University.

Koehler, M. J. (2002). Designing case-based hypermedia for developing understanding of children's mathematical reasoning. *Cognition and Instruction, 20,* 151–195.

Landry, S. H., Anthony, J. L., Swank, P. R., & Monesque-Bailey, P. (2009). Effectiveness of comprehensive professional development for teachers of at-risk preschoolers. *Journal of Educational Psychology, 101,* 448–465.

Markussen-Brown, J., Juhl, C. B., Piasta, S. Bleses, D., Højen, A., & Justice, L. (2017). The effects of language- and literacy-focused professional development on early educators and children: A best-evidence meta-analysis. *Early Childhood Research Quarterly, 38,* 97–115.

Martinez-Beck, I., & Zaslow, M. (2006). The context for critical issues in early childhood professional development. In M. Zaslow & I. Martinez-Beck (Eds.), *Critical issues in early childhood professional development* (pp. 1–16). Baltimore, MD: Brookes.

Mashburn, A., Justice, L. M., McGinty, A., & Slocum, L. (2016). The impacts of scalable intervention on the language and literacy development of rural pre-kindergartners. *Applied Developmental Science, 20,* 61–78.

Myers, D., & Dynarski, M. (2003). Random assignment in program evaluation and intervention research. Washington, DC: Institute of Education Sciences, U.S. Department of Education. Retrieved from http://www.ed.gov/offices/IES/NCEE/qa.html

Neuman, S. B., & Cunningham, L. (2009). The impact of professional development and coaching on early language and literacy instructional practices. *American Educational Research Journal, 46,* 532–566.

Neuman, S. B., & Wright, T. S. (2010). Promoting language and literacy development for early childhood educators: A mixed-methods study of coursework and coaching. *The Elementary School Journal, 111,* 63–86.

Lonigan, C. J., Farver, J. A. M., Phillips, B. M., & Clancy-Menchetti, J. (2011). Promoting the development of preschool children's emergent literacy skills: A randomized evaluation of a literacy-focused curriculum and two professional development models. *Reading and Writing, 24,* 305–337.

Perry, N. E., Walton, C., & Calder, K. (1999). Teachers developing assessments of early literacy: A community of practice project. *Teacher Education and Special Education, 22,* 218–233.

Pianta, R., Hamre, B., Downer, J., Burchinal, M., Williford, J., LoCasale-Brouch, J., ... Scott-Little, C. (2017). Early childhood professional development: Coaching and coursework effects on indicators of children's school readiness. *Early Education and Development, 28,* 956–975.

Pianta, R. C., Mashburn, A. J., Downer, J. T., Hamre, B. K., & Justice, L. (2008). Effects of web-mediated professional development resources on teacher-child interactions in pre-kindergarten classrooms. *Early Childhood Research Quarterly, 23,* 431–451.

Powell, D. R., & Diamond, K. E. (2011). Improving the outcomes of coaching-based PD interventions. In S. B. Neuman & D. K. Dickinson (Eds.), *Handbook of early literacy research* (Vol. 3, pp. 295–307). New York, NY: Guilford.

Powell, D. R., Diamond, K. E., Burchinal, M. R., & Koehler, M. J. (2010). Effects of an early literacy PD intervention on Head Start teachers and children. *Journal of Educational Psychology, 102,* 299–312.

Powell, D. R., Diamond, K. E., & Koehler, M. J. (2010). Use of a case-based hypermedia resource in an early literacy coaching intervention with pre-kindergarten teachers. *Topics in Early Childhood Special Education, 29,* 239–249.

Powell, D. R., Steed, E. A., & Diamond, K. E. (2010). Dimensions of literacy coaching with Head Start teachers. *Topics in Early Childhood Special Education, 30,* 148–161.

Raver, C. C., Jones, S. M., Li-Grining, C. P., Metzger, M., Champion, K. M., & Sardin, L. (2008). Improving preschool classroom processes: Preliminary findings from a randomized trial implemented in Head Start settings. *Early Childhood Research Quarterly, 23,* 10–26.

Sheridan, S. M., Edwards, C. P., Marvin, C. A., & Knoche, L. L. (2009). Professional development in early childhood programs: Process issues and research needs. *Early Education and Development, 20,* 377–401.

Vernon-Feagans, L., Gallagher, K., Ginsberg, M., Amendum, S., Kainz, K., ... Burchinal, M. (2010). A diagnostic teaching intervention for classroom teachers: Helping struggling readers in early elementary school. *Learning Disabilities Research and Practice, 25,* 183–194.

Vernon-Feagans, L., Bratsch-Hines, M., Varghese, C., Bean, A., & Hedrick, A. (2015). The targeted reading intervention: Face-to-face vs. webcam literacy coaching for classroom teachers. *Learning Disabilities Research and Practice, 30,* 135–147.

Vescio, V., Ross, D., & Adams, A. (2008). A review of research on the impact of professional learning communities on teaching practice and student learning. *Teaching and Teacher Education, 24,* 80–91.

Wasik, B. A. (2010). What teachers can do to promote preschoolers' vocabulary development: Strategies from an effective language and literacy professional development coaching model. *The Reading Teacher, 63,* 621–633.

Wasik, B. A., Bond, M. A., & Hindman, A. (2006). The effects of a language and literacy intervention on Head Start children and teachers. *Journal of Educational Psychology, 98,* 63–74.

Wasik, B. A., & Hindman, A. H. (2011). Improving vocabulary and pre-literacy skills of at-risk preschoolers through teacher professional development. *Journal of Educational Psychology, 103,* 455–469.

Wayne, A. J., Yoon, K. S., Cronen, S., & Garet, M. S. (2008). Experimenting with teacher professional development: Motives and methods. *Educational Researcher, 37,* 469–479.

Wesley, P. W., & Buysse, V. (2006). Building the evidence base through communities of practice. In V. Buysse & P. W. Wesley (Eds.), *Evidence-based practice in the early childhood field* (pp. 161–194). Washington, DC: Zero to Three Press.

23

Assessing Teacher–Child Relationships

A Cultural Context Perspective

Athanasios Gregoriadis, Vasilis Grammatikopoulos, Nikolaos Tsigilis, and Evridiki Zachopoulou

Introduction

The broad aim of this chapter is to prompt reflection on attachment theory and teacher–child relationship research, on one hand, and the influence of cultural contexts in the development and interpretation of these relationships, on the other hand, by discussing relative conceptual and empirical contributions. In other words, the goal is to tackle the question about the central role sociocultural processes and cultural contexts play in the way adult-child and teacher–child relationships are assessed, perceived and interpreted in different cultural settings.

This chapter is structured in the following way: the first section describes key findings about the significance of teacher–child relationships, especially in early childhood settings. Afterward, we present in brief the most common techniques for assessing early teacher–child relationships. The third section introduces key aspects of attachment theory to demonstrate the central role it holds in conceptualizing teacher–child relationships. The fourth section describes main points of criticism regarding the universality of attachment theory and also summarizes in brief literature findings about the influence, the role and the characteristics of cultural contexts. In addition, the example of the construct of dependency is presented in detail, in order to build the case for the influence of the cultural context, while measuring teacher–child relationships. The last section attempts to present some conclusions and proposals for future research efforts.

Importance of Teacher–child Relationships

A few weeks prior to the preparation of this chapter, one of the authors had an interesting conversation with a kindergarten teacher with more than 30 years of teaching about what matters the most for a child's success in early childhood education. Among other things, the experienced kindergarten teacher mentioned that "I can't imagine a young child doing well in school, without having a good relationship with his/her teacher".

To further support this opinion, there are experts who suggest that a preschooler's relationship with at least one caring adult might be the single most important element for smooth development and academic success (e.g. National Research Council, 2004; Sabol & Pianta, 2012). In several occasions, especially for children who are facing multiple risks in their lives, this adult can be the teacher (Gambone, Klem, & Connell, 2002; Pianta, Hamre, & Stuhlman, 2003).

A positive and warm relationship with a teacher can help the child feel emotionally secure and accepted (e.g. Baker, 2006; Pianta, 1999), and promotes a positive attitude toward exploring the school environment and engaging in classroom's life more actively (Hamre, Hatfield, Pianta, & Jamil, 2014). Especially for the younger children who spend their whole day with one or only a few teachers, a supportive relationship can promote their socio-emotional adjustment in the preschool center (e.g. Glüer & Gregoriadis, 2017; Pianta & Stuhlman, 2004) and their learning (Drugli & Hjemdal, 2013). For example, teacher–child relationships that are characterized by warm and affectionate interactions have been associated with increased task completion (Ahnert, Milatz, Kappler, Schneiderwind, & Fisher, 2013) and improved academic performance (Spilt, Hughes, Wu, & Kwok, 2012).

On the other hand, a negative or less positive teacher–child relationship can affect both children's academic performance and their behavior (Solheim, Berg-Nielsen, & Wichstrøm, 2012). Children whose relationships with their teachers are characterized by low quality often become disengaged or distant from classroom activities and may display negative attitudes toward school (Cadima, Doumen, Verschueren, & Leal, 2015; O'Connor, 2010). High levels of conflict have been shown to associate with antisocial behaviors and social withdrawal (Doumen, Verschueren, Buyse, Germeijs, & Soenens, 2008; Murray, Murray, & Waas, 2008; Rudasill & Rimm-Kaufman, 2009), and with poor performance in language and math skills (Doumen et al., 2008; Hamre & Pianta, 2001; Palermo, Hanish, Martin, Fabes, & Reiser, 2007).

To summarize insofar, during the last two decades a growing body of literature has generated ample and solid evidence about the impact of teacher–child relationships on children's emotional, social, cognitive and academic development especially in early childhood education (e.g. Anders et al., 2012; Curby, Rimm-Kaufman, & Cameron Ponitz, 2009; Hamre et al., 2014; Murray et al., 2008). This well-documented knowledge has led several governments, international organizations and policy-making institutions, such as EU, OECD, UN and UNESCO, to place the quality of teacher–child relationships in the epicenter of their key priority targets and educational policies (European Council, 2009; Eurydice/EACEA, 2014; OECD, 2015). At the same time, the increasing recognition of the importance of teacher–child relationships on children's development, school adjustment and academic trajectory raises the demand and emphasizes the need for even more accurate and precise assessment and measurement of the quality of these relationships (Tsigilis, Gregoriadis, Grammatikopoulos, & Zachopoulou, 2018).

Assessing the Quality of Teacher–child Relationships

Assessing the quality of teacher–child relationships is by nature a demanding effort, due to the fact that it is difficult to best conceptualize and describe these relationships. A wide range of methodological traditions (e.g. person centered, variable centered) and methods have been engaged in this demanding task, but despite the increasing volume of available literature, the well-validated techniques, especially in early childhood education, are still limited.

Up until the late 1990s, the majority of the studies assessing teacher–child relationships were mostly based on teacher-reported measures, parents' perceptions or classroom observations. Especially for studies in early childhood education, researchers usually avoided involving young children either because they considered developmentally inappropriate to ask them about their feelings for a specific relationship, because there seemed to be a consensus that children below six years of age were not reliable sources of information (Harcourt & Einarsdottir, 2011) or simply because there were not a lot of instruments available at the time. However, from a methodological standpoint, the evaluation of teacher–child relationships is much better informed when it includes multiple perspectives and mainly both the insider's and the outsider's view (Pianta, 1999). The beginning of the new century revealed a gradual shift in several researchers' mindsets, by designing developmentally appropriate measures for young children and by also incorporating children's representations in their research designs (Papadopoulou & Gregoriadis, 2017). Thus, new "avenues" of information were starting to open, adding new tools to the effort to fully understand

teacher–child relationships. Below, there is a brief presentation of recent assessment techniques regarding teacher–child relationships in early childhood settings.

Teachers' Perspectives. Addressing young children to examine their representations about their relationship with their teacher is important and can enhance our understanding about these relationships' mechanisms. However, the teacher continues to be the most valuable source of information for researchers, when it comes to assessing teacher–child relationships, due to the asymmetric nature of this relationship. As an adult, the teacher bears a disproportionate responsibility for the well-being of the child and the quality of their interactions (Howes & Hamilton, 1992) and is in possession of extensive information about the child's behavior and performance and the overall picture of their relationship.

The most frequently used and popular methods for assessing teacher–child relationships from the teacher's view include questionnaires or interviews, despite the existing limitations of using self-report measures. Nevertheless, there are not a lot of instruments available for examining teachers' perceptions about their relationships with young children. The few available measures that assess teachers' perceptions about classroom relationships in early childhood education (or at least these that are briefly described here) draw heavily from literature about parenting and attachment theory (Sabol & Pianta, 2012).

One instrument is the Index of Teaching Stress (ITS; Greene, Abidin, & Kmetz, 1997), a teacher-reported scale with 90 items that consists of two subscales, "Teacher's Response to Student Behavior" and "Perceptions of Interactions and Self-Efficacy". Another instrument is the Teacher Relationship Interview (TRI; Pianta, 1997). TRI is a semi-structured interview that aims at eliciting teachers' representations of relationships with children four to six years old. It consists of three dimensions (Content, Affect, Process) and includes 13 questions about a general description of the relationship with a specific child. Teacher Reinforcing Scale (TRS; Hughes, Cavell, & Jackson, 1999) is a brief scale that examines teachers' perceptions and includes nine items. Teacher-Student Relationship Inventory (TSRI; Hughes, Luo, Kwok, & Loyd, 2008) is another measure assessing teachers' perceptions about relationships with young children. It includes 22 items that assess the dimensions of Support, Conflict and Intimacy. Finally, one of the most widely accepted instruments that assess teachers' perceptions of their relationships with individual children is the Student-Teacher Relationship Scale (STRS; Pianta, 2001). It is a 28-item questionnaire based on attachment theory and research on parent-child and teacher–child interactions. The STRS evaluates teachers' relationships with children from preschool to Grade 2 (ages four to eight) and contains three subscales, which in turn assess three relational dimensions: Closeness, Conflict and Dependency.

Children's Perspectives. As was mentioned earlier, until a few years ago there were several doubts from researchers whether young children could describe their emotions and their experiences in a reliable and consistent way (Harcourt & Einarsdottir, 2011). Apart from the children's oral difficulty to describe things accurately, there were also objections about the consistency and stability of preschoolers' perceptions and feelings. However, recent literature has shown that not only children can provide reliable information for many aspects of their social and school life, but also they can offer an alternative "insider" perspective of their relationships (Einarsdottir, 2011; Gregoriadis & Grammatikopoulos, 2014; Vervoort, Doumen, & Verschueren, 2015). In addition, other researchers showed that young children can reliably report their feelings and their experiences (Storksen, Thorsen, Overland, & Brown, 2012), express their moral judgments (Weller & Lagattuna, 2014) and recognize socially unacceptable behaviors (Hennessy, Swords, & Heary, 2008).

Researchers were able to report all these findings due to the "paradigm shift" that occurred the last years regarding the assessment of young children's perceptions. New measures that were more child-friendly were developed aiming at eliciting children's representations about their relationships (Fargas-Malet, McSherry, Larkin, & Robinson, 2010). Studies that included young children as participants used various child-friendly techniques to elicit children's representations like, for example, puppet interviews (Arseneault, Kim-Cohen, Taylor, Caspi, & Moffitt, 2005; Measelle, Ablow, Cowan, & Cowan, 1998), story completion tasks (Laible, Carlo, Torquati, & Ontai, 2004), drawings and photographs (Einarsdottir, 2007, 2011) and visual materials like computer software, applications or illustrated cards (Spilt, Koomen, & Mantzicopoulos, 2010). These techniques allowed researcher to address in a more developmentally, age-appropriate and ethical way children's linguistic and cognitive abilities, to overcome their attention-span difficulties and to examine their thoughts and feelings (Arsenault et al., 2005).

Yet, despite these methodological advances, the available measures for assessing the quality of early teacher–child relationships based on children's perceptions continue to be limited. One instrument addressing young children's perceptions is the Young Children's Appraisals of Teacher Support (Y-CATS; Mantzicopoulos & Neuharth-Pritchett, 2003). Y-CATS consists of three subscales that assess three relational dimensions (Warmth, Conflict and Autonomy) and a total of 31 items. A second measure which assesses young children's feelings about the teacher and attitudes toward the school is the Feelings about School (FAS; Valeski & Stipek, 2001). FAS consists of four subscales (perceived competence about math, perceived competence about literacy, children's attitudes toward school and children's feelings about relationship with the teacher) and a total of 12 items. Another instrument assessing young children's perceptions about their relationship with their teachers is the Children's Feelings about Their Teachers (CFATT; Salmon, 1998).

CFATT is an 18-item scale that explores children's emotions about their teacher. The development of its items was based on attachment theory and the attachment Q-set (Waters & Deane, 1985). CFATT consists of 18 items, eight of which assess the dimension of Closeness and six for the dimension of Conflict between teacher and child. There are also four filler items destined to reduce salience of the questions about teacher–child relationships and check for response bias. Another brief measure is the Teacher Acceptance interview (Harrison, Clarke, & Ungerer, 2007) that consists of five items. Finally, a more recent measure is the Child Appraisal of Relationship with Teacher Scale (CARTS) developed by Vervoort et al. (2015). CARTS is a 16-item instrument that evaluates six- to ten-year-old children's perception about the quality of teacher–child relationships. Apart from the sound psychometric properties, CARTS has the advantage that it assesses the same attachment-based relational dimensions as the STRS does: Closeness, Conflict and Dependency.

Observational Measures

There are several observation measures available for observing teacher–child relationships and for assessing the quality of their interactions in early childhood education settings. In general, these observation measures can be divided into two categories: (a) the first category includes those observation instruments that focus on various dimensions of the early childhood education environment and that also assess some dimensions of teacher–child interactions. These "omnibus observation systems however" do not typically focus solely, "or in a targeted fashion, on teacher–child relationships and are not very comprehensive or detailed with respect to this relationship" (Pianta, 1999, p. 101). (b) The second category includes classroom observation systems that are more relationship focused and contain items and codes for teacher–child interactions.

The Early Childhood Environment Rating Scale: Revised edition (ECERS-R; Harms, Clifford, & Cryer, 2005), and the Early Childhood Environment Rating Scale: Third Edition (ECERS-3; Harms, Clifford, & Cryer, 2015) are observational rating scales that assess the global quality of an early childhood program. The ECERS-R consists of seven subscales (space and furnishings, personal care routines, language-reasoning, activities, interaction, program structure, parents and staff) and 43 items. The ECERS-3 contains 35 items while the "parents & staff" subscale was omitted. Another, well-recognized observation scale is the Classroom Assessment Scoring System (CLASS; Pianta, La Paro, & Hamre, 2008). The CLASS focuses on the quality of classroom interactional processes. It is organized to assess three broad domains of interactions among teacher and children: Emotional Support, Classroom Organization and Instructional Support. These three domains include 11 dimensions that assess the extent to which teachers are effectively supporting children's development, both social and academic. Finally, the Teacher Attachment Q-Set (Howes, Hamilton, &

Matheson, 1994; Howes, Matheson, & Hamilton, 1994) is an adaptation of the Attachment Q-Set (Waters & Deane, 1985) which was originally designed to assess the mother-child attachment organization. The Q-set methodology has been used mostly in early childhood settings. The Teacher Attachment Q-Set consists of 90 descriptions of child behaviors based on attachment theory and reflects different aspects of the child's attachment (Howes et al., 1994).

The existence of validated instruments from all sources (teachers, children, observation, parents) is an important aid for researchers examining teacher–child relationships. Combining teacher-report, child-report and observational methods of assessment can offer a multi-perspective approach than may lead to a more spherical and thorough examination of these relationships.

The quality of teacher–child relationships in early childhood education is defined by a variety of dimensions. Characteristics like age, gender, race and socioeconomic status have their share in explaining the variation in the quality of teacher–child relationships (Jerome, Hamre, & Pianta, 2009). Relationships are multicomponent systems that involve attributes of the participants and reciprocal, bidirectional processes embedded in constant interactions with the early childhood settings and the community (Pianta et al., 2003). In addition to the existing level of complexity, when it comes to assessing teacher–child relationships, one should also consider how structural aspects of early childhood education settings (e.g. quality of environment, child-teacher ratios, teacher training) contribute to the emotional and social quality of interactions among teachers and children (NICHD Early Child Care Research Network, 2002).

How can researchers examine such a multifaceted assortment of teacher, children, classroom, preschool center and community influences? Pianta et al. (2003) suggest that focusing on teacher–child relationships as a key unit of analysis rather than on discrete characteristics of the participants can provide a useful mean to understand processes that have been difficult to study.

Finally, researchers should take under consideration the potential influence of the cultural context in the development, interpretation and quality of teacher–child relationships. The majority of studies in the field, even those who examine how multiple dimensions interact and influence relationships, often omit looking for sociocultural influences (Sabol et al., 2012). However, an increasing number of recent international studies have challenged the cultural universality of specific teacher–child relationship constructs like autonomy, dependency, etc. (e.g. Bao & Lam, 2008; Gregoriadis & Tsigilis, 2008; Joshi, 2009; Mesman, van IJzendoorn, & Sagi-Schwartz, 2016; Solheim et al., 2012; Tsigilis, Gregoriadis, Grammatikopoulos, & Zachopoulou, 2018; Webb & Neuharth-Pritchett, 2011). Thus, an important issue that requires attention is the extent to which sociocultural context can influence the quality of teacher–child relationships in early childhood settings.

Teacher–child Attachment Relationships and Cultural Context

During the past decades, several theoretical models (e.g. ecological culture theory, developmental systems theory, attachment theory) have been developed to conceptualize and analyze teacher–child relationships. However, it is widely accepted by scholars that attachment theory is the most influential conceptual framework for teacher–child relationships that has shaped both academic research and real-life situations (Morelli et al., 2017).

Bowlby (1982) focused his attention on the way emotional bonds between parent and child function and how they are organized. He described attachment as the critical relationship that keeps the primary caregiver close to the young child, and makes the child seek the attention of the caregiver in times of distress. He also emphasized on the regulating mechanism of secure attachment that makes the child feel safe, comforted and accepted (McKenna, 2009). Attachment theory provided the necessary framework to understand that children form working models of attachment based on their early experiences with their primary caregivers and other adults (Ainsworth, Blehar, Waters, & Wall, 1978). In other words, the association the quality of parent-child relationship has with the quality of teacher–child relationship provides strong support to Bowlby's suggestion that the experiences and representations of the mother-child relationship are subsequently carried forward and affect future relationships with other caregivers/adults, like the teacher (Sabol & Pianta, 2012; Sroufe, 1983).

Upon entering an early childhood setting, a young child acquires new relational experiences, feelings and beliefs with the teacher. Constructing differentiated models of relationships with the teacher compared to those with their parents may offer unique opportunities to buffer previous poor attachment histories (Sabol & Pianta, 2012; Verschueren & Koomen, 2012). Relational models are open systems: the acquired experiences, while defining, are open to change based on new relational schemata (Morelli et al., 2017; Pianta et al., 2003; Verschueren & Koomen, 2012). Recent studies have shown that supportive and high-quality teacher–child relationships can support children who are at risk for behavior problems, reduce the intensity of the problems, and in some occasions even intercept completely children's unfortunate attachment histories (e.g. Baker, 2006; Ladd & Burgess, 2001). For example, Berry and O'Connor (2010) reported that teacher-perceived warmth and closeness are associated with improved social skills, and O'Connor and McCartney (2007) that a supportive teacher–child relationship facilitates social-emotional success in school.

In addition, the main constructs used to define children's attachment quality contributed also in identifying the basic components and dimensions required for a high-quality teacher–child relationship (Pianta et al., 2003). Verschueren and Koomen (2012) suggest that the affective quality of teacher–child relationships in early childhood and early primary settings is basically defined in terms of the relational dimensions of Closeness, Conflict and Dependency.

Criticism to Attachment Theory and the Role of Cultural Context

Despite the wide acceptance of attachment theory and how it conceptualizes teacher–child relationships, there have been various critics in the literature. The most widespread, perhaps, criticism of attachment-based studies is the one that refers to "cultural blindness" to alternative interpretations or conceptions of basic relational constructs (Mesman et al., 2016; Rothbaum, Weisz, Pott, Miyake, & Morelli, 2001; van IJzendoorn & Sagi, 2001). This criticism was based mainly to the way the concept of attachment and relational security is perceived in the Japanese culture, where the idea of "*amae*" (Doi, 1992) is the most prominent construct in describing and interpreting adult-child and family relationships (Bornstein, Cote, Haynes, Suwalsky, & Bakeman, 2012; Emde et al., 1992; Mesman et al., 2016; van IJzendoorn & Sagi, 2001). "*Amae*" basically focuses on relational dependence, the desire for interpersonal closeness and relying on others implying a sense of psychological dependence, but also being a concept that is not necessarily perceived always as a positive characteristic or procedure (see for details Behrens, 2004; Doi, 1989; Morelli et al., 2017).

Another point of criticism for attachment theory was that it is basically a theory of independence focusing its attention on autonomy, self-reliance and exploration (Harwood, 2006; McKenna, 2009; Rothbaum et al., 2001) without taking under consideration the perspectives of non-Western societies. Adults and children behaviors in different ethnic contexts may not correspond to the attachment relationships categories that are based on assessments and principles of Western societies(McKenna, 2009).

In their seminal review regarding the cross-cultural patterns of attachment, Mesman et al. (2016) have provided descriptions of attachment relationships in different geographical areas (e.g. Africa, Asia) and different types of societies (e.g. from modern urban societies to hunter-gatherer societies with seminomadic groups and fluid social structure). In their analysis of cross-cultural attachment research, they describe the "importance of including variations in the socioeconomic context within countries, so that attachment patterns can be elucidated from both a cultural and a resource perspective" (p. 809).

However, defining the term "culture" in cross-cultural studies is by nature a demanding task. It is very difficult to determine and describe which parameters should be used in order to include or exclude populations in a specific cultural framework or group (Carlson & Harwood, 2003) and to map how the value system and attitudes of a specific cultural context is influencing relationships. For example, it is common practice in humanistic studies to perceive Western (Caucasian European or American) populations as one distinct culture, even though it is a heterogeneous group (McKenna, 2009).

When researchers conceptualize and examine attachment relationships based on the value system and attitudes of their own culture, to different culture groups it is not methodologically sound to conclude about the universality of a model or a behavior. For example, in some occasions of cross-cultural attachment studies, the variations found in attachment classifications or associations among attachment categories were interpreted as deviating from the hypothesized norm or unclassified cases (Bornstein et al., 2012; van IJzendoorn & Sagi, 2001). But such an approach hinders the danger of overlooking valuable information regarding the way adult-child relationships are perceived and interpreted in the non-Western context (Morelli et al., 2017).

So there seem to be several arguments, evidence and a logical basis to challenge the universality hypothesis of attachment relationships, or at least that which will not take under serious consideration the influence of the cultural context factor in the way attachment relationships are formed. But how does the sociocultural context influence the way teacher-child relationships are developed and perceived? As is mentioned earlier, young children's internal working models of relationships with their primary caregiver and other caregivers, and their individual characteristics constitute a solid base for developing attachment bonds and relationships with adults. Yet, it is together with the cultural context in which they function that jointly influence development and the way relationships are perceived and experienced (Ladd, 1996). For example, Van IJzendoorn, Sagi and Lambermon (1992) reported lower percentages of avoidant attachment in a group of Chinese studies compared to those of avoidance found in Western studies. However, Mesman et al. (2016) mention that the lower rates of avoidant attachment in Chinese studies agree with those of other studies in non-Western cultures, thus reflecting the cultural influence in parent-child relationships.

A possible explanation of the way the cultural context influences how attachment relationships are perceived can be attributed to the intergenerational transmission of attachment (Hesse, 2016). As was mentioned earlier, the sociocultural framework can partially define the way basic constructs of attachment are viewed and interpreted. This influence is then transferred to the daily parenting practices of adults. It is possible that parents' experiences and mental representations of their past attachment relationships influence their parenting style and behavior and in turn the quality of their children's attachment (Bowlby, 1982). To further support this line of reasoning, Van IJzendoorn (1995) found a concordance rate of about 75% in Western societies between parents' mental representations of attachment and their children's attachment category.

Similar to this rationalization, other researchers (Verschueren, Doumen, & Buyse, 2012) described the existence of intervening mechanisms that might explain the sociocultural impact on attachment relationships and adversely on teacher–child relationship quality. Attachment researchers have proposed pathways or mechanisms explaining the link between the quality of adult-child attachment relationships and the way a sociocultural framework interprets specific relational constructs (Thompson, 2008; Verschueren et al.,

2012). For example, a core element of attachment theory is the development of an attachment pattern that allows the child to explore the environment using the secure base as a resort in time of distress. But if the social conditions and the cultural niche are not normal (e.g. in time of war, in time of economic crisis) then the avoidant attachment pattern may become normative (Simpson & Belsky, 2016), thus showing the potential impact the context can have.

From the many dimensions a culture or a cultural group can be categorized into, the most fundamental is perhaps the individualism-collectivism typology (Hofstede, 1980; Oyserman, Coon, & Kemmelmeier, 2002; Triandis, 1989). Individualism and collectivism are described by Triandis (1995) as cultural syndromes that reflect values, beliefs and shared attitudes organized around a central theme. These cultural syndromes are found among individuals who speak a particular language and live during the same historical period in a specified geographic area.

The term "individualism" refers to a social pattern that consists of "loosely linked individuals who view themselves as independent of collectives" (Triandis, 1995, p. 2). In individualistic cultures typical attributes are autonomy, competition, achievement orientation and self-reliance. Individualists are described as having control over and taking responsibility for their actions (Green, Deschamps, & Paez, 2005), usually placing their personal goals on top of the goals of the collective, especially if they don't match, and dropping a relationship if the costs are greater than the enjoyments. In sum, personal freedom from the social pressure and the weight of conformity is of highest value for individualism (Oyserman et al., 2012; Triandis, 1989).

The term "collectivism" refers to a social pattern that includes "closely linked individuals who see themselves as parts of one or more collectives (family, co-workers, tribe, nation); are primarily motivated by the norms of, and duties imposed by, those collectives" (Triandis, 1995, 2). Collectivism is mainly associated with an emphasis on behavior determined by social norms, a sense of duty toward one's group, interdependence with others and conformity with group norms. Collectivists usually maintain their relationships unless the relationship is extremely unpleasant or dysfunctional.

To examine anew how do cultural contexts influence teacher–child attachment relationships in terms of individualism and collectivism, there are various factors that contribute to how a social pattern like collectivism or individualism operate. There are various factors like social conditions, geographic region, religion and language that reflect specific "subjective cultures" (Triandis, 1995, p. 6). These subjective cultures are better described as common attitudes, shared values, norms and beliers among speakers of a specific language. The individuals who live in a specific region and share a common language usually "imbibe" and internalize a common cultural system.

However, this does not mean that all the people of a specific cultural context behave in the same manner. Triandis (1989) concludes that tendencies toward collectivism and individualism exist within every individual and every society. Within each country there are people who behave more like individualists or like collectivists. In every cultural context there are individuals who are allocentric – who act and behave much like collectivists – and individuals who are idiocentric – who act and behave like individualists (Oyserman et al., 2012; Triandis, 1989). Also, people may be individualist and collectivist at the same time (Green et al., 2005). But the general social pattern shows that the majority of the population of a specific cultural context usually behaves in an analogous way (Triandis, 1995), thus allowing for cross-cultural examinations.

In addition, literature has suggested that there are various in-between types of cultural contexts-societies and not only individualistic and collectivistic. For example, Cozma (2011) describes a typology of four constrained cultural context combinations: horizontal individualism, vertical individualism, horizontal collectivism and vertical collectivism. So generally speaking, collectivistic and individualistic cultures include different social behaviors. These differences are usually more clearly visible regarding human relationships and especially adult-child relationships in different cultural settings (e.g. Japan and the United States) (Green et al., 2005).

The next section aims at emphasizing how these differences are displayed in teacher–child relationships in early childhood settings and more specifically it will present the example of the construct of dependency and dependent relationships.

The Example of the Construct of Dependency. As was mentioned earlier, in the last years the affective quality of early teacher–child relationships is mainly assessed in terms of the relationship dimensions of closeness, conflict and dependency (Verschueren & Koomen, 2012). These dimensions have most frequently been assessed with the Student-Teacher Relationship Scale (STRS; Pianta, 2001).

The STRS is one of the most widely used instruments to evaluate teacher's perceptions of their relationships with individual children. The STRS is a 28-item questionnaire based on attachment theory and research on parent-child and teacher–child relationships (Pianta, 1999). It assesses teachers' perceptions of their relationships with individual children and their perceptions about children's behavior and feelings toward them (Pianta & Nimetz, 1991). The STRS contains three subscales which assess the relational dimensions of closeness, conflict and dependency. The closeness subscale evaluates positive affect and the degree of personal communication of teachers and children. The conflict subscale includes items that show that the teacher and the child are frequently at odds with each other. The dependency subscale measures the level of inappropriate developmental dependency a child might have with his/her teacher (Pianta, 1999).

Research on teacher–child relationships using the STRS has been applied in various countries with different cultural settings (e.g. Germany, Greece, Italy, Norway, Spain, Sweden, Turkey, the United States) and mixed findings have been reported regarding its psychometric properties, especially for the dimension of dependency (Tsigilis, Gregoriadis, & Grammatikopoulos, 2018).

Beyazkurk and Kesner (2005) found that Turkish students described being closer to and more dependent on their teachers than did their colleagues in the United States. They attributed these differences in closeness and dependency dimensions to the different underlying family structures existing in the two cultures and to the more collectivistic orientation of the Turkish society (Oyserman et al., 2012).

In the same period, a Greek study (Gregoriadis, 2005) reported a significant positive association between closeness and dependency. This finding showed that Greek kindergarten teachers, in contrast with most of their colleagues in other Western countries, didn't consider dependent behaviors and dependency as a negative construct. Four subsequent studies in the Greek early childhood settings, with the last one in a nationally representative sample, showed again significant moderate to small positive association between closeness and dependency (Gregoriadis & Grammatikopoulos, 2014; Gregoriadis & Tsigilis, 2008; Tsigilis, Gregoriadis, & Grammatikopoulos, 2018; Tsigilis, Gregoriadis, Grammatikopoulos, & Zachopoulou, 2018). These repeated findings, which do not agree with findings from other countries like Germany, Italy, the Netherlands, and the United States (e.g. Fraire, Longobardi, Prino, Sclavo, & Settani, 2013; Glüer & Gregoriadis, 2017; Koomen, Verschueren, van Schooten, Jak, & Pianta, 2012; Milatz, Glüer, Harwardt-Heinecke, Kappler, & Ahnert, 2014; Webb & Neuharth-Pritchett, 2011), supported the claim that the cultural context could be influencing the way dependency is perceived, interpreted and measured in teacher–child relationships (Tsigilis, Gregoriadis, Grammatikopoulos, & Zachopoulou, 2018).

Apart from these findings, other researchers have described cultural differences in teacher–child relationships (Sroufe, 2005) and have challenged the universality of constructs like autonomy or dependency (e.g. Webb & Neuharth-Pritchett, 2011). In a Norwegian study, Solheim et al. (2012) mention that "the meaning and interpretation of a dependent relationship may be subject to cultural differences" (p. 206). Gregoriadis and Tsigilis (2008) have attributed the cultural differences found in the way dependency is perceived to the differences between individualistic and collectivistic or semi-collectivistic (like Greece) cultures. For a more collectivistic society like Greece, interdependence and reliance on others, as well as dependency are not necessary considered as negative traits or behaviors. The authors of that study conclude by suggesting further examination of the issue.

Conclusion

High-quality teacher–child relationships are the cornerstone of smooth development and school success, even under conditions of risk (Pianta, 1999). Secure attachment relationships between a teacher and a child can even compensate for previous poor attachment histories. The wide volume of relevant literature offers ample evidence that a core element of attachment theory, like the need of the child to become securely attached, is universal (Mesman et al., 2016). However, the same authors acknowledge that even though secure attachment seems to be the norm across cultures, there are variations in the rates reported in Western and non-Western contexts, which in turn emphasize the significance of socioeconomic conditions for parenting patterns.

For instance, even characteristics that have recently been found to play an important role in the quality of parent-child relationship, like the primary caregiver sensitivity (e.g. Sabol & Pianta, 2012), can display variations according to the way each cultural setting translates this behavior. The behavior and the parenting patterns of caregivers surely depend on specific arrangements that are common in a specific cultural context. In some cultures, the appropriate responding to infants' cry or call usually is stroking and comforting the child, while in other cultures it is to smile at the infant or talk to it (Kartner, Keller, & Yovsi, 2010). Moreover, there are studies showing that even infants' manners to express attachment vary depending on cultural norms (Marvin, VanDevender, Iwanaga, LeVine, & LeVine, 1977). So, can we claim with certainty that mothers from a semi-nomadic hunter-gatherer society in Africa, a traditional middle-class Japanese family, a Greek rural family and an upper-class American family all interpret, perceive and display sensitivity in the same way? Another example to support this argument refers to studies in Israeli kibbutz, where contextual factors like communal sleeping seemed to override the influence of parents' attachment representations and parenting behaviors (e.g. Oppenheim, Koren-Karie, & Sagi-Schwartz, 2007; Sagi, Van IJzendoorn, Aviezer, Donnell, & Mayseless, 1994). Such a finding could highlight the limits of a context-free, cultural-free universal mode of attachment relationships.

To conclude, in the current chapter we propose that an alternative conception of assessing teacher–child attachment relationships needs to be adopted. As Morelli et al. (2017) suggest, the central role of sociocultural processes and structures in the relationships and the attachments children develop need to be emphasized. Moreover, Bornstein et al. (2012) support that even different caregiver behaviors can have the same function in different cultural contexts.

Narrow-focused examinations of teacher–child relationships based on one cultural perspective are less likely to yield a comprehensive understanding of the dynamic, multilevel interactions of young children with their teachers. It is our firm belief that a greater understanding of the developmental significance of the influence of cultural settings on teacher–child relationships can result in an increased understanding of the mechanism of creating secure teacher–child relationships in early school settings across and within cultures.

One proposal for researchers could be to adopt a culturally inclusive set of attitudes/items, when examining culturally appropriate attachment-based adult-child relationships. It is significant for academic researchers to develop culturally sensitive research designs by understanding how different cultural practices and values fit into the field of teacher–child relationships. Promoting studies or interventions based on one cultural approach (usually the Western perspective) can lead to overlooking valuable information about teacher–child relationships. Unless certain cultural issues regarding the assessment of teacher–child relationships are better examined and understood, there is a risk that research findings will underserve populations with different cultural backgrounds, over-identify poor attachment adult-child relationships and misinterpret attachment relationships of children's at-risk populations due to cultural beliefs and practices (e.g. Berg, 2003; McKenna, 2009; Melendez, 2005). This is a pressing issue for research practices both for across and within cultures.

In terms of future research efforts, there are still several areas of uncharted water that needs to be thoroughly examined. First, regarding the assessment field, researchers should examine if the available teacher–child assessment measures are valid in all cultures. For example, the current literature could use a valid and reliable measure for assessing dependency and dependent behaviors without cultural limitations. Second, a vital priority would be to expand the limited cross-cultural database in order to comprehend and map in more detail how attachment relationships and non-Western cultural contexts intertwine. Third, another point of interest for researchers could also be to adopt rigorous research designs that would obtain less correlational and more longitudinal and experimental data in order to establish causality. Finally, drawing from the example of social epidemiology, future studies should examine the effects of socio-structural factors on social experiences and adult-child relationships (Honzo, 2004). Children's academic trajectories are the result of complex interactions among various characteristics (e.g. children growing up in poverty) (Mckinnon, Friedman-Krauss, Roy, & Raver, 2018) or school-related variables (e.g. subjective attitude toward school) and it is essential to take into account the broader social context in which they are developing (Kim, 2015).

As a final message, it is our belief that attachment and teacher–child theorists and researchers must widen their perspectives to a more pluralistic and flexible view of attachment relationships – one that will manage to acclimatize the various cultural influences and the diversity that exists in the daily lives and interactions of children.

References

Ahnert, L., Milatz, A., Kappler, G., Schneiderwind, J., & Fischer, R. (2013). The impact of teacher–child relationships on child cognitive performance as explored by a priming paradigm. *Developmental Psychology, 49*, 554–567. doi:10.1037/a0031283

Ainsworth, M. S., Blehar, M. C., Waters, E., & Wall, S. (1978). *Patterns of attachment: A psychological study of the strange situation.* Hillsdale, NJ: Erlbaum.

Anders, Y., Roßbach, H.-G., Weinert, S., Ebert, S., Kuger, S., Lehrl, S., & von Maurice, J. (2012). Home and preschool learning environments and their relations to the development of early numeracy skills. *Early Childhood Research Quarterly, 27*, 231–244. doi:10.1016/j.ecresq.2011.08.003

Arseneault, L., Kim-Cohen, J., Taylor, A., Caspi, A., & Moffitt, T. E. (2005). Psychometric evaluation of 5- and 7-year-old children's self-reports of conduct problems. *Journal of Abnormal Child Psychology, 33*(5), 537–550.

Baker, J. A. (2006). Contributions of teacher–child relationships to positive school 16 adjustment during elementary school. *Journal of School Psychology, 44*, 211–229.

Bao, X.-H., & Lam, S.-F. (2008). Who makes the choice? Rethinking the role of autonomy and relatedness in Chinese children's motivation. *Child Development, 79*(2), 269–283.

Behrens, K. (2004). A multifaceted view of the concept of amae: Reconsidering the indigenous Japanese concept of relatedness. *Human Development, 47*, 1–27.

Berg, A. (2003). Beyond the dyad: Parent-infant psychotherapy in a multicultural society – Reflections from a South African perspective. *Infant Mental Health Journal, 24*(3), 265–277.

Berry, D., & O'Connor, E. (2010). Behavioral risk, teacher–child relationships, and social skill development across middle childhood: A child-by-environment analysis of change. *Journal of Applied Developmental Psychology, 31*, 1–14.

Beyazkurk, D., & Kesner, J. E. (2005). Teacher–child relationships in Turkish and United States schools: A cross-cultural study. *International Education Journal, 6*(5), 547–554. Retrieved from https://eric.ed.gov/?id=EJ855008

Bornstein, M. H., Cote, L. R., Haynes, O. M., Suwalsky, J. T. D., & Bakeman, R. (2012). Modalities of infant–mother interaction in Japanese, Japanese American immigrant, and European American dyads. *Child Development, 83*, 2073–2088.

Bowlby, J. (1982). *Attachment and loss: Vol. 1. attachment.* New York, NY: Basic Books. (Original work published 1969).

Cadima, J., Doumen, S., Verschueren, K., & Leal, T. (2015). Examining teacher–child relationship quality across two Countries. *Educational Psychology: An International Journal of Experimental Educational Psychology, 35*(8), 946–962. doi:10.1080/01443410.2013.864754

Carlson, V. J., & Harwood, R. L. (2003). Attachment, culture, and the care-giving system: The cultural patterning of everyday experiences among Anglo and Puerto Rican mother-infant pairs. *Infant Mental Health Journal, 24*(1), 53–73.

Cozma, I. (2011). How are individualism and collectivism measured? *Romanian Journal of Applied Psychology, 13*(1), 11–17.

Curby, T. W., Rimm-Kaufman, S. E., & Cameron Ponitz, C. (2009). Teacher–child interactions and children's achievement trajectories across kindergarten and first grade. *Journal of Educational Psychology, 101*, 912–925.

Doi, T. (1989). The concept of amae and its psychoanalytic implications. *International Review of Psychoanalysis, 16*, 349–354.

Doi, T. (1992). On the concept of amae. *Infant Mental Health Journal, 13*, 7–11.Doumen, S., Verschueren, K., Buyse, E., Germeijs, V., Luyckx, K., & Soenens, B. (2008). Reciprocal relations between teacher–child conflict and aggressive behavior in kindergarten: A three-wave longitudinal study. *Journal of Clinical Child and Adolescent Psychology, 37*, 588–599. doi:10.1080/15374410802148079

Drugli, M. B., & Hjemdal, O. (2013). Factor structure of the student–teacher relationship scale for Norwegian school age children explored with confirmatory factor analysis. *Scandinavian Journal of Educational Research, 57*, 457–466. doi:10.1080/00313831.2012.656697

Einarsdottir, J. (2007). Research with children: Methodological and ethical challenges. *European Early Childhood Education Research Journal, 15*(2), 197–211.

Einarsdottir, J. (2011). Reconstructing playschool experiences. *European Early Childhood Education Research Journal, 19*(3), 387–402.

Emde, R. N., Plomin, R., Robinson, J., Corley, R., DeFries, J., Fulker, D. W., Reznick, S., Campos, J., Kagan, J., & Zahn-Waxler, C. (1992). Temperament, emotion and cognition at fourteen months: The MacArthur longitudinal twin study. *Child Development, 63*(6), 1437–1455.

European Council. (2009). *Council conclusions of 12 May 2009 on a strategic framework for European cooperation in education and training-ET2020*

(OJ C119 of 28.5.2009, pp. 2–10). Retrieved from http://eur-lex.europa. eu/legalcontent/EN/TXT/?uri=URISERV%3Aef0016

Eurydice/EACEA. (2014). *Eurydice policy brief: Early childhood education and care.* European Commission: Education, Audiovisual and Culture Executive Agency. Retrieved from http://eacea.ec.europa.eu/education/ eurydice/ documents/thematic_reports/Eurydice_Policy_Brief_ECEC_ EN.pdf; doi:102797/52737

Fargas-Malet, M., McSherry, D., Larkin, E., & Robinson, C. (2010). Research with children: Methodological issues and innovative techniques. *Journal of Early Childhood Research, 8*(2), 175–192.

Fraire, M., Longobardi, C., Prino, L. E., Sclavo, E., & Settanni, M. (2013). Examining the student-teacher relationship scale in the Italian context: A factorial validity study. *Electronic Journal of Research in Educational Psychology, 11*, 851–882. doi:10.14204/ejrep.31.13068

Gambone, M. A., Klem, A. M., & Connell, J. P. (2002). *Finding out what matters for youth: Testing key links in a community action framework for youth development.* Philadelphia, PA: Youth Development Strategies, Inc. and Institute for Research and Reform in Education.

Glüer, M., & Gregoriadis, A. (2017). Quality of teacher–child relationship and preschoolers' pro-social behaviour in German kindergartens. *Education 3–13, 45*(5), 558–571. doi:10.1080/03004279.2016.1140802

Green, E. G. T., Deschamps, J.-C., & Paez, D. (2005). Variation of individualism and collectivism within and between 20 countries. *Journal of Cross-Cultural Psychology, 36*(3), 321–339. doi:10.1177/ 0022022104273654

Greene, R. W., Abidin, R. R., & Kmetz, C. (1997). The index of teaching stress: A measure of student-teacher compatibility. *Journal of School Psychology, 35*(3), 239–259.

Gregoriadis, A. (2005). Interpersonal relationships in kindergarten: Teachers' and children's perceptions about their relationships (Unpublished Doctoral Dissertation). Aristotle University of Thessaloniki, Thessaloniki, Greece [in Greek].

Gregoriadis, A., & Grammatikopoulos, V. (2014). Teacher–child relationship quality in early childhood education: The importance of relationship patterns. *Early Child Development and Care, 184*(3), 386–402.

Gregoriadis, A., & Tsigilis, N. (2008). Applicability of the student–teacher relationship scale (STRS) in the Greek educational setting. *Journal of Psychoeducational Assessment, 26,* 108–120. doi:10.1177/ 0734282907306894

Hamre, B. K., Hatfield, B., Pianta, R. C., & Jamil, F. (2014). Evidence for general and domain-specific elements of teacher–child interactions: Associations with preschool children's development. *Child Development, 85,* 1257–1274.

Hamre, B. K., & Pianta, R. C. (2001). Early teacher–child relationships and the trajectory of children's school outcomes through eighth grade. *Child Development, 72,* 625–638. doi:10.1111/1467–8624.00301

Harcourt, D., & Einarsdottir, J. (2011). Introducing children's perspectives and participation in research. *European Early Childhood Education Research Journal, 3*(19), 301–307.

Harrison, L. J., Clarke, L., & Ungerer, J. A. (2007). Children's drawings provide a new perspective on teachers' child relationship quality and school adjustment. *Early Childhood Research Quarterly, 22*(1), 55–71.

Harms, T., Clifford, R. M., & Cryer, D. (2005). *The early childhood environment rating scale: Revised edition.* New York, NY: Teachers College Press.

Harms, T., Clifford, R., & Cryer, D. (2015). *Early childhood environment rating scale* (3rd ed.). New York, NY: Teachers College Press.

Harwood, R. L. (2006). Multidimensional culture and the search for universals. *Human Development, 49,* 122–128.

Hennessy, E., Swords, L., & Heary, C. (2008). Children's understanding of psychological problems displayed by their peers: A review of the literature. *Child: Care, Health and Development, 34*(1), 4–9.

Hesse, E. (2016). The adult attachment interview: Protocol, method of analysis, and empirical studies. In J. Cassidy & P. R. Shaver (Eds.), *Handbook of attachment: Theory, research, and clinical applications* (3rd ed., pp. 552–598). New York, NY: The Guilford Press.

Hofstede, G. (1980). *Culture's consequences: International differences in work-related values.* London, UK: Sage.

Honzo, K. (2004). Social epidemiology: Definition, history, and research examples. *Environmental Health and Preventive Medicine, 9,* 193–199.

Howes, C., & Hamilton, C. E. (1992). Children's relationships with caregivers: Mothers and child-care teachers. *Child Development, 63,* 859–866.

Howes, C., Hamilton, C. E., & Matheson, C. C. (1994). Children's relationships with peers: Differential associations with aspects of the teacher–child relationship. *Child Development, 65*(1), 253–263.

Howes, C., Matheson, C. C., & Hamilton, C. E. (1994). Maternal, teacher, and child care history correlates of children's relationships with peers. *Child Development, 65*(1), 264–273.

Hughes, J. N., Cavell, T. A., & Jackson, T. (1999). Influence of the teacher-student relationship on childhood conduct problems: A prospective study. *Journal of Clinical Child Psychology, 28*(2), 173–184.

Hughes, J. N., Luo, W., Kwok, O. M., & Loyd, L. K. (2008). Teacher-student support, effortful engagement, and achievement: A 3-year longitudinal study. *Journal of Educational Psychology, 100*(1), 1–14.

Jerome, E. M., Hamre, B. K., & Pianta, R. C. (2009). Teacher–child relationships from kindergarten to sixth grade: Early childhood predictors of teacher-perceived conflict and closeness. *Social Development, 18*(4), 915–945.

Joshi, A. (2009). What do teacher–child interactions in early childhood classrooms in India look like? Teachers' and parents' perspectives. *Early Child Development and Care, 1,* 1–19.

Kartner, J., Keller, H., & Yovsi, R. D. (2010). Mother–infant interaction during the first 3 months: The emergence of culture-specific contingency patterns. *Child Development, 81,* 540–554.

Kim, H. H.-S. (2015). School context, friendship ties and adolescent mental health: A multilevel analysis of the Korean Youth Panel Survey (KYPS). *Social Science & Medicine, 145,* 209–216

Koomen, H. M. Y., Verschueren, K., van Schooten, E., Jak, S., & Pianta, R. C. (2012). Validating the student–teacher relationship scale: Testing factor structure and measurement invariance across child gender and age in a Dutch sample. *Journal of School Psychology, 50,* 215–234. doi:10.1016/j.jsp.2011.09.001

Ladd, G. W. (1996). Shifting ecologies during the 5–7 year period: Predicting children's school adjustment during the transition to grade school. In A. Sameroff & M. Haith (Eds.), *Reason and responsibility: The passage through childhood* (pp. 363–386). Chicago, IL: University of Chicago Press.

Ladd, G. W., & Burgess, K. B. (2001). Do relational risk and protective factors moderate the links between childhood aggression and early psychological and school adjustment? *Child Development, 72,* 1579–1601.

Laible, D., Carlo, G., Torquatti, J., & Ontai, L. (2004). Children's perceptions of family relationships as assessed in a doll story completion task: Links to parenting, social competence, and externalizing behavior. *Social Development, 13*(4), 551–569.

Mantzicopoulos, P., & Neuharth-Pritchett, S. (2003). Development and validation of a measure to assess Head Start children's appraisals of teacher support. *Journal of School Psychology, 41*(6), 431–451.

Marvin, R. S., VanDevender, T. L., Iwanaga, M. I., LeVine, S., & LeVine, R. A. (1977). Infant–caregiver attachment among the Hausa of Nigeria. In H. Mc-Gurk (Ed.), *Ecological factors in human development* (pp. 247–259). Amsterdam, The Netherlands: North-Holland.

McKenna, Y. E. (2009). *Cultural influences on attachment behaviors* (Unpublished Master Thesis). University of Lethbridge, Faculty of Education, Lethbridge, Alberta.

McKinnon, R. D., Friedman-Krauss, A., Roy, A. L., & Raver, C. C. (2018). Teacher–child relationships in the context of poverty: The role of frequent school mobility. *Journal of Children and Poverty, 24*(1), 25–46. doi:10.1080/10796126.2018.1434761

Measelle, J. R., Ablow, J. C., Cowan, P. A., & Cowan, C. P. (1998). Assessing young children's views of their academic, social, and emotional lives: An evaluation of the self-perception scales of the Berkeley puppet interview. *Child Development, 69*(6), 1556–1576.

Melendez, L. (2005). Parental beliefs and practice around early self-regulation: The impact of culture and immigration. *Infants & Young Children, 18*(2), 136–146.

Mesman, J., van IJzendoorn, M. H., & Sagi-Schwartz, A. (2016). Cross-cultural patterns of attachment: Universal and contextual dimensions. In J. Cassidy & P. R. Shaver (Eds.), *Handbook of attachment: Theory, research, and clinical applications* (3rd ed., pp. 790–815). New York, NY: The Guilford Press.

Milatz, A., Glüer, M., Harwardt-Heinecke, E., Kappler, G., & Ahnert, L. (2014). The student–teacher relationship scale revisited: Testing factorial structure, measurement invariance and validity criteria in German-speaking samples. *Early Childhood Research Quarterly, 29*, 357–368.

Morelli, G. A., Chaudhary, N., Gotlieb, A., Keller, H., Murray, M., Quinn, N., … Vicedo, M. (2017). Taking culture seriously: A pluralistic approach to attachment. In H. Keller & K. A. Bard (Eds.), *The cultural nature of attachment: Contextualizing relationships and development* (pp. 139–170). Boston, MA: The MIT Press.

Murray, C., Murray, K. M., & Waas, G. A. (2008). Child and teacher reports of teacher–student relationships: Concordance of perspectives and associations with school adjustment in urban kindergarten classrooms. *Journal of Applied Developmental Psychology, 29*, 49–61. doi:10.1016/j.appdev.2007.10.006

National Research Council. (2004). *Engaging schools: Fostering high-school students' motivation to learn*. Washington, DC: National Academy Press.

NICHD Early Child Care Research Network. (2002). The relation of global first grade classroom environment to structural classroom features, teacher, and student behaviors. *Elementary School Journal, 102*, 367–387.

O'Connor, E. (2010). Teacher–child relationships as dynamic systems. *Journal of School Psychology, 48*, 187–218. doi:10.1016/j.jsp.2010.01.001

O'Connor, E., & McCartney, K. (2007). Examining teacher–child relationships and achievement as part of an ecological model of development. *American Educational Research Journal, 44*, 40–369. doi:10.3102/0002831207302172

OECD. (2015). *Starting strong IV: Monitoring quality in early childhood education and care*. Paris, France: OECD Publishing. doi:10.1787/9789264233515-en

Oppenheim, D., Koren-Karie, N., & Sagi-Schwartz, A. (2007). Emotional dialogues between mothers and children at 4.5 and 7.5 years: Relations with children's attachment at 1 year. *Child Development, 78*, 38–52.

Oyserman, D., Coon, H. M., & Kemmelmeier, M. (2002). Rethinking individualism and collectivism: Evaluation of theoretical assumptions and meta-analyses. *Psychological Bulletin, 128*, 3–72.

Palermo, F., Hanish, L. D., Martin, C. L., Fabes, R. A., & Reiser, M. (2007). Preschoolers' academic readiness: What role does the teacher–child relationship play? *Early Childhood Research Quarterly, 22*, 407–422. doi:10.1016/j.ecresq.2007.04.002

Papadopoulou, E., & Gregoriadis, A. (2017). Young children's perceptions of the quality of teacher–child interactions and school engagement in Greek kindergartens. *Journal of Early Childhood Research, 15*(3), 323–335. doi:10.1177/1476718X16656212

Pianta, R. C. (1997). *Teacher relationship interview*. Charlottesville: School of Education, University of Virginia.

Pianta, R. C. (1999). *Enhancing relationships between children and teachers*. Washington, DC: American Psychological Association.

Pianta, R. C. (2001). *STRS, student–teacher relationship scale, professional manual*. Lutz, Germany: Psychological Assessment Resources.

Pianta, R. C., Hamre, B., & Stuhlman, M. (2003). Relationships between teachers and children. In W. M. Reynolds, G. E. Miller, & I. B. Weiner (Eds.), *Handbook of psychology: Volume 7 – Educational psychology* (pp. 199–234). Hoboken, NJ: Wiley.

Pianta, R. C., La Paro, K., & Hamre, B. K. (2008). *Classroom assessment scoring system manual: Pre-Kindergarten*. Baltimore, MD: Brookes.

Pianta, R. C., & Nimetz, S. L. (1991). Relationships between teachers and children: Associations with behaviour at home and in the classroom. *Journal of Applied Developmental Psychology, 12*, 307–322.

Pianta, R. C., & Stuhlman, M. (2004). Teacher–child relationships and children's success in the first years of school. *School Psychology Review, 33*, 444–458.

Rothbaum, F., Weisz, J., Pott, M., Miyake, K., & Morelli, G. (2001). Deeper into attachment and culture. *American Psychologist, 56*(10), 827–829. doi: 10.1037/0003-066X.56.10.827

Rudasill, K. M., & Rimm-Kaufman, S. E. (2009). Teacher–child relationship quality: The roles of child temperament and teacher–child interactions. *Early Childhood Research Quarterly, 24*, 107–120. doi:10.1016/j.ecresq.2008.12.003

Sabol, T. J., & Pianta, R. C. (2012). Recent trends in research on teacher–child relationships. *Attachment & Human Development, 14*, 213–231. doi:10.1080/14616734.2012.672262

Sagi, A., Van IJzendoorn, M. H., Aviezer, O., Donnell, F., & Mayseless, O. (1994). Sleeping out of home in a kibbutz communal arrangement: It makes a difference for infant–mother attachment. *Child Development, 65*, 992–1004.

Salmon, J. (1998). *Kindergarten teachers' and children's perceptions of the teacher–child relationship* (Unpublished Doctoral Dissertation). University of Virginia, Charlottesville, Virginia, VA.

Simpson, J. A., & Belsky, J. (2016). Attachment theory within a modern evolutionary framework. In J. Cassidy & P. R. Shaver (Eds.), *Handbook of attachment: Theory, research, and clinical applications* (3rd ed., pp. 91–116). New York, NY: The Guilford Press.

Solheim, E., Berg-Nielsen, T. S., & Wichstrøm, L. (2012). The three dimensions of the Student-Teacher Relationship Scale: CFA validation in a preschool sample. *Journal of Psychoeducational Assessment, 30*(3), 250–263. doi:10.1177/0734282911423356

Spilt, J. L., Hughes, J. N., Wu, J. Y., & Kwok, O.-M. (2012). Dynamics of teacher-student relationships: Stability and change across elementary school and the influence on children's academic success. *Child Development, 83*(4), 1180–1195.

Spilt, J. L., Koomen, H. M. Y., & Mantzicopoulos, P. Y. (2010). Young children's perceptions of teacher–child relationships: an evaluation of two instruments and the role of child gender in kindergarten. *Journal of Applied Developmental Psychology, 31*(6), 428–438.

Sroufe, L. A. (1983). Infant–caregiver attachment and patterns of adaptation in preschool: The roots of maladaptation and competence. In M. Perlmutter (Ed.), *In The Minnesota symposium in child psychology* (Vol. 16, Development and Policy Concerning Children with Special Needs, pp. 41–83). HillsDale, NJ: Lawrence Erlbaum.

Sroufe, L. A. (2005). Attachment and development: A prospective, longitudinal study from birth to adulthood. *Attachment & Human Development, 7*(4), 349–367. doi:10.1080/14616730500365928

Storksen, I., Thorsen, A. A., Overland, K., & Brown, S. R. (2012). Experiences of daycare children of divorce. *Early Child Development and Care, 182*(7), 807–825.

Thompson, R. A. (2008). Early attachment and later development: Reframing the questions. In J. Cassidy & P. R. Shaver (Eds.), *Handbook of attachment. Theory, research, and clinical applications* (2nd ed., pp. 348–365). New York, NY: The Guilford Press.

Triandis, H. C. (1989). The self and social behavior in differing cultural contexts. *Psychological Review, 96*, 506–520.

Triandis, H. C. (1995). *Individualism and collectivism*. Boulder, CO: Westview.

Tsigilis, N., Gregoriadis, A., & Grammatikopoulos, V. (2018). Evaluating the student–teacher relationship scale in the Greek educational setting: An item parcelling perspective. *Research Papers in Education, 33*(4), 414–626. doi:10.1080/02671522.2017.1353675

Tsigilis, N., Gregoriadis, A., Grammatikopoulos, V., & Zachopoulou, E. (2018). Applying exploratory structural equation modeling to examine the student-teacher relationship scale in a representative Greek sample. *Frontiers in Psychology, 9*, Article 733. doi:10.3389/fpsyg.2018.00733

Valeski, T. N., & Stipek, D. J. (2001). Young children's feelings about school. *Child Development, 72*, 1198–1213. doi:10.1111/1467-8624.00342

van IJzendoorn, M. (1995). Adult attachment representations, parental responsiveness, and infant attachment: A meta-analysis on the predictive validity of the adult attachment interview. *Psychological Bulletin, 117*(3), 387–403.

Van IJzendoorn, M. H., & Sagi, A. (2001). Cultural blindness or selective inattention? *American Psychologist, 56*, 824–825.

van IJzendoorn, M. H., Sagi, A., & Lambermon, M. W. E. (1992). The multiple caretaker paradox: Data from Holland and Israel. *New Directions for Child Development, 1992*(57), 5–24.

Verschueren, K., Doumen, S., & Buyse, E. (2012). Relationships with mother, teacher, and peers: Unique and joint effects on young children's self-concept. *Attachment & Human Development, 14*, 233–248.

Verschueren, K., & Koomen, H. M. Y. (2012). Teacher–child relationships from an attachment perspective. *Attachment & Human Development, 14*(3), 205–211. doi:10.1080/14616734.2012.672260

Vervoort, E., Doumen, S., & Verschueren, K. (2015). Children's appraisal of their relationship with the teacher: Preliminary evidence for construct validity. *European Journal of Developmental Psychology, 12*(2), 243–260.

Waters, E., & Deane, K. E. (1985). Defining and assessing individual differences in attachment relationships: Q-methodology and the organization of behaviour in infancy and early childhood. *Monographs of the Society for Research in Child Development, 50*(1/2), 41–65.

Webb, M.-Y. L., & Neuharth-Pritchett, S. (2011). Examining factorial validity and measurement invariance of the student–teacher relationship scale. *Early Childhood Research Quarterly, 26*, 205–215.

Weller, D., & Lagattuta, K. H. (2014). Children's judgments about prosocial decisions and emotions: Gender of the helper and recipient matters. *Child Development, 85*(5), 2011–2028.

24

New Information on Evaluating the Quality of Early Childhood Education Programs

Dale C. Farran and Kimberly T. Nesbitt

In 2017, about 69% of the four-year-old children in the United States were enrolled in some form of early childhood education center-based program, almost the same percentage as in 2000 (IES, NCES, 2019). Center-based care includes publicly funded programs such as Head Start, state- and/or Title I-funded prekindergarten (pre-k), and non-profit and for-profit child care centers. The primary shift from 2000 has been in where four year olds are receiving care. According to the 2018 report from the National Institute for Educational Research (NIEER), many states are now educating a large portion of their four year olds in state-funded pre-k programs (Friedman-Kraus et al., 2018). This relatively recent extension of public education into the preschool years makes early childhood settings the first introduction for many children to the world of more formal learning in a group setting. These early experiences are critical for establishing learning and social-emotional dispositions that may affect children's interactions with students and teachers in classrooms for years to come. Over the years, however, there have been competing perspectives for the purpose of early childhood education and the relative importance of "care" versus academic learning for young children.

Historically, the purpose of caring for young children was to allow impoverished parents to work: "Day care was founded, therefore, as a necessary social service to alleviate the child care problems of parents who had to work and to prevent young children from wandering the street" (Scarr & Weinberg, 1986, p. 1141). In World War II, the federal government invested heavily in childcare with the Lanham Act to allow mothers to work for the war effort (Herbst, 2017). "The Act funded programs that served both white and African American children, increasing employment for women of both races" (p. 5, Johnson-Staub, 2017). Immediately after World War II, working mothers were replaced by returning veterans and childcare centers almost immediately closed. Subsequently, mothers began entering the labor force at higher rates to preserve their families' middle-level incomes and therefore they needed care for their children.

Concurrent with this surge of mothers entering the labor force was a growing concern for the quality of the alternative care the children received. In 1980 a group of professionals from different agencies and universities developed and proposed a national set of standards for childcare that would cover educational aspects, as well as the health and safety issues, states were ordinarily concerned with (Scarr & Weinberg, 1986). These standards were never adopted, and since then there has not been a uniform, agreed upon set of standards for the care of children before formal schooling. While all states have regulations concerning health and safety and these sometimes also include educational requirements for teachers and regulations about teacher-child ratios and group size, many states have developed their own standards, reviewed in the section on Quality Improvement Ratings Systems (QRIS).

In addition to concerns about the quality of child care, many believe in the importance of intervening early to prevent the pernicious effects of poverty environments (see Parker, Workman, & Atchison, 2016). Thus, another motivation for programs for young children prior to formal school entry has been compensatory education. Public funding for compensatory early childhood education began with Head Start in 1965 (Farran, 2007; Scarr & Weinberg, 1986) and continued with the 1987 amendment to the Elementary and Secondary Education Act that allowed Title I funds to be used for whole school program improvement, ushering in the creation of Title I-funded prekindergarten classes in many school districts (Ewing & Matthews, 2005).

There are primary differences between early childhood programs developed to care for children and support families and those programs with a compensatory focus. A major difference is in the hours of care each covers. Head Start, Title I, and most state-funded programs provide five to six hours of care a day, nine months of the year, or what is essentially a school year calendar. A second difference is that these compensatory programs are primarily meant to prepare children for school entry, and thus they serve four year olds, or sometimes threes and fours. Third, these programs have various admission requirements with most being means tested. Parents have to be at or below a certain income level to be eligible. Finally, compensatory programs are often administered by different agencies from those responsible for community childcare. The different purposes, programs, and agencies involved in early childhood education have exacerbated the difficulty in finding a common quality measure that is suitable for all types of program. The search for quality measures that can serve all programs is explored in the next section.

Definitions of Quality by Programmatic Purpose

The purpose of community child care programs is to care for children whose parents work, or to care for children whose parents are themselves in school or whose parents want their children to have a socialization experience before formal school. The quality concerns related to this purpose center on ensuring safe and appropriate environments for children who are young and vulnerable and therefore dependent on adults to create their environments. Moreover, when other adults, outside of "kith and kin," are responsible for children, they may be unknown to the parents, at least initially. Thus, regulatory agencies become involved. Childcare centers are supposed to be licensed to meet a state's health and safety regulations and are inspected by agencies tasked with those regulations, usually Departments of Health and Human Services.

In contrast, programs whose primary purpose is compensatory education may be quite separate from programs for which caring is primary. Head Start, for example, began with the mission to compensate for deprivations children from low-income families were presumed to experience in their home environments. In 2007, that mission was affirmed more specifically: Head Start's purpose is to "promote the school readiness of low-income children by enhancing their cognitive, social and emotional development" (https://eclkc.ohs.acf.hhs.gov/policy/head-start-act/sec-636-statement-purpose). Because of its history, the Office of Head Start, within the Administration for Children and Families (ACF), US Department of Health and Human Services (DHHS), administers Head Start programs. This administrative structure links Head Start to other childcare programs within a state and means that Head Start classrooms are usually under similar regulatory obligations.

Prekindergarten programs funded by Title I or by state funds, on the other hand, are often located in public school buildings or connected to Local Education Agencies (LEAs). Historically these programs have been resistant to coming under the supervision of the state departments of Health and Human Services and daycare regulations. A proposal during the George W. Bush administration, for example, argued for moving Head Start under the Department of Education (DOE), thereby combining all programs for young children that had an academic focus (Bumiller, 2003). Such a move, strongly resisted, would have made it more likely that a similar quality evaluation measure could have been developed for all programs with a compensatory focus.

Confusion on the focus and administrative home for programs intended to prepare children for school and primarily serving children from low-income families continues. In December 2014, then Secretary of Education Arnie Duncan announced that $226 million had been awarded to 18 states under the Preschool Development Grants (PDG) program. The goal for these programs was to close the "opportunity gap" (https://www2.ed.gov/programs/preschooldevelopmentgrants/index.html). Programs funded through this means were required to be administered by the State Education Agency and were housed primarily in public schools. In 2015, however, the Every Student Succeeds Act (ESSA) established a new PDG program to be under the auspices of *both* the US DOE and the ACF in DHHS (First Five Years Fund, 2018). The lead department for states would no longer be the state's education agency, but instead the state's health and human services department in partnership with education. The purpose of the program broadened to cover birth through age five services in the state. Issues of quality and how to measure it remain, however; it will have to be determined if the new preschool development programs must meet each state's child care requirements.

Outcomes Related to Differences in Programmatic Goals

Measures of quality logically should be related to the types of outcomes desired; those desired outcomes, as we have seen, differ for child care and compensatory programs. In the general literature, quality is described in terms relating to excellence, value, conformance to specifications, and/or meeting customer expectations (Reeves & Bednar, 1994). Since the expectations for these two types of programs are different, it has been difficult to find a single measure to capture the quality of both.

For the caring mission, the emphasis has been more on *preventing* the presumed deleterious consequences of poor-quality care. The original version of the frequently used Early Childhood Environmental Rating Scale (ECERS) was the Day Care Environmental Rating Scale (Harms & Clifford, 1983, p. 264) and, as the name implies, it was intended to be used in daycare settings. The assumption behind the ECERS then and in its present form is that by assuring that child care environments are safe, organized, material-rich,, and filled with positive teacher-child interactions, children should develop typically. From the beginning, efforts were made to link ECERS scores to cognitive and academic outcomes as well as social-emotional ones (see McCartney, Scarr, Phillips, Grajek, & Schwartz, 1982), again with the primary goal of assuring that typical development was not endangered by poor care.

For compensatory education programs, however, the goal is for development to be accelerated, improved over what would have occurred without the program experience. In the United States, these programs were specifically established to prevent school failure for children from poor families. School readiness for kindergarten is the immediate goal, and the long-term expectation is that enhancing early skills will ultimately close the achievement gap for poor children. Therefore, determining which proximal outcomes at the end of prekindergarten will be associated with long-term school success is important.

One source of useful guidance are studies that have longitudinally examined early skills and their predictive relations to later achievement. A heavily cited analysis of data from six major longitudinal studies from the United States, Canada, and Great Britain found that early measures of children's math skills predicted later reading and math (Duncan et al., 2007). Indeed, early measures of math were somewhat more predictive of later reading achievement than were early measures of reading skills. These findings have been confirmed by analyses from additional longitudinal studies (Hooper, Roberts, Sideris, Burchinal, & Zeisel, 2010; Watts, Duncan, Siegler, & Davis-Kean, 2014). In addition, Duncan et al. (2007) found measures of cognitive self-regulation (i.e., attention) to be a significant correlate of later achievement; they did not find early social-emotional skills to have any relation to later academic achievement. In a more recent effort to examine the relations between skills at kindergarten entry and later achievement in grades 3 and 5, Pace, Alper, Burchinal, Golinkoff, and Hirsh-Pasek (2018) found that the most important early skill for predicting later achievement, especially in reading, was language development.

The conclusions from these studies are fairly consistent: the best skills to effect in compensatory prekindergarten programs are those related to math, reading/language, and attention/cognitive self-regulation in that order. It must be acknowledged that the types of skills currently being measured and included in longitudinal studies limit our conclusions about important school entry skills. There may well be more foundational, underlying competencies for which the field has no assessments. However, given the state of our knowledge at this time, these outcomes can provide a lens through which to judge measures of quality; the utility of a quality measure for classrooms with a compensatory mission should be judged by its association with gains for children in the three areas of math, language, and attention.

The most comprehensive attempt to regulate early childcare quality has recently been the development of Quality Rating Improvement Systems (QRISs). Many states have such systems and they typically include the primary quality assessment measures used for both caring and compensatory education programs. QRIS work will be described next.

Quality Rating and Improvement Systems

QRIS Background

Childcare centers are supposed to be licensed to meet health and safety regulations and are inspected by those agencies. A growing concern with the inability of these standards to capture actual quality coupled with the fact that federal funds through subsidies were likely supporting poor-quality programs led to the development in many states of QRISs (Cannon, Zellman, Karoly, & Schwartz, 2017). The development of QRISs began in the late 1990s; as of 2017, 49 states have a QRIS either implemented, piloted, or planned.

> The basic QRIS approach is to establish quality standards at successively higher levels, measure the quality level that programs reach given those standards, provide supports and financial incentives for programs to achieve and sustain higher levels of quality, and disseminate objective information about quality that parents can use in selecting an ECE [early childhood education] program.
>
> (Cannon et al., 2017, pp. 1–2)

> QRIS[s] are founded on the assumption that the quality of early childhood programs can be measured, that the results from the measurements are credible, and that differences between programs that are measured through the QRIS are accurate and associated with meaningful outcomes.
>
> (Hestenes et al., 2015, p. 200)

Through a quality rating process, the QRIS categorizes programs based on a multidimensional set of components including teacher education, program policies, curriculum, and performance on rating measures of classroom quality resulting in overall scores from poor to excellent. These quality scores are also used by the policy world in decisions about program funding and childcare reform. Currently, many states assess childcare quality to determine the amount of money that is allocated to childcare programs in state support for the care of children from low-income families ("tiered reimbursement"). This process effectively ties a program's score to, among other things, the salary of the program's staff. This type of real-world consequence in the use of a quality measure lends urgency to a determination of the validity of such measures.

QRISs were developed in individual states primarily by local early childhood experts relying on their beliefs about what constitutes best practices (Cannon et al., 2017); they have not been evidence based. Beginning with the 2008–2011 Quality Rating Systems project, the Administration for Children and Families (ACF) of the US Department of Health and Human Services (DHHS) created the QRIS Compendium (now the Quality Compendium, https://qualitycompendium.org) to provide states a location where QRISs could be compared. Components of state QRISs are documented in a QRIS Compendium 2016 Fact Sheet available from the site.

In 2016, 41 states had fully completed QRISs. All states include requirements for staff qualifications, typically an associate's or bachelor's degree. Nearly all states include indicators of program administration, including written operating policies, and most include health and safety evaluations focused on physical activity, nutrition, and staff first aid certification. More than half also include requirements for group size and staff-child ratios. Many states further include an environmental rating scale (ERS) assessment such as the ECERS or the Classroom Assessment Scoring System (CLASS) although the ways they are implemented vary, with some states using self assessment and others using independent observations of randomly selected classrooms. For some states, like North Carolina, the use of an ERS (ECERS or other version of environmental rating scales such as the Infant Toddler Environmental Rating Scale) is optional but provides extra points on the quality indicator scale (Hestenes et al., 2015).

QRIS Evaluations

The motivation for states to create a QRIS is to improve outcomes for children through improving classroom and program practices (Hestenes et al., 2015). But that goal makes a rigorous evaluation of the effectiveness of any QRIS very difficult to enact. Enrollment in childcare programs is not on a random basis; parents choose the care situations for their children. Their choices are often based on what they can afford to pay and location. It is almost impossible to disentangle the effects of parent selection from the effects of the quality of the program, hence potentially confounding effects of the program with family characteristics such as socioeconomic status. Thus, none of the validation studies has been a true experiment. Cannon et al. (2017) report that as of 2017 there were 12 published validation studies covering QRISs in 11 states. Evidence from these studies was contradictory and no firm conclusions about the utility of QRISs could be drawn. Focusing on a somewhat more rigorous design, Herbst (2018) found three longitudinal studies of QRIS that included controls for family and community characteristics; only one found a positive association between program quality and child outcomes and that only modestly on literacy.

Another problem is that the differences in quality between one ERS rating level and the next are small and may not, in fact, be linear (Hestenes et al., 2015; Votruba-Drzal & Miller, 2016), bringing into question their utility for QRISs that classify programs into star levels or other hierarchies. Another issue is the reliability of observers. Louisiana, for example, bases its entire QRIS on ratings from the Classroom Assessment Scoring System (CLASS; Pianta, La Paro, & Hamre, 2008). Yet in a recent study, independent researchers and local observers rating the same classrooms placed almost half into different QRIS categories, a finding with significant policy implications (Vitiello, Bassok, Hamre, Player, & Williford, 2018).

Although QRISs began with the goal of improving child outcomes, without systematic measures of children's development, the focus shifted to quality-related goals such as greater professionalization of the early childhood care and education workforce and higher wages and reduced turnover of the staff. Many states now provide technical assistance to child care programs to help them improve their quality and thus their QRIS rating. However, there appears to be little consistency in what should be covered in the professional development related to quality. A recent review of 62 studies

examining professional development activities and/or technical assistance in states found that the most frequently used indicators of the quality of the training were the providers' perceptions of the value of the activity and the number of times it occurred (Smith, Dong, Stephens, & Tout, 2017). Three-fourths of the studies did not measure the content covered in the professional development nor whether changes in classroom practices resulted from the training.

One intermediate goal of QRIS ratings is to improve quality by increasing salaries to attract more highly skilled workers and to reduce staff turnover in child care settings. Herbst (2018) conducted an ambitious study of the effects of QRIS on workforce salaries and turnover. He compared a large number of databases in states that varied in the degree of participation in QRIS between the 1990s and 2012. The institution of QRIS in a state increased the number of both newly hired and separated child care workers, thus leaving the overall supply of child care workers unaffected. Less skilled and less experienced workers had both rising compensation and more turnover. Those systems that included a wage compensation program had lower staff turnover and increased salaries substantially more than states with a QRIS that did not have a wage incentive program. Herbst concluded that financial incentives may be essential if QRISs are to be effective in attracting and retaining higher skilled workers; the downside is that his data also suggest these changes may attempt to improve quality at the expense of pricing low-income families out of the market.

The following sections examine the primary components of QRIS systems. These same components have been used to examine the quality of prekindergarten programs administered by state and local education agencies and are included in state policies regulating the programs. Typically, prekindergarten programs are not included in a state's QRIS system, though there are some exceptions (e.g., Louisiana). However, many of the QRIS components have been examined in all the various settings serving young children, including childcare, Head Start, and prekindergarten programs. We begin with structural features and then examine the research on the observational components.

Structural Features as Measures of Quality

Structural features are prominent in requirements for programs with a childcare mission as well as being important for programs with a compensatory education mission. Until recently they were the key components of the National Institute for Education Research (NIEER) Benchmarks being used as the guidelines for states establishing prekindergarten programs for children from low-income families including class sizes and ratios, teacher qualifications, and program hours (Friedman-Krauss et al., 2018). One reason these structural characteristics are appealing is that they are easy to regulate; 62% of QRIS systems include those requirements (QRIS Compendium Fact Sheet, 2016). Many state-funded prekindergarten programs also include policies for class size, ratios, and teacher qualifications.

An ambitious and comprehensive study of the relation between structural characteristics and child outcomes was reported by Mashburn et al. (2008). Mashburn et al. created individual measures of the NIEER Benchmarks for the 671 classrooms included in the study. Because these were state-funded prekindergarten programs, many of the benchmarks were met by 70% or more of the programs; for example, most tended to have teachers with bachelor's degrees, to have class sizes of 20 or under, and to have student-teacher ratios of 10:1. They served meals and provided family supports (though the latter is not always specified in detail). They were somewhat less likely to use a comprehensive curriculum, offer health services, or require their assistant teachers to have a Child Development Associate credential.

Associations were examined between gains in language, literacy, and math measures and the benchmarks, collectively and individually. The total NIEER benchmark score was related to none of the outcomes. Similarly, none of the individual benchmarks predicted gains on the outcomes with the exception of a negative relation between serving meals and gains in receptive vocabulary, likely a function of the fact that programs serving poorer families are required to serve meals. These findings were duplicated in a follow-up publication (Sabol, Hong, Pianta, & Burchinal, 2013).

The relation between teacher credentials and child outcomes has been the focus of intense study over the past few years. The same Mashburn et al. (2008) dataset provided more detailed data on teacher preparation (years of teaching, highest degree earned, whether the teacher had a bachelor's degree or licensure) and found no effects on children's gains in language and literacy for any of the teacher preparation measures (Early et al., 2006). The only outcome for which teachers' education had a positive effect was a small one on math skills. Exploring the issue of teacher credentialing further and in samples with much greater variation in teachers' educational status is an analysis of data from seven major studies, the majority of which involved prekindergarten or Head Start programs (Early et al., 2007). The overwhelming conclusion across these seven studies is that neither the presence nor absence of a bachelor's degree, having a teaching license, or majoring in early childhood education was related to children's gains on either language/literacy or math measures. A recent thorough investigation of credentialing and early childhood education coursework for teachers conducted by Lin and Magnuson (2018) found negative effects on classroom quality and child outcomes only for teachers who had a high school degree and no early childhood education coursework. However, they found no variation in quality linked to the higher end of preparation (i.e., having a bachelor's degree and taking many early childhood education courses).

The surprising lack of relation between structural measures of quality, especially teacher credentials, requires careful reflection. A belief in the importance of both structural characteristics and teacher credentials has been strong at least since the publication of *Children at the Center* (Roupp, Travers, Glantz, & Coelen, 1979); the requirement that teachers have a bachelor's degree is the primary recommendation of the National Research Council's 2001 report on preschool education. One possible explanation for the lack of relations is two-pronged – children are not making a great deal of gain in these prekindergarten programs, especially in the areas of language and math (Howes et al., 2008; U.S. Department of Health and Human Services, January, 2010), and teachers are not observed delivering very high-quality instruction in their classrooms (e.g., Farran, 2016; Farran, Meador, Christopher, Nesbitt, & Bilbrey, 2017; Justice, Mashburn, Hamre, & Pianta, 2008). It appears that having a bachelor's degree is not sufficient to prepare teachers to be effective in classrooms where the purpose is to work specifically with children whose school entry skills are low.

Teaching young children who are developmentally quite different from each other has many challenges (see Farran, 2005); working with children who are enrolling in formal education for the first time and who are there because they do not possess school entry skills is the most formidable challenge of all. It is not clear where teachers would have been expected to learn these unusual, multidimensional instructional skills, nor has there been sufficient research to determine if these skills could be obtained through professional development activities, especially since individualization is hardly addressed in professional development (see Smith et al., 2017).

The following sections explore in some depth the two primary environmental rating systems included in QRISs as well as in various evaluations of publicly funded programs, the ECERS and CLASS.

Environmental Rating Scales as Measures of Quality

Early Childhood Environmental Rating Scale (ECERS)

Background. The ECERS (Harms & Clifford, 1980) – and its subsequent versions (ECERS-R, ECERS-3) – is perhaps the most widely used measure to evaluate program quality (Brunsek et al., 2017; Sakai, Whitebook, Wishard, & Howes, 2003). ECERS and ECERS-R focus on the materials available in the classroom and the way the day is structured, with some attention to interactions. Primary guidance for the original ECERS came from Thelma Harms. Describing the evolution of the scale (Frank Porter Graham, 1999, p. 11), Harms indicated that based on her 20 years' experience as a teacher and classroom observer she concluded that

> in order to provide care and education that will permit children to experience a high quality of life while helping them develop their abilities, a program must provide for the three basic needs of children:
>
> - Protection of their health and safety
> - Building positive relationships
> - Opportunities for stimulation and learning from experience

The definition of quality adopted by the ECERS-R is thus consistent with both the NAEYC [National Association for the Education of Young Children] program accreditation standards as well as with the Child Development Associate requirements that focuses on the professional knowledge teachers need to facilitate high quality classrooms.

(Setdoji, Schaack, & Le, 2018, p. 159)

The ECERS-R contains 43 items in seven subscales (Space and Furnishings, Personal Care Routines, Language-Reasoning, Activities, Interaction, Program Structure, and Parents and Staff). Each item is rated from 1 (inadequate) to 7 (excellent) and is behaviorally anchored, based on indicators that must be checked under the 1, 3, 5, and 7 ratings. Overall, there are 470 indicators within the scale. Concerns have been raised about how these indicators are arranged and problems with the "stop rule" which requires an observer to give the rating at the first place where all indicators are not checked (Gordon et al., 2015). Thus, quality indicators may be achieved by programs at higher rating levels but are not credited. The ECERS-R requires a classroom observation that lasts two to three hours and includes an interview with a classroom teacher, often to complete ratings of practices not observed during the visit. Scores of up to 36 of the 43 items are often scored from the teacher interview, which has a strong effect on achieving higher ratings (Hestenes et al., 2019), especially when the observation period is as short as two hours (Hofer, 2010).

Although there are subscales and 43 items, a number of psychometric analyses suggest that the ECERS and ECERS-R are unidimensional measures of quality, while others have reported a two-factor solution of (1) appropriate activities and materials, and (2) learning interactions (Setdoji et al., 2018). No studies have validated the seven different subscales.

The ECERS-3 published in 2015 is a substantial revision (Harms, Clifford, & Cryer, 2004). At the higher rating levels, much more attention has been given to the instructional behaviors of teachers (Early, Sideris, Neitzel, LaForett, & Nehler, 2018). In addition, the teacher interview has been eliminated in the ECERS-3, and the requirement for direct observation increased (Hestenes et al., 2019). The ECERS-R is currently the observation tool most often included in the QRISs developed by states (Harms, Clifford, & Cryer, 2015). It is less often used in observations of prekindergarten programs administered by state and local education agencies, especially if the classrooms are housed in public elementary schools. The following sections examine the connection between ECERS scores and various important domains of children's development. Because some of the studies are older, the scale will be referred to generally as "ECERS" even though most of the studies have involved the ECERS-R.

ECERS and Child Outcomes. One outcome of interest is improving social-emotional development in young children, or at least preventing negative behaviors. A direct linear relationship between ECERS scores and social-emotional outcomes has not been demonstrated across studies as shown in a recent systematic review and meta-analysis (Brunsek et al., 2017). In the studies reviewed, social skills were primarily assessed through teacher ratings; ratings also included problem behaviors and "approaches to learning" (self-regulation skills in the classroom). There were virtually no associations between ECERS total or subscale scores and any of these social outcomes.

In terms of academic outcomes, Brunsek et al. found somewhat higher associations for math outcomes with ECERS though the direction of effects was not consistent with some studies citing positive associations while others were negative. Positive relations between language outcomes and ECERS-R scores were found but only in a single dataset. Small effect sizes on academic gains – if any effects are found – are usual in studies with the ECERS (Gordon, Fujimoto, Kaestner, Korenman, & Abner, 2013; Weiland, Ulvestad, Sachs, & Yoshikawa, 2013), including the newest version of the scale, the ECERS-3 (Early et al., 2018).

One issue of interest is whether instead of a linear effect there might be a threshold effect for ECERS. Perhaps a minimum threshold of quality must be reached and once reached, further improvements will not be related to outcomes. Setodji et al. (2018) used data from the Early Childhood Longitudinal Study-Birth Cohort sample to examine effects on a social-emotional composite score. They found a threshold effect of 3.4 for ECERS (out of a 7-point scale) such that between an ECERS score of 1.0 and 3.4 there were significant associations between the score and social-emotional outcomes. Beyond a score of 3.4 there was no further effect. This work has important implications for where states set their cut points on the ECERS in their QRISs. Making setting cut points more difficult, Setdoji et al. report a different and higher threshold effect in states like Colorado that have had many years of experience with the ECERS.

The predictive utility of these global measures has been relatively unsuccessful in predicting academic outcomes for children. While one could argue that the original intention of child care programs was not to improve these types of outcomes, measures like the ECERS have been used for just this sort of investigation. In studies that do not use *gains* in children's achievement, there is a strong relationship between child care quality scores and children's skill levels (e.g., Hestenes et al., 2015). This association is not surprising given that parents are the ones who choose and must pay for the programs. Few studies have examined change over time to relate the amount of change in children's skills to measures of child care quality.

As noted, child care is not an experience that lends itself easily to random assignment. When random assignment and group design are not utilized, however, differences in study groups, both before and after attrition, and differences in the experiences of those participants in study classrooms can be great. Descriptive studies of this type have been more common than experimental ones in the area of child care because in early childhood research it is really impossible to experiment with variations in the quality of care young children receive.

The following section provides information about another environmental rating scale, one that is increasingly being included in QRISs and also applied to programs administered by the public schools.

Classroom Assessment Scoring System

Background. Environmental rating scales commonly focus on the structural features of the furnishings, materials, and activities available to children as well as the proximal process characteristics of the social and instructional aspects of children's interactions with teachers, peers, and materials (e.g., Howes et al., 2008, Pianta et al., 2008). Initially, aspects of structural quality were presupposed to be the distal aspects of quality that lead to higher process quality and subsequently to better child outcomes (Vandell et al., 2010) and as we indicated, these features are easily regulated. More recent attention has turned to classroom *processes*. The predominant observational measure to assess the effectiveness of interactions among teachers and students in prekindergarten classrooms is the Classroom Assessment Scoring System (CLASS; Pianta et al., 2008). The ACF Office of Head Start is required by legislation to utilize the CLASS as a component of the Head Start program monitoring system, and currently, 19 states include the CLASS as a component of their QRIS (16 states use the CLASS in combination with the ECERS-R).

The CLASS rating system is structured differently from the ECERS; observers watch interactions within the classroom for cycles of 15–20 minutes and then give ratings of 1–7 on 10 scales grouped into three dimensions. The CLASS ratings can also be completed from videotapes. In either case, total observation time can range from two hours to all day. As with the ECERS, the focus of the observation is on the classroom as a whole, and the CLASS concentrates particularly on the behavior of the teacher.[1]

The three CLASS dimensions include Emotional Support (ES; comprised of positive climate, negative climate, teacher sensitivity, and regard for student perspectives scales), Classroom Organization (CO; behavior management, productivity, and instructional learning formats scales), and Instructional Supports (IS; concept development, quality of feedback, and language modeling scales). Mirroring the confusion with ECERS cut scores, states utilizing the CLASS as part of their QRIS vary widely in how they use the dimension scores to assign ratings, including cutoff values. For example, as of November 2017, for their highest Level 5-star rating, Nevada requires ES scores above 6, CO scores above 5.5, and IS scores above 3.5 and has established minimum CLASS scores for Levels 3 and 4, while Oregon requires ES, CO, and IS scores all above 5 to receive their highest rating and does not use CLASS scores for lower ratings (The Build Initiative & Child Trends, 2017). There is no empirical evidence for any cut score.

CLASS and Child Outcomes. To justify the use of a given observational measure of early childhood care and education quality, it is vital that scores on the measure are associated with intended positive outcomes, including aspects of language, cognition, and social-emotional functioning. A recent meta-analysis of associations between the CLASS and child social-emotional outcomes found significant but small relations between CO scores and children's inhibitory ability and between IS scores and social skills (Perlman et al., 2016). No associations were found between the three CLASS dimensions and children's receptive vocabulary, letter and sight word identification, and math skills.

Data available from several individual longitudinal studies of prekindergarten quality have found small and mixed effects for CLASS quality on language and literacy gains over the prekindergarten year. Several publications using data from the National Center for Early Development and Learning (NCEDL) and the State-Wide Early Education Program (SWEEP) 11-state evaluation of prekindergarten programs (Early et al., 2005) found modest to no associations between the Emotional Support (ES) and Instructional Support (IS) dimensions and the PPVT (Burchinal et al., 2008; Burchinal, Vandergrift, Pianta, & Mashburn, 2009; Howes et al., 2008; Mashburn et al., 2008), with the most recent analysis by Keys et al. (2013) indicating a significant but small effect for IS (1 point increase in IS ratings associated with a 0.04 SD increase on the PPVT).[2]

More recent studies of the relation between CLASS and language outcomes have yielded inconsistent findings. Hamre, Hatfield, Pianta, and Jamil (2014) reported positive effects of IS but not for ES and Classroom Organization (CO) on vocabulary (PPVT and Woodcock-Johnson Picture Vocabulary composite). On the other hand, others have found no relation between gains in PPVT and all three dimensions of the CLASS (Weiland et al., 2013).

The CLASS dimensions were also examined for their effects on gains in literacy skills, including letter and sight word naming and writing, rhyming, print awareness, and oral language skills (Anderson & Phillips, 2017; Gosse, McGinty, Mashburn, Hoffman, & Pianta, 2014; Guo, Pianta, Justice, & Kaderavek, 2010; Howes et al., 2008). There were similar, small effects (Cohens *ds* < 0.10 *SD*) on these outcomes for IS and ES for most of the outcomes; the exception was gains in Woodcock-Johnson Spelling scores where there was no relation (Anderson & Phillips, 2017). Overall the gains in children's skills were small in these studies, although there was some classroom variation in how much children gained.

As an alternative to using the ratings as linear dimensions, the CLASS observations have been explored through the creation of profiles of teachers (LoCasale-Crouch et al., 2007). Profile 1 was labeled the "highest quality" – the teachers in this cluster had the highest CLASS scores on ES; these classrooms also had the highest ECERS scores. The profile with the lowest CLASS scores across all the dimensions was Profile 5. Profile 5 also had the lowest ECERS scores, included the most Head Start classrooms, and enrolled the highest proportion of poor and minority children. In a follow-up study, Curby and colleagues examined the fall and spring academic gains for children who were taught by teachers in each of the profiles (Curby et al., 2009). Children taught by Profile 2 teachers made significantly greater gains on the PPVT than children taught by teachers in Profile 5 ($d = 0.21$). Teachers in Profile 2 were not as warm or emotionally supportive as teachers in Profile 1, but they had the highest scores on the CLASS scale Concept Development of any of the profile clusters. Concept Development is one of the items scored under IS on the CLASS.

Despite the fact that Duncan et al. (2007) and Hooper et al. (2010) listed math skills as important skills to affect in prekindergarten programs (followed by reading and attention), little is known about what facilitates the development of skills in this area for young children. Unlike language and literacy skills where there are multiple measures, one primary test of skill development dominates the research done in early math, the Woodcock-Johnson III Applied Problems subscale. Anderson and Phillips (2017) examined the effects of Tulsa's school based-universal prekindergarten program on gains in Applied Problems as predicted by CLASS scores. No significant main effects were found between scores on the three CLASS dimensions and math, but a marginally negative effect was found between the EC dimension and math gains for boys only.

Small effect sizes of the same magnitude as literacy gains have been found between gains in children's math skill and CLASS dimensions. Ratings on the CLASS IS subscale predicted gains in Applied Problems (Mashburn et al., 2008) with the most recent analysis by Keys et al. (2013), indicating a significant but small effect for IS (1-point increase associated with a 0.06 SD increase on Applied Problems). The Curby et al. (2009) profile approach to examining the CLASS also found that children who had teachers in Profile 2 (Individual Instruction profile), the profile with the highest Concept Development scores, made more gains in math. The effect size of 0.19 on Applied Problems between children who had Profile 2 teachers and those whose teachers were Profile 5 is one of the largest obtained in this set of studies.

As we have pointed out, social skills and self-regulation are difficult areas to measure reliably and validly. Teacher ratings of children's self-regulatory skills taken during the prekindergarten year are difficult to use as an outcome measure against which to investigate the effects of quality. This is especially the case if teachers are aware of the focus on dispositions and would like their children to make improvements. An attempt to connect changes in teacher ratings of self-regulation to CLASS scores was conducted by Dominguez, Vitiello, Maier, and Greenfield (2010). They had 29 Head Start teachers who rated children's "learning behaviors" three times over the prekindergarten year. There was considerable variation among the classrooms in the rate of change in learning behaviors portrayed by the teachers; CO was the only CLASS dimension related to these ratings,

accounting for 1% of the variation in the rates of change in learning behavior.

Social competencies and problem behaviors have more often been investigated although these are not the behaviors so far shown to have long-term significance for school achievement. The NCEDL-SWEEP study included measures of social skills and problem behaviors in the children. During the prekindergarten year, changes in teacher ratings of children's social skills were predicted to a small degree by CLASS ratings of ES (not IC and CO) (Mashburn et al., 2008). While the Keys et al.'s (2013) reanalysis of the same data found no associations between IC and social skills, but there was a small but significant relation between IC and problem behaviors with a 1-point increase on the scale actually associated with a 0.05 SD increase in problem behaviors.

Other studies have sought to understand the relations between CLASS scores and executive function skills (inhibitory control and working memory) and attentiveness but with mixed and very small effects when found. Weiland et al. (2013) found no main effects for any of the three dimensions of the CLASS on inhibitory control and working memory, while Hamre et al. (2014) found small positive associations between the CO dimension and both inhibitory control and working memory and a negative association between inhibitory control and the ES dimension of the CLASS. In a somewhat longer-term study, Anderson and Philips (2017) found no relations between the prekindergarten CLASS scores and children's attentiveness in kindergarten.

Findings presented thus far on the associations between CLASS scores and children's outcomes have focused exclusively on main effects averaging across the levels of quality. Just as with the ECERS, there is a growing body of research seeking to identify levels or thresholds in quality that relate child outcomes. As we noted with ECERS threshold investigations, these analyses have clear implications for the cutoff scores assigned by states for the various levels of their QRIS. The original source of information on threshold effects comes from the data using the pilot version of CLASS. Burchinal, Vandergrift, Pianta, and Mashburn (2010) found that the CLASS higher ranges of the IS dimension were more strongly related to language, reading, and math skills (range = 3.25–7). Also, the ES dimension was more strongly related to higher social skills and lower behavior problems, when quality was high (range = 5–7) rather than low (range = 1–4.99). Subsequent analyses of the data from a part of this dataset found similar threshold effects for language and literacy outcomes, but not for math, social skills, and problem behaviors (Burchinal et al., 2016). These higher thresholds indicate that very high scores on CLASS dimensions would have to be achieved before any effects on child outcomes would be found.

In another short-term study of quality thresholds related to immediate prekindergarten effects, Weiland et al. (2013) found threshold effects for inhibitory control (not working memory) when IS quality was high (range = 3.90–7; $d = 0.19$) but negatively related when quality was low (range = 1–3.89;

$d = -0.20$). A similar pattern was also found for the relation between the ES dimension and language skills in the study, with ES negatively related to the PPVT when quality was low (range = 1–5.12; $d = -0.13$) but not when quality was high (range = 5.13–7). Taken together, this suggests a complex picture of how to define quality and the need for measures that not only consistently relate to intended child outcomes, but that, if benchmark or cutoffs are to be assigned for the various levels of a state's QRIS, the chosen scores should be consistently supported by empirical evidence.

Using the more recent version of CLASS and being one of the few studies to investigate long-term relations between prekindergarten quality and outcomes, Anderson and Phillips (2017) followed children who had been in Tulsa prekindergarten classrooms into middle school. Their results are somewhat baffling and indicate that much more discussion is needed of CLASS as a measure of quality in prekindergarten classrooms. They found quadratic relations between CLASS Instructional Support (IS) quality indicators and middle school Letter Word outcomes – meaning that students at the lowest and highest rating levels of IS had the *poorest* outcomes. Also intriguingly the effects of IS differed by the income level of the children's parents. Although only 20% of the children in the sample came from higher-income families, their middle school outcomes were higher in classrooms with *lower* IS ratings. This is an important study, one of the few, to examine long-term effects of the quality of prekindergarten classrooms and to examine how subgroups of children might be affected differently by different classroom quality.

Summary

For both ECERS and CLASS, research results from various studies have found minimal relations to children's short- and long-term gains in all child outcome measures including achievement domains (language, literacy, math), self-regulation (inhibitory control and working memory), social skills ratings from teachers, and problem behaviors noted by teachers. Routinely, the term "high quality" preschool is used in legislation, such as the 2014 Preschool Development Grant RFA, in state initiatives, and in the writings of advocates and researchers. The term is easy to agree with but has proven incredibly troublesome to define. Early et al. (2018) offer three reasons for the minimal to no effects between our current measures of quality and child outcomes: either the quality tools we are using are too imprecise, they are too broad, or our child outcomes are not measured well enough. Later in the chapter, we will offer our interpretations of the problems with these kinds of global environmental measures. First, we will provide some information on alternative measures of quality currently under development.

Alternative Observation Measures of Quality

There are several quality instruments such as the ones that are described below.

Optimizing Learning Opportunities for Students' Early Learning Observation System

Supported by funding from the Institute of Education Sciences, the Early Learning Network (http://earlylearning-network.unl.edu/) is currently in the process of developing a multidimensional observational system for preschool and early elementary general education classrooms, the Optimizing Learning Opportunities for Students' (OLOS) Early Learning Observation System. The system aims to capture structural and process quality generally as well as the quality of instruction in specific subject matter areas. The OLOS system is built upon the Individualizing Student Instruction/Pathways (Connor et al., 2009), Creating Opportunities to Learn from Text (Sparapani, Carlisle, & Connor, 2018), and the Quality of the Classroom Learning Environment Rubric (Connor et al., 2014). By capturing both individual children and global aspects of teaching quality, the system aims to capture the types (e.g., literacy, numeracy, math, and science learning) and amounts (in minutes) of instruction occurring in classrooms, children's participation in learning opportunities, teacher-student interactions, teacher responsiveness, and classroom management and emotional environment.

A key feature of the system is the technology being employed to capture the data on classroom quality (http://isilearn.net/olos/) and generate reports that provide feedback to principals, coaches, and teachers to improve practice. Currently in development and undergoing field testing in early childhood programs and elementary schools, including establishing an association between quality as assessed by the system and children's language, literacy, math, and self-regulation skills. The comprehensive and user-friendly nature of the OLOS system offers great promise as a tool to provide not only an avenue to capture reliable and valid classroom quality data but also an effective and efficient system for informing programs about their quality and supporting their engagement in continuous quality improvement. However, in all caution, no research with this tool has taken place, especially in its application to the preschool classroom setting.

Child Observation in Preschool and Teacher Observation in Preschool

Developed by Farran and colleagues specifically for use in prekindergarten classrooms, the Child Observation in Preschool (COP; Farran, & Son-Yarbrough, 2001; Farran, Son-Yarbrough, Silveri, & Culp, 1993) and the Teacher Observation in Preschool (TOP; Bilbrey, Vorhaus, & Farran, 2007) are observation protocols designed to quantify child and teacher behaviors. The COP/TOP uses a systematic behavior-sampling procedure – also known as a snapshot procedure. The COP captures information regarding children's listening and verbalizations, learning setting, interaction state (e.g., parallel, cooperative, associative) with teacher and peers, activity–task demands, level of involvement in learning activities, and the learning focus of activities. The TOP captures information regarding teacher and other classroom adults' listening and verbalizations, learning setting, schedule, task type (e.g., instruction, management, assessment), level of instruction, emotional tone, and the learning focus of activities. The system begins with observers first coding the teacher and then the assistant(s), followed by each child in the classroom in succession. Upon completion of all class members, the coder returns to the teacher to start the observation coding process over. The observation tends to be conducted over the entire school day and yields approximately 20–24 separate instances, or sweeps, of each classroom participant across the school day. The system provides a picture of the classroom as a whole by aggregating scores from the individual children. Alternatively, analyses can be conducted with children's individual scores nested within classrooms.

The COP and TOP are organized so that researchers can examine contingent probabilities and allow for a dynamic picture of the school day. Studies that have employed the system have found a variety of associations between observed classroom behaviors and children's literacy, math, and executive-function development (Farran et al., 2017; Fuhs, Farran, & Nesbitt, 2013; Hofer, Farran, & Cummings, 2013; Nesbitt, Farran, & Fuhs, 2015; Spivak & Farran, 2016). For example, in a large study of an early mathematics curriculum enacted in prekindergarten and Head Start classrooms, talking while engaged in math was relatively rare, but significantly associated with gains in math across the prekindergarten year (Hofer et al., 2013). Prekindergarten children's level of involvement in learning activities and engagement in sequential or goal-driven behaviors have been found to positively predict literacy and math gains in prekindergarten, while unoccupied and disruptive behaviors negatively predicted children's gains (Nesbitt et al., 2015). With regard to teacher behaviors, behavior approving, emotional tone, instructional focus, and level of instruction have been found to relate to children executive function gains (Fuhs et al., 2013) as well as gains in literacy and math (Farran et al., 2017).

COP/TOP is a research instrument requiring extensive training and field-based reliability assessments before observers can code independently. Versions of each have also been created to use in kindergarten through second grade (COPG and TOPG – children and teachers' observation in primary grades). This kind of measure is unlikely to be used broadly due to the demands placed on data collection and data synthesis. In an effort to make the instrument more practitioner friendly, the National Science Foundation provided funding in 2018 for the development of a coaching tool that would focus on the classroom interactions from COP/TOP that various studies have found to be linked to gains (Christopher & Farran, 2018). This simplified measure will be ready for experimental field testing in 2020.

Emerging Academics Snapshot

The Emerging Academics Snapshot (Ritchie, Howes, Kraft-Sayre, & Weiser, 2002), sometimes just referred to as "Snapshot," focuses on the individual children in the classroom.

It is a time sampling instrument designed to capture children's exposure to instruction and engagement in academic activities, including teacher responsiveness. The measure captures information about activity setting (e.g., routines, centers, whole group time), content focus (e.g., letter/sound reading, math, science, aesthetics), and teacher interactions with students (e.g., scaffolds, didactic). Each Snapshot instance coded consists of 20 seconds of observation, followed by 40 seconds of coding. A few children are selected from each classroom and then observed in succession and when all children are observed, the coder starts over with the first child and repeats the coding process. The Snapshot system was included as part of the NCEDL and SWEEP studies and was found to have a modest, positive association with the ECERS (Early et al., 2005; Pianta et al., 2005) and also to be significantly related to children's language and literacy outcomes but not math (Howes et al., 2008).

Issues in Measuring Quality in Early Childhood Classrooms

The Use of Observer Ratings

The primary measures of the quality of child care and prekindergarten classrooms rely on observer ratings. For the following reasons, the use of ratings may, in fact, contribute to the fact that the findings from the use of these measures have been mostly disappointing.

First, ratings require a judgment, and judgments have a subjective component. It is exceptionally difficult for raters to adopt the shared perspective necessary to ensure that they are all rating the same qualities of teacher and child behaviors and classroom organization. Because of the difficulty of agreement, many studies reviewed in this chapter count as "agreement" when raters come within one point of each other. This tendency effectively reduces the scale metric; one rater's score of 3, for example, on CLASS and ECERS, could be counted as an agreement with another observer who rated either 2 or 4. Scores of 2 and 4 on both instruments are assumed to have quite different meanings.

Compounding the problem with the way agreement is determined is the fact that in many studies, reliability is only established during the training phase using videotapes provided by the scale developers. This practice has at least two flaws: first in the problem of observer drift. Training reliability should always be followed up by field reliability with multiple checks across the length of the data collection period to prevent observer drift especially in subjective ratings. Second, reliability should always be established in the type of setting in which data will be collected. A videotape is not the same stimulus as a live classroom; if observers are going to collect data in live classrooms, classrooms must be the places where reliability is obtained. Classrooms themselves are quite varied, especially across different funding agencies; observers in the actual settings in which data will be used simply must obtain reliability.

Another problem with ratings is their instability. Many recent investigations of both ECERS and CLASS have found great instability in ratings across the day and within a single observer (see Mashburn, 2017) and also related even to the season in which data were collected (see Buell, Han, & Vukelich, 2017). Using the ECERS, Rentzou (2017) found that programmatic items were relatively stable (materials available, room organization, etc.) but that items related to interactions, the key classroom component, were much less stable. She argues that a one-day visit may capture the former classroom characteristics but will be insufficient to measure the more dynamic aspects of classroom interactions. These instability issues are important for QRISs; it is hard to systematize and equate when the environmental measures will be taken during the year.

Third, rating scales begin with the assumption that qualities of classrooms can be described on a continuum from poor to exemplary along prespecified dimensions. Because not enough empirical work has determined which particular behaviors of teachers and aspects of classroom organization are related to child outcomes of interest, rating scales have emerged from ideological beliefs of the developers. The ECERS reflects a perspective that the materials in the classroom, the ways they are organized, and the amount of time children are allowed to explore them freely are critical quality features. The new ECERS-3 has changed the exemplary end of each subscale to focus on instruction following changing perceptions in the field of what is important (Early et al., 2018). The empirical work to determine which aspects of organization, which and how many types of materials, and how to facilitate children's focus during free play has not occurred. CLASS, on the other hand, proceeds from a perspective that the emotional atmosphere of a classroom and the teachers' interactions with children are the critical quality features.

The point is not to call these ideological perspectives into question but to demonstrate that these are *beliefs* and not empirically determined measures of quality demonstrated to link to the outcomes of interest to the programs. Reliance on beliefs is what has led states to develop such various quality rating systems (Cannon et al., 2017). Curby et al. (2009) concluded their investigation of quality in prekindergarten classes by remarking, "Given their [prekindergarten programs] explicit intention of changing students' school readiness and performance trajectories, it is important to identify classroom practices that promote student learning and, thus could serve as a target for intervention" (p. 364) and, one might add, could serve as the basis for the development of a quality observation scale.

Child Perspective versus a Teacher/Classroom Perspective

Most of the current measures of quality focus on the classroom as a whole, in effect, investigating the classroom from the "top down." A "bottom up" or child perspective might provide a different picture of classroom quality (e.g., Farran et al., 2017; Powell, Burchinal, File, & Kontos, 2008). Examining only what the teacher does can be misleading as it does not provide the observer with information about how children are actually responding. In an intense study of 26 classrooms over four years, Farran and colleagues (2017) found only one global top-down measure to be related to children's outcomes, the amount of time spent in transitions. Instead, the predictors of better outcomes for children consisted of a mixture of specific children's behaviors (associative interactions, level of involvement in learning) and teacher behaviors (listening to children, providing higher-quality instruction).

The national evaluation of Early Reading First (ERF) is a good example of the problems in taking a teacher-only perspective (Jackson et al., 2007). Teachers in classrooms funded by ERF were observed and rated on literacy practices that would seem to reflect the types of instruction that should lead to strong literacy growth in children. The rating scales used were the ECERS and the Teacher Behavior Rating Scale (TBRS; Landry, Crawford, Gunnewig, & Swank, 2004). Teachers in ERF-funded classrooms were rated significantly higher on both ECERS and TBRS than prekindergarten teachers in non-funded classrooms. Despite these large and significant differences in teacher behaviors, no differences were found in child outcomes between those children who had been in ERF classrooms and those who had not. Observing how the children were actually reacting to the increased literacy instruction would have been an informative supplement to these global quality ratings of teacher practices.

More recently, several studies have examined the effects of a coaching program developed by Pianta and colleagues, My Teaching Partner, and found similar effects. With sustained coaching, teachers' practices as measured by their CLASS scores improved (see Early, Maxwell, Ponder, & Pan, 2017). More recently, Ansari and Pianta (2018) found no effects on any child outcomes from My Teaching Partner intensive coaching in 401 Head Start classrooms (though there were indications of age moderation). Few studies of intensive interventions to change teacher behaviors on current rating scales have found related effects on child outcomes.

A global rating of the classroom by definition blurs individual differences among the children and assumes that the impact of the practices studied will be uniform. The importance of examining individual child classroom interactions is demonstrated in a paper by Bratsch-Hines, Burchinal, Peisner-Feinberg, and Franco (2019). They report that the language interactions individual children had with their teachers predicted gains in expressive language. These kinds of data demonstrate the wide variability in children's experiences within the same classroom. A global measure of quality will not capture what is happening to individual children. Similarly, unfortunately, choosing only a few children to observe for their interactions may not be a sufficient index of the experiences of all. The *quality* of a prekindergarten classroom must be concerned with its connection to the needs of the children, even when those needs are quite varied. It may be possible to design a quality measure for early childhood that combines both a classroom and a child perspective, but to date, researchers seem to focus pretty exclusively on one or the other.

Summary

This chapter updates a prior review on efforts to measure quality in early childhood classroom settings. The conclusion remains that finding a measure that can evaluate the quality of early childhood education has been complicated by the very different histories and missions of programs in this field. The caring mission involves a heterogeneous group of children and families. Children are cared for by adults other than their families away from their homes for large portions of the day. The original measures of quality developed to assess these environments, such as the ECERS, helped to bring attention to the needs of young children and made states aware of their responsibilities to do more than just make these locations healthy and safe. These quality measures have not, however, been effective in establishing a relation between their quality perspective and either short- or long-term gains for children in important developmental domains.

According to current wisdom, the academic outcomes most important for later school success are math, reading (language/literacy), and attention. None of the quality measures currently in the field have shown much capacity for identifying classrooms that are more effective in helping children learn those skills. We argue that the first step in developing an effective measure of classroom quality has got to be empirical investigations of the behaviors of teachers and children demonstrated to be linked to gains in those three skill areas. The importance of determining appropriate and valid measures of quality has become urgent with the 2018 publication of the results of an experimental evaluation of Tennessee's Prekindergarten program (TNVPK) (Lipsey, Farran, & Durkin, 2018). Despite initial improvements in school readiness outcomes of the size obtained by most state-funded programs, by third grade, those children randomly assigned to attend TNVPK were scoring lower than the comparison group on both individually administered and state high-stakes tests. This study is the only randomized controlled evaluation conducted to date on scaled-up state prekindergarten programs. The need to find measures of quality to assess these classrooms as they are instituted widely is essential.

As Hughes (2010) asserted, "The identification of specific classroom transactions or processes that predict the growth in skills that enable children to make a successful transition to kindergarten and first grade is critical to realizing the promise of preschool education" (p. 48). Only observational measures that reliably describe the specific behaviors of teachers and children and then examine those behaviors in relation to child growth on important outcomes in long term will be useful in the identification of these important classroom transactions.

Notes

1. The CLASS has a related child-focused measure, the Individualized Classroom Assessment Scoring System (inCLASS, Downer, Booren, Lima, Luckner, & Pianta, 2010), that evaluates children's interactions with teachers, peers, and tasks, though it is not currently being used by any state as part of their QRIS system.
2. To understand this effect size, it is helpful to remember that Instructional Support is a 7-point scale whose average score across studies is less than 3.0. On the other hand, the PPVT standard deviation is 15 points, so 0.04 of a PPVT SD would equal a gain of less than 1 point on this receptive language measure.

References

Anderson, S., & Phillips, D. (2017). Is pre-K classroom quality associated with kindergarten and middle-school academic skills? *Developmental Psychology, 53*(6), 1063–1078. doi:10.1037/dev0000312

Ansari, A., & Pianta, R. (2018). Effects of an early childhood coaching intervention on preschoolers: The role of classroom age composition. *Early Childhood Research Quarterly, 44*, 101–113. doi:10.1016/j.ecresq.2018.03.001

Bilbrey, C., Vorhaus, E., & Farran, D. (2007). *Teacher observation in preschool.* Unpublished instrument available from D.C. Farran, Peabody Research Institute, Vanderbilt University, Nashville, TN.

Bratsch-Hines, M., Burchinal, M., Peisner-Fineberg, & Franco (2019). Frequency of instructional practices in rural prekindergarten classrooms and associations with child language and literacy skills. *Early Childhood Research Quarterly, 47*, 74–88. doi:10.1016/j.ecresq.2018.10.001

Brunsek, A., Perlman, M., Falenchuk, O., McMullen, E., Gletcher, B., & Shah, P. (2017). The relationship between the early childhood environment rating scale and its revised form and child outcomes: A systematic review and meta-analysis. *PLoS ONE, 12*(6), e0178512. doi:10.1371/journal.pone.0178512

Buell, M., Han, M., & Vukelich, C. (2017). Factors affecting variance in Classroom Assessment Scoring System scores: Season, context, and classroom composition. *Early Child Development and Care, 187*, 1635–1648. doi:10.1080/03004430.2016.1178245

Bumiller, E. (2003, July 8). Bush seeks big changes in Head Start, drawing criticism from program's supporters. *The New York Times.* Retrieved from https://www.nytimes.com/2003/07/08/us/bush-seeks-big-changes-in-head-start-drawing-criticism-from-program-s-supporters.html

Burchinal, M., Vandergrift, N., Pianta, R., & Mashburn, A. (2009). Threshold analysis of association between child care quality and child outcomes for low-income children in pre-kindergarten programs. *Early Childhood Research Quarterly, 25*, 166–176. doi:10.1016/j.ecresq.2009.10.004

Burchinal, M., Vandergrift, N., Pianta, R., & Mashburn, A. (2010). Threshold analysis of association between child care quality and child outcomes for low-income children in pre-kindergarten programs. *Early Childhood Research Quarterly, 25*, 166–176. doi:10.1016/j.ecresq.2009.10.004

Burchinal, M., Xue, Y., Auger, A., Tien, H. C., Mashburn, A., Peisner-Feinberg, E., ... Tarullo, L. (2016). III. Testing for quality thresholds and features in early care and education. *Monographs of the Society for Research in Child Development, 81*, 46–63. doi:10.1111/mono.12238.

Burchinal, M. R., Howes, C., Pianta, R., Bryant, D., Early, D., Clifford, R., & Barbarin, O. (2008). Predicting child outcomes at the end of kindergarten from the quality of pre-kindergarten teacher–child interactions and instruction. *Applied Development Science, 12*, 140–153. doi:10.1080/10888690802199418

Cannon, J., Zellman, G., Karoly, L., & Schwartz, H. (2017). Quality rating and improvement systems for early care and education programs: Making the second generation better. *Perspective: Expert insights on a timely policy issue*, The Rand Corporation. Retrieved from www.rand.org/t/pe235

Christopher, C., & Farran, D. (2018). Development and validation of a mobile, web-based coaching tool to improve pre-k classroom practices to enhance learning. Proposal to DRL – Discovery Research K-12, National Science Foundation. Funded 7/1/18.

Connor, C. M., Morrison, F. J., Fishman, B., Ponitz, C. C., Glasney, S., Underwood, P. S., ... Schatschneifer, C. (2009). The ISI classroom observation system: Examining the literacy instruction provided to individual students. *Educational Researcher, 38*, 85–99. doi:10.3102/0013189X09332373

Connor, C. M., Spencer, M., Day, S. L., Giuliani, S., Ingebrand, S. W., McLean, L., & Morrison, F. J. (2014). Capturing the complexity: Content, type, and amount of instruction and quality of the classroom learning environment synergistically predict third graders' vocabulary and reading comprehension outcomes. *Journal of Educational Psychology, 106*(3), 762–778. doi:10.1037/a0035921

Curby, T., LoCasale-Crouch, J., Konold, T., Pianta, R., Howes, C., Burchinal, M., ... Barbarin, O. (2009). The relations of observed pre-k classroom quality profiles to children's achievement and social competence. *Early Education and Development, 20*, 346–372.

Dominguez, X., Vitiello, V., Maier, M., & Greenfield, D. (2010). A longitudinal examination of young children's learning behavior: Child-level and classroom-level predictors of change throughout the preschool year. *School Psychology Review, 39*, 29–47.

Downer, J. T., Booren, L. M., Lima, O. K., Luckner, A. E., & Pianta, R. C (2010). The Individualized Classroom Assessment Scoring System (inCLASS): Reliability and validity of a system for observing preschoolers' competence in classroom interactions. *Early Childhood Research Quarterly, 25*, 1–16. doi:10.1016/j.ecresq.2009.08.004

Duncan, G. J., Dowsett, C. J., Claessens, A., Magnuson, K., Huston, A. C., Klebanov, P., & Japel, C. (2007). School readiness and later achievement. *Developmental Psychology, 43*(6), 1428–1446.

Early, D., Barbarin, O., Bryant, B., Burchinal, M., Chang, F., Clifford, R., ... Barnett, W. S. (2005). *Pre-kindergarten in eleven states: NCEDL's Multi-State Stud of Pre-kindergarten and State-Wide Early Education Program (Sweep) Study*. Retrieved from https://fpg.unc.edu/sites/fpg.unc.edu/files/resources/reports-and-policy-briefs/NCEDL_PreK-in-Eleven-States_Working-Paper_2005.pdf

Early, D., Bryant, D., Pianta, R., Clifford, R., Burchinal, M., Ritchie, S., ... Barbarin, O. (2006). Are teachers' education, major, and credentials related to classroom quality and children's gains in pre-kindergarten? *Early Childhood Research Quarterly, 21*, 174–195.

Early, D., Maxwell, K., Burchinal, M., Alva, S., Bender, R., Bryant, D., ... Zill, N. (2007). Teachers' education, classroom quality, and young children's academic skills: Results from seven studies of preschool programs. *Child Development, 78*, 558–580.

Early, D., Maxwell, K., Ponder, B., & Pan, Y. (2017). Improving teacher-child interactions: A randomized controlled trial of making the most of classroom interactions and my teaching partner professional development models. *Early Childhood Research Quarterly, 38*, 57–70. doi:10.1016/j.ecresq.2016.08.005

Early, D., Sideris, J., Neitzel, J., LaForett, D., & Nehler, C. (2018). Factor structure and validity of the Early Childhood Environment Rating Scale – Third Edition (ECERS-3). *Early Childhood Research Quarterly, 44*, 242–256. doi:10.1016/j.ecresq.2018.04.009

Ewing, D., & Matthews, H. (2005). *The potential of Title I for high quality preschool*. Washington, DC: The Center for Law and Social Policy.

Farran, D. (2016, February 25). We need more evidence in order to create effective pre-K programs. *Evidence Speaks, 1*(11). Washington, DC: Brookings.

Farran, D. C. (2005). Developing and implementing preventive intervention programs for children at risk: Poverty as a case in point. In M. Guralnik (ed.), *A developmental systems approach to early intervention: National and international perspectives* (pp. 267–304). Baltimore, MD: Paul Brookes Publisher.

Farran, D. C. (2007). Is education the way out of poverty? A reflection on the 40th anniversary of Head Start (with commentaries by James King and Bernard L. Charles), *Monographs of the Center for Research on Children's Development & Learning*, No. 3 (50 pages, ISBN: 0-9727709-2-5).

Farran, D. C., Meador, D., Christopher, C., Nesbitt, K., & Bilbrey, L. (2017). Data-driven improvement in prekindergarten classrooms: Report from a partnership in an urban district. *Child Development, 88*, 1466–1479. doi: 10.1111/cdev.12906

Farran, D. C., & Son-Yarbrough, W. (2001). Title I funded preschools as a developmental context for children's play and verbal behaviors. *Early Childhood Research Quarterly, 16*, 245–262.

Farran, D. C., Son-Yarbrough, W., Silveri, B., & Culp, A. (1993). Measuring the environment in public school preschools for disadvantaged children: What is developmentally appropriate? In S. Reifel (Ed.), *Advances in early education and day care, 1993* (pp. 75–93). Greenwich, CT: JAI Press, Inc.

First Five Years Fund. (2018). Every Student Succeeds Act (P.L/ 114–95): High level comparison of ESSA's Preschool Development Grants program with the Legacy Administration Preschool Development Grants program. Retrieved from https://ffyf.org/wp-content/uploads/2016/02/PDGvsESSAPDG_020316.pdf

Frank Porter Graham Child Development Institute. (1999). Building blocks: Research that led to new quality assessment tools & changed personnel preparation programs. *Early Developments, 3*(3), 11–13. Retrieved from https://fpg.unc.edu/resources/early-developments-vol-3-no-3

Friedman-Krauss, A. H., Barnett, W. S., Weisenfeld, G. G., Kasmin, R., DiCrecchio, N., & Horowitz, M. (2018). *The state of preschool 2017: State preschool yearbook*. The National Institute for Early Education Research, Rutgers University. Retrieved from http://nieer.org/state-preschool-yearbooks/yearbook2017

Fuhs, M., Farran, D., & Turner [Nesbitt], K. (2013). Preschool classroom processes as predictors of children's cognitive self-regulation skills development. *School Psychology Quarterly, 28*, 347–359. doi:10.1037/spq0000031

Gordon, R., Fujimoto, K., Kaestner, R., Korenman, S., & Abner, K. (2013). An assessment of the validity of the ECERS-R with implications for assessments of child care quality and its relation to child development. *Developmental Psychology, 49*, 146–160.

Gordon, R., Hofer, K., Fujimoto, K., Risk, N., Kaestner, R., & Korenman, S. (2015). Identifying high-quality preschool programs: New evidence on the validity of the Early Childhood Environment Rating Scale-Revised (ECERS-R) in relation to school readiness goals. *Early Education and Development, 26*, 1086–1110. doi:10.1080/10409289.2015.1036348

Gosse, C. S., McGinty, A. S., Mashburn, A. J., Hoffman, L. M., & Pianta, R. C. (2014). The role of relational and instructional classroom supports in the language development of at-risk preschoolers. *Early Education & Development, 25*, 110–133. doi:10.1080/10409289.2013.778567

Guo, Y., Piasta, S., Justice, L., & Kaderavek, J. (2010). Relations among preschool teachers' self-efficacy, classroom quality, and children's language and literacy gains. *Teaching and Teacher Education, 26*, 1094–1103.

Hamre, B., Hatfield, B., Pianta, R., & Jamil, F. (2014). Evidence for general and domain-specific elements of teacher–child interactions: Associations with preschool children's development. *Child Development, 85*, 1257–1274. doi:10.1111/cdev.12184

Harms, T., & Clifford, R. (1983). Assessing preschool environments with the Early Childhood Environmental Rating Scale. *Studies in Educational Evaluation, 8*, 261–269.

Harms, T., & Clifford, R. M. (1980). *The early childhood environment rating scale*. New York, NY: Teachers College Press.

Harms, T., Clifford, R. M., & Cryer, D. (2004). *Early childhood environment rating scale*, revised edition (ECERS-R). New York, NY: Teachers College Press.

Harms, T., Clifford, R. M., & Cryer, D. (2015). *Early childhood environment rating scale*, third edition (ECERS-3). New York, NY: Teachers College Press.

Herbst, C. (2017). Universal child care, maternal employment, and children's long-run outcomes: Evidence from the US Lanham Act of 1940. *Journal of Labor Economics 35*, 519–564.

Herbst, C. (2018). The impact of quality rating and improvement systems on families' child care choices and the supply of child care labor. *Labour Economics, 54*, 172–190. doi:10.1016/j.labeco.2018.08.007

Hestenes, L., Kintner-Duffy, V., Wang, Y., La Paro, K., Mims, S., Crosby, D., ... Cassidy, D. (2015). Comparisons among quality measures in child care settings: Understanding the use of multiple measures in North Carolina's QRIS and their links to social-emotional development in preschool children. *Early Childhood Research Quarterly, 30*, 199–214. doi:10.1016/j.ecresq.2014.06.003

Hestenes, L., Rucker, L., Wang, Y., Mims, S., Hestenes, S., & Cassidy, D. (2019). A comparison of the ECERS-R and ECERS-3: Different aspects of quality? *Early Education and Development, 30*(4), 496–510. doi:10.1080/10409289.2018.1559681

Hofer, K., Farran, D., & Cummings, T. (2013). Preschool children's math-related behaviors mediate curriculum effects on math achievement gains. *Early Childhood Research Quarterly, 28*, 487–495. doi:10.1016/j.ecresq.2013.02.002

Hofer, K. G. (2010). How measurement characteristics can affect ECERS-R scores and program funding. *Contemporary Issues in Early Childhood, 11*(2), 175–191. doi:10.2304/ciec.2010.11.2.175

Hooper, S., Roberts, J., Sideris, J., Burchinal, M., & Zeisel, S. (2010). Longitudinal predictors of reading and math trajectories through middle school for African American versus Caucasian students across two samples. *Developmental Psychology, 46*, 1019–1029.

Howes, C., Burchinal, M., Pianta, R., Bryant, D., Early, D., Clifford, R., & Barbarin, O. (2008). Ready to learn? Children's re-academic achievement in pre-kindergarten programs. *Early Childhood Research Quarterly, 23*, 27–50.

Hughes, J. (2010). Identifying quality in preschool education: Progress and challenge. *School Psychology Review, 39*, 48–53.

IES, NCES (February, 2019). *The condition of education: Preschool and kindergarten enrollment.* https://nces.ed.gov/programs/coe/indicator_cfa.asp

Jackson, R. McCoy, A., Pistorino, C., Wilkinson, A., Burghardt, J., Clark, M., ... Swank, P. (2007). *National Evaluation of Early Reading First: Final Report*, U.S. Department of Education, Institute of Education Sciences, Washington, DC: U.S. Government Printing Office.

Johnson-Staub, C. (2017). *Equity starts early: Addressing racial inequities in child care and early education policy.* The Center for Law and Social Policy. Retrieved from https://www.clasp.org/sites/default/files/publications/2017/12/2017_EquityStartsEarly_0.pdf

Justice, L., Mashburn, A., Hamre, B., & Pianta, R. (2008). Quality of language and literacy instruction in preschool classrooms serving at-risk pupils. *Early Childhood Research Quarterly, 23*, 51–68.

Keys, T. D., Farkas, G., Burchinal, M. R., Duncan, G. J., Vandell, D. L., Li, W., ... Howes, C. (2013). Preschool center quality and school readiness: Quality effects and variation by demographic and child characteristics. *Child Development, 84*(4), 1171–1190. doi:10.1111%2Fcdev.12048

Landry, S., Crawford, A., Gunnewig, S., & Swank, P. (2004). *Teacher Behavior Rating Scale (TBRS).* Houston, TX: Center for Improving the Readiness of Children for Learning and Education, Unpublished Research Instrument.

Lin, Y.-C., & Magnuson, K. (2018). Classroom quality and children's academic skills in child care centers: Understanding the role of teacher qualifications. *Early Childhood Research Quarterly, 42*, 215–227. doi:10.1016/j.ecresq.2017.10.003

Lipsey, M., Farran, D., & Durkin, K. (2018). Effects of the Tennessee prekindergarten program on children's achievement and behavior through third grade. *Early Childhood Research Quarterly, 45*, 155–176. doi:10.1016/j.ecresq.2018.03.005

LoCasale-Crouch, J., Konold, T., Pianta, R., Howes, C., Burchinal, M., Bryant, D., ... Barbarin, O. (2007). Observed classroom quality profiles in state-funded pre-kindergarten programs and associations with teacher, program, and classroom characteristics. *Early Childhood Research Quarterly, 22*, 3–17.

Mashburn, A., Downer, J., Hamre, B., Justice, L., & Pianta, R. (2010). Consultation for teachers and children's language and literacy development during pre-kindergarten. *Applied Developmental Science, 14*, 179–196. doi:10.1080/10888691.2010.516187

Mashburn, A., Pianta, R., Hamre, B., Downer, J., Barbarin, O., Bryant, D., ... Howes, C. (2008). Measures of classroom quality in prekindergarten and children's development of academic, language, and social skills. *Child Development, 79*, 732–749.

Mashburn, A. J. (2017). Evaluating the validity of classroom observations in the Head Start designation renewal system. *Educational Psychologist, 52*(1), 38–49. doi:10.1080/00461520.2016.1207539

McCartney, K., Scarr, S., Phillips, D., Grajek, F., & Schwarz, J. C. (1982). Environmental differences among day care centers and their effects on children's development. In E. F. Zigler & E. W. Gordon (Eds.), *Day care: Scientific and social policy issues* (pp. 126–151). Boston, MA: Auburn House.

National Research Council. (2001). *Eager to learn: Educating our preschoolers.* Committee on Early Childhood Pedagogy, B. T. Bowman, M. S. Donovan, & M. S. Burns, Commission on Behavioral and Social Sciences and Education (Eds.). Washington, DC: National Academy Press.

Nesbitt, K., Farran, D., & Fuhs, M. (2015). Executive function skills and academic achievement gains in prekindergarten: Contributions of learning-related behaviors. *Developmental Psychology, 51*, 865–878. doi:10.1037/dev0000021

Pace, A., Alper, R., Burchinal, M., Golinkoff, R., & Hirsh-Pasek, K. (2018). Measuring success: Within and cross-domain predictors of academic and social trajectories in elementary school. *Early Childhood Research Quarterly, 46*, 112–125. doi:10.1016/j.ecresq.2018.04.001 [online access].

Parker, E., Workman, E., & Atchison, B. (2016, January). *50 state review. States pre-k funding for 2015–16 fiscal year: National trends in state preschool funding.* Denver, CO: Education Commission of the States.

Perlman, M., Falenchuk, O., Fletcher, B., McMullen, E., Beyene, J., & Shah, P. S. (2016). A systematic review and meta-analysis of a measure of staff/child interaction quality (the classroom assessment scoring system) in early childhood education and care settings and child outcomes. *PLoS One, 11*(12), e0167660. doi:10.1371/journal.pone.0167660

Pianta, R. C., La Paro, K., & Hamre, B. (2008). *Classroom Assessment Scoring System (CLASS) manual, Pre-k.* Baltimore, MD: Paul Brookes.

Pianta, R., Howes, C., Burchinal, M., Bryant, D., Clifford, R., Early, D., & Barbarin, O. (2005). Features of pre-kindergarten programs, classrooms, and teachers: Do they predict observed classroom quality and child-teacher interactions? *Applied Developmental Science, 9*(3), 144–159.

Powell, D., Burchinal, M., File, N., & Kontos, S. (2008). An eco-behavioral analysis of children's engagement in urban public school preschool classrooms. *Early Childhood Research Quarterly, 23*, 108–123.

QRIS Compendium, 2016 fact sheet. National Center on Early Childhood Quality Assurance. (2016). Fairfax, VA: Early Childhood National Centers. Retrieved from https://childcareta.acf.hhs.gov/resource/qris-compendium-fact-sheet-indicators-quality-ratings

Reeves, C. A., & Bednar, D. A. (1994, July). Defining quality: Alternatives and implications. *Academy of Management Review, 19*(3), 419–445.

Rentzou, K. (2017). Using rating scales to evaluate quality early childhood education and care: Reliability issues. *European Early Childhood Education Research Journal, 25*, 667–681. doi:10.1080/1350293X.2017.1356599

Ritchie, S., Howes, C., Kraft-Sayre, M., & Weiser, B. (2002). *Snapshot.* Los Angeles: University of California, Los Angeles.

Roupp, R., Travers, J., Glantz, F., & Coelen, C. (1979). *Children at the center: Final results of the National Day Care Study.* Cambridge, MA: ABT Books.

Sabol, T., Hong, S., Pianta, R., & Burchinal, M. (2013). Can rating pre-k programs predict children's learning? *Science, 341*, 845–846.

Sakai, L. M., Whitebook, M., Wishard, A., & Howes, C. (2003). Evaluating the Early Childhood Environment Rating Scale (ECERS): Assessing differences between the first and revised edition. *Early Childhood Research Quarterly, 18*, 427–445.

Scarr, S., & Weinberg, R. (1986). The early childhood enterprise: Care and education of the young. *American Psychologist, 41*, 1140–1146.

Setdoji, C., Schaack, D., & Le, V. (2018). Using the early childhood environment rating scale-revised in high stakes contexts: Does evidence warrant the practice? *Early Childhood Research Quarterly, 42,* 158–169. doi:10.1016/j.ecresq.2017.10.001

Smith, S., Dong, X., Stephens, S., & Tout, K. (2017, November). *How studies of QRIS measure quality improvement activities: An analysis of measures of training and technical assistance.* Child Care & Early Education Research Connections. Retrieved from www.researchconnections.org

Sparapani, N., Carlisle, J., & Connor, C. (2018). Observations of vocabulary activities during second-and third-grade reading lessons. *Education Sciences, 8*(4), 198. doi:10.3390/educsci8040198

Spivak, A., & Farran, D. (2016). Predicting first graders' social competence from their preschool classroom interpersonal context. *Early Education and Development, 27*(6), 735–750. doi:10.1080/10409289.2016.1138825

The Build Initiative & Child Trends. (2017, November). *Quality compendium: A catalog and comparison of quality initiatives* [Data System]. Retrieved from http://qualitycompendium.org/

U.S. Department of Health and Human Services, Administration for Children and Families. (2010, January). *Head Start impact study. Final report.* Washington, DC.

Vandell, D. L., Belsky, J., Burchinal, M., Steinberg, L., Vandergrift, N., & NICHD Early Child Care Research Network. (2010). Do effects of early child care extend to age 15 years? Results from the NICHD study of early child care and youth development. *Child Development, 81,* 737–756. doi: 10.1111/j.1467-8624.2010.01431.x

Vitiello, V., Bassok, D., Hamre, B., Player, D., & Williford, A. (2018). Measuring the quality of teacher-child interactions at scale: Comparing research-based and state observation approaches. *Early Childhood Research Quarterly, 44,* 161–169. doi:10.1016/j.ecresq.2018.03.003

Votruba-Drzal, E., & Miller, P. (2016). Reflection on quality and dosage of preschool and children's development. In Burchinal, M., Zaslow, M., & Tarullo, L. (Eds.), *Quality thresholds, features, and dosage in early care and education: Secondary data analyses of child outcomes. Monographs of the Society for Child Development,* pp. 100–113. Retrieved from http://onlinelibrary.wiley.com/doi/10.1111/mono.v81.2/issuetoc

Watts, T. W., Duncan, G. J., Siegler, R. S., & Davis-Kean, P. E. (2014). What's past is prologue: Relations between early mathematics knowledge and high school achievement. *Educational Researcher, 43,* 352–360. doi:10.3102/0013189X14553660

Weiland, C., Ulvestad, K., Sachs, J., & Yoshikawa, H. (2013). Associations between classroom quality and children's vocabulary and executive function skills in an urban public prekindergarten program. *Early Childhood Research Quarterly, 28*(2), 199–209.

Weiland, C., Ulvestad, K., Sachs, J., & Yoshikawa, H. (2013). Associations between classroom quality and children's vocabulary and executive function skills in an urban public prekindergarten program. *Early Childhood Research Quarterly, 28,* 199–209. doi:10.1016/j.ecresq.2012.12.002

25

Rethinking Quality in Early Education

Practices that Advance Children's Cultural Strengths

Bruce Fuller, Margaret Bridges, and Claudia Galindo

Overview – Competing Conceptions of Quality

Debate persists over how to define key elements of quality in early education settings, animated by the kaleidoscope of individual caregivers and pre-k programs that emerged over the past half-century. Uneven long-term benefits of some preschool efforts – especially when quality lags – bring educators and scholars back to the question of *which ingredients of quality* can boost sustained benefits for children.

After all, policy makers hear varying claims about what quality elements will raise children's early growth: increasing teacher wages or credentials, putting more adults in classrooms, or strengthening learning activities. The struggle manifests in state efforts to pinpoint indicators for quality rating systems that actually predict children's growth (Cannon, Zellman, Karoly, & Schwartz, 2017). Faith fades in tinkering with material inputs (say, class size), while scholars debate the caregiver sensitivities or classroom practices that allegedly pay off for young children (Phillips & Lowenstein, 2011).

Typically missing from this conversation is how the learning aims of culturally diverse parents, set against mainstream pedagogical practices, may conflict with mostly White and middle-class conceptions of child-rearing. We fail to first ask: what cognitive skills and social practices do young children learn, as they become competent members of *their* communities?

Many educators and policy makers realize that over one-fourth of the nation's preschool-age children are of Latino heritage (Krogstad, 2019). We know that Latino preschoolers lag behind White peers, on average, on preliteracy and math assessments, even as they enter kindergarten (Guerrero et al., 2013; Reardon & Portilla, 2016). We habitually cite the need for more bilingual teachers, and greater understanding of immigrant kids and families.

This chapter urges that we go deeper, to learn about the culturally situated contexts and competencies of young children, as practitioners and policy activists seek to define and improve the quality of child-care and preschool settings.

To vividly see the power of cultural socialization, one need only watch White boys pepper pre-k teachers with questions or perform with quick responses, while Latina girls meld into the background; or observe a Latina in-home caregiver heaping *cariña*-rich affection in Spanish, while her White counterpart earnestly refreshes play centers, encouraging autonomous exploration (Holloway & Fuller, 1997; Rogoff, 2003; Tobin, Hsueh, & Karasawa, 2009).

This chapter advances how to widen the debate over early education quality, to consider how caregivers and teachers can prepare young children to become competent members of their immediate community, along with developing the cognitive and social agility for a variety of other settings. We first back-up to review the field's conceptual shift from structural facets of quality to process dimensions. Researchers, of late, have found consistent benefits from caregivers who pair warm, responsive exchanges with cognitively demanding language and learning activities (Zinsser, Shewark, Denham, & Curby, 2014).

Once the quality discussion centers on the character of adult-child interaction, language, and cognitive fostering, we must necessarily learn about the cultural assets and forms that young Latino children bring to nonparental home and pre-k settings. Teachers often inquire about what their children know, or the behavioral norms to which they abide. But lack of familiarity with a child's language and social norms makes this inquiry less likely among White or majority-culture teachers, who may make uninformed inferences about young Latino children.

Second, these developments invoke past decades of empirical work on the culturally situated home contexts and competencies of Latino toddlers and preschoolers, one expanding case of cultural difference (and internal variety) in the United States. We highlight how the wisdom around "high quality care," or contemporary work on the social organization of learning activities, at times departs from Latino children's everyday competencies, discourse conventions, and behavioral norms.

We review findings, mounting over the past half-century, on how many Latino children are socialized to become *bien educado*, to demonstrate *buen comportamiento*, and to signal the primacy of the family collective (*familismo*)—not necessarily one's own performances or interests. The cognitive frames and knowledge required to become a competent member of their own group remain couched in activities and tacit routines, which may come to conflict with the pre-k classroom's cognitive demands and expected performances.

This evidence brings into focus the cultural turn in social psychology and cognition that distinguishes universal from culturally bounded dynamics of child development (e.g., Fuller & García-Coll, 2010; Velez-Agosto, Soto-Crespo, Vizcarrondo-Oppenheimer, Vega-Molina & García-Coll, 2017). Beyond the shared necessities of health and nutrition, maternal attachment, and the capacity to thrive, toddlers and preschools apprentice within particular cultural contexts, including the home, kin networks, and child care as distinct social settings. To the extent quality implies building children's academic skills and knowledge base, child care and pre-k will fail to scaffold from cultural strengths and means of belonging.

Finally, we detail several promising practices to improve children's early education experiences. By engaging parents and understanding what Latino children are learning at home, teachers can develop practical steps that help to scaffold from their cultural assets.

In short, this chapter points to a *culturally situated* understanding of how young children learn that may not entirely overlap with traditional conceptualizations of quality. Scholars rightfully focus on the sensitivity of caregivers or teachers, their capacity to support children's cognitive challenges or motivate learning activities (e.g., *instructional support*, Pianta, Hamre, & Allen, 2012). But we talk about each regardless of culture, as if sensitivity or cognitive fostering occurs without the particular meanings, linguistic conventions, and scripted social norms that young children observe, imitate, and learn inside their immediate social contexts.

Conventional Notions of Quality

The contemporary rise of child-care and pre-k programs stems from two important movements: importing the German and Swiss model of kindergarten by New England activists in the mid-nineteenth century, and widening government support of child welfare agencies in the early twentieth century. Indicators of quality from both movements – serving government's desire to efficiently regulate child-care settings – became tied to attributes of facilities, group sizes, and caregiver credentials (Bliss, 1957). These markers remain relevant to ensure children's safety and the presence of caring adults, as well as to assess appropriate class sizes or the adequacy of teacher training.

The quality of child care or pre-k is typically defined in terms of *structural* or *process dimensions*. The empirical search for potent elements of quality is motivated by the

pursuit of greater predictive validity and increasing the magnitude of sustainable benefits on children's cognitive and social-emotional development. By examining this varied body of work, we discover how adults foster early learning and socialization, then how their efficacy might increase as they learn more about the culturally situated nature of children's growth.

Structural Dimensions of Quality

Originally, the quality of early education was signaled by structural and organizational factors, such as group size, the teacher-child ratio, and teacher education levels. These aspects of quality seemed important; intuitively, many people sensed that having a smaller group of three- and four-year-olds in a class would probably be a calmer, more enriching environment than one with a larger group. With a class of 24, one might assume that children would be more comfortable having three adults to guide activities, rather than having one attending to all of the youngsters. Similarly, most people would assume that teachers with more education would provide higher-quality care than those with less education.

By the 1990s, however, modest changes in these structural gauges of quality failed to predict variation in young children's developmental gains. Predictive validity could be established for extreme characteristics, such as excessively high class sizes or untrained teachers. Yet, regulatory tinkering with the ratio of children per adult in pre-k classrooms, for example, was not consistently predictive of children's growth curves in cognitive or social-emotional domains (e.g., NICHD, 1996; Perlman et al., 2017). The appeal of teachers having four-year college degrees remains strong, but unless training includes rigorous study of child development, the bachelor's degree holds slight, if any, benefits for children (Early et al., 2007; Fuller, 2011).

Social Processes Defining Quality

More promising findings have emerged regarding the importance of process dimensions of quality. The character of interactions between teacher and child, for instance, has come to be viewed (and empirically substantiated) as fundamental, including the adult's sensitivity to the child's language, gestures, and emotional reactions, or how the caregiver or teacher organizes learning activities. This *process* domain of quality is not entirely divorced from structural facets: poorly staffed classrooms, decrepit facilities, and teacher turnover all contribute to the quality of interactions among adults and children (Phillips, Mekos, Scarr, McCartney, & Abbott–Shim, 2000).

Still, this shift toward interactions among teachers and children has highlighted the micro practices and agility of caregivers as they engage individual children. The process dimensions of quality are manifest in both adult-child interactions and how caregivers and teachers craft the social organization of learning or play activities.

Teacher-Child Interaction. The interplay of caregiver sensitivity and the skilled fostering of cognitive and language growth have attracted considerable scholarly attention in recent years. "Across all types of settings, young children whose caregivers provide ample verbal and cognitive stimulation," one review notes, "are sensitive and responsive, and give children generous amounts of attention and support are more advanced in all realms of development" (Phillips & Lowenstein, 2017, p. 487). For example, when teachers attend and respond to children, make eye contact, and respect their autonomy, children feel more comfortable and are more receptive to learning. The field has come to view this relationship between the adult and the child as fundamental, as several careful studies find how sensitivity, responsiveness, and skilled cognitive fostering through rich language and inquisitive dialogue with children advance at least cognitive dimensions of child development (e.g., Hamre, Hatfield, Pianta, & Jamil, 2013). Fortunately, most early childhood teachers are warm and engaged: just one in five caregivers, in a large, national study, was observed as detached from the children being served.

Social Organization and Learning Activities. How teachers engage young children with rich language and arrange educational activities – offering cognitive challenge and emotional support for tasks – represents a complementary facet of process quality. The cognitive and linguistic richness of learning activities also predicts stronger child development when "characterized by teachers' sensitivity to individual needs, support for positive behavior, and stimulation of language and cognitive development" (Pianta, Downer, & Hamre, 2016, p. 119). A summary of recent work appears in Yoshikawa et al. (2013), who argue for the importance of "interactions that help children acquire new knowledge and skills… elicit verbal responses and reactions from them, and foster engagement in and enjoyment of learning" (2011, p. 1).

We also know that idle time in child-care or pre-k settings slows children's learning growth; in contrast, time spent on rich oral language and engaging preliteracy activities predicts stronger cognitive growth among three- and four-year-olds, with no discernible decrement to social development (Burchinal, Vandergrift, Pianta, & Mashburn, 2010; Fuller, Bein, Bridges, Kim, & Rabe-Hesketh, 2017; Loeb, Fuller, Kagan, & Carrol, 2004).

Engaging and emotionally supportive activities focused on math concepts also appear to yield positive effects on early growth. Teachers who arrange instructionally rich tasks appear to foster stronger cognitive development (Bridges et al., 2019; Hamre & Pianta, 2005; Stipek, 2017). That said, few teachers consistently offer this type of care; among those attending to infants or toddlers, only one in four caregivers was deemed "moderately" to "highly" stimulating of cognitive growth (NICHD, 1996).

Next, we will place this evolving focus on social-process elements of quality alongside the *cultural turn* in social psychology and child development. The nation's rediscovery of race and poverty in the 1960s exposed differing forms of parenting and child socialization, often stigmatizing Black or Latino families as enmeshed in a dismal "culture of poverty," beset by material misery, harsh discipline, and little respect for the young child's potential for growth. Economic poverty became broadly associated with poor parenting.

Culturally Situated Dimensions of Quality

It is difficult to imagine how human-scale processes inside child-care or pre-k settings could *not* be mediated by children's culturally acquired forms of cognition, language, and social norms. Take, for instance, the perennial debate over whether young children learn best through (variably structured) play, borne from culturally assumed proclivities to explore and take risks, or via "school readiness" activities, focused on letter and word recognition and advancing knowledge of math concepts (Denham & Burton, 2003; Fisher, Hirsh-Pasek, Newcombe, & Golinkoff, 2013; Fuller et al., 2017). Early educators and scholars alike make tacit assumptions about how the classroom agenda should fit parents' preferences and/or dominant institutional and economic demands.

Scholars of child socialization have consistently focused on preparing young children for the cognitive requirements and social routines of school, then the workplace and salient structures of opportunity. So, pre-k and early schooling tends to focus on the individual child's growth, conventionally defined as "the habits, values, goals, and knowledge" that ready the new student for regimented institutions and the generalized "society" (Macoby, 1980, p. v). How preschool organizations prepare Latino youngsters for their immediate community, then bridge to wider social settings, is one facet of socialization that is asked less frequently.

Culture and Poverty

When non-White or culturally distinct children arrive to U.S. classrooms, they have long been seen as somehow lacking needed attributes or skills—and since the 1960s viewed as inevitably impaired by a corrosive "culture of poverty" (Lewis, 1968). Many of these children – whether of Latino, African, or Asian heritage – certainly experience cultural activities and practices inside their homes that depart from White, middle-class ones.

This attention to children's varying contexts a half-century ago, as opposed to hereditary notions of intelligence or fixed traits, would help spur the rise of cultural psychology and novel ways of understanding child development. As Bloom (1963) argued early on, children's early social experiences and situated learning trump any static notion of personality. Then, pioneering research among Black families in poor parts of Chicago began to illuminate how parenting practices – varying among and within racial groups – shaped young children's early language and preliteracy skills (Hess & Shipman, 1965).

Meanwhile, the new field of cultural psychology, inspired by the early work of Mead (1931), along with Whiting J. & Whiting B. (1975), detailed widely varying parenting goals and practices from around the globe, including Spanish-speaking societies. By 2006, Richard Shweder and colleagues detailed a rich array of research that revealed "one mind but many mentalities." Scholars were detailing the immense variation in how different families approached raising their young children. As Markus et al. noted (1996),

> the communities, societies, and cultural contexts within which people participate provide the interpretive frameworks – including the images, concepts, and narratives as well as the means and practices and patterns of behavior – by which people make sense of… and organize their actions.

Cognitive Growth in Cultural Bounds

Cultural psychologists highlight two discrete breakthroughs that moved the field of child development beyond the acultural assumption of universal home practices that result in normatively uniform child outcomes (be they cognitive processes or social competencies). First, the influence of the child's immediate contexts leads to tacit cognitive demands and social norms, apprenticed from birth forward, long before entry to school (e.g., LeVine et al., 2001). That is, the child's earliest development involves not only near-universal physiological dynamics, but also learning and membership within a particular set of cognitive requirements and social-behavioral expectations (that is, *cultural* in character).

Second, when such child-rearing ideologies or practices become highly instantiated, they shape what members must "know, think, feel, want, value and hence… decide to do to carry forward the normal practices of their society" (Shweder et al., 2006, p. 730). In short, "thinking depends on features of the context, not just on the mental activity of brains" (Correa-Chávez & Rogoff, 2009, p. 7; for a review, Kagitcibasi, 1996). Young children learn within an ecocultural network of adults and peers, which holds particular meanings, language, social scripts and roles, and everyday social practices (Weisner, 2002).

One theoretical piece related to the culturally instantiated nature of learning comes from how children observe and mimic the behavior of adult or peer "models," what became known as social learning theory (Bandura, 1977). Departing from behaviorist reinforcement, these cognitive theorists emphasized how the child self-consciously reflects on one's "trial behavior," then observes the reactions of others in the local social setting. In this way, children learn how their utterances and actions hold efficacy within their immediate social norms.

These ideas lent theoretical clarity to the work of cultural psychologists, who began to argue that the mind devises schema, frameworks, or categories that lend automaticity to the mind's interpretation of everyday information and social cues (D'Andrade & Strauss, 1992). Thus, cognitive

structures are socially shaped in two ways: how informational or behavioral demands encouraged by parents and adults are interpreted by children, and how the child makes meaning of, and adapts to, normative feedback within daily practices. Our cognitive apparatus frames belief and behavior as a web of tacit social scripts, language, and meanings, "culture in mind," as psychologist Brad Shore (1996) argues.

The child's implicit mimicry of another's behavior, along with the desire to feel efficacious in one's immediate context, helps to further animate culturally situated views of cognition. Rogoff & Callanan (2016) focus on what they term informal learning: "It's non-didactic; is embedded in meaningful activity; builds on the learner's initiative, interest, or choice (rather than resulting from external demands or requirements); and does not involve assessment external to the activity." For example, Mexican-heritage children often display strong collaborative skills and initiative, fostering support of peers and cooperative norms (Cabrera, 2013). More broadly, the middle-class aspiration that ties school success to upward mobility may be discounted by Latino families who instead emphasize family and community well-being (Lutz & LeVine, 1982; Rosado-May, Urrieta, Dayton, & Rogoff, in press).

Rogoff and colleagues have demonstrated the high level of informal learning mastered by Guatemalan and indigenous Mexican children, simultaneously attending to multiple events around them (López, Correa-Chávez, Rogoff, & Gutiérrez, 2010). Young children glean important abilities from observing the more skilled members of their community. Children routinely work in "skilled coordination" with extended family, deftly blending priorities and taking initiative in contributing to household duties without being asked (Alcalá & Rogoff, 2017; Silva, Shimpi, & Rogoff, 2015).

We will return to how the cultural expectations and cognitive demands in the home may differ from those in traditional U.S. classrooms—a disconnect that speaks to how we conceive quality in care and pre-k settings. But first, we focus on how young Latino children acquire the skills and understanding that renders them competent in their immediate contexts – what this process looks like inside many Latino families, in terms of both parenting approaches and behavioral practices; and how research has transformed the field of social cognition, which alters how we think about children's early learning.

Cultural Strengths of Latino Children

To better understand how children's culturally derived strengths or "assets" play out in the early education classroom, we draw on the accumulating literature on child-rearing inside Latino families. Traditional aspects of quality – the dimensions of structure and process – are likely conditioned by the cultural assumptions made by teachers and whether institutionalized scripts in classrooms recognize the social practices children have acquired at home and inside their communities. We briefly review the research that has illuminated the cultural assets of Latino children, and how the disconnect with assumptions held by caregivers or teachers may have far-reaching effects on children's cognitive and social-emotional growth.

Cultural Assets

To identify the cultural strengths that Latino children bring to pre-k and early-elementary school, researchers examine the "apprenticing practices" and immediate contexts through which young children learn to become competent members of their immediate communities (Cabrera, Beeghly, & Eisenberg, 2012; Fuller & García-Coll, 2010; Moll, 2015; Rogoff et al., 2017). Young children may arrive in the classroom with complex language skills, recognition of text, cooperation skills, and expectations regarding adult authority – competencies shared across or particular to specific cultural groups or social classes.

Epidemiologists first discovered the embedded cultural practices of immigrant Latina mothers that resulted in surprisingly positive child health outcomes (for review, Mendoza, 2009). These researchers noted how rates of infant mortality and low birth weight among babies born to first-generation Mexican mothers in the U.S. rival, and at times fall below the corresponding rates for their White, middle-class peers. These Latina mothers displayed healthier prenatal practices – less smoking and drinking, higher consumption of fresh fruit and vegetables – compared with White mothers (Escarce, Morales, & Rumbaut, 2006; Guerrero et al., 2013).

This has become known in scholarly circles as the "immigrant paradox," where the heritage culture hosts practices that shape stronger child outcomes than the poor or middle-class norms adopted by many second- and third-generation families. This paradox motivated research into how social practices and expectations, generally fostered in the home, shape the early growth and school performance of young Latino children (García-Coll & Marks, 2012). Our team, for instance, has shown how Latino-heritage children – especially those of Mexican origin – arrive in kindergarten with social skills that rival or exceed levels reported by parents or teachers for their White, middle-class peers, despite the fact that many come from low-income households (Guerrero et al., 2013; see also Crosnoe, 2006).

The comparatively strong capacity of Latino children to cooperate and focus on instructional tasks in kindergarten classrooms predicts their relatively strong performance in knowledge of math (Galindo & Fuller, 2010). Similarly, Fuligni and colleagues have shown how adolescents who identify more strongly as Latino, and respect obligations to the well-being of their families, demonstrate higher levels of achievement in school (Fuligni & Pedersen, 2002), and display more robust mental health (Telzer, Tsai, Gonzales, & Fuligni, 2015).

So, which cultural assets, drawing from this line of research, could directly inform the social organization of pre-k and early-elementary classrooms? We consider parents' discrete *practices* found inside homes, including: (1) high expectations for proper behavior and supporting collective obligation; (2) apprenticing and commitment to foster learning; and (3) emphasizing respect for authority, as reflected in language.

Expecting Respectful Behavior and Shared Obligations. Scholars have detailed how many Latino parents ensure that their children are properly brought up (literally "well educated" or *bien educado*) by displaying respect for adults (*con respeto*), commitment to family (*familismo*), and positive comportment (*buen comportamiento*; Bridges et al., 2012; Halgunseth, Ispa, & Rudy, 2006; Jensen, Reese, Kenyon, & Bennett, 2015).

Children learn about social roles, tools, and requisite knowledge through their daily activities. In the home, this may involve chores, helping with siblings, preparing meals, and watching television or playing outside. Language and cognitive demands are embedded in such daily routines at home and inside classrooms. Pre-k teachers, for instance, may establish predictable routines for young children with little curiosity about how they compare with what is happening inside children's homes. So, while young Latino children may spend less time than White peers in parent-arranged instructional activities (e.g., reading, online tasks), the former appear to spend more time assisting parents with younger siblings, attending to household guests, and helping at meal times (Bridges et al., 2015; Livas-Dlott et al., 2010).

Young children often enjoy emotional support and cognitive facilitation in their everyday activities at home. That is, adults foster the cognitive requirements needed for displaying competence in highly valued activities. Early educators, however, often fail to consider *"how meaningfully classroom interactions are instantiated, that is, the extent to which they incorporate children's local knowledge and experiences outside the classroom"* (Jensen, Grajeda, & Haertel, 2018, p. 3).

In contrast, Reese et al. (2014) found that California teachers switched to Spanish, their children's home language, when they verbalized emotional support, to provide comfort, praise, or rectify problems experienced by the children. Similarly, current efforts to gauge the cultural fit of classroom activities – drawing on children's own cultural assets and norms – emphasize activities that "explore and value aspects of students' out-of-school lives in order to make personal connections with classroom content" (Jensen et al., 2018, p. 4).

The emphasis placed by many Latino parents on the child's obligation to the collective, from exhibiting the family's virtues and maintaining its reputation, to contributing to its economic security later on, has long been reported by scholars and writers (e.g., Calzada et al., 2014; Urrea, 2018). Latina mothers often express worry that their young children are getting too selfish or individualistic (*egoísta*; Holloway & Fuller, 1997; Jaramillo, Pérez, & González, 2013).

We earlier detailed how the cooperative skills of Mexican-heritage kindergartners, including a ready eagerness to engage shared classroom tasks, pay off in terms of acquired comprehension of math concepts (Galindo & Fuller, 2010). Early educators could take explicit advantage of collectively oriented notions of competence. Instead, teachers often act from a highly individualized notion of child psychology, emphasizing steady assessment of the lone child's behavior, parceling out praise and personalized guidance. It is the child's curiosities and self-esteem that become salient in these classrooms, normative expectations that may feel foreign to many immigrant or second-generation Latino children.

Apprenticed Learning at Home. A second set of cultural assets is tied to Vygotsky's (1978) realization that children's competencies in cognitive and social domains are built from the material conditions of their everyday lives, whether they grow up on a farm, factory town, or Manhattan apartment. Children "apprentice," practicing elements of language and discourse conventions, their role in the family or neighborhood, and their influence in a variety of collective, social settings. For many Latino children, this means apprenticing as one member in a family, whose integrity and well-being comes first, primary to their interests.

Ample research has demonstrated the strong commitment of Latino families to support the learning experiences of their children. For example, Galindo, Sonnenschein, and Montoya-Avila (2019) found that Latina mothers of different education levels use multiple approaches to help teach their children math. Similarly, Civil and Andrade (2002) showed that Latina mothers support the development of math skills at home by involving their children in daily tasks that require basic mathematics.

Respect for Authority. Latino children often are raised to respect adult authority – ranging from those more distant to close family and kin. Richard Rodriguez (1992), the Latino essayist, talks of "the world of *tú*," his own network of warm and familiar kin members, compared with more formal adult acquaintances, for whom everyday verbs must be conjugated differently. Or, he notes the derogatory word, *pocho*, used to describe an English-speaking cousin who had lost proficiency in speaking respectfully in Spanish to his grandparents.

Early field work tended to classify Latino child-rearing as authoritarian in character (Halgunseth, Ispa, & Rudy, 2006). More recently, research reveals many parents who display steady affection and encouragement, in addition to firm rules enforced with direct language. Our team studied discourse inside Mexican-heritage families over a 14-month period, yielding data on nearly 1,500 attempts by mothers to achieve behavioral compliance from their four-year-olds (Livas-Dlott et al., 2010). Direct commands characterized the majority of these utterances, yet often they incorporated an explanation or strategy to gain the child's cooperation. Reliance on firm commands was less frequent among better-educated or acculturated mothers – revealing widening variation in cultural contexts.

How Latino children tacitly understand adult authority – especially a teacher who behaves in a foreign manner – may not serve them well. After tracking three-year-olds from home to school over a two-year period, Tudge, Odero, Hogan, and Etz (2003) found that children who initiated conversations with the teachers, and participated more frequently, were perceived to be more competent by their teachers. But if first-generation Latino children are raised to respect adults – which includes not questioning grown-ups –youngsters may appear to be less engaged or lacking in language skills. And the propensity of young Latino to speak-up or publicly demonstrate competence is further ordered by gender (Caughy, Peredo, Owen, & Mills, 2016; Cristofaro & Tamis-LeMonda, 2008).

Cultural Mismatch – Children and Early Educators

Although Latino families bring ample cultural strengths, the extent to which these assets are embraced by early educators remains unclear. We often observe wide cultural distance between early educators and many of the Latino families they serve. This concern is manifest in basic data about the teachers of our nation's diverse young children: about 80% of elementary-grade teachers are White (Taie, Goldring, & Spiegelman, 2018), although half of all students come from other ethnic backgrounds (NCES, 2017). Currently, about 11% of pre-k teachers are Latino, which maps onto about 25% of the children. Representation of Latino teachers in the pre-k workforce is likely growing, as federal Head Start and state programs attempt to hire classroom aides and lead teachers. One-fifth of preschool teachers reported gaining certification to serve English learners (ELs) – most of whom are Latino (Garcia, 2018).

Preschool is the first institution that Latino parents confront locally, embedded in wider expectations and hopes of upward mobility. It can be quite a cultural shock for immigrant and even second-generation parents – many worried about the individualistic tone of *Americano* youngsters. Latino parents report strong enthusiasm for education, while remaining wary over the institution's behavioral expectations, delivered in a foreign language with strange social conventions (Suárez-Orozco & Suárez-Orozco, 1995). Yet, American pre-k, as noted above, typically manifests social rules – from celebrating learning through play to praising the performance of individual children – which may not fit the social-historical heritage of Latino families (Fuller, 2007).

Why does it remain so difficult – despite widening rhetorical enthusiasm for children's cultural assets – for early educators to learn about embedded social behaviors and norms, and adjust classroom practices to better support Latino children? This final section reviews what is known about the organization of preschool and early-elementary classrooms, along with attributes of teachers, both of which mitigate against recognizing what children already know, and how they expect to behave in school. Then, we close by reporting on several examples of best practices, where teachers and policy leaders have figured out how to scaffold from children's cultural backgrounds.

Institutionalized Pedagogy

The scarcity of instructional activities and rich language exchanges with teachers, and the abundance of unstructured time, in many classrooms appear to constrain young children's early growth – troubling in the context of stark delays in Latino children's oral language, preliteracy, and cognitive processing skills at entry to kindergarten (Fuller et al., 2017; Pianta et al., 2016; Reardon & Portilla, 2016).

Worry over the lack of cognitive demands recurrently surfaces in a field that often assumes young children thrive when their curiosities are fostered through play, advanced by stimulating environments (Fuller, 2007). Yet, many Latino parents view pre-k as the first year of formal schooling, anticipating that teachers will advance children's language and early literacy skills (Holloway & Fuller, 1997). (We are not taking a normative position, yet emphasizing the lack of dialogue with parents situated in diverse cultural groups.)

Set against the policy backdrop of school accountability, there's strong pressure on teachers and school officials to ensure preschool is an effective "intervention." So instructional coaches or inservice training focus on the (important) pragmatics of instructional activities, and the virtues of "guided play"; children and families remain the objects of intervention, not the sources of novel input on how they are socializing kids. In this context, it becomes much less likely that teachers will pause to inquire about how Latino children are being raised, tacit expectations for activities with peers, and the behavioral priorities held by their parents.

More broadly, the policy priority to improve the skills of pre-k teachers builds from a classic human capital framework. If the field can agree upon the competencies displayed by high-quality teachers, then infuse the workforce with these proficiencies – presumably predictive of children's growth – then gains in children's growth will follow. But this implies a return to universal forms of pedagogy or activity structures that: (a) complement the strengths and social norms that children bring to pre-k, and (b) assume a singular form of pre-k that imparts the same cognitive and social forms to all children, independent of their local communities. Does such regimentation, for instance, encourage teachers to respect how many Latino parents conceive of children's subordination to the collective good, or discourse rules embedded in the Spanish language?

Diverse Mix of Pre-K Organizations

The policy struggle over what mix of agencies can best operate pre-k organizations – whether run by local schools or nonprofits – offers another institutional juxtaposition that serves to recognize or discount cultural variety in the upbringing of young children. Over four-fifths of Head Start preschools, for example, are run by community action agencies, originating from their Great Society ideals. Local school districts operate just one in six early childhood centers nationwide (Alamillo et al., 2018).

This structuring of early education through federal and state funding streams supports a variety of diverse caregivers and organizations, reflected in staff composition, languages spoken, and cultural sensitivities – setting in motion a variety of culturally situated facets of child-rearing. One ripe area for future research is to learn how this variety of pre-k centers, operated by school districts or community-based nonprofits, can recruit more diverse teachers and offer greater cultural variety in their classrooms and ties with parents.

Whether or not pre-k teachers attend to each individual child, for example, or encourage the child's obligations to the group likely varies across cultural groups and locations. The comfort level of young Latino children in speaking back to adults is conditioned by home practices, as reviewed above. Indeed, the degree of emotional facilitation perceived by a child is likely affected by the language in which such interaction occurs.

The social and verbal interplay portrayed in recent work on classroom quality may feel a bit foreign for Latino parents, some of whom worry about their children becoming too "cheeky" or disrespectful (Greenfield & Quiroz, 2013; Urrea, 2018). That is, the learning or developmental aims that we value, along with interwoven pedagogical practices, are embedded in the cognitive requirements, discourse patterns, and social norms that cultural or social-class communities believe to be natural.

Culturally rooted differences may go misunderstood at the cost of non-mainstream children, such as when Latino children refrain from asking questions to demonstrate respect for the teacher, and dramatically backfires when it conveys a lack of engagement. These disconnects may generate distance between Latino preschoolers and their teachers – a relationship that consistently predicts children's learning in preschool (Pianta & Stuhlman, 2004).

Conversely, children's adoption of cultural practices consonant with their preschool teachers may disconnect them from their families, language, and cultural identity. Valenzuela's (1999) work on "subtractive schooling" argues that schools can erode social foundations that Latino children learn at home, while handicapping them in acquiring the majority culture's dominant way. So, how the institution of nonparental child care and pre-k is organized – governed by which communities and civic leaders – will condition which young teachers are hired, how public support is distributed, and the odds of cultural and linguistic consonance inside these organizations in which America's diverse children are nurtured.

Racial Segregation and Difference

Racialized signs of status and segregation may better explain the likely disconnects between families and early educators described above. It is not so much innocent naiveté of cultural variety or missing the tacit strengths of non-mainstream children; instead, teachers and early education officials simply make race-based judgments about kids and families, or fail to address the persisting segregation of children. This is the argument made by critical analysts of early education. At times certain indicators – most recently the documented suspension rates of Black children from *preschool* – suggest racialized markers are at play with distressing results (e.g., Gilliam, Maupin, Reyes, Accavitti, & Shic, 2016).

Additional research is required to understand whether the residue of "culture-of-poverty" accounts leads teachers and education officials to punish young children for their materially impoverished origins, and whether this plays out differently among Black, Latino, and Asian neighborhoods within the U.S. context. Our research team has shown that Latino kindergartens have generally entered racially segregated schools, even among ethnically diverse school districts, with little progress over the past generation (Fuller et al., 2019). And children of foreign-born parents enter more segregated schools, further isolated from White or middle-class Latino peers.

To the extent that boundaries of cultural groups are vividly demarcated by racial characteristics, Black and Latino children may remain even less well understood inside care settings and classrooms. Ironically, these disconnects may be greatest in integrated settings. This, of course, holds implications for the early education workforce, as discussed above. Racial or cultural consonance would at least increase the likelihood that teachers will pause to listen and learn from young children, perhaps considering how the social organization of classrooms and learning activities can build from the strengths, not the stigmatized attributes, of children.

Advances in Methods and Measurement

A variety of developmentalists and sociologists have progressed in defining the cultural assets of young children with ecological validity, along with how pre-k teachers can recognize and scaffold from these strengths. Bridges et al. (2012) have built a tool by which parents or teachers can rate the social competencies of Latino children, drawing on earlier ethnographic studies of how parents (variably) value their children's affectionate qualities, positive comportment, respectfulness, communication, and self-reliance (maturity expectations). These dimensions, derived from item-response theory, are based on scales that show internal consistency for the Mexican American Socialization (MAS) Scale, but as yet have not been tested for predictive validity.

Complementary efforts assess the capacity of teachers to observe the cultural knowledge and social practices of young children inside the classroom. Jensen et al. (2018) have conceptually specified three major domains in which teachers recognize, accommodate, and teach from children's culturally situated understandings (not limited to Latino-heritage

children). These domains of teaching practice and social organization include Life Applications (language use, appreciation of difference, equitable participation), Self in Group (competition, cooperation, social motivation), and Agency (child's autonomy in the classroom, role flexibility, equitable expectations of children). The instrument shares the aims of acultural classroom observation measures, while attending to how teachers recognize and organize classroom activities in ways that accommodate and value cultural variety among children.

The designers began with 138 observable markers of 38 indicators set in the four domains, called the Classroom Assessment of Sociocultural Interactions (CASI), and conducted measurement studies to improve internal consistency and simplify the observational protocol (Jensen, Rueda, Reese, & Garcia, 2014). They have established strong construct validity and inter-rater reliability within classrooms of Mexico and the United States. Similar to the MAS scale for young children's competencies, the next step for the CASI observation tool is to assess its validity in predicting differences in children's early learning.

Promising Practices – Scaffolding from Cultural Strengths

Caregivers and teachers often cite examples of young children's strengths or skills, apparently woven into their cultural fabric: respect for adult authority, eagerness to cooperate with peers, or hesitancy to ask questions or stand out. Volumes continue to fill with appeals to practitioners for culturally responsive teaching (e.g., Ladson-Billings, 1995). But how can caregivers and teachers inquire mindfully about the cultural strengths of children, then craft pedagogical practices that build from these social and cognitive assets? This section reports on four promising strategies.

Fostering Bilingual Skills and Discourse Conventions

A review by the National Academies of Science (2017) highlights the importance of rich language in English *and* Spanish in fostering preliteracy and higher-order thinking skills (Gándara, 2013). The Academy's authors urge early educators to arrange classroom activities in ways that promote oral language proficiency (e.g., receptive and expressive oral language, phonology, oral vocabulary, grammar, discourse features), including frequent interaction between ELs and those whose home language is English. A high-quality pre-k classroom encourages thoughtful oral language among *all* children and adults.

August and Shanahan (2006) similarly argue that limited oral proficiency in pre-k and elementary classrooms constrains young children's early learning, especially in building reading skills. Again, pedagogical practices and the structuring of activities tacitly incorporate or marginalize the competencies of young ELs in the classroom. For example, the careful grouping of children, each assuming a different, active role (e.g., reading, listening, or helping another), can facilitate wide engagement (Fuchs, Fuchs, & Burish, 2000). Research has demonstrated that peer-assisted learning facilitates English-language development as well (Francis & Vaughn, 2009). It provides Latino youngsters, and other ELs, structured opportunity to practice language, demonstrate comprehension, and expand their linguistic repertoire with peers (Martin-Beltrán, 2014).

Organizing Culturally Relevant Pedagogy

This strategy requires classroom staff to frame curricula in ways that incorporate the culturally embedded social forms and discourse norms that young children acquire at home (Ladson-Billings, 1995). Recognizing holidays and historical episodes does validate the heritage of a particular group. But deeper connections are made through classroom activities that draw on home language, children's indigenous knowledge, norms of cooperation, and engagement with culturally relevant materials.

Classroom activities have been designed that foster Latino children's academic development and simultaneously support cultural competence by scaffolding from their linguistic and social norms (Scanlan & López, 2015). Teachers who use this *culturally relevant pedagogy* (CRP; Ladson-Billings, 1995) uphold high learning expectations and build from culturally relevant content (Aronson & Laughter, 2016). When teachers implement CRP in pre-k classrooms – validating and scaffolding from children's cultural heritage – youngsters may gain a sense of belonging, experiencing equal standing with classmates, and feel more deeply connected to their teachers (Wanless & Crawford, 2016).

Classrooms and allied programs serving the specific needs or cognitive strengths of ELs appear to accelerate their early growth (Gándara & Contreras, 2009; Suárez-Orozco, Suárez-Orozco, & Todorova, 2008). These benefits may be mediated by teachers or aides who hold bilingual competence and cultural sensitivities, and better understand children's strengths and local challenges. Dual-language immersion preschools are proving popular among parents in California and other states, although the child-level benefits, relative to conventional pre-k settings, remain largely unknown (Buysse, Peisner-Feinberg, Páez, Hammer, & Knowles, 2014). Various strategies are employed by teachers to build from children's cultural knowledge and language, including the use of Latino-heritage literature and storytelling within structured activities. This promotes cognitively demanding and validating interactions among and between children and teachers (Nathenson-Mejia & Escamilla, 2003).

One rendition of CRP comes from the well-known funds-of-knowledge approach by which teachers draw on parents' knowledge and heritage narratives (González, Moll, & Amanti, 2005). These scholars, for instance, offer one commonplace example that holds visceral meaning for many children: selling Mexican candy. By asking even young children

to inquire of street vendors, González and colleagues report how they enjoyed the activity, which tapped into their intrinsic motivation, lived experience, and social networks – in turn fostering growth in reading and writing skills, research inquiry, and everyday mathematics.

Professional Learning Communities

Many teachers hold little expertise in working with young ELs, the majority of whom come from Latino backgrounds (Hopkins, Lowenhaupt, & Sweet, 2015). Even recently certified EL teachers report feeling unprepared to work with these children (Herrera & Murry, 2006; López, Scanlan, & Gundrum, 2013). One promising strategy is to form a professional learning community (PLC) among teachers to learn more about their young students and experiment with promising practices.

DuFour and DuFour (2010, p. 11), for instance, define an "ongoing process in which educators work collaboratively in recurring cycles of collective inquiry and action research to achieve better results for the students they serve." The PLC model emphasizes how teachers can work together, inquiring about the communities they serve and sharing knowledge of classroom activities that invite children to express their cultural knowledge and forms of social participation (Hopkins et al., 2015). Such teacher networks, within or among schools, strive to diagnose learning challenges facing Latino children, and how to create sustainable and effective classroom practices (Hord & Tobia, 2012; Stoll, Bolam, McMahon, Wallace, & Thomas, 2006).

Family and School Partnerships

Fostering closer relations with families offers an obvious means for learning about children's culturally embedded strengths, then for building learning activities that complement home practices (Galindo & Sheldon, 2012; Schulting, Malone, & Dodge, 2005). The aim remains the same: weaving children's particular ways of knowing into the social organization of classrooms, devising methods for advancing cognitive and social-emotional growth. As Epstein (2010) argues, schools and families offer *overlapping* spheres of influence that can reinforce pro-learning activities in both settings.

Family-school collaboration can deepen via differing mechanisms. The interchange between early educators and parents can serve to support learning activities in the home, widen parents' own social networks and resources, offer an inviting school climate, and enrich the cultural identity and familial ties that benefit young children (Montoya-Ávila, Ghebreab, & Galindo, 2019). Parent training and informal get-togethers can bring new material resources and friendships that buoy parents (Small, 2011). Family and school engagement appear more potent and sustainable when well-integrated into a pre-k center and everyday curriculum, moving well beyond episodic festivals and holiday celebrations (Galindo & Pucino, 2012).

Pro-Learning Home Activities

Latino parents typically report a strong commitment to their children's formal schooling (e.g., Jiménez-Castellanos, Ochoa, & Olivos, 2016), even though many have attained little formal schooling. Home reading and allied learning activities – rising in prevalence among children of color in recent decades (Reardon & Portilla, 2016) – still occur less frequently in low-income households (Guerrero et al., 2013; Montoya-Ávila et al., 2019). So, meaningful parent-teacher partnerships can help, linking the family's everyday activities to pedagogical work occurring inside the child's preschool. This may include telling stories, cooking and baking practice, or tying vocabulary and math concepts to household chores.

Civil, Bratton, and Quintos (2005), for instance, developed a program – Math and Parent Partnerships in the Southwest (MAPPS) – to engage Latino parents in learning mathematical concepts inside the home. These developers created workshops for parents and educators (working together) on how young children can practice math in everyday activities, synched between home and classroom, to advance children's sense of competence and practical relevance. Lopez and Donovan (2009) similarly implemented Family Math Nights to embed math practices within families (also, Hawkins and Graue, 2008).

Overall, these four strategies offer theoretical frames and practical activities, inside classrooms or homes, to recognize what young children are learning within their immediate social contexts, then advance cognitive or social agility via organized learning activities. Parts of these models imply clear intentionality around learning, even for very young children, along with coaching and emotional support from caring adults.

What's intriguing is the challenge of how to "intervene" in the home and school to augment implicit learning that already takes place. Teachers and parents discover how to scaffold from culturally embedded routines in ways that advance deeper learning and wider social agility, building from *and* extending beyond the indigenous arenas in which young children first learn. Few scholars argue that we should take as sacred the tacit routines found in the homes of diverse Latino families, many struggling with the exigencies of poverty.

Still, these promising pedagogical methods recognize and build from what Latino children already know, the cognitive requirements and social forms that mark their membership in the family and immediate community. These models also serve to enrich how we gauge the quality and contributions of early education organizations and less formal caregivers.

Summary – Diversifying Notions of Quality

We do not intend to lodge unfair criticism at educators or policy makers, who earnestly seek to lift the quality and effectiveness of this growing sector. No one intends to disregard the knowledge or social norms that toddlers and preschoolers implicitly learn at home, becoming competent members of their immediate communities. After all, Western conceptions of human development since the Enlightenment have prized the potential of young children, nurtured by kind and respectful adults. The sacred individual's growth and capacity for self-determination have long been central tenets of humanist philosophy, then modern psychology.

Still, legitimate authorities have proposed universal theories about the factors that seem to drive the healthy growth, skills, and behaviors that propel each generation into a structure of opportunities. But this affection for universal conceptions of child-rearing is limiting in cosmopolitan societies that respect and learn from plural cultures. The field now debates whether learning through play best leverages the "natural" curiosities of young children, or should pre-k explicitly teach preliteracy skills and math concepts? Perhaps it is religious dictates or proper discipline that should be privileged; no, it is dual-language immersion that universally advances cognitive agility.

What is difficult about listening carefully to children and parents, untangling how their social practices and cognitive demands differ from one's own, is that we must set aside our penchant for simple theories about how young children learn and grow along the same pathways. Of course, we should not discard universals, especially when it comes to the biological determinants of robust births and early health of infants and toddlers. But when it comes to socially embedded cognition and the acquisition of normative behaviors, we quickly find ourselves raising young children within cultural bounds.

It falls on the shoulders of caregivers and early educators in large part to acquire the language of their young charges – literally and figuratively – to understand what they know and their strengths (and blind spots). Still, highly institutionalized practices mitigate against culturally sensitive conceptions of pedagogy and organizational quality. When the classroom's dominant tongue ignores children's home language, there's an institutional problem. Or, when stakeholders require bachelor's degrees for all caregivers and teachers, it might advance professional status *and* further distance them from culturally different parents and their offspring.

The rise of dual-language pre-k classrooms is but one signal of the widening respect for cultural variety. Or take the spread of publicly funded vouchers for a panoply of individual caregivers – mainly to serve infants and toddlers, and provide greater legitimate differing parental choices. California spends nearly a billion dollars on this array of caregivers each year, offering a variable quality of care about which we know little.

The spread of cultural pluralism and cosmopolitan variety, from adult lifestyles to how parents variably raise their children, manifests a dramatic shift in contemporary society. Yet, how we organize settings for young children – then narrowly define the quality of this burgeoning institution – ignores a wide range of cognitive and social competencies that soon a majority of America's families will experience each day and warmly embrace.

Acknowledgments

We thank Cynthia García Coll, Bryant Jensen, and four anonymous reviewers, who helped to clarify the core thesis and sharpen our prose. Special thanks to Olivia Saracho for guidance along the way. Our team has been supported most recently by the Heising-Simons, Packard, and Spencer foundations.

References

Alamillo, J., Aikens, N., Moiduddin, E., Bush, C., Malone, L., & Tarullo, L. (2018). *Head Start programs in spring 2015: Structure, staff, and supports for quality.* Washington, DC: Mathematica Policy Research.

Alcalá, L., & Rogoff, B. (2017). *Collaboration as shared thinking or dividing roles: Cultural differences* (Unpublished manuscript). University of California, Santa Cruz.

Aronson, B., & Laughter, J. (2016). The theory and practice of culturally relevant education: A synthesis of research across content areas. *Review of Educational Research, 86,* 163–206.

August, D., & Shanahan, T. (2006). Synthesis: Instruction and professional development. *Developing literacy in a second language: Report of the National Literacy Panel,* Washington, DC: National Academies Press. 321–335.

Bandura, A. (1977). *Social learning theory.* Upper Saddle River, NJ: Prentice-Hall.

Bliss, L. (1957). *A survey of state regulations relating to certification of teachers in nursery schools and day care centers.* Thesis submitted for Master's degree. Corvallis: Oregon State College.

Bloom, B. S., Englehart, M. D., Furst, E. J., Hill, W. H., & Krathwohl, D. R. (1956). *The taxonomy of educational objectives, the Cognitive domain.* New York: McKay Co.

Bridges, M., Cohen, S. R., McGuire, L. W., Yamada, H., Fuller, B., Mireles, L., & Scott, L. (2012). Bien educado: Measuring the social behaviors of Mexican American children. *Early Childhood Research Quarterly.* doi: 10.1016/j.ecresq.2012.01.005

Bridges, M., Cohen, S. R., Scott, L., Fuller, B., Anguiano, R., Mangual-Figueroa, & Livas-Dlott, A. (2015). Home activities of Mexican American children: Structuring early socialization and cognitive engagement. *Cultural Diversity and Ethnic Minority Psychology, 21,* 181–190.

Bridges, M., Cohen, S. R., Anguiano, R., Fuller, B., Livas-Dlott, A., & Mangual-Figueroa, A., & Scott, L., (2019). *Purposeful parenting by Mexican American mothers: Advancing school readiness through social-emotional skills?* Manuscript submitted for publication.

Burchinal, M., Vandergrift, N., Pianta, R., & Mashburn, A. (2010). Threshold analysis of association between child care quality and child outcomes for low-income children in pre-kindergarten programs. *Early Childhood Research Quarterly, 25,* 166–176.

Buysse, V., Peisner-Feinberg, E., Páez, M., Scheffner-Hammer, C., & Knowles, M. (2014). Effects of early education programs and practices on the development and early learning of dual-language learners. *Early Childhood Research Quarterly, 29,* 765–785.

Cabrera, N. (2013). Positive development of minority children. *Social Policy Report, 27,* 2. Monograph of the Society for Research in Child Development.

Cabrera, N. J., Beeghly, M., & Eisenberg, N. (2012). Positive development of minority children: Introduction to special issue. *Child Development Perspectives, 6,* 207–209.

Cannon, J., Zellman, G., Karoly, L., & Schwartz, H. (2017). *Quality rating and improvement systems for early care and education: Making the second generation better.* Santa Monica, CA: RAND.

Civil, M., Bratton, J., & Quintos, B. (2005). Parents and mathematics education in a Latino community: Redefining parental participation. *Multicultural Education, 13*(2), 60–64.

Correa-Chávez, M., & Rogoff, B. (2009). Children's attention to interactions directed to others: Guatemalan mayan and european american patterns. *Developmental Psychology, 45*(3), 630.Crosnoe, R. (2006). *Mexican roots, American schools: How children from Mexican immigrant families make the transition into the American educational system.* Palo Alto, CA: Stanford University Press.

D'Andrade, R., & Strauss, C. (1992, eds.). *Human motives and cultural models.* Cambridge, England: Cambridge University Press.

Denham. S. A., & Burton, R. (2003). *Social and emotional prevention and intervention programing for preschoolers.* New York, NY: Kluwer-Plenum.

DeParle, J. (2019, February 4). Cleaner classrooms and rising scores: With tighter oversight Head Start shows gains. *New York Times.* Retrieved from https://www.nytimes.com/2019/02/04/us/politics/head-start-preschool.html

DuFour, R., & DuFour. R. (2010). *Learning by doing: A handbook for professional communities at work: A practical guide for PLC teams and leadership* (2nd ed.). Bloomington, IN: Solution Tree Press.

Early, D. M., Maxwell, K. L., Burchinal, M., Alva, S., Bender, R., Bryant, D., ... Zill, N. (2007). Teachers' education, classroom quality, and young children's academic skills: Results from seven studies of preschool programs. *Child Development, 78*(2), 558–580. doi:10.1111/j.1467-8624.2007.01014.x

Epstein, J. L. (2010). *School and family partnerships: Preparing educators and improving schools* (2nd ed.). Boulder, CO: Westview Press.

Escarce, J., Morales, L., & Rumbaut, R. (2006). The health status and health behaviors of Hispanics (pp. 362–409), in *Hispanics and the future of America,* edited by M. Tienda & F. Mitchell. Washington, DC: National Academies Press.

Fisher, K., Hirsh-Pasek, K. Newcombe, N., & Golinkoff, R. (2013). Taking shape: Supporting preschoolers' acquisition of geometric knowledge through guided play. *Child Development, 84,* 1872–1878.

Francis, D. J., & Vaughn, S. (2009). Effective practices for English language learners in the middle grades: Introduction to the special issue, *Journal of Research on Educational Effectiveness, 2*(4), 289–296.

Fuchs, D., Fuchs, L., & Burish, P. (2000). Peer-assisted learning strategies: An evidence-based practice to promote reading achievement. *Learning Disabilities Research and Practice, 15*(2), 85–91.

Fuligni, A. J., & Pedersen, S. (2002). Family obligation and the transition to young adulthood. *Developmental Psychology, 38*(5), 856.

Fuller, B. (2007). *Standardized childhood: The political and cultural struggle over early education.* Palo Alto, CA: Stanford University Press.

Fuller, B. (2011). College credentials and caring: How teacher training could lift young children. In E. Zigler, W. S. Gilliam, & W. S. Barnett (Eds.), *The Pre-K debates* (pp. 57–63). Baltimore, MD: Brooks Publishing.

Fuller, B., Bein, E., Bridges, M., Kim, Y., & Rabe-Hesketh, S. (2017). Do academic preschools yield stronger benefits? Cognitive emphasis, dosage, and early learning. *Journal of Applied Developmental Psychology, 52,* 1–11.

Fuller, B., & García-Coll, C. (2010). Learning from Latinos: Contexts, families, and child development in motion. *Developmental Psychology, 46,* 559–565.

Fuller, B., Kim, Y., Galindo, C., Bathia, S., Bridges, M., Duncan, G., & Garcia Valdivia, I. (2019). Worsening school segregation for Latino children? *Educational Researcher, 43,* 407–420. Online: https://journals.sagepub.com/ doi/abs/10.3102/0013189X19860814.

Galindo, C. & Fuller, B. (2010). The social competence of Latino kindergartners and growth in mathematical understanding. *Developmental Psychology, 46,* 579–592.Galindo, C., & Pucino, A. (2012). Family diversity and school-family relationships. In J. A. Banks (Ed.), *Encyclopedia of diversity in education* (pp. 885–889). Thousand Oaks, CA: Sage Publications, Inc.

Galindo, C., & Sheldon, S. (2012). School and home connections and children's kindergarten achievement gains: The mediating role of family involvement. *Early Childhood Research Quarterly, 47,* 90–103.

Gándara, P. (2013). Meeting the needs of language minorities. In P. L. Carter & K. G. Welner (Eds.), *Closing the opportunity gap: What*

America must do to give every child an even chance (pp. 156–168). New York, NY: Oxford University Press.

Gándara, P., & Contreras, F. (2009). *The Latino education crisis: The consequences of failed social policies*. Cambridge, MA: Harvard University Press.

Garcia-Coll, C., & Marks, A. K. (2012). *The immigrant paradox in children and adolescents: Is becoming American a developmental risk?* Washington, DC: American Psychological Association.

González, N., Moll, L. C., & Amanti, C. (Eds.). (2005). *Funds of knowledge: Theorizing practices in households, communities, and classrooms*. New York, NY: Routledge.

Guerrero, A., Fuller, B., Chu, L., Kim, A., Franke, T., Bridges, M., & Kuo, A. (2013). Early growth of Mexican-American children: Lagging in pre-literacy skills but not social development. *Maternal and Child Health Journal, 17,* 1701–1711.

Halgunseth, L. C., Ispa, J. M., & Rudy, D. (2006), Parental control in Latino families: An integrated review of the literature. *Child Development, 77,* 1282–1297.

Hamre, B., Hatfield, B., Pianta, R., & Jamil, F. (2014), Evidence for general and domain-specific elements of teacher–child interactions: Associations with preschool children's development. *Child Development, 85,* 1257–1274.

Hamre, B. K., & Pianta, R. C. (2005). Can instructional and emotional support in the first-grade classroom make a difference for children at risk of school failure? *Child Development, 76,* 949–967. doi: 10.1111/j.1467-8624.2005.00889.x

Hawkins, M., & Graue, E. (2008). Working with linguistically and culturally diverse families. In T. Good (Ed.), *21st century education: A reference handbook.* (pp. II-392–II-401). Thousand Oaks, CA: Sage Publications, Inc.

Herrera, S., & Murry, K. (2006) Accountability by assumption: Implications of reform agendas for teacher preparation, *Journal of Latinos and Education, 5,* 189–207.

Hess, R., & Shipman, V. (1965). Early experience and the socialization of cognitive modes in children. *Child Development, 36,* 869-886.

Holloway, S., & Fuller, B. (1997). *Through my own eyes: Single mothers and the cultures of poverty.* Cambridge, MA: Harvard University Press.

Hord, S. M., & Tobia, E. F. (2012). *Reclaiming our teaching profession: The power of educators learning in community.* New York, NY: Teachers College Press.

Jensen, B., Grajeda, S., & Haertel, E. (2018). Measuring cultural dimensions of classroom interactions. *Educational Assessment.* doi.org/10.1080/10627197.2018.1515010.

Jensen, B., Reese, L., Kenyon, K., & Bennett, C. (2015). Social competence and oral language development for young children of Latino immigrants. *Early Education & Development, 26,* 933–955.

Jiménez-Castellanos, O., Ochoa, A. M., & Olivos, E. M. (2016). Operationalizing transformative parent engagement in Latino school communities: A case study. *Journal of Latino/Latin American Studies, 8,* 93–107.

Kagitcibasi, C. (1996). *Family and human development across cultures.* Mahwah, NJ: Erlbaum.

Krogstad, J. (2019). A view of the nation's future through kindergarten demographics. Washington, DC: *Pew Research Center.* https://www.pewresearch.org/fact-tank/2019/07/31/kindergarten-demographics-in-us/.

Ladson-Billings, G. (1995). Toward a theory of culturally relevant pedagogy. *American Educational Research Journal, 32,* 65–491.

LeVine, R. A., LeVine, S. E., & Schnell, B. (2001). "Improve the women": Mass schooling, female literacy, and worldwide social change. *Harvard Educational Review, 71,* 1–50.

Lewis, O. (1968). *La vida: A Puerto Rican family in the culture of poverty.* New York, NY: Vintage.

Loeb, S., Fuller, B., Kagan, S., & Carrol, B. (2004). Child care in poor communities: Early learning effects of type, quality, and stability. *Child Development, 75,* 47–65,

López, A., Correa-Chávez, M., Rogoff, B., & Gutiérrez, K. (2010). Attention to instruction directed to another by U.S. Mexican-heritage children of varying cultural backgrounds. *Developmental Psychology, 46,* 593–601.

López, F. Scanlan, M., & Gundrum, B. (2013). Preparing teachers of English Language Learners: Empirical evidence and policy implications. *Education Policy Analysis Archives, 21*(20). Retrieved from http://epaa.asu.edu/ojs/article/view/1132

Lopez, C. O., & Donovan, L. (2009). Involving Latino parents with mathematics through family math nights. *Journal of Latinos and Education, 8,* 219–230.

Lutz, C., & LeVine, R. A. (1982). Culture and intelligence in infancy. In M. Lewis (Ed.), *Origins of intelligence* (pp. 1–28). New York, NY: Plenum.

Macoby, E. (1980). *Social development: Psychological growth and the parent-child relationship.* New York: Harcourt Brace.

Markus, H., Kitayama, S., & Heiman, R. J. (1996). Culture and "basic" psychological principles (pp. 857–913), in *Social psychology: Handbook of basic principles* edited by E. Higgins & A. Kruglanski. New York: Guilford Press.

Martin-Beltrán, M. (2014). "What do you want to say?" How adolescents use trans-languaging to expand learning opportunities. *International Multilingual Research Journal, 8,* 208–230.

Mead, M. (1931). The primitive child. pp. 669–687 in *A handbook of child psychology* edited by C. Murchison. Worcester, MA: Clark University Press.

Mendoza, F. (2009). Health disparities and children in immigrant families: A research agenda. *Pediatrics, 124* supplement, S187–S195.

Moll, L. (2015). Tapping into the 'hidden' home and community resources of students. *Kappa Delta Phi Record, 51,* 114–117.

Montoya-Ávila, A., Ghebreab, N., & Galindo, C. (2019). Towards improving educational opportunities for Black and Latino young children: Strengthening family-school partnerships. In S. Sonnenschein & B. E. Sawyer (Eds.), *Academic socialization of young Black and Latino children: Building on family strengths* (pp. 209–231). New York, NY: Springer.

Nathenson-Mejía, S., & Escamilla, K. (2003). Connecting with Latino children: Bridging cultural gaps with children's literature. *Bilingual Research Journal, 27*(1), 101–116.

National Academies (2017). *Promoting the educational success of children and youth learning English.* Washington, DC: National Academies of Sciences, Engineering, and Medicine.

National Institute of Child Health and Human Development (NICHD) Early Child Care Research Network. (1996). Characteristics of infant child care: Factoring contributing to positive caregiving. *Early Childhood Research Quarterly, 11,* 269–306.

Perlman, M., Fletcher, B., Falenchuk, O., Brunsek, A., McMullen, E., & Shah, P. (2017). Child-staff ratios in early childhood education and care settings and child outcomes: A systematic review and meta-analysis. *Plos One.* https://doi.org/10.1371/journal.pone.0170256.

Phillips, D., & Lowenstein, A. (2011). Early care, education, and child development. *Annual Review of Psychology, 62,* 483–500.

Phillips, D., & Lowenstein, A. (2017). Early care, education, and child development. *Annual Review of Psychology, 62,* 483–500.

Phillips, D., Mekos, D., Scarr, S., McCartney, K., & Abbott–Shim, M. (2000). Within and beyond the classroom door: Assessing quality in child care centers. *Early Childhood Research Quarterly, 15*(4), 475–496.

Pianta, R., Downer, J., & Hamre, B. (2016). Quality in early education classrooms: Definitions, gaps, and systems. *The Future of Children, 26*(2), 119–137.

Pianta, R., Hamre, B., & Allen, J. (2012). Teacher-student relationships and engagement: Conceptualizing, measuring, and improving the capacity of classroom interactions. In S. Christenson (Ed.), *Handbook of research on student engagement* (pp. 365–386). New York, NY: Springer.

Pianta, R. C., & Stuhlman, M. (2004). Teacher-child relationships and children's success in the first years of school. *School Psychology Review, 33*(3), 444–458.

Reardon, S., & Portilla, X. (2016). Recent trends in income, racial, and ethnic school readiness gaps at kindergarten entry. *AERA Open, 2,* 1–18.

Reese, L., Jensen, B., & Ramirez, D. (2014). Emotionally supportive classroom contexts for young Latino children in rural California. *Elementary School Journal, 114,* 501–526.

Rogoff, B. (2003). *The cultural nature of human development*. New York, NY: Oxford University Press.

Rogoff, B., Coppens, A. D., Alcala, L., Aceves-Azuara, I., Ruvalcaba, O., Lopez, A., & Dayton, A. (2017). Noticing learners' strengths through cultural research. *Perspectives on Psychological Science, 12*(5), 876–888.

Rosado-May, F. J., Urrieta, L., Jr., Dayton, A., & Rogoff, B. (in press). The pedagogy and innovation involved in indigenous knowledge systems. In N. S. Nasir, C. D. Lee, & R. Pea (Eds.), *Handbook of the cultural foundations of learning*. London, UK: Routledge.

Scanlan, M., & López, F. (2015). *Leadership for culturally and linguistically responsive schools*. New York, NY: Routledge.

Schulting, A., Malone, P., & Dodge, K. (2005). The effect of school-based kindergarten transition policies and practices on child academic outcomes. *Developmental Psychology, 41*, 860–871.

Shore, B. (1996). *Culture in mind: Cognition, culture, and the problem of meaning*. New York: Oxford.

Shweder, R., Goodnow, J., Hatano, G., LeVine, R. Markus, H., & Miller, P. (2006). The cultural psychology of development: One mind, many mentalities (pp. 716–792), in *Handbook of Child Psychology, Sixth Edition*, edited by R. Lerner. Hoboken: Wiley & Sons.

Silva, K. G., Shimpi, P. M., & Rogoff, B. (2015). Young children's attention to what's going on: Cultural differences. *Advances in Child Development and Behavior, 49*, 207–227.

Small, M. L. (2011). How to conduct a mixed method study: Recent trends in a rapidly growing literature. *Annual Review of Sociology, 37*, 57–86.

Stipek, D. (2017, July). Playful math instruction in the context of standards and accountability. *Young Children, 72*(3), 8–12.

Stoll, L., Bolam, R., McMahon, A., Wallace, M., & Thomas, S. (2006). Professional learning communities: A review of the literature. *Journal of Educational Change, 7*, 221–258.

Suárez-Orozco, C., Suárez-Orozco, M., & Todorova, I. (2008). *Learning a new land: Immigrant students in American society*. Cambridge, MA: Harvard University Press.

Taie, S., Goldring, R., & Spiegelman, M. (2018). *Character of public elementary and secondary teachers in the United States from the national teacher and principal survey, 2015–16*. Washington, DC: National Center for Education Statistics.

Telzer, E., Tsai, K., Gonzales, N., & Fuligni, A. (2015). Mexican American adolescents' family obligation values and behaviors: Links to internalizing symptoms across time and context. *Developmental Psychology, 51*, 75–86.

Tobin J., Hsueh, Y., & Karasawa, M. (2009). *Preschool in three cultures revisited*. Chicago: University of Chicago Press.

Valenzuela, A. (1999). *Subtractive schooling*. Albany: State University of New York Press.

Velez-Agosto, N., Soto-Crespo, J., Vizcarrondo-Oppenheimer, M., Vega-Molina, S., & Garcia- Coll, C. (2017). Bronfenbrenner's bio-ecological theory revision: Moving culture from the micro to the macro. *Perspectives on Psychological Science, 12*, 900–910.

Yoshikawa, H. (2011). Immigrants raising citizens: Undocumented parents and their young children. New York, NY: Russell Sage.

Wanless, S., & Crawford, P. (2016). Reading your way to a culturally responsive classroom. *Young Children, 71*. Retrieved from https://www.naeyc.org/resources/pubs/yc/may2016/culturally-responsive-classroom

Weisner, T. (2002). Ecocultural understanding of children's developmental pathways. *Human Development, 45*, 275–281.

Whiting, J., & Whiting, B. (1975). *Children of six cultures*. Cambridge, MA: Harvard University Press.

Zinsser, K. M., Shewark E. A., Denham S. A., & Curby T. W. (2014). A mixed-method examination of preschool teacher beliefs about social–emotional learning and relations to observed emotional support. *Infant and Child Development, 23*, 471–493.

26

Early Childhood Education Programs in the Public Schools

W. Steven Barnett and Allison H. Friedman-Krauss

Although overall enrollment in preschool classrooms seems to have plateaued beginning around 2000, the percentage of children enrolled in public programs has continued to increase, driven entirely by increases through the public schools (U.S. Department of Education, 2018a, 2018b). By 2017, state and locally funded pre-K programs served most of the four-year-olds enrolled in some type of preschool and a substantial (though much smaller) percentage of three-year-olds (Friedman-Krauss, Barnett, Weisenfeld, Kasmin, DiCrecchio, & Horowitz, 2018). Not all these children are enrolled in public schools, as states and local education agencies often contract with private providers to deliver the service, but all these services may be viewed as part of the public education system.

Although state pre-K initiatives take a variety of different forms across the United States, they share two common features (Friedman-Krauss et al., 2018). First, they are funded and administered by state government, following specified state regulations. Second, they focus primarily on children's education, rather than custodial child care during the work day to support parental employment. Of course, they sometimes also serve as child care, and they can offer before- and after-school care to enhance their ability to meet this need. By fall 2017, state pre-K initiatives enrolled more than 1.5 million children across 43 states, the District of Columbia, and Guam – an increase of nearly 830,000 children, or 120%, since fall 2001. Total state spending on these initiatives topped $7.6 billion, with additional commitments of local and federal funds bringing the total to $8.65 billion. State spending on pre-K has increased by $3.88 billion, nearly tripling since 2001 (adjusting for inflation).

This chapter provides an overview of early childhood education programs supported primarily by state and local education agencies. Most often these are under the aegis of the public schools, though some states have created separate agencies to administer these programs. As noted earlier, not all of these are physically located in public schools. We begin with a discussion of the research base on the effectiveness of these public preschool programs. Next, we describe trends in access, quality standards, and spending for state-funded pre-K nationally and state by state over the last 15 years. Unfortunately, comparable data simply are not available for programs operated by local agencies including public schools without state support, but we describe some aspects of what appears to be a growing part of the field. We conclude with a discussion of policy issues related to state and locally funded public preschool education programs.

Early Evidence of Effectiveness

Typical goals of preschool education programs, including state pre-K initiatives, include improving language and early literacy skills to build foundations for reading and writing success, as well as developing knowledge and skills that relate to math, science, and the physical and social world. Also important is the development of social-emotional skills including attitudes, habits, dispositions, and social skills. Beginning in the 1960s rigorous studies found that preschool education programs could produce substantive gains in learning and development for disadvantaged children at high risk of poor achievement and school failure. These gains persisted through the school years and led to pervasive improvements in the adult lives, affecting employment and earnings, delinquency and crime, and health-related behaviors like smoking and health.

The earliest of these studies is the well-known randomized trial of the High/Scope Perry Preschool study (Schweinhart et al., 2005). Most children participated in the Perry Preschool program for two years, beginning at age three, though a few had only participated for one year at age four. Although operated by a local public school and similar in some ways to today's public pre-K programs, there were notable differences. The teacher-child ratio was much more intensive 1:6 or 1:7. Weekly visits were made to tutor the child at home. Teachers were well paid and supported by strong pedagogical leaders. The initial effects of this intervention on children's language and cognitive abilities were very impressive, about 0.90 standard deviations. Though effects on IQ were not persistent, there were persistent effects in literacy and math, as well as other positive outcomes such as better teacher-reported classroom and personal behavior, fewer special education placements, and higher high school graduation rates (Berrueta-Clement, Schweinhart, Barnett, Epstein, & Weikart, 1984; Schweinhart, Barnes, & Weikart, 1993).

The second study was conducted by the Institute for Developmental Studies (IDS; Deutsch, Deutsch, Jordan, & Grallow, 1983; Deutsch, Taleporos, & Victor, 1974; Jordan, Grallow, Deutsch, & Deutsch, 1985). In the IDS study, 402 children were randomly assigned to a one-year pre-K program in the public schools beginning at age four, or to a control group. Classes of 17 children were staffed by one teacher and one aide. By the end of the pre-K year, estimated effects on measures of cognitive and language abilities were more than 0.40 standard deviations. An estimated effect of 0.20 standard deviations in these areas remained evident at least through third grade. Later follow-ups suffered from severe attrition, so it is unknown to what extent these gains were sustained beyond third grade.

The third rigorous study of public school preschool focused on a larger initiative – the Chicago Child Parent Center (CPC) study (Reynolds, 2000). CPC programs operated within Chicago's public schools, and study participants attended half-day preschool programs for two years starting at age three or one year starting at age four during the 1980s. The CPC program also included kindergarten and elementary school follow-on components. Classes of 18 children were staffed by a certified teacher and a teacher assistant; parent outreach and support were also provided. Although much larger in scale than the two programs described above, the CPC program was not implemented city-wide, presumably because it was costlier than the typical approach.

Initial effects of the CPC program by kindergarten varied by outcome measure, in the range of 0.35–0.77 standard deviations (with effects of 0.20–0.65 standard deviations for a single year of attendance). Long-term positive impacts of the CPC program included higher test scores through middle school, increased high school graduation rates, better mental health, and reduced rates of arrests and special education placements (Reynolds, Ou, & Temple, 2018). Findings from the CPC study are especially important because they qualitatively replicate the findings of the Perry Preschool study in the context of a more broadly available, somewhat less intensive, public school program. The smaller size of most outcomes suggests a possible dose-response relationship, though differences in the scale, population served, and context could also explain smaller impacts.

Recent Evidence of Effectiveness

Many other studies provide evidence relevant to the impact of preschool education programs (Barnett, 2011a; Camilli, Vargas, Ryan, & Barnett, 2010; Duncan & Magnuson, 2013; Kay & Pennucci, 2014). However, relatively few have evaluated the effects of state and local preschool programs and many of those studies suffer from serious methodological weaknesses (Gilliam & Zigler, 2000, 2004). Overall, recent studies find much more modest effects for large-scale public programs, including those in the public schools compared to the earlier studies discussed above. They also find that effects decline after children exit preschool and enter primary school. Average effects in the primary grades are less than 0.10 SD (Kay & Pennucci, 2014).

Although disappointing, the much smaller effects are hardly unexpected. Large-scale public programs are much less intensive and shorter in duration than those that produce the largest gains in the earlier research. Earlier programs also had stronger supports for strong practices, a point to which we will return later. Moreover, increased participation of comparison and control groups in other types of preschool programs over time is strongly implicated in the smaller initial effects for contemporary programs. Less clear is what explains the convergence in achievement after entry to primary school, though research suggests this may be better described in some cases as catch-up than fade-out with the quality of both pre-K and primary schools relating to lasting impacts (Barnett, 2011a; Ansari et al., 2017).

Insights into the importance of pre-K quality are provided by recent studies employing a type of regression discontinuity design that leverages the strict age cutoff for entry to most public school preschool programs to control for possible selection bias (Barnett et al., 2018; Gormley, Gayer, Phillips, & Dawson, 2005; Gormley, Phillips, & Gayer, 2008; Weiland & Yoshikawa, 2013; Wong, Cook, Barnett, & Jung, 2008). Effect sizes vary considerably across these state and school district operated programs indicating substantial differences in immediate impacts. Yet, across all of them there was a pattern of very large effects on simply literacy skills (e.g., print awareness), moderate effects on mathematics, and relatively small effects on language development. The modest effects on language contrast sharply with much larger impacts in the Perry and Abecedarian studies, for example. One suggestion based on these findings is that public programs today may focus too much on simple, easily attained skills relating to letters and numbers and too little on more fundamental and less constrained knowledge and skills such as language that might provide a basis for more sustained gains (Barnett et al., 2018).

Recent studies of long-term achievement effects for large-scale pre-K reveal remarkable heterogeneity behind the near zero average effect size. Although many effects are between 0 and 0.10, one major study found negative effects, while others find larger positive effects (Ansari, 2018; Ansari et al., 2017; Barnett & Frede, 2017; Dodge, Bai, Ladd, & Muschkin, 2017; Hill, Gormley, & Adelstein, 2015; Lipsey, Farran, & Durkin, 2018; Yoshikawa et al., 2013). Researchers differ in the extent to which they attribute these variations in outcomes to differences in pre-K and primary schools or to differences in research methods. As we explain below, we conclude that the former is more important.

As the only randomized trial of large-scale public school pre-K (in Tennessee) found that initial positive effects gave way to later negative effects, and a large randomized trial of Head Start found few indications of substantial lasting effects, some now question whether any public preschool programs can produce positive lasting gains at scale (Lipsey, Farran, & Durkin, 2018; Whitehurst, 2018). We do not believe this is supported by the evidence. Meta-analyses of preschool effectiveness studies find that the randomized trial design is not associated with smaller effect sizes (Camilli et al., 2010; Shager et al., 2013). In addition, earlier nonexperimental studies of the Tennessee pre-K program found the same pattern of initial positive results followed by negative outcomes found in the randomized trial (Strategic Research Group, 2008). The Tennessee program is an outlier in its long-term effects regardless of the methodology used. Understanding what goes wrong in Tennessee should be a high priority. Over-referral of children from Tennessee's preschool program into special education may be a partial explanation and is something for other public school pre-K programs to avoid, but even accounting for that leaves a substantial negative effect unexplained (Strategic Research Group, 2008).

As we explore in depth in subsequent sections, there are substantial variations among states in pre-K policies relating to funding and standards for staffing and operations. These influence implementation quality in ways that may affect initial and later outcomes (Pianta, Barnett, Burchinal, & Thornburg, 2009). In addition, they affect the amount of pre-K children receive. Newer studies find that both length of day and number of years of pre-K (starting at age three) may have substantive effects on program outcomes (Atteberry, Bassok, & Wong, 2018; Barnett & Frede, 2017; Robin, Frede, & Barnett, 2007).

As funding and structural features are increasingly recognized as relatively blunt policy instruments, research and policy have become more focused on direct supports for strong practice. This includes an increased emphasis on teacher-specific coaching, curriculum selection and supports for strong implementation of curriculum, and continuous improvement systems that incorporate aligned standards, curriculum, and assessments of children and teachers (Egert, Fukkink, & Eckhardt, 2018; Pianta et al., 2017; Weiland, 2016). Similar efforts may be undertaken to improve K-3 practices to better support persistent gains from pre-K (Jenkins et al., 2018).

Unfortunately, public education generally has very limited capacity at either state or local levels to develop and support policies that directly affect practice from teacher preparation (outside their purview) to curriculum selection and development (often left to individual teachers or schools) and curriculum implementation (Smith, Moffitt, & Cohen, 2017). If anything, this capacity is even weaker at the pre-K level in many states (Weisenfeld, Frede, & Barnett, 2018). Developing even a portion of this capacity for public school pre-K is a substantial task, but comprehensive models have been developed and tested (e.g., Reynolds et al., 2017; Barnett & Frede, 2017). Documented successes have relied upon extensive systems of data collection and evaluation to provide feedback for continuous improvement as there seem to be few guarantees. For example, two years starting at age three

compared to one year at age four has not always performed significantly better, but some programs have found it to double achievement gains while not improving other indicators of school progress (e.g., Barnett & Frede, 2017). Given the many unknowns, state and local education agencies cannot assume success, but must collect data on child progress through the early primary grades to determine whether a specific pre-K program in a specific state (or even an individual school district) performs as expected.

Access

By the 2017–2018 school year, 1,523,410 children were enrolled in state-funded pre-K education programs. These initiatives were available in 43 U.S. states, the District of Columbia, and Guam, and some states offered multiple distinct pre-K initiatives aimed at different groups of children. By 2018–2019, two additional states had begun state-funded pre-K education programs (Montana and North Dakota). Nearly 90% of the children enrolled in state pre-K were four-year-olds – representing 33% of all four-year-olds in the country – but only 5% of the nation's three-year-olds were enrolled. Overall enrollment figures in state pre-K continued a trend of annual increases dating back to at least the 2001–2002 school year, when we began collecting this type of data (Friedman-Krauss et al., 2018). During the ensuing 15 years, enrollment more than doubled, driven primarily by an increase in enrollment of four-year-olds and state spending on pre-K increased three-fold from $2.4 billion in 2002 to $7.6 billion in 2017.

Enrollment Levels and Eligibility Criteria

Age is the primary eligibility criterion for state pre-K initiatives, and all state pre-K programs offer enrollment to four-year-olds who will be eligible for kindergarten the following year. The District of Columbia served the greatest percentage of its four-year-old population during 2016–2017, with 88% of all four-year-olds in the District enrolled, followed by Florida which served 77% of four-year-olds. Eight other states[1] served at least half of their four-year-olds: Vermont (75%), Oklahoma (73%), Wisconsin (72%), West Virginia (65%), Iowa (63%), Georgia (60%), New York (52%), and Texas (50%). At the other end of the spectrum, seven states served no children in state pre-K and 12 states with state pre-K programs served less than 10% of four-year-olds.

Twenty-nine of the 44 states with pre-K initiatives also offered enrollment to three-year-olds, though always to a lesser degree than they offered enrollment to four-year-olds. States that enrolled the greatest percentages of three-year-olds were DC (66%) and Vermont (60%). New Jersey and Illinois both served approximately 20% of their three-year-olds. Arkansas (19%), Nebraska (15%), West Virginia (11%), and California (11%) were the only other states to serve more than 10% of their three-year-olds in state pre-K (Friedman-Krauss et al., 2018). Table 26.1 provides state-by-state enrollment information for each state offering a pre-K initiative.

Table 26.1 **Access to and Spending for State-Funded Pre-K Programs in 2016–2017**

State	Total Number of Children Enrolled, Fall 2016 (All Ages)	Percentage of Four-Year-Olds Enrolled in State Pre-K (%)	Percentage of Three-Year-Olds Enrolled in State Pre-K (%)	Total State Spending ($)	State Spending per Child ($)	All Reported Spending per Child* ($)
Alabama	14,032	23.9	0.0	64,462,050	4,594	6,990
Alaska	358	3.5	0.0	2,000,000	5,587	5,587
Arizona	5,285	3.9	2.1	18,972,738	3,590	3,590
Arkansas	20,285	31.4	18.5	111,000,000	5,472	7,696
California	235,651	36.6	10.9	1,490,527,786	6,325	6,501
Colorado	21,622	23.1	8.3	59,948,508	2,773	4,095
Connecticut	14,778	30.2	8.3	115,514,745	7,817	10,020
Delaware	831	7.4	0.0	6,149,300	7,400	7,400
District of Columbia	13,077	87.9	66.0	222,257,368	16,996	18,054
Florida	174,252	77.3	0.0	397,698,606	2,282	2,282
Georgia	80,874	60.0	0.0	348,959,814	4,315	4,315
Hawaii	376	2.1	0.0	2,500,000	6,649	6,649
Illinois	72,007	26.0	20.4	304,314,676	4,226	4,852
Indiana	1,792	2.1	0.0	10,079,418	5,625	6,250
Iowa	26,310	62.8	3.0	83,791,732	3,335	3,437
Kansas	8,011	20.5	0.0	17,583,501	2,195	2,195
Kentucky	19,435	25.8	9.5	91,637,785	4,715	8,083
Louisiana	19,054	31.1	0.0	89,665,275	4,706	4,796
Maine	5,440	38.6	0.0	18,775,709	3,451	8,285
Maryland	31,382	37.2	4.9	108,517,098	3,458	7,597
Massachusetts	12,657	8.1	5.3	41,634,101	3,289	3,530
Michigan	38,371	33.4	0.0	243,900,000	6,356	6,356
Minnesota	4,603	5.6	1.0	28,982,528	6,296	7,339
Mississippi	1,642	3.4	0.7	4,000,000	2,436	5,832
Missouri	2,646	2.5	1.1	9,703,786	3,667	3,667
Nebraska	12,864	31.7	14.6	25,054,777	1,948	5,178
Nevada	1,870	4.5	0.5	4,838,875	2,588	5,130
New Jersey	53,370	29.8	20.7	653,333,890	12,242	12,478
New Mexico	10,379	35.4	4.2	52,310,000	5,040	5,040
New York	122,871	51.6	1.5	791,700,144	6,443	6,647
North Carolina	27,019	22.3	0.0	143,419,198	5,308	7,748
Ohio	15,942	11.2	0.3	63,768,000	4,000	4,000
Oklahoma	41,264	73.3	3.6	144,470,607	3,501	7,428
Oregon	9,456	12.3	7.7	90,146,488	9,533	9,533
Pennsylvania	28,833	13.2	6.5	209,159,001	7,254	7,254
Rhode Island	1,008	9.0	0.0	5,149,554	5,109	9,812
South Carolina	24,079	40.6	0.0	71,513,051	2,970	3,258
Tennessee	18,640	21.6	1.0	86,200,000	4,624	6,019
Texas	224,114	49.4	6.9	862,035,287	3,846	3,901
Vermont	8,943	75.1	59.7	61,505,762	6,878	7,209
Virginia	18,023	17.5	0.0	69,296,590	3,845	6,100
Washington	11,691	8.3	4.5	96,325,951	8,239	8,239
West Virginia	16,300	64.7	11.4	98,007,376	6,524	9,501
Wisconsin	51,973	71.8	0.8	195,864,098	3,769	5,858
National Total/Average	1,523,410	32.7	5.3	7,616,675,173	5,008	5,691
Guam	71	2.2	0.0	357,700	5,038	5,038

Note: Data are derived from Friedman-Krauss et al. (2018). Seven states are omitted because they did not offer state pre-K during the 2016–2017 school year. They are Idaho, Montana, New Hampshire, North Dakota, South Dakota, Utah, and Wyoming.

*Not all states were able to report funding from federal and local sources, but funding from these sources is included in calculations when data are available.

Figures 26.1 and 26.2 demonstrate how enrollment of three- and four-year-olds in state pre-K has changed in each state between 2002 and 2017. In these figures, progress is represented by how far a state is to the right from the diagonal. Clearly, progress has been uneven across the states. In addition, although a handful of states have begun pre-K programs since 2002, as of 2017, seven states still served no children in state-funded pre-K. Florida experienced a large increase in enrollment of four-year-olds in state pre-K,

serving no children in 2002 but 77% by 2017, emerging as a leader in access for four-year-olds. Vermont, Iowa, and Wisconsin, all committed to providing universally available pre-K for four-year-olds, also increased enrollment of four-year-olds by more than 50 percentage points between 2002 and 2017. Unfortunately, a few states have moved backward, serving a smaller percentage of four-year-olds in 2017 than in 2002, and other states have remained relatively stagnant. Turning to three-year-olds, Vermont and DC are the only two

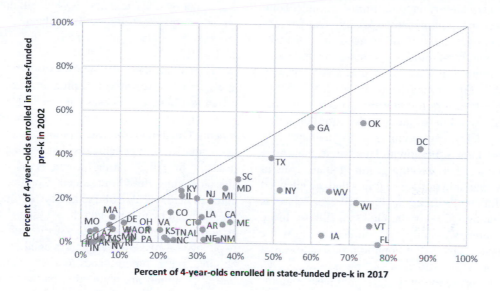

Figure 26.1 Percent of four-year-olds enrolled in state-funded pre-K in 2002 and 2017.

Note: States that did not serve four-year-olds in state-funded pre-K in both 2002 and 2017 are excluded. Progress in serving more four-year-olds in state-funded pre-K is represented by how far a state is to the right of the diagonal.

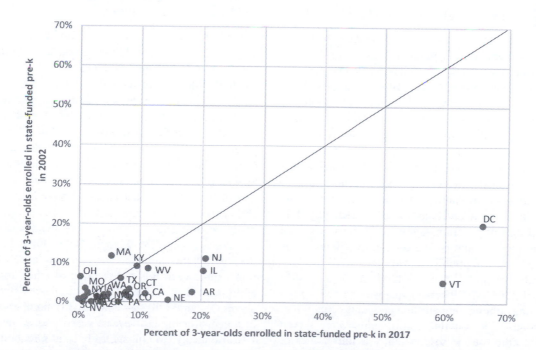

Figure 26.2 Percent of three-year-olds enrolled in state-funded pre-K in 2002 and 2017.

Note: States that did not serve three-year-olds in state-funded pre-K in both 2002 and 2017 are excluded. Progress in serving more three-year-olds in state-funded pre-K is represented by how far a state is to the right of the diagonal.

states to make great progress in this area, each increasing enrollment of three-year-olds by more than 45 percentage points. Arkansas, Nebraska, and Illinois each increased by more than 10 percentage points. Others moved in the wrong direction, reducing the percentage of threes served (those to the left of the diagonal). Many states continue to serve no three-year-olds in state pre-K, providing funding only for four-year-olds.

In determining eligibility for publicly funded early childhood programs, most states also use factors other than the child's age. Family income limits are most common, as states set maximum income levels to target programs to the most financially disadvantaged. In at least 27 of the 44 states with pre-K initiatives, state income limits are used to determine eligibility for at least some subset of the enrolled children (Friedman-Krauss et al., 2018). Some states use other risk factors to determine pre-K eligibility as well, such as low levels of parent education, disability or developmental delay, and having non-English-speaking family members (Barnett, Friedman, Hustedt, & Stevenson Boyd, 2009). A small but growing group of states aims to offer universally available pre-K programs that are intended (now or in the future) to be available to all four-year-olds statewide – including DC, Florida, Georgia, Illinois, Iowa, New York, Oklahoma, West Virginia, and Wisconsin. While many of these states have made notable progress toward a universal program, others still have a long way to go. DC, Vermont, and Illinois are the only states that have committed to providing a universally available state pre-K program for three-year-olds, but only DC and Vermont come close to doing so.

State Pre-K Programs in Public School Settings

Although state pre-K initiatives are all publicly financed, and are controlled and administered at the state level, states frequently partner with private organizations to operate state pre-K programs. This takes advantage of existing early childhood facilities and staff, as well as the ability of the private sector to grow quickly. Most state-funded pre-K initiatives allow both public schools and private providers to receive state pre-K funds. The types of private agencies involved (e.g., Head Start, private child care providers, faith-based agencies) and the degree to which private agencies participate vary from state to state. However, most participants in these initiatives do attend classrooms located in public schools. A handful of programs allow children to be served only in public schools; and on the flip side a few programs serve children in only nonpublic settings.

We estimate that 60% of all children enrolled in state pre-K during the 2016–2017 school year were served in public school settings (though not all state programs could report this information). The remainder of children were served in Head Start, other public settings such as universities or government agencies, or private settings (including child care). There has been a slow but steady decline in the percent of children in state pre-K served in public school settings. During the 2003–2004 school year, 76% of all state pre-K enrollees attended classrooms in the public schools, and by 2008–2009 this number had decreased to 67% (Hustedt & Barnett, 2011) and is now even lower. This continued decrease reflects a national trend toward growing enrollment levels in private settings as state pre-K programs become more widely available across the United States. For example, in 2004, Michigan served nearly 80% of all enrolled children at public school sites (Barnett, Hustedt, Robin, & Schulman, 2004), but by 2017 less than 60% of children enrolled were served in private settings. This changed occurred as the program expanded enrollment by 50% (Friedman-Krauss et al., 2018).

While some states distinguish between the standards that apply to public school pre-K programs and those offered in private settings, others make no such distinction and may even consider private settings an extension of the public schools. Oklahoma is a case in point. It allows public schools to collaborate with private providers by placing public school teachers in collaboration programs at community-based sites, including Head Start centers. Children in these sites are enrolled in the local public school system and receive the services offered by that public school system. Also, teacher salaries in collaboration settings must be equivalent to salaries in public schools. West Virginia is another example. In West Virginia, pre-K funding goes directly to public schools, but half of programs are required to partner with Head Start or private agencies and standards are the same for all programs (Friedman-Krauss et al., 2018).

Other Public Programs: Special Education and Local Preschool Initiatives

Special education programs are another important component of access to early childhood education initiatives in the public schools. During the 2016–2017 school year, more than 450,000 children received publicly funded special education services at ages three and four, though at least one-quarter of these children were also enrolled in state pre-K programs and are included in the state pre-K enrollment counts reported previously (Friedman-Krauss et al., 2018; U.S. Department of Education, Office of Special Education Programs, 2016). Special education programs are funded through a combination of federal, state, and local sources. There is great variability from state to state in percentages of children served, likely because states do not use identical sets of eligibility guidelines (Hustedt & Barnett, 2011). Overall, we estimate that 3% of the nation's four-year-olds and 3% of the nation's three-year-olds receive special education services in addition to those already counted as part of state pre-K programs (Friedman-Krauss et al., 2018), numbers that have not changed over the last several years. A few states, including DC, Kentucky, Michigan, Nebraska, Oklahoma, Vermont, West Virginia, and Wisconsin, serve nearly all special education children in their state-funded pre-K programs.

Another component of access to publicly funded early childhood programs involves programs that are designed and administered at the local level, including local programs that make use of Title I and other federal funding streams. It is difficult to estimate the number of children enrolled in locally developed programs because such programs are not required to report their preschool enrollment to state or federal agencies.

Over the last several years, major cities as diverse as New York City, Boston, Cleveland, Dallas, Seattle, Philadelphia, San Francisco, and San Antonio have made their own strides toward high quality pre-K. Some cities like Boston and Philadelphia have established pre-K programs independent of their respective states' pre-K programs. New York City worked with New York state to establish high-quality, full-day preschool for all four-year-olds in New York City with plans to extend the program throughout the entire state. Pre-K for All in New York City also offers another example of a public pre-K program utilizing community-based providers to serve more children than the school districts could easily accommodate (Barnett et al., 2016).

Quality Standards

Research on early childhood educational programs has found links between quality and positive effects on children's development, academic success, and other outcomes that yield economic benefits to society. In establishing and expanding early childhood programs, decisions must be made about program standards that will facilitate the provision of high-quality learning environments to all children. However, often the standards that may lead to the highest quality environments are also the most costly to implement, such as teacher qualifications and professional development and teacher-child ratios. Other quality standards such as having comprehensive early learning and development standards and conducting health screenings and referrals are less costly to provide.

Early childhood programs in public schools vary greatly in their policies regarding quality standards. The National Institute for Early Education Research (NIEER) conducts an annual survey that tracks ten quality standards which were updated in 2017 to reflect newer research. We identified common features of early childhood programs that have produced large and lasting improvements on children's learning and set benchmarks for *policies* relating to each. These ten policy standards and the benchmarks for "adequate" performance on each policy are presented in Table 26.2 (Friedman-Krauss et al., 2018). It is important to note that these quality standards and benchmarks are not judged to be of equal importance nor are the areas of focus all-inclusive. However, each of these standards for policy is judged to contribute to the educational effectiveness of an early childhood program. We consider them necessary for a high-quality learning experience, though they do not guarantee high quality.

Table 26.2 Quality Standard Benchmarks

Early Childhood Program Policy	Quality Standard Benchmark
Early learning and development standards	Comprehensive, horizontally and vertically aligned, supported, and culturally sensitive
Curriculum supports	Supports for curriculum selection and implementation
Teacher degree	At least a BA
Teacher specialized training	Specializing in pre-K
Assistant teacher degree	CDA or equivalent
Staff professional development	At least 15 hours/year of PD, individualized PD plans, and coaching for lead and assistant teachers
Maximum class size	20 or lower
Staff-child ratio	1:10 or better
Screening/referral	Vision, hearing, health
Continuous Quality Improvement System	Structured classroom observations; data used for program improvement

Note: Benchmarks are derived from Friedman-Krauss et al. (2018).

It is useful to distinguish between NIEER's benchmarks for policies and program quality standards that have been developed for individual programs and practices as implemented. For example, the National Association for the Education of Young Children (NAEYC, 2018a) has articulated ten program standards relating to NAEYC Accreditation. These are applied to individual programs and are more generally stated but overlap with eight of NIEER's ten benchmarks as they address: aligned standards (which children should learn, how they should be taught, and assessment), curriculum, health, staff qualifications, professional development, and continuous improvement. Elsewhere, NAEYC suggests as "best practice" for preschool a 1:10 ratio which corresponds to the other two NIEER benchmarks (NAEYC, 2018b).

Teacher Qualifications in State Pre-K Programs

While findings may not be conclusive, there is a considerable body of research indicating that children whose lead teachers have bachelor's degrees and specializations in pre-K education have better academic outcomes (Barnett, 2003a; Burchinal, Cryer, Clifford, & Howes, 2002). Notably, the recent Institute of Medicine and National Research Council (2015) *Transforming the workforce for children* report concluded that all teachers of children birth through age eight should have a teacher with at least a bachelor's degree and specialized training in ECE. However, some researchers suggest that the evidence indicates teacher qualifications do not strongly contribute to preschool student learning, for a variety of reasons (Early et al., 2005; Mashburn et al., 2008). Others emphasize that only programs employing highly educated, well-paid teachers have been found to produce very large gains for students on broad measures of learning and development in randomized trails (Barnett, 2011b). Furthermore, continued teacher professional development is crucial for success in the classroom including both in-service professional development opportunities and continuous coaching and mentoring (Weiland, 2016). To support these high levels of teacher qualifications in public early childhood programs, states typically need to offer supports and incentives, such as higher salaries, scholarships, and mentors to encourage teachers to obtain the necessary degrees. This often is costly, and states vary in their emphasis placed on teacher training and degrees as evidenced in current policies for public pre-K programs.

While most state-funded early education programs have policies requiring pre-K specialization and professional development, many states still do not require teachers to have bachelor's degrees. Out of the 61 distinct state-funded pre-K initiatives offered in 43 states, DC, and Guam during the 2017–2018 school year, only 34 (56%) initiatives required all lead teachers to have a bachelor's degree while 52 (85%) required specialization in early childhood. This difference reflects the fact that many states not requiring a bachelor's degree do require a Child Development Associate (CDA) credential, which is a specialization in early childhood. In comparison, in 2002, 45% of programs required all lead teachers to have at least a bachelor's degree and 86% of programs required specialized training in ECE. Although more than half of all state-funded initiatives require lead teachers to have bachelor's degrees, only nine of the 61 state pre-K initiatives require *all* teachers to be paid on the public salary scale (including the same starting salary and same salary schedule as K-12 teachers). Another 19 initiatives require teachers to be paid on a public school scale if they are in a public setting, but not if they are in a nonpublic setting (Barnett et al., 2017).

Though public early childhood programs continue to increase (albeit slowly) the education and training requirements for lead teachers, very few programs have strict educational requirements for assistant teachers. As with lead teachers, there is an evidence-based rationale for supporting improvements in assistant teachers' qualifications in conjunction with other policies to raise their effectiveness in the classroom (Barnett, 2003b; Bowman, Donovan, & Burns, 2001; Burchinal et al., 2002). During the 2016–2017 school year, only 19 (31%) state-funded prekindergarten initiatives required all assistant teachers to have at least a CDA or equivalent, compared to 24% of programs in 2002. Progress in this area has been slow, and many programs require assistant teachers to have only a high school diploma.

A total of 50 (82%) state pre-K initiatives required lead teachers to have at least 15 hours per year of professional development (meeting the old NIEER quality standard benchmark for professional development), compared to 83% of programs in 2002. However, only nine (15%) programs require all lead *and* assistant teachers to have at least 15 hours per year of professional development, to receive ongoing coaching or classroom-embedded support, and to have annual individualized professional development plans (meeting the new NIEER quality standard benchmark). Thirty-four (56%) programs require all assistant teachers to have at least 15 hours per year of professional development and only 24 (39%) programs require all classrooms to receive classroom-embedded support.

Teacher Qualifications in Public School Pre-K Settings

When examining state-funded pre-K programs, in general, policies and program standards apply equally to all types of auspices in which the program is located. However, in some states there are key differences in educational requirements for teachers depending on location. Twelve states have pre-K initiatives with different educational requirements for lead teachers in public settings compared to teachers in nonpublic settings. Although each state requirement differs slightly, all 12 require lead teachers in public school to have a bachelor's degree, whereas for nonpublic settings degree requirements vary including an Associate's degree (AA), CDA, or high school diploma. Eight of these twelve initiatives also have different certification and/or specialized training requirements for lead teachers based on whether they work in public or nonpublic settings. However, only two programs do not meet the teacher specialized training benchmark due to these differences. Of the programs that apply the same degree requirements to lead teachers in both public and nonpublic settings, some require only a minimum of a CDA or an AA for all teachers while many require a BA for all. In six of the states, while the degree requirements are the same, certification requirements differ by program location. Lastly, there are a few state-funded pre-K initiatives that currently operate either only in public school settings or in nonpublic school settings. Except for Guam which requires an AA in ECE, all programs that only operate in public settings require lead teachers to have bachelor's degrees. Three programs operate in only nonpublic settings; one requires all teachers to have bachelor's degrees.

For assistant teachers, almost all state-funded pre-K initiatives require the same educational requirements regardless of program location. Only five states have initiatives where there are distinct differences – Connecticut School Readiness Program, District of Columbia, Massachusetts Inclusive Preschool Learning Environments (IPLE), New York, and Virginia.

Other Program Standards in State Pre-K

In addition to teacher qualifications and professional development, it is important to understand what other standards are in place to determine the quality of a program. As of the 2016–2017 school year, all 61 state pre-K initiatives had comprehensive early learning and development standards (ELDS). Early learning standards provide a framework for programs to ensure that children's learning and development across multiple domains are covered in the classrooms. Comprehensive early learning standards should cover all areas as identified by the National Education Goals Panel (1991) – children's physical well-being and motor development, social/emotional development, approaches toward learning, language development, and cognition and general knowledge. Only 52 programs had ELDS that were comprehensive, vertically aligned with other state standards, horizontally aligned with child assessments, supported by the state, and culturally sensitive (meeting the new, enhanced NIEER benchmark).

In 2016–2017, 53 (87%) state pre-K programs had in place supports for curriculum decision-making and implementation. Based on recent research regarding the importance of a strong, well-implemented curriculum for children's learning, NIEER added a new quality standard benchmark; to meet this new benchmark, states must have in place an approval process or guidance to help programs select a curriculum model and then provide supports such as training or technical assistance to help programs implement the selected curriculum. Further, 26 (43%) programs have a list of comprehensive curricula approved for use in their state-funded pre-K programs.

Other aspects of program structure such as class size and staff-child ratios are important determinants of program effectiveness, though not independently of other program features including teacher and leader quality and supports for strong practice (e.g., planning time and coaching). Research suggests that young children perform better in classrooms with fewer students and low staff-child ratios, especially disadvantaged children (Barnett, 1998, Bowman et al., 2001; Frede, 1998). Smaller classes with more adults present allow for more teacher-child interactions and individualized attention, resulting in both short-term and long-term academic and social/emotional gains. It is recommended that to enhance program quality and in turn effectiveness, early childhood programs should have a maximum class size of 20, with at least two adults in the classroom, creating a 1:10 staff-child ratio or lower. For the 2016–2017 school year, 49 (80%) state-funded pre-K initiatives met the class size benchmark, 51 met the ratio benchmark, and 48 met both benchmarks. Texas and Pennsylvania's K4 program do not set limits on maximum class size and staff-child ratios while California's State Preschool Program does not limit class size (but does limit staff-child ratios). Both class size and staff-child ratios are locally determined in Wisconsin's 4K program. Arizona, California Transitional Kindergarten, Georgia, Indiana, and Ohio set limits, but they do not meet the recommendations of 20 or fewer children and a 1:10 staff-child ratio. Florida does not meet the 1:10 staff-child ratio and the Kansas State Pre-K program does not meet the requirement for 20 or fewer children per classroom. In DC, the District's class size and staff-child ratios meet these requirements, but these do not apply to the public charter schools which serve more than half of the children.

The percentage of programs requiring screenings and referrals for problems that can impair learning and development is one of the areas in which states have made the most progress over the last 15 years. About half (52%) required vision, hearing, and health screenings in 2002. By 2017, 43 state pre-K initiatives (70%) required screenings and referrals for at least vision, hearing, and health for children enrolled in those initiatives.

Lastly, while it is important to have policies in place regarding quality standards, it is critical to continuously monitor programs to ensure that they are correctly and successfully implementing these standards and providing high-quality learning environments. Equally important is having a system in place to provide programs and teachers with frequent feedback based on data collected to support program improvement. Unfortunately, unless programs are held accountable, not all of them will take the necessary steps to create high-quality learning environments for young children. NIEER's revised quality standard benchmark requires that data on classroom quality are systematically collected each year and that both the state and local programs use that information for program improvement practices. In 2016–2017 only 35 (57%) state pre-K initiatives had policies in place that met these requirements.

Over the last 15 years, public early childhood initiatives have worked to increase levels of quality in their classrooms through implementing new policies. However, as noted above, some states are making more progress and reaching their goals faster than others, and improvement is easier in some areas than others. It is important that all public pre-K programs provide the necessary resources to create high-quality learning environments for young children so that all children have a chance to reach their potential.

Resources

The amount of resources a state allocates to pre-K affects the accessibility of the program (including availability as well as the types of services provided), and the quality standards that can be put in place. Without enough funding, a program can lack the ability to implement required quality standards or may subvert quality by making unwise trade-offs, which in turn may have an impact on children's learning and development. Or, a program may require high standards but lack enough resources to serve more than a small percentage of children in the state.

State Investments for Pre-K Programs

State government investments in pre-K are substantial, totaling more than $7.6 billion across the 43 states, DC, and Guam that offered pre-K initiatives during the 2016–2017 school year. Spending on public pre-K has consistently climbed over the last 15 years from $2.4 billion during the

2001–2002 school year. Adjusting for inflation, this represents a 100% increase in state funding for pre-K. However, progress has not always been steady and 2016–2017 marked a slowdown in the growth rate compared to the prior year's increase. Progress has also been uneven across the states: while several states have started funding state pre-K, others have demonstrated inflation-adjusted decreases in their support for pre-K. Additionally, while there has been a national trend toward increased spending, there are marked differences in spending patterns between individual states (Friedman-Krauss et al., 2018).

There are also large differences between individual states in their spending for pre-K, ranging from $2 million in Alaska to $1.49 billion in California. Although state population has a strong influence, differences in program coverage and in funding per child to support both quantity and quality account for much of the variation. These disparities in total state contributions to pre-K have increased over the last 15 years as many states have made large strides in increasing their investments while other states continue to provide no funding at all for state pre-K.

To accurately understand a state's investment in pre-K, accessibility and enrollment levels must also be considered. For example, Texas spends over $760 million for its state pre-K initiative, while New Jersey spends over $550 million. However, because Texas is a much larger state and enrolls over 170,000 more children than New Jersey, the picture is quite different when looking at per child spending. Texas spends $3,846 per child, while New Jersey spends $12,242 per child. Therefore, when comparing state-allocated resources in public programs, it is useful to look at funding amounts per child enrolled, as well.

The average state spending per child in 2016–2017 was $5,008. Although this represents a small increase from the previous year, in inflation-adjusted dollars, it was a slight decrease since the previous year. Further, state spending per child has failed to keep up with inflation over the last 15 years: spending per child in 2016–2017 is nearly $400 lower than it was in 2001–2002. State spending per child also varies widely across states. For example, in 2016–2017, New Jersey spent more than $12,000 per child and six other states spent at least $7,000 per child. On the flip side, seven states spent less than $3,000 per child, some of which do not require a local match. Inequality in state pre-K investments per child has increased over the last 15 years.

Figure 26.3 demonstrates the change in per child spending between 2002 and 2017 in 2017 dollars and shows a very mixed picture. As in the previous figures, distance to the right of the diagonal indicates how much progress has been made and distance to the left indicates how much some states have fallen behind what they spent in 2002. Compared to the access picture, there has been much more backsliding on spending per child. Several states invested $0 in pre-K in 2002 but did invest in pre-K by 2017; the largest increase in spending per child was seen in Hawaii. Other states like New Jersey had high per child funding levels in 2002 and have sustained those levels with only small increases over the ensuing 15 years. Twenty-one states decreased spending per child on pre-K when adjusting for inflation.

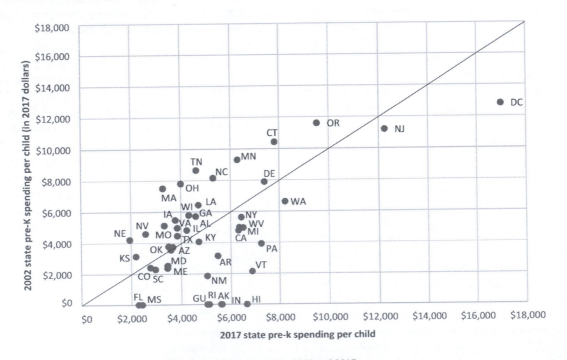

Figure 26.3 State spending per child on state-funded pre-K in 2002 and 2017.

Note: All dollar amounts are in 2017 dollars. States that did not operate a state-funded pre-K program in both 2002 and 2017 are excluded.
Progress in spending per child is represented by how far a state is to the right of the diagonal.

Additional Resources Used in Pre-K

In addition to state-allocated resources, most state pre-K programs employ other sources of funding such as federal and local funds. These funding streams can substantially increase the total amount of funding for a public program and, when available, can be used as a better gauge to determine total funding levels for a program. When states were asked to report all sources of funding the nationwide total rose to nearly $8.66 billion. For example, in West Virginia, state spending per child is $6,524 but when all reported resources (including both local and federal dollars in this case) are added, the total jumps to $9,501. Several other states also use federal Preschool Development Grants (PDG) to increase enrollment in or improve the quality of state-pre-K. For example, Rhode Island spent $5,150 per child in state dollars on their pre-K program but spending per child rose to $9,812 when including the state's federal PDG funding. However, many states lack a complete accounting of dollars spent at the local level, including funds raised by local public schools and federal Title I dollars allocated to state pre-K initiatives at the local level. It is difficult to compare *total* spending across all the states as some are better able than others to count federal and local dollars spent.

In Table 26.1 information is provided on total state spending and state spending per child enrolled. Additionally, data on per-child spending including all reported resources are provided for states that can report additional federal and local funds used in their pre-K programs. When identical dollar amounts are listed for both state per-child spending and all reported per-child spending, this means that a state either does not use additional resources for its program or is unable to report the additional amounts from federal and local sources.

The lack of solid information on funding to support pre-K programs in the public schools in many states means that it is much more difficult to ascertain the extent to which funding is adequate and equitable as is commonly done for K-12 spending. We can draw some limited conclusions. Many state programs target children in low-income families which tend to focus spending on disadvantaged children in lower income communities. However, rarely is variation in local capacity and local need taken into consideration in setting the state funding amounts. As a result, schools with weak tax bases and high concentrations of eligible children might choose to serve less of the eligible population or not participate at all. Exceptions are states that use the school funding formula to automatically incorporate adjustments they commonly use that change allocations depending on local fiscal capacity and needs (Barnett & Kasmin, 2018).

Conclusions and Policy Issues

Publicly funded pre-K in general, and state pre-K initiatives in particular, expanded significantly over the past two and a half decades. However, there is tremendous variation from state to state with respect to availability, quality, and spending, as well as progress over the last 15 years. While some states, such as West Virginia, have model programs that succeed in combining wide availability, high standards for quality, and adequate funding, these states continue to be the exception (Friedman-Krauss et al., 2018). Obama era efforts to incentivize states to move in this direction have been rolled back and the future federal role is uncertain. Current federal policy appears to emphasize reducing Head Start enrollment at ages three and four to provide higher quality and expand services for children under three. Increased funding for the Child Care and Development Fund has increased financial support for child care. On balance, the importance of state and local education agency policy in pre-K has increased, both because of the need to expand their services and to manage blending and braiding of child care funding with education funds.

As public education's pre-K programs continue to expand, there are several key questions that must be addressed. First, how will states manage collaboration and coordination across public programs that currently have distinct missions – including special education, Head Start, child care, and state pre-K? It is crucial that public schools fully participate in this process. State-funded pre-K programs have the potential to serve as a hub for services pooling resources across the various programs even if these are contracted out to providers operating under different auspices. Second, how will publicly funded early childhood programs create the collective capacity needed to deliver coherent, highly effective educational programs across the preschool and early primary years to produce lasting gains that contribute to increased excellence and equity? And finally, what lessons will be learned and adopted by public education systems about the design and implementation of highly effective pre-K programs? In part, this can be fostered by increasing the amount of research supported and conducted aimed at developing principles that can be adopted for the provision of highly effective practice at scale. Yet, given the diversity across states in their populations, values, and resources, state and local education agencies will also have to become more adept learning systems generating their own knowledge through continuous improvement systems. The larger p-12 education systems may learn from these efforts, just as pre-K can learn from progress at solving problems in the larger systems.

Note

1. Consistent with U.S. government statistical reporting practices, the District of Columbia will be referred to as a "state" throughout this chapter.

References

Ansari, A. (2018). The persistence of preschool effects from early childhood through adolescence. *Journal of Educational Psychology*, 10(7), 952–973.

Ansari, A., López, M., Manfra, L., Bleiker, C., Dinehart, L. H., Hartman, S. C., & Winsler, A. (2017). Differential third-grade outcomes associated with attending publicly funded preschool programs for low-income Latino children. *Child Development, 88*(5), 1743–1756.

Atteberry, A., Bassok, D., & Wong, V. C. (2018). *The effects of full-day pre-kindergarten: Experimental evidence of impacts on children's school readiness.* Charlottesville, VA: Curry School of Education, University of Virginia.

Barnett, W. S. (1998). Long-term effects on cognitive development and school success. In W. S. Barnett & S. S. Boocock (Eds.), *Early care and education for children in poverty: Promises, programs, and long-term results* (pp. 11–44). Albany, NY: SUNY Press.

Barnett, W. S. (2003a). Better teachers, better preschools: Student achievement linked to teacher qualifications. *Preschool Policy Matters, 2.* New Brunswick, NJ: National Institute for Early Education Research.

Barnett, W. S. (2003b). Low wages = low quality: Solving the real preschool teacher crisis. *Preschool Policy Matters, 3.* New Brunswick, NJ: National Institute for Early Education Research.

Barnett, W. S. (2011a). Effectiveness of early educational intervention. *Science, 333,* 975–978.

Barnett, W. S. (2011b). Minimum requirements for preschool teacher educational qualifications. In E. Zigler, W. S. Barnett, & W. Gilliam (Eds.), *Current debates and issues in prekindergarten education.* Baltimore, MD: Brookes Publishing.

Barnett, W. S., & Frede, E. C. (2017). Long-term effects of a system of high-quality universal preschool education in the United States. In H.-P. Blossfeld, N. Kulic, J. Skopek, & M. Triventi (Eds.), *Childcare, early education and social inequality: An international perspective* (pp. 152–172). Cheltenham, UK: Edward Elgar Publishing.

Barnett, W. S., Friedman, A. H., Hustedt, J. T., & Stevenson Boyd, J. (2009). An overview of prekindergarten policy in the United States: Program governance, eligibility, standards, and finance. In R. C. Pianta & C. Howes (Eds.), *The promise of pre-K* (pp. 3–30). Baltimore, MD: Brookes Publishing.

Barnett, W. S., Friedman-Krauss, A. H., Gomez, R. E., Horowitz, M., Weisenfeld, G. G., & Squires, J. H. (2016). *The state of preschool 2015: State preschool yearbook.* New Brunswick, NJ: National Institute for Early Education Research.

Barnett, W. S., Friedman-Krauss, A. H., Weisenfeld, G. G., Horowitz, M., Kasmin, R., & Squires, J. H. (2017). *The state of preschool 2016: State preschool yearbook.* New Brunswick, NJ: National Institute for Early Education Research.

Barnett, W. S., Hustedt, J. T., Robin, K. B., & Schulman, K. L. (2004). *The state of preschool: 2004 state preschool yearbook.* New Brunswick, NJ: National Institute for Early Education Research, Rutgers University.

Barnett, W. S., Jung, K., Friedman-Krauss, A., Frede, E., Nores, M., Hustedt, J. T., … Daniel-Echols, M. (2018). Effects of eight state prekindergarten programs on early learning: A regression-discontinuity analysis. *AERA Open, 4,* 1–16.

Barnett, W. S., & Kasmin, R. (2018). Fully funding pre-K through K-12 funding formulas. *Standard, 18*(1), 22–29.

Berrueta-Clement, J. R., Schweinhart, L. J., Barnett, W. S., Epstein, A. S., & Weikart, D. P. (1984). *Changed lives: The effects of the Perry Preschool Program on youths through age 19.* Ypsilanti, MI: High/Scope Press.

Bowman, B. T., Donovan, M. S., & Burns, M. S. (Eds.). (2001). *Eager to learn: Educating our preschoolers.* Washington, DC: National Academy Press.

Burchinal, M. R., Cryer, D., Clifford, R. M., & Howes, C. (2002). Caregiver training and classroom quality in child care centers. *Applied Developmental Science, 6,* 2–11. doi:10.1207/S1532480XADS0601_01

Camilli, G., Vargas, S., Ryan, S., & Barnett, W. S. (2010). Meta-analysis of the effects of early education interventions on cognitive and social development. *Teachers College Record, 112*(3), 579–620.

Deutsch, M., Deutsch, C. P., Jordan, T. J., & Grallow, R. (1983). The IDS program: An experiment in early and sustained enrichment. In Consortium

for Longitudinal Studies (Eds.), *As the twig is bent: Lasting effects of preschool programs* (pp. 377–410). Hillsdale, NJ: Erlbaum.

Deutsch, M., Taleporos, E., & Victor, J. (1974). A brief synopsis of an initial enrichment program in early childhood. In S. Ryan (Ed.), *A report on longitudinal evaluations of preschool programs. Volume 1: Longitudinal evaluations* (pp. 49–60). Washington, DC: Office of Child Development, U.S. Department of Health, Education, and Welfare.

Dodge, K. A., Bai, Y., Ladd, H. F., & Muschkin, C. G. (2017). Impact of North Carolina's early childhood programs and policies on educational outcomes in elementary school. *Child Development, 88*(3), 996–1014.

Duncan, G. J., & Magnuson, K. (2013). Investing in preschool programs. *Journal of Economic Perspectives, 27*(2), 109–32.

Early, D., Barbarin, O., Bryant, D., Burchinal, M., Chang, F., Clifford, R., … Barnett, W. S. (2005). *Prekindergarten in eleven states: NCEDL's multi state study of pre-kindergarten & study of state wide early education programs (SWEEP)* (NCEDL Working Paper). Chapel Hill, NC: National Center for Early Development & Learning.

Egert, F., Fukkink, R. G., & Eckhardt, A. G. (2018). Impact of in-service professional development programs for early childhood teachers on quality ratings and child outcomes: A meta-analysis. *Review of Educational Research, 88*(3), 401–433.

Frede, E. C. (1998). Preschool program quality in programs for children in poverty. In W. S. Barnett & S. S. Boocock (Eds.), *Early care and education for children in poverty* (pp. 77–98). Albany, NY: SUNY Press.

Friedman-Krauss, A. H., Barnett, W. S., Weisenfeld, G. G., Kasmin, R., DiCrecchio, N., & Horowitz, M. (2018). *The state of preschool 2017: State preschool yearbook.* New Brunswick, NJ: National Institute for Early Education Research.

Gilliam, W. S., & Zigler, E. F. (2000). A critical meta-analysis of all evaluations of state-funded preschool from 1977 to 1998: Implications for policy, service delivery and program evaluation. *Early Childhood Research Quarterly, 15,* 441–473. doi:10.1016/S0885-2006(01)00073-4

Gilliam, W. S., & Zigler, E. F. (2004). *State efforts to evaluate the effects of prekindergarten: 1977 to 2003.* New Haven, CT: Yale University Child Study Center.

Gormley, W. T., Jr., Gayer, T., Phillips, D., & Dawson, B. (2005). The effects of universal pre-K on cognitive development. *Developmental Psychology, 41,* 872–884. doi:10.1037/0012–1649.41.6.872

Gormley, W. T., Jr., Phillips, D., & Gayer, T. (2008). Preschool programs can boost school readiness. *Science, 320,* 1723–1724. doi:10.1037/0012–1649.41.6.872

Hill, C. J., Gormley Jr, W. T., & Adelstein, S. (2015). Do the short-term effects of a high-quality preschool program persist? *Early Childhood Research Quarterly, 32,* 60–79.

Hustedt, J. T., & Barnett, W. S. (2011). Private providers in state pre-K: Vital partners. *Young Children, 66*(6), 42.

Institute of Medicine and National Research Council. (2015). *Transforming the workforce for children, youth through age 8.* Washington, DC: The National Academies Press.

Jenkins, J. M., Watts, T. W., Magnuson, K., Gershoff, E. T., Clements, D. H., Sarama, J., & Duncan, G. J. (2018). Do high-quality kindergarten and first-grade classrooms mitigate preschool fadeout? *Journal of Research on Educational Effectiveness, 11*(3), 339–374.

Jordan, T. J., Grallow, R., Deutsch, M., & Deutsch, C. P. (1985). Long-term effects of early enrichment: A 20-year perspective on persistence and change. *American Journal of Community Psychology, 13*(4), 393–415. doi:10.1007/BF00911216

Kay, N., & Pennucci, A. (2014). *Early childhood education for low-income students: A review of the evidence and benefit-cost analysis* (Doc. No. 14-01-2201). Olympia: Washington State Institute for Public Policy.

Lipsey, M. W., Farran, D. C., & Durkin, K. (2018). Effects of the Tennessee Prekindergarten Program on children's achievement and behavior through third grade. *Early Childhood Research Quarterly, 45*(4), 155–76.

Mashburn, A. J., Pianta, R. C., Hamre, B. K., Downer, J. T., Barbarin, O. A., Bryant, D., … Howes, C. (2008). Measures of classroom quality in prekindergarten and children's development of academic, language, and social skills. *Child Development, 79*(3), 732–749. doi:10.1111/j.1467–8624.2008.01154.x

NAEYC. (2018a). *NAEYC early learning program standards.* Washington, DC: Author. Retrieved February 8, 2019 from https://www.naeyc.org/sites/default/files/globally-shared/downloads/PDFs/accreditation/early-learning/overview_of_the_standards.pdf

NAEYC. (2018b). *Staff-to-child ratio and class size.* Washington, DC: Author. Retrieved February 8, 2019 from https://www.naeyc.org/sites/default/files/globally-shared/downloads/PDFs/accreditation/early-learning/staff_child_ratio.pdf

National Educational Goals Panel. (1991). *The Goal 1 Technical Planning Subgroup report on school readiness.* Washington, DC: National Educational Goals Panel.Pianta, R., Hamre, B., Downer, J., Burchinal, M., Williford, A., LoCasale-Crouch, J., … Scott-Little, C. (2017). Early childhood professional development: Coaching and coursework effects on indicators of children's school readiness. *Early Education and Development, 28*(8), 956–975.

Pianta, R. C., Barnett, W. S., Burchinal, M., & Thornburg, K. R. (2009). The effects of preschool education: What we know, how public policy is or is not aligned with the evidence base, and what we need to know. *Psychological Science in the Public Interest, 10*(2), 49–88.

Reynolds, A. J. (2000). *Success in early intervention: The Chicago Child-Parent Centers.* Lincoln: University of Nebraska Press.

Reynolds, A. J., Hayakawa, M., Ou, S. R., Mondi, C. F., Englund, M. M., Candee, A. J., & Smerillo, N. E. (2017). Scaling and sustaining effective early childhood programs through school–family–university collaboration. *Child Development, 88*(5), 1453–1465.

Reynolds, A. J., Ou, S. R., & Temple, J. A. (2018). A multicomponent, preschool to third grade preventive intervention and educational attainment at 35 years of age. *JAMA Pediatrics, 172*(3), 247–256.

Robin, K. B., Frede, E., & Barnett, W. S. (2007). *Is more better? The effects of full-day vs. half-day preschool on early school achievement.* New Brunswick, NJ: National Institute for Early Education Research, Rutgers University.

Schweinhart, L. J., Barnes, H. V., & Weikart, D. P. (1993). *Significant benefits: The High/Scope Perry Preschool Study through age 27.* Ypsilanti, MI: High/Scope Press.

Schweinhart, L. J., Montie, J., Xiang, Z., Barnett, W. S., Belfield, C. R., & Nores, M. (2005). *Lifetime effects: The High/Scope Perry Preschool Study through age 40.* (Monographs of the High/Scope Educational Research Foundation, 14). Ypsilanti, MI: High/Scope Press.

Shager, H. M., Schindler, H. S., Magnuson, K. A., Duncan, G. J., Yoshikawa, H., & Hart, C. M. (2013). Can research design explain variation in Head Start research results? A meta-analysis of cognitive and achievement outcomes. *Educational Evaluation and Policy Analysis, 35*(1), 76–95.

Smith, K. B., Moffitt, S. L., & Cohen, D. K. (2017). The influence of practice on policy. In D. E. Mitchell, D. Shipps, & R. L. Crowson (Eds.), *Shaping education policy* (pp. 172–196). New York, NY: Routledge.

Strategic Research Group. (2008). *Assessing the effectiveness of Tennessee's pre-kindergarten program: Annual report 2008–2009.* Columbus, OH: Strategic Research Group. Retrieved October 11, 2018 from http://www.comptroller.tn.gov/repository/re/srgannualreport08-09.pdf

U.S. Department of Education. (2018a). *The condition of education at a glance.* Retrieved October 11, 2018 from https://nces.ed.gov/programs/coe/indicator_cfa.asp

U.S. Department of Education. (2018b). *Digest of education statistics.* Retrieved October 11, 2018 from https://nces.ed.gov/programs/digest/d17/tables/dt17_202.10.asp

U.S. Department of Education, Office of Special Education Programs (2016). *Number of Children with Disabilities (IDEA) Receiving Special Education and Related Services by Age: Fall 2016. Table generated from 2016 Part B Child Count and Educational Environments data in the EDFacts reporting system.* Retrieved January 2, 2018 from https://www2.ed.gov/programs/osepidea/618-data/state-level-data-files/index.html

Wong, V. C., Cook, T. D., Barnett, W. S., & Jung, K. (2008). An effectiveness-based evaluation of five state prekindergarten programs. *Journal of Policy Analysis and Management, 27*(1), 122–154. doi:10.1002/pam.20310

Weiland, C. (2016). Launching preschool 2.0: A road map to high quality public programs at scale. *Behavioral Science & Policy, 2*(1), pp. 37–46.

Weiland, C., &Yoshikawa, H. (2013). Impacts of a prekindergarten program on children's mathematics, language, literacy, executive function, and emotional skills. *Child Development, 84*, 2112–2130.

Weisenfeld, G.G., Frede, E.C., & Barnett, W.S. (2018). *Implementing 15 essential elements for high quality pre-k: An updated scan of state policies.* New Brunswick, NJ: National Institute for Early Education Research.

Whitehurst, G. J. (2018). The positive impacts of public pre-K fade quickly, and sometimes reverse: What does this portend for future research and policy? *Early Childhood Research Quarterly, 45*(4), 183–187.

Yoshikawa, H., Weiland, C., Brooks-Gunn, J., Burchinal, M., Espinosa, L. M., Gormley, W. T., … Zaslow, M. (2013). *Investing in our future: The evidence base on preschool education.* Ann Arbor, MI: Society for Research in Child Development.

Index

Note: Bold page numbers refer to tables; *italic* page numbers refer to figures

accommodation 19–20
active start, physical activity 7, 77, 78
administration for children and families 335
aggregate lens 103
aggressive behaviour: peer relations 36
Albertini, G. 139
Almeda, M. 93
Amendum, S. J. 317
American Educational Research Association 5
Anagnostou, E. 24
Anderson, J. 117
Anderson, S. 340, 341
Andrade, S. 353
Angold, A. 212
Anning, A. 141
Ansari, A. 343
Aral, N. 171
Arnheim, R. 141
Arranz, E. 19
art education 134; context 137–9; curriculum 140–2; development, traditional views 135; pictorial turn 142; social context and child art 139–40; sociocultural perspectives 137; standard of realism 136–7
Asia-Pacific Journal of Research in Early Childhood Education 5
Association of Childhood Education International 5
Atkinson, D. 136, 139, 142
attachment theory 326–7
attention deficit hyperactivity disorder 23, 49, 188
attitude development 279
August, D. 355
Austin, P. 88

baby family and child experiences survey 225
Baddeley, A. 23
Badzinski, D. M. 106
Barker, A. 127
Barr, R. 201
Barrett, M. 154
Beck, I. L. 315
behavioral attractors 70
Bekkus, M. 169
Berk, L. 167
Berry, D. 325
Beyazkurk, D. 328
Big Search 124
Bilingual Education Act 256–7

bilingualism: benefits 234–235; children in preprimary programs 239; demographic overview 236; early childhood population 240; elementary and preschool 240; inconsistent data gathering 242; K-12 population 236–237; limited assessment in languages 242; number and percentage distribution 237; policy requirements 243–245; public K-12 students 238; public school students 238; reclassification policy conflicts 246–247; score differences, fourth grade 240; score differences, kindergarden 240; terminological distinctions 235–236; workforce policies 246
Bird, J. 166
Björkvold, J. 156
Blanchet-Cohen, N. 169
Blau, D. 222
Blaye, A. 107
Bloom, B. 350
Bockmeyer, C. 170
Bodrova, E. 166
Borge, A. 169
Bornstein, M. H. 328
Bowles, R. P. 23
Bowlby, J. 325
Boyatzis, C. J. 139
Branscombe, A. 128
Bratsch-Hines, M. 343
Bratton, J. 357
Brendgen, M. 169
Bridges, M. 355
Broadhead, P. 167, 168
Brooks-Gunn, J. 224
Bruner, J. 21, 108
Bryant, P. 106
Burchinal, M. 340, 343
Burke, R. 179
Bus, A. G. 91, 93

Cabell, S. 117
Calderon, M. 259
California's current approach: approach to assessment 260; early learning foundations/curriculum frameworks/professional development 260; preschool program guidelines 260
Calvert, S. L. 201
Cantor, J. 106
Caputa, F. 117
Carlson, S. M. 24
Carruthers, E. 101
case value lens 103
Casey, B. 24
Casey, M. B. 86
Ceder, I. 86